THE PAPERS OF

Andrew Jackson

·

DANIEL FELLER
EDITOR-IN-CHIEF

THE PAPERS OF

VOLUME VII, 1829

DANIEL FELLER

HAROLD D. MOSER

LAURA-EVE MOSS

THOMAS COENS

EDITORS

•

THE UNIVERSITY OF TENNESSEE PRESS
KNOXVILLE

Frontispiece: Andrew Jackson, 1829. Oil sketch on panel by Thomas Sully.
Courtesy of The Historical Society of Pennsylvania Collection, Atwater Kent
Museum of Philadelphia.

This book is printed on acid-free paper.

Library of Congress Cataloging in Publication Data
(Revised for vol. 7)

Jackson, Andrew, 1767–1845.
The papers of Andrew Jackson.
Vol. 2 edited by Harold D. Moser and Sharon MacPherson.
Vol. 6 edited by Harold D. Moser and J Clint Clifft.
Vol. 7 edited by Daniel Feller, Harold D. Moser, Laura-Eve Moss,
and Thomas Coens.
Includes bibliographical references and indexes.
Contents: v.1. 1770–1803. —v.2. 1804–1813 —[etc.]
—v.6. 1825–1828. —v.7. 1829.
1. Jackson, Andrew, 1767–1845.
2. United States—Politics and government—1829–1837—Sources.
3. Presidents—United States—Correspondence
I. Smith, Sam B., 1929– .
II. Owsley, Harriet Fason Chappell.
III. Moser, Harold D.
IV. Feller, Daniel.
V. Title.

ISBN 0-87049-219-5 (v. 1: cl.: alk. paper)
ISBN 0-87049-441-4 (v. 2: cl.: alk. paper)
ISBN 0-87049-650-6 (v. 3: cl.: alk. paper)
ISBN 0-87049-778-2 (v. 4: cl.: alk. paper)
ISBN 0-87049-897-5 (v. 5: cl.: alk. paper)
ISBN 1-87049-174-7 (v. 6: cl.: alk. paper)
ISBN 978-1-57233-593-6 (v. 7: cl.: alk. paper)

Advisory Board

Publication of
The Papers of Andrew Jackson
was supported by funding from
THE COLLEGE OF ARTS AND SCIENCES OF
THE UNIVERSITY OF TENNESSEE, KNOXVILLE
THE NATIONAL HISTORICAL PUBLICATIONS
AND RECORDS COMMISSION
THE LADIES' HERMITAGE ASSOCIATION
THE TENNESSEE HISTORICAL COMMISSION
and
THE NATIONAL ENDOWMENT FOR THE HUMANITIES

Contents

For the page number on which each document
of The Papers begins, see the Calendar.

How to Use This Volume

HISTORY AND SCOPE OF THE PROJECT

This seventh volume of *The Papers of Andrew Jackson* marks a new beginning in two ways. It inaugurates the core of the series, the portion covering Jackson's tumultuous two terms as president of the United States. With this volume also, a new editorial team headed by Daniel Feller assumes the helm, while Harold Moser, who as editor shepherded the previous five volumes and the microfilm edition through to completion, succeeds to a well-earned retirement.

With the start of Jackson's presidency, the nature of his papers changes even as their bulk multiplies. These changes dictate some modest adjustments in editorial method. By way of introducing these, it seems fit to review the project's history and overall strategy.

Our aim is to systematically present Andrew Jackson's full extant literary remains. We define "papers" broadly, to mean everything written to, by, or for Jackson, or annotated by him—every piece of paper, so to speak, on which Jackson left his fingerprints. This includes incoming as well as outgoing correspondence, official documents, drafts, memoranda, and financial and legal records. (For a fuller definition, including some exclusions particular to Jackson's presidency, see "What Is a Jackson Document?" below.)

The project began more than thirty years ago with a worldwide canvass for Jackson papers. The search yielded photocopies of some 100,000 documents held by hundreds of libraries, archives, and private owners. The two largest caches are both in Washington, D.C. The Library of Congress holds the bulk of Jackson's surviving retained personal papers, while the National Archives has many Jackson documents distributed among its holdings of records of the various branches of the federal government.

In 1967 the Library of Congress produced a 78-reel microfilm edition of its entire Andrew Jackson Papers collection. The National Archives has also filmed many Jackson documents on its M and T series microfilms of government records. In 1987, when our project's initial document search was complete, we produced a 39-reel Microfilm Supplement containing all Jackson items that were not already on the National Archives or Library of Congress films. (We also included some Library of Congress documents that were misdated or otherwise unfindable on the Library's own film.) As of 1987, then, every known Jackson document had been microfilmed by the Library, the Archives, or this project. To provide unified access to them all, the project published *The Papers of Andrew Jackson: Guide and Index to the Microfilm Editions* (Scholarly Resources, Inc., 1987), which listed every document alphabetically by name of author or recipient, with the microfilm location for each. (For a full listing of microfilms pertinent to this volume, see "Microfilm Series" below.)

Meanwhile the project embarked on its plan to publish a carefully chosen selection of Jackson's papers in sixteen chronological volumes: six pre-presidential, one for each presidential year, and two post-presidential. This volume is part of that series. Presenting the most significant documents in full annotated text, and summarizing the rest in calendar form, the volumes are designed both to stand on their own as a compilation of Jackson's most important papers and to offer those who wish to delve further an easy window into the full corpus of papers available on microfilm.

Newfound Jackson documents continue to surface. Those discovered in time are incorporated into the chronological volumes, including this one, as they appear. At the project's conclusion, all the documents unearthed since 1987, and therefore absent from the existing microfilms, will be collected in a final microfilm or electronic supplement.

WHAT IS A JACKSON DOCUMENT?

The following types of papers lie within our corpus:

Documents written or signed by Jackson, except those excluded below.

Documents composed for Jackson, such as drafts of his messages.

Documents addressed, written, or delivered to Jackson.

Documents annotated, inscribed, or endorsed by Jackson.

All documents in the Library of Congress Jackson Papers. These were, with few if any exceptions, papers received and kept by Jackson even if not addressed to him.

Other items that were microfilmed and included in the *Guide and Index,* especially some civil commissions signed by Jackson and job applications and recommendations addressed to his private secretary, Andrew Jackson Donelson. Even if these do not meet our present definition of Jackson documents, they are retained herein to preserve, as much as possible, a one-to-one correspondence between the listings in the *Guide and Index* and the volume. On the other hand, a very few items that were included as Jackson documents in the microfilm and the *Guide and Index* not by a variant definition but by simple mistake have been omitted.

We exclude the following:

Routine official documents bearing Jackson's signature as president (unless appearing in the microfilm and *Guide and Index,* as above). These are often printed forms with handwritten insertions. They include civil and military commissions, land patents, proclamations of federal land sales, diplomatic credentials, consular exequaturs, and ship passes.

Reported utterances, conversations, or remarks by Jackson, unless made from a written text.

Communications made by others in Jackson's name, such as a letter from a government official beginning "the president directs me to say. . . ."

Published materials ostensibly addressed or inscribed to Jackson or to the president, unless known to be sent to him or seen by him.

Spurious documents. One of these deserves special mention: a January 1829 letter from Martin Van Buren, complaining of railroads and proposing an Interstate Commerce Commission. The text of this purported letter, of which no manuscript original exists, surfaced in the mid-twentieth century and has obtained wide currency. It is a transparent fraud.

ORGANIZATION AND PRESENTATION

Like its predecessors, this volume contains three component parts. Its main body presents full texts of Andrew Jackson's most significant papers from 1829 with explanatory footnotes. Following the text is a calendar—a chronological listing of *all* the papers, with a brief content synopsis for each item not printed in full. Together, the text and calendar account for every 1829 Jackson document falling within our definition of his papers. The index at the back provides full coverage of document authors, recipients, and contents for both text and calendar.

The volume text, calendar, and index can be used in tandem with each other and with the microfilms and microfilm *Guide and Index* to pursue almost any kind of research inquiry. If the subject is a person, say John Doe, the *Guide and Index* will give dates and microfilm locations for all letters he wrote to, or received from, Jackson. Each letter will also be either printed in the appropriate volume or summarized in its calendar. If Doe is mentioned in a letter by someone else, that mention will appear in the volume index. Reaping the full benefit of a volume requires consulting calendar as well as main text, and using the index as a guide to both.

Selection of Documents for Printing

About one-fifth of Jackson's 1829 papers are presented here in full text; the rest are calendared. We have selected for printing what we judge to be the most significant papers, defining significance by the widest possible criteria—those documents that most illuminate Jackson, his presidency, his country, and his times. In general we have made our selection irrespective of a document's previous publication history, if any. However, Jackson's public papers—his official presidential addresses, messages, and proclamations—constitute a special case.

Jackson's Official Papers

Jackson's presidential public papers in 1829 include his inaugural address, his first annual message to Congress, several proclamations, and a number of special messages to Congress, sometimes transmitting documents or reports. These papers have all been published in one or more of three official series. First, many messages with their attachments were immediately printed by order of the House or Senate and included in the consecutively numbered volumes of congressional documents known as the Serial Set. Secondly, messages that Jackson sent to the Senate in executive session, concerning treaties or nominations to office, were later collected and published in the fourth volume of the *Journal of the Executive Proceedings of the Senate of the United States of America.* Lastly, at the end of the nineteenth century James D. Richardson published under congressional authorization *A Compilation of the Messages and Papers of the Presidents 1789–1897* in ten volumes, the second and third of which included Jackson's presidency. Richardson's compilation was itself included in the Serial Set (House Miscellaneous Document 210, 53d Congress, 2d session, Serial 3265) and was reissued in several later editions. (These editions were variously repaginated. All page citations herein are to the original, official Serial Set version.)

Today all three publications are widely available, not only in libraries but through electronic media. (As of this writing, the *Senate Executive Proceedings* and portions of the Serial Set have been posted to the Library of Congress website, American Memory: A Century of Lawmaking for a New Nation.) Their texts are reliable and authoritative. There seems to be no point to reproduce in this volume previously published documents that readers can find at their fingertips; and to do so would consume much precious space. Accordingly we have determined not to print the final, official texts of any presidential papers that appeared in the Serial Set, the *Senate Executive Proceedings,* or Richardson. The manuscript originals of these documents, residing now generally in the National Archives, were microfilmed by the project and listed in the *Guide and Index;* they are calendared here, and their publication in official series is uniformly noted. But they are not printed. However, we do print drafts, where such exist and differ significantly from the final versions. Readers may track the evolution of, for instance, Jackson's inaugural address or first annual message to Congress by comparing the drafts in this volume to the final texts in Richardson.

For a full listing of Jackson's 1829 public papers with their publication history, see the table "Jackson's Presidential Public Papers" below.

Ordering of Documents

The general order of documents, both in text and calendar, is chronological. Inferred dates are given in brackets; estimated ones are preceded by c (*circa*). Items within a month, or within the year 1829, that cannot be dated more precisely go at the end of the month or year respectively. Documents with spread dates, such as running financial accounts, are placed at their opening date. Within each day, letters from Jackson, arranged alphabetically by recipient, come first, followed by letters to Jackson alphabetically by author, then other Jackson documents, and lastly third-party correspondence. However, where a chronology can be established within a day—an exchange of notes back and forth, for instance—the documents composing it are grouped in sequence.

A special case concerns the private memorandum book Jackson began keeping in April 1829. Many of its entries are brief and undated, and to break them out individually as separate items, or not to print them, would obscure the book's distinctive character. Conversely, to print the book as a unit at any one point would place many entries far out of proper sequence. We have, accordingly, broken the 1829 portion of the book into several chunks and printed them, close to their likely time of composition, at the end of April, beginning of June, end of June, end of September, and end of November.

Transcription

Each document printed here is presented in full. Most are transcribed from handwritten originals. Where the original is itself a printed text, for instance in a newspaper, its appearance and typography have been reproduced as exactly as possible.

Converting handwriting to print is an inexact process. It requires rendering a nearly limitless array of pen marks into a finite set of typographic characters. In Jackson's era, even polished writers often punctuated sentences with marks that lay somewhere between clear dashes, periods, commas, or semicolons; and they formed letters such as *c, m,* and *s* not simply in upper or lower case but in a variety of styles and gradations of size. Jackson, for instance, had at least three, not two, distinct ways of making an *a* and a *t.*

That said, within the limits of the medium, our policy is to reproduce the original text as closely as possible, retaining its peculiarities of grammar, spelling, capitalization, and punctuation. When Jackson reversed "the" and "they," as he sometimes did, we have transcribed just what he wrote, without comment or *[sic]*. The following are exceptions. Inadvertent word repetitions ("and and"), nonfunctional dashes following other punctuation, and addressees' names at the end of a document have been omitted. Superscript characters have been brought down to the main line. Dates placed at the bottom of a document have been moved up to the top, and interlined or marginal additions have been inserted in the text at the spot marked by the writer. Significant cross-outs have been preserved, trivial ones omitted. Interpolated readings of missing or obscured text are bracketed; where conjectural, they are also italicized. Complimentary closings to letters ("your obedient servant") have been run onto the preceding text. Unpunctuated spacings between sentences are retained.

Annotation

Each printed document is followed by a source note that identifies its type, its repository or owner, its location on microfilm (in parentheses), and whether it has been previously published, as shown in the example below. Where more than one version of a document exists, the one we print is listed first.

> ALS, DNA-RG 59 (M179-67). AL draft, THi (12-1456); LC, DLC (60). *Niles,* January 18, 1830; *Doe Papers,* 18:243.

In this sample case, our printed text is from an Autograph Letter Signed (ALS)—a letter handwritten and signed by its sender—housed in Record Group 59 of the National Archives (DNA-RG 59) and filmed on Reel 67 of National Archives microfilm series M179 (M179-67). There is also an unsigned draft of the letter in the sender's hand (AL draft) in the Tennessee Historical Society (THi) and filmed on Reel 12, frame 1456, of the Microfilm Supplement produced by this project; and also a Letterbook copy (LC) held by the Library of Congress (DLC) and filmed on Reel 60 of the Library's Jackson Papers microfilm. The letter was published contemporaneously in *Niles' Weekly Register* and again in the modern *Papers of John Doe*.

For lists and explanations of document types, repositories, microfilm series, and publication titles, see "Codes and Symbols" below. In general, our policy in noting previous publication is to cite the first or earliest known contemporary publication, and the most authoritative modern one. For items we print, we do not cite previous appearance in John Spencer Bassett's *Correspondence of Andrew Jackson,* which our publication supersedes.

The source note also presents information germane to or explanatory of the document as a whole, such as the author's identity if not previously given. Numbered footnotes, keyed to callouts in the text, give further information on particular points. In general, our policy is to offer only what facts are necessary to make a document intelligible and to place it in immediate context, leaving the rest to the reader. Where possible, we have briefly identified, with birth and death dates, each person named in the volume at the point of their first significant appearance.

We have not routinely employed cross-referencing footnotes to link up related items in the volume, as these may be located by using the index and calendar. When Jackson writes to Smith, "I have received yours of the 17th instant," that letter, if extant, will appear in the calendar at its proper date ("instant" means this month; "ultimo" means last month) and it, with all other mentions of Smith, will be indexed under his name. Nor have we used the citation "not found" for documents mentioned in the text which are not extant or not known to us. We have looked as hard as we could and included everything we found. If it is not accounted for here, we didn't find it.

Calendar

In the calendar, entries for documents printed in the volume are italicized, with page numbers. The calendar thus also functions as a table of contents. For documents not printed in the volume, calendar entries present the same identifying and locating information as a text source note (see Annotation above), followed by a brief synopsis of contents. To save space, we have in a few cases merged the entries for substantively identical documents of the same date. Routine Jackson notations on incoming documents—for instance, referring a letter to one of the executive departments—are not mentioned in calendar descriptions. However, we have noted substantive Jackson endorsements, and also those on third-party letters where the endorsement is what makes the item a Jackson document. (For an example covering both cases, see John Mullowny to Martin Van Buren, October 15, 1829, p. 764.)

Codes and Symbols

DOCUMENT TYPES

Abbreviations

A   Autograph—written in the author's hand
D   Document—a manuscript document other than a note or letter
L   Letter—a manuscript letter
LC   Letterbook copy—a handwritten copy recorded in a letterbook
N   Note—a brief informal manuscript message or memorandum
S   Signed—bearing the author's signature

Other Notations

Abstract   A précis of a document
Copy   A handwritten copy
Draft   A handwritten draft
Duplicate   A document created in identical multiple versions
Extract   A copied or printed excerpt from a document
Fragment   A partial document
Printed   A printed document

Sample Combinations

AL   Autograph Letter—an unsigned sent letter, written by
           the sender
ALS   Autograph Letter Signed—a sent letter, written and
           signed by the sender
ALS copy   Autograph Letter Signed copy—a copy of a sent letter,
           written and signed by the sender
ALS draft   Autograph Letter Signed draft—a draft of a sent letter,
           written and signed by the sender
LS   Letter Signed—a sent letter, signed by the sender but
           written in another hand

REPOSITORIES

AFLau	Office of the Judge of Probate, Lauderdale County, Florence, Ala.
ArLTR	Historic Arkansas Museum, Little Rock
CLjC	James S. Copley Library, La Jolla, Calif.
CSmH	Henry E. Huntington Library, San Marino, Calif.
CtHi	Connecticut Historical Society, Hartford
CtNlCG	United States Coast Guard Academy, New London, Conn.
CtY	Yale University, New Haven, Conn.
CU-BANC	Bancroft Library, University of California, Berkeley
DCU	Catholic University of America, Washington, D.C.
DGU	Georgetown University, Washington, D.C.
DLC	Library of Congress, Washington, D.C.
DNA	National Archives, Washington, D.C.

RG 11, General Records of the United States Government
RG 15, Records of the Department of Veterans Affairs
RG 26, Records of the United States Coast Guard
RG 28, Records of the Post Office Department
RG 39, Records of the Bureau of Accounts (Treasury)
RG 45, Naval Records Collection of the Office of Naval Records and Library
RG 46, Records of the United States Senate
RG 49, Records of the Bureau of Land Management
RG 50, Records of the Treasurer of the United States
RG 56, General Records of the Department of the Treasury
RG 59, General Records of the Department of State
RG 60, General Records of the Department of Justice
RG 75, Records of the Bureau of Indian Affairs
RG 76, Records of Boundary and Claims Commissions and Arbitrations
RG 77, Records of the Office of the Chief of Engineers
RG 84, Records of the Foreign Service Posts of the Department of State
RG 92, Records of the Office of the Quartermaster General
RG 94, Records of the Adjutant General's Office
RG 99, Records of the Office of the Paymaster General
RG 107, Records of the Office of the Secretary of War
RG 108, Records of the Headquarters of the Army
RG 125, Records of the Office of the Judge Advocate General (Navy)
RG 127, Records of the United States Marine Corps

	RG 153, Records of the Office of the Judge Advocate General (Army)
	RG 156, Records of the Office of the Chief of Ordnance
	RG 192, Records of the Office of the Commissary General of Subsistence
	RG 206, Records of the Solicitor of the Treasury
	RG 217, Records of the Accounting Officers of the Department of the Treasury
	RG 233, Records of the United States House of Representatives
F	Florida State Library, Tallahassee
FPeE	Escambia County Historical Documents Section, Pensacola, Fla.
G-Ar	Georgia State Department of Archives and History, Atlanta
ICHi	Chicago Historical Society, Chicago, Ill.
InHi	Indiana Historical Society, Indianapolis
InU	Indiana University, Bloomington
KyLoF	Filson Club, Louisville, Ky.
KyU	University of Kentucky, Lexington
LNT	Tulane University, New Orleans, La.
LU	Louisiana State University, Baton Rouge
MA	Amherst College, Amherst, Mass.
MB	Boston Public Library, Boston, Mass.
MdHi	Maryland Historical Society, Baltimore
MH-H	Houghton Library, Harvard University, Cambridge, Mass.
MHi	Massachusetts Historical Society, Boston
MLexM	Museum of Our National Heritage, Lexington, Mass.
MNS	Smith College, Northampton, Mass.
MoSM	St. Louis Mercantile Library Association, St. Louis, Mo.
NBuHi	Buffalo and Erie County Historical Society, Buffalo, N.Y.
Nc-Ar	North Carolina Office of Archives and History, Raleigh, N.C.
NcD	Duke University, Durham, N.C.
NcU	University of North Carolina, Chapel Hill
Nh-Ar	New Hampshire Department of Administration and Control, Division of Archives and Records Management, Concord
NHi	New-York Historical Society, New York, N.Y.
NIC	Cornell University, Ithaca, N.Y.
NjMoHP	Morristown National Historical Park, Morristown, N.J.
NjP	Princeton University, Princeton, N.J.
NjR	Rutgers University Libraries, New Brunswick, N.J.
NN	New York Public Library, New York, N.Y.
NNMu	New York Municipal Archives, N.Y.

NNPM	Pierpont Morgan Library, New York, N.Y.
NPV	Vassar College, Poughkeepsie, N.Y.
OCHP	Cincinnati Historical Society, Cincinnati, Ohio
OClWHi	Western Reserve Historical Society, Cleveland, Ohio
OkTG	Thomas Gilcrease Institute of American History and Art, Tulsa, Okla.
PHi	Historical Society of Pennsylvania, Philadelphia
PPAmP	American Philosophical Society, Philadelphia, Pa.
PPPrHi	Presbyterian Historical Society, Philadelphia, Pa.
PPRF	Rosenbach Foundation, Philadelphia, Pa.
PPT	Temple University, Philadelphia, Pa.
PSt	Pennsylvania State University, University Park
PU	University of Pennsylvania, Philadelphia
PWbW	Wilkes College, Wilkes-Barre, Pa.
RP	Providence Public Library, Providence, R.I.
ScCleU	Clemson University, Clemson, S.C.
ScLan	Lancaster County Library, Lancaster, S.C.
ScU	University of South Carolina, Columbia
T	Tennessee State Library and Archives, Nashville
THer	Ladies' Hermitage Association, Hermitage, Tenn.
THi	Tennessee Historical Society, Nashville
TNDa	Davidson County Archives, Davidson County Court, Nashville, Tenn.
TNJ	Vanderbilt University, Nashville, Tenn.
TU	University of Tennessee, Knoxville
TxU	University of Texas, Austin
UkLPR	Public Record Office, London
UkOxU-As	Oxford University, All Soul's College, Oxford, England
ViHi	Virginia Historical Society, Richmond
ViNC	Chrysler Art Museum, Jean Outland Chrysler Library, Norfolk, Va.
ViW	College of William and Mary, Williamsburg, Va.
WHi	State Historical Society of Wisconsin, Madison

MICROFILM SERIES

Microfilm citations (in parentheses) are of four types:

37	The Library of Congress Andrew Jackson Papers microfilm, listed by reel number (reel 37). For contents of reels cited in this volume, see below.
M179-67 or T967-2	National Archives microfilms, listed by publication series and reel number (series M179, reel 67, or series T967, reel 2). For series titles cited in this volume, see below.
12-1456	*The Papers of Andrew Jackson* Microfilm Supplement, listed by reel and frame number (reel 12, frame 1456).
mAJs	Items acquired since 1987 and therefore not included on the Library of Congress, National Archives, or project microfilms. These will be collected in a microfilm or electronic addendum at the project's conclusion.

Library of Congress Andrew Jackson Papers Reels, 1829

36–38	General correspondence
60	Letterbook
64	Memorandum book
72	Correspondence
75	Correspondence, including a volume of copied letters regarding the Eaton affair
76	Presidential message drafts
78	Bank and record books

National Archives Microfilms

M6	RG 107: Letters Sent by the Secretary of War Relating to Military Affairs, 1800–1889
M21	RG 75: Letters Sent by the Office of Indian Affairs, 1824–81
M22	RG 107: Registers of Letters Received by the Office of the Secretary of War, Main Series, 1800–1870
M23	RG 59: Despatches from U.S. Consuls in Algiers, Algeria, 1785–1906
M25	RG 49: Miscellaneous Letters Sent by the General Land Office, 1796–1889

M27	RG 49: Letters Sent by the General Land Office to the Surveyor General, 1796–1901
M30	RG 59: Despatches from U.S. Ministers to Great Britain, 1791–1906
M34	RG 59: Despatches from U.S. Ministers to France, 1789–1906
M38	RG 59: Notes to Foreign Ministers and Consuls in the United States from the Department of State, 1793–1834
M40	RG 59: Domestic Letters of the Department of State, 1784–1906
M46	RG 59: Despatches from U.S. Ministers to Turkey, 1818–1906
M49	RG 59: Notes From the Brazilian Legation in the United States to the Department of State, 1824–1906
M54	RG 59: Notes From the Mexican Legation in the United States to the Department of State, 1821–1906
M60	RG 59: Notes From the Swedish Legation in the United States to the Department of State, 1813–1906
M65	RG 77: Letters Sent by the Office of the Chief of Engineers Relating to Internal Improvements, 1824–30
M73	RG 59: Notes From the Chilean Legation in the United States to the Department of State, 1811–1906
M77	RG 59: Diplomatic Instructions of the Department of State, 1801–1906
M78	RG 59: Consular Instructions of the Department of State, 1801–34
M97	RG 59: Despatches from U.S. Ministers to Mexico, 1823–1906
M124	RG 45: Letters Received by the Secretary of the Navy: Miscellaneous Letters, 1801–84
M125	RG 45: Letters Received by the Secretary of the Navy: Captains' Letters, 1805–61
M127	RG 107: Letters Sent to the President by the Secretary of War, 1800–1863
M149	RG 45: Letters Sent by the Secretary of the Navy to Officers, 1798–1868
M175	RG 56: Letters Sent by the Secretary of the Treasury to Collectors of Customs at All Ports, 1789–1847
M178	RG 56: Correspondence of the Secretary of the Treasury with Collectors of Customs, 1789–1833
M179	RG 59: Miscellaneous Letters of the Department of State, 1789–1906
M205	RG 45: Correspondence of the Secretary of the Navy Relating to African Colonization, 1819–44

M209	RG 45: Miscellaneous Letters Sent by the Secretary of the Navy, 1798–1886
M221	RG 107: Letters Received by the Secretary of War, Registered Series, 1801–70
M222	RG 107: Letters Received by the Secretary of War, Unregistered Series, 1789–1861
M234	RG 75: Letters Received by the Office of Indian Affairs, 1824–81
M235	RG 217: Miscellaneous Treasury Accounts of the First Auditor (Formerly the Auditor) of the Treasury Department, 1790–1840
M273	RG 125: Records of General Courts-Martial and Courts of Inquiry of the Navy Department, 1799–1867
M472	RG 45: Letters Sent by the Secretary of the Navy to the President and Executive Agencies, 1821–86
M531	RG 59: Letters of Application and Recommendation During the Administration of John Quincy Adams, 1825–29
M565	RG 94: Letters Sent by the Office of the Adjutant General (Main Series), 1800–1890
M567	RG 94: Letters Received by the Office of the Adjutant General (Main Series), 1822–60
M625	RG 45: Area File of the Naval Records Collection, 1775–1910
M639	RG 59: Letters of Application and Recommendation During the Administration of Andrew Jackson, 1829–37
M664	RG 59: Notes From Foreign Consuls in the United States to the Department of State, 1789–1906
M688	RG 94: U. S. Military Academy Cadet Application Papers, 1805–66
M699	RG 60: Letters Sent by the Department of Justice: General and Miscellaneous, 1818–1904
M733	RG 56: Letters Sent by the Secretary of the Treasury Relating to Public Lands ('N' Series), 1801–78
M735	RG 56: Circular Letters of the Secretary of the Treasury ('T' Series), 1789–1878
M800	RG 59: Reports of Clerks and Bureau Officers of the Department of State, 1790–1911
M857	RG 108: Letters Sent by the Headquarters of the Army (Main Series), 1828–1903
M873	RG 59: Letters of Application and Recommendation During the Administrations of James Polk, Zachary Taylor, and Millard Fillmore, 1845–53

M1329	RG 49: Letters Received by the Secretary of the Treasury and the General Land Office from the Surveyor General for Mississippi, 1803–31
T33	RG 59: Despatches From U.S. Ministers to Colombia, 1820–1906
T61	RG 59: Despatches From U.S. Consuls in Tangier, Morocco, 1797–1906
T181	RG 59: Despatches From U.S. Consuls in Antwerp, Belgium, 1802–1906
T229	RG 59: Despatches From U.S. Consuls in Puerto Cabello, Venezuela, 1823–1906
T238	RG 59: Despatches From U.S. Consuls in Smyrna, Turkey, 1802–1906
T412	RG 60: Opinions of the Attorney General, 1817–32
T494	RG 75: Documents Relating to the Negotiation of Ratified and Unratified Treaties With Various Indian Tribes, 1801–69
T967	RG 59: Copies of Presidential Pardons and Remissions, 1794–1893
T1223	RG 59: Presidential Proclamations 1–2160, 1789–1936

PUBLICATION SHORT TITLES

Bassett	John Spencer Bassett, ed., *Correspondence of Andrew Jackson.* 7 vols. Washington, D.C., 1926–35.
Burke	Pauline Wilcox Burke, *Emily Donelson of Tennessee.* 2 vols. Richmond, Va., 1941.
Calhoun Papers	W. Edwin Hemphill and Clyde N. Wilson, eds., *The Papers of John C. Calhoun.* 28 vols. Columbia, S.C., 1959–2003.
Clay Papers	James F. Hopkins et al., eds., *The Papers of Henry Clay.* 11 vols. Lexington, Ky., 1959–92.
Hamilton *Reminiscences*	*Reminiscences of James A. Hamilton.* New York, 1869.
Heiskell	Samuel G. Heiskell, *Andrew Jackson and Early Tennessee History.* 3 vols. Nashville, Tenn., 1920–21.
HRDoc	U.S. Congress, House of Representatives, *House Documents.*
HRRep	U.S. Congress, House of Representatives, *House Reports.*

Jackson Papers	Harold D. Moser et al., eds., *The Papers of Andrew Jackson.* 7 vols. to date. Knoxville, Tenn., 1980–.
John Ross Papers	Gary E. Moulton, ed., *The Papers of Chief John Ross.* 2 vols. Norman, Okla., 1985.
Nat. Intelligencer	Washington, D.C., *Daily National Intelligencer.*
Niles	*Niles' Weekly Register.*
Papers of George Washington	Philander D. Chase, ed., *The Papers of George Washington: Revolutionary War Series.* 16 vols. to date. Charlottesville, Va., 1985–.
Parton	James Parton, *Life of Andrew Jackson.* 3 vols. New York, 1860.
Polk Correspondence	Herbert Weaver, Paul H. Bergeron, and Wayne Cutler, eds., *Correspondence of James K. Polk.* 10 vols. to date. Nashville and Knoxville, Tenn., 1969–.
Register of Debates	U.S. Congress, *Register of Debates in Congress.* 14 vols. Washington, D.C., 1825–37.
Richardson	James D. Richardson, ed., *A Compilation of the Messages and Papers of the Presidents, 1789–1897.* 10 vols. Washington, D.C., 1896–99.
SDoc	U.S. Congress, Senate, *Senate Documents.*
Senate Executive Proceedings	*Journal of the Executive Proceedings of the Senate of the United States of America.*
TPUS	Clarence E. Carter and John Porter Bloom, eds., *The Territorial Papers of the United States.* 28 vols. Washington, D.C., 1934–75.
US Telegraph	Washington, D.C., *United States' Telegraph.*
Van Buren Autobiography	John C. Fitzpatrick, ed., *The Autobiography of Martin Van Buren.* Washington, 1920.
Writings of Sam Houston	Amelia W. Williams and Eugene C. Barker, eds., *The Writings of Sam Houston, 1813–1863.* 8 vols. Austin, Texas, 1934–75.

Lists and Tables

1829 CHRONOLOGY

Jan 1 — Senator John H. Eaton of Tennessee marries the recently widowed Margaret (Peggy) O'Neale Timberlake

Jan 18 — Jackson departs Nashville for Washington

Feb 11 — Jackson arrives in Washington. Congress tallies the electoral vote for president, making his election official

Feb 26 — *United States' Telegraph* announces Jackson's Cabinet

Mar 4 — Jackson is inaugurated as seventh president. Senate convenes in special executive session to receive nominations

Mar 6 — Jackson nominates John McLean for the Supreme Court and Martin Van Buren and Samuel D. Ingham for the State and Treasury departments

Mar 9 — Jackson nominates the remainder of his Cabinet; all are confirmed

Mar 12 — Van Buren resigns as New York governor to become Secretary of State

Mar 17 — Senate adjourns

Mar 18 — Ezra Stiles Ely writes Jackson charging Margaret Eaton with promiscuity; Jackson responds March 23

Mar 21 — Jackson replaces Treasury officers William Lee, Richard Cutts, and Tobias Watkins with William B. Lewis, Isaac Hill, and Amos Kendall

Mar 23 — Jackson addresses the Creeks, urging their assent to removal. Eaton similarly addresses Cherokees on April 18

Apr 6 — Jackson meets with the diplomatic corps at Washington

Apr 16 — Samuel Houston resigns as governor of Tennessee

Apr 24 — Jackson appoints Samuel Swartwout customs collector at New York City

Apr 30	Tobias Watkins is arrested in Philadelphia for embezzlement
July 8–14	Jackson visits Fortress Monroe, Norfolk, and Portsmouth, Va.
July 22	Jackson leaves Washington to visit elder statesman Charles Carroll in Maryland, returning July 25
July 29	Chippewa, Ottawa, and Potawatomi delegations sign a land cession treaty at Prairie du Chien; a Winnebago treaty follows August 1
Aug 12	Louis McLane and William C. Rives, Jackson's ministers to Britain and France, depart New York City on the *Constellation*
Aug 14	Tobias Watkins, convicted in federal court, is sentenced to nine months in prison
Aug 19	Jackson leaves Washington to vacation at the Rip Raps, returning September 1
Aug 25	Secretary of State Van Buren instructs minister to Mexico Joel R. Poinsett to initiate negotiations for the purchase of Texas
Sept 1	Presbyterian minister John N. Campbell reveals himself to Jackson as the source of information against Mrs. Eaton
Sept 3	Jackson further interviews Campbell in presence of Andrew J. Donelson and Nathan Towson
Sept 10	Jackson confronts Campbell before his entire Cabinet (except Eaton), Donelson, and Ely
Sept 16	Jackson offers John Randolph the mission to Russia
Oct 4	Jackson appoints John Coffee to determine the historic Creek-Cherokee boundary line in Georgia, disputed between the Cherokees and the state
Oct 16	Tennessee legislature elects Felix Grundy to replace Eaton as U.S. Senator
Oct 17	Jackson recalls Joel Poinsett and appoints Anthony Butler chargé d'affaires to Mexico
Nov 15	Bank of the United States president Nicholas Biddle presents a plan to expedite payment of the national debt
Nov	Jackson collects advice on an alternative to the Bank of the United States
Dec 7	Twenty-first Congress convenes in first regular session
Dec 8	Jackson sends his first annual message to Congress

JACKSON'S PRESIDENTIAL PUBLIC PAPERS, 1829

DATE	DOCUMENT TYPE	RECIPIENT	RICHARD-SON[1]	*JEPS*[2]	SERIAL SET[3]	*PAJ*[4]
Mar 2	Letter	John C. Calhoun	436			
Mar 4	Inaugural Address		436–38			74–79
Mar 6	Nomination	Senate	439	6		
Mar 6	Nomination	Senate		6		
Mar 6	Treaty	Senate	439	7		
Mar 9	Nomination	Senate		8		
Mar 9	Nomination	Senate		8		
Mar 9	Nomination	Senate		8		
Mar 9	Nomination	Senate		9		
Mar 10	Nomination	Senate		10–12		
Mar 10	Nomination	Senate		13		
Mar 11	Nomination	Senate		12–13		
Mar 11	Nomination	Senate	439	13–14		
Mar 11	Nomination	Senate		14–15		
Mar 11	Nomination	Senate		15–16		
Mar 12	Nomination	Senate		18–19		
Mar 12	Nomination	Senate		19		
Mar 12	Nomination	Senate		20		
Mar 12	Nomination	Senate		20		
Mar 12	Nomination	Senate		20		
Mar 12	Nomination	Senate		20		
Mar 12	Nomination	Senate		22		
Mar 13	Nomination	Senate		22		
Mar 14	Nomination	Senate		24		
Apr 8	Executive Order		442			
May 11	Proclamation		440			
Jun 3	Proclamation		441–42			
Dec 8	First Annual Message	Congress	442–62		*SDoc* 1, Serial 192	601–30
Dec 14	Nomination	Senate		28		
Dec 14	Message	Senate	463	28		

DATE	DOCUMENT TYPE	RECIPIENT	RICHARD-SON[1]	JEPS[2]	SERIAL SET[3]	PAJ[4]
Dec 14	Treaty	Senate	463	28		
Dec 14	Nomination	Senate		29		
Dec 15	Message	House	463			637–38
Dec 15	Nomination	Senate		29		
Dec 15	Message	House	464		HRDoc 7, Serial 195	
Dec 22	Treaty	Senate	464	30		
Dec 29	Treaty	Senate	464	30		
Dec 30	Message	House	464			
Dec 30	Nomination	Senate		31–32		
Dec 31	Nomination	Senate		33–34		
Dec 31	Nomination	Senate		34		
Dec 31	Nomination	Senate		34–35		

1. Page numbers in vol. 2 of James D. Richardson, ed., *A Compilation of the Messages and Papers of the Presidents, 1789–1897* (Washington: Government Printing Office, 1896), House Miscellaneous Document 210, 53d Cong., 2d sess., Serial 3265.

2. Page numbers in vol. 4 of *Journal of the Executive Proceedings of the Senate of the United States of America* (Washington: Government Printing Office, 1887).

3. House and Senate documents of the 21st Congress, first session.

4. Page numbers for drafts printed in this volume of *The Papers of Andrew Jackson*.

The Papers, 1829

PRINCIPAL CHARACTERS OF
JACKSON'S FIRST PRESIDENTIAL YEAR

The Cabinet

Secretary of State Martin Van Buren, of New York
Secretary of the Treasury Samuel Delucenna Ingham, of Pennsylvania
Secretary of War John Henry Eaton, of Tennessee
Secretary of the Navy John Branch, of North Carolina
Attorney General John Macpherson Berrien, of Georgia
Postmaster General William Taylor Barry, of Kentucky

In Washington

Vice President John Caldwell Calhoun, of South Carolina
John Nicholson Campbell, minister of the Second Presbyterian Church
Margaret O'Neale Timberlake Eaton, wife of the Secretary of War
George Graham, Commissioner of the General Land Office
Duff Green, editor and publisher of the *United States' Telegraph*
James Alexander Hamilton, adviser and interim Secretary of State
Isaac Hill, Second Comptroller of the Treasury
Amos Kendall, Fourth Auditor of the Treasury
William Berkeley Lewis, Second Auditor of the Treasury
Thomas Loraine McKenney, Superintendent of Indian Affairs

Family

Andrew Jackson, Jr., Jackson's adopted son
Andrew Jackson Donelson, Jackson's nephew and private secretary, and
    his wife and cousin—
Emily Tennessee Donelson, Jackson's niece and White House hostess
Samuel Jackson Hays, Jackson's nephew
Andrew Jackson Hutchings, Jackson's grandnephew and ward

Confidants

Richard Keith Call, of Florida, former comrade-in-arms
John Coffee, of Alabama, former comrade-in-arms
Hardy Murfree Cryer, near the Hermitage
Reverend Ezra Stiles Ely, in Philadelphia
Samuel Houston, governor of Tennessee
Charles Jones Love, near the Hermitage
John Christmas McLemore, in Nashville

January

Andrew Jackson handily defeated incumbent John Quincy Adams (1767–1848) in the presidential election of 1828. Jackson and his wife Rachel (1767–1828) received the news at their Hermitage plantation home outside Nashville. On December 18, Rachel suddenly fell ill. She died four days later. The year 1829 began with Jackson mourning Rachel while preparing to assume his post as the seventh president of the United States.

Jackson departed from Nashville on Sunday, January 18. He traveled by steamboat to Louisville and Pittsburgh, then by carriage overland to Washington. He was accompanied by his late wife's nephew and niece: Andrew Jackson Donelson (1799–1871), son of Rachel's brother Samuel Donelson; and Andrew's wife and first cousin Emily Tennessee Donelson (1807–36), daughter of Rachel's brother John Donelson. The couple would live with Jackson in the White House, with Andrew serving as the president's private secretary and Emily as official hostess.

To Francis Preston Blair, Preston Samuel Loughborough, and Charles Scott Bibb

HERMITAGE, Jan. 1st, 1829.

GENTLEMEN:

I had the honor to receive, through Mr. Campbell, on the 30th December, the letter of "congratulation and invitation," which, as the organ of the Central Jackson Committee, you addressed to me on the 5th of that month: and I beg you to accept my thanks for your kind and flattering expressions.[1]

Were my heart susceptible of other emotions, than those with which a recent calamity has filled it, I should be very unwilling to forego the proud and peculiar satisfaction of exchanging salutations with my fellow-citizens of Kentucky, and of participating in the celebration of the 8th of January, at the metropolis of a State whose valor and patriotism signalized that day.[2]

But, for me, the present season is sacred to sorrow, and that which approaches must be devoted to duties, justly represented by yourselves, as complex, delicate and arduous. Concurring with my private feelings, for the mention of which their nature must be my apology, they constrain me to decline the honor of meeting at Frankfort your Committee, and our mutual friends; to whom, as well as to yourselves, Gentlemen, I offer the assurance of my best wishes, and grateful consideration. Your obedient servant.

ANDREW JACKSON

Printed, Frankfort *Argus of Western America,* January 28 (mAJs). Blair (1791–1876) was an associate of Amos Kendall on the pro-Jackson *Argus*. He established the *Globe* in Washington in 1830. Loughborough (1802–52) was a Frankfort lawyer who moved to Washington later in the year to work in the General Post Office. Bibb (1801–32) was also a Frankfort lawyer.
    1. Arthur Lee Campbell (1780–1838) had edited the *Louisville Gazette,* a Jackson paper, during the 1828 campaign.
    2. January 8 was the date of AJ's victory at the Battle of New Orleans in 1815.

Bill of Sale of Slaves from James Rucker Donelson

I have this day sold & delivered to Andrew Jackson of the county of Davidson and state of Tennessee, a certain negro woman slave named Candis about twenty five years old, with her child named Betsy, about three years old—& in and for the consideration of four hundred & fifty dollars to me in hand paid, the receipt whereof I hereby acknowledge, do bind myself my heirs &c &c &c, the right title & property of the said negro woman slave & her child Betsy to warrent & defend to the said Andrew Jackson his heirs & assigns forever. Witness my hand & seal the 2nd day of January 1829—

James R. Donelson (seal)

Test   William Donelson
          Stockly Donelson

DS in AJ's hand, DLC (36). The signatories were all Rachel Jackson's nephews. James R. Donelson (1805–29) was the eldest son of her brother Severn Donelson. The two witnesses, William Donelson (1795–1864) and Stockly (or Stockley) Donelson (1805–88), were sons of Rachel's brother John Donelson and his wife Mary Purnell. AJ owned Candis's husband Titus and had listed her with him on his inventory of slaves at the Hermitage in January 1825.

To *Katherine Duane Morgan*

Hermitage January 3d 1828.

Dear Madam.

Your kind letter of the 6th December last, addressed to the dear companion of my bosom, it is my sorrowful task to thank you for. It pleased God to take her from this world on the night of the 22d December, and by this solemn dispensation of his Providence, to deprive me of my stay and solace whilst in it. I bow to the decree, but feel in its afflictive power, how weak are the sentiments of Philosophy without the aid of divine Grace—that grace which enables it to pierce the veil of futurity, and find in the convulsions here, an immortal birth in that *hereafter* where the good unite again, and the wicked "disturb not."

My journey to the Federal city will most probably carry me thro' your Town. In that event, I will not fail to call upon you, and avail myself of the opportunity to manifest more forcibly than I now can, the obligations due to you & Mr Morgan for your kindness to my dear wife, and for the feeling language with which you have pointed to the results of the recent election. Mr & Mrs Donelson will accompany me, and will also feel honored by an opportunity to pay you once more their personal respects.

As the friend & early acquaintance of your Father, be pleased to present me respectfully to him; and accept for Mr Morgan & yourself these assurances of my friendship & esteem. Your Obt & Humble servant

Andrew Jackson

LS in AJ Donelson's hand, OClWHi (12-0438). Morgan (c1787–1855) was the daughter of Philadelphia *Aurora* editor William Duane (1760–1835). Her husband Thomas Morgan (1784–1855) was a lawyer and former state legislator who edited the pro-Jackson *Democratic Eagle* in Washington, Pa.

From *Edward Livingston*

New Orleans 3d. Jany 1829

I write you my dear General to express my own affliction; not with the vain endeavor to alleviate yours. I should be insensible to the worth of your excellent Lady, and ungrateful for the uniform kindness and friendly attention with which she honored me; if I did not feel her loss as a personal misfortune; even if it were possible for me to consider it as unconnected with the operation it must have upon your mind

The common topics of consolation would be on this occasion as much misplaced as they are in others ineffectual. At another period I should have feared the effect which this cruel misfortune might have upon your mind; but now your country in whose defense you have so often risqued your life demands a more difficult exertion of energy. She requires you for her welfare to abandon your just grief, to tear yourself from the indulgence of regrets which would be a virtue in a private individual, but to which you are not permitted to yield while so much of her happiness depends upon your efforts in her service; and she promises you the noblest of all consolations, that which is found in promoting her welfare. While patriotism offers this recompense here, religion holds out the certain hope of a reunion in a better world with her who so faithfully performed its precepts in this. Knowing the force these considerations will have upon your mind, I do not participate in the fears of those, who considering only the magnitude of your loss, apprehend an indulgence of your feelings injurious to the public good and to your private peace

That these and all other effectual consolations may lessen your grief, and a nations prosperity reward your sacrifice of private feelings to promote it is the devout wish of Your Affectionate Friend

Edw Livingston

ALS, DLC–Donelson Papers (12-0435). Livingston (1764–1836), a Louisiana lawyer and congressman, had served as AJ's volunteer aide at New Orleans. He was later his secretary of state.

To *James Ronaldson*

Hermitage January 4th 1829
Dear Sir,
    Your kind letter of the 7th ulto. has been received, and I sincerely thank you for the hints which it contains. They should have been acknowledged earlier, but for the painful situation in which I have been placed by the loss of the dear companion of my bosom, and which yet forces me to decline the agitation of political questions. All that I can now say on this part of your interesting letter, is the expression of my concurrence with you, that the favorable association of my name with the triumphs of the principles involved in the recent contest, is to be ascribed to the partiality of the people—and that the high station to which it has called me must be devoted to their happiness and good. So far as this desireable result can be anticipated from my humble abilities, be assured, they will be dedicated with zeal, and honesty of purpose, to its attainment.

I am gratified to receive your testimony in favour of Mr Duane; and will take it as a favor to be informed of your views in relation to any measures which you may deem useful & proper.

With the assurance of my great regard for your character, I pray you to accept my best wishes for your health & happiness, & believe me yr. very obt. srvt.

Andrew Jackson

LS in AJ Donelson's hand, TNJ (12-0442). Ronaldson (1770–1841) was a Philadelphia manufacturer and philanthropist. His December 7, 1828, letter proposed publicly exposing those men who recommended unfit characters for office. He also recommended William John Duane of Philadelphia (1780–1865), son of *Aurora* editor William Duane, for U.S. attorney in Pennsylvania.

To William Polk

Hermitage January 5th. 1829

Dear Sir,

Your kind letter of November last apprising me of the state of the Polls in the recent election, and your subsequent congratulations on the general result, have been received: I tender you, Sir, my sincere thanks for the favorable language with which you are pleased to anticipate my agency in the future prosperity of our beloved country.

You will have heard how suddenly I have been deprived of the dear companion of my life, before this reaches you. It was a severe stroke—one which leaves me without a solace; but I bow to it with calmness as the decree of divine Providence, by whose grace I trust her gentle spirit is conducted to a better & happier world.

Fully sensible that no words can be a suitable return for the friendly support yielded me by the people of your state, all that I can now say can only be an acknowledgement of my accountability to the high station to which I am called by their free suffrage, and the dedication of my humble abilities to its arduous duties.

As a friend, it will afford me much pleasure to be possessed of your views on any public question which you may deem important to the country. I pray you to present me respectfully to Mr Badger & his lady,[1] & accept for yourself & your amiable family the assurances of my friendship and great regard yr. obt srvt

Andrew Jackson

LS in AJ Donelson's hand, DLC-Polk Family Papers (12-0447). Polk (1758–1834), of Raleigh, was a Revolutionary colonel, a leading North Carolina Jacksonian, and a relation of Tennessee congressman and later president James K. Polk.

1. George Edmund Badger (1795–1866), a Raleigh lawyer and later U.S. senator, had married Polk's daughter Mary Brown Polk (1808–35).

Inventory of Hermitage Slaves and Property

[This inventory, including the last extant full list of Jackson's slaves made during his lifetime, was entered in a Hermitage account book begun in 1817. The ordering of slave households roughly paralleled that of a previous enumeration made in January 1825 for tax purposes (Jackson Papers, 6:3–5). However, these and later partial listings contain many unresolvable discrepancies in slave names, ages, and family relationships.]

The names and ages of the negroes on Andrew Jacksons Farm, Hermitage this 5th of Janry, 1829

	No.
Old Hanah aged about 59 years of age—	1
Her son George aged about 22 years of age	1
Ned & Betty his wife, Ned 28 & Betty 36 years—	2
Alfred, Bettys son, aged about 16—[1]	1
Charles & Charlotte, Charls about 35 & wife=30—	2
Charlottes Children—the first Aggy about 5 years	1
The second Jane about 3 years old. the 3d Maria=1 year[2]	2
Aron & his wife Hanah, Aron about=40, wife=23=	2
Hanah Children, Byron=9— Rachel=5=Charlotte 3=	3
The Last one Moses about=2 years=[3]	1
Tom & wife Molly—Tom about 40=wife, 30. years=	2
Molly children, Camel=22=Isaac=20—Moses=18=	3
The 4ᵈ Canseur=15=Sam=12, Malinda=14=	3
The 7ᵈ William=9=Daniel=6. The last Ben=4=[4]	3
Prissy & family. Prissy=59 children, Grace=20=	2
The second=Littleton=19=Orange=17=Essex=15=	3
The 5ᵈ Anny=13=Nathan=11=Sarah=8=[5]	3
Ben & wife Creasy,=Ben about=35=wife about=30=	2
children=Sally=15=Anaca=12—Eady=8=	3
The 4ᵈ Julius=4—The Last Disa 2=[6]	2

Squire & wife Gincy Squire about=30=wife=18 years=   2
children, the 1st Morgan=4—Betty=2=Agness=about one week old=[7] 3

Alabama Sally & family, Sally about=30 years old=   1
children, John=15—Mary=5—Henry—3 years=   3
The Last one Elizabeth=about 8 months old=   1

Polladore & wife Sally Polladore about=40— wife. 25=   2
children, Adaline=5=Toney=3—Phillip=2=   3
The Last one Prissy about one month old=[8]   1

Aron & wife Mary, Aron about=40. wife. 40=   2
children, Smith about=12. Reuben about. 8=[9]   2

Titus & wife, Candis, Titus about—40 wife= 25=   2
Candis children, only one—Bettsy=2=[10]   1

Sampson & wife Pleasant, Sampson=50, wife=50=   2
children—George=16 years old=[11]   1

Argile & wife Creasy—Argile=35—wife—30=   2
children Eliza=13—William=7—Milly=6=   3
The 4d Lucinda=3. Lewis=2 years old=[12]   2

Jim & wife Hanah, Jim, about=35, wife=30=   2
children—1st Sam=12, Nancy=9, Jim, 6=   3
The Last Poll about=3=years old=[13]   1

I have mentioned Grace on the other side but not her children.
The first is named
Sylva about=5. Franka=3. Dick—2=   3
The Last one named Allen about 1 year—   1

Old Sampson aged about 40 years=   1
Dunwooda aged about=50 years=   1
Old Ned aged about—55 years=   1
Old Penny aged about=50 years=[14]   1

Big Tom aged about 35 years old=[15]   1

Peter & family, Peter aged about=50 years old=	1
His children, Jack=17—Jacob—15. Joe. 13=	3
The Last one Elick about 9 years old=[16]	1

A List of the Stock of horses, mules, cattle Hoggs and Farming utensils, Left on this farm, under the superintendance of Mr. Steele. and in the above statement showing the number of Negroes belonging to the said Farm of Andrew Jackson.

Left, four Brood mares, Six young Colts Two studs. 3 young mules. and 15 work horses. with one mule, which makes—16 in all=And in the 1828 the number of Horned Cattle stood thus= 102, Sheep=145 stock of hoggs=250=Corn cribbed 288 = waggon loads, 5 barrels pr load—which makes 1440 barrels. Pork killed to the ammount of 18,900 pounds. The number of Ploughs stands thus, 14 single Ploughs 8 Double ones, 10 Bull Tongue Ploughs 6 scrapers 3 coulters—Axes 22, weeding hoes 30 Grubbing hoes 11, Iron wedges 7, Mechanics & Plantation tools, one Cross cut Saw 2 frows, 4 Sithe cradles & one blade 4 waggons, 3 spades 19 pieces of Leather in Tan Vat 10 Dry Hides 15 pair of gears 15 single trees 8 pair stretchers 13 clivises 4 log chains 5 cotton wheels, 2 fan wheels 1 loom & gears 1 spining machine, 1 water wagon 2 pair of stilyards 1 pair of ballances 1 glass Lantern.

D, THer (38-0001).

1. AJ bought Old Hannah and her daughter Betty in 1794. They were in succession the Jackson family cooks. Ned was one of five young men purchased for AJ in Portsmouth, Va., in January 1820. Betty's son Alfred (d. 1901) was a longtime family retainer who resided at the Hermitage until his death. George (d. 1865) was AJ's personal servant and accompanied him to Washington.

2. Charles was a carriage driver and AJ's former military servant.

3. Aron (c1785–1878), purchased in 1791, was a blacksmith. Hannah (b. c1801) had been a personal servant to Rachel Jackson and was head of the household staff.

4. Tom and Molly (d. c1846) were field hands.

5. AJ purchased Prissy in 1805.

6. Ben was later identified as caretaker of the plow horses and a ginner, and Creasy as a weaver. Anaca died in 1833.

7. Squire, the son of Old Hannah, had been AJ's military servant. He was later listed as the field foreman, and Gincy as a spinner.

8. AJ had captured the escaped slave Polydore in Florida in 1818, took him into his household, and formally purchased him in 1822. His wife may have been the Sally AJ bought in Washington in 1819.

9. AJ had purchased Aaron, a "half Blacksmith," from Elizabeth R. Donelson in 1823.

10. Titus (d. 1833) was purchased in 1820 in Portsmouth, Va. AJ had just bought Candis and Betsy from James R. Donelson on January 2.

11. Sampson or "Big Sampson" (d. 1833), Pleasant (d. 1847), and their son George (d. 1830) were bought as a family in Mobile in 1814.

12. Argyle was purchased in 1820 in Portsmouth, Va.

13. Jim (d. 1829) had been AJ's military servant and a family messenger. Hannah and Sam may have been a mother and son by that name whom AJ purchased in Mobile in 1814.

14. Old Sampson (c1770–1833), probably bought from the Samuel Donelson estate in 1804, was the gardener at the time of his death. The 1825 inventory listed him as Prissy's husband. Dunwoody (c1770–c1845), whom AJ purchased in 1806 to accompany the horse Truxton, was the trainer of AJ's racing stock. AJ had purchased Penny in 1816.

15. Big Tom was bought in 1820 in Portsmouth.

16. AJ purchased Peter, his wife Rachael (d. 1816), and their infant son Jack in Knoxville in 1810. Jack died in 1829, Joe and Elick in 1830.

From Benjamin Pierce

Hillsborough, N.H. 12th Jan. 1829.

Dear Sir,

Permit me to congratulate you upon the result of the recent Presidential election. Such a decided expression of an intelligent and reflecting people, while it must be flattering to your feelings, will gladden the heart of every patriot. There has indeed been a glorious triumph of principle; and the contest, although it brought along with it much to regret, will undoubtedly be of the greatest service to the country. It will form an epoch in our political history. Those who were on the stage of action at the birth of the Republic, and who cannot expect much longer to witness its rapid advancement, will be animated in their decline with renewed confidence in the permanency of our institutions. The next generation will recur to it as the present does to that of 1800.[1]—I feel a pride in introducing to you the bearer, the Hon. Isaac Hill, because the devotion with which he has ever embraced the cause of the people, and the distinguished aid he has rendered it, entitle him to the consideration of all who love their country: he has not been a "fair weather" politician, always with the dominant party—having early come forth as a decided republican, he has never forfeited that character, but shone most conspicuously at times when a strong arm has most been needed. Possessing an uncommon power for intense and continued application, he has added to the first order of talents untiring industry. As a member of our State Senate he has held a high rank, but has been preeminently dis[tin]guished as editor of one of the ablest political journals of the day, in which capacity he has long officiated, the able and fearless advocate of the Republican cause. Please to accept the assurance of my best wishes: may you long live to enjoy the confidence of a people whom you have served so faithfully.

With sentiments of the highest respect, I have the honor to be your obedient servant,

Benjamin Pierce

Copy in Isaac Hill's hand, DLC (36). Pierce (1757–1839), father of President Franklin Pierce, was governor of New Hampshire, 1827–28 and 1829–30. Hill (1789–1851) was editor of the Concord *New Hampshire Patriot*.

1. In 1800 Thomas Jefferson defeated Federalist incumbent John Adams, father of John Quincy Adams, for president.

Receipts from Ralph Eleazar Whitesides Earl and George Ament

Tomb Stone for Mrs. R. Jackson from Mr Solomon Clark $100
For cutting, lettering frame & putting up to Mr Ement   <u>72.25</u>
                                                              $172.25

Recd. from Andrew Jackson for the use of Mr Solomon Clark, to pay over to Major William B. Lewis, for him as pr contract, one hundred dollars
Hermitage January 17th. 1829 $100
                                                    R. E. W. Earl

Recd. from Andrew Jackson the sum of seventy five dollars twenty five cents, for cutting, lettering, frame, & putting up, tomb stone over Mrs. R. Jacksons grave at the Hermitage, the sum of Seventy two dollars twenty five cents, which is in full for said work—January 17th. 1829—
                                            <u>$ 72.25</u>
                                            $172.25
                                      George Ament

DSs in AJ's hand, DLC (36). Solomon Clark was a Nashville brickmason. Ralph E. W. Earl (1788–1838) and William Berkeley Lewis (1784–1866) were AJ intimates. Earl, widower of Rachel's niece Jane Caffery, was an artist who painted many AJ portraits. Lewis was AJ's political factotum and traveled with him to Washington.

To John Coffee

                                        Hermitage Janry 17th. 1829—
My dear Genl
   I have this day got my dear Mrs. J. Tomb, compleated, and am notified that the Steam Boat will be up tomorrow for me, of course, we will leave here tomorrow evening, or monday morning. Whether I am ever to return or not, is for time to reveal, as none but that providence, who rules the destiny of all, now knows, be this as it may, I leave for you, & your amiable wife & family my sincere prayrs, for your wellfare & happiness in this, & the future world, and as rational beings it behoves us so to live, to be prepared for death when it comes, with a reasonable hope of happiness hereafter through the atonement made by our blessed saviour on the cross.
   I have been trying to wind up all my business before I left the country—but two debts remain unpaid, except what I owe to Nichol & Hill[1]. The two debts are one to the estate of Capt Henry Thompson deceased, for a

horse bought at one hundred & thirty five dollars due on the 25th. day of December last, the other to Albert Ward for a horse imposed upon me for a gentle good conditioned horse, at one hundred & thirty dollars, this is due on the first of March next, tho, when the contract was made I was assured, if inconvenient then to pay he would wait until next fall—now he says he has made engagements & he must have the mony—it is the first & I am sure it will be the last contract I will ever have with him.[2]

Mr. Eastin tells me Mr Griffin was in when he left you, if he has paid the debt he owes me, I wish you to send to Mr William Donelson the amount of the note due Thompsons, which is $135 with interest from 25th. of december last until you forward it, and $130 due Albert Ward, with a request that he pay it over to the Executors of Henry Thompson, to wit, James P. Thompson & take up my note—and to pay $130 to Albert Ward & take up my note. Should the debt due from Griffin not be recovered, I have to request so soon as you make sale of A. J. Hutchings cotton you will remit to Mr William Donelson the amount of the aforesaid two notes with the request above, & when griffins debt is received, place to the credit of the amount sent me the principle & interest so sent. I have promised that this sum will be paid by the first of april next. I am anxious that it be so paid, which will clear me of all claims that can be rightfully set up against me, but that of Hill & Nichol. do my dear Genl attend to this for me.[3]

I never have had time to search over my papers for the Bonds of the commissioners of Florence for the Lotts, I think you have them If you have not sold the Lott please close the contract with the man spoken of, keeping a lien on the lott as security for the consideration mony, and have the debt of Judge Fulton secured by morgage on his Lotts, it will be serving him & securing me.[4]

I inclose you Mr Wm Crawfords note for $400 dollars, due 1st. of May 1828 & 1829[5]—it may be convenient for him next fall to pay one half the debt, if he can it will aid me in meeting Mr Nichols debt—if you find it not in his power, why he must be indulged another year, but the truth is, I owe Mr Nichol & I must pay him next fall, & my expences for the last four years have exausted all my means, & I must begin to collect my debts to enable me to meet mine.

My mind is so disturbed, & I am even now perplexed with company that I can scarcly write, in short my dear friend my heart is nearly broke. I try to summons up my usual fortitude but it is vain, the time, the sudden & afflictive shock, was as severe as unexpected, adieu my dear Genl, and give my love to Polly & all the children, to Capt Jack & Eliza and believe me yr friend

Andrew Jackson

P.S. I shall expect to see you & Mr Earle at the city in the spring. A. J.

ALS, THi (12-0457). Coffee (1772–1833) was perhaps AJ's closest friend. He married Mary ("Polly") Donelson (1793–1871), daughter of Rachel Jackson's brother John, and served with AJ throughout the Creek and Gulf campaigns. John ("Capt Jack") Donelson (1787–1840) and William Eastin (1784–1829) were Coffee's brothers-in-law: Donelson was Mary Coffee's brother, and Eastin was the widower of her sister Rachel. John Donelson's wife Eliza Eleanor (1791–1850) was the daughter of Edward Butler.

1. William Nichol (1800–1878), son of Nashville merchant and banker Josiah Nichol (1772–1833), and Harry Rufus Willie Hill (1797–1853). AJ paid the firm $5,500 on August 4.

2. Henry Thompson (d. 1828) of Wilson County and Albert G. Ward (d. 1840), nephew of AJ's neighbor Edward Ward.

3. William Griffin (c1780–c1839) still owed AJ for the purchase of a slave, George, in 1823. Andrew Jackson Hutchings (1811–41) was AJ's ward, the son of Rachel's nephew and AJ's former business partner John Hutchings. AJ and Coffee were executors of the Hutchings estate. Coffee paid Ward and Thompson on June 1. James P. Thompson was Henry's son.

4. AJ was an original investor in the Cypress Land Company, which founded Florence, Ala., in 1818. He gave Coffee power of attorney to sell his Florence lots on December 30, 1828. William Savin Fulton (1795–1844) had served as AJ's private secretary in the 1818 Seminole campaign. He secured his $400 debt to AJ for Florence property by a trust deed on February 21. AJ appointed him secretary of Arkansas Territory on April 8.

5. William White Crawford was the son of AJ's cousin James Crawford, Jr. His note to AJ was dated January 30, 1827.

To Mary Middleton Rutledge Fogg

Hermitage Janry 17th. 1829

My Dear Madam

I have received by the hand of our mutual friend Mrs McLamore,[1] the inestimable book which you were kind enough to present to me, to console me under my present affliction. I thank you kindly for this precious gift, & receive it as the highest evidence of your friendship, not only for me, but the dear partner & solace of my life, who, providence has taken to that clime where the wicked disturb not, "and the weary are at rest."

Could this world compensate her loss, it might be found in the reflection, that her virtues, her piety & christianity, has ensured her that future happiness, which is promised to the deciples of Christ. The valuable book you have presented teach me, that the feeling of resignation to the dispensation of providence, is only the feeling of despair, when unsupported by his grace—that grace which has taken from me the dear partner of my bosom, and admonishes me by its sudden, solemn, & afflictive influence that I must soon follow her—your invaluable present will aid me in my preparation to unite with her in the realms above never to be seperated.

I pray you to accept my sincere thanks for your kind present, with the assurance of my high respect friendship & esteem

Andrew Jackson

ALS, PHi (12-0461). Fogg (1800–1872) was the wife of Nashville lawyer Francis Brinley Fogg. She had sent AJ an inscribed copy of James Abercrombie, ed., *The Mourner Comforted* (Philadelphia, 1812), a compilation of Christian writings and prayers on the topics of death and mourning.

1. Elizabeth Donelson McLemore (1796–1836) was the daughter of Rachel's brother John Donelson and the wife of Nashville businessman John Christmas McLemore (1790–1864).

Contract with Graves W. Steele

This memorandum of agreement between Andrew Jackson & Andrew J. Donelson of the one part, and Graves Steele of the other part, both of the County of Davidson and State of Tennessee, Witnessth, that the said Andrew Jackson and Andrew J. Donelson have employed the said Steele to oversee their negroes and manage the affairs of their plantations during the year 1829, and as such have placed him in possession of the working tools, the horses & stock of every description, and whatsoever else appertains to the land as necessary to its cultivation and protection, with obligations to bestow upon them the attention & care usually expected from the most faithful, diligent and industrious overseers. And further the said Steele is left in charge of their dwelling houses and the buildings attached to them, and is obligated to devote to them the care necessary to their preservation, and the furniture within them; and to do whatever else the said Andrew Jackson and Andrew J Donelson may point out relating to the correct disposition and management of their interests on their plantations. And in consideration of these services the said Andrew Jackson and Andrew J Donelson are obligated to pay to the said Graves Steele at the end of the year the just and lawful sum of six Hundred dollars.

It is also stipulated by the parties that this agreement is to be continued for four years unless one or the other give notice of his wish to dissolve it, thirty days before the close of the year. It is also stipulated that the Brother of said Steele is to be engaged as assistant in the performance of the duties of overseer, the said Jackson & Donelson charging him nothing for his board.

In testimony whereof the parties have hereunto subscribed their names and affixed their seals this 19th January 1829, having signed duplicates.

Andrew Jackson

Test B. F. Currey

Andrew J. Donelson
Graves Steele

DS in AJ Donelson's hand, DLC-Donelson Papers (12-0463). Steele (d. 1838) served as Hermitage overseer until 1832. His brother was Nathaniel Steele (d. 1838). Benjamin Franklin Currey (d. 1836) was an AJ associate and nephew of former Nashville postmaster Robert B. Currey.

From Charles Coffin

Knoxville Janry. 21. 1829.

Respected Sir,

Among the many feeling addresses pouring in upon you, in condolence for the loss of your amiable and pious companion, I have not the vanity to imagine, that the expression of my own lively sympathies, awakened as they have been by a very distinct and gratifying recollection of the deceased, can administer to you any considerable relief from your desolating experience of bereavement. May the God of all grace and consolation be with you and support you; and give you good hope of spending a blessed eternity with her, after the trying scenes of mortality shall [h]ave passed away forever.

Permit me, however, to remark, that from the time it was made clear, what an overwhelming majority of the American people had called you to the high and responsible office of their first magistrate, I have felt an ardent desire to address you by letter on the great good you might do them, and the inward satisfaction and undying honour you might receive, by setting them, in your elevated sphere of action, the precious example of a conscientious observance of the Lord's day. A general effort is making by American Christians, to rescue the sabbath from profanations which have mournfully abounded. In regard to some desirable changes in the times of business at the Post Offices and in the carrying of the mail, a memorial to Congress goes on to Washington by the next mail from this place; which, in a few days, was more generally signed here, than almost any other public paper is known to have been in so little time.[1] We hope the time is come, when, in a season of national peace, and on the eve of a new administration, the post offices will be closed, and the mail carriers will rest on the sabbath, in consequence of an appropriate law, purging our national code from even the appearance of hostility to the fourth commandment. This, I am aware, may not be postponed long enough for any official aid from you. But probably it did not escape your notice that there were some grievous public breaches of the sabbath on certain occasions by your immediate predecessors which pained the hearts of all pious people;[2] and tended powerfully to break down in our country that holy reverence for the sacred day, which, more than all civil law, sustains our liberties; and which could no sooner disappear, than the curse of the God of nations would make us feel to the quick. There are many prayers, that your example may be of an opposite character. Your respect for the institutions and ministers of religion I had an early opportunity to know and prize, and I calculate on your having the moral courage, at the head of the nation, to act it out in your own conduct. It will assist you in this momentous duty, to refresh your mind with the contents of the 17. &

18. chapters of Jeremiah; and to observe anew, how certainly the curse of God will afflict a sabbath-breaking nation, and how certainly his blessing will prosper a nation that hallows the day which he has set apart for his own honour and the spiritual welfare of mankind. The public enticements and entanglements which already begin to surround you will easily and inoffensively be got over by a seasonable & uniform plan; but in no other way. Let it be silently resolved in your own mind, with your wonted firmness, that you will decline receiving congratulatory addresses, public dinners and attentions on the Lord's day; and the least hint delicately communicated, however informally, by a judicious friend, will always be sufficient for one day's postponement, or anticipation. Begin your journey in proper season for the execution of this plan, and you will have no further difficulty. Should you be the happy example to a whole nation of keeping the sabbath, as the Lord's day, instead of making it a day of journeying, of visiting national ships, of receiving political and civil honours, and of preconcerted meetings for distinguished conviviality, you will exert an indescribable influence to reform the morals and perpetuate the prosperity of this extensive people. You will in this way give much animation, concert and effect to the prayers of Christians, that your civil admin*[istration]* may prove a still greater blessing to your beloved *[country for]* which you have so willingly and so often risqued *[your life]*, than your high, successful & far-famed military command has been. I may be permitted to add, that to a less intrepid spirit I might have urged, that the weeping remembrance of a Christian companion, just gone to heaven, is reason enough to a thinking community for claiming uninterrupted sabbaths; but I shall not be forbidden to say to you, that the sabbath's peculiar privileges, for your aid in following her along the sacred path to the skies, can never be exchanged, without inconceivable loss, for all that earth can present.

You will be sufficiently aware, that there is nothing of politics in the design of this letter. My office, as a minister of Christ, and as president of a literary institution, has for years induced me, to know no party but my country, and no patron but my God.

Yet in the undissembled friendship, which our former acquaintance guarantees, I congratulate you on your past usefulness, and pray heaven that your greatest usefulness may be yet to come. Most respectfully yours,

Charles Coffin.

ALS, DLC (36). Coffin (1775–1853) was a Presbyterian minister and president of East Tennessee College (later the University of Tennessee), 1827–32.

1. The Knox County memorial, a printed form with eighty-five signatures, urged a cessation of all postal operations on the Sabbath (DNA-RG 233). Tennessee congressman Pryor Lea submitted it to the House on February 9. A Senate committee chaired by Richard M. Johnson on January 19 and a House committee on February 3 had already reported unfavorably. No legislation ensued.

2. John Quincy Adams had been criticized in the press for traveling on the Sabbath.

From Thomas Gillespie

Xenia Ohio January 26th. 1829

Dr Sir,

The bearer Colo. Watson a member of the central Jackson committee of the District of Columbia arrived in this place yesterday on his way from Columbus to Cincinati, there to perform a special trust, confided to him by the Republican members of the Legislature of Ohio and Citizens of Columbus—but on his arrival in Xenia had the mortification to hear you left Cincinati for Wheeling; he therefore, was under the painful necessity of returning to Columbus, without haveing the pleasure of seeing you or performing the important trust, assingned him.

I have seen with pleasure the recommendation of Jeremiah McClene Secretary of the state of Ohio and the Republican Senators, and other citizens in favour of Colo. Watson for Governor of the Territory of Huron.[1] From what I have seen and heard of Colo Watson and his activity in our late Presidential Canvass, I most Cheerfully cooperate in lending my mite in recommending him to you for that appointment. We have had a severe campaign. But a Glorious victory not inferior to that of New Orleans. I have a few days since returned from Washington City, where I had the pleasure of delivering to the Vice President the sixteen votes of Ohio. Need I say to you that it was (Politically speaking) the proudest hour of my life. As early as March 1824 I set myself up as a target to be shot at by every aristocratic paltroon in the state of Ohio by offering myself puclickly in a news paper published in this place as a candidate for Elector of President and vice President of the United States. I was defeated by a small majority in the first, but succeeded in the second Canvass. It is my deliberate opinion that our political friends if found capable should fill the most important Offices in the gift of the Executive and on this account I would particularly recommend Colo. Watson to your special notice.

And my Dear Genl. while I have the pleasure of Congratulating you on the splendid Majority in your favor for Chief Magistrate—allow me the priviledge of Condoling with you on your late bereavement. I am with due esteem your friend

Thomas Gillespie
one of the Electors of Ohio and late
messenger to Washington City

ALS, DNA-RG 59 (M639-25). Gillespie (1776–1856) was on the Ohio slate of Jackson electors in 1824, when Henry Clay carried the state, and in 1828. AJ appointed him register of the land office at Tiffin in 1830. Joseph Watson (1772–1836) operated a land agency and was a member of the Jackson Central Committee in Washington, D.C.

1. Jeremiah McLene (1767–1837) was Ohio secretary of state, 1808–31, and later congressman, 1833–37. The bill to establish Huron Territory passed the House in January, but not the Senate. In March Watson was appointed inspector of the land offices in Ohio and Michigan.

From Ingoldsby Work Crawford

Union (Conn.) January 27, 1829.

Sir,

A citizen of Connecticut who has never had the honor of your personal acquaintance, but who has long cherished sentiments of admiration for your talents, and of gratitude for your public services, would offer his humble congratulations on your recent election to the highest office in the gift of a free people. He hopes and believes that this event will tend to correct many abuses in the administration of the government, and will impart new vigor to its republican principles. To produce these results with the more ease, it is presumed that some of the friends of the President elect in this State will be placed in such official stations as will enable them most effectually to cooperate in those measures which may be adopted to promote the general welfare.

We desire not the removal of any man from office merely for his having prefered an unsuccessful candidate for the Presidency, or for his having honestly exercised his own rights of opinion, without invading the equal rights of others; but we do hope that we shall be delivered from the tyranny of those officers who have made their own temporary personal interest the sole object of their ambition, and who have prostituted their official influence to the vile purpose of traducing the characters, disturbing the domestic repose, and crushing the honorable hopes of every man who had too much patriotism and firmness to fall down and worship the image which they had set up. We trust that the offices which have been so abused will be transfered to worthier hands.

Impressed with these feelings, Sir, I would respectfully recommend Asa Child Esqr. of Norwich as a suitable Candidate for the office of Attorney for the District of Connecticut. He is a man of distinguished talents, liberally educated, and regularly bred to the profession of the law. His diligence and faithfulness in business are unquestioned. He is now in the prime and vigor of life. He has been open, bold and zealous in his exertions for the election to the Presidency of "the man who had filled the measure of his Country's glory"[1]—and on that account he has had his share in the common sufferings here. His appointment to the office named would be very grateful to the feelings of his numerous friends, and would add a powerful support to the government.

For the office of Collector of customs at the port of New Haven it is presumed there will be several Candidates. A very worthy and respectable one is William H. Ellis Esqr. the present surveyor. He is a genuine republican without guile. He hazarded the loss of office by his early and persevering opposition to the measures of Mr. Clay and his partisans. He is extensively known and beloved—is well acquainted with the duties of Collector—and would undoubtedly execute them with perfect fidelity, and to the full satisfaction of the public.

Devoutly imploring the Supreme Ruler of the universe that your future days may be as happy as your past ones have been glorious, I am, with the highest considerations of respect, your Excellency's most obedient servant.

Ingoldsby Work Crawford.

ALS, LU (mAJs). Crawford (1786–1867) presided over Connecticut's Jackson state convention and was a Jackson candidate for elector in 1828. In 1831 AJ appointed him customs collector at New London. AJ appointed William H. Ellis as New Haven customs collector and Asa Child (1798–1858) as district attorney for Connecticut.

1. The phrase, often invoked in the 1828 campaign, derived from Thomas Jefferson's toast to AJ at Lynchburg, Va., in November 1815: "Honor and gratitude to those who have filled the measure of their country's honor."

From Ezra Stiles Ely

Philadelphia Jan. 28th. 1829.

My Dear & Honoured Sir,

You will impute, I hope, the liberty which I take in writing to you, to my strong attachment to you, and the earnest desire of my heart that you may prove the best President who ever acted as Chief Magistrate of our nation. My principal design at present is to give you the copy of a letter which I have to-day received from the Rev. Lyman Beecher, D. D. of Boston, the most distinguished divine at present living in Massachusetts, if not in New England: from which you will learn the sentiments of many of the thousands of your friends, & of your countrymen who wish you the highest honour, usefulness, & happiness in your exalted station. I feel confident that both your sense of duty & your desire to gratify a numerous class of your firm supporters, would prevent you from publicly travelling on the Lord's day, *except in a case of mercy or necessity*. If ascending a river in a boat, you would of course, & with propriety, proceed in it; but when on land, if the stage of Monday would carry you in season to the place of destination, I feel confident that you would set an example of resting on the day previous. You are not ignorant of the effect produced by the needless excursion of Mr. Adams, and that will explain to you the letter which follows.

copy. "Boston Jan. 20. 1829.

"Rev. Dr. Ely,–Brother,

A fear has been expressed here that as Genl. Jackson sets out for Congress only till after notified officially of his election, he may be tempted, inadvertently, to ride on the sabbath, at a time when it might injure both us & him greatly: and as you have seen & corresponded with him, I was requested to suggest to you our wish that you would write a line to the General, and put him on his guard in this thing: for as *Nobody*, almost, loved his predecessor, or regrets the election of Jackson, and all seem to be prepared to give him a candid trial, he possesses a fine opportunity by a virtuous & independent example to secure the confidence & affection of all the friends of virtue in the nation. If nothing happens to prevent, I should apprehend that he may become one of the most popular men who have set at helm, and a great blessing to the civil & religious interests of the nation. He possesses a noble opportunity to distinguish himself as a patriot and friend of good men, and not the head of a party. I am affectionately yours,

Lyman Beecher."

This coming from Boston, & one of the most influential men in it, deserves regard; & I rejoice to know that New England will yet be as well pleased with the Patriarch of the Hermitage, as with any former President. We do not wish, dear & honoured Sir, to seem to prescribe your course of conduct. We are not bigots, but believe "the sabbath was made for man, & not man for the sabbath."[1] I have travelled on that day, & expect to do it again, when duty calls; but the papers, unhappily in this instance, *publish* the arrivals of our great men, & do not give the religious public the reasons for their journeying on the sabbath, although they might in some cases be satisfactory to the strictest moralist. It was lately published that Mr. Calhoun arrived, for instance, in Washington on the sabbath, and it created a prejudice against him immediately in many of our citizens.[2] On this subject I need say no more, for I expect this letter will not reach you until you will have arrived in W. I send it to the Hermitage because Dr. Beecher seems to think, with many others, that you will not leave home until the 20th of Feb. next.

Something of the public voice may be learned from the numerous & most respectable petitions which have lately been sent to Congress on the subject of transporting the mail on the sabbath in the time of peace. I saw one in Albany lately subscribed by 7000 names. We do not wish any national legislation about any holy days or religious matters; but merely that our Government should not instruct their agents to violate the sabbath, [and] set an ungodly example in this matter. [No] civil laws should enforce the religious [obs]ervance of any day; and at the same time no Christian ruler of a Christian people should do violence to his own professed, personal principles. This I say again, I am confident you will not do.

My wife sends her kind regards to you, and says that she shall feel little interest in W. since the death of your beloved companion. Many who love you, will still regard W. much as you will; as a place of pilgrimage. Old Mrs. Calhoun, the mother-in-law of the Vice President will miss your dear wife more than any one there. She said that she would spend another winter there if you should become President, "that she might see a President who would go to church." When I was there a few years since, several said to me, "Genl. Jackson & Mrs. Colhoun are the only independent characters here."[3]

May the Lord bless & keep you my dear & much esteemed friend

Ezra Stiles Ely.

ALS, DLC (36). Ely (1786–1861), long acquainted with AJ, was minister at the Seventh Presbyterian Church in Philadelphia. During the campaign he had averred, in an appendix to *The Duty of Christian Freemen to Elect Christian Rulers: A Discourse Delivered on the Fourth of July, 1827, in the Seventh Presbyterian Church, in Philadelphia* (Philadelphia, 1828), that AJ was a friend to Christianity and Rachel "an eminently pious" woman. Lyman Beecher (1775–1863), a celebrated Congregational preacher, was minister at the Hanover Street Church in Boston. He was a leader of mission and Bible societies and of crusades against dueling, intemperance, and Sabbath-breaking. AJ had left home before Ely wrote. He traveled on Sundays on the steamboat portion of his journey to Washington, but not when going overland.

1. Mark 2:27.
2. John Caldwell Calhoun (1782–1850) of South Carolina had been congressman and secretary of war before being elected vice president in 1824 as candidate on both the Adams and Jackson tickets. He was re-elected as AJ's running mate in 1828.
3. Ely's wife Mary Ann (c1792–1842) was the daughter of AJ's late friend, Philadelphia merchant Samuel Carswell. Floride Bonneau Colhoun (1765–1836), mother of John C. Calhoun's wife Floride, was the widow of South Carolina senator John Ewing Colhoun.

Resolutions of the Louisiana Legislature

Copy,

Resolved by the Senate, and House of Representatives, of the State of Louisiana, in General assembly convened, That our Senators in Congress be instructed, and our Representatives be requested to solicit from the General Government, that Detachments of United States Troops be stationed at different points on the Mississippi, and Red River, at such places as may be deemed most important, and *Especially at, or near New Orleans.*

Signed, A. B. Roman,
Speaker of the House of Representatives,
Ad Beauvais, President of the Senate,
Approved, January 28th. 1829
P. Derbigny, Governor, of the State of Louisiana.

[Endorsed by AJ:] refered to the Secretary of War—This was handed by Messhrs Livingston Johnston, White & Genl Overton—with a request that Troops should be stationed in orleans to deter insurrection which is threatened. A.J.

Copy with AJ ANS, DNA-RG 94 (M567-42). André Bienvenu Roman (1795–1866) was later governor of Louisiana, 1831–35 and 1839–43. Arnaud Julie Beauvais (1783–1843) was acting governor, 1829–30. Pierre Auguste Charles Bourguignon Derbigny (1767–1829) had been elected governor in 1828. Edward Livingston and Josiah Stoddard Johnston (1784–1833) were Louisiana senators and Edward Douglass White (1795–1847) and Walter Hampden Overton (1788–1845) were representatives in the new Congress that began March 4. Fears of slave insurrection prompted the legislature's request. On March 25, Secretary of War Eaton responded through former congressman William L. Brent, explaining the disposition of federal troops in the area, their readiness for immediate service if needed, and the impracticability of quartering them at New Orleans (DNA-RG 107, M6-12).

From Joseph Saul

New Orleans 29th January 1829

My dear Sir

I did myself the pleasure by two opportunities for Nashville and took the liberty of troubling you with one of my Pamphlets which justice to myself and family compeld me to publish.[1]

Soon after writing you we recd in this City the dreadful tidings of the death of Mrs. J—be assured Sir many sincere friends here regret her loss, and condole with you on the melancholy event, and none more sincerely than myself and family.

The time is now fast approaching when you will have to occupy the Presidential chair, and I regret that it may not be in my power to be at Washington at the time of your Installation—in addition to the pleasure I should derive from personal considerations towards you, it will be a proud day to myself, and every true republican in the Nation—I therefore mean if I possibly can to be present.

The office of District Atty has lately become vacant by the resignation of Mr John W Smith who has been appointed Judge of our Criminal State Court.[2] In hopes the office may not be filled by Mr Adams permit me to take the liberty of naming to you Mr. John Slidell—I know him to be capable, and a high minded honorable Gentleman—no one laboured more zealously than Mr Slidell did in the good cause, and to his uncommon personal exertions added to those of Mr. Gordon[3] may in a great measure be attributed the success of the election in this City. Mr Slidell is entitled to the patronage of the Government on another score, to defeat the various machinations of the Adams party, he had frequently to throw himself in opposition to some of the Merchants on whom he had relied for professional patronage—I can from my own personal Knowledge say, that no one had greater inducement to act with caution from personal considerations—& yet no one ever acted a more independent or honorable part.

I congratulate you and the Country on the election of our friend Livingston to the Senate—every effort was resorted to by the Adams party to defeat his election. it was a hard trial, & on that account I feel the victory the greater.[4]

You must now my dear Sir permit me to take the liberty of calling your attention to my own situation—you will learn from my pamphet which I hope you have found leisure to read, that I have been, to serve party purposes, deprived of my office, & that after a service of 32 in that line. our friends Livingston and Gordon can give you some information on that head. my object in calling your attention to this fact is to state to you, that if there is any situation in which I can be useful to your administration no one will enter on the duties of Office with more zeal for the public good than I will, and to be candid with you (put down as I have been by party) the respectability of the office wod be more an object with me than salary, provided it only affords me decent support.

This latter subject I have not mentioned to a soul living prefering to address you direct, & if you can find leisure from your many occupations & engagements to drop me a few lines it will afford me much satisfaction, in the interim believe me Dear Sir with the condolence and esteem of my family—your sincere friend & Obd Ser—

Jos Saul

ALS, DNA-RG 59 (M639-21). As cashier of the Bank of Orleans, Saul (c1771–1856) had advanced funds for AJ's New Orleans campaign of 1814–15. In 1831 AJ appointed him consul at Tripoli, but he declined. John Slidell (1793–1871), later a prominent Democratic senator and Confederate diplomat, was a New Orleans lawyer and businessman. In 1828 he had run unsuccessfully for Congress on a Jackson ticket. AJ appointed him U.S. district attorney.

1. In his pamphlet, *A Letter to the Stockholders of the Bank of Louisiana, and to the Public; With a Delineation of the Characters and Conduct of Certain Bank Directors, &c. in New-Orleans* (New Orleans, 1828), Saul claimed that he had been driven into bankruptcy and ousted as the bank's cashier by its president, Benjamin Story, and counsel, Samuel Livermore, for resisting their scheme to profiteer on the sale of state bonds.

2. John Witherspoon Smith (1778–1829) had been federal district attorney for Louisiana since 1821.

3. Martin Gordon (c1773–1852), president of the Orleans Navigation Company, had hosted AJ in his January 1828 visit to New Orleans and run unsuccessfully for the legislature on a Jackson ticket. In April AJ appointed him collector of customs.

4. On January 12 the Louisiana legislature elected Edward Livingston senator on the fifth ballot, defeating incumbent Charles Dominique Joseph Bouligny and former senator and governor Henry Johnson.

From Thomas Patrick Moore et al.

TO GEN. JACKSON.

Sir:—The underwritten your friends, take the liberty of expressing in a manner which cannot admit of any evasion hereafter on their part, their confirmed and sincere opinion of the worth of Amos Kendall of Ky. both as a citizen, and as a public champion of the purity, simplicity and republican features of our constitution and Government. His merits they confidently trust, are not altogether unknown to yourself. Kentucky or the better half of Kentucky hear and are yet ready to acknowledge them, and the Republican party in every part of the United States, which has found in you a leader in every way so worthy of itself, is not unwilling to recognise the claims of Mr. Kendall to some of the rewards which a greatful country likes to bestow upon her faithful sons. The *Five letters* and their effects can never be forgotten by those who lost or those who gained by them. Mr. Kendall, we all *believe,* and some of us have had an acquaintance with him which authorizes us to say, *we know* is a man of exemplary purity in his private life, and we challenge the annals of party warfare for the instance of a man conducting so efficient a public journal as he has done, who has maintained a character more highly distinguished for probity, consistency and a uniform devotion to the best interests of his country than himself.

The under written would be highly gratified if the President elect would appoint Mr. Kendall auditor in case of a vacancy.

(Signed.)
T. P. MOORE,
H. DANIEL,
C. A. WICKLIFFE,
THO. CHITTON,
JOEL YANCY,
ROB. M'HATTON,
JOSEPH LECOMPTE,
JOHN ROWAN,
CHILT'N. LYON,
RH. M. JOHNSON.

The above is a true copy of the original on file in the office of the President's Private Secretary.

Andrew J. Donelson.

May 23d 1829.

Printed, Lexington *Kentucky Gazette*, May 31, 1834 (mAJs; 12-0418). Rowan and Johnson were Kentucky senators, and the others Kentucky representatives, in the Congress that ended March 3. Amos Kendall (1789–1869) was editor of the Frankfort *Argus of Western America*. From September 26, 1827, to October 1, 1828, he had addressed six letters in the *Argus* to Henry Clay, charging him with a corrupt bargain to make Adams president in 1825.

February

Jackson arrived in Washington on February 11 amid mounting speculation over the personnel of the new administration. His election marked the first partisan change in the presidency since Jefferson's defeat of John Adams in 1800. In addition to naming a new Cabinet, many expected Jackson to make sweeping removals among the commissioned federal officeholders, including Treasury bureau chiefs, land office registers and receivers, customs officers, territorial officials, Indian agents, and district attorneys and marshals. All of these were presidential appointments requiring Senate confirmation. Under the Tenure of Office Act of 1820, most high civil officials were commissioned for terms of four years but were still "removable from office at pleasure." Jackson also had vacancies to fill, including one on the Supreme Court, resulting from the Senate's refusal to act on some of John Quincy Adams's nominations in the lame-duck session of 1828–29.

Jackson's first task was to assemble a Cabinet. On February 26, six days before the inauguration, the Washington United States' Telegraph announced his choices. Edited by Duff Green (1791–1875), a journalist and entrepreneur from Missouri, the Telegraph had orchestrated the Jackson press in the 1828 campaign and now spoke as the incoming administration's authorized voice.

Martin Van Buren (1782–1862) of New York headed the Cabinet list as secretary of state. A key architect of Jackson's electoral coalition, he had been a U.S. senator since 1821 and had just been elected governor of New York. Pennsylvania congressman Samuel Delucenna Ingham (1779–1860) was named secretary of the Treasury. John McLean (1785–1861) of Ohio, postmaster general under Monroe and Adams, was to be retained and his office raised to Cabinet rank. Senator John Branch (1782–1863) of North Carolina was to be secretary of the Navy, and Senator John Macpherson Berrien (1781–1856) of Georgia attorney general. For secretary of war, Jackson chose Senator John Henry Eaton (1790–1856) of Tennessee, his former aide, biographer, and confidant of many years.

From Thomas Marshall

Frankfort February 1st 1829

Dear Sir

I have enclosed to you the Recommendation of Mr John Pope as Attorney General of the united States, with the assureance that your appointing him to that office, or that of Judge of the supreme Court of the United States (the vacancy not being filled)[1] will meet the most cordial approbation not only the representatives of the people who have affixed their signatures to the enclosed recommendation, but with the mass of your friends throughout the state

The persons who have signed the enclosed are the active friends of your election; and include with a few exceptions, the Jackson representaton in the present Legislature of Kentucky

Mr Popes talents are too well known to you, to require any representation from me   during the late presidential controversy no individual exerted himself with more effect or displayed more magnanimity, always surrendering his own Just claims to promotion rather than produce a division in the ranks of your friends. I alude particularly to the gubernatoria[l] election, and I may add the late senatorial election in either instance I have little doubt of his success had he pressed his pretentions[2]

as a Matter of policy I shall take the liberty of urgeing the appointment of Mr Pope in preference of any other person in this state

he belongs to the party that is known by the name of the old court[3] it carries with it a majority of one fourth of the population of this state or nearly   a great proportion of that party have adheared to the administration of Mr Adams many of whoom are anty Clay men and if you should select Mr Pope or give a shew of your confidence to prominent men of that party you will produce accession from H Clays party–this effects of this old party feeling has been very sensibly felt during the present seshion of our legislat[ure] and Mr Clays friends make strong calculations from anticipating that a preference will be given to the new court party, by the ensuing administration, which will create zealousies and discontent in their ranks, the appointment of Mr Pope will have a strong tendency to unite the anty Clay old court Adams men to your administration, at the same time it will keep the anty Adams men who are at hart Clay men from disuniting and joining the ranks of Clay that now rank as Jackson men I have given these crude remarks more with a view that you may understand the situation of parties in this state than with an expectation of its effecting any thing for my friend Pope   The Eliments of a prodigious struggle are preparing for next summers campain   yours respectfully

Thomas Marshall

ALS, DNA-RG 59 (M639-18). Marshall (1793–1853), a nephew of Chief Justice John Marshall and later brigadier general in the Mexican War, represented Lewis County in the Kentucky house of representatives. The recommendation he enclosed for John Pope, dated January 22, was signed by sixty-seven Kentucky legislators headed by John T. Johnson. Pope (1770–1845) was a former U.S. senator and current Kentucky state senator. AJ appointed him governor of Arkansas Territory on March 9.

1. In December 1828, after the election, President Adams had nominated John J. Crittenden to the Supreme Court to replace the late Robert Trimble. The Senate tabled the nomination.

2. At the state Jackson convention in January 1828, Pope had refrained from pressing his claims for the gubernatorial nomination against William T. Barry. In the senatorial election in December, Pope and other Jacksonians withdrew, allowing the party to unite on and elect George M. Bibb.

3. The Kentucky court battle erupted after the legislature enacted a controversial law to relieve debtors in the wake of the Panic of 1819. In 1823 the state Court of Appeals invalidated the act. The legislature retaliated by abolishing the court and creating a new one. The two courts vied for legitimacy until the Old Court prevailed in 1826. The controversy prefigured political alignments in 1828: Adams and Clay men had generally supported the Old Court, while most leading Kentucky Jacksonians, Pope excepted, had backed the New Court.

From Henry Marie Brackenridge

Pensacola Feb: 4t. 1829

dear General—

I mourn with you, the loss of one, in whom, so many have lost the kindest friend, and to you irreperable. As long as I exist, I will cherish the remembrance of that benevolent disposition, which sought to render so many happy. But the subject is painful, and I will not dwell upon it. I had flattered myself with the pleasing idea of seing her again, and recalling the memory of other days—but she has passed away, and it must be only for a season, that we shall remain behind.

While I rejoice at the honours the American people have bestowed upon you, I think with pain and solicitude, on the laborious and anxious duties you are about to enter upon, and of the injustice, and ingratitude, that will attend your best and wisest measures. One of your maxims often recurs to me, "to please yourself and then you will be sure of pleasing at least one man." I must however, beg you to forgive the presumption on my part, in throwing my glowing warm light, on the difficult path you are about to tread. The maxim of Mr. Monroe, to prepare in time of peace, for war, I think is wise, both for the sake of economy and safety. A state of complete preparation, takes away the temptation to attack, and when it comes, is the best reliance for victory. It would be unpopular to suggest an increase of the trifling force now on foot, so inadequate to national purposes; not more than sufficient for our Canada frontier alone; but you are the only man who would have the courage to recommend it.[1] When at Charleston and Savanna, last year, I was astonished to find those important cities entirely unprotected by any military works, and not as much as a company of soldiers within a hundred miles of them. The general goverment is only felt in these important places, by the withdrawal of immense sums of money to be expended elsewhere. No fortifications are going on there—no ships building, no money expended, by which the good will of the inhabitants might be conciliated. Our confederacy is so much of a compromise, bargain, or partnership, that *mutual benefit,* may be regarded as its very foundation. Is not this neglect a more natural cause of disatisfaction than the effect of the tariff? Say, that in the general plan of defense, the ingineer looking only to this, should not consider it necessary at present, to undertake any thing of the kind at Charleston and Savanna; but is there not a wider view of the subject? What signifies the returning of a half million of dollars, even on a decent pretext, to the place whence it was originally drawn, if in doing so, the great interests of the nation can be advanced? And can there be any thing more important than to sooth the feelings and concilitate the goodwill of so large a portion of the Southern States?[2] I disapprove of the rebelious spirit, and rebelious language used by the politicians of those parts of those states near the seaboard—but I beleve the great mass of the Southern population, and for which we must look to the Western parts of those states, are truly and sincerely attached to the Constitution, and a very large, and increasing portion of them friendly to the tariff—at least to what they would consider a proper one. In the back parts of the southern states, *farming* and planting, go together, they must have towns to afford a domestic market, and those towns must have manufactures, and those require protection. The mere planter who has every thing within himself, is independant of the country around him—he looks to a foreign market for the sale of his crop and for his supply—the ship owner, looks to every part of the world for employment—hence it is, we find that these two classes are most loud against the tariff. But I am writing you a tedious letter which you will not have time to read—let me therfore tender you my best wishes for your success and happiness. With sentiments of respect I remain your most obt st—

H. M. Brackenridge

ALS, DLC (36). Brackenridge (1786–1871) was the son of writer Hugh Henry Brackenridge and an author of histories and travel narratives. He had served as a secretary and interpreter to AJ as governor of Florida Territory and was now a federal district judge there.

1. In 1821 Congress against the wishes of President James Monroe had reduced the regular army to just over 6,000 men. AJ did not recommend an increase in his first annual message in December.

2. Passage of a highly protective tariff in 1828 had aggravated southern complaints of sectional oppression and prompted the South Carolina legislature in December to issue an *Exposition and Protest.* Secretly drafted in part by John C. Calhoun, it declared the tariff unconstitutional and asserted the right of state nullification.

From Ratliff Boon et al.

Boonville, Indiana, February 5th 1829

Sir,

We The Undersigned, have used our utmost exertions to procure your election to the Office of Presidency, not only as a Reward for your Patriotic Services; but with the hope, that in your election, the Republicans of our common Country, would (for a considerable time) have a sufficient guarantee against the progress of those Aristocratic principles, which have been so openly avowed and supported, by a large portion of our Fellow Citizens; and especially, by most of those holding offices under the General Government—

Most of our State Officers, have also taken an active part in favor of the Aristocracy, and have waged an exterminating *political War*, against your *friends* in Indiana, nor has their *Vindictive* and *persecuting* spirit abated since your election; but the *People* will in due time, apply to *them* the *proper Correctiv*—

We conceive that we have the Right to Appeal to *you* for the protection of your *friends* in Indiana, against the improper interfereance of Government Officers in our State elections, and we do not hesitate to say, that unless a timely corrective is applied, by the *Executive,* (as well as by the People), the *proscription of your Active friends here is inevitable*—The Active and persevereing exertions of the Hon. T. P. Moore have contributed much to the success of our cause in Indiana—By forwarding from time to time suitable documents, and correct information to your friends here, he enabled them to counteract the numerous slanders propagated against you by the Tribe of Office holders dependant on Messrs Clay and Adams—We have the Honor to remain with sentiments of the highest consideration your Friends

R. Boon	B. K. Burns
Thos. Fitzgerald	John Hargrove
Thomas Lowe	John D. Day
Jefferson W. Ramsey	Thomas McCool
Daniel Y. Hudson	John S Camp
Henry L. Talbott	Garret C. Young
	James T. Denton

LS, DNA-RG 59 (M639-16). The signers were residents of Warrick and neighboring southwest Indiana counties. Ratliff Boon (1781–1844) was a Jackson elector in 1828 and congressman, 1825–27 and 1829–39. Thomas Fitzgerald (1796–1855) was a former state legislator and later U.S. senator from Michigan. John Hargrove (1799–1874) later served in the legislature. John S. Camp (1784–1848) was a minister and farmer. Thomas Patrick

Moore (1797–1853) had been a Kentucky congressman since 1823. AJ appointed him minister to Colombia on March 12.

From Robert Punshon

Cincinnati Feby. 6th. 1829.

Dear Sir

An act of justice to our mutual friend Moses Dawson Esqr. of this city, is my only apology for this intrution. It ha[s] long been contemplated, that the public printing in this City, will be removed from the present incumbent Charles Hammond of the Gazzette. I have understood that application have been made by others from this City while the extreme delicacy of Mr Dawson has prevented him from making any application; When I concider his large family consisting of five sons and two daughters, and who from his devotion to the great cause in which we are engaged; has exposed himself to the obliquity of our adversaries to such an extent as to prevent him from realizing any support from his public paper; I could not refrain from expressing to you that I have assertained from him: that the printing of the Laws, the Post Office blanks for the western country, the monthly list of letters in post office &c in Cincinnati: would be gratefully received and duly apperciated by him: this I have found my indispencible duty in *justice to him* to com[mun]icate to you, and to tender to you my heartfelt gratification on your safe arrival at the seat of government, as our future chief magistrate

accept, Dr. Sir the prayers of the late Grand Chaplin of the Grd. Lodge of Ohio, for your present and eternall happiness With respect and esteem

Robt. Punshon

[Endorsed by AJ:] Revd R Punshon recommending Mr M. Dawson as public printer for Cincinnati—to be attended to—

ALS, DNA-RG 59 (12-0485). Punshon (c1776–1848) was a Cincinnati Methodist minister and Masonic officer. Moses Dawson (1768–1844) was editor of the pro-Jackson *Cincinnati Advertiser*. In December his paper was given the public printing in place of the *Liberty Hall and Cincinnati Gazette*, whose stridently anti-Jackson editor Charles Hammond (1779–1840) had attacked AJ's marriage during the 1828 campaign.

From Micajah Harrison

Ky M Sterling 10th Feby 1829

Dear Sir,

I hope you will excuse the liberty which I take, to inform you that I solicit the appointment of Marshal of this state.

Almost all the Offices in *these* days are held by *your* enemies, and in *my* Opinion, by the enemies to the *republick*. Now, that they find *their places* in danger, they begin to fawn & *bow* to the powers, that will *soon be*—After their *hawking* about every vile *slander,* they have the daring *impudence,* to expect, or say they expect a Continuance in Office.

The Coalition have *claimed* the right, of being the true *Jeffersonian* republicans—I hope that you will give them the same rights, which Mr Jefferson gave the enemies of his Country when he came in to Office, by turning every *man* of them *out,* and supplying their places with its friends.[1]

In the State of Tennessee, there was scarcely any Contest; so that your friends there could scarcely be aware, of the slanders and Opposition to you—but in Kentucky, the battle was hard fought—The forged letter of Harris—Coffin handbills, and every sort of meanness was resorted to by the Coalition in Order to carry their point—bribery &c&c&c—[2]

In fact, although I had long personal friends of that party, yet I do not know One single One, that I could wish to have, or be Continued in Office—your friends here, have no idea upon earth that you will Confer a single favour more, than their protection as Citizens of America—

I should not be this plain were I a *mere Child* of *yesterday*—I am a grand father, and tho' not as old as you are yet am in my 53d year.

I have lived in Ky upwards of 40 years—I know something of the distresses and privations of *early* days—I commenced the early Campaigns against the Indians the year I was 16 years old—I was with Genl Wayne throughout his Campaigns of 1793 & 4 and I feel some claims, when put in Competition with persons who were not *born,* when I was fighting the battles of my Country, particularly when my qualifications should be *equal* & perhaps superior to *theirs.* I came off better than the Chickasaw Ambassador, for I kept my *hide* hold—[3]

The present marshal, has held the Office, for 10 or 12 years—and I am told was Commissioned by Mr Adams in January 1828 for 4 years which, if permitted to stand, will pretty well run through your first term—Indeed Mr Adams might supply the whole union with Officers & save you the trouble—no doubt, but that he would gladly do so.[4]

For my Character, qualifications &c I will refer you to the Hon. George M. Bibb with whom I have been intimately known for 30 years— Also to Mr. Daniel, Colo R. M. Johnson, Mr Rowan, Majr T. P. Moore, Mr Chilton, Mr Yancey, Genl McHatton—Hon: Jno McKinley, from Alabama.[5]

I have written to them & expect they will name me to you. I am poor and needy—I have been in *unprofitable* publick business for 30 years.

The latter gentlemen named, except Mr Daniel, I have only that passing acquaintance with, usual to publick men yet they [know] me & my Capacity for business.

In Conclution, be pleased to accept my most unfeigned & heart felt Condolence for your late bereavement of your amiable Wife—I thank the Lord, that in his goodness, he permitted her to stay in this world of trouble & sorrow, until she saw a brave and generous people, prostrate your enemies at *both* your feet.

Please to accept my best wishes and prayer to Heaven, that He will give you wisdom & discretion to preside over the people with Judgment, Justice & mercy. I remain with great respect & Esteem your most obt Servt—

Micajah Harrison

ALS, DNA-RG 59 (M639-10). Harrison (1776–1842) was the father of Albert G. Harrison, later a Missouri congressman. On May 23 AJ appointed John M. McCalla marshal in Kentucky, removing incumbent Chapman Coleman.

1. Jacksonians called their opponents "the Coalition" in reference to the supposed "corrupt bargain" between John Q. Adams and Henry Clay (1777–1852) that made Adams president and Clay secretary of state in 1825.

2. In the 1828 campaign, Adams presses had circulated both a handbill depicting the coffins of six militiamen executed under AJ's orders in 1815 and a spurious letter in which one of the six, John Harris, pled for mercy.

3. General Anthony Wayne (1745–96) defeated northwest Indians at the battle of Fallen Timbers in 1794. The "Chickasaw Ambassador" was Leslie Combs (1793–1881), who visited the Hermitage in 1828 to question AJ about his 1818 Chickasaw negotiations. Combs had been wounded and taken prisoner in the War of 1812.

4. Chapman Coleman had been appointed marshal by James Monroe in 1823 and reappointed by Adams for a four year-term beginning January 6, 1827.

5. George Mortimer Bibb (1776–1859) was former chief justice of the Kentucky Court of Appeals and a senator in the incoming Congress. John McKinley (1780–1852) was a senator from Alabama.

To Joel Blanckenship

WASHINGTON CITY, Feb. 14, 1829.

SIR:

The Hon. Speaker of the House of Representatives has this day presented me a Hickory Cane, the growth of Virginia, mounted and embellished by your own hands. I accept it, Sir, as a token of your respect, not the less gratefully, because of your not being a voter in Virginia. The sentiments of patriotism, altho' generally invigorated by the possession of this privilege, do not take their source from it, and in many cases, exhibit the noblest sacrifices in the defence of liberty, without it.

I pray, you, Sir, to be assured of my best wishes for your health and happiness, and believe me, Your Ob't. Serv't.

ANDREW JACKSON

Printed, *Richmond Enquirer,* June 5 (mAJs; 12-0510). The cane had an ivory cap with AJ's initials and a silver band engraved with a plough, a plane, a sheaf of wheat, and the words "It's Hickory." The *Enquirer* identified Blanckenship as an "ingenious Mechanick" of Richmond and an admirer of AJ though not a voter, perhaps because he did not meet Virginia's property qualifications for the suffrage. Other ceremonial gifts to AJ in 1829 included a giant cheese, a barrel of whiskey, dressed meats, a live bald eagle, and various edible delicacies and objects made of hickory.

From William Claggett

Portsmouth, N H. February 14th. 1829

Sir—

It would have afforded me inexpressible pleasure to pay my respects to you upon your arrival at the City of Washington, and there to participate in the general joy which will animate a large assemblage from different sections of the Union upon that auspicious event, which will elevate you to the highest station in our country. Circumstances rendering the journey impracticable at this time, I take the liberty, without having the honor of your acquaintance, to request my friend, the Hon Jonathan Harvey, one of the Representatives in Congress from Newhampshire, to hand you this note—And to satisfy you that you may place confidence that my political sentiments are in unison with those which you have ever espoused, I also take the liberty to present you with a copy of our Address, intended to promote your election, which I made at a State Convention of Republican Delegates in June last—the call for which convention I take much satisfaction in saying originated with myself. Although Newhampshire gave you more votes than any other of the New England states, yet, Sir, the Republicans of this state sensibly feel their disappointment in having been overpowered by their political opponents.[1] They, however, have a right to, and will join in the grand national jubilee—they will render thanks to that All-wise Providence, which, by placing in your hands the principal direction of our public affairs, has secured the triumph of Liberty, & given additional safeguards to the equal rights and privileges of the people. Your accession to the Presidency will form a new epoch in the history of our beloved country. And I doubt not but that your administration of the government will be characterized by a strict adherence to the republican policy and the sacred principles upon which the Constitution is founded

Permit me, Sir, to congratulate you upon your election, as being one of the most auspicious events that has ever occurred. And as I have, for seventeen years since I have been upon the political stage, been engaged in an arduous struggle in the defence of the republican cause against a powerful New England faction, and have been assailed by the venomous weapons of that faction in consequence of my exertions to promote your election, I will frankly say, that no one in this section can have more abundant cause for rejoicing at the glorious result than myself.

Please, Sir, to excuse these prefatory remarks The object I have in view in now addressing you is to recommend to your particular notice the Hon Levi Woodbury, one of the Senators of the U States from this state. Having been intimately acquainted with him from early youth, I have had an opportunity to acquire a full knowledge of his eminent virtues and qualifications. Should you see fit to select any one from the Eastern states to take charge of one of the public Departments, I hesitate not to express my belief that the qualifications of Mr Woodbury would give him the preeminence over any other republican citizen in New England. As a classic scholar, no one stands higher in this quarter. He has a strong & vigorous constitution, which enables him to pursue whatever he undertakes, with unremitted assiduity. At about the age of twenty one, he was admitted to the Bar, and such were his talents and profound legal knowledge, that at the age of twenty six, he was appointed a Judge of our Supreme Judicial Court, the duties of which office he performed with great ability & honor & to the public satisfaction, until the year 1823, when he was elected Governor of this state; and two years afterwards he was elected a Senator of the United States. Mr Woodbury is now aged about Forty. And I believe that as a Statesman he holds a high rank in the Union. But such are his talents & application to business, that should he be placed in any station, he would soon acquire a full knowledge of his official duties & all subjects connected with the same. His integrity moral and political, cannot be called in question—and I need not say that he sustains a pure moral character. Although vials of wrath have been poured forth upon his devoted head by the leaders of the federal party in this section of the Union, yet those leaders are unable to substantiate a solitary fact impeaching his moral character. I will only remark that the abuse heaped upon him originated from the same party motives, which gave rise to the unfounded calumnies, with which the same faction vainly attempted to undermine your honest & immortal fame. The noble stand which Mr Woodbury has taken in your support and in defence of the great cause of our country justly entitles him to the gratitude of [the] great republican family; and I can entertain no do[ubt] of your disposition to reward merit. Mr Woodbury has been spoken of in many of the republican journals as a gentleman well qualified to perform the duties of Secretary of the Navy. Should you deem it adviseable to call him to that or any other station in the Cabinet, which you are about to form, I have full confidence that he would perform his official duties to your entire approbation & to the public satisfaction. You may, perhaps, consider it as presumption in me thus to address you. If so, I can only hope, that you will excuse me, as I have no other motive than to promote the common cause which has ever commanded my devotions, and the just pretensions of a highly distinguished individual. I have the honor to be, Sir, with the highest respect, yr most obt Servt

William Claggett

ALS, DNA-RG 59 (M639-27). Claggett (1790–1870) was a Portsmouth lawyer and some-time state legislator. Levi Woodbury (1789–1851) was a U.S. senator, 1825–31. In April AJ offered him the post of minister to Spain, which he declined. He became secretary of the Navy in 1831 and of the Treasury in 1834.

    1. Jonathan Harvey (1780–1859) served in Congress, 1825–31. Claggett's address is in *Proceedings, and Address of the New-Hampshire Republican State Convention of Delegates Friendly to the Election of Andrew Jackson to the Next Presidency of the United States, Assembled at Concord, June 11 and 12, 1828* (Concord, N.H., 1828). AJ lost New Hampshire in 1828, but his popular vote total and percentage there were his highest in New England.

From Richard Montgomery Young

Kaskaskia, Illinois, February 14th. 1829

Dear Sir,

    Altho personally unacquainted with you, I have at the earnest desire of some of my friends, to whom I am under obligations, presumed to address you on a subject of much delicacy, both as it regards myself, the individual concerned, and perhaps still more so in relation to yourself. Altho I have uniformly given you my feeble support in this State, as well in the former, as latter contest for the Presidency, yet it is not my disposition to take merit to myself, for having so done, much less to claim or expect any thing in return. What I did was freely done for what I conceived to be for the public good, and the result so far has fully compensated me for my exertions. My wish has uniformly been, to see you as little embarassed, by ill-timed applications from your friends as possible, and I would on that account alone, if upon no other, have gladly avoided saying any thing on the present occasion, if I did not consider it due to those who have solicited me so to do. Sidney Breese Esq. a Citizen of this place is at present the District Attorney of the United States for this State, and is desirous of retaining his present situation, if his continuance should meet your approbation, and his friends who are also friends of mine, wish me to say to you, which I do not hesitate to do, that he is a gentleman of good moral character, and well qualified for the Station. Mr. Breese does not wish the fact disguised that in the late contest he was the friend, and supporter of Mr. Adams. In the first election I think he was for you, but being subsequently well pleased with the administration of Mr. Adams, he prefered his continuance in office to any other person, whose views in relation to several leading features in our domestic relations had not been so fully developed. As to the Course it may be proper for you to pursue towards your late political opponents, in respect to appointments, it is not for me to advise; I do not feel competent to the task, even if it were my disposition so to do. But I have no doubt that a certain degree of liberality (to what extent I cannot say) will be at least satisfactory, if not looked for, by many of your best friends. By such a course you would still retain your old friends (at least those worth retaining), and make such inroads into the quarters of your late political rivals, as effectually to destroy, or render harmless, their opposition as emanating from a party, and to paralize any efforts which may be made from that quarter to embarrass your administration. Whatever you may conceive to be your duty in this respect, I am prepared to believe that you will act in accordance with your best judgment, to secure individual justice, and to promote the public good. I am with sentiments of high consideration, and esteem your most obt. servt.

Richard M Young

ALS, DNA-RG 59 (M639-3). Young (1798–1861) was an Illinois judge, a Jackson presidential elector in 1828, and later a U.S. senator. Sidney Breese (1800–1878) was appointed district attorney for Illinois in 1827. In April AJ removed him for Samuel McRoberts.

To Martin Van Buren

Washington City Febry 15th 1829—

Sir

I am now at the seat of Goverment, ready to enter on the high duties that my country has so flatteringly assigned me. My first and strong desire, is to have associated with me in the discharge of my responsible trust, men, in whom, under all exigencies, I can repose—I have thought of you; and trusting in your intelligence & sound Judgment, my desire is that you shall take charge of the *Department* of *State*. Do me the favor to say, if you will undertake it? were you here, I should defer any enquiry on the subject, untill the end of this month[,] but being at a distance my solicitude is to k[now] forthwith, if I may calculate on your aid.

If consistant with your feelings; it would afford me great pleasure to have you here early as possible, that I may consult with you on many & various things purtaining to the general interest of the country[.]

As early as possible I shall be glad to he[ar from] you, & to know your determinati[on; and if] leisure permits, to know your opi[nion of the] time when you can be at the city of Washi[ngton.] very respectfully

Andrew [Jackson]

ALS (torn), DLC-Van Buren Papers (12-0514); LC, DLC (60). Missing characters in the ALS are supplied from the LC.

From Henry Baldwin

Washington 15 February 1829

Sir

You come into office strong in the confidence and affection of the Nation, and want no political alliance to enable you to administer the Government with usefulness and efficiency: you come here pure and free, no party or cabal has selected you as its head and forced you into power against the voice of the people, or intrigued you in without their confidence—without pledge or promise to politicians or Candidates they have no claims to urge no contract to enforce upon you—none can say to you pay me the stipulated or understood price—and you can truly and proudly say to any aspirant for office at this or any future election I owe you nought, am not here at your bidding or subservient to the views of the proudest among you—The Nation had a task to accomplish and sought a man who never feared to do his duty, failed to perform it or returned to his country an unfinished trust in a time of emergency—the man was found and is now placed at their head by the generous confidence of the people and with the full assurance that their interest would alone be the object of his cares & his labors that as an agent of their spontaneous selection sent directly by themselves no one would question your authority and you be under no necessity of strengthening it by any coalition—none can add to or impair the moral force which public opinion has placed in your hands—On the coat of arms of my native state there is a motto which ought to be yours as peculiarly appropriate to your present situation—The power which planted will protect[1]—In thus attaining the chief Magistracy untrammelled by any political hand you are also free from the influence which private obligations or injuries may sometimes bring to bear on the firmest minds and soundest judgment—your only obligations are to the people; to your personal friends you owe none for they could do no more than discharge a portion of what they owed you—your personal injuries have been nobly avenged by the Nation which has identified yours with the character of the country and which it will protect as its proudest monument next to its first honored Chief—Look around you to your enemies who now fill the highest stations in the Government and who are so low as they? victims to their own passions and ambition they are writhing in all the tortures of self reproach & self immolation their political death is convulsed with more pangs than any enemy could inflict no blow has fallen on their heads from your hands while your triumph is complete their Chief dare not return to the land and house of his fathers and the people have put a mark on his subordinates which no waters can wash out and no time efface—Retributive justice has done its work

In preparing for the commencement of your great work the first object is the selection of your assistants and the inquiry is now with you is as it was with the people before the election—where can the greatest means of public usefulness be found—in your choice you are as free and will be as unbiased as they were—I have on this subject no remarks to make no advice to offer—if you want my opinion you will ask it I would thus endeavor to make it respected but could not indulge that hope if it was volunteered—

As to myself your kindness has more than filled the measure of all my hopes and my highest ambition—I feel that I have your confidence and you shall feel that it is not bestowed upon an ingrate—I have now a legacy to leave to my son more precious than any politician can bequeath to his—your friendship your good opinion & confidence the more dear to me because acquired by no acts or extraneous aid and the prouder triumph because it is my own work—My conscience an old and true friend with whom I never differed and who never reproached or deserted me tells me that I have used no unworthy means and that in my whole conduct in relation to yourself either here or at home among the people I have been governed by a sense of the highest public duty due my country and that the most acceptable services which could be rendered by me for that portion of the confidence of the public which had been awarded to my exertions—was to persuade the people to avail themselves of the benifit of yours—It would be however uncandid in me to say that this was the only motive which impelled me for impressing on the public your claims to their confidence and honor I could unite the zeal of friendship to the duties of patriotism and with the same union of public & private feeling shall always endeavor to continue my efforts in the joint cause of country and friend whenever called on or occasion may require

You have asked me what are my wishes—employment at home or abroad—my answer is at home or abroad wherever I can best serve my friend and country—but neither at home or abroad unless I can serve both—My choice is at home and by your side, come weal come wo—If however you think that abroad I could perform any definite service for the public better than another person—my time my labor my best efforts are now or hereafter, at any and all times at your volition. As a station of distinction of rank or honor a foreign appointment has no value in my eyes when I could contribute more to the common good at home—and while enjoying your confidence a title to my name would be as little a matter of ambition as the accompanying ornament to my person

At home I could serve you in no station where a controul could be exercised over me by any person but yourself—of the five which are confidential ones there are but two for which I am qualified   In the discharge of the duties of the other three my only promise to you would be fidelity. I would not add public usefulness to the pledge because I doubt my ability to redeem it

But in either of the other two I could promise you the fulfilment of every attendant duty and without any consciousness of any want of the requisite capacity—Should experience teach me that I have mistaken my own powers none will discover it sooner than myself and whenever that happens the appointment will be returned to him who gave it—

I have now answered your inquiry with that freedom and candor which was promised and which should never be wanting between friend and friend—refusing nothing concealing nothing and not fixing any interpretation of motives or expressions unworthy of the feelings which have hitherto subsisted between us you see my views and wishes in plain intelligible language—you see me on paper as you will find me on trial—the same out as in office my course as respects my friends my principles the measures of Government & the int— of the country is and ever will be uniform consistent and fearless   With politicians I have no connection no one is answerable for my political conduct and the merit of no ones is imputable to me   It is my good fortune to have many kind and valued friends I have a home among the people of my state and have no fear of returning to them with diminished confidence in any possible event—

As to yourself take my assurance solemn & sincere that every wish of my heart has been gratified—no office can bind me by a tie so strong as your kind expressions—no time or circumstance can ever weaken it and our acquaintance when it ceases with time will end as it began in mutual respect and mutual esteem—Should you decline to give me any appointment you must remember that you reject no application and refuse no favor it will give me no offence and wound no feeling—you have given me what is more valuable than any office in your disposal and you have made me happy—remember too that you have given me no pledge—that nothing which has passed between us is so considered or can be so considered by me—you are as free as when we met on the Ohio and if any friend of mine should mention my name to you with a design to produce any effect on your mind you have my word that it is wholly unauthorized by me

I had intended to say something on the attempt to influence you against me but your good opinion has placed me so far above my enemies that they are worthy of no notice now—when you have decided you will know who they are—what has made them so and my opinion of them—I have only to add that the bitterest among them shall never say that in private or public life—at home or here my path has ever been stained by the vices of a Candidate[.] yours with esteem

Henry Baldwin

[Endorsed by AJ:] Mr. Baldwins letter to be preserved

ALS, DLC (36). Baldwin (1780–1844) was a Pittsburgh lawyer and former congressman and an early supporter of AJ. Baldwin had met AJ in Pittsburgh on his way to Washington, and newspapers had named him as a likely Cabinet prospect. AJ appointed Baldwin to the Supreme Court in 1830.

1. The state motto of Connecticut, *"Qui transtulit sustinet"* (He who brought us here will sustain us).

To Littleton Waller Tazewell

[Congress officially tallied the electoral votes for president on February 11, recording 178 for Jackson and 83 for John Quincy Adams. A joint committee, chaired by Senator Littleton Waller Tazewell (1774–1860) of Virginia and including Representatives John Bell (1797–1869) of Tennessee and James Hamilton, Jr. (1786–1857) of South Carolina, was appointed to notify Jackson of his election. The committee met Jackson formally, probably on February 16. Tazewell read a short congratulatory address and Jackson replied. The committee reported back to Congress on February 17, and the next day the United States' *Telegraph carried a verbatim report of the exchange.*

Two manuscripts of Jackson's reply to Tazewell survive, both in his own hand and both printed below. The first is evidently a draft. The second matches the wording reported in the Telegraph.*]*

Sensible that I owe what public consideration I possess to the confidence reposed in me by my fellow citizens of these United States—feeling a concious inability to discharge this debt of gratitude, I have made it an undeviating rule of my conduct not to decline any situation that it was the pleasure of the people to call me to fill. I had retired from the bustle of public life to my farm, there to repair an enfeebled constitution, worn out in the service of my country. The people of their own mere will brought my name before the nation for the office of President of these U. States. They have sustained me against all the torrents of slander that corruption & wickedness could invent, circulated thro subsidised presses and every other way supported by the patronage of the government; and by a large majority of the virtuous yeomanry of the U. States have elected me to fill the presidential chair. Such call, under such circumstances, I cannot hesetate to obay, I accept the office given me by the free & unbiased suffrage, of a virtuous people, with feelings of the highest gratitude.

Allow me to assure you I feel the great responsabity of the duties I am called on to perform and I appreciate as I ought the honor they people have confered on me, and that I will enter upon the duties of the office to which I am called, with that zeal the confidence in me has inspired, supplicating the throne of grace, to guide me in the duties of my office, that my administration may redound to the harmony, prosperity, & happiness of these united States.

Permit me to assure you of the sensibility I feel of the kind manner you have been pleased to make known to me the result of the peoples will in the election of their chief Magistrate.

AD draft, DLC (12-0504).

Sir

The notification that I have been elected President of the united states for four years from the 4th of March next, which by the directions of the Senate and House of Representatives you have so politely presented, is received with feelings of the deepest sensibility.

I desire you to communicate to the respective Houses of Congress my acceptance of the high trust which has been conferred by my fellow citizens, with an acknowledgement of the responsibility which it enjoins; and that I can make no suitable return for so flattering a proof of their confidence and attachment. All that I can offer, is my willingness to enter upon the duties which they have confided to me, with an earnest desire to execute them in a manner the best calculated to promote the prosperity and happiness of our common country; and to the attainment of these objects shall my unceasing efforts be directed.

I beg you, Sir, to convay to the Senate and House of Representatives assurances of my respect & regard

Andrew Jackson

ADS, PPRF (12-0502). *US Telegraph*, February 18.

From Caleb Atwater

Circleville Feb. 16, 1829.

My Dear sir,

I sit down, for the purpose of performing a very unpleasant, but what is laid upon me, as an *imperious duty*. Several members of our Legislature, have made an attempt, to divide all the offices, for this state, among themselves, and although, in a general meeting, that attempt was put down, by more than three fourths of all present, as unauthorised, highly impolitic, unjust and ruinous, to the party, in Ohio, yet those who voted in the majority, inform me, by letters and otherwise, that for 8 days *before the close of the Session,* papers of recommendation, were in circulation for signatures, and several, who disapproved of the men, as incompetent for the offices they aspired to, yet they signed the papers, as they would a remonstrance against the appointment, believing such bargains of rec- ommending, *each other,* would be viewed, by yourself, in their true light. I remark briefly, that not one of the appointments, would satisfy one hundred friends of your's in Ohio. The man recommended for Dist. Judge, has not *now,* and *never had,* even *one suit in the dist. or Circuit court!* never had, ten suits, in his life, so far as I know—is destitute of a moral character, and so malignant in his disposition, that he speaks evil of every man not present. His days are spent in rioting, drunkenness and gambling and I have seen him intoxicated in the streets. The whole bar would rise up in one mass against that appointment. The man recommended for a foreign mission is wholly unfit for one—he never voted for you, I know— was not in the state at the last election and who opposed you in 1824. When elected to the Senate, no one knew on which side he was, nor did we ever know until your election was achieved when he began to show his name in every paper as your warm friend.[1]

The Collector of the Port of Detroit (recommended as such) is on the limits of Cincinnat[i] jail—has spent $10,000 in gambling and is notorio[usly] and habitually intemperate.[2]

The marshall (recommended) brother in law to J. C. W. has voted the Adams ticket for congress—for the legislature & every thing else every year since 1824—and tho' a candidate for elector in '24 yet of so doubtful a character that we unanimously rejected him as an elector on the 8 Jany '28.[3]

The man recommended for Indian Agent i[s sh]eriff of a county near me—a man of property, and does not need it—he drinks to excess very often and although, his removal from an office by the Gov. is attributed to political grounds yet, had he been a temperat man, that removal would not have taken place.[4]

My heart sickens, at the attempted imposition upon *you,* and I allude to no more, of them, but, say seriously, that not even one of the men is at all qualified for the station he aspires to, and their appointment would prostrate us in Ohio, at one blow. I was in favor of a prompt removal of *all the officers in Ohio, instantly,* on your coming in to office; I now see, clearly that it must be a work of some little time—that great caution is necessary. Permit me to add, that the self made officers have *dispatched a messenger* to Washington who is *now with you posibly,* and who is recommended for a high office, one indeed, that Col. R. M. Johnson of Ky. would best fill, perhaps.[5]

My request is, that this state may remain untouched, until the 1st of May, next. In the meantime I will collect the sense of your friends, honestly, correctly and impartially and lay it before yo[u] in person, if I can, or by letter. By such a dela[y no] injury will be done, but absolute ruin prevent[ed.] We who have watched over, the flock, ever since it had a being—wish you to have a fair opportunity of doing as you really wish to do, of making no appointment until you are correctly informed of all the circumstances belonging to the case. I shall not apply in the usual mode for any thing, choosing rather to submit my case, without, any recommendation, unless, some friend, like Maj. Lewis, say something for me.

Nor will I directly or indirectly, be concerned in any bargain, with any candidate for office.

The marshall of Ohio, is the <u>*son in law*</u> of Jer. McLene, Secy of state, as true a friend as you have—one of the *first*, most *firm* & *quite efficient* too. The marshall himself, lay perfectly still, last summer and fall, as I believe—his time expires perhaps, in Decr next. Let that be, until *then*.[6] The printers, I would locate in Cleaveland, Columbus & Cincinnati. Let Olmsted at Columbus remain, until Decr. next—remove Hammond—remove Wilson instantly.[7] Tiffin Surveyor Genl immediately, ie early in May. Indian Agent then too.[8] With profound respect & esteem I am dear sir, your's truly

Caleb Atwater.

Should you see fit to appoint me Dist. Judge, and should I not be able to give satisfaction to the bar and the public, I would resign the appointment, so as to give you an opportunity to appoint another, and in the meantime, it should always be my most anxious endeavor to do justice to all and no injustice to any one.

I may be misinformed, but if I can believe what I am told by those attornies who have voted for you, my appointment would give better satisfaction, than any other one.

If our senators were sincerely of the opinion that Thos Morris would be appointed if I were not, I think they would not object to me. It is easy to see, that the coalition have placed more than one senator in the senate to oppose your best friends, in Ohio. This would not be the reason of their opposition to Morris, but an old quarrel, as old as this state, operates still I suppose. I prefer Mr. Creighton to most of those who claim the appointment on political grounds.[9]

Judge Scott is with you—he wants to be judge, but he has come over to us too recently—has belonged to every party in the state—has not the confidence of any one, and is too unstable in all things. He is rather too old to be appointed to an office for life, and understands only one branch of law, (the Va land laws) and has practised in no other cases. Justice compels me to add, that he is a gentlemanly man, and a moral one, but he would be indolent and is too well off in his circumstances to need it.[10]

I presume he wants to be Sup. Judge, yet that may be a cover for his attempt to obtain the lesser appt. As a party man he has no claims and when a candidate for assembly after his conversion he did not receive one half the Jackson votes of Ross co. He sometimes preaches, and sometimes pleads law and at others follows his trade of a tailor. I state nothing but facts, I assure you Sir. I am aware, that it does not follow, because I have recd a public education—have regularly studied law and followed that profession and nothing else for a living for nearly 30 years, that I am qualified for Dist. Judge, in preference to others—nor does it follow, that because others beset your path by night and by day—enter into bargains to recommend each other for office, that therefore they ought to be preferred.

All I ask is, that you will deliberate on an appointment of great importance to the public, and use your best judgement in filling it. And as I said in the beginning of this half sheet, should I be so fortunate as to meet with your preference, I will exert every power and every faculty to serve the public and to do honor to your choise, and whenever I cease to give all reasonable satisfaction, I will instantly resign it.

I have a large family to support—am literally poor and really need some appointment from the general government; and after a life of half a century, devoted as mine has been, to honorable and useful pursuits, with a character, so far as I know, fair and spotless, am I not Sir, entitled to a favorable notice, without any other recommendation?

[In margin:] The common enemy knows nothing of these things.

[In margin:] When a change is made in the marshall, Charles Colerick is the man.[11]

ALS, DNA-RG 59 (M639-1). Atwater (1778–1867) was a lawyer, antiquarian scholar, public school advocate, and former state legislator. In May AJ appointed him commissioner to treat with the Winnebago Indians.

1. Elijah Hayward (1786–1864), recommended for judge, was a Cincinnati lawyer, editor, state legislator, and chair of the state Jackson committee in 1828. In 1830 AJ appointed him commissioner of the General Land Office. John Hamm (c1777–1861) of Zanesville, recommended for a foreign mission, was a state senator and former federal marshal for Ohio. AJ appointed him chargé d'affaires to Chile in 1830.

2. Andrew Mack (1780–1854), a Cincinnati hotel keeper and state senator, had been detained at the Hamilton County jail on two writs of execution in favor of the Bank of the United States. AJ appointed him collector of customs at Detroit.

3. John Patterson of Steubenville, an 1824 Jackson candidate for elector, was appointed federal marshal for Ohio in April. Atwater erred in calling him brother-in-law to anti-Jackson congressman John Crafts Wright (1783–1861).

4. Franklin County sheriff John McElvain (1789–1858) had been a Jackson candidate for elector in 1824 and a Jackson elector in 1828. He had been dismissed as adjutant general by Governor Allen Trimble. AJ appointed him Indian agent at Piqua.

5. Joseph Watson.

6. William Doherty (1790–1840), a Franklin County lawyer and husband of Jeremiah McLene's daughter Eliza, was appointed Ohio marshal by James Monroe in 1822 and reappointed by John Quincy Adams to a term running to March 1830. AJ removed him for Patterson.

7. Philo Hopkins Olmsted (1793–1870) published the Columbus *Ohio State Journal* and James Wilson (1787–1852) the Steubenville *Western Herald*. Both were anti-Jackson. The Jackson administration gave the public printing to the *Cincinnati Advertiser*, Cleveland *Independent News-Letter*, and Columbus *Ohio Monitor*.

8. Edward Tiffin (1766–1829), a former Ohio governor and U.S. senator, was appointed surveyor general of public lands for Ohio, Indiana, and Michigan by James Madison in 1814 and reappointed by Monroe and Adams. AJ removed him in May for William Lytle. Indian agent John Johnston was removed for McElvain.

9. John Quincy Adams had named William Creighton, Jr. (1778–1851) to the Ohio district judgeship vacated by the death of Charles Willing Byrd, but the Senate tabled the nomination. AJ appointed former congressman John W. Campbell on March 6. Thomas

Morris (1776–1844) was a Jacksonian state senator and later U.S. senator, 1833–39. Both of Ohio's U.S. senators in 1829, Jacob Burnet and Benjamin Ruggles, were anti-Jackson.

10. Thomas Scott (1772–1856) was a former judge of the Ohio supreme court. AJ appointed him register of the Chillicothe land office on March 9.

11. Charles Colerick (d. 1838) was a Knox County state legislator.

To Richard Rush

Washington City Februay 17th. 1829.

Sir,

Your letter of yesterday has been received. In reply I have cordially to confess to you, that during the angry-political contest which has just terminated, I have at no time understood that you pursued any other course than that which was the undoubted right of every freeman—an expression of your opinions and preferrences, candid & decorous. Independent of the avowal in your letter, my knowledge of your character precluded the idea that you could have adopted a different course.

Your kind wishes for my private and public happiness in the duties before me, are thankfully received. I am aware that they are surrounded with many difficulties; but called to them by the flattering preferrence of my fellow citizens, I can only assure you that my constant efforts shall be devoted to their proper performance.

I offer you my best wishes for a speedy restoration of your impaired health, and am, Sir, with great respect yr. obt svt

signed, Andrew Jackson

LC, DLC (60). Rush (1780–1859) had been Treasury secretary under John Quincy Adams and was his vice-presidential running mate in 1828.

Account with William O'Neale

City of Washington
1829 Feby. 18

Genl. A Jackson
   To Wm Oneale   D.

To livery for three Horses
from 18 Feby. till 13 March
three weeks @ 3 $ each ℔ week $27.00

To livery for two Horses
from 13 to [22] March one and
half week @ 3$ each ℔ week   9.00

To livery for one horse from
22 March to 27 ²/₃ week   2.00
                                 $36.00

Recd pay. 13 April 1829

                                      Wm ONeale

[Endorsed by AJ:] Major Wm Oneals receipt for horse keeping March &
april 1829.

DS, DLC (36). William O'Neale (c1751–1837) was the proprietor of a Washington boardinghouse and father of Margaret O'Neale Timberlake Eaton. AJ appointed him an inspector of
the District of Columbia penitentiary in March.

From John Pope

                          Frankfort February 19th 1829—
Dr Sir
    I have just returned from Louisville where I learnt from our friend
Worden Pope your enquiry as to my disposition to take a seat in the
national Judiciary[1]—The Jackson members of both houses of our general
assembly almost unanimously had a few days before forwarded to you
at Washington City an address pressing me on your consideration for the
office of attorney Genl—A few of our partiular friends at Louisville had a
private conference on the subject & all concurred that the office of Judge
would be most advantageous to me but most of them believed that as
regarded the party and the effect on the cause here & in the west generally
the office of atto general ought to be preferred and I was strongly inclined
to this opinion but our friend Worden Pope & another friend dissented
and he has made known his view of the subject to you—He is a sincere
& disinterested friend of ours & his opinion is entitled to high regard—I
gave my opinion with the reasons for it in two letters to your friend
Judge White of the Senate with a request that he would submit them to
your perusal[2]—It is gratifying to me to believe that I have a place in your
friendship & confidence—Your better judgment upon a view of the whole
ground will settle the question and I will cheerfully accept whatever situation your partiality may assign me—I have never before solicited an office
from the executive of the state or the nation nor would I now obtrude
myself upon your notice but for some late indications of your regard &
confidence & a conviction that some distinguishing evidence of it is necessary to my political advancement & that it will add much to my power &
influence to sustain your administration & our party in the west—I will
not affect indifference to your favour because upon you my political fate
& prospects depend—

I hope you will excuse the solicitude of one who has had to encounter opposition at every step of his political march—a public & decisive evidence of your confidence will lessen to a great extent the difficulties in my way—our friends in congress from kentucky at an early period of the session were for presenting me to you for a place in the Cabinet but I now understand that by some magic influence they have abandoned their first plan & that amos kendall & these gentlemen have made some other arrangement—that I am to be excluded & my family satisfied with some small offices & my friend Duff Green who was pressing me all last year to permit Colo Johnson to be reelected & to look to some high station under your administration after I have yielded to Barry Johnson Bibb &c what they were under the highest obligations to concede to me writes that it is doubtful whether I can be promoted because I did not have Colo Johnson elected & voted for the confirmation of Judge Robinson[3]—whether this little fry of managers at washington shall control my fate in defiance of the will & judgment of the President & that of near seventy members of our General assembly & the will of the people of kentucky is for you to decide—I have neither the motive or disposition to indulge bad feelings towards our members from kentucky—I have fought the good fight with them in the great struggle in which we have been associated & have certainly given them no cause of complaint—I am at home & have no means of counteracting the artful machinations against me at washington—I suspect some invisible hand has been operating on these men—It may be that political aspirants of other states imagine that I will not subserve their objects of ambition—our friends here who have been eyewitnesses of my public conduct here are entitled to be heard in my favour in preference to mr kendall who went from here in december my warm friend & the members of congress if they have changed their opinions since the commencement of the session—Give to my exertions in the common cause my talents & reputed integrity a due estimate & award me what your judgment approves—Be assured I would not consent that you should sacrifice the public good to gratify me or advance my interest—In my letters to Judge white who I have ever understood had your good opinion & a considerable share of your confidence I mentioned the name of mr Van Burin of new york not with reference to his merits or demerits but to effect on that state—I had no preference for him over other distinguished men on the list of your friends—I have no personal acquaintance with that gentleman & his public career has not furnished sufficient data to enable me to form a satisfactory opinion of his pretensions to public consideration as a statesman & patriot—I regret that I cannot have a personal interview with you on the commencement of your administration—you will not I know doubt my sincerity when I assure you that no man feels more solicitude for the success of your administration & that it may furnish additional evidence of elevated patriotism & devotion to the prosperity & glory of your Country—I have a special desire to converse with you on the subject of removals from the subordinate offices of the government—It is one of peculiar delicacy difficulty & embarrassment & demands a calm & dispassionate consideration uninfluenced by the host now pressing you for places from every quarter of the union—In this business pardon me for suggesting that you should proceed with caution & the process should be gradual—A too sudden & violent shock ought not to be given to public feeling & sentiment—Remember that the hope of office will secure you more support than the enjoyment of it—By the removal of a good officer of character you not only array him & his friends against you but a portion of the disinterested part of the community & if you secure the man substituted you offend twenty or more disappointed expectants—As regards yourself & the strength & stability of your administration it is a losing game unless managed with consummate skill & judgment and yet to a certain extent it must & ought to be done & especially where influential political men hold office which afford them power to annoy you & your friends—Pardon my freedom in making these remarks which are merely intended to guard you against the importunities of members of congress & others who are more engrossed with their little selfish & electioneering projects than zeal for your fame or the success of your administration—you should bear in mind that a large portion of the members of congress have less moral weight & political influence than many of their constituents—such I know to be the case in relation to the members from kentucky—most of them have good managing electioneering sense & local popularity but none have extensive weight & influence in the state—not more than one in twenty probably in one hundred are office holders or office hunters & you have been placed in power not by the aspiring politicians & busy partisans but by the affections & confidence of the great body of the people who feel no other concern than that the government may be administered by the man of their choice & upon just & honest principles—Elevated like Washington by the will of the nation rather than party for your patriotism & distinguished public servi[c]es you should look to the moral force & sound intelligence of the country for support & not to the mere creatures of party—The sound sense & intelligence of the people is the only rock upon which a great public man can build a lasting fame, every other foundation is temporary & evanescent—Policy however requires him to be mindful to a certain extent of mere partisans and while on this subject permit me to call your attention to one here Wm T. Barry Esqr who deserves nothing from me & but little from you—He & his friends have lost us the state administration & had nearly lost you the state—He is not fit for any station which requires great intellecual force or moral firmness but he is a gentleman in his deportment & amiable in his private relations—He is nearly insolvent & has the sympathies of many of the new Court men & is more a favourite with them than any other—They want something done for him & as a measure of policy I would gratify them to a reasonable extent—give him the attorneyship for this District if vacant or make him Governor of arkansa & public sentiment might bear his being sent to some of the south american states[4]—Of our senators I will say nothing—you know them—Dick Johnson & his family connections I like generally, although very wild & violent occasionally in politics they are warm hearted & efficient—Governor metcalf & some other of Clays friends are I think endeavoring to separate them from your other friends here. Let me advise you to treat old Dick and his brother John T. Johnson who voted for you with kindness & attention—Henry Daniel is a bold efficient man in his quarter. Thomas P Moore is an efficient man of sense & management & although he has not much moral weight & has not done for you one tenth part of what is pretended, yet he has fought the battle with zeal & boldness—He regards neither truth nor principle to carry his point—as a matter of policy I advise you to treat him as well as you can—but dont give him too much influence with you—Charles Wickliffe has done his duty—He is a cool calculating man to whom I stand indifferent. Chilton shoots at random now & then but has good popular talents—of the rest of our delegation it is unnecessary to speak—It will be well if they can be elected & vote with you—I fear that our members in relation to me may be influenced by ambitious men from other states—In this I may be mistaken—I am sorry to send this letter in my own hand writing as it may give you more trouble to read it than it is worth—Please to consider it a substitute for a free confidential conversation & when you have read it I would prefer that you should commit it to the flames. Permit me to tender to you assurances of my respect & sincere regard—[5]

John Pope

[Endorsed by AJ:] (Confidential to be preserved carefully—to be filed with my *private* papers—

ALS, DLC (36).

    1. Worden Pope (1772–1838), John's cousin, was a Louisville bank president and active Jacksonian.

    2. AJ's friend Hugh Lawson White (1773–1840) had succeeded him in the Senate in 1825.

    3. Kendall and Green each admonished Pope that his recent conduct in the state senate had forfeited his claims for the Cabinet. Pope had opposed the effort to reelect Richard Mentor Johnson (1780–1850) to the Senate, and he had voted to confirm George Robertson (1790–1874), a Clay man, for the Kentucky Court of Appeals (Kendall to Pope, Jan 11, Blair-Lee Papers, NjP; Green to Pope, Jan 2 and 26, Green Papers, DLC).

    4. William Taylor Barry (1784–1835), a former congressman and senator and New Court chief justice, was the unsuccessful Jackson candidate for governor in 1828.

    5. Thomas Metcalfe (1780–1855) had defeated Barry for governor in 1828. Richard M. Johnson's brother John Telemachus Johnson (1788–1856) was a former Kentucky congressman. Henry Daniel (1786–1873) and Charles Anderson Wickliffe (1788–1869) were Kentucky congressmen.

From Martin Van Buren

Albany Feby 20t. 1829

Sir

Your favour of the 15t instant proposing to assign to me the Department of State in the administration about to be formed under your auspices, was received yesterday. With an expression of my gratitude for the favourable opinion you have formed of me & the very flattering manner in which you have expressed it, I have to say that I accept your invitation with no other hesitation except such as is derived from a distrust of my fitness for the high Station to which you have been pleased to call me. Allow me to assure you that the hope of being able to assist you in some small degree, to realize the expectations of a people, who, under the most trying circumstances have evinced a degree of patriotism & fidelity that would have done honor to the proudest days of the Republic, induces me to quit the elevated & truly honorable Station confered upon me by my immediate constituents.[1] Associated as I shall doubtless be in your Cabinet with so great a portion of the intelligence & virtue of the Country and having constantly & only in view the success of your administration, I cannot doubt of our ability to fulfil the public expectation. My movements in regard to my repairing to the Seat of Goverment will be entirely controuled by my new duties, and subjected to no farther delay than is strictly unavoidable. Of that character my dear Sir will be the necessity of waiting the receipt of information of the confirmation of my appointment by the Senate. a few moments reflection will satisfy you that however, desirable & agreeable it might be, that I should be with you sooner, a different course would be subject to insurmountable objections. Although I am satisfied that the great body of my leading friends in this State, look to the result that is about to take place, as probable & are prepared to approve it there are thousands and tens of thousands who have never bestowed a thought upon the subject. With such particularly & indeed in a greater or less degree with all, the fact of my soon leaving the Station to which I have been raised by their favour, in the midst of a busy & very interesting session of the Legislature, cannot fail to create a strong sensation unless it be done with the utmost propriety. To go off without communicating with the Legislature & leave the Goverment to devolve in the first instance silently upon the Lieut. Governor would not do. The first direct notice that my constituents are to have of my intention should be an address to the Legislature resigning my office and assigning my reasons for doing so. In the discharge of that duty (which I am satisfied public opinion will require of me) it is due to the Senate of the United States that I should avoid the presumption of taking the confirmation of my nomination for granted. Independent of the unpleasant reflections that an opposite course would give rise to, in relation to me personally, & by which my future use-fulness might be impaired, it is scarcely to be doubted that the appetites of your enemies for detraction would be re-excited, and that we should be charged through their presses with disrespect towards the Constitutional rights of an other department of the Goverment. Hoping that my views upon this subject thus hastily expressed will be satisfactory, I have only to add that no time will be lost after the receipt of my appointment. The resignation and delivery over of what belongs to the office &c will of course take a day or two & I may want a few days to shut up house &c not to exceed a week in all as I shall leave the final arrangement of my domestic affairs for a period when it can be done under circumstances more consistent with the public service. My friend & aid Col. Hamilton of this State is now with you, & will take the trouble to ascertain as far as that can properly be done, how long a time may without prejudice to the business of the office be allowed to me to pack up, and upon confering with you will communicate to me the result.[2] Accept Sir the assurance of my great respect and kindest regard

M. V. Buren

ALS, DNA-RG 59 (12-0543). AL draft, DLC (12-0553); Bassett, 4:9–10.
    1. Van Buren had been elected governor of New York in November 1828 and took office on January 1, 1829. He was nominated and confirmed as secretary of state on March 6 and resigned as governor on March 12.
    2. James Alexander Hamilton (1788–1878), a lawyer and son of Alexander Hamilton, served as acting secretary of state from March 4 until Van Buren's arrival on March 27.

From Zalegman Phillips

Washington Febry 21 1829

Dear Sir,
    In presenting to your perusal and consideration the enclosed recommendation from a few Republican Gentlemen of known character and standing, I avail myself of the occasion to express to you my wishes and feelings on an unpleasant duty which among the other arduous ones you are called upon to perform will I am satisfied be fulfilled with justice impartiality and honour to the country at large. I allude to the selection to office from the numerous candidates who will be placed before you. As a father and the only parent of a large and unprotected (and I think I may add of a virtuous & moral) family of children there are duties imposed upon me which I have never hesitated to perform and however unpleasant is the task I now undertake of throwing myself upon you in the midst of the struggle that will be made for office still it is one that a just regard for the welfare of my children entirely dependent upon me obliges me to perform.[1] I respectfully and earnestly solicit from you the appointment of "Attorney of the United

States for the Eastern District of Pennsylvania," now and for the last fourteen years in the tenure of Charles J. Ingersoll.[2] It is an office the duties of which from education habits of industry and a long course of professional experience I could discharge with fidelity to the government and I think I can add with satisfaction to the public at large particularly in the city of Philadelphia whose citizens are not unacquainted with my professional standing. For this office I believe there will be many applicants from whom and their numerous friends supporting them I must expect to encounter great opposition. I stand alone   I do not know that I have any one to press my pretensions and if I had five hundred friends if I know myself, I would not permit them to be placed before you in any other light than that of the purest and simplest truth. Of all the Gentlemen offering for this situation I am the oldest at the bar and I believe in years. As to being equal in point of legal qualifications and experience to any of my competitors it would be indecorous for me to say, this you no doubt will be informed of by others; of my claims on the score of Democracy I will yield to no one in the United States, and on the score of pure original and unaffected attachment to yourself and persevering zeal in your cause I am proud to say & will carry the recollection with satisfaction to my grave, there is no one of my competitors that can approach me. For any service that so humble an individual as I may have rendered I claim no merit; I only did my duty as a citizen. In advocating your election I was serving the cause of my country and benefitting my children by giving the little aid I possessed to render secure to them the blessings of an uncorrupted and incorruptible Republican Administration. But Sir as far as I was able I did all in my power, whilst some of the gentlemen who are or will be pressed upon you, were not only looking on with unconcern but others were warmly engaged in support of their own candidate and in opposition to your cause. It may not be considered right that in urging my own claims I should attempt to detract from the merit of my competitors, but standing alone, with so many in opposition to me and no one to press my application but myself I do not consider that I violate any private rights in saying that if I have an opportunity of being heard I can satisfactorily shew that from the list of candidates that will be presented before you I am not one who ought to be overlooked. I am aware that my religion will be urged against me by some; but in our country where the constitution secures the blessings of toleration such an objection I think cannot be successfully urged against me. I am a Jew; it is the religion of my forefathers in which I was born and bred, in which I have lived all my life time and as an evidence of the estimation in which my Jewish brethren hold me permit me to say that I am now and have been for eight successive years elected President of the temporal concerns of the Hebrew Congregation of the City of Philadelphia. I am also and have been from its commencement President of the United Hebrew Beneficent society of Philadelphia, both of which institutions are incorporated by the Laws of Pennsylvania, and yet notwithstanding all this, I have always lived in the strictest bonds of honesty and charity with my christian brethren who have not refused me their confidence and esteem nor made my religion a matter of reproach. In the revolution of 1776, and the war of 1812 our people took their station with their christian brethren they fought side by side, and I believe in this country they have always been considered as pure patriots and as good citizens as those of any other creed. The christian religion in all its forms and bearings is respected by the jews; it is considered a system of the most excellent morality; our children are taught no doctrines inconsistent with it; humility to the Supreme being and a strict observance of the laws of God and man are inculcated in their minds from the earliest period of their lives; the foundation of which is in the most beautiful moral precept of Christ "do unto others as ye would others should do unto you." I have thought it my duty thus to place myself before you because as I have already said in this contest I stand almost alone and unsupported. I trust and hope that I may not be unsuccessful, and that no suggestions unfavorable to the kind feelings you may entertain towards will be sustained untill an opportunity is afforded me of removing any which if they are raised I can satisfy you have not truth or justice for their support. Any result to this my application to your patronage will never change the unfeigned respect & sincere attachment of your Always devoted friend and Obedient Servant

Z phillips—

ALS, DNA-RG 59 (M639-18). Phillips (1779–1839), a graduate of the University of Pennsylvania, was a criminal lawyer, early Jackson supporter, leader in Philadelphia's Jewish community, and uncle of New York City Jackson editor Mordecai M. Noah. He enclosed a February recommendation from Henry Horn and other Philadelphia Jacksonians praising his talents and principles (M639-18).

1. Phillips's wife Arabella Solomons bore nine children before her death in 1826.
2. Charles Jared Ingersoll (1782–1862), a lawyer and former congressman, had been district attorney since 1815.

From Samuel Smith

Capitol Hill 21 feby. 1829

dr. Sir

I am about to ask a most particular favor *personal to myself.* It is, that you will renominate George Harrison, Navy Agent for Philadelphia. I have been on terms of intimate friendship with him for 35 years. He is a Gentleman, highly estimated by all the most respectable people of the City, independent in his Circumstances, and with whom the public money is perfectly safe, a consideration of no Small importance, as I shall show. Mr. H. has held the Office for 30 years, during which time he has rendered Entire satisfaction, his Accounts have been Clear and regularly returned—He has ever been a federalist, and has probably voted with that party, but he has never acted as a partizan. he has simply exercised the right of a freeman, which Evinces his independence, and for which I Esteem him the more. you will be told "That he attends little to the duties of his office" This I unhesitatingly say is untrue, and I refer with confidence to the testimony of every Captain of the Navy who has Commanded at Philadelphia, to the Commissioners of the Navy Board, to the Navy department, and particularly to the Chief Clerk of the 4t Auditor whose duty it is to audit the accounts Mr. Gilliss (the Chief Clerk) has held that Office for nearly twenty years. he is a Capable honest man, is competent to give Correct information and will do so fearlessly.[1] If the Charge "that he is inattentive to his duties" be predicated on his seldom visiting the Navy yard, It may be true, for he has no more business there than I have—the Commanding Office would resent any interference and tell him to mind his own business. The duty of a Navy Agent is, to purchase such articles as may be wanting, either under the Orders of the Secretary, or the Commanding Officer, to keep his Accounts Clear, and to return them once a quarter.

I did the duty of Secy of the Navy for Mr Jefferson for 4 months at my own expense, and understand the Business of that department *well*

Until the year 1809 (I think) Navy Agents were Merchants of high Character who purchased for the Use of the Navy under the Orders of the Navy dept. on a Commission, and from whom the business Could be taken at any moment, under that system not a dollar was lost—I opposed the Change, I thought I could foresee what has occurred that they would be appointed because they were poor and had families to support (a very bad reason where money is to pass to a large amount) or because they had influential friends &c &c—It was however determined that they should be Officers of the govt. the consequence was defaults to a large amount, in N. York $90.000[2]

Whilst Congress was in Philada—a Mr. Sitgreave rose and said, "That separated as the Federalists and Democrats were in politicks, it was high time to separate in social intercourse, and that he hoped all private association would be abandoned"[3] It took immediately. my federal acquaintances all *Cut me,* except Mr. Harrison. A deputation Called on and told him, "That he must relinquish all intercourse with democrats, and particularly with General Smith, or the business of the Navy would be taken from him." He answered, Go back, and say, That be the consequence what it may I will not give up my acquaintances that I am a federalist, I trust a gentleman, that I will associate with whom I please, and would not relinquish my friendship for Gen. Smith for any consideration, tell them that I will ask him to dine with me tomorrow, and he did so

Mr. Harrison was Continued by Mr Jefferson, was appointed by Mr. Madison as an Officer, was reappointed by Colo. Monroe, and confirmed by the senate, altho: his term expired on the 3 march, and has been renominated by Mr. Adams but not acted on, because his four years terminated on the 3 march. I have the honour to be with the highest respect your devoted friend

S. Smith

[Endorsed by AJ:] recommending Mr H as a fit person for Navy agent Philadelphia—to be handed to the Sec of ~~Treasury Mr Ingham~~ Navy, Govr Branch with other

ALS, RP (12-0566). Smith (1752–1839), a senator from Maryland, had served in Congress since 1793. He unofficially administered the Navy Department for several months at the beginning of Jefferson's administration in 1801. George Harrison (1762–1845) had been Philadelphia navy agent since 1799. On February 16 the Senate postponed his nomination by Adams for a new four-year term. He was renominated by AJ on March 12 and confirmed the next day.

    1. Thomas Handy Gilliss (1768–1851) was chief clerk in the fourth auditor's office.

    2. Navy agents became presidential appointees in 1809. The first two in New York, John Bullus and Robert Swartwout, compiled arrearages exceeding $80,000.

    3. Samuel Sitgreaves (1764–1827) was a Pennsylvania Federalist congressman, 1795–98.

From Charlton Hunt

Lexington Febry. 23. 1829

Private

Dear Genl

    This letter will find you engaged in duties which I apprehend you will find both arduous and responsible. Those friends who have aided in elevating you to your present office owe it to you and to the good of the Country to place within your reach such facts as will enable your judgment to decide upon circumstances that may arise during your administration: it is to this feeling of duty to you that I must ascribe the trouble the reading this epistle may occasion.

    The vacancy upon the Bench of the Supreme Court of the U. S. will require of you the duty of appointing some individual qualified to fill that office. Anterior to the Senatorial election last Jany public sentiment was undivided in the opinion that Geo M Bibb would be nominated as the successor of Judge Trimble. This expectation arose from the exalted estimate in which Mr Bibb's legal attainments and private virtues were held; and from the belief that you would appoint to office the most worthy and talented of your friends. The result of the Senatorial election, by placing Judge B. in the U. S. senate for six years has created a doubt here as to the course it would be proper for you to pursue in relation to that gentleman. It is regarded as all important that you should retain a majority of friends in the Senate; and it is by no means certain, that Mr Clay will not be enabled by his wiles and intrigues to secure the ascendancy in the next Legislature of Ky. which will place a man of different politics in the Senate. I consider Judge Bibb the best qualified man in our State for the office; but should it be considered unwise to remove him from his present situation; there is no man who from his transcendant talents his virtue and integrity and his important services to the republican party, deserves more at the hands of the President than Maj. Barry. His legal attainments are inferior to Judge Bibb, but they are very respectible, and his genius and application will render him in a short time a distinguished member of the Bench. He is poor; and has been assailed by the taunts: and bourn down by the insulting oppression of haughty aristocrats who would have lavished their smiles and money upon him, had he consented to compromise his honor and political principles for wealth and power. Your friends are very desirous that a man who has suffered so much should be placed in an eligible situation by which he can at the same time serve both himself and his Country.

I have one other friend to present to your consideration; and I will have closed this letter. The Office of U. S. Atto. for the Ky district will, I apprehend be vacated by the removal of Jno J Crittenden; should that event occur; Col John Speed Smith of Madison County, Speaker of the House of Representatives in the years 1827.8. would be an extremely acceptable appointment to the great majority of our friends. whether he is considered, as a lawyer, a courteous and agreeable gentlemen, a talented and eloquent advocate or an honorable man he will be found most eminently qualified for the duties of that office.[1] Residing in the most aristocratic part of the State, he was enabled to sustain a respectable opposition by his great personal popularity and his generous and extravigant expenditures, indeed he has been subjected to pecuniary embarrassment by the heavy sacrifises he made to keep up the party in his County.

Wishing that the close of your career may be as brilliant and useful as we have every reason to believe it will be, I subscribe myself, Your friend

Charlton Hunt

ALS, DNA-RG 59 (M639-2). Hunt (1801–36), a lawyer and later mayor of Lexington, was the eldest son of Lexington pioneer and merchant John Wesley Hunt.

1. John Jordan Crittenden (1786–1863), a former and future U.S. senator and Adams's unconfirmed nominee for the Supreme Court vacancy, had been appointed federal district attorney for Kentucky in 1827. On May 23 AJ removed him for John Speed Smith (1792–1854), a former congressman and speaker of the Kentucky house.

From Stephen Simpson

WASHINGTON, Feb. 23d, 1829.

Dear Sir—

The difficulty of obtaining a private interview for any length of time, has induced me to address you in this form, prior to my departure for Philadelphia. If I stood alone on this occasion, I should perhaps be the less solicitous to obtain from you, an explicit avowal of the feelings and sentiments that you may cherish towards me and my friends—an avowal which I am the more desirous of being favored with, since the appointment of Mr. Ingham at the instance of the sixteen.[1] That gentleman has ever stood in an attitude of hostility to me and my friends—it becomes a question between us, whether his adoption as a cabinet minister, will transfer to you a portion of his enmity, or that general feeling of partiality which he may cherish for a party opposed to that mass of our democrats which I have the honor to represent, and whose sentiments I now express in common with my own. I am aware that you are elected for the good of the whole people; but all *general* principles must eventually find their illustration and their practice, in special measures and individual preferences. The democrats of Pennsylvania that I represent, or rather in whose behalf I can speak, are well known to you for their early and steadfast adhesion to your fame and your cause. It is not necessary, I trust, that I should recall to your mind, the long and intimate correspondence that has subsisted between us, in order to explain the solicitude I now feel, under the circumstances of Mr. Ingham's appointment. Allow me, therefore, to ask the question distinctly, and solicit the favor of an explicit reply—will that appointment *exclude* my representations in favor of your *early friends in Pennsylvania*—and will it change for the worse, the friendly relations in which we have so closely stood for seven years past?

This question, my dear sir, is put thus frankly, in order to save you all future embarrassment, and from a warm-hearted desire, to render smooth and tranquil the remainder of your life; to shed flowers in the path of your presidential toils, and to render *harmony* among your friends the characteristic feature of your administration. The candor of this communication will find an apology in the fact, that the people look to their President for a free and liberal reciprocation of confidence and regard. Any profession of friendship on my part, at this late hour, would be equally unnecessary and formal. We know one another I trust, to well, too cherish a distrust of the sentiments that may naturally actuate us. Surrounded by enemies, I am prepared to disregard their machinations, and thus throw myself upon your candor, that you will not listen to detraction, without affording me an occasion of justification, and an opportunity for *truth*. It would be a new era in the history of the human heart, if your political friends were to incur proscription, and your foes were to be nestled in the warmth of your bosom: it would be a still more marvellous event, if such an era could find an author in you.

Allow me once more to impress upon your mind, sir, that I stand at the head of a party, whose feelings may be highly excited by the cabinet appointment for Pennsylvania. I recall the circumstance to your recollection merely to show the importance of *conciliation* in our own party, *by that gentleman*. With sentiments, &c.[2]

Printed, Philadelphia *United States' Gazette*, August 9, 1831 (mAJs). Simpson (1789–1854) was editor of the *Philadelphia Mercury*. He had served under AJ at New Orleans, and as editor of the Philadelphia *Columbian Observer* in 1822–25 had early supported him for president. Simpson was politically opposed to the "Family Party," the Pennsylvania Jackson faction headed by Samuel D. Ingham and George M. Dallas. In 1831 Simpson published this letter within a series tracing his troubled relationship with AJ. Simpson then claimed that he had met with AJ in February 1829 and was reassured by him that the Cabinet was still undecided. Hearing minutes later from Pennsylvania congressman James S. Stevenson that the Cabinet was "fixed," Simpson went to his hotel and wrote this letter.

1. Simpson's 1831 account related that William B. Lewis told him before he met AJ that AJ had first intended the Treasury for Henry Baldwin, but changed his mind after a delegation of sixteen Pennsylvania congressmen voiced a preference for Ingham. Baldwin himself wrote Simpson on February 26 that AJ said he felt compelled to withdraw the offer of the Treasury after hearing objections from eleven Pennsylvania congressmen (*Hypocrisy Unmasked!*, Philadelphia, 1832). The Philadelphia *Democratic Press* of March 18, 1829, reported that sixteen congressmen had met with AJ, but only eleven from Pennsylvania.

2. According to Simpson, AJ Donelson replied by inviting him to call that evening. He met with AJ, who admitted that the Cabinet was decided but pledged that Ingham should have no influence over Pennsylvania appointments.

Memorandum on Appointments

Outline of principles submitted to the Heads of Department.
Feby 23d. 1829

The late political struggle exhibited the people acting against an improper use of the patronage in the hands of the executive branch of the General Govt. A patronage whose tendency was a corruption of the elective franchise, in as much as it sought to mould the public sentiment into an acquiescence with the exercise of power acquired without the sanction of that sentiment. It follows as a consequence, that the president of the people is to reform the abuses of which they complained, and repair, as far as he can, the individual and public injury produced by them; and that it becomes his duty in conformity with this principle to dismiss all officers who were appointed against the manifest will of the people, or whose official station by a subserviency to selfish & electioneering purposes was made to operate against the freedom of state elections

The same principle will also require of every Head of Depart., a strict examination into the state of his Dept., and a report to the President; stating what retrenchments can be made without injury to the public service, what offices can be dispensed with, and what improvement made in the economy and dispatch of business.

Connected with the character of the administration are the moral habits of those who may be entrusted with its various subordinate duties. Officers in their private and public relations should be examples of fidelity & honesty; otherwise the interests of the community will require their removal, and they will have to be removed. A strict adherence to this rule will increase the scope of the rotative principle in office, and contribute in this respect to elevate the character of the government, and purify the morals of the country. This principle will be regarded as a fundamental one by the President, and as the best check for the evils arising out of the growing propensity for office.

LC and AD fragment, both in AJ Donelson's hand, DLC (60; 12-0573).

John Hopkins Houston
to Andrew Jackson Donelson

Washington.
23rd. Feby. 1829.

My dear Sir;

Aware that your time must necessarily be very much occupied, I would not now break in upon it, but that the object I have in view, as you will perceive, must be effected, before the Old Cheif writes his Inaugural address. If you will run your eye over an article in the enclosed paper, headed the "New Cabinet," written by a personal freind of mine, you will see it is the desire of the writer of the article, who is the Organ of the Democratic party of the State, at Harrisburg, that Genl. Jackson should be a candidate for reelection. I have heard from him on the subject, and he is extremely anxious that Genl. Jackson should not, in his Inaugural address, decline a reelection, but is afraid to approach him on the subject, at the same time wishing that I could let him know it, by some means or other. I yesterday recd a letter from my Father, a Senator in the Pena Legislature, to nearly the same effect.[1] Under the hope that Genl. Jackson may not revert to the Subject in his Inaugural address, I at the same time could not presume to say a word on the subject to him, directly, but have taken the liberty to drop you the paper, with what I have informed you, and request you, if you think it would be decorous or proper, to let him know the sentiments and wishes of his *original* freinds in my native State. I must rely on your own judgement to decide whether there is anything improper in this request, and if you think there would be, to attribute it to the zeal of some of the Genls. warmest supporters. In great haste, I remain yr. frd. & sevt.

John H. Houston

ALS, DLC (36). Houston (1796–1870) was a clerk in the fifth auditor's office. The article he enclosed appeared on February 20 in the Harrisburg *Pennsylvania Reporter, and Democratic Herald,* published by Samuel C. Stambaugh. It hailed AJ's election, urged him to serve two terms, and recommended Ingham for the Cabinet.
1. Houston's father Samuel (1767–1842) represented Lancaster County, 1828–32.

From Spencer Darwin Pettis

Saint Louis
Feby 25. 1829.
Sir,
   The political relation which I have the honor to bear towards the friends of republicanism and of reform in the State of Missouri compels me to yield to the solicitation of many gentlemen and write you directly on the subject of several appointments. I should have addressed myself to the several Departments without taking the liberty of writing to you but for the fact that a considerable time will elapse before it can be known here who will be appointed to the cabinet
   I do not presume Sir to point out a course to be pursued by you in relation to matters of so much delicacy as appointments to office; nor do I desire to obtrude my opinions on that subject, but I beg leave to state it as my belief that a very large majority of the people of this State confidently expect that *many changes* will be made   This expectation cannot I think be considered unreasonable when it is borne in mind that during Mr. Adams' administration none were appointed to office except the *known* friends of that administration, and when it is remembered that (as I before advised you) almost all the federal officers in this State, during the late contest threw their whole might & influence in the scale of Messrs. Adams & Clay—many indulged in violent abuse of all those who opposed their favorites and left no effort untried by which to accomplish their views The great body of the people remained firm to their principles, and permit me to say that next to the Kentuckians no people deserve more credit than do the people of Missouri, for the part they have acted. I confess sir that I participate freely in the feelings of the good people of my state and consider the change which they expect essential to a fair and impartial administration of the affairs of government—I feel some solicitude on another account. Our opponents in the late struggle, reproachfully represented that our candidates, (from the candidate for the Presidency down to that of a member of the State Legislature) were wholly unqualified for office.

The people have given some of us an opportunity of disproving this assertion and I feel anxious that some of them shall have a like opportunity

I have therefore enclosed you a list of the names of gentlemen who are well qualified in every respect for the appointments mentioned, and I earnestly recommend them to your most favorable consideration. without entering into a special commendation of each individual, permit me to remark that I have recommended none who will not do honor to the stations to which they have been named. I trust I have too much regard for the proper administration of the government—too much respect for yourself and my own standing lightly to recommend persons for appointments.

In conclusion sir I tender you my best wishes for the success of your administration—that it may be so directed as to disappoint even the least violent of our enemies and equal the expectation of the most sanguine of our friends. As the prototype of the Jeffersonian Administration I trust in God that it may tend to the prosperity of the people and to the perpetuation and preservation of the only free government on earth

With sentiments of the highest respect and of the greatest confidence I have the honor to be sir your Obdt Servt

Spencer Pettis

ALS, DNA-RG 59 (M639-18). Pettis (1802–31) was a newly elected Missouri congressman. His "List of appointments recommended" (DNA-RG 59, M639-20) named John F. Ryland for Missouri district attorney, Finis Ewing for marshal, and twelve others for land offices, Indian agencies, and postmasterships.

From John Johnston

Washington City
Feby 26. 1829.

Sir,

The circumstances under which I find myself placed here, will I trust plead my apology for troubling you with this communication

I came to this City under the orders of the War Department, on the 31 ultimo for the purpose of settling my accounts, and I have ascertained thro' a member of the Ohio Delegation in Congress, that applications are already here, from Citizens of that state, for the office which I now hold, and I presume there is no cause alleged against me, save that of having in the late election, given a preference to Mr. Adams. I hope this will not be considered sufficient to remove me from office, thereby disolving a connexion subsisting between myself and the Indians for a period of near thirty years, and which I trust has not been without considerable benefit to the United States

I respectfully ask a continuance in the service on the following grounds.

I have served the United States long, and faithfully and I might add with a zeal which never knew abatement. I have a large and encreasing family, thirteen children living, my eldest an officer in the Navy now in the Mediteranean, and my salary is now more necessary to their support, than at any former period[.][1] My health has been greatly impaired by exposure in the open air, lying out in every season of the year for near thirty years now past, and am too far advanced in life to commence new pursuits.

I am removing some of the Indians from ohio to the west of the Mississippi every year. in the ensuing autumn I expect to remove all the Senecas, a few years more and the Agency will cease altogether[.] a stranger could not so well accomplish the views of the Government in this matter, nor give satisfaction to the natives. under a change the business must necessarily stop for a time.[2]

Altho' my preference was for Mr. Adams, and this from no motives of interest whatsoever, for I never asked, expected or received a favour from him in all my life. I did not interfere with the opinions or motives of others. many persons dependant upon me for their daily bread including my two hired domestics, and my own Brother, were among your supporters. And Mr. Henry Barrington your Elector in my District, could not have kept a House, nor paid the postage on the correspondence to which he was exposed, were it not for the pecuniary aid received from me.[3]

I have been for many years a member of the Canal Board of Ohio, and was honored with several other marks of confidence there, to none of which however has there been any compensation attached, save the expences actually incurred.[4] this has led me often to Columbus the seat of Government. In the winter of 1827–8 The Secretary of State General M.Lene, a warm supporter of yours, whose term had expired, came up for reelection.[5] he was an old and faithful officer, it was a time of high party excitement. He had all the interest and support which I could give him. He was elected, altho' the administration party in the Legislature was by far the strongest.

I therefore pray for that liberality in my case which I have invariably extended to others.

The enclosed sheets will shew in what light my services have been viewed by those most competent to judge of them. I beg leave further to refer to Mr. Calhoun, the Post Master Genl. & his Brother of the House of Representatives, and to Gov. Cass[.][6]

The situation and circumstances of a large dependant family, and the peculiar situation of the Indians of my Agency will I hope plead my excuse for trespassing upon your time with these details

I have the honor to remain with very great respect Sir, yr. mo. ob. st.

John Johnston
Indian Agent in Ohio.

My family is settled in the U.S. forty years, having emigrated from Ireland at the close of the Revolutionary War. I had Relatives both by Father and mother, some of them field officers in the Pennsylvania line, during the whole of that contest.[7]

J. J.

ALS, DNA-RG 107 (12-0594). Johnston (1775–1861) served as factor and Indian agent at Fort Wayne, 1802–11, and as Indian agent at Piqua, Ohio, 1812–29. AJ removed him for John McElvain.

1. Stephen Johnston (1803–48) was in 1829 a Navy midshipman.

2. Johnston had long been treating with Ohio Indian nations for the purchase of their lands and removal to the West. His replacement, McElvain, negotiated a Delaware removal treaty in August 1829, and in 1831 Ohio Senecas signed a treaty in Washington for their removal to Oklahoma.

3. Henry Barrington (c1771–1839) was a Jackson presidential elector in 1828.

4. Johnston served on the Ohio Canal Commission from 1825 to 1836.

5. Jeremiah McLene.

6. John McLean's brother William McLean (1794–1839) was an Ohio congressman, 1823–29. Lewis Cass (1782–1866) was governor of Michigan Territory, 1813–31.

7. Johnston's father, Stephen Johnston, emigrated with his family from Ballyshannon in northern Ireland to Cumberland County, Pa., in 1786.

From *William Whiteley et al.*

Annapolis February 26th 1829

The undersigned members of the Legislature of Maryland on reviewing the late contest which has terminated in the complete triumph of the Jackson Party and the difficulties amidst which its cause was sustained in the State of Maryland, cannot permit the occasion to pass by without presenting to the consideration of the President Elect the distinguished services of one Individual whose efforts whilst they were followed by more individual sacrifices have produced more beneficial results to the cause of the Party than those of any other of its members within the State

It is well known that when the late contest was commenced in Maryland, it was conducted on the part of our Party in the face of the Patronage both of the General and State Governments and in opposition to nearly all the Established Presses of the State. All that Power could do to intimidate, all that Patronage could effect by cajoling, all that misrepresentation could produce through subservient presses were put in requisition to prostrate the People's will. To breast all these and to exhibit to the People the true character and circumstances of the Election by Congress[1] required extraordinary firmness, zeal, energy and intelligence and an entire reliance upon the integrity of the People and the Justice of our cause; and all these were displayed by Dabney S Carr Esquire when he established the Baltimore Republican as the organ of the Party within the State. All admitted the necessity of such a Press to resist the combined efforts of Power, Patronage and Misrepresentation: and yet few if any were willing to risk the consequences and hazard the sacrifices which were necessarily incident to its Establishment at the moment when Mr Carr threw himself into the onset for the general benefit, actuated solely by a regard for the general interests of the Party

Although established at a comparatively late period, its successful results are well known and have been experienced in every county of this state and are abundantly demonstrated by the firmness with which the Jackson cause was upheld and by the triumph with which it was followed in the City of Baltimore.[2] During the progress of the contest there were many dark and gloomy moments which threatened the downfall of an Establishment against which all Power and Patronage were arrayed and which could only be sustained through good and through evil report by individual exertions and sacrifices on the part of Mr Carr which but very few would have undergone. Yet he rose superior to all and did not hesitate to jeopard all for the rewards which follow a course of manly adherence to principle

Aware of this the undersigned, although unsolicited by Mr Carr yet deem it their duty to offer their humble Tribute to his Merits and to express the hope that he has not relied in vain upon the Justice of his Party for the proper rewards of a course of principle characterised throughout by extraordinary individual efforts for the general good

Wm. H. Marriott	William Whiteley
J C Herbert	Jno. T. Rees
Kensey Harrison	U S Heath
Tho. Kennedy	of the Senate

[Signatures of 27 members of the Maryland House of Delegates follow on next page.]

DS, DNA-RG 59 (M639-4). Dabney Smith Carr (1802–54) established the *Baltimore Republican and Commercial Advertiser* in 1827. In April AJ appointed him naval officer at Baltimore, removing William B. Barney.

1. Jacksonians charged corruption in John Quincy Adams's election as president by the House of Representatives in February 1825.

2. In 1828 Jackson carried Baltimore by 9,565 to 8,629, although Adams outpolled him narrowly statewide. Maryland's electoral vote was split with six for Adams and five for Jackson.

From Caleb Atwater

Circleville Feb. 28, 1829.

Dear Sir,

I wish to inform you, that I have made particular enquiry as to the family of my lamented friend DeWitt Clinton, with a view to turn your attention to them. All of them, appear to be provided for, except the eldest son, Charles A. Clinton. He is by profession a lawyer, and about 30 years of age, has received a liberal education, studied law regularly, and has practised law several years. The Profession is crowded, and his friends have procured for him, the appointment of clerk of the city court; an office, which confines him to the city and does not afford him a competent support. I have ascertained, that neither he nor his friends feel anxious to obtain any high station for him, at present, and that they would be perfectly satisfied with the office of Dist. Atty. for the southern district of New York, for which he is fully competent.[1]

John Duer Esq. is the present incumbent, whose history is briefly as follows, viz. He was bred up in a federal, aristocratic family, and continued to be openly on that side, until after the close of the war of 1812, when he, and James Hamilton, Verplank and others, to the number of 40 or more, pretended to dissolve the federal party! and from the most violent, persecuting federalists, became as violent persecuting Bucktails and *Duer*, true to the principles in which he was bred, supported Adams in 1824 and ever since, with great violence and virulence, assailing your character on all occasions in a tone and to an extent exceeded by none.[2]

My Dear Sir, such men can have no sympathies in common with us, the old republicans, and I am satisfied, that altho' Verplank, James Hamilton et alii, who were once federalists & turned around to the Bucktails together, may feel some sympathy for Mr. Duer, yet I do not believe that one Democrat, in New York state, wishes Duer continued in office, nor do I believe one would object to the appointment of Charles A. Clinton in his stead. If I knew that Duer would be removed, and I know he ought to be removed, I would advise Col. Clinton's friends to apply for the appointment forthwith, for him. On the whole, I hope and fervently pray, that some honorable place may be given to Mr. Clinton. It will produce a great deal of good, every where, and no harm. History will do justice to your motives in making such an appointment, and the present age will applaud it. I have thus, to the best of my poor ability, discharged a debt of gratitude due to my deceased friend, and to yourself.

Col. David Robb, member of the Senate of this state, has written to me the enclosed letter, which in your possession, will not injure him, and I have forwarded it. Col. R. was the *first man*, that came out for you, in Guernsey co. O. in 1823, I think, and to him and his unceasing labors we are indebted for the support you obtained in that county. Col. R. publishes, a newspaper, "the Guernsey Times" at Washington, Guernsey county Ohio. From long conversations with him, at Columbus, recently, I suppose, that if a few advertisements could be sent to him for insertion, in his paper by members of your cabinet, he would be satisfied—some little notice from Gen. Jackson.[3]

Of similar letters, I have recd recently, great numbers, not only from your friends in Ohio, but in other states, and as soon as the health of my family, will permit, I will, mention several of your friends to you, who wish to prove by me, their early, continued and faithful friendship towards yourself. In complying with their several requests, I do but perform a duty towards yourself and them, though it costs me both time and money, and is without any personal benefit to myself or family.

In this state, great caution is necessary, and every step, *at first,* ought to be cautious. Fifty persons [b]y turning around from us to our opponents in each county, would destroy us, as a party, perhaps, forever. Every officer of the U. S. government, 4 postmasters, excepted, are against us—every officer of the state government (civil ones) Secy of state, keeper of the Pen[i]tentiary (a brother of J. McL. and like him, on both sides[)] and 3 judges of common Pleas, excepted, are all all opposed to us!![4] One single bad appointment, to start upon, (and every one is such an one, where the applicant has gone around for signers, like Hayward, and co. and Ohio is lost to us. Spare us, My Dear Sir, awhile—send home the hosts around you, from Ohio, who would ruin all, to gratify their unholy ambition. April or May will be early enough, to begin on Ohio. *If posible,* I will visit the city in April or May and bring with me, the sense of your friends, in this state, as to appointments and removals. Wishing you Sir, success in your arduous and Herculean labors and many, very many years of happiness, without alloy, I am, Dear Sir, Your's ever

Caleb Atwater

ALS, DLC (36).

1. De Witt Clinton (1769–1828) had been four-term governor of New York and leader of the state political faction opposed by Martin Van Buren's Bucktails. His son Charles Alexander Clinton (1798–1861) was a New York City lawyer.

2. John Duer (1782–1858), son of William Duer, was appointed district attorney by Adams in 1828. AJ removed him for James A. Hamilton. Gulian Crommelin Verplanck (1786–1870) was a Jacksonian congressman.

3. David Robb served in the Ohio senate, 1819–20 and 1827–29. He edited the *Washington Republican* in Guernsey County.

4. Nathaniel McLean (1787–1871), brother of John McLean, was keeper of the Ohio penitentiary, 1823–30. He had been an Adams candidate for elector in 1824.

From Stephen Simpson

Philadelphia February 28. 1829.

Dear Sir,

We arrived here last night; & I will candidly confess, that at one time I had resolved not to trouble you with my advice; but when I came to reflect, that you *now* were more in want of a candid & Sincere friend than ever, I gave up my punctilios, & determined to let you hear from me. It has occurred to me, that you must have placed your confidence in some one, to an extent not warranted by the fallibility of the human heart; & that the person so much confided in, is less solicitous for your glory, than his own advancement. Look about you, my Dear Sir, & See if none such are not favoured with too much of your confidence! You may have had a friend as Andrew Jackson; but believe me it is very difficult, *as President of the U.S.* to have a *true one*. I did intend to write you a long letter, but the enclosed reflections, which are cut from the *Philada. Gazette,* a paper that has been your steady friend, will supercede what I designed to Say. It is worthy of your marked attention. I respond cordially to all its sentiments; & be assured, my dear Sir, that *none* but a *disinterested friend,* could have written, or could respond to such Sentiments; which emanate from the heart of the Bishop of Geneva. The article that precedes it, was written by the Editor of the paper, a Mr. Gouge. Excuse this frank letter, & believe me with high consideration, your friend & Servt.

S. Simpson

ALS, DLC (36). Simpson enclosed two extracts from the *Philadelphia Gazette* of February 27. The first, by editor William M. Gouge (1796–1863), defended AJ's failure to call on President Adams on arriving in Washington. Gouge later wrote the influential *A Short History of Money and Banking in the United States* (1833). The second item complimented AJ's moral courage and quoted the admonition of St. Francis de Sales (1567–1622), Bishop of Geneva, to "follow your own path, be guided by your own taste and judgment, and do not seek to conform to the caprice of all your audience."

Memorandum on Administration Policy

Mr. R__ e__ R__ va.

1rst.   a strong constitutional att. genl
2nd.   a genuine old fashioned Cabinet to act together & form a counsel consultative
3rd.   no Editors to be appointed

4th.   no Members of Congress, except heads of Departments or Foreign ministers to be appointed

5th.   no Foreign mission to be originated without the senate &c &c—

6th.   The Public debt paid off, the Tariff modified & no power usurped over internal improvements

7th.   a high minded enlightened principle in the administration of the Govt. as to appointments and removals. These things will give a brilliant carreer to the administration

[Endorsed by AJ:] memorandom of points to be considered in the administration of the government: to be filed—

AD (at Dec 9, 1828), DLC (36). This undated document in AJ's hand probably summarizes the views of *Richmond Enquirer* editor Thomas Ritchie (1778–1854).

March

Andrew Jackson was inaugurated on March 4, 1829. Before he had been in office a month, he was enmeshed in two difficulties that would do much to shape his presidency.

The first concerned relations between the federal government, the states, and the Indian nations within their borders. By 1829, the Indian tribes that remained east of the Mississippi faced intensifying threats from white encroachments upon their lands and from state challenges to their sovereignty. Within the limits of Georgia, Alabama, and Mississippi, the Creek, Cherokee, Choctaw, and Chickasaw Nations occupied and governed dominions that were secured to them by treaty with the United States. But the federal government had also promised, in an 1802 compact with Georgia, to extinguish the Indian title within that state "as early as the same can be peaceably obtained on reasonable terms." Between Jackson's election and his inauguration, all three states formally asserted jurisdiction over their Indian domains—Georgia in December 1828, Alabama and Mississippi in January and February 1829. Faced with these competing imperatives, Jackson signaled from the outset that he would not defend tribal treaty rights at the expense of state sovereignty, and that the only solution lay in the Indians' removal west of the Mississippi where they would be beyond state jurisdiction.

The other issue concerned the personnel of the administration. The Cabinet Jackson named upon taking office was the same the Telegraph had announced in February, with one exception: John McLean was nominated on March 6 to the vacancy on the Supreme Court, while William T. Barry became postmaster general. Jackson's Cabinet was widely derided by both friends and foes. The appointment that came under greatest fire was that of Senator John Henry Eaton to be secretary of war.

On January 1, 1829, Eaton had married Margaret O'Neale Timberlake (1799–1879). Margaret, or Peggy, was the daughter of William O'Neale, proprietor of a prominent Washington boardinghouse where both Jackson and Eaton had lodged while serving in Congress. In 1816 she had married John Bowie Timberlake, a Navy purser. Timberlake died at sea on the USS Constitution in April 1828, an apparent suicide. Margaret's marriage to Eaton just a few months later ignited a scandal, and some leading Washingtonians determined to exclude the couple from their society.

Meanwhile, as foretold in his inaugural address, Jackson commenced his reform of the officeholders, replacing some long-serving government functionaries with such active partisans as Amos Kendall and Isaac Hill. Controversy over Jackson's policy deepened as the removals continued on through the spring.

To John Marshall

March 2d. 1829

Genl Jackson presents his respects to Chief justice Marshall and would be gratified to be informed by him whether it will suit his convenience to administer the oath prescribed by the Constitution for the President of the United states before he enters upon the duties of office, on Wednesday next at 12 oclock, and at such place as the senate may designate.

LC, DLC (60). John Marshall (1755–1835) was Chief Justice of the United States, 1801–35.

From William Polk et al.

Washington, 4th March, 1829.

GENERAL ANDREW JACKSON—

SIR: We, a few of the surviving officers and soldiers of the army of the Revolution, now convened at this place, most respectfully solicit the honor of forming your escort to the Capitol, where you are about to be inaugurated as President of the United States.

Former events, and our advanced ages, preclude the idea that this is designed to be a military pageant; no, Sir, it is far otherwise; having fought in the defence of the sacred rights of man, and for the liberty, sovereignty, and independence of these United States, now happily bound together, as we fondly hope, by an indissoluble chain, we feel desirous to avail ourselves of the opportunity of being present when the guardianship of these invaluable benefits shall be deposited in your hands.

The valor, the judgment, the independence of mind, the prudence, the firmness and the true patriotism of our great commander, Washington, led us triumphantly through the Revolutionary war, and the nation through the first periods of the Federal Constitution; and we have entire confidence that the exercise of the same transcendent virtues, will, under God, preserve inviolate our liberties, independence and union, during your administration;—and it is our most ardent prayer that they may be perpetual. May your days be long and happy—may increasing honors multiply on your head—and, like your first predecessor, may you add a civic monument to your martial glory; and like his, may they be imperishable!

We have the honor to be, With the highest respect, Your most ob't ser'ts.

WILLIAM POLK, *Chairman.*
JOHN NICHOLAS,
AARON OGDEN,
ABRAHAM BROOM,
ROBERT BOLLING,
ELNATHAN SEARS,
ROBERT KAENE,
J. WOODSIDES,
PHILIP STEWART,
ARMISTEAD LONG,
JNO. M. TAYLOR,
JOHN BROWNE CUTTING,
CALEB STARK,
WILLIAM GAMBEL,
JACOB GIDEON, Sr.

Printed, Washington *United States' Telegraph,* March 5 (mAJs; 12-0854). The signers had served in the Revolution in various capacities. Aaron Ogden (1756–1839) was a former senator and governor of New Jersey, Philip Stewart or Stuart (1760–1830) a former Maryland congressman and member of the Washington Jackson Central Committee in 1828, and John Browne Cutting (c1755–1831) a War Department clerk.

To *William Polk et al.*

[March 4]

Respected Friends.

Your affectionate address awakens sentiments and recollections which I feel with sincerity, and cherish with pride. To have around my person, at the moment of undertaking the most solemn of all duties to my country, the companions of the immortal Washington, will afford me satisfaction and grateful encouragement. That by my best exertions, I shall be able to exhibit more than an imitation of his patriotic labours, a sense of my own imperfections, and the reverence I entertain for his virtues forbid me to hope.

To you, respected friends, the survivors of that heroic band, who followed him so long & so valiantly in the path of Glory, I offer my sincere thanks—and to heaven my prayers that your remaining years may be as happy as your toils & your lives have been illustrious

AD draft, DLC (36). *US Telegraph*, March 5.

Inaugural Address

[On March 4, in a ceremony at the Capitol, Jackson was inaugurated as seventh president of the United States. Chief Justice Marshall administered the oath of office, and Jackson delivered an inaugural address. The address was widely published in newspapers and later in James D. Richardson, ed., A Compilation of the Messages and Papers of the Presidents, 2:436–38.

Jackson's papers at the Library of Congress contain three manuscripts of the address. One, nearly identical to the official published text, is a copy by William B. Lewis (DLC–60). The other two, both printed below, are drafts, the first by Jackson and the second by Andrew Jackson Donelson. Jackson endorsed the latter "Inagural address as delivered." However, a comparison with the published version shows a number of minor adjustments and two very substantive changes. In the published text, the seventh paragraph of the Donelson draft, proposing a distribution of the surplus revenue, was omitted after the first sentence. Also, a new tenth paragraph was inserted following that on the Indians. Beginning with "the recent demonstration of public sentiment inscribes on the list of Executive duties, in characters too legible to be overlooked, the task of reform," it announced Jackson's intention to overhaul the federal patronage in order to safeguard the freedom of elections and remove power from "unfaithful or incompetent hands."]

Fellow Citizens

About to enter upon the duties to which as President of the United States, I have been called by the voluntary suffrages of my country, I avail myself of this occasion to express the deep and heartfelt gratitude with which a testimonial of such distinguished favor has been received. To be elected under the circumstances which have marked the recent contest of opinion to administer the affairs of a goverment deriving all its powers from the will of the people—a goverment whose vital principle is the right of the people to controul its measures, and whose only object and glory are the equal happiness and freedom of all the members of the confederacy, cannot but penetrate me with the most powerful and mingled emotions of thanks, on the one hand, for the honor conferred on me, and on the other, of solemn apprehensions for the safety of the great and important interests committed to my charge.

Under the weight of these emotions, unaided by any confidence inspired by past experience, or by any strength derived from the conscious possession of powers equal to the station; I confess, fellow citizens, that I approach it with trembling reluctance. But my Country has willed it, and I obay, gathering hope from the reflection that the other branches of the

Govt with whom the constitutional will associates me, will yield those resources of Patriotism and intelligence, by which the administration may be rendered useful, and the honor and independence of our widely extended Republic guarded from encroachment; but above all, trusting to the smiles of that overruling Providence, "in the hollow of whose hand," is the destiny of nations, for that animation of common council and harmonising effort, which shall enable us to steer, the Bark of liberty, through every dificulty.

In the present Stage of our history, it will not be expected of me on this occasion to enter into any detail of the first principles of our goverment— The atchievements of our fathers, our subsequent intercourse with each other, the various relations we have sustained with the other powers of the world, and our present attitude at home, exhibits the practical operations of these principles—all of which are comprised in the sovereignity of the people. This is the basis of our system, and to its security from violation and innovation must our practice and experience as a goverment be dedicated. To the administration of my illustrious predecessors I will be permitted to refer as mirors, not so much for the measures which m[a]y be demanded by the present state of the country, but as applications of the same principles to the various exigencies which have occurred in our history, and as shedding light upon those which may hereafter arise—It is thus the great moral race we are running, connects us with the past, and is tributary to the events which are to come: thus, that every period of our goverment is useful to that which follows, not as the source of principles, but as guides on that sacred fountain to which we must often go for the refreshment of our laws, and the invigoration of the public morals. It is from this source that we derive the means of congratulating ourselves upon the present free condition of our country, and build our hopes for its future safety—In fine, Fellow Citizens, this is the bulwark of our liberties.

Among the various and important duties that are confided to the President, there are none of more interest than that which requires the selection of his officers. The application of the laws, and the management of our relations with foreign powers, form the chief object of an Executive, and are as essential to the welfare of the union as the laws themselves—In the discharge of this trust it shall be my care to fill the various offices at the disposal of the Executive with individuals uniting as far as possible the qualifications of the head & heart, always recollecting that in a free goverment the demand for moral qualities should be made superior to that of talents. In other forms of goverment where the people are not regarded as composing the sovereign power, it is easy to perceive that the safeguard of the empire consists chiefly in the skill by which the monarch can wield the bigoted acquiesence of his subjects. But it is different with us. Here the will of the people, prescribed in a constitution of their own choice, controuls the service of the public functionaries, and is interested more deeply in the preservation of those qualities which ensures fidelity and honest devotion to their interests.

Provisions for the national defence form another class of duties for the Representatives of the people, and as they stand in delicate connection with the powers of the general & state Governments when understood to embrace the protection of our own labour, merit the most serious consideration. Legislation for this object encouraging the production of those articles which are essential in the emergencies of war, & to the independence of the nation, seems to me to be sanctioned by the constitution, as lawful & Just. The general safety was the great motive for the confederation of the states, and never could have been effected without conferring on the Federal Government the power to provide those internal supplies which constitute the means of war, and which if left to the ordinary operations of commerce, might be witheld at a time when we most needed them. Judicious Tariff imposing duties high anough to insure us against this calamity will always meet with my hearty cooperation. But beyond this point, legislation effecting the natural relations of the labour of the states are irreconcileable to the objects of the union, and threatening to its peace and tranquility.

Recollecting that all the states are equal in sovereignity, and in claims to the benefits accruing from the confederation, upon the federal principle of providing by taxation for the wants of the Goverment, it seems Just that the expenditures should be distributed regard being first paid to the national debt, and the appropriations for the support of the Government, and safety of the union The necessity of conforming more closely to this principle is illustrated by the dissatisfaction which the expenditures for the purposes of improvement has already created in several of the states. The operation of the principle, as fixed on this equitable basis, will give to the states the fisical prosperity of the nation, and secure harmony by removeing the grounds of Jealousy.

Between the powers granted to the general government, and those reserved to the states and the people, it is to be regretted that no line can be so obviously drawn as that all shall understand alike its bounderies—There will be a teritory between them which must be governed by the good sense of a nation always ready to resist oppression, and too high minded to forget the rights of the minority. It is the inheritance of that sentiment of conciliation, and spirit of compromise which gave us the constitution, and which is to enable us in the progress of time to amend such defects in the system as experience may detect—Fully sensible of the necessity which I shall have for the exercise of this spirit on the part of my fellow Citizens, I shall notice with pleasure an unreserved examination of the measures of my administration, and shall be the last to cry out treason against those who interpret differently from myself the policy, or powers of the government.

Some of the Topics which shall engage my earliest attention as intimately connected with the prosperity of our beloved country, are, the liquidation of the national debt—The introduction and observance of the strictest econonomy in the disbursments of the Government, a Judicious tariff, combined with a fostering care of commerce & agriculture, and regulated by the principles before adverted to, a Just respect for state rights and the maintainance of state sovereignity as the best check of the tendencies to consolidation; and the distribution of the surplus revenue amonghst the states according to the apportionment of representation, for the purposes of education & internal improvement—except where the subjects are entirely national—With the accomplishment of these objects I trust the memorials of our national blessings may be multiplied, and the scenes of domestic labour be made more animating and happy.

[Endorsed by AJ:] Rough draft of inagural address—

AD draft, DLC (36).

Fellow Citizens—
About to undertake the arduous duties that I have been appointed to perform by the choice of a free people, I avail myself of this customary and solemn occasion to express the gratitude which their confidence inspires, and to acknowledge the accountability which my situation enjoins. While the magnitude of their interests convinces me that no thanks can be adequate to the honor they confer, it admonishes me that the best return I can make, is a zealous dedication of my humble abilities to their service, and their good.

As the instrument of the Federal Constitution it will devolve on me, for a stated period, to execute the laws of the United States, to superintend their foreign and their confederate relations, to manage their revenue, to command their forces, and by communications to the Legislature to watch over and to promote their interests generally. And the principles of action by which I shall endeavor to accomplish this circle of duties, it is now proper for me briefly to indicate.

In administering the laws of Congress, I shall keep stedfastly in view the limitations as well as the extent of the Executive power, trusting thereby to discharge the functions of my office without transcending its authority. With foreign nations it will be my study to preserve peace and to cultivate friendship on fair and honorable terms; and in the adjustment of any differences that may exist or arise, to exhibit the forbearance becoming a powerful nation, rather than the sensibility belonging to a gallant people.

In such measures as I may be called on to pursue in regard to the rights of the seperate States, I hope to be animated by a proper respect for those sovereign members of our union; taking care not to confound the powers they have reserved to themselves with those they have granted to the Confederacy.

The management of the public revenue, that searching operation in all governments, is among the most delicate and important trusts in ours, and it will of course demand no inconsiderable share of my official solicitude. Under every aspect in which it can be considered, it would appear that advantage must result from the observance of a strict and faithful economy. This I shall aim at the more anxiously, both because it will facilitate the extinguishment of the national debt—the unnecessary duration of which is incompatible with real independence—and because it will counteract that tendency to public and private profligacy which a profuse expenditure by the government, is but too apt to engender. Powerful auxiliaries to the attainment of this desireable end, are to be found in the regulations provided by the wisdom of Congress for the specific appropriation of public money, and the prompt accountability of public officers.

With regard to a proper protection of the subjects of impost with a view to the collection of the revenue, it would seem to me that the spirit of equity, caution and compromise, in which the constitution was formed, requires, that the great interests of agriculture, comerce, and manufactures, should be equally favored; and that the only exception to this rule should consist in the peculiar encouragement of any products of either of them, that may be found essential to our national independence.

The subjects of internal improvement and of popular education, so far as they can be promoted by the constitutional acts of the federal Government, are of high importance. After liquidating the national debt the national income will probably exceed the ordinary expenses of Government, in which event the apportionment of the surplus revenue among the states according to the ratio of their representation for these purposes, will be a fair, federal, and a useful disposition of it. Every member of the Union, in peace and in War, will be benefitted by the improvement of our inland navigation, and the construction of highways in the several states. And the Representative principle, upon the virtue of which our state and federal governments are founded, can reach its *maximum* value, only by a wide and effcacious diffusion of instruction—knowledge and power being in this respect coexistent qualities.

Considering standing armies as dangerous to free Governments in time of peace, I shall not seek to enlarge our present establishment, nor disregard that salutary lesson of political experience which teaches that the military should be held subordinate to the civil power. The gradual increase of our navy; the preservation of our forts, arsenals and dock yards; and the introduction of progressive improvements in the discipline and science of both branches of our military service, are so plainly prescribed by prudence that I should be excused for omitting their mention, sooner than for insisting on their importance. But the bulwark of our defence is the national militia, which in the present state of our intelligence and population must render us invincible. As long as our Government is administered for the good of the people, and is regulated by their will; as long as it secures to us the rights of person and of property, liberty of conscience and of the press, it will be worth defending; and so long as it is worth defending a patriotic militia will cover it with an impenetrable aegis. Partial injuries and occasional mortifications we may be subjected to; but a million of armed freemen possessed of the means of war, can never be conquered by a foreign foe. To any just system, therefore, calculated to strengthen this national safeguard of the country, I shall cheerfully lend all the aid in my power.

A humane and considerate attention to the rights and the wants of the Indian tribes within our limits, consistent with the habits of our government, and the feelings of our people, it will be my sincere and constant desire to observe. A just and liberal policy is due to their dependent situation, and to our national character.

In the performance of a task thus generally delineated, I shall endeavor to select men whose talents and integrity will insure in their respective stations, able and faithful cooperation—depending for the advancement of the public service, more on the ability and virtue of the public officers, than on their numbers.

A diffidence, perhaps too just, in my own qualifications, will teach me to look with reverence to the examples of public virtue left by my illustrious predecessors, and with veneration to the lights that flow from the mind that founded, and the mind that reformed our system. The same diffidence induces me to hope for enlightenment and aid from the coordinate branches of the Government, and for the indulgence and support of my fellow citizens generally. And a firm reliance on the goodness of that power, whose providence mercifully protected our national infancy, and has upheld since, our liberties in various vicissitudes, encourages me to offer up my ardent supplications that he will continue to make our beloved country, the object of his divine care and gracious benediction—

[Endorsed by AJ:] Inagural address as delivered—

Draft by AJ Donelson, DLC (36). The manuscript bears a number of pencilled alterations, not shown here, none of which were incorporated in the final text.

From Daniel W. Wright

Hamilton, Monroe County, Mississippi
4th. March 1829

Dear Sir

During the recent session of the Genl. Assembly of this State, a committee was raised (of which I was chairman) with directions to enquire into the Constitutional right and power which this State possessed, to extend her legal process into, and to exercise jurisdiction over, that portion of territory now occupied by the Chickesaw and Choctaw tribes of Indians embraced within her chartered limits. Without entering into a detail of the reasons by which the committee was actuated, they reported a bill which passed into a law declarative of the right. The committee with a view, that no collision of power, policy or interest, as respects the powers of the Genl Government, contrasted with States' sovereignty should take place—and knowing that the present policy of the Government, is, to remove, at as early period as possible, those tribes west of the Mississippi river, requested me to address you on the subject of their removal, which, I trust, will be a sufficient apology for this communication—

It was believed by the committee, and is the general opinion of those best acquainted with the present feelings and condition of those tribes, that if a delegation of their Chiefs and some of their principal head men, were called, by your Excellency to the city of Washington, during the ensuing summer, that a treaty or cession of their country may be made with them, favorably to the interest of the Government. A few designing individuals among them (that class of people called Missionaries not being the least conspicuous) operate most powerfully in thwarting the policy of the Govt. relative to their removal.

It is believed, that even at this time, if a suitable person were empowered, and sent among the Choctaws, who was authorized to give a reasonable price for their improvements and surplus cattle, two thousand of them, (at least) could be induced to remove before the first of December next—

There is another subject, to which I would respectfully call your attention, to wit, the importance of establishing a Port of entry at the Pascagola Bay in this state, for the purpose of protecting the revenue Laws of the United States. I have recently heard, that the Govt. contemplates appointing a revenue Officer to be stationed at that place; If the appointment of such an Officer become necessary or expedient, I take the liberty of presenting to the favorable consideration of your Excellency, an application (through me) by Colo William Dowsing of this County. his qualifications are ade*[quate]* to the discharge of the duties of the Office[1]

As an evidence of the high estimate in whi*[ch the]* citizens of this State hold Colo. Dowsing, I *[will]* refer you to the vote of our last electi*[on for]* electors of President and Vice Preside*[nt of the]* United States, by which you will asc*[ertain]* that he was one of the successful candida*[tes. I]* also refer your Excellency to our Senators *[and Rep]*resentative in Congress for further par*[ticulars]* relative to the respectability and qualific*[ations]* of the Colo. I will remark however, *[that]* Office is an object to him; he has a v*[ery nu]*merous family of children, and his view *[in]* settling in that section of the State wou*[ld]* be greatly promoted by the appointment.

I hope sir, you will pardon the liberty I have taken, in addressing to you the foregoing in regard to the pretentions of Colo. Dowsing, as my acquaintance with you was at a period of life when my years were so few that I expect you scarcely recollect me—

I am sir, with sentiments of the highest respect, and friendly considerations, your Excellency's most Obt Sert.

D. W. Wright

[Endorsed by AJ:] refered to *the Sec. of War*

ALS, DNA-RG 75 (M234-432). Wright (1795–1844), a lawyer, represented Monroe County in the Mississippi house. The law of February 4 extended state legal process over Chickasaw and Choctaw lands in Mississippi.

    1. Dowsing (1784–1854), of Washington, Monroe County, had been a state senator and 1828 Jackson presidential elector. In 1833 AJ appointed him register of the land office at Columbus.

From Samuel Rogers

Ennis Ville 5th. March 1829
Huntingdon County Pennsylvenia

Deare General—

Sir I adress you Respecting my son David Rogers who was stolen from me in october 1826 the first act. I had from him was in the begining of November Last he is now on Bord the U S Scooner Alert at Norfolk whare he states to me he was shiped for three years by a Certain Leutenant Mont Gomery[1] the Boy was but 14 years of age at that time I had him at School a Distance from home when he was Felloneously Decoyed from me with out my Knowladge or Consent I made Complaint to the Sacretary as soon as I heard whare he was but Recd no answer   I then wrote to Mr John Mitchel of Centre County a Member of the House of Represntatives for his Interfarence he answered my Letter with the answer of the Sacretary which I send Enclosed to you[2] by which it apears he is to be Detained until he is out of Debt and then to be Dis Charged a Distance of Four Hundred miles from home whare he was taken & is now this would be a poore way of Redressing me for the Injuries I have sustained by the absence of my son for more than two years and five or six months I Recd. Letter from my son a few days since he states to me that Comadore Barron[3] tells him he will Discharge him as soon as he is out of Debt I should be Glad if Comadore Barron Could give a satisfactory act. how my boy become inDebted to the united states or wheather Contracts or Bargins made with Miner Children of his age are valid my Lit*[tle]* son states to me In a Letter that Leutenant J H Montgomer got his money from him at Carlisle

Previous to his going to sea with Promise to Deposit it in the Bank at Ca[rlisle] for him untill he would Return from sea he wrote to me to get it on Enquiery at the *[Bank]* there apears no Deposite of any money ma[de] by montgomery for David Rogers Children *[are]* Easely Imposed on and Probabely if a Fair Investigation was made it would turn out that all his wages has been swindled from him in the same way—

Deare genral I Earnestly solicite your atention in my Case in giveing sutch orders as you shall think Proper and Consistent with the Laws of our Cuntry those who misaplyes the Publick money by Bargening with Children aught in my opinin to be made acountable I wish to have my Little s*[on]* sent Home safe & a Suteable Redress for the ti*[me]* the have Detained him from me with sincere wishes for your wellfare and Happyness I am your Friend & Humble Svt.

Saml. Rogers

[Endorsed by AJ:] Saml Rogers letter recd. March 25th. 1829—complaining that his son was stolen from him two & half years ago, & is detained on board the U. States Schooner, Alert, at Norfolk—& praying that his son may be restored to him, with damages, for his detention—

This refered to the Secretary of the Navy, that enquiry may be made, & if the boy is detained from his father wrongfully, that he may be restored to him, & Justice be done. A. Jackson

ALS, DNA-RG 45 (M124-117). Samuel Rogers (d.1831) was a Revolutionary veteran. According to Navy records, David Rogers did not enter service until June 1828. Samuel's initial complaint had prompted Adams's Navy secretary Samuel L. Southard in November 1828 to order David discharged once he repaid the three-month advance on his pay. On May 8, 1829, Navy secretary John Branch wrote Rogers that his son had been discharged in January and his whereabouts were unknown (DNA-RG 45, M209-6).

1. John Berrien Montgomery (1794–1873) of New Jersey was a Navy lieutenant.
2. Southard to John Mitchell, January 10, 1829. Mitchell (1781–1849) was a Pennsylvania congressman, 1825–29.
3. James Barron (1768–1851) was commandant of the Gosport Navy Yard at Norfolk, Va.

From John Ross et al.

Williamson's Hotel, Washington City
March 6th. 1829

Respected Sir,

We respectfully beg leave to inform you that the present U.S. Agent for the Cherokee Nation (Colo. H. Montgomery) in his official acts does not give that satisfaction to the nation as will inspire the confidence which should be placed upon an Officer of the Genl. Govt. and however much this is to be regretted, we can assure you that this want of confidence is not without *good causes.*

We therefore earnestly solicit & hope that another will be appointed in his stead; and were we permitted to express our opinion, we would say, that, if Colo. Thos. C. Hindman of Tenee. was appointed to the office, the instructions & Orders of the Genl. Government would be executed with promptness and fidelity, as well as afford more general satisfaction to the Nation—Our reason for introducing this Gentleman's Name is because we have been informed that he is desirous, in case of a vacancy, to receive the appointment—Confiding in your magnanimity and justice to our Nation we hope you will take the subject into consideration. Very Respectfully Yr. Obt. Servts.

> (Signed) Jno Ross
> Richd. Taylor
> Edward Gunter
> Wm. S. Coodey

Copy, OkTG (12-0868). *John Ross Papers,* 1:157–58. Ross (1790–1866) was the principal chief of the Eastern Cherokees. In November 1828, the Cherokee National Council appointed Ross, Richard Taylor (1788–1853), Edward Gunter (1789–1842), and William Shorey Coodey (1806–49) to go to Washington to present grievances and claims against the federal government. The delegation arrived in January and remained through April. On February 27 they protested to Congress against Georgia's extension of jurisdiction and the federal government's efforts to induce Cherokees to emigrate west of the Mississippi (*HRDoc* 145, 20th Cong., 2d sess., Serial 187; *John Ross Papers,* 1:154–57). Hugh Lawson Montgomery (1767–1852), Cherokee agent since 1825, continued to serve until 1835. Thomas Carmichael Hindman (1793–1856) of Knoxville had been an Army lieutenant under AJ in the War of 1812.

From Roley McIntosh et al.

> Western Creek Nation
> March 7th. 1829

To Our Father The President

We the chiefs head men and warriors of the Creek Nation now in council assembled—petition the President of the United States to take into consideration the complaints which we lay before you—against Col. Brearley U. States Agent for the Creek Nation—It is with reluctance that we complain—and Nothing but necessity—and repeated injustice compel us—we have been deceived by the Government—things which were promised to us are now denied us—We under stood by the Treaty that we were to receive on our arrival in the Territory of Arkansas at our place of residence Thirty dollars a head—beaver traps—Guns—Brass kettles butcher knives and blanketts—the Thirty dollars have not been paid—nor beaver traps—and many have not had their Guns Kettles nor blanketts—and many others not paid for improvements[1]—Col. Brearley promised us that fifty days after his departure from this place the money should be paid—his son[2] and Capt. Thos. Anthony now acting as a Sub Agent—were the two appointed to pay us at the expiration of the fifty days—we attended at the Agency for the purpose of receiving our money but we were disappointed—and received for answer that no instructions nor money had been left by the Agent We have lost all confidence in Col Brearley and we regard him no more as our Agent—we sincerely hope that our Father the President will send us a man in whom we can place confidence and who will do us justice—we will rely upon him as to the choice he may make

Father, you are well aware that the Laws prohibit men who are in the employ of the Government from speculating in any manner whatsoever—Col. Brearley seems to put your Laws at defyance—for he has to our knowledge purchased all the cattle and hogs in the country—and he has sold and continues to sell to the Indians at a verry extravagant advance—Flour—at ten dollars ℔ barrel (which we believe he received from the Asst. Com. Of Subsistence at Cantonment Gibson)—also spirituous Liquors—which are most strictly prohibited by the Laws,[3] the first party that came were well furnished with beef & Pork this year Col. Brearley has taken the contract—the contract was not let out as is generally done to the Lowest bidder—but was taken by Col. Brearley at three & half cents for beef—when their were persons offering to furnish us at two and two & half cents ℔ pound—Col. Brearley having taken the contract and giving instruction to his son to take out all the Lard—and after selecting all the choice pieces for his own use the balance are Issued to us—the Lard taken from the hogs afterwards were sold to us for ten cents ℔ pound[4]—Col. Brearley never attends our Councils to advise us—we frequently called upon him But Generally found him intoxicated so that no satisfaction could be obtained for the business which caused our Visit—his Sub Agent Capt. Anthony is far worse than himself so as to render him totally unfit for business of any kind—we could say much more about this Gentleman but we regard it as a loss of time—Father we could say much more but we will trouble you no Longer with our complaints —and we rest satisfyed that you will pity our situation—that you will have justice done us for justice only we demand—We have to call your attention again on a subject which we cannot pass over in Silence—The Emigration will certainly cease from the old Nation should the news of the imposition practised upon us reach their Ears—and the ill treatment which we received—the party that came by water came as far as fort Smith and the boat their stopd. and a great portion of their property was left and destroyed[5]—Col. Brearley said he had got the people at their place of residence and they might get their property as they could

Accept Father the Sincere wishes of your Children for your health and Prosperity

      1 Roley   X   McIntosh
      2 Chilly McIntosh
      3 Foshatchee   X   Micco
        William   X   Miller
      5 Micco   X   Charles

[Forty-eight additional names follow.]

We the undersigned do witness the three first, and fifth signatures to this paper. Cantonment Gibson 9th March 1829.

       N. G. Wilkinson Capt 7 Infy
       John Stewart Capt. 7t. Infy
        E. S. Hawkins Lt. 7 Inf
        Th. Johnston Lt 7 Inf.

DS, DNA-RG 75 (M234-236). Roley (c1790–1863) and Chilly (c1800–1875) McIntosh were the half-brother and son of late Creek chief William McIntosh (1775–1825), who was slain by tribal order for signing the disputed removal Treaty of Indian Springs. By the 1826 Treaty of Washington, which voided the previous year's agreement, the Creeks ceded most of their Georgia lands and the McIntosh faction of the tribe arranged to remove west of the Mississippi at federal expense. President Adams appointed New Jersey native and former U.S. Army colonel David Brearley (1786–1837) as agent to the emigrants. In 1828, two parties comprising about 1200 Creeks emigrated to the Verdigris River near Fort Gibson in present-day Oklahoma.

    1. The Treaty of Washington pledged the United States to compensate the emigrants for improvements on their former lands, defray all removal expenses, furnish a year's subsistence in their new home, and pay a cash sum of up to $33.33 per emigrant.

    2. Joseph H. Brearley worked as a surveyor in the Arkansas territory and assisted with affairs at the Western Creek Agency.

    3. The 1802 Indian Intercourse Act barred agents from having "interest or concern in any trade with the Indians" and also forbade "vending or distribution of spirituous liquors" to them. The assistant commissary was Francis Danielly, who had accompanied Brearley and the emigrating Creeks west.

    4. The contractors Mark (1794–1862) and Richard Henderson (c1799–1859) Bean, who since April 1828 had been supplying the Creeks with beef, ceded the contract to Brearley for a period of four months.

    5. The first emigrating party had split into two groups at Memphis. One, consisting mostly of warriors and accompanied by Brearley, completed the journey by land; the other, comprised of women, children, and the elderly, came by boat on the Mississippi and Arkansas rivers. Both groups were hampered by heavy rains and high water.

From James Alexander Hamilton

[In repeated efforts over many years, the American and British governments failed to reach agreement on where to locate the northeastern boundary of the United States pursuant to the Treaty of Paris ending the Revolutionary War. In 1827 the two countries signed a convention to submit the matter to a friendly sovereign for arbitration.]

Department of State
Washington 9th. March 1829.

The Acting Secretary of State has the honor, respectfully, to report to the President of the United States, all the information at this Department of what has been done to carry into effect the first Article of the Convention between the United States and the British Government concluded at London on the 29th September 1827, a printed copy whereof accompanies this Report.

The ratifications of this Convention were exchanged at London on the 2nd of April, 1828.

By the instructions of this Government to their Chargé d'Affaires at St. James', Mr. W. B. Lawrence, dated 20th. February, 1828, (copy annexed) he was required to proceed to the fulfilment of the first Article of the Treaty, and, in pursuance of the instructions therein contained, after various interviews with Lords Dudley and Aberdeen, on the 14th. June 1828, they fixed upon the King of the Netherlands as the Arbiter, and, on the 19th. of the same month, it was determined between Mr Lawrence and Lord Aberdeen that the communication to the selected Sovereign should be made by the Ministers of the United States & Great Britain in separate notes addressed to his Minister of Foreign Affairs. The form of the note to be used by the respective Governments, in making that communication, was submitted by the British Minister, communicated to this Government, adopted, and used in making that communication. Copies of these notes and of the instruction to Mr Hughes, Chargé d'Affaires at the Hague, are annexed.[1]

No information has, as yet, been received at this Department whether His Netherland Majesty has accepted this arbitrament, or not.

By the instructions referred to, it will be perceived that the choice fell upon the last named Sovereign, who was least desirable to this Government to be the Arbiter.

Under these circumstances the course of this Government, in my opinion, ought to be directed by the anticipation that the King of the Netherlands will accept the trust confided to him, and every measure, on our part, ought to be ~~tried, at least,~~ taken, to secure to us his favorable consideration.

The King of the Netherlands has, for about four years past, been represented near this Government by a Minister Plenipotentiary. During the same time, the United States have been, and still are, represented by the inferior grade of Chargé d'Affaires, thus subjecting that Court to the mortifying reflection of being esteemed by us as a mere secondary Power.

Although from the personal character and habits of His Netherland Majesty we have a right to believe that he will, himself, examine the statements and arguments of the respective Parties, and the representations which may be made in regard to them, by the Officer of this Government who may be charged with the subject, yet it may reasonably be supposed that much would be gained by the assiduity of a judicious Envoy.

I find that it was contemplated by the late President, at the proper time, to send Judge Preble, who is perfect master of the whole subject, as Agent of this Government to Brussels and the Hague, in order that he may give such explanations as may be required by the Arbiter in the course of his examination.[2]

Under these circumstances, I am clearly of opinion that it would be proper to send a Minister Plenipotentiary to represent this Government at that Court.

James A. Hamilton

DS, DNA-RG 76 (12-0903). Hamilton *Reminiscences*, pp. 115–16.
 1. Secretary of State Henry Clay had instructed William Beach Lawrence (1800–1881), American secretary of legation in London and acting chargé d'affaires, that the United States would accept as arbiter the Emperor of Russia, the King of Denmark, or the King of the Netherlands, in that order of preference. John William Ward (1781–1833), Earl of Dudley, was succeeded as British foreign secretary in 1828 by George Hamilton Gordon (1784–1860), Earl of Aberdeen. William I (1772–1843), King of the Netherlands, agreed to undertake the arbitration on January 22, 1829. Christopher Hughes (1786–1849), American chargé d'affaires to the Netherlands, had been nominated by Adams in December 1828 to the higher grade of envoy extraordinary and minister plenipotentiary, but was not confirmed by the Senate.
 2. William Pitt Preble (1783–1857) had left the Maine supreme court in 1828 to help Albert Gallatin prepare the American case for the Northeastern boundary arbitration. On June 1 AJ appointed him envoy extraordinary and minister plenipotentiary to the Netherlands.

From Richard Mentor Johnson

Ohio River Steam Boat
9th. March 1829

Dear Sir,

I have nothing to prevent me from congratulating you & the Country upon the manner in which you acted the part assigned you on the 4th. I am happy to find that in all difficulty & trial you fill the measure of your own honor & your Countrys glory—I brought with me your inaugural address & it was sought & read with avidity. The frends were pleased with its conciseness and dignifyed energy—It manifested to them a determination for fewer words & more action—The opposers observed a respectful silence: It is my opinion that there is an inclination in the great body of the people to support you—I discovered some disposition, generally, to find fault or rather to express disappointment in the Cabinet. But confidence however, in your judgement, produces perfect acquiescence & to judge the tree by its fruits. I think you have a strong, high minded amiable & honorable Cabinet; a business Cabinet; & for such chiefs of deparments the Country has been suffering—I hope, *now,* the central committee of the dist. will not be known any longer, as an association, whatever may be their individual worth—I find the existence of that Committee, the canvass being over, gives offence to frends as well as foes. The people say that you stand in no need of any organized bo[d]y to sustain you, or to enlighten your Councils, or to give you information upon which to form correct opinions of men & things[1]—I was very appehensive when I left the City, that Judge McLean entertained some fears as to his position & was rather desireous to leave his department, if you would make him the judge—I hope however he has not changed his Position as he is a most excellent office & Every where I find great confidence expressed in him as a head of a department

I hope you may look at his situation with kindness—if it should so turn out that he may not in the application of your rules extend it to some cases supposed to be embraced by them. It is natural to suppose this state of case, arising partly from the peculiar situation in which he has been heretofore placed[2]—I again repeat that even at this distance from the Seat of Empire the central committee is odious & let it not be known as a body to Genl. Jackson—I have been your frend in good & in evil report, & as I am, so like a plain blunt man, I speak—I have not left you, in seven troubles & so far as I have any power I shall not leave you in the seventieth; no ansr expected. As ever yours.

Rh. M. Johnson

ALS, DLC (36).

1. Jackson men in Washington had formed a Central Committee in 1827 to promote his campaign. Chaired by banker and former New York congressman John Peter Van Ness (1770–1846), it included Henry Ashton, Thomas Corcoran, Duff Green, William Jones, Henry Mason Morfit, Henry C. Neale, Thomas Sim, Philip Stewart, and Joseph Watson. The committee continued to operate after the election, assuming direction for AJ's welcome in Washington and for the inaugural celebration.

2. John McLean was understood to have balked at carrying out AJ's removal policy.

From John Brown

Wellsburgh Brooke County Va. March 10th 1829

(Dear Sr)

I hope you will pardon the freedom in a stranger in addreessing a few Lines to you: Especially: when I inform you: that I am an old revelutonist: one of your warmest friends: and an induvidual of the near 200-000 freemen which I hope have taught congress a Lesson not soon to be forgotten: some twenty years ago I had the pleasure of takeing Breakfast with you at a Hotell in the villedge of genava: I did flatter myself that I should again had the pleasure of a short interview with you as you passed up the ohio river to Pittsburgh but as the Boat barely touched at the shore I had no oppertunity of seeing you; I must inform that your friends are much plased with you; on account of your refuseing to recived publick addresses publick Dinners and other publick perade: on your way to City washington: I have ever thought it very improper conduct in the citizens of these united states so to act: and that no truly wise man could have any pleasure in reciving such flattering useless and pompous perade how evever it might tickle the voletile fancy of a Frenchman: we know we had a circle of such perade not many years since; but I am informed that genl. La Fiatte did not approve of such conduct and to his honour be it spoken[1]; your truly and Exampleary conduct relative to these matters have imboldened me; (not by way of Dictating) but only to call to you consideration an other kind of perade Viz what is commonly called the Presidents levees I never was at one of these kind of meetings but I am informed by those who have been spectators at such a place that it is the most useless and unnessary and unmeaning assemblege on Earth I do not know how or when or by whom they ware intro dused[2] I have thought that such a perade: was antirepublican in its nature banefull in its consequnces and of bad precident to the nation Court Ettiquett and pompous perade in my humble opinon are not congenial with Republican goverment: when I consider the privations hardships and dangers that our forefathers and many that are yet Living have indured in setling the colinies under the monarcy in setling the western and souther states and teritories and above all when I think of the year 1776 and of many occurences in those times; a small Brokendown army not propcrly supplied with the munitions of war Clothing or provitions Marching on the frost till their footsteps might be traced by the Blood isuing from the gashes made in their naked feet: togather with the sufferings of our armies during the Last war: an the massacree and murder of fronteir settlements: I say when I contrast these Events and the genious of Republican goverment: with the court at Washington City: (perhaps the most pompous court on Earth) I conclude that there is much room and much need of reform; your friends:

are much pleased: with the selection; of your Cabinet: Even your Enimies have Little fault to find Dear sir you will Looked up to by your friends for retrenchment and reform of abuses: and I feel confident that they will not be Disappointed as you have never been in the habit of Doing Business by the halvs; your Enimies cannot attribute it to covetousness or penurious-ness as Every offical of your whole Life gives unequivocal Evidence that such charges are falce: Be aware of the old federal faction (or I would say more properly if speaking in the tecnical terms of the revolution) the old Tory faction: I have been watching them ever since the days of Jno. Adams the first they are now throughout these united states Lying Like snaks in the grass; and I do firmly believe that they have done more serious injury to these states than all forreign Enimies: be assured that they would ruen your admistaton blast your character and Blow you to attoms if in their power but why should I further add believeing that you are fully apprised of these matters; and been thinking of reform in more instances then I am able to point out; do not attribute my freedom to arigance but to friend-ship: from your fellow citizen and well wisher most Respectfully

Jno. Brown

[Endorsed by AJ:] Jno. Brown, an old Revolutionary Soldier—a friendly letter—worth reading—*Private*

ALS, DLC (36).
　　1. The Marquis de Lafayette's tour across the United States in 1824–25 was marked by countless dinners, parades, and public celebrations.
　　2. Critics had complained of President George Washington's regular public levees as smacking of monarchism. His successors discontinued them, but continued to host public receptions on special occasions such as New Year's Day.

From Mary Conner

Philada: March 10. 1829.

Respected Sir
　　On Saturday morning last my husband James Conner enlisted in this place in the U.S. army—he was intoxicated the evening before and says now that he did it under the Influence of liquer and the persuasions of some idle associates—he has always been industrious and respectable tho' poor—he has been for many years lame from a fracture which he some years since received in the lower part of one of his legs—he has also for years past been aflicted with "fits—" and hence has been the care and solicitude of his anxious wife and family—I should hope that a man thus situated would be relieved and that his family would not be left to indulge in the most fearfull apprehensions for his safety—when thousands can be readily obtained for the service—if it was a time of war I would not

complain for I would willingly consent that his feble strength should be devoted to the defence of his Country—under the circumstances I pray you Sir to order his discharge

The Lieft. told me my husband could be cleared by getting a Substitute—but I cannot get one without money and I am poor & have none—my husband has been sick all winter and we have almost suffered for the necessaries of life—I am teling you sir the plain Truth and beg that you will order his discharge—I should have written to the secretary at war but was told that you had not yet appointed one yet

Respectfully I am yours most Sincerly

Mary Conner

My husband has from the fits he has been troubled with and much sickness been for years almost blind in one eye—I live at the corner of 12th: & South streets

M.C.

ALS, DNA-RG 94 (M567-42). Conner's letter was referred on March 25 to Major General Alexander Macomb, commander of the Army.

From John Forsyth

Executive Department Georgia
Milledgeville 11th March 1829

Sir

I transmit to you a Copy of An Act of the General Assembly of this State passed at the last Session in consequence of repeated injuries suffered during the preceding year from the Creek Indians—and copies of three letters received yesterday at this Department on the subject of a recent outrage committed by four of that Tribe, and of the danger to which the Citizens of the State are exposed notwithstanding the provisions of the enclosed Act.[1] As soon as a satisfactory description of the authors of the recent murder can be obtained it is my intention to demand them through the Agent—if not delivered immediately to apply to the commander of the United States Troops near Fort Mitchell to arrest them & hand them over to the Civil Authority of the State. If he declines making the arrest I shall send a party from Georgia to perform that service.[2] In communicating these papers for your information I request that you will take into consideration, as early as the pressing engagements of your high place will permit, the condition of the people of the frontiers of Georgia, and cause such Instructions to be given to the Creek Indian Agent as will prevent him from giving, except in cases of actual business, permits to the Indians to cross into this State.[3] Their frequent visits on hunting expeditions inevitably lead them into disorders which duty to the people will not permit us to pass unpunished & from the commission of which every principle of humanity requires that we should as far as practicable carefully guard them. I am Sir with consideration & respect yr. obt. servt.

John Forsyth

LS, DNA-RG 75 (M234-222); LC, G-Ar (12-0946). Forsyth (1780–1841), a former congressman and senator, was governor of Georgia, 1827–29. Secretary of War Eaton replied to Forsyth on March 24, promising full federal cooperation in apprehending the murderers and halting Indian intrusions (DNA-RG 107, M6-12; DNA-RG 75, M21-5).
    1. "An Act to protect the frontier settlements of this State from the intrusion of the Indians of the Creek Nation," signed December 20, 1828, prohibited Creeks from entering Georgia territory without a pass from their agent. The enclosed letters complained that on February 18 Indians had murdered Elijah Wells at his house in Marion County (DNA-RG 75, M234-222).
    2. On March 25, Adjutant General Roger Jones ordered Brevet Major Philip Wager, commanding at Fort Mitchell, Ala., to cooperate with Georgia authorities in apprehending the murderers (DNA-RG 94, M565-7).
    3. Eaton so instructed agent John Crowell on March 27 (DNA-RG 75, M21-5).

From Katherine Duane Morgan

Washington City March 11th. 1829

    Mrs Katherine Morgan tenders her acknowledgements to General Jackson for the ring (handed by his son) containing a lock of hair which once adorned the "dear partner of his bosom"—The gift is received with feelings of grateful sensibility "as a memento of the respect and affection entertained for her" by the best of women, and with prayers to Heaven that no subsequent act of her life will cause her to forfeit "the high regard for her character" which the General has so kindly expressed, and which she so highly estimates.

[Endorsed by AJ:] Mrs. C. Morgan letter acknowledging the receipt of a mourning ring set with my dear departed wifes hair as a momento of the regard she had for Mrs. Morgan—

AN, DLC (36).

From John Rowan

Washington March 11th 1829.

Sir
    I have recd letters from divers citizens of Kenty relative to the office of Marshall in that state. Genl. James Allen, Tho C. Slaughter, William

McBride, and Tandy Allen, severally wish to obtain that appointment—They are Excellent men, and each of them, well qualified to discharge its duties.[1]

Such a group of meritorious aspirants, is well calculated to embarrass choice—I at first thought of transmitting to you the letters, which I had recd upon that subject, without encountering the difficulty, and responsibility, of attempting to designate the one, who in my judgmt ought to be preferd. But in almost all the letters, that subject is mixd up with other matters, not intended for the public eye—Besides I have a preference, and I ought not to be unwilling to avow it—my preference is not one of feeling—my feelings towards each of the gentlemen are of the kindest cast—But in my *judgmt,* the cause of reform in our state, woud be most strengtend by the appointment of General Allen—He resides in Buckners district[2]—He has done much, and can still do a great deal for the cause, in that region of country; By receiving the appointmt, He will be enabled to do much throughout the state—He is not one of the many, to whom the fervor of the late contest, by throwing Him on the surface, has given a Temporary conspicuity—He belongs to that stable mass of population, in whose keeping are the destinies of this country; and to the power of whose will, is to be ascribed the late signal Triumph of correct principal—so do the other gentlemen—I woud not disparage their claims—But Genl. Allen's unpretending cast of character, his having been for very many years a member, and Elder, of the Presbyterian Church—and the affectionate regard, in which he is held by other religious denominations, fit him imminently for efficiency, & usefulness, in the great cause, to which I have alluded—

I have heard Mr Taylor, a relative of Colo. Johnston's, spoken of for this appointment—He is a clever man, and woud, no doubt make a good officer; but not better than either of the four[3]—and there are many reasons, why either of them shoud be preferrd to him; in my humble judgement—But I shall not fatigue you with them—your choice, let it fall upon whom it may will have my acquiescence—nor do I wish the preference, which I have thought it my duty to express, to have any embarrassing effect whatever, upon your agency in this matter—I have expressd it, because I thought candor requird that I shoud do so—and because I believe that the representative, instead of throwing upon the Executive the entire responsibility in such cases, shoud meet and incur his share of it—I have the honor to be with sincere respect yr obt

J. Rowan

P.S. Genl Allen is now in the senate of Ky for a second Term—Mr. McBride is the Brother of Mrs Priestly of Tennessee—He, & his family have renderd much service, & sufferd much in our indian wars—He is, I believe the only male survivor of two families, the Heads, & most of the members of which, fell under the Tomahack—Mr. Slaughter is the Brother-in law of my Colleague Mr Bibb—Tandy Allen is the son of the late Judge Allen of our state—J R.[4]

[Endorsed by AJ:] Judge Rowan of U.S. Senate, Ky—recommending Genl Allen & others for the marshal of Ky   when this subject is taken up this to be particularly attended to—

ALS, DNA-RG 59 (M639-1). Rowan (1773–1843) was a U.S. senator from Kentucky, 1825–31. James Allen (1769–1836) of Greensburg had been a militia brigadier in the War of 1812 and was now a state senator. AJ appointed John M. McCalla marshal on May 23.
    1. Thomas Smith Slaughter (1778–1838) of Logan County and Tandy Allen (1790–c1833) of Bourbon County were both Jackson presidential electors in 1828. William McBride (1771–c1844) of Woodford County had solicited the marshalship from AJ on January 24.
    2. Richard Aylett Buckner (1763–1847) of Greensburg was a Kentucky congressman, 1823–29.
    3. Benjamin Taylor (1784–1850) of Woodford County had run for Congress in 1827 and was a Jackson elector in 1828. His wife's aunt was Richard M. Johnson's sister-in-law.
    4. In the Revolution, the War of 1812, and the intervening Indian wars, William McBride lost his father, uncle, brother and two cousins. His sister Sarah (1766–1829) was the widow of James Priestly (c1751–1821), former president of Cumberland College. Slaughter was married to Lucy Booker Bibb (1786–1848), sister of George M. Bibb. Tandy Allen's father, John Allen (1749–1816), had been a Bourbon County judge.

From James Akin

Philadelphia March 13th, 1829.

Respected and Honoured Sir,

God be praised that you are (in spite of a wicked opposition,) President of the United States. Were it no other gratification to me, I feel that sufficient to reward my feeble Efforts before and during the late election, to attain that object.

I, Sir, had the honour to paint three exceeding large transparencies on that eventful occasion, representing you a general, a President, and a Farmer, which we exhibited in Philadelphia in October last.[1]

A burst of universal Approbation was the result, and the people manifested their joy in loud huzza's! For this, the enemies of the Jackson cause, have meted me full measure, all injuries which was in their power to inflict! It is peculiarly embarrassing to endure it! if for myself I should care but little, but I have an Amiable and tender wife, whose affections causes her to share in my afflictions!! I am therefore prompted to seek means of alleviation, and I now ask a situation which I formerly enjoyed, in the Elder Adam's administration, and was removed on account of my politicks.[2]

My petition was addressed to you, Sir, but changed to Mr Van Beuren out of respect to that Gentleman, who properly appoints to Office, the Superintendent of the Patent Office; the place for which I apply.[3]

It was my intention to have waited on you, a second time, after I had the honor of an interview when my letter of introduction from the Revd. Doctor Ely, was delivered to you; but seeing the great press of business upon you, and the daily crowd of visitants, I was governed from motives of respect not to obtrude myself too often upon you, and gave preference to this course, which I hope meets your approbation.[4]

I have the honor Sir to claim birthright from the same state with yourself, a Carolinian; hitherto my residence has been Philadelphia, am a relation of the late, brave, Genl. Marion, and a descendant of a Revolutionary Soldier.[5] My efforts have long since been directed to serve my country's cause, and it is painful to see strangers from foreign lands, enjoying honours & trusts to the Exclusion of those who are not only natives of the soil, but whose political feeling is consonant with the spirit of the Constitution & laws of our Country.

Should you, Sir, be pleased to honor me with your notice in any way you may think proper, to aid my success, in my application It will be to me one of the most fortunate events of my life, and the greatest proof of your good opinion, for which I shall be ever grateful. God grant you health and make you revered, and truly happy. I am Respected Sir, With the greatest considerations, your most obt Servt.

James Akin.

ALS, DNA-RG 59 (M639-1). Akin (c1773–1846), a Philadelphia engraver and caricaturist, had published a pro-Jackson cartoon, *Caucus Curs in full Yell,* in 1824. He did not receive an appointment from AJ and later turned against him, producing an anti-Jackson pamphlet, *The House That Jonathan Built,* in 1832.

1. Akin's transparencies were exhibited in front of Bradshaw's and Hollahan's taverns on October 14, 1828, as an electioneering device for the state and city elections held that day.

2. Akin married Eliza Cox (d. 1834) in 1797 and worked in the State Department under secretary Timothy Pickering, 1795–1800.

3. John Polhemus et al. to Van Buren, December 10, 1828, recommending Akin for the Patent Office, was originally addressed to AJ (DNA-RG 59, M639-1).

4. Ely had written AJ to introduce and recommend Akin on February 2.

5. Revolutionary general Francis Marion was famed for his guerrilla exploits against British troops in South Carolina.

From Naw-Kaw

Fort Winnebago.
Portage of the Fox & Ouisconsin
March 14th. 1829

My Father

In my late visit to Washington, I understood that a Treaty was to be held with our Nation next summer, for the purpose of purchasing that part of our Country now occupied by your white Children.[1] I did not know until I arrived at Chicago that the Treaty was to be at the mouth of Rock River. I am not pleased with this arrangement and if the Treaty should be there neither myself nor any of the principal men of our Nation will be able to attend it.

We are unable to understand, why we are required to go upon the lands of other people to transact our own business.

We therefore respectfully request that the Treaty may be held at Prairie du Chien, a place convenient to our whole nation, and where we have long been accustomed to transact our Public business.

This request I make for myself, and all the Chiefs of the Winnebagoe Nation.

(Signed) Naw-Kaw his   X   mark The wood

In presence of
D. E. Twiggs Majr. 1st. Infy.
W. V. Coobs Capt. Ist. Infy.
Thos. P. Gwyne Lt. [Sup] Asst. Com. Sub[2]

The above Signed Chief Naw-Kaw is a principal Chief of the Hoa-chain-ga-raw or Winnebagoe Nation

John Marsh U. S. Sub. Ind Agt.
Pierre his   X   mark Paquette. Interpreter[3]

Copy, DNA-RG 75 (T494-2). Naw-Kaw or "The Wood" (c1734–1833) was a leading Wisconsin Winnebago chief. In an August 1828 treaty at Green Bay, he and other representatives of upper Mississippi tribes had agreed to reconvene in a year to treat for the cession of valuable mineral lands. The meeting location was changed after this protest from Rock Island, Ill., to Prairie du Chien. Naw-Kaw attended and signed a Winnebago cession treaty on August 1.

1. A Winnebago delegation headed by Naw-Kaw and accompanied by Michigan Governor Lewis Cass had visited Washington and met with President Adams in the fall of 1828.

2. Major David Emanuel Twiggs (1790–1862), Captain Waddy Vine Cobbs (d. 1848), and Lieutenant Thomas Page Gwynne (d. 1861), assistant commissary of subsistence, were stationed at Fort Winnebago at Portage, Wisc.

3. John Marsh was Indian subagent at Prairie du Chien. Pierre Paquette (1796–1836), son of a French father and a Winnebago mother, resided at Portage and was also an agent of the American Fur Company.

To John Branch

Washington
March 16 1829.

Sir.

Your note of this date enclosing a statement shewing the present disposition of the United States vessels of war in commission agreably to my verbal request has been received—

I enclose to you statements of piracies recently committed and call your attention particularly to that committed near *Matanzas* on the 22d February last—

These atrocities will require prompt and energetic measures on the part of the Government in order to put them down—

You will find from the statement of Mr Shoemaker Consular Commercial Agent of the U.S. at the Port of Matanza's that, that Port has not been visited by any of our armed vessels since August last—[1]

You will please to furnish me with information—Whether there are any of our small vessels of war now in ordinary or undergoing repair in our ports? and if so—In how short a time they could be fitted out for this service? And also in how maney days the *Natchez* now in New York could put to sea? your obt Servt

[Andrew Jackson]

LS (signature removed), DNA-RG 45 (M124-117); LC, DLC (60). The enclosures (M124–117), presented to AJ earlier that day by James A. Hamilton, reported piracies against American vessels off Cuba, including the slaughter of the crew of the brig *Attentive* on February 22. Branch replied on March 17 that the *Natchez*, an 18-gun sloop of war, could sail in twenty-four hours.

1. Lewis Shoemaker (c1795–1838) was American commercial agent at Matanzas. AJ appointed him consul in 1831.

To Ralph Eleazar Whitesides Earl

(private)

Washington March 16th. 1829—

My Dr. Sir

I have not recd. a line from you, or any other of my friends, since I left you—my time has been so engrossed with crowds of hungry expectants, and the necessary business of my situation, that I have no time to devote to friendship—This is the only letter I have written to a friend, except one to McLamore, from Pittsburgh, since I left Nashville, & the Senate being still in session, I have but a few moments to spare.[1]

It seems to me from the thousands that Press for office, that every man who voted for the cause of the people, think they ought to be rewarded with office, having but few offices to bestow, compared with the many that apply, many must go away dissatisfied—This gives me but little concern, I will do what my Judgtment tells me is right, regardless of consequences, trusting to my god to guide & direct me in all things for the best, and suplicating him, for a blessing upon my country—There was an attempt to get up a great excitement here, to prevent me from appointing Major Eaton to the War Dept—and this too, by some of my Tennessee friends, who were made the dupes to my designing enemies—The object was to destroy him—I sustained him as I ought, fearlessly, and I have no doubt but his Department, which has been left in the utmost confusion & disorder, will be soon systematised, and well directed

I have been crowded with business thrown upon me by the Senate, and the Departments all vacant, until I filled them, I had an arduous task, but my friends tell me, I have thus far met it with much satisfaction to my real friends.

I find myself very loansome, I wish you were here—My late bereavement has left a solemn gloom upon me, with which I am oppressed when alone, in your society, I would find some solace to my grief—My Dr friend, visit the Hermitage & write me, whether the overseer has secured the Tomb, as I had directed.[2]

I shall expect you on in June   for the present adieu, yr friend

Andrew Jackson

ALS, NN (12-1017).
   1. John C. McLemore.
   2. Earl replied on April 3 that overseer Graves W. Steele was "making a new house over the Tomb."

To John Henry Sherburne

Washington City
March 16th. 1829—

Sir

The life of J. P. Jones which you have so kindly presented to me, is received, and I shall undertake with pleasure the perusal of it as soon as I can obtain a little respite from the business now pressing upon me—The incidents of the life of so meritorious and distinguished a man, cannot fail to be interesting and useful; and the opportunity to become familiar with them is gratefully acknowledged.

I beg you, Sir, to accept assurances of my great respect & believe me yr mo. obdt. Servt.

Andrew Jackson

ALS, PWbW (12-1020). Sherburne (1794–1852) was a writer and former Navy Department clerk. His biography of Revolutionary naval hero John Paul Jones was titled *Life and Character of the Chevalier John Paul Jones* (Washington, 1825).

To John Branch

March 17th. 1829

Sir,

Your's of this date with a letter of the commissioners of the Navy containing the information desired in my note of yesterday has been received.

You will forthwith order Comodore Ridgely, the commanding officer of the West India squadron, to keep one of his small vessels of War on the coast of cuba, and never to be absent from it longer than a week at a time.[1] That the Matanzas, and the inlets near to that port, and all others on the coast where there may be reason to believe that Pirates are concealed, may be well guarded, urge upon the Comodore the necessity for the utmost vigilance and energy. The dictates of humanity and the honor of our flag require that the piracies in those seas should be suppressed.

Be pleased to dispatch orders embracing these views by mail, and by the sloop of War Natchez, with instructions to the commander of this sloop to proceed to the coast of cuba and unless he finds the trade sufficiently protected by the squadron under the command of Comodore Ridgely, to scour the coast until he meets some one of the U states vessels, with which the dispatch may be left. It is expected that the Natchez can perform this service and return to New York in the course of five or six weeks.[2] yrs. Respectfully

Andrew Jackson

LS, DNA-RG 45 (M124-117); Draft and LC, DLC (60).
1. Captain Charles Goodwin Ridgely (1784–1848) commanded the West India squadron, consisting of four sloops and two schooners.
2. The *Natchez,* under Commander William Branford Shubrick (1790–1874), sailed from New York on March 28 and returned May 13.

To *James Alexander Hamilton*

March 17th. 1829

The President of the United States will thank the acting Secretary of State, Col J A Hamilton to cause to be made for him a synopsis of our foreign relations as it regards navigation commerce and friendship with foreign nations—With the names and residence of our ministers of the first grade and also of our ministers of the second grade, or Chargés, their residence and names; our consuls or commercial agents, their names & places of residence—

LC, DLC (60). Hamilton replied with a lengthy report on March 26.

From *John Caldwell Calhoun*

Washington 18th March 1829

Dear Sir,

I omitted accidentally in my last conversation to bring to your notice, a friend whose name I had been requested to present to you. I refer to George M. Dallas Esqr present Mayor of Philadelphia. I have known him long and intimately, and do not hesitate to state, that few men in the state are his superiors in talents, acquirements and integrity. Of his standing his present office, which he owes to the confidence of the Republican party in the city in his worth, affords the highest proof. It is generally believed that the present District Attorney will not be continued in office. Should such be the fact, I feel satisfied that no appointment could be made, which would be more acceptable to the state. To me personally it would be very gratifying. Sincerely

J. C. Calhoun

ALS, DNA-RG 59 (M639-6). *Calhoun Papers,* 11:13–14. George Mifflin Dallas (1792–1864), son of former Treasury secretary Alexander James Dallas, was mayor of Philadelphia and leader of Pennsylvania's powerful "Family" faction. AJ appointed him district attorney on April 7, removing incumbent Charles J. Ingersoll.

From Ezra Stiles Ely

Philadelphia March 18th. 1829.

(Private & Confidential)

My dear General

With deep regret I now approach you, because I dread the thought of giving you pain: judge whether I do not love you and dearly love the memory of your sainted partner, and if you should think me obtrusive, forgive me for her sake; for it is chiefly *on her account* that I have consented, after long deliberation in my own mind, to make this communication. When I left this city I knew nothing of Mrs. Eaton; but some vague reports; and when I had a little conversation with you on the nomination of her husband, I did not believe any thing could be substantiated against her. Soon after, however, I found that all parties in Washington, male and female, with the exception of good Mr. Ryland's family and a gentleman who boarded at Mr. O'Neale's had but one language concerning her: they all said that she was a woman of ill fame before Major Eaton knew her; and had lived with him in illicit intercourse.[1] On this account the nomination of Mr. E__ I found distressing to all your friends, of every name: but I concluded that Mrs. E__ was not to be the Secretary, and that it would be requiring too much that all the wives of your officers should be above suspicion: I therefore said nothing on the subject.

On my return home, I was delayed in Baltimore untill Monday. There a merchant of the first respectability, whom I had long known as your warm supporter, Mr. J. Campbell, who seeks no office, told me that on account of Mrs. Eaton "the most influential Jackson men could not lift up their heads".[2] I told him that Mr. Eaton had no doubt made the best of his case to you, and that you thought her an injured woman. He was satisfied, as all of your friends, I believe are, that you had no knowledge of her notorious infamy. Before I left Baltimore I was earnestly solicited by several of your warm admirers to write you a full disclosure on this subject; and finally I determined to do it, for this reason, *the name of your dear departed and truly pious wife is stained through Mrs. Eaton.* In a meeting of the Directors of a Bank in Baltimore it was publicly said "its too bad but what could you expect better: its only supporting Mrs. Jackson," or words to that effect. This rouses my indignation; and I cannot endure it, that Mrs. Eaton should be named in connexion with your ever to be honoured and lamented wife. Your friends all say, as they ought, and will, that these persons have no similarity of character; but the public who generally believe Mrs. E__ to have been a licentious woman for years, will consider her elevation to society through the influence of the President as a reflection upon the memory of Mrs. J__. It is uttered by a thousand malicious tongues, "*he* could not make an objection to Genl. E on account of his wife."

Now my dear Genl. I have told on what I believe to be good authority, that Mrs. Jackson when in Washington did not return the call of Mrs. Timberlake; and she did not fear to put the seal of her reprobation on such characters. You will find, on enquiry, that this was the fact in relation to Mrs. J__. She was too pure to countenance such a character as Mrs. T__ then sustained.

I do not presume to ask my venerable friend any thing more than this, *that you will not expect Mrs. Donelson and Miss Easton, your lovely nieces, to return the civilities of Mrs. Eaton.*[3] I wish to be able to say, and to have all your friends who are spoken to on this subject say, that your family follow the example of Mrs. Jackson in relation to this unhappy woman. They cannot resist the power of public sentiment on this subject; for few persons of any political note in Washington and Baltimore are ignorant of the bad fame of Mrs. E__.

With great love and respect I feel compelled to state the following reasons for desiring that you would excuse your family from calling on and entertaining her, until *time* has enabled her in some measure to redeem her character.

1. Whether with truth or not, Mrs. E is generally spoken of in Washington and Baltimore as having been a lewd woman, excluded from society, before her *first* and *second* marriage.

2. The ladies of Washington are so fully persuaded of the truth of the reports against Mrs. E__ that they have refused to return her calls, and do still refuse. I could name to you many of the first ladies of W__, that if they met Mrs E__ in a public place they would speak with civility to her, if she spoke to them, but would never receive her to their houses; or be on visiting terms, because she was notoriously infamous. Their husbands have said they will support their wives in this course, if it should cost them their places.

3. At the public table at Gadsby's, on the day after Mr. Vaughan's party, a man whom I shall not call a gentleman, said in the hearing of four persons, "Mrs. E__ brushed by me last night and pretended not to know me. She has forgotten the time when I slept with her." My authority was Mr. John E. Hyde of New York, then at Gadsby's, whom I know to be a gentleman of high standing.[4]

4. A gentleman now in Washington told me that Mrs. E__ had been heard, I think by himself, telling her servant not to call her children by the name of *Timberlake,* but *Eaton,* because they were his: and Mr. Timberlake, when he last left W__ told this gentleman with tears, "that he would never return to this country," on account of Eaton's seduction of his wife.

5. A clergyman of Washington besought me to tell you, that when Timberlake had been gone more than a year from this country, Mrs. T__ had a miscarriage, as was currently reported, and as her attending Physician told him was the case.[5]

6. A lady and gentleman of excellent character, who urge the kind treatment of Genl. E__ and feel gratified with his appointment now he and his wife are married, *told me* that during one session of Congress Mr. Eaton's friends got him to board at Mr. Coyles for the express purpose of getting him free from Mrs. Timberlake.[6]

I could add to this sad catalogue, but I forbear to say more than this, that members of Congress have seen the name of Mr. and Mrs. E__ entered at public houses as man and wife before they were married; that a boarding house in N. York caused them to remove because Mr. E__, not being able to find the key, had the lock removed from a door between Mrs. Timberlakes room and his own; and that another boarding house in N. York refused to receive them a second time because their intimacy disgraced their house; and that I have reason to think Mr. E__ has heard, even from intimate friends, of all, or most of these reports.

I have been requested also to say to you that the opposition prints will drag these things before the public and that your friends, while they honour the kindness of your heart and the purity of your motives cannot pretend to defend Mrs. E__. With the exception of Mr. Ryland's family and Mr. Bradford above refered to, who boards at Mr. O'Neill's, I have not found one Jackson man who doubts the truth of the reports against Mrs. E__. On board of a Steam Boat, on our way home, Mrs. Ely triumphantly vindicated Mrs. Jackson's honour; when a lady the wife of President Kirkland turned to her and said, "and pray Madam do you also defend Mrs. Eaton?"[7]

Dear General, I have seen enough of Mrs. Eaton to confirm these reports in my own mind, and I am no judge of human nature, or else Mrs. Eaton rules her husband in such a way that he is a very miserable man. If she would let him, I believe he would save you from all trouble on his account; for he is naturally a man of fine feelings. She will do more to injure your peace and your administration than one Hundred Henry Clays.

I have now done what I believe duty and friendship to the most honoured man in our nation required; I have discharged my tender duty to the memory of dear Mrs. Jackson; and I hope, my venerated friend, that I have not deserved to lose your esteem.

As a minister of God, as a man, and a christian I would forgive Mr. and Mrs. E__ and do them all the kindness in my power; but forgiveness does not imply that a woman of lewd character for years should on marriage be received, at once, into chaste society.

Mr. Eaton cannot, or he would clear the character of his wife. I wish he were to go to France, and he might live away from Washington long enough for his wife to prove her reformation.

Need I apologize for this long letter? My hearts desire and prayer to God for you is, that you may have the happiest presidency, and heaven at last.

(Signed) E. S. Ely.

Copy, DLC (75).
1. William Ryland (1770–1846), pastor of the Methodist Ebenezer Church in Washington, had officiated at the Eatons' wedding. In May AJ appointed him a naval chaplain. The gentleman boarder was Philadelphia publisher Samuel Fisher Bradford (1776–1837). Ryland on September 28 and Bradford on October 10 (below) furnished written testimonials to Mrs. Eaton's good character.
2. James Campbell was a partner in the firm of Campbell and McIlvain and a director of the Union Bank of Maryland.
3. White House hostess Emily Donelson was Rachel Jackson's niece. Her companion Mary Ann Eastin (1810–47), daughter of William and Rachel Donelson Eastin, was Emily's niece and Rachel's grandniece.
4. John Gadsby (c1766–1844) kept the leading hotel in Washington at this time. Charles Richard Vaughan (1774–1849) was British minister to the U.S., 1825–35. John Ellsworth Hyde (1781–1844) was a New York City import merchant. On November 26 he denied telling this story.
5. The clergyman was John Nicholson Campbell (1798–1864), whose Second Presbyterian Church AJ attended. The physician was Elijah Richardson Craven (1796–1823), professor of botany at Columbian College.
6. Eaton boarded at the establishment of Treasury clerk John Coyle (c1764–1831) during the first term of the Seventeenth Congress, 1821–22, but returned to O'Neale's the next session.
7. John Thornton Kirkland (1770–1840), president of Harvard, 1810–28, had married Elizabeth Cabot (1785–1839) in 1827.

To John Coffee

Washington March 19th 1829—

My Dr. Genl,

Since I have been here my time has been constantly employed with a press of business left undone by the preceding administration, and many things done by them, intended no doubt, to embarrass the present—This, with my late afflictive bereavement on my mind, has been as much as my debilitated constitution could well bear, still I have to thank my god, my health still enables me to attend to my duty, and I trust in him, will enable me to perform it, to the satisfaction of my country.

great exertions have been made by Clays friends to raise a clamour about my taking Major Eaton into my cabinett, and some of my friends from Tennessee weak anough to be duped by the artifice, were made instruments; the object was to intimidate me, from the selection, & thereby destroy Major Eaton—I had to assume sufficient energy to meet the crisis—I did meet it—and Major Eaton will become one of the most popular men in the Departments, be a great comfort to me, and will manage the Dept. of war well

I intended to have written you by Col Mc.Kinley he called, & finding me engaged, left his card and took leave, to him I must refer you for the current news here—say to Judge Fulton I will provide for him shortly

I Just have heard that my Dr little Hutchings has been suspended at college, & I fear expelled—my Dr Genl, attend to him, he is an orphan, and altho a head strong & ungovernable boy, I have his prosperity & good name much at heart—I was fearful to leave him without some person to control & council him, and I am happy I did not bring him on with me, as here he would have been ruined; I must send Saml Hays from here, and when I can find a good place, my son also—They must be seperated or both ruined—by idleness.[1]

When you have leisure, I would be glad to hear from you—shall we have the pleasure of seeing you here in the summer with Mr McLamore—we shall have a bed for you & him—we are enjoying tolerable health, say to Mr Easton Mary enjoys good health & all Join in respects and good wishes to you & your amiable family—write me how Hutchings overseer does[2]—In a few days we will send you a civil Engineer to lay out your canal, & on the application of Col McKinley and Col King a commission to you to superintend it.[3]

I shall write you again the first leisure

accept the assurance of my friendship & esteem, & present me kindly to Capt Jack & Elisa, and my friend Savage,[4] & all other friends[.] yours

Andrew Jackson

ALS, THi (12-1052).
1. Andrew J. Hutchings had been suspended from the University of Nashville for striking a professor with a chair. Samuel Jackson Hays (1800–1866) was Rachel Jackson's nephew, the son of her sister Jane and Robert Hays. AJ's son was Andrew Jackson, Jr. (1808–65), one of twin boys born to Rachel's brother Severn and his wife Elizabeth Rucker Donelson. AJ and Rachel adopted him in infancy.
2. George J. Jordan was the overseer of Hutchings's Alabama farm.
3. In 1828 Congress had granted 400,000 acres of land to Alabama to improve steamboat navigation at the Tennessee River shoals. On April 7, Army engineer James Kearney was detailed to locate the work. William Rufus Devane King (1786–1853) and John McKinley were the senators from Alabama.
4. Samuel Savage (d. 1837) was a north Alabama planter.

From Tuskeneah et al.

Creek Nation
Tuckabatchee March 20th. 1829

Sir

We the chiefs and Head men of the creek nation in Council now assembled congratulate you upon your late appointment as President of the United States. We wish to call your attention to a subject that is painful to us, and to our nation at large—It produces feelings of the greatest excitement and uneasiness throughout our Country. We are sorry to find the white People in the State of Alabama so inimical and unfriendly to ourselves, our interest and our future prosperity as they wish to drive us from our Land and our Homes by enacting laws extending the Jurisdiction of said State over the creek nation   To this *measure we do most solemnly protest against* it, and we humbly call upon your Excellency as the President of the United States to interfere in our behalf, to put a stop to such unlawful measures as it is contrary to the provissions of the late Treaty made and concluded at Washington City.[1]

In *that* Treaty, the *Goverment* of the United States *guaranteed* to the creek nation *forever* all the Lands we now hold with a perpetual annuity of Twenty thousand Dollars   It is unnecessary to recite any other of the provissions of said Treaty as by your refference to it, you can judge of its contents your Self—all we want, all we expect and all we ever desire is the *complete fulfilment* of that Treaty. as the most enlightened people of the present age say and contend that Treatys thus made and thus Sanctioned and ratified by all the constituted authorities of both nations does most absolutely become the *Supreme Law* of the Land and can not be broken, by the whim or caprice of any State Legislature and as our nation gave up to the Genl Goverment for the use of Georgia all the Land she claimed we then expected peace and happiness and the goverment told us that they would not ask us for any more Lands—and of late and since the ratification of that Treaty so solemnly made and concluded *our Country* has and is still annoyed by the appearance of whitemen under the garb and character of agents, sub agents &c, &c, persuading, bribing and by all the arts of deception endeavor to get our people to go to that inhospitable clime, near the borders of the Rocky mountains and some of these whitemen under the character of assistant agents or employers carry on their blasphemous conduct still further, in endeavouring to *seduce* our wives and our Daughters[2] Now Sir we the chiefs and Head men of the creek nation have deliberated upon all these matters herin embraced as great grievances to our peace, Happiness and prosperity and we have unanimously agreed to address you this letter under the firm belief that you will remedy the evils herin complained of—as such conduct is inconsistent, and contrary to the Treaty made at Washington and contrary to many promises made us by the officers of the Goverment of the United States and contrary to the principles of free goverment which the United States so much boast of—We repeat again, and hope that the evils herin complained of, will be remedied and a fulfilment of the treaty be reccognized and viewd as the Supreme Law of the Land, and let us receive that *kind* treatment from the United States that has been promised us, and that *Justice* so loudly calls for. for further proof of our great annoyance and trouble we enclose for your inspection several writs that has been served upon us by the Sheriff of Montgomery County of the State of alabama and we would also beg of you to read the late enactments passed by the Legislature of said State extending her Jurisdiction over our Country.[3] In closeing this communication we humbly beg you as the Father of our Country and as the great chief of the United States to have the rongs, the injuries and impositions that have for a long time been practised, upon us, *redressed,* and our future Generations, will have the pleaseing consolation to know that *you* have been the *Saviour* of our Country and the *protector* of our rights, We beg you to accept the warmest feelings of our friendship, wishing you a long and happy administration of the public affairs, both as regards the white People and the Indian Tribes in all their respective rights, as guaranteed to each Nation by Solemn Treaty.

Tuskenahaw his X mark
Neharhoboy his X mark
Cosa Tuskenega his X mark

[Eleven more signatures follow on next page.]

LS, DNA-RG 75 (M234-222). Tuskeneah, whose name was spelled variously, was the son of Big Warrior, late head chief of the Upper Creeks. Tuckabatchee, on the Tallapoosa River in Alabama, was the largest of the Upper Creek towns.

1. An Alabama statute of January 29, 1829, formally extended state jurisdiction over the territory of the Creek Nation. In the 1826 Treaty of Washington by which the Creeks relinquished lands in Georgia, the United States had guaranteed Creek title to "all the country, not herein ceded, to which they have a just claim" and pledged a perpetual annuity of twenty thousand dollars.

2. Since 1826, Indian agents and subagents including John Crowell, David Brearley, Thomas Triplett, and William Walker had been encouraging Creek emigration from Alabama.

3. The writs, issued in February and March 1829, summoned Creek headmen Opothle Yoholo (a signer of this remonstrance) and Jim Boy to answer actions for assault and debt before a Montgomery County court. Despite the defendants' denial of state jurisdiction, the assault case went to trial and plaintiff James B. Reed was awarded $4,500 in damages. One of the writs for debt was from David R. Mitchell, who wrote AJ about his case on June 16 (below).

To John Coffee

Washington March 22nd 1829—

My Dr. Genl

I have Just received your letter of the 1rst. instant, enclosing me one from Doctor Lindsley to you, convaying the unpleasant information of my little ward Hutchings having been suspended from college, & having gone to the Hermitage where he now is—This is information, of the most distressing kind to me, but upon the best reflection I can give the subject I have determined to send him to Mr. Otte at Franklin who, if any man can, will controle, & preserve him, and carefully attend to his morales. I have just written a short letter to Mr Wm. Donelson, requesting him to have Hutchings immediately, on the receipt of my letter, sent to Mr. Otte and advise you of it—and I beseech you to address Mr Otte, requesting his particular attention to him, and to his morales, enquiring of him the amount of tuition, & board, and transmit Mr Otte the amount—& dealing to Hutchings but little funds.[1]

I wish him taught penmanship, arithmatic, & Book keeping, algrebra, and some other branches of mathematics, moral philosophy, belles letters, & such other branches that may be profitable to him as a farmer, & private gentleman

I have lost all hope of making him a classic scholar, and do not wish him to touch the languages, except to review those Books, of latin & Greek, that he has read, but wish him to understand his gramer well. These are only useful to him as a farmer, or a politician, and should he ever form a taste for reading & improvement being well versed in the branches named, he has it in his power to become useful to himself and country—If Mr Ote cannot control him, then sir I know not what to do with him, as I have determined never, whilst I hold my present office, to place one of my young relatives, either in the military school, or the navy. I hope & trust Mr Ote will be able to controle him, I shall leave him to your direction under the observations made—I shall write him under cover to William.

I shall refer you to the papers and other channels of information for news of this place, since the 4th. I have been crowded with thousand of applicants for office, and if I had a tit, for every applicant to suck the Treasury pap, all would go away well satisfied, but as theer are not office for more than one out five hundred who applies, many must go away dissatisfied, all I can do is, to select honest & competant men, this I will do, as far as I can be informed, & reform & retrenchment will be made, as far as sound principle will warrant it.

Much pains was taken to prevent me from taking Mr Eaton into the Cabinet, his wife was assailed secretly, in the most shameful manner, &

every plan that Clay and his minions, could invent to deter me, in hopes I would be intimidated and drop Eaton, which would have been destruction to him, under those circumstances I could not, nay I would not, abandon an old & tried friend—I sustained him, and I have no doubt he will become the most popular of the heads of the Departments and the war office will be well directed.

My labours have been great, my health is not good, but if my constitution will bear me up for one year I have no fear but I will make such an expose to the nation that will be satisfactory to the peopl—The late administration has left every thing in such a state as to embarrass me but you know when I am excited all my energies come forth.

I would be delighted to see you and yr daughter here with Mr McLamore & his in June—we will have but a small family—I send Saml Hays to Judge Tuckers law school[2] in a few days & will put my son here to learning French we will have but Andrew & Emily Miss Mary & Major Lewis, & perhaps Emily & Mary would go on with you to Philadelphia—There are many reasons why I am anxious to see you here—

I hope you may do well with your Cotton & Hutchings—still the prospects appear dull, but the shortness of crop must raise the price—I will be happy to hear from you often   My labours will prevent me from writing many letters to my friends—present us all affectionately to your whole family & believe me yr friend.

Andrew Jackson

ALS, THi (12-1074).
    1. Philip Lindsley (1786–1855) was a Presbyterian clergyman and president of the University of Nashville. James Hervey Otey (1800–1863) was an Episcopal clergyman and master of Harpeth Academy in Franklin, Tenn.
    2. Henry St. George Tucker (1780–1848), a jurist and former congressman, kept a private law school at Winchester, Va.

To William Donelson

Washington March 22nd. 1829—

My Dr. Sir
    I have Just received from Genl Coffee a letter enclosing one from Doctor Lindsley to him informing that Hutchings has been suspended from College, & is now at the Hermitage Idle—This intelligence is a sore grief to me, and one from his pledge to me, of good behaviour, & application to his Book, and strict adherence to the rules of the university, & the orders of they professors, I was not prepared to hear—I was not prepared you may say to him to hear of his disgrace, which I had taken so much pains, by my frequent admonitions to prevent, nor did I believe he would so far forget himself, as to inflict such a wound in my feelings; if he was

regardless of his own—But it is so, and I must adopt such measures, as will yet preserve him from ruin, & myself from disgrace.

On the receipt of this my dear friend can I ask the goodness of you, forthwith to take him & enter him with Mr Otey at Franklin, & advise Genl Coffee thereof, & draw upon him for the amount of Tuition & Board in favour of Mr Otey—I have this day wrote Genl Coffee that I would thus direct you, & he will be prepared to meet your draft for Hutchings board & tuition.

say to Mr Otey I wish him instructed in writing & arithmatic, so that he may become a good Book keeper, as I find it useless to attempt to make him a good classic scholar; and all I now hope for is, to give him an education to fit him for a farmer—If he can be restrained & governed, I would wish him to study algebra & some branches of mathematics, with Bells letters, & natural & moral Philosophy—and review his greek & latin which he has read.

My Dr Sir write me on the recept of this and let me know how your dear little Elisabeth is, & whether *poor poll* the favorite bird of my *dear wife* is still living—present me affectionately to Elisabeth to your father & mother, and all our relations,[1] say to them that we are all well & all send their love to them & believe me respectfully your friend

Andrew Jackson

ALS, DLC–Charles C. Hart Autograph Collection (12-1078).
    1. Elizabeth Anderson Donelson (1809–41) was William's wife. AJ had purchased Poll the parrot in 1827.

From Benjamin Chew Howard

Baltimore March 22st. 1829

My dear Sir

I have understood that an expression has escaped from you with regard to one of the Baltimore Appointments, which has cast a censure upon myself in common with some others of your friends. The remark was that you had been "*deceived* by your friends respecting Captn. Philips."[1]

That I should be charged with voluntarily deceiving you (and the general nature of the remark leaves it open whether the deception was voluntary upon my part or not) excites feelings of deep mortification. There is in your character a trait which I have always admired, that of placing confidence in those whom you believe to be your friends and the correspondent willingness to be treated by them with similar frankness. To have been supposed capable of perverting and misusing this unsuspecting and generous reliance and of advancing the interest of private friends at the expense of the popularity of your administration, is a charge which you must allow me to meet with an instant and peremptory negative. Asking nothing for myself, expecting nothing from government, all that remains to me as the result of my efforts, sacrifices and risks, is the consciousness of having promoted the welfare of my country, and the security, until now undoubted, that I enjoyed your good opinion. I cannot suffer myself to be stripped of the latter possession without a protestation that I should have been prevented from voluntarily deceiving you as much by a feeling of self-respect as a desire to advance the honor of that administration with whose success all my political character is identified. Having much to lose and nothing to gain as regarded myself, I threw into the struggle all the little reputation which I had earned and it would now be an act of political suicide to throw obstructions or difficulties in your path—As long as I shall live, the character of your official champion before the people will rest upon me and I have thereby staked myself as a guarantee that your high powers will be so exercised as to conduce to the welfare of the nation. You have therefore every tie upon me that can bind a man of honor.

I fear that I speak too plainly for our relative situations: but if (which I hope is not the case) any expression is found in this letter betraying more sensibility than you may suppose the occasion calls for, my apology will be found in the unexpected circumstances in which I am placed when I find the overwelming influence of your name used to destroy the standing which I have acquired in this community by my private and public life—

I will not enter into a detail of the circumstances which have probably produced this unfortunate misapprehension more than to remark that after my name had been affixed to the recommendation of Captn. Philips, I learned that he had been a decided supporter of Mr. Adams after his election, a circumstance which my memory had not retained; and in consequence of the information remarked in conversation and in a letter to a friend in Washington written chiefly for other purposes, that I would not have signed my name had I remembered it—You will readily perceive however that this did not amount to such a disqualification for office as to render the withdrawal of my signature necessary.

~~I am conscious that my private affairs or feelings constitute but a small subject for the occupation of your time or thoughts. If however you have treated any one of your friends with unmerited unkindness, there is something in your disposition that will induce you to repair the injury—~~I am Sir with the highest respect your obt. sert.

Benjn. C. Howard

ALS draft, MdHi (mAJs). Howard (1791–1872) was a Baltimore lawyer and civic leader, elected to Congress as a Jacksonian in October 1829.

1. AJ had nominated Isaac Phillips (d. 1833) for navy agent at Baltimore on March 12. Phillips was a former Navy captain, dismissed in 1799 for allowing a British officer to board his ship, the *Baltimore,* and press fifty-five of its crew. In 1825 he had unsuccessfully petitioned Congress for reinstatement.

To the Creek Indians

March 23rd. 1829.

Friends & Brothers,

By permission of the Great Spirit above, and the voice of the people, I have been made a President of the United States, and now speak to you as your father and friend, and request you to listen. Your warriors have known me long. You know I love my white and red children, and always speak straight, and not with a forked tongue; that I have always told you the truth. I now speak to you, as to my children, in the language of truth—listen.

Your bad men have made my heart sicken and bleed, by the murder of one of my white children in Georgia. Our peaceful mother earth has been stained by the blood of the whiteman and calls for the punishment of his murderers, whose surrender is now demanded under the solemn obligation of the treaty which your chiefs and warriors in council have agreed to. To prevent the spilling of more blood, you must surrender the murderers, and restore the property they have taken. To preserve peace, you must comply with your own treaty.[1]

Friends & Brothers, listen: Where you now are, you and my white children are too near to each other to live in harmony and peace. Your game is destroyed and many of your people will not work and till the Earth. Beyond the great river Mississippi, where a part of your nation has gone, your father has provided a country large enough for all of you, and he advises you to remove to it. There your white brothers will not trouble you; they will have no claim to the land, and you can live upon it, you and all your children, as long as the grass grows or the water runs, in peace and plenty. It will be yours for ever. For the improvements in the country where you now live, and for all the stock which you cannot take with you, your father will pay you a fair price.

In my talk to you in the Creek nation, many years ago, I told you of this new country, where you might be preserved as a great nation, and where your white brothers would not disturb you. In that country, your father, the President, now promises to protect you, to feed you, and to shield you from all encroachment. Where you now live your white brothers have always claimed the land. The land beyond the Mississippi belongs to the President, and to none else; and he will give it to you for ever.

My children, listen: The late murder of one of my children in Georgia shows you that you and they are too near to each other. These bad men must now be delivered up, and suffer the penalties of the law for the blood they have shed.

I have sent my agent, and your friend, Colonel Crowell, to demand the surrender of the murderers, and to consult with you upon the subject of your removing to the land I have provided for you west of the Mississippi, in order that my white and red children may live in peace, and that the land may not be stained with the blood of my children again. I have instructed Colonel Crowell to speak the truth to you, and to assure you that your father, the President, will deal fairly and justly with you, and whilst he feels a father's love for you, he advises your whole nation to go to the place where he can protect and foster you. Should any incline to remain and come under the laws of Alabama, land will be laid off for them, and their families in fee.

My children, listen: My white children in Alabama have extended their law over your country. If you remain in it, you must be subject to that law. If you remove across the Mississippi, you will be subject to your own laws, and the care of your father, the President. You will be treated with kindness, and the lands will be yours for ever.

Friends & Brothers, listen: This is a straight and good talk. It is for your nation's good, and your father requests you to hear his counsel.

Andrew Jackson

DS, THer (12-1080); LCs, DLC (60) and DNA-RG 75 (M21-5). *Niles,* June 13. Secretary Eaton enclosed this talk to Creek agent John Crowell on March 27, with instructions to convene the Chiefs, read the talk, demand the murderers of Elijah Wells, and urge the Creeks to remove, stressing the president's "utter inability" to protect them where they were. Eaton remarked that the "murder altho' much to be lamented, may be turned to advantageous account, by pressing it as an inducement for the entire Creek Nation now to remove west of the Mississippi" (DNA-RG 75, M21-5).

1. The Creek obligation to deliver up murderers of whites dated to the 1790 Treaty of New York.

To Ezra Stiles Ely

Washington City March 23d. 1829.

Dear Sir

Your confidential letters of the 18th. and ____ Inst. have been received in the same spirit of kindness and friendship with which they were written.[1]

I must here be permitted to remark that I sincerely regret you did not personally name this subject to me before you left Washington, as I could in that event, have apprised you of the great exertions made by Clay and his partisans here and elsewhere, to destroy the character of Mrs. Eaton by the foulest and basest means, so that a deep and lasting wrong might be inflicted on her husband. I could have given you information that would at least, have put you on your guard with respect to anonymous letters containing slanderous insinuations against female character. If such evidence as this is to be received, I ask where is the guarantee for female character, however moral—however *virtuous.*

To show you how much you have been imposed on, and how much Mrs. E__ has been slandered, I am warranted in the positive contradiction of the very first charge made against her—"that she was in ill fame before Mr. Eaton ever saw her," from the united testimony of the Hon. Jno. Rhea, Dr. Hogg and others who had boarded with Mr. ONeale, long before Mr. Eaton was a member of Congress.[2] If you feel yourself at liberty to give the names of those secret traducers of female reputation, I entertain no doubt, but they will be exposed, and consigned to that public odium which should ever be the lot of those whose morbid appetite delights in defamation and slander.

As to the information of Mr. Campbell of Baltimore, I will barely remark that he may be a respectable man, but surely you will agree with me that a charge so malignant in its character unless accompanied with indubitable evidence of the criminality of the act, should not have been made, and shews him, at once, to be destitute of those just, manly and charitable feelings which should be—characteristic of every good and virtuous man. In contradiction of Mr. Campbell's information to you I have many letters from Baltimore, Pensylvenia, Ohio and other States congratulating me, and the nation, on the selection of Mr. Eaton as one of my Cabinet. Beside these, many members of Congress, and among them the leading members of the New York delegation, expressed personally their high gratification at his appointment—You were assuredly justified in stating to my friends that I have no information, or ever had on which any reliance ought to be placed, of any infamous conduct of Mrs. Eaton.

One observation on the Bank conversation. The place where the remark was made is sufficient evidence, to my mind, that it emanated from Clay or his satalites with a view of completing what he had *here* begun. I am fully warranted in charging Mr. Clay with circulating these slanderous reports, from information derived from a very inteligent lady who met Mr. Clay and his wife[3] on her way to this City. This lady says Mr. and Mrs. Clay spoke in the strongest and most unmeasured terms of Mrs. Eaton. She enquired of them to know upon what grounds these charges rested—*rumour mere rumour* was the answer. So far from this attempt to injure Mr. Eaton on the part of those personages, having the effect which it was intended, the lady as soon as she arrived, sought to become acquainted with her and Mr. Eaton. Now my dear Sir, justice to female character, justice to me, and justice to Mr. Eaton require that those secret agents, in propogating slander, should be made known to Mr. Eaton that he may be enabled to defend the character of his wife against such vile and unprincipled attacks. Would you my worthy friend, desire me to add the weight and influence of my name, whatever it may be, to assist in crushing Mrs. Eaton who, I do believe, and have a right to believe, is a much injured woman and more virtuous than some of her accusers? It is due to me to be made acquainted with the names of those Bank directors who have dared to throw an imputation on the memory of my departed wife. Men who can be base enough to speak thus of the dead, are not too good *secretly* to slander the living; and they deserve, and no doubt will receive, the scorn of all good men. Mr. Eaton has been known to me for twenty years—his character, heretofore for honesty and morality, has been unblemished, and am I now for the first time, to change my opinion of him, because of the slanders of this City? We know, *here* none are spared; even Mrs. Madison was assailed by these fiends in human shape—Mrs. Commodore Porter has also been singled out as a victum to be sacraficed on the altar of defamation, because she left this City and travelled precisely in the way agreed on by Com: Porter, but did not promulgate it to the gossips here. I speak advisedly in relation to this matter, for I have seen a letter from Com: Porter giving an expose of this whole transaction, justifying his wife's conduct and vindicating her innocence. He expresses a determination, when he returns to this Country, to investigate the affair and punish the defamers of his wifes character—and I sincerely hope he may live to do it, for I am disgusted even to loathing at the licentious and depraved state of society—it needs purifying.[4]

You were badly advised, my dear Sir, when informed "that Mrs. Jackson, while in Washington, did not fear to put her seal of reprobation on such a character as Mrs. Eaton." Mrs. Jackson to the last moment of her life believed Mrs. Eaton to be an innocent and much injured woman so far as relates to the tales about her and Mr. Eaton, and none other ever reached her or me. As Mrs. J__ has been introduced into this affair, and as she loved truth while living and she and myself have always taken the _____ and _____ Psalm for our guide, to which I refer you, I will give you a concise history of the information which I and Mrs. Jackson possessed upon this subject. First let me remark, that Major Oneal is a mason, Mr. Timberlake was a mason, and Mr. Eaton is a mason; therefore every person who is acquainted with the obligations of masons must know, that Mr. Eaton as a mason could not have had criminal intercourse with another mason's wife, without being one of the most abandoned of men. The high standing of Mr. Eaton as a man of moral worth and a mason, gives the lie direct in my estimation, to such a charge—and ought to do it, unless the facts of his alledged guilt shall be clearly and unequivocally established, when, should that be the case, he ought and would be spurned with indignation.

I became acquainted with Major Oneal in this City before Congress even sat in it. I never saw him again until 1819 when I visited his house to pay my respects to Mr. Eaton who in Decr. preceding, took his seat in the Senate for the first time.[5] In 1823 I again visited the City in the character of Senator from Tennessee, and took lodgings with Mr. Eaton at Major Oneal's, when and where I became acquainted with Mr. and Mrs. Timberlake. I was there when Mr. Timberlake left this country for the Mediterenean, and present when he took leave of his wife, children and the family; he parted with *them* in the most affectionate manner, as he did also with myself and Mr. Eaton. Between him and the latter gentleman, there appeared to be nothing but friendship and confidence from the first time I saw them at Major Oneal's until the day of his departure. From the situation and proximity of the rooms we occupied, there could not have been any illicit intercourse between Mr. Eaton and Mrs. Timberlake without my having some knowledge of it; and I assure you Sir, that I *saw* nothing—*heard* nothing which was calculated to excite even the slightest suspicion.

Shortly after Mr. Timberlake left Washington for the Mediterreanean, I was told in *great confidence* that it was *rumoured* in the City, that Mr. Eaton and Mrs. Timberlake were too intimate. I met it as I meet all slanders, with a prompt denial, and enquired from what source this rumour came, and found it originated with a female against whom there was then as much said, as is now said against Mrs. Eaton. This report came to the ear of Mrs. Jackson through the same channel; but to the day of her death she believed it a base slander, as I do at this day—As to what servants may have said about her telling them not to call her children Timberlake, but *Eaton,* it is matter of regret to me that you have named it. My dear Sir, if the tales of servants who become offended by being dismissed, are to be believed, what security has your dear wife for her virtuous character—or that of any other lady.

It is reported that Mr. Timberlake declared he would never again return to this country in consequence of Mr. Eaton having seduced his wife. How can such a tale as this be reconciled with the following facts. Whilst now writing I turn my eyes to the mantle piece, where I behold a present sent me by Mr. Timberlake of a Turkish tobacco pouch, which was accompanied by a Turkish pipe, about three weeks before his death, and presented through *Mr. Eaton* whom in his letter, he calls "*his friend.*" Now Sir, could this be so, if he did really believe Mr. Eaton had injured or wronged him! No I am sure you will say, *it is impossible.*

I have not the least doubt but that every secret rumour is circulated by the minions of Mr. Clay for the purpose of injuring Mrs. Eaton and through her Mr. Eaton; but I assure you that such conduct shall never have my aid. When Mrs. E__ visits me (she has not done so since the 4.) I shall treat her with as much politeness as I have ever done, believing her virtuous, at least as much so as the female who first gave rise to the *foul tale,* and as are many of those who traduce her. As to the determination of the ladies in Washington, I have nothing, or will I ever have any thing to do. I will neither persuade or, dissuade any of them from visiting Mrs. E__, leaving Mrs. Eaton and them to settle the matter in their own way; but I am told that many of the ladies here have waited on her.

The villian who could have used such an expression at a public table, as has been related to you by Mr. Jno. E. Hyde of N. York, ought to have been instantly kicked from the table; and that Mr. Hyde did not thus treat him, instead of telling you of it, does not elevate him much in my estimation. A man who could be so base and wanton in his conduct, would not hesitate to slander the most virtuous female in the country—nay even our Saviour were he on earth. With regard to the tale of the Clergyman, it seems to me to be so inconsistent with the charities of the Christian religion, and so opposed to the character of an embassador of Christ, that it gives me pain to read it. Now my dear friend, why did not this Clergyman come himself and tell me this *tale*, instead of asking you to do it. His not having done so, convinces me that he did not believe it, but was willing through other sources to spread the vile slander. If he had been told this by the attending physician himself he had nothing to fear from giving his name provided he was a person of responsibility—if he derived it from any other source than the Doctor, he himself became a slanderer—the New Testament contains no such uncharitable examples as given by our Saviour while a sojourner on earth—I pray you write this Clergyman and remind him of the precepts contained in the good old Book—if he *reads* it he will know where to find them.

I am authorised to say, it is untrue that Mr. Eaton ever changed his lodgings, from the first time he went to Major ONeal's to the present day, except for a few weeks, which was in consequence of his being on several committees, much pressed with business and making it necessary for him, a short time, to be near the Capitol. I should like to know the names of the Members of Congress who saw the names of Mr. and Mrs. Eaton entered on the Tavern Register, as man and wife and the dates of those entries. If my memory serves me correctly Mr. Eaton never travelled in company with Mrs. Timberlake but once and then her husband was along—nor do I believe they went as far as New York; but in this I may be mistaken—But suppose it to be true, are we to infer guilt from that circumstance? If the Owner of the house, or his Bar-keeper were to place upon their register the names of Mr. and Mrs. Eaton, what would that prove—why only that they supposed the lady with him, on his arrival at the Inn, was his wife—a mistake, I will venture to say that very often occurs. There is, I expect, about as much truth in this story, as the one that informed you on your return to Philadelphia, that Mrs. Eaton was to preside at the Presidents house; or the one that represented her as intending to visit your City in company with Major Lewis to assist in purchasing furniture for the Presidential Mansion. Now my dear sir, when such a barefaced and unfounded misrepresentation as this can meet you in the teeth, I set down all that has been told you as unworthy, entirely of credit;

Major Lewis will go on shortly to see his daughter at school in Phila.[6] and Mrs. Eaton, for aught I know, may go with him to purchase furniture for her own house, as I am told she and Mr. Eaton intend keeping house. I suppose she has a right to travel, as well as any other person, if she chooses to do so—and if she desires to go under the protection of Major Lewis, if he, nor her husband object, I do not think any other person has a right; but I do not know that she designs going at all—I am inclined to think she does not. Mrs. Eaton has not been in my house since I moved into it, but should she do so the same attention and respect will be shewn to her that are shown to others. On my nieces I lay no restrictions—I only enjoin it on them to treat *all* well who may call to see them; they are required to visit none but those they may think proper.

Permit me now my dear and highly esteemed friend to conclude this hasty and I fear unintelligible scrawl. Whilst on the one hand we should shun base women as a pestilence of the worst and most dangerous kind to society, we ought on the other to guard virtuous female character with vestal vigilance. Female virtue is like a tender and delicate flower; let but the breath of suspicion rest upon it and it withers and perhaps perishes for ever. When it shall be assailed by envy and malice the good and the pious will maintain its purity and innocence untill guilt is made manifest—not by *rumours* and *suspicions;* but by facts and proofs brought forth and sustained by respectable and fearless witnesses in the face of day. Truth shuns not the light; but falsehood deals in sly and dark insinuations and prefers *darkness* because its deeds are evil—the Psalmist says "the liars tongue we ever hate, and banish from our sight." [Your friend,

Andrew Jackson][7]

Copy, DLC (75). Parton, 3:186–91.

1. Later copies and printings of this letter, including Parton's, have AJ referring to only one Ely letter, that of March 18; but Ely on April 4 acknowledged writing two.

2. Tennessee congressmen John Rhea (1753–1832) and Samuel Hogg (1783–1842) boarded at William O'Neale's during the first session of the Fifteenth Congress, 1817–18. Eaton joined them when he entered the Senate for the second session, 1818–19.

3. Lucretia Hart Clay (1781–1864).

4. During Jefferson's administration, stories circulated accusing James Madison's wife Dolley Payne Todd Madison (1768–1849) of having affairs with the president and with foreign diplomats. David Porter (1780–1843) was an American naval officer. Court-martialed in 1825 for his over-aggressive actions in suppressing West Indian piracy and for subsequent insubordination, he resigned his commission in 1826 and accepted command of the Mexican navy. His wife Eveline (or Evelina) Anderson Porter (1791–1871) remained in Washington, and in late 1828 rumors charged her with infidelity. Porter returned to the U.S. in the fall of 1829.

5. O'Neale had located in Washington in 1794. AJ passed through on trips to Philadelphia, where he sat in Congress and had business in the 1790s. He returned in 1819 to defend his 1818 Seminole campaign, which was under investigation by Congress.

6. Mary Ann Lewis attended Madame Sigoigne's school in Philadelphia.

7. From Isaac Watts's rendition of Psalm 101: "The liar's tongue I ever hate / And banish from my sight." AJ's closing, missing from the DLC text, appears in later copies and in Parton.

To Benjamin Chew Howard

Washington March 23d. 1829

Dear Sir,

I am happy to have it in my power, in answer to your letter of yesterday, to correct the expression which has been ascribed to me on the subject of the appt of Capt Philips, viz, "that I had been deceived by my friends." This expression has no doubt been fabricated by some malicious person for the double purpose of changing your feelings towards me, and of rendering as odious as possible the name of Capt Philips.

The fact is, that seeing your name with that of Messrs. Winchester, McKim, Taney & others, attached to the application in behalf of Capt Philips, I did not hesitate to nominate him; and after his confirmation by the senate, when it was stated by some one that the appointment had not been acceptable to the citizens of Baltimore, did remark that my confidence in yourself & the other Gentlemen had induced me to nominate him, and that the same confidence would not permit me to doubt his capacity & honesty. I also observed that if a recommendation with your names could not be relied upon, I had as well burn all the papers of recommendation which had been presented to me.[1]

Expressions indicating my great respect for you, I have no doubt made, Sir, on many occasions subsequently, and in reply to objections made to the appointment of Capt Philips, have possibly made reference to the improbability of *your having been deceived in his character.* But the idea that you had deceived me is one which I have never entertained, and one, I assure you, that I could never express in the manner represented.

For the prompt and frank avowal of your feelings on this occasion, permit me, Sir, to offer you my thanks, and to assure you that I appreciate it as the characteristic of a noble and generous heart. yr. friend

Andrew Jackson

LS in AJ Donelson's hand, MdHi (12-1086).

1. George Winchester (1787–1840) was a Baltimore lawyer and railroad promoter, later appointed by AJ as a commissioner to settle American claims against Denmark. He had importuned AJ in Phillips's behalf in 1825. Alexander McKim (1748–1832), a Baltimore judge, was a former congressman and a Jackson organizer in 1824 and 1828; his nephew Isaac McKim (1775–1838) was a leading Baltimore merchant and also a congressman, 1823–25 and 1833–38. Roger Brooke Taney (1777–1864), later a Cabinet officer and Chief Justice of the Supreme Court, was the attorney general of Maryland.

From John Pemberton

Philadelphia March 23rd. 1829

Dear Sir,

your enquiries of me relative to Geo. M. Dallas Esq has induced me in justice to him, to occupy a few moment of your time, to give you all the light on the subject, the Political sphere I have moved in will enable me to do—

Mr Dallas since Feby. 1824 (the time his friend J. C. Calhoun was withdrawn,) has been a faithful, efficient, and untiring supporter of the democratic candidate in the late Presidential contest; and the open vindicator on all occations of you and yours—Mr. D. stands high in the estimation of the dominant party in Penna. and should he be selected to fill the situation, at present occupied by Chs. J. Ingersoll, I sincerely believe you could not make an appointment, that would give more pleasure to the pure Democracy of this State.

It would be wormwood to the monster of the Press, nor would Mr. S. Simpson, and his friends, or the body of the *Federal* party be pleased with the appointment of Mr. D.[1]

Since my return I have first heard from Mr. Dallas his views on the subject, I find it would be highly gratifying, and a proud day to him, should he be appointed by you, District Attorney of the US. for the District of Philadelphia.

Should Mr. D. resign the Mayoralty of this City, Mr. Wurts, or Mr. Wm J. Duane, would I have no doubt be chosen to fill the residue of the term—[2]

The selection you have made from those before you, for the Collectorship of this Port, has given almost universal pleasure.[3]

If I can be of service to you in any way, it will be a source of duty, and pleasure for me to perform it—I am Dear Sir most respectfully, your friend

John Pemberton

[Endorsed by AJ:] Mr Pembertons Letter—*Private*

ALS, DNA-RG 59 (M639-6); Copy, PHi (12-1090). Pemberton (1783–1847) was a Philadelphia merchant. In April AJ appointed him naval officer for the Philadelphia customs district.

1. The "monster of the Press" was probably John Binns (1772–1860), anti-Jackson editor of the Philadelphia *Democratic Press* and original publisher of the coffin handbill.

2. Duane declined the mayoralty, and Dallas was succeeded by Benjamin Wood Richards. John Wurts (1792–1861) was a lawyer and former congressman.

3. On March 10 AJ had appointed James Nelson Barker, a playwright and former mayor, as Philadelphia customs collector.

From Edward Digges

City of Washington D.C.
March 24th. 1829

Honble. Sir,

The liberty I take in addressing you this letter will I trust be attributed to that cause which induces a Husband and Father, who is bound by the Ties of Nature to Exert every nerve to Shield his family from Extream Indigence and want, (a reprsentation of which you will see on the other side &c.) At this time I am out of Employ and destitue of means to relieveing the distresses of my family, who are in want of the Necessarys for subsistance no means to procure them or to Shield the small remnant of property which I have saved from the wreck of my advese fortune which I have experianced for the last Three or 4 years and I have nothing left to Console us in our Indigent state but that of an unblemished Charecter either in public or private life, (and that of being one of the decendants of the most respectable Famile of Maryland & amongst the first emegrants to that State under Lord Baltimore)

I have been an aplican for a situation under the former administration and was promised one by the former Secretery of State the first situation which be vacant in his office after that promise onc did Take place & I calld on him in Company Mrs Digges and I was Treated by Mr H. Clay with all his Viperous indignity for no other Fault but that of giveing my entire Support in defending, The brave, and Truly Virtuous, Partiot of my Cuntry to whome alone we are indebted for the dignity, we possess as a Great Nation=Trusting in your generosity and liberality of heart that you will forgive me for the remark I am about to make on the former and present State of our offices.[1]

It is Truly distressing to ye feeling of an american who is in a state Extream want to see Englishmen (not Naturalised) Scothmen, and Negroes, put in office to ye Exclusion of Americans of family & Talant, Equal, if not Superior to them who have had a preference; at this time there is a Negro man Chief Messenger to ye Secretery of State department a place that woud be verry acceptable to me next to that of A Clerks place.[2] it woud be truly greatful to my feeling to have the pleasure of an Interview with your Excellency and to receive that Hand which weilded the Sword of destruction to ye foes of our beloved Cuntry will Contribute to gratify one of the Greatest Wishes of a poor man who depends on his Cuntry for his & familys Existance. With Great Respect and Esteem I am your Excelancy Most Obdt. Hmble Servt

Edward Digges

P.S. It wou'd Contribute to ye relieve the distress's of my mind to hear from your Excellency early as possible Convenient by the door Keeper.

Edwd Digges

[Endorsed by AJ:] Edward Digges application for office & recommendation of Genl. Stewart & other respectable gentlemen in his favor—refered to the War Department for employment

ALS, DNA-RG 107 (12-1096). Digges enclosed a March 20 letter from Philip Stewart and five other members of the Jackson Central Committee recommending him for employment because of his honesty, poverty, and service as "an ardent and zealous Jacksonian during the late presidential contest" (DNA-RG 107). Digges had been a constable of the District of Columbia. He apparently did not secure an appointment.
    1. Solicited by Mrs. Digges, Louisiana congressman William L. Brent had recommended Digges for a State Department job in April 1826. Clay replied that he was willing but had no vacancies. In August 1827, seeking a messenger's post, Digges and his wife annoyed Clay by calling on him at home, an intrusion for which Digges afterward apologized (*Clay Papers*, 5:213; DNA-RG 59, M531-2).
    2. Joseph Warren (c1789–1844), the chief messenger for the State Department, retained his position.

From John Crowell

Washington City
March 25th. 1829

Sir

I proceed in pursuance of *[your request]* to state to you some of my views on the subject of removing the Creek Indians west of the Missisippi.

These Indians number about twenty thousand. I will premise that in my opinion some new relations are required to be established with those people before their removal can be effected upon peaceable terms. Indians are to be moved upon by the opperation of one or the other of the most powerfull of influences; I mean Love, or fear, and unfortunately the latter passion has been the one hitherto two often appealed to by those engaged in the business of removal, and not having either the means or the authority to coerce them, it has resulted in a fixed hate on the part of the great body of the Creek Nation, from this feeling has sprung apparently, a settled obstinacy of purpose not to comply with their future demands or requests.

They say the Treaty of 1826 stipulated the period in which the Agents for the emigrating Creeks was to be priviledged to travel over their Country, that period has expired, and they ask to know why these Agents are yet permited to remain among them.[1]

Here then in my view of the subject is the great obsticle. If in the removal of it another power can be brought to bear upon them in an appeal to their best interest by one on whose protection and friendship they rely, a new influence would be felt which in my opinion would be opperative & prove in the end succesfull. The means to be used in this new appeal, I respecfully suggest should be, first The views of the Government upon the subject of their removal should be made known to them, and let them understand that the Country set apart for them shall be in fee simple & that they will not again be required to remove from it, that the Government will protect them against the encroachment of the whites & hostile tribes of Indians.

Second. Entire power should be given to the person employed to remove them, to exercise a sound discression in all matters, necessary & proper to effect the object; that person should have the entire confidence of the Indians, he should be authorised to select his sub Agents, they too should have the confidence of the Indians; one of those should remain in ~~my~~ his absence at the Agency in Alabama & one other at the Agency west of the Missisippi, or change as might be advisable, by occasionally moving through the Indian Country and going with the emigrating parties.

Third   The Indians should be paid full & fair value for their improvements, they should be paid a fair value for their stock & such other articles not moveable; which could be again sold to reemburs the Government, they should be fed from the time of enrolment and for one year after they arrive in their new Country—each Warrior should have a rifle gun & Kettle, each individual a Blanket.

These helps with such others as the Governmt have in their power to give, placed in my power to offer; & the Government backing me in the faithfull application of them; I have but little doubt of being able to effect their removal in a few years.

My first step would be to convene a general council & explain to them the views of the Government and endeavour to effect an arrangemt with the whole nation allowing them a reasonable time to prepare for removal, This failing I should endeavour to weaken the opposition of the chiefs by profers of reservations in fee simple & other matters suitable to induce their acquiesance. This failing I should move upon them by Towns & families & by leading the way with such as I could carry, I have but little doubt they would all ultimately follow, should all my efforts fail the Governmt shall be regularly apprised of it and the causes, with such suggestions as may seem proper;

The entire cost of this removal I am not now prepared to estimate, but apart from the [*cost of their improve*]ments & their stock and their equipments &c &c, the cost would be for rations, while going and for a year afterwards, for ferriages, transportation &c &c. all of which is respecfully submitted, for your consideration

Jno. Crowell
Agt for I. A

[Endorsed by AJ:] Col. Crowal letter containing his views on the subject of the removal of the Creek Indians—to be considered

ALS, DNA-RG 107 (M222-25). Crowell (1780–1846), a former Alabama congressman, served as agent to the Creek Indians from 1821 to 1836.
1. The 1826 Treaty of Washington stipulated that the emigrating McIntosh Creeks were to leave within twenty-four months. It made no provision to continue recruiting for emigration thereafter.

To John Branch

March 27th. 1829

Sir,
The evening post published at New York on the 25th instant announces that the Natchez sloop of War had not then sailed. You will please make prompt inquiry into the cause of this delay, and report the same to the President.

Piracy can only be kept down and prevented by prompt movement and energetic measures. This is expected from our Navy, and the expectation must not be disappointed.

(Signed) Andrew Jackson

LC, DLC (60). On March 31 Branch reported that the *Natchez* had sailed on the 28th. On April 3 he submitted papers explaining the delay: the ship's crew was shorthanded, and the messenger carrying its orders had been held up leaving Washington because the stages were full.

To Samuel Delucenna Ingham

The Secretary of the Treasury will give the following directions, by circular, to all the Collectors.

That they use *great vigilence & care,* that in every case, the payment of the import duties be *well secured by solvent endorsers,* that no individual be taken as endorser for a greater sum, than *two thirds* of his clear estate.

Hereafter no collector to be allowed any percentage on any dues that may be lost to the goverment.

Sent to Mr Ingham March 28th. 1829—for consideration

Andrew Jackson

ADS copy, DLC (12-1166). On June 5 Ingham issued a circular to customs collectors cautioning them to obtain ample security from importing merchants and their endorsers for the payment of customs bonds, while leaving the particulars of each case to their discretion (DNA-RG 56, M735-2).

From John Macpherson Berrien

Attorney General's office
28th. March '29

Sir,

In the earliest interview which I had with you, after you did me the Honor to communicate your wish, that I should take upon myself the office of the Attorney General of the United States, I took occasion to mention to you, that I had entered into certain professional engagements, with some of the Claimants of lands, in the territory of Florida, which I should be bound to fulfil, and consequently that it would become necessary to engage counsel to represent the interests of the United States in these cases. You thought, as I did, that this circumstance presented no difficulty, and I acquiesced in the call with which you had honored me.

It now becomes necessary to act upon this. The District Attorney of East Florida, has transmitted to this office certain documents relating to the claim of Arredondo & son and others, to a tract of land in that territory, on which he asks advice.[1] The Court sits in Augustine, on the first Monday in May, and it will consequently be desirable that no time should be lost in providing Counsel to represent the United States in this matter.

I beg leave to suggest that as cases of this sort will probably occur frequently, it may be of importance that some professional gentleman in this vicinity should be selected to prepare the cases for trial on the part of the United States, and that the magnitude of the cases, as well as the novelty of some of the questions involved, will make it important to secure to the Government professional talents of the highest order. I have the Honor to be Very Respectfully Sir, yr. obt. st.

Jn Macpherson Berrien

LCs, DNA-RG 60 (M699-1; M699-2). *TPUS*, 24:175–76. Florida land claimants were seeking confirmation of their titles derived from grants that Spain had purportedly made before ceding the province to the U.S. Spanish records concerning some grants had been removed to Havana and withheld from American inspection, and American officials believed many of the claims to be defective or spurious. Berrien represented two of the largest and most suspect claims, those of Arredondo and Son, of nearly 300,000 acres, and of John Forbes and Company, for around 1.2 million acres. AJ immediately engaged William Wirt (1772–1834), former attorney general under Monroe and Adams, to handle the cases for the government. In the 1830s the Supreme Court upheld both grants.

1. U.S. attorney Thomas Douglas (1790–1855) had written for instructions on the Arredondo case on February 4. Wirt answered on April 1 (*TPUS*, 24:167–69, 178–81).

From Littleton Waller Tazewell

Norfolk. March 30th. 1829.

Dear Sir,

I reached this place on the 23d. Instant, after a very disagreable journey, from all the effects of which I have not yet entirely recover'd. Ever since my return home, I have devoted every moment I could spare, to such an investigation of my domestic concerns and private affairs, as might enable me to form a prompt and satisfactory judgment of my situation, with a view to ascertain the propriety of complying with your kind wishes towards me. Altho' I have not yet completed this examination, yet I have progressed on it so far, as to satisfy myself that I could not possibly justify, either to my own feelings, or to the interests and prospects of my numerous family, the acceptance of any situation, which might oblige me to leave Virginia for any length of time, and at a great distance. The obstacles which prevent me from doing so are numerous, and insurmountable, certainly during the present year; and I cannot now foresee enough of future events, to promise myself with any degree of assurance, that they will not continue for a much longer period than that to which I have referred. It becomes my duty therefore, to give you early information of my situation; and while expressing my very grateful acknowledgments, for the many evidences you have given me, of your very kind and friendly consideration, to beg of you to disregard me altogether, in the selection you may feel yourself constrained to make, of one qualified to perform such duties, as it was your wish that I should undertake. In making this communication, I beg leave to assure you, Sir, that I have labor'd for the accomplishment of your wishes, with a most sincere desire, and very anxious wish, to reconcile the duties which I owe to others, with a ready compliance with your kind solicitude in my behalf. Even the apparent difficulties which at first presented themselves, did not deter me: but after overcoming many, I at last encounter'd others, of a kind which nothing but time itself can remove. To such alone do I submit; and to these, only because in their very nature they are insurmountable by mortal means.

I have now redeemed the promise which I made, when I last had the honor to converse with you upon this subject; but before I part with it, I hope you will pardon me, if I avail myself of the privilege in which you have sometimes indulged me, of making to you some suggestions in relation to this matter, that may perhaps be found worthy of more reflection, than you have had occasion yet to bestow upon it. I present these to your own eye *only;* and shall speak of them with the frankness that becomes one always to use, and in that spirit of candor, which will ever dictate what I may take occasion to say to you upon any subject.

I have reason for believing, that owing either to the practices of those who have preceded you in the administration, or to some wounded pride but badly concealed, or to some other cause, which it is not worth while even to conjecture, the Statesmen of Great Britain, view your accession to the place you now hold, with no very kind feelings; and that if they do not seek to embarrass you, they will at least treat with much indifference any overtures made by the U. S. to re-open a negotiation with them—Should this impression of mine be found to be correct, it is very obvious, that any direct offer to negociate at this time, must be productive of some mortification, if not of future mischief.[1] The first care of our Minister therefore, should be, to remove any false impressions that may exist in England in regard to this country, and especially in respect to the views and policy of your administration. Until this object shall be accomplished, any attempt to negociate, would be much worse than useless—Even after the Minister has succeeded however, (and there is no doubt but by a prudent course he will succeed) it would be still impolitic to make any direct offer to treat, until he was assured that such an overture would be received with satisfaction, and met with cordiality. The native character of British Statesmen constitutes a very strong obstacle to the acquisition of any certain information upon this point. They are all cautious cold and reserved by nature, and must be stimulated by some excitement, before they will allow themselves to express what they really feel, and what the interests of their own Country requires that they should utter. Mere general declarations of the disposition of the U. S. to adjust with them all the differences existing between the two countries, may not be sufficient to break the ice, with which a British statesman is always encrusted. Some more special, and therefore more powerful stimulant may be requisite, to make him move promptly, and speak decidedly. This can easily be supplied, by opening a negociation for a commercial treaty with France. Let the Minister of the U. S. in England be informed of this fact, with directions to hint at it, upon some fit occasion, in the presence of the British Minister, and my life upon it, the tone and temper of the British cabinet towards us, will be at once changed. That Cabinet will then no longer regard with indifference, our general declarations of an amicable temper towards them; but will reciprocate such declarations, with an earnestness and cordiality, the very rarity of which will be a strong pledge of its sincerity. The negociation may then be commenced, with happy auspices of its successful termination. But if commenced before, it will very probably drag on heavily, if it does not soon come to such a rupture, as may do mischief both at home and abroad—I would suggest to you then the propriety of dispatching a Minister to France, previously, or certainly simultaneously with one to Great-Britain; and the necessity of instructing the former, to open a negociation for a liberal commercial treaty with France, and to communicate freely and promptly with the latter, as to his progress in this negociation—Let the Minister to Great Britain be apprised of these instructions, before he leaves this country; and be directed to govern himself in his intercourse with the British Ministry, according to the effects they may produce, should circumstances seem to require it—

The preceding remarks will sufficiently shew, if indeed you required any such proof, that it is all-important, that the Minister to Great-Britain should be a man high in the confidence of this government, and known to the world so to be—That he should be one of much intelligence, of amiable manners, and of quick and sure observation—In one word, that he should possess not less of tact than of judgment; and of sufficient discretion to discriminate accurately and properly, when he should rely upon the one or the other of these qualities most—In casting my eye around the circle of our friends, to find one who might answer this description, I can think of none to whom it applies more truly, than to the Attorney General Mr. Berrien. His present situation marks him to the world as one high in your confidence; and the appointment of one of your cabinet, will be the best pledge you can offer to Great Britain, of the zeal and sincerity of your wishes towards her—It will be quite unnecessary for me to enlarge before you upon the other qualifications of Mr. Berrien, you know him as well as I do, and will probably concur with me in opinion, that you can find no person better suited to the service which you wish performed—You can find no difficulty in filling the place of the Attorney General, altho' you will probably be much perplexed to find one better qualified than Mr. Berrien to fill the other situation—

I have felt it my duty to make these suggestions to you, under the hope, that you will not think me trespassing too far on your goodness, while offering such unasked for advice—To this let me add, that if at any time, or in any way, you may think I can be of service to you, I hope you will freely command me, under the assurance, that there is nothing which may be within my power to perform, that I will not readily do. With very high respect, and much esteem and regard, I have the honor to be, Sir, yours very truly.

Littn. W Tazewell

ALS, DLC (36). AJ had offered Tazewell the post of minister to Great Britain.
    1. A protracted dispute over colonial trade regulations culminated in 1826 with Britain closing its West Indian ports to American ships. In a series of newspaper articles later republished as *A Review of the Negotiations between the United States of America and Great Britain* (London, 1829), Tazewell had criticized Adams's diplomacy.

From Martin Van Buren

March 31—1829.

My dear Sir

On my return from your house last evening I found the enclosed among some letters which I had not before been able to examine. Upon a careful consideration of its contents, I find it to be so evidently written for your perusal as to make it something like a duty on my part to lay it before you; and I do that the more readily from an entire consciousness that you wish to hear all that may be said with decency in respect to your administration, by those interested in its success. I have known Mr Ritchie long and intimately, and am well satisfied that there is not a man of purer public spirit in the Country. The disinterestedness of his views, with the great ability that has characterized his paper, have given it an influence infinitely greater than any other press in the Union. Whatever you may think of the wisdom or justice of the opinions expressed by such a man, I am quite sure that they will receive from you a liberal and respectful consideration.

not being certain from the great press that is made upon me that I shall be able to see to you to day, I have thought proper to enclose it, & will receive it again at your perfect leisure— Yours affectionately

M Van Buren

[*Endorsed by AJ:*] Mr Van Burens note 31rst March enclosing Mr Richie—answrd 31 of March 1829—

ALS, DLC (36); ALS draft, DLC-Van Buren Papers (12-1189). Van Buren *Autobiography,* pp. 245–46.

[*Enclosure: Thomas Ritchie to Van Buren*]

March 27, 1829

Dear *Sir*

This is in all probability the last Letter I shall have the honor of addressing you for many years to come. Our respective situations, though vastly different from each other; make such a Correspondence delicate on both sides. A Secretary of State has his own duties to perform, and so has an Editor, however humble he may be. I need not be more explicit—but I cannot reconcile it to myself to remain altogether silent, amid the Scenes which I have witnessed. You are the only member of the Administration with whom I am acquainted. I therefore address myself to you. If there be any thing in this letter, which you may think it proper to submit to Gen. Jackson, you are authorized to lay it before him—and him only. In truth, I would have addressed myself directly to him, but for my anxiety to preserve even the *appearance* of that respect, which I sincerely feel for his Character & himself.

You, Sir, or perhaps Gen. J. if he should see this Letter, may charge the writer with arrogance, impertinence, call it what you will, for intruding my opinion, unasked & unacceptable, upon the grave matters of which it proposes to treat. I am content to abide by your severest censures, as I am satisfied with my own motives. This letter is dictated by the most friendly feelings. It is from a sincere desire that you should be possessed of the state of pubic opinion in this part of the country, that I break through all the Rules of Etiquette. You know how anxiously I desired the election of Gen. Jackson. My most intimate friends have witnessed the joy which his success inspired. I regarded it not simply as the downfall of a party which had corrupted the purity of Elections and abused its power for its own little purposes, but as a new epoch in the history of our Country; as opening a bright prospect of wise and constitutional principles. I need not say, Sir, that I had nothing to gain, except as one of ten millions of people. I have nothing to ask—the Administration has nothing to offer which I will accept.

Why this bright prospect is somewhat clouded over within the short Space of thirty Days, I will not enter into a long Recapitulation to explain. I pass over the Cabinet. It has disappointed many of the sincerest of the President's friends. In the same proportion that it dispirited them, has it raised the hopes of their enemies. They have already raised the standard of opposition; and a rival, who was abandoning all his views in utter despair, was immediately animated to enter the lists again.[1] I do not speak at random, when I make these assertions. The admirable Inaugural Address, however, counteracted these effects in some degree. It gave us all additional spirits. But, I speak it with profound regret, the subsequent appointments have thrown a cloud over our friends, which it will require some time and great wisdom to dispel. We are sorry to see the personal friends of the President appointed. We lament to see so many of the Editorial Corps favored with the patronage of the Administration.[2] A single Case would not have excited so much observation—but it really looks as if there were a systematic Effort to reward Editorial Partizans—which will have the effect of bringing the vaunted Liberty of the Press into a sort of Contempt. I make allowance for the situation of these Gentlemen. I know most of them are able and qualified men. They have fought manfully, to put out a corrupt Coalition. They have fought with the halter round their necks; and not, as I have done, so much in the country of friends, as of enemies. I allow for all these things—and still the Truth cannot be disguised, that the press, which shrinks like the sensitive plant from the touch of Executive Power, has been heedlessly handled. Invade the freedom of the Press and the freedom of Election, by showering patronage too much on Editors of newspapers and on Members of Congress, and the rights of the People themselves are exposed to imminent danger. I know that this was not the *motive* of such appointments; but I argue about *effects;* effects too, not to be brought about by *this* administration, but by less worthy ones which are to succeed it.

There is some difficulty under all new administration's, to know whom to *put out* and whom to *put in*—and it is the right use of patronage under such circumstances that constitutes one of the most delicate operations of government. We should suppose that one pretty good rule was, for the Chief Magistrate to consider offices, not as made for himself, the gratification of his own feelings and the promotion of his own purposes, but as a public trust to be confided to the most worthy. I throw out this suggestion, because I have seen too much stress laid upon the personal feelings of the President, by some who did not sufficiently estimate the high station which he occupies. There is another thing. I go for reform—but what is reform? Is it to turn out of office all those, who voted against him, or who decently preferred Mr. Adams? Or is it not rather those, who are incapable of discharging their duties; the drunken, the ignorant, the embezzler, the man who has abused his official facilities to keep Gen. Jackson out—or, who are so wedded to the corruptions of Office, as to set their faces against all Reform? Is it not to abolish all unnecessary Offices, and to curtail all unnecessary Expences? It surely is not to put out a good & experienced officer, because he was a decent friend of J. Q. Adams, *in order* to put in a heated partizan of the election of Gen. Jackson, which partizan choses to dub himself on that account the friend of Reform. I trust that such a spirit of Reform will not come near to us in Virginia. Should any one be seeking the loaves & fishes of federal office in Virginia, I hope the Administration will be very careful *whom* they may put out, to serve such an Office-Seeker. There is no man, whom I would touch, in this City.

The course of appointments at Washington is calculated to cool and alienate some of our friends. The enemies of the Administration are on the alert—they are availing themselves of all our errors—while we are so situated, that we are unable to justify & defend them. You can scarcely conceive the uneasiness which prevails

Will you excuse me for troubling you with the following extract, which I have received from Washington, from a profound Observer of Men & things—He is a warm friend of the President—and no Virginian:[3]

"I can read the History of this Administration more clearly than I did the late one, and I was in no respect disappointed in my views respecting its course and termination. Under the profession of Reform, changes will be made, to the public injury. Let the rule be once known, and every man who was not an active partizan of Gen. Jackson, will be brought within it. A great number of violent men, alike destitute, I fear, of principle & intelligence, will be thrown into conspicuous positions, in the excitement, and placed in Offices of trust. High-minded and talented men, in such a result, will for a time, be thrown into the shade. The contest will be for Office, and not for principle. This will impair the moral force of our Institutions, at home and abroad, and may eventuate in their destruction.

Should the present Administration go down, as I fear it will, and should Clay come into power, *on his system*, I tremble for the Union. A scene of violence, reckless of Consequences, will then be the order of the Day. This is a gloomy Picture, and I wish to God, I could persuade myself it is too highly coloured. I see, and understand perfectly all the movements made."

My heart aches as I make this Extract. Sincerely do I trust that its gloomy anticipations may be defeated—and that Gen. Jackson may lay down his power amid the loudest acclamations of a grateful people. I would do any thing, that was honorable & proper, to lead to this Result— But, I have done.

I beg you to make no answer to this Letter. I write in haste, and with pain—Perhaps I ought not to write it at all, I am, sir, Respy.

Thomas Ritchie

ALS, DLC-Van Buren Papers (12-1192). Van Buren *Autobiography*, pp. 246–48.
1. At a March 7 farewell dinner in Washington, Henry Clay made remarks intimating his willingness to stand for the presidency (*Clay Papers*, 8:4–6).
2. On March 21, AJ had appointed his close friend William B. Lewis and editors Amos Kendall of the *Argus of Western America* and Isaac Hill of the *New Hampshire Patriot* to be respectively second auditor, fourth auditor, and second comptroller of the Treasury.
3. The writer was almost certainly John McLean, who privately censured the adminis- tration to Ritchie and others. McLean used phrasing very close to this in an April 4 letter to James Monroe (Monroe Papers, DLC).

To Martin Van Buren

March 31rst. 1829

I have read the enclosed letter with attention, and if the facts adverted to would warrant the conclusion, the objections would be well founded.

There has been as yet, no important case of removal except Genl Harrison; and I am sure if Mr Richie has read the instructions given to our ministers, who were sent to Panama, he must think the recal of Genl Harrison, not only a prudent measure, but one which the interest of the country makes indispensibly necessary.[1] I have refered to the case of Genl Harrison only, because I cannot suppose Mr Richie has any allusion to the Auditors & Comptroller, who were dismissed, not so much on account of their politics, as for the want of moral honesty.[2]

The Gentleman who has been selected to supply the place of Genl Harrison is, I believe as well qualified, if not better, than any other who would have undertaken the mission to that country.

I would advise the answering of Mr Richie's letter; and, in the most delicate manner, to put him on his guard with respect to letter writers from Washington. The letter he has extracted from, instead of being from my *friend*, must be from some disappointed office hunter—one who merely professes to be my friend; or perhaps, from a friend of Mr Clays in disguise. How could this letter writer, know what changes were to be made? How can he pretend to *foretel*, without knowing who are to be appointed, that the changes will be injurious to the public interest? you may assure Mr Richie that his Washington correspondent knows nothing of what will be the course of the President in appointments, or he would have known that the President has not, nor will he ever, make an appointment but with a view to the public good, and the security of the fiscal concerns of the nation. He never has, nor will he, appoint a personal friend to office, unless by such appointment the public will be faithfully served. I cannot suppose Mr Richie would have me proscribe my friends, merely because they are so. If my personal friends are qualified and patriotic, why should I not be permitted to bestow a *few* offices on them? For my own part I can see no well founded objections to it. In my Cabinet, it is well known that there is but one man with whom I have had an intimate and particular acquaintance, tho' they are all my friends, and in whom I have the greatest confidence. But even if it were as Mr Richie supposes, I have only followed the examples of my illustrious predecessors, Washington and Jefferson. They took from their own state, bosom friends and placed them in the Cabinet. Not only this, but Genl Washington went even farther—besides placing two of his friends from Virginia near him, he brought into his cabinet Genl Hamilton with whom, if possible, he was upon more intimate terms than I am with any member of my Cabinet.[3] I have drawn your attention to these facts because I apprehend that our friend Mr Richie had not reflected upon the subject, or he would not have suffered himself to be so easily alarmed. I have, I assure you, none of those fears, and forebodings, which appears to disturb the repose of Mr Richie, and his Washington Correspondant. I repeat, it would be well for you to write Mr Richie and endeavour to remove his apprehension of dificulty, & danger. Say to him, before he condemns the Tree, he ought to wait and see its fruit.[4] The people expect reform—they shall not be disappointed; but it must be *Judiciously* done, & upon *principle*. yours respectfully

A. Jackson

ALS, DLC-Van Buren Papers (12-1198); LS copy, DLC (36). Van Buren *Autobiography,* pp. 248–49. Pursuant to AJ's suggestion, Van Buren wrote Ritchie on April 1 to thank him for his candor and assure him of AJ's pure intentions (Van Buren Papers, DLC; Van Buren *Autobiography,* pp. 249–50).
1. On March 12, AJ had replaced Adams's minister to Colombia William Henry Harrison (1773–1841) with Thomas P. Moore. Henry Clay's instructions of May 8, 1826, and March 16, 1827, to the U.S. delegation to the international Panama Congress (*Clay Papers,* 5:313–41, 6:311–13) had been transmitted to Congress by Adams on March 3,

1829, and published in the Washington *National Journal* on March 20. They included assessments of various diplomatic prospects involving Colombia, Mexico, and Spain. On March 30 the *US Telegraph* lambasted their publication as insulting to the three countries and a deliberate embarrassment to the new administration's diplomacy.

2. AJ had removed second auditor William Lee (1772–1840), fourth auditor Tobias Watkins (1780–1855), and second comptroller Richard Cutts (1771–1845) for Lewis, Kendall, and Hill. All three were appointees of James Monroe, Lee and Cutts in 1817 and Watkins in 1824.

3. Washington appointed Virginians Thomas Jefferson as secretary of state and Edmund Randolph as attorney general. Treasury secretary Alexander Hamilton had served as Washington's secretary and aide-de-camp in the Revolution.

4. The Biblical injunction to judge a tree by its fruit was, as AJ remarked in 1817, "a favourite adage with me" (*Jackson Papers,* 4:81).

To Morgan Lewis

Confidential,

My Dear Sir,

your high standing and the confidence I have in your candor, induces me to write to you.

I have laid it down as a rule in my appointments to office to look for honesty and integrity, and talents sufficient for the execution of the trust reposed. And when these are obtained to govern the selection of individuals as nearly as I can by the wishes of the people immediately interested in the discharge of the duties.

For the collector's place in the Port of New York Mr S. Swartout has been presented to me as a fit character. It is admitted by all that he is a man of strict integrity, honor, and capacity; but it is alledged that he is poor. I have always thought an honest man the noblest work of God, and that in most of the operations of life there could be no safety without integrity of character.[1] Will you have the goodness to state to me whether Mr Swartouts standing in the city is such as will enable him to give the necessary security, and his popularity such, as will permit him to get on with the duties pleasantly should he receive the appt—

Be pleased to give me your opinion as early as you can, which I shall regard as confidential should you require it. yr. obt. & Humble svt

Andrew Jackson

LS in AJ Donelson's hand, Mills Mansion State Historic Site, New York (mAJs). Lewis (1754–1844) was a former governor of New York, a major general in the War of 1812, and a leading New York Jacksonian and presidential elector in 1828. Samuel Swartwout (1783–1856) had been an intimate of Aaron Burr and was tried and acquitted for his role in the Burr conspiracy of 1806. Long familiar with AJ, he served as a political confidant and operative in the 1824 and 1828 campaigns.

1. "An honest man's the noblest work of God" was a widely quoted phrase from the fourth Epistle of Alexander Pope's *An Essay on Man* (1744).

April

From Jehiel Brooks

Washington April 1. 1829

Sir,

I enclose a letter addressed to you by Mr. E. Hayward; of Cincinnati, which letter, in connexion with those now on file in the War Dept., from Gentlemen of Louisiana, and from Senators and members of Congress, &c., form a connected statement of the character I have supported, from the time I quit the Army, down to the present.[1]

I beg leave further to state, that, since my health would permit, I have been in almost daily attendance at the War Office, without having yet obtained an interview with the Secretary, during which time, I am informed, that others have come to Washington, vacancies have been made in the Indian Department, filled by them, and they gone to the performance of their duty; while I remain utterly ignorant whether those letters, which I returned to the War Dept. by your direction, have even been read by the Secretary.

After having waited here, Sir, for nearly four months—defeated in my application for the Indian Agency on Red River, before the late administration, on account of my political creed; defeating in turn the nomination of Mr. Adams to that office, and being again defeated in the same application after your succession, and contrary too, as I humbly conceive, to those immutable principles of abstract justice, which form the polar star to all your actions, public or private; and which dictated those favorable expressions to me, on the 13th. *Ultimo*—I say, Sir, after all this delay and disappointment—the sacrifice of my professional hopes at Natchitoches, which I have been for upwards of two years building there, with no little labour and expense, together with present embarrassment; I hope it will not be thought unreasonable, improper, or impertinent that I now solicit you, Sir, to do something in my behalf.

I understood from Major Armstrong of Alabama, Majr. B. F. Smith, and others (all of whom left the City during my late indisposition) that there would be vacancies soon in the Osage, and other Indian Agencies west of the Mississippi and that they thought one of them would be appropriated to me.[2] I will only further add, that if such is to be the case, or if any other situation is to be awarded me, and the great perplexities which have constantly attended me during my long sojourn here, entitle me to immediate consideration, it is most anxiously solicited by—Your obedient, and most devoted humble Servant,

J. Brooks

[Endorsed by AJ:] Mr. Brooks enclosing the recommendation of Mr Hayward for Indian agency—refered to the sec. of war.

ALS, DNA-RG 107 (12-1221). Brooks (1797–1886), a Cincinnati lawyer and former Army lieutenant, had moved to Natchitoches, La., in 1826. The Red River agency at Natchitoches, which oversaw relations with the Caddo and Quapaw nations, was vacated by the death of George Gray in November 1828. Brooks applied to President Adams, but he in December nominated former Orleans Territory Indian agent John Sibley. The Senate did not act on the nomination. AJ appointed Thomas Griffith of Kentucky to the Red River agency on March 12, 1829. After Griffith died, AJ appointed Brooks in March 1830.

    1. Elijah Hayward's letter was dated April 1. Previous recommendations for Brooks included letters from New Orleans and Natchitoches and one from ten congressmen and senators headed by John Woods and Benjamin Ruggles of Ohio (Brooks-Queen Papers, DCU).

    2. Francis Wells Armstrong (1783–1835) was federal marshal in Alabama, 1823–30. Benjamin Fort Smith (1796–1841) was Chickasaw agent, 1823–30.

To Susan Wheeler Decatur

Washington April 2d. 1829

Dear madam.

    Your note of yesterday is before me. In reply, permit me to assure you that your situation interests my warmest wishes, and will not be forgotten.

    In reference to the claims of Mr Ridgely, I can only say that they must await the action of those general principles by which the administration is to be governed. offices cannot be created by it, nor can incumbents be removed to make room for others without an enquiry establishing their incompetency, and even where this enquiry produces a vacancy it must be remembered that the numerous applicants for it have, each, a conviction of superior claim, and demand from the President an impartial hearing.

    It is a source of sincere regret with me that congress disappointed your appeal to its justice and magnanimity. I am satisfied however, that the disappointment was not the result of an unfriendly feeling, or of a conviction that your claim was not well founded; and that at the next session you may calculate upon a favorable decision. In the mean time I assure you that whatever I can do with propriety for your relief will be cheerfully done.[1] yr. obt svt

Signed A. J.

Copy by AJ Donelson, DLC (36). Decatur (c1776–1860) was the widow of naval hero Stephen Decatur (1779–1820). She had aided AJ in the 1828 campaign by repudiating stories of ill feeling between him and her husband in 1819, and was now seeking a better position for William G. Ridgely (c1788–1861), who was chief clerk to the Board of Navy Commissioners.

1. Decatur had petitioned Congress for prize money for the frigate *Philadelphia*, which after being captured by Barbary pirates was destroyed in Tripoli harbor in a raid led by her husband in 1804. In the previous Congress a bill in her favor had passed the Senate but not the House. AJ endorsed the claim in his first annual message in December (Richardson, 2:462), but no bill passed.

From Ezra Stiles Ely

Philadelphia April 4th. 1829.

(Private and Confidential.)

My dear General

Your generous and noble disposition merits the best of friends. Of this, your last letter, if I had wanted proof would have been the best evidence. It has given me what I desired, the best reason to say, to those *friends* who may speak to me on the subject, that you had no knowledge of any evil in Mrs. Eaton and believed her an injured woman. If your opponents speak to me about the matter, I shall say the same; although their accusations scarcely need any longer to be answered at all. You have granted too, in relation to *the ladies* all which I asked; and I had no desire that you should add the weight of your influence to crush an injured female; while I did earnestly wish that your nieces might not visit any one whom the most respectable families in Washington could not.

Permit me to do justice to James Campbell, a merchant in Baltimore, by saying that he repelled the slander uttered in the meeting of certain Directors of a Bank; and expressed his persuasion that you knew nothing of the common rumour against Mrs Eaton. Still the reports against Mrs. E. had been so general and of so long continuance in B__, that many of the most respectable Jackson men felt, he said, "as if they could not hold up their heads." I wish you not in your thoughts, through me, my dear Sir, to do Mr. Campbell injustice, for he is an honourable man, and a sincere friend to that man of the people whom millions delight to honour. Mr. Clay, he and I both believe to be as unprincipalled and base a politician as ever lived.

I did not ask the name of the Bank nor of the Directors of which he spoke; although I think he told me that he was the only Jackson man amongst them, I then had no disposition to trouble you on the subject. I would write to him and learn their names, and then communicate them to you, were it not for some considerations which I shall directly state. Several other persons in Baltimore, and among them some ladies of high standing, one of whom had known Mrs. E__ from her youth, said in my hearing that her character did not stand fair before she knew Genl. Eaton. It was this general rumour in Baltimore which was the source of mortification; and to me of indignation, when it was made to bear against the triumphantly vindicated fame of your precious wife. I cherish her memory with delight.

My object, dear General, is not now to convince you of any thing against Mrs. E__; and, could I make you believe as I have been compelled to believe, I should not advise any present change in the War Department: I rather write for the sake of explanation, and perhaps self-vindication; for having written to you on the subject.

The reports concerning Mrs. Madison I am fully convinced were unqualified lies: I wish the same could be said of Mrs. Porter; whose brave husband I should be glad to see restored to his standing in the Navy by our gallant Jackson. It was a mean, time-serving policy which induced the last administration to sacrafice Capt. Porter. But my excellent friend, if Porter would punish the authors of the rumours against his wife, he must begin with her own father, Mr. Anderson of Chester Pa.[1] who doated on his child; with her mother, who had originated the story that Mrs. Porter was insane, and so accounted for her conduct; and with his own sister at Elkton;[2] and then he must be avenged on the unutterable anguish which they have often expressed on the subject. Some of these things I had from his friends at second hand only from these near relatives. Mr. Anderson is a man of property and gave his daughter a fine establishment in Chester: the Commodore cannot excuse her not returning to her father, if she needed any thing; he cannot convince *her own family* of the purity of her conduct, but if he believes her innocent he may possibly re-establish her at a distance from her native place. He is a doating husband; and may believe what he wishes to believe: (and from his letters to Jos. P. McCorkle,[3] a very worthy clerk in the Naval Commissioners' office, I should be ready to think that he did regard her as faithful to himself. Her conduct, however, ought not to hinder his restoration to the American Navy.) From your letter I began to think her a slandered woman myself; but on calling on a person intimate with the family I heard such evidence stated as makes me confident that if he can satisfy his and her own relatives there will be no difficulty with any body else.

When I first heard rumours in Washington against Mrs. E__ I did not credit them; and for some time I had thought of sifting them to the bottom; and if I could not find any good ground for them, of calling on Mrs. E__ with my wife, that we might make our respects to her. It was my purpose also to put her husband in the way of vindicating her character;

but in prosecuting my object, I learned that Mr. Eaton had been told by a gallant man of these rumours; that this friend of Genl. Eaton had told *him* that he made you accquainted with the fact that such rumours were in circulation; and that another of the most intimate friends of Mr. Eaton and of yourself believed in the reports to be true. In this state of things I clearly saw, that I should probably be the occasion of a duel between persons long and well acquainted, if I proceeded; and I was determined if I could not make matters better, to make them no worse.

Yet when I did write my two first confidential letters I could not refrain for my spirit burned within me. I would *now* push this matter, did I not know that some manly cheeks which have been watered with tears on this subject, would be in great danger of becoming cold in death; and that Genl. Eaton, to effect any thing, must fight half Washington, if he should not be killed himself. I am rejoiced that you intend dear General, to let Time and the Ladies work the right issue. My wife was waited upon by a friend of Mrs. Eaton's and solicited to undertake with me an investigation, and we should have made the effort but for the reasons above stated. Except in this matter of temptation, I think Genl. E. a very amiable, capable, clever fellow: and in this matter I consider *him* tempted as Joseph, without the religious principle of Joseph to make resistance.[4] My heart's desire is that he may be a true penitent, confess *to God,* become happy, and find salvation. The same blessing I implore for his wife.

If I have committed any offence by being full and frank, I am sure that your kindness will impute it to the right motive, and esteem, yours,

(Signed) E. S. Ely.

Copy, DLC (75).
    1. William Anderson (1762–1829), a former Pennsylvania congressman, was a customs inspector in Philadelphia.
    2. Mary Porter (b. c1785), of Elkton, Md.
    3. Joseph P. McCorkle (c1790–1834) was a Navy clerk from 1819 until his death.
    4. In the Book of Genesis, the patriarch Joseph resists seduction by the wife of Potiphar, suffering imprisonment rather than commit adultery.

From James Payne Clark

Nashville April 5th. 1829.

Dear Sir,

I pray your forgiveness for this, my present intrusion, upon your privacy or business—more particularly, as it is a *selfish* application, I am about to make to you—

Mr. Fletcher, informed me a few days since, that he had resigned his office of *Atto Gen.* for the U. S. in this District

If I am thought worthy and capable of discharging the duties of the office, I should like to get it—

I have not thought it necessary, to procure a long string of recommendations—for you have known me, from my youth up, and by that knowledge am I willing to be tested—

My competitors are all respectable, and capable of discharging the duties of the office—and rest assured, sir, be the result what it may—that my feelings towards you, will be, as they have been, true and faithfull—

In my letter to friend Andrew, a few weeks ago, I expressed a hope, that no *recreant* son of Tennessee would be found attempting to create any difficulties in your administration—[1]

I regret much that in this reasonable hope, I was mistaken—

P. M. Miller Esq. has declined running for Congress, and has given his *reason* for so doing, in the Jackson Paper, which I presume you will see, tho I hope, it will not be read—tho should it be, I have no dowbt, but that you will recognise it to be the "worthy offspring of a worthy sire[."] To one, who has long known, *Miller* it would appear *farcicle* to hear him making a noise about *Principles*—and yet, that is his Theme—[2]

your friends are well. accept my best wishes for your Prosperity and happiness—yours respectfully

J. P. Clark

ALS, DNA-RG 59 (M639-4). Clark (1797–1863) was a Nashville lawyer. Thomas H. Fletcher (1792–1845), appointed attorney for the western district of Tennessee by Adams in 1827, resigned April 7. AJ replaced him with James Collinsworth.

1. Clark had used this phrase in remarking on signs of political unrest in Tennessee in a March 23 letter to AJ Donelson (Donelson Papers, DLC).

2. Pleasant Moorman Miller (1773–1849), a former congressman and state legislator, had authored the 1822 Tennessee legislative caucus resolution that first nominated AJ for president. In a letter in the *Jackson Gazette* on April 4, Miller withdrew as a candidate for Congress, saying he could no longer support AJ because AJ's appointment of congressmen to the Cabinet belied his previous professions and invited electoral corruption.

From Henry Lee

Washington 5th. April 1829

dear Genl.

In recommending to your favourable consideration Mr. Rives the bearer of this letter, I am doing an act so strictly within the bounds of truth and justice, that I feel a confidence not common to the solicitors of favour.

He has served his country as a regular officer during the last war—in which capacity I became acquainted with him—and since the peace, as a republican editor and politician—in which last character he is well known to the nation. During the great struggle which terminated in the downfall of the coalition There was no combattent on our side who wielded a brighter or a sharper spear than Mr. Rives—as the Earl of Empty Barrels—Prince Hal—Uncle Toby—the Kickapoo ambassador, and other worthies of that class, well remember.[1] When the people were tired of argument, Mr. Rives enlivened them with wit, and it is my firm belief that his dialogues & dramatic pieces in the Telegraph did more good to the Republican cause than the gravest and most elaborate essay effected. I know I have seen your risible faculties highly excited by them, and have heard your approbation of their talent and felicity often expressed. I therefore hope you will agree with me that when the Danl. Doughheads—Charley Nurslings &c are permitted to walk out of office, Mr Rives who has contributed as much to their fame as he has to their expulsion, ~~will~~ shall be ~~permitted~~ invited to walk in.[2]

His talents and qualifications are above any post to which he aspires, & he will be content with one which, while it will afford him a decent support and laudable occupation, will prove to his friends that the party he so greatly served, has not been forgetful of his merit. I am dear Genl. Yr faithful svt.

H Lee

ALS, DNA-RG 59 (M639-20). Lee (1787 1837), son of Revolutionary hero "Light-Horse Harry" Lee and half-brother of Robert E. Lee, was an author and AJ's campaign publicist and prospective biographer. AJ appointed him consul general to Algiers on April 8, but the Senate rejected him unanimously in March 1830. John Cook Rives (1795–1864) wrote for the *United States' Telegraph* in the 1828 campaign. He obtained a clerkship in the fourth auditor's office, and later became Francis P. Blair's partner in the Washington *Globe* and publisher of the *Congressional Globe*.

1. Rives bestowed these epithets on AJ's opponents in his *Telegraph* pieces. The "Earl of Empty Barrels" was Adams's secretary of war James Barbour (1775–1842); "Prince Hal," after Henry V, was Henry Clay; "Uncle Toby," after a character in *Tristram Shandy,* was Tobias Watkins; and the "Kickapoo ambassador" was Thomas L. McKenney, head of the Bureau of Indian Affairs.

2. "Charley Nurseling" was Charles Josephus Nourse (1786–1851), chief clerk in the War Department and son of register of the Treasury Joseph Nourse. He was replaced in early May by Philip G. Randolph. "Daniel Doughhead" was Daniel Brent (1774–1841), chief clerk in the State Department, who remained until 1833 when AJ appointed him consul at Paris.

From Martin Van Buren

SUNDAY MORNING
April 5th, 1829.

DEAR SIR

In conversation last evening with Mr. Huygens he made a suggestion which I think deserves consideration.[1] I mentioned to him, as I had before done to Sir Charles Vaughan, that as the only object of the introduction tomorrow was to relieve them and yourself from the embarrassments resulting from the very irregular interviews which had previously taken place, it could not be necessary to have anything like formal addresses. To this both assented and Mr. Huygens added that an impression had been made in Europe of an unfavorable character in respect to your dispositions in respect to our foreign relations; that they (the Diplomatic Corps) had already seen sufficient to relieve whatever apprehensions might have existed upon that point and were strongly disposed by their reports to do all in their power to effect the same result at their respective courts; that the invitation for to morrow was very proper in itself and had been well received and that if you should choose to submit a few observations to them of a general character and advancing only the same sentiments as those contained in your inaugural address, it would, he thought, enable them to do great good at home.

I submit to you whether avoiding anything like a set speech, and without designing it for any other publication than would be given to it by the Ministers, in their reports, and by common fame, you might not say to them, with advantage, that the sentiments you expressed in your inaugural address in regard to the foreign relations of the Country you now repeat to them; that your opinion now is and always has been that the true interests of this Country would always be best consulted by preserving the relations of peace with all the world, and an intercourse founded upon principles of fair reciprocity; that you entered upon the trust committed to you without foreign prejudices or predilections and with personal feelings of the most friendly character towards every nation with whom we have intercourse, and that it should be your endeavour as it was your sincere desire to promote the interests of your own Country, without doing injustice to the rights of others, by the most frank, friendly and sincere negotiations.

I shall have the pleasure of seeing you either this evening or in the morning. Yours truly

Printed, *The Autobiography of Martin Van Buren*, pp. 261–62 (12-1273). AJ met the diplomatic corps on April 6.

1. Christiaan Diederik Emerens Johan Bangeman Huygens (1772–1857) was minister from the Netherlands to the U.S., 1825–32.

To Littleton Waller Tazewell

Washington April 6th. 1829

My dear Sir,

On the 3d inst. I received your letter of the 30th. ulto. and am filled with regret by the causes which prevent your acceptance of the mission to the court of Great Britain. The settlement of our differences and the formation of a commercial Treaty with that power on the broad principles of justice and reciprocity, are objects which I have much at heart, and I know of no one so well qualified in every respect to effect them as yourself.

I sincerely thank you for the views which you were pleased to take of our present relations with great Britain. They are sound, and will profit me. And the conclusion of your letter gives me room to hope that if here-after it may become necessary to ask your aid in establishing them upon a more just and friendly basis, I may have it.

I have to add that I have adopted your suggestion of sending out Judge Berrien, and have accordingly written to him, at New York, to be informed whether he will accept it. I am with great respect &c yr. obt svt

Andrew Jackson

LS in AJ Donelson's hand, NjMoHP (12-1288); LC, DLC (60). AJ offered the post to Berrien the same day.

From John Jack and Isaac Solomon

Wilmington (Delaware) April 6, 1829

Sir

The two undersigned individuals, citizens of this Borough, have taken the liberty of addressing you relative to the office of Marshal of this State. It has been generally expected that Mr Brobson the present incumbent will not be reappointed; he has been a warm supporter of Messrs. Adams and Clay, and indeed his son has been the principal writer of all the abusive articles that flowed from the Coalition news papers of this State during the late contest.[1] If you conclude to make a change in this office, the undersigned would respectfully recommend Samuel Harker, the Editor of the Delaware Gazette, in this Borough; he has been a warm supporter of your election, and has suffered much persecution on that account, to go into particulars, would encroach too much on your time; suffice it to say that nearly all the moneyed men, in and about this place, have resorted to every means in their power to put down his paper; they have been known to stoop so low, as to personally wait, on individuals and solicit them to discontinue his paper; the master manufacturers (particularly the Duponts) have been known to take their workmens papers out of the post office, and withhold them from them.[2] The said Samuel Harker has been much persecuted by the state Government. Mr Clayton at present Senator in Congress, and lately Secretary of State of this State, during the late contest, commenced a suit against Mr Harker for a libel, for no cause but that he expressed his sentiments, on Mr Clayton's conduct as a public man, this suit Mr Clayton commenced in his own county so as to put Mr Harker to the expence of taking a journey of about fifty miles, during Court term, though there is not much probability of it been brought to a trial[3]

If you would deem it necessary to appoint Mr Harker it would we believe give general satisfaction, it would invigorate the friends of the present administration, and teach the aristocracy a lessen, that they cannot do just as they please. The office is very little in a pecuniary point of view, we believe.

You will please excuse this intrusion, we have been the humble, but constant supporters of your election; we have suffered so many frowns and contempts from the affluent and the haughty, within the last few years, that we have but lately got into heart

We will conclude by stating that Mr Harker knows nothing of our writing this letter, we were impelled to it by a desire of seeing a poor but a worthy man rewarded[.] We are with great respect Your Obedient Servants

John Jack
Isaac Solomon

LS in Jack's hand, DNA-RG 59 (M639-10). Solomon (c1762–1842) was a grocer. James Brobson (1756–1834), a Revolutionary veteran, had been Delaware's federal marshal since 1809. His term expired in December, and AJ appointed David C. Wilson. Samuel Harker (1792–1850) edited the *Delaware Gazette* from 1820 until 1830, when he sold it to his brother.

1. William P. Brobson (b. 1784) was a lawyer. In 1833 he became editor of the *Delaware State Journal.*

2. The family firm headed by Eleuthère Irénée du Pont (1771–1834) ran the country's leading gunpowder works near Wilmington. Workers were housed and fed by the company.

3. John Middleton Clayton (1796–1856) was Delaware's secretary of state, 1826–28, and became a U.S. senator in 1829. The *Gazette* had pilloried him for his politics and for his conduct as defense counsel in an 1828 murder trial, where Clayton called his own mother and sister to testify against the credibility of a family slave who was a witness in the case. Clayton commenced suit for slander against Harker in July 1828.

From John Ross et al.

Williamsons Hotel, Washington City
6th. April 1829.

Honoured Sir,

In our communication of the 6th. of March we informed you that the present U.S. Agent for our Nation (Colo. Montgomery) in his acts did not give that general satisfaction to the nation as to inspire the confidence which should ever be maintained by the officers of the Genl. Govt., therefore, earnestly solicited the appointment of another. In justice to our people as well as to ourselves, we deem it proper to state some of the reasons which has given rise to this want of confidence. Firstly: complaints having been made to the Secretary of War against the Agent permitting a

Mr. Cowan to reside in the nation as a public house keeper, and the opening of a farm to cultivate our lands. The Sectry. of War gave instructions for the removal of Mr. Cowan, which was executed by Colo. Montgomery, but no sooner done than he, (Colo. M.) placed Mr. Hardwick (his own son-inlaw) in possession of the premises from which Mr. Cowan had been removed, who still continues to live there and to cultivate the lands of the nation.[1]

Secondly, Colo. Montgomery, independent of the priviledge which he has a right to exercise, to cultivate as much land adjacent to the Agency as may be necessary for his own temporary use, did, without the consent of the nation take possession of, and occupy, another farm on the chatahoochie river (a distance upwards of 100 miles from the Agency,) by placing hands on it under the charge of his son or some other connexion, who lived on the opposite side of the river, in Georgia, in consequence of these proceedings, no doubt, and under the natural influence of the desires of man to exercise equal priviledges with his countrymen, some of our frontier white neighbours were induced to intrude on our lands, and when removed by the Agent under the orders of the Genl. Govt. some of the citizens of Geo. under the spirit of retaliation crossed the river in the night and cut down part of the crop of corn that was growing on the farm cultivated by the Agent.[2]

Thirdly. He has neglected after having instituted suits against citizens of the U. States in behalf of Cherokee individuals under instructions from the War Deptmt, to attend to them, in consequence of which neglect they have been dismissed by the court, to the no small injury of the Cherokees, and expense of the United States. He has in other instances manifested a relaxation in discharging the duties required of him under his general instructions from the War Department, by referring plain & common cases to the Department for new instructions.[3]

Colo. Mc.Kenny has informed us that in consequence of the Agent's apparent incompetency to discharge his duty, he had repeatedly remarked to the Head of the Department, that our business might as well be managed altogether in the office of Indian Affairs at Washington City as to continue Colo. Montgomery as agent in the Nation.[4]

In thus communicating some of the grounds which has destroyed the confidence of our people in Colo. Montgomery as a public officer, we hope that you will not harbour an opinion, from the frankness with which we have stated them, that we have been in any degree influenced by personal or private unfriendly feelings towards our agent. We have none to cherish—and however painful it may be to communicate these facts, we are conscious of having discharged an imperious duty due to our nation in presenting them before you. We hope and trust that you will upon consideration view our application for a new Agent as reasonable, and that the wishes of our people will be granted.

With considerations of the highest respect and Esteem, we have the honor to be, Sir, Yr. Obt. hble Servants.

Jno Ross
R Taylor
Edward Gunter
Willm. S. Coodey

[Endorsed by AJ:] refered to the sec. of War for enquiry & report thereon. A. J.

LS, DNA-RG 75 (M234-73); Draft, OkTG (12-1283). *John Ross Papers*, 1:159–60.
    1. A May 1824 War Department order forbade renting out any part of the Cherokee agency's square-mile allotment of land for farming or commercial purposes (DNA-RG 75, M21-1). In 1825 Cherokee agent Hugh L. Montgomery evicted James Cowan, who had a farm and public house on agency land, paying him for his improvements, and turned over management of the property to John Wesley Hardwick (1797–1852), who was married to Montgomery's daughter Jane.
    2. Ross's draft of this paragraph concluded with the struck-out sentence: "Owing to this, or for other reasons, it is said that the Agent has since been compelled to discontinue the cultivation of the farm on Chatahoocha." Montgomery had rented a Cherokee farm and worked it with two slaves. In 1826 a posse led by Montgomery expelled eleven white families from Cherokee lands on the Georgia frontier, cutting down crops and burning houses and fences. Whites retaliated by destroying Cherokee crops and stealing livestock.
    3. On April 16, Thomas L. McKenney, head of the Bureau of Indian Affairs in the War Department, instructed Montgomery "that as agent for the Cherokees, it is within the sphere of your duties always to listen to, and take, or advise measures to secure justice to them" (M21-5). On June 24, Ross forwarded to AJ records of suits brought on behalf of Cherokees who had been forcibly dispossessed of reservations of land granted them under an 1817 treaty. The suits were dismissed in 1828 when Montgomery failed to appear.
    4. In repeated letters over several years, McKenney had sharply chided Montgomery for referring to Washington matters that he should have handled himself (M21).

To Martin Van Buren

[April 7]

you will find the following the substance if not the precise language of my address to the foreign ministers on yesterday

Gentlemen
    I am happy that an occasion has presented itself which enables me to reiterate to you Gentlemen respectively, those sentiments expressed in that part of my inaugural address concerning our foreign relations and to add that I am sure the true interest of my country will be best promoted by preserving the relations of peace with all nations, when this can be done without impairing the honor of my own, and by an intercourse founded on principles of fair reciprocity—That I had entered upon the high trust com-

mitted to me, without prejudice to, or undue partiality for any nation, or people, and with personal feelings of the most friendly character towards all, and altho with a determined purpose to promote the best interests of my country, I had no desire to impair the rights or interests of others, and that I would endeavour to effect these objects by the most frank, friendly & sincere negotiations; and where differences did exist or hereafter might arise I would desire to settle them on the most fair & honorable terms in that spirit of frankness so congenial with my nature, and the spirit of our goverment.

Should any ~~thing~~ error exist in the above, from your & Col Hamiltons recollection, it can be corrected—please inform me by Major Donelson if it is correctly remember by me, as above written. yrs respectfully

Andrew Jackson

ALS, NN (12-1297). Texts of AJ's April 6 address nearly identical to this were recorded in the presidential letterbook kept by Donelson and later published in the press.

From Enoch Parsons

Near Claiborne 8th April 1829

My Dear friend.

Perhaps for the honor of corresponding with a President, I am partly induced to write, yet I have other views. I know of the many appointments, the President, has to make, he must in part rely upon the information of others, and that his administration, for good, or bad, rests greatly on the appointment of officers, and I presume my recommendation will pass for what it is worth.

I understand you have to appoint a Marshall, for the Northern District of Alabama. Genl James Carroll of Huntsville is the deputy Marshall in that quarter and is well qualified, and desires the place, and I hope you will appoint him. I think a better will not take it, and that a better need not be looked for.[1]

Your inaugral address accords with the feelings and disposition of your friends in this quarter, and is a document which in my opinion will last through all time.

I know divided as the nation is by different and conflicting interests, that the Tariff is to distract and divide the country for years to come. And possibly but I hope not dissolve the union. Your view of it is just, and will one day be the settled opinion, or the union must fall, and this fair and great empire totter to ruin, and liberty not have a home upon the Earth. When I so freely sanction your views, I would be understood as making with due deference one exception, that is I believe all articles ought to fall within your Genl class, and that no necessaty can justify the imposition of duties, which operate to the injury of agriculture and commerce, and to the benefit of manufactures a minor interest compared with either.[2]

The idea of paying off as speedily as possible the national debt, is as it should be. The army navy & militia all right. The state rights and constructive powers all, as I think they are placed in the constitution and I think Col Bentons Resolutions offered on the 6th of Jany, in relation to the Sinking fund, and public debt, are worthy of the high consideration of the Executive, and the Congress.[3] I would not write so freely, but I know the thoughts of an old friend, whether right or wrong, when well intended will by you be well received.

For your late misfortune, I have not language to express my sorrow.

I hope your health is good, and I hope you will find use in high offices for Tazwell, and, P. P. Barbour. I do not expect, crowded with business as you are that you can reply to my letter, but hope you can find time to read it, and to accept the good wishes of myself & wife.[4] Yours with great respect

Enoch Parsons

P.S. as to the cabinet, it is able, and I am delighted to see Messrs Barry & Pope noticed, I would have proposed Mr Tazwell for Premier, & P. P. Barbour for the war Department. I am glad to see north Carolina, have an officer in the counsels of the nation.[5]

And I know that scarcely any man in this great nation would fall upon the same six persons for high office,

Enoch Parsons

ALS, DNA-RG 59 (M639-4). Parsons (1781–1841), a former Tennessee legislator, represented Monroe County in the Alabama legislature and was a Jackson elector in 1828.

1. James G. Carroll (c1800–1854) was adjutant general of the Alabama militia. On April 20 AJ appointed Benjamin T. Moore marshal.

2. AJ's inaugural suggested that in framing a tariff "the great interests of agriculture, commerce, and manufactures should be equally favored," but that an "exception to this rule should consist in the peculiar encouragement of any products of either of them that may be found essential to our national independence."

3. Resolutions introduced by Senator Thomas Hart Benton (1782–1858) of Missouri on December 23, 1828, called for the entire Treasury surplus to be applied to debt payment, demanded that the Bank of the United States compensate the government for its use of public funds, asserted that the public debt could be paid off in four years, and urged a reduction in tariff duties once the debt was paid. The Senate discussed the resolutions on January 6 and later referred them to the Finance Committee, which reported unfavorably on February 20.

4. Philip Pendleton Barbour (1783–1841) was a Virginia congressman. AJ appointed him a district judge in 1830 and Supreme Court justice in 1835. Parsons had married Kitty Kain in 1813.

5. Secretary of the Navy John Branch was the first Cabinet officer from North Carolina.

To Martin Van Buren

(Confidential)

Sir

I have thought, since Mr Tazwell declined the mission to England, that it would be proper to offer the office of Treasurer to Virginia—My best reflection has fell upon Col John Campbell of the council, va, as being a fit person to fill it—his standing is good, & his connection large & respectable. This is but "a small loaf," as Genl Root would say, but all we have at present to give.[1]

I submit to your Judgtment, whether it would not be pleasing to Mr Richie to consult him, confidentially, on this subject, & if the selection of Col Campbell is approved by him, to ask him to say to Col Campbell from me, if he will accept it, to come on forthwith to this city when his commission will be made out for him, as it is important that no *hint* of the *intent* to *remove* the present incumbent should be made, until his successor should be ready, to take charge of the office

Mr Richie might be asked whether any other character would be prefered to Col. C. Mr Pollard has been highly recommended, but as it has been intimated he has been unfortunate in trade, he may be encumbered with debt—This, the Treasurer must be free from, & in every way confidential.[2]

Should this view be approved by your Judgt. will you write Mr Ritchie confidentially on this subject this evening, requesting an early reply.[3] yrs respectfully

A. Jackson

ALS, DLC-Van Buren Papers (12-1309). John Campbell (c1788–1866) of Abingdon was a member of the Virginia Council of State. AJ appointed him Treasurer on May 26, removing William Clark (1774–1851), appointed by Adams in 1828.

1. Erastus Root (1773–1846) was a former New York congressman and militia general.

2. Richard Pollard (1790–1851), whom AJ later appointed chargé d'affaires to Chile, was a Lynchburg merchant.

3. Van Buren wrote Ritchie, who informed Campbell. Campbell balked at first because he had supported Nash Legrand for the post, but then accepted. While reporting this to Van Buren, Ritchie continued to complain of AJ's removals (Apr 9–21, Van Buren Papers, DLC).

From John Macpherson Berrien

New York 9th. April 1829—

Dear Sir,

Your letter of the 6th inst. reached me this morning. If any thing had been wanting to convince me, how much I am, and am destined to remain, your debtor, for a confidence as gratuitous, as it is gratifying, that evidence is now afforded me. I beg you to be assured my dear Sir, that as no one of your political friends attaches a higher value to your good opinion, so I would yield to no one in the devotion of my very humble powers, to the success of your administration—to the advancement of those two objects which I consider identified your personal fame, and the public welfare. With the view therefore, which you are pleased to take of my capacity to render service in the station to which you have invited me, it is matter of unfeigned regret to me, notwithstanding my distrust of my competency to discharge the duties of this highly important mission, that the situation of my private affairs forbids its acceptance—

Torn as your own heart has been by calamity, I need not enter upon the detail of my private sorrows, to convince you, that my duty to the little children of whom I am now the sole surviving protector, would not justify the separation, which the duties of this mission would inevitably demand. The state of my professional engagements, and the situation of my planting interests, would also make it extremely injurious to me, to leave the United States during the present year—Mr Tazewell intimated his wishes to me on this subject, on the contingency of his being unable to accept, in the last conversation we had before he left Washington, and I endeavored to explain to him fully and more in detail, than the limits of a letter admit, why I could not undertake this service—I regret extremely that he has declined it—

I propose to proceed to *Savannah* in a vessel which sails on the eleventh inst. Any commands, which you may have for me there, shall be promptly attended to—Meanwhile allow me to repeat the assurance of the respect and gratitude with which I am Dr sir yr mo obt st

Jn Macpherson Berrien

ALS, DLC (36). On April 15 Van Buren offered the British mission to Senator Louis McLane (1786–1857) of Delaware, who accepted.

To *Ezra Stiles Ely*

Washington City April 10th. 1829.

My dr Sir

I have just received your friendly and frank letter of the 4th. Instant; and, finding that you have been badly advised as to some matters on the subject under consideration, I am induced, once more to write you. And first I must remark that I have always thought *repentance* presupposes the existance of *crime*—and should have been gratified, had you pointed to the proof of Mr. Eaton's criminality before you recommended repentance.

In your letter you say, you had been assured by a gallant man that the rumours of which you speak had been communicated to Mr. Eaton and myself—this is not true unless in *confidence,* or the information having been given by a lady as stated to you in my last letter. If I am right in my conjectures, as to the *gallant man* alluded to, he never did see any thing criminal of Mrs. Eaton, as he has always positively assured me: and the rebuff this *gallant gentleman* met with, if he had related it, would have convinced you that Mrs. Timberlake was not of such easy virtue. From that time to the present period, they have been unfriendly. I think I well know the gentleman alluded to; and if I am not mistaken, altho' I entertain a high opinion of him, yet I do know there is no man whose prejudices run higher.

I will relate a circumstance which has lately occured, and then you can judge whether attempts have not been made to destroy Mrs. Eaton's character upon mere rumour, *unfounded* and under *secrecy.* Soon after Genl. Call returned from Philadelphia he communicated to me that he had received, *confidentially* from a *high minded honourable man,* "information of a correspondence, in writing, between Mr. Eaton and Mr. Timberlake, which fixed on Mr. and Mrs. Eaton positive criminality—and that *he* had seen it." I replied, as I always had done to the Genl., that this was a positive and unfounded slander, and that he ought to give up the name of such a *villian;* for, said I—pointing to the "tobacco pouch,"—*that* with the note which accompanied it, is my evidence that Mr. Timberlake had the utmost confidence in Mr. Eaton to the day of his death.[1] I insisted that it was due to Mr. Eaton to give him the name of this man, as he was determined to have justice done himself and lady. But, as has always been the case, the name of this man could not be had—*it was confidential.* It is thus, my dear Sir, this and all other slanders are circulated and promoted.

I have since obtained a power of Attorney, a copy of which I enclose you—besides this, there are letters, of a more recent date, expressive of the highest confidence and of the most friendly feeling: Yet it has been stated and *confidently circulated* that the conduct of Mr. Eaton was the cause of

Mr. Timberlakes cutting his throat! Can any man disposed to do justice and support truth, believe such tales, after reading the enclosed power of attorney and the letters refered to?[2] They afford to my mind the most satisfactory evidence of the entire confidence reposed in Mr. Eaton by Mr. Timberlake up to the period of his death. Instead of communicating these slanderous tales to Mr. Eaton, they are concealed under the *pledges of confidence* by those who *profess* friendship for him. I do not wish to be understood as saying that these reports have never reached his ear; but I *do say*, that no one, so far as I am advised, has ever said to him, that *such a gentleman of high standing* has taken upon himself the responsibility of charging either Mr. or Mrs. Eaton with any act of *criminality* or even *impropriety*. I am sure our friend Genl. Call has not; but to *me* he has *said* such rumours were in circulation, and when investigated were traced to the female alluded to in my last letter. In all Genl. Call's conversations with me, and they have been frequent and *confidential*, he never did intimate any knowledge of Mrs. Eaton's conduct which was calculated, in my opinion, to cast even a shade of suspicion upon her virtue. The very act, which gave rise to *his* suspicions, was one which, in my judgement, should have given him a more exalted opinion of her chastity.

Mr. Eaton has very recently understood that the wives of two gentlemen in this City, have been speaking disrespectfully of himself and Mrs. Eaton and he has, as it has been intimated to me, with promptness attended to the matter, and I doubt not that their lips will be hermetically sealed for the future.[3] I have often reflected upon myself with some severity for ever having received, confidentially, any communication prejudicial to the character and standing of Mr. Eaton. I have known him for twenty years, without a speck upon his moral character, and my friend Genl. Call has always united with me in expressions of his great moral worth. I would then ask you, if such confidence existed between Mr Eaton and Mr. Timberlake to the day of the death of the latter, as is conclusively shewn by the enclosed power of Attorney, and the other evidences refered to, would not Mr. Eaton have been the basest man on earth to have violated his confidence and severed the ties that exist between Masons? His general character forbids the idea, and his having taken her as his wife, is conclusive to my mind that he knew her to be virtuous. If he had been base enough to violate the confidence reposed in him by her husband, and to burst the bonds of Masonry, he would have left her in disgrace and misery, instead of taking an object so *vile* and so *loathsome* to his bosom. Permit me now to say to you, in the language of sincerity, that I do not believe there is a being, worthy of belief, that can or will dare to state *a single fact* going to shew criminality or a want of virtue in her. Why then will not these secret slanderers, if they believe what they propagate, and have the proof, why not come out boldly, and like men armed with truth, be responsible for what they are daily in the habit of *secretly* and *confidentially* circulating? Truth fears not the open day, but Falshood and *vile slander* delight in darkness, and under the garb of Friendship and in the name of *confidence,* circulate their poison.

I question very much if any one ever told Mr. Eaton more, than that rumours were afloat, injurious to his character, until lately. No individuals ever were pointed out, as speaking disrespectfully of Mr. Eaton & his wife, except the two ladies mentioned above; and, from my knowledge of the man, I feel confident, that so soon as he can trace these slanders to any *responsible* source, he will make the individual answerable to him, be him whom he may. I know he has been most cruelly treated by two men, who, to his face, have been always most friendly; and yet by inuendos behind his back, have added to these slanders.

The opinion I had of Mrs. Porter when I last wrote you, I still entertain. After reading Com: Porter's letter to Mr. Skinner of Baltimore, I could not give credence to the reports which had been circulated about her, and my belief of her innocence has since been strenghtened by corroborating statements made to me here.[4] If her father is really wealthy, as is stated to be the case by you, he is unworthy of confidence; for in an application which he has made to me for office, he assures me it is made in consequence of his poverty! Again you say, "if Porter would punish the authors of the rumours against his wife, he must begin with her own father &c." Now permit me to say, that unless you have it from Mr. Anderson's own lips, you ought not to believe *he* has been instrumental in circulating these rumours about his daughter. I have received a letter from him, in his own hand writing, in which he speaks in the most indignant manner of the authors of the slanders against his child, and solemnly declares his firm conviction of her innocence. I have been thus explicit, my dear Sir, knowing that you love Truth, but believing that you have opened your ear to *tales,* which, if I judge rightly of the *high character* you allude to, should never have been repeated to you—for he has either acted treacherously to *me,* or told *you* of things which have no existance. In short he has told me himself that he never did see any act of Mrs. Eaton which was improper, though he believed her a thoughtless, volatile woman—I have written to the gentleman, informing him of the power of Attorney, letters, &c, &c, refered to above. From this evidence of confidence, on the part of Mr. Timberlake in Mr. Eaton, I ask, can you believe such Tales without some *direct* and *positive* proof of criminality, and that too from the lips of individuals whose standing in society entitle them to credit? Where is the witness who has thus come forth in substantiation of these slanderous charges? None has yet done so, nor do I believe any will; for *I believe* the reports are *entirely destitute* of foundation. It puts me in mind (if I may be permitted to refer to the circumstance by way of illustration) of a tale circulated here the other day, to wit, "that I was seized with spasm in the stomach, which would have occasioned my *instant death* but for the immediate assistance of a Doctor Henderson, who was at hand and saved me." This was asserted to be an *indubitable* fact, and from the lips of Dr. Henderson himself. Now my worthy friend, the truth is I had no spasms nor had I ever seen or heard of Dr. Henderson before to the best of my recollection. But still the tale was told and confidently believed to be true. It was repeated in the presence and hearing of my friend Mrs. Love who promptly contradicted it, but she was met with the reply, "I have it from the mouth of Dr. Henderson himself—it must be true."[5] Thus it is with most of the *tales rumours* and *surmises* which are put in circulation by the gossips of the world. Unless I am greatly mistaken, when *all* the facts and circumstances connected with this attempt to destroy Mr. Eaton; and blast the reputation of his wife, are brought to light, it will be found in point of malignity and wickedness to have few paralell cases.

Please present me most kindly to your amiable wife, and believe me to be sincerely Your friend

(Signed) Andrew Jackson

Copy, DLC (75). Parton, 3:192–95.

1. Richard Keith Call (1792–1862), a former military aide to AJ, had boarded with him and Eaton at O'Neale's while serving as Florida Territory delegate to Congress, 1823–25. Shortly before his death, Timberlake had sent Eaton a tobacco pouch to present to AJ.

2. AJ enclosed a power of attorney from Timberlake to Eaton, November 13, 1826 (DLC-75).

3. The two women were Harriet Love Sim (d. 1831), wife of AJ's Washington physician Thomas Sim (1770–1832), and her niece Jane Love Watson Graham (1799–1869), wife of George Graham (1770–1830), the Commissioner of the General Land Office. Harriet and Jane were respectively the sister and daughter of Rachel Jackson's friend Elizabeth Courts Love Watson.

4. John Stuart Skinner (1788–1851) was Baltimore postmaster and editor of the *American Farmer*.

5. Thomas Henderson (c1789–1854) became an Army surgeon in 1833. Frances Peyton Dixon Love (1785–1833) was the wife of AJ's Tennessee neighbor Charles Jones Love (c1773–1837).

To *William Savin Fulton*

Washington April 11th. 1829.

Dr. Sir

I have appointed you Secratary to the Territory of Arkansa, your commission was signed on the 8th. instant, and will be forwarded by the Sec of State—It will be proper that you should, if you accept it, proceed forthwith to Arkansa, as it may be, that Mr Pope may not have accepted the appointment as Governor, and until you arrive there will be no person to administer the Goverment.[1]

Present me to your lady & all friend, respectfully—and say to Genl Coffee that I have written twice lately, and would be happy to hear from him[2]   I am very respectfully yr mo obdt. servt.

Andrew Jackson

ALS, KyLoF (12-1317).
1. Newspapers in early April reported incorrectly that John Pope had declined the governorship of Arkansas Territory. On May 11 Pope wrote AJ that he was leaving for Arkansas.
2. Fulton married Matilda Frances Nowland (1803–79) in 1823.

To Martin Van Buren

April 11th. 1829—

I was waited upon yesterday by the Gentleman who had presented the charge against the Marshal of this District, & requested to add to the number of witnesses The name of John K. Smith, & Sabret. E. Scott of George Town—you will please call for their statement.[1]

I enclose a recommendation forwarded to me, in favor of Mr Langdon as publisher of the laws Xenia ohio.[2]

I sent you the appointment of Major Lee, vice, Mr Shaler resigned, on yesterday—please inform me whether it reached you[.][3] yrs respectfully

Andrew Jackson

ALS, DNA-RG 59 (M179-67).
1. On April 2, AJ had directed Van Buren to investigate charges of taking illegal fees and other misconduct against District of Columbia marshal Tench Ringgold.
2. William Burke, Robert Punshon, and Moses Dawson of Cincinnati wrote AJ on March 28 to recommend Richard C. Langdon, editor of the *Farmers' Record and Xenia Gazette,* for public printer. AJ endorsed their letter "refered to the Secretary of State with this remark the gentlemen recommendg Mr Langdon are worthy of all confidence."
3. William Shaler (1773–1833) had been consul general at Algiers since 1815. Returning home in 1828, he asked for and received appointment by AJ as consul at Havana.

Introduction for Allan Ditchfield Campbell

The bearer, the Revd. A D. Campbell of Pittsburgh Pa., being about to visit Scotland and England, I take pleasure in recommending him to the attention of the pious and good with whom he may be, by chance or otherwise, associated, as a Presbyterian Minister eminently beloved at home for his private virtues, and respected for his talents and efficiency as a preacher.

He is an agent of the Western Theological Seminary in the United States, and undertakes this journey with a hope that the truly religious of every sect will befriend an institution devoted alone to the Gospel and a more general diffusion of its blessings.

Given under my hand this 13th. day of April 1829. at Washington City

Andrew Jackson

DS in AJ Donelson's hand, Steven G. Barnett (12-1330). Campbell (1791–1861) had been pastor of the First Presbyterian Church in Nashville, 1820–27, before removing to Pittsburgh. He sailed for Britain May 1 and returned in November. AJ had served in 1825 on the committee to find a site for the Western Theological Seminary, which located in Allegheny, Pa.

From Churchill Caldom Cambreleng

My dear Sir,

I have abstained from writing you on the subject of our collectorship under an apprehension that I might interfere with arrangements which could not be revoked. Indeed the declarations of Mr. Swartwout and his friends were so positive that I deemed any interference indelicate if not improper. Believing however that no appointment has yet been made and that it is the desire of the President of the United States to possess all the information on ~~any~~ every question involving the public interest ~~which he may be called upon to decide,~~ I cannot, as one of the Representatives of this City and County, refrain from frankly expressing my opinions, knowing that no one will more kindly or justly appreciate my motives.

Towards Mr. Swartwout I entertain none but the most friendly feelings and whenever he may ~~seek~~ solicit an office which it would become him to seek and be proper for the President to grant, he shall receive my most cordial support. ~~But until recently it never occurred to me I could not persuade myself to believe that he would be a candidate for an office for which I had not supposed that Mr S would aspire to an~~ The office in question in not ~~such~~ one, which Mr. S. ~~ought to~~ would have aspired to, had he consulted his own qualifications, his residence, the interest of his friend and patron or the public good. It is the duty of the collector of Newyork to receive annually for the government about fifteen millions of revenue—he is invested with an absolute discretion to receive or to reject such bonds as may be offered. It is due to you Sir, to truth and justice to say that I do not know a man less fitted ~~in habits~~ to be entrusted with such a vast discretion and authority—~~and pardon me when I say I should look with apprehension~~ Should he be appointed to that highly responsible office I should look with apprehension at the result. There is no man more sensible than Mr. S. himself must be ~~that~~ from the unfortunate management of his own concerns and the speculative eccentricity of his career that he is not qualified to discharge the duties of the office with justice to himself and to his Country.

Besides it cannot be presumed that a stranger to our commercial concerns and a citizen engaged in large and unfortunate speculations in another state for more than ten years past can be a proper judge of the responsibility of principals and sureties to bonds to the amount of more than two thirds of the whole revenue of the Country.

The appointment of Mr. S.— to some other office involving less responsibility—and such a one I sincerely hope he may receive—could not but be acceptable to our friends—but ~~in giving him~~ should he receive the appointment which he now solicits the public mind would be instantly carried back—to the history of John ~~& Robert~~ Swartwout late Marshall and defaulter of this District—and to the more recent case of Robt. Swartwout—Navy Agent—the influence of such recollections and the conclusions resulting are irresistible.[1] The appointment wold not only injure us here but throughout the State, with the politics of which these names were intimately associated.

The effect of this appointment would be bad generally in our State but particularly so in our city. It would be thought extraordinary that amidst a population of 200,000 people no one could be found competent to fill the highest office in this State within the patronage of ~~a President~~ government and that it should be necessary to select one who had been more than ten years a citizen of another State.[2] Our politicians would be apt to consider it a poor compliment to a district which triumphed so victoriously over our adversary. The three Representatives from this district in Congress dare not sustain his application. Indeed my impressions are that the appointment of Mr. Swartwout under all the circumstances of the case would revolutionize this city and county, turn us all out of office and transfer the power to the partizans of Mr. Clay. One thing is certain his appointment to the office would be a signal ~~of~~ for general rejoicing among our adversaries.

You will pardon me, my dear Sir, for taking the liberty of addressing you on this occasion. I know how much you must be harrassed with ~~appointments~~ candidates for office and I sincerely regret that ~~I have felt it my public duty~~ my duty towards my constituents has compelled me to tresspass for a moment on your valuable time. I have been also induced to do so from a knowledge that many letters in favor of Mr. Swartwout have been recently forwarded to Washington. It is quite unnecessary for me to state by what means and through what earnest personal solicitations these letters have been obtained. I ~~fear~~ am only ~~that~~ anxious that you may ~~you might~~ not receive them as an evidence of public sentiment here. They are generally written by the relations or personal friends of Mr. S.— and of various other persons to whom he has promised offices under him in our custom House. It is principally my knowledge of these movements which has induced me to address you on this occasion. Were it not an ungracious office for private citizens to oppose any mans application you would readily receive hundreds against his appointment. Allow ~~in~~ me in conclusion to express a hope that Mr. Swartwou will receive from you such an appointment as he may justly expect from your confidence and patronage—but not such a one as would do an injury to his best friend and to the common and as I sincerely believe the righteous cause in which we are engaged.

One word with regard to Mr. Post who I understand has been at Washington soliciting an appointment. He was the Cashier of the Franklin Bank which about a year ago was discovered to be bankrupt. the whole of the stock gone—and not even sufficient funds left to pay the deposits and notes issued. In the mean time however the Bank had continued to make regular dividends. That this case may be thoroughly understood before any appointment is made, I have transmitted to the Secretary of the Treasury an important document relating to the affairs of that Bank which were placed under the ~~control~~ management of Mr Post and are now in the hands of the Chancellor of the State.[3]

I am aware Sir, that pains may be taken to induce you to believe that some of us may be unfriendly to applications made by the friends of the late Mr. Clinton. I trust I am incapable of indulging any such illiberality and I shall most cheerfully aid them if I know them to have been faithful to our cause and whenever I believe them to be worthy of your confidence and patronage. All who are so know me too well not to apply to me. But sir ~~none of them have any excuse for~~ even if they were so, they have no excuse for not applying to my colleague in the next Congress Campbell P. White Esq who was a devoted friend of Governor Clinton.[4]

[Endorsed by Cambreleng:] Rough draft of a letter to Genl. Jackson 15 April 1829

AL draft, DLC-Van Buren Papers (12-1354). Cambreleng (1786–1862) had represented New York City in Congress since 1821 and was a close confidant of Van Buren. Van Buren prompted this and other remonstrances against Swartwout in an undated letter to Cambreleng and New York City mayor Walter Bowne (Van Buren Papers, DLC).

1. John Swartwout (1770–1823) and Robert Swartwout (1778–1848) were Samuel Swartwout's brothers. John was appointed marshal for the district of New York by Jefferson in 1801, but removed in 1806 for undermining the government's prosecution of Samuel C. Ogden and William S. Smith for filibustering. Robert was appointed navy agent at New York City in 1818. He resigned in 1823 and was found in arrears of $67,358.06.

2. Swartwout's business activities since the War of 1812, including ferrying, banking, and land development, had been centered in New Jersey.

3. Henry Post, Jr. (1774–1847), a confidant of De Witt Clinton, had sought a consulship in Liverpool or Paris or a position in the New York custom house. He had written on April 5 to complain of Van Buren's proscription of AJ's Clintonian friends. Post was cashier and then

· April 1829 ·

president of the Franklin Bank, which closed in May 1828. New York's Court of Chancery transferred control to Chancellor James Kent.

4. Campbell Patrick White (1787–1859) served in Congress, 1829–35.

From Charles Jones Love

Mansfield 15th April 1829.

Dear Sir

Mr. Steel will finish planting corn today except the new ground and commence the cotton to morrow, young Hutchins is very much in the way at the Hermitage, he rode one of the brood mares away the other day and got her eye put out; I think she is called Deanna, a letter from you to him might be of service; Mr. Steel is anxious he should leave the place unless it is your wish for him to stay there

Our friend Houston has seperated from his Wife; and will resign to morrow and leave the state Immediately for the Arkansas Territory to reside among the Indians. There is a hundred reports about the cause of seperation; he gave her Father a certificate that she was virtuous[1]   I lament his unfortunate situation most sincerely his hopes for happiness in this world are blasted forever his effigy was burned in Gallatin on Saterdy night last; be so good as make my best respects to your family and my friend Majr. Lewis I am dr Sr. your friend

Ch J Love

ALS, DLC (36). Mansfield was Love's plantation near the Hermitage.

1. Samuel Houston (1793–1863), former congressman and present governor of Tennessee, had married Eliza Allen (1809–62), daughter of Sumner County planter John Allen (1776–1833), on January 22. He resigned as governor on April 16, citing "sudden calamities" that compelled his departure. The certificate was likely Houston's April 9 letter to John Allen, which described coldness in the marriage but affirmed that Eliza was "a *virtuous & chaste* wife" (Houston Papers, DLC).

Decision concerning Daniel Turner

Washington
April 15th. 1829.

The Presidents decision upon the Case of the Culling out the Schooner Federal from St. Barts by Captn Turner of the U.S. Ship Erie.[1]

This act of invasion of the Territorial rights and Jurisdiction of the King of Sweden must be disavowed by the Government of the U.S. and assurances must be given to the Government of his Swedish Majesty through his Chargé d affaires at Washington that Captain Turner will be arrested & tried.[2]

2d.   That as the B A. Privateer the Federal is under adjudication her restoration must await the decision of the Court—[3]

3   Our Consul at St. Barts must be directed to Call upon the Government of the Island of St Barts to hold the Property taken out of the Nymph for a reasonable time in order to afford the owners of that property an opportunity to lay claim to it and to have their claims judicially investigated   By a subsequent note Bar[on de] Stackleburgh must be requested to direct the authorities of St Barts [to] hold the property in the manner [and] for the purposes above stated[4]

                                        Andrew Jackson

DS, DNA-RG 59 (M179-67); LC, DLC (60). Missing text in DS supplied from LC.
    1. On December 5, 1828, Commander Daniel Turner (1794–1850), commanding the sloop *Erie* in the West Indies, seized the privateer *Federal* in the port of Gustavia, St. Bartholomew. Sailing under the flag of Buenos Aires (now Argentina), the *Federal* had raided the American vessel *Nymph* carrying goods from Brazil, with which Buenos Aires was recently at war. Swedish authorities in St. Bartholomew had allowed the *Federal* into port to repair damages and had refused Turner's demand to turn over the ship and cargo. On April 16 Van Buren wrote Berndt Robert Gustaf (1784–1845), Baron de Stackelberg, the Swedish chargé d'affaires, to express AJ's "deep regret" over the incident and explain that Turner had "from a mistaken zeal in the service of his Country, overstepped the bounds of his duty." Van Buren promised an investigation (DNA-RG 59, M38-4). A naval court of inquiry was convened and reported on April 9, 1830. Approving the report, AJ on April 17 determined that Turner had misinterpreted his orders but that no action was required beyond expressing "strong disapprobation" of his conduct (DNA-RG 125, M273-23).
    2. In the LC, AJ replaced "arrested & tried" with "subjected to Judicial investigation."
    3. Turner had sent the *Federal* to Pensacola, where it was condemned for piracy and sold at public auction.
    4. Van Buren wrote Stackelberg on April 22 that U.S. consul Robert Monroe Harrison had been instructed to ask the authorities at St. Bartholomew to hold the cargo stolen from the *Nymph* and unloaded from the *Federal* before its seizure, to give the rightful owners an opportunity to reclaim it (DNA-RG 59, M38-4).

To Martin Van Buren

[In 1827 the Cherokee Nation adopted a formal constitution of government. Modeled on the U.S. Constitution, it asserted sovereign authority over the domain previously guaranteed to the Nation by treaty with the United States. In December 1828 Georgia passed a law to annex the Cherokee lands to five existing counties and to extend state jurisdiction over them as of June 1830. The implicit conflict between tribal and state sovereignties was thus directly joined.

In February 1829, a Cherokee delegation in Washington headed by Principal Chief John Ross protested Georgia's "wanton usurpation of *power" to outgoing Secretary of War Peter B. Porter. John Eaton sought Jackson's advice on a reply on April 13. This undated note followed.]*

The President send the enclosed for the perusal of Mr Van Buren and asks him to say whether the constitutional *law* embraced therein is consistant with his views. The P. will thank him to return it with his remarks on the paper this evening, as the chiefs of the Cherokees are awaiting this reply[.] yrs.

A.J.

ANS, DNA-RG 59 (37-0287). Eaton, speaking for AJ, replied to the Cherokee chiefs on April 18 (DNA-RG 75, M21-5; *Niles*, Jun 13). He denied that the Cherokees had ever exercised sovereignty over their domain in Georgia. Rather, sovereign authority had passed directly from Great Britain to the state during the Revolution. The Cherokees, said Eaton, had no intrinsic right to their lands and occupied them merely by state sufferance. Their insupportable claim to self-government had itself compelled Georgia to assert its jurisdiction. The United States had no power to arrest the legitimate authority of a state within its own borders. Therefore the only remedy was for the Indians to remove west across the Mississippi and beyond the states, where the federal government would afford them full protection. Eaton's "talk," which AJ later spoke of as his own, was widely published in tandem with AJ's address to the Creeks of March 23.

From George Hay

Oak Hill, Loudon April 16. 1829

Dear Sir

During my late visit to Washington, where I arrived on the 4th. and which I left on the 11th. inst: I called, three times, at your residence for the purpose of seeing you. My failure to see you, was occasioned, obviously, by the crowd, constantly in attendance.

I mention this fact as furnishing an apology for seeking to obtain by letter, that information, which might have been orally communicated in a very few minutes.

You will recollect, I am confident, a conversation which passed between yourself and me, during an interview, on the morning of the first Tuesday, after your occupation of the Presidential residence. I think that my recollection of it is perfect. You took the trouble to state to me the principle or rule by which you meant to be governed in dismissions from Office. Your exposition on this subject, was produced by my reference to the rumors at that time current, which gave me some inquietude, as to my son Charles Hay, then and for several years before Chief Clerk of the Navy Department. I was about to state to you, and did in part state to you, his claims and his situation: but you interrupted me, earnestly, tho' kindly, for the purpose of denouncing rumor, which you did denounce in terms, as correct as they were emphatic. You then proceeded to state, "that freedom of opinion and of speech, was a natural right: guarantied by the constitution: for which you had fought and were willing to fight again: The exercise of that right could furnish no ground of complaint against any officer of the government: but where such officer had employed his official power and station to promote party purposes he should be dismissed. This rule would be indiscriminately applied, unless indeed the ruin of a family would be the result."

Convinced that this rule thus laid down by you, could not be applied to my Son, and that even if it could, he might claim the benefit of the exception, I retired immediately: persuaded that he would be permitted to remain where he was: and left the city in compliance with the unexpected and distressing summons which called me to this place.[1]

You can conceive then what were my mortification, astonishment and distress, when I found that on the 1st. April, my Son had received from the Secretary of the Navy, a note containing a single sentence, announcing that his commission as Chief Clerk of the Navy Department was thereby revoked.

Presuming that this revocation, could not have taken place, without some communication from the secretary to you, I have taken leave now to call what formerly passed to your recollection. I hope that I shall not be charged with doing more than a friend & father ought to do, when I ask to be informed, on what ground this dismission, so injurious in its effect, so humiliating in its manner, was pronounced. If my Son has done officially wrong, let him suffer. But if he has done no act imputable to him as a fault, let him, and his parent, and his friends, some of whom are among the most distinguished men in this country, enjoy the consolation of knowing that his integrity is not impeached, let them feel that as they have heretofore given, so they may again, confidently, give their support to his character, whenever it may be required, in furtherance of any scheme or plan which he may devise for the purpose of gaining bread for himself, his wife, his infant child, and his future offspring.

I will take leave to remind you, that the mention of my Son's name to you, in the conversation to which I refer, was not the sole nor even the principal object in the interview during which it passed—I have the honor to be with high respect Yr. mo. ob. se.

(Signed) Geo. Hay

Copy, DNA-RG 45 (M124-118). George Hay (1765–1830) was a federal district judge in Virginia and son-in-law of James Monroe. Charles Hay (c1793–1833) became a Navy Department clerk in 1819 and chief clerk in 1823. He was replaced on April 6 by Richard H. Bradford, who a month later was succeeded by former North Carolina congressman James W. Clark.

1. In February, James Monroe at his Oak Hill estate had suffered a fall from a horse and subsequently caught cold, leaving him bed-ridden for three weeks.

To *the Marquis de Lafayette*

(Copy)

Washington April 17th. 1829

My Dear Sir,

I have just received your letter of the 26t. February last, and feel a melancholy pleasure in knowing that the dispensation of Providence which has thrown over my future days the mantle of sorrow, has engaged your sympathies. The reflections which they inspire are consolotary as a tribute to the memory of my dearly beloved wife, and as a proof of your friendship for me. They are also cheering as another evidence of the goodness of your heart, which, amidst the vicissitudes of life in a distant land, does not cease to look with a parents eye upon the private as well as public concerns of the people of the United States.

With my prayers for the continuation of your health and happiness allow me to offer you the grateful recollection of Mrs Donelson and every other member of my family, and subscribe myself Your Sincere friend

Signed Andrew Jackson

Remember us if you please to Mr Lavossiur and the whole family of La Grange[1]

LS copy in AJ Donelson's hand, DLC (37). AJ had become acquainted with Lafayette during the latter's American tour in 1824–25.
1. Auguste Levasseur, Lafayette's secretary, had accompanied Lafayette and published an account of his tour. La Grange was Lafayette's estate outside Paris.

From *Charles J. Jack*

Phil. April 17. 1829—

Sir,

I addressed for your use and perusal, several papers relating to my application for the situation of Marshall of the Eastern District of Pennsylvania, To the Care of A. J. Donalsen, and the Honorable John H. Eaton, requesting them to inform me of their reception by them, and of their delivery to you. *I have never received any answer, whatever, from either!* The entire want of decorum in this conduct is too evident not to merit your disaprobation. If the men who sacrificed their all to sustain you, are to be treated in this way, *disapointment,* will not be the only feeling which must fill their bosoms. I respectfully request from you intelligence, wether you have been put into possession of the papers forwarded. Very Respectfully your obt st

C. J. Jack

[Endorsed by AJ:] Mr Donelson will read & give it such a laconic answer as it merits—

ALS, TNJ (12-1378). Jack (b. 1798), a Philadelphia lawyer, sometime newspaper editor, and early AJ supporter, had visited Washington around the time of the inauguration, but was unable to secure an interview with AJ. Before leaving he entrusted to Donelson a letter to AJ asking to be appointed marshal. Jack wrote Donelson twice more in March, and he continued to urge his claims in later letters to AJ and Van Buren. AJ retained former congressman John Conard as marshal.

From Edward Livingston

Private

Philada. Apl 17. 1829

Dear General

After thanking you which I do most sincerely for the new proof you have given me of a confidence which it has always been my pride to possess and my earnest desire to merit I wish to make to you some confidential communications on the subject   It is my earnest desire to accept the mission to France for many reasons but principally and without the fear of being thought vain because I think I can render my country service and do credit to your administration, and I should without further delay accept it but for reasons which I am now about to detail. I have much private business to arrange but the greater part might be done by the time mentioned in Mr. Van Burens letter as the period at which you wish me to embark. Circumstances however may possibly occur in one of them which may render it impossible for me to go. and this can not be determined in less than a fortnight or three weeks from this time so that if I should accept, and the circumstances should occur I shall have lost my seat in the Senate, and be deprived of any chance of supporting your administration either there *or elsewhere* in any other public station—on the contrary should I decline the mission under an apprehension of the possible contingency, It may not happen, and I shall then deeply regret that I have deprived myself of the opportunity of serving you where I could do it most effectually.

I will explain myself more fully. It is generally known that my Sister who died while I was absent decreed to me the greater part of her Estate[1] I have received an intimation that one who has married her niece, intends to dispute the will on account of some alledged informality. Whether he will do so or not, I can not certainly know in a shorter time than I have mentioned—should this end in a serious lawsuit it will be impossible for me to leave the country in less than six months and I must of course decline, should it terminate as I hope, and believe it will in an abandonment of pretentions which I can demonstrate to be frivoulous & unjust I shall with pleasure accept.[2]

Since I am taking the liberty of writing to you in this friendly and confidential manner there is another subject which I will submit to your ~~friendly~~ consideration not to be put in competition with any public interest but to have its weight only if that should not stand in the way

a cause of prodigious magni

AL draft fragment, NjP (mAJs). Van Buren had offered Livingston the post of minister to France on April 6 (Van Buren Papers, DLC).

1. Livingston's sister Joanna (1759–1829), wife of New York politician Peter R. Livingston, had died on March 1.

2. An "X" is inscribed over this paragraph.

From Henry Mason Morfit

Washington 18th. April 1829

Sir

The Consulate at Havre being an Office which from public opinion I am led to believe will be vacated, I present myself as a candidate for that appointment   Whatever specific charges might be brought against the present incumbent I shall not presume to say, as the indignation which was felt at his conduct to our citizens in Dartmoor is still alive and furnishes sufficient reason without any new allegations[1]   Not descending therefore to urge any thing against the character of this gentleman I would rely more particularly upon the popular rule, that rotation in Office after a reasonable time is one of the elementary principles of our government, a principle which the people look to as an essential point in the system of reform anticipated from the present administration

Perhaps there is no greater anomaly in the scheme of a Republic whose very term implies equal rights, than that of changing the chief and material agents to give place to the pretensions of others, while those farther removed from the labors and honors of government though as closely connected with its emoluments, are suffered to remain and acquire a prescriptive and perpetual right to office in exclusion of all other citizens

In the establishment of our Constitution when its peculiarly new form required much argument to reconcile and explain its character to the people, the material feature which produced the effect was that by which the whole government with all its rewards was thrown open to the enjoyment of every class in the community; and the most beautiful illustrations in the letters of "Publius" written at the time, are those which represent Offices of trust as apples of gold upon plates of silver, to be presented to every worthy member of the Republic.[2]

The incumbent in question has been about thirty years receiving the profits of various Offices, and, if there is any limit to the enjoyment of public patronage even where it is not assailed by general clamours and reproach, it is at that period when the individual has become estranged and expatriated by length of absence, and when even an acquaintance with the laws and institutions of his own country are absorbed or obliterated in the alliances he has made abroad

The pretensions which I have to the favourable consideration of the President are simply those which accompany every respectable citizen who has taken a proper part in the recent contest, superadded to which I may say, that for many years I have been his warm advocate even long before his name was fully presented to the people as a candidate for the Presidency; and when the moment arrived in which the public voice could render justice to his past good services, I became one of the first to lend my efforts to this object.

The sphere in which I could operate it is true appeared at first circumscribed and powerless, as Washington is but an isolated place, with all the materials of government in its centre few of its benefits and *none* of the franchises common to the citizens of other parts of the Union   But with all this a few of us as a Central Committee were enabled to hold up such lights and beacons as we had to the people at a distance, at least to cheer them in their labours, endeavouring in some remote degree to realize the predictions of Patrick Henry, that from the people of this District will emanate the means to prevent an increase of power in the few, or tear down the faction which sustains them. What estimate is to be put upon the labors of these few individuals who were thus associated they will not seek to know, though they could very well foresee that if the election had terminated differently they would have been exposed to the contumely of their enemies, who with the rods of power and the places of patronage in their hands would have driven almost as exiles from their homes

With these remarks such as they may weigh I submit myself to the consideration of the President for the Office I have named

Henry M Morfit

[Endorsed by AJ:] Mr Morfit applying for the consulate at Havre—& giving reasons why the incumbent ought to be removed—and his claims upon government for its favor—

ALS, DNA-RG 59 (M639-16). Morfit (1793–1865) was a lawyer and a member of the Washington Jackson Central Committee. In 1836 AJ appointed him a special commissioner to report on conditions in Texas.
    1. Reuben G. Beasley (d. 1847) was appointed consul at Havre, France, by President Madison in 1816. During the War of 1812 Beasley had served as agent to look after American captives in England. He was widely criticized for negligence after seven Americans

were killed and dozens wounded in a riot at Dartmoor prison in 1815. AJ did not remove Beasley, who remained consul at Havre until his death.

2. "A word fitly spoken is like apples of gold in pictures of silver" (Proverbs 25:11).

To George Hay

Washington April 19th. 1829—

Dear Sir,

your note of 16th. instant has been received. In reply, I have to inform you that the Secretary of the Navy is now absent, but will be here in a few days, when, should you apply to him, he will give you the reasons for the removal of his chief clerk.[1] The were such as I approved, and are perfectly consistant with those general principles which I stated in the conversation with you on the subject of removals, but which you have only partially quoted. No personal considerations, or sentiments of unfriendlyness to the family connections of your son operated against him: on the contrary, so far as these could be consulted, I know that the formed a claim upon Mr Branch, as well as myself, which it would have been truly gratifying to have favored. I am respectfully your mo. obdt. servt.

Andrew Jackson

P S. Please present me kindly to Mr & Mrs. Monroe—[2]

ALS, DLC-James Monroe Papers (13-0072); Copy, DNA-RG 45 (M124-118).

1. Hay wrote Branch on May 13, and Branch replied on May 16 that because of the confidential relationship with his chief clerk, he wanted a man whom he knew better than he did Charles Hay (DNA-RG 45, M124-118 and M209-6).

2. Elizabeth Kortright Monroe (c1763–1830).

To Samuel Delucenna Ingham

I have recd your note with Mr. C.[1] and Mr. R.[2] letters enclosed. you will find a remark made by me at the bottom of Mr. R. letter.

I have read Mr. C. letter & have barely to remark that I was aware of his feelings, but Mr. C. is deceived, Mr. S.[3] is more *strongly recommended* than he is aware of—I thank you for the perusal, will consider well, & then decide for *myself* & country.

I send Mr Rs. & Mr. C. letter is returned, enclosed.

A. J.

ANS, TU (13-0074). This note may have been written anytime between April 20 and 24.

1. Churchill Cambreleng.

2. Probably Henry Rutgers (1745–1830), philanthropist and former state legislator. Van Buren had urged Cambreleng to get him to write against Swartwout.
    3. Samuel Swartwout.

To Martin Van Buren

April 20th. 1829—

Dr. Sir

your note of last evening was handed me as I was going to bed, with the letters to Mr Livingston & Mr Woodbury inclosed, which I examined, sealed & forwarded, by this mornings mail.[1]

I recd. last evening a private letter from Mr. Livingston, for reasons therein named, asking three weeks to determin on accepting the mission, but expressing at the same time his *great desire to do so,* if he can arrange some private business. I have wrote him the necessity of a speedy answer of acceptance, as I wish, for reasons assigned, that he should go out in the same vessel with Mr McLean.[2]

I will see you with pleasure at 11 oclock a.m. today, on the business proposed. yours respectfully

Andrew Jackson

ALS, DLC-Van Buren Papers (13-0080).
    1. The enclosed letters of April 19 were Van Buren to Woodbury (Woodbury Papers, DLC; Van Buren *Autobiography,* p. 254) requiring him to leave for Spain no later than August 1 should he accept as minister, and Van Buren to Livingston (Van Buren Papers, DLC), urging him not to delay his decision.
    2. William B. Lewis wrote for AJ to Livingston that day, promising "every indulgence" but stressing the need for a prompt decision (Livingston Papers, NjP). On May 3, Livingston wrote to Van Buren (Van Buren Papers, DLC) and AJ that his unsettled affairs precluded his accepting.

To Martin Van Buren

April 20, 1829.

Dr. Sir

I have this morning sent to Mr. Ingham the papers in relation to the New York Customs, requesting him after he examines them to hand them to you. Will you also have the goodness to look at them and give me your opinion in writing on the relative merits of the several applicants specifying at the same time the offices to which you would appoint them, and how far the principles we have adopted would justify dismissals from office in that Port? I wish now to act promptly on a subject which has a good deal worried me.

In addition to the papers sent Mr. Ingham this morning I have a few more confidential letters, for the most part in favor of Mr. Swartwout. The two Senators from New York, also, verbally recommended Mr. Swartwout.[1] I am, very respectfully Yrs &c

ANDREW JACKSON

Printed, *The Autobiography of Martin Van Buren*, p. 263 (13-0082).
    1. New York's senators were Charles Edward Dudley (1780–1841), elected to fill the seat vacated by Van Buren in December 1828, and Nathan Sanford (1777–1838).

From William Pope Duval

Tallahassee April 21st 1829

Dear Sir

I am in commond with your friends in this Territory solicitous that the benefits resulting from the salutary reform which you have commenced should also be extended to Florida pray inquire what claim, either the Marshall of West Florida or the Navy agent has to your forbearance so far as they had influence, it was used to the utmost in the abuse of your character, or they are greatly belied. The Attorey of the united states, at Key West Mr McRea to my knowledge ought to be removed no man could have been more indecently abusive of you.[1]

The Indian Agent Coln. Humphreys who ought long since to have been removed for misconduct in his office and Judge Smith of the Eastern district, a man who was dismissed with disgrace from our army, as to vile to hold any command, is thought pure enough to grace the ermine for this Territory[2]—Sir we look to you as the father of this Territory it is truly the child of your own creation—It was the success of your arms that first, induced to spain to surrender a country that she found it too dangerous to maintain. When you consented to become the Governor of Florida you were promised that your friends should be provided for it was a long time ere they were noticed and then, very partially[3] I beg of you to remember them now and aid us in giving a character to our Territory is richly deserves—Their is not one man in 50 throughout the Territory that does not revere you for your virtues & services, and yet nearly two thirds of all the appointments made by the Late adminstration, were in direct opposition to the wishes of the People. Believe me sir it is from no influence of any vindictive feelings that I call your attention to these facts—The honor interest and character of the Territory and can with truth add, its prosperity will in a great degree depend on the changes that shall be made.

In this district we have an able and invaluable judge the Secretary of the Territory is a capable, firm and valuable officer, and our Marshall Majr Adair is esteemed and valued by all who know him[4] I solicit from you for

Coln. James W Exum, the office of Marshall for West Florida. The present incumbent, is nether intitled to confidence or ever possessed the esteem of the People, his business or much of it is transacted by deputy, who is most obnoxious to the people, and whom I know to be destitute of every honorable feeling or principle[5]   I am with sincere respect & esteem Your friend

Wm. P. Duval

ALS, DNA-RG 59 (M179-67). *TPUS,* 24:197–98. Duval (1784–1854), a former Kentucky congressman, was governor of Florida Territory, 1822–34.
1. In May, AJ removed Adam Gordon as marshal of the western district of Florida and replaced Pensacola navy agent Nathaniel Amory with Charles P. Tutt. On April 20 he had appointed John G. Stower attorney for Florida's southern district, removing William Allison McRea (c1804–29). Gordon, Amory, and McRea were all Adams appointees.
2. AJ removed Gad Humphreys (1786–1859), a former Army officer, in 1830 and replaced him with subagent John Phagan. Humphreys had been charged with illicit slave dealing and other abuses. Joseph Lee Smith (1776–1846), a former Army colonel, had been a Florida federal judge since 1822. AJ replaced him when his term expired in 1832. In an 1820 court-martial arising from a dispute with General Alexander Macomb, Smith was found guilty of contempt of authority and conduct unbecoming an officer. He was sentenced to be cashiered, but received clemency and remained in service until honorably discharged in 1821.
3. AJ had felt aggrieved at the first civil appointments in Florida Territory in 1821, which ignored his recommendations (*Jackson Papers,* 5:52–53).
4. AJ retained and in 1831 reappointed middle district judge Thomas Randall (1792–1877) and marshal Alexander Adair (d. 1831). Territorial secretary William Mason McCarty (c1789–1863) resigned in June.
5. AJ appointed James W. Exum (d.1838) to replace Adam Gordon. Gordon's deputy was Sears Bryan (b. c1788).

Memorandum

From the Sec of State—to be *attended to*—
    read, & *duly considered*—the commercial agent is intemperate, & disliked by his countrymen, as reported—enquiry is directed—but the source from which the information comes, is creditable, *& believed*—& his removal determined upon—
    Genl Chandlers letter contains sound sense & good ideas, on the subject to which it relates

AN, ICHi (13-0086). A clerk's endorsement reads "Rec. 21 April, 1829." John Chandler (1762–1841) was an Army brigadier general in the War of 1812 and U.S. senator from Maine, 1820–29. AJ had appointed him customs collector at Portland in March.

From Duff Green

Confidential.

Washington, 23d April, 1829.

Dear Sir,

Please to read this yourself & oblige D Green

After the conversation which passed between us on the subject, I am much at a loss to find terms to express to you the solicitude which I feel in behalf of Mr. Meehan. I would not, under other circumstances, mention my own sacrifices or my losses—but when they are brought in aid of the proper claims of a valued friend, I trust they will be considered worthy of consideration. My *personal* acquaintance with him commenced in the spring of 1826, when I found him the Editor of the Telegraph. He then relinquished the establishment to me, and accepted a salary of $1200 per annum. I have found him to be an able auxiliary, a faithful friend, and one of those men rarely to be found—a strictly conscientious and pious Christian. His ardent attachment to you, and his devotion to the great principles upon which you have been elected, is surpassed by those of no other individual. He is the father of an amiable family, who are entirely dependant upon his earnings for support. He is a good scholar, a printer and publisher by profession, and of the most amiable and conciliatory manners. He has not, that I know of, a single enemy—yet no man has more firmness. So much for the man.

As for myself, I have now devoted five years and more of my life, almost exclusively to your election. I have expended about $15,000 in cash, and am $20,000 in debt. I have, it is true, some little property, and have my office to show for these expenditures and this labor. It is true that I am also the printer to Congress, and believe that prudence and industry will make me independent—but it requires economy, and it is as important that I should retrench my expenditures, as it is that your administration should be economical.[1] I cannot propose to reduce Mr. Meehan's salary, because it formed part of the condition of his sale to me; yet I can get an assistant to discharge his duties for $800 per annum. His appointment would, therefore, be a saving to me of $400 per annum.

Is it said that Mr. Meehan is already well provided for? Or is it said that by his contract with me he has guarded against loss? This objection is not good, because my ability to pay him his salary depended upon my success in business, and he is involved beyond that by his endorsement on my notes in Bank, because he has heretofore been my sole endorser, with the exception of one or two small notes in the Bank, and a larger note in the Bank of the U. S. which is endorsed by Gen. Van Ness, who is secured by a *lien* upon my press.[2] My failure would therefore have involved him in ruin—and when you look to his situation, you see that his services have been poorly requited.

I mention these things, that, by combining his claims with mine, you may see no individual can present such a case for the office he asks. I mean no disparagement to others—but I ask you to look around, and see if there be one individual who will accept *that* office, who has done more for the party. As to his qualifications and personal merits, he has no superior.

In relation to Gen. Van Ness, I am the last individual on earth that would come in contact with him for your favor for myself; but permit me to ask you to compare his claims with those of Mr. Meehan. Of boundless wealth, he has never put his name to paper on account of funds for party purposes, unless he was first well secured. Yet there are few who have done so much as he—few who could be prevailed on to commit themselves in money matters upon good security. Gen. Van Ness is wealthy, and *he* can aid his nephew, or he can obtain for him other and better employment.

As to the removal of Watterston, I know that he has no claims to your favor. He never was your friend—and, permit me to say, that no situation under the government affords greater facilities for an adversary to operate upon. That he belongs to, and acts with the little knot of *corrupt* aristocrats who have brought this city to the verge of bankruptcy, ought to form cause enough, without any other argument for his removal.

I know, my dear Sir, that there are things in this letter which those who are disposed to cavil might find fault with, but it is written for your own eye. I have disguised nothing from you. You never have had cause to consider me wanting in respect for you. You must respect the motives which induce me to press the appointment of Mr. Meehan, as an act of justice to him, and of favor to myself; and I cannot believe that, when you come to consider the whole ground, you will hesitate to make the appointment. I trust that you will not consider me as saying a word to the disparagement of Gen. Van Ness. I introduce his name because I consider him as having strong claims; and because I do not know how I can illustrate Mr. Meehan's claims better than to prove them to be stronger than it is possible for Mr. Van Ness to urge. Your sincere friend,

D. G.

LC, DLC-Duff Green Papers (13-0105). John Silva Meehan (1790–1863) had edited Baptist newspapers before launching the *United States' Telegraph* in February 1826, which Green purchased from him four months later. On May 28, AJ appointed Meehan librarian of Congress in place of George Watterston (1783–1854), who had served since 1815. Watterston wrote for and later edited the anti-Jackson Washington *National Journal*.

1. Green had been elected printer for the upcoming Congress by both House and Senate.
2. John Peter Van Ness.

From Thomas Loraine McKenney

Department of War,
Office Indian Affairs,
23rd. April, 1829.

Sir,

An Article in the Telegraph of the evening before last, having been shewn to me by one Gentleman, and my respected and venerable friend Doctr. Worthington having, last evening, at my house, again called my attention to the subject, and stating that it was understood as implicating me in similar acts as those attributed to the late 4th. Auditor,[1] I feel called upon to give you a simple statement of so much of that article as relates to this bureau.

The pre-emption right holders of lands in New York, held by the Seneca Indians made as is usual, under the auspices of the General Government some two years ago—a purchase of certain portions of those lands. A party at the head of which is the famous Red Jacket, remonstrated against the means resorted to in the negotiation of the Treaty. The memorials being transmitted to this office, thro' the Department proper, I read them, and looking upon them as the fruit of some dissatisfied or meddling white man, and to Red Jackets known enmity to the party which governed in making the Treaty, I put them on file as not, in my opinion, meriting the action of the Department. Some time afterwards Red Jacket came to Washington, had an interview with President Adams, and referr'd to the papers he had sent on.[2] The President never having seen them was led to send for them. Upon examining them, and hearing Red Jacket, he deemed the subject worthy of investigation; and thro the Secretary of War, ordered it. The Secretary of War made this known to me, and I was directed to prepare suitable instructions for the occasion, for his signature, which I did, and direct them to R. M. Livingston, Esqr, of New York—a Gentleman then, for the first time *heard* of by me. The compensation for his services I was also directed to make, in the instructions, equivalent to that paid to a Commissioner. I accompany this with a copy of these instructions.[3]

Mr. Livingston did not seek the trust judging from a recent letter of his to the present Secretary of War, and as far as I know, never heard a word of it, until he received Secretary Barbour's letter.[4] He engaged in it, and fulfilled it, with considerable ability—and possessed the Department of much valuable information on the subject of the great excitement among portions of the New Indians arising out of their religious feuds, and the Treaty.

He sent on his account. It was made out on the basis of so may days attendance at Council; and so many miles travel. It came without the usual certificate. It was sent back to him, with the usual form of one—He returned it, signed. No "vouchers" were required. His "mileage" was to embrace all his expenses. The present Secretary of War acted upon it, & in fulfilment of the Executive obligation, allowed it—referring its payment to the provision for the year 1828.[5] I notified Mr. Livingston accordingly—and further than this I had no agency in the affair, *which the* Telegraph would have the public believe was a thing got up by me for political ends, and paid for through me, by some hocus-pocus process, adverse to my honor, and the interests of the Government. At least such is the interpretation put upon the article by my friends. You, Sir, can now judge of the justice of such implications.

I avail myself of this occasion, respectfully to state, that whilst I deeply regret the existence of a spirit in some individuals to hunt me down, that I am prepared to meet any charge, and of any sort, that they may in the execution of their settled purpose to unoffice me, prefer—a purpose that has broken out in assertions, backed by bets that it *shall* be done—and if I am at any one point, either as an officer, or a man of honor touching either my public, or private acts, deficient, I will abide, with cheerfulness, the decision that shall pronounce me so.

I am well aware that many assertions have been made in regard to this office calculated to render it obnoxious; and much excitement even has been felt in the accounting branch of it—and which has borne hard upon it—but I am prepared to show, at any moment, that all this has arisen out of a want of a proper conception of *the relations it bears to other branches of the Government;* and that in no *one* instance has the proper action of this office been withheld, delayed, or misapplied, to objects referr'd to it—but that in every instance the evils complained of by many (*as all are concerned who have sought information*) arise after the subjects are acted upon here; and in their passage through other Departments of the Government; and this is owing to the deficiency in the organization of this office, and its necessary dependence, in its present state upon others. Still I consider the organization to be as perfect as Executive power can make it; and what remains to perfect it, refers itself to the Congress. Mr. Calhoun, to whom the War Department owes its organization, formed and fashioned this office; and in my Commission defines my duties. I act, only, within the circle drawn by his hand.[6] My services were saught by Mr. Calhoun. The place was not solicited by me, nor did I consent to accept the offer *until* a third interview, when he gave me assurance, (as far as he could,) that it should be organized, and the Salary made equal to its duties, in the sum, as agreed upon, received by Auditors. In a letter from him on this subject he wrote to me thus:—

"No one better knows than myself how inadequate your Salary is, (1600$) as a compensation for the varied services, and important public duties of your office. *There is no branch of business in the War Department which requires more minute and laborious attention, or to which greater responsibility is attached.* I would rejoice to see your compensation placed on a more respectable footing."[7]

I refer to this, to show that I have been four years *trying* to live on about half pay—lived every year by the hope that the promised organization and compensation would take place, and not without grounds of hope, since every Congress, but one has brought forth a bill prepared by myself, and approved by Mr. Calhoun, with the promised compensation in it. The subject is now, in a more extended form, before Congress—in certain compilations &c, with the same bill, in part, and as far as it goes, by Messrs. Cass and Clark, and will doubtless be acted on at the next Session.[8]

I meant when I began this letter to confine it to the implications in the Telegraph, which I feared might make a wrong impression on you. I have added, however, what follows, and trust to your goodness to excuse the details; & with assurance of my great respect &c, I have the honor, to be, your obedt. Servt.

Thos. L. M'Kenney.

LC, DNA-RG 75 (M21-5). McKenney (1785–1859) was Superintendent of Indian Trade from 1816 until the office was abolished in 1822, and then head of the Bureau of Indian Affairs from its creation in 1824 until 1830, when AJ removed him. The item in the April 21 *US Telegraph* charged that the Adams administration had employed an "electioneering agent in the State of New York," sent on the pretext that he was "to visit a tribe of Indians at Buffalo."

1. Tobias Watkins. Charles Worthington (1759–1836) was a Georgetown physician.
2. The Ogden Land Company had secured the pre-emption rights to purchase all Seneca lands in New York in 1810. The 1802 Indian Intercourse Act required that purchase of Indian lands "be made by treaty or convention" and under the supervision of a representative of the general government. In August 1826, at a treaty at Buffalo Creek, N.Y., in the presence of U.S. commissioner Oliver Forward, the Ogden Land Company purchased about 80,000 acres of Seneca land. Seneca Chief Red Jacket (c1758–1830) had been instrumental in defeating previous attempts at purchase by the Company in 1811 and 1819. Leader of the so-called "Pagan party," he also opposed missionary efforts among the Senecas. Red Jacket helped author several remonstrances against the Buffalo Creek sale, alleging that the chiefs had been bribed and intimidated into signing. Red Jacket met with President Adams on March 7 and 24, 1828.
3. Richard Montgomery Livingston (1787–1838) was a lawyer from Saratoga, N.Y. Secretary of War James Barbour's instructions of May 9, 1828, ordered Livingston to visit the Senecas "and ascertain and report all the facts in the case." His pay was to be $8 for every twenty miles traveled and $8 for every day spent among the Senecas (DNA-RG 75, M21-4). Livingston met with the Senecas for about ten days in June and July 1828.
4. Livingston to Eaton, March 26, 1829 (DNA-RG 75, M234-808).
5. Livingston was paid $1,477.60 on April 6, 1829.
6. Secretary of War John C. Calhoun created the Bureau of Indian Affairs in 1824 by administrative action. Because no law defined or funded McKenney's position, he was classified and paid as a War Department clerk. McKenney's duties, which Calhoun outlined on March 11, 1824 (*Calhoun Papers*, 8:575–76), were to take charge of the Department's management of Indian affairs, including expenditures for tribal annuities, claims, and expenses.

7. According to McKenney's *Memoirs, Official and Personal* (New York, 1846), Calhoun wrote this letter after leaving the War Department in 1825 in response to one from McKenney complaining of his "unrequited labors" (p. 58).

8. A House bill, reported in March 1826 and again in January 1828, would have created a General Superintendent of Indian Affairs in the War Department at a salary of $3,000. In February 1829, Secretary of War Peter B. Porter submitted to Congress a proposal by Michigan Governor Lewis Cass and William Clark (1779–1838) of St. Louis to overhaul the management of Indian affairs, including the creation of a Commissioner with a salary of $3,000.

From Martin Van Buren

Washigtn April 23 1829.

Sir

In compliance with your request that I should look at the papers sent to me in relation to the Newyork Customs, & give my opinion in writing on the realitive merits of the several applicants, specifying at the same time the offices to which I would appoint them, & how far the principles we have adopted would justify dismissals in that port I have carefully examined the documents & have the honor to submit this my report upon the subject. The first & most important question relates to the office of Collector, & the first consideration that naturally presents itself is the propriety of dismissing the present incumbent. I have been long and intimately acquainted with Mr Thompson, believe him to be a strictly honest man, & to have discharged the duties of his very difficult and highly responsible office with integrity & fidelity. I am however constrained to express my belief, that the manner in which he has disposed of the patronage of his office, (including the application of a great portion of it to his own family) with a personal demeanor far from conciliatory, (as it is said by those who have business intercourse with him) superadded to his course in reference to the recent struggle in which the whole country has been involved, have excited a current of public feeling adverse to his continuance in office that deserves the respect of the Goverment; & that under the circumstance his dismissal would be justifiable upon the principles we have adopted; provided a successor can be selected who possesses in an ample degree the public confidence. Justice to my own feelings requires that I should add that the early and uniform Republican character & course of Mr Thompson, my respect for his private virtues, and our long and unbroken personal friendship, makes this act of public duty a source of deep regret on my part.[1]

The prominant candidates for that office are Jeromus Johnson and Samuel Swartwout.

I know Mr Johnson intimately & believe him to be a worthy & highly deserving man, & it would give me great pleasure to see him placed in some office which would be agreeable to him, & for which his talents are adapted. He is a merchant of respectability, and has strong claims upon us. I do not believe that his capacities, (respectable as they are,) qualify him for that difficult & extremely responsible station, & for that sole reason cannot recommend his appointment.[2]

I have known Mr Swartwout for many years although not intimately. I have always regarded him as a generous, warm hearted & high spirited man, influenced by kind feelings to his friends, & have consequently never entertained any other than friendly feelings towards him personally. Politically; he has never been, and is not now, in a situation, to make his opinions the excuse of either prejudice or solicitude with me. It is my clear & decided opinion, (and a firmer or better grounded conviction I never entertained in my life,) that the appointment of Mr Swartwout to the office of Collector of the port of Newyork, would not be in accordance with public sentiment, the interests of the Country, or the credit of the administration. Deeply impressed with the peculiar importance of this appointment, and anxious fully to discharge the duty imposed upon me by your request, & the relation in which I stand to you, I feel it my duty to add, that his selection would in my judgment be a measure that would in the end be deeply lamented by every sincere & intelligent friend of your administration throughout the Union.

I have examined the recommendations of Mr Swartwout carefully & from my local knowledge would have no difficulty in presenting to you a just estimate of their amount. That there are individuals of much personal worth who have expressed a desire for his appointment I cheerfully admit; but so far forth as the documents profess to establish a favourable expression of either the commercial or political sentiment of the City they are extremely deceptive and deficient; and fall far short, of what I had, under the circumstances, been led to expect. I have reason to believe that this subject is somewhat irksome to you, & it is assuredly not a pleasant one to me. I shall therefore not press the explanations which I am prepared to make unless your view of the matter should induce you to think them necessary. For the present allow me barely to add, (and aver that I would not do were it not for the circumstance that you must unavoidably be ignorant of most of the men who have addressed you upon the subject;) one or two observations. Several of the gentlemen who urge Mr Swartwouts appointment also speak in the very highest terms of the character & claims of Henry Post, whose character is now well understood; & whose appointment (had it been possible) would have filled the minds of every sincere friend of yours with the deepest sorrow. In some of the cases this arises from a want of discretion, & in others from a want of principle. An attempt is made to impress you with the belief that Gnl. Lewis is in favour of Mr Swartwouts appointment, & the reason given for his not writing is that he did not allow himself to recommend in any case. I do not know the gentleman who makes this statement & have no wish or cause to impeach his correctness but waiving the consideration of the weight that ought to be given to this opinion of Gnl Lewis if correctly given, it is worthy of remark that among the papers will be found two recommendations of Gov Lewis for other persons. It is alledged that Mr Astor (who though a good merchant is no politician) is in favour of Mr S. In addition to the letter from Mr Cambreling, which I read to you, I have rcd one from him yesterday, in which he informs me that he had called on Mr Astor, who informed him that he had been twice applied to to write in favour of Mr S. but had refused, and repelled the idea of his being in his favour.[3] I have mislaid Mr Cs. letter but can hunt it up if material. Mr. Governeur (the Postmaster) sends a recommendation from a Mr Richard Hatfield as entitled to much consideration—now this is the same Mr Hatfield who our friends in Nyork wish to turn out of the office of Clerk for his conduct during the last election—and to put Mr Noah in his place they have had two meetings upon the subject & will I hope & trust do it.[4] But I find I am going into the very explanation I propose to avoid & will therefore desist with this single remark. I do not understand from your note whether our Senators recommended Mr Swartwout for the office of Collector in particular, or for some place generally & am strongly impressed with the belief that it must have been the latter. I have however written to Mr Dudley & will have his and Mr Sanfords views in a few days.[5]

I believe that the appointmt of either John Ferguson or Saul Alley would satisfy the public mind and secure the public interest. Neither of those gentlemen have made any communication to me in the form of application upon the subject. In regard to the removal of the Surveyor & appraisers there is no difficulty.[6]

All three of the members of Congress from the City, together with the prominent & influential men of the Republican Party, including the minor sections of it which have formerly broke off, have concentrated their support upon *Johnathan I Coddington* for Surveyor, & there is no doubt that his appointment is generally desired & expected by the great body of those whose wishes next to your own ought to govern in the matter.[7]

The same may be said of Mr Coe for appraiser. If the recommendations are looked into it will be found that his name is almost universally one. He has been secretary of the General Republican Committee for a great many years, is a popular Alderman of the upper wards, & his disappointment would be more severely felt in that strong hold than that of any other man.[8]

The other appraiser I would select from the following list—Jeromus Johnson, (if nothing better is done for him) Alderman Messerole, Abrm B. Meade, Oliver Drake, & I would say Hector Craig with great pleasure if he resided in the City. Mr Craig is an honest worthy man who has strong claims for his fidelity. I wrote to him before he came to Washington, that I would cheerfully comply with his request by uniting in a recommendation in his favour for any place out of the City, that would be adapted to his capacity & situation; but that I had united in condemning the conduct of Mr Monroe in sending Genl Swift as Surveyor of the port to Nyork—that I knew the effect of such appointments, to be, to offend a whole community, instead of individuals only, as is the case where you make a selection between individuals in the same place, & therefore could not now advise a different course.[9] Mr Craig is now elected to the next Congress & I wish he could be satisfied to serve out his time & trust to a future & just estimate of his merits. I hope you will excuse me for sending you this rough draft—I have no time to occupy but will ask your permission to do so hereafter—very respectfully your Obednt servant

M. VanBuren

ALS, DLC-Van Buren Papers (13-0114).
  1. Jonathan Thompson (1773–1846) had been collector for the port of New York since 1820. AJ removed him for Swartwout.
  2. Jeromus Johnson (1775–1846), who had served in Congress 1825–29, was appointed an appraiser of goods.
  3. John Jacob Astor (1763–1848) was a wealthy New York merchant and fur trader.
  4. Samuel Laurence Gouverneur (1799–1865), a son-in-law of James Monroe, served as New York City postmaster, 1829–36. Richard Hatfield (1785–1833) was a New York City attorney and clerk of the criminal court. AJ appointed Mordecai Manuel Noah (1785–1851), editor of the pro-Jackson *New-York Enquirer,* surveyor of the port of New York.
  5. Replying to Van Buren's query of April 20, Dudley on April 25 denied that either he or Sanford had recommended Swartwout (Van Buren Papers, DLC).
  6. In March AJ had reappointed John Ferguson (c1777–1832) as naval officer for the port of New York, a post he had held since 1813. Saul Alley (c1777–1852) was a New York merchant. In 1832 AJ appointed him a director of the Bank of the United States.
  7. New York City's congressmen were Churchill Cambreleng, Gulian Verplanck, and Campbell P. White. Jonathan Inslee Coddington (1784–1856), a merchant, received no appointment at this time. AJ appointed him postmaster in 1836.
  8. AJ appointed William S. Coe, a New York City merchant, an appraiser of goods for the port of New York.
  9. Bernard J. Meserole, a merchant and alderman of New York City's tenth ward, became assistant appraiser of goods. Abraham B. Mead, a New York City merchant, was appointed an appraiser in 1830. Hector Craig (1775–1842) of Orange County served in Congress, 1823–25 and 1829–30. AJ appointed him surveyor of the port in 1833, after Noah resigned. Joseph Gardner Swift (1783–1865) had been surveyor, 1818–26.

To James Alexander Hamilton

April 24th. 1829—

(private)

Dr. Sir

I have recd a note from Mr Ingham last evening, in which he requests me to give to Mr Dickins an "acting power," in his absence, wishing to do this, and that uniformity should be seen in all the powers granted I turned my thoughts to the copy of yours, which I was sure, had been copied in my record Book—This I find not the case, & it has been somehow mislaid so that I cannot lay my hand on it.

Will you have the goodness to send me a copy of the acting power I gave you over the State Department—your compliance will much oblige yr mo. ob. servt.

Andrew Jackson

ALS, NcD (13-0135). Asbury Dickins (1780–1861) was chief clerk of the Treasury Department. AJ gave him temporary charge of the department the same day. AJ entered a draft and copy of the appointment on separate pages of his memorandum book.

To Martin Van Buren

April 24th. 1829.

Dr Sir,

I have looked over your views and expositions as to the appointments in the customs of New York with great attention and care; and with the best lights afforded to my judgement have settled in the determination to place Mr Swartout in the office of Collector. It will be matter of regret to me, if our friends in New York shall complain of the selection; but from the strong and highly respectable recommendations presented in his favor, I cannot suspect that any greater dissatisfaction will be produced than would be towards almost any other who might be selected: perfect and entire unanimity towards appointments is not to be expected. respecting Mr Swartout all agree, and many have spoken, that he is a warm hearted, zealous and generous man, strictly honest and correct in all his dealings and conduct; none has impugned his integrity or honor. He is reputed to be poor; but as an honest man is the noblest work of God, I cannot recognise this to be an objection to any man. Mr Jefferson's creed, "was he honest, was he capable," I have always admired.[1] This being the case of Mr S. from his recommendations, and it appearing that he can give the necessary security required of him, I have thought proper to appoint him. your friend

(signed) Andrew Jackson

LC, DLC (60). Van Buren *Autobiography*, pp. 264–65.
    1. Thomas Jefferson, writing to Elias Shipman et al., July 12, 1801, to defend the appointment of Samuel Bishop as collector of New Haven, said that he looked forward to the day "when the only questions concerning a candidate shall be, is he honest? is he capable? is he faithful to the constitution?"

To Martin Van Buren

April 24th 1829

MR. VAN BUREN.

Respecting the appointment at Nashville (Attorney) I shall leave that to you; fair reciprocity is always right, and as I have given you, in your State, a Collector, I leave you, in mine, to give us an Attorney; asking nothing more than that you will give us as qualified a man. I have directed all the recommendations to be sent you for the applicants for this office. Yours &c

ANDREW JACKSON

Printed, *The Autobiography of Martin Van Buren*, p. 265 (13-0136).

From Martin Van Buren

W. April 24 1829.

Dear Sir.

If it is perfectly agreable to you it would be particularly so to me to be permitted to send your letter to Mr Cambreleng with a view to its being shewn to a few of my friends in New York. If you have the slightest objection to the course I propose I hope you will do me the favor to inform me of it.

If you allow it to be sent it will be inclosed in the within (which was written before I received it) & of course with a prohibition against its publication.[1] I shall cheerfully do what you may desire in regard to the appointment at Nashville but as I have not the slightest choice between the Candidates and no personal knowledge of either of them save Mr Balch & that very superficially, I should be in no small degree embarrassed in the execution of a trust you have in so kind & flattering a manner committed to me   But we shall converse on this subject further when I have the pleasure of seeing you[2]   Your friend

M Van Buren

I return the letter with a view to give you an opportunity to alter it (if you think it advisable to have it sent upon which point I repeat my wish that you should not suffer your sense of propriety to be in the least influenced by your desire (of which I am well satisfied) to gratify me   you will observe that in the word *capable* the *pa* is through inadvertance omitted. The whole letter to Mr Cambreling is subject to your opinion as to its propriety. If you doubt the policy of sending it I will suppress the whole & leave the matter to take its course without explanation.

Copy (partly in Van Buren's hand), DLC-Van Buren Papers (13-0138).
    1. Van Buren had composed a letter to Cambreleng, dated April 23, warning of Swartwout's likely appointment. Enclosing AJ's letter making the appointment, Van Buren added that although AJ had acted "against my decided & earnest remonstrance," Van Buren more than ever respected "the purity of his motives" (Van Buren Papers, DLC).
    2. Alfred Balch (1785–1853) was a Nashville lawyer. AJ appointed James Collinsworth (1806–38) district attorney on April 30.

To Martin Van Buren

[April 24]

My Dr. Sir
    your note, enclosing one intended to be sent to Mr Camberlig, has been recd. and read with attention, & I thank you for the perusal. I have not the least objection to your inclosing mine to Mr Camberlig under the injunction imposed—Indeed, I think it proper that you should, and wish it. I would write my letter over again, but I have not time & my head is very painful, & as it is *only* for the *eye of friends*, I return it, correcting the omission your were kind anough to note. I herewith send the letters enclosed, yr friend

Andrew Jackson

[Endorsed by Van Buren:] The letter refered to in the above was intended for my perusal only

ALS, DLC-Van Buren Papers (13-0144).

To Henry Conwell

WASHINGTON CITY, April 25th, 1829

Dear Sir—
    I have the honor to acknowledge the receipt of your letter of the 1st of January last, and to tender to you my thanks for the engraving of his Holiness Pope LEONE the XIIth, and the impression of yourself, which last you had the goodness to send with your congratulations to Mrs. Jackson. I feel a melancholy pleasure on accepting them, for we have accounts of the death of the Pope, and shortly before the date of your letter, Divine Providence took from me the dear companion of my bosom. So that within this brief period we have both been subjected to the heaviest

calamities, and what you have designed as tokens of respect for the living, can only be accepted as memorials of their departed worth.

Allow me, Sir, to express a hope that nothing will occur in the selection of the successor at Rome, to detain you long from your country—to which I wish you a safe and prosperous return. With the assurance of my greatest respect, I am your most obedient Servant,

ANDREW JACKSON.

Printed, Charleston *United States Catholic Miscellany,* January 16, 1830 (mAJs). Draft by AJ Donelson, DLC-Donelson Papers (13-0150). Conwell (c1747–1842), Bishop of Philadelphia since 1820, had written on January 1 to congratulate AJ on his election. Pope Leo XII (1760–1829), elected in 1823, had died on February 10 and was succeeded by Pius VIII.

To John Christmas McLemore

Washington City, April [26]th 1829

Dear Sir,

Major Donelson has read me part of your Letter Just received. I have also recd. one from my old friend Judge Overton, which I will answer so soon as a Leisure moment occurs.[1] I am much engaged—*a rat* that has been marauding on the Treasury, finding that he was detected, left this place, and I am engaged preparing legal process to pursue & arrest him.[2] It may be that the Late Secry. of the Navy is concerned in the frauds. The presumption is *strong,* still, he may be able to explain   this for your self, and your confidential friends; a few days will give publicity to this transaction, but all must be still until the principal is arrested, and until the ExSecry of the Navy explains, for which I have directed a call to be made upon him in writing, which is done, and I presume he will forthwith answer; should he hesitate he will be called on by a Judicial inquiry, and be put upon his defence.[3] Should a Jury find him guilty, The punishment a Penitentiary offence, as to the guilt of *Tobias Watkins* in this fraud upon the Treasury, There can be no doubt. but he has disappeared.

[4]I beg my friends in Tennessee to have no fear; I will go on in the same even tenor of my ways in harmony with my Cabinet, (which is one of the strongest, as I believe, that ever have been in the United States) cleansing the Augean Stable.[5] My Cabinet is gaining upon the popularity of the nation daily, and my deceitful enemies in Tennessee will fall in to utter disgrace and contempt, not in Tennessee alone, but in the whole union. I am aware of the base conduct of some of our Tennessee friends towards Eaton—I heard some of the most unfounded lies ever propagated, that must have been circulated by some members of Congress, be them, whom they may, if Eaton can trace it to a source worthy of notice, they will feell the chastisement that such base conduct and secret slander deserves

merit—he has already paid his respects to two gentlemen *here,* for the tales of their wifes, and I suppose their tongues will be hereafter sealed.[6] I have heard, that it has been circulated in Tennessee, that Timberlake cut his throat on account of his jealousy of Eaton. There never was a *baser Lie told.* To the Last moment of his life, he had every confidence in Eaton, & in Novembr 1826 sent him a full power of attorney to attend to all his business, by which Majr Eaton has saved from the rack of his fortune, about $25,000, which he has willed to his wife & children. Read the two letters enclosed.[7] They are from two Gentlemen that were with him, on the whole cruise, intimate friends of his and who closed his eyes in death, and then recollect, that Timberlake was a mason, Major Eaton, a mason, & Majr Oneal, The Father, a mason & must he not be a Villain, who could ascribe to Majr Eaton, such base conduct, and violation of every virtuous obligation; I would enclose you a copy of the Letter of Attorney, but time will not permit, I have had it in my possession, it is authenticated in due form, at Giberalter.

I have Long ago intended to do something for Genl Carroll, I will give him a charge de affairs to South America, if he will accept it, so soon as one is open—It is all that can be done for him, as we are trying to curtail our Diplomatic Corps, at Least of Ministers of the first Grade, and our predecessors has left us without funds.

I fear nothing that clay or such treacherous friends as *Miller* & others can do. These are the men who cry out principle, but who are on the scent of Treasury Pap. And if I had a *tit* for every one of these *pigs* to suck at, they would s[t]ill be my friends. They view the appointment of Eaton as a bar to them from office, & have tried here, with all the tools of Clay helping them on, to alarm & prevent me from appointing him. I was elected by the free voice of the people, I was making a Cabinet to aid me in the administration of the government, agreeable to their will. Majr Eaton was necessary to me to fulfill the expressed will of the people, he was *my friend,* I knew his *worth,* & Like Washington, Jefferson, & Madison, I took him from my own state. I was not making a Cabinet for Genl Desha, Isaacs, Mitchel & Miller, I was making a Cabinet for my self, as I told them, I did not come here to make a Cabinet for the Ladies of this place, but for the nation, and that I believed, & so I do, that Mrs. Eaton is as chaste as those who attempt to slander her.[8] assure my friends we are getting on here *well,* we labour night & day, & will continue to do so, until we destroy all the rats, who have been plundering the Treasury—I am not in good health, but as Long as I am able, I will Labour to fulfill the expectations of the nation. The press *here* for offics exceeds every thing known before, and it seems that almost every man that voted for me, Lays in his claims for some office or other, not having time to say more at present, remember me affectionately to your Lady and the dear Little ones, to all friends, and accept of my wishes for your future welfare & prosperity. I remain your sincere friend

Andrew Jackson

I have this moment heard a rumor of poor Houstons disgrace—My god, is the man *mad*

P.S. say to my friend Earle I have recd his letter & will answer it soon—

LS with postscripts in AJ's hand, NHi (13-0156); AL draft, DLC (37). Date taken from the draft.

1. Tennessee lawyer and jurist John Overton (1766–1833) was AJ's longtime friend and political supporter. McLemore had written Donelson on April 5 to report "much dissatisfaction" over Eaton's appointment and to warn that an opposition party in Tennessee might coalesce around the popular William Carroll (1788–1844), a former three-term governor now seeking a new term. McLemore urged offering Carroll a federal appointment to cement him and his friends to the administration (Donelson Papers, DLC).

2. Tobias Watkins, late fourth auditor of the Treasury, had embezzled funds by filing fraudulent requisitions for the navy agents at New York and Boston. Watkins left Washington in mid-April. Formal charges against him were filed April 26, and he was arrested in Philadelphia on April 30. In August he was convicted on three charges and sentenced to nine months in prison and a $3,050 fine.

3. Navy Department chief clerk and acting secretary Richard H. Bradford wrote former Navy secretary Samuel Lewis Southard (1787–1842) for explanations on April 25. On May 4 he informed Southard of the charges against Watkins (DNA-RG 45, M209-6). Responding on May 13, Southard professed ignorance of Watkins's frauds but pledged to cooperate with the investigation (DNA-RG 45, M124-118). No charges were filed against him.

4. At this point in the draft, AJ wrote and then struck out the following: "Now, whilst those friends of mine, who dragged me from my peaceful Hermitage, as they then said, it was necessary for me to make the sacrafice, for the sake of principle, now because I did not bring them into office why I have abandoned principle, and they virtuous souls, must abandon me—be it so, but I will go on in the even tenor of my ways, unrobe, first, their chief managers here, and the people will leave them on their native dunghills there."

5. The mythical fifth labor of Hercules was to clean King Augeas's stable, which housed thousands of oxen and had not been cleaned in thirty years. The phrase was used to connote a place of great filth or corruption.

6. Thomas Sim and George Graham.

7. Thomas Norman to Margaret Eaton, dated April, and Elie Augustus Frederick Vallette to Margaret Eaton, April 18 (DLC-75). Norman, the purser's steward on the *Constitution,* wrote that he was with Timberlake at his death and that he "on every occasion spoke of Mr. E__ as his best friend." Vallette (1789–1862), a lieutenant on the *Constitution,* affirmed that Timberlake always spoke of his wife and Eaton with trust and affection.

8. Robert Desha (1791–1849) of Gallatin, Jacob C. Isacks (1767–1835) of Winchester, and James Coffield Mitchell (1786–1843) of Athens were all Tennessee congressmen.

To Martin Van Buren

April 28th. 1829—

Dr Sir

I have recd. your note of this day enclosing Major Moors private letter.

I have read it with the feelings of a friend—Those feelings would say the indulgence asked ought to be granted—Humanity would say, indulge him until he hears the fate of his wife—*What says the duty we owe our country, and the principles we have adopted to guide us through our administration.* one of the charges against our predesessors was, that they appointed ministers and permitted them to remain here, and traverse the country on electioneering tours, neglecting the great interests of our Foreign relations—*true,* these ministers were receiving their salary, not so ours, as nothing is to be paid, as salary, until they set out on their mission; still we are liable to the charge of neglecting the great interests abroad, & if in one case we grant indulgence, we must extend it to others. The 15th. of July, appears to me, to be as bad a season as he could select, and altho I would not hazard his life still it would seem to me, the 15th. of June would be as long as we could indulge him, and surely he must hear of Mrs. Moor before long, so that he could make arangements to set out by that date. If he does not hear from her, soon, he would surely like to leave home by the 15th of May and touch at Veracruze to enquire for her The Major could be permitted to sail from Neworleans, for this purpose, and by descending the Mississippi, would be certain to meet her—I am respectfully yrs.

Andrew Jackson

P.S. upon reflection, if you think we would not be sacraficing our principles for the convenience of our friends, the indulgence may be granted[1]

It would be important that we should hear from Bolivar before the meeting of Congress & that Harrison should be recalled to put an end to his salary[2]

I enclose Mr Moors letter yrs A. J.

ALS, DLC-Van Buren Papers (13-0175). Endorsed by James A. Hamilton, "The Prest decision is clearly right   This appt was made early in March the outfit was immediately paid Mr Harrison must be considered as recalled or Moore's appt was unconstitutional recalling Harrison & having no minister there would be *very inexpedient* under existing circumstances." Thomas P. Moore had written Van Buren on April 16 that he was awaiting his wife's return from Matamoros, Mexico, where she had gone to recoup her health. Moore asked to postpone his departure for Colombia until after July 15 (Van Buren Papers, DLC, 13-0178).

1. Van Buren wrote Moore on April 29, urging him to leave before June 15.

2. Simón Bolívar (1783–1830), famed liberator of South America, was the dictator of Colombia. On June 9, Van Buren informed Harrison of his recall and Moore's appointment.

From Richard Keith Call

Tallahassee 28th. Apl 1829—

My Dear Genl.

I have the satisfaction to acknowledge the receipt of your letter of the 7th. Inst. which I have read with deep interest.

So soon as I can leave my wife who will be confined in a few days I shall set out for Havanna, and will there attend particularly to your instructions relative to Mr Rodney.[1] There is however no doubt but this man should be removed. He is a disgrace to his country. I have it from the lips of a most respectable and worthy Gentleman who visited Cuba last Fall, that he heard him at a public Table among americans and foreigners speak of you in the most disrespectable manner, and declaired that if elected you would have to employ some one to write your messages, and that he took all occasions to speak of you in the terms of abuse. This Gentleman represents him as being obnoxious to all americans who visit the Island. If you think proper to wait I will give you more particular information on my return from Cuba. If you should remove him which I doubt not you will do, I hope you will provide for your old friend Vincent Gray, who I understand is universally esteemed by all the americans, and has been on all occasions your steadfast friend.[2]

I have read Dear General with great interest that part of your letter which relates to our friend Eaton, and hope sincerely that your impressions with regard to him may be correct. None would rejoice in the beliefe more than myself. You misunderstood me with regard to the person from whom I recd my information relative to the correspondende between Eaton and Timberlake. The Gentleman who gave this information is incapable of making a mistatement on any subject but he had recd it from one who said he had seen the papers, of this second person I know nothing, and he may have told a false-hood, I hope he did. I am sure Genl you cannot mistake my motives in mentioning this subject to you. I feel too deeply what ever concerns you not to speak when I believe you are imposed on, and I fear you are still deceived with regard to the Majors domestic relations. I do not wish to prejudice you against your friend, who I consider has one blemish and a thousand virtues. But I do believe Mrs E is an unworthy associate for the ladies of your household. While living in the same house I had such evidences of her conduct, as to convince me of her want of virtue. You will pardon me Genl for speaking plainly to you on this subject. I do believe and I have the *most conclusive reason to believe,* that as early as 1824 an *aggreement* existed between the parties that they would marry in the event of the death of T. This added to other circumstances which I mentioned to you have left me without a doubt on this subject. I wish it were otherwise, but the convictions of my mind are too strong to be removed. Your friends all believe this story, but they do you the justice to believe that you entertain a different opinion. Yours is certainly the most charitable belief, and one which I would embrase if I could. I do fear Genl that this Lady will create a difficulty among some of the members of your cabinet. I tell you in confidence and I think you will find me correct. She will not be recd. in the families of the other members of your Cabinet. But I have trespassed to long on your time. I hope your health is restored, and that the blessings of heaven may decend on you is the sincere prayer of your friend

R. K Call

[Endorsed by AJ:] This letter to be filed with my private papers, as an evidence of the falibility of man & how far he will be carried by his prejudices—There was not an act of Mrs. T. for the whole time I lived about the huse of Major Oneal, with Genl Call, that created the slightest suspicion on my mind of the impressions of Genl. Call as now expressed by him, & I have been & ever will remain stedfast in the opinion of her innocense & the falshood of the charge. A.J.

ALS, DLC (37).
    1. Mary Letitia Kirkman (c1801–36) had married Call at the Hermitage in 1824. AJ had commissioned Call on April 3 to obtain Spanish documents at Havana regarding the disputed Florida land claims. Thomas McKean Rodney (1800–1874) had been consul at Havana since 1825. AJ removed him for William Shaler.
    2. Vincent Gray was an American merchant long resident in Havana, who claimed credit for informing AJ of British invasion plans in 1814.

Review of Abram Rall Woolley's Court-Martial

The President of the United States approves the Sentence of the General Courtmartial Whereof Colo. Clinch is president—

    The court has recommended him to the clemency of the Executive in hopes his ungovernable temper may be reformed for the reasons given (insert them in the order) But the prisoner has been found gui[l]ty of punishing a soldier with lashes is such a flagrant breach of positive law that the Executive cannot extend his clemency to excuse—Every soldier before he enlist is a freeman, & when he enters into his enlistment he believes himself protected by the laws of his country from personal injury & personal degradation by stripes or lashes even by the sentence of a court-martial and still more f[rom] the tyrany and abuse of his officer whose duty it is to be his protector in all his legal rights, and to watch over him with the Justice & care of a father—

The Sec of War will order the sentence to be carried into effect—[1]

AD, DNA-RG 107 (M222-24). Lieutenant Colonel Woolley (1784–1858) was court-martialed at Jefferson Barracks, Mo., on March 14 for severely whipping a private and for abusive conduct toward junior officers. Colonel Duncan Lamont Clinch (1787–1849) presided. Woolley was found guilty and sentenced to dismissal from the service, but the Court recommended clemency in the stated hope that the trial had taught him to control his temper.

1. Eaton ordered Woolley dismissed on April 28 (DNA-RG 153).

From Samuel Swartwout

New York 29th. April 1829

Dear Sir,

I avail myself of the only moment afforded me since the receipt of the comptroler's letter yesterday, enclosing my commission, to express to you my heart-felt acknoledgements for this evidence of confidence and friendship. No event of my life has afforded me so much happiness. As an evidence of personal regard not to be shaken by the base and the insideous, nor by the noisy clamours of the interested, I shall esteem it the proudest triumph of my life. I am aware Sir, that any other person than yourself, might have been induced to abandon a friend through the arts and misrepresentations of unprincipled men. But you could not be intimidated nor imposed upon; the pleasure which I experience, in receiving this appointment at your hands, under those circumstances, is, therefore, infinitely enhanced.

I am fully sensible of the importance and great responsibility of the situation confered upon me, I shall dwell no longer upon the subject, however, than to assure your excellency, that diligence, zeal, fidelity and courtesy shall mark my conduct in the discharge of its duties. As vigilence and courtesey are not incompatable in a public officer, I shall strive to guard the interests of the government, whilst no effort shall be spared to facilitate and accomodate the business of the merchants.

I cannot close my letter without repeating to your Excellency that I am duly sensible of the extent of your friendship, and of the great responsibility which you have assumed in making this appointment. It will be my pride and my interest both, so to deport myself in office, as to call forth from the public an expression of their entire approval.

With every sentiment of veneration and respect I remain your Excellency's most obt. Sevt.

Saml. Swartwout

ALS, NjP (13-0184). Swartwout served as New York City customs collector until March 1838. Soon after leaving office he was found to be in default for an estimated $1,374,119.

Memorandum on Appointments

Genl Duncan, in the room of Dr Gentworth survayor[1]—Dallas atto. for District E. Pa. vice Ingersol removed—

Mr Handy. Indiana applies for—Register—*be careful*

Mr Ross of the marines, applies through Mr Davis S.C. for messenger to carry dispaches to Europe[2]—

Jacob R. Brooks Georgia DeCalb *County*[3]

Truman Becher collector Detroit to be removed & Col *Mack in his room*[4]

Col. Randall—worthy of appointment, well educated—lives in Baltimore—

Mr. Buchannan—recommended for sec of Foreign leg—to be remembered in our Foreign appointments—[5]

AD, DLC (12-1204).
    1. In April, AJ appointed William Duncan (1772–1864) surveyor and revenue inspector at Philadelphia in place of Revolutionary veteran James Glentworth (d. 1839), appointed in 1814.
    2. Andrew Ross (d. 1836) was a Marine lieutenant. Warren Ransom Davis (1793–1835) was a South Carolina congressman. Henry S. Handy (c1804–46) had edited the pro–Jackson Salem, Ind., *Annotator of News, Politics, and Literature.*
    3. Jacob R. Brooks (b. c1787) of DeKalb County, Ga., had been a contractor's agent during AJ's 1818 Seminole campaign.
    4. AJ removed Detroit customs collector Truman Beecher (1796–1850), an Adams appointee, for Andrew Mack.
    5. James Madison Buchanan (1803–76) of Baltimore had been extensively recommended for secretary of legation.

Memorandum Book

[In April 1829 Jackson began a presidential memorandum book. He made entries irregularly and not in strict order, sometimes going back to fill in space on a previous page with a later note. Printed here are the opening pages of the book, written mostly in April and May with one later entry from July.]

[On inside cover:]
Doctor George Fleming   Louisia V.a.[1]

The Bolmar plum, from Mr Hagner with the Green guage—The seed of the ½ dozen of each to be sent & planted on the Hermitage[2]

[Beginning on first leaf:]
Private—
Memorandom Book of A. Jackson commencing in April 1829—

April 18th. enclosed to the sec of State Mr Noval's letter complaining of the unjust treatment of Mr Rhea our Consul at Brazill, for his enquiry & report, that instructions might be given to our minister at that court on the subject.[3]

Wyandott & Seneca stock to be noted in message to next congress. A. J.[4]

April 24th. 1829—

Sir
    you are appointed to take charge of the Treasury Department ~~of the Treasury~~ and to perform the duties of that office from this time until Mr Ingham returns to this city yr mo obdt ~~servt~~

Andrew Jackson[5]

Dr Richard H Bradford appointed to take charge of the Navy Dept. in the absence of Mr Branch, dated April 8th. 1829. A. J.[6]

I appoint Thomas H. Gillis to take charge of the office of 4th. Auditor during the absence of Mr Amos Kendal   July 29th. 1829—

Private.
    Instructions to our minister who goes to France to be friendly, decorous, & peaceful, but firm, demanding a final answer to our complaints so often and so Justly reiterated, and to which their magnanimity & Justice as a great nation requires a prompt reply
    The claims known to be Just and which by every principle known to international law ought to be paid, to be selected & placed in one aggregate and fixed as a basis upon which we will close this long controversy— setting off all other claims against those raised against us by France, and which is considered not to be founded in Justice—all claims on both sides prior to the 30th. of Septbr. 1800 is considered to come within the above rule—[7]
    Our minster instructed to propose to France a commercial Treaty on the broad basis of Just reciprocity—opening all her ports, colonial included, to our merchant vessels &c &c &c

The minister to France to be charged with obtaining information on the subject of the modification & improvement of artillery as suggested in a work of Mr. Paixhans which was transmitted by Mr Gallatine to Mr Adams sec of State U. States, under date of the 10th. of July 1822 (recd 30th of August) What experiments have been made, and the result of those experiments—Whether favorable to the modification, & experiments of Mr. Paixhans plan or otherwise, & transmit the same to the President of the U. States.[8]

The maxim, provide for war in time of peace, a good one[9]—let us profit by all experience we can obtain. that appears, Mr Paixhans book sent by Mr. Gallatine is lost, or mislaid, that it cannot be found.

Judge Preble & Vaness or Woodbury to be sent to the Netherlands next fall, if Congress will appropriate—Hughes to be then provided for by being raised to Minister of first grade & sent to some other place[10]

Washington April 24th. 1829

Sir

you are appointed to take charge of the Treasury Department and to perform the duties of that office from this time until the return of Mr Ingham to this city yr. ob. servt.

Asbury Dickens Esq

Andrew Jackson[11]

To keep peace on our Borders, the priviledge of British Traders, entering our Territory & trading with The Indians ought to be done away[12]

Our criminal code as it respect counterfeit, Silver, coin defective—It ought to be a criminal offence to put into circulation any base Silver coin—This, from our proximity to Texas, is absolutely necessary for the safety of our citizens, & our revenue—[13]

The claims for military Services, in New england, during the late war to be examined, and if any services have been rendered, and in other States, for similar services have been paid, to be recommended to congress at their next Session to be paid—but none other to be recommended to be paid, as it would be a premium offered to our citizens to commit Treason in time of war—[14]

Washington May 13th. 1829

Mr Enoch Reynolds

sir you are appointed to take charge of the office of the second comptroller of the Treasury & perform the duties thereof from this time until the return of Mr Hill to this city yr mo obdt servt.

Andrew Jackson[15]

A Frigate to be put in readiness to carry out the ministers to London France & Consul to Algiers & then relieve the Java which is to be ordered on her return to touch at Liberia, & scour the coast of africa near that station—Then proceed to the United States. The sec of the Navy directed to carry into effect the above May 18th. 1829 The Fr—e to be ready by the first of July next.[16]

The diplomatic dress at Ghent ~~abr~~ordered by the President—abrogated, and a *plain dress directed*[17]

May 21rst 1829. recd. from Genl Duff Green an extract of a letter (Doctor Marable to Genl G) containing declarations of Govr. Houston late of Tennessee, that he would conquor Mexico or Texas, & be worth two millions in two years &c—Believing this to be the efusions of a distempered brain, but as a precautionary measure I directed the Secretary of war to write & inclose to Mr Pope Govr. of Arkansas the extract, and instruct him if such illegal project should be discovered to exist to adopt prompt measures to put it down & to give the Goverment the earliest intelligence of such illegal enterprise with the names of all those who may be concerned therein—[18]

Early attention to be paid to the boundery between the U. States and Mexico—The line must be altered as by it part of our citizens are thrown into the Province of Texas, & the Cadow tribe of Indians to whom we have been paying an annuity for years—Mr Duns letter—This to be brought before congress[19]

There has been a great noise made about removals—This to be brought before congress with the causes—with the propriety of passing a law vacating all offices periodically, then the good can be reappointed, & the bad, defaulters left out without murmurs—now every man who has been in office a few years, believes he has a life estate in it, a vested right, & if it has been held 20 years or upwards, not only a vested right, but that it ought to descend to his children, & if no children then the next of kin—This is not the principles of our government. It is rotation in office that will perpetuate our liberty.[20]

ANS, DLC (64).
    1. George Fleming of Louisa County, Va., wrote AJ from Tennessee on April 13 with a report that the Chickasaws and Choctaws were prepared to cede their lands to the United States.
    2. The Bolmar and the Green Gage were two varieties of plum. Peter Hagner (1772–1850) was the third auditor of the Treasury Department.
    3. On March 17, newspaper editor John Norvell (1789–1850) wrote AJ on behalf of Joseph Ray of Pennsylvania, late consul at Pernambuco, Brazil. Charged with abetting Brazilian rebels, Ray had been removed as consul in 1819 at the request of the Brazilian government. He continued to aid the dissidents and in 1825 was expelled from the country and his property seized. Norvell asked AJ to help Ray recover his property and to reappoint him consul at Pernambuco, which AJ did in 1836.
    4. Under treaties of 1797 and 1805, the president held $100,000 in trust for the Seneca Indians and a smaller sum for the Wyandots, from which the tribes received annuities. Invested at one time in stock of the first Bank of the United States and later in six per

cent government bonds, the Seneca fund had for many years produced an annual payment of $6,000 to the tribe. On March 18, responding to a query from AJ to Eaton, War Department chief clerk Charles Nourse reported that the present investment in three per cent bonds (the six per cents having been retired) yielded much less than $6,000, and that President Adams had been making up the difference out of general funds without congressional authorization (DNA-RG 75, M234-808). On April 22 AJ gave Secretary of War Eaton power of attorney over the Seneca fund. That fall the War Department tendered the Senecas only $3,385.60, the fund's current annual return, which the tribe refused. Both Eaton's annual War Department report and AJ's annual message to Congress in December addressed the issue (Richardson, 2:456). In 1831 Congress fixed the payment to the Senecas at $6,000.

5. This entry, which is crossed out with vertical lines, is an apparent draft of Asbury Dickins's temporary appointment.

6. Richard Henry Bradford (1770–1835) served as chief clerk of the Navy Department from April 6 to May 4. Secretary Branch left for North Carolina on April 8 to arrange his family's move to Washington.

7. The U.S. had pressed France for indemnity for American ships and cargoes seized during the Napoleonic wars under Napoleon's Berlin (1806) and Milan (1807) decrees. France had lodged a counterclaim for alleged American violations of the eighth article of the 1803 Louisiana Purchase treaty, which granted France most-favored-nation trading status in Louisiana ports. The French had attempted to link the two issues. In May AJ appointed Virginia congressman William Cabell Rives (1793–1868) minister to France. Van Buren instructed him on July 20 to make every effort to improve commercial relations and that resolving the spoliation claims was "of the most immediate concern and greatest importance" (DNA-RG 59, M77-54). The claims were finally settled in 1836. In the convention of September 30, 1800, ending the "quasi-war" with France, the U.S. had dropped its claims against France for previous spoliations. Merchants with such claims continued to pursue them with the American government.

8. In *Nouvelle Force Maritime: et Application de Cette Force à Quelques Parties du Service de l'Armée de Terre* (1822), Henri-Joseph Paixhans (1783–1854) proposed arming French warships with guns that could shoot exploding shells. Albert Gallatin (1761–1849), then American minister to France, had sent a copy to the State Department and recommended investigating the subject (DNA-RG 59, M34-24). On May 1 AJ asked Eaton to look for the lost book in the War Department.

9. A variation on the aphorism of the Roman author Vegetius (fl. c400): "Igitur qui desiderat pacem, praeparet bellum" (he who desires peace will prepare for war).

10. Cornelius Peter Van Ness (1782–1852), former governor of Vermont, had served as commissioner to settle the northeastern boundary under the Treaty of Ghent. AJ and Van Buren contemplated sending him with Preble to present the American case for arbitration by the King of the Netherlands. He was appointed minister to Spain on June 1 after Woodbury declined. On April 14 Van Buren recommended moving Hughes to a less responsible post.

11. This entry matches the text of Dickins's April 24 temporary appointment. Secretary Ingham left for Pennsylvania on April 25 to arrange his family's removal to Washington. Dickins served as acting secretary until May 26.

12. In the wake of the War of 1812, Congress in 1816 had passed a law that forbade foreign nationals from trading with the Indians without express presidential permission.

13. Under an 1806 law, making or circulating counterfeit coins was a felony punishable by fine or imprisonment. Congress also periodically specified those foreign silver coins to be deemed legal tender and regulated their value. AJ was either unaware of these laws or deemed them inadequate. Texas at this time was a province of Mexico, a major source of silver.

14. In the War of 1812, Federalist governors of Massachusetts, Connecticut, and Rhode Island had sometimes ignored federal calls on their militias or refused to allow them to serve under regular officers. After the war Massachusetts sought federal reimbursement for her

own militia expenses incurred under state authority. AJ's annual message did not mention these so-called "militia claims," which were pursued for many years after.

15. On May 12, second comptroller Isaac Hill asked leave to visit New Hampshire on personal business. Enoch Reynolds (1776–1833) was Hill's chief clerk.

16. The frigate *Constellation* left New York on August 12, carrying Louis McLane and William C. Rives. She then cruised the Mediterranean until 1831. Relieved in January 1831 by the *Brandywine*, the *Java* was ordered to return via the Cape Verde Islands and Liberia to aid in suppressing the illegal slave trade. She called at Monrovia in February.

17. AJ so instructed Van Buren on May 18.

18. Houston had already written AJ on May 11 to deny this report. John Hartwell Marable (1786–1844) was a Tennessee congressman, 1825–29.

19. The 1803 Louisiana Purchase from France failed to define a boundary with Spanish Mexico. Article Three of the Adams-Onís Treaty of 1819 drew a line north from the Gulf of Mexico along the Sabine River and then west along the Red River. The Caddos resided mainly in Louisiana, but with a scattered presence in Texas. AJ acknowledged the letter of "Mr. Dunn," possibly Michael C. Dunn (1770–1853) of Nashville or his son John R. Dunn (1803–36) of Natchitoches, in writing to John Overton on June 8.

20. AJ's annual message in December defended his removals and recommended putting all federal officials on four-year terms (Richardson, 2:448–49).

Memorandum

A Fr[igate to] be put in readiness to take out the ministers to England & France, & the Consul to algiers—Touch at Liberia scour the african coast, & then repair to the Mediterranean & relieve the Java &c &c.

order for a court of enquiry on Capt Turner of the Navy, for capturig of the Columbian vessel in a Danish harbour, & bringing her out under the fire of the Ft—2d. charge, not Sustainin[g] the honor of his flag when fired upon—

The Subject of the removal & appointment of officers in Florida to be taken up so soon as the Sec of the Treasurer returns—See Govr Duvals letters, James W. Exum recommended as Marshal for West Florida &c &c—

The appointment of Marshal & attorney for Kentuckey, &c &c—& alabama

The officers of Indiana, of Illanois, and Misouri, to be passed in review—and those of Va. Norfolk collector, complaints against him—enquire

The Columbian Ship cut out of the Danish port by Capt Turner—The Danish Minister has required to be restored—*quere*, as she is under adjudication will not the act of restoring her be a direct censure on the act of Capt. T. & may prejudice him on the enquiry—and if the court of enquiry acquits Capt Turner on the ground that the vessel was really *piratical*, would it not give our enemies [go]od ground to censure *[the act]*—would it not *th[en be]* [p]rudent to let the vess[el] *[go under?]* trial—

AN, DLC (13-0349).

May

From Ezra Stiles Ely

Philadelphia May 2nd. 1829.

My dear Geneneral

The copies of the Power of Attorney and of the two letters which your last favour enclosed gave me unfeigned pleasure; and from them I feel fully convinced, that the report of Mr. Timberlakes being jealous of and dissatisfied with Mr. Eaton is false; and that the gentleman in Washington who told me the former departed with a broken heart, and wished never to return; must have mistaken the cause of his depression of spirits, or must have told me an untruth. He was a clerk in Washington, whom I casually met in a morning call on one of my friends; and he is the same individual who told me the story of the children. I do not remember his name; but, I could point him out at once were I in your city: and I shall let him know, so soon as I can, that I consider his representations to have been untrue. He made no injunction of secrecy; and I am not therefore bound to conceal his name, when I can command it; but I would rather convince him of his error, than expose him to be removed from his place, for foolishly volunteering to give me, while a stranger to him, slanderous representations.[1]

In a few days I expect to visit New York, and if I can, I will know the truth relative to the boarding houses there; without making myself known as an enquirer after scandal: for I should delight to serve the injured.

The reported declarations of a dead physician I know ought not to be regarded as sufficient proof to convict any one of crime; and that physician may have been a slanderer. If I live to visit Washington again, as I hope to, I shall have a thorough examination made into his character for veracity; and if his testimony ought not to be regarded, I hope to convince the clergyman *who told me what the physician told him,* that he ought to do every thing in his power to repair the injury done Mrs. Eaton.[2]

An apology my wife thinks due for the liberty which I took in sending you a lithographic print of myself, and she would suggest that it was procured to be executed as a charity to the industrious and worthy American artist who had lived on bread and molasses for a week, and who wrought every part of it, with his own hands: but I must honestly say, that I sent it to your Excellency from what some would call a *romantic,* but what I trust is *a truly christian attachment* to you; for I wish to visit you, by letter, and otherwise, in your own chamber as a friend; and I thank you, sincerely, for receiving it kindly, and giving it the desired location. I should be sorry to see it any where else in the Presidents house. Kings, Emperors, Presidents, and Generals, and prints of coronations and battles may occupy your dining halls with propriety; and I should like to see there a good representation of March 4th. 1829, from the eastern view of the capitol; but if my *shadow* may be familiar in your bed chamber; and I may now and then say to you, "dear General, the spirits of the departed are as the angels; and the angels are ministers of God, sent forth to minister to those who shall be heirs of salvation; consider the practical and evangelical faith of your dear, departed companion; serve the Saviour that she loved, and be prepared to meet her in everlasting blessedness." this, this is the honour that I desire.

It is not likely that the remainder of your life will be as fully occupied with busy and momentous cares as any former part of it: may your labours be the sources of lasting benefits to our country: and may all of your fellow citizens honour you as I do in my heart: still let me say honoured friend, *many things* are convenient, desireable, lovely, of good report, but *"one thing* is needful."[3] I know, indeed, that you are not insensible of the realities of the eternal world; but in the midst of honours & pleasures and toils, and vexations, who does not need to be reminded, that he is living for eternity?

May the lord be your light and your defence. May he give you abundant grace to walk humbly before him in the presence of our highly gifted nation; and when you have finished your earthly course, gather you to the spirits of the just made perfect.

Mrs. Ely and Mrs. Carswell frequently speak of you and yours with great affection.[4] Please to make our friendly compliments to Mr. and Mrs. Donelson, and to your son. We should be delighted to have any and all of your family domesticated with us for a month. Yours with the best wishes

(Signed) E. S. Ely

Copy, DLC (75).

1. Ely's informant was Navy Department clerk Thomas Fillebrown, Jr. (1794–1873), a former neighbor of the O'Neales and friend of John B. Timberlake. In three letters to Eaton on September 15, 16, and 22, 1829 (DLC-75), Fillebrown gave his version of his interview with Ely. He said that Ely, not he, had instigated the conversation, and that he had told him, truthfully, that Timberlake had been despondent over his wife's reputation and had left the country vowing never to return. Fillebrown acknowledged informing Ely of the stories about Mrs. Eaton but denied that he had either vouched for their accuracy or himself ever believed them to be true.

2. John N. Campbell was the clergyman; Elijah Craven was the physician.
3. Luke 10:42.
4. Margaret Means Carswell, widow of Samuel Carswell, was Ely's mother-in-law.

To Philip Lindsley

Washington May 3d. 1829

Dear Sir,

I have recd. your letter of the 16th. ulto. and have to regret in my reply to it, that it has not been in my power to gratify the desire of your Brother to be appointed Surgeon for the Penitentiary established in this district. His application was presented by Mr Donelson with authority to refer to me as entirely satisfied with his testimonials: to which was added an expression of his own wishes that he might be appointed. To have said more than this would have been interfering with the discretion of the Inspectors to whom the Law had assigned the selection of the surgeon, and would have subjected your Brother to those unpleasant imputations which are sure to be suggested by a jealousy of power and as a proof of which I need only state to you the fact, that the Gentleman who receved the appointment (a distinguished Physician of this place, Dr Sim) would not accept it, until he had waited upon Mr Donelson and asertained from him that in presenting the recommendation of Mr Lindsly we had no other wish than that of submitting his pretensions to a fair comparison with those of others.[1]

If any future occasion should allow me to favor the views of your Brother, I need not assure you, Sir, that it will be embraced with the confidence due to your evidence in his behalf, and to the friendly interest which you take in the prosperity of my administration. With great respect yr. obt. sert.

Andrew Jackson

LS in AJ Donelson's hand, Anonymous (mAJs). Lindsley had written AJ on April 16 to recommend his brother, Harvey Lindsley (1804–89), for physician at the District of Columbia penitentiary.

1. A law of March 3, 1829, vested oversight of the District penitentiary, including the selection of a physician, in five inspectors appointed annually by the president. Thomas Sim was AJ's Washington physician and a member of his Washington Central Committee in the 1828 campaign.

To John Christmas McLemore

Washington May 3rd. 1829—

My Dr. Sir

I have this day recd. a letter from A. J. Hutchings which informs me, that my Dr young friend Elizabeth Donelson was very sick and the Doctor told him she could not recover   This has filled me with much sorrow, and my prayers are offered up for her recovery   I pray you write me how she is, as I will be in grief until I hear of her recovery.[1]

We have Just recd. the Governors resignation—Houston must be deranged, or what is worse bewitched—be his disorder what it may, he is prostrate forever—my heart bleeds for his fate occasioned by his own folly.

Mr Tobias Watkins was lodged in Jail last evening for frauds, by forgery & false requisitions on the Treasury by which he drew large sums in open violation of the statute in that case made & provided, if found Guilty, it is a penitentiary offence—his examination will take place tomorrow.

I find my son made a mistake in the name subscribed to one of the letters I enclosed to you the other day, he mistook Lt. Elie A. F. Vallette, for Wallette the F being Joined to the V. you will please note this mistake & correct it—The letter is from Lt. Elie A. F. Vallette, a highly respectable Lt. in the Navy, and which gives the lie direct to the slanders circulated about Major Eaton & Mrs. Eaton—If you see Genl Desha, or any other who has been thus speaking; you are at full liberty to shew them the copies of the letters I enclosed to you—Major Eaton is now popular, & will become one of the most popular of all the heads of Departments—Indeed I am highly pleased with my executive council, they are able amiable men, and the greatest harmony prevails—the prime movers of the secrete slanders against Eaton have been silenced by the firm & energetic stand taken by Eaton. he has never yet been able to trace it to a Gentleman, it has been circulated by Females, & he took the stand to make husbands answerable for the sayings of their wifes, & called upon two of them—when both the wife & the husband declared that they never had heard or knew any thing disrespectful of Mrs. or Major Eaton—Now I do know that one of them was the first originater of the falshood, & I have no doubt were the source from whence Houston Desha & others got their information   But these satelites of Clay, who has duped some of our Tennessens, are falling into the pitts dug for Major Eaton, and their slanders are recoiling upon their own heads—There is no respectable strangers who do not call upon Mrs. & Major Eaton and Major Barry is now living with them; the cloud is blowing over—altho it has cost me some pangs—But the world was mistaken in me—The attempt was made to induce me to abandon my friend, *it failed*—I would sink with honor to my grave, before I would abandon my friend Eaton—I will support him, he is a well tried friend, and now, an efficient aid to me, in the administration of the Govt. I have no fear but it will be found that I have around me as able a cabinet as ever administered this goverment—give my respects to my friend Judge Overton, say to him, I will write him soon—give my compliments to Mr. Hume, Earle, Purdy, Barryhill, Armstrong, Parish & all friends,[2] present me affectionately to Betsy and all yr sweet children, we are all getting well here, yr friend

Andrew Jackson

P.S. Rumour says here, you are going to Have Genl Hall a candidate for the office of Governor—& that East Tennessee is going to bring him out—is this true—[3]

ALS, NHi (13-0247).
   1. Probably Elizabeth Hays Donelson (1819–50), daughter of Rachel's brother William (1758–1820), or Elizabeth Anderson Donelson.
   2. Presbyterian minister William Hume (1770–1833), federal marshal Robert Purdy (d. 1831), merchant William McLean Berryhill (1785–1836), merchant and postmaster Robert Armstrong (1792–1854), and Joel Parrish, Jr. (d. 1834) were Nashville friends of AJ.
   3. William Hall (1775–1856) was speaker of the Tennessee senate and briefly became governor upon Houston's resignation. He was not a candidate in the regular August election, won by William Carroll.

To Martin Van Buren

May 3rd. 1829—

Dr. Sir
   I have recd your note of today—read, and approve the letters to Mr Woodbury & Genl Lyman and have as you requested forwarded them.[1]
   I have duly noted your ideas of the proposals sugested to be made to Govr. Vaness on his arrival here—they are such as I approve—and I would suggest the propriety of Sending him to Spain as soon as our means will permit, least Mr. Woodbury might suppose us uncandid with him, when we said our interests with Spain required an early attention to it. yr friend

Andrew Jackson

Mr Woodburys letter I return enclosed

ALS, DLC-Van Buren Papers (13-0251).
   1. Woodbury had written Van Buren on April 27 to decline the Spanish mission. Van Buren's letters were to Woodbury, May 3, accepting his decision with regret, and to Theodore Lyman, Jr. (1792–1849) of Boston, May 2, offering the post of secretary of legation at London (Van Buren Papers, DLC). Lyman declined, and AJ appointed the celebrated author Washington Irving on June 1.

From Elizabeth Williams

City of Washington May 3rd 1829

Respected Sir,

According to your orders I called on Mr Ringgold the Marshall and requested him to pay my claim against the U States for work done the jail, or if he refused so doing, to call on you, he told me this morning that he had a conversation with you on the subject, the result of which was nothing, now this is very curious, to be plain sir, it is the wish and will of Mr Ringgold to trifle with me from time to time without any real foundation to build upon—I would humbly desire you at this time to render me that justice that is in the sight of *God* and man due me, I ask no more to whom can I go but you, I know not   the gratitude of a great nation has placed you at the head of affairs, to render to evry citizen that justice that has ben long held from them by their cruler oppressors, my humble opinion is and it is the opinion of several others that Mr Ringgold has made u[se] of this mony for his private purpo[se] and thereby wishes to deprive of support [a] large and helpless family. I ask not for charity, but justice, notwithsta[nding] to many evil tales Mr Ringgold may attempt to offor without the least shaduow of evidence I pray you wi[ll] take this petiton seriously into consideration and render strict an[d] impartial Justice I ask no more[.] with due Respect I [. . .] your &c

Elizabeth William[s]

[Endorsed by AJ:] The sec of state will [. . .] into the case of Mrs. Williams, and the Marshal—The Marshal states that the record will shew that she is not entitled to her demand against him, & that he is not liable for this debt—call, if you please, for the record, & make report to me of the facts of this case, and your opinion of the Justice of her claim. A. Jackson.

ALS, DNA-RG 59 (M179-67). Tench Ringgold (1776–1844) was marshal for the District of Columbia, 1818–31. Elizabeth Williams was the widow of Thomas Williams (c1768–1825), an Irish immigrant blacksmith. In 1818 Thomas posted $300 bond for a horse thief named George Ackle. Ackle fled and Williams's bond was forfeited. To offset the debt, Williams did $285 worth of ironwork for Ringgold on a wall around the jail. After President Monroe granted Williams a remittance of the forfeiture in 1821, Williams asked for payment for his work, but Ringgold refused. Elizabeth Williams petitioned Congress for redress in February 1830 (*HRRep* 188, 21st Cong., 1st sess., Serial 200). An act of May 29 awarded her $285.

To Stephen Simpson

Washington May 4th, 1829

SIR—

You letter marked confidential April 30th. 1829 has been received. I had supposed the letters of Major Lewis, and Donelson would have proved satisfactory as to the friendly feelings which were entertained towards you; and for the present that things would have rested there. Finding it not to be the case, and that in connexion with you own complaints, the name, and remarks of Mr. Miller of Tennessee, are obtruded upon me in your Letter, I can be at no loss to draw the conclusion, that you and he have been actuated by similar motives; and because I did not forthwith appoint persons to office, as you and he believed I showed, that therefore your enmity is to flow as a consequence. Those who pretend to be friends, little understand me, if they have pursuaded themselves that I am to be operated upon, by any such considerations: *my own time and manner of doing things, now,* as *has ever been the case,* WILL BE MY RULE OF ACTION *I assure you.*

You charge me to be UNDER THE INFLUENCE OF MR. INGHAM; it is quite a modest imputation, and one that would merit no consideration, had you manner of addressing me been different. JUSTICE TO HIM *compels me* to say that IN NO INSTANCE DID HE EVER ATTEMPT ANY SUCH A THING AS YOU HAVE IMPUTED. There is not an appointment at Philadelphia, *one excepted* which as far as I am advised, and do believe, WAS THE FIRST CHOICE OF MR. INGHAM; *and had you* REALLY KNOWN AS MUCH ABOUT THIS GENTLEMAN AS YOU PROFESS this fact would have suggested itself to you. But what of those appointments, with which you are pleased to find so much fault? *Are they not all of them,* HONEST AND CAPABLE MEN? And *if so of what consequence can it be what* HAS BEEN THEIR POLITICAL OPINIONS. The *country requires faithful* agents, and these being obtained I shall feel quite contented and happy, although some may be found who will complain. All I have to say is, be it so.

It is altogether unnecessary for you, to talk further of *my fame and success;* and of your efforts to maintain both. Whatever you have done under the government of principle, has been well done, and your country for it, may feel itself your debtor,—what may have been the result of motive, and self is for yourself to appreciate. Upon this, can only remark, *that I was at home,—the Hermitage, where it was my highest ambition to continue. Contrary to any wish ensertained by me, my name was brought before the country.* Mr. Miller, whom you have named, was one who commenced it, and you supported it, acting as you have both asserted and maintained, upon principle. I regret to find, and it is painful to me to admit, that both of you have been actuated by other considerations then to serve those great Republican principles, which were professed as your rule of action. Give me leave to say, that office when demanded, as the consideration of rendered service, stands stripped of all the honour that should attach, and which only can attach, when bestowed apart from such demand presented and pressed.

I have thought it right and proper to make this reply to you,—extorted by your own reiterated complaints and letters,—*presented in the most objectionable and dictatorial form.* You must cease to think you have done any thing for me, or to serve me.—If in your exertions any thing shall arise to benefit the nation, then you will be entitled to its thanks, and *to mine also, and your reward remain I hope, in whatever may follow.* But when the contest is ended to insult me, is neither congenial with my feelings, nor is it in accord with that action which *professes to lean itself upon principle and the general good.* It is impossible therefore under a review of the circumstances, for me to refrain asking you to *forbear any further communication to me, until you* can conclude to write with that *propriety and becoming moderation, which is at all times becoming.* Until this can be the case, you will be good enough to trouble me with no further communications. I am thankful to my friends for *their kindness and good opinion,* and shall ever be glad of their suggestions on public matters; but cannot feel any obligation when they become dictatorial and authoritative. I am, sir, very respectfully, Your most ob't. serv't.

ANDREW JACKSON

Printed, Philadelphia *Pennsylvania Whig,* December 21, 1831 (mAJs). Simpson, then editor of the *Whig,* printed this letter within an article series entitled "Illustrations of Jacksonism."

To James P. Turner

Washington May 4th 1829

Sir,

Mr James Allison, principal deputy surveyor for the S En district of Louisiana having forwarded a complaint to me that he had been turned out of office without sufficient cause, and having accompanied his complaint with the most respectable vouchers of good conduct and attention to duty, it becomes necessary for me to call your attention to the subject, and require forthwith from you a report of the causes which led to his removal.

Among the vouchers alluded to is the following affidavit of Mr A B Sterritt, stating "that you had been directed by George Graham commissioner of the Genl Land Office to discharge James Allison, principal deputy surveyor of the South Eastern district of La, and to appoint another in his stead, and in case of refusal to do so you would be removed from office yourself. And that in compliance with this order you had appointed William Fulson to the office of principal deputy surveyor."[1] This information Mr Sterritt says he obtained from you, and in regard to it, it may be well to remark that Mr Graham denies having issued such order. very respectfull &

(signed) Andrew Jackson

This letter was sent sealed to Mr Graham, with a request that he would forward it to the surveyer Genl Mr Turner.

Andrew J. Donelson

LC, DLC (60). Turner (1782–1843) was appointed surveyor of public lands for Mississippi and Louisiana by President Adams in 1828. His predecessor, George Davis, had appointed James Allison of Tennessee as principal deputy surveyor for the southeastern district of Louisiana in 1827. On October 3, 1828, Turner informed Graham that he was removing Allison for "inattention to the duties of the Office" (DNA-RG 49, M1329-4). On April 25 AJ forwarded Allison's complaint of his dismissal to Graham. Graham replied to AJ on April 28 that Turner was authorized by law to select his deputies, and that while he (Graham) had previously complained of inefficiencies in the surveyor's office and ordered the removal of incompetent deputies, he had not instructed Turner to dismiss Allison (DNA-RG 49, M25-23). Meanwhile, Turner wrote Graham on April 7, accusing Allison of making fraudulent locations of land claims (M1329-4). Graham showed the letter to AJ, and AJ ordered that Turner substantiate and Allison respond to the charges. Graham accordingly on May 5 wrote to Allison (M25-23) and also to Turner, enclosing with the latter this sealed letter from AJ (DNA-RG 49, M27-4). Turner responded directly to AJ on May 29 (below).

1. Alexander B. Sterrett (b. 1787), a deputy surveyor in the southeastern district of Louisiana and brother-in-law of Jim Bowie, was later sheriff of Shreveport, La. William Fulsom (c1789–1842) of West Feliciana, La., resigned as principal deputy surveyor in July.

From Joseph Scott

Bellefonte State of Alabama Jackson County
May 4th 1829

Andrew Jackson President of the United States—

When the suffrages of a great and powerful people called you to the highest office known in the annals of nations, I had not the least idea of obtruding myself upon your notice, as an applicant for any office of honor or emolument.

But my situation in life is changed and I hope it is for my advantage—

It is my desire to fill the office of district attorney for the United States for North Alabama—

The gentleman Mr Thornton who now holds this office is an Adams man and the office was confered on him by the firm Adams, Clay &

Co—This office is a *sinecure* and the friends of the "*Milatary Chieftain*" had as well have it as his enemies.[1]

If there is any merit in being the warm and desided friend of Gen Jackson, I shall be treated with respect in this my application for public confidence—

From principle I have adhered to you and your friends   In Knoxville Tennessee my vote was always Counted in the day of battle, on the side of democracy and reformation—I may likewise add that I have not a relation in Virginia *Kentucky* or Tennessee, who have ever given the least countenance to the circulators of Coffin-handbills and other slanders which prudence and respect for your feelings forbids me to mention—

It is my deliberate conviction that the friends of a corrupt coalition deserve no quarters—Besides the removal of Mr Thornton would neither injure *you* nor the *government*—

If I should obtain the object of my ambition, it will be the means in all probability of opening to my view scenes of wealth prosperity and distinction—For "*Their is a tide in the affairs of men which taken at the flood leads on to fortune*"[2]   But if I should fail in this application, it is my sincere desire that the present incumbent be turned out and some worthy friend of yours take his place and if the idea is prohibited that I shall never "walk abroad" in the fields of promise and the gardens of pleasure, I shall still find consolation—It is this. I shared in the glorious political acheivement in putting down men who came into power by fraud, and who wished to sustain themselves by falshood—

In fine: This is the first letter I have ever written to any man high in authority. Perhaps I have said some things amiss: If I have; you will excuse the impetuosity inherited from my fathers—yours with sincerity

Joseph Scott

Mr Eaton will lay before you some evidence of my charater and qualifications—[3]

Jo Scott

I have been settled and been living in this County for the last five months
Jo Scott

ALS, DNA-RG 59 (M639-21). Scott (b. 1802) was the son of Tennessee judge Edward Scott of Knoxville. Adams had appointed Harry Innes Thornton (1797–1861) district attorney for northern Alabama in 1826. AJ removed Thornton and appointed Scott on June 6.

1. Henry Clay had famously branded AJ a dangerous "military chieftain" in justifying his support for Adams in the 1825 House election (*Clay Papers*, 4:45).

2. Shakespeare, *Julius Caesar*, 4.3.252–3.

3. On April 25, Scott had written Eaton that he had been a lawyer for five years and that his father was a political and personal friend of AJ (M639-21).

From Samuel Delucenna Ingham

New Hope 8th May 29

my dear sir

I had the pleasure of receiving Mr Donelsons letter of the 3rd yesterday—and am exceedingly gratified with the information that you are disposed to appoint my very worthy friend Mr Craig to the superintendence of the Patent office, altho I feel perfectly confident that he will do credit to your administration, yet I must regard it as an additional obligation of gratitude to the many you have already confered on me—I have written to Mr Craig agreeably to the suggestion of Mr Donelson, but since my letter went to the P. office it has occurred to me that the Patent office is considered as an appendage of the State Departt., I ought therefore in strictness to have waited for the communication to pass first from Mr Van Buren—It is not perhaps a matter of much importance but desiring to act with scrupulous delicacy for the feelings of my associates, I must beg the favor of you to mention the appointment of Mr Craig to him in such way as may be ~~thought~~ best—

I am busily engaged in putting my business in order for a long absence and hope to be able to leave here by the last of next week and reach Washington by the 20th or soon after—

accept my very best respects for yourself and family—and believe me sincerely yours

S D Ingham

The appointment of Mr Swartwout so far as I hear goes off very well, and public opinion is highly gratified with those in Philada.—

ALS, DNA-RG 59 (M639-5). John D. Craig (1766–1846) was an educator and scientist who had helped found the Ohio Mechanics Institute in Cincinnati in 1828. Thomas P. Jones (1774–1848), a former professor at the Franklin Institute in Philadelphia, had been superintendent of the Patent Office since April 1828. AJ selected Craig not knowing that Van Buren, believing the appointment lay with him, had promised Jones he would be retained. On May 14, AJ Donelson forwarded Ingham's letter to Van Buren (M639-5). Van Buren, in reply the same day, informed Donelson of the mishap and warned that "the Literati of Philadelphia & Virginia" would regard Jones's removal "as an act of Vandalism." Fearing "we shall be involved in some unpleasant embarrassment upon the subject," Van Buren asked that AJ "consider what can & ought to be done" (Donelson Papers, DLC).

From Henry Mason Morfit

Washington 8 May 1829.

Sir

Mr *Cary Selden* Naval Storekeeper at this place has within the last few days felt much apprehension in consequence of a report that there is an individual making great exertions to obtain his Office   Whether there is any truth in the rumor he cannot Say, but a duty to his family as well as a desire to place himself in the true position before the President has induced him to call on me as an old friend, a long resident of this City, and a member of the Jackson party to express whatever opinion I may entertain of him

I have known this gentleman for twenty years during all which time both in our native State Virginia and in this District he has maintained in every respect the character of a gentleman a man of business & integrity; and my intimacy with him has been of that kind that no deviation could have taken place without its being known to me.

As regards his political course I may say it has been entirely neutral with the single exception that the fact of having derived his present Office from Mr Adams created that fair feeling towards his benefactor which is always due from gratitude

The system of removing political opponents as called for by our party I know should be universal, nor would I suffer private friendship to inter-fere in making any individual exemption, but when an honourable man is placed in the situation of owing an obligation there is some excuse if his moral feelings influence his judgment and induce the simple expression of thankfulness to the hand that has sustained him   Thus far I believe and no farther has Mr Selden gone in any of his expressions and if the circum-stance of mingling temperance and propriety of conduct can entitle a man to the friendly considerations of our party Mr Selden has placed himself in the situation to merit them. Respectfully

Henry M Morfit

ALS, DNA-RG 45 (13-0265). Selden (c1783–1843), appointed in 1826, retained his position until his death.

From Lucius Bolles

Washington May 9. 1829

Sir,

By treaties with the Osage and Kanza tribes of Indians, lands have been reserved for education purposes, to be applied under the direction of the President of the U.S.[1] The Baptist Convention for the U.S. have authorized me to inform you, that in the application of those lands to their object, they wod be glad to be honoured with the trust.

Their views relative to the collocation of the tribes west of the state of Missouri & territory of Arkansaw, perfectly agree with those of the Government, an expression of which they made to Congress in a memorial in 1827.8.[2] Mr. McCoy who accompanied the late exploring expedition, has, in conjunction with another agent, been appointed by them, again to visit that country, to select a suitable situation for the settlement of the fruit of their schools, & for education establishments, & to procure such information relative to the country as may be serviceable to the next Congress.[3]

They beg leave respectfully to submit to your consideration, the propriety of establishing within the Indian territory, so called, a superintendency, that may tend to the judicious location of the tribes, which may be settled there. They would further suggest with due respect, the probability, that shod an expedition be sent next spring to the Camanches & others in the west, at present at war with the Osages, menacing to emigrating Indians and mischievous on the Santa Fee road, they wod be rendered peacable.[4]

For reasons for the above suggestions relative to a superintendency, and to the expedition, they wod respectfully refer to pages, 19, 20, 21, & 22 of the Report to the Secretary of War, of Mr McCoy, herewith submitted.[5] With the highest respect I am Sir Your Obt Servt

Lucius Bolles, Cor Sec'y

[Endorsed by AJ:] The application of the Baptist society to have an agency established within the Osage & Kansa tribes of Indians & to have the land reserved for the education or sold—This to be attended to—& a report to be hand from the Comissioner of the land office on the subject of those lands, & the sec of war.

ALS, DNA-RG 75 (M234-774). Isaac McCoy, *History of Baptist Indian Missions* (Washington, 1840), pp. 385–86. The Baptist General Triennial Missionary Convention, which met at Philadelphia from April 29 to May 7, 1829, sanctioned this communication and appointed Bolles (1779–1844) and two others to present it to AJ in person. A minister from Salem, Mass., Bolles served as corresponding secretary of the Baptist General Convention for Foreign Missions from 1826 to 1842.

1. The treaties, signed June 2 and 3, 1825, at St. Louis, called for the sale of fifty-four and thirty-six sections of land to fund the education of Osage and Kansas children, respectively.

2. In December 1827, the Baptist General Missionary Convention petitioned Congress for permission to form, under federal patronage, a settlement west of the Mississippi for Indians who wished to emigrate, with land to be allocated for missionary establishments. An April 1828 report by the House Committee on Indian Affairs approved the Convention's "benevolent designs" but declined framing a specific measure.

3. The 1829 Triennial Missionary Convention appointed Isaac McCoy (1784–1846) and Johnston Lykins (1800–1876), both Baptist missionaries, to examine lands west of Missouri and the Arkansas Territory for possible settlement. In 1828 McCoy had accompanied a similar expedition sponsored by Congress.

4. The thousand-mile Santa Fe road, used primarily by traders, connected the Missouri River with the Mexican province of New Mexico. Depredations on the road were frequent; in 1828, thirty-three Americans were killed by Comanche and other Indians.

5. Bolles enclosed *HRRep* 87, 20th Cong., 2d sess. (Serial 190), which included McCoy's report of January 29, 1829, to Secretary of War Peter B. Porter urging the creation of a western Indian superintendency.

From Thomas Scott

Greenville Jefferson Co. Mississippi
May 10— 1829—

Sir,

As an injured citizen, I have thought proper to lay before you a statement of the following facts respecting the depredations of a band of Cherokees, and to request that such proceedings may be ordered thereupon as you may judge just and expedient. About thirty six years ago William Scott a resident of this country was returning from S. Carolina in company of several other persons. As they were descending the Tennessee river, they were attacked near the Muscle Shoals by a band of Cherokees and were all murdered.[1] The Indians possessed themselves of their slaves and other property. Of these slaves & property thus taken, the heirs, of whom I am one, could never obtain any certain information as to what had been done with them,[2] till about seven months ago, when a *converted* Cherokee voluntarily gave the following information respecting them—viz—that several of the negroes taken as aforesaid were long since sold to the whites, but that a considerable part of them and their descendants, about 60, are still in possession of some wealthy half breeds living in the Cherokee nation on the Arkansaw river.[3] This communication he made solely, as he said, that justice might be done to the injured. There are two other Cherokees who are also willing to give testimony to the same purport, one of whom was at the massacre. It may be necessary to observe that this information was given under promise of secrecy, lest the life of the informant should be put in jeopardy. Besides this testimony of the Indians, and what may be obtained from the old negroes, some of whom are still living, we can prove our right to these slaves by persons living in this country. The principal reason why I have thought proper to make this communication to you at this time in particular is this—I have just seen an account in a paper published at Little Rock Arkansaw Terr. stating "that a citizen of that country had set up a claim to some of the negroes taken on the Tennessee river upwards of thirty years ago, and that he had forcibly taken eight of them from the Indians—and that the Indians were about to apply to the government to have the slaves restored to them."[4] And I supposed that if the Indians should apply to the executive for redress, Commissioners would be appointed to examine into the affair, and that now would be a proper time to make my grievances and the justice of my claim known to the government. This statement I submit to your consideration, with the advice and consent of the other heirs, and request that Commissioners be, if they have not already been, appointed to examine this business, before whom the different claimants whether whites or Indians should be cited to appear and make proof of their title. We wish not merely to obtain the slaves still in the nation, but also an indemnification for their services, an equitable price for those that have been sold to the whites & the value of the other property taken from the boats at the time of the massacre. Whatever course of proceedings you may order concerning this business, I wish to have timely information thereof, and of the time when and the place where the Commissioners are to meet, if any should be, or have been, appointed. I have the honour to be very Respectfully yours &c

Thomas Scott
Son & Heir of the aforesaid William Scott

P.S. Who "the citizen of Arkansaw" is or on what title he founds his claim to some of the negroes, the paper does not state. I am inclined to think as most probable that he is an heir of one of the persons who were killed at the same time with William Scott. T.S.

P.S. The heirs once applied to Congress for a remuneration for these negroes, but their petition was never finally acted on, their agent Alexander Scott of S. Carolina having died before the business was brought to a close, and a mass of evidence respecting it is still in the Office of the Indian Agent at Washington or in that of the Committee of Indian Affairs. It was before Congress from 1818 to '22.[5] TS

ALS, DNA-RG 75 (M234-77).

1. The party led by William Scott included James and John Pettigrew of the Darlington District of South Carolina, three white women, four white children, and some twenty black slaves. They were attacked around June 9, 1794.

2. Scott's status as a claimant was contested by Samuel Nesmith. Nesmith held that William Scott's purchase of the slaves from the estate of Alexander McKnight before the massacre was invalid, and that he as McKnight's heir was entitled to any redress for their loss.

3. In 1832 Edwin T. Clark, an agent for the Nesmith and Pettigrew families, reported on about eighty blacks linked to the captured slaves. Some were freed and many dispersed, including two in Arkansas Territory, seven in the Chickasaw Nation, six in Missouri, and five in Mississippi.

4. Scott paraphrased an item from the Little Rock *Arkansas Gazette* of January 20. In December 1828, Jesse Burton of Crawford County, Arkansas Territory, led an armed party into the Cherokee country, seizing eight slaves valued at $3,300. Cherokee subagent Pearson Brearley reported the episode to acting territorial governor Robert F. Crittenden, who ordered the slaves returned. They were restored early in 1829 (*TPUS*, 20:821).

5. Alexander Scott of South Carolina was a nephew of William Scott. Congress rejected a petition for relief of Alexander Scott and other heirs in 1805, reasoning that the government was not "bound to guaranty the possession of negro slaves to individuals passing for no public purpose through the country of hostile savages." A law of July 14, 1832, authorized payment of $9,750 plus interest to the Pettigrew heirs and $2,120 plus interest to the McKnight heirs.

To Martin Gordon

Washington 11th. May 1829

Dr. Sir,

Suffer me to call to your attention the situation of my friend Co Peire, and to request if there be any cumfortable office within your gift in the customs of New Orleans that you may bestow it upon him. The situation of weigher or gauger would, as I am informed be acceptable to him. yr. &c

Andrew Jackson

LC, DLC (60). Henry Duvivier Peire (c1777–1848) of Louisiana had served under AJ at New Orleans. On May 16 Gordon offered him a position as weigher or gauger, but Peire declined both, explaining in a letter to AJ that they were "entirely out of my line and indeed incompatible with my habits." He asked instead to be made consul at Havre or Havana. On June 15 AJ introduced Peire to Van Buren as "a particular friend of mine" and urged his appointment to a consulate.

From Samuel Houston

Little Rock A. T.
11th May 1829.

Genl Jackson,

Tho' an unfortunate, and doubtless, the most unhappy man now living, whose honor, so far as depends upon himself, is not lost, I can not brook the idea of your supposing me capable, of an act that would not adorn, rather than blot the escutcheon of human nature! This remark is induced, by the fact, as reported to me, that you have been assured that I meditated an enterprize calculated to injure, or involve my country, and to compromit the purity of my motives. I do not distinctly understand the extent of the information, or its character, but I Suppose it was intended to complete my ruin in irremediable devastation of character. To you any suggestions would be idle, and on my part, as man; ridiculous—You Sir, have witnessed my conduct from boyhood thro life—You saw me, draw my first sword from its scabbard—you saw me breast the fore front of Battle, and you saw me, encounter successive dangers, with cheeks unblenched, and with nerves, which had no ague in them! You have seen my private, & my official acts—to these I *refer* you—To what woud they all amount, and for what would I live? but for my own honor, and the honor and safety of my country? Nothing! And now that domestic misfortune; of which I say nothing; and about which there are ten thousand imputed slanders; has come upon; as a black cloud at noonday I am to be *hunted down!* What am I? an Exile from my home; and my country, a houseless unshelter'd wanderer, among the Indians! Who has met, or who has sustained, such sad and unexpected reverses? Yet I am myself, and will remain, the proud and honest man! I will love my country; & my friends—You Genl. will ever possess my warmest love and most profound veneration! In return I ask nothing—I would have nothing, within your power to give me! I am satisfied with natures gifts—*They* will supply natures wants!!

When in this section of the country if in my power to give information at any time of matters, that concern either your feelings, or your administration I will be proud & happy to do so, and in my *individual* capacity, if I can keep peace among the Indians, & between them & the *whites* I will cheerfully do it. If I find your favors *abused,* and injustice done to the Indians, by their agents, I will feel bound, to let you know facts.

Two days since I arrived here I have had the pleasure of seeing Colo Crittenden the acting Governor of the Territory, and I am happy to assure you that, my opinion in relation to many reports about his hostility to you have changed. On the subject I have heard him speak, more than once. He is satisfied that he will be; if he is not already removed from office. And he says that he has ever; and does at this moment retain for you the most perfect respect & veneration; and that he has ever since Seminole campaign, cherishd feelings not less than those of filial regard towards you. He has no doubt but many representations, have been made to you respecting him—and he says that "any representations, which may have been made contrary to these sentiments, are unqualifiedly, false and designed for mischievous purposes."[1]

In two hours I will leave here, for my old friend Jollys, of the Cherokees; and will from thence start on a Buffaloe (summer) hunt; so soon as I am rested! If at any time you should feel, for me the personal regard that woud induce you to write to me, I will get it from Cherokee Agency.[2] You have much employment, and little time for private purposes, and I woud not tax you, with the labour of writing; unless it is perfectly convenient—tho' I will always be happy to hear from you. I need not tell how sincerely and truly I wish you a successful and glorious administration of the Goverment of the U. States.

May you live long, and my your days be as happy, as your life has been glorious, and useful to your country. Farewell

Sam Houston

[Endorsed by AJ:] Governor Houston letter—to be answered—answered 21rst. of June 1829—

ALS, DLC (72). *Writings of Sam Houston,* 1:132–34.
1. Robert F. Crittenden (1797–1834) had served under AJ in the 1818 Seminole campaign. He was appointed secretary of Arkansas Territory in 1819, and as such became acting governor on George Izard's death in 1828. AJ had already appointed William S. Fulton to replace him.
2. John Jolly or Oo-loo-te-ka (1776–1838), Houston's adoptive father, was a principal chief of the Western Cherokees. He resided near the mouth of the Illinois River in present-day Oklahoma. The Cherokee agency was located near Fort Smith in Crawford County, Arkansas Territory.

From William Robinson

Washington May 11 1829

D Sir,

I returned to this place from Westmoreland County yesterday. On scaning over the different dismissals, and appointments since I last had the pleasure of seeing you, I have become if possible more anxious to be numbered among your auxiliaries. Remembring the old proverb "Spare to speak, and spare to speed" I have resolved once more to call your attention to the subject. I have the vanity to believe I am both "honest and capable" to discharge the duties of any situation already applied for, or that may have been suggested by yr. self. I am sure you never had a more devoted friend from the moment you were announced as a candidate for the Presidency; and indeed before that time, I defended you from the foul aspersions of your implacable enemies, with the most *untired* zeal, and often declared in public and in private that your merits and qualifications when better known, would ensure the event wch. has taken place. I have innumerable witnesses to testify for me: they are the people of my County & Dist. and you may have heard of me as your defender, and friend throughout the contest   I was among the first movers of the Fredericksburg Convention, and was appointed one of the delegates from Fairfax County   It was there that effectual efforts were made to organize a party friendly to your election, and it was then, and there determined, that a Central Committe should be established at Fredericks.g. and auxiliary Committies in every county through out the state of Virginia, to ensure the wished for result, and to counter act the diabolical falshoods wch. had been industriously circulated by an organized party of men, to ruin your reputation by base and dishonourable means.[1] Soon after the Convention at Fredericksg I removed to the County of Westmoreland and found no efficient means or that any exertions had been made to further the cause; but this did not abait my ardour and perseverance, and it was with *great* difficulty I could get together a sufficient number of respectable Gentlemen to form a committe of correspondence, & vigilence   No expence, or exertion was spared on my part, in Conjunction with a few choice spirits (among that number there was no one more conspicuous than Doct. Rob: Murphy: the most talented, and eloquent Gentleman in the County; and for his zeal in your behalf no one has been more persecuted and slandered.) to convince the people of your merits &c &c. We did succeed, we did triump contrary *to all* expectation.[2] For my activity and zeal Governor Giles did me the honour to appoint me as one of the inspectors of the electoral election, and I never did leave my post until I had fulfil'd my trust.[3] I do believe if the same ardour had been evinced in the other counties of the Dist. there would have been majorities in all.

Your notice of me among the number of your appointments will be highly gratifying; besides an office at this time will open a way by wch. I shall be enabled to impart the little means I have in another quarter, and without an accident, will I trust remuncrate me for the many losses I have sustained. I hope you will pardon my too frequent importunities. I am conscious I intrude on your time, but my anxiety to receive some testimonial of *your* confidence must plead my apology—I shall feel myself at liberty as a friend to pay my respects to you in person at hours of your leasure; but I shall never again presume to address you on this subject wch. so much occupies my mind at present. I leave it to your decision without further effort to inspire you with a belief that I am worthy or that I am entitled to your consideration   My Sister Mrs. Ann W. Rose the Mother of Doct. Wm R Rose came up on a visit to our friends in this vicinity. It would gladen her heart to see her son in some office on a Salery sufficient to support him as his health is too delicate to practice his profession.[4] On presenting your kind regards to my mother, she was pleased to say, she felt her self much honoured by your recollection of her, and can never feel sufficiently grateful for the kind solicitude, and attentions shewn by yourself and Mrs. Jackson to her Grand Daughter Mrs. Lee.[5] The mention of this venerated ladies name will call to your remembrance an epoch in your life truly to be lamented; but let it be a consolation to you my Dr Sir, to know that Mrs. Jacksons life had been *truly* exemplary. She filled the various relations that appertained to her, as became a Christian; and her numerous duties as a wife, a relation and a friend were uniformly discharged under the benign influence of that religion, in wch. she "lived, moved; & had her being."[6] My prayer is that you may be happy: and that the close of your administration may inspire the people wth. that admiration, and gratitude, in a *greater degree* than ever has been evinced by them for your *past* and *most distinguished services*

Accept the reiterated assuran[ces] of my respect and esteem[.] your most Ob. St.

Wm. Robinson

ALS, DLC (37). Robinson (1782–1857), a Virginia planter, had in 1824 presented AJ with a pair of pistols once belonging to George Washington. According to Thomas L. McKenney's *Memoirs* (pp. 204–6), AJ in 1829 offered Robinson the post of superintendent of Indian affairs, but he declined it as too demanding. In 1833 he was appointed a clerk in the War Department, where he served until 1839.

1. Robinson was one of two delegates representing Fairfax County at the July 28, 1824, Jackson convention at Fredericksburg, Va.

2. Robinson, Robert Murphy, and seventeen others served on Westmoreland County's Jackson corresponding committee in 1827–28. AJ narrowly outpolled Adams in the county, 101 votes to 95.

3. William Branch Giles (1762–1830) was Virginia's governor, 1827–30.

4. Robinson had written AJ on March 12 seeking an appointment as librarian for his nephew, William Robinson Rose (d. 1861).

5. Robinson's mother was Margaret Williamson Robinson (b. 1756). Ann Robinson McCarty Lee (1797–1840), Henry Lee's wife, was Robinson's niece.

6. Acts 17:28.

To Thomas Miller

Washington May 13th. 1829.

Dr. Sir,

I have recd. your letter of the 4th inst., and must plead my numerous & varied engagements as an apology for not responding to it at an earlier period.

The remarks you have offered, require no explanation or apology on your part—they are of that friendly, frank character as to deserve my thanks.

Mr. Tazwells reasons for declining the mission offered him, were of so candid a nature, that while the loss of services so valuable were matter of regret, it was impossible for me to do otherwise than appreciate motives which induced his decision.

Upon other matters touched upon in your letter, relative to the appointment of Editors to office, I am constrained to disagree with you. It is true as suggested, that the press being an important essential in the maintenance of our republican institutions, its freedom & purity can not be too carfully guarded. But while we are reasoning upon the policy of a measure, it is proper that all the circumstances in connection with it, should also be duly weighed. I agree with you, that considerations of no sort, neither hopes nor fears, should be held out by Government to Editors of papers, nor indeed to any description of men, to induce a course of conduct not sanctioned by principle, and by their unbiassed judgement. But is this the case under the present posture of affairs?

You will recollect that in the recent political contest it was said & truly said, to be a struggle between the virtue of the american people & the corrupting influence of executive patronage. By no act, by no solicitation of mine; and apart from any interference of myself, did the people in their kindness, present me as their candidate. The different presses of the country acting upon their own impulses, espoused one side or the other, as judgement or other causes operated.

Those who stept forward and advocated the question termed the side of the people, were apart of the people & differing only in this that they were the proprietors & conductors of the press—in many cases purchased by themselves expressly for the purpose of aiding in the "grand cause." And to what motive other than the love of country & the exercise of a sound judgement could their course be ascribed? I was not abroad seeking popularity, nor did I tramel or commit myself by pledges to reward partizans in the event of success—no one has ever accused me of doing so, & hence we are bound to believe that they were disinterested in their support of me. Many maintained & believed, and especially the politicians of the country, that no efforts of the people, would be found sufficient to counteract the subsidizing influence of government. Upon this ground then, whatever motive could arise founded on self, was of a character to invite chiming in with the powers that were then in existence. Yet many Editors did not, & hence can we resist the impression that they were actuated by the same generous & patriotic impulse that the people were?

If these suggestions be founded in truth, why should this class of citizens be excluded from offices to which others, not more patriotic, nor presenting stronger claims as to qualification may aspire?

To establish such a precedent would I apprehend, have a powerful tendency to place the control and management of the press into the hands of those who might be destitute of principle; & who prosecuting their profession only as means of livelihood & lucre, would become mercenary, & to earn their penny would abandon principle, which ought to be their rule of action.

The road to office & preferment, being accessible alike to the rich & the poor, the farmer & the printer—honesty, probity & capability constituting the sole & exclusive test, will I am persuaded, have the happiest tendency to preserve, unimpaired, freedom of political action; change it & let it be known that any class or portion of citizens are & ought to be proscribed, (and) discontent, and dissatisfaction will be engendered. Extend it to editors of papers, and I reiterate, that men of uncompromising & sterling integrity will no longer be found in the ranks of those who edit our public journals—I submit it then, to your good sense & calm reflection, what must be the inevitabl result of things in this country, when the press & its freedom shall become so depressed & degraded as to be found altogether under the control of men wanting in principl & the proper feelins of men! I am very respectfully yr. mo. obt. sevt.

Draft, DLC (37). Thomas Miller was a Powhatan County, Va., legislator. The draft is mistakenly marked "T. L. Miller," evidently from a misreading of Miller's "Th Miller" signature.

From Martin Van Buren

W. May 14 1829

My dear Sir

I send you a very interesting dispatch from Mr Barbour.[1] Also a private letter which you will readily perceive was, not written for your eye but the perusal of which so far as it goes to shew the sound state of public opinion in NY. will gratify you & the other parts will throw some light upon that (to strangers) incomprehensible subject, NYork politics; but in respect to which the truth is known by all at home but they will not let it be known abroad. Mr Throop is now our acting Gov—he has been my intimate & confidential friend from our boyhood & if I am not egregiously disappointed, we shall elect him Govr. at the next election agt. all opposition by at least twenty thousand majority. You will be amused to find how prone all my friends are to suspect me of too great liberality to my opponents whilst they on the other hand wish it to be believed that I am intolerant. Throop is a cool clear headed honest man. Jenkins whose appointment appears to be only difficulty he has met with since I left NYork is a respectable man well calculated for the situation for which Gov. Throop nominated him. Still the prejudices arising from the repeated charges to which Mr Clinton unfortunately for him & them exposed his friends, are so strong that the Senate; two thirds of whom are the Govs devoted friends would not act upon his appointment[2]—very truly yours

M. Van Buren

P.S. Please to destroy Gov Throops letter when you have read it—

[Endorsed by AJ:] The letter burnt as directed A. J.

ALS, DLC (72). Enos Thompson Throop (1784–1874), elected lieutenant governor of New York in 1828, assumed the governorship on Van Buren's resignation in March. He was reelected in 1830.

1. James Barbour, previously Adams's secretary of war, had been appointed minister to Britain in 1828. His March 29 dispatch from London offered a wide-ranging commentary on affairs in Europe (DNA-RG 59, M30-32).

2. Elisha Jenkins (1769–1848) was a former mayor of Albany and ally of New York governor De Witt Clinton. Throop had nominated him for bank commissioner.

From Preserved Fish et al.

To ANDREW JACKSON, President of the United States of America, the memorial of the subscribers, a committee appointed at a general meeting of the citizens of New York having claims upon France for spoliations committed on their property, respectfully showeth:

THAT during the late general war in Europe, the merchants of New York, in common with the merchants of other parts of the United States, were engaged in the shipping business and carrying trade. In the prosecution of this business, they endeavoured strictly to conform to the laws of nations, and of the respective countries with which they traded, and confidently relied upon the protection, which every civilized nation feels bound to extend while engaged in their lawful pursuits. It is unnecessary, to state in detail the measures adopted by the great belligerent parties to that war against the commerce of neutrals, by multiplying the pretexts of seizure and confiscation. The official records of the government show, that they were carried to an extent of which history had not, until then, afforded an example, and were sought to be justified upon principles which no civilized nation had before dared to avow. It cannot now be doubted, that the measures to which we refer, were intended chiefly to operate upon the commerce of these United States, and to control the policy of their government. The grasping spirit of European monopoly attempted to impose upon us new shackles in place of the colonial fetters that had been shaken off, and displayed itself in continual efforts to cripple the commerce it could not prohibit—lessen the resources it was not permitted to appropriate—and retard the growth of the prosperity it had no longer the power to crush.

After a long submission to a series of aggressions continually advancing in mischief and enormity, the period finally arrived when it was decided, that further acquiescence would be a surrender of national independence. The last remedy for national injuries was resorted to against one of the belligerent parties, and the settlement of our claims upon Great Britain placed on the arbitrament of arms. By this extreme remedy, the accounts between the governments were closed; but the beneficial effects of the contest are still felt, not only in the elevation of the national character, but in the security of our fellow citizens, when on the ocean, from the visitation of armed vessels, and in the silent abolition of pretensions which, if not expressly renounced, we venture to predict will not again be advanced.

The claims on Spain have also been enforced by the government, and satisfied by the cession of Florida.[1]

From France, however, one of the chief violators of our neutral rights, not the slightest redress has been obtained. Its government does not deny, that millions of dollars belonging to the citizens of the United States were appropriated to the use of the former government of that country. It does not deny, nor can it deny, that by the laws of nations, and by express treaty at the late restoration, the present government is bound to fulfil the obligations, and responsible for the public acts, of its predecessors; yet, notwithstanding this solemn obligation, not in a single instance has the Minister of the United States resident at that court been able to obtain satisfaction for the numerous spoliations upon our commerce. Twelve years of fruitless remonstrance and negotiation have elapsed, and redress has not only been withheld, but the representations of the United States have not been deemed worthy of a specific answer. The claims of the citizens of other countries for similar outrages have been acknowledged and paid; but those of our citizens, whether arising from the numerous seizures under the Berlin and Milan decrees; or originating in the sequestrations by France of American property in order to control the policy of this government; or in the wilful destruction of our vessels at sea without any pretext, are contemptuously rejected.

This preference for the claims of the European subjects over American citizens, has indeed been so strongly manifested, that it would seem as if the French government meant to inculcate, in the most striking manner, the maxim, that a nation which is wanting to itself, is not entitled to an equal measure of justice. Your Memorialists will not offer any comment on these facts.—The distinctions which they imply, the inferences which they justify, are deeply injurious to our national character, and call loudly for the energetic interposition of the government, to vindicate the honor of the country.—The fruitless efforts of resident Ministers have obtained nothing but neglect and insult—for in no other than an insulting light can be regarded the demand of France to connect the settlement of our claims, and the redress of insults offered to our flags, with her claim for the admission of her vessels into the ports of Louisiana upon the same footing as British vessels.

Your Memorialists will not here discuss the futility of the grounds upon which this claim has been preferred.

To prefer it under any circumstances, was to insult the sagacity and integrity of the American government; but to require its allowance, as an equivalent for our indisputable demand for justice, is trifling with its remonstrances, and is not so much an evasion of our claims as a denial of our rights.

No country which values its honor and independence, can submit to a connection between questions affecting national character, and those growing out of the construction of treaties.

It is this principle which every government, that, while respecting itself, has commanded the respect of other nations, has constantly asserted; and its surrender would imply a voluntary degradation, to which your Memorialists cannot suppose the government of a free people will ever submit.

The idea of co-ercing the United States into the admission of unfounded claims, by refusing to settle claims of the paramount nature of those of our citizens upon France, could only have originated in an erroneous estimate of the spirit of the American people, and the character of their government. France must have presumed, that the forbearance, too long extended to her arbitrary and unjustifiable course, was not yet exhausted: that a government, which had only resorted to unheeded remonstrance against the systematized plunder of its citizens; to neglected complaints on account of treaties violated and public law infringed; and to unanswered letters asking for the liquidation of undisputed claims, long after the subjects of every other civilized nation, and even of the piratical state of Algiers, had received full indemnity for similar losses, would never be driven from its submissive pacific policy, but would prefer a fruitless negotiation to an implicit assertion of its rights.[2]

It must have been believed, that a government which depended upon, and was regulated by, popular sentiment, would not venture to enforce the rights of your Memorialists by any manifestation of the national power. But even the proverbial forbearance of a republican government may be carried too far.

There are some injuries to which a nation cannot submit, without degradation and loss of honor. These wrongs cannot be estimated by any pecuniary standard. They refer directly to that national feeling which is the best support of the republic in great emergencies, and which has carried the country through the war of the revolution, and its subsequent conflicts for American rights, to an elevation among the powers of the earth, that induces its citizens to claim, with pride, the protection of their national character.

Your Memorialists cannot so far forget their character of petitioners, as to prescribe the measures which the dignity of the country, and the peculiar nature of their claims, would seem to require. Submitting themselves, however, entirely to the wisdom of the government, they may be permitted to suggest, that experience has demonstrated that nothing is to be gained or expected from a course of ordinary negotiation. An explicit and final answer, your Memorialists are compelled to believe, will not be obtained from the goverment of France, until a Minister shall be appointed, whose sole and special duty it shall be made, to enforce the demands of justice, that have so long been urged in vain.

> PRESERVED FISH.
> ABM. OGDEN.
> DAV. CLARKSON.
> GEO. GRISWOLD.
> J. BLUNT.
> LEWIS HAMERSLEY.

JAS. J. ROOSEVELT, Jr.
PETER A. JAY.
BENJ. BAILEY.

Printed, *New-York Evening Post*, May 15 (mAJs); *Niles*, May 23. Fish (1766–1846) and the other signers were prominent New York merchants. An April 22 public meeting chaired by Fish had authorized this memorial. Similar appeals were addressed to AJ from Portland, Maine, on May 4 and from Baltimore around May 19. Speaking for AJ, Van Buren replied to this and the Baltimore memorial on June 4, saying that the administration would vigorously pursue settlement of the spoliation claims, but through regular diplomatic channels rather than a special mission (DNA-RG 59, M40-21; *New-York Evening Post*, Jun 16).

1. In the 1819 Florida cession treaty, the U.S. assumed its citizens' claims against Spain up to $5 million.

2. In 1820 France had agreed to pay compensation for wheat supplied by Algerian merchants to the revolutionary Directory government in the 1790s.

To Hardy Murfree Cryer

Washington May 16th. 1829—

My Dr. Sir

Your kind letter of the 20th. ult. has been some days before me—The great press of business has prevented me from attending to it sooner, and even now I can only say to you as it regards our mutual friend Mr Gwinn that he had better remain where he is, untill you hear from me again.[1] There is more distressed people here, than any person could imagine who were not an eye witness to the various applications for relief—my feelings have been severely coroded by the various applications for relief, and as far as real charitable objects presented themselves, I have yielded my might to their relief—would you believe it, that a lady who had once rolled in wealth, but whose husband was overtaken by misfortune & reduced to want, and is, & has been an applicant for office, & well recommended, applied to me with tears in her eyes, soliciting relief, assuring me that her children was starving, & to buy them a morsal of bread she had to sell her thimble the day before—an office I had not to give, & my cash was nearly out, but I could not withold from her half of the pittance I had with me. I name these things to bring to your view, that from the extravagance of this place, how small a prospect is *$1000* pr anum for the support of a family here, & the moment they are out of office, starvation presents itself to the view—

We have not had leisure yet, to make the necessary arrangements of reform—we are progressing, and such is the press for office, & the distress here, that there are for the place of messengers (for the Departments) at least twenty applicants for each station, and many applicants who have been men of wealth & respectability—still if our friend Gwinn wishes to come on here, when we finally organise the Departments, and turn out the spies from our camp, I will preserve an office for him—but we are now having a thorough investigation, into the situation of all the Departments, and the enquiry will be made how many, if any clerks, can be dispensed with.

I wrote my overseer the other day on the subject of sending my mares to Stockholder—I would like to hear how many colts I have from Sir william—I learn that the Cotton mare, & Major Donelsons, has not proved with foal.[2]

In the day I am laboriously employed, and it is only when late in the night I retire to my chamber, that I have time to think of, or write to, my friends—It is then I feel the great weight of the late affliction of providence in the bereavement I have been visited with in the loss of my dear wife—I find myself a solitary mourner, deprived of all hope of happiness this side the grave, and often wish myself at the Hermitage there to spend the remnant of my days, & daily drop a tear on the tomb of my beloved wife, & be prepared, when providence wills it, to unite with her in the realms above—But providence has otherwise ordered, & to his will I must submit.

present me affectionately to your amiable wife & family & believe me yr friend

Andrew Jackson

ALS, THi (13-0336). Cryer (1792–1846), of Sumner County, Tenn., was a minister and horse-breeder. He married Elizabeth L. Rice (1794–1833).

1. Samuel Gwin (c1794–1838) was the son of James Gwin (1775–1841), a Methodist minister from Sumner County. In August he was given a $1000 clerkship in the Post Office Department at Washington.

2. Stockholder was a stallion belonging to Cryer. AJ had sent eight mares to Sir William, a stud horse in whom Cryer had an interest, for the 1828 breeding season. The "Cotton mare" was one of two sent to AJ by the horse-breeder Henry Cotten (d. 1828).

From Mushulatubbe

May the 16th. 1829 Choctaw Nat.

Dear friend and Brother

as I Consider it my Duty to write to you my best Respects to you and Inform you how myself and the people of My Nation Generally are gratified on hearing of your Elevation to the presidency I am the man that has Ever been willing to Do any thing that was Reasonable and in the bounds of my power when I was acting chief in my Nation to vissillitate your veiws or the Veiws of your Goverment when I was acting chief we made a treaty in the year of 1820 at Doaks Stand wherein there was a Stipulation Saying that I Should Receive annually from the Goverment of the United States one hundred and fifty Dollars During my Natural life which I have

Regularly Recd. Ever Since but now I understand I am not to Receive any more and that it is to be paid to the Acting Chief of the District I think his taking my office from me Dont give him any Claims to my money I have Ever Respected you as a brother we have been together in war and pease when you was Engageed in war with the Creek Indians I was always Subject to your order and willing to aid and assist you we were together in Washington City in 1824 where we were very friendly therefore my Dependance is on you to see that I get my Right one hundred and fifty Dollars is not much to a man that has plenty but a great Deal to me that has but little therefore I contend for my money that I know I ought to have I wish you to answer me as Quick as convenient. I am with Respect your most obedient Servt.

Mushuletubbee

I Certify the above to be truly Interpreted and wrote by me
M Mackey US Intr.[1]

ALS by proxy, DNA-RG 75 (M234-169). Mushulatubbe (d. 1838) had ruled the Northeastern district of the Choctaw Nation as one of its three so-called "Medal Chiefs." AJ had served as commissioner at the 1820 Treaty of Doak's Stand, by which the Choctaws exchanged lands in Mississippi for a tract west of the Mississippi River. Article Fourteen granted Mushulatubbe a lifetime annuity of $150. In a subsequent treaty at Washington in January 1825, a Choctaw delegation headed by Mushulatubbe traded a part of their western domain upon which whites had already settled for a perpetual $6,000 tribal annuity. Mushulatubbe was criticized for this, and in 1826 he was replaced as chief by his rival David Folsom. A $150 annuity payment was made to Mushulatubbe in July 1829.

1. Middleton Mackey, a native of South Carolina, served as interpreter for the Choctaw Nation.

From Martin Van Buren

W. May 18 1829

Dear Sir

Finding that Mr. Southard when he wrote his last letter was in possession of Watkins's Statement to the Navy Agent at Boston & reflecting upon your suggestion of the other evening Col. Hamilton & myself incline agt. putting any specific queries to Mr Southard; but think it best under the circumstances to send him a letter like the enclosed; if it should meet your views and those of the Secty. of the Navy.[1]

Every thing that was required of you has we think been already done, but as the object of the original letter was to give Mr S. an opportunity to explain—as he avows his willingness to do so but states his bad health &c as a reason why he does not come down & desires to be further informed and as the original letter was somewhat general we think it advisable to give him the charges; leav[ing] the fitness of his course, as to visiting the seat of govermt, & as to the chara[cter] of the information to be given (as it before stood) to his own choice and resting upon his own responsibility[.] your friend

M Van Buren

Navy Department
Wash. May 18 1829

Sir.

Your letter of the 10 Int.[2] has been submitted to the President—It is a source of regret that you should be prevented by any circumstances but particularly those to which you refer from availing yourself of the best if not the only adequate ~~sources of possessing yourself fully~~ means of acquiring a full knowledge of the acts of the late 4 Auditer which are made the subject of complaint

I am dircted by the President to say in reply to your enquiries that the charges against Tobias Watkins in relation to the warrnts of which a statement has been furnished you First That the same appear to have been fraudulently obtained and under the pretext that the money was for the public service when in fact it was for his own private purposes. *Secondly* That in the perpetration of these frauds & for the purpose of concealment—he withdrew from the office vouchers connected with the transactions & necessary to their being correctly understood—suppressed information intended to be given & which by the Course of business ought to have been given to the officers of the Government who were made accountable for the said monies—and falsified by altering and obliterating Items of the orignal accunts of those officers which had been sent to this department for settlement

ALS, DNA-RG 45 (M124-118). Acting Navy secretary Richard H. Bradford had informed Southard of the charges against Tobias Watkins on May 4. Southard in reply on May 13 said that he still did not understand Watkins's offense and pled ill health and family concerns as reasons for not coming immediately to Washington. On May 16 John Branch drafted a letter demanding Southard's answers to a series of detailed queries (M124-118), to which Van Buren proposed this alternative. Southard came to Washington in July and testified at Watkins's trial.

1. Watkins's April 27 letter to Richard D. Harris, navy agent at Boston, upheld his innocence, claimed Southard's approval for all his transactions, and blamed his successor Amos Kendall for malignant persecution (*The Trial of Tobias Watkins* [Washington, 1829], pp. 144–45).

2. Actually May 13.

To John Branch

Sir

I have just recd from the Secratary of State the enclosed, which I send, for your consideration & reflection.

I approve the suggestions made by the Secratary of State—they are those which occurred at the time we first conversed upon the subject—If any alteration or adition suggests itself to you, you will please add it—I think well of the outlines of the answer proposed.

I am very respectfully yr friend

Andrew Jackson

ALS, DNA-RG 45 (M124-118). AJ enclosed Van Buren's letter of May 18, above.

To Richard Keith Call

Washington 18th of May 1829—

Dear Genl

yours of the 28th. ult. has been received, I hope before this reaches you, your dear wife may have been safely delivered, & have presented you with a fine son, or daughter.

I am anxious to hear of your safe return from the Havanna, with such documents as may enable the United States to detect all frauds that has been attempted to be practised against her in Florida—

you will have seen from the Public Journals that we have been ferreting out some gross frauds practised against the United States in the Navy Department by the late 4th. auditor Mr Watkins—The Grand Jury altho 18 out of 23 Mr Seaton of the number are the most violent partizans of the late administration have found a presentment against him, but I have no doubt, if they could they would shield him from disgrace—whether this investigation may not produce facts well calculated to throw around the late Sec. of the Navy, strong suspicions of a participation in the guilt of Watkins, a few days will determine—[1]

On the subject of our friend Eaton I will make a few remarks, to shew how you must have been imposed upon by the information you have recd. and how unfounded must be the rumors of a hostile correspondence ever having taken place between Mr Timberlake & Major Eaton—The proof which I now inclose you Lt Vallette & Thos. Normans letters); with those heretofore refered to must be conclusive to prove to all unprejudiced minds the falshood of the statement—The friendly seperation between Mr Timberlake and his family to which I was an eye witness 1824 This was

conclusive that they parted on the most friendly & confidential terms—
The power of att. Executed at Giberalter in Novbr. 1826, shew that until
that period, no diminution of friendship & confidence could have taken
place—The purchase of the Tobaco pouch & Turkish pipe but two weeks
before his death & sent to me "Through his friend Major Eaton," was
conclusive to my mind, that until that period no information could have
reached him that could have lessened his confidence in Major Eaton.
The copies of two letters from gentlemen of high standing in the Navy,
now inclosed—men who sailed with him, and remained with him, until
they closed his eyes in death, gives the lie direct, to the information of
your secrete informant—nay more, his leaving all his estate to his wife
& two children shews that your informant has been imposed upon, or
like those that you, & Govr. Houston first obtained your information
from; when called on the *other day,* has positively declared, that they
neither ever knew, or said any thing disrespectful of Mrs. Timberlake,
now Mrs Eaton, or Major Eaton, and I have very little doubt whenever
your informant is called upon he will be like those above alluded to—or
like my friend Mr. Ely, who got his information, from a clergyman, whose
name is not given, & who had his information from an unnamed dead
Doctor—and from one of the cleıks in the Departments whose name is
not recollected, but who I suppose was Mr Henshaw, who it is believed,
when he found an enquiry was set on foot, *cut his throat* whether this
was in part or in whole the cause, you will understand is only conjecture,
as it is believed, he had an agency in circulating this foul & unfounded
slander[2]—I will add one notorious fact—it is this, that Major Eaton by his
disinterested friendship to Mr Timberlake, has saved by his advances, out
of the wreck of his Mr T. fortune the sum of $25,000, which is willed to
Mrs. Timberlake & her two children[3]—now let me ask, should any thing
but the most positive proof, when the moral character of Eaton stands
throughout life so fair; when standing in the relative situation that he did
to Mr Timberlake & Major Oneal, be received as evidence even to raise
suspicions against him—and my Dear Call *you* have a right to believe that
Mrs. T. was not a woman of *easy virtue* your own declarations is *proof of
this*—& if you have said any thing to the contrary to Genl Polk or Mr Ely,
it is due to yourself & to major Eaton upon the receipt of the Testimony
I now enclose you, which as stated to me, are both Gentlemen of high
standing in the Navy to say to them, that from proof furnished you lately
believe your information was incorrect—you ought at once to reflect how
unjustifiable your informants were to give you such information of your
friend and enjoin you to secresy—the very injunction, with the slanderous
information, *that cannot be true,* is criminal in the highest degree, and the
man that would be guilty in one case, would traduce you or me *secretely*
if it entered into his wicked designs

As to my female family I exercise no control over them—They have
visited Mrs. Eaton—But you are Badly advised as to those who visits Mrs

Eaton Major Barry is one of his family   I well know Mrs. Hamilton & her daughter visitted her—Miss McLean from Dalaware by the instructions of her father visitted her, and The lady of Major Bender, visitted her, & all respectable strangers visit her as I am [informed]   I happened to be present at the parting between her and Mrs. Bender which was most affectionate & friendly, & the character of Mrs. Bender stands as fair as any lady in america[4]—Justice to truth & to my friend, & your friend, Major Eaton requires this statement—Major Eaton has taken a proper stand & his firmness, we both know, are equal to the task, & all my wish is that my friends may not in the investigation, be found acting incorrectly or on *secrete* information, the weapon of all detraction.

AL draft, DLC (37).
   1. On May 16 and 18, a Washington grand jury issued presentments against Tobias Watkins. William Winston Seaton (1785–1866) was co-editor of the Washington *National Intelligencer.*
   2. John H. Henshaw, a Massachusetts-born Treasury clerk, killed himself on April 22. Reports also attributed his suicide to rumored involvement in frauds against the government or to despondency over the prospect of removal from office.
   3. Mary Virginia (b. 1819) and Margaret Rosa (1825–55).
   4. Postmaster General Barry lived with the Eatons. Mrs. Hamilton was likely Mary Morris Hamilton (1790–1869), wife of James A. Hamilton. Rebecca Wells McLane (1813–93) was the eldest daughter of Louis McLane. George Bender (c1785–1865) of Massachusetts, a brevet major serving in the quartermaster general's office, married Mary Briscoe of Washington in 1816.

To Martin Van Buren

May 18th. 1829—

The dress of an american minister as fixed by the mission to Ghent, and adopted by the Department of state being extremely ostentatious and probably equal in expense to one eighteenth part of the outfit allowed to a minister of the highest grade, the order prescribing it is henceforth abrogated. But as it is considered necessary that our ministers should be distinguished by their dress while at Foreign courts from unofficial personages, I am willing to prescribe one which shall conform to the simplicity of our government founded upon, and guided as it is, by pure republican principles.

I therefore direct when the minister thinks proper to wear a court dress, that it shall be a Blue coat with american Artillery buttons, a gold star on each side of the collar near its termination—the under clothes to be black[1] blue or white at the option of the wearer—a three cornered Chapeau de Bras, a black cockade and eagle, and a steel mounted sword with a white scabbard.

Andrew Jackson

DS in AJ Donelson's hand, DLC (37); LC, DLC (60); DS in Donelson's hand, DNA-RG 59 (M179-67). The second DS (Bassett, 4:34) is dated June 15 and labeled "Executive Order." The court uniform for American diplomats since the 1814 mission to Ghent included a silk-lined blue coat with embroidered collars and cuffs, a gold-embroidered cape, white breeches and silk stockings, and gold knee and shoe buckles. In instructions to ministers abroad, both Adams and Clay as secretary of state had remarked that this dress "is, in no case, prescribed by this Government, and every Minister of the United States abroad, may wear, at his discretion, any dress conformable to the customs of the place where he may reside" (*Clay Papers*, 4:183). In instructions pursuant to AJ's order, Van Buren likewise stressed that the new costume was not required but suggested "as an appropriate and a convenient uniform dress" (Van Buren to William C. Rives, Jul 20, DNA-RG 59, M77-54).

1. AJ inserted "black." In the later DS the underclothes are black or white, the coat color changed to black, and the reference to buttons omitted. Van Buren's instructions followed the two latter changes but reinserted blue as an option for the underclothes.

To Martin Van Buren

May 18th. 1829—

Dr Sir

I return the Despatches from France. I have read them with much interest, & am happy to find the clear our brave officers from the least censure in this unfortunate & disgraceful affair.

When we meet we will converse on the subject whether any reply is necessary—

furnish the sec of the Navy with a copy as early as convenient   yr friend

Andrew Jackson

ALS, Gallery of History (mAJs). In dispatches of March 23 and 26, American minister to France James Brown reported about an affray on February 15 at Mahon on the Mediterranean island of Menorca between French and American sailors, the latter on shore leave from the frigate *Java*. A French officer and at least one American died. Inflammatory French newspaper accounts blamed John Downes, captain of the *Java*, for failing to control his crew. Responding to Brown's complaint, French officials published a correction acquitting Downes and his officers of any fault in the affair (DNA-RG 59, M34-26).

From John Donelson

may 19th. 1829

Dear Sir,

I receved your kind and affectioned letter some time ago. and with grief and sorrow. I read it tho the apostle Paul says sorrow not as others that have no hope[1] but o yes we have a Bright hope that she was receved into the Bosum of hur lord and saviour and is one of his Jewels and this to be sure is and aught to be a great consolation to hur friends but to sorrow not it is not in our nature we cannot avoid it for when we loose a Beloved friend and relation I think it is right to sorrow I think I may say with proprity that there never was a Human Being that had a Better Hart then she had all of hur friends and piticular hur own family can Bare Witness of that and more especially the younger Branches of hur family. there is not one I think of hur nephews or nieces But what can Bare Witness to the goodness of hur Hart. hur council, hur money and meat was Bestowed upon them with a liberal Hand. and they in piticul aught to remember hur as long as they live on the earth, nearly the last time she was at our House after dinner I wint out and was gone some time and when I was coming to the House she and my old lady had got out to the carriage was standing talking. seeing me a comming she turned to my old lady saying every time I look at Brother Johnny I am almost ready to cry, O why sister Jackson why, O she says he has neglected and still is neglecting the one thing needfull his here after) when we went into the House my old lady toald me what she had sayed; it struck me like a flash of lighting is it possable that she has been more conserned for me then I have been for myself it has rung in my ears ever since   I am now one foot in the grave and the Other on the Brink and am still neglecting the One thing needfull. I am ready to cry out mercifull lord what shall I do. the cares and trouble of this world has been Heavy upon me and still perplexing my mind sometimes I am almost ready to say I will turn my Back and have nothing more to do with it still something coming in Vew, I cannot do as I would do. therefore I must submit and do the Best I can perhaps I aught not write as I do now to you but I think I know your good sense and fortitude will Bear you up agaist all misfortune that can happen you; I wish now to say something about Andrew Hutching   I should have wrote you Before but was waiting to know how he was to be disposed of after I got your letter I sent for him let him read the letter have had him at my House several times since soon discovered his sentiment about the Business. Billey Doctor Hogg and myself done every thing we could with him the day Before yesterday Billey got him on as farr as Nashville there it seems he took the studs but still promis that he would go. Billey returned home and left him in Nashville he promised Billey that he would go the next day to Lemuels and he and Lemuel would fix the Business Billey is of the appinion that he will not go. we will hear in a few day, convinced I am he never will go. and now I give my friendly advise never to let him go into a school House again for if he is forced he I think will run away and perhaps be his ruin he seems to wish to be a farmer let him have his wish. he was asked some time ago what he intended to be his answer was a D rich old farmer like the rest of his kin Folks[2]

Billey I suppose will write you again in a few day about Andrew. you I suppose Frequantly hear from your farme we have at present the greatest prospect of a fine crop I must say to you that Mr. Hume comes preaches for us the [la]st sunday after sermon we all came down to your house went into garden, Mr Steel has Built a nice little framed house. a round the tomb there has been a good maney ladys and some Gentleman has been to visit the plaice at severl different times I have no news to give; all things almost as you left us perhaps this may be the last letter you will ever get from me not that I think I may die shortly tho it may be the case but I would not wish you to take up your time reading my le[tter] my old lady Joins me in love to you (and I pray almighty god to give you Health and strength to accomplish the great task set Before you[.] your sincer friend

John Donelson S[r]

ALS, Mrs. W. R. Stevens (mAJs). Extract, Burke, 1:194. John Donelson (1755–1830) was Rachel Jackson's older brother, husband of Mary Purnell Donelson (1763–1848), and father of thirteen children including Mary Coffee, Elizabeth McLemore, and Emily Tennessee Donelson.
    1. 1 Thessalonians 4:13.
    2. William ("Billey") and Lemuel Donelson (1789–1832) were John's sons. Former congressman Samuel Hogg was a neighbor physician who had treated Rachel.

From Francisco de Paula Santander

Bocachica Castle May 19, 1829

Sir,
    A son of Columbus's hemisphere, burdened with misfortunes, has the honor of directing his voice to the illustrious American whose eminent virtues and distinguished services to his country have elevated him to the highest office. My ardent love of American liberty, my faithful adhesion to the fundamental laws of my country, and my loyal submission to the duties she assigned me when I was entrusted with the office of the Vice Presidency of the State, have brought me persecution, torment, and the hard imprisonment that I suffer in this fortress. Proceeding with haste in the case brought against me for the Conspiracy of Bogotá of September 25 of last year, depriving me of the right to defend myself, not permitting testimony from some of the witnesses on my behalf, circumventing all of the rules that serve as guarantees of honor and life for all citizens, violating the laws and what is most sacred, they sentenced me to the ultimate penalty and declared me a conspirator. President Bolívar, for reasons which are not to be examined here, commuted this unjust sentence, imposing instead that of exile from Colombia, for as long as he wishes. But to the scandal of just men and in outrage against public morale and the good faith of the government, instead of fully complying with divine providence, they have reduced me to captivity within this fortress, subjecting me to severe restrictions, without knowing the cause of this arbitrary proceeding and without the ruling having been pronounced by any court. It cannot be concealed from Your Excellency's wise and prudent notice that in all these

hardships nothing operates but the spirit of party, which seeks to punish me, and the steadfast opposition, which, within the space of three years, has effected the establishment of a military dictatorship over the ruins of our fundamental laws. I daresay that in me has been reproduced in part, and for the same causes, the scenes of Barneveld in Holland and of Sydney in England.[1]

Sir, in drafting this confusing sketch of my current hardships, I know that the internal affairs of a state fall outside the domain of foreign governments, although not outside that of public opinion. I am consequently very hesitant to attempt to compromise the supreme authority of Your Excellency, or your public character. My only object is first to make these remarks to an illustrious defender of liberty and a fierce soldier against tyranny, and to preserve in his good opinion whatever I may deserve by my services to Colombia, through 18 years of warring for her independence and the seven years I exercised supreme power—After this, it is my desire to request of Your Excellency that, through private means and in the form of a recommendation, you would help to interest the Liberator President Bolívar in granting me my liberty on the condition of leaving Colombia, as the same President decreed on November 12, 1828. I assure Your Excellency on my word of honor, that nothing has occurred other than that which I have related thus far. The personal recommendation of a man as illustrious as Your Excellency in favor of an unfortunate Colombian who has taken up arms for 18 years in defense of a worthy cause on behalf of humanity, and who earned the privilege of governing his country for seven years—it appears to me that such an action will be effective and that it will honor eternally the memory of Your Excellency. Compassion and humanity are virtues belonging to valorous warriors, to the friends of liberty, and to the rulers of a wise, free and virtuous people. This confidence has moved me to seek protection from my disgrace in the magnanimity of Your Excellency, without in any way jeopardizing the order and dignity that pertain to you. Will Your Excellency reject my supplication? No, it is not possible that Your Excellency would forfeit either the pleasure of performing an honorable and beneficial action or the right that action will give you to have history say: "Gen. Jackson has increased his claims on the admiration of the philosophical world by pleading for the liberty of a Colombian, a constant friend of public, civil and religious liberty."

I ask that Your Excellency would conceal the excess of confidence which the direction of this letter shows, and I entreat you as well, to please keep it secret, as I have written it in violation of the order that I was not to write to anyone. When I am able to publish the true story of my persecutions and hardships, then Your Excellency may make use of this paper as you see fit. But to do so beforehand would irritate the authorities and injure myself. For this same reason, I have declined to have printed a long defense which I sent from here to the Liberator President, dated

December 13 of last year, in which I have successfully refuted the unjust sentence pronounced against me.[2]

Please, Your Excellency, accept the respectful and distinguished consideration of an unfortunate Colombian, but one who always has admired the civic and military virtues of Your Excellency and who has the honor of calling himself your most humble and obedient servant,

Francisco de P. Santandér
Former Vice President and
General of Colombia

Translated from ALS (in Spanish), DLC (37). Horacio Rodriguez Plata, *Santander en el Exilio* (Bogotá, 1976), pp. 184–86. Santander (1792–1840) served as a general under Simón Bolívar in the wars of South American independence and as vice president and *de facto* chief executive of Gran Colombia from 1821 until 1828. On September 28, 1828, there was a failed attempt on Bolívar's life known as the "Conspiracy of Bogotá." Associated as he was with Bolívar's political opponents, Santander was charged with complicity in the attempt and sentenced to death by military trial. On November 12 Bolívar commuted the penalty to exile, but Santander remained imprisoned until June 1829. Following his release he traveled to Europe and the United States, where he met AJ in 1831. Santander returned to Colombia in 1832 and was president of New Granada until 1836.

1. Johan Van Oldenbarnevelt (1547–1619) a leader in the Dutch struggle for independence from Spain, was later tried and executed by domestic enemies. Algernon Sydney (1623–83), an English politician and republican theorist, was executed for treason by the government of Charles II. Both were famed republican martyrs.

2. On August 28, outgoing minister to Colombia William H. Harrison forwarded to the State Department a translation of Santander's December 13, 1828, memorial to Bolívar (DNA-RG 59, T33-5). It was later published in Santander's *Proceso Seguido al General Santander* (Bogotá, 1831).

To Stephen Pleasonton

May 20th 1829
Washington City

Sir,

It being considered proper that the amount of Tea imported in the ship Mariah from Canton, should be forthwith sold at auction for cash, and the balance of the cargoe handed over to the Marshal to be subject to his levy in behalf of the United States, you, as 5th auditor and agent of the Treasury will instruct the Marshal to sell the same at a credit of six months subject to the advice of the attorney for the southern district of New York and the attorney of the United states for the district of New Jersey.[1]

You will instruct the attorney of the United States for the southern district of New York (Mr Hamilton) *confidentially* to employ an agent on behalf of the U S. to purchase in the property for the benefit of the U S. if from the claim or conduct of Mr Bruen it should be about to sell under its value or from any other cause be about to be sacrificed; so that it may be sold by the U states thereafter for a fair price, and as much of the debt due the U S. be made out of the property as it is fairly worth. I am respectfully & yr. obt svt

Copy in AJ Donelson's hand, DLC (37). Pleasonton (c1775–1855) was fifth auditor of the Treasury from 1817 until his death. The *Maria* was owned by the China trading house of Thomas H. Smith & Son. The firm failed in 1828, owing about $700,000 in back customs duties. The U.S. filed suit against the firm's trustees and won judgments in December 1828 and March 1829. On April 17, 1829, then U.S. Attorney John Duer ordered the seizure of the *Maria*, whose cargo of teas, silks, and other valuables was estimated at about $350,000. Matthias Bruen (1766–1846), a wealthy Perth Amboy, N.J., merchant, was the father of George W. Bruen (1795–1849), Smith & Son's sole surviving partner after Smith died in September 1828. Before his death, Smith assigned the *Maria* and its cargo to Matthias Bruen in an attempt to shield it from seizure. Claiming that the *Maria* was his personal property and therefore not subject to confiscation, Matthias Bruen filed for a writ of replevin and succeeded in forestalling the sale of the cargo. Legal wrangling continued until 1835 when a compromise was reached and Bruen paid the U.S. $200,000.
   1. In April AJ had appointed Garret Dorset Wall (1783–1850) and James A. Hamilton as U.S. attorneys for New Jersey and the southern district of New York respectively.

From Charles Jones Love

Nashville 20 May 1829

My Dear Sir
   I wrote you last week and mentioned that Jack was very ill he is since dead
   In future I think Dr Hogg had better be sent for when a physicion is necsay, of that you will please address me   If you were at home dissernment might answer
   The weather is warm and we have just had a very fine rain which will Improve the crops very much   I will visite the Hermitage next week and give you a statement of the affares there[.] I am your hbly

Ch J Love

ALS, DLC (37).

From Martin Van Buren

W. May 21 1829

Dr Sir
   I can see no solid objection to the course recommended by Mr. Hamilton although my judgment in such matters is not worth much. If it should afterwards appear & be so decided that the Goverment have taken the property wrongfully it will have to make good the whole loss. Common

prudence would therefore require that every allowable step be taken to prevent a sacrafice which is other wise almost certain. I know of nothing to prevent the goverment from purchasing in property which is sold on its account. A question has been made whether it can hold lands except for the purposes specified in the constitution but that steers clear of this case and even in those respects the constant practice of the govermt has been to purchase whenever the land was sold upon Execution in favour of the U. States & no other purchasers appeared.

The agent ought to be instructed to purchase only in the event of an evident & great sacrafice & the property sold again as soon as that can be done to advantage. So the mater strikes me—Much would depend upon the character & discretion of the agent. No one could make the selection with more discretion than Mr Hamilton on the spot—Your friend

M Van Buren

[*Endorsed by AJ:*] Mr Hamilton on the subject of the ship Maria & cargo of teas—to be attended to with great deliberation

ALS, DNA RG 206 (13-0368).

To Willie Blount

Washington May 22d. 1829

Dear Sir,

It gives me great pleasure to acknowledge the receipt of your friendly letter of the 27th. ulto., and to thank you for the indulgent retrospect which you have been pleased to give to my administration thus far. Whether I shall succeed in accomplishing all that can be expected from good intentions and the best exercise of my humble talents depends upon too many contingencies not within my reach, to justify the sanguine anticipations which you have formed. Short of them, however, under the guidance of Providence, there is room enough for my highest ambition, which will be gratified in the preservation of the good opinion of my friends, and the maintenance of those republican principles upon which the Govt is founded.

The extraordinary course of Mr Miller[1] is a subject of regret chiefly on account of its effects upon himself. He seems not to have considered that in the formation of my cabinet it was my duty, as well as my right, to consult the interests of the people, rather than his will, or his interpretation of the obligations of consistency & propriety. I have no doubt, before this, he must be satisfied of his folly.

My health is improving, and it gives me pleasure to learn that yours is so strong as to enable you to give 10 hours of the day to the work of history & politics. May you long be blessed with it is the sincere prayer of your friend.

Andrew Jackson

P.S. I should like to see your labours in print.

LS in AJ Donelson's hand, T (13-0371). Blount (1768–1835) had been governor of Tennessee from 1809 to 1815 and a Jackson presidential elector in 1824 and 1828. In retirement he labored on a history of Tennessee that was never completed.
 1. Pleasant M. Miller.

From Felix Grundy

(private)

Nashville, May 22nd 1829—

Dear Sir,

A few days since, I receivd your esteemed favor of the 2nd instant, and now proceed to answer—All are now satisfied with the appointment of Mr Collinsworth as atto for this District—I conversed with Judge Brown & Mr Clark[1] fully and freely on that subject—I also conversed with Govr Carrol on the subject, named by you, he appeared much gratified at the fact of your noticing him in the way you did, and spoke very freely & in strong terms of commendation & friendship of you & your administration and at my request furnished the inclosed answer to my inquiry—From it, you will discover, that it is inconsistent with his situation and views at present to accept of such appointment as is contemplated[2]—he I have no doubt entertains a hope, that at some future period, it will be found consistent with the public interest to provide for him, in a suitable manner—I hope so too—the military is certainly the place for him—and as he will be Governor of the State, things need not be hurried, events can be waited for—On the subject of the National Bank, you have in view—I admire the project and beleive, that the president of the U States, who shall accomplish it, will have atcheived more for his Country, than has been effected by any act of Legislation, since the foundation of the Government—I will furnish as early as I can my views at large on that subject—agreeably to your request—

You ask, If I will come to the Senate? I answer, I will If I can—and when I tell you truly, that I have more strength, than any man who can or will oppose me, it would seem strange that any doubt should exist—still there is doubt. I account for it in this way—Wm E Anderson, your friend & mine who is the very last man, I should have expected to oppose me-has been prevailed onto be a Candidate—he has resided in East Tennessee, which gives him an advantage in that quarter—and should Judge White aid him, he will get an almost unanimous vote in that end of the State—In the western District, pleasant M Miller, will do what little he can for him—that will not amount to much—There are at all times, you know a few dissatisfied men in the Assembly, who would most probably unite on any other man rather than myself—[3]

I have been thro a part of the Western District on a trip to Kentuckey lately—I found great solicitude existed with those who had thought of the subject, that I should go to the Senate & more especially so as Mr Miller was opposed to it—I consider Miller at present a desperate politician, ready for every sort of mischeif—Brown will not be a Candidate and will support me—If Carrol goes into the matter heartily, the danger is over— you have heard the report probably that Lyon of Kentuckey had declared in favor of Clay as next president—I heard him deny it in a public speech at the Ironbankes in his District—[4]

I am sorry to inform you, that Malvina's father in law Mr peter Bass our old friend died at the mouth of Cumberland three days since—My family is well, and Mrs Grundy unites with me in wishing you health & prosperity[5]—yr friend

Felix Grundy

ALS, DLC (37). Grundy (1777–1840) was a Nashville lawyer and a former congressman.

1. William Little Brown (1789–1830), a former legislator and judge, and James P. Clark.

2. Grundy enclosed a May 21 letter from Carroll (DLC-37) declining an appointment in light of his expected election as governor, but pledging AJ his "honest and faithful support."

3. William Evans Anderson (1791–1841), a Jackson elector in 1824, was a chancery judge in West Tennessee. On October 16 Grundy was elected over Anderson and Brown to the Senate seat vacated by John Eaton.

4. Chittenden Lyon (1787–1842) was a Kentucky congressman.

5. Malvina Chenault Grundy (c1809–63), Felix's daughter, had married John M. Bass on January 7. His father Peter (1769–1829) operated a Nashville tannery before moving to Missouri in 1816. Grundy's wife was the former Ann Phillips Rodgers (1779–1847).

Order of Pardon

Having duly considered the memorial & petition of John Allen & John Polk, natives & residents of the state of Delaware, & the libel against the american ~~ship~~ schooner Anna Maria seized by the collector of the port of Norfolk and libelled in United States Court held for the Eastern Distrit of Virginia refered to in said memorial[1]—and it appearing that the penalty against the owners of said vessel & against said vessel have been incurred without any fraud, or participation or knowledge of the said owners—Let a pardon be granted as to the owners of the vessel, & a remission of the penalty against the said schooner Anna Maria—and

I am willing that all suits & prosecutions against the said vessel for this offence be stayed & the vessel discharged—

AD draft, DLC (13-0382); LC dated May 22, DLC (60); DS in AJ Donelson's hand dated May 23, DNA-RG 59 (13-0383). The *Anna Maria* arrived at Norfolk on April 15. The ship was seized and captain Jonathan Cathell arrested for bringing from St. Bartholomew Jose Emanuel Gonzales, a black man, for the purpose of selling him into slavery in violation of federal law. Pleading ignorance of Cathell's action, owners John Allen and John Polk petitioned AJ after failing to gain relief from the district court or secretary of the Treasury. The formal pardon was issued May 23. Cathell was released for lack of evidence, and Allen took custody of Gonzales with the aim of returning him to St. Bartholomew.
    1. Allen and Polk to AJ, cMay 20. Moses Myers was customs collector at Norfolk.

To Martin Van Buren

May 23rd. 1829—

Sir

    I return the papers you have sent for my perusal with this remart on Mr Moors letter—at the time his appointment was made, it was urged that the recal of the minister was necessary to shew to Bolivar & the world, my disapprobation of the insulting expressions contained in the instructions which had been so imprudently published, and which, no doubt was intended to emberrass the present administration[1]—To counteract this, and to shew to Bolivar & Europe my disapprobation of some of those sentiments, contained in the instructions the minister was recalled & Mr Moor appointed with the intention that Mr Moor should carry out the recall, & that it should reach Bolivar as soon as the publicity of these instructions, & the sloop of war Natchez was ordered to be in readiness to take him out—nothing has occurred to alter the necessity of his early departure, and you will so write Mr Moore—

    I am very unwell, but having taken medicine & hope to be about in a few hours—yrs &c

Andrew Jackson

ALS, DLC-Van Buren Papers (13-0405). Thomas P. Moore had written Van Buren on May 9 that his wife had arrived and that, although preferring to wait until fall, he was ready to depart for Colombia as soon as directed. Van Buren wrote back on May 23 enclosing AJ's decision (Van Buren Papers, DLC). Moore sailed from New York on the *Natchez* on July 7 and reached Bogotá on September 21.
    1. Henry Clay's second instructions in 1827 to the U.S. delegation to the Panama conference, made public by the outgoing Adams administration in March 1829, had referred to "the ambitious projects and views of Bolivar" (*Clay Papers*, 6:312).

To Martin Van Buren

(private)

Washington May 23rd. 1829—

Dr. Sir

I enclose, as requested, Mr Woodburys letter—I regret to see he is wavering, as it respects his continuance in his present public station—I had suspected, from Mr Hills observations to me, that *he* expected, Mr. W. might *resign* & he will be his successor—Mr Hill is gone home to be at the meeting of the Legislature—

A gentleman from Boston introduced to me yesterday by Genl Vaness, says; all things are getting on *well in Boston,* they appointments *all* generally *approved* and that Mr Clay has sunk never to rise again, & surely Mr Adams cannot transfer Mr Clay any great support, from which I would infer Mr. W. is more alarmed than real facts would warrent—To sustain ourselves we have only to continue in the course we have commenced—taking principle for our guide, & public good our end, the people will sustain us—yr friend

Andrew Jackson

ALS, DLC-Van Buren Papers (13-0411). Woodbury had written to Van Buren that he might soon resign his Senate seat. He also warned of strong opposition and of Jacksonian divisions in New England (Van Buren Papers, DLC).

From William Carroll

Nashville, May 25th. 1829.

Dear General

I should have written to you before now, but I was perfectly aware that you were so much occupied with the various duties of the high station you occupy, that little, if any time was left for private correspondence.

As was reasonable to expect, in the estimation of those who were apposed to your election, you can do scarsely any thing that is right; but no one could have thought that those who had been for years your professed friends should be the first to raise a clamour against your Cabinet appointments. It is nevertheless true however, that such was the fact *even* here. I am no tale bearer, nor shall I mention names; but it was extraordinary to hear the bitterness of opposition from those of whom you would have expected better things. A few of us took the ground that your Cabinet officers were confidential advisers, that it was prudent and right that you should select persons, in whose honesty and private friendship you had every confidence—that you were responsible to the nation for all your acts—that if you appointed incompetent individuals to office you were accountable for it—that fault should not be found unless that incompetency [becomes manifest] and at all events it was highly improper in Tennessee to be among the foremost to find fault with the first acts of her own distinguished citizen to whom she had made such professions of devotion for many years. The steam was gradually let off and now, an expression of apposition is scarsely ever uttered.

You owe but little to the leading polititions for your present elevation—It was the act of the honest Yeomenry of the country—the great body of the American people—You therefore owe but few individual obligations and in the selection of officers for public trust, need have an eye only to the great interests and growing prosperity of our happy Union. that you will be thus actuated your public life has given abundent proof in the previous stations you have heretofore occupied.

Our local elections in some parts of the State begin to make a noise, but generally the contests will be carried on without much bitterness of feeling. You have doubtless seen the ridiculous reasons of Pleasent M Miller for withdrawing his name as a candidate for congress. The true reason for his [conduct], as is universally believed is, that he would have been beaten by Crocket by a large majority. Be it as it may, he is completely down in Tennessee, and cannot again rise politically. Marable and Johnson are exerting themselves to the utmost, and the result is extremely questionable.[1]

A good deal is said about a successor to Major Eaton, and various persons are mentioned as probable candidates[.] I think myself the contest will settle down between Grundy and Anderson, but who will be most likely to succeed, I cannot now give an opinion to be relied on   If Judge White goes for Grundy he could influence a sufficient number of votes in East Tennessee to secure his election, but if he is neutral the chances are in favor of Anderson. It is very natural that from your own State, and especially from your own neighborhood, that you should desire to have a Senator in whose ability and discretion you could have every confidence. Such an one we will indeavour to give you; but should you have a preference, candor obliges me to say that an expression of that preference will require some degree of prudence, otherwise it may have a contrary effect to the one desired.

The fate of Houston must have surprised you as much at Washington as it did us here. His conduct, to say the least, was very strange and charity requires us to place it to the account of insanity. I had always looked upon him as a man of weak and unsettled mind, without resources, and incapable of manfully meeting a reverse of fortune, but I confess I was not prepared to see him act as he did. A letter was received from him yesterday, dated at Little rock, stating that he was in good health and spirits—that he was about setting out for the Cherekees accompanied by Haroldson—a newly imported Irishman and four large dogs—that he expected to be ingaged in hunting the Buffaloe before mid-summer—that he had not shaved his beard since his departure from Nashville and that it should be permitted to grow the balance of his days.

With an expression of a desire to hear from you, if leisure permits, and a tender of my best wishes for your health and happiness. I am, with esteem and regard, Most respectfully

Wm. Carroll

ALS, DLC (37). Envelope, ICHi (13-0415).
1. Incumbent congressman David Crockett (1786–1836) easily won reelection in August, while Cave Johnson (1793–1866) defeated incumbent John H. Marable.

From Enoch Parsons

Claiborne Aa. 25th May 1829

Dear Sir

The Town of Claiborne, which I reside near, is as a central South Alabama considered, as any Town in South Alabama. And we have a news paper published in the Town. The Editor of the paper, is Wm. B. Travis. Esq. a young Lawyer, and who I believe to be a worthy young man, and who has a family, and is poor. If Mr Travis could have the printing of the laws of the U. S. it would aid him materially and I should be much gratified. I believe Mr Travis would faithfully perform the duty, Candor compels me to say his paper; does not circulate as much, one or two others, but if the laws are published in the Claiborne paper, it will at once circulate more freely. The present Editor has but a short time conducted the paper, and the predecessor being intemperate, lessened the use of the paper.

If upon my recommendation and request you will, or can say to the Secretary of State, something in favour of my favorite, you will oblige me.

I see you are yet the subject of slander and detraction, but now, I care not, you are placed in a station, to expose to the world that you are a good and great man, and have by your works conclusive refutations, of the ten thousand falshoods, party heat and party heat. And the *Hand* of war, pestilence, & famine, has conjured up.[1]

I know your manner of rule, and that the administration will be republican, and brought nearer home to the hearts of the people, than the light Houses of the Skies &c,[2] And so far, I am satisfied except one or two of the appointments, I think might have been better. And I would have preferred fewer printers, and members of Congress, but I know you act for the best, and possess more information upon the subject than I can. and therefore I merely in the spirit of friendship speak my sentiments.

My family are well & Mrs P & myself present to you, the respects of your friends, I am Sir your humble servant

Enoch Parsons

ALS, DNA-RG 59 (13-0424). William Barret Travis (1809–36), later famed as commander of the Alamo in Texas, edited the Claiborne *Herald.* He did not get the government printing, which went to papers in Huntsville, Mobile, and Tuscaloosa.

1. In a May 1828 campaign speech, Henry Clay said he would rather see the country visited "with war, with pestilence, with famine, with any scourge other than military rule or a blind and heedless enthusiasm for mere military renown" (*Clay Papers,* 7:273).

2. In his first annual message to Congress in 1825, President Adams urged federal sponsorship of science and education. His characterization of astronomical observatories as "light-houses of the skies" was widely ridiculed by Jacksonians.

From Rosewell Saltonstall

Newyork May 25th 1829
Monday Morng 7 oc'lock

Revered Sir

Holding an internal consciousness of Purity and belonging to the family of the *Self voted,* whose inward Monitor seldom makes Self error, I congratulate your assuming & entering the Presidental Chair, which I advocated and for which I voted among a sett of friends Vizt Samuel Swarthout Esqr Collector Thomas Hertell Esqr Doctor *[Sl]* Ackerly Doctor N Brush[1] &c &c &c Inwardly satisfied you Rule the Chair of State and that your native Talent and Inward Rectitude will guide the Union Right and into Prosperity & felicity, I always Honord Sir, owe Duty filial obedience, and Respect to the Elections I join in of the Land of our Nativity Hail Columbia happy Land Produces the Enligtened and Heros of a glorious Band. Past Valor is not unseen by Human optic, under that Part of the Heavens where dwells N.O. Millions for Defence not one Farthing for Tribute the commercial World will then understand he who this side the Transatlantic is First will have Respected the Eagle. this Bird Registers Deeds among the Recording Angels. May the Heros of America find the above Haven. 3 Cheers of Andrew and his ancestor the Immortal Columbus

I have wanted to hear from the President and from my own Introductory I endeavored to call the Respected and Honororable Secratary of War, Treasury, and Navy to my aid that I might be serviceable to the Union to the *Arts & Sciences* and to Longitude Naval Courses & Discoveries and to the Machanical world. I have appealed to the Sire of my Country President Jackson that his Enlightened mind might view what I transmitted the three above Secrataries for the President's inspection. I Petitioned his aid. But the Multiplicity of his immergencies has not wafted me his Reply. with filial Pleasure I await his answer

I have also Petitioned the Honorable Secretary of Treasury for an appointment under Samuel Swarthout Collector Sanction by him and the President and doubt not the favorable Result at their Leasure unless they are Convulsed with Remonstrances about the Custom House that Keeps Convulsed the Transactions of Regular appointments   May I not with Candor ask and appeal to the Dignity of him I address, That under Republican forms, People cannot Expect Hereditary or to abide During life or Twenty years in a Custom House. if this was adopted the last President would be President beyond dooms day and never adjourn. I Pray your considerations on me, and my appointment by the Dictates of your generous Self voted Heart my Duty & fidelity is never sold all Remonstrances on Earth cannot make him Deviate who is First and acts for Common good   If the President has a Consulship in Spain or South America or in the West Indies St Kitts, I shall be grateful therefor. Antisipating a Reply from the President when at Leasure I subscribe your Respectful obedt Servant &c

Rosewell Saltonstall—

This will be handed by the Honorable Secratary of War J H Eaton—

[Endorsed by AJ:] Salstonstal. *is* he not *deranged*

ALS, DLC (37). Saltonstall (1778–1841) wrote again on June 1 to request a consulship and to solicit help in publishing his scriptural explanation of the tides. He did not receive an appointment.
    1. Judge Thomas Herttell (1771–1849) and physicians Nehemiah Brush (1787–1843) and either Samuel Akerly (1785–1845) or George Ackerley (c1797–1842), all of New York.

From Susan Wheeler Decatur

Union Hotel, May 26th 1829—

My Dear General,
    I have requested the favor of Major and Mrs Donelson and the other members of your family, to come and take a social cup of Tea with me tomorrow afternoon, or the first afternoon that might be more convenient to themselves; and I shou'd be particularly gratified if you wou'd have the kindness to class me among the few friends whom you permit yourself to visit—The late Administration, in consequence of the *political* sentiments of my intimate friends and associates, not only broke of their acquaintance with me, themselves, but they moreover endeavor'd to prevail upon my friends of the Diplomatic corps to drop my acquaintance also, and finally succeeded with the French[1] and the Dutch Ministers; and it wou'd be a satisfaction to me to be able to shew them that I am in some degree restor'd to Executive favor!

I beg you to believe me, My Dear General, very sincerely and respectfully Yours

S. Decatur

ALS, DLC (37).
1. The Baron Durand de Mareuil (1769–1855) was French minister at Washington from 1824 to 1830.

From David Campbell

Pleasent Grove Wilson County Ten—
May 29—1829

Dear Sir

I went to see you a few days after the death of Mrs Jackson, but your having left home for Nashville a short time before I arrived at your house prevented me from having the pleasure of seeing you—I assure you sir I feelingly sympathised with you on that melincholy event—but it was the will of God and it is the duty of his rational creatures to be resigned to his will—but I hope it will still be consoling to your feelings when you reflect that she is now in happiness with her blessed Redeemer, enjoying a happiness vastly greater than she could possibly enjoy here, and this happiness will never end—yea I believe that all who were well acquainted with her will not hesitate to accord with this hope and I do sincerely hope that her pious example will have a good effect on her dear friends that she left behind her

My oldest son of my present family G W Campbell became ailing about the middle of November last with a breast complaint[1]—kept declining through the course of the winter, and on the 27th. of March died, apparrently quite resigned to his fate and to have strong confidence of making a happy change—he was in the 24th year of his age

My son Genl John Campbell went with me when I went to your house and would have been glad to have seen you—he is now preparing to move to the Arkansaw Teritory next fall—he would esteem it as a great accommodation if some Governmental appointment should be confered on him—he has been rather unfortunate became somewhat embarrasd and his property considerably sacrificed to pay his debts—he is now poor—he conceives his claims to the patronage of the Government some what considerable—when he was quite young at the time we lived in the station he risked his life for nine years—and perhaps was as much and often exposed to danger as any other person in that part of the county—and when he was about eighteen or nineteen years old he went into the army and served in it eighteen years—was in some hard fighting—and I have always understood was considered among the best disciplinarians in the army—and perhaps as useful as any officer of His rank in training the new part of the army after the war commenced—he has an amiable wife[2]

If you should find it convenient and Judge it proper to use your influence to promote his obtaining some suitable appointment it would be gratifying to me[3]

I sincerely wish you may enjoy health and happiness that your administration may be pleasent and comfortable to yourself and advantagious and agreeable to the nation over whom you preside[.] I am with high esteem Yours

David Campbell

ALS, DNA-RG 46 (13-0492). David Campbell (1753–1832), long a friend of AJ, had fought in the Revolution and served in the North Carolina and Tennessee legislatures. He established the frontier post of Campbell's Station west of Knoxville around 1787.

1. David Campbell had married Margaret Campbell (1748–99) in 1774 and Jane Montgomery Cowan (c1770–1840) in 1803.

2. John Campbell (1777–1858) was an Army officer from 1797 to 1815, rising from ensign to lieutenant colonel. He was later a general of militia. He had written AJ on May 10 asking to be appointed secretary of Arkansas Territory. He married Mary E. Cowan (1798–1880) in 1822.

3. AJ forwarded this letter to Eaton on September 8 and recommended Campbell. Campbell was commissioned Creek agent the next day and nominated to the Senate in February 1830, but AJ withdrew his name when he learned that he was a public defaulter. After coming to Washington and clearing his debts, Campbell was renominated and confirmed in March 1831.

From James P. Turner

A copy

Surveyor's Office Washington Miss
29th May 1829

Sir,

Your favour of the 4th instant forwarded by Mr Graham the Commissioner of the Genl Land Office has been received by this morning's mail.

In reference to the complaint of Mr Allison I have but to inform you that I was appointed to take charge of this office, by a Commission from the President bearing date the 28th day of February 1828 for the term of four years from the 24th May ensuing. Upon my entering on the duties assigned me I found every part of the business in this district in confusion and more particularly that part of the District, the Surveys in which were to be executed under the Superintendence of Mr Allison. I first endeavoured to discover the causes of delay in the business, and very soon discovered that the defect was not in the Laws or a want of the necessary appropriations on the part of the Government—but wholy owing to the negligence and mal-conduct of Mr Allison and his predecessors in Office. I immediately urged on Mr. Allison the necessity of a promp attention to the discharge of the duties that devolved on him as an Officer acting under the authority of the Government, but all advice and remonstrance for four or five months on my part was in vain—there was nothing done in his office for the time above stated, save the making out of an Account in favour of Mr A. B. Sterrett a Deputy Surveyor, for work which had been executed one year previously. An Amount of labour which is usually performed by one of the clerks in this office in less than two days. And it is here proper to remark that Mr Allison during the term which he acted as principal Deputy Surveyor, which was about twenty months—he did not complete a survey either of a Private Claim or any part of the public Lands and make return of the same in any manner, so that the Government could either issue a Patent to the Claimants or proclaim any part of the public lands for sale.

A short time before Mr Allison's dismissal from Office, I was informed from the most respectable sources that Mr. Allison had been engaged in making locations of fraudulent claims & giving his santion to them in opposition to his express instructions from this Office relative to this matter. And further that he had made other locations of claims, that were valid in themselves, if confined to the special calls contained in the descriptions of the Confirmation—but they have in several instances been removed from five to twenty miles from the point where they should have been located.

There is one other fact which has come to my knowledge since my letter was written to Mr. Graham dated 7th April ulto. (To wit) when Mr Allison found that he was dismissed from office, he destroyed several of the certified plats of survey which he had approved of fraudulent claims that had been confirmed on fraudulent papers before he delivered the papers of the office to Mr. Fulsom, but he had not destroyed all of such approvals—but about the time of his departure from Louisiana, which was in last month, and I presume the same time that he was about to make his complaints to you for his removal from office he called at the Office of the pr. Dep. Surveyor at Donaldsonville, & wished access to the papers of the office in order that he might be permitted to destroy some other papers which he well knew had been illegally approved by him—which he was not permitted to do.

The facts stated in the first part of this letter are the only reasons that influenced my conduct towards Mr Allison, and I conceived that they were ample grounds for his removal—for in the first place negligence and inattention to the discharge of this duties as an officer, surely disqualified him for the station; & secondly, his disobedience or refusal to comply with his instructions in locating and approving fraudulent Claims, was surely good cause for removal. but if Mr Allison should plead ignorance or that he was in error, this again would disqualify him for the place—and from every view that could be taken of the case, I was compelled to resort to the painful alternative of dismissing him from the Office.

In relation to the affidavit of Mr Sterrett it is not true that I informed him that Mr Graham had urged me to remove Mr Allison; but it is true, that in conversation with Mr Sterrett on my way from Opelousas last October, he (Sterrett) informed me of two or three Cases in which Mr Allison had made illegal locations, to which I replied that I had been informed of the fact, and had made it a reason of his removal from Office, and at the same time recited a part of Mr. Graham's instructions, dated August 1824, to my predecessor in Office, & further observed to Mr Sterrett, that agreeably to the Laws and instructions that had governed in all similar cases, that I should be unworthy of the Confidence of the Government, if I continued Mr. Allison in Office.[1] Mr. Sterrett must have laboured under a great mistake if he understood me to say that I had removed Mr Allison under express instructions to me from Mr Graham to that effect.

I have forwarded an original letter from Mr. Sterrett dated the 4th instant in which you will perceive that he has applied for a clerkship in this office, which I could not give him on account of incapacity & his frequent habit of gambling. I had not the most distant idea, that Mr Sterrett had made an affidavit (the contents of which are wholy misrepresentations) respecting Mr Allison's official conduct, until I received your letter stating the fact.

I regret that Mr. Allison has left Louisiana for Tennessee, and I have been informed that it is not his intention to return—as I wish him to be present in taking the testimony to prove that he was removed from Office for negligence and misconduct.

The testimony in support of the above facts will be forwarded to the Genl Land Office in a few days.

It is a matter of regret to me that Mr Allison could not be satisfied without compelling me to expose his conduct as an Officer—but painful as it may be, he has now rendered this course necessary in justification of my own conduct towards him. I am, Sir, with great respect Your Obt Servt

(Signed) James P. Turner

Copy, DNA-RG 49 (M1329-4). On June 10 Turner forwarded evidence to Graham that Allison had taken bribes to change the locations of land claims. On August 14 Allison in turn charged that Turner was persecuting him for making locations that conflicted with claims in which Turner's brother, John C. Turner, was interested (M1329-4). On September 8 AJ removed Turner for William S. Hamilton. Hamilton declined on November 5 (below), and on December 14 AJ appointed Joseph Dunbar.

1. On August 27, 1824, Graham had instructed Turner's predecessor, George Davis, that "should you find on due investigation that your Principal Deputy Surveyors are not qualified or are inattentive to their duties, you should remove them" (DNA-RG 49, M27-2). Graham too had quoted this language to AJ on April 28 as the likely source of Sterrett's allegation.

To John Coffee

(Private)

Washington May 30th. 1829—

My Dr. Genl.

yours of the 7th. & 12th. of May are just recd. I have had no recent intelligence from my little ward Hutchings—I recd. a letter from him dated in april and wrote, advising him of my wishes, that he might forthwith repair to Frankling and enter himself as a student with Mr Ote—I also wrote Capt John Donelson senr. to see, & admonish him on the propriety of his yielding to my request, & forthwith to repair to the school at Franklin—I also wrote Mr William Donelson to have the goodness to go with, & enter him with Mr. Ote—since the date of these letters I have heard nothing from him, nor have I recd. a sigle line from one of my friends, but yourself & Mr McLamore since I left home—

From the circumstance of Mr Charles J Love, & Mrs. Love, not naming Master Hutchings in their letters of the 11th. instant Just received, & who had visited the Hermitage, I take it for granted he has gone to Franklin—I am more inclined to this belief, as Thomas Donelson has wrote Andrew on the 11th. instant, and does not even mention him[1]—I cannot well account for the silence of our friends on this subject, nor for the silence of Hutchings who I had requested to answer my letter on its receipt—when I am informed where to address him, I shall write him often—His situation claims my serious attention—I have his welfare much at heart, & I still hope to make him a valuable member of society—I shall in the course of next year; if I live, bring him on, & place him at the college here—in the mean time, I wish him with Mr. Ote, who I am *sure,* will preserve his morals as well as the can be, by any superintendant

I am happy to learn that Hutchings crop of cotton is sold—The proceeds except the amount to Thompson & Albert Ward, I wish you to take care of in such way as you may believe will be most profitable to Hutchings—and I wish you to write to William Crawford to have the debt collected from Griffin & the amount advanced for me to Thompson & Ward refunded, so that the accounts with the Estate may stand closed— please, in your next, to inform me whether a recovery has been had against Mr Griffin & what prospect there are to obtain the debt.

It is pleasant to be informed that Mr Jourdon is doing well, I hope he may continue so to do, & that there may be no cause for a change until Andrew J. Hutchings comes of age.[2]

I am happy to hear that Judge Fulton has set out for Arkansas—he has now a fair prospect to do well in that new country, to grow with its growth & prosper—I have always held him as a upright & worthy man, & if he can add a little more energy to his composition, he will do well, and I am sure it will be a pleasing reflection to me, that I had it in my power to serve him.

I am happy to learn that the Engineers has reached you, & are engaged in the duties assigned them—I have given a spurr to industry in every department, and I hope the nation will soon feel the benefit of the change—The war Department is better filled *now,* than it has been since the days of Genl Knox[3]—But My Dr. Genl, I have to thank my god for that energy with which he has endowed me—There never was a more insidious attempt to intimidate me & to destroy a man, than there was to destroy Eaton, & with him myself; & strange to tell, the art of *Clay,* whose project it was, brought into action many who had ostensibly been his Eatons bosom friends, & who he had often served—some of our Tennessee friends in the ranks—The most unblushing, & unfounded slanders were daily, *in confidence* circulated against his wife, I took a stand worthy of *friendship,* & I hope, I may be permitted to add, worthy of myself, & he will triumph over his enemies & become, if not already, one of the most popular members of the cabinet—The Major has taken a stand such as he ought, and I am happy to say to you, that every charge that calumny has set on foot against Mrs. Eaton has vanished on enquiry and those who has secretely propagated them has denied ever hearing or knowing any thing improper ascribed to her—and she has the respect, & is visited, by every respectable lady who visits this city, and Major Barry is now living with Major Eaton as one of his family & the calumnies are recoiling on the heads of her calumniators—I have had an arduous, and dificult duty to perform, in organising the Goverment, but I trust in a kind providence to direct me, and pursuing that Judgt. that he has endowed me with, and acting with deliberation, & great caution, taking principle for my guide, and the prosperity of our country my end, I hope I shall pass through my administration of the Goverment with satisfaction to myself, & the approbation of the people—My first object is, *in all things that I may possess an approving conscience,* & then, if the acts of my administration, meets with the approbation of my country, it will be a gratification to me, & tend to hand me down to my grave in peace.

The most disagreable duty I have to perform is the removals, & appointments to office—There is great distress here, & it appears, that all who possess office, depend upon the emoluments for support, & thousands who are pressing for office do it upon the ground, that they are starving, & their families, & must perish without they can be relieved by the emolument of some office—These hungry expectants, as well as those who enjoy office, are dangerous centinels over the public purse, unless possessed of the purests principles of integrity, and honesty, and when any, & every man can get recommendations of the strongest kind, it requires great circumspection to avoid imposition, and select honest men.

you will see from the public Journals we have began to reform, & that we are trying to cleans the augean Stable, & expose to view the corruption of some of the agents of the late administration—But whether from the defect of the law, or the malladministration of the law, Watkins may escape that punishments that his acts merit, is not for me to decide—that the grand jury & court would shield him from that just punishment that his conduct merits is believed by many here—and should he escape, it will be at once saying that every fraud may be practiced on the Treasury that any of its officers have the power to commit, and it can only be viewed as a breach of trust—The act of congress is as broad as language can make it, & still, the grand Jury could not be brought to present the acts, as contrary to the statute—with such a grand Jury, and court—vigilence can drive the rats from their nests in the Treasury, but cannot punish them, and being worth nothing, the goverment must loose the amount of which it has been defrauded, & the culprit go unpunished—The court has not yet decided on the demurrer, but as the Telegraph is publishing a report of the case *at length* you may rest assured, it is believed by him that the court will shield Watkins if it can find a legal shield to cover them from that indignation that must fill the breast of every honest man, be his preferences in politics, what they may.[4]

My health has not been good, my mind has been sorely afflicted, with the bereavement I have met with—added to this the labour & scenes that have surrounded me, has been as much as the best fortitude I could muster could sustain—My days have been days of labour, & my nights, have been nights of sorrow—but I look forward with hope once more to return to the Hermitage and spend some days near the Tomb of my dear departed wife—This is now the only ~~hope~~ thing that makes life desirable added to the hope, that I may, in some small degree, realise the expectations of my country, and by *reform* lay a foundation upon which the liberty of my country may be perpetuated.

We are all now in tolerable heath, Emily in the family way—The young people of my family enjoying themselves in the social circles of this great city, & Jackson growing finely—he is a fine boy.[5]

I am fearful we will not be gratified with a visit by you & Mr McLamore and your amiable daughters this summer   This will be a serious disappointment to us all, & to me in particular—It would have been to me, a source of great pleasure to have seen you here, & had an opportunity to have conversed with you freely upon many subjects—I hope it may be convenient for you to come on in the fall & spend with us the winter, this would be gratifying to the young ladies, and I need not repeat the gratification it would be to me to have you & Mr McLamore with me a few weeks.

Present us all affectionately to Polly & all your sweet family and receive for yourself our best wishes for your welfare & happiness & believe me your friend

Andrew Jackson

P.S. I have no time to copy this hasty scrall, for you must know, that I have no time for corresponding with a friend, but in the night when I get leave to retire—A. J.

ALS, THi (13-0499).
1. Thomas Jefferson Donelson (1808–95), son of Severn Donelson, was Rachel's nephew and the twin brother of AJ's adopted son Andrew Jr.
2. George J. Jordan.
3. Henry Knox (1750–1806) was Washington's secretary of war, 1789–94.
4. The grand jury investigating Tobias Watkins did not charge him under the 1823 federal statute that made defrauding the government a felony. Instead it indicted him on May 21 for a misdemeanor at common law. Watkins's lawyers responded with a general demurrer, arguing that he was at most liable to a civil suit. The *US Telegraph* began reporting Watkins's trial on May 29.
5. Emily T. Donelson gave birth to a daughter on August 31. "Jackson" was Emily and AJ Donelson's son Andrew Jackson Donelson (1826–59).

From Ezra Stiles Ely

Philadelphia May 30h. 1829.

Dear and Honoured Friend

I fear that my frequent communications may be troublesome to you; but when a gentleman of the first standing in our city writes me such a letter as the enclosed, I can do no less than forward it is you.

It gives me pleasure to inform you that I have ascertained to my satisfaction, that most of the reports against Mr. Eaton and Mrs. Timberlake in relation to some boarding houses in N. York, are untrue; and that nothing more than imprudent familiarity could be asserted against them; and that, perhaps by a lady who may have been fastidious. Yours most Sincerely

(Signed) E. S. Ely.

Copy, DLC (75).

From Frances Walton Pope

[May 30]

You will no doubt be surprised, to be again addressed by me in an epistolary way; but such is my confidence in your good feelings and highmindedness, that I cannot for a moment believe, my letter addressed to you last winter ever reached you: or the President of the United States would even condescend to have taken notice of a letter addressed to him, in so good a cause as I then embarked in, and still conceive it is not presumable that the President can be acquainted with the private character of every subaltern that fills the different offices under government: but at the same time let me assure you, you can have no idea of the integrity, honesty and good principles of the man you have prostrated, and literally taken the bread out of the mouths of a helpless wife and two small children. Such unfortunately has been the lot of Mrs: Hawkins! Yet for your cause, not even now, can she be tempted to turn against you, or utter a word of disapprobation against your course, whilst her eyes are swimming in tears, she adds "I cannot turn against Genl. Jackson!

I who was the cause of my husband's many and powerful exertions in your favour (which he has long since acknowledged) could not be made to believe, you would not have granted me one small request—when in fact and reality it would have been a step greatly in your favour to have retained Mr. Hawkins in his petty office, which his highmindedness would have long since made him resign, had it not been, that it was a support for his helpless family:

If charges have been alleged against Mr. H. and sent on to your Cabinet, rest assured they have originated in the imaginations of designing sycophants: for never has a similar circumstance came under my knowledge, that has excited more universal sympathy than this one, even among your own ranks: and I may also venture to say it has and will turn many Jacksonians.

I still must believe that my letter of last Winter was not recd. by you, or your general politeness, for which you have ever been charecterized, would, notwithstanding your power and preferment, induce you to return the common courticies of life, to a Lady, who was induced by the best feelings of philanthropy to address you last Winter: And should I not receive an answer to this, through some medium, I must still suppose my epistles are intercepted, or kept from your eyes, again I repeat it, if I do not receive an answer to this, I must resort to some other conveyance than that of mail. I must intrust some friend to present my next to you personally. I expect to remain in Frankfort until the first of July.

I have the honour to subscribe myself with all due Respect and Regard

F. Pope

[Endorsed by AJ:] Mrs. John Pope letter with the answer—Sent this 8th. of June 1829—To be filed—A. J

ALS, DLC (13-0509). Pope (c1772–1843), daughter of Henry Watkins of Virginia and widow of Matthew Walton, married John Pope in 1820. James Wood Hawkins (1786–1830) was dismissed as Frankfort postmaster and replaced by Benjamin B. Johnson on May 12. James's wife was Francis R. Hawkins (1796–1855).

From Worden Pope

(Confidential)

Louisville May 31st 1829

My dear Sir

I came home last evening, from Shepherdsville, and my little son put into my hands, your interesting & gratifying letter, to me of the 9th Instant. Having for a long time distrusted the fidelity of Post-Masters, where I could not rely on the influence of private friendship, and over whom Mr. Clay exercised *political charms,* I have avoided, as much as possible, all correspondence by *mail!* I allow no one, to take my letters out of the post-office. I do not even allow my *sons* to open my letters in order to prevent *indiscreet* or *thoughtless* conversations to which the most *prudent* young men are liable. Indeed, I consider almost four fifths of mankind to be very *leaky vessels;* and therefore unfit to be trusted, with any thing more, than what *we wish to be known.* These views have kept me from the post-office for nearly six weeks, hence the reason why the receipt of your letter, has not been sooner acknowledged.

As between *you and myself* the explanation in your letter was wholly unnecessary—There is no man living or dead in whose candor frankness veracity, and honor, I more confide than I do in those of Andrew Jackson; and I have good reason to belive that his opinion of Worden Pope is the same. I will say to *you,* and to *you alone,* that I have for a long time had *good reason to be dissatisfied* with Gen. Duff Green. If it had not been for the lamented death of the patriot *statesman* Clinton, he would have been a Candidate for the Vice-presidency and coming in with *you* and your friends he would have been the master-spirit of the Republican party; he would have been your successor, and have wielded the power which he had so largely contributed to put into your hands.

I justly feared a bad effect from nominating the Candidates for President & Vice-president from the slave-holding states; and was disgusted with the determination of Mr Calhoun and the measures taken to *force* him on the Republican party, instead of Gov. Clinton for the Vice-presidency. In that business, Gen. Green acted the political Gladiator, and Vassal of Mr Calhoun. He made rude attacks upon Gov. Clinton, which greatly disgusted me. He *pressed* his communications on that subject upon me, and I was reduced to the necessity of cutting the Comb of his vanity. Much to my satisfaction, the Cord of our correspondence was cut for some time.[1]

I knew that Mr Calhoun could bring South-Carolina *alone* to the *great battle,* which was to decide the destinies of North-America; that from Gov. Edwards and Gen. Green as Zeniths down to their common Nadir, they are the Vassals of Mr Calhan resting on *his basis* for power and wealth; that those men were not *heart-Christians* towards Andrew

Jackson and John Pope; and that at a time when *your friends*, were fighting a *rude battle* with Mr Clay and the South on the subject of the Tariff,
Mr Calhoun *writes* and Gen. Green *publishes* an *Anti-Tariff* letter.[2] This
was well-calculated to injure our *cause* and *purposely intended* to make
Mr Calhoun, the *head* and *leader* of the *opposition* in the South and New-
England. Now, sir, under all these circumstances, augmented, by attempts
to impress, a belief, that Gen. Green was a great man, and his voice strong,
with *you*, in the distribution of *Offices*, I submit it to your own discriminating and sound judgment, if Gen. Green ought to have *renewed* his correspondence with me, but more especially about Mr. John Pope. My letter
to Gen. Green, was in reply to one received from him on the subject of the
appointment of Mr. Pope as Gov. of Arkansas. It was *intended* for Gen.
Green's *own* consideration and reflection; and I cannot *divine* his *motive*
for laying it before *you*. Most certainly, I had not the least expectation or
desire that he would make such an use of it.[3] Having the liberty to address
you *directly*, I do not feel myself, at all, constrained to adopt or take any
indirect or oblique arts or course to make you acquainted, with such facts
& speculations, which, as your friend, I feel it my duty, to let you know.
From a close perusal of your letter, I fear that you had not received one
from me of previous date, in which the precaution was taken, of enclosing
it in one, to your inflexible and incorruptible friend Majr. Eaton. That letter, excludes the presumption, that *I am dissatisfied with,* *your* relation to
Mr. Pope; and sir, if you had seen Gen. Green's letter to me, to which mine
that he laid before you, is a reply, your upright mind, would have given
it, a *different* interpretation. Suffice it to say, for the present, and future,
that *I am not,* but declare that I have *no cause* to be *dissatisfied* with *you*.
I am incapable, even, for one moment, of believing, that *you* are capable
of acting with duplicity towards any man, or to gain any object. Your life
has been nearly spent in active struggles for principle; and you have not
"Climbed over the Wall," but have "come in at the Door" to your present
exalted station. You have always been a Cato but with a better destiny.[4]
On no occasion, have you used, duplicity, fraud, intrigue, or corruption
to elevate yourself; and this well-earned character shields you, from the
mere suspicion that you will be induced by any consideration to pursue
a dark and crooked course of policy towards even your *enemies,* much
less your friends. And I will end this part of my remarks, by assuring you
that I place unlimitted confidence, in every thing you say; that your own
principles and persecutions have endeared men of like character to you,
and that you are sensible that the Glory of your administration, greatly
depends upon, confiding in and employing such men.

Mr John Pope is my blood relation. He is a real patriot, and a virtuous
and highly talented man, and therefore, I love him with a brother's affection. He is a *statesman,* but not much of a *politician.* Morality and judgment enter largely into his opinion, of a proper public character. Against
my Judgment he stept on the political arena, at too early a period. It was

his misfortune to encounter a drilled corps of united, intriguing corrupt, St. Tamany *politicians*. He was seduced by Messrs. Madison & Gallation, as well as his own opinion of the public interest to advocate the renewal of the charter of the old Bank of the Ustates. From a conviction of our *unprepared*, condition for such an appeal, with such a *prepared* and powerful enemy, and the severe test which it would give to our republican institutions, Mr John Pope voted against the late war.[5] The patriotism pride and ardour of the people of Kentucky were seized upon by those politicians to prostrate him. I advised him to withdraw from political life, and turn his whole force to the pursuit of his profession   I exacted a promise from him not to oppose Mr Clay, on the subject of the compensation Bill; but he yielded to the wishes of his friends who had been identified and persecuted with him.[6] I had at the age of nineteen, a splinter, and almost a dwarf, let go the Ax, Hoe, and Plough, with but about 27 months of Common schooling, and embarked, in the pursuit and attainment of almost a mechanical profession and therefore my opinions upon abstruse political subjects and policy, had not, and were not entitled to much weight with him. It was his misfortune to find out and feel his error. He was the Hoop that kept the Barrel of his enemies together, and his struggles at Lexington were like opposing France in the Netherlands. I advised him to leave Lexington, because as long as that place was *Hell*, Mr Clay would be *King* of it.[7] We are both of about the same age and have been residents of Kentucky, the land of blood, danger, faction and trouble, ever since about the first of May 1779. And I have looked with hope to the period of your success when he could give his aid in the administration of the National Government, to a man of virtue, firmness, patriotism, and wisdom, sustained by the first confidence and affections of a free and enlightened people.

Now sir, I freely, admit that the office of Governor of Arkansas, *under you*, is "an important and honorable station." It was so to *you* and to your *Country* when you were Governor of Florida. But sir, it was so only, because *you administered* the Government in *person*. It would not have been the case, had it been by *Deputy*. Whilst Miller & Izard were Governors of Arkansas it was governed by Deputy—whilst the Governors resided out of the Territory and were seldom there, it was little better than a *Sinecure*—And pardon me sir, when I say that I considered their administration neither important nor honorable.[8] In order that the office, filled by Mr Pope, shall be *honorable to himself* and *important to his Country*, he ought to *reside* in the Territory, and hence I could not advise him to take it. Considering his own and his wife's age, the size of his family and easy condition, in life—and the strong wishes and inclinations of Mr Pope to a contrary field of action, I extremely regretted that the office was bestowed upon him; and that he had not been passed over, in silence. It would have filled the measure of his own and my *wishes*, if there had been a liberal consent and concert of the Jackson-party, to make him Senator or a Representative in Congress from the District in which he lived. This would have been an act of justice, and sound policy. Mr Pope *wished* to be in Congress, where he could gratify his own feelings and give the most efficient service in his power to your administration. He desired the place of Senator but would take no measures, as a Candidate, in order to defeat Colo. Johnson. I was at Frankfort, on professional business, a week before the meeting of the Legislature, and continued until the evening of the 23d of Decr 1828; And I assure you, that the Representation made at Washington that Mr John Pope was the cause that Colo Johnson, was not elected Senator, is *base and false*. The Clay-party were beaten, and in a small minority; but to produce effect abroad, they were bent on the *defeat* of Colo Johnson. He had recommended Crittendon for Judge of the Supreme Court of the United States; and Owsley for a Judge of our appellate court. This was a direct interference with the designs of the Jackson-party and reduced his friends to a minority; and put it compleatly in the power of the Clay-party to kill Johnson. I aver that as much as the Clay-party hate Mr Pope, they preferred him to Colo Johnston; and it was in the power of Mr Pope to make terms with the Clay-party and have been the Senator. The Clay-party talked of Colo Johnsons peculiar Domestic Situation, and were anxious to go to the people on his defeat. This was the *real* cause of Colo Johnson's failure.[9] Our party owed much to John Pope; and when they saw that they Could not elect Colo. Johnson, every principle of justice, duty and policy demanded that Mr. Pope should be selected and elected Senator instead of Mr Bibb. In his election the New Court-party overshot themselves. That election was intended to get for Mr Bibb the office of Judge of the Supreme Court of the UStates which he *wanted* and *needed*; and which Mr Pope neither *wanted* nor *needed*. After securing that office for Mr Bibb, the New Court-party, intended to fill the vacancy of senator with another of their party. And this is the true explanation why neither Colo Johnston nor Mr Pope was made senator. While I was at Frankfort I saw much personal and political depravity; but I little thought, that it would go Office-hunting from Kentucky to Washington and there explode, in treachery, falsehood & denunciations towards your original sincere and continued friends. I was well-aware that certain men from Kentucky, the old friends and tools of Mr Clay, mercenaries and political Gladiators, would surround and press upon you for office; but I felt the strongest indignation at their lies, treachery and denunctions towards your best and most useful friends. Like cunning Rats, they were afraid of the Clay-storm and sought *office* by any means, to shelter themselves from his influence and resentment. I wish most heartily that the Hon. T. P. Moore was at Bogota. He has kindled a flame in his District and will travel off by the light. In his plan to elect his relation Colo McAfee he has produced an incurable division of the Jackson-party, in that quarter.[10] Be assured that he is a *little gostering man*, and fights for plunder, not principle. He was one of Mr Clays tools, and made it the "sine qua non" of republicanism to be for Clay & of Toryism and Federalism to be for you. There is such a thing as a man overacting his part; and I feel it to be a high duty of friendship to say to you, that nothing is so disapproved of, as his appointment, by *friends* as well as *enemies*. I have vindicated it, and hope that I shall make no complaint against any appointment. We all expected, in the nature of things, *some bad* appointments, but we place such confidence, in you, that we believe, that as soon, as you discover, that you have been deceived into such selection, that you will, forthwith, remove the incumbent. The removal of an unworthy officer is expected and desired by the people, but no honest man is prepared for the appointment, of an unprincipled scoundrel. It is essential, that your friends; men of merit and character should be the objects of choice and selection.

Mr Wickliffe and Major Rudd are out for Congress; and I have no fears for the election of Wickliffe. But I wanted & solicited Guthrie to be a candidate, because he would, better than Mr Wickliffe have secured, Jackson members to the Legislature from Jefferson, Oldham, Bullitt and Nelson Counties which compose the District. I deemed it due to Judge Oldham to *invite* him, before Wickliffe was *called* and *pressed* out. This neglect of Oldham is the effect of selfishness and mean jealousy.[11] A little New Court knot of Gladiators without integrity, power or influence, already cry "Pope faction" because my relation, Worden P. Churchill, has declared himself a candidate for the Legislature; and although they know that his friends are the body and life of the success of their own men. Such conduct is really insupportable and detestable. Mr Churchill, was one of your original friends; and is still so. He is a young man of Education, talents, wealth and influence; and was zealous, active and bold, and freely used his *purse,* in your cause. These fellows want a convention, the *real* object of which is to abolish debts, divide property and obtain offices.[12] They also want to revive the Court-question, in order to have some little consequence, in the general excitement. All men of sense and prudence are sick of the Court question; and all men of property principle and patriotism, abhor and dread the project of a convention, and the promoters of it. It is an object with those men to use your popularity, in favor of those projects, and identify your administration with them, than which nothing can be more dangerous and fatal. It is a fact, that Majr Barry has been a factious man, but now he has power, distinction, and high prospects and does not need, the services of violent men. I feel sincerely disposed to see him possess the confidence and affections of the nation, and therefore wish that he would silence his partizans on the subjects of the Court question and a convention. With the highest respect & friendship I am your obedient servant,

Worden Pope

[On envelope:] Majr Barry, will please, deliver this letter personally to Gen. Jackson

ALS, DLC (37).

1. On January 4, 1828, Duff Green wrote Pope deprecating De Witt Clinton and urging Calhoun's retention as Jackson's running mate (Duff Green Papers, DLC). Among other things, he accused Clinton of being unsound on the issue of slavery. Before Clinton's death in February 1828, Green sent similar letters to other Jackson leaders including William B. Lewis, William T. Barry, Richard M. Johnson, and Samuel Swartwout.

2. Ninian Edwards (1775–1833) was governor of Illinois and Duff Green's brother-in-law. On July 12, 1828, the *US Telegraph* published a letter from Calhoun calling the tariff "by far the most dangerous question that has ever sprung up under our system." As reprinted in *Niles* and elsewhere, the letter included a spurious paragraph denouncing the tariff as unconstitutional and demanding its repeal (*Calhoun Papers*, 10:392–93).

3. Pope had written Green that John Pope deserved a better post than governor of Arkansas. Green read part of the letter to AJ. Learning of this from AJ, Pope accused Green of trying to injure him, and Green replied on August 15 that he had only acted to counter Thomas P. Moore's "machinations" and that he had done all he could for John Pope, whose own political blunders had destroyed his chance for higher office (Green Papers, DLC).

4. John 10:1–10. The Roman Cato the Younger (95–46 B.C.), a symbol of austere virtue and probity in public life, killed himself rather than submit to Julius Caesar.

5. As a senator from Kentucky, John Pope in 1811 had supported the Madison administration's unsuccessful bid to renew the charter of the original Bank of the United States. In 1812 he opposed declaring war against Britain, on the grounds that it should be declared on France as well. Both votes stood counter to instructions from Kentucky's legislature and to prevailing sentiment in Kentucky.

6. In 1816 John Pope unsuccessfully challenged Henry Clay for Congress. He and his backers made an issue of Clay's support for the unpopular Compensation Act of 1816, which raised congressional salaries.

7. An echo of Satan's determination in John Milton's *Paradise Lost* that it was "Better to reign in Hell, than serve in Heaven."

8. James Miller (1776–1851) was the first governor of Arkansas Territory, 1819–24, and George Izard (1776–1828) was the second, 1825–28. For much of their terms the territory was administered by its secretary, Robert F. Crittenden.

9. William Owsley (1782–1862) served on Kentucky's old Court of Appeals, 1812–28. Richard M. Johnson, who was unmarried, had two daughters by a mulatto slave, Julia Chinn, whom he treated as his wife.

10. Robert Breckinridge McAfee (1784–1849), a New Court politician and former Kentucky lieutenant governor, was Thomas P. Moore's brother-in-law. He was among several put forth at a Jackson meeting at Harrodsburg on May 9 to succeed Moore in Congress. McAfee did not stand in the August election, won by John Kincaid.

11. Charles Wickliffe won reelection over Richard Rudd (b. c1794), a Bardstown lawyer. James Guthrie (1792–1869), later a U.S. senator, represented Jefferson County in the Kentucky legislature. John Pope Oldham (1785–1858), a former judge and legislator, was appointed Louisville postmaster on May 13.

12. Worden Pope Churchill (1804–30), a cousin of Worden Pope, narrowly lost the election for state representative from Jefferson County. Some New Court adherents had proposed a state constitutional convention to limit the power of judicial review. A bill authorizing a convention referendum was defeated in December 1828.

To Andrew Jackson Donelson

Please call on the Comptroller of the Treasury, and request him to send me an official statement of the defalcation of Mr Nourse: and also request him to apprise me whether there are any others in the offices who are defaulters.[1] yr.

Andrew Jackson

[In AJ's hand:] P.S. It being intimated that Mr Vansant has been recommended To the Treasurer for appointment in his office—Mr Donelson will please say to Major Campbell, that this man has been twice turned out of office, as is reported to me, & that he must not be brought into office again as it would be painful to have to remove him immediately on his appointment, to prevent which this intimation is given—

A. J.

NS in AJ Donelson's hand, DLC (13-0513). Joseph Nourse (1754–1841) was appointed register of the Treasury by George Washington in 1789. On May 30 AJ removed him for Thomas L. Smith. The government's reckoning of his accounts showed Nourse in arrears, while he claimed a balance in his favor. A federal court found for Nourse in 1831, and in 1848 his heirs were paid $12,331.96 to settle the claim.

Nicholas Biddle Van Zandt (1780–1863) had served under John Beckley as clerk of the House of Representatives and librarian of Congress. Beckley died in 1807, and Van Zandt's bid to succeed him failed amid charges that Van Zandt had divulged secret proceedings of the House. He was later a clerk in the General Land Office, 1816–17. In 1830 he received a clerkship in the comptroller's office and was appointed by AJ as a justice of the peace in Washington.

1. Former Tennessee senator Joseph Inslee Anderson (1757–1837) was first comptroller of the Treasury.

To Samuel Delucenna Ingham

complaint being made that the collector at Alexandria V.a. keeps his own Negroes employed in his office & to keep the lights in lighthouse &c &c sec. to write to the Deputy collector Mr Chapman—who can give information—[1]

Weatherburn Survayor of the Port, *worthless & ignorant,* violent in the late canvass, Thornton the uncle of weatherburn—

Mr Jas. Mcguire presented as the survayor of the Port—[2]

[Endorsed by AJ:] for the Sec of T. Memorandom from C. Mc.g. relating to the collectors of Alexandria & some improper conduct there employing slaves &c &c—

AN, PU (13-0219).
    1. Humphrey Peake (1772–1856), customs collector at Alexandria since 1820, resigned on June 15 under the threat of impending removal and was replaced by George H. Brent. Brent reported to Ingham on July 11 that it had been the practice to employ only blacks as boatmen, which he recommended continuing (DNA-RG 56, M178-1). Charles T. Chapman (c1776–1834) was the deputy collector.
    2. William Wedderburn (c1762–1837), surveyor at Alexandria since 1827, was the uncle of William Fitzhugh Thornton (1789–1873), who edited an Adams newspaper in the 1828 campaign. AJ removed him for James McGuire.

June

Memorandum Book

[These notes, begun in early June, appear together out of chronological sequence at the rear of Jackson's memorandum book.]

Brevet. rank—The marine corps, & their emoluments—To be submitted to the atto. Genl for his opinion.[1]

This 6th. of June 1829. Mr Whitehead verbally reported that the Honble. Mr Webb Judge for the District of Key west, resides at St, Andrews, Florida, holds his court but twice a year, passes in a public vessel, and is absent all the year except in term time, and when a *wreck* happens, & possession is taken by the marshal there is no authority to adjudicate the case, from which, great delay & injury accrues to the owners—on this report, I have directed the sec of State to write to Judge Webb that he must remove to & reside at Key west or give up his commission[2]

A.J.

June 9th. gave written instructions to tender the vessel that takes out major Moor to So. America to Genl Harrison & Mr Tayloe to bring them home—[3]

It has been reported by the Gentlemen of the Navy & Mr Eckfort, that the Columbus and Independence, are, in their present condition, good for nothing, must be cut down to Frigates, The Washington & Frankling, *Defective*
William Doughty Naval architect at Washing $2200 James owen at $1500 Mr Hart at Newyork $2200—[4]

Does not the Executive Legislate by approving the Estimates presented to Congress, when Congress app[r]oves them—quere, is this not reversing the constitutional order of Legislation—would not the true view of this subject be, that the head of the Different departments being required by the comittees to make out an estimate for their informati[on] and the only approval by the president his signature to the appropration bill—Then, taking the law for his guide, there would no occasion for implication on the subject—

AN, DLC (64).

1. AJ queried Berrien on June 11 (below).
2. John Whitehead (c1797–1864) resided at Key West. James Webb (1792–1856) was appointed judge of Florida's southern district in 1828. On June 6, AJ wrote Van Buren to instruct Webb to remove to Key West, and Van Buren did so on June 9 (DNA-RG 59, M40-21). Webb retained his judgeship and was reappointed in 1832.
3. Van Buren to AJ, and AJ to Van Buren, June 9 (below).
4. Henry Eckford (1775–1832) was a renowned naval architect and shipbuilder. The *Columbus, Independence, Franklin,* and *Washington* were 74-gun ships of the line authorized during the War of 1812 and completed between 1814 and 1819. William Doughty (c1772–1859) and Samuel Hartt (c1782–1860) were prominent naval shipbuilders.

From Tomlinson Fort

[This letter is available only in typescript. It is printed here verbatim, with corrections of obvious misreadings supplied in italic brackets.]

Milledgeville, Ga., June 1st, 1829

Sir:—

It was my intention before leaving Washington to have performed for my constituents the final duty of presenting the names of some of them to your attention for countenance and favour. But I was prevented by the press of similar applications with which I understood you were perpetually teased. I regret, the more, not having been able to obtain a private interview with you because the people I represent stand on a peculiar ground, and although they ask or desire but little, the obstacles thrown in their way to the obtainment of that little are of a kind peculiarly vexatious. That I might have an opportunity of explaining these circumstances I returned to Washington a month after the inauguration but could not obtain an interview without becoming in my own views considerably importunate. I therefore take this method to perform a duty which I feel bound to perform however painful.

For myself or anyone related to me I desire nothing in the gift of the Government. I can therefore speak with less reserve the sentiments of those who elected me to an honorable station. Since my return to Georgia, I have endeavored to understand their views and feel assured that I represent them truly in this communication. You are apprised that from the close of the late war you have had in this state a party devoted to run *[ruin]* as a political leader. The attempt to destroy you by a provision of your act, in the Florida campaign gave rise to the first trial of their strength. The defeat of Mr. Cobb was the consequence.[1] With him your enemies fell, but they arose with Mr. Crawford in the struggle which soon followed. I need not remind you of the scurrility which teemed from their presses against you. You have forgiven them and taken into your Cabinet one anyway, as a politician, identified with their base and illiberal slanders.

Every one must approve the magnanimity you have shown in thus overlooking the misdeeds of your most powerful adversaries. Although some of us may not be able to discover what could have directed a particular election *[selection]*. It is my purpose to recall the circumstance that Georgia was the first field on which your pretentions were truly canvassed, that the question has caused amongst her people the most bitter party sessions; that having one of her own citizens a competitor with you for the highest office in the figt *[gift]* of man, the party opposed to you arose to power on the strength of his name and that by an uncommon turn of events, your old and steadfast friends have witnessed your complete triumph and with it the staff of office and the echo of triumph raised by those who as they express themselves, have supported you as an alternative; or to use the phrase of their most influential writer they *"have taken the Tartar in preference to the Spicac."*[2]

Your old and uniform friends in the meantime mix in festivities which they cannot conceal from them the part *[fact]* that the fruit of their exertions is to be gathered by others, and that the channel of communication which ought to remain free between us, has a cross it an impassable barrier. You will pardon me if I go a little farther with detail. The right of office in this state has been steadily against you till the somerset of the Troup party in the late contest. The patronage of the General Government in the contest with Mr. Crawford and probably caused the loss of that election.

From the year 1815 there has been in Washington a vigilence which never slept and a power which never failed to exclude from office any man known to have been friendly to you in the times above alluded to. So absolute and prevading has been this principle that I doubt whether a single individual who was known to be friendly to you in the contest with Mr. Crawford has received even a petty post office appointment since the year 1818. Exceptions may exist where the office is valueless but scarcely in a single case besides. There are probably twenty thousand voters in this state who advocated your election in 1824, who are placed in this drastic point of view before the Community in which they live.

It might be expected that since all parties have been united in your final election, these feelings of hostility would cease, and that before the new administration the question discussed with regard to individuals would be, who is worthy and if length of friendship gave no permanence, lateness of conversion should at least give no preference. Now, Sir, allow me to say that I have not the least doubt but your wishes would go even handed with justice and that your feelings towards your old friends are unaltered. But looking to you through the office of your Cabinet selected from this state and supposing that the influence ordinarily accompanying such a selection to exist, I am bound to apprehend the same system of pre-scription *[proscription]* will continue unless controlled by your personal knowedge and interference. Magnanimity is a rare quality and I may be excused for supposing Mr. Berrein could never imitate your example in selecting him, nor can he do otherwise than throw the whole weight of his influence into the continuance of a system so long continued here. There is not the least appearance of a cessation of party strife in this state. The animosity engendered by a bitter contest does not cease with the triumph of a party. The actors must pass away, and painful as the reflection is, it is yet true that the struggle of 1818 has kindled in the heart of our citizens enmities which can close only in the grave.

Under this state of things I beg permission to ask whether in our appli-cations to you for countenance or favor Mr. Berrein will be referred to as a source of information with regard to our standing or qualifications. The peculiarity of our situation here and the strength of the passions con-cerned, induce me to hope you will deem the case worthy of particular consideration, and I will add that I have shown this letter to many of your old friends who unanimously concur in the views.

I have said that for myself or anyone related to me I desire nothing in the gift of the government. If the plain language I have used is deemed improper I trust it may not be suffered to result in any injury to those I advocate. But I must be allowed to say that although at present almost totally excluded from every mark of favor by the General Government my political friends can never submit to have their pretentions canvassed by one whose prejudices and party views, will operate to reduce them to a contemptuous standard.

Hoping that I shall not be thought to have taken an improper ground towards the President of the Union and trusting that the highly respectable portion of the community whose views I represent will entitle this letter to some regard, I am, sir, With great respect Your o'bdt. Svt.

TOMLINSON FORT

Note: Several persons have applied to me for letters of recommendation, for favors of some kind. I mention at this time only Maj. R. R. Ruffin, who I suppose you will remember. His worth of character is known to you, his necessities entitle him to your sympathy. He deserves the place of Post Master in Augusta, which, I understand, is at present filled by a man invalid from disease but fortunately rich from the fruits of office, and although a Troup man, as they are here called like many others amongst us, friendly to the late administration—Any other equal station would doubtless be honorably filled by Maj. R. The Collector of the Port of Savannah I understand desires to retire, and the Marshall is another invalid as I am informed.[3]

T. F.

Typed copy, NcU (13-0536). Fort (1787–1859) had been a Georgia congressman, 1827–29. Two factions had long dominated Georgia politics, one founded by former governor John Clark, a Jackson ally, and the other headed by former Treasury secretary William Harris Crawford (1772–1834) and by governor and senator George Michael Troup (1780–1856). The Crawford and Troup men had condemned Jackson's Seminole campaign of 1818 and backed Crawford against him for the presidency in 1824. Both factions supported Jackson in 1828. Attorney general John M. Berrien had been a Crawford man.

1. Georgia congressman Thomas Willis Cobb (1784–1830) had sponsored resolutions to censure Jackson's Seminole campaign in the session of 1818–19. He was defeated for reelection in 1821.

2. Ipecac and tartar were common emetics. Criticizing AJ's appointments, the Milledgeville *Georgia Journal* on May 11 said that "the choice between him and Mr. Adams was a choice between ipecac and tartar."

3. Robert R. Ruffin (c1788–1830) had been an aide to General Edmund P. Gaines in the Seminole campaign. Augusta postmaster James Frazer was replaced by William C. Micou in January 1831. AJ reappointed Savannah customs collector John Stevens (d. 1832) and Georgia marshal John H. Morel (c1781–1834) when their terms expired in 1830.

To Martin Van Buren

June 2nd. 1829.

Dr. Sir

If you have not seen Mr. Jones on the subject we conversed on yesterday, I wish you to have the interview as soon as it will meet your convenience— Mr. Craigg is here waiting with some anxiety—Having wrote, and informed you yesterday, to Mr Ingham to invite him on here, I feel, & I have no doubt Mr Ingham feels, in a delicate situation on this subject—and it appears that you are also from what you said yesterday—we must get out of this delicate situation somehow and shortly—If Mr. Jones will agree to take some other situation it will at once relieve us all—and I do think the talents of Mr Craigg in the Patent office, & being there, we can command them, if *wanted,* on other subjects, is of such importance, that he ought to be retained here by placing him at the head of the Patent office.

My Dr Sir let me hear from you on this subject soon, I am yr friend

Andrew Jackson

ALS, DLC-Van Buren Papers (13-0553). John D. Craig was appointed superintendent of the Patent Office, and Thomas P. Jones accepted a State Department post as clerk in charge of consular correspondence.

To Martin Van Buren

June 2nd. 1829

your quere within has been recd. and I answer the atto. for the District ought to be written to for his opinion before I can with propriety act, and he ought to add to his opinion a request, that a nole prosequi, be entered against them—

I return the papers & request you to address the District atto. on this matter—when his opinion is recd. I will act upon it[.] yrs.

Andrew Jackson

ANS, DNA-RG 59 (M179-67). In September 1827, Elias Henry Merryman (b. c1804) of Baltimore went to sea aboard the privateer *Bolivar* as its surgeon and purser. Its crew was American, British, and Spanish, and it preyed primarily on Spanish and Portuguese shipping. In July 1828, sailing under an expired Buenos Airean commission and the name *Las Damas Argentinas*, it captured the British merchantman *Carraboo* off Gibraltar. The *Bolivar* was afterwards apprehended, and twenty-eight of its crew were tried by a British Admiralty Court on the island of St. Christopher (St. Kitts), convicted, and put to death. Merryman and one other man testified against their shipmates in return for immunity. On Merryman's return to the United States, a Baltimore grand jury investigated him for prosecution under American law, but concluded that he deserved clemency. On June 1, U.S. district attorney Nathaniel Williams (1782–1864) sent to Van Buren the grand jury's recommendation for a nolle prosequi for Merryman (M179-67). Van Buren suggested to AJ that Williams's opinion be requested in writing, to which this note is a response. Van Buren notified Williams the same day (DNA-RG 59, M40-21), Williams duly wrote AJ on June 3 endorsing the grand jury's request, and on June 4 AJ ordered the nolle prosequi.

To Martin Van Buren

June 4th. 1829—

Dr. Sir

Mr Meehan has Just informed me that he has applied for possession of the Library, and has received for answer from Mr. W. the late incumbent, that he will not give possession until he is relieved from the obligation of his bond—will you write Mr. W. a note informing him that Mr. Meehan has been commissioned, & has given bond & security agreable to law, and request, that he deliver to Mr Meehan possession of the library, with an Invoice of the Books therein contained—on such a note being delivered, & a proper demand made by Mr Meehan, should Mr. W. still refuse, you will please direct Mr Meehan to apply to the court for a quo warranto, or a mandamus. I am respectfully yrs

Andrew Jackson

ALS, DNA-RG 59 (M179-67). AJ had appointed John S. Meehan librarian of Congress on May 28, replacing George Watterston. The 1802 law governing the library stated that a new librarian before taking charge had to give a bond whose amount and security had been approved by the President of the Senate and Speaker of the House. Congress not being in session, AJ directed on May 30 that Meehan furnish bond to the same amount as his predecessors. To clear himself of responsibility, Watterston declined giving up the library until his own bond, held by the secretary of the Senate, was returned. As AJ directed, Van Buren wrote Watterston on June 4 (DNA-RG 59, M40-21) and entrusted his message to Ebenezer J. Hume for delivery. Watterston finally surrendered the library key to AJ in person.

From Samuel Craig Lamme

Independence Jackson County June 5 1829

Dear Sir

I am just on the eve of leaving the upper settlements & bound for Santa-Fe the company of traders in number will be, (when collected) about fifty, waggons thirty, this is but a small company in comparrison to what has formerly gone to that country, but owing to the depredations committed on the road, and the anticipated dangers from those tribes of Indians on the heads of Missouri & Arkansas Rivers & bordering on the Mexican Teritory, that it has detered all most all from trading to that country, except a few enterprising men, who have been engaged in that trade for some years past & have considerable interest in that country at this time, & are compelled in order to get that, to risque their lives & property for sake of same & to keep up the trade to the country not so much an advantage to the traders as to Our Country as we find all of our Circulating medium are of the new spanish coin

The appropriation made by government is very deficent for its protection, as it will afford little or no security to the traders as they (the troops) are only ordered to that point where the danger only commences, & Should there be any danger between here & that point, it would afford us no security unless by great detention on the road, in consequence of the means of transportation which is drawn by oxen entirely, which (in my opinion & those who are better & more experianced) will not be able to get half way through that scorching & dry country that we have to travel unless very [tardiouly]; but hoping they may answer the purposes anticipated

My object of communicating at this time (principally) is to ask the favour of you to transmit to me, at Santa-Fe a pasport for a citizen of U. S. to travel through that country as I expect to return by the way of the South & could not with safety do it without, & time would not of permited me to of got it here before I would be off. My age is twenty Eight full faced & stout built & five feet 9 Inches hight tolerable fair hair, another one in company five feet 6 inches high slender made & slim features & 22 years of age with a black wart on his right hand & by name William Gaw &

from my residence Franklin M¹   your attention to the above request will greatly oblige a friend & a Santa-Fe trader[.] Yours very respectfully And most Obt Servt.

S. C. Lamme

NB. If we are fortunate we will get to Santa Fe in 60 or 65 days from this time by which time a communication from you will reach that country—by that time or shortly afterward, any advancemt to the traders in that country Accompaning the pasports which you will inclose to me will be kindly received &c.

I am engaged in this country in the merchantile business & have been for some time & still expect to be & find this trade of a singular advantage to our country & hope in another year we will have ample protection for the safety of our traders to & from that country unmolested which cant be done without the aid of government yours &c— S. C. Lamme

any information requisite I refer you to Shaw Tiffany & Co Baltimore T. C. Rockhill Philadelphia—Merchants of those places.²

ALS, DNA-RG 59 (13-0574). Lamme was a Franklin, Mo., merchant with stores in Independence and Liberty. The Santa Fe overland trade, exchanging American dry goods for Mexican coin, had burgeoned in the 1820s. Indian attacks on the trade in 1828 brought appeals for federal protection. The 1829 trading caravan of 38 wagons, less than half the size of the preceding year's, was escorted to the Arkansas River border by four companies of infantry under Major Bennet Riley. A few hours after the traders left the troops and crossed into Mexican territory on July 11, they were attacked by Indians and Lamme was killed.

1. William Gaw was a partner with John Bird in the merchant firm of Bird & Gaw.

2. William C. Shaw and his partners Osmond C. Tiffany (1793–1851) and Comfort Tiffany (1797–1879); Thomas C. Rockhill (d. 1855).

To John Donelson

(private)

Washington June 7th. 1829

My Dr. Sir,

your letter of the 19th. ult is Just received. What satisfaction to me to be informed that you & Mr Hume had visited the Hermitage & Tomb, of my dear departed wife, how distressing it has been to me to have been drawn by public duty from that interesting spot, where my thoughts delight to dwell, so soon after this heavy bereavement, to mingle with all the bustle, labour, & care of public life; when my age, my enfeebled health and constitution forwarned me, that my time cannot be long here upon Earth, and admonished me that it was time I should place my earthly house in order and prepare for another, & I hope a better world—my Dr wife had your *future state,* much at heart, she often spoke to me on this interesting subject in the dead hours of the night, and has shed many tears on the occasion—your reflection upon the sincere interest your Dr. sister took in your future happiness are such, as sound reason dictates—yes my friend it is time that you should withdraw from the turmoils of this world, & prepare for another & better—you have well provided for your household, you have educated your children, and furnished them with an outfit into life sufficient, with good management and oeconomy, to build an independence upon—you have sufficient around you to make you & your old lady independant & comfortable during life, & when gone hence, perhaps as much as will be prudently managed, and if it should be imprudently managed, then, it will be a curse, ruther than a blessing to your children—I therefore Join in the sentiments of my deceased & beloved wife, in admonishing you to withdraw from the busy cares of this world, & put your house in order for the next, by laying hold "of the one thing needful"—go read the Scriptures, the Joyful promises it contains, will be a balsame to all your troubles, and create for you a kind of heaven here on earth; a consolation to your troubled mind that is not to found in the hurry & bustle of this world. Could I but withdraw from the scenes that surround me, to the private walks of the Hermitage, how soon would I be found in the solitary shades of my garden, at the tomb of my Dr wife, there to spend my days in silent sorrow & in peace from the toils & strife of this world, with which I have been long since surfeited—but this is denied me—I cannot retire with propriety—when my friends draged me before the public, contrary to my wishes, and that of my Dr wife, I foresaw all this evil—but I was obliged to bend to the wishes of my friends, as it was believed, it was necessary to perpetuate the blessings of liberty to our country, & to put down misrule—My political creed, compelled me to yield to the call, and I consoled myself with the idea of having the counsel & society of my Dr wife, & one term would soon run round, when we would retire to the Hermitage & spend our days in the service of our god—But o, how fluctuating are all earthly things—at the time I least expected it, & could least spare her, she was snatched from me, and I left here a solitary monument of grief, without the least hope of any happiness here below, surrounded with all the turmoils of public life and no time for recreation, or for friendship—from this busy scene I would to god I could retire, & live in solitude.

How much the conduct of A. J. Hutchings corodes my feelings   I have Just read a letter from him to Saml Hays, in which he says there is a vacancy at the Franklin academy & promises to write me—If he does not go to school, I will withdraw from him all supplies, that may indulge extravagance, & confine him to such means as with oeconomy will keep him decent.

We are all in tolerable health, Emily in the family way, little Jackson growing finely, & all Join in our best wishes to you & your amiable lady & all our connections & good neighbours; your friend

Andrew Jackson

P.S. Mr Steel has written me but one letter say to him to write me how much crop he has in, how many coalts, lambs & calves and how my last years coalts are—and of the health of my Negroes—I learn old Ned & Jack are both dead—Jack was a fine boy, but if he was well attended to, I lament not—he has gone the way of all the earth—[1]

A. J.

ALS, THi (13-0589); Cover, Mrs. W. R. Stevens (mAJs).
 1. Old Ned (c1770–1829) and Jack (c1809–29) were Hermitage slaves. Ned died on April 13. Jack, stepson of Peter, died on May 8.

To John Overton

Washington June 8th. 1829—

My Dear Sir

I have received your letters of the 22nd. & 26th. ult. and after noting their contents have disposed of them as usual—

I have duly noted the contents of the letter of Mr Dunn, I have long since been aware of the importance of Texas to the United States, and of the real necessity of extending our boundery west of the Sabine as far west as the sandy desert, which is a good natural boundery—It is fortunate that our boundery has not been run and marked, and from the deranged state of the finance of Mexico, I hope we may be able to obtain an extension of our Southwestern limits as defined by the late Treaty with Spain, so important to the safety of Neworleans—How infatuated must have been our councils who gave up the rich country of Texas, for the Floridas, when the latter could have been obtained for the sum we paid for it in mony—It surely must have been with the view to keep the political ascendency in the north, and east, & cripple the rising greatness of the west—I shall keep my eye on this object, & the first propitious moment make the attempt to regain the Territory as far south & west, as the great Desert.[1]

I intend in due time to notice Govr. Carroll—The only thing at present I had to offer him, the charge de affairs at Brazil, I find he will not accept, and as I know he is needy, I have directed the Secratary of War to give him the appointment of agent to visit the cherokee & creek Indians, and give them my talk on the subject of their removal to the west of the Mississippi and to use his influence in conjunction with the agent to enforce upon their minds the necessity of their adopting this course, as the only means we have in preserving them as nations, and of protecting them. The State of Georgia having extended their civil Jurisdiction over them, makes it desirable that the Indians should remove to a Territory over which no State has any right to the soil—and to which, the u states can give the Indians a *perfect right*—The course pursued by Georgia is well calculated to involve her & the United States in great dificulty, unless the Indians can be got to remove west of the M. you see we are employing the Govr. beneficially, as I believe, few men will have more influence with the Indians than he—[2]

I am sorry you are to have a contest between Judge Anderson & Grundy for the senate—They are both my friends & I doubt whether you can spare Jud[g]e Anderson from the Bench, and if you do, where & by whom can you fill his place with so much talent & safety to the State—Anderson is poor and I am apprehensive, if he leaves the bench, & comes to the senate, it will injure him in his pecuniary concerns, as it must take one third of his pay to meet his expence here, which will leave but one thousand or eight hundred dollars, to support his family & himself at home.

They are both enlightened men but Grundys knowledge of men, would make him better adapted to the atmosphere of Washington than Judge Anderson for a while, & he would be better calculated to aid Judge White & myself in the change of the present incorporated Bank to that of a National Bank—This being the only way, that a recharter to the present U. S. Bank, can be prevented, & which I believe is the only thing that can prevent our liberties to be crushed by the Bank & its influence; for I find from the various applications for removals, many are requested on the ground of the injurious effect the interference of the directors of the Bank had in our late election which if not *curbed,* must destroy the purity of the right of Suffrage—

I intend to write Judge White shortly and draw to his view, the importance if possible to keep Judge Anderson on the Bench, he is of more importance to the state where he is than he can be in the senate—and take him from the Bench & by whom will you replace his integrity & talents—except Judge Brown would accept it, I am at a loss to point to the character that would fill it with equal talents & integrity & in whom the people have confidence—But as I never interfere in elections, I leave it to the wisdom of the Legislature, and would regret to see Judge Anderson taken from the Bench.

We are getting on pretty well here—every few days discovers more delinquencies, and of course a *removal* and the Journal & Intelligencer of course tell the world what virtues the delinquent possessed & the cruelty exercised in turning him out—But I have but little doubt, when all things are exposed to the people, they will call out *"well done good and faithful servants"*—[3]

Major Barry' family have reached the city, and are living with Major Eaton, Col Morgan & his family also, The cloulds are passing away—and I can say with truth there never was a man more cruelly treated than Major Eaton, & by some of *my friends*—my situation has been an unpleasant one—How much pleasure it would give me to see you here where, & when, I could speak freely to you, & when, I could have your advice upon many weighty matters

When I take a view of my situation, behold myself left here alone, without any hope of any *happiness here below* toiling night, & day, a constitution already worn out in my countries service, and daily assailed by the wicked & ambitious, I cannot but exclaim to myself why this toil & labour; & why sacrafice myself thus when I have no hope of pleasure here—the only consoling reply; *my country has required it,* and it is a duty I owe to that *country to yield to its wishes*—But how hard my situation, when my mind is torn to pieces by the severe bereavement I have met with, and when I have done all I can do by making use of my best exertions to have the constitution amended,[4] a National Bank established, our western boundery enlarged, and our affairs with england & France arranged, even then, I am forbid to withdraw until the tedious four years run out, which in my state of health, gives me serious forebodings that I shall not spend much of my time in this world on the silent walks of the Hermitage.

My Dr friend I am interrupted & have to close this hasty scrall—with our best wishes to you & your family believe me yr friend

Andrew Jackson

ALS, T (13-0595).
1. In the 1819 Adams-Onís Treaty, Spain ceded East and West Florida while the United States assumed American citizens' claims against Spain up to $5 million. The treaty drew a line to the Pacific between the United States and Spanish Mexico, with the Americans relinquishing their claim to Texas. AJ at the time approved the treaty, saying in 1820 to Secretary of War Calhoun that "I am one of those who believed, and still believes, that our Treaty with Spain as it respected our limits and the possession of the Floridas, was a good one—Texas for the present we could well do without" (*Jackson Papers,* 4:410). A boundary survey stipulated by the treaty had not yet been run.
2. William Carroll was commissioned as a special Indian agent on May 27.
3. Matthew 25:21 and 25:23. The Washington *National Intelligencer* and *National Journal* were leading anti-Jackson papers.
4. As a candidate and as president, AJ favored amendments to ensure a popular choice for president and to restrict congressmen's eligibility for appointive office.

To Frances Walton Pope

Washington June 8th. 1829

Dear Madam
    your letter of the 30th. ultto. has been received, and I embrace the first leisure moment since, to explain to you the reasons which produced the removal of Mr Hawkins. Acting upon the information contained in your first letter on the subject, I felt a pleasure in the supposition that he could be retained without violating a proper regard for the duties of my office, or for the opinion of the great body of the people interested in that which he filled. This pleasure I assure you, Madam, was heightened by the

respect which I entertained for your wishes; and it was not without much pain that I felt constrained to act upon the belief that you had mistaken his true character. Unquestioned authority has been lodged in the department of the Postmaster General for the assertion that Mr Hawkins ~~intemperate~~ habits disqualify him, in a great degree, for the personal discharge of the duties of the office, and that he had been in the custom from this cause, of intrusting its keys to individuals obnoxious to the community in many points of view. an extract of the memorial on this subject I inclose for your satisfaction

I have thus candidly stated the considerations which compelled me to approve of the removal of Mr. Hawkins; and hope that you will have no dificulty in reconciling them to a sincere indulgence of those sentiments of friendship & respect, which are due from me both to yourself, and to your distinguished husband.

It is a painful duty to be the instrument of lessening the resources of a family so amiable as that of Mr Hawkins; but when the public good calls for it, it must be performed. As a private individual, it would give me the greatest happiness to alleviate their distresses, but as a public officer, I cannot devote to this object the interests of the Country[.] Accept the assurance of my great respect and Esteem, & believe me Dr Madam yr mo obdt. servt.

Andrew Jackson

ALS, DLC (37).

From Martin Van Buren

W. June 9t 29

Dr Sir

Would it not be well to offer Genl. Harrison & Mr Taylo the privilege of returning in the vessel that takes Mr Moore out.[1] I am not advised of the nature of the Service on which she is to go so as to judge of the degree of inconvenience that would result from what is suggested.

Please to let me know as we are preparing the letter of recall—yours truly

M Van Buren

[*Endorsed by AJ:*] directions given to offer the vessel that carries out Mr Moor to Genl Harrison to bring him home to be noted in memorandom Book—June 9th. 1829

ALS, DLC (72).
1. Edward Thornton Tayloe (1803–76) of Virginia had been appointed secretary of legation in Colombia in 1828.

To Martin Van Buren

June 9th. 1829

Dr Sir

Returning from the Navy yard I recd. your note of this morning

I view it proper that a tender of the vessel taking out Major Moor should be made to Genl Harrison & Mr Tayloe to bring them home—on this subject I had, on yesterday, some conversation with the Sec, of the Navy—The only dificulty is the detention of the Vessel at the port at which Major Moor may land.

I presume Bolivar will be at Bogota, the nearest port to that place is carthagena which is 400 miles, Maracaibo is about 500—it will take say 30 days at least for Major Moor to reach Bogota & Genl Harrison to reach the port, this in that climate will be a long time for our seamen to remain in port—I will see the Secratary of the Navy, perhaps he may have orders to send to our Brazilian squadron, if the vessel can be employed on that duty—I will direct the secratary of the Navy to prepare his order that the vessel Either wait in Port or return at a given day, & recei[ve] Genl Harrison & Mr Tayloe, and you can prepare the letters accordin[gly] yr friend

Andrew Jackson

P.S. It is possible the Genl would prefer returning in a private vessel—if so, it will be well to [ask] him, to advise the Capt of the Natchez by letter that he may leave the Port forthwith—

ALS, DNA-RG 59 (M179-67). On June 30, Navy secretary Branch ordered Alexander Claxton, commanding the *Natchez*, to deliver Moore to his port of preference, continue to Rio de Janeiro to drop off the new commander of the Brazilian squadron, and then stop back to pick up Harrison (DNA-RG 45, M149-18). Harrison missed the *Natchez* and returned on the private brig *Montilla*, which reached New York in February 1830.

From Henry McKenny

[June 10]

I made application for admision as a midshipman in the *Navy*, but thear was too much patronage. Str. Benton Filed my appication. I hope as you are disposed to giv Evry on a Equil Chan according to merit, you will give my appication due attention. I am decidedly of the opinon that, a reform is nesessary in our Republican Govermt Your &C.

Henry McKenny

ALS, DNA-RG 45 (mAJs). McKenney (b. 1811), an orphan from St. Charles, Mo., did not receive a berth. On June 26 he wrote to Secretary Branch asking if his application was neglected "because I am not a son of some member of Congress." He had earlier applied for admission to West Point.

To John Macpherson Berrien

June 11th. 1829—

The question arises under the laws of the 6th. July 1812 and 16th. April 1818, how far and to what extent can Brevet pay, and double rations be rightfully allowed?

Where Brevet rank gives positive command then the Brevet pay and emoluments must be allowed. But where lineal rank entitles the officer to the command it would seem that the pay and emoluments of the Brevet cannot be legally claimed. For instance, a Lieutenant in the Line being a Brevet Captn., and acting with his own Regiment, should his captain be absent, the Lieutenant being then the oldest officer of the company commands it by virtue of his lineal rank and of course does not acquire the Brevet emoluments. The law of 1812 gives the President the power to confer Brevet rank and restricts the command under it to detachments, separate posts or districts; and the law of 1818 without diminishing this restriction seems to have been designed to express it in more certain and positive terms, and may be thus read—*That at no other time shall Brevet rank give pay and emoluments, except when on duty commanding a separate post, district or detachment, and then commanding according to Brevet rank.*

Doubts also exist as to the right of the Surgeon & paymaster Generals to extra pay and emoluments. As salary officers I incline to the opinion that a fair interpretation of the law is against any other allowance than that which is designated as the salary.

The whole subject is referred to the atty. Genl for his opinion

The report of the 4th. Auditor on the subject of the pay and emoluments of the marine corps from which they have appealed to the President, appears to be well founded. as its sanction however will reverse a rule adopted by the late administration, the President requests its consideration also by the attorney Genl. that he may be well advised before he acts upon it.[1]

Andrew Jackson

DS in AJ Donelson's hand, DNA-RG 60 (13-0624). Berrien replied at length on July 18. The 1812 Army law said that brevet rank did not entitle officers to "additional pay or emoluments, except when commanding separate posts, districts, or detachments." The 1818 law said that officers should receive brevet pay and emoluments "when on duty, and having a command according to their brevet rank, and at no other time." Berrien held that the War Department in 1827 had indeed exceeded the law by allowing brevet pay to officers who were commanding units smaller than their brevet rank entailed. He upheld the right of the surgeon general and paymaster general to allowances for fuel and quarters.

1. Kendall's report of May 28 to Navy secretary Branch complained that Marine officers were drawing excessive pay and allowances without any statutory authority (*HRDoc* 107, 21st Cong., 1st sess., Serial 198). Berrien's opinion upheld the legality of the payments as conformable to apparent congressional intent and to parallel usage in the Army. But he joined Kendall in recommending reform of the practice, either by law or executive action.

From Hinton McKinney

Raleigh Jail 11th. June 1829

To his Excellency Andrew Jackson President of the united States.

The humble Petition of Hinton Mc.Kinney, Your Petitioner with a feeling of deep humiliation represents That on the first day of August 1825 he was arrested on a charge of having Stolen money From the mail of the united States which was under his charge as the Driver of a public Stage, and That in the month of May following he was Justly convicted by a Jury of his Country of having committed This mean and atrocious crime, Your Petitioner dares not to utter a Word in extenuation of his offence, the [enor]mity of which he Now perceives as distinctly as any individual of the community, But your petitioner when the fatal deed was committed had Received little or no education, was a wild and wreckless, youth and had associated with companions who regarded Them Selves as having nothing at Stake in the welfare of Society and as deriving no benefit from the laws, in the Solitude of confinement he has been kindly furnished with The means of instruction and has endeavoured to avail Himself of Them, Reflections has been followed by the Deepest contritions for his offence and a firm determination, Should he be restored to Society, to atone for his past Misconduct by a virtuous and useful life,

Under these circumstances he presumes to approach the Chief Magistrate of the united States and to Supplicate For the remission of the unexpired term of his imprisonment, and being taught, That the brave are ever the more humane he can not but indulge the hope, That his humble and Earnest prayer will not be disregarded.

H Mc.Kinney

ADS, DNA-RG 59 (13-0780). As he had in other cases of mail robbery, President Adams in December 1828 refused a plea for McKinney's release supported by federal district attorney Thomas P. Devereux. Devereux appealed again to Van Buren on June 11. A June 12 petition to AJ, signed by officials including federal marshal Beverly Daniel, district judge Henry Potter (who had presided at McKinney's trial), and North Carolina governor John Owen, urged clemency for McKinney and particularly praised him for apprising the keeper of dangerous "plots and combinations" among the prisoners.

From John Simpson

Geo.town June 11th. 1829

Hon. Gen.

If you will afford me an opportunity of putting into action, my native genius, in making a grand piano Forte, for your Mansion; it would be to me, the most gratifying circumstance that ever occurred—my mind is fill'd with it—let my first and grand effort, be for you. The Instrument shall be of entire new construction, both inside and out, and if I do not excel, any Instrument, that ever was made in Europe, or America; in tone, touch, variety, and beauty, both interiour and exteriour, (all which may be left to connoisseurs) I promise not to present it to you. The Instrument shall contain ten Octaves, and in the centre of a drawing room, will make a splendid appearance. With the highest esteem, your most Ob. Hum. serv.

J. Simpson

[Endorsed by AJ:] Mr Simpson on the subject of a *piano*—I want none for myself—

ALS, DLC (37). Earlier, Simpson (c1780–1850) had offered a "new invented square horizontal Grand Piano Forte," which he called the "Jackson Piano," for the White House. Asked by AJ to examine it, AJ Donelson deemed it "not unworthy" to occupy the East Room.

From William W. Lyon

New York June 12th. 1829.

Sir

During the excursions of the British on Long Island at the time of the Revolutionary War, they cut down the most valuable timber. From a stump of a Hickory tree a sprout shot forth, and after the lapse of nearly fifty years grew into a solid mass which formed a natural pitcher or can. I have had it properly mounted, and beg you will do me the honour to accept it, as a slender homage to your worth and services, and particularly to that important crisis to which the country has applied the now favored title of Hickory.

Rude as it appears, it is still a massive emblem of the simplicity and republican characteristics of our Revolutionary fathers, who frequently had no softer place as a pillow for their aching heads.

May you long enjoy health and happiness, and live long to see our Country prosperous under your administration[.] Your friend and fellow Citizen

Wm W. Lyon

LS, DLC (37).

To Richard Keith Call

Washington City, June 13th. 1829

My Dear Sir

I have received your letter of the 30th. ulto. and regret for the cause assigned, that it has not been in your power to set out to Havana before the date of your letter. It appears from Mr Whites communications to Majr Graham, that he is anxious that these suits in Florida should come on for trial in October next, this must be prevented if possible, until all the documents from the Havana can be obtained[1]—I enclose you a note just recvd. from Mr Ingham, from which *[you will]* see, that it is considered altogether important to obtain & have at the trial, copies of certain reports of the Spanish Governors in Florida, and of treaties made with the Indians, whilst, Florida belonged to England—I agree with Mr. Ingham, if the trial can be put off, that you may safely remain until the sickly season is over, but if it is intended to bring the suits on in Octbr.—which if Mr White attends as council in behalf of the United States & he consents, they may be brought on, then the papers are all important, and you must proceed to Key West, & if you find the yellow fever at Havana, then you must communicate in the best way you can with the Authorities at that place, so as to have a copy of these necessary papers—I do not wish you to risk your health, but I repeat if the causes are presented for trial in Octbr. next, these papers must be had if possible—you being on the spot can be informed on this subject better than we can here, & I leave it to your own Judgement to decide—With my best respects to Mary and the children, & best wishes for you and their welfare believe me your friend,

Andrew Jackson

LS, DLC (37). *TPUS*, 24:237–38.

1. Joseph M. White (1781–1839), the Florida Territory delegate in Congress since 1825, had been appointed assistant counsel for resolving the Spanish land claims in 1828.

To Andrew Jackson Hutchings

Washington June 13th. 1829

My Dear Hutchings

I have Just received your affectionate letter of the 25th. ultimo, & hasten to answer it.

I am pleased to find you are determined to adopt, & follow my advice—I gave it with the feelings of a father, and I am sure it will bring you into life happily, and be the means to carrying you through life with respectability & honor.

I have a great wish that you should go to Mr Otte, because I know him to be a religious, moral, & honest man, capable of teaching you those branches that I have recommended to your study, & a man who will guard your morales both by precept, & example—But as you appear to have such unwillingness to go to Mr. Otte, and has chosen Mr Williford as your Teacher, should you not have Joined Mr. Otte before this reaches you, I yield my consent that you may go to Mr. Williford—but if you have entered with Mr Otte, you must on no account, leave him before your session terminates[1]—If you should, having been suspended from College, you never can regain your character—and now is the time for you to obtain an education, which if you neglect, the day will come when you will sincerely regret your present mispent time—In a few years now, you will be of age and without an education, unless you attend better to your learning, than you have heretofore—I must again i[m]press upon your mind the great [value] of an education, and urge you for y[our] own benefit, to great application in you[r] studies so that you may at least be a good mathematician, as well as master of arithmatic, and that you learn to write a good hand, and become well acquainted with orthography, in which I find that you are at present, very defectiveficient.

When I review the great expence I have been at to give you an education how many admonitions I have bestowed upon you, urging you to proper industry in your studies, and application to your book, & now find you approaching to manhood without an education, having spent your time in idleness & folly, the tear trickles down my cheek, a[nd] I supplicate my god, that he may [guide] & direct you better for the fut[ure] and console myself with the p[romise] in your letter now before me, that my advice will be followed by you for the future—if it is, I freely pardon what is past, & will foster, & cherish for you in my boosom, those parental feelings for you that I have always had, & will bring you on here so soon as I find you have laid the foundation of a good education where you now are, when you can spend with [me] a few months, & become acquainted with your grand Uncle Judge Smith now in the Senate of the U. States.[2]

Write to me on the receipt of this informing me where you are, and the studies that you are engaged in—and inform General Coffee who will furnish the funds to pay your board, schooling & cloathing.

Andrew & Samuel, send their respects to you, in which Capt A. J. Donelson Emily, & Mary Easton unite with Major Lewis your cousin Andrew has written to you some time since, you must write to him often as well as to me—

give my respects to Thomas J. Donelson & Mr Steel—and to all my friends in the neighbourhood of the Hermitage—Tell the negroes *all* howde, for me—that I am glad to hear that they are well treated, & happy, that I wish them all to behave well & they shall be well treated & that I supplicate a throne of grace for them. I wish you to write me often, follow my advice & believe me yr affectionate father & Friend

Andrew Jackson

ALS, NjP (13-0654).
    1. William L. Williford ran an academy in Columbia, Tenn.
    2. William Smith (c1762–1840), senator from South Carolina, was the brother of Hutchings's maternal grandfather.

To John Coffee

Washington June 13th. 1829—

My Dr. Genl
    I have recd. your letter of the 25th. ult. marked confidential, with the one enclosed in favor of your Voluntary aid at Neworleans—The office solicited had been filled before the receipt of your letter—on a future occasion, his merits will be duly considered.[1]

I have recd. a letter from my little friend Hutchings & answered it to day—he requests to be permitted to go to Mr Williford at Columbia—he appears to have great objections to go to Mr Otte—should he not have entered with Mr. Otte let him go to Mr Williford least he might runaway from Mr. Otte which would ruin him for ever, but if entered with Mr Otte, on no account, let him leave that school until his session is out.

I write you at Nashville expecting it will meet you there on your way hither, with your daughter, we are all delighted here with the thought of seeing you & Mr McLamore with your two daughters here shortly   we will have rooms for you prepared, & hope Mr. Earle is with you

Present us to all friends, affectionately & believe me yr friend—I have been writing for four hours & am obliged from debility to stop

Andrew Jackson

ALS, THi (13-0651).

1. Coffee on May 25 had recommended Neil B. Rose for marshal in Alabama, but AJ had already appointed Benjamin T. Moore.

From Mary Chase Barney

[Jackson's removals from office sparked bitter criticism. In April 1829 Jackson removed William Bedford Barney (1781–1838) as naval officer (a customs post) for the port of Baltimore, replacing him with Dabney S. Carr. Barney had been appointed in 1818, succeeding his father, Joshua Barney, a naval hero of the Revolution and War of 1812. Mary Chase Barney (1785–1872) was William Barney's wife and the daughter of Samuel Chase, a signer of the Declaration of Independence and later Supreme Court justice. Her letter below circulated widely and was published in 1830. Barney continued her criticism of Jackson in The National Magazine; or Lady's Emporium, *which she published in 1830–31.]*

Baltimore June 13th. 1829

Sir,

Your note of the 22 April last addressed to me through your private Secretary accompanying the return of my papers, which expresses your *"sincere regret that the rules which you had felt bound to adopt for the government of such cases, did not permit the gratification of my wishes,"* affords no palliation of the injury which you have inflicted on a meritorious officer and his helpless family—It is dark & ambiguous.[1] Knowing that the possession was not alone sufficient justification for the exercise of power; unwilling that your character for firmness should suffer by the imputation of caprice, or that your reputation for humanity should be tarnished by an act of wanton cruelty, you *insinuate* a cause; you *hint* at a *binding rule,* and *lament* that my husband is within its operation. If it were not unworthy the character of *Genl. Jackson,* I ask you, was it not beneath the dignity of the *President* of these United States to *insinuate,* if bold assertion had been in his power. When you had adopted for your government this *inexorable rule* was it not cruel in you to conceal it from those on whom it was to operate the most terrible calamities? Why should the President of a free country be governed by *secret rules?* Why should he wrap himself up in the black robes of mystery, and like a volcano, be seen and felt in his effects, while the secret causes which work the ruin that surrounds are hid within his bosom? Is this *rule* of which you speak a law of the land; is it a construction drawn from any articles of the constitution, or is it a section of the articles of War? Is it a rule of practice, which having been acted upon by any of your illustrious predecessors, comes down with the force of *authority* upon you? Did it govern the conduct of that great Man in whose mould (according to your flattere[r]s) *you* were formed? If so, why should you conceal it? The constitution and the laws, civil and military, will justify you, and all who obey *them;* and the robes of power which *you* wear cannot be stained by an act which finds a precedent in the conduct of any of your predecessors. Is it any old principle of new application in the art of government which having escaped the searching mind of Washington and the keen vision of succeeding Presidents, has been grasped by your gigantic mind? Or is a new, wholesome principle patented to you and for which you alone are to receive all the rewards of (glory at least) which succeeding ages never fail to bestow on the first inventor of a public blessing?

The Office Harpies who haunted your public walks and your retired moments, from the very dawn of your administration, and whose avidity for office and power made them utterly reckless of the honorable feelings and just rights of others, cried aloud for *Rotation* in Office. Is that magical phrase, so familiar to the Demagogues of all nations, and of all times, your great and much vaunted Principle of *Reform?* If it be, by what kind of rotary motion is it, that men who have been but a few years, or a few months in office, are swept from the boards, while others (your friends) remain, who date their official Calends, perhaps from the time of Washington? What sort of adaptation of skill to machinery is that which brushes away those only who were opposed to your election, and leaves your friends in full possession?

Your official ~~confident~~ Organ would impose upon the public the belief that you had adopted the Jeffersonian rule of honesty, and capacity, and that incumbents, as well as applicants were tested by that infallible touchstone. The alleged delinquecis of one or two public officers have for this been made a colour; and the dye of their avowed iniquity has been spread with industrious cunning over the skirts of everry innocent victim. Even of those few who have been thus charged, their misconduct (reported) was unsuspected, until the prying eyes of their *successors* came to inspect the official records of their proceedings, when *their delegated ingenuity* as in duty bound, could do no less, than find them guilty, and therefore could not have been the *cause* of their dismissal. Your's therefore is not the Jeffersonian Rule—You ask respecting incumbents and applicants *other* questions, than, "is he *honest,* is he *capable?*" and the answer to your questions decides the applicability of your Rule. By thus ascertaining what your secret rule is *not,* we may easily come to the discovery of what it *is.* Supposing you serious when you say you are *controulled by a rule,* and that you do not move blindly like other storms, but that you have eyes which see, and ears which hear, and hence that I have not yet described your rule; there remains however but one motive which could possibly have governed you, *"punishment of your political opponents and rewards for your friends."*[2] This is your *rule* and however you may wish to disguise it, or to deceive the world into the belief that your secret principle, is something of a nobler sort, the true one is visible to every eye, and like a red meteor beams through your midnight administration, portending and working mischief and ruin—It was prescribed to you before you had the power to pursue it, by one to whom you are allied by a happy congeniality; whom you have neither the ability nor the wish to disobey, before whose omnipotent breath your presidential strength lies nerveless as infancy; who, while he suffers your heart to pursue its wonted palpitations, seems to have locked up the closet which confines your *intellect*. In this imprisonment of your mental powers, you see with his eyes, and hear with his ears. It is a misfortune for this great nation that *You* were born for him, and *He* for you. At one and the same time he is your minion and your Monarch; your priest, and your demon; your public counsellor and your bosom friend. I blush for my country when I see such unnatural formations, such a cancerous excrescence fastened upon the body politic, and the footstool of the President converted into a throne for a slave.

The injustice of your new principle of "*Reform*" would have been too glaring, had it been at once boldly unfolded, and hence is it, that it was brought out by degrees—At first it was pretended that those only who had made use of office as an engine for electionering purposes, were to be "reformed away." But when it was discovered that there were in place very many of your own friends who had been guilty of this unconstitutional impropriety as you have been pleased to call it, who contrary to any feeling of gratitude or sence of duty, had stung the bosom which warmed and the hand which fed them, making use of their office in the gift of Mr. Adams as the means of furthuring your designs upon the presidency to his exclusion, and that *your rule* was a "two edged sword" which if honestly born would "cut upon both sides;" it was soon carefully withheld, and finally, gave way to a much more comprehensive scheme of *reform*.

It was next declared that those in office who in violence of opposition had offended you in one particular (I need not name it)[3] should meet with *condign punishment*. Indeed you intimated in your private conversation with my husband that those who had passed that Rubicon had sealed their destruction—But the misfortune attending this rule was that there were none in office upon whom it *could* operate. Has the charge alluded to been fixed upon any individual of the multitude of those who have been *reformed* away? Was it ever even whispered in regard to my unfortunate husband. You know that it was not.

But I boldly declare that such a rule is altogether unworthy the Presidential office of a magnanimous nation! What! wield the public vengeance for your private wrongs? Hurl from the armory of the nation the bolt of destruction on your private foes? Was the power, dignity, and wealth of the Union concentered in your person to be so misused? Had a foreign Prince or Minister committed a like offence, with the same propriety might you have made it a cause of public quarrel, and sent from the ocean and the land hecatombs of appeasing ghosts.

The whole circumference of your *rule* at length expanded itself full to the public view; the reign of terror was unfolded, and a principle unprecedented even in the annals of tyranny, like a destroying angel, ranged through the land blowing the breath of pestilence and famine into the habitations of your enemies. Your *enemies* Sir, No. Your political opponents? You called them *enemies,* but were they so? Can there be no difference of opinion without enmity? Do you believe that *every man* who voted for Mr. Adams and who had not receiv'd from you some personal injury preferred him because he hated you? Think you, Sir, that there is no medium between idolatry and hate? It is not because you think there is no such medium, but because your elevated ambition will allow of none. This makes you look upon all those who voted against you, as your bitter foes. I most firmly believe that, saving those whom you had personally made your enemies, every honest man in giving his suffrage to Mr. Adams, obeyed the dictates of his judgement, and that many did so in violence to their warmer feelings towards you.

My husband, Sir, never was your *enemy*—In the overflowing patriotism of his heart, he gave you the full measure of his love for your *military* services. He preferred Mr. Adams for the Presidency, because he thought him qualified, and you unqualified for the station. He would have been a traitor to his country, he would have had even my scorn, and have deserved yours, had he supported you under such circumstances. He used no means to oppose you—He did a patriots duty in a patriots way—For this he is proscribed—*punished,* Oh how punished! My heart bleeds as I write. Cruel, Sir! Did he commit any offence worthy of punishment against God, or against his country or even against you? Blush while you read this question; speak not, but let the crimson negative mantle on your cheek! No, Sir, on the contrary, it was one of the best acts of his life. When he bared his bosom to the hostile bayonets of his enemies, he was not more in the *line of his duty* than when he voted against you; and had he fallen martyr on the field of fight, he would not more have deserved a monument, than he now deserves for having been worse than martyred in support of the dearest ~~birthright~~ priveledge, and chartered right of American freemen.[4] Careless as you are about the effects of your conduct, it would be idle to inform you of the depth and quality of that misery which you have worked in the bosom of my family. Else would I tell a tale that would provoke sympathy in any thing that had a heart, or gentle drops of pity from every eye not accustomed to look upon scenes of human cruelty "with composure." Besides you were apprised of our poverty, you knew the dependence of eight little children for food and raiment upon my husbands salary. You knew that advanced in years as he was, without the means to prosecute any regular business, and without friends able to assist him, the world would be to him a barren heath, an inhospitable wild—You were able therefore to anticipate the heart rending scene which you may now realize as the sole work of your hand—The sickness and debility of my husband *now call upon me to vindicate* his and his childrens wrongs—The natural timidity of my sex vanishes before the necessity of my situation, and a spirit, Sir, as proud as yours, although in a female bosom—demands justice—At your hands I ask it—return to him what you have rudely torn from his possession, give back to his children their former means of securing their food and raiment, shew that you can relent, and that your rule has had at least one exception. The severity practised by you in this instance is heightened, because accompanied by a *breach of your faith solemnly pledged to my husband*—He called upon you, told you frankly that he had not voted for you—What was your reply? It was in substance this, "that every citizen of the United States had a right to express his political sentiments by his vote." That no charges had been made against Major Barney, if any should be made, he should have justice done, he should not be condemned unheard—Then holding him by the hand with *apparent* warmth you concluded "be assured, Sir, I shall be particularly cautious how I listen to assertions of applicants for office." With these assurances from you, Sir, the President of the United States, my husband returned to the bosom of his family—With these, rehearsed, he wiped away the tears of apprehension—The President was not the Monster he had been represented—They would not be reduced to beggary, haggard want would not be permitted to enter the mansion where he had always been a stranger—The husband and the Father had done nothing in violation of his duty as an officer. If any malicious slanderer should arise to pour his poisonous breath into the ears of the President, the accused would not be condemned unheard, and his innocence would be triumphant, they would still be happy. It was presumable also that possessing the confidence of three successive administrations (whose testimony in his favor I presented to you) that he was not unworthy the office he held, beside the signatures of a hundred of our first mercantile houses, established the fact of his having given *perfect satisfaction* in the manner he transacted the business of his office—In this state of calm security, without a moments warning—*like a clap of thunder* in a clear sky your dismissal came and, in a moment, the house of joy was converted into one of mourning—Sir, was not this the refinement of cruelty? But this was not all—The wife whom you have thus agonized, drew her being from the illustrious Chase whose voice of thunder early broke the spell of British Allegiance, when in the American senate, he swore by Heaven, that he owned no allegiance to the British Crown; one too, whose signature was broadly before your eyes affixed to the Charter of our Independence—The husband and the father whom you have thus wronged, was the first born Son of a hero, whose naval and military renown brightens the page of your Country's history from seventy six to 1815, with whose atchievements posterity will not condescend to compare your's; for he fought amidst greater dangers, and he fought for Independence.

By the side of that Father in the second British War fought the Son, and the glorious 12th. of September bears testimony to his unshaken intrepidity[5]—A wife, a husband thus derived; a family of Children drawing their existence from this double revolutionary fountain—You have recklessly, causelessly, perfidiously, and therefore inhumanly, cast helpless and destitute upon the icy bosom of the world, and the children and grand children of Judge Chase & Commore Barney are poverty stricken upon the soil which owes its freedom and fertility in part to their heroic patriotism.

Sir, I would be unworthy the title of an American Matron, or an American wife, if I did not vindicate his, and my children's wrongs. In this happy land the panoply of liberty protects all without distinction of age or of sex. In the severity practised towards my husband (confessedly without cause) you have injured me and my children—You have grievously injured them, without atchieving any correspondent good to individuals, to your country or yourself—Silence therefore would be criminal even in me, and when the honest and regular feelings of the people of this country (who cannot be long deluded) shall have been restored, and when Party Frenzy, that poison to our national happiness, liberties and honour, shall have subsided, I have no doubt that the exterminating system of "Reform" will be regarged as the greatest of tyranny, though now masked under specious names, and executed with some of the formalities of Patriotism and of liberty. It is possible this communication from an unhappy Mother, and from a female, who until now had many reasons to love her country, will be regarded by you as unworthy of notice; if otherwise, and your inclination corresponds with your power, you have still the means of reparing the injury you have done—I am Sir Yr. Obt Sevt.

Mary Barney

ALS, DLC (37). *Niles*, May 15, 1830.
1. AJ Donelson had used this language in an April 22 note returning to Mrs. Barney letters she had submitted urging her husband's retention (Washington *National Journal*, May 13, 1830).
2. Duff Green had declared in a November 3, 1828, *US Telegraph* editorial that "We know not what line of policy Gen. Jackson will adopt. We take it for granted however, that he will reward his friends, and punish his enemies."
3. Criticism of Rachel Jackson.
4. Barney served as a Maryland militia major in the War of 1812.
5. At North Point near Baltimore on September 12, 1814, Maryland militia engaged a British force, inflicting heavy casualties and stalling its advance.

From Duff Green

Private & confidential

Washington 14th. June 1829

Dear Sir

Mr John Green, a clerk in the Navy Commissioner's office called on me, in great distress to advise about what course it is his duty to pursue in relation to some contracts which he believes were fraudulently entered into greatly to the loss of the United States—The facts which he discloses deeply affect the character of some of your personal & political friends, but it is no less your duty to examine into them on that account   Mr Green has a family dependant upon his salary and is unwilling to provoke the illwill of the board. In his difficulty I have taken the liberty to advise him to see you personally

I trust that you will excuse the liberty I have taken[.] your sincere friend

D Green

[Endorsed by AJ:] private & confidential.

ALS, DLC (37). John Green had been a Navy Department clerk since 1815.

[Memorandum on reverse by AJ]

Contract in Baltimore McDonald & Ridgley for groceries—is extravagant —John Nexsen offered to furnish whiskey at $^{10}/_{100}$ lower than the contract[1]—

Mr Broadhead, contract with the Navy Board, for Slop; the same, see contract filed in 2nd. auditors.[2]

Compare the above contracts with those made by the former *[board]*[3]

Warrington bought of Mr Ridgley his Clerk a quantity of powder—

Mr. Sickles. a clerk in one of our vessels died, mony drawn in his name after he was dead & given to the Secratary of the Board—

The accounts of Mr Beaty Navy agent B. to be examined[4]

AN, DLC (13-0658).

1. The Baltimore firm MacDonald & Ridgely had contracted to provide groceries, including whiskey, molasses, peas, rice, flour, and sperm oil, to several navy yards and the Baltimore naval station. John Nexsen was a New York naval supply contractor.

2. Daniel Dodge Brodhead (1802–85) of Boston had contracted to deliver slop clothing and hair mattresses to navy yards. AJ appointed him navy agent at Boston in 1830.

3. The Board of Navy Commissioners consisted of three senior naval officers appointed by the president and confirmed by the Senate. It had charge of naval procurement. Its members in 1829 were Lewis Warrington (1782–1851), Daniel T. Patterson, and John Rodgers, all appointed by Adams.

4. James Beatty (1770–1851) had been navy agent at Baltimore since 1810. He was renominated by Adams in January 1829 but not confirmed. AJ appointed Isaac Phillips in March.

To Charles Carroll

Copy

June 16th. 1829

Dear Sir,

It affords me the highest pleasure to thank you for the kind invitation with which myself and family are honored in your note of the 14th instant, by your Grandson Mr Harper. In the course of the summer we shall try and avail ourselves of it.

I am more than happy to know that you are gratified with the situation which has been assigned to Mr Harper. It is one that he will find agreeable, and in the service of which he may be prepared for much higher duties hereafter, an anticipation which his talents enables us to form with much confidence, and which I trust will reconcile you to his absence.

Accept, Sir, the assurances of my sincere regard and esteem

signed A Jackson

LS draft in AJ Donelson's hand, DLC (37). Carroll (1737–1832) was the sole surviving signer of the Declaration of Independence. On June 1 AJ had appointed his grandson Charles Carroll Harper (1802–37) secretary of legation at Paris. Carroll wrote on June 14 to thank AJ for the appointment and invite him to visit his Carrollton estate near Frederick, Md.

To Martin Van Buren

June 16th. 1829—

Dr. Sir,

I enclose you the opinion of Mr Berien on the question "Can the President *legally* under the act of Congress of the 31rst. of Janry. 1823 make an advance to the minister of the U. States about to be sent to Columbia beyond the amount of his outfit."

Mr Berien having answered this question in the afirmative you will make such reasonable advance to Major Moor as the fund on hand will authorise, keeping in view that we cannot, nor must not, in any instance exceed the appropriation, and keeping in view the advance to be made to the ministers to be sent to England, France & Spain[.] yr friend

Andrew Jackson

ALS, Sinclair Weeks, Jr. (13-0672). AJ had sought Berrien's opinion on June 13 because the 1823 law governing disbursements stated flatly that "no advance of public money shall be made in any case whatever" except to military and naval personnel on distant service.

Replying on June 15, Berrien reasoned that Congress did not intend the law to apply to diplomatic expenditures, and that these in any case fell under the president's discretionary power to conduct foreign diplomacy.

From Joshua Noble Danforth

Washington, June 16. 1829.

To His Excellency the President,

Permit me, Sir, to present to your notice, as the friend of the poor & the patron of learning, the subject of Infant Schools. When I had the honour of waiting on you a few days since in company with the Rev. Dr Griffin of Massachusetts & Col. Towson, I had no opportunity from the urgency of your business to unfold the subject.[1] I speak, I venture to say, only your own sentiments when I say the President of the United States is never engaged with more dignity & utility than when patronizing the education of his people. An Infant School at the seat of Government is deemed of preeminent importance. We wish to establish an experimental school to try the good effects in this city, as they have been tried in the other cities of the Union. The first school is to be principally a Charity School, though no children will be excluded until the full number (100) is made up.

Should the President desire further information on the subject besides that which he will obtain through the papers of today, I shall be ready to wait on him at any hour he may name for the purpose of communicating it.[2] Should the President be satisfied with the information already given, he will confer a favour on the Committee, the Community & the Cause by granting us the sanction of his name with any donation that will be agreeable.

There is no distinction of denomination in our enterprise. Among the names of the Committee are Maj. Gen. Macomb[,] Col. Jones, Rev. Messrs. Campbell, Post, Brown, Johns & Hawley, Dr Laurie & others.[3]

I will call at your house, Sir, tomorrow morning at ten o clock to receive any answer you may please to give this letter, unless you should prefer some other mode of communication. I am very respectfully, Your Excellencys obedt Servant,

J. N. Danforth
Pastor 4th Presb. Church &
Secy & Gen. Agent of Committee

ALS, DLC (37). Danforth (1798–1861) had led a church in Delaware before moving to Washington in 1828. He headed a committee of fifteen to organize a school for children aged two to seven, along recent models in London and Philadelphia.

1. Presbyterian minister Edward Dorr Griffin (1770–1837) was president of Williams College. Nathan Towson (1784–1854) was paymaster general of the Army.

2. An article by Danforth appearing in the *National Intelligencer* and *National Journal* on June 16 and the *US Telegraph* on June 17 described the benefits of infant schools and announced the intent to seek contributions.

3. Alexander Macomb (1782–1841) was commanding general of the Army, and Roger Jones (1789–1852) was adjutant general. Reuben Post (1792–1858) was pastor of the First Presbyterian Church. Obadiah Bruen Brown (1779–1852), a clerk in the post office, was pastor of the First Baptist Church. Henry Van Dyke Johns (1803–59) and William Hawley (d. 1845) were rectors of Trinity and St. John's Episcopal churches in Georgetown. James Laurie (1778–1853), a clerk in the register's office, was a Presbyterian minister at the F Street Church.

From David Reed Mitchell

State of Alabama Montgomery County June 16th 1829

Dr. Sir

I have sent on to John H Eaton coppys of two bills of sales with a copy of a letter from Opothohola head man of the Creek Nation and a statement of facts relitive to said buisness as they hapened[1] this debt I purchesed from my brother James Mitchell (who died here in 1825) as you will see some time in 1820 I took his Children and reared them and schooled them and heave neaver recd. the first cent yet but have spent near seven hundred dollars in cash and more then two year of time riding after this business you will see from the head mans letter and the memerandum of facts how I been treated I understand they have sent on the writ that was served on him and a protest against said Writ with several other communications[2] and when you see all the facts relitive I hope you will direct the agent Colnl. Crowel to force him to a settlement or direct said head man to settle this debt immediately or have the negroes secured so I can get them it is William Walkers intention to swindle me out of this debt if possable as he said a few days since when he started to the arkensaw with the imegrating Indians that when he got to Arkesaw he intended to take them himself when he got there which you will see by my statement to the secetary at war and Walker is an agent in the imigrating party and has the power which I have no hesitation in saying he will make use of if not provented[3] this business has reduced me to an imbaresed situation and I hope you will take it into consideration and let me know your appinion as early as possable as I am anxious to return home I have been waiting here on the promises of this head man better then nine months I live near Columbia Maury County Tennessee and as to my charactor I would refer you to Coln. James K Polk Coln William Pillow Samuel Olophant Esqr who lives in two mile of me when at home or Majr John Gorden[4] I shall wate here for your decision which I hope will be as early as possable which will much Obblige your humble servent

D. R. Mitchell

ALS, DNA-RG 75 (M234-222). In 1820 James Moore, an Alabama Creek, gave notes of $1,469.45 for purchases from the merchant James Mitchell (1782–1825). Mitchell signed over the debt, which was secured by four of Moore's slaves, to his brother David (c1797–1853) for the support of James Mitchell's two children. After James Mitchell's death in 1825, David Mitchell tried to recover the debt. For two years, Moore and the Creek headman Opothle Yoholo (c1798–1862), to whom Moore consigned his property, stalled him with promises to pay. Moore emigrated west in 1828, and Opothle Yoholo refused to settle. Under Alabama's new law extending jurisdiction over the Creeks, Mitchell had a writ served on him on March 6, 1829, for a debt now reckoned at $2,325. Opothle Yoholo refused to give security for his appearance in court and did not attend the subsequent trial, but was represented by counsel. On September 14, Mitchell obtained a judgment in Montgomery County circuit court against him for $2,097. The case became a judicial test of state jurisdiction over the Creeks.

1. On June 15 Mitchell sent Eaton documents sustaining his claim against Opothle Yoholo (DNA-RG 75, M234-222).

2. Tuskeneah and the Creek chiefs enclosed a copy of Mitchell's writ with their March 20 appeal to AJ (above).

3. William Walker (c1774–1836), an Army captain under AJ in the War of 1812 and son-in-law of the Creek chief Big Warrior, was a Creek subagent charged with encouraging and organizing emigration across the Mississippi. Walker at this time was preparing a Creek emigrant party from Alabama to Arkansas Territory. In his June 15 letter to Eaton, Mitchell accused Walker of taking Moore's slaves west to put them out of Mitchell's reach with the intention of keeping them himself.

4. Congressman and later president James Knox Polk (1795–1849), William Bonaparte Pillow (b. c1801), Samuel Oliphant, and John Gordon all resided in Maury County, Tenn.

To Joshua Noble Danforth

Washington June 17th. 1829

Dear Sir,

I have recd. your letter of the 16 instant, and in answer I pray you to accept of the enclosed (5 dollars) as my mite in behalf of the infant school which it is proposed to establish in this district. It is needless to add my conviction of the utility of such schools when properly managed, or my hope that, in the organization of this, nothing will be omitted which experiments elsewhere have proved to be beneficial, and necessary to its success. yr. obt sert.

A. J.

LS draft in AJ Donelson's hand, DLC (37).

To Martin Van Buren

June 17th. 1829

My Dr. Sir

When I enclosed you Mr Beriens opinion the other day, I really did not like to yield to the opinion, seeing that it would open a door to a precedent that I always wished to avoid, & that nothing could excuse only the necessity of the case—Being informed by Mr Ingham that an arrangement has been made by which Mr Moor & Mr Pickett[1] can be accomodation, I have to request that you will return me the order I have sent you, to make a reasonable advance to major Moor &c &c—as I am sure we will be able to avoid any infringement of positive law for the future[.] yr friend

Andrew Jackson

ALS, MHi (mAJs). Van Buren followed up the same day by requesting authority to make advances under several specific appropriations.

1. James Chamberlayne Pickett (1791–1872) was the newly appointed secretary of legation in Colombia.

From Stephen Simpson

(Private)

Philadelphia June 18. 1829.

Sir,

As your avocations are so oppressive & multifarious, I will not add to your labours, by making this a long letter; the object of it being merely to request a favour, which I feel confident your friendship & generosity will equally incline you to grant; & that is merely, an answer to a direct and Single question—to wit, whether what has passed between us is of such a character, in your estimation, as to preclude me from the continuance of your friendly & favourable consideration?

I am *anxious* for a Reply to this, as a friendship of Seven years continuance, & other cares & labours, would render me most unwilling to have the kind ties between us severed by a temporary difference of opinion. I have the honor to be, Sir, Your obt. hble. Servt.

S. Simpson

ALS, DLC (37).

To Joseph Elgar

Washington June 20th. 1829—

Sir

In your communication of yesterday you inform me "that from the advanced state of the work at the Capitol, & from the skill and experience of the workmen employed, you are induced to believe that the services of an architect are no longer required;" and as congress, by an act passed at its last session, authorises the President of the United States to continue in office "the architect of the capitol," so long *only* as may be necessary for the completion of the work for which appropriations were made, you will please pay the architect up to the end of the present quarter, and notify him that his services will be no longer wanted. I am very respectfully

Andrew Jackson

ALS copy, DLC (60). Elgar (c1773–1854) was the commissioner of public buildings for Washington, D.C. Charles Bulfinch (1763–1844) of Boston had been architect of the Capitol since 1818. In 1828 Congress had set the office to expire on March 4, 1829, but a law of March 3 authorized continuing it until repairs were completed. The office was abolished on June 25.

To William Pitt Preble

Washington June 20th. '29

Dr. Sir,

I take the liberty to introduce to your acquaintance & polite attention Maj Devazac, who will hand you this.

The Major during the campaign of 1814–15, before New Orleans, acted as one of my volunteer aids, & Judge advocate to the army and it affords me pleasure to say that his chivalrous conduct on that occasion deserved & received my warmest approbation   He is the brother in law of the Honble. E. Livingston of Louisiana, of the U.S. Senate, and is a gentleman of brilliant talents, & classical education—a member of the bar by profession, speaks the French & Italian languages fluently, and has expressed a great desire to attend you as Secy. of Legation to the Netherlands.

You will find the Major possessed of fine talents & agreeable manners—one who in a foreign country could render you great services. Should you be pleased with the Major, & intimate a wish to have him with you—we will with pleasure gratify you in his appointment[.] very respectfully yr. obt. servt.

Andrew Jackson

Photocopy of LS, THer (13-0690). Auguste Genevieve Valentin Davezac (1780–1851) was a New Orleans lawyer. His sister Louise had married Edward Livingston in 1805. AJ appointed Davezac secretary of legation on August 11.

To Samuel Houston

[This letter survives only in printed versions.]

WASHINGTON, D.C., June 21, 1829.

My Dear Sir:

Your letter of the 11th ult. has been received, and I seize the first leisure moment to reply.

My affliction was great, and as much as I could well bear. When I parted with you, on the 18th of January last, I viewed you on the brink of happiness and rejoiced. About to be united to a beautiful young lady of accomplished manners, of respectable connections and of your own selection, you—the Governor of the State—holding the affections of the people. These were your prospects when I shook you by the hand and bid you farewell. You can well judge of my astonishment and grief at receiving a letter, dated at Little Rock, A. T., 11th of May, conveying the sad intelligence that you were then a private citizen, in exile from your country. What a reverse of fortune! How unstable are all human affairs!

It is useless to attempt to philosophize on this sudden change of fortune. The act is done and cannot be recalled. I would it were otherwise. But now we must look to the future and forget the past, unless we review it to prevent a recurrence of evil from the same source for the future.

Surely it is a dream. It cannot be possible you have taken the determination to settle with the Indians and become a savage. I hope you have not formed such an improper determination, unless, indeed, you have determined to study theology and become a missionary amongst them. Thus you might apply your talents beneficially by teaching them the road to happiness beyond the grave. This might produce a benefit to the heathen and might be gratifying to your aged and pious mother, when it must also break her heart to hear that you have united yourself with the Indians and become one of their tribe.[1]

But I think a moment's reflection will tell you a better plan will be to settle in Kansas, pursue your profession, by which you can procure a competency, and in that new country try and regain your fallen fortune; but never let it be said that you have joined the Indians and become identified with the savages.

It is true, I have heard, and it has been communicated to me, that you had the illegal enterprise in view of conquering the Texas; that you had declared you would, in less than two years, be Emperor in that country by conquest. At the same time it was communicated that you were mad; and

I really must have thought you deranged to have believed you had such a wild scheme in contemplation, and particularly when it was communicated that the physical force to be employed was the Cherokee Indians. Indeed, my dear sir, I cannot believe you have any such visionary scheme in view. Your pledge of honor to the country is a sufficient guarantee that you will never engage in any enterprise injurious to your country, or that will tarnish your fame. I sincerely thank you for your kind expressions and wishes toward me   I will always be happy to hear from and of your prosperity   May Providence have you in His holy keeping and support your spirit under your misfortunes, and make you eminently useful to your country and yourself, is the prayer of your friend

ANDREW JACKSON.

Printed, *St. Louis Daily Globe-Democrat,* October 4, 1880 (13-0696).
    1. Elizabeth Paxton Houston (c1757–1831).

From David Reed Mitchell

State of Alabama Montgomery County June 21st 1829
Dr. Sir
    Parden me for intruding on you agane on a subject I but a few days since addressed you on as some information reletive to my case onely came to my knowledge yesterday. I was in company with the Counsel for Opothohola the head man of the nation and he stated that he had made him an offer if he would clear him of the case or reather if he would make the law unconstushenal that he would give him Five thousand dollars my debt is only about Twenty three hundred dollars The intention of this is that he wishes to make the law of the State Void and then they think they will Tamper with goverment as long as they please and to do this he will pay an attorney Five thousand dollars rather then pay my debt he should have paid three year ago there is a great meany men who live round the nation on the line and some in it who wish to make fortunes of them who are doing every thing in their power to prevent them from immegrating and I have no doubt but goverment is mistaken in some of his Officers. I am a long ways from home and not many acquentenances and in distressed circumstances from the way he has treated me and it is impossable for me to employ counsel to Compete with the Creek Nation and a great meany desineing men. I hope you will take it into consideration and say something decisive as it is out of my power to support a law suite against the whole Creek Nation for seaveral year which is intinded to be taken to the supream court. I know not wheather the state of Alabama will assist me or not (althouthe it is a popular measure) as I am a perfect stranger— you will confer a great favour by litting me know your mind as early as

possable as I wish to return home to Tennessee as soon as I can get my business settled your attention will obblege friend and humble sevant—

David R. Mitchell

NB This head man has not gave sicurity yet and I expect he intends if he cannot get clear of it by law he will by putting his property out of the way as has made it all over

D. R. Mitchell

ALS, DNA-RG 75 (M234-222). In the September trial, Opothle Yoholo's lawyers moved unsuccessfully to transfer the case to federal court. The Alabama Supreme Court upheld the 1829 state law extending jurisdiction over the Creeks in *Caldwell v. the State* (1832). From 1834 to 1840 Mitchell repeatedly petitioned Congress, without success, to compensate his costs in pursuing his suit against Opothle Yoholo.

From Roley McIntosh et al.

Council Ground of the Western Creeks
22d. June 1829.

To General Andrew Jackson President of the United States

The Chiefs, Headmen & Warriors of the Creek nation, in full council assembled, cannot overlook the unhappy situation, in which they are placed, and deeply impressed with their misfortunes, believe it their duty to complain to a man, whose Ears have always been open to hear the complaints of the Wretched, and whose Hand has always been swift to redress the wrongs of the injured—

We have before set forth complaints, but we are fearful they have not reached the President and least that should be the case, we will repeat some of our complaints, and make new ones, not without a cause.

General Jackson knows the circumstances under which we emigrated to this Country; He heard the groans of the Mackintosh Party in the old nation—We talked to him at a distance and he told us to come to this Country—In War and in Peace, we have always taken his counsel; In coming to this Country an agent was given to us, but not by General Jackson—That agent has not tried to make us happy—He has done bad things towards us, and when he saw he could do us good, and help us, he shut his Eyes, to our necessities, folded his arms and would not reach out his Hand to help us—He has made us promises and has not performed them—We will state the causes of our sorrows—

1st. Col Brearly has failed to pay us the bounty promised us by the Treaty and we have reason to believe that money was placed in his Hands by the Government for that purpose.[1]

2d. He made a Private Contract to furnish us with provision at 3½ cents per pound for Beef, when we believe it could have been obtained for $ 2½—He purchased up all the Cattle and Hogs of the Country, and then took the Contract from Mr. Bean, whilst it was at 3½ cents per pound, slaughtered and issued the Beef to the Indians, thereby profiting by his own contract from his official station and assuring Mr. Bean, that the Contract should be renewed with him on terms of equal advantage—

3d. He has connived at the introduction of spirituous liquors into the Creek nation if he has not participated in the benefit of their sale—

4th. He has speculated on the necessities of the Indians, through his clerk, by permitting him to sell flour to the Indians at the enormous price of $10 the barrell—

5th. Intoxication and disrespectful language to the chiefs whilst in that state.

6th. Injustice to Emigrants, in this that he represented to the Government, that the Country selected by the Creeks was that lying between the Arkansas and Verdigris, when he well knew that the Country selected by them, was that lying between the Arkansaw and Canadian for immediate settlement, and for future settlers that lying between the Arkansaw and Verdigris, and that they would have made immediate settlement between the Arkansaw and Canadian, had it not been that Col. Brearly refused to deliver them provision at the point selected—[2]

7th. He has failed to remunerate the Indians for money expended for the purchase of forage, while removing to this Country—

8th. By his neglect the Indians sustained considerable loss by property left at Fort Smith for want of Transportation, which he refused to furnish.

9th. He has failed to pay for the improvements in the old nation, according to their Valuation—He notified the holders of claims to repair to the agency on a certain day, to receive pay for their improvements, and when they arrived, he informed them, he was just about starting to Washington had packed his trunk and would not unpack it for the purpose of paying them and without offering them any satisfaction left them—

10th. His Sub-Agent has recently taken receipts for Bounties due to Emigrants and has given certificates of the amount due to each one in lieu of the money, in his own name thereby prejudicing the Emigrants, inasmuch as they cannot pass these certificates off for Cattle in the cherokee nation or elsewhere to meet their necessities and they are of depreciated Value in the Creek nation, whereas the money would afford them all the facilities contemplated by the Treaty granting the Bounty. The chiefs are greatly fearful that some imposition is intended either towards their nation or against the Government, inasmuch as the Sub-Agent declares he has no authority from Col Brearly to take receipts and has placed them in the Hands of Joseph Brearly son to the agent for safe keeping. The Chiefs requested the sub-agent to have the receipts placed in the Hands of Col Arbuckle, for safe keeping, so that no injury might grow out of the transaction, but when they called for that purpose Joseph Brearly refused to place them in the hands of Col Arbuckle or any other person until the return of his father.[3]

11th. The agent has not furnished the nation with a mechanic as stipulated in the Treaty—[4]

The chiefs feel sensible that Col Brearly does not regard them or their people in the light contemplated by the Government and that his sole object is *speculation* regardless alike of the interest of the Indians or of that of the United States—Under these circumstances it cannot be thought amiss by the President, situated as we are that we should solicit the removal of this man and request the appointment of some Individual, whose Moral Conduct honesty & good feeling, will ensure to the Indians happiness, and to the President the faithful execution of his orders—Another subject of deep sorrow to us, is the information that Col Crowell is to be sent to us as our agent—[5]

This we hope is not true, nor can we believe that Genl Jackson would make us so unhappy—He well knows the sorrows that we suffered in the old nation! He has not forgotten the murder of Mackintosh—He knows that his blood yet lies on the ground unburied—

Mackintosh was a Warrior of Genl Jackson's—The Genl. told him he would protect him, but Jackson was far off—Col Crowell near at hand—He whispered to the enemies of Mackintosh—he pointed at him and he perished—Mackintosh has friends and children yet living—they cannot be happy when they think of his death—nor can they ever receive the man who caused—If he were amongst us, the same men are yet living that killed Mackintosh and the agent might point at another Mackintosh—whenever we think of Col Crowell our Hearts are sorrowful—we hope Genl Jackson will not make us miserable and that he will keep this man from among us—

our miseries in the old nation drove us from the land of our fathers and we hope Genl Jackson will make our new Homes happy—Division amongst us at this time would prevent the old nation from coming and if a good agent is given to us and we are happy, the people of the old nation will flock to us to share our happiness—

The chiefs will add one request of the President to permit a Delegation of Six to visit Washington City, that their lines with the Cherokees may be settled and the creeks know what land belongs to them, and for other purposes which will be made known when they see the President and take him by the Hand[6]

> Roley McIntosh his X mark
> Chilly McIntosh
> Fush hatcha Micco his X mark
> Hottley Marter Tuskenuggee his X mark
> Benjamin Derrisaw X

[Nineteen additional names follow, along with the signatures of witnesses: Army officers Mathew Arbuckle, John Stewart, James Low Dawson, Lawrence F. Carter, and Gabriel James Rains; interpreter Benjamin Hawkins; and Samuel Houston.]

Done at Cant. Gibson in the presence of the subscribed Witnesses at an adjourned Council

John Wynn Clerk of the C.N.

LS, DNA-RG 75 (M234-236). This memorial was forwarded by Houston on June 24, and referred by AJ to Eaton. AJ had already ordered David Brearley's removal on June 10. Eaton answered the Creeks on August 3. He acknowledged their complaints, informed them of Brearley's removal, and reiterated AJ's urging that all the Indians remove beyond the Mississippi "where alone he thinks they will be able to find repose and happiness" (DNA-RG 75, M21-6).

1. Writing to Eaton on June 15, Brearley defended his conduct of the agency and blamed the delay in paying the bounty on difficulties in settling the Indians' accounts for previous advances (DNA-RG 75, M234-237).

2. Brearley had reported on May 28 and July 20, 1827, that the exploring party for the emigrating Creeks preferred the land north of the Arkansas River, between it and the Verdigris, to that southward between the Arkansas and the Canadian (M234-237).

3. Colonel Mathew Arbuckle (1776–1851) commanded at Cantonment Gibson. Subagent Thomas Anthony had issued due bills to the Creeks for the bounty owed them, taking their receipts. The Indians sold the due bills to traders or made purchases with them at depreciated value. In 1830 Houston charged that due bills had been issued for about $21,000 and that the Indians had lost around one-third that sum (*Writings of Sam Houston*, 1:159).

4. The Treaty of Washington promised the emigrants a blacksmith and a wheelwright.

5. John Crowell, agent to the eastern Creeks. AJ appointed John Campbell of Tennessee to replace Brearley on September 9.

6. Eaton's reply of August 3 promised a settlement of the boundary but declined to invite a delegation to Washington.

From Joshua Noble Danforth

Washington, June 23. 1829.
Marblehead

Mr Danforth begs leave to inform the President that, if agreeable, a Class of Infant Children from Alexandria with their Teacher will wait on him at his house tomorrow afternoon about five or six oclock & in an half hour or an hour will present to the President and his family a more perfect view of this wonderful system of instruction than they could otherwise obtain.

Should the President be disposed to invite the Secretaries, or any other friends, to witness the exhibition, the Teachers will endeavour to make it interesting, so as not only to afford a pleasant relaxation from the fatigues of business, but also to enable parents to judge of the propriety of placing their children in schools of this character. Most respectfully,

J. N. Danforth
Secy & Gen. Agent of
Committee on Infant Schools

[Endorsed by AJ:] Mr Donelson will answer the enclose[d] by Mr Danforth on Thursday 11 oclock the Infant children with their preceptor will attend at the president House—the Heads of Departments with their families are requested to attend—Mr Donelson will address a note to each head of a Department—including the attorney Genl—

ALS, DLC (37). Danforth brought his pupils to the White House on June 25. AJ and family, Eaton, and Berrien attended. AJ and Danforth exchanged remarks and the children performed their exercises (*US Telegraph,* Jun 26).

From John Forsyth

Copy,

Executive Department Georgia
Milledgeville June 23d. 1829.

Sir,

I have the honor to transmit to you by this days mail a copy of the map of the true line between the Creeks and Cherokees according to the testimony forwarded to the War Department with my letter to the Secretary of War of the 19th. Ulto.[1]

In obedience to the instructions of the General Assembly of Georgia I request that you will have all and every Indian whether Creek or Cherokee who may be found residing below the line discribed in the Map between the Chattohoochee River and the boundary line of Georgia and Alabama immediately removed.[2] I am Sir with great Respect Your obt. Servt.

John Forsyth

Copy, DLC (37); LC, G-Ar (13-0699). In 1821 the Cherokees and Creeks had defined the boundary between their Georgia domains. Georgia officials claimed that this agreement wrongfully gave to the Cherokees an area of some one million acres in northwest Georgia that had been recognized by federal treaty as belonging to the Creeks, and that therefore belonged to Georgia after the Creeks ceded the last of their Georgia lands in 1827. A resolution of the Georgia legislature, signed December 20, 1828, authorized the governor to mark the correct boundary and ask the president to immediately remove Indians from state land.

1. Forsyth had sent Eaton documents supporting Georgia's claim on May 19 (DNA-RG 75, M234-73).

2. This letter miscarried and did not reach AJ. Forsyth wrote Eaton again on July 27 (DNA-RG 75, M234-222) to complain of Indian depredations and press for an answer about removal. Eaton's reply on August 5 (DNA-RG 75, M21-6) promised to deter Indian hostilities but did not address the boundary issue.

Order for Remission of Penalties

June 25th. 1829—

The act of the 2nd of March 1819 under which arise the penalty & forfeiture of the British vessel Wm. Shand (wm Bowell master) is founded in considera[tion] of humanity. The policy of the law is, that imigrants and passengers should not be so crouded in vessels as to induce the apprehension of suffering & inconvenience at sea. In the present instance neither appears to have been the case: The passengers show that they were treated kindly, & every thing wanted, liberally furnished, and that they were not crouded, & thereby incommoded.[1] Altho under the letter of the law, the forfeiture might be insisted upon, yet it does not appear to be a case within the spirit & policy of the act. Let therefore the penalty be remitted, & the forfeiture of the vessel set aside; on payment of any costs to the officers that may have been incurred by the seisure.

Andrew Jackson

ADS, DNA-RG 59 (13-0732). The penalties were formally remitted on June 27. The *William Shand*, under master William Boswell, was carrying immigrants from Rye, England, to New York City. It had 147 passengers, 33 more than permitted under an 1819 law that limited vessels to two passengers for every five tons of weight. Violators were liable to a penalty of $150 for every excess passenger and to forfeit the vessel if the excess reached twenty.
    1. John Arnold and twenty-two other passengers so deposed on June 17 (13-0721).

To Stephen Simpson

(copy)

Washington June 27th. 1829

Sir,
    I received your confidential note of the 18th. inst in due time, and designed to have answered it immediately but incessant calls upon my ~~time~~ attention prevented me until now.
    You desire to know whether any thing has passed between us which I consider as precluding you from my friendly consideration. I answer, nothing. In my public and private capacity, bound in both to take care of the interests of the country, and my own character, you must perceive the

necessity for cautious deliberation in every step which I take concerning either. Responsible to the country, I must look for information to all fair sources, reserving at all times the right to weigh it, and the independence to follow the dictates of my best judgement in the course of action which may be the consequence of it. But feeling that you had not been disposed to accord to me this freedom of action, I indulged no other sentiment on account of it than that of regret, that one who expressed so much disinterestedness of support for me should be among the first to menace me with consequences injurious to the country, and threatening to the purity of my motives. If I misunderstood you, be assured I am ready to revive the same intercourse which formerly prevailed between us. I cherish no unfriendly feeling toward you, and will always be glad to hear of your prosperity, and when I can, to promote it. Very respectfully yr. obt. sevt.

signed Andrew Jackson

[Endorsed by AJ:] copy to S. Simpson June 27th—1829—

LS draft in AJ Donelson's hand, DLC (37).

From Logan Davidson Brandon

Huntsville June 27th. 1829

Dear Sir;

   Although my acquaintance with you is very limited, yet the friendship I have ever evinced and still feel toward you, will in some sort excuse the liberty I have taken in addressing you—

   Your friends in this section of the state are dissatisfied with the appointment of Mr Joseph Scott to the office of District attorney, though generally pleased with the removal of Mr Thornton—Mr S. is said to be by those who know him best, intirely incompitent—He has not been residing in the State but a few months and is unknown except to those who knew him in East Tennessee—There are several persons here who have a kind of introductry acquaintance with him—such an one I have myself with Mr S. tho not sufficient to form a correct Idea of his talents, though I am certain from what I know myself and from what I have heard others say who deserve to be credited, who have long known Mr. S., and who are uninfluenced by any unfriendly feelings toward that gentleman, that you must have been much imposed upon by those who recommended Mr S. otherwise he could not have obtained the appointment—If it had been known that Mr T. would have been removed, there are men in this district who stand deservidly high in the estimation of the community and who have always been your warm friends and supporters, that could have presented themselves before you with the best recommendations from men of the highest legal and moral respectability—But they have been deprived of this, by modesty and nothing else, while another who perhaps could not have obtained a letter from a gentleman *in this state* has been success-ful—While ever the incumbant remained quietly in office it was deemed a matter that involved the most refined delicacy to presume to forward recommendatory documents to remove him and place another in his sted and therefore men of ordinary modesty were precluded from presenting their claims—I do not wish to say anything against Mr S. as a gentleman or otherwise but I declare to you most *sincearly* that I never have seen more dissatisfaction manifested in all my life than is appearant on the present occasion—It is a matter of much regret to your friends and a mat-ter of rejoi[c]ing in the highest to your enemies except to the few personal friends of Mr. Thornton—I had a conversation with the Editor of the Democrat[1] this morning on the subject of Mr S. appointment and he is of opinion that you will upon being made acquainted with the talents of Mr S. recind the appointment and that will shew to the world you have been misled by the representations of the friends of Mr S.—Candour compells me to say to you that I have a relation known to you, who is or will be an applicant for that appointment—and you may think I am induced to this course by motives of interest—but sir I declare to you most solemnly I am actuated by no other motive than a wish to see the present administration prosper and flourish under your guidence and direction and to sustain you and myself *[also]* I have had some conflicts in my life with men in this place on your account who are yet my enemies and they will seize upon this as an auspicious era of triumph—I am in great hast your sincear friend &c

Logan D. Brandon

ALS, DNA-RG 59 (M639-21). Brandon (1803–55) was a native of North Carolina. In February 1830 AJ superseded Scott's recess appointment by nominating Brandon's older brother, Byrd Brandon (1798–1838), as attorney for Alabama's northern district.

    1. The Huntsville *Democrat,* a Jackson paper, was edited by Philip M. Woodson (1791–1869) and Thomas J. Sumner (1798–1881). Woodson protested Scott's appointment to AJ on June 29.

To Judith Page Walker Rives

Washington June 28th. 1829.

Dr Madam

    Having been informed by Mrs. Donelson that you have a desire to be possessed of a sample of my Autography, I furnish it with much pleasure. Accept the assurance of my great respect and esteem,

Andrew Jackson

The within ve[r]ses are respectfully presented to Mrs. Rives. J.

> Now to my tent, O God, repair,
> And make thy servant wise;
> I'll suffer nothing near me there,
> That shall offend thine eyes.
> The man that doth his neighbour wrong,
> By falsehood, or by force,
> The scornful eye, the slanderous tongue,
> I'll banish from my doors.
> I'll seek the faithful, and the Just,
> And will their help enjoy;
> These are the friends, that I shall trust,
> The servants, I'll employ.

Andrew Jackson

ALS, DLC-William C. Rives Papers (13-0737); ALS draft of June 26, DLC-Donelson Papers (13-0717). Rives (1802–82), who later attained note as an author, had married William C. Rives in 1819. AJ's verses were from Isaac Watts's version of Psalm 101.

To *Ezra Stiles Ely*

Washington June 29th. 1829.

My Dr. Sir,
  This will be handed to you by my son, who is charged to present our kind salutations to you, your amiable family, & Mrs. Carswell & hers— My son[1] goes to spend two or three days in your city before he returns to Tennessee; whilst in the city, I place him under your kind protection, & guardianship. I am very respectfully yr friend,

Andrew Jackson

ALS, Dr. Harry L. Wechsler (13-0746).
  1. Andrew Jackson, Jr.

From *William Carroll*

Nashville, June 29th. 1829.

Dear Sir:
  I have received from the Secy. of war several communications on the subject of visiting the Cherokee and Creek Indians for the purpose of inducing them to remove west of the Mississippi. In answer I have stated to him that I shall leave here about the 15th. of August for the purpose of carrying into effect your wishes. I delay until the time mentioned because there seemed to be no great necessity for going sooner; and because I

wished to remain for some time at home to rid myself of a very afflicting disease, with which I have been occasionally attacked for the last eighteen months. Should it be your desire that I should set out earlier, I will do so, unless prevented by ill health.

I am induced to believe, from what I have lately heard, that your correct and humane intentions with regard to the Southern Indians can be carried into effect without much dificulty. Mississippi, Georgia and Alabama having extended their Jurisdiction over their Territorial limits owned by the Indians will be a strong inducement for them to remove. They cannot bear the execution of our criminal laws. I was in South Alabama a short time since, when three or four Indians were tried and found guilty of horse-stealing in a county near Fort Strother.[1] The sentence of the court was immediately carried into effect, and the red brethern gave abundent proof of their dislike to a whipping post and the laws of civilized society. I cannot but hope, that I can induce both the Creeks and Cherokees as directed by the Secretary of War to agree to hold treaties in which event, the means of success will be found in assailing the averice of the chiefs and principal men. I think that I can move among the Cherokees without exciting their suspicion. My avowed object will be to get them to agree to let the waters of Tennessee and Coosa be united by means of a canal and to assure them, in a delicate way, that Tennessee will, at the next session of the Legislature extend her Jurisdiction over them   These, and the employment of other means which may present themselves, I trust will enable me to succeed.[2]

I see that Doctor Watkens is more disposed to rely on a demurrer than on the Justice of his cause. His conduct if there was no proof against him looks bad.

I believe we have nothing of a domestic character worth communicating

With a tender of my sincere wishes for the prosperity of your Administration, and for your own health and happiness I am dear Sir most respectfully your Obt Servt.

Wm. Carroll

ALS, DNA-RG 75 (M234-113); Copy, DNA-RG 46 (13-0743). *SDoc* 512, 23d Cong., 1st sess., vol. 2, pp. 76–77 (Serial 245). Carroll had been commissioned as a special Indian agent on May 27. Eaton instructed him on May 30 to meet privately and informally with influential Cherokees and Creeks, "not as a negotiator, but friend," and induce them to support removal by stressing the dangers of their position and the advantages of the West. He was authorized to spend up to $2,000 on presents (Eaton to Carroll, May 27, May 30, and Jun 1, DNA-RG 75, M21-5). Carroll reached the Cherokee country on August 13 and met with many of the chiefs, but failed to persuade them to remove. Illness prevented his visiting the Creeks (*SDoc* 1, 21st Cong., 1st sess., pp. 178–82 , Serial 192).

1. Fort Strother, erected by AJ before the Battle of Talladega in 1813, was located on the Coosa River in what is now St. Clair County, Ala.

2. The Tennessee legislature discussed extending state jurisdiction over Cherokee lands in 1829, but did not do so until 1833.

From Wewelino et al.

Crooked Creek, Arkansas Territory
The 29th. day of June. 1829

Father

We send you Our Talk, Hopcing you will hear our complaints as, well, as Our desires—some Time aftar the Close of the War, in your Country Cause (in which you ware Inguaged) with Great Britton, we seperated ourselves from Our Shawane's Brothers, & Exchanged our Lands, removed To Whiteriver, in Arkansas Territory, where we ware Told, Land would be given To us, whereon we would live in peace & Happiness, with such necessaries as was Stipulated by Treaty—but by some fatality, our Expectations has been Disappointed, but this we cannot Comprehend, Thence, About Two or three years ago, we ware Told—That Land ware Laid off for us on Kansas River a Branch of the Missouri River with Instructions, To send a Deputation To this Land & point out a place, whereon, To remove our woman & Children, with an Assurance that there we should Live forever undisturbed—Nevertheless, this being a Third time, that Assurances To the same Effect was Imposed on us some of Our Chiefs & young men attended The Escort, & was conducted To Kansas River & directed To Chose, or, point out Our situation, there again was Our Expectations Disappointed

Father, we desire you will hear & listen To Our Talk

During the last War with Great Briton, several of us your Children Entered in the servis of the United states & served under the Orders of Genl. Harrison wher many of our best men, & near relations, fell, fighting for & in behalf of the United States—Nevertheless, we, at the Close of the War Agreed To the Exchange of Land—we have now at this time Not one foot of Land we can Call Our Own, Unless we remove To Kansas River, where we are very Certain we Cannot Live[1]   On Kansas River the soil is good, but the winter season is Too Cold; the Country without Timber, or, nearly so, nether Game or Winter range, & under such sircumstances we will All Die of Hunger, & the small Quantity of Horses & Cows we now Possess will parrish the first Winter Season—

Father listen—when we seperated Ourselves from Our Shawne Brothers, It was our Intention never to Unite with them, Or any Other Indian Nation, but to become Citizens of the United states & To Conform Ourselves To their government & Laws believing (as we do) in their mildness & Justice & with a Sincare desire, That Our Children under their Administration may be Taught the princibels of Civilized Life, & be pertakers of the very great Blessings & Advantages resulting therefrom—Father,

In this way we have often spoke, but we have not been heard

Father,

we rejoice you have become Our Father

you are a Great Captain in war & Knows how to Appreciate the merrits of a brave soldear who has Assisted you to fight & Conquor the Enemies of your Country, there is between Twenty &, Thirty, families belonging to our Party, Therefore, Father,

We desire To be Taken & Admitted as Citizens of the United States as aforesaid, & To have a small Portion of Land Alotted Sufficient, by, attention To agriculture to support on, Lying & being so convenant to Our White Brethern, That we may not Only profit by their Example, but have the benefit of their Counsil in the Direction & Management of Our Concerns. the Land whereon we now live, ware we alowd, we would make Choice of, Generally, Known by, Shawane town, on Crooked Creek Father,

We are now without a prospect, you are all, & the Only One That is Able To help us, & we hope the great spirit Will Bless you & give you Mercy & power to Extend it To us your Children, & when you read this Our Talk, we desire you To write us your answer & Direct To Izard Court House Arkansas Territory—

Father

We Ask the great spirit Above, to Love you & make you Happy

Signed
Wewelino, Capt. Tomhalk
Petiethwa, Capt. Read
Mithapesika—Capt. John
Myawaskaha
Psapowcta
Elowpesikah, Capt. Henry
Squabisuka, Capt. Bob
Linewahpesika

D, DNA-RG 75 (M234-300). Shawnee Town was at the site of present Yellville in northern Arkansas. Groups of Shawnees had moved west over the years, some settling in Missouri and with the western Cherokees in Arkansas. In the 1825 Treaty of St. Louis, they ceded their Missouri holdings for cash and 50 square miles of land to be located either just west of southern Missouri or further north along the Kansas River. The Shawnee presence in Arkansas Territory was undercut in May 1828 when the Cherokees ceded their lands there and agreed to vacate within fourteen months. As late as 1831 about 300 Indians remained at Shawnee Town, but an 1832 treaty required their removal to the Kansas River.

1. Shawnees had fought with William Henry Harrison on the northwest frontier in the War of 1812 and signed an 1817 treaty by which the Wyandots and other tribes ceded lands. Some Shawnees remained in Ohio.

To John Branch

Washington June 30th. 1829—

Sir

A Ship having been chartered agreeable to an appropriation of the last Session of Congress, to remove to the coasts of Africa certain Africans who were wrecked on the coasts of Florida & brought within the Jurisdiction of the United States; and orders having been sent to the Marshal of the Eastern District of Florida for their delivery—The vessel thus chartered will proceed in a few days for the Port of St. Augustine or Fernandina to receive said Africans—Mr Smith Marshal of the Eastern District of Florida, has Just arrived, & is now in this city; and as it is important that no delay should be met with, as the owner of the Ship if detained will claim Demurrage; you will Issue your order to the Marshal forthwith to proceed to Florida, & have the whole of the Africans ready to be embarked on board the Ship Nautilus, _____ Commander on the first day of august next, so that on no account, shall the said ship be detained in port more than ten days after her arrival—you will make enquiry which of the ports, St. Augustine or Fernandina will be most convenient for the embarkation of the Africans, and give orders accordingly to the captain of the ship chartered.[1] I am very respectfully yr mo. obdt. servt.

Andrew Jackson

ALS, DNA-RG 45 (M124-119); ALS draft, DLC (37). In December 1827 the Spanish brig *Guerrero,* carrying more than 500 slaves from Africa, was chased by a British warship and wrecked in the Florida Keys. About 120 of the Africans were brought to Key West, after the Spanish crew commandeered two rescue ships and fled to Cuba with the rest. The naval appropriations act of March 2, 1829, allocated $16,000 to transport the Africans and to reimburse Waters Smith (c1779–1831), the marshal for Florida's eastern district, for his expenses in keeping them. Not knowing that Smith was coming to Washington, Branch had written him on June 15 and 27 to ready the Africans for sailing on August 1 (DNA-RG 45, M205-1).

1. On July 1 Branch ordered Smith to have the Africans ready to sail from Fernandina on August 15 on the brig *Nautilus,* hired from John McPhail of Norfolk. The *Nautilus* proved unseaworthy, and after further delays the Africans embarked from Fernandina on September 30 on the schooner *Washington's Barge,* chartered from Richard Churchward of New York. It did not reach Africa but put into Barbados in distress. In January 1830 the Africans returned to Baltimore.

From James G. Carroll

Huntsville, June 30th 1829—

Respected Sir,

Upon the appointment of Mr. Moore, to be Marshal of the Northern District of Alabama, I did myself the honor to address a letter on the subject to Mr. Van Buren, which I requested him to lay before you— should business, or any other cause, have prevented his compliance, I now respectfully ask you to inspect it—[1]

In that letter, I informed him, that I held a deputation for this District from Maj. Armstrong, Marshal of the State & was watching the progress of the Law authorizing the Appt. of a Marshal for this District, with the intention of making application for it, should the Law pass—From the caption of the acts of Cong—and from various other sources, I learned that it did not pass—and became quiet in my apprehension on the subject—

I stated also that I had given general Satisfaction to the people—that I had been your firm, original & abiding friend in the struggle, in which you have so gloriously triumphed—and to shew the consideration in which I was held by those who know me best, I remarked, that I held the appointment of adjt. General of the State of Alabama—to which I was elected, at the session of the legislature, before the last—which is however without a salary adequate to my actual expenditure in discharging its functions—

In regard to Mr. Moore, who had received the appt, I remarked among other things, that I had strong ground for believing that he was the silent friend of Mr. Adams—that the two young men with whom he had written in the Clerk's office, had never heard him say for whom he intended vote or with whom his wishes & his feelings were—that he was young & the associate of boys—rather than men—that Messrs. Hopkins & Birny, who I was informed, had recommended him, among others, altho' distinguished lawyers, were "Adams men"—and one of them his Candidate for elector—that Genl. Brahan, who had also recommended him had done so, at the instance of one of those young clerks, without any personal knowledge of him—and finally inquired, what effect, these facts if proven, could have, and whether it might not twist the stream of patronage from him to me—[2]

Not having received any reply, I have concluded to take the liberty of addressing you, personally—in as much as I have the honor of an acquaintance—

In my original and continuing support of you, I was influenced by regard for your person—& admiration & gratitude for your services to the republic—I did never know—nor did I ever expect to be an applicant for any favour, which success might enable you to bestow—My father & 3 brothers, were I presume, actuated by the same motives—Our frienship was not needed, but still it constituted a part of that great Majority, by which you are now enabled to wield the destinies of this great nation—We claim no credit for it, but that which is due for conscientiously discharging our duty as freemen—I beg leave to observe therefore, that, I do not ask a reconsideration on that account, but Mr. Moore's father voted for your opponent—he himself, was silent—and I humbly think, that, respect to yourself and to the great cause in which your *friends* & yourself have been successful—should designate *them* where they possess equal or superior qualifications, as the proper recipients of those favours, which that success has enable you to bestow, in preference to those, who folded their arms in indifference & silently awaited the result of the great struggle, prepared, to ask of Adams, if successful, any office, within his gift, with the same propriety & *shew* of *friendship* &c that they can now ask you   this I believe to be the fact in regard to Mr. Moore—

I have written to several of the most [dis]tinguished of your friends & *acquaintances* in this *[place]* to obtain letters, which I shall forward as soon as *[I can—]* this would have been done earlier, but I awaited a reply from Mr. Van Buren—*I have written you now* that you may be prepared to understand those letters when received, and because Maj. Smith is at Washington, with whom I have some acquaintance & by whom these things are in part unknown—³

The arrival of the mail, has just brought three letters—from Dr. Gid. G. Williams, Maj. Kellough & Col. Winston, together with *a paper,* signed by many of your friends & acquaintances—all men of the first respectability⁴ —I ask a reply—(confidentially). I am with all respect & regard your friend—

Jas. G. Carroll

ALS, DNA-RG 59 (M639-4). On April 20 AJ had appointed Benjamin T. Moore (c1803–70) marshal for the northern district of Alabama. Moore had previously been employed by the clerk of the Circuit Court at Huntsville, Lemuel Mead. He was the son of Edward Moore (1770–1855) and nephew of former congressman Gabriel Moore, elected governor of Alabama in 1829. The 1824 statute creating a second Alabama judicial district had not provided for a marshal, and a bill to authorize one in the last Congress did not pass. Moore's appointment was consequently revoked in August. A law of May 5, 1830, authorized a marshal, and AJ appointed Benjamin Patteson.

1. Carroll had written Van Buren on May 20 (M639-4).
2. Huntsville attorneys James Gillespie Birney (1792–1857) and Arthur Francis Hopkins (1794–1865) had recommended Moore to Senator John McKinley on March 20 (M639-16). Birney, later a famous abolitionist, was an Adams candidate for elector in 1828. John Brahan (1774–1834) of Huntsville had recommended Moore to AJ on March 22.
3. Benjamin F. Smith.
4. Anthony Winston (1782–1842), David Keller (1788–1837), and Gideon G. Williams of northern Alabama recommended Carroll to AJ on June 11, 13, and 15, as did John J. Winston and twenty-seven others in an undated letter.

From Nathaniel Amory

Pensacola

Sir

Circumstances which have recently come to my knowledge relative to my removal from office induce me to address you this Letter. I hope & confidently trust that the peculiar nature of the case will be deem'd by you an acceptable apolgy for thus intruding upon your valuable time.

It has been stated from a source that cannot be doubted that you were pleased to name as a reason for depriving me of the Navy Agency here, that you wish'd the Office fill'd by a person in whom you could place confidence, leaving it to be infer'd that I was unworthy the trust that had been confided to me. The loss of my office situated as I am, was I must confess a sad disappointment, an event I consider'd hardly within the range of possibility, being conscious of having perform'd the duties thereof with zeal & fidelity, with perfect acceptation to the late Secretary & the Board of Navy Commissioners. I was also free from all political connexions, having through life felt a distaste for such pursuits, the favorable consequence of which has been a most satisfactory & confidential intercourse with valuable friends throughout the Union whose politics have been opposed & I truly believe that I enjoy the confidence & friendship of as many highly respected & conspicuous Individuals were favorable to your Election as of those who were opposed to it. True it is, I feel a personal friendship for your Predecessor & I feel truly grateful for his kindness & confidence in confering the favor & honor of my appointment. It is no less true, that I have always entertain'd for yourself sentiments of the highest respect & I may add gratitude, since it was to your noble exertions & brilliant success at New Orleans that I was indebted for the preservation of an ample fortune which I once possess'd. I must confess that the loss of my office grieved me much, I had held it Eighteen months only when I learnt that a Successor had been appointed, the expences were heavy attending my coming to this distant part of the Country and the necessary arrangements for a residence, my return home will be equally so, independent of my detention here on account of the Season—still I have never complained—I consider'd it a course of policy you were pleased to pursue in your administration of the General Government and I should not now trouble you with this communication but from a sense of duty to myself & friends; it is not with a view of restoration to my Office, it is merely a restoration of my good name which I ask & which appears implicated by the reason you assign'd for removing me. I fear your Ear has been abused, I respectfully solicit the means of defence by a knowlege of what I am accused; in the power of effecting this most desirable object I have the fullest confidence; such is the knowledge of my own rectitude & such my perfect assurance of the generous magnanimity of your character.

For the last thirty years I have taken a great & increasing interest in the prosperity of our Navy which led to an intimacy & friendship with almost every Officer of distinction in the Service, to these Gentlemen I could appeal if appeal were necessary for the respectability of my standing & character and I beg leave more especially an appeal to Como Ridgely, who is about to leave this command, for the propriety of my conduct as a public Officer.

I beg you to believe Sir that it is with great reluctance that I have thus tresspass'd with such length—I hope my motive will be duly appreciated & that you will have the goodness to devote as early as your convenience will permit a few moments in reply directed Post Office Pensacola. I have the honor to be most respectfully Your ob Servant

[Endorsed by AJ:] copy of Mr Emorys letter—To be placed on file—relating to his dismissal from office   Col Hamiltons private letter enclosed—have an interview with the sec of the Navy—

AL Copy, DLC-Gideon Welles Papers (13-0517). Amory (1777–1842), a Massachusetts native and Harvard graduate, had operated a mercantile business in New Orleans for many years. Adams appointed him navy agent at Pensacola in January 1828. In May AJ had replaced him with Charles P. Tutt.

Memorandum Book

[These June and July entries in Jackson's memorandum book directly follow those above from April and May.]

The System of Smuggling entered into by our citizens with the British manufacturers is alarming to us, & must be injurious to our revenue, every exertion & vigilence by our officers & agents must be resorted to, & the aid of the manufacturers called in, whose interests are so much affected by it, & ruin to their establishments inevitable if smuggling cannot be put down—English goods are now selling in Newyork &c &c, 33⅓ prct. lower than the fair american merchant can afford to sell his goods for—

The attention of Congress must be drew to a Judicious revision of the Tariff—note, whenever any branch of labour is ~~too well~~ protected more than another, it converts so much capital to that branch, that it is sure to destroy itself, the competition reduces the price of goods below their real cost, stocks & glutts the markett, & bankrupts the manufaturer—June 20th. 1829—Mr Swartwout instructed as to smuggling, to have it detected A. J[1]

The Honble Mr Nobles letter on the subject of the suspension of the sales of public land—on a consultation with Major Graham on this day (23rd June 1829) we unite in opinion that there can be no necessity for prolonging the sales of forfeited or relinquished land—all who wish, can get land, at the minimum price by entry, so soon as they lands are offered for sale— and it is probable, after the lands are offered for sale, that which remains unsold, and are not entered in a short space of time will be graduated in price—The country has been much injured by the suspension of the sales, particularly in alabama, where the emigration to it has been suspended by reason, that those moving there cannot obtain titles to land & will not settle on land not their own—[2]

Instructed Mr. Ingham Sec. of Treasury to engage Mr McLane to obtain in London correct weights & measure, & pendulum &—

This 3rd. July gave instructions to Sec. of the navy to pay Marshal of E Florida—Waters Smith $4000 out of the appropriation for expences of Africans wrecked on the Florida coast within U States—

appointed Doctor Shepherd to supperintend the Navy Dept. in the absence of the Secratary of the Navy[3]

July 8th. 1829–

appointed Major Wm. B. Lewis to superintend the war Dept. in the absence of the Sec. of War.

July 8th. 1829—

Directed the agent of the Treasury Mr Pleasonton to examine how it has happened that Collector Dr Peak, Default has been, without the knowledge of him or any other officer of the Revenue & report thereon, that measures may be taken that the like again cannot must not take place and also that he report how much is due on Judgts. to the U. States, when recovered, and the probability of the debt being made & how much is in the hands of the different marshals, &c &c &c—How much is due by Defaulters to the Goverment and not in suit & how long since the debt became due; & at what time audited—Either by Legislation, or by the establishment of rules, where the president & his secrataries are cloathed with by proper Legal enactment to make them, must be made to secure the collection of the public dues that no officer belonging to, or having connection with the recovery of the public debts, can have mony in his hands without it being known at the public proper office—A rule to be established, so far as it can be, to close all accounts of two years standing—[4]

An order to be taken to preserve the live oak growing on the land of the United States, agreable to the 3rd. Section of the act approved 3rd. of March 1827. and also as to the dry docks at Gosport— &—Charleston Massachusetts—note written to Major Graham for a report on this subject. July 16th. 1829—[5]

Massachuthets—her claims for payment of her militia for services in the last war to be brought before Congress—and such part of the militia services recommended to be paid, as has been for like services to other states recommended to Congress to be paid, the ballance not, as it would hereafter in time of war be holding out to the unfaithful to our goverment a premium to oppose it, & to commit Treason

AN, DLC (64).

1. Swartwout had reported widespread smuggling in New York in letters to Ingham of June 10 and June 20, the latter penned in Washington (DNA-RG 56, M178-17).

2. James Noble (1783–1831) was a senator from Indiana. Under the cash sales system established in 1820, federal lands after being surveyed were first offered for public sale at auction with a minimum price of $1.25 per acre, and if unbid there were afterwards available for "private entry," or direct purchase, at the minimum price. Under the previous system of credit sales, abolished in 1820, some purchasers, especially in Alabama, had bought large tracts at high prices during the land boom of 1817–19 and then defaulted on their later payments. They had either forfeited their purchases or, under a series of subsequent relief laws, were allowed to take an extended credit or to relinquish a portion of their holdings and apply the payments already made thereon to complete purchase of the rest. The forfeited and relinquished lands were to be reoffered for sale. Thomas Hart Benton's bill to graduate or reduce the entry price for lands not taken at the auction was first introduced in 1824. It passed the Senate in 1830 but did not become law until 1854.

3. On July 8, AJ appointed Richard H. Bradford acting secretary of the Navy.

4. In July 1829, former Alexandria, Va., customs collector Humphrey Peake was thought to have defaulted for at least $17,000. On August 21, Eaton relayed to auditor Stephen Pleasonton AJ's request for a full accounting of individual debts and claims against the U.S. (DNA-RG 206). Pleasonton reported back to AJ on October 21.

5. "An Act for the gradual improvement of the navy of the United States" authorized the president to preserve live oak timber on federal land for naval construction and to reserve live oak lands from public sale. The law also authorized construction of two dry docks, one north and one south of the Potomac. The ship yards of Gosport (also called Norfolk) in Portsmouth, Va., and Charlestown, Mass., were selected in 1827. Land office commissioner George Graham reported to AJ on July 16 that measures had been taken to stop timber-cutting on federal live oak lands in Florida, but that none had yet been reserved from sale.

July

From Stephen Simpson

Philadelphia July 1. 1829.

My Dr. Sir,

Your esteemed favour of the 27th. ultimo, was recd. yesterday; and its contents afforded me that pleasure, which a good understanding between us, & the long attachment I have borne to you, ought to, & were calculated to inspire. I have certainly been misunderstood, if it was ever thought that I intended to interpose an obstacle to your perfect freedom of action, in all your measures & appointments; but it is with undissembled pain that I perceive, that my reception of any favour at your hands, would come within the limits of those actions which might prove detrimental "either to the interests of the country, or to your character." Yet I must frankly confess, that since your hesitancy to avow to the world a reciprocity of esteem & confidence, I have looked upon myself with more distrust & diffidence, than I ever imagined to be possible; so that I have no confidence left but in my *humble* integrity, & concur with you in opinion that as it respects talents I might prove alike discreditable to your character for discernment, & to the interests of the country. I say this in undissembled sincerity of heart; for, as you know Sir, nothing teaches humility so effectually as the school of affliction; especially when to the sufferings of adversity is superadded, what I have certainly experienced—a disappointment in the return of friendship; a disappointment not altogether the result of official disregard, but the fruit of apparent want of confidence. Bear with me, Sir, while I merely express the regret, which such a state of feeling on your part, as I conceived, was naturally calculated to produce. But you *now* assure me, that I am possessed of your friendship; & under that assurance, I am bound to do justice to your generous feelings, & for what you have always been extolled for—your magnanimous heart. Upon those feelings, & that heart, I must throw myself. It is not for me to solicit, or to distrust. As you remark, you are bound to preserve your fame & to consult the interests of the Country—God forbid that I should ever tarnish the one, or injure the other. Yet, what, Sir, would be your opinion of me, if I could accept your friendship under the condition, that my character could possibly discredit your reputation, or injure the Country in an official station? Surely you could not avoid thinking meanly of a man, who could patiently concur in an opinion that might, even by implication, bring a cloud upon his honour; so, that while I perfectly agree with you, my great & good friend, that you owe it to yourself & to your country, to act with all possible caution in relation to both—I cannot agree with you, that such a rule of action could apply to *me individually;* & I am induced to express this dissent, as I before observed, not from any feeling of vanity, but a sense of honour, which I know you will not condemn, because you, of all men, know best what honour is. There is now standing in Chesnut Street, a large house built by my Grandfather. It was called in the *Revolution,* "the *Whig House*!!" & is still known by name to our old citizens. He emptied his Chests of 40.000 pounds of *Gold,* to forward that Revolution; a large fortune in those days, & he lost it all, but cheerfully, because in the cause of freedom. Our old friend who died lately never tired of talking of the "*Whig House*"; I mean old Allen Mc.Lane, who often wished he might live to see you—but his wish was fruitless. I mention the *Whig House,* merely to say that the Grandson of that *Whig,* & the son of one equally ardent & honorable, is not, I hope, destined to discredit his country. Excuse this length. Pray do me the favour to present my most respectful compliments to your amiable & interesting family circle.[1]

Accept the assurance of my profound respect & regard; & beleive me to be Your most obt. humble St.

S. Simpson

[Endorsed by AJ:] To be answered friendly manner

ALS, TNJ (13-0786).
 1. Simpson's grandfather, Samuel Simpson (1720–89), was a wealthy shoemaker who headed Philadelphia's radical Committee of Privates, 1775–76. His father, George Simpson (1759–1822), was an assistant commissary general during the Revolution and later cashier of the first Bank of the United States. Allan McLane (1746–1829), father of Louis McLane and a noted soldier of the Revolution, died May 22.

From Alphonso Wetmore

Washington City July 1. 1829.
Sir
 Having understood that the office of marshal of this district will soon be vacant, I have taken the liberty to ask your perusal of the following sketch of my claims as an applicant for this appointment. They consist principally in the services I have rendered in the army during a period of the last seventeen years: in the field during the war, and in the staff since

the peace. My person bears some marks of war service, and the paymaster General, to whom I beg leave to refer you can speak of my services in the pay Department.

There are some passages in my Father's political history which give him strong claims upon the consideration of the government at this time, and which are not irrelevent when considering the application of a member of his family. During the existence of the sedition law in the administration of the elder president Adams, in addressing the people he protested in strong terms against the constitutionality of that law; and for this act he was arraigned and punished, in a fine & costs to the amount of five hundred Dollars. The same undeviating political course he has all his life continued to pursue—and this course it was that enabled him and all his sons, & grandsons to rejoice in the triumph of the people at the late general election. He is a farmer in Montgomery county, New York, and not much known abroad. But he is one of three, who first dared to avow in his native state (connecticut) those principles which eventually elected Mr. Jefferson. Mr. Secretary Vanburen knows my Father.[1]

I mention these things because I believe my Father has rendered services to his country in a political point of view, and to add at the same time an expression of my belief, that the success of my application would enable him to forget his pecuniary losses, and his toils in the support of our institutions.

During the late canvass there were various opinions entertained in regard to the course proper for those citizens who held office. Some insisted that we were bound to support the cause of the then existing administration—and *suited the action to the word*. I exercised my opinion freely—and when the candidate for the presidency which I prefered was villified and represented as a military despot, I wrote and published that essay which went to show that general Jackson had proved, in the achievement of "a tearless victory," that the militia may be relied on for national defence—and that consequently regular forces, so much feared, are less essential.

I am sensible of the labor that applicants for office impose on you, and will not extend this communication—but refer you, as I have permission to do, to my friend Genl. Green, who has known me many years, and who can give you an idea of my standing in Missouri. Reference may also be had to the letters from *Governor Miller* and *Senator Benton* which I handed you yesterday.[2] As I have intended this for your own observation, I give it as I have roughly sketched it in my own hand. I am Respectfully your obedt Servt

Alphonso Wetmore

[Endorsed by AJ:] Mr Wetmores letter, applies for the Marshals office D. Columbia—

ALS, DNA-RG 59 (M639-26). Wetmore (1793–1849) had joined the infantry in 1812 and lost an arm while fighting the British. An Army paymaster stationed at Franklin, Mo., he was also an author and booster of the Santa Fe Trail. He wrote AJ twice more in July to request the superintendency at Harpers Ferry, but AJ gave him no appointment. Tench Ringgold remained as marshal until his commission expired in 1831.

1. In 1802 Seth Wetmore (1761–1836) was convicted of sedition under Connecticut state law for declaring at a town meeting that every adult man enjoyed a natural right to vote. He was sentenced to pay a $100 fine and court costs.

2. Duff Green, Missouri governor John Miller, and Thomas H. Benton.

Order of Pardon

July 1rst. 1829—

The case of Hinton McKinney of Raleigh North Carolina, who prays for a remission of the residue of his confinement.

This petition is signed by the Judge before whom he was tried, and the Governor, Judges, Secretaries, and many of the most respectable lawyers and citizens of the state, who say that the prisoner was arrested in August 1825, tried, convicted, and sentenced to ten years imprisonment, and has been in close confinement ever since—that his conduct during this period has been so exemplary as to excite a general sympathy in his behalf, and a conviction that his reformation is thorough and sincere—that since his imprisonment he has never been known to drink to excess, or conduct himself improperly—that his time has been devoted with great assiduity to the cultivation of his mind by useful reading, and the acquirement of a mechanical trade; and that on several occasions his timely information to the keeper of the prison has conduced to his personal safety and prevented the escape of other prisoners: all which give evidence of his reformed character and is accompanied by the letter of the Atty for the U S who prosecuted the prisoner to conviction, also favoring his discharge.

As the object of all punishment is the reformation of the criminal, and, by the force of its example, to deter others from the perpetration of similar crimes, the exercise of the Executive clemency should never be permitted to impair it. It is believed, however, in this case, altho' the crime is one of the deepest kind, and without any circumstances of extenuation but those which arise from youth and the want of moral instruction, that this object will be advanced by granting the petition. The high and respectable source of the evidence leaves no doubt that, in regard to the individual, all the ends of punishment are fully accomplished; and the other consideration, in which the force of example as a general rule requires that the whole measure of the penalties of the law should be felt, it seems, will be sustained by making this an exception.

His meritorious conduct throughout the confinement, and the calamities which his fidelity to the keeper of the prison averted, furnish motives for his liberation which should be indulged, as having their origin in the love of good actions, and making it probable that their influence will hereafter strengthen his reformation, and have a useful effect upon the discipline of the prison.

The President therefore orders that the residue of the imprisonment be remitted and the prisoner liberated upon the payment of costs.

Andrew Jackson

DS in AJ Donelson's hand, DNA-RG 59 (13-0776). Raleigh *Star*, July 16; *Niles*, August 1. The formal pardon was issued July 3.

To Amos Kendall

July 2nd. 1829—

Dr. Sir

I have read with great pleasure the enclosed, & now return it—It is always pleasant when our course is approved by such enlightened minds, as Mr. Tazewells—So long as we take the law for our guide, & Justice the end in view, we will meet with the support of the people. yrs respectfully

Andrew Jackson

Photocopy of ALS, THer (13-0806).

From Gabriel Poillon Disosway

New York July 2. 1829

Dear Sir,

In common with the mercantile community of this city, I cannot but regret that the Administration, by its Post Master, should have issued new instructions to the Post office here, of such a nature, as no precedent will justify nor does the public good demand   Great and universal complaint prevails on account of what has already become a serious greivance to those of us, whose correspondence from our mercantile pursuits, embraces every part of our extended country. No assurances of honor, not even of an oath, are sufficient, to obtain a mitigation of its injustice, the world of letters received by some houses, render it impossible, under the present arrangements of the Post office in this city, to break open, every letter, immediately under the eyes of the Post Master, or those in the Post office building.

You are elevated, to our chief Magistracy, We have placed you there, that the rights of our citizens may be equally protected—and to you we appeal on this subject, for suitable redress, from this act of injustice and oppression. "Vox populi, vox Dei." Yours &c

Gabriel P. Disosway

ALS, DLC (37). Disosway (1798–1868) was a New York City merchant. Under the 1825 law governing the Post Office, postage on letters was paid by the recipient at a rate based on the number of sheets. The postmaster at the mailing office determined the proper charge by external inspection. In a case where the envelope on delivery proved to have fewer sheets than supposed, it had been customary at New York and elsewhere to allow a refund on the recipient's oath that he had been overcharged. In a May 18 circular, William T. Barry invoked the language of the 1825 law to rule that overcharges could be refunded only if the recipient opened his mail in the presence of the postmaster or clerk. Responding to protests, Barry reiterated his stance in letters of June 25 (printed in the July 2 *New-York Evening Post*) and July 28. Barry noted that although undercharges were more common than overcharges, undercharged customers never returned to pay the extra postage due.

From William Berkeley Lewis

Washington July 2d. 1829.

D. Sir,

You request me to inform you of the remarks made by Genl. Call to me, relative to a misunderstanding which is said to have taken place between him and Mrs. Timberlake, in the spring or winter of 1824. I will do so as concisely as I can; but I must be permitted to make a few preliminary observations by way of explanation.

What Genl. Call said to me upon that subject was perhaps, intended by him as confidential—at least it was so considered by me and, acting under that impression, I have no recollection of ever having named it to a single individual except yourself—and not then until I discovered you had knowledge of the circumstance. I was then, as I am now, upon the most intimate and friendly terms with both Major Eaton & Genl. Call, and altho' I was greatly mortified at what had been related to me concerning the former gentleman; yet I never spoke of it to him or any other person, in connection with Genl. Call's name; nor does he, even to this day, know that, that gentleman ever made such representations to me. In consequence of what had been said to me by Genl. Call and another gentleman, then also a member of congress, I was led to believe that possibly there might be some truth in the report concerning Major Eaton and Mrs. Timberlake, and accordingly wrote to him in the summer of 1824, urging him to leave Washington, if he had not already done so, and return without delay, to Tennessee. Before, however, I mailed the letter, I enquired of you concerning Mr. Eaton's movements and was informed that you did not doubt, from what he told you at parting with him in Washington, but that he was then on his way home. This information prevented me from sending the letter, and I recollect having seen it in my Secretary not long before I left home, where it yet remains.

With regard to the particular transaction to which you have drawn my attention, I will state that in one of the conversations had with Genl. Call he said, "that he and Mrs. Timberlake were one day alone, and believing that she and Major Eaton were *unwarrantably* intimate, and having no doubt on his own mind that she was a woman of easy virtue, made propositions of a certain discription to her himself, which she, he said, with much seeming indignation rejected. This, however, he said, he considered as mere affectation, and did not change his previous opinion of her."

I do not pretend to recollect the precise words of Genl. Call; but, unless my memory has greatly failed me, what he said on that occasion, is substantially correct as stated above; nor do I know whether what I have related accords with what you have heard upon this subject from others. *You*, I am sure, my dear sir, will not attribute what I have said to any disposition to reflect on Genl. Call, a man for whom you know, in common with yourself, I have always entertained feelings of personal regard. I am with much respect, your obt. srvt.

W. B. Lewis

ALS, DLC (37).

To William Taylor Barry

July 3rd. 1829.

Dr. Sir

The bearer Major Nathan Reid, who is the son of Major Nathan Reid an old revolutionary officer va, and a particular friend of mine, will hand you this, who I beg leave to introduce to your kind attention.

Major Reid is an applicant for the office of Postmaster at Linchburgh Virginia—& every way *qualified* & *worthy* of that office—I must add he is the brother of my aid de camp Major John Reid, deceased. yr friend

Andrew Jackson

ALS, DLC (37). Nathan Reid, Jr., was an attorney from Campbell County, Va. His father, Nathan Reid (1753–1830), was a captain in the Revolution. John Reid (1784–1816) had died before finishing a biography of AJ that was completed by John H. Eaton and published in 1817. Barry did not remove Lynchburg's postmaster, John D. Marrell.

From Ezra Stiles Ely

Philadelphia July 3d. 1829.

Very Dear General,

I first caught a glimpse of your son on Wednesday morning, while he was passing to the Navy Yard. On the evening of the same day he went to Wilmington; and no opportunity presented of showing him any such kind attentions as we would wish until yesterday afternoon. It would have been very pleasing to my wife & myself had he come, without ceremony, to our house, as his Philadelphia home, in which he would have been as welcome as at your hospitable Hermitage. We hope that he will do so, when he shall again visit our city; but we excuse him now, on the ground of his having been *captured* on his way from Washington by Com. Stewart, who appropriated him to himself & friends as his *lawful prize*.[1] It would afford us no ordinary pleasure to receive any of your family as our guests; and if the *Military* & *Civil Cheiftain* of our country will honour us with a visit, we should be able I am sure to make him feel at home with his friends.

In the midst of your important national affairs, I feel confident that your immortal soul frequently visits, intellectually, the pious dead; and that you derive more pleasure from anticipating future communion with one of the saints in light, than from all your worldly greatness. I lend you, venerable friend, the enclosed letter, for a few days, when I beg you to return it to me; for I should be very unwilling to part with it. The friendly *left* hand which wrote it, is, indeed, motionless, for the present, in the cold grave; but, blessed be God, the truly Christian spirit which dictated to that hand what sentiments to express is full of holy thought, activity & bliss.[2]

The spirits of the departed friends of Christ are as the angels, & there is joy among them at our repentance & improvement in piety: I flatter myself, therefore, that one celestial being [clo]ser to you than any other, except her *[God &]* Saviour, knows, with gratitude to the God of all grace, that you are a different being in relation to spiritual & eternal matters, from what you was in 1819; and that you have since that time, begun to be one of the humble followers of Christ; more distinguished by any one Christian virtue, than by the Presidency over the happiest & most flourishing nation on the globe.

May the peace of God be your pillow in sleep; your staff in old age; and your portion for ever.

E. S. Ely

[Endorsed by AJ:] Dr Ely of Phila. Private to be carefully preserved & filed away   A J

ALS, DLC (37).
1. Navy captain Charles Stewart (1778–1869) had commanded the *Constitution* in the War of 1812.
2. Ely enclosed a letter (now lost) from Rachel, probably in reply to his of October 22, 1819, in which Ely hoped that AJ would become "a humble disciple of Jesus Christ" (DLC-28).

From Alexander Hamilton

New York July 4th. 1829.

Dear Sir

From motives of delicacy, I have heretofore declined to obtrude myself on your attention, to solicit a participation in the patronage of the Government, forseeing that you would be seriously embarrassed, with applications from your early confidential friends and from those of more recent date, who may have rendered you essential services. I do not claim, either of these distinctions, and it would be only to anticipate posterity in the enjoyment of a patriotic and grateful feeling to have been among the first admirers of your military achievements and sincerely to honor you for the several important responsibities you have assumed for your country's welfare. In justice, nevertheless, to my own feelings, I take the liberty to remark, that with the exception of *my friend* Swartwout, with whom, I cooperated in Albany at the Session of 1824, as the representative of your friends, there has not been in this section, a more public or constant advocate of your success and with censure from those, who under more favourable circumstances now affect to be violently attached to your interests. In the early stages of my preference, I should have been unwilling to have advanced any pretentions, my support was disinterested and your election advocated, with determined and honest pride, but a change of times and considerable losses require from me new arrangements   To the distinguished fidelity with which I have performed an important public trust I appeal with great confidence to the Genl Land Office and without hesitation assume the merit of rescuing the United States, from the grossest impositions, by forcing from the archives of Florida, (preserved by your own promptness), the criteria to determine the validity of all Land grants. In this course, I found myself unsupported by the Executive and resigned, with a full exposition of my motives, which were subsequently submitted to Congress by Special Message from Mr Monroe. At that early period, I had the honor to refer to *your conduct* with marks of distinction officially.[1]

If in your disposal, there is any station of respectability, and permit be to refer to the Consulate at Havre, the Navy Agency in this Place, that you could consistently confer on me, I should esteem it a favour worthy of every respect. I communicate to you directly, knowing that you will appreciate the delicacy of the motive which dictates this course and add that if essential, I can procure the very best recommendations.

As it may be a source of satisfaction to you, permit me to remark that such has been the conduct of our new Collector, that he has become extremely popular and the appointment with candid men is generally much esteemed. Mr Noah performs the duties of his office with industry, intelligence and civility.[2]

It is much to be regretted that Mr Barry has arrested the discretionary administration of the law relative to overcharged postage in this City; the rigid adherence to the letter of the law is extremely vexatious and subjects the clerks to much abuse and the government to very unnecessary censure. The law must be general and it would be bad legislation to create legal discretionary exceptions, such practice, should alone be the result of circumstances and rest on the responsibility of the Officer. The revenue is not advantageously affected by the restriction, if, I am correctly informed, the apprehension of overcharging is increased in proportion to the embarrassment and the dissatisfaction. I have had Mr McLanes letter in corroberation of Mr Barrys construction of the law reprinted from the Telegraph—[3]

In the course of this letter, I have refered to Florida, to which I again call your attention, for the express purpose, of advising the dismissal of Govr. Duval, who was esteemed by all respectable, disinterested men there, a low, vulgar, heartless fellow—To his songs, ribaldry and duplicity was he indebted for his elevation and Florida degraded by his presence, to the exclusion of the claims of the present Secretary of the Navy. This man is as much your friend as he is that of Mr Adams and if he thought it politic, would be first to cry out for the champion of the American System—The vulgarity and profanity of this personage has been so disgusting, that I have frequently cautioned him against its effects on the public and he was well aware, I was always answerable for these sentiments.[4]

I have been urged and solicited to make this application by those who are honestly attached to you personally and if disappointed, I must beg you to divide the responsibility between us. In the hope that your patriotic Laurels may long continue to be encircled with the civic wreath I have the honor to remain with much esteem and regard Your Obt Sert

Alexander Hamilton

ALS, DNA-RG 59 (M639-10). Son of Treasury secretary Alexander Hamilton and older brother of James A. Hamilton, Alexander Hamilton (1786–1875) was an infantry captain in the War of 1812 and federal district attorney for East Florida, 1822–23. AJ did not give him an appointment.

    1. In 1823 Hamilton was appointed one of three commissioners to ascertain Florida land claims and titles. Convinced that the commission was proceeding irregularly and that fraudulent claims were being allowed, he resigned and submitted a lengthy report to President Monroe, who sent it to Congress on May 18, 1824 (*HRDoc* 158, 18th Cong., 1st sess., Serial 103). Hamilton's report drew on Spanish documents that AJ had secured

in 1821 while serving as U.S. commissioner for the transfer of Florida. In an official letter protesting his colleagues' methods, Hamilton remarked that for the evidence to adjudicate claims "the United States are principally indebted to the detention of the public documents . . . by the order of General Andrew Jackson" (*HRDoc* 156, 18th Cong., 1st sess., p. 103, Serial 103).

2. Samuel Swartwout; Mordecai Noah.

3. On June 30, the *US Telegraph* printed a December 12, 1828, letter from former Postmaster General John McLean holding, as did Barry, that overcharges could only be refunded on letters opened in the presence of the postmaster or clerk.

4. AJ retained Duval and appointed him to a new four-year term in 1831. In 1824, Henry Clay had dubbed his economic development program of a protective tariff and federal internal improvements the "American System."

To Richard Keith Call

(Copy) (Private)

Washington July 5th. 1829—

My D Sir,

Your letter of the 12th. Ultimo has been recd. To that part relating to your journey to Cuba I have to refer you to mine in answer to your former letter. From it you will find that we have no wish you should endanger your health by proceeding to the Havana during the sickley season, unless the suits should be attempted to be brought on this Fall at St. Augustine. Whenever these suits shall be tried, it is believed by Mr. Wirt, as reported to me, that the documents and papers named in my former letter to you, are absolutely necessary for the safety of the U. States—To that letter you are refered for your government on this subject.

The other part of your letter, as you observe, refers to a very delicate subject; as such I always viewed it, and thought silence ought to have been observed by all justly apprciating female character, or who had any regard for me; taking into consideration the circumstances with which I was surrounded at the time the communications were made to Dr. Ely & Lady, who I know, had previously entertained a good opinion of both Major Eaton & his Lady, Dr Ely having in a note recommended the appointment of Major Eaton in the warmest terms. On Sunday they told me they intended to visit them the *next day*, and you can judge of my astonishment after Mr. Ely's having expressed the most favourable opinion of those two individuals, & his determination to visit them, when I received his letter from Philadelphia stating to me numerous base acts attributed to Mrs. Eaton which had been *confidentially* communicated to him, and in confirmation of these charges the declirations of my dear departed wife had been refered to, but which I knew she had never uttered. This brought from me a reply to Dr. Ely, such as truth and justice required and respect for the memory of my dear wife demanded, whose name had been so unjustly associated with a set of vile and secret slanderes.

From the tenor of the Doctors letter to me as well as from other sources it was intimated that *some* of the information he had received was from you, and believing that in all probability an investigation would take place, and if you were implicated in giving information to Mr. Ely it might lead to an exposure of your own declirations with respect to Mrs. Eaton, which you made to Major Lewis in 1824 shortly after ~~your~~ our return to Tennessee. These declirations, made known to me by Major Lewis on my requesting him to inform me upon what grounds you rested your belief of the guilt of Mrs. Eaton, so far as he had heard you speak upon the subject, I did believe would place you, in the discussion before the public, should one take place, in a very unpleasant situation. But you say you never made such declirations. Now my dear friend, what an unpleasant predickament this denial would place you in, if investigated; for you certainly did make to Mr. Lewis shortly after our return to Tennessee, substantially the following remarks—"that you and Mrs. Timberlake were one day alone, and believing that she and Major Eaton were *unwarrantably* intimate, and having no doubt but she was a woman of *easy virtue,* you made propositions to her of a certain discription, which she with seeming indignation rejected &C &C"—and you must recollect that from the day you and she had the quarrel, she never again appeared at our table and complained, as well as some other members of the family, that you had grossly insulted her. Knowing these things as I did and foreseeing the angry passions that might arise, I thought it my duty to bring them to your recollection. In doing this I thought you would be sensible of having injured your friend Major Eaton, and would have magninimity and liberality enough to have informed Genl. Polk[1] and Mr. Ely that the rumors of an angry correspondence—Timberlake having cut his throat from jealousy—dire[c]ting locks to be taken off doors at boarding houses in New York; and passing for man and wife &C &C—were all vile slanders so far as you knew or believed; and it was to give you correct information with regard to a part of these things that I sent you copies of two letters from Officers who sailed from this country with Mr. Timberlake and were with him until his eyes were closed in death.

Genl. you cannot regret more than I do that you assisted in giving currency to any reports about Major Eaton and his wife at the time you did. That the hired slanderers of Mr. Clay should have attempted to destroy Major Eaton and through him to reach me, was neither astonishing or unexpected; but that my own personal & confidential friends should have aided in such an unhallowed work by lending their countenace to such unfounded falsehoods as were put in circulation about Mr. & Mrs. Eaton & when it was well know too he was to form a M. of my *[Cabinet]* I must confess that I was both astonished and mortified. But my dear Genl however much I may regret your course, on this occasion, you and I will not quarrel about it. You well know that we always differed about these slanders, circulated to the prejudice of Mrs. Timberlake now Mrs. Eaton—I have ever believed her a virtuous and much injured Lady—it appears you have thought differently, but as you have given me no evidence, entitled to any weight, in support of your opinion, I must be excused for still adhering to my own opinion.

Several letters have passed betw[een] Mr. Ely and myself upon this unpleasant subject. He caused the most minute enquiry to be made about the New York story, and in his letter of the 30th. May last he says— "It gives me pleasure to inform you that I have ascertained to my satisfaction, that most of the reports against Mr. Eaton & Mrs. Timberlake, in relation to some board'g houses in New York *are untrue;* and that nothing more than some imprudent familiarities could be asserted against them, and that perhaps by a Lady who may have been fastidious" Major Bradford of Phila. who made the enquiry at the request of Dr. Ely, informs me that the Lady who kept the boarding house refered to, told him the report was an unfounded falsehood—that no improper conduct had ever taken place in her house, and the only impropriety, as she conceived, was their travelling together in a steam boat from New York to Albany and back again, leaving Mr. T. who was indisposed; but who insisted on his wife's taking the trip. Major B. also informed me that the lady related a circumstance of Mrs. Timbrlake that did her much honor, and would do honor to *any wife* in any Country or age. Thus you see every charge, when investigated, vanishes; and I have no doubt but that the balance of the information given to Dr. Ely is equally unfounded, and if enquired into will be traced to *dead* Doctors, or *other nameless* persons. I will name another report put in circulation a few days ago—It is this—a short time ago Mr. Lewis McLane and his daughter visited this City. While here Miss McLane, with the approbation of her father, waited on Mrs. Eaton, but that on her return home studiously concealed it from her mother. Mr. & Mrs. McLane[2] were in Washington for a few days, and as they passed through Baltimore Mrs. McLane for the first time learned that her daughter had called on Mrs. Eaton, and so great was the shock that she had well nigh fainted—*this is the story.* Mrs. Eaton must surely bear about her some unaccountable charm, for this same Mrs. McLane, who *fainted* at hearing her daughter *had visited* her, also called to see her while here; so also has Mrs. Rives. What a ridiculous attitude must the conduct of such ladies as these place those in, who think *they* are too *good* to visit Mrs. Eaton. I assure you Sir, that there are few respectable ladies who visit this City, that do not call on Mrs. Eaton; and I repeat, does it redoun to the credit of any gentleman or lady, to have his, or her name associated with such a group of gossips as I have described, & whose principle business it is to run about the Country and point to the mote in their brother or sister's eye without being conscious of the beam that lirks in their own.[3]

Having done what concieved to be my duty as the friend of yourself and Major Eaton, I will drop this delicate, and, I assure you to me, unpleasant subject, with this remark—I will never abandon an old and well tried friend for new ones, for slight or trivial causes—nor will I ever be *silent* when female character is wantonly assailed and my name, or those of my family, falsely introduced to give weight as to the truth of the charge.

I am happy to have in my power to assure you that your fears are groundless with regard to Major Eaton's appointment having a tendency to embarrass my administration. The War Department is conducted with more ability than it ever has been since the days of Knox, and the Head of that Dept. is gaining popularity daily. I am entirely satisfied with the way, manner, and ability with which it is conducted; and as all the Members of the Cabinet were acquainted with each other and approved the appointment of each, no cause can arise for dissatisfaction among them that did not exist at the time they took their seats in the Cabinet. But if I am, or should be mistaken in this, I have, I assure you, still energy enough to relieve myself from any such embarrassment, let it arise from what quarter, or source it may: I am not so blind as to believe that there are not other men in the U. States possessing as clear heads and as true harts as those, or a part of those, who compose my Cabinet.

Present me affectionately to Mary and the sweet little children and as usual believe me, Your friend.

Signed Andrew Jackson

LS draft in the hand of William B. Lewis, DLC (37).
1. William Polk of North Carolina.
2. Catherine Milligan McLane (1790–1849).
3. Matthew 7:3 and Luke 6:41.

To John Overton

Washington July 5th. 1829—
My Dr. friend
I lift my pen merely at present to acknowledge the receipt of your kind letter of the 20th. & to say to you how much pleasure it afforded me whilst reading *[it.]*

My son will set out in a few d[ays] for home & will see you shortly after this letter reaches you, to whom I refer you for the news of this place—all things however are going on smoothly, and the trial of Mr Watkins will be entered upon during the present week—it has been too long delayed by the tecnicalities of lawyers, sustained by the court, untill public sentiment complains of uncessary delay—Mr. W. cannot escape punishment of some kind.

The prospect of fine crops in Tennessee are quite cheering, & the health and harmony in your society must make you quite happy & add much to your health & years.

I fondly cherish the hope to see you here, I am sure it would add to my health & length of days—no happiness on this earth can excell the pleasure of the meeting of old friends after a long absence, & particularly at an advanced age—This brings to my view that exquisite & pleasing sensations we must experience on meeting with our departed friends beyond the grave—It is *this* that makes life *now* tolerable to me. The duty I owe my country, the cheering idea of meeting my Dr wife beyond, & you in this side the grave, alone buoys up my depressed & troubled mind, added to the hope of meeting you with her beyond the grave when we both fulfil the course allotted to us here below.

We are still very busily employed   Our ministers to England & France will sail in a few days, and I have reasons to believe we will be able to accommodate our commercial difference with England on the basis of a Just reciprocity.

My son will be directed to call on & communicate to you freely

Present me affectionately to yr Lady[1] & family & believe me yr Friend.

Andrew Jackson

ALS, THi (13-081 /).
 1. Mary McConnell White May Overton (1782–1862), sister of Hugh L. White and widow of Francis May.

From Mordecai Manuel Noah

New York July 6 1829

Sir,
    Mr Charles Rhind long a respectable and intelligent merchant of this City visits the seat of Government in order to have some conversation with your Excellency in relation to securing the trade of the Levant. Mr. Rhind is personally acquainted with the Turkish policy and with that Country generally and carries with him such testimonials of character from this City as cannot fail to give weight to his representations. This subject has occupied my attention for many years and I can say with confidence that obtaining the free passage of the Dardanelles and the Black Sea will open a new channel to our commerce which, while it will give us a majority of the Carrying trade, will open a new market & a profitable one to our surplus manufactures   It is before the difficulties are adjusted between Russia and the Ottoman Porte that this privilege must be obtained because the dispositions of the Divan are of the most friendly character towards us—When peace shall be established the influence of Great Britain and the European powers generally may be brought to bear against us.[1] From several conversations which I have had with Mr Rhind

during the last seven years we are confirmed in the belief that a treaty to that effect can be cheaply obtained but at all events a permission can be obtained at little cost to navigate the Black Sea for five years which in effect will be perpetual

I do not hesitate to say that a more valuable trade cannot be obtained for our Country and no act would be better received by the people or would render the administration more popular with the Eastern States[.] I have the honor to be very respectfully your Excellencys obediant Servant

M M Noah

ALS, DNA-RG 59 (M639-20). In August AJ appointed Charles Rhind (1779–1857) consul at Odessa, a Russian port on the Black Sea. In September he was named to a three-man commission that concluded a commercial treaty with Turkey granting the United States most-favored-nation status and opening the Black Sea to American shipping.

1. The Russo-Turkish War of 1828–29 ended in September with the Treaty of Adrianople.

From John Hanson Good

Cascade Farm near Wheeling July 10th. 1829

Dr Sir

I wave the delicacy that caused the apology I made to you in Fby 1828 in a letter associated with Mr Stinerod I was then unknown to you and am Still so as to my person but presumeing as a Jackson Man you may have heard of me but If you have not my own political feelings are a Justification for this address and under this influence I have taken the libirty of requesting Mr King[1] to present it to your Excellency for the purpose that he may be known to you he is a firm friend and does pursue the undeviating Jackson principles supporting the administration in to too he was one of the Jackson ~~Central~~ committee for Ohio County to correspond with the Jackson Central Committee at Richmond he is of tryed Integrity and their is no alloy of Clay in him he is not a Rufus King but one that will assert the necessity of reformation[2] If it would not be an intrusion on your time to have some conversation with him I anticipate a mutual satisfaction would result—I will use the freedom of speaking of Carter Beverly Esqr. his writing the Faettvill letter to his friend which was not intended for publication but his friend as eager for your success as himself it came out to the public what you had said in your Own House respecting Mr Adams Election he spoke it publicly at wheeling those observations you had made and their were nothing new in all that was said it was well understood and generally spoken of before[3] for myself I claim nothing but what every Man of small experience might have known that when their partie had influence and strength enough to make Right of Ohio Chairman of a committee that where to prepare the rules for the House Voting for the President they would make Mr Adams President in dispite of the vote of the people[4] all this was known at wheeling before Mr Beverly spoke of it but to assail Mr Beverly to come at you to injure your Election and assit Mr Clay was the grand object you have seen as I expect what was publised in the papers about Beverly Zane & Clay by the aid of some of your friends Mr Beverly came out honorable and had the ascendancy over Mr Zane to the great mortification of the Clay partie to give you the whole history of Mr Beverly conduct while at Wheeling in advocating your Election and repelling every thing said against your consort was praise worthy as a politician and Christian and would comprise a History of not an ordaniary size—not presuming but with humble solicitude I would ask for some appointment for Carter Beverly Esqr. which would be a gratification to your friends in this section of Western Virginia[5]—I regret that our friend Stinerod has passd over the Rubicon for he told Mr Doddridge the other day in my presence that he was the first Man that brought him out for Congress I had heard in time of the canvass for the Election that he was electionering for Mr Doddridge I called on him and pointed out the impropriety of such a course he denied to me and said he was only Jokeing with the people but at last voted for neither for he did not go to the Election doddridge told him he would have been glad to have seen him an Mr Zane at the Election—Mr King Mr Pemberton and a few other of your friends useing their best endeavours to keep Jackson Men from amalgamating and imbibeing Clay principles[6]   The artfull Clay Men soon after your Election was over began to say Genl Jackson is now Elected we must now send the best talented Men to Congress I belive some of the incautious Jackson Men have committed themself unreflectingly in voteing for Mr Doddridge I hope the reformation may extend to every unjust man in office that they may be ousted and their places filled with honest industrious Men[.] I am respectfully your Obdt Servt

John Good

P.S. Mr Stinerod still expresses a great regard for you I must try and get some able Jackson Man to reform him at least not to bring out another Clay Man he was useful in your Election and I want him such with your friends

J G

[Endorsed by AJ:] Mr Good—introducing Mr King

ALS, DLC (37). Good (1765–1844) operated a farm near Wheeling in Ohio County, Va. On March 8, 1827, Good and Wheeling tavern keeper Daniel Steenrod (1784–1864) had written an adulatory letter to AJ, which he answered.

    1. Solomon King (b. c1788) resided in Wheeling.

    2. Rufus King (1755–1827), for many years a Federalist senator from New York, had served as minister to Britain during the Adams administration.

3. In March 1827, Carter Beverley (1774–1844) of Virginia wrote to Richard S. Hackley of Fayetteville, N.C., that AJ, in conversation at the Hermitage, had revealed that Clay's agents approached him before the February 1825 House election with a promise to make him president if AJ would agree not to retain John Q. Adams as secretary of state. Beverley's account was published and angrily denied by Clay; Beverley called on AJ for confirmation, and in his response AJ spelled out his charge against Clay (*Jackson Papers*, 6:329–32). Beverley showed AJ's letter to Noah Zane (1778–1833), a Wheeling merchant, who showed it to Clay. Clay repudiated AJ's charge on June 29, 1827, in a public address and again in a July 12 speech at Lexington. The controversy went on from there, with AJ naming James Buchanan as Clay's alleged emissary and with subsidiary debate, particularly in the *Wheeling Gazette*, over the propriety of the conduct of Beverley and Zane.

4. Congressman John C. Wright of Ohio, a Clay man, chaired the committee appointed on January 18, 1825, to prepare the rules for the House election for president.

5. Beverley did not receive an appointment.

6. Philip Doddridge (1773–1832) was elected to Congress in April, defeating Joseph Johnson. James Pemberton (1777–1839) had been a deputy sheriff.

From Richard Gilliam Dunlap

Knoxville Tennessee
July 12th. 1829

Dear Sir

A few days since I received a letter from Gover. Houston of the 29th of May last from the Osage nation. He was on a visit to this tribe and was to return (to his adopted father's Jolly, the King of the Arkansas Cheerokees) in *one mon*. He speaks of his *exile* from society with the mild and elevated calmness of a phylosipher. I mourn his fate—T'is the wreck of more than fair hopes—and has to some extent deranged our state matters. Majr McClellen, the agent for the Osage nation, is dead—will this place not suit Houston?[1] He solicits nothing in his letter—but *past* friendships urge me to mention to you this fact—while I well know your heart yearns over his misfortune with the kindness sorrow; I still feel assured that *Houston* is *one* of the *men* in this nation that you would like to rescue from almost promised ruin—If he will again begin the discharge of publick duties, hopes of better times may dispel the gloom that seem to surround his fortune—His letter shews no despondency but his *novel change* foretels much, I fear   I hope you will excuse this importunity for my friend—He deserves a better fate and a higher destiny than to be the agent of a savage tribe according to the friendship of my views—He directs me to write him at Cantoonment Gibson Arkansas Territory. We have a most shamefull canvass between Lea & Arnold—This foolish & wicked disorganiser seems to have inspired the *people* with the promise of great things and that he is the chosen agent to bring them to pass—[2]

Dr. John C. Gunn, (who is my opponent for the legislature with no prospects but with the view to aid Arnold), declared yesterday in a stump speech, that you told him in Gove. Houston's presence, that you did not intend to serve longer that four years. The object is to shew, that the

Jackson question has nothing to do in this canvass for congress—This is very much laboured—I have written to Houston but can not hear from him in time. Did you ever tell Dr Gunn so or not? He is a perfect Jaybird and hardly worth notice, but his faulsehoods seem to take with *some effect*, with the uninfor[med] part of society. The success of su[ch] petty maneuvers proclaims the want and utility of a general system of popular education—will not the money arising from the immediate sale & settlement of the publick lands be better appropriated in this way than any other? The popular will is the paramount rule of political action within this union; and it begins to claim its empire in Europe. Is it not then all important that it should be well informed, so that *its aim* may *always* be for the *good* & *glory* of our country. I am your friend

R. G. Dunlap

ALS, DLC (37). Dunlap (1796–1841) was a Knoxville lawyer. In August he won election to the Tennessee house, defeating physician John C. Gunn (c1800–1863).

1. William McClellan (1779–1829) of Tennessee, a former Army officer who served under AJ in the War of 1812, had died May 24. Since 1825 he had been agent to the Choctaws (not the Osage) in present-day Oklahoma. His brother David succeeded him as subagent.

2. In the August congressional election, Pryor Lea (1794–1879), the pro-Jackson incumbent, narrowly defeated Thomas Dickens Arnold (1798–1870).

To Andrew Jackson, Jr.

Washington July [1]4th. 1829—

Dear Andrew

I have Just returned from my visit to Fortress Monroe, the Navy yard at gossport &c and recd a letter from Colo. Charles J. Love of the 27th. ulto. advising me of the death of my negroman Jim, and the manner of it.[1] I pray you my son to examine minutely into this matter, & if the death was produced by the cruelty of Mr Steel, have him forthwith discharged—But as you are young, advise with Col Love upon this matter—My negroes shall be treated humanely—When I employed Mr Steel, I charged him upon this subject, & had expressed in our agreement that he was to treat them with great humanity, feed & cloath them well, & work them in moderation, if he has deviated from this rule, he must be discharged.

Since I left home I have lost three of my family—Old Ned, I expected to die, but I am fearful the death of Jack, & Jim, has been produced by exposure & bad treatment—your Uncle John Donelson writes, that *Steel has ruled with a rod of iron*—This is so inconsistant to what I expected, that I cannot bear the inhumanity that he has exercised towards my poor negroes, contrary to his promise and has impaired my confidence in him—Unless he changes his conduct, dismiss him, and employ another.

I write in haste that it may go by to nights mail & meet you at Nashville—Consult with Colo. Love & Doctor Hogg about Mr Steel & whether he ought to be discharged. I am your affectionate father

Andrew Jackson

ALS, DLC (37). On July 8, AJ and a large party had left Washington on the steamboat *Potomac* for Fortress Monroe at Old Point Comfort, Va., near the mouth of the James River. In the next few days he toured the area's military facilities and public works and visited Norfolk and Portsmouth. AJ returned to Washington on July 14.
   1. Jim, or James, AJ's former military servant, died June 16.

To John Henry Eaton

July 18th. 1829—
Dr. Sir
   I recd. the other day from Genl Plache Neworleans a letter requesting that a cadets warrant should be granted to his son; I have had search made for it, but cannot find it, and suppose it has been sent to your office—If there is any vacancy in Louisiana, it will be proper to appoint young Plache, as his father has claims upon his country—yr friend

Andrew Jackson

ALS, DNA-RG 94 (M688-63). Jean Baptiste Plauché (1785–1860), long a friend of AJ, had commanded a battalion of volunteers at New Orleans. His son John Baptiste Plauché (1815–61) was admitted to West Point. He enrolled in 1831 but was dismissed two years later.

From Richard Keith Call

Tallahassee 18th. July 1829
My Dear Sir
   The enclosed article taken from the Telegraph of the 23rd. Ult. has been read with sensations of pain and regret which I cannot easily describe.[1]
   The many acts of disinterested kindness which I have received at your hands, the long and intimate friendship which had *[subsisted]* between us, and the knowled[ge]

on the altar of public censure? Have I betrayed your confidence? Have I made false representations against an inocent man? no, I have done neither. If I have erred it was in defending you with too much zeal from charges which I though were calculated to do you a serious injury where ever the history of the Florida land claims is known.
   It is proper that I should explain to you the manner in which I became engaged [in] this controversy. Mr White in an add[ress]

must reserve to myself the privilege of fulfilling my pre existing professional engagements among which I *enumerated the claims for Florida Lands*."[2]

In my reply to Mr White I observed, "I undertake to say emphatically and positively that the President did not know that Mr Berrien was of counsel for the claimants when he appointed him atty Genl of the United States."[3]

Now Sir I appeal to you to say who is right and who is wrong in the respective state[men]ts made by Mr Berrien and myself. If

is no less dear to me than his fame to him.

Permit me to ask sir did Mr Berrien *enumerate* to you his pre existing engagements in the case of Forbes & Co, in the case of John Forbes individually, in the case of John Forbes & Co west of the appalachicolas, in the two cases of Arridonda and Son, in the case of Clark and several others which claims embrace the best portion of this Territory. Did he tell you that he was of counsel *[for]* Forbes & Co when he procured the

silence the lash of public censure, or whether I shall be permited to defend my reputation by a fair and candid statement of facts. For the last four years sir your friends in this Territory have been oppressed by the partizan *[. . .]* administration

matter of controversy to your impartial judgment, and have only to request you will at a leasure moment give it that consideration which it may seem to merit. I can only add that to me it is a subject of vital importance.

I am Dear Genl very sincerely your friend

R K Call

[Endorsed by AJ:] Genl Call to be acknowledged A.J.

ALS fragments, DLC and ICHi (13-0883). The first four fragments and AJ endorsement are from DLC, the other two from ICHi.

A controversy had erupted over whether John M. Berrien had adequately divulged his interest in Florida land cases when AJ appointed him attorney general. Florida congressional delegate Joseph M. White, appointed by President Adams as U.S assistant counsel against the claimants, had recused himself from the Arredondo and Forbes cases, and in March AJ appointed Call to handle them. An anonymous writer in the Tallahassee *Floridian* then charged Call himself with an interest in Florida claims. Call attributed the piece to his rival White and replied in the *Floridian*. In the course of his defense, Call claimed that AJ did not know when he appointed Berrien that he was employed as counsel for the Forbes and Arredondo claimants, which "engagement is incompatible with his duties as attorney-general of the United States" (*Niles,* Jun 13). On June 20, the *US Telegraph* declared on "unquestionable authority" that Call's charge was "founded in misapprehension," and that "we are, moreover, authorised to state" that Berrien had fully disclosed his interests and that AJ was "perfectly satisfied" with his candor. Editor Duff Green told Call three years later, in letters of June 26 and August 22, 1832, that the article was published at Berrien's behest and with his assurance of AJ's approval (Green Papers, NcU).

1. The article appeared in the June 20 daily *Telegraph*. The paper also published a semi-weekly national edition.

2. A piece signed "William Tell" in the May 12 *Pensacola Gazette*, responding to Call's *Floridian* publication, quoted a letter from Berrien saying "In the acceptance of my present situation, I announced to the President, that I must reserve to myself the privilege of fulfilling my pre-existing professional engagements, among which, I enumerated the claims for Florida lands."

3. From Call's *Floridian* publication, which he requoted in the *Floridian* of April 13, 1833.

To Andrew Jackson, Jr.

Washington July 20th. 1829.

My Dr. son

I am gratified by the receipt of your affectionate letter of the 16th. instant, Just recd.

I was fearful from information received of the low state of water in the ohio river, that you would be compelled to travel overland thro' Ohio to Kentucky—your letter has dispelled this fear & shews that you have been fortunate in getting a Boat to cincinnati, from there to Louisville you will no dificulty in getting a Boat, & I trust you will reach home in safety without much injury to your Horses.

I have recd. since you left me a letter from Col Charles J Love informing of my negro man James death—I was fearful that his death might have been produced by the illtreatment of the overseer and wrote you immediately on the subject to enter upon an enquiry & if you found it did, to remove him

This letter you will have recd. before this reaches you, and as I have received another letter from Col Love which speaks of Mr. Steel in warm terms, I wish you to consult with him & Dr. Hogg upon this subject—I hope Mr. Steel will treat my negroes with humanity as I have requested him   I have confidence in him, have no wish to remove him, if he will only treat my slaves with hummanity.

On the other parts & objects of your visit home I pray you to act with circumspection—you are young, and now for the first time distant from me, but I have confidence that you will steer clear of evil company, & all kind of disapation   Our family enjoy health, & you will be particular in presenting us to all our friends & relatives affectionately—we had a pleasant tour to the Point & all have returned in good health—say to your uncle John & aunt Mary that Jackson is one of the finest boys of his age—we are about to take a trip to visit the venerable patriarch Mr Carroll of Carrolton where we will be absent a few days—Present us kindly to Col

Ward, Sanders, Mrs. Ward Mr Watson & all our neighbours[1]—write me often and believe me affectionately your father

Andrew Jackson

ALS, DLC (37).
1. Edward Ward (d. 1837) had been AJ's friend and neighbor since 1804, when he purchased AJ's Hunter's Hill plantation. William Saunders (c1776–1846) operated the Fountain of Health spa near the Hermitage. Mrs. Ward was probably Sarah, widow of AJ's former neighbor William C. Ward. William Watson, a shoemaker, resided near the Hermitage.

To John Coffee

Washington July 21rst. 1829—

Dear Genl

I have received your letter of 24th. ult on the subject of my ward Hutchings, & his conduct has filled me with sincere regret—I know not what to do with him—I cannot think of letting him be lost, & have concluded to bring him here, and place him at the College at George Town under the controle of the Catholics—it is an excellent instution, & perhaps under my own eye, I might be able to controle him & convince him of the impropriety of his ways—When I reflect on the charge given me by his father on his dying bed, and the great anxiety he had about him, I am truly distressed, & have determined to make the trial by directing him to come on with my son, who has left me some days ago, for Tennessee, & to whom I write by this mail on this subject[1]—It will be, perhaps, more expensive to have him here, than in Tennessee, but it appears, if left to himself there, he must be lost—If it therefore meets your approbation I have to request that you will furnish him with the means to bring him on—my son will be able to give you the amount of the expence of his travel to this place, & you will be able to Judge of what will cloath & school him for one year, after which I hope to be able to spare as much from my other expences, as will meet his expence whilst here—I have given out all idea of giving him *now* a liberal education, and will direct the professors of the college to confine his studies to Arithmetic, Orthography, and Mathematics—and by the time he is of age I hope by counciling him I can bring him to the knowledge of the benefit of a proper course of conduct—If left to himself at the Hermitage he must be lost—Here, I will have the aid of his uncle Judge Smith Senator from the State of South Carolina to controle and govern him—five hundred dollars I think will bring him on, & meet his expences for one year.

I have read you letter respecting the Gentlemen, Engineers, ordered to the Mussle Shoals to lay out & locate your Canal, with much pleasure—I have had an interview with the Secratary of war & the chief Engineer &

they assure me the report & plan shall be made out with the estimate of the expence of the work, at as early a day as possible, and forwarded to you—It is grateful that the citizens on both sides are well pleased with the location of the Canal—The report will reach you in due time for the Legislature—[2]

On the subject of entering the land for Hutchings on the west & &c I will write you fully my opinion in a few days   I have been very much afflicted with a pain in my head for a few days past so much so that my eyes are much affected so that I can scarcely see, & we are about to visit Mr Carroll of Carrolton to day where I expect to spend two days—I shall return on saturday & the first leisure will write you again—My present opinion would be that part of the school land ought to be annexed to his tract.

We all unite in Love to you Polly & the children yr friend

Andrew Jackson

[Endorsed by Coffee:] I wrote to Andw. Jackson Jur, to Nashville, 8th. Agt. 1829 And to Genl. Jackson the 16th. August—

ALS, THi (13-0906).
　　1. July 22, below.
　　2. Coffee had written AJ Donelson on June 24 (THi) to compliment the work of the engineers surveying the Muscle Shoals canal. Coffee hoped their report would prod the Alabama legislature, which had previously balked, into starting construction on the canal when it convened in November. James Kearney, head of the survey team, submitted his report in January 1830. The Army's chief engineer was Brevet Brigadier General Charles Gratiot (1786–1855).

From John Macpherson Berrien

Office of the Attorney General US
21st July 1829—

Sir,

I have examined the petition and accompanying documents in the case of A B Fickle an applicant for pardon, which you have done me the honor to refer to me—and find it difficult to come to a conclusion, which is entirely satisfactory to my mind—

The petitioner was an assistant post-master, and to possess himself furtively of the property of another, violated the confidence which his country had reposed in him in this responsible station—

When we consider how numerous this class of officers is—how indispensable to the security of the monied transactions of the country, their fidelity is—and how comparatively mild is the punishment which the law imposes, it is difficult to convince ourselves that Executive clemency ought to be interposed in such a case, where the guilt of the party is clearly established, under any circumstances short of a perfect conviction, that confinement would prove fatal to the health and life of the party.

On this point I do not find that the evidence is satisfactory—Indeed it does not seem to be chiefly relied upon—

It is the refusal of the prisoner to avail himself of the means of escape, when it was in his power to do so—his industrious habits—his deep and apparently sincere contrition and penitence—the entire conviction on the part of the petitioners, among whom is the prosecutor himself, that the work of reformation has been thorough in the bosom of this unfortunate man, which has induced these benevolent individuals to supplicate your clemency in his behalf—Certainly the appeal is a strong one—You are convinced of the correctness of the facts, which are stated, You see then that the law has done its good work in behalf of this unfortunate man—that it has brought him to a sense of his guilt—and has inspired him with new and better thoughts—that he is in truth a reformed man—and fitted to mingle again with society, with advantage to himself and to the community—It is the apprehension that his pardon will diminish the terror of his example to others, which alone opposes its allowance. Unquestionably this is a very strong consideration—but perhaps it ought to yield in this case, to the thorough conviction which is felt of the entire reformation of the prisoner—

I return the papers sent to me, and I have the honor to be Very Respectfully Sir Yr Obt St

Jn. Macpherson. Berrien.

ALS, DNA-RG 59 (13-0988); LC, DNA-RG 60 (T412-3). *HRDoc* 123, 26th Cong., 2d sess., p. 707 (Serial 387). Abram B. Fickle (b. c1799), whose father died when he was young, was raised by Robert Preston of Abingdon, Va., and married a niece of former Tennessee congressman John Rhea. He was serving as deputy to Blountville, Tenn., postmaster James Rhea when arrested and convicted in 1825 for stealing banknotes from the mail. He was sentenced to ten years' imprisonment. AJ received a number of pleas for Fickle's release, including one from John Goodson Eason (1794–1837), the Jonesboro merchant whose money Fickle had stolen. The petitions cited Fickle's complete reformation, his good behavior and refusal to escape during two prison breaks, and his ill health from prison conditions. AJ decided to pardon Fickle, endorsing a June 29 appeal from Tennessee congressman John Blair, "Let the prayer of the petioners be granted on the payment of costs—It appears that the punishment has already produ[ced] the reformation of prisoner, which was the good work intended by the law—Therefore let him be pardoned." The official release was issued July 29. When Fickle proved unable to pay costs, Blair again petitioned, and AJ released him unconditionally in January 1830.

To Andrew Jackson, Jr.

Washington July 22nd 1829

My son

In my last I forgot to say any thing about my little ward Hutchings—I have wrote Genl Coffee if he still refuses to go to school there, to furnish him the means to bring him on to me—you will consult my little ward Hutchings who I learn is still at my House, whether he will go to school there or prefer coming on here—If he prefers coming on here, you will write Genl Coffee advising him thereof & requesting the Genl to forward you the means, to bring him here—five hundred dollars will bring him here & meet his expences I think for one year—This sum if furnished by Genl Coffee you will recollect I am chargeable with & you will keep an account of how it is expended, and take receipts for all payments made for A. J. Hutchings so that I may be able to settle with the court—

I am not well, I have been severely attacked with head ache since I returned from old point from which I am not entirely free, & it has affected my vision—I wish you to return to me as early as you can—But you must await the convenience of old Mrs. Eaton—you must attend to her as a mother if she consents to come on here[1]—say to Hutchings I would have wrote him but he has not answered my letters therefore I have not wrote him believing it useless—say to him I never expected that he would prove ungrateful to me—I have spent many an anxious thought about him—I, together with his deceased aunt, has often admonished & councilled him for his good, and I still hope he will not disgrace himself, but will be advised, & adopt, & follow, a course that will eventuate in his respectability & prosperity—If he consents to come on here with you this fall—you will write Genl Coffee to furnish you with $500 for his use—Hutchings & Mr Earle will come with you—If the ohio is not up you will have to send Hutchings by the mail stage—However, when I return from Mr Carrolls of Carrolton whither I go to day I will write you again on this subject, expecting on your arrival at the Hermitage you will loose not a moment in writing me—My Dear give me a true relation what attention has been paid to your mothers Grave, whether any Flowers, as I requested, has been planted—let me know how the servants are and how they have been treated—how my stock have been attended to & particularly my Coalts &c &c &—

I have but one word to add on the subject you communicated to me—As you have fixed your affections on Miss ____ say to her, you have known each other from your childhood and it is useless to delay[2]—an answer you expect & a candid one, to which you [will] submit without murmurming[. If it] should be adverse to your wishes [you have] too good an opinion of her to be[lieve] she would wish to coquett you [but] put it not in her power—have a *[categori]*cal answer—present me to Mrs. M*[aria &]* Doctor Shelbys family & all ou*[r]* friends—your affectionate fat[her][3]

Andrew Jack[son]

ALS, DLC (37).
    1. Elizabeth Eaton (c1753–1843), mother of John H., lived in Franklin, Tenn.
    2. AJ Jr. was courting Mary Florida Dickson (b. c1810), the youngest daughter of late Nashville physician and congressman William Dickson and the ward of AJ's neighbor Edward Ward. She married Henry Baldwin, Jr., in 1830.
    3. John Shelby (1785–1859) was a Davidson County physician; his wife was the former Anna Maria Minnick (1793–1873) of Philadelphia.

From Richard Keith Call

Tallahassee 23d. July 1829—

My Dear General
    Your letter of the fifth Inst. has been recd. and read with great attention, and though the subject to which it relates is one which I would most willingly permit to slumber in oblivion, yet the duty I owe myself requires I should give it further attention.
    I must acknowledge Sir that your letter has given me more pain, and inflicted on my feelings a deeper wound than they have ever before experienced. From the general tenor of your remarks it is evident that you have been induced to believe that I have been the slanderer of Mrs. Eaton that I have given currency to the reports circulated against her and that I prevented the Dr and Mrs. Ely from payin her a visit while at Washington. Your letter is private and I presume confidential. I must therefore request your permission to communicate to Dr Ely that part which relates to any conversation I am supposed to have had with him on this subject. I believe him a man of truth and I know he will not say that his impressions with regard to Mrs. & Mr Eaton were derived from me. I met with the Dr and his Lady the 2d evening after my arrival at Washington. They mention the subject themselves and spoke of the general impression which prevailed in society against those individuals. To them I did not disguise my feelings and opinion, which corresponded with their own. They had heard every thing almost which I had heard and much more. While at Philadelphia I did inform the Doctor of some circumstances which passed within my own observation which confirmed my belief in the guilt of those two individuales. I advised him to write to you because I believed you had been imposed on and I conceived it to be the duty of your friends to undeceive you.[1]
    I am much mortified to find Sir that you have been induced to class me among your enemies, for doing that which could only have been dictated by the most devoted friendship. What other motive could have prompted

me to speak to you on that subject. I knew the confidence you had in Eaton. I knew I should make him my Enemy, and should run the risk of incurring your lasting displeasure. I have every thing to looss and nothing to gain by the course I pursued. Prudence would have dictated a different course, and policy would have suggested the madness, of provoking the enmity of men in power, for sooner or later that power is certain to be felt. But when I met with your old friends from all parts of the Country and witnessed the deep regret and consern they expressed at the appointement of Maj Eaton I determined not to be governed by the cold and selfish dictates of policy, but resolved to inform you of what was generaly thought of his domestic relations. Genl you have but little idea of the mortification expressed by your friends on that occasion. I speak not Sir of the newly converted friends who surrounded you, but of your old and well tried friends, from the West and South West of the Union, among those there was a universal expression of regret. I discharged faithfully what I considered to be my duty to you, and I must abide the issue let it be what it may.[2]

You speak General of an investigation of this affair and of the unpleasant situation it would place me in. I hope and trust Sir that no investigation will be avoided on my account. If I am a slanderer, if I have traduced the reputation of a virtuous female, If I am capable of telling a malicious falsehood to gratify the most wicked feelings of the human heart, it is proper that I should be exposed to the world that I may be shuned by all honest and virtuous men. But if I have told the truth let censure rest where it is due. For my own part I fear nothing from an investigation.

I wish not Genl to make you the medium of communication between Maj Lewis and myself, though what I have to say of him is neither secret or confidential, on the contrary I wish him to know, and if ever we meet, he shall know, the expressions I make, and the opinion I entertain of him. You say Sir that I "certainly did make to Maj Lewis shortly after our return to Tennessee the following remark, "that myself and Mrs. Timberlake were one day alone and believing that she and Maj Eaton were *unwarrantably* intimate, and having no doubt she was a woman of easy virtue I made proposals to her of *a certain* description which she with seeming indignation rejected &c" In reply Sir I say that *I certainly did not make any such statement* I do hope that you have not understood Maj Lewis correctly for if he has made this statement, I hesitate not in saying, that he *has told a wicked malicious, and willful falsehood.*

I have a perfectly distinct recollection of the conversation I had with Maj Lewis on this subject 1824. I remember the time and place, and the motive which induced me to mention it to him. I must now Sir speak in defence of my own reputation and I hope you will bear with me when I go back to a period anterior to our departure from Washington. I did believe as I stated in a former letter that a criminal intercourse existed between Maj Eaton and Mrs. T. I believed it first because I was told so by several members of Congress who had lived in the same house with the parties, and I afterwards believed it from a variety of circumstances which occurred within my knowledge. I mentioned my belief to Maj Eaton, and charged him with unkindness to you in carrying you to live in a house which he himself had brought into disrepute. He denied that any impropriety of conduct had ever existed between him and Mrs. Timberlake, and observed to me if you think so badly of her why do you not try her yourself. I laughed and replied to him you do not give me an opportunity, Sir, but if you will go to Baltimore and stay three days on your return I will make a faithful report to you. I have always believed that this conversation was communicated by Maj E to Mrs. T. For she some time after told me privately not to look at he[r] so hard at Table for the Maj would take notice of it. A short time previous to our departure from Washington I invited Maj Eaton in to my room one night, and had a long conversation with him on that delicate subject. I told him that the supposed intercourse existing between him and Mrs. T was bringing him rapidly in to disrepute. I advised him as a friend to fly from her as the only means of avoinding distruction. I entreated him to make an effort and accompany you to Tennessee he became very serious and finally promised me he would do so. The next morning while at breakfast the Maj informed you of his determination, at which you expressed great satisfaction. Maj O'Nile was siting at table at the time, and as I supposed informed the family, for we had not been at the capital more than a half hour when the maj recd. a note, he returned to O'Niles as I understood, where he spent the whole day, thoughs this was but a few days before the adjournment of Congress, and the most important part of the session. When you and I returned home we found him melancholy and dejected, and Mrs. T looked as if she had wiped her eyes out. The next morning at day light you entered my room, and informed me that Maj Eaton had declined going with you to Tennessee, and you requested me to get up and prepare to go with you. This I did   we set out a few days after leaving the Maj behind.

After our arrival in Tennessee, in riding from the Hermitage to Nashville with Maj Lewis, I mentioned to him as a mutual friend the unhappy situation of Eaton. I communicated to him my belief and the facts on which it was founded. I intreated him to write to Eaton, and to leave nothing undone to get him a way from Washington. I ashured him of my belief that he would be a lost man in a short time if he did not resist the control that this woman exercised over him. Lewis replied that he had heared of this affair before, and promised to write to Eaton. This is the history of the case and if Lewis has told you a diffent story I without hesitation say he has *lied willfully and corruptly*. If any other person Genl tels you that I ever made an attack on the chastity of Mrs. T I have the same epithet to apply to them. I never did, and the remark made to Maj Eaton about going to Baltimore for three days was only intended to disgust him with a woman who I thought would destroy him.

Again Sir you say that I must recollect that from the day I and Mrs. T. had the quarrel she never again appeared at our table, and complained as well as some of the family that I had grossly insulted her." Now Sir I have no such recollection. Mrs. T and myself quareled so frequently, I cannot remember either the time or the cause of our first disagreement, but I know it was not from my galanttry towards her. If I mistake not it was from my refusing to wait on her in publi[c]   you mention the communication I made to Col Poulk. If I am not greatly deceived I think you will learn on inquiry that Lewis was the first man that ever mentioned this subject to Col Polk. I believe more over that some of Lewises letters may be found in North Carolina which would place him in a very unpleasant situation.[3]

I have gone in to the history of this unpleasant affair not with a view of doing others an injury but in justification of myself, and in that light I hope you will consider it.

I am happy to learn Sir that your war minister has evinced so much ability in discharging the duties of his office. He is a man possessed of many virtues, and considerable talent, and whatever may be my opinion with regard to a *certain matter,* no one will rejoice at the success and prosperity of your administration more than myself.

I know not Genl what may be the opinion you may hereafter entertain of me, whether you will view me with distrust or with confidence, but I am consoled in the belief that I have acted with fidelity to my friend. That I have warned you of a danger which I believed to threaten you, and shall be happy indeed to find that my fears were immaginary. Genl I risked much in what I have done, I have told you of that which thousand and thousands of your friends daily speak of in the various parts of the Union, but who wanted confidence to approach you on the subject. Perhaps you will say they are not your friends who entertain those opinions, but in this you are mistaken they are your friends, for I hold no communion with your enemies. that I have been actuated by the most pure and disinterested motives in making this communication to you I appeal to him who knows the secret feelings of the human heart. I have no malice against Maj Eaton, but I have said what I believed, and what I thought as a friend you ought to know.

You say Genl we will not quarrel, I am happy to find Sir there is one subject on which we can agree. No Sir we will not quarrel. For however sensably I may feel the severity of your remarks, and the deep wo[u]nds they have inflicted on my feelings, I can never forget the obligations, the duty and the respect I owe to General Jackson. I never can forget the happy days I spent at the Hermitage, and the more than parential kindness, I experienced within its bosom. I never can be otherwise than the friend, the devoted friend of Genl. Jackson, and though my enemies may endeavour to impress him with a different belief, should an occasion ever be presented, he will find me no less faithful than they.

My Wife and children are in good health and desire to be affectionately presented to you.

Adieu Dear Genl and believe me most sincerely yours

R. K Call

[Endorsed by AJ:] Private Genl. Calls, the time when the comt. made to Dr. Ely was not the act of friendship—it was calculated to injure me, it was in cojunction with the cry of my enemies & laid hold of by them &c &c—Major Lewis did make the communication to me in Tennessee shortly after Genl Call made as he said to him, & then or now I have no doubt but you made it to him   A. Jackson.

ALS, DLC (72); AL draft, F (mAJs).
 1. In Call's draft, the last sentence of this paragraph reads: "I advised Dr Ely to address you on the subject because I believed you had been imposed on and I thought you would listen to him with more attention than you would to me."
 2. Call's draft of this paragraph concludes: "I have no doubt Sir that Maj Eaton and his suborned witness Maj Lewis will induce you to believe that all the reports prejudicial to the former have been circulated by me. They may impose this belief on you Sir but they cannot on any other person who has spent a winter in Washington within the last ten years. For I repeat again that the galantry of Maj Eaton with Mrs Timberlake was talked of at Washington as publickly as the meeting of Congress. this was well known to Mr Eaton, and to every other member of your cabinet."
 3. The rest of Call's draft reads: "you speak Genl of my having assisted in giving currency to the reports against the Maj and Mrs. Eaton. Now Sir I deny having ever mentioned this at Washington to any one who had not heard of it before, for be assured Sir I am not mistaken when I say this matter has been talked of for at least ten years. To you and to your devoted friends only, did I mention this subject, with your enemies I held no intercourse, and it was at the urgent solicitation of many of your best and warmest friends that I approached you on the subject. I now regret having done so not because I believe I have sade or done any thing improper, but because I have given you displeasure, without rendering you the service I intended. I have created enemies amonge men in power, whoes enmity I expect to feel when ever an opportunity is . . ."

To Andrew Jackson, Jr.

(Confidential)

July 26th. 1829—

My son
 Having your happiness at heart more than my own, for since I have been deprived of your dear mother, there is no happiness or contentment for me this side the grave, none but what your society, and your welfare & prosperity, and that of your family, should you have one, can afford, added to the love I have for yr cousin Andrew & his, who I have raised as a child.[1] You can Judge of the anxiety I have that you should marry a lady that will make you happy which would add to mine, seeing you so—You are very young, but having placed your affections upon Miss Flora, I have

no desire to controle your affections or interfere with your choice—early attachments are the most durable, & having been raised together in the same neighbourhood, I have only to remark—that no good can flow from long courtship; Therefore I would recommend to you to be frank with her, say to her at once the object of your visit & receive her anser at once—Under your situation this I think will be right, and you have a claim upon her to meet you with Frankness, and should her reply be adverse to your wishes, you ought not to be offended, but continue to treat her as a friend—so soon as you see & converse with her write me & write me with candor the truth on this important subject to yourself & no less to me as your father and friend—Should Miss Flora not favour your wishes, then my son, I have one request to make of you, that is that you will give out all idea of marriage for the present, until you see & advise with me. yr affectionate father

Andrew Jackson

ALS, NN (13-0935).
   1. AJ Donelson.

Statement by Barnard O'Neill

Portsmouth Virginia—27th July 1829—

A Summary Statement of the way and manner the Public Business is carried on and conducted at the navy yard and other places on this Station. Vizt.

When northern pine plank is to be furnished One who keeps a Lumber yard in Portsmouth, a Mr. ____ goes on to Baltimore and purchases sometimes 7 or 8 to 10 or 15 Vessel Loads of lumber at about 10$ per thousand, and sells at 30$ prM. to the navy yard, (by a previous understanding)   When Other requisitions are made for lumber that can be furnished in this part of the Country the Navy Agent sends for his friends and privately contracts with them also, and then sometimes advertizes it afterwards, and when appyed to by persons wishing to contract for it, his answer is (it is contracted for Sir)   But the private leting out the contract of the navy yard Wall and other public (works such as the magazine lately built) and other Houses &c caps the Climax. It is thought that at least One Hundred Thousand dollars might be saved, if it had been put at fair competition   The condemned Plank and Timber of all kinds in the navy yard is given away to favourites for nothing, which if sold at auction would bring a large amount annually—From the large number of Horses and Oxen belonging to the Navy yard a large quantity of manure is sold and it would be well to know what becomes of the money—In the Dry

Dock the same game is going on—Mr Singleton the superintendant not content with 100$ pr. month for his Own services, besides a number of hands employed he has Two Horses and Carts of his Own also at the rate of One & half dollars pr. day each

Throughout the year, to the exclusion of the rest of the Community and the excavations of the dock being laid down from wheel barrows within a short distance of where it is intended to be placed, gives work for his Horses & Carts the year through. And the following names are the persons that it is actually necessary should be discharged from public employ at this Station Vizt.

*James Jarvis, Inspector of Lumber &c in the Navy Yard.[1]
Charles, A, Grice, Master Black Smith.   Ditto.
William, Bishop, Clerk in the navy Store.   Ditto.
Leml, Langley, Master Joiner.   Ditto.
Henry, Singleton, Superintendant Dry Dock.
John, Cox, Keeper of Magazine.
Jesse, Nicholson, Post, Master, Portsmouth.
William, Tee, Master of Light Boat off Craney Island.
John, B. Sayles, Master of Light Boat, Hampton Roads.

*Perhaps there is no man in the united States who (by the influence of his office) has gone Greater lengths in proscription and other conduct too disgracefull to mention. And the above persons with others of this place who have equally forfeited their claim to Public confidence, Have gone all lengths to Villify and destroy the Character and reputation of the present administration during our struggle; were the very persons, (through Capt. Barron) to intrude themselves on the president and suite while among us, which had the effect (as they intended) to prevent many *real* friends from participating in the enjoyment of their Company while in Portsmouth.[2]

It may not be improper to mention the names of some of our early and well tryed friends. In case of Vacances in this place and the situation in which they are capable of giving satisfaction

Capt John Bayne whose name is already known to, and recommeded to Mr. Branch, as one of our first and best friends.

Capt. Doggett a gentleman well known as a respectable ship master for upwards of thirty years in this place and would be well calculated to take charge of One of the light Boats at this place

The Reverend David M. Woodson would do credit to and be well worthy of the situation of Chaplain to the Naval Hospital Building at this place

[*Endorsed by AJ:*] abuses at Navy yard Gosport or portsmouth, va. The secratary of the Navy will see the bids of the different bidders for the Navy yard, the magazine &c at Gosport—and note whether lower bids were not made than that at which the contract was let—who was the agent letting this work & the price at which it was *let*—

AD, DNA-RG 45 (M124-119). O'Neill had previously complained to John Branch on June 13 that Norfolk navy agent Miles King was privately awarding padded contracts for construction at the navy yard.

1. AJ noted next to Jarvis's name: "a proper person to be removed—says M O Neil—(coffin handbill) threatened to turn men out of employ if they did not vote for Adams."

2. AJ had been in Portsmouth on July 10.

To Daniel Brent

Washington July 30th. 1829

Sir,

The President has been informed this evening that John Jackson of North Carolina appointed consul for the Island of Martinique is supposed to be the Mr John Jackson who has resided some time in this city. This is not the fact as was understood by the President at the time the commission was signed. You will therefore please withold the commission from this latter Gentleman, or if delivered, call for its return to the State Dept. until further advised. yr ob. sevt

Andrew Jackson

LC, DLC (60). John Jackson (1787–1854), formerly from Washington, N.C., was a merchant residing in Alexandria, D.C. He had applied unsuccessfully for several positions under Adams. He was commissioned as consul at Martinique on July 27, and the *US Telegraph* announced the appointment on July 30. Brent informed him of AJ's retraction on July 31.

To Richard Keith Call

[July 31]

with me, & I sincerely regretted it, because I knew the great exertions making here by our enemies was to produce a split in Cabinet, that they might profit by it, which I was determined to prevent; and from the confidence I had in Mr Berien rectitude, I did believe & still do believe should it become necessary from any motives of delicacy toward himself or the Executive he would withdraw from his situation, or abandon the suits. I therefore cannot permit myself to be dragged into a political newspaper quarrel and all the confidential chitchat before my own fireside to be incorporated into it.

My Dr. Sir I regret exceedingly the indiscretion that has sought to bring my name into a political contest. When you well knew that if any blame could attach it was to myself in not making the special inquiry into what suits Mr. B. was engaged when he made the exception from the official duties about to be assigned him by the office confered. Lastly I can assure you, that I never heard or suspected that Judge Barien had been concerned directly or indirectly in the large grants in Florida until he was appointed, and the first & only intelligence I had on the subject was from yourself[1]—since his return from Georgia he has conversed with me upon this subject & seems confident that he named to me the particular suits. I can only say, that I have at no time had any recollection of it—if he did it entirely escaped me amidst the hurry & confusion of the time. My belief tho is that he did not state any particular suits, and your own recollection will furnish you with the information I gave you when you made your communication to me of his interest & engagement in the Florida grants.

We are all in our usual health & desires to be affectionately presented to Mary & the sweet little children and believe me as usual your friend

Andrew Jackson

P.S. Doctor Bailer of the army is now here & requests to be presented to you—he left Houston on the Arkansa.[2]

Houston poor fellow has sent me an Indian tobacco pouch & pipe he is with his adopted father Capt Jolly of the cherokees

ALS fragment, CtY (13-1019).

·1. Call quoted three passages from this letter in an address to the public in the Tallahassee *Floridian,* April 13, 1833 (13-1021). This sentence was the third. The first two were as follows: "When J. M. Berrien was notified of my intention, by offering thro' a friend, the office of Attorney General of the United States, he waited upon me and said, he would accept the appointment, observing at the same time, it was a duty he owed, to inform me, that he was engaged in two or three (or he might have said several) cases against the United States, that he must reserve the right to appear in.—Knowing as I did, that there was no eminent lawyer practising in the courts of the United States, but what was engaged in suits against the United States, and it never entering into my mind, that J. M. Berrien was engaged in the large land claims in Florida; I gave him the appointment. It was made and had got before the public. The information from you was the first I ever heard, and you were the only individual who gave me the idea, that he was concerned in those large land claims." "I had not heard that suits were instituted for the recovery of the Florida lands, and had received Mr. B's remarks as referring to suits then pending in the Supreme Court of the United States."

2. John Walker Baylor (1782–1835) was an assistant surgeon in the Army.

From Mahlon Dickerson

Suckasunny (N. J.) 31st. July 1829.

Sir,

John L. Leib Esq. formerly of Philadelphia now of Michigan is anxious to obtain the place of Secretary of that District—In the years '98 '99 & 1800 Mr. Leib at Philadelphia was among the most active politicians who brought about the change that placed Mr. Jefferson in the presidential chair, and gave a check to aristocracy at that time—During the late war he removed to Michigan, since which I have known but little of him, but have kept up a correspondence with him so far as to know that he remains faithful to his former principles.

As I do not easily forget those with whom I was associated in '98, I feel much interest in favor of Mr. Leib—& take the liberty of soliciting for him the office of Secretary or of attorney of the Michigan District—I am with profound respect your obdt. & Very Huml. Servt.

Mahlon Dickerson.

ALS, DNA-RG 59 (M639-14). *TPUS*, 12:58. Dickerson (1770–1853) was a U.S. senator from New Jersey. John L. Leib (c1767–1838), brother of late U.S. senator Michael Leib of Pennsylvania, was a Michigan lawyer and judge. AJ appointed him territorial marshal in 1830, but the Senate rejected him.

Memorandum

Brarely has not paid the due bills for articles to be furnished by the Traty—requests that these due bills should not be paid.[1]

Let the treaty be examined, what has not been performed, *let it be—*

They want their land survayed—that they may know where to sleep they want a new agent—

Genl Ridgely at Williamsons invite him to dine—[2]

Mr. Wear says there is a ballance of $165.33 of his $2000—that he cannot receive it without giving receipt in full—enquire why this is so—Let this ballance be paid—

Genl Irwin recommends Mr Buchanan of Pittsburgh for atto. u. states. in place of Mr. B. if removed—Colo. Evans for Sec. Foreign legation—Mr. James. B. minister abroad.
Mr. Finley recommended for atto. u. state, has been appointed Depty atto. for the state—[3]

Armstead Beckham chief armorer H. Ferry—recommended by Maj Peter & Mr. Wilson—an invaluable man[4]

Mr. M.Gee. Coorad. A. Tenyeck—for marshal—This man is not a moral a man, as a gambler swindler & immoral man[5]

AD, DLC (38).
    1. Roley McIntosh et al. to AJ, June 22, above.

2. Perhaps Charles Carnan Ridgely (1760–1829), a former Maryland governor and brigadier general of militia, who died July 17. Williamson's was a Washington hotel.

3. Thomas Irwin (1785–1870) was a Pennsylvania congressman. In 1830 AJ removed western Pennsylvania district attorney Alexander Brackenridge for George Washington Buchanan (1808–32). George's brother James Buchanan (1791–1868) was a prominent Jacksonian Pennsylvania congressman who in 1831 was appointed minister to Russia. Samuel Evans, a former state legislator, was an applicant to be secretary of legation in England. James Findlay (1801–43) was a Greensburg attorney.

4. Armistead Beckham (1786–1858), master armorer at Harpers Ferry, was implicated for corruption in a War Department investigation in May. He refused to resign, and in 1830 was reassigned to the Allegheny arsenal at Pittsburgh.

5. Conrad Anthony Ten Eyck (1789–1845) was the county clerk and former sheriff of Albany County, N.Y.

August

From John Jackson

Washtn City Aug. 1s 1829

Sir

On thursday last I had the honor to receive a Communication from the State department advising me of your having appointed me Consul of the United States for the Island of Martinique, accompanied with my Commission as such, instructions &c—On the evening of the same day, my appointment was Officially announced to the public, by your order in course (I presume) issued through the State Dept. Yesterday (and I crave your pardon for the remark) I with unfeigned surprize, received a Communication from same source, stating that you had "directed" that I should be requested to return the Commission I had recvd. the day before, to the dept. of State, it having been granted under a "misapprehension of the person *intended* to be appointed"[1]—this very novel & extraordinary course of proceedur is to me inexplicable! Will you have the goodness Sir, to explain to me the cause for it—stating the accusations that have been made against me, if any, and by whom, that an opportunity may be afforded me of acknowledging their Correctness, or of refuting the Calumniator, & of treating him (if such he should turn out to be) as he deserves—

The nature of the charge, the pit of infamy from which it eminated, is as at present advised, nothing more than Conjectur—but be it what it may, and coming from the source it did, I cannot find language to express my astonishment, that the President of the US. should so promptly have acted upon it, without knowing it to be true or false, as on the instant, to revoke his deliberate act of the day before, on a subject which had been before him for four months & more particularly when that act was founded on the representations of above forty as respectable Citizens as is to be found in the US. evry one of whom; would stand as gold seven times refined, when Contrasted with your informant or a host of such miscreants—That you might act understandingly upon the subject of my application, I stated in a Communication I had the honor to make to the Hon: Secretary of State the following, "Altho the Office I solicit is not one of political trust, influence or that has Salary attached to it, I deem it due to Candour & fair dealing to state for the information of the President that in the last Presidential Canvass, I advocated the re-election of Mr Adams." And again "In procuring testimonials I had no regard to the political opinions held by the Gentlemen who I applied to, their high standing & respectability, in attesting to my character being the only Consideration, being content to rest my claims to office on my character & fitness, deeming political opinions of minor importance—My own opinions however were well known & fearlessly expressed, when occasion called forth an expression, or it was my pleasure to express it   And further, I stated I had been an applicant for office under the administration of your distinguished predecessor & that I had been honored with strong testimonials of Character & Capacity from many the most distinguished Gentlemen in the State of No. Ca. (some 50–60 in number) & which I would submit to your inspection if desired, & that perhaps an equal number of them were your political friends—

The testimonial addressed to your Excellency which accompanied my application, was signed by above forty of the most respectable inhabitants of Alexandria (my former residence) and Certified by one of your stanchest friends to be so, as well, as, of both political parties, among whom, you must have recognised the names of many of your friends[2]—Altho differing with you in opinion, if I have not greatly mistaken your character, justice to me, & yourself, will I think, & trust, induce you to Comply with my request, to give me the charges prefered & the author of them—it is but reasonable—

Pardon me for my presumption in addressing you & for any expression that may appear to you to be exceptionable—I have felt myself agrieved & unjustly treated without cause being shewn, which are circumstances calculated to produce excitement & warmth, and which must be my apology—I have the honor to be, most respectfully Sir Yr Hb Ser

Jno Jackson

ALS, DNA-RG 59 (M639-12). Washington *National Journal,* August 25. In a public letter to AJ in the *National Journal* on August 21, Jackson had accused the Washington Central Committee of scuttling his appointment and blasted AJ for imbecility, wickedness, and tyranny. The *US Telegraph* replied that same evening that Jackson's appointment had been retracted when he was identified, not by a Central Committee member, as the author of scurrilous writings against AJ. AJ commissioned John S. Meircken as consul at Martinique on August 21.

1. Daniel Brent to John Jackson, July 31, DNA-RG 59 (M78-3).

2. Alexander Hunter et al. to AJ, April 18, a copy of which was published with this letter in the *National Journal* on August 25. Hunter (1791–1849), an Alexandria justice of the peace whom AJ later appointed marshal for the District of Columbia, retracted his endorsement of Jackson in the *US Telegraph* of August 27 on account of his "gross and unbecoming" publications against AJ.

To [F. J. Naylor?]

August 7th. 1829

Sir,
Your letter of the 4th inst is just recd. Of the two Africans named in your letter, I have no information except that contained in your letter. Arrangements were made for taking several Africans from Baltimore in the vessel preparing to take those from St Augustine provided they would pay for their passage. They were accidentally brought in, and were represented to be anxious to return to Africa. I will just add that there is no power vested in the President to order to be sent out of the country any free person; and the writ of *habeas corpus* will always relieve where a freeman is deprived of his liberty contrary to law and his consent, yr. &c

Andrew Jackson

Norfolk Va.

LC, DLC (60). In January two African men, Caesar and Pompey, aged about twenty, had been sent by customs officials in Mobile to Baltimore and placed under custody of federal marshal Thomas Finley for return to Africa. Arrangements were made for them to sail with the shipwrecked Africans from Florida, despite their protests that they did not wish to go. On August 18 Finley wrote Navy secretary Branch that in compliance with instructions he had sent them to Norfolk for boarding (DNA-RG 45, M124-120).

From John Miller

City of Jefferson
August 8th. 1829.

Sir
On the 20th. ult. I received information by express, that a party of Indians, supposed to be Ioway and Sacks, had attacked and killed three of our citizens and wounded three or four others. The attack was made about 150 miles north west of this place, and within perhaps 20 or 30 miles of the northern boundary of the State   the circumstances which led to this outrage as communicated to me, and which, I believe may be relied on as correct, are; that a party of Indians entered the settlements of the whites, on the head waters of the river Chariton, some time in the month of June last; remained there hunting until the rupture between them & the frontier inhabitants; in their intercourse with the whites they became insolent and abusive, ordered them from their farms and the country, killed their stock and finally collected and drove off a number of cattle.

The whites, in numbers about twenty six men, pursued the Indians to their camp, demanded the stock, and satisfaction for previous outrages committed by the Indians—this was refused; an Indian, (one of the perpetrators) was seen to cock and present his gun to fire, on which a conflict immediately ensued and terminated in the death of three of our citizens and three wounded. The whites were soon compelled to retreat, as the Indians were greatly superior in numbers—After the conflict three Indians were found dead on the ground. The number of Indians engaged in this affair, were in the first instance, reported to me, to consist of from 150 to 200; but subsequent information, represent their number at from 50 to 60 warriors.

Immediately on receiving the foregoing information, I ordered a detachment of about 250 men, to march to the defence of the frontier, to bury the dead and pursue and punish the offenders, if found within our limits. When the detachment reached the ground where the engagement took place, they ascertained that the Indians had fled in the utmost haste and precipitation—they were pursued 25 or 30 miles, in the direction of the Sack Village, situate on the east of the Mississippi river; to which nation or tribe, I have no doubt, the greater part of this lawless banditti belong.

With the view of giving security and confidence to our frontier settlers, and prevent them from abandoning their property and seeking security by moving into the interior of the State—other detachments of militia were ordered to the frontier for a few days; the whole force however, have been recalled and discharged for the present

The state having been invaded and murders and other depredations committed on her citizens by the Indians before mentioned, it is confidently expected and believed, that the government of the United States, will defray the expenses incurred by this State, in organizing a military force, to repel the invaders, and give Security and protection to her citizens.[1]

Genl Levenworth passed up the Missouri river on the 1st. inst with a detachment of United States troops, for the Ioway villages with the view of ascertaining whether that nation had any agency in the late murders &c. and to treat them as circumstances might require—On enquiry, should it be found that they are innocent, he will immediately proceed to the Sack villages, having the same object in view. I hold in readiness to march, when required, a strong and respectable force of mounted men, to join Genl. Levenworth, in the event of its becoming necessary and he desire it. The Genl. deserves the highest credit and has my thanks and acknowledgements for the prompt manner in which he marched to the protection of our frontier, immediately on being informed by me, of the outrages committed. I flatter myself, and at the same time, do most earnestly request, that orders will be given to the officer commanding the United States troops in this department, to cause the nation to whom the offending Indians belong, to be severely chastised, if they refuse to surrender them, on being demanded to do so.[2]

Before I close this communication, permit me to call your attention to the late abandonment, by the troops of the United States, of cantonment Levenworth. There is no part of the extensive frontier of the United States more exposed to Indian depredation, than is the South western frontier of this State; allow me therefore, to solicit the reoccupation of this highly important post, by a military force, sufficiently respectable in point of numbers, to keep the numerous and powerfull tribes of Indians in that quarter, effectually in check. I flatter myself that it will be convenient to order the reoccupation of this post during the ensuing fall[.][3] I have the honor to be with the highest considerations of respect, Sir, your obt. Servt.

John Miller

ALS, DNA-RG 94 (M567-45). Miller (1781–1846) was governor of Missouri, 1826–32. The clash he described occurred on July 17 in Randolph County, Mo. Brevet Brigadier General Henry Leavenworth (1783–1834) commanded the Third Infantry Regiment at Jefferson Barracks near St. Louis. In mid-August he met at Cantonment Leavenworth with chiefs of the Iowa, Sac, and Fox Indians, who gave hostages for their good behavior and agreed to help apprehend the Iowas believed to be involved. In October, Iowa chief Big Neck and several warriors surrendered to Indian subagent Andrew S. Hughes. In March 1830 they were tried and acquitted on evidence showing that the whites had started the fight.

1 In 1831 Congress appropriated $9,085.54 to cover Missouri's militia expenses.

2. Brevet Brigadier General Henry Atkinson (1782–1842) commanded the Western Department, headquartered at Jefferson Barracks.

3. Cantonment Leavenworth was built in 1827 on the west bank of the Missouri River above current Leavenworth, Kans. Finding the post unhealthy, expensive, and too remote to offer effective protection, the War Department had ordered the garrison withdrawn to Jefferson Barracks in March 1829 (Eaton to Miller, Jul 29, DNA-RG 107, M6-12). The cantonment was reoccupied in November by troops returning from Santa Fe escort duty. It became Fort Leavenworth in 1830.

From William Ingalls

(Copy)
To the President of the United States.

Boston Aug. 9th. 1829.

Respected Sir,

The enclosed is submitted to your consideration without comment, as, it is presumed all comment is unnecessary. With the assurance of my highest regard.

signed William Ingalls

[Enclosure: Charles Harrison Stedman to Ingalls]

(Copy)
To Dr. Wm. Ingalls

Chelsea Aug. 8th. 1829.

Dear Sir,

The following, according to the best of my knowledge & recollection, is the conversation & the circumstances attending it that I had with Mr. David Henshaw of Boston. On the 2d day after I entered upon the duties of my office (2d May 1829) I had occasion to obtain some medicines for the Hospital, & for this purpose I called at the store of Mr. J. Henshaw in India St. After informing Mr. H. what articles I wanted, he asked me to whose account they should be charged, I told him to the U. S. Marine Hospital. Mr. David Henshaw who was present, then said in words to this effect—that I had better let another person a friend, Dr. Ingalls for instance obtain the medicines for me so that I might make a little profit upon them—charging government a little more than my friend gave & thus obtain "perhaps" to use his own worlds, "25 per cent on the medicines you purchase—which will be a very pretty thing for you." "Dr. Townsend did so—did he not?"[1] I told him I did not know and directly left the store.

The above are facts which I am ready to substantiate by oath at any time if called upon. Yours Affectionately

signed Chas H. Stedman

Copy, DNA-RG 46 (13-1053). David Henshaw (1791–1852), a wholesale druggist, was co-founder of the *Boston Statesman* and a leading Boston Jacksonian. AJ had appointed him collector of the port; he was narrowly confirmed by the Senate in April 1830 and served through AJ's presidency. His brother John Henshaw (b. 1798) was also a druggist. William Ingalls (1769–1851) was a noted physician and politically associated with a rival Boston Jacksonian faction. Charles Harrison Stedman (1805–66) was a physician at the Charlestown, Mass., marine hospital and Ingalls's son-in-law. In another letter to Ingalls, which Ingalls also forwarded to AJ on August 9, Stedman said that he had taken no profit on medicines as Henshaw suggested.

1. David Townsend (1753–1829) and his son Solomon Davis Townsend (1793–1869) were physicians at the Charlestown marine hospital.

From David Henshaw

SIR:

The recent publication of a report and resolutions, adopted by a meeting of merchants in this city, and forwarded, as I am informed, to you, animadverting on my official conduct, impels me, in duty to myself and for the respect I bear the government, which has honored me with its confidence, to address you in reply.

The report and resolutions bear against me for the removals I have made generally, but more particularly for that of Mr. Johnson, a clerk in the Custom House, the cause of which they quite gratuitously ascribe to his political opinions.[1] I am unwilling to admit as sound, the doctrine which seems to be advanced by the committee, that an officer is, impliedly, entitled to his place so long as he discharges its duties ably and faithfully. If this were the case, it would change entirely the tenure by which offices are held, the appointments could last during good behaviour or for life, in opposition to the spirit of our institutions and in violation of the express law of the land.

In great political revolutions, after contests as embittered as that through which we have recently so happily passed, many changes are expected, and the violent but unsuccessful partisan, ought to submit, without repining, to the natural consequences of defeat. He ought to know that an administration elected by the people will naturally rely for support on its friends, and not on its opponents. However justifiable, then, it might be to displace officers for their political opinions, a rule almost always followed by the people, and adopted on a scale more or less extended by all parties, and every administration; still I have made no changes that ought not to have been made independently of these considerations—such as I have made were reported according to law, to the chief officer of the Treasury Department, who has not, I am gratified in saying, disapproved of any of them.

Mr Johnson is the last case that ought to have called forth the severe animadversions of any respectable meeting. Independently of the fact that he has been a heated politician, and to the extent of his power, has attempted to prostrate the influence of all opposed to his political opinions —independently of the fact that he has been in office more than twenty years, and on the principle of rotation in office ought to give place to another; for, if the office were a burden to him he has borne it long enough; if a privilege he has had a fair share of it; independently of these considerations, he ought to have been removed: For, I had reasons which induced me to believe that he had accepted, if not demanded, fees or gratuities from merchants and others doing business with the office which were prohibited by a provision of the act of 1822, which provision I have been informed was adopted expressly, though it seems ineffectually, to suppress abuses existing in this Custom House.[2] Under these circumstances, I felt unwilling to be longer responsible in my reputation or property for his conduct, for I believed that any one who would accept of a gratuity for doing his duty, might one for neglecting it.

As a public servant, I feel myself responsible to the government and the people for the prompt and faithful discharge of all the duties appertaining to the appointment with which you have honoured me; but when men of good characters, urbane manners and ample qualifications, are placed in office, and all their duties are promptly and faithfully performed, I am unable to discern the propriety of the interference of political opponents in the arrangement of clerks on political grounds. The meeting urge no complaint against Mr. Johnson's successor. I was notified the day after Mr. Willard's appointment, before it had been seen how he discharged his new duties; and it consequently appears that the opposition was determined on without knowing or caring whether or not the change was an improvement. There is not only no charge against Mr. Willard or any other of the newly appointed officers, but on the contrary, the majority and the most respectable members who were chosen on the committee, and who declined serving, say in their [n]ote appended to the published proceedings of the meeting, that "they are not aware of any deficiency among the officers recently appointed in the performance of their duties."[3] Personal feelings and private griefs may have operated in producing the meeting. Mr. Blake, the Chairman of the committee, who made the report, is brother to George Blake, Esq. late district attorney. In the course of my official duty a short time since, I caused two delinquent bonds against one, who took an active part in the meeting, to be sued. I am unable to account for the hostility of this individual in any way satisfactorily, except by supposing that this circumstance may have caused it.[4]

In discharging the duties of the office confided to my care, my object has been to obtain trusty and efficient officers. The removals have not been confined to political opponents, and so far from being operated upon by feelings of political intolerance, there are now in office double the number of political opponents, that there were of political friends when I received my commission. I have endeavored to divest myself of all personal considerations, of every feeling of prejudice or partiality, and to look solely to promoting the public interest and the credit and honor of your administration.

The complaints, however, as you will perceive, seem not to be exclusively against the removals which I have made, but extend generally to the system pursued by the administration, and particularly embrace that of the late Naval Officer at this port, whom they assert to be the patriot who has come down to us from the "revolution, with every claim of public gratitude and private respect, in the midst of his usefulness, and with all the advantages of mature experience, has been only the more conspicuous object for the indignity by which *his* sacrifice has been made the reward of some political intriguer." This complaint will appear the more extraordinary, when it is known that the Secretary of this meeting was one who signed the petition and procured others to sign it, recommending the appointment of his uncle, the present Naval Officer, and of course the removal of the late Naval Officer.[5]

A large proportion of those who signed to have Mr Johnson retained, have their names attached to a similar request now on the files of the Treasury Department, to have the late Collector of this port retained, and were equally anxious to have the late administration retained. Among this number, are some, who in a public circular recommended to the patronage of the people the "Massachusetts Journal," a paper that outraged the feelings of decency and truth, and which this meeting chose as the organ of its communication to the public, of its proceedings.[6] I have the names of many of them recommending some one of their friends to places within my gift, to comply with which, it would have been necessary to make removals, but it would seem that their horror at these changes would have been much less distressing, if their friends could have derived the benefit resulting from them. I dwell the longer on these facts, that you may be the better able to estimate the value that ought to be placed upon the *opinions* of these people. Those who now talk loudest against what they term proscriptions, but which are changes and reforms demanded by the unequivocal and overwhelming voice of the people, are themselves of the most intolerant cast. They never have voted, nor never will vote, for any one whose political opinions they dislike. In their bigoted and factious course they have trampled down the principles of honor and moral honesty to reach those who have opposed their opinions. The last year the editor of the Boston Statesman was refused a job of printing to which he was fairly entitled, under the plighted faith of the city, avowedly because his political opinions were obnoxious; and the most boisterous now against what they term the proscriptions of your administration, are those who voted for this unjust and dishonorable act, and those who approved of the measure.[7] That men who have left no effort unessayed to prevent the great civil revolution which the people have decreed, that they who in their intolerance have been unrestrained by love of country or love of justice, should now step boldly forward to denounce salutary official changes, under the plea that they are proscriptive, if it cannot move our anger, must at least excite surprise.

I am constrained to ask, who and what are the men who assume, without right and without truth, to speak the voice of "nine-tenths" of the people of this place? Some of the most prominent among them, have within a few years emerged in affluence from bankruptcies that involved in losses, distress or ruin their confiding creditors. Go, Sir, upon an exchange, and ask the respectable merchants of Boston, if they would accept the characters of these men as standards by which to estimate our mercantile worth, and they would tell you that the very suggestion was a libel upon the reputation of our city. Some who have risen to distinction in this business were, at the commencement of the late war, undistinguished in that mass of opposition, which displayed its patriotism in mobbing the officers of the revenue, or in tearing from our shipping, flags raised in honor of the national valor. They are the men who have grown gray in opposing the national administration, who from Jefferson's first election to the present period, could find but one era in that lapse of time congenial to their feelings and principles—the past four years. They are those who, while you, under every privation, encountered difficulties and dangers, and covered

yourself with glory in the vast wilds of the south in combatting and sub-
duing a savage foe, and his more savage allies, were singing Te Deums in
honor of the victories of our enemies, and resolving that it was unbecoming a religious and moral people to rejoice in our own.[8]

While you were raising an imperishable monument of your fame on
the banks of the mighty Mississippi, and were shedding a lustre upon the
character of this nation, which will shine as long as her history is known,
they were deliberating to meet the enemy under the white flag, or were
plotting the dismemberment of the Union.

Such, Sir, are the character and claims of those who insist that I ought
to follow *their opinions* in preference to my own, in selecting officers
under my direction.

With sentiments of profound respect and veneration, I have the honor
to be your obediant servant,

DAVID HENSHAW.

Printed, Washington *United States' Telegraph,* September 15 (mAJs); AL draft, MHi (13-
1059). Boston merchants opposed to Henshaw's removals at the custom house had met at
the Exchange Coffee House on July 21. Benjamin Rich presided. The meeting appointed a
committee of thirteen to draw up a report. Their report, adopted by a reconvened meeting
on July 27 and circulated in the anti-Jackson press, accused Henshaw of outraging public
sentiment and violating public trust by his "system of proscription, unbounded and unspar-
ing" (*National Journal,* Aug 14).
    1. The merchants' report named Henshaw's removal of John Johnson as chief clerk of
the coastwise department as an egregious offense against the wishes of nine-tenths of the
community. Johnson himself addressed a public protest to AJ (*Niles,* Oct 10).
    2. The 1822 act regulating compensation for customs officers barred them from accept-
ing any fees or rewards not provided by law.
    3. Henshaw had appointed Paul Willard (1795–1856), then clerk of the state senate,
to replace Johnson. Seven of the men originally named by the July 21 merchants' meeting
to the committee of thirteen had declined to serve, some saying in a note published with
the committee's report that they regretted the removals but saw no grounds for formal
complaint.
    4. Joshua Blake (1779–1844) chaired the committee of thirteen. AJ had replaced his
brother George Blake (1769–1841) with Andrew Dunlap as federal district attorney for
Massachusetts on March 6. Henshaw's draft named Samuel Ellis, secretary of the July 21
meeting, as the delinquent merchant.
    5. Thomas Melvill (1751–1832), a participant in the Boston Tea Party and grand-
father of author Herman Melville, had worked at the Boston custom house since 1789
and been naval officer since 1814. In April AJ appointed John Parker Boyd (1764–1830),
a brigadier general in the War of 1812, to replace him. Boyd was Samuel Ellis's uncle by
marriage.
    6. Henshaw's predecessor as collector was Henry Alexander Scammell Dearborn
(1783–1851). The *Massachusetts Journal* was edited by David Lee Child. The May 20,
1828, circular, signed by Dearborn and others, had commended the paper for its support
of the Adams administration and opposition to AJ. The circular and a Jacksonian critique
appeared in *Political Extracts from a Leading Adams Paper, the Massachusetts Journal*
(Boston, 1828).

7. Jacksonians had charged in 1828 that *Boston Statesman* editor Nathaniel Greene (1797–1877) was refused the city of Boston's annual printing contract for political reasons despite submitting the lowest bid.

8. In 1813 the Massachusetts senate passed a resolution declaring it "not becoming a moral and religious people" to celebrate military victories in a war waged for "conquest and ambition."

To Martin Van Buren

August 12th. 1829—

Dr. Sir

I have decypered the Genls. (Smiths) letter as well as a severe head ache will permit—I am pleased with the arrangement & choice of Sweden by Mr Hughes—There is no dificulty in removing the present incumbent.[1]

I concur with you that it would not be proper to send the Commission before a positive acceptance—The precedent would be one, out of which, much inconvenience & michief might arise—any arrangement you may think proper to make respecting his return to america, I will approve, expecting that no aditional expence to the U.S. States may be incurred thereby.

I am pleased with the document you sent me respecting Texas, and will be happy to see you & Colo Butler whenever it may suit your convenience[2]—The constitutional question can be easily gotten over, two millions added to the one already offered will amend the Mexican Constitution[3]—and to obtain it to the west of the Nueces to the grand prararie or desart, I would go as far as five millions rather than leave a foreign power in possession of heads of our leading branches of the great Mississippi on its west, as it appears, and has always so appeared to me, that the whole of the western branches of the M. was necessary for the security of the great emporium of the west, Neworleans, and that the god of the universe had intended this great valley to belong to one nation—yr friend

Andrew Jackson

P.S. I return Genls Smith letter that it may remain on file.

ALS, DLC-Van Buren Papers (13-1113).

1. On August 10, Samuel Smith wrote Van Buren that he had inquired of his son-in-law Christopher Hughes, recently displaced in the Netherlands, whether he would prefer a new posting in Mexico or as chargé d'affaires to Sweden, the latter possibly sparing him a return from Europe. Thinking Hughes would choose Sweden, Smith asked Van Buren to send him a commission (Van Buren Papers, DLC). AJ recalled John James Appleton (1792–1864) and appointed Hughes chargé in February 1830.

2. Anthony Butler (1787–1849) was an old AJ acquaintance who had served in the Kentucky and Mississippi legislatures. At about this time, Butler wrote AJ describing Texas at length and urging its acquisition by the U.S.

3. The Adams administration had tried to buy Texas for $1 million, but was rebuffed on the grounds that relinquishing territory would violate Mexico's constitution.

Notes for Instructions to Joel Roberts Poinsett

The line agreed upon in the Spanish Treaty with the U States, leaves new orleans unprotected in a state of War.[1] Its defences can be turned by approaches to the Mississippi thro the La Fourche and other bayous to the west. To counteract the evils growing out of the surrender of that part of Louisiana west of the Sabine, and East of the Rio del Norte or Grand river, it is proposed to open a negotiation for the retrocession of the same to the U States, upon a plan of which the following is the outline.

Instruct Mr. Poinsett to feel the Mexican Govt upon the subject. The threatened invasion of Spain, connected with the deranged condition of the finances of Mexico, makes the time a very propitious one for the ascertainment of her views in regard to this territory, as Mr P can give his enquiries the character of individual solicitude for her welfare, and a desire to relieve her embarrassments, rather than turn them to the advantage of his own country.[2] He might say to her, I see the depressed situation of your revenue, and in the course of a discussion upon the impracticability of defending the republic against foreign invasion without it, or even preserving the harmony of its own citizens who have numerous claims upon its common treasure; he might find occasion to suggest, as an evidence of his reliance upon the friendly disposition of this Government towards that, a project for their relief embracing the retrocession of the territory mentioned. In support of which might be added the fact that a portion of our citizens from a misapprehension of the range of the eastern boundary line, as defined by the T[r]eaty with Spain, are already located beyond it; and the confident anticipation that this Government for the double purpose of advancing Mexican interests, and guarding in future against all causes of collision between the two countries, on account of the unsettled state of their boundery lines, would with great pleasure accede to a plan so well calculated to attain these desireable objects. Governing himself by the drift of feeling and sentiment which these suggestions may elicit, he might in the event of their favorable character go further, and propose to guarantee the payment of bills for the purchase of the Territory drawn at 1. 2. & 3 years for 3 millions, and at 1. 2. 3. 4. & 5, for 5 millions of dollars, to be paid after and subject to the ratification of the President and Senate. Or as it is probable that tho' unwilling to surrender as far as the Rio Grand, and yet willing to do so as far as the district running west of the river Nuesis Mr. P. in that event might close a favorable bargain making the middle of that district which is a desert, the dividing line until it strikes our south Boundary running west to the Pacific as defined in our treaty with Great Britain, in 1783, and the Treaty of Ghent in 14. & 15: The maximum limit of purchase in both cases to be 5 millions.[3]

This acquisition is all important to the United States. If ever the present boundary is run, it will be found to approach us much nearer on the west than was anticipated at the time of its establishment, and the effect of a discussion to which it will give rise, will be to augment the value of the Territory in the eyes of the Mexican Govt. And in proportion to its n[e]cessity to us, will be their unwillingness to cede it. In the present state of that frontier, many of our citizens being already on the Spanish side of the line, and near whom will be gradually concentrated the most of our Indian tribes, it is easy to percive that the causes of collision with the Mexican authorities, will be constantly increasing, and if they are not obviated in a short time by the purchase of the Territory as far as the desert west of the Nuesis, our national safety must pay for it herafter an immense price, peaceably or forcibly. Believing however that this is the most favorable time to obtain it on reasonable terms, I would propose such an instruction to Mr Poinsett as that which has been recited.

He ought to be able to make a strong argument on the case. The friendly feelings of the U States to that Governmt—The d[e]ranged condition of their revenue—the unsettled boundary between us—the real security which both Governmets would derive from a desert on their frontier that will afford no population, and forever banish those sources of discord which so uniformly attend a crow[d]ed population on an imaginary line—are all points which he can use with force and sincerity.

The distance from our boundary to the river Nuesis is supposed to be about 450, or 500 miles, on the west of which is the desert spoken of.

[*Endorsed by AJ:*] project, for the acquisition of province of Texas—

D in AJ Donelson's hand, DLC-Van Buren Papers (13-1116). Poinsett (1779–1851), a former congressman from South Carolina, had been minister to Mexico since 1825.
1. The Adams-Onís Treaty of 1819.
2. King Ferdinand VII of Spain still contemplated the reconquest of Mexico. In July an armed force from Havana, secretly prompted from Madrid, seized Tampico and proclaimed Spanish control over Mexico. Poinsett had been reporting for several months that the Mexican government's bankrupt finances threatened the breakup of the country.
3. Neither the Treaty of Paris (1783) nor the Treaty of Ghent (1814) defined a boundary for the United States west of the Mississippi. The Adams-Onís Treaty had established a southern boundary on the forty-second parallel from the Rockies to the Pacific.

To Martin Van Buren

August 13th. 1829—

The inducements to be presented to the Mexican goverment for the cession of Texas to the United States.

1rst.   The advantage of having a natural boundery over the one which is now imaginary and unsettled.

2d.   The aid which the consideration she will receive for it, will give her in repelling such attempts upon her Sovereignty as that recently organized at Havanna; in providing a Navy, and the means of vigorous defence

3rd.   The removal of those collisions which must grow out of the intercourse of her citizens with ours, seperated as they will be from the efficient control of their respective goverments: and liable to all the excitements natural to the neighbourhood of conflicting laws, habits and interests.

4th.   Its real necessity to us as a guard for our western border and the protection of Neworleans—furnishing a motive for the cession which will be honorable to the republican character of Mexico, and worthy of that reciprocal spirit of friendship which should forever characterise the feelings of the two goverments toward each other

5th.   The Probability of its being settled chiefly by the citizens of the United States, who under a different system of Govt. may become turbulent and dificult of controul, and taking advantage of their distance from Mexican authority might endeavour to establish one independant of it—an event that will be sure to make this Govt. the object of Jealousy, and in conjunction with other causes unavoidable on an imaginary line of boundery of manny hundred of miles might seriously weaken those bonds of amity and good understanding which it is the interest and duty of both Republics to cherish

Objects of the United States in obtaining it.

1rst.   The Safety of Neworleans. The present boundery would enable an enemy on the Sabine, Red, & Arkansas rivers, to organise a force which by *a coup de man* might reach the Mississippi and thereby prevent the interposition of one by us sufficient for its protection   This disadvantage can only be overcome by having within our possession all the Territory washed by the branches of the Mississippi.

2nd.   The acquisition of additional territory for the purpose of concentrating the Indians, adopting a more effective system for their goverment, and relieving the states of the inconveniences which the residence within their limits at present affords

3rd.   The procurement of a natural boundery—one that cannot become the subject of dispute hereafter, and near to which a dense population on either side can never can be settled.

These purposes will be accomplished by obtaining a cession to the Grand Prarie or desert west of the Nueces, beginning at the Gulf, and following the courses of the centre of that desert, north to its termination on the mountain, thence with a central line on the Mountain, dividing the waters of the Rio del Nort from those that run Eastward of them in the Gulf, to the 42d degree of North latitude until it strikes our present boundery on that parallel. This line is a natural seperation of the resources of the two Nations. It is the centre of a country uninhabitable on the Gulf, and on the mountain so difficult of access and so poor as to furnish no inducement for a land intercourse, and of course no theatre for those causes of difference that belong to a neighbourhood of commercial interests. an advantage which would be lost if we were to stop short of it, either at the Brassos or the Trinity. Beyond either of these rivers and this line on the Gulf is a section of fine land.

For these reasons I wish Mr Poinsett to be instructed to open a negotiation for the purchase of this Territory, and be authorised to offer as high as five millions subject to the conditions mentioned in my former note

Andrew Jackson

Note The condition alluded is, that he shall consider five million as the maximum, and in the event of success to obtain first the ratification of their constituted authorities, before it is submitted for ratification to this Govrt.—and to get it as low as possible—and if the limits cannot be obtained—To obtain to the Brassos or to the Trinity agreably to the ratio of the maximum stated—and if cash should be preferred to payment by instalments (*and cash I suppose* would be a great inducement) let cash be stipulated to be paid after ratification by our goverment, as we can in a few days raise it by creating stock

A. J.

ADS, DLC-Van Buren Papers (13-1123); LC, DLC (60). AJ Donelson headed the LC "Suggestions to Mr. Van Buren of views that might be presented to Mexico as inducements for the surrender of Texas, upon which were founded the dispatches entrusted to Col Butler." On August 25 Van Buren issued detailed instructions along these lines to open a negotiation for Texas (DNA-RG 59, M77-152). Anthony Butler carried the instructions to Poinsett.

To Martin Van Buren

August 14th. 1829.

My Dr. Sir

I forgot in my note of yesterday to bring to your view the necessity of instructing Mr Poinsett, if he obtains a cession, that the United States shall not be bound to ratify or confirm any grant or grants in the Territory ceded, the conditions of which has not been complied with. This I think necessary for the safety & peace of our country

I gave you a memorandom the other day on the subject of Mr Shaler having been appointed commercial agent to Cuba, in 1810, and of his removal from that place at the instance of the Spanish authorities; for enquiry to be made   I would like to see you about one or two oclock if convenient, & I would thank you to have the enquiry made about Mr Shaler so that we could converse on that & other subjects.[1] yr friend

Andrew Jackson

P.S. Say in answer whether it will be convenient for you to see me today & at what hour

A. J.

ALS, DLC-Van Buren Papers (13-1131).
    1. William Shaler was commissioned consul at Havana on September 8. In 1810 the Madison administration had sent him to Havana, ostensibly as a commercial agent, with secret instructions to report on prospects for Cuban independence. Spanish authorities ordered him out of the country in November 1811.

From Eli Baldwin

New York, August 14, 1829.

Sir,

The condition of the Indian tribes, and their present relations to the General and State Governments, have occasioned among the friends of these interesting people, feelings of deep anxiety; and awakened a disposition among various citizens of the Union, to harmonize, if possible, the present discordant relations, and in a way that shall secure to the Indians peace and prosperity for the future. Participating in this common feeling, an Association of citizens of various denominations has been formed with the view of contributing to ends so important.

The principles on which this Association proposes to act and be governed, are disclosed in the accompanying documents, which embrace the preliminary proceedings, the origin of the Association, and the Constitution of the Board.

By a resolution therein, you will perceive that it is made my duty to communicate for the information, and with a view to obtain the approbation and co-operation of the Executive, a copy of those proceedings to you.

The Board looks with confidence to the Executive of the United States for such patronage as it may have the power to bestow; and with deep anxiety to the Congress, to whom it doubts not the Executive will submit the subject for those ways and means upon which reliance is placed for the promotion of its benevolent intentions.[1]

I am, most respectfully, Your obedient Servant,

ELI BALDWIN
Corresponding Secretary of
the Indian Board, &c.

Printed, *Documents and Proceedings Relating to the Formation and Progress of a Board in the City of New York, for the Emigration, Preservation, and Improvement, of the Aborigines of America* (New York, 1829), pp. 44–45; *National Intelligencer,* September 7 (13-1129). Baldwin (1791–1839) was a Dutch Reformed pastor in New York City. The Indian Board, composed largely of Protestant clergy, was organized in New York in July with the help of Thomas L. McKenney to promote the Indians' "final and speedy removal" from the states as the only means of securing their preservation and improvement.

1. Eaton replied for AJ on August 25, thanking the Board for its support and defending the government's policy of encouraging, though not compelling, the removal of Indians from Georgia (*Documents and Proceedings,* pp. 45–48). In September the government contributed $200 for the Board to begin operations, under authority of an 1819 law for civilizing the Indians (McKenney to Eaton, Sep 15, and to John Clark, Sep 16, DNA-RG 75, M21 6).

From Easter Charco Micco et al.

Little Rock   A Territory August 14 1829

Dear Father

we have the Pleasure to wright you a few lines this day our agent Capt walker who you authorise to take us to our new country has treated us well gave us a plenty to eat and we are sorry he is going to Leave us this day he has used us all well one know better than another he holds the orphan child by the hand he has brought us in boats we came down the rivers in flat boats to the mouth of white river he there got a steam boat to take us up the arkansaw river it could not go far the warter was so low he then got boats and horses for the sick people and fetched us this far we have lost some of your red children by sickness but if we where at home the Almightty would take some of us away we had some of our freinds that went to our new country and came back to us and told us it was a good country we took there talk for we beleifd them to be straight men we have not got there yet but as far as we have come we have seen good land and are much pleased with the country this far dear father we old men did not come to this country for our own good but for our children who loves to hunt we find plenty of game more than we can destroy. we have not got all our Rifles yet but have every reason to beleif we will get them soon Great Father we hope you will be pleased with few Lines about our agent Cap. walker for we are well pleased him

Easter Charco   X   mickco
Tustenuge   X   Thlockco
Easter Sharco   X   Hargo
Powes   X   mickco
Tuskenahah   X
Holatter   X   mickco
Coe   X   Marthter
Hollatter   X   Shlackco
Tusttenuge   X   Chopco
Daniel   X   Perriman
Coe   X   Hargo

DS, DNA-RG 75 (M234-237). Subagent William Walker had led a large party of Creeks bound from Alabama to the Western Creek Agency near Fort Gibson in Arkansas Territory. In early August the steamboat *Virginia,* carrying about 900 Creeks, ran aground sixty miles below Little Rock. Walker procured boats for the Indians' baggage and for those who could not walk, while most of the Creeks continued on foot along the Arkansas. Some died of sickness on the march. Walker left Little Rock on August 15 to return to Alabama.

To Martin Van Buren

Dear Sir,

I have read with much attention Mr Burnetts views of Texas, and find my first impressions strengthened by them. Now is the time for the extension of the western boundary of Louisiana as far as the western side of the river Nuesis making the large desert the boundary. This desert is from one to one Hundred and fifty miles wide, and extends north beyond the Rocky mountains, and will add to Louisiana and Arkansas all the country watered by the red river. The intervening country on the Gulf will afford a dense population, sufficient for its protection in the worst of times, and leaving room for our Indians and free people of color in the country north to the settlements on the Columbia river.[1]

Mr. Burnett appears to have consulted sectional feelings, and the jealous anticipations of the politician, rather than the general prosperity and security of the union as prospectivly to be affected by this purchase. We must look only at the latter, and if we can ascertain their true basis, do all that we can to strengthen it and leave to others the consequences of a failure.

This cession will unite the Gulf with the Pacific. It will give to the western border the power to defend itself against a greater force than will probably ever be brought against it. The wants and habits of the people who will be settled upon it will be similar to those of the people of Louisiana, whose trade and intercourse with the Atlantic states is so necessary and advantageous to both that it may be regarded as one of the strongest bonds of our union. It will besides cut off forever the communication between Canada and the Gulf, and diminish in this respect the motives for the occupation of Cuba, which no doubt the British Govt at present cherishes.

Consider these things, and say whether they do not indicate the present as the time to acquire this country, or at least to make the attempt. yr Sincerely

L in AJ Donelson's hand, DLC-Van Buren Papers (13-1142). David Gouverneur Burnet (1788–1870), later interim president of the Texas Republic, had written Van Buren on April 10 (TxU) to recommend acquiring Texas as far as the Trinity River, well east of the Nueces and Rio Grande. He advised against going further because of expected Mexican opposition and because a large addition to slaveholding territory might disturb "the present happy equipoise of our several sectional interests." This undated response by AJ might have been written any time thereafter.

1. Various proposals had been made over the years to colonize American free blacks in the west.

From Samuel Swartwout

New York 15th August 1829

Dear Sir

The accompanying letter has just this moment been handed to me by the enterprizing and inteligent writer of it, with a request that I would forward it to you. Mr Burrows has not his equal, in our City, for commercial enterprize. You will readily perceive on perusing his communication, the extent and utility of the proposed line of communication between different and very distant parts of South America. It is really surprising that a gentleman, single handed and without the aid of the Government, should have projected and actually carried into execution such an extensive and very important operation. But his zeal is not surpassed by his perfect independence of character. It was intimated to him a year or two ago, that Goverment felt so deep an interest in this affair, that they would be willing to contribute largely towards its completion, but Mr. Burrows being a gentleman of fortune and great pride of feeling, said no. He preferred the whole expense and the whole credit of it and he will not swerve from that determination. All the aid he requires from Government, is the appointment of Mr Everitt as consul at Panama, where there never was one before and where there are no americans residing at present. This appointment is important to him, for the single reason, that he knows that his commercial agent, if Clothed with Consular dignity & authority, will be more respected in that country particularly, than if he went there as a mere merchant. The person selected, Mr Everet is active & inteligent and a warn & zealous friend of the present administration.

Independently of the merit of this Enterprize, Mr Burrows is considered, universally in our city, as one of the most upright, honorable and gentlemanly men in the community. I am personally known to him, and I can assure your Excellency that no man possesses more of my confidence & esteem than Mr Burrows. As this gentleman has already done a great deal for that country, which cannot fail to benefit his own, and which has in fact, already benefitted it exceedingly, he certainly merits the countenance of Government   The Steam Vessel which he has sent thither and which I visited in company with Mr Moore our minister, before his departure, cannot fail to increase the facilities of communication to an extent certainly never before contemplated by its inhabitants or by strangers. and whilst we have a minister there or an agent of Government of inferior rank, this little Boat alone will be worth thousands of dollars annually to our Government & its citizens.[1] The request, therefore, of Mr Burrows that Mr Everet may be appointed a consul where there never was one before, and where it is important that Mr Burrows, should have an agent & where the Government of the United States will also soon require one, is a very small request & I feel persuaded your Excellency will consider it so reasonable and proper, as to give it your immediate sanction. I have the honor to be your Excellencys most obt Humbl. Servt.

Saml. Swartwout

LS, DNA-RG 59 (M639-7). Swartwout enclosed a letter from Silas Enoch Burrows (1794–1870). Burrows reported on his progress in establishing monthly packet service to Colombia and, via a transit at Panama, to Peru and the Pacific, a project that former Navy secretary Southard had proposed the federal government undertake. To further his aims, Burrows solicited the appointment of merchant Silas Kendrick Everett (1801–66) as consul at Panama. AJ appointed Everett in October, and Burrows announced regular service to Panama in November.

1. Burrows had built the steamboat *Liberator* and sent it to run from the packet at the port of Cartagena up the Magdalena River to near Bogotá.

From *William Gordon*

Teton River Upper Missouri
Aug 16th 1829

Dear Sir:

Having lately learnt with the most heartfelt satisfaction that you have been called by the voice of a free and grateful people most emphatically and decisively expressed to preside over the government of our country, I am emboldened to offer to you for your information a true account of our situation and of the general condition of the fur trade of this country—

This trade which might be so beneficial not only to the individuals immediately engaged in it but to the nation at large must at some not distant period be abandoned unless some salutary measures are taken by the Government for its protection

Already have the affairs of this country arrived at that crisis when the life of an American citizen is taken with the greatest impunity possibly to be imagined; and it is my decided opinion and I believe that of every other gentleman engaged in business that the trade will ere long be brought to a disastrous termination unless some decisive step be taken by the government —the indian mistake the forbearance and lenity of our government, for inability to chastize or regulate them, and boast in the most open manner of their powers to treat us as they please and ridicule the idea of our government to protect us or redress our wrongs—this Sir is and should be mortifying to every lover of his country, and of justice—The property of persons engaged in this trade has been taken and is frequently taken without provocation, and afterwards the owners tantalized with an exhibition of his property and dared to touch it—not a year passes but the lives of American citizens are taken most wontonly—within the last six weeks I myself have witnessed three and how many more are yet to be heard of time alone will develope

These circumstances which are not aggravated but on the contrary might be enlarged an hundred fold by entering into particulars are the precise features of the present condition of this trade—these same things should and perhaps have been reported by the Indian Agents for this country—If they have not been the Agents are certainly blameable for not doing so—and I can without consulting them safely and fearlessly refer you to them for the truth of what I say—and I must be further allowed to say that I conceive that under existing regulations they are entirely inadequate to answer what must have been the intentions and expectations of the Government in appointing them—At this time when surrounded with difficulty and insult there is not an Agent nearer than St Louis nor has there been for eight months

Colonel Benton to whom I shall also shortly write on the subject will from his local residence and the information he must constanly receive be able more *[ful]*ly and ably to explain the true situation of *[our affa]*irs—

As you are Sir at the head of this nation and its Government I have thought proper to make directly to you this plain expose of facts, knowing that you will not regard with indifference (as has been too long the case) the sacrifice of the lives of our citizens however humble their condition, or of the seizure of or depredation upon their property whilst prosecuting a business legally authorized—With sincere wishes for your health and prosperity I am Your friend & Servt

Wm Gordon

ALS, DNA-RG 107 (M222-25). Gordon was a fur trader operating out of St. Louis. A War Department assessment of the trade in 1832, forwarded by AJ to Congress, included a report from Gordon complaining of Indian depredations and the depletion of the beaver by British competition. To deter the former he recommended mounting the frontier garrisons for greater mobility (*SDoc* 90, 22d Cong., 1st sess., pp. 26–30, Serial 213).

To Andrew Jackson, Jr.

Washington August 18th. 1829—

My Dr. Son

When you left me I charged, & you promised, to write me every week during your absence—forty days have passed away since you left me, and the only letter I have recd. from you is one from Wheeling Eight days on your Journey—had it not been from a letter from Albert to his wife, & one from your Uncle J. Donelson informing that you had reached home & in good health I would have concluded you were sick or even dead; but to account for your silence, having reached the Hermitage on the 25th. ult. I am entirely at a loss.

I write you by Mr Lafayett Sanders, who will see you, and to whom I refer you for the news of this place. Saml Hays has been absent a month, with young Mr Van Buren;[1] I have expected him for a fortnight, but I find his mind too unstable to profit here by reading, he cannot nor will not confine himself to his Book, his mind wandering on other & trivial subjects, unprofitable to improvement—He will permit the year to pass without benefit to his mind, & with an exausted purse   Idleness my son is the mother of all evils and how you can reconcile your neglect in not writing me I cannot imagine   I have always impressed upon you the rule, of punctuality in engagements, never make a promise until well considered, & then be sure to comply with it. I have been very unwell since you left me, am now better, with my salutations to all friends I am yours affectionately

Andrew Jackson

ALS, DLC (37).

1. Lafayette Saunders (c1790–1848) was a Louisiana judge and husband of Rachel's grandniece Mary Smith. Hays was in upstate New York with Martin's son Abraham Van Buren (1807–73).

To Martin Van Buren

[August 18]

Dr. Sir

I have carefully looked over Mr. Lawrence's papers and return them, with the following remarks which have occurred, on turning to the law, & comparing it, with the facts in this case.

The law, in extending out-fit to a minister, or Charge de affairs, does not look to it, as Salary, but as an advance to cover the expences of going abroad; for the language of the act is, "on going from the United States, to any foreign Country; evidently looking to the expences to be incurred on account of the Journey to be performed. Mr Lawrence did not proceed from the United States, or from any other place as Charge de affairs, *but as Secratary of legation,* and hence cannot under the law claim an outfit: The act of 1810 forbids it. He assumed this office at the court where previously he was Secratary of legation.[1]

This appointment of Charge de affairs was to continue during the absence of a minister. On the arrival of a minster there, that commission ceased, and he became again Secratary of legation

It would seem upon the score of pay, Mr Lawrence is entitled to it, as Charge de affairs from the date of his appointment, 4th. of October to the period when by the arrival of Mr Barber, the Minister, his functions ceased, wh[ich] appears from Mr Barbers letter of the 5th of September 1828, to have been the 3[d], the day on which he was presented to the Earl of Aberdeen: at this period then, the Commission of charge de affairs ceased, and he again assumed the office of Seratary of legation, in which latter capacity, he is entitled to one quarter Salary for his return.[2]

As this is a transaction however of my Predecessor, and Mr Lawrence can produce the authority of the late secratary of State for the acceptance of his outfit, I am willing to regard it as one of those cases which ought to be referred to the Legislative power of the Goverment. I consider the law, as it now stands, too imperative to admit the payment of the ~~account~~ claim upon the ground of precedent or usage, and therefore order its suspension.[3] I am very respectfully yrs.

Andrew Jackson

ALS, DNA-RG 59; Copy fragment, DNA-RG 233 (13-1169); LC with variant wording, DLC (60). *HRDoc* 66, 21st Cong., 1st sess., p. 14 (Serial 197). William B. Lawrence, appointed American secretary of legation at London in 1826, had served as acting chargé d'affaires in the interval between the departure of minister Albert Gallatin in October 1827 and the arrival of his successor James Barbour a year later. On May 17, 1828, Henry Clay informed Lawrence that President Adams would allow him "the usual salary and outfit of a chargé d'affaires," which Lawrence duly collected (*Clay Papers*, 7:279). In reviewing Lawrence's accounts in 1829, fifth auditor Stephen Pleasonton questioned the legitimacy of both salary and outfit. Lawrence wrote Pleasonton on August 10 in justification.

1. The May 1, 1810, statute set salaries for diplomatic officers and authorized the president "to allow to a minister plenipotentiary or charge des affaires, on going from the United States to any foreign country, an outfit, which shall in no case exceed one year's full salary."

2. Lawrence held that he acted as chargé until he left England on October 15, 1828, and was entitled to salary to that date and a chargé's return pay. Barbour had arrived in London and met with Aberdeen in early September but was not formally presented as minister until November.

3. Pleasonton forwarded AJ's decision to Lawrence on August 20. On September 14 Lawrence rejoined that AJ had misinterpreted the 1810 law and that any attempt to make him return his earnings would provoke a judicial contest. On January 26, 1830, AJ asked Congress to clarify the laws governing compensation for diplomats, citing the Lawrence case as an example (*HRDoc* 37, 21st Cong., 1st sess., Serial 196). On February 18, in response to a House resolution, he transmitted the Lawrence correspondence to Congress (*HRDoc* 66, 21st Cong., 1st sess., Serial 197).

From Chesed P. Montgomery

Washington City August 18th 1829

Dr. Sir

I enclose you the $30 you loaned me, if you will not assist me more liberally I do not want that small sum & I intended at the time of taking it that if you would not loan me a greater amount that I would return it & you know very well that I in a very pathetic manner requested you to loan me a greater amount, you refused. I then stated to you that I understood you had 2 horses for sale & that I would be gratified you would let me have one of them, you refused to grant me that favour. I told you then I would have to walk, to which you readily approved & told me not to stop till I got above the mountains in Va. I stated to you that it had cost me $100 to come here by the way of the stage, that tuition was so low in Va. that I did not wish to go there, that I inte[n]ded to go to Lou. or Miss. where I could get reasonable pay for my services but your generosity only prompted you to loan me the small pittance $30. Supposing you had of happened at my Father's house & on foot, when he had his wealth would he not have offered you a horse without making the request would he not have granted you any favour you wanted. When you & my Father boarded at the same house Salisbury N. C. for a considerable time, did you ever ask him for any favour at that time, or at other period of your intimacy & friendship with him, that he did not grant. Supposing my Father & Uncle Campbell had not of exerted their influence & voted for you, for Major Genl. would you have been elected?[1] You were only elected by one vote with all their exertions. If they had not of exerted their influence & voted for you & by that means elected you, you never would have been the Hero of Neworleans & consequently never the President of the U. S. You will perhaps say that it is vain & weak in me to remind you of those services, on the score of gratitude, but did not your advocates & I among the rest remind the nation of the services you rendered your country & that it would be the dictates of policy & gratitude to elect you.

Immediately after your election & before you left the Hermitage I wrote to you from Jacksborough E. Ten. about 200 miles from your residence. I sent you by mail 3 letters 2 of which you received, the last letter probably you did not receive as you may have left Nashville before its arrival. In the 1st letter I stated to you that I never had been actuated to support you through self interest, that if you were determined not to assist me, to write immediately & let me know & that I would cheerfully submit, that I would go to the Miss. or Lou. but a southern Climate did not agree with my health & that my parents were opposed to my going there. In a few days after I sent you the 2d letter & after communicating to you what I did in the 1st. I stated to you that if you did not write I would conclude your were determined to assist me & therefore I would meet you at this place. In the third letter I stated to you that I had an Idea of chastising a certain Editor in Ten. who had cast some reflections own your amiable, pious & excellent companion relative to her death, he stated it was a "providential act" & great many other slanderous expressions & I stated to you if you thought it prudent that I would go immediately & chastise him or die trying. I received no answer to any of those communications & from your not writing & also from the intimate correspondence that we have carried on for several years & the assurances & pledges of friendship which you have given in those commu[ni]cations, any rational being would have concluded that you were determined to assist me, my friends had no doubt of it & members of Congress who recommended me to you told me there was no doubt but that you would give me that assistance I wanted. The Hon. John Blair stated in his recommendation to you that "I needed pecuniary aid to go on with my studies" & also told me that you could now loan it to me, if he thought it would be improper in you, or that it would answer no good purpose, for you to loan me the sum necessary to go on with my studies, he would not have mentioned it in his recommendation & he also stated that "I was an applicant for a clerkship & that he had no doubt that if I should be employed that I would acquit myself with credit" &c.[2] The Hon. G. Moore of Ala. who will be the next Governour of that State gave a similar recommendation to you.

On my arrival here, you assured me when a vacancy occured I should occupy it, a great many vancancies have occured & you have made a great many appointments & your pledge has not been redeemed yet & I have been here more than 5 months. 2 or 3 months since you notified me that you had obtained an appointment for me, that Mr. Branch would give me an appointment in his office. I went to Mr. Branch & he said he had determined on giving me an appt. & to prepare to enter on the duties of it the next day, that evening he notified me to my great astonishment & mortification, that he had declined giving it to me. I then had an interview with you & you told me that your mind was unaltered on the subject that you still wished me to have the appt. I communicated that fact to Mr. Branch, he told me that my friends had advised him not to give it to me, but that he still would comply with their wishes. I had another interview with you & you contradicted Mr. Branch's statement I went & saw Mr. Branch again but he still refused to give me the appt. Do you conceive that there is any honour to be attached to a procedure of this kind, violating solemn pledges, deceiving me & sporting with my feelings.

I have communicated to you since I have been here the wretched & needy condition of my parents & that my principal design in getting assistance was to make them comfortable, but poor & wretched as they are—their condition does not excite thy sympathy, not withstanding the services my Father has re[n]dered you. If brother Lemuel had of lived who sacrificed his life in the defence of his country under your command in leading his men to the charge at the battle of the horse Shoe I should not have made this request of you, either on account of myself or parents, which you well know & from the copy of his will which I have enclosed to you heretofore, shows what great solicitude he had for the welfare of his parents brothers & sisters & makes use of the following pathetic expression in his will "to protect & advise an unfortunate family." And you know what an irreparable loss the family have sustained in his death. In consequence of his death the family have been reduced to wretched-ness & want. The man who is eminently useful both to his relatives & his country who sacrifices his life in the defence of the liberties of his country & thereby his dear relatives sustain a great loss have not the rela-tives of such a man superiour claims on the government to those persons who never have rendered any services to their country nor their relatives. Notwithstandging this important republican principle which should actu-ate you in the discharge of your duty, you do not appreciate it. Foreigners & others who have no claims on the government have received lucrative appointments. Mr. Brady Gadsby's bar room clerk who has emigrated to this country since the war who is scarcely naturalized has received a lucrative appointment & a certain horse Jockey & trainer, for his services render in that way to A. J. D. in W. Tennessee has received a fine appoint-ment. I have observed to you before that brother Lemuel was the only one of the family that ever had a good opportunity, he being the older child of the family received his education when my Father was wealthy, furnished with every thing necessary to prosecute his profession, he was our only dependance & at the time of his death we were all young & in a helpless condition, my Father at that time insolvent. I have had to labour for my own education & support & I have been the means of giving 2 younger brothers all the education they have received, by dividing my funds with them &c. and contributing to the comfort & support of my aged, dis-tressed & indigent parents. One of those brothers that I assisted has lately commenced the practice of the Law & I am told he is succeeding well for a young attorney. I could also have been practicing Law long since but the advice of my Preceptor Judge Haywood was not to be in too great a hurry but be well prepared & that I would finally succeed better. I have but one more proposition to make to you, if you have not the command of your offices I hope you have of your purse. After the death of Judge Haywood of Ten. I communicated to you, that I had met with a great loss in the death of that famous & distinguished Jurist, who without any solicitation from me, offered me the use of his library which is the best in the State, my board, all the instruction he could give me, all without pay. I told him that I would not receive it in that way that when I got able I would compensate him, he then repeated that he would not have any compensation.[3] This letter I left at the P. O. Nashville, I received your written reply, left at the office   From this letter I will take a few extracts. It is dated Hermitage Jan. 15th 1827. "I have just received yours of the 13th instant having duly noted its contents I have to reply that it gives me regret to be compelled to say to you that I am entirely unable to comply with your request I have not the command of $100 at present" "had I the means, your request should be readily granted, as it is, I can only regret the want of them."

You cannot regret that you have not the means at the present time, the means are ample, & you can command the amount I want very easily. I do not want you to make me any presents, although you have made a great many to other people. I want you to loan me the small sum of $1000 & I will return it to you ag[ain] before you complete your administration. I will give you yo[ur] personal & political friends as security, who are men of property & punctual in their payments, or I will give you a mortgage on my property in Ten. both personal & real, left to me by the will of my brother. It is estimated to be worth $1000 & probably it will be worth more when a division takes place among the heirs. The personal estate consits in a negro woman & 3 or 4 children. My Father & Mother have a life estate in the property, it is of no advantage to me at present & very little to my Father & Mother as his unfeeling creditors sell the products of the farm. They talked about selling the crop, when I left home last winter & I calculate they have done it & if they have Oh! my God in what a wretched condition they must be in their old age. They sold the crop last summer & left them without the common necessaries of life. I have not written to them since I have been here, because they expected assistance from me & which they sincerely believed I would get & I have been disappointed & I know it would create very unpleasant sensations & add to their distress if I was to communicate to them the harsh treatment that I have received, from those whom they thought were my best friends & one in particular in which great intimacy & friendship existed between my Father & him in the days of their youth & continued to exist at their last parting & whom my Father was ready to do any favour by merely making it known. You prefer to assist those who are in comfortable circumstances; surrounded with property who did not need your aid

to the indigent & distressed & who are neither distinguished for qualification nor merit & also a great many eleventh hour men who have no
claims on you or the government & who gave you severe abuse in the first
canvas for the Presidency & discovering that they would not receive any
thing from the late administration & that probably you would be elected,
actuated by self interest they supported you, in the expectation that they
would be rewarded & although having no friendship for you & who do
not prefer you to this day & notwithstanding all this they have received
lucrative appointments for their hyprocrisy & deceit. I could obtain the
certificate of a distinguished & talented clerk in one of the offices that
I am better qualified to discharge the duties of a clerkship than a great
many who are now in the employment of the government & who are
getting lucrative salaries. Owing to the way in which my feelings have
been sported with, most solemn pledges violated, deceived, wavering,
& want of confidence, I would not receive the best appointment within
your gift. If I was to receive an appointment under existing circumstances,
some secret & curtain slanderer would make accusations against me &
which he would be afraid to do publicly & knowing at the same time they
were false & he could not sustain them. Notwithstanding the slanderer is
believed & when I ask for his name contrary to every principle of justice
his name cannot be given up.

If you grant this small request, after paying my small debts, I will
enclose the greater part to my indigent & distressed parents & with the
remainder I will proceed immediately to the University of Va. where I will
complete my education & profession. I am convinced that you will not
comply with my request, A. J. Donelson as usually will prevent you, if it
is in his power, he will no doubt conclude that it will be something out of
his pocket, he is expecting another bril[l]iant present a $20000 plantation
or the money.[4] What has A. J. Donelson done for you? that you lavish
your presents so extensively on him; was he an ornament of the Bar of
his State, did his eloquence & writing elect you President. He has had as
good an opportunity to become a distinguished man as any man in the
U. S. What great display of talents has he made? does his fame extend
from the Atlantic to the pacific ocean. It is probable that if he had not of
possessed this covetous disposition to amass wealth & paid more attention to the cultivation & expansion of his mind that he might have made
some display of talents & attracted the attention of the nation. I think
what you have done for him, ought to appease his craving disposition &
the property he has in Ten. is sufficient to furnish him with every comfort
& necessary in this transitory life but the avaricious never can, nor never
will be satisfied.

A. J. D. called to me 2 or 3 months since, on the pavement near the
department of State after I had passed him, for I was determined never to
speak to him again as he had insulted me & assailed my character, that
I could get the letter of Mr. Blair that I had previously made application

to you for, but I did not get it but it is consolatory to me that I recollect the contents of it. He observed that I had been brawling about him in the Street. I denied his assertion & inquired of him the auther, which he refused to give. It is true I censured his conduct & I think justly to a few of my friends & they recommended me to cane him. But who brawled 1st as he has made use of the word I will repeat it. A few days after you had taken possession of the Presidents mansion I called to see you & not A. J. D., he came into the dining room where I was siting & observed to me that I had acted imprudently in coming on here, that I ought to have waited untill I was invited & at another time he observed, if I expected you to support me & in pompous manner one morning, he observed to me in the presence of Mr. Robison of Va. what I expected you to do for me now.[5] If you comply with my request & prefer it I will leave here immediately & no person shall know how I obtained the money & I will give you a mortgage on my estate or I will give you your personal & political friends as security. I do not calculate that you will comply with my request, but that you will be influenced & prejudiced against me by A. J. D. but if you fail to comply, those who have insulted me, injured my prospects & assailed my character they shall suffer for it. You may think that I make those assertions for the purpose of bullying you into measures, I have no such Idea I know that you are not to be scared, but it is the course after long deliberation that I am determined to pursue, it will be in vindication of my character & wounded feelings which is dearer to me than my life & I believe that if I was to submit to it that the departed spirit of my brother would haunt me. I calculate on being sacrificed, but I will glory in that sacrifice to my last breath & I am satisfied that my relatives & friends who are your friends will approve of the act. A. J. Donelson observed that I had complained, about you not giving me an appointment, my friends were the first that complained; & there is no Jacksonian that I have conversed with about it, but what says I have been treated cruelly.

I have never gave A. J. D. any cause of offence, unless it was by communicating to you when I lived in Ala. during the canvass for the Presidency, that S. Donelson your nephew & who is my cousin, observed to me that you did not write your resignation as senator to Congress, directed to the Legislature of Ten. & that I replied to him that I believed that you did write it & that I thought it necessary for you to remonstrate with him, to be cautious how he conversed & that he being a nephew & the assertion emanating from him, would have a tendency to injure your election & that I had not communicated to any person but yourself &c.[6] If this communication has given offence to A. J. D. he cannot be a true friend of yours, for it ought to given him an additional esteem for me.

I asked A. J. D. if he did not tell you? that I was not qualified for office, he said he did not, he has been an enemy of mine ever since I have been here & in the last drama he acted behind the curtain.

The small pittance I requested of you, to carry me away from here, where I can get into lucrative business, I have other friends here who will cheerfully furnished it to me, when ever I want it & I knew that I could get it when ever I become acquainted. But I intend to stay here till I punish those malicious men who have injured my prospects & assailed my character without provocation. Any malicious attack that any man has made against my reputation calculated to injure my prospects in life I can prove to be false by the letters & certificates of the most honourable & conspicuous men in the nation at every place where I have lived & I have a pamphlet prepared to establish that fact   Mr. Branch has observed to me, that I was injured from another source, he must give me the author or I shall hold him responsible. I have demanded of him the author several times he still refuses to give me his name. I have always been your warm & zealous advocate & as much attach to your reputation & person as any man in the nation & you must be convinced of that fact from the communications that I have made to you at various periods & are you then to be influenced to violate the most solemn pledges both written & verbal by any person whatever, if you are I then have mistakened your character. I have always had & I hope to God I always will have the same respect for my word as my bond & if there is no confidence to be placed in what a man solemnly pledge[s] himself to do what kind of a man do you conceive him to be? If you will not assist me to the extent of my request do not offer me any pitiful assistance. I will not accept of it. The last interview I had with you, you said something about beging, that would prompt any man of honourable feelings to enclose you the small pittance you loaned me, but I always intended that if you could not treat me no better than a beggar that I would be under no obligations to you & you are the first man that has ever applied that unfeeling expression to me. I have made use of more solicitation to some of my friends for favours, than I ever did to you & they never replied in that insulting manner & you know that I have not made use of half the solicitation that a great many have, who have succeeded in obtaining offices. You have given a great deal of liberal assistance, loans & presents to those who could have got along very well without your assistance. Gov. Blount informed me this last summer that you made a present to Dr. Hog of 2 or $3000 & that the Doctor offered you a note or something to that purpose, which you refused to take.[7] Dr. Hog is an excellent physician & has a great practice & could have lived very well without your assistance. I send you a copy of my Preceptor's guide (Judge Haywood) to his students, you do not appear to be actuated by the same motives of this great man to assist the needy & distressed.

If you persist in the course you have taken, or comply with my request let me know by sending a letter to the City Post-office tomorrow evening & if you do not write I will conclude that you are determined to persist & in that event if A. J. Donelson will accept of a challenge, he shall have it immediately & if he will not accept, I must have a street fight. If he determines on a street fight, I will not take any private advantage but I will make the attack publicly after giving him due notification. I have never had a combat with a relative or a man that has married a relative of mine on that account I shall regret that his harsh treatment should compell me to vindicate my character & wounded feelings   This harsh treatment that I have received from you & your private secretary, was the cause of me, being overwhelmed with grief so frequently in your presence but that grief is banished & my indignation is excited. Provided you persist in the course you have taken, you cannot condemn me, you have never suffered any man during your life to assail your character, injure your prospects, insult you, or sport with your feelings with holding him responsible. I shall keep a copy of this communication (provided you persist) it will constitute a part of my defence, of the course I intend to take, in vindication of my character & wounded feelings, which will come before the public. You may think that I have taken this course for political effect but I disclaim all such intentions as I have stated, I do it in vindication of my character & if you comply with my request, I will leave here immediately my name will not be brought before the public & I shall have no combat with A. J. D. & here the affair will end. I wish to God I had never come on here & if I had of had any Idea of the cruel treatment that I have received since I have been here, I would never have come & my relatives & friends urged me to come on here & they had no doubt but that you would give me that assistance that I wanted & as I have come one here & received such harsh treatment & that without provocation I am determined not to leave here untill I see myself righted & if I was to leave here without seeing myself righted, I never would be satisfied and my friends would blame me. The situation you promised me was not a very desireable one but you intimated to me when Mr. Ingham returned from Penn. that I should have a more lucrative appt. & I knew I could soon exhibit my capability & demonstrate that I deserved a better appt. & also some of the most conspicuous men the nation ever produced had occupied less deserving stations. If this affair should ever come before the nation the public will discover that I have not wantingly sought a contest, that I have a long time patiently submited to, what a great many men would not have done & that I have given you this opportunity to avoid a contest with A. J. D. & comply with your pledges. I am very respectfully your friend

C. P. Montgomery

ALS, TNJ (13-1151). Montgomery was the son of Hugh (d. 1833) and Euphama Purnell Montgomery (d. 1834). His brother, Major Lemuel Purnell Montgomery (1786–1814), served with Jackson in the Creek War and was killed at Horseshoe Bend. Chesed was a first cousin of AJ Donelson's wife Emily, whose mother, Mary Purnell Donelson, was his mother's sister. Montgomery enclosed this letter in a note requesting an immediate reply. He also gave notice that he might later polish the letter for publication. On August 21 he sent a "corrected" version to AJ Donelson.

1. Hugh Montgomery had been a companion of AJ's in Salisbury in 1786–87, when AJ was preparing for the bar. David Campbell, whose second wife was Hugh Montgomery's sister, had supported AJ's successful candidacy for major general of the Tennessee militia in 1802.

2. John Blair (1790–1863) was a Tennessee congressman.

3. John Haywood (1762–1826), a legal scholar and historian, was a Tennessee Supreme Court judge from 1816 until his death.

4. In 1824, AJ gave AJ Donelson a wedding gift of nearly 350 acres of land near the Hermitage, which became part of Donelson's Poplar Grove (later Tulip Grove) plantation.

5. William Robinson.

6. Likely Stockley Donelson, Emily's brother and Montgomery's first cousin. AJ resigned from the Senate in a letter of October 12, 1825 (*Jackson Papers*, 6:108–11).

7. AJ wrote Samuel Hogg around June 1, 1828, offering to accept a note payable in two years for Hogg's debt to the Hutchings estate, which AJ reckoned at more than $1,500.

To Andrew Jackson, Jr.

Washington August 19th. 1829—

My Dear Son

I have this moment recd. your letter of the 1rst. instant from the Hermitage, being the first I have recd. from you since you left Wheeling. My dr. I was very uneasy at your silence, and hope hereafter you will write every week even if it is only to tell me you are well.

I am pleased that you found all well at the Hermitage, and that Mr Steel has done his duty and has treated my Negroes humanely. So long as he treats my Negroes well, I have no wish to remove him; I have confidence in his honesty, & industry, and I well know, negroes, will complain often, without cause—The death of Jim was a mortifying circumstance to me, and if it had proceeded from the cruel treatment of the overseer, he must have been discharged. It gives me pleasure to learn from you, that Dr Hogg & McCorkle have said, that jims death was occasioned by poison, & in nowise, by the chastisement given him by the overseer.[1]

you have not informed me how much cotton Mr. Steel has this year in culture—nor have you told me which of the mares colts, has got injured by the conduct of Dunwodie—I hope it is not my oscar bay mares colt—in your next, inform me on these two subjects, as well as all others interesting[2]

I am about to leave here this evening for the Rip Raps, to spend some days in sea bathing   I have been unwell but am recovered but a little debilitated,[3] therefore must close this letter with a request that you will present me affectionately to all our relations, & particularly to James, John, & Thomas, who, I am glad to hear, are at the Hermitage—make them comfortable my son, & particularly your sick brother James.[4] was your mother alive she would attend to this—yours affectionately

Andrew Jackson

Andrew, Emily & son with Mary Easton & Saml Hays send there love to you—I suppose Saml will marry before you return[5]

A. J

present me affectionately to Col. Love & family & all my neighbours
A. J.

ALS, DLC (37).
1. Miles Blythe McCorkle (d. 1869) was a Davidson County physician.
2. AJ owned several horses sired by Oscar, a bay that was undefeated as a racer before retiring to stud.
3. AJ left Washington with a few companions on August 19 for the Rip Raps, an artificial island housing Fort Calhoun (later Fort Wool) across Hampton Roads from Fortress Monroe. He remained until the end of the month. The seclusion of this visit, contrasted with his busy public tour in July, prompted speculation in the opposition press about the state of AJ's health.
4. James R. Donelson, John Donelson (c1807–79), and Thomas J. Donelson were the natural brothers of Andrew Jackson, Jr. James died of consumption on August 18.
5. In August Samuel J. Hays proposed to Frances P. Middleton.

To Chesed P. Montgomery

August 19th. 1829
Sir,
I have received the letter enclosing me the amount of money which I gave you early in the spring to enable you to reach Tennessee.

My only object in writing to you is to correct the impression that Mr. Donelson has endeavored to injure your character, or to prevent the success of your application for an office. Such is not the fact. If you apply to Mr. Branch, you will ascertain from him that his disposition to serve you grew out of the friendly statements of Mr. Donelson in your behalf: And that his determination not to give you the office named in your letter was the result of a conviction that you were not qualified for it. Mr. Donelson has on all occasions expressed the greatest concern for your situation; but it has not been in his power to serve you.

Your letter is in other respects a tissue of falsehood. I was never under obligations to your Father. He was my companion and friend in our early life; and as such I have always cherished for him the most favorable regard. Neither am I under obligations to you, altho it would have given me pleasure to have been instrumental in advancing your interests. I have only to add that your whole letter is sufficient proof of the correctness of the opinion of you & decision upon your case by Govr. Branch[.] In haste yr. &c &c

A. Jackson

LS in AJ Donelson's hand, DLC (72). Montgomery responded on August 21 by challenging Donelson to a duel and threatening to assault him if he refused.

To Andrew Jackson, Jr.

On board the Steamboat Potomac
august 20th. 1829. C. Bay.

My Dr Son

I wrote you yesterday a hasty scrall, being then pressed with business & surrounded by a croud—being retired on board this boat I have sat down to day again to write you.

In your letter altho' you have informed me of your visit to your dear mothers tomb, still you have not informed me of its situation, & whether the weeping willows that we planted around it, are growing, or whether the flowers reared by her industrious, & beloved hands, have been set around the grave as I had requested—Mr. Dr. Son inform me on this subject, you know it is the one dearest to my heart, & her memory will remain fresh there as long as life lasts.

you say, you will return to me soon, I therefore shall not write you again until I am informed by you at what time you will leave Tennessee least you might have left there before my letter would reach you.

In your letter you have not given any information of the health of my neighbours, or whether Col Ward has removed to the Western District &c. Should this reach you & you not be on the eve of setting out on your return, inform me on this subject and of the health of all my neighbours, & whether Miss Flora is still living with Col Ward, her guardian.

I have heard that Mr J Martin has become deranged &c—please advise me, correctly, on this unpleasant subject[1]—Present me to Col. Love, & Dr Hogg, & both their families, & request them, both, to write me—say to Mr. Earle it would afford me great pleasure to hear from him, I would be glad to see him at Washington, give me a distinct account of the situation of my stock, & farm the amt. of horses, & cattle, that have died, & the amt. of cotton, & corn, &c &c, cultivated, whether any, & if any, how much timothy, Mr Steel has sowed, & how much grass he has cut, & if any, how many brick he has made—urge him to attend to the getting out his cotton, by setting all hands to picking, the moment each hand can pick thirty pounds a day, keeping them at it, until the crop is Housed—I would like to hear how you have settled your matter with Miss. F. she is a fine girl, but you being young she may try to keep you within her toils, without giving you a definitive answer—permit this not to be the case—have a final and positive answer, & let it be as it may, close the matter finally with her—if favorable, marry, & bring her on with you, if unfavorable, wish her happy, cherish her as a friend, but have it understood that hereafter you remain her friend without any other views—and I beg you my son, that you enter into no more love affairs, until you see me—you have many years yet for the improvement of your mind, & to make a selection of a companion—Remember my son, that you are now the one solace of my mind, & prospects of my happiness here below, & were you to make an unhappy choice it would bring me to the grave in sorrow—My *Dear & Sincere friend Major Eaton is with me—he is worthy to be called friend*—See my friend Judge Overton & McLamore and greet them kindly for me, attend to *James,* yield him all the comfort you can—Present me to all friends & believe me affectionately yours

Andrew Jackson

ALS, DLC (37).
1. James Glasgow Martin (1791–1849), stepson of Rachel Jackson's brother Stockley Donelson (c1759–1805), married Rachel's niece Catherine Donelson (1799–1836) in 1815. The two had recently separated because Martin was drinking heavily and abusing his wife, but they soon reunited.

To Andrew Jackson Donelson

Rip Rap August 20th. 1829—
Dr Andrew
We arrived here at 2. p.m. had a pleasant passage but today, cold, damp & disagreable, not very congenial with the improvement of my health—however I am as well as when I left you—Tommorrow we commence Batchellors life, where we will be in perfect retirement, Surrounded by a delightful water view, made more pleasant by the constant din of improvement with which we are surrounded. It is now night, every thing is perfectly still & silent as tho we were the only inhabitants of this spot—such is the order of the place, & shews what system can produce, where the superintendant is acquainted with human nature, & possessing talents to benefit from that knowledge.
I cannot say how long I shall remain here—write us daily by the way of Baltimore & send us the newspapers until you are advised when we will leave here—present me kindly to Emily Mary, & Major Lewis, & all the heads of Dept & their families & believe me affectionate yours.

Andrew Jackson

P.S. If Mr Hill Lady & Harriet Barryhill is with you present me kindly to them, say to Harriet I sent by son to her the promised ring.[1]

ALS, DLC-Donelson Papers (13-1178).
1. Harriet Craig Berryhill (c1810–64), daughter of William M. Berryhill, had been a friend of Rachel's.

From Henry Lee

New york 20th. August 1829

dear Genl.

We were certainly to have committed that impracticable act of getting off in an American vessel of war, to day, with a fair wind a fine ship, capital officers, and a lively crew; when late last evening our Captain recd. an order from Commodore Chauncey, directing him to transfer to the navy yard here, 20 of his men. As these men had entered the service on the express condition that they were to serve their time in the Ontario—and as the officers, who are now to transfer them, are the very gentlemen who made this condition with them, & in some instances with their parents—as this very condition was suggested by you yourself in my presence to Capt. Stevens, and through him and his officers was communicated to these gallant tars, as a kind and paternal regulation introduced into the service by you, you may conceive that our surprise was not greater than our mortification at this late & embarrassing order of the Comre. Capt. Stevens has gone over to the N. yard, to remonstrate against it; but I fear his remonstrance will be without effect. Lt. Dupont who enlisted most of these men, declares that if the order is persisted in, he shall give the men a certificate stating the conditions on which they entered the service & the consequence will be that they will all be lost to the navy, and disgusted with the Govt. He told me last night that there had not been a dry eye among them from the time they heard of the order—for they are all youths. If the order is persisted in we shall be detained at least 2 days longer, as the accts. of the purser, which were just settled up, will all have to be resettled.[1] Every body thinks it strange the Comre. should have deferred this measure until the last moment. Mr. Tazewell says the system prevailing in the navy is d__n bad & I agree with him. I wrote you the other day recommending James McCrea, a friend of Register Smith, as Naval Store Keeper at this yard. Since that letter was written, Mr. McCauley our purser has told me that the present incumbent Craven, has been the cause of great difficulty and delay in our getting off—that he is frequently absent from his residence on fashionable excursions, & as frequently absent from the yard when he is at home, being as he expresses it, too great a gentleman to attend to business. The sailing Master Mr. Davis, a very clever young man confirms and indeed aggravates this acct. of him. If you wish to have any thing like efficiency in this important station, for Gods sake, remove the Store Keeper, and supercede the Commander.[2]

Genl. Armstrong is about publishing a brief historical summary of the last war, and he had the goodness first to offer it to me, as a material for my promised history of your life; which offer I was compelled to decline, inasmuch as you took back the memo. you once gave me, and never did shew me the confidential correspondence with Monroe. I therefore advised the genl. to publish his own sketch. I had time to read the first few pages & found it beautifully executed. I enclose you a letter I have recd. from him since I was at his house to which I have replied that by writing to Major Lewis or Capt. Donelson I thought he would get answers to any *specific* enquiries respecting your public life that he might make. You will see that the letter is confidential, & of course shew it to no one but Donelson & Lewis.[3]

Your withholding materials from me, has involved me in another difficulty, for Green (who was to bear my expenses in Tennessee & then share the profits of the book) has called on me to refund. I shall have to refuse him or give him an order on the Dey of Algiers, which ever he likes best. You remember Donelson took back the sketch you once gave me, & I have not since seen it or a copy.[4]

Swartwout gives universal satisfaction as far as I can learn. Tazewell looks well, talks well (but too much) praises you very much, but admires himself more, and is going on a tour to Quebec. The packet ships from & to Liverpool & Havre some of them as large as the Ontario, come in occasionally Unload & load and are off in 8 days. Such is the comparison between the Stimulus of private interest & public duty.

With the affectionate remembrances of Mrs. Lee for Mr. & Ms. Donelson I am dear Genl. your attached friend and humble sert

H. Lee

P.S. I must repeat the expression of my regret that Lynch did not succeed in his application   I have seen much of him here, and have found *[new]* reasons to admire his talents attainments and good feeling both private & political. Middletons return will of course leave a vacancy for the appt. of a new Secretary of Legation at St. Petersburg—It is the only place of the kind now to be had or given worthy of his acceptance. I wish you would give it to him Genl. as he is every way qualified for it.[5]

ALS, DLC (37). The 18-gun sloop *Ontario,* under Commander Thomas Holdup Stevens (1795–1841), was to carry Lee to Algiers en route to service in the Mediterranean. It sailed August 22.

1. Captain Isaac Chauncey (1772–1840), a veteran naval officer, was commandant of the New York navy yard. Lieutenant Samuel Francis Du Pont (1803–65) later became a Union admiral in the Civil War.

2. Lee had written AJ to recommend James McCrea for naval storekeeper at Brooklyn in place of Tunis Quick Craven (1781–1866). McCrea's brother John McCrea was a Philadelphia merchant and former associate of AJ in Florida and Alabama land dealings. Thomas Lilly Smith (1787–1871) of New York had recently been appointed register of the Treasury. Francis G. McCauley was a naval purser, and Charles Henry Davis (1807–77) a passed midshipman who later became a Union naval commander in the Civil War. Despite urging from Lee and others, Craven was not removed.

3. Lee enclosed an August 14 letter (DLC-37) from John Armstrong (1758–1843). Secretary of war in 1813–14, Armstrong later published a two-volume *Notices of the War*

of 1812. His letter pressed Lee for confidential details about AJ's difficulties with the War Department under James Monroe during the New Orleans campaign.

4. Duff Green had planned to publish Lee's biography of AJ, begun during the 1828 campaign but never finished.

5. New York attorney Jasper Lynch had applied to be secretary of legation at London or Paris. In 1830, American minister to Russia Henry Middleton (1770–1846) was replaced by John Randolph, and John Randolph Clay was made secretary of legation.

To Andrew Jackson Donelson

Rip Raps August 22nd. 1829

Dr Andrew

Since I have left Washington, I have understood that our Steward does all his business with a man by the name of Coburn, a former Steward of Mr Monroe, & who, it is believed, did him much injustice—Be this as it may, there is a Mr. Bartcroft who lives opposite to Major Barrys who is represented to be a very honest, & excellent man, by whom our wants can be supplied faithfully—as soon as the present month is out, go to Mr Bartcroft & make an engagement with him for a supply of such grocries as we may want, & direct the Steward to apply to him for our supplies— furnish the Steward with a book similar to a bank book, & instruct him to make Mr Bartcroft enter every thing in that book, that is got, & at the end of the month it will be a check by which our account can be settled with him, & a check upon our Steward—The beef account I expect has been too high, & more than the markett   The Capt of the Steam boat informs me that the choice pieces has not been over from 6 to 8 cents this Season, if we at any time have paid more, he says, it must be an imposition, on board his Boat, we had as good beef as I ever saw in markett, for which he had paid six cents.[1] I name this that you may examine our account, & if charges are made higher than 6 & 8 cents, have our Butcher changed—It is easy for you to send Gowen to markett, & let him enquire of the prices & report to you—From what Major Eatons marketting has cost, & his groceries laid in at Mr Bartcrofts, we must have been paying at least a third more than him, & worse fair—By making our Steward keep a small book as before stated, which is the proper rule, we will save at least $200 pr month—Major Eaton does not think Coburn an honest man, if so, it is easy to account for our heavy bills, each month—Therefore at the end of the month, let our Grocer be changed, & a trial made with Mr Bartcroft, who Major Eaton says he knows to be a very honest man, we will save much by it.

If the funds in Major Lewis hands are not sufficient to meet the expence of the current month, please inform me, & I will send you a blank check.

I cannot yet determine whether I will be benefitted by the salt water bath. it is very cold, tho' this day is clear & fine. present me affectionately to Emily & Mary, to Major Lewis & the heads of Depts. and if any thing occurs worthy of note please communicate it to me, & believe me very affectionately yrs

Andrew Jackson

ALS, DLC-Donelson Papers (13-1193). John Coburn and John Barcroft both sold goods to the White House in 1829. AJ's steward was Michael Anthony Giusta, who had filled the same position for John Quincy Adams.
  1. Uriah Jenkins (c1784–1837) captained the *Potomac.*

From David Twopence

Gallatin 24th. August—1829

Dear General

I Now Glory in the happiness of writing to you that I am still living in Gallatin I don't know whether you will recollect me or Not—you will I am in hopes recollect the little Barber that went the rounds with you from Wilson to Smith and Hartsville By the Name of David Twopence[1] I proposed buying of a lot from you once in florence Alabama when I lived there I left there because I was not allowed a vote and after I came here I gave you that support which the Laws of the state allow'd me as a colourd man by voting in one of the electors[2] therefore that you will permit me to put up this servant prayer to you for help for I am poor when times was good, all I made I put it to good use in buying my father and I think that if you will give me a spot of Ground in florence that I hope that God will Bestow a Blessing on you for supporting the Needy. Dear General I wish you to write to me when you receive this excuse me for taking this liberty of writing to you for I hope it will do you No harm General Desha has resign'd and Mr. Andrew Donalson and Colonel Guild are Candidates for the Office and I am electionering hard for Donalson although I am Not allow'd a vote in that[3] Nothing More but remain your most humble devoted friend and servant

David Twopence

ALS, DLC (37). Twopence was a barber in Gallatin, Tenn. His father was William Twopence.
  1. In July 1828, AJ attended successive public dinners near Gallatin at Lebanon in Wilson County, Carthage in Smith County, and Hartsville.
  2. Free blacks could vote in Tennessee before 1834, when a racial qualification was added to the state constitution. Alabama's 1819 constitution required voters to be white.
  3. Daniel Smith Donelson (1801–63), brother of AJ Donelson, won election to succeed congressman Robert Desha as brigadier general of the militia for Sumner, Smith, and Wilson counties. Colonel Guild was probably Josephus Conn Guild (1802–83), a Gallatin lawyer.

From John Branch

Washington City
Augt. 26th. 1829

My dear Sir

A weeks absence has produced a thousand kind enquiries on the part of your many friends and not a few malignant speculations, on the part of those who rely on the, *chances* and who have nothing to hope from the existing state of things. Some of the latter have rather tended to excite mirth, others contempt & abhorence.[1]

Our friend Hill arrived here on Friday last & left us this morning for Philadelphia from whence he will probably return about the middle of next week under a confident belief that he will meet with you

Genl D. Green called to see me about King's removal and after a careful examination of the causes expressed a desire to submit them to the public. I convinced him that it was better to wait a while and thereby shew to the world that we were disposed to *forbear* untill *forbearance ceases to be a virtue*[2]

You will doubtless often see Com. Barron. It is desirable to avert if possible an open rupture between him and Com. Rogers. The temper of the present correspondence passing between them is well calculated to lead to consequences, that we ourselves individually and the Country generally might deplore.[3]

That Com Barron has some cause of complaint is probable enough, but say to him *confidentially* that while we are not at liberty to avenge his past wrongs, he must know that he will at least receive *justice* at our hands

I have appointed Cap. Elliot to the command of the West India squadron and fondly hope that in this as well as every other official act, I may be so fortunate as to receive your approbation[4]

Accept my best wishes for your health & happiness and believe me to be your friend

Jno Branch

ALS, DLC (37). *North Carolina Historical Review,* 14 (1937): 366–67.

1. The opposition press suggested that AJ was in seclusion to hide his ill health, to shield him from public discontent, or, as the *National Journal* said on August 24, "to keep him a prisoner, in order that he may be coerced into any measures which his ministers may desire to carry into operation."

2. Miles King (1786–1849) had been navy agent at Norfolk, Va., since 1816. AJ appointed him to a new four-year term in March, but then replaced him with Nash Legrand on August 10 after receiving complaints of King's malfeasance and word from Branch of irregularities in his accounts. Opposition papers criticized the removal, even suggesting it was for King's failure to render "servile adulation" during AJ's July visit to Norfolk (*National Journal,* Aug 26). Duff Green defended it in the *US Telegraph* on September 4. In 1830 the

House of Representatives inquired into King's case, and Branch submitted a report implicating him in fraud (*HRDoc* 115, 21st Cong., 1st sess., Serial 198).

3. Captain John Rodgers (1773–1838) was the Navy's senior officer and head of the Board of Navy Commissioners. He had presided at the court-martial that convicted James Barron for neglect of duty as commander of the *Chesapeake* in its 1807 encounter with the British ship *Leopard*. The episode crippled Barron's naval career and poisoned his relations with fellow officers, leading to an 1820 duel in which he killed Stephen Decatur. On August 13, Rodgers had written Barron insinuating that he had been negligent in not rejecting defective brick and timber delivered for construction at the Gosport navy yard under contracts made by Miles King. Barron in reply accused the Navy commissioners of mismanaging the project and of trying to foist the blame on him after deliberately depriving him of authority to intervene. On August 22 he forwarded the correspondence with a remonstrance to Branch (DNA-RG 45, M124-120).

4. Navy captain Jesse Duncan Elliott (1782–1845) commanded the West India squadron until 1832.

To Joel Roberts Poinsett

Rip Raps Virgina
27. Augt 1829

Sir

Col. Butler an old acquaintance and friend of mine proceeds to the Capital of Mexico, charged with dispatches to yourself   The business on which he comes, renders it unnecessary to remark to you, that he is entitled to your entire confidence

The instructions forwarded will shew you what is desired. It is a matter of high consideration that you should be successful; & full confidence is entertained of your zeal, & caution in bringing about a treaty

You will find Col. Butler well informed as to the topography of the Country, & may prove of material service to you in the negotiation with which you are charged

Wishing you success; & health & happiness I am with great respect Yo Mo Obt

Andrew Jackson

LS in John H. Eaton's hand, PHi (13-1208).

From Thomas B. Laighton

Portsmouth N H. August 31. 1829.

Sir,

Conceiving that the interests and welfare of the people, over whom you have the honor to preside, to be the first object of your care and solicitude, I have taken the liberty of addressing you upon a subject that involves in its consequences some of the dearest rights, and proudest privileges of freemen. You may deem me presumtious in this attempting, unsolicited, to express the wishes of my fellow citizens, but believing, you are ever ready to listen to the voice of public opinion, and to be put in possession of those facts that will tend to the correction of unintentional error; I am emboldened to proceed. A sacred regard to truth, and a confidence in the soundness & purity of my motives, have combined to inspire me with confidence in this undertaking, and enabled me to overcome that delicacy of feeling, which is very naturally created in the mind of a private citizen, at the idea of addressing one who has been raised to the enviable dignity of reigning in the hearts, and presiding over the affairs of a free people, proverbially jealous of their rights.

Soon after your acceptance of the high station to which the confidence of a free people had elected you, a petition was sent from this town, signed by about 300 of its independent republican voters, in favor of the appointment of Abner Greenleaf Esquire, to the office of Collector of the Customs for this district, and yet, by a train of circumstances, to us inexplicable, Mr. John P. Decatur was appointed to that very important situation, contrary to the wishes of your Petitioners and the citizens generally, who were too well acquainted with his conduct and character to repose any confidence in him. In connexion with this subject, I would observe, that the petitioners were the *"bone and muscle"* of the Portsmouth Democracy.[1] They had risen from a fearful minority, to a great and powerful majority, by mere dint of exertion and an untiring activity. They were the practical champions of those doctrines of equal rights which had for their advocate your illustrious predecessor Thomas Jefferson, and supposed they were defending the violated maxim, that *"the will of the people, is the will of the law."* But the event would almost justify them in a contrary opinion. When the result of their application was anticipated, they remonstrated against the appointment of Mr. Decatur, and were powerfully seconded by a similar measure in the State Capital, which was signed by the most prominent Republicans of that place, such for instance, as William Pickering now Treasurer, Dudley S. Palmer, now Secretary of State, Francis N. Fisk, now Counsellor for Rockingham, Charles Walker, Joseph Walker, John George, David Davis, Horatio Hill, and many others, all gentlemen of the first respectability, and unwavering patriotism.* (*This remonstrance was directed to Mr. Hill at Washington.)[2] These gentlemen well knew the effect that would succeed this unpopular measure, and were urged to the act by their ardent solicitude to present unbroken the solid colum of Democracy, that their labor and perseverance had called into action. When Mr. Decatur returned from the seat of government, loudly vaunting of his influence over you, and of having defeated the will of the people, all the energies of our republican citizens appeared to be paralized, and they viewed each other with silent astonishment. When they saw the individual crushed whose elevation they had been seeking, and whose whole soul was wrapped up in their interests, and a man elevated, in whom they had not the least confidence; who had rendered himself odious for his lack of good faith and want of attachment to principal, as well as the malignant propensities of his heart; they were confounded and overwhelmed. It was then indeed, their enemies obtained an advantage over them, which they failed not to improve, by dark insinuations and open vile attacks upon your character and firmness. Yet the confidence of your friends, even at this trying moment, was unshaken. The believed that you had been decieved; that you were unacquainted with the facts, and that you knew not the real character of him, who was thus unexpectedly designated to fill a station in direct opposition to their expressed wishes.

I will not trespass upon your patience by dwelling longer upon the effects of this unpopular measure, but proceed at once, to point out to you the events that led Mr. Decatur to seek this appointment with so much solicitude. I will however premise, by saying, that I have no predilections in favor of Mr. Greenleaf, more than for any other gentleman possessed of sterling honor, and sound practical principles. I have long entertained the same feeling toward him, as will more fully appear by reference to an address to this gentleman, which appeared in the N. H. Gazette in February last, signed by me and thirty nine others, and of which I was the author.[3] I make these remarks that you may not suppose me actuated by improper and unworthy motives, which, from my situation in the Post Office would appear both natural and plausible. But enough of this: one appeal to my fellow citizens would exonerate me from so unjust an imputation.

Mr. Decatur, once professed to be the warm friend of Mr. Greenleaf, and was as much opposed to Mr. Cushman, who like himself, never had the confidence of the republican party in this town.[4] But, in consequence of some events that show the high toned principles of Mr. Greenleaf in proportion as they exhibit the mean and hypocritical conduct of Mr. Decatur, he became his most bitter and untiring enemy; and to defeat the expectations of Mr. Greenleaf's friends, he proceeded to Washington, and, as is generally supposed, by a train of deception of the most detestable character, succeeded in accomplishing his design, and gratifying the natural malignancy of his disposition.

Some of the circumstances that led to this breach of friendship, it will be well enough to notice. Mr. Greenleaf it is well known assisted in managing the editorial department of the Newhampshire Gazette, and contributed to its colums, in a tenfold degree, more than any other man throughout the late presidential campaign, and possessed the confidence of the editor and proprietor. Mr. Decatur was sometimes disposed to dabble in short communications, which were generally marked with his usual want of discretion (to say nothing of their crudities, vulgarities and want of point and talent). These communications sometimes failed to appear, and in all such cases, he imputed the cause to Mr. Greenleaf. Impatient of revenge, that his spirit of dictation should be thus checked, he joined his efforts with those of Mr. Cushman who had always been the secret enemy of Mr. Greenleaf, and viewed his political progress with a jealous eye, to destroy his popularity; but it had only the effect to make the conspirators themselves still more unpopular. On the eve of the Presidential election, Mr. Decatur wished to publish in the Gazette, some forged letters, purporting to have been received from distant parts of the State, containing accounts of the unparalled success of Republican principles, and offered to write them himself; and he even proposed publishing an account, purporting to be from the South, stating that Mr. Adams had been suddenly attacked with the palsy, and that his friends dispaired of his life. Mr. Greenleaf with his characteristic promptitude and decision, expressed his unqualified disapprobation of such unprincipled baseness, and it need not be added, that it was rejected by all your friends, who were in the secret, with indignation and abhorrence. Inflamed with resentment at being thus thwarted in his nefarious schemes, he, with the natural revengeful feeling alone known to minds of little worth, turned short upon the man who had so nobly taught him the genuine principles of true honor, and in language not suited to the delicacy of social intercourse, protested that he would take care to prevent Mr. Greenleaf from obtaining any office under the Government whatever. The friends of Mr. Greenleaf smiled at this idle ebulition of his spleen, not supposing he could carry his purposes so completely into effect. It was at this period he seriously talked of abandoning the office that he then held, in expectation of another. The office of Naval Store Keeper, at this station which he then held, combined in an eminent degree, the advantages of ease and profit; it being worth, if his testimony can be relied on, the hansome sum of nineteen hundred dollars, per annum. He seldom was confined by its duties, but amused himself, the larger portion of his time in the sports of the field. This office you well know, he resigned, to assume at once, all the responsible and arduous duties of Collector of Custums. Did you know the man, you would readily accord with me in opinion, that he is rendered, both by nature and habit, notoriously unfit to fulfil the duties of this highly responsible situation. As a further illustration of the position, that Mr. Decatur was actuated by the mean principle of revenging a supposed injury, before his departure from Washington, he waited upon Daniel P. Drown Esquire, a gentleman who is regarded as the guardian genius of Democracy by the citizens of this town, and offered him the situation he then held, indirectly hinting that its price must be the withdrawal of his friendship for Mr. Greenleaf, at the same time observing, that you would do as he said. Mr. Drown knew the man, and scorned to barter away his friendship for a gentleman with whom he had breasted the heaviest portion of the political storm. He declared to Mr. Decatur, that the course he was pursuing was ungenerous and unmanly.

With this brief statement of facts before you, can you believe that the public were satisfied with the appointment of Mr. Decatur. They never had reposed any confidence in him, nor ever trusted him with their views or policy. His frequent indiscretions, kept your friends constantly on the alert, guarding against their evil consequences. As a specimen of his duplicity and weakness, he proposed to bring twenty men to the polls, from the State of Maine, and solicited the aid of Mr. Drown, the person I have before mentioned, who was the Town Clerk to assist him in getting them through, which he probably might have done, had not honor forbade it, as it was his duty to check the names of the voters, as they passed. This proposition was rejected on all hands with the indignation it merited.[5] Mr Decatur was ever considered as an incubus which the Democracy of this town would gladly have shaken off. They have been more than once reproached by their political enemies upon the very floor of their elective hall, with the crying sin of having their ranks poluted with such men as Decatur and Cushman. On the contrary, the steady virtue and uncompromising patriotism of Mr Greenleaf had enshrined him in the hearts of his fellow citizens. He had long labored under the concomitant evils of poverty, persecution and sickness, yet he shrunk not from what he concieved to be his duty. Under these circumstances, the ultimate notice of Government, in behalf of this Gentleman, operated as a balm to their wounded feelings. They infered that you had, at length, become possessed of the true situation of affairs in this section of the union, and had partially repaired the injury done to their feelings, by the munificient attention bestowed upon him. Yet the public are far from being satisfied. They would see many such men as Mr Greenleaf sacrificed 'ere they could regard the appointment of Mr. Decatur as a wise and politic measure.

These facts, with a train of others too numerous to note within the prescribed limits of a single epistle, will be laid before the Honorable Senate of the United States, in order that they may the better judge what will restore the confidence and esteem of their constituents.

I have thus far, with the fearless frankness of a citizen of the United States, endeavoured to exhibit to you, some of the evil effects that have arisen from an appointment, in which the feelings and wishes of your Republican friends, were not consulted.

In concluding this lengthy epistle I would respectfully solicit you, if the arduous nature of your duties will permit, to inform me, if you ever received the petition and remonstrance to which an allusion is had in the above. Here it has been generally supposed that you never saw them. With sentiments of the sincerest respect, I have the honor to subscribe myself, your fellow citizen

Thomas B. Laighton.

Copy, DNA-RG 46 (13-1211). Laighton (1805–66) was a clerk in the Portsmouth post office and later a New Hampshire state senator. Abner Greenleaf (1785–1868), a coppersmith, had been elected to the state senate in March and appointed Portsmouth postmaster in April. John Pine Decatur (1786–1832), brother of naval hero Stephen Decatur, had been naval storekeeper at Portsmouth since 1818. In April, AJ had removed Portsmouth customs collector Timothy Upham and appointed Decatur, who was recommended by Isaac Hill and others.

AJ Donelson replied to Laighton on September 5 that his letter had been referred to Treasury secretary Ingham. Laighton sent further complaints about Decatur to AJ on October 21 and November 14. AJ nominated Decatur to the Senate on January 13, 1830. He was rejected on March 29 by a vote of 43 to 1.

1. The petition urging Greenleaf's appointment (DNA-RG 46) was dated March 1829 and addressed to Treasury secretary Ingham.

2. Pickering (1778–1850) was appointed collector at Portsmouth after the Senate rejected Decatur. Dudley S. Palmer (c1800–1886) was New Hampshire secretary of state, 1828–31. Francis N. Fisk (1780–1870) served on the state executive council. Charles Walker (1765–1834), brother of Joseph Walker (1782–1833), was a lawyer and former Concord postmaster. John George (d. 1843) was an attorney. David Davis, Jr. (1799–1882) was an aide to New Hampshire governor Benjamin Pierce. Horatio Hill (1807–93) was Isaac Hill's brother and succeeded him as editor of the *New Hampshire Patriot*. On March 9, Daniel P. Drown, Laighton, and nine others of Portsmouth had remonstrated to AJ against Decatur's appointment (DNA-RG 46).

3. The address, drawn up at the behest of a meeting of Portsmouth Jacksonians, commended Greenleaf's editorial labors in the 1828 campaign. It had appeared in the Portsmouth *New Hampshire Gazette* on February 24.

4. AJ had appointed Samuel Cushman (1783–1851), a former Federalist, as district attorney for New Hampshire in April. The Senate rejected him by 36 to 9 on the same day it rejected Decatur.

5. Responding to a solicitation from Laighton and others, Daniel Pickering Drown (b. 1784) confirmed this accusation on October 10. In a later letter he also confirmed that Decatur had offered him the post of naval storekeeper if he would turn against Greenleaf. The *New Hampshire Gazette* printed both letters on February 16, 1830. AJ appointed Drown collector at Portsmouth in 1834.

To James Hamilton, Jr.

Copy to Col James Hamilton

My Dear Sir

I beg leave to make known to you my nephew, Mr. Saml J. Hays, who will hand you this.

Mr. Hays has just mentioned to me that he has formed an attachment to the Miss Middleton of whom you are the guardian. Upon which information I have stated to him the propriety of acquainting you with his intentions, and of waiting upon you for this purpose   This he will do in a proper manner, I hope.

I can assure you that Mr. Hays is a young man of unblemished character and good morals, and that his family is respectable. His Father had once a fortune, but like many others he died insolvent. His mother, one of the most amiable of her sex, has by her industry and prudent management, obtained an independence, and lives cumfortly on a farm in West Tennessee which she owns. So that you will perceive ~~that~~ her son is not a man of fortune, being dependent upon his profession as a Lawyer, and the share he will have in his mother's estate ~~which will be~~   I have taken some pains with his education in aid of his amiable mother, and trust that it will secure success in his profession.

To you Sir, the guardian of the young lady, this explanation was due that she might marry Mr. Hays for his merits, and not for his fortune. I trust, tho, that my nephew's candor has made this known to her. Accept the assurance of my great respect & esteem.

signed A. Jackson

LS draft in AJ Donelson's hand, TU (mAJs). Frances Pinckney Middleton (1811–65) of South Carolina was the daughter of John Middleton, a cousin of James Hamilton, Jr. After Middleton died in 1826, Frances became Hamilton's ward. In July and August, Hays accompanied Frances and her mother at Saratoga and Ballston Spa, N.Y., and then at Northampton, Mass., where in late August he proposed. Hamilton enclosed his reply to AJ's "very handsome Letter" to Martin Van Buren on August 30, saying "I have signified to the General my ready consent in as civil terms as I can and I assure you I am right well pleased to transfer my amiable ward to the protection of one whom I believe to be a gallant & amiable youth, & who of course is not the less acceptable to me, for his connection with the sturdy old Hickory Tree. The Genl.'s Letter was quite satisfactory" (Van Buren Papers, DLC). Hays and Middleton were married on November 24 in Charleston, S.C.

September

From Chesed P. Montgomery

Washington City Sept. 1st 1829

Dr. Genl.

I have discovered by a dispassionate & thorough inestigation of the subject that I ought to have been more mild in my communication to you that I sent you a few days since & you have replied to that communication in a very harsh manner. I am satisfied that you would have done me justice long since if it had not of been for the false representations of my enemies. I have never been an advocate of John Q. Adams & Henry Clay & I never will be. I am no patron of intrigue, bargain & corruption. The coalition since you left here hearing of the difference that existed between A. J D. & myself requested interviews with me in which they have endeavoured to purchase me but if they were to give me millions it would not induce me to advocate a corrupt cause. If I had of consented to a publication of your letters & at a future period to support Henry Clay for the Presidency I could have obtained the sum of money I requested you to loan me one of their party shook the money at me but it did not tempt me the least. I have always had more regard for my honour than for money obtained by such base means. I replied to their interrogatory very mildly & told them I would think about it. I have an idea (provided you will do me justice) of entraping them by getting Proof of their proposition & blowing them sky high. I am afraid that they noticed my contemptuous look at their proposition which I could not suppress. They thought to take advantage of my distressed & vexed situation but I would suffer death before I would agree to such a base proposition. They are very anxious that I should attack A. J. D. but they say I ought to attack you first that you have given me more provocation & I have no doubt that if I would agree to assassinate you that I could obtain thousands.

My determination to punish A. J. D. has resulted from a conviction that he deserves it, for a wanton & unprovoked attack on my character & insulting language of which I have given you an account of. It will be extremely gratifying to the coalition if I should make an attack on A. J. D. but the public will perceive by this letter to you that they have had no agency or concern in forming my determination. I want to know whether you will comply with my request or not, in your letter to me, you do not mention any thing about it. If you comply with my request here this contemplated combat between A. J. D. & me will end & I will leave here immediately, after giving the coalition a blowing up. If you will not comply I intend to attack A. J. D. the first time I meet him in the Street. I have already notified him of my intention all I want is a fair & equal combat. I have a few genuine friends here that never belonged to the ranks of the coalition who conceive that I have been cruelly treated & they are anxious to have justice done to me.

You say in your reply to me "Your letter is in other respects a tissue of falsehood." My Father informed me before I left home that he voted for you as Major Genl. in addition to that I have ventured to assert my belief that if you ever asked of my Father a favour that he never denied you, for I never knew him to deny a friend a favour. I wish you would do me the justice to examine my letter & your reply & if you have made a mistake to inform me.

A. J. D. since I notified him of my intention by letter & since you left here has made indirect overtures to me through his friends which I have rejected & which is demonstrable evidence of his guilt. I have adopted it as a rule when a man insults me, assails my character & injures my prospects without provocation never to be friendly with him again or to place myself in his power to do me a greater injury or to blast my reputation for ever. I can forgive him but I never can forget his base treatment toward me.

I have thought it necessary to make this communication to you in case there should be a combat between A. J. D. & me the public will perceive that I have not united with the coalition. You will please to send your reply immediately to the Post office. Excuse haste   I am very respectfully your friend

C. P. Montgomery

ALS, TNJ (13-1223).

Account with Pishey Thompson

Washington Decr. 15 1829

Andrew Jackson Esq.
Bot. of Pishey Thompson
Bookseller Stationer & Music Seller
PENNSYLVANIA AVENUE

1829

Sept. 2d	1 Telemaque	$1.50
"	2 Songs	.50
Oct. 17	1 Bible, (extra binding)	9.25
"	1 Boyer's Dictionary—4to	12.00
Nov. 6	1 Sevigne's Letters 3 vols	2.25
		$25.50

Received payment for P. Thompson

Franck Taylor.

17 December 1829

DS by Franck Taylor (1811–73), DLC (37). Thompson (1785–1862), an antiquarian and bookseller, had emigrated to the United States in 1819 from England. Francois Fénelon's novel *Telemaque* (1699) chronicled the adventures of the son of the Greek mythological hero Odysseus. The French-English *Royal Dictionary* of Abel Boyer (1667–1729) was first published in 1699. The posthumously published *Letters* of the aristocrat Madame de Sévigné (1626–96) to her daughter and friends discussed life in Paris and at the French court.

To Ezra Stiles Ely

(private)

Washington Septbr. 3rd. 1829—

My Dr. Sir

On the 1rst. instant, the Revd. Mr. Campbell requested an interview with me, and to my great astonishment, informed me that he was the Presbetarian Clergyman who had given you the information derived from the dead Doctor, respecting the miscarriage &c &c[1] Never having even suspected, or even heard it lisped that the Revd. Mr Campble was the individual, I was truly astonished for reasons I will give you when we meet—The more this thing is investigated the more I am convinced, of the wicked combination to Slander, and to destroy the female alluded to—In the course of Mr Cample's relation of the information given him by this *dead Doctor*, I found it necessary for my satisfaction to ask Mr Campble what date was given by this dead Doctor of this transaction; viewing the date altogether important to the guilt, or innocence of the ~~lady~~ female concerned. Mr Campbell gave me the year 1821—I then brought to his view, the dilemma that the information given to him by this dead Doctor & which he had propagated & become the avowed author, if it should turn out upon investigation that Mr Timberlake, was not absent in the year 1821 from the U. States; the statement being that Mr. T. had been so long absent from Mrs. T. that he could not be the father—and I assured him such was my opinion & impressions[2]—Mr Campble replied he, Mr. T. from information, must have been absent—I again repeated my ~~belief~~ opinion that he could not, & gave him my reasons; that about that time he had been sued by the United States, Judgt recovered & that he was petitioning congress for relief &c &c &[3]—Still Mr Campbell insisted that he certainly was absent in that year—we parted I made a memorandom of the date that I might make the necessary enquiry into this fact so important to the truth or falshood of this Slander—believing if I found the fact as I believed it was, that upon communicating the proof to Mr Campble he would be ~~at once~~ convinced of the wickedness of the slander at once ~~first~~ say to Mrs. Eaton, & acknowledge to the world, that he was now convinced of the injustice done her—& that he regretted ever having named it even confidentially—On the 2nd. instant, so soon as my public engagements would permit I entered on the enquiry—and ~~was informed~~ found that Mr. T. had been engaged in merchandize here & that his Books were in possession of Mrs. Eaton. I ~~went & asked~~ applied for a sight of the Books and upon examining them found entries in Mr. T. own handwriting, as was stated by those whom I asked the question, & was present; I took a copy of two entries with the dates, to shew Mr. Campble to convince him of the dilemma he was in, and the wickedness of this secrete Slander[4]—I had an interview this morning with Mr Campble—in the presence of Col. Towson[5] & Major Donelson and when I had made the statement & produced copies of the entries with the dates as proof to shew that Mr. T. was here he then said I must have mistaken him as to dates—I told him I could not for I had called the date given by him to his view and pointed out the dilemma he would be in upon proof of this fact—He still had the hardihood to state I must have mistaken him, I again assured him I could not—and called upon him then to ~~state a date~~ name the time given to him by the deceased Doctor; but no, no date ~~would~~ could be named—you can as easily Judge of the impressions such conduct made upon my mind as tho I ~~repeated~~ were to repeat them—Mr Campble ~~still adhered~~ said he had employed council and would defend himself—poor deluded man, he has forgot that he has assumed the affirmative, and if he do not produce other proof, that his reputation as an embassador of christ is gone forever—What course Major Eaton may adopt I know not, but I have often heard him say, that my Christian mothers advice was a good one, never to sue a man ~~for slander~~ or indict him for slander—

The object of this letter is to give you hint how matters are here is to say to you, that I wish is, & I think it necessary that you to come on here as soon as you can—it is proper that you should for many reasons—and one, tho last not least, you may save Mr Campbell from public exposure—I have your promise that you will visit me & shall expect you on as soon as your convenience will permit & I shall expect you to stay with me—with compliments to your amiable lady and all yr family & connections & believe sincerely your friend

Andrew Jackson

[Endorsed by AJ:] Roug copy of a letter to The Revd. E. S. Ely Dated 3rd. of Septbr. 1829—This private—

ALS draft, DLC (37).
    1. Ely had reported this story to AJ on March 18.
    2. Timberlake had been purser aboard the schooner *Shark,* which sailed from Washington on July 15, 1821, and was at sea until May 1824 except for port intervals at New York in January and February, 1822, Norfolk from December 1822 to February 1823, and New York from July to October, 1823.
    3. Besides their official duty as paymasters, Navy pursers sold goods to sailors on private account, advancing credit against their pay. In the War of 1812 Timberlake was purser on the frigates *United States* and *President,* both commanded by Stephen Decatur. He suffered losses from crewmen who deserted and from the British capture of the *President* in January 1815, and fell in arrears to the government for more than $23,000. A suit to collect the debt was initiated in 1818, suspended in March 1820, and revived in November 1821, after Timberlake petitioned Congress unsuccessfully for relief. The debt remained unresolved at his death in 1828.
    4. AJ's memorandum of his September 2 inspection reads: "Doctor Sims account up to the 15th. July 1821—Wm Oneals up to the the 12th of Septbr. 1821 from March 20th. & In February 1822—entry all in the hand of Mr. Timberlake   AJ."
    5. Nathan Towson, Army paymaster general.

Statement of an Interview with John Nicholson Campbell

Be it remembered that on tuesday evening the 1st. of September 1829, I was in my parlour when the door-keeper came to, and informed me that the Revd. Mr. Campbell wanted an interview with me in my office. I went immediately up to my office, where I found Mr. Campbell and Major Donelson. Mr. Donelson having retired, Mr. Campbell observed he supposed I knew his business, or the object of his business with me. I assured him that I did not. He then said, that he had received a letter from Dr. Ely, which made it proper for him to inform me that he was the Presbyterian preacher or Clergyman, alluded to in Dr. Ely's letter to me, as having given the information relative to the *tale* of the deceased Doctor upon the subject of the miscarriage of Mrs. Timberlake, now Mrs. Eaton, in the absence of her husband under circumstances which made it manifest that the child could not be his, as related to me in a letter from Dr. Ely. I was much astonished at this avowal, and replied, that it was the first intimation I ever had, that he was the Presbyterian Clergyman who gave currency, through Mr. Ely, to this *vile tale,* and assured him that I never had the least suspicion of his being the author; and that in passing the subject through my mind, I had done injustice to another, for which I was sorry, although I had never named him to any one.

Mr. Campbell then read to me part of Dr. Ely's letter, and entered into an explanation of his motives for not having made his communication directly to me; he said he knew Dr. Ely was my friend, and he wished me to be informed of those charges against Mrs. Eaton, before I appointed Major Eaton a member of my Cabinet; that he had enjoined on Mr. Ely secrecy—that he considered it confidential, and charged him, that if he did not give it to my own ear, not to lisp it to any one. It was upon this condition alone that Mr. Ely was authorised to give up his name to me, he complained that Dr. Ely had not treated him well in communicating the information to others, and particularly to Mrs. Eaton. To which I replied, I regretted that either he or Dr. Ely had not come directly to me with the *tale* before Dr. Ely left Washington. If they had done so, I told him, I could have easily shewn them the falsehoods of some of the charges contained in Dr. Ely's letter to me, and would have pointed out to them, some of the unhappy consequences that must now inevitably take place. I told him that I never had heard of this *tale* circulated as coming from a dead Doctor, before I read it in Dr. Ely's letter; that I was surprised Dr. Ely had not told him he had advised me in a confidential note the Saturday before he lef Washington, not to be drawn from my determination of appointing Mr. Eaton a member of my Cabinet, as his talents and my confidence in him, made it necessary for me to have him near me. This I had determined on, and when next I saw him, told him that I could not be shaken in my purpose, that Major Eaton came into my Cabinet by my persuasion, and not from his own choice; that I knew him intimately for twenty years and upwards, and believed his moral character to be without a blot.

Mr. Campbell then detailed the information derived from this dead Doctor whom he called by the name of Craven.[1]

The manner of his relating the circumstances drew my particular attention, and I observed to him, as soon as he had gotten through, that this dead Doctor's *tale* was, to me, in itself, incredible. As related by Mr. Campbell, it is substantially as follows. "The Doctor told him that he had been called into Mrs. Timberlake as a physician in consequence of her having been thrown from her carriage and much hurt; that when he entered the room where Mrs. Timberlake and an old woman were, they broke out in a loud laugh, and told him he was too late—that Mrs. Timberlake had miscarried, and he lost his job; that Mr. Timberlake had been so long absent from home, that it was well known that the infant could not have been his." I drew Mr. Campbells attention to the absurdity of this story as related, and asked him if he had ever thought of the dilemma in which the dead Doctor would be placed for *telling* such a *tale,* and he for believing and reporting it. I asked him if he did not know, that Doctors were prohibitted by law from revealing the secrets of a sick bed, and if he did not suppose this dead Doctor would be considered a base man and unworthy of credit, the moment this story was presented to the public.[2] I told him the honorable moral and religious part of the community would have no confidence in the representation of such a man, and that he would be held responsible for it, inasmuch as he had avowed himself the author of its circulation. Mr. Campbell then observed, he believed he (the Doctor) had stated, he accidentally happened in, and had not been sent for as a physician. I told Mr. Campbell it was *still more* absurd to suppose that a married woman, so long absent from her husband that every one must know the child could not be his, would so wantonly publish her own disgrace and infamy to the world, when she had no need of a physician in her private chamber. This version of the story, I observed to him, was too absurd and ridiculous, as well as inconsistent with every principle and feeling of human nature to be believed even by the most *credulous:* and that I was astonished a man of his good sense could, for one moment give credence to it, and particularly as it involved the character of a lady. I then enquired of Mr. Campbell what date the dead Doctor had given to this transaction—the date being important. He replied in 1821. I asked him if he was aware of the situation he would be placed in if, on enquiry, it should appear that Mr. Timberlake was in this country and never out of it in all the year 1821. I told him I was under the impression that it would so appear, whenever examined into; that I was induced to believe he had not been absent from the United States from the close of the war until 1824; that I had understood he was detained here prosecuting a claim against the Government for property thrown overboard by Commodore Decatur, previous to the capture of the Frigate President—having lost his vouchers he was unable to settle his accounts, and therefore being considered a defaulter, could not get public employment.[3]

Mr. Campbell replied that Mr. Timberlake, from the information of the Doctor, must have been absent in that year. I answered it was my opinion he would find himself mistaken, and it would be well for him to make enquiry, and as a christian and preacher of the gospel, it would be his duty, if he found he had been mislead by this information to repair the injury he had done female character, by saying to Mrs. Eaton, and to the world, that on enquiry he found there was no truth in the tale of his dead Doctor. Justice and christianity, I told him, demanded this of him.

After some further conversation on the subject of Mrs. Timberlakes visiting his family, and the visit being returned, and that a friendly intercourse was kept up between the two families until Doctor Craven gave him the information relative to the abortion, when all intercourse ceased;

I asked Mr. Campbell why he did not, when he received this information, and before he terminated the friendly relation which had subsisted between his family and Mrs. Timberlake, go to her and inform her of this *vile tale* and the name of the person from whom he had received it, and say to her that she must remove this stain upon her character, or all intercourse between them must cease. This I told him, was what I thought he as a christian ought to have done—pursuing the golden rule of doing to others as we would they should do unto us. This would have given to her an opportunity of shewing her innocence; or if she failed, then with a clear conscience he and his family could have withdrawn from her society.

The date having been given by Mr. Campbell, as stated by the dead Doctor, its being an important fact by which to judge of the truth, or falsehood of this *story*, I at once determined to have enquiry made as to where Mr. Timberlake was in all the year 1821, and whilst ruminating on this subject Major Wm. B. Lewis came into my office and enquired relative to Mr. Campbell's business with me, (he having been in the parlour below, when the door-keeper told me the Revd. Mr. Campbell wished to have a private interview with me.) I told him Mr. Campbell came to avow himself to be the Clergyman alluded to in Dr. Ely's letter to me, who had informed him (Ely) of the reported miscarriage of Mrs. Timberlake when it was well known the child could not be her husbands, in consequence of his long absence from the country; and that Mr. Campbell had affixed to this transaction a date—1821.—This, I observed, was tangible, and by it the truth or falsehood of the *tale* might be tested. I requested Major Lewis, to ascertain, if it was practicable to do so, where Mr. Timberlake was in all that year, assuring him that I was convinced in my own mind, and had so said to Mr. Campbell, that Mr. Timberlake was here during the whole year of 1821, that I had never heard of his leaving the United States until the spring of 1824, that I had seen him at Mr. Oneal's in the winter of 1823 and 1824, and was there when he took leave of his family preparatory to a cruise up the Mediterreanean.[4]

On the evening of the 2nd. September instant Major Lewis informed me that he had made the enquiry, as requested by me, and had learned that Mr. Timberlake was a merchant in this City about that time, and that his Books were now in the possession of Mrs. Eaton, which if looked into would, in all probability, shew where he was during the year 1821.[5] I resolved to go, and examine the books myself, and on the same evening, 2nd. Septr. I accordingly went up to Major Eaton's. On entering the parlour, I found no one there but John Henderson, Major Eaton's nephew, who informed me that his uncle was up stairs with his aunt who was very sick.[6] I desired him to go up and request his uncle to come below, as I wanted to see him. Major Eaton came down and invited me to walk up and see Mrs. Eaton—I did so, and found her very ill and in bed. After a short conversation with her, and being informed of an interview had with Mr. Campbell on that day, I asked Mrs. Eaton if she had the mercantile

Books of Mr. Timberlake in her possession. She said she had—I desired to know if she would permit me to see them—She said not only me, but any one. I then went down stairs to the parlour, where the Books were brought to me, and I examined them. I soon found from entries, said to be in the hand writing of Mr Timberlake, that he was in this country, and *in this City,* throughout the year 1821. Before leaving Major Eaton's I took extracts from the Books, of Dr. Sim's and Major Oneal's accounts, to shew Mr. Campbell, and to prove to him, that Mr. Timberlake must have been here in that year, and as late as February 1822, as the entries were made in his own hand writing. I was convinced, in my own mind, that on exhibiting this proof to Mr. Campbell, he would, at once, see the cruelty of this charge as made by his dead Doctor, and the injustice done Mrs. Eaton, and would so declare to Mrs. Eaton and all others. I, therefore, on my return home, requested Major Donelson to wait upon Mr. Campbell, and having heard that Col. Towson, by request of Mr. Campbell, was present at the interview between the latter gentleman and Major Eaton and his lady, on the 2nd. Instant, I desired Major Donelson to request the Col: to accompany Mr. Campbell and be present at the interview I wished to have with him.

Agreeably to my request the Revd. Mr. Campbell called at my office on the morning of the 3rd. Inst. When an interview was had in the presence of Col: Towson and Major Donelson. After stating to Mr. Campbell and Col: Towson, the reasons which had induced me to request this meeting, it being in consequence of a conversation had with Mr. Campbell, at his own request, on the 1st. Instant, I stated the result of my enquiry as to the fact, where Mr. Timberlake was in the year 1821, and having the proof in my hand, observed that it evidenced beyond all contradiction, that the *tale* of the dead Doctor could not be true.

I further observed that if any doubts existed, as to the entries being in the hand writing of Mr. Timberlake, the Books could be seen, and that fact clearly ascertained. Mr. Campbell then said I must have misunderstood him as to the date—I replied I could not; he must recollect, at the time he made the statement, how earnestly I brought to his view the dilemma in which he would be placed, if, at the date given to this transaction, Mr. Timberlake should be proved to be in this country—Notwithstanding this he (then) still persisted in the declaration of Mr. Timberlake's absence in that year. He however *now* maintained that I had mistaken *him,* as to the date—I again told him as positively I *had not.* I then asked him to give a date to the transaction, if it was not in 1821. He refused—I again replied, that the date being all important, for on this depended the innocence or guilt of the lady, I requested he should give to it a date. He did not, and would not. After taking out some papers and looking over them, he said Mr. Timberlake was absent, from his memoranda, in the autumn of 1822. I observed to him that there was neither justice nor christianity in making a charge, which goes to the destruction of female character without affixing to it a date, by which truth or falsehood could be tested. Still, however, Mr. Cambell in his last interview positively refused to give a date, although in his first he had given 1821, and insisted that Mr. Timberlake must have been absent. Col: Towson and Major Donelson being present, their written statement is referred to, as explanatory of what was further said at this interview—being on the 3rd. Instant.

I will barely add, in conclusion, that Mr. Campbell stated he had employed Mr. Key as counsel, who had told him his proof was sufficient. He further said his statement would be corroborated by the evidence of the Mother and Wife of Dr. Craven.[7] I cautioned him not to be too sanguine with regard to his proofs. He said that he and Col: Towson had seen the Mother and Wife of Doctor Craven that morning, &c, &c, &c. This statement is made from memoranda in writing, taken immediately after the conversations took place, from day to day; and although the very words may not be given, I am certain the whole as far as I have attempted to state the conversation, is substantially correct. September 3rd. 1829.

(Signed) Andrew Jackson.

P.S. I requested Mr. Campbell to explain his motives in coming to me, to avow himself the author of this secret slander against Mrs. Eaton, but this he has failed satisfactorily to do. It was well known that I had been long and intimately acquainted with Major Eaton, knew his worth, and was satisfied that a blemish did not rest upon his moral character. Why he did not go to Mr. Eaton with it, who was here I cannot tell; he was the person who should have been informed of this slander, and especially, as both Mr. Campbell and Dr. Ely acknowledged to me in the presence of my Cabinet Mr. Van Buren, Mr Ingham, Mr. Branch, Mr Barry and Mr Berrian, and also Major Lewis and Major Donelson, that they entirely *accquitted Major Eaton* of the charge of improper or *criminal* conduct.[8]

Why this persecution of Mrs. Eaton—of the motives which induce to such conduct I leave to the decision of the moral and christian world. Mrs. Eaton is the wife of Major Eaton, which is the strongest evidence he can give in her virtue. Does Mr. Campbell wish to seperate man and wife by his false tales? Surely this is not the doctrine taught by our Saviour, and which if he reads his bible, he may find in every page of that sacred Book.

(Signed) Andrew Jackson.

Septr. 4th. 1829 Washington City.

The foregoing statement has been read by me and, so far as it relates to a conversation between Genl. Jackson and myself, is correct.
(Signed) W. B. Lewis.

Copy, DLC (75); AD fragment, DLC (13-1235). Parton, 3:197–202. Text of the Copy almost identically matches the surviving portions of the AD.

1. Elijah R. Craven.

2. Doctor-patient confidentiality was enjoined by the Hippocratic Oath and protected by English common law.

3. Decatur had jettisoned Timberlake's trade goods to lighten the ship during the British pursuit of the *President*. Timberlake's account books, showing the sums owed to him by crewmen, were seized with the ship.

4. Timberlake shipped aboard the *Constitution* as its purser in June 1824.

5. Before sailing with the *Shark,* Timberlake had sold dry goods from a store adjoining William O'Neale's establishment.

6. John Eaton Henderson (c1813–36) was the orphaned son of Eaton's sister Ann.

7. Francis Scott Key (1779–1843), author of "The Star Spangled Banner," was a Georgetown attorney. Craven's mother was Nancy Richardson Craven (c1754–1840); his widow was the former Sarah Eccleston Landreth (1798–1885).

8. This postscript was added on or after September 10, when AJ assembled Ely, Campbell, and his Cabinet to discuss the Eaton affair.

Memorandum by Andrew Jackson Donelson

Memorandum of an interview held by Genl Jackson and the Revd. Mr. Campbell in the presence of Col. Towson and Andrew J Donelson on the 3d. Septr. 1829

This interview being the result of a previous disclosure by Mr. Campbell of certain transactions implicating the character of Mrs. Timberlake, now Mrs. Eaton, made on the evening of the 1st. September to Genl Jackson, it is proper that I should state the substance of a conversation previously held with me by Mr. Campbell on the same subject, on the night of the 29th. August at my office, as giving a more full view of the understanding and motives of all the parties to this interview.

Mr. Campbell having called upon me as stated, remarked, that as I was the relative and intimate friend of the President he felt it his duty to say in confidence to me, that during Mr Ely's visit to Washington City last winter, governed by feelings of the most sincere friendship for the public and private character of the Presidt, as well as a sense of duty to religion and the interests of the society in which he was performing the services of a Pastor, which he apprehended were about to sustain an injury by the appointment of Majr. Eaton to the cabinet, he was induced to relate to Mr Ely a fact which, in connection with the general belief of Mrs. Es bad character, if communicated to the President, might satisfy him, or enable him to judge of the justice of that apprihension. This fact was this. That some time after he settled in this city Mrs. Timberlake visited his family, some member of which returned the call as was usual, but soon hearing reports very unfavorable to the character of Mrs. T who then lived in the family of Mr. Oneale, he was induced to make application to Dr. Craven to ascertain their cause, when the Dr. gave him the following information

—that he, the Dr., had been called upon on a certain occasion as he, Mr. C, understood in his professional character to go to the house of Mr. Oneale, which he obeyed, and, upon entering it was met and accosted by one of the ladies in the presence of Mrs. Timberlake in language like this, *you have lost a job Dr.—Mrs. T had fallen from her carriage, but it is now all over—to all which Mrs. T assented*. Mr. Campbell continued, that the respectability of Dr. Craven, and the great confidence he reposed in his integrity and goodness of character, left him no alternative but the belief of this circumstance: and that from the knowledge which he seemed to possess of dates and the situation of the family, it was impossible they could be true and Mrs. T be a chaste and virtuous lady—that adopting this conviction he determined henceforward to have nothing further to do with the subject, and would have adhered to this determination had he not been well apprised that the community from various other reasons had formed and long acted upon the same opinion of her want of character—that meeting with Dr. Ely whom he knew to be a valued friend of Genl Jackson and full of the same apprehensions that disturbed him, *this remote origin of his* was mentioned with the expressed understanding that it might be communicated before the formation of the cabinet; and that he never had been informed until now told so by me, that it had not been till after this event.

He added in conclusion that Mr. Ely had now called upon him to give up his name to Genl Jackson, at the instance of Mrs. Eaton who had been lately at Philadelphia for this purpose, which he had been always ready to do, and indeed had authorised Mr. Ely so to do originally. And he wished me to apprise the President of these facts, and to appoint an interview at as early a period after his arrival from the Rip Raps which was on the first of Septr. as would be convenient. I declined a conversation with the President on the subject, but concurred in the propriety of his waiting upon him, and making such explanations of his motives as he thought due to them and the delicate situation in which he was placed.

This call he made on the 1st. of September.

The interview which succeeded in the presence of Col Towson & myself on the 3d. was introduced by the President, who, referring to the subject of his last conversation with Mr. Campbell, remarked that he understood the facts in regard to the miscarriage to be located some time in the year 1821—that he had been therefore particular in looking over some accounts which were thought to be in the handwriting of Mr. Timberlake, and if so, proved that he was in Washington during that year—that there was besides strong reason for the belief that he did not leave the city until some time in the year of 1824, as he had seen him in the winter of 23–24, and was informed he did not go to sea for some period after. Mr. Campbell replied, that the President had misunderstood him—that it was impossible from the time of his own arrival in the city, and the delay to which he was subject in furnishing his house,[1] that he could have located these facts in the year before, or at any time preceding the occupation of his house, in the parlour of which the conversation with Dr. Craven occurred. The Prest. reiterated his conviction that he had been positive in fixing the transaction in the year 1821; and asked if he would now give it a date—Mr. Campbell would not positively, but related again the circumstances with some memoranda from the sea books placing dates in the year 1822, which he thought would determine Mr. Timberlakes absence for at least a sufficient time to give to the statement of Dr. Craven, the possibility, if not the certainty of truth.

The President then went further and spoke of the improbability of Dr. Cravens not having left with his family some impressions of his distrust of Mrs. T's virtue, and mentioned also the substance of an interview which Mr. Eaton & lady had had with old Mrs. Craven and daughter, wherein they had disavowed any knowledge of such a circumstance as that related by Mr Campbell. Mr. C replied that Col Towson and himself had also an account of that interview from the ladies themselves, which the Col related substantially in these words—that, Mrs. Eaton went privately to the bed chamber of the daughter, and referring to Col. Towson as having requested the interview she was about to hold with her, proceeded to state the transaction ascribed by Mr. Campbell to the authority of Dr. Craven. After having done which she mentioned the importance of her denying it; as otherwise blood might be spilt, a challenge having already passed, and at least a suit would grow out of it which might embarrass their estate—that the lady answered, she knew nothing about law, but in the event of her being called upon to speak in court she would tell the truth. That the old lady being questioned by Mr. Eaton told him, that Mr. Timberlake had been in the habit of unbosoming himself to Dr. Craven, that he had left impressions on his mind not favorable to the character of Mrs. T, and in this spirit had told him he must go to sea—that reports of this kind had long existed, and it was singular she should now be called upon to do away their prejudices which he must know had been of long standing—and that Mr. Eaton said in reply *man born* of *woman is full of trouble.*[2]

Mr. Campbell also related the substance of an interview with Mr. & Mrs. Eaton at which Col Towson was present. In this Mr. Eaton expressed his determination to punish his levity, contradicted Mr. C's account of the ~~transaction~~ conversation they had previously held together, but not until Mrs. Eaton had asked in terms of much surprise if he permitted any one to speak thus. Mr. C said he maintained the accuracy of his recollection and his determination not to be driven from the truth by the terrors of blood &c.

The President concluded with a very animated comment upon the delicacy of Mr. C's situation, the danger of listening to the reports of the malevolent, or to the verbal statements of dead men when intended to injure the character of the living. He said that he had done his duty, that his confidence in Majr Eaton had never been shaken, nor would it be by any thing but the most unquestioned evidence, and he would now leave to his own reflection the course which his sense of justice to himself, to Majr Eaton, and to christianity recommended.

Mr. Campbell remarked that he was ready and anxious to vindicate himself before any competent tribunal, that he had taken the advice of Mr. Key who had no doubt of his ability to sustain himself, and who entertained great fears of a prosecution as likely to disturb the administration, and do infinite injury to the reputation of Mr. Eaton. Col. Towson also brought to the Presidents recollection a conversation held with him previous to the formation of the cabinet, in which he stated his conviction that in consequence of reports in circulation injurious to Majr Eaton his appointment would be a most unfortunate one—that such was his own opinion and that of the Presidents friends generally, and that he had expressed the same personally to Majr Eaton at a party given by Mr. Vaughan. But he also said neither then nor now did he assume the truth or falsity of any charge either against him or Mrs. Eaton.

In this detail the substance and meaning of the parties are written as accurately as my memory would permit me. The particular speech, and the many repetitions, and interruptions, that would occur in a dialogue of this nature have not been preserved.

3d. Sept. 1829
Andrew J Donelson

P.S. I had omitted as immaterial the manner of the communication made by Mr. Campbell to Dr. Ely, as to its being confidential or private; and the conversation that turned upon it, in the above interview. In the first conversation with me, I told Mr. Campbell that I believed Mr. Ely had not given the information at the time desired by him, & that therefore I inferred there would be a contrariety in their account of it. As Dr. Ely did not also give up Mr. Campbells name with the information derived from him when he first conveyed it to the President, I formed an expectation on this point too that the Dr. having not felt himself at liberty to view the information in any other light than that of confidence, would be found to disagree with him, which I expressed. In answer as well as I now remember, Mr. Campbell stated to me positively that Dr Ely was authorised by him to give up his name with the information, and that it was to be considered confidential only until it was conveyed to the President; and he indulged in some terms of complaint against the Dr. if a different impression were to grow out of any thing that he should hereafter say, or had now done.

The same ground was taken by the President on this subject in the interview at which Col Towson & myself were present, and Mr Campbell expressed a corresponding complaint against the Dr

Sept. 25th 1829
Andrew J Donelson

[Endorsed by AJ:] Major A. J. Donelson statement, of the inview had with Mr. Campbell in the presence of him and Col. Towson on the 3rd. Septbr 1829—

ADS, DLC (37). ADS draft, DLC (72); Bassett, 4:68–72. Donelson evidently composed and then later rewrote this memorandum, retaining the original date but adding the September 25 postscript. The two versions do not differ in substance.
    1. In 1822, according to the ADS draft.
    2. Job 14:1. On this same day, Reverend Obadiah B. Brown called on the Craven women and submitted a statement to AJ that both denied ever hearing the miscarriage story from Craven (DLC-75). Brown said further that Craven had habitually confided with him on sensitive matters, yet never mentioned this story or spoke critically of Mrs. Eaton.

To Andrew Jackson Donelson

Major Donelson will recollect to add in his statement my reply to Col Towsons remark stated to have been made at Gadsbys   Answer—I recollect it well, & replied, I had not come here by the peoples will to make a Cabinet for the fashionable ladies, but for the benefit of my country—& that I had long been acquainted with Major Eaton, he had my confidence and twenty years acquaintance with him insured me there was not a speck upon his moral character.

A J—

ANS, DLC (13-1239).

From John Nicholson Campbell

Washington City Sept. 5th. 1829.
Dear Sir
    Being unable to foresee how the very unpleasant affair in which I have been involved, solely by my desire that the honor of my country's government might be sustained under your administration, and that the best interests of morality and religion might be promoted, may terminate; at this stage of the business, I feel it to be my duty to submit to your consideration, whether, in the difficulty which exists between me, a minister of

the gospel and the Secretary of War, it be not due both the character of the President of the United States, and also as an act of justice, to myself, that you do not throw the weight of your authority and influence into the scale against me. Very respectfully Your friend

(Signed) J. N. Campbell.

Copy, DLC (75).

To John Nicholson Campbell

Washington at night [Sept. 5th. 1829.]

My Dr. Sir

I have recd. your note of this date, and hasten to reply to it. you are well aware that I have had no act, or part, in producing the unhappy difference between you & the secratary of war, nor do I intend to have any, unless when called upon, if called upon at all, to speak the truth; and how you should take up so injurious an idea as that of my intending to interfere in my official character, I cannot divine. If you converse with Mr Key, you will have evidence of my christian feelings and conduct toward you[.] very respectfully Sir your most obedient Humble Servant.

Andrew Jackson

ALS, PHi (13-1257); Copy, DLC (75). Date taken from the copy.

From John Nicholson Campbell

Washington Sept 5th. 1829.

Dear Sir

I cannot refrain from expressing to you how highly I am gratified by the note I have just received from you in reply to mine of this evening, that part of it I mean especially which refers to the christian feelings you entertain towards me. You have not precisely apprehended the tenor of my note I should presume—but it matters not—I am fully satisfied by what your note contains, that what ever apprehensions had been, by circumstances, suggested to my mind are altogether unfounded. Very Respectfully Your friend

(Signed) J. N. Campbell.

Copy, DLC (75).

From Chesed P. Montgomery

Washington City Sept. 5th 1829

Sir

Your object is to destroy my reputation by approving of a combat between A. J. D. & me for political effect & not to do me justice & then say that the opposition to your administration caused me to make the attack although I have communicated to you by letter that such is not the fact   If you will communicate to me that you will make use of no such stratagem or publication then I will make the attack on A. J. D. I shall make no publication of your conduct toward me nor publish your private letters to me. A. J. D. is very anxious for a fight he called on me yesterday evening with his friend when I was alone for an attack but it must have been apparent to every person present that he acted cowardly I dared him to give me a fair fight he refused to meet me I told him I would fight him in any way I did not care how desperate. I will venture to assert that you never refused to meet an enemy on those terms during your life. A. J. D. designed to take some private advantage & not give me a fair fight as he discovered I was not prepared. If he will communicate to me that he will meet me at Barnards Hotel at 5 o'clock this evening upon the terms I have stated I will chastise him or die trying.[1] If I should receive no communication from him at the Post office at 2 o'clock I will conclude that he has declined fighting. In haste

C. P. Montgomery

ALS, TNJ (13-1259). No fight between Donelson and Montgomery ensued.

1. The Mansion House hotel at Pennsylvania Avenue and 14th Street was operated by Frederick Barnard (d. 1838).

From Anthony V. Carr

Franklinsville Farm near Saint Louis September 7th 1829

Sir

I hope you will pardon this Communication in as much as I make it from the purest of motives, and at the Same time wish to Sustain the present Administration as much as it lies in my power. In doing this I have been put to the trouble of Travrsing Several Counties in This State for the purpose of obtaining Signers to An adress which you will find enclosed, the original of which is in my possession, I therefore Send you a Copy but should have Sent the orriginal, only it was So much defaced and blotted, I Can assure you Sir it Comes from Some of the best Republicans in the State, many of whom are known to Gentlemen living at Washington City, most especially Genl D. Green who is well acquainted with the R[eput]ation and Standing of a large majority [of peti]tioners to the Ad[ress in] question and Some [are k]nown to the Hon[orable] William T. Barry the present Post master General, there is the name of one Gentleman who resides in Callaway County an old and tryed Republican of the Jeffersonian School, I mean Majr Jamison, who was in the Senate of the State of Kentucky, and he informed me he was well acquainted with Judge Barry[1]—The Cause of this trouble, to obtain Signers to the Adress, is the Extraordanry Cou[r]se Taken by our Governer, John Miller in recommending—Some of the most voilent men belonging to the late Coalition to be retained [in] office, among the number was Majr. Richard Graham late United States Indian Agent, and Wilson P. Hunt Esqr. now Post master at Saint Louis, Contrary to the well known wish of the Republican party of this State,[2] you will find upwards of one thousand names to this Adress men who well understand the nature of the late firery Contest, I went Through Eleaven Counties, and I know I speak the Truth when I tell you that I Could have obtained as many more in the Said Counties, Ther is Twenty County now in the State, the vote of which Stood as follows for President as nigh as I Can recollectt Cooper, County Jackson 350. Adams & Clay 200. Saline County Jackson 150. Adams 21—Lafayette County Jackson 180. Adams 41—Jackson County. Jackson 200. Adams 21—Clay County Jackson 250. Adams 150. Ray County Jackson 150. Adams 28. Chariton County Jackson 220. Adams 110. Howard County Jackson 450 Adams 281. Ralls County Jackson 100. Adams 76 Marion County Jackson 220 Adams 125 Jeffeson County Jackson 171. Adams 115. Washington County Jackson 350. Adams 237. Madison Jackson 180 Adams 98. Saint Franis County Jackson 140 Adams 110. Wayne Jackson between 200 & 300 Adams from 5 to fifteen Perry County Jackson 100 Adams 60. St. Genevive Jackson 140 Adams 110 this is the County the Honerable Mr. John Scott lives in[3] Scott County Jackson 125 Adams 65. Cape Girardeau County Jackson beteen 3 and 400. Adams from one to Two hundred New Madrid Jackson had a majority of thirty or forty, thus you see how the State Stands the majority Through it was a few under Five Thousand votes, with all the Advantage of the best officers of the State and nearly all under the General Government, [on the] side of the Coalition, [and still now all the o]fficers belonging—to Land office except one [whi]ch was said to be doubtfull, and that was Majr. Christy However, Majr. Benjamin OFallon our Elector for this District informed me he did not vote   They have had, untill very lately, the marshall and District Attorny, They have the Indian Department with the exceptions of a few Subagencies and Capt Vashon who was lately appointed to Succeed Majr. Graham,[4] The watch word of the Jackson Party was Jackson and *Reform,* from Maine to Missouri, and the victory has been Complet   Thank *God* the Aristocracy of the Land has been put down, there never has been the Son of a Farmer put in any office, in this State, by the Frederal Government, I mean a farmer of missou yet the farmers are the men that have always Sustained the Republican Party, I know the Situation I am placed in in taking this Stand against the Coalition, but it was the Stand I took during the Contest. I had more Slander heaped upon me during the Canvass than any Ten men in the [state] all the Low and vulgar abuse was Thrown at me but it did not move me from my purpose the Statements I have here made Can be Sustained by the best men in the State for your Satisfaction I will name a few Genl Danl Bissell Col Th. H Benton Col George f Strother Judge George Shannon Honbl Spencer Pettis Col Lawless Col Dunklin and many others that might be named but I deem it unnessary[5]—if I had had time to Traverse the State I could have got Five Thousand Signers to the Adress this I know the Republican Party want [these] well dressed beggars put out of office, the Clay party together with what friends Mr. Adams had are more voilent than ever. Mr Clay is there Candidate, and they are Still abusing yourself and the Cabbinett, as much as ever. I hope you will excuse my uncorrected Scrall an[d bad] Spelling as I had a Severe attack   [. . . bowel] Complaint yesterday and a[m much] debilitated, [howe]ver I was determined [to] Adress you [in] person I know different Statements will be made to you by the trimmers of the Town of Saint Louis. I hope therefore you will pardon the libberty I have taking in Adressing you as the Chief of our Republican Government, your fellow Citizen

A [V] Carr

NB I refer you to Genl D. Green as to the Correctness of my Statements

ALS, DNA-RG 107 (M222-26). Carr (d. 1830), a former Florissant, Mo., postmaster, was appointed subagent to the Osage Indians in July 1830. The petition he enclosed, dated July and bearing more than a thousand names, hailed AJ's election and urged the immediate removal of all Adams and Clay men from federal office in Missouri.

1. John Jameson (c1770–1834), formerly of Kentucky, settled in Callaway County, Mo., in 1824.

2. Richard Graham (1780–1857), a former Army officer, had been an Indian agent since 1818. Wilson Price Hunt (c1782–1842), commander of the Astoria expedition in 1811–12, had been postmaster since 1822. A marginal note, perhaps in AJ's hand, reads "postmaster obnoxious requested to be removed," but Hunt retained his post.

3. John Scott (1785–1861) was Missouri's first congressman, 1821–27. He had cast the state's vote for Adams in the House election in 1825.

4. William Christy (1764–1837) was register of the St. Louis land office. Benjamin O'Fallon (1793–1842) was a fur trader, former Indian agent, and Jackson presidential elector in 1828. George Vashon (1785–1835), a former Army officer and a Jackson elector in Virginia in 1824, was appointed in April to replace Graham as Delaware and Shawnee agent. AJ had removed Missouri marshal John Simonds, Jr., and district attorney Beverly Allen.

5. Daniel Bissell (1769–1833), a career soldier and brigadier general in the War of 1812, had served in the postwar Army under AJ. George French Strother (1783–1840) had been a Virginia congressman and receiver of the St. Louis land office. AJ appointed former

Kentucky legislator George F. Shannon (1787–1836) Missouri district attorney in place of Beverly Allen. Luke E. Lawless (1781–1846) was a St. Louis lawyer. Daniel Dunklin (1790–1844) was lieutenant governor of Missouri, 1828–32, and governor, 1832–36.

From John Henry Eaton

7. Sept 29

Dear Sir

Yr opinion is always of more value & consideration to me, than that of any other in the world   I shall accordingly act as you have requested[.] Yrs truly

J. H. Eaton

[Endorsed by AJ:] Major Eatons answer to my note of the 6th. Septr 1829 *requesting* him in consequence of an interview I had with Mr. Key, who waited upon me, as the l̶a̶w̶y̶e̶r̶ friend of peace to try to have the matter between Major E, & the Revd. Mr Campble settled—I wrote major E, the note to which the within is an answer   A. J.

ALS, DLC (37).

From William Savin Fulton

Little Rock September 7th. 1829.

My Dear General,

I wrote you, soon after my arrival here, and as I do not expect regular answers from you, I shall from time to time, communicate to you, such information from this quarter, as I may consider of sufficient importance to merit your attention.

By a law passed at the last session of Congress, the expenses of the next session of the Legislature of this Territory are to be paid by the United States. The session of our Legislature commences on the first Monday in October next; and, as the members must be paid at the close of the Session, it will be necessary, that the funds appropriated for this purpose, should be immediately forwarded. There will be 40 members in the two houses—their pay is three dollars per day as fixed by law. I understand that Governor Pope, will not return to the Territory, until about the first of October, when it will be, too late for him to make the requisition himself. I have therefore (as I am but just commencing public life) preferred addressing myself directly to you, in order that such steps may be taken by the Treasury Department, as may be deemed most advisable, in compliance with the law.[1]

I find my duty, as prescribed by law, requires me "to record and pre-serve, all the proceedings and papers of the Executive &c"—"and to transmit authentic copies of the same, every six months, to the President of the United States." I would be glad to receive some instructions, as to the extent of this duty. Does it comprehend all the correspondence of the Governor with the Departments at Washington, and with different individuals upon official business in the Territory? Does it require of me, to make out and forward, a list of all Territorial Executive appointments, both civil and military? And am I required to forward copies of all drafts, upon the Treasury of this Territory? I wish to be particularly informed, in order that I may not be accused of any neglect of duty; and at the same time, so as not to burden my communications with matter which would be considered unimportant and unnecessary.[2]

I feel it my duty to mention to you, that there are many suspicious circumstances, connected with the adjudications of the vast number of Spanish claims to lands; which have been confirmed, by the courts of this Territory; and that most persons here, believe that those claims are fraudulent. The claims are themselves suspicious; but that, *all* the Spanish claimants, should *still be alive;* and should have *each one,* taken, the very *same witness with them,* when they made the transfer of their right, to their claims, (after they were confirmed here, by the court;) and that, *this witness,* should have proved this transfer in *every instance,* before the *same Notary Public* in Louisiana, appears to me to be so incredible, that I am compelled to believe, that the whole of these claims, have emanated from one source; *and* that they are *all,* parts of the same grand scheme, to cheat the United States, out of their lands in Arkansas. These transfers or assignments have been received at our land offices; upon which, enter-ies have been made, and then forwarded to the General land Office, for patents. If fraud has been attempted, it is now almost too late to prevent its consumation, without violating the public faith, which may be con-sidered as pledged, to the bona fida purchaser: as the transfers, have in many instances, passed through several hands. The fact, that it is the same individual, who proves the transfer in every instance, may be ascertained, from an inspection of the papers, in the office of Mr. Graham. No patents have yet been received here, and I would certainly recommend, that none should issue, until an effort is made to detect the fraud, and correct the evil, if possible.[3]

I am under the impression, from the peculiar nature of this subject; and also, that, of the Indian Superintendency, that it is highly importat to the welfare of the Territory, that you should be confidentially and fully advised, concerning them, by a personal communication, with some one who can be relied upon, I have no doubt, but that Governor Pope would cheerfully undertake a visit to Washington, if you thought it necessary and adviseable; and I confidently believe, that in a personal interview, he could give you much valuable private information. I believe this, from the circumstance, that altho' he was here, but a few weeks, yet even in that short time, he became convinced, that there were many things relating to the Territory which ought to be placed before the Government in their proper lights. I shall therefore, in order to satisfy you that my views are not erroneous, request Govr. Pope, to write you upon this subject, immediately after he returns to this Territory.

The duties which have devolved upon me, in the absence of Govr. Pope, have been faithfully attended to. I have as yet met with no difficulties. I have had no sickness of consequence in my family. Mrs. Fulton desires to be remembered to her friends, as I also do to mine and believe me to be truly yours

William S. Fulton.

[Endorsed by AJ:] To be laid before the secratary of the Treasury— & the commissioner of the Genl Land office for their perusal and notation—Then before the sec of State that he may answer that part of it, that relates to the Dept of State. A. J

[Endorsed by AJ Donelson:] done accordingly, & returned by Mr. Dickins for file in this office AJD

ALS, DLC (13-1260). *TPUS*, 21:67–69.
1. AJ endorsed this paragraph "sec of the Treasury." A May 1828 law set salaries for Arkansas territorial legislators; on March 2, 1829, Congress appropriated $6,130 for the expense. John Pope arrived in Arkansas with his family on October 7.
2. AJ endorsed this paragraph "Secretary of State." Fulton's description of his duties as territorial secretary is from the June 1812 act establishing a government for Missouri Territory. When Arkansas was separated from Missouri in 1819, Congress assigned its secretary the same duties.
3. AJ endorsed this paragraph "Secretary of the Treasury and Comr. of the Genl land office." On commissioner Graham's recommendation, AJ had already on August 6 appointed Isaac T. Preston to investigate the Arkansas land claims. Graham informed Fulton of this on October 13 (*TPUS*, 21:61–65, 81–82). Ingham submitted Preston's report to AJ on November 9.

From John Coyle

Septr. 8, 1829.

Capt. Coyle, in answer to the note of the President of the United States of this morning, begs to inform him that the Price of the Pew in Mr Post's Church is $26. p An. the time spoken to was about the first of April last.

[Endorsed by AJ Donelson:]

2.　　10.　　$20
1.　　5.　　5
Silvr　　—　　1
This amount enclosed in a letter to Capt. Coyle this 8t. Sept.

Andrew J Donelson

AN, DLC (13-1265). Treasury clerk John Coyle was a ruling elder of Reuben Post's First Presbyterian Church. AJ had previously attended John N. Campbell's Second Presbyterian Church.

To John Nicholson Campbell

Washington Septbr. 10th. 1829.

Dr. Sir

After our interview in the presence of Col. Towson & Mr Donelson, Mr. Key sought one with me, in which he submitted certain propositions as the basis of an accommodation ~~of the difficulty~~ of the difference between you & Major Eaton, the result of which was nothing more than an agreement to suspend any further action upon the subject until the arrival of Mr. Ely who was to be requested to visit this place immediately. Mr. Ely has since arrived but I do not perceive, notwithstanding your failure to sustain the charge against Mrs. Eaton' Character, that you are disposed to make those acknowledgements which it occurs to me an embassador of christ ought on such an occasion to render. This being the fact; and finding, from your letter of the 5th. and from insinuations from Mr. Ely in regard to the supposed reluctance of certain clerks to testify in the case, that my relation to it has been, or may be, misconceived, I have determined to call my Cabinet together at 7 oclock this evening when I have asked Mr Ely to attend, and will be happy also if you will, for the purpose of disclosing to them what has happened, so that whatsoever may be the course of the affair hereafter no misunderstanding of my motives, or agency in it, may exist.

Having ever entertained the highest regard of the moral character of Major Eaton, I brought him into my Cabinet with a full pursuasion that the cause of virtue & religion, which it has been my pride through life to support, would be benefitted by it. I wanted no information to satisfy me of the purity of his character. As my friend, years of intimacy and experience with him supplied the most abundant evidence of it; but a different sentiment entertained by others has been obtruded upon me in a manner which I must say invarably excited my distrust of its sincerity. In this I may be wrong, but the golden rule which requires us to do to others what we would others should do unto us, seems to me so plainly to have required that the cause of such a sentiment, should have been first communicated to Mr Eaton that I cannot yet give up this distrust. It can only be removed by the compleat establishment of the facts upon which they have professed to rest there belief of his criminal intercourse with Mrs. Timberlake. and until this is done Justice to him, myself and the Country, requires that after the proposed counsil with my Cabinet, I shall hold no future conversations with yourself or any one else in relation to this subject. I am very respectfully yr mo. obdt. servant—

Andrew Jackson

ALS, PHi (13-1291); Copy, DLC (75). Parton, 3:202–3. According to Martin Van Buren's account to James A. Hamilton (Hamilton *Reminiscences,* pp. 146–48), AJ's entire Cabinet, Eaton excepted, attended the meeting that evening. AJ Donelson related AJ's correspondence with Campbell and his own interview with Campbell on August 29. Ely recanted his report of the Eatons' misbehavior in New York and praised AJ's handling of the controversy. AJ closed by condemning the stealthy attacks on Eaton and reaffirming his faith in him. He declared "his entire conviction that Mrs. Eaton was a virtuous and persecuted woman" and vowed to wash his hands of the dispute.

To William Berkeley Lewis

Washington Septbr. 10th. 1829—

Dr Sir

youre note of the 8th. instant is before me—To the enquiry in your note whether, "in the spring of the year 1824 at the time when myself Major Eaton & Genl Call were boarding at Major Oneals, & before Congress adjourned, Mrs. Timberlake who lived at her fathers at the time, complained to me of being grossly insulted by Genl Call &c &c"—I reply Mrs. Timberlake did, one day before congress rose in the spring 1824, come to me much agitated and overwhelmed in tears, & complained with much feeling & bitterness that Genl Call had grossly insulted her, by making to *her & urging upon her,* very indelicate propositions, & attempting to inforce them by *great rudeness,* which she was compelled to extricate herself from, by seizing a pair of tongs, or shovel, &c &c. I endeavoured to calm her into silence, by assuring her, I would speak to Genl Call & put an end to a repetition of such conduct, &c &c—on which she became calm & promised to be silent—accordingly, the first opportunity I had, I did speak to Genl Call, and *admonished him* upon the *great impropriety of his conduct,* and from that period Mrs. T. & Genl Call, as far as I know, never spoke to each other—before this happened Mrs. T. & Miss Mary oneal, now Mrs. Randolph, alternately sat at the breakfast table, & dished out the coffee & tea, for us—after this, Mrs. T. never appeared at our table.[1]

When I spoke to Genl Call on this matter he did admit, that believing she was a woman of easy virtue & familiar with others, *whom he named* he had made the advance upon her, which she had firmly resisted, but *he believed* her resistance was merely from *mock modesty*, & not from a sense of virtue—on which, I gave him a *severe lecture* for taking up such ideas of *female virtue* unless, on some positive evidence of his own, of which he acknowledged he had none, only information—and I inforced my admonition by refering him to *the rebuff* he had met with, which I trusted for the future, would guard him from the like improper conduct.

Thus, this matter, as far as I was concerned, rested in my own boosom, until after my return to Tennessee in the spring 1824, when you made certain enquiries of me about Major Eaton & Mrs. Timberlake, and after asking you wherefore you made the inquiry of me, & being informd by you that it was occasioned by information you had Just recd. from Genl Call. I then told you, & have ever since repeated, that I had never seen or heard aught against the chastity of Mrs. Timberlake that was calculated to raise even suspicion of her virtue in the mind of any one who was not under the influence of *deep prejudices, or prone to Jealousy*—that I believed her a virtuous & much injured female—and upon your having communicated to me the intelligence given you by Genl Call, I related to you the complaint made to me by Mrs. T. of the attempt upon & rudeness of Genl Call to her, substantially as I have heretofore stated, & the admonition I had given him, by which I had calmed her feelings & kept Mrs. T. silent on that occasion, as she had threatened to expose him—From the time of that conversation with you, until the late cruel & unprecedented persecution by a combined few to destroy Major & Mrs. Eaton, I have never named it to any one, but lately, first by letter to Genl Call,[2] & then to yourself, & very lately to two or three individuals in confidence[.] yr mo obdt. servt.

Andrew Jackson

ALS and Copy, NN (13-1294); Copy, DLC (37).
1. In October 1824 Mary B. O'Neale (d. 1831), Margaret's sister, had married Philip Grymes Randolph (1801–36), an Army surgeon and later chief clerk in the War Department under AJ.
2. AJ to Call, July 5, above.

From Thomas Tenant et al.

Baltimore 10th. September 1829
Sir
The underwritten Merchants of the City of Baltimore, beg leave, with all due respect, to submit the following Statement to the Executive of the United States.

It is known that a Spanish Force, proceeding from Havana has invaded the Territory of the Mexican Republic, and taken possession of the Town of Tampico, with the avowed design of conquering, or revolutionizing that Country, and reannexing it, if practicable, to the Spanish Monarchy. The Independence of Mexico having been acknowleged by our Government, we have been in the habit of trading freely, & extensively, with it; in the confidence, that the Persons, and property, of American Citizens, would receive all due and proper protection. The amount now exposed to the perils of War, belonging to Citizens of this place, as near as we can estimate, exceeds a Million of Dollars. Its fate is painfully uncertain; and we are impressed with the opinion that much, if not all, may be rescued from danger, and perhaps destruction, by the interposition of Government in the firm and energetic manner which the occasion requires and the Law of Nations will justify. Far be it from us to suggest the measures that it may be necessary to adopt in this emergency—But we have witnessed with pleasure the activity and success of our Squadron in the West Indies in suppressing Piracy, and are persuaded, if they can be spared from this service, that some of our Ships of War may be usefully employed on the Mexican Coast. This we would respectfully solicit, and any other and further protection it may please you to grant to our jeopardized property. We need not intimate that the Danger is imminent, and we are confident a prompt relief will be granted, so far as it is necessary and proper[.] We have the honour to be with profound respect Sir Your humble Servts.

Thos. Tenant
Mattw Bathurst
Mezick & Johnson
D'Arcy & Didier
Saml Etting
Edmd. Didier

[Thirty-one more signatures follow on next page.]

LS, DNA-RG 59 (M179-67); Copy, DNA-RG 45 (M124-120). Tenant (c1768–1836) was a Baltimore merchant trading to Tampico. On July 26 about 4,000 Spanish soldiers from Havana landed in Mexico. They captured Tampico and proclaimed the renewal of the vice-royalty of New Spain. Mexican troops under Antonio López de Santa Anna attacked the Spanish and forced their surrender on September 11. On September 21 Van Buren informed the memorialists that AJ had already ordered available naval forces to the Mexican coast (DNA-RG 59, M40-21; *US Telegraph*, Sep 26).

To James Alexander Hamilton

(Private)

Washington Sept. 11t. 1829

Dear Sir,

It gives me pleasure to acknowlege the receipt of your favor of the 3d. inst. and to thank you for the friendly concern which you have expressed for the state of my health. The fine air & pleasant bath at the Rip Raps have so much braced it, that I feel quite sure I shall have no apology on this score for any inattention to the public business, whatever the world may say or think about me.

It is my steady object to administer the government *according to the laws,* and to advance the good of the country by a faithful discharge of my duty; And should Providence enable me to succeed, or rather to terminate my career far short of your favorable anticipations, I shall be amply rewarded for the cares and labours which it imposes upon me.

My family, who are all now in good health with the exception of Mrs. D. recently delivered of a fine daughter,[1] join me in the most respectful regard to you & your amiable lady & daughter, yr. friend & obt. sert

Andrew Jackson

LS in AJ Donelson's hand, NN (13-1302). Extract, Hamilton *Reminiscences*, p. 144.
 1. Emily T. Donelson gave birth to Mary Rachel (later Mary Emily) Donelson (1829–1905) on August 31.

To John Branch

Secret and Confidential
Washington 12 Sept: 1829

Sir

A sum of twenty thousand dollars from the Contingent fund for foreign intercourse, will be placed at your disposal to be remitted to the Navy Agent of the U. States at Gibraltar. For an amount not exceeding that sum, you will, by a secret instruction to Captain James Biddle, Commander of the United States' Squadron in the Mediterranean, authorise him to draw upon the said Agent to defray the necessary expences incurred under the letter addressed to him, under date the 12th. instant, by the Secretary of State. You will direct him to keep an exact *secret* account of all his expences under that authority, and to transmit the same, in duplicates, to the President of the United States, under a blank cover addressed to the

Secretary of the Navy; and you will, yourself, keep a secret and separate account of this fund, and of all expenditures under it, to be settled under my certificate at the Treasury.

You will please to furnish me, from time to time, with copies of all the instructions and other papers from the Navy Department relating to this subject. I am respectfully Your Obedt. Servant

Andrew Jackson

LC, DNA-RG 59 (M77-162); Copy, DNA-RG 233 (mAJs). *HRDoc* 250, 22d Cong., 1st sess., pp. 74–75 (Serial 221). This same day, Navy captain James Biddle (1783–1848), diplomat David Offley (1779–1838), and Charles Rhind were commissioned to negotiate a commercial treaty with Turkey. Van Buren put Biddle in charge of the commission's expenses, and Branch wrote Biddle and navy agent Richard McCall pursuant to AJ's instructions (Serial 221, pp. 69–76).

From James Gray

Pittsburgh. Septr 13th 1829

Sir

about one month since I made Complaint to the Treasury Department relative to Mr Brackenridge's Conduct as attorney of the United States for this district. my Complaints has been attended to & I have no doubt of the Proffs of the facts being full & satisfactory, as Judge Wilkins yesterday heard the Witnesses to whom I refered & pronounced at once the Horrid Turpitude of Sutch offences[1]—it will next be my duty to apprise you as farr as my observation & Experience Enables me without the Vannity of Persumeing to dictate who Should in all Probabillity be his successor. I have a personal knowledge of most of the Barr in our Western Countys I know a good deal how the Public mind are now Engeanged the virtuous & good of all Parties are Pleased with the Course Pursued—*as to what are sneeringly Termed by your adversaries reform* viz the removals. Some disaffection in Your own camp arrising from Disappointment are uniting with the Clay Partie in Pennsylvania and are Every day ringing in the Peoples Ears a destruction of the Tarriff. another Partie has it, a Philadelphia Partie influence calld *a Sutherlend Dallas & King influence,*[2] in order to Guard against that Extending here I would Beg leave to recommend a young Gentleman Mr Geo W. Buchanan Esqr. a Brother to the Honorle James Buchanan a Representative in Congress from Lancaster. he has resided here Better than a year is very Inteligent Gentlemanly in his manners & Popular with the People as well as his Brother in the middle Counties of the State. I know all from this County Washington & Butler are or may likely apply & I do Candidly assure you his qualifycation are as good or Better & his Popularity very far in advance of any of them—I have taken this Liberty from a desire I have to see your administration

Popular as will as I believe it will be Just. I am no applicant. I have no relatives to recommend—I was Born in the Swett little Isle of the ocean. I feel attachd. to my adopted Country & I Trust I see a guaranty in your administration of returning to our primitive Plainness in the affairs of our Happy Countrey. the good sense of the People will sustain you Hitherto in the removals and I hope & Pray for a Continuance of this sallutary remedey for Purgeing the Chaff from the Wheat, it was not Gripeing necessity that inducd Mr Brackenridge to Play this Part in the Govemnt it was their Coveteousness, Love of money, about 10 years ago he Commencd the Practice of the Law here without mony his father left him nothing. he married a Lady worth 9000 Dollers he never was able to Conduct or Plead an important suit without Employing an assistant. Yet he is now worth 50 or 60 thousand Dollers—these are facts I beg you Excuse me in drawing inferances.[3] I have deemd it my duty this far to recommend or inform you of what I have above stated hopeing if you Judge it irrelavent you will Excuse the Liberty I have taken, wishing you the Enjoyment of all that is Dear To one who so ardently Loves his Countrey[.] I am your Excellency Devoted Servt.

James Gray
4th Street—

ALS, DNA-RG 59 (M639-3).

1. Gray had leveled charges of misconduct against Alexander Brackenridge (1792–1870), federal district attorney for western Pennsylvania and son of Hugh Henry Brackenridge. Gray claimed that Brackenridge had improperly released two men as securities to the United States for the debts of Nathaniel Plummer, deceased, and had then purchased Plummer's farm at the estate sale for a price below its value and the debt due the United States. A Pittsburgh magistrate took depositions on the charges in October. William Wilkins (1779–1865) was the federal district judge for western Pennsylvania and a witness in the case. Brackenridge vehemently denied all charges (DNA-RG 59, M639-3). AJ removed him for Buchanan in October 1830.

2. Congressman Joel Barlow Sutherland (1792–1861), George M. Dallas, and Philadelphia judge Edward King (c1794–1873).

3. Brackenridge married Mary Porter (1804–57).

To [John Christmas McLemore]

My Dear Sir

I promised before this, to send you an account of the refutation of the various slanders *secretly* circulated by a wicked combination, to destroy Major Eaton & his wife—as I expected Major Eaton comes forth like double refined gold, and Mrs Eaton without a single speck upon her virtue—I would have sent it before now but having no person but Saml Hays to copy, and his engagements to the north *lately,* has prevented him from finishing it—This may be well, for *at last Major Eaton* has traced the slander to a responsible source & is carrying on, *it is said,* a serious correspondence with this individual, that from hints given me (for I have no coversation with any on this subjeck) must close shortly—I will just add that in all my life I never read of such a wicked persecution, & so unfounded.[1]

Let Eaton die, or live, he will leave an unspotted character behind him

We are all well, the little daughter growing finely & little Jackson a none such, & all Join in love to you & your amiable family—yr friend

Andrew Jackson

Please give my best respects to my Dr. old friend Judge Overton, & say to him how much I was disappointed in his not getting on here, perhaps providence had a hand in it, *& he orders all things well:* say, with my compliments to her father & family, to Miss Berryhill that Mr Moss arrived here a few days after she left us, & made many enquiries after her, & expressed many regrets in not overtaking her here &c &c &c—present me to Mr Hill & all friends[2]

A. J.

ALS, NHi (13-1314).

1. On September 12, Eaton wrote John N. Campbell demanding that he either prove or retract his story of Mrs. Eaton's miscarriage. Campbell in reply refused to speak except in a court of law, where he would appear "with perfect confidence as to the result." Responding on September 16, Eaton scorned the idea of settling a personal wrong with a lawsuit and branded Campbell a liar and a coward (DLC-75).

2. John Overton had left Nashville for Washington in early September, but turned back at Knoxville when his horse gave out.

To Martin Van Buren

Septbr. 15th. 1829—

The secratary of State will address Mr Poinsett a letter upon the subject of the illegal seisure of our citizens effects & the murder of our citizen—you can inform Mr Poinsett that we have augmented our Naval force in those seas; & on the West India Station[.] yr friend

Andrew Jackson

ANS, DNA-RG 59 (M179-67). Before evacuating Tampico to the Spanish invaders, Mexican troops had reportedly seized the money of foreign merchants and arrested and killed Francisco Mazas, a Spanish-born U.S. citizen accused of communicating with the Spanish army. Van Buren instructed Poinsett on September 18 to confirm the facts and, if true, demand redress from Mexico for this "wanton outrage" (*HRDoc* 351, 25th Cong., 2d sess., pp. 34–35, Serial 332).

To Samuel Delucenna Ingham

Septbr. 16th. 1829—

My Dr. Sir

I now send for your consideration a project for adding security to our revenue, & at the same time improveing our Navy of which I spoke to you, the other day—would like to know, whether you think the change profitable, and whether in your opinion, it ought to be adopted—I have thought it would be an improvement, & therefore suggest it to you.

The project.

The Revenue Cutters to be built in our Navy yards & not by contract—When the Secratary of the Treasury wants a Cutter, to make requisition on the Navy department, the expence of which to be charged to the revenue service. The Cutters ought to be the very best sailers, & to be such, must be on the very best model, and can be built out of the refuse timber left from our seventy fours, Frigates, & Sloops of war; this would be oconomy; besides it is alledged our Cutters are of a poor class & dull sailers, which must be injurious to the safety of our revenue, as it is reported to me, that they are outsailed by all bay craft, and our merchantmen—Lieutenants of the Navy ought to be given the command of our Cutters, & they subordinate officers taken from the midshipmen of our Navy, and when detailed for this duty, to be under the exclusive controle, command, & orders of the Secratary of the Treasury. This would be giving a *stronger guard* to our revenue than the present mode, whilst we are improving our Navy, the strong arm of our national defence—Whilst by this change we are making a saving to the nation, we are extending employment to our naval officers, where they will be improving in seamanship, and gaining a knowledge of our coasts, Inlets, & harbours, & when not employed in the active duty of guarding our revenue, can be usefully employed in surveying the coast, Inlets, & harbours of their respective cruising grounds. respectfully submitted for the consideration of the Sec of the Treasury

Andrew Jackson

ALS, CtNlCG (13-1317). Before writing Ingham, AJ composed a draft of this project in his memorandum book (below). Thirteen new revenue cutters of the larger, faster *Morris* class were built between 1830 and 1833 at New York and Washington. The Treasury Department began placing Navy officers on cutters in 1830 but dropped the experiment in 1832.

To John Randolph

Washington Septr. 16th. 1829

Dear Sir

The office of Envoy Extraordinary & Minister Plenipotentiary to Russia will soon become vacant, & I am anxious that the place should be filled by one of the most capable and distinguished of our fellow citizens.

The great & rapidly increasing influence of Russia in the affairs of the world renders it very important that our representative at that Court should be of the highest respectability, and the expediency of such a course at the present moment is greatly increased by circumstances of a special character. Among the number of our statesmen from whom the selection might with propriety be made, I do not know one better fitted for the station, on the score of talents and experience in public affairs, or possessing stronger claims upon the favourable consideration of his country than yourself[.] Thus impressed, and entertaining a deep & grateful sense of your long & unceasing devotion to sound principles & the interest of the people, I feel it a duty to offer the appointment to you.

In discharging this office I have the double satisfaction of seeking to promote the public interest whilst performing an act most gratifying to myself on account of the personal respect & esteem which I have always felt and cherished towards you.

It is not foreseen that any indulgence as to the period of your departure, which may be required by a due regard to your private affairs, will conflict with the interests of the Mission: & I sincerely hope that no adverse circumstances may exist sufficient to deprive the country of your services. I have the honour to be with great respect your mo. ob. Sert.

(signed) Andrew Jackson

Copy in Randolph's hand, DLC-John Randolph Papers (mAJs). Draft in Martin Van Buren's hand, DLC; Copies, NcD, Nc-Ar, PHi (13-1327). A longtime congressman and senator from Virginia, Randolph (1773–1833) had been a strident critic of the Adams administration. He wrote back accepting the mission on September 24. He was nominated and confirmed as minister to Russia in May 1830, replacing Henry Middleton.

To Martin Van Buren

Septbr. 16th. 1829—

My Dr. Sir

I enclose the letter to Mr. John Randolph of Roanoke open, that you may read, seal, & forward it to him, with such sentiments in a letter of your own & explanatory, as you may deem proper to ensure his services. yr friend

Andrew Jackson

ALS, DLC-Van Buren Papers (13-1342). Van Buren wrote Randolph on September 17, urging him to accept the Russian mission and pledging "any facilities &c which the state of your health, or private affairs may require" (Randolph Papers, DLC).

From Thomas Sisk et al.

To the president of the United States—

Your memorialist citizens of Jackson county State of Alabama, and occupants of lands belonging to the genl. Government, above the age of twenty one years, have with some concern ascertained that it has been intimated by the commissioner of the Genl. land office at Washington to the genl. Surveyor of Alabama, that the lands on which they reside will be offered for sale sometime in the month of next February—Your memorialists have with much pleasure marked the annual increase of the number of supporters of the bill which was introduced, and has been so ably advocated by the Hon. Thos. H. Benton, and which amongst other salutary measures contemplates pre-emption rights to occupants of public lands—From the progress of the bill at the several successive sessions, at which its measures have been advocated, and its near approach to a final passage at the last, your memorialists with strong ground of hope anticipate its passage at the next—Your memorialists settled on the lands which they now occupy if not with the express approbation of government, at least with its connivance and implied consent, and have at all times in this situation been recognized as citizens, and as such have discharged all demands made on them by the genl. & state governments—They have converted the wilderness into cornfields, and do now feel desirous to continue proprietors of the improvements made with their own hands, if the lands can be obtained for a fair price—Their means with which to purchase are limited, and they are liable to be oppressed if thrown upon the mercy of speculators under the auction system—your memorialists would therefore gladly participate, in the benefits resulting from a change of the auction, for the pre-emption right and entry system, and do respectfully ask as president of the United States, having the control of the time of selling public lands, that you do not advertise those on which they reside for sale, until it be ascertained whether or not the next congress will change the system, and if so that the advantages of the change may be extended to them—Your memorialists are not sensible of any injury which would result to the government from a postponement of the sales of those lands for the short space of one year, and therefore ask such postponement with an expectation that it will be unhesitatingly granted—

Thomas Sisk
Hiram Sisk
Wm. Morgan
James Duncan
Henry McElyea

[More than 700 additional names follow.]

Copy, DNA-RG 49 (13-1337). This petition was forwarded to AJ on September 16 by Samuel B. Moore, who represented Jackson County in the Alabama senate. AJ referred it to George Graham. Graham wrote Moore on October 6 declining to postpone the Jackson County sale, partly on grounds that the proceeds were obligated by treaty to the support of schools for Cherokee children (DNA-RG 49, M25-24). The sale was proclaimed on October 5, 1829, and held February 15, 1830.

Pre-emption was the policy of allowing those who had settled on public lands that were not yet open for sale to purchase their holdings at the minimum price in advance of the public auction. Although such settlers were technically trespassers, Congress had granted pre-emption rights in some particular circumstances, and agitation for pre-emption had risen in connection with Benton's graduation proposal to reduce land prices. A general law that for the first time granted a 160-acre pre-emption right to every current occupant of public lands passed Congress in May 1830, too late for the Jackson County squatters.

To Martin Van Buren

Sept 1829—

no complaint has ever been made that I recollect of against Governor Cass, nor has the administration any idea of removing him, unless, on the settlement of his accounts, he should prove a defaulter, & you know the rule is, friend or foe, being a defaulter, must go—I have ordered all accounts to be settled & audited—I have not heard it even suggested, that Govr. Cass is a defaulter[.] yr friend

Andrew Jackson

[Endorsed by AJ:] no such thing has ever come to my knowledge   A. J.

[Endorsed by Van Buren:] Mr Van Buren will review the enclosed from the President at his convenience. There is no such application that Mr V Buren knows of—Sept 17th. 29

ANS, DLC-Van Buren Papers (13-1349).

To Isaac Wayne

Washington Septb. 17th. 1829—

My Dear Sir,

A letter this day recd. from our mutual friend the Honble. James Buchannon of Lancaster Pa. has brought to my recollection the inestimable present which you made me of the likeness of your renowned father, Major Genl Wayne, with a specimen of his autography as early as the 3rd. of July 1777. It has given me much pain to learn that you have not received my acknowledgement of a present which I so highly prize—I thought I had written it shortly after the receipt of your letter, but if I did, it must have miscarried, or have been omitted to be mailed.

On turning to your letter I found the following endorsement upon it. "Col Wayne of chester County Pa. enclosing a striking likeness of his father, Genl Wayne, and his autographical letter dated July 3rd. 1777, to be respectfully answered, and carefully preserved as an evidence of the sincere respect I entertain for the donor, as well as the veneration in which I hold the memory of his deceased Father Genl. Wayne."

They deserve Sir, and shall have a place by the side of some remembrances of Genl. Washington with which I hav[e] been honored by the kindness of his friends.[1] Having fought together for the independence and liberty of their country, posterity will delight to have the opportunity which such remnants will afford, of contemplating their conduct, and venerating their memories.

Accept Dr. Sir, the assurances of my best wishes for your health and future happiness, and believe me very respectfully yr Servant

Andrew Jackson

ALS, PU (13-1353). LS draft in AJ Donelson's hand dated September 16, DLC (37). Isaac Wayne (1772–1852), son of Revolutionary general Anthony Wayne, was a lawyer and a Pennsylvania congressman, 1823–25.

1. While a U.S. senator in 1823–25, AJ had been presented with a telescope, a china plate, and a pair of pistols once belonging to George Washington.

To Chesed P. Montgomery

Sept. 19.

Sir

your letter enclosing your recommendation is recd. and notwithstanding your very improper conduct to myself and Major Donelson, still you have nothing to fear from any opposition of ours, against your obtaining employment as a teacher or clerk—To err is human, to forgive is divine, & we freely forgive you in hopes of good conduct in future—yrs respectfully

AL copy, DLC-Donelson Papers (13-1365). On September 16 Montgomery had written asking AJ's help in procuring a government office and enclosing a recommendation.

From Samuel Houston

Cherokee Nation.
19th Sept 1829.

My dear Sir,

I am verry feeble, from a long spell of fever, which lasted me some 38 days, and had well nigh closed the scene of all my mortal cares, but I thank my God that I am again cheered by the hope of renewed health. I would not write at this time but that I can not deny myself the pleasure of tendering to you my heartfelt acknowledgement for your kind favor, which reached me, when I was barely able to peruse its contents.[1] It was a cordial to my spirits, and cheered me in my sickness. From the course which I had pursued in relation to the cause of my abandoment of society—my absolute refusal to gratify the inquiring world—my entire silence, because it comported, with my notions of honor, and a willingness to sacrifice myself, rather than do violence to my principles—I had a right to suppose that, the world would acquiesce in the sacrifice, nor could I of right claim of you, a departure from what I supposed the general influence of my destiny. You have acted upon the great scale which prescribes no limits to true greatness, but boundless benevolence, and universal philanthropy. Had a Sceptre been dashed at my feet, it would not have afforded the same, pleasure, which I derived from the proud consciousness, not only that I deserved, but that I *possessed your* confidence!

The elevation of your station, and your renown, which could acquire no additional lustre from official distinction; contrasted with that of a man, who had ceased to be all that he ever had been, in the worlds eye; was such as would have justified you; in any inference, the most damning, to his character, and prejudicial to his integrity of heart! You disregarded the standard, calculations of mankind, and acted from an impulse, peculiar to yourself!

The solicitude which you have so kindly manifested, for my future welfare can not fail to inspire me with a proper sense of additional obligation to you. To become a missionary among the Indians is rendered impossible, for a want of that Evangelical change of heart, so absolutely necessary, to a man who assumes the all important character, of proclaiming to a lost world, the mediation of a blessed Savior! To meliorate the condition of the Indians, to suggest improvements to their growing institutions—to prevent fraud, and peculation, on part of the Goverments Agents among them; and to direct the feelings of the Indians in kindness to the Government, and inspire them with confidence in its justice, and magnanimity towards the Red People; have been objects of my constant solicitude, and attention, since I have been among them!

Your suggestion on the subject of my location in Arkansas has received my serious attention, and I have concluded, that it would not be best for me to adopt the course. In that Territory there is no field for distinction—it is fraught with *factions;* and if my object were to obtain wealth; it must be done by fraud, & peculation upon the Government, and many perjuries would be necessary to its effectuation! Were I disposed to abandon my present seclusion, I would submit to you, if it would not be more advantageous, for me to locate in Natchez. I am well-known to the first men of that state—I was presented there under your kind auspicies, on your last visit to that country, and I would rally around me very many Tennesseeans who have migrated thither![2] You can think of all the advantages presented by me, and the many more, which will present themselves to your mind!

When I left the world I had persuaded myself that I would lose all care, about the passing political events, of the world, as well as those of my own country, but it is not so—for as often as I visit Cant. Gibson, where I can obtain news Papers, I find that my interest is rather increased than diminished—It is hard for an old Trooper, to forget the *note* of the *Bugle!* Having been so actively engaged for years past in politics, it is impossible to lose all interest in them for some time to come, should I remain in my present situation! I am not so vain as to suppose, myself so important to the world, or to my own country, as to believe that my location on earth can, have any important influence upon its destinies, and therefore the claims, of Patriotism and duty to the land of my birth rest easy!

If we are to judge of the future by the past, it might so happen, were I settled in a state; that I might render my aid in some future political struggle between usurpation, and the rights of the people, in wresting power from the hands of a corrupt usurper, and depositing it, where the spirit of the constitution, and the will of the people would wish it placed. These considerations are not without their influence, for I must ever love that country and its institutions, which give Liberty and happiness to my *kindred,* and *friends!* And these blessings can only be preserved by vigilance and Virtue!

I am rejoiced that you have cleaned the stalls of Washington, as well as others! Get rid of all the *wolves* and the barking of Puppies, can never destroy the *fold!* It amuses me to see the leaden pointed arrows shot at you by Gales & Co[3]—I trust in God, the Edifice which you have so nobly reared, and are now finishing, will receive, your own peculiar impress, and be worthy of your renown!

I pray you to salute your family for me, and be assured, of my sincere devotion & friendship. Truly your friend

Sam Houston

P.S. I hope to take, and send you, between this and christmas, some fine Buffaloe meat for your Christmas dinner, or at furthest, by the 8th of Jany!

H.

ALS, DLC (37).
1. AJ to Houston, June 21, above.
2. AJ, Houston, and other dignitaries visited Natchez on January 4, 1828, on their way to a celebration of the Battle of New Orleans.
3. Joseph Gales, Jr. (1786–1860) was co-publisher with his brother-in-law William W. Seaton of the anti-Jackson *National Intelligencer.*

From Marcus Morton

Taunton Mass. Sept. 19. 1829

Sir,
   You have many friends desirous to promote your personal & political welfare and willing to labour in support of your Administration; but I fear very few who have independence enough to inform you of its dangers and to point out its errors. This I deem the highest attribute of friendship.
   I have no reason to expect that the communication which I am about to make will derive any weight from the name of its author. I do not flatter myself that my person or character has any place in your recollection. This I do not regret, for I wish that my suggestions should rest solely upon their own merits. My object is to benefit you and I intend to state only what I know to be true and what I believe to be both just & reasonable.
   Altho many of my remarks will apply to the other New England States as well as to Massachusetts yet my intention is to confine them principally to the latter. I have as good an opportunity to know the feelings and opinions of the Citizens of this State as any man in it. My official duty carries me thro. every part of it, once or twice a year. I am favourably situated for observation; and I trust am not an inattentive observer. I desire no favour from the Government for myself or my friends. I am influenced solely by an ardent wish to see our Country & its Democratic Institutions flourish under your Administration; and especially to see that conducted on principles in themselves righteous & which of course will ensure its prosperity & glory.
   Although upon your election a great majority of the people of this Comth. were opposed to you; yet they were governed principally by local feelings and had no settled hostility to yourself or your friends.[1] They saw

your elevation with a secret hope that in your Administration they should find good cause to be satisfied with it and to change their opposition into support. They were disposed to look upon its measures with favour & I confidently anticipated that within one year a majority of Mass. wd. be its friends. A class of politicians determined to oppose it at all events predicted a course of violence & proscription, while its friends expected one of dignified moderation as well as energetic firmness. The latter trust that a falsification of their predictions would be the sure means of raising your friends into popular favour. It would be aside from my principal purpose to make any remarks upon the general course of your measures. I have no reason to doubt that yourself & your Cabinet understand the genius of the people and the wishes of your Friends throughout the Union, a thousand times better than we can here. It is however the duty of real friendship to suggest that there is a strong impression among your friends in this Section of the Country that those who have made personal applications have been too successful, and that we cannot but fear that sometimes the noise of hungry Office seekers and the clamour of brawling Editors of Newspapers have in some degree been mistaken for the sober voice of the people.

But in relation to Mass. you will permit me to assure you that the voice of the Jackson party in many cases has been unheard & their wishes disregarded.

It was the general wish of this party & the expectation of both parties that the Collector of Boston, the Attorney of the District—the Post-Masters of Boston & Salem should be removed. There were not only strong political, but other strong reasons for this. The selection of their successors was judicious.[2] Although it may be the very best man who could be found was not appointed in each case; yet in view of all circumstances the Government could not have done better. With these changes the public would have been satisfied. Here prudence would have dictated a pause. It is true there were a very few other cases in which for local or other special reasons, changes might have been justifiable & perhaps expedient. But every step which *has* been taken beyond these has been an injury to your friends and a benefit to your enemies—a source of joy to the latter & of grief to the former.

To illustrate my remarks, I must beg leave to refer you to particular instances which have occurred under my immediate observation & in relation to which I personally know every fact which I am about to state. I refer to these cases not only for illustration but in entire confidence that the gross errors which have been committed will be corrected.

The County of Bristol in which I reside contains more than one twelfth of the population of the State. In it a large proportion of the men of talents, education, wealth & general respectability were your decided friends. And we anticipated, that at the first election after your Administration had gone into operation, we should have commanded a majority. But what has been our disappointment. Instead of advancing we have retrogaded. This is owing to the removals & appointments among ourselves. In these we have been disappointed & mortified.

There are, in the County, four offices only deemed of any importance. The Collector of N. Bedford the Collector of Dighton—the Post Master of New Bedford & the Post Master of Taunton. In relation to three of these, it was the wish of the Jackson party—in which they were nearly unanimous—that there should be no removals. There were very strong reasons for the removal of the Collector of Dighton and had he been removed or retained, had there been no other removal, no complaint would have been heard from any quarter.

The Post Master of New Bedford has not *yet* been removed and so far there is not the slightest complaint.[3]

The Post Master of Taunton gave general satisfaction and altho. he had prefered Mr Adams to yourself yet he never had been violent or abusive and it was the unanimous wish of the Jackson party that he should be continued   He has recently been displaced without our knowledge and a man altogether more objectionable than himself appointed in his stead.[4]

The Jackson party in this town, are at least as respectable as their opponents. They pay at least one half the postage   Had they known or suspected that a removal was necessary or intended they would promptly have reccommended a candidate as competent & respectable as the one appointed.

It is said the cause of the removal of the late Post-Master was delinquency in rendering accounts or paying over money. Of this we know nothing. If it be so the removal cannot be complained of. And we do not now, in any event request the restoration of the late Post-Master. But we most earnestly complain of the appointment of Mr Lord. We object to him solely on political grounds. He was distinguished for his opposition to all the Republican Administrations of our Country; for his support of the election of Mr Adams for his violent opposition to the late war—for his support of the Hartford Convention its members & friends, for his personal abuse of General Jackson & his lamented Lady and for his active exertions against the Jackson electoral ticket at the last election.[5] There is no reason to believe that he has changed his sentiments on any of these points. We think the P. M. General has been grossly imposed upon & that when disabused he will correct the mistake. But if we are mistaken in this and the Administration have determined that we must have such a man for our P. Master we will submit to it and will support them as well as we can wherein they are right & make the best apology we can for them wherein they are wrong. But we must not be asked to justify such appointments nor expected to prevent the alienation of the affection & confidence of the mass of the people.

The appointment of the Collector of N. Bedford is no more justifiable. The former Collector was an old & tried Republican of the Jefferson

School. He had supported all the Republican Administrations; actively supported the war & resisted the Hartford Convention. He was particularly friendly to yourself & uncommonly active & successful, in conversation & in writing in defending all your conduct & in extolling your memorable & praiseworthy deeds. It is true that he gave a moderate support to the late Administration & in the election preferred Mr Adams to yourself; but had he been continued in Office, I have no doubt, he would have given a reasonable support to your Administration and wd. have done altogether more to aid it than his successor can or will. But he is displaced and while we deeply regret the act, we think it would be unreasonable to ask his restoration. We will only say that there were not five Jackson men in the County nor ten in the State who wished his removal. I believe their wishes were communicated but seem to have been overlooked.

The appointment of his successor was peculiarly unfortunate. Had the selection been made with a view to render your Administration unpopular, I do not believe another competent man could have been found who would have so effectually done it.

Mr Williams always was of the old federal School—opposed all the Republican Administrations & the war—supported the Hartford Convention its members & friends, and opposed your election till just before the contest was over and untill your success had become certain. To give you a view of the merits of this shuffling politician & of his claim to your confidence, I must beg you to bear with me while I refer to some details, in themselves uninteresting but illustrative of his character.[6]

It was a great object with the Adams party to elect Mr Webster into the U. S. Senate. In 1827 the House repeatedly elected Mr Webster and the Senate elected & persisted in electing John Mills a staunch Republican and Friend of the Administration. The two branches being unable to agree no election was completed that year. It became necessary for Mr Adams Friends to procure a change in the majority of the Senate   The County of Bristol was selected as the principal scene of operations and Mr Williams as the proper agent for the work. He never had the confidence of the people and could not by any fair means have obtained one quarter of the votes. But intrigue & artifice were resorted to. There was a violent local contest in the County as to the place of holding the Courts. By pledging himself to the North to aid them and to the South to aid them and by giving repeated pledges to support Mr Adams, he succeeding in getting nearly one half of the votes. No one having a majority of the whole as our constitution requires, he was elected by the Legislature. With his aid Mr Webster was elected. He supported Mr Adams election awhile, but before his year expired, avowed himself an advocate for your election and has since professed to support your Administration. The indignation at this double breach of trust was universal and neither party has any confidence in him. Such is the man whose appointment to the most important office in the County your friends are called upon to justify. Upon his appointment he dismissed all the subordinate Officers who were old Republicans and filled their places with ultra federalists.[7]

The supporters of your Administration in this State and in New England are almost to a man Jeffersonian Republicans. With the exception of some dozen or half dozen highminded honourable Federalists, who have acted with us from principle, all the men of that description who have joined us are needy, unprincipled Office seekers—the filth and scum of their party.

The great body of Republicans who have laboured in your support amidst discouragement abuse and persecution, cannot well brook the appointment of men of this description. They have not yet become sufficiently established in their attachment to your Administration and in their confidence in its democratic principles to see such men as Lord & Williams preferred to the veterans of their own party without manifesting pretty strong indications of disaffection.

The effect of appointments of this description upon the people may be seen in our neighboring States. In Vermont we have retrogaded. In Maine where the local appointments have been more judicious than any other State in New England, unless New Hampshire be an exception, and where but for some disappointment and disaffection at the course of appointments among our Friends we should have had a decided majority, I have great reason to fear we shall loose the election. But our near neighbours of Rhode Island have been entirely broken down by the selection of a list of desperate unprincipled office seeking Federalists to fill the Providence custom House &c. Last spring we got one half the votes, but last month only one quarter.

The plain truth is that the Democrats and the Democrats alone in New England can be relied upon to give any efficient support to your Administration. And they cannot be brought to approve of the appointment to office of the worst part of the federal party.

We know not by what means or through what influence Mess. Williams & Lord obtained their appointments. But the interest of the Republican party and the unequivocal voice of all your friends here require the recal of these appointments. We know it will be a disagreeble act; but at the same time we also know that it will be an act of magnanimity which will shed lustre upon any character & that a high minded man when imposed upon needs only to be informed of the deception to correct the error.

I will only add one word in relation to the Dighton Office. It is of less importance than either of the others. But why this Officer should be retained while the others were removed has seemed to us unaccountable. He is not a man of character standing or respectability. He has been unceasing in his opposition to your election and in his gross & vulgar abuse of yourself and all your friends. The man recommended to succeed him, is now a respectable member of our Senate, a man of high character & great worth & respectability, and ever has been an old school Republican & an early & uniform supporter of your election

Why such men as Freeman & Hodges should be removed and such a man as S. Williams retained is to me incomprehensible. But still more incomprehensible & extraordinary is it that such men as Lord & Williams should be selected and such a man as Wood neglected.[8]

I must now beg you to pardon this unreasonable intrusion upon your attention and to be assured that my sole motive has been to benefit yourself and your friends and my sole object to give you correct information on which to exercise your own sound judgement. With sentiments of the highest respect and the most sincere regard I am Your faithful Servant

Marcus Morton

LC, MH-H (mAJs); Photocopy of LC, MHi (13-1367). Morton (1784–1864) was a justice of the Massachusetts Supreme Court, a former congressman and lieutenant governor, and a member of the Henshaw faction of Massachusetts Jacksonians. He was the Jacksonian and Democratic candidate for governor every year from 1828 to 1843, winning in 1839 and 1842.

1. Adams carried Massachusetts in 1828 by a margin of nearly five to one.

2. These changes were made in March and April. AJ supplanted Boston collector Henry Dearborn with David Henshaw and district attorney George Blake with Andrew Dunlap (1794–1835). Boston postmaster Aaron Hill (c1758–1830) was replaced by Nathaniel Greene, and Salem postmaster Joseph E. Sprague (c1783–1852) by Ebenezer Putnam

3. Richard Williams was postmaster at New Bedford.

4. Joseph Lyman Lord was appointed Taunton postmaster in August, replacing David C. Hodges.

5. The Hartford Convention met in December 1814 during the War of 1812, attended by delegates from the five New England states. Unaware of the just-signed Treaty of Ghent, the convention condemned the Madison administration, the war, and southern domination of the government, presented a list of grievances and proposed constitutional amendments, and recommended another convention if its demands went unmet. With the peace, the convention became a symbol of nearly treasonable ultra-Federalism.

6. AJ had appointed Lemuel Williams (1782–1869) collector at New Bedford in place of Russel Freeman (c1780–1842). Williams declared his support for AJ at a March 7, 1828, meeting of "Jackson Federal Republicans," a rival faction to Henshaw's.

7. Daniel Webster was elected senator in June 1827 after a deadlock in the previous legislative session between the pro-Adams incumbent Elijah Hunt Mills and opposing candidate John Mills (1787–1862) had left the seat temporarily vacant. A contest between New Bedford and Taunton over the Bristol County seat led to an 1828 law providing that court sessions would alternate between the two.

8. In October, AJ removed Dighton collector Seth Williams and appointed state senator William Wood (c1772–1833).

To John Coffee

Washington Septbr. 21th. 1829—

My Dr. Genl.

I have recd. your letter of the 6th instant convaying the malancholy intelligence of the death of your sweet little daughter Emily—permit me to tender to you & Polly, my sincere & heartfelt condolence on this mournful occasion—we ought not to mourne for the dead, but the living, for he that giveth life hath aright to take it away, and on all such occasions we ought to be prepared to say, blessed be the name of the lord—you ought to be perfectly resigned to her death, when you recollect the reply of our saviour to his deciples, "let (says he) little children come unto me, for such is the kingdom of heaven."[1] She is a little angel, now with my Dr wife (her aunt) in the boosom of our saviour enjoying that exquisite happiness, bought by the death & sufferings of our dear redemer on the cross, an atonement made for sinners, that they might not perish, but have eternal life, by repentance & belief in him—what a cheering thought to all the afflicted here below, & the only one that makes life supportable to me under my afflictions, & arduous labours; that I am hastening to that bourne, from whence no traveller returns,[2] with a hope, that I shall unite again with my Dear Sainted wife in bliss, in the mansions of the skies, "where I will bath my troubled soul, in seas of heavenly ~~bliss~~ rest, & not a wave of trouble roll, across my peaceful breast."[3] I hope & trust that you will find consolation in the reflection that your dear little Emily is in paradise in the boosom of her saviour, enjoying all that happiness with her aunt that *the presence* of *her saviour gives, which must be unutterable.* It gives me much pleasure to hear that my dear little namesake,[4] has perfectly recovered, & that your family now enjoy health.

I had retired a short time since to the Rip Raps, for the benefit of my health, which had become impaired from the weight of my labours, and distress of mind—I returned with much improved health, in an absence of thirteen days, but the accumulated ~~labour~~ business in my absence has kept me so much confined since my return, that it is beginning to effect my health again—still I trust in a kind providence, that he will sustain me under my labours & other troubles, & carry me through the duties assigned me to the glory of his kingdom, & the prosperity & happiness of our country—& whensoever my god may call me hence, I will be prepared to obay his call with perfect submission to his will. My troubles have been great, my bereavement at the time it was afflicted, as much as I could bear—if my Dr wife had lived she would saved me from much disquietude & embarrassment, both of body, & of mind—but my god willed it, & I yield to his decrees with all due submission—But my Dear Genl, If he will permit me once more to retire to the Hermitage, I will spend the ballance of my days in perfect retirement, at the tomb of my dear departed wife.

I sincerely regret the untoward conduct of Hutchings, and the company & council he has got into, I well know, will not improve him—all things considered, I think you had better send him on to me, & I will endeavour to controul him by placing him at the Roman Catholick College in George Town—I have Just recd. a letter from my son from Nashville—he says he & Mr Earle will set out about the 18th. of next month, for this place, & he says he will try to bring Hutchings on with him—I write my son by this days mail on this subject & have requested him to notify you of his departure from Nashville and I have to request, if you reach Nashville before my son & Hutchings sets out, to place in Hutchings hands, *Just* as much as will serve him for pockett mony untill he gets *here,* placing the ballance in the hand of my son, who I have desired to receipt for it in my name and as my agent as guardian to be applied to Hutchings education—we must act with great care, for from his disposition shewn, & the company he now keeps, we may expect dificulty in settling the estate with him—Therefore for your safety, as well as my own, I wish the receipt for the $500 dollars I have requested you to furnish my son to bring Hutchings on here, to be specifically mentioned for his expences here & for his education—

I am much pressed with business and must close this letter, requesting my warmest affection to be presented to yr poor afflicted wife, & all your family—We are all well, poor Mary has felt her bereavement severely, but I have tendered to her all the consolation in my power "that I would be a father to her as long as I lived"[5]—Emily is doing well, is up, & her daughter Mary Rachel is a fine child & growing well—nothing could give me more pleasure than to see you, I trust, providence will permit this before I die—affectionately yr friend

Andrew Jackson

private
PS. Our young friend Saml. J. H. is to be married in the month of Novbr. next at charleston So. C. Mrs. Genl Thos. Pinckney, the granmother of Miss M., wishing it there—all parties fully consenting—he is doing well—A J.[6]

ALS, NcD (13-1393). Coffee's infant daughter Emily (1828–29) had died on August 7.
   1. Matthew 19:14 and Luke 18:16.
   2. *Hamlet,* 3.1.89–90.
   3. From the Isaac Watts hymn, "The Hopes of Heaven our Support under Trials on Earth."
   4. Andrew Jackson Coffee (1819–91).
   5. Mary Ann Eastin's father William had died on August 23.
   6. Frances Motte Middleton Pinckney (1763–1843), grandmother of Samuel J. Hays's fiancée Frances Middleton, had married as her second husband Thomas Pinckney (1750–1828), South Carolina statesman and AJ's commanding general during the Creek War.

To Joel Henry Dyer

Washington City Septbr. 21rst. 1829—
Dr Sir
   I have received your letter of the 1rst. instant, asking me to Join in a memorial to the Legislature to release the debt of the State against your deceased father: were it proper in my present situation to do so, it would

afford me pleasure. But placed as I am, exception might be taken to any interference by the Executive chief magistrate with the local concerns of the State. The Service your father so cheerfully rendered in the most critical times of the late war, the privations & wounds that he met & suffered without dismay or cowering under them, endeared him to me, as a gallant and servicable officer. The State of Tennessee has cause to remember him with pride and pleasure; and if, consistantly with propriety & public duty, her Representatives can do any thing to assist & releive his bereaved wife and children, I have every confidence that it will with cheerfulness be done.

With my kind regard to your mother and family, & kind solicitations to you, & your family. I am very respectfully yours &c

Andrew Jackson

[Endorsed by AJ:] Copy of a letter to Major R. H. Dyer in answer to his of the 1rst. instant—answered 21rst. Septbr. 1829—

ALS draft, DLC (37). In 1825 Robert Henry Dyer (c1744–1826), who had commanded Tennessee volunteers in the Creek and Seminole campaigns, borrowed $3,000 from the state to build a canal. AJ mistakenly addressed this draft to him rather than to his son Joel Henry Dyer (1801–66), a lawyer. Robert's widow Susan Mitchell Dyer (b. 1779) had made a similar plea to AJ in 1827. In 1833 the Tennessee legislature authorized Joel to raise $6,000 by a lottery to support Robert's heirs and repay the loan.

To Andrew Jackson, Jr.

Washington Septbr. 21rst. 1829—

My Dr Son

I had the pleasure this morning to receive yours of the 1rst. instant, and am happy to find that you & Mr Earle will be on about the 18th. proximo—and that all things on my farm are going on well—I regret to hear the great loss of horses & oxen, I would like to have a full statement on this subject, for if it has happened from neglect in the overseer, I will have a Just deduction from his wages—if not from neglect, but from unavoidable accident, then am I willing to submit to it—but if from Mr Steels neglect, he as a Just man, will voluntarily make an offer of such deduction of wages, as he thinks this neglect has produced to me. god forbid, that if his neglect or acts has not been the cause of the losses sustained, if he offered it, I should not accept it—Therefore I have written Mr Steel some time since on this subject & requesting a Just statement of the horses & oxen lost. This I want him to furnish, & you to bring on with you, that I may Judge myself of the matter—Stockly Donelson says his neglect produced this loss, as some of the oxen fell dead in the waggon halling grain from Winstons place.[1]

I expected the result you name with Flora[2]—she is a fine little girl—the daughter of my deceased friend & I esteem her much—but as I told you she has give herself up to coquettry & I warned you of the fact—treat her with all kindness, but I assure you I am happy at the result; as I seldom ever saw a coquett, make a good wife, & when you marry, if ever, I wish you to marry a lady who will make a good wife, & I, a good daughter, as my happiness depends much upon the prudence of your choice—Therefore I am happy you are clear of your little engagement with Flora—and all I have to request is, that you will engage in no other without first obtaining my advice—I had no wish to interfere with your choice, & particularly when you stated, there had been some little engagement—you know I have councilled you from your childhood, to make no promises, or engagements, but what you punctually perform, therefore before engagements are formed, or promised made, it ought to be on mature reflection, and when made religiously performed—I will only add I am happy you are now free from all engagements & I trust you will keep so untill you advise with your father on this interesting subject on which your peace & happiness throt. life so much depends.

I have recd. a letter from *my friend* Genl Coffee This morning, which makes it necessary that Hutchings be brought on, he cannot be governed there, and he has got into such company as I am sure will not profit him much by their council—I have therefore said to Genl Coffee furnish you $500 for his expence here & his education during the ensuing year   I wish you to give Genl Coffee a special receipt as my agent as guardian for this five hundred dollars & when you give to Hutchings any Pockett mony out of it take his receipt & keep an exact acpt of his expences hither—This is the last letter I will write you to Nashville   present my respect to Mr Earle & say I shall certainly expect to see him on with you next month—present me kindly to Mr MLamore & family your unkle Jonny & family, yr uncle Alexander,[3] william & family Mr Martin Stockly & their families & all my good neighbours and believe me yr affectionate father

Andrew Jackson

P.S. I have written to Mr Steel to have the Negro Houses placed where the old ones stands—if he has not recd it, direct him to place them there—but urge him as to getting my cotton early Hou[se]d   A J

ALS, DLC (37).
1. This was probably the farm of Anthony Winston (1750–1827) that AJ had acquired after his death.
2. Mary Florida Dickson.
3. Alexander Donelson (1751–1834) was Rachel Jackson's brother.

To John Henry Eaton

Washington Sept. 23d. 1829

Dr. Sir,

The case of the seizure by Col. Arbuckle of the goods of Cairns & Co in the cherokee nation, I have carefully considered. Col. Arbuckle's instructions and the act of congress regulating intercourse with the Indian tribes fully authorise this seizure—the mere fact of the spirits being found within the Indian Territory without the license of the Governmet, was *prima facie* evidence of the illicit objects of those who had introduced them   The design is a matter of subsequent inquiry, for the purpose of ascertaining which, we are at liberty to look at the facts, and if we think they acquit the owners of the goods of any intention to violate the law, we may recommend such steps as justice and fairness to both parties dictate. Upon this principle, being convinced from the smallness of the quantity of spirits, that the Messrs Carnes & Co, did not design to make them a subject of traffic with the Indians, I would order Col. Arbuckle to deliver up the goods, provided they receipt to him a release from all damages for the seizure & detention. Further than this the Government cannot interfere, and if the Messrs. Carnes & Co. do not consent to it, Col. Arbuckle must retain the goods until the Judiciary decides the case. Be pleased to make this known to them and oblige yr. friend

Andrew Jackson

[In AJ's hand:] P.S. Before you give the order to Col. Arbuckle to deliver the goods take from Messhrs. Carnes & Co. a compleat release to Arbuckle for their seisure & detention, least our interference might work an injury to that faithful officer.[1]

A. J.

LS in AJ Donelson's hand, THi (13-1410). Federal law forbade selling liquor to Indians and made violators liable to forfeiture of all their trade goods. In May 1829, Colonel Mathew Arbuckle, commanding at Cantonment Gibson, searched the goods of Peter A. Carnes and William Duval, licensed traders to the Western Cherokees. He found barrels of cognac, rum, and port, and seized their trade goods valued at up to $10,000. Carnes protested to Eaton, contending that the liquor was intended for medicine, not trade. Fearing that the seizure would not hold up in court, the traders would sue Arbuckle, and the government would wind up paying damages, Eaton on September 23 proposed to AJ the compromise endorsed here.

1. Eaton conveyed AJ's decision to Arbuckle on September 24 (*TPUS,* 21:70–72). Carnes and Duval duly freed Arbuckle from liability for the seizure, but pursued a claim against the War Department for more than $6,000 in alleged injury to their goods. Rebuffed by Eaton, they took their case to Congress, which awarded them $3,828.49 in 1831.

To *Samuel Delucenna Ingham*

Septbr. 24th. 1829—

Dr. Sir

Mrs. McPherson sister in law of the late clerk, Mr Lewis, deceased, waited upon me last evening with a tale of woe & distress, that aroused all my sympathy—She says her brotherinlaw Mr Lewis has left to her charge two small orphan children without any means of support, & applied for the office vacated by the death of Mr Lewis to be filled by her brother Robert T. Washington—I had Just recd. your letter, upon which I told her that office would not be filled—she requested me to make known to you her distress & ask your influence in behalf of her brother who says if he can get an office, he will take, & raise the children. Judge Anderson speaks well of the young man, but it appears that his father & brother are both in office here, & there is dificulty in the way, as our rule is not to permit any family to monopolize office—still charity speaks aloud in favour of these little orphans, & I have said if we cannot appoint this young man, that until some provision can be otherwise made, if she will make known to me their wants, I will supply them—Having promised, I have here made known their situation to you, & will Join with you, in any arangement for their support[.] yr friend

Andrew Jackson

ALS, PHi (13-1421). Edward Simmons Lewis (1794–1829), a clerk in the third auditor's office, died on September 23; his wife, the former Susan Jean Washington (1795–1829), had died on July 2. Their orphaned children were Elizabeth (c1818–45) and Edward Augustus Lewis (1820–89). Susan's sister Mary Elizabeth Washington (1800–1874) had married Navy lieutenant Joseph Stout MacPherson (c1789–1824) in 1819. Robert T. Washington (1805–32) began work as a clerk in the third auditor's office on November 19. His father, Lund Washington, Sr. (1767–1853), was a clerk in the office of first comptroller Joseph I. Anderson; his brother, Peter Grayson Washington (1798–1872), was chief clerk in the Treasurer's office.

Statement by Mary B. O'Neale Randolph

Sep. 25

I do not understand what Dr. Ely means by "this admitted instance of miscarriage," as there was nothing passed on the subject but what I told you, & I have the most distinct recollection, of our, (Mrs. E & myself) mentioning no other than that referred to before Mr. Eatons acquaintance with the family—Upon a trip to Blad[1]—with Mr. Tim—the horse took fright & she jumped from the Carriage, was carried to the Toll House & sent for by Her Father. On her return home Dr. Sim was called, but the feared accident prevented—I also perfectly recollect that Dr. E. remarked the conversation with Mr. Campbell & Himself was in the presence of Mrs. Ely & Her Brother. Dr. Craven's name was to me first mentioned.

Mary B. Randolph—

[Endorsed by AJ:] Mrs. Randolph statement of a conversation between Mrs. E. & Mr Ely—

ADS, DLC (37).
  1. Bladensburg, Md.

From John England

Convent of the Visitation
Georgetown Sep 26—1829

Sir

As an American citizen and a Bishop of the Roman Catholic Church, I take the liberty of drawing your attention to the following facts, & presenting the annexed request.

The spiritual & ecclesiastical supremacy of the Pope who is Bishop of Rome is an essential portion of the Roman Catholic religion; any attempt to overawe this head of the Church in the exercise of his Spiritual or ecclesiastical authority is believed to be such an interference with the Roman Catholic religion, which is that of a large body of Citizens, as the constitution forbids to Congress. It is believed that no officer of the general government could constitutionally do that which is thus forbidden to the representatives of the people & the representatives of the States.

The said head of the Roman Catholic Church happens at present to be a temporal Sovereign, and to have civil dominion in a large portion of Italy; but it is clear that this dominion does not extend to this country, nor does he claim to have such power here. And if he did so claim, the Roman Catholic citizens of this Union would feel themselves called upon effectually to resist the same. And should the Pope either for the enforcement of his Spiritual or ecclesiastical decrees, or in furtherance of any temporal claim attempt to use any physical force, the constituted authorities of the several States are fully competent and well disposed as they are bound to protect their citizens from such usurpation and aggression. It appears to be their duty to do so to the exclusion of the general government; unless from want of power, which is a ridiculous supposition, they should be compelled to have constitutional recourse to the Federal executive for protection

It does not appear that any State has found it necessary to make such a call upon the executive of the Union, and therefore there does not appear to have been any constitutional ground for its interference; yet it is believed that such interference has taken place, at least in two distinct instances.

The first related to a decree of Pope Pius VII. regarding a dispute between the then Archbishop of Baltimore and a certain corporation of Catholic clergymen concerning the possession of a farm: upon which the Pope, as arbiter, pronounced in favour of one party, and the other applied to the department of State, & procured, as it is believed that instructions should be transmitted to one of our ministers residing abroad in 1824 or 1825 to interfere in such a manner as to exhibit the opposition of the Federal government to the Papal decree. Whereas it is conceived that the proper mode would have been to leave the question of property to be decided by the court having proper jurisdiction in that part of Maryland where the farm lay.[1]

The second case is more recent; it occurred last year. Two priests in Philadelphia were accused of causing trouble in the church of that city: the See of Rome (now its government) was called upon to take cognizance of their conduct: the Pope directed all parties concerned in the dispute to leave that city; so as thereby to restore peace, the Bishop retired in obedience to the decree: the two Priests applied for protection to the department of State: the President directed a letter to be written from that department, in which the cause of those priests is countenanced by the government in such a manner as to interfere with the freedom of agency of the Spiritual head of the Roman Catholic Church; & to cause several citizens to dread that the repetition of such conduct would be the commencement of an Union of Church & State as well as an unconstitutional intermeddling with the affairs of our ecclesiastical body, productive of serious mischief to ourselves, and a just cause of jealousy to our fellow citizens of other religious denominations.[2]

I have therefore humbly to request, that your Excellency will cause enquiry to be made in the office of the Secretary of State for such documents as might there exist relating to those or any similar cases, and, also direct that copies thereof should be furnished to me for publication; so that the citizens at large should be satisfied that no private and unconstitutional interference in religious concerns shall be permitted by the President of the United States.[3] I have the honor to be Respectfully Your Excellency's obedt. humbl. Servant

John, Bishop of Charleston

Doctor England will have the honor of paying his respects to his Excellency on Monday morning[4]

ALS, DNA-RG 59 (M179-67). *United States Catholic Miscellany,* September 4, 1830. England (1786–1842), a native of Cork, Ireland, was Bishop of Charleston and co-editor with his sister of the *United States Catholic Miscellany.*
1. In a Bull of July 23, 1822, Pope Pius VII (1740–1823) had ordered Maryland Jesuits to turn over White Marsh farm or another farm of comparable value to Baltimore Archbishop Ambrose Maréchal (1764–1828).
2. Seeking to quiet dissension in the Philadelphia diocese, Pope Leo XII in 1828 summoned bishop Henry Conwell to Rome and ordered two Philadelphia Dominicans, William Vincent Harold and John Ryan, to remove to Cincinnati. Both were Irish immigrants, Harold a naturalized citizen. The two appealed to the State Department for protection against what they construed as a papal threat of civil as well as religious penalties if they disobeyed. Through American minister to France James Brown, the Adams administration queried the Vatican, which denied claiming any other than a spiritual authority over Harold and Ryan. Ryan sailed for Ireland in August 1829, followed by Harold in September.
3. Van Buren furnished the correspondence regarding Harold and Ryan to England, who published it in the *Catholic Miscellany* in August and September 1830.
4. In publishing this letter, England noted that at their interview on September 28 "his Excellency expressed his co-incidence with the views in the letter, and gave the necessary directions for furnishing the documents."

To [Samuel Swartwout?]

(private)

Washington Septr. 27th. 1829—

(copy)

My Dr. Sir

In your letter of the 21rst instant, marked confidential you are pleased to inform me, that information has reached you through a channel on which relience can be placed, that a "few ladies of this place, *Washington* with a Reverand Genleman at their head, has formed a determination to put Mrs. Eaton out of socieety, & who for that purpose are circulating by themselves, & *their secrete agents,* the most foul & malicious slanders, some, if not all, *I* know from investigation to be basely false, & that my family have attached themselves to this secrete inquisition, who are to admit, or not admit into society in this place, such Ladies, & only such as they may think worthy"; & enquire, *& hope,* it is not true, as it respects *my family*—To which *I answer, as to my family I believe, and trust, it is not true;* and pledge myself, so far as my advice can govern, that it shall not be the case—

you do me but Justice when you say, that I took major Eaton into my Cabinet of my own free choice, *where,* but for his friendship for (you) (*me*) he would not have gone into it, that all the Cabinet was harmonious in the whole selection, & to abandon him, before *all sides are heard* would be so injurious to him, & *to me,* that my friends believe I am incapble of such a course—*And you have so declared, that Eaton is the last man on earth I ought,* or *would abandon*—You have Judged rightly of me; The world in truth, cannot say that I ever abandoned a friend, without on such grounds, that a righteous course founded upon the principles of that gospel, which I not only profess to believe, but do religiously believe, or when they abandoned me without cause—you know my opinion of the purity of Eaton, I believe, & ever have believed that his morale character was without a blemish, & had the other day the pleasure to hear the clergyman who give currency to the *tale* of the dead Doctor & the Revd. Gentleman from Philadelphia to whom you allude declare in the presence of the sec of State, the Treasury war, Navy, atto. Genl. Postmaster General, Major Lewis, & Major Andrew Donelson, that in all their inquiries, they were free to declare, there was nothing to impeach the moral character of Major Eaton—and I am sure from the Testimonials I have seen, that there is nothing that *can*, or ought to *attach the least Stain upon her Virtue*—I am free to declare to you, that I do think Major Eaton, & Mrs. Eaton more unjustly, & cruelly slander than history has ever recorded in any other instance & a short time will prove it & all this by tales circulated in the most secrete manner & under strict confidence. How then could the unjust world for a moment suppose I would abandon him—I would sooner *abandon life*. I have long knew the vallue of the man, & his high standing both in Newyork, Pensylvania, & the west, & as far as Justice, & truth, will authorise, I will sustain him. you could not shudder more at the depravity of morales, than I have, that would sanction a system, that a clergyman detailing the *tale* which he says he received from a deceased Doctor, & who has been dead nearly if not upward of six years, unsupported by any other testimony, should be sufficient to destroy female character—I am too well acquainted with the religious part of our country & the high minded & honorable, to believe the moment this slander is placed before the world, & the manner of its being circulated, but, the whole people will spurn the wicked slander, & prostrate the slanderer.

I will only now add—That if this combination of which you speak, is really in existence, The virtuous, morale & religious world will begin and enquire, by what authority These ladies with their clergyman at their head has assumed for themselves this holy allience & secrete inquisition to pass in secrete upon the conduct of others, & say, who shall, & who shall not be permitted into society. If it does exist, the enquiry will go farther, it may extend to the enquiry into their own immaculate characters, & their divine right to assume such powers, & I would not for the Presidency be in their places—The indignation is arising here, as well as with you, and the moment it is known, must arise over the christianised world—for the matron, the daughter, the father will all cry out, where is the safety for our characters, if it is placed within the pale of a vindictive clergyman, who from the act, shews he has no religion, who may get displeased with a fair & virtuous female, who has nothing to do, but put forth the saying of a dead man, & the female character is gone forever—I can assure you that the morales & virtue of our country is not prepared to support or countenance such things as this, & I am happy to hear, that the indignation of your citizens has become so much arroused at the mere recital of the conduct here—it will have a good effect—it must in the end, put down gossipping here, & chasten society every where, and give a greater respect to female character, & an utter detestation of slanderes—Then will society enjoy peace, & harmony, & character be secure from secrete & unfounded calumnies—*our society wants purging here*—When you write to your distant friends present me to them kindly & believe me yr friend—

signed A. J.

ALS draft, DLC (37). Addressed "To Mr. S. N.y."

To John Christmas McLemore

(private)

Washington Septbr. 28th. 1829.

Dr. Sir

you may recollect the visit of Col Combs to the Hermitage as the agent of Genl. Shelby Just before the election for the last president, to obtain from me evidence to exonerate his deceased father from the lies of his son Thomas, or in other words to insult me. If Mr. Clay & the secratary of war had been men of either truth or honor, they would have furnished to the world a copy of my letter & Governor Shelby to the secratary of war which went on with the treaty. But as those men, concealed every thing like truth, & spread nothing but falshood, I enclose to you a copy of our letter to the sec. of war J. C. Calhoun dated 30th. of Octbr. 1818 that you may use it as your own Judgt. may direct—If published, let they *names* of the *Colberts* be omitted, as I do not want their names to be known to the chikesaw nation—I wish this letter shewn *P.S. shew this copy to my friend Judge Overton, & take his advice what to do with it—give my love to him & say I will write him soon—* to Col. Douglass & his associates who performed the honorable service of lackeys to Col Comb, waited on, ~~Mr James Jackson,~~ and gave a certificate of the interview with Mr Jackson to the Chickasaw embassador—I believe the *honorable Mr Tanyhill* was Col Douglass associate in this ~~duty~~ honourable business—shew the letter to him, but do not let it be known who sent it to you—Major Lewis has sent one to Genl Coffee; & Major Barry, has sent another to Lexington certified by him that the signature Isaac Shelby is in his, Shelby's own proper hand writing, I wish you to shew it to my friend Doctor Shelby & Judge Overton.[1]

you will see by the papers the attack made on Major Barry, by the Bradly's—I have no doubt but an alarming defalcations will be discovered in that department, and they Bradleys wanted to alarm Major Barry but he is made of too stern stuff, I cautioned Major Barry against these men some time since—and the moment that Barry made the arrangements to secure the revenue of the postoffice, that has for twenty years been at the will of Mr Bradly who, was recever, Treasurer, & disburser they became restive, & Barry removed him—from the attempt to intimidate Barry I have no doubt, but Mr Bradley feels himself on the brink of exposure, & his corruption for twenty years exposed: a few days will unfold this matter —As we progress we are daily unfolding the corruption of the past, & endeavouring to have an honest administration in every department of the goverment, for the future—[2]

Every thing I think will *now* go on *well* here—The system of gossipping & slander will be put down soon, when female character will not be secretely assailed by fiends, aided by hypocritical preachers detailing dead Doctors slanders—The time is hastening on, when it will be enquired by the moral & religious portion of our country, what divine right six females with a clergyman at their head have, to establish a secrete inquisition, and decree who shall, & who shall not, come into society—and who shall who be sacraficed by their secrete slanders—and when it will be enquired whether they have not been subject to the keen & envenomed shafts of slander themselves—I have had an arduous, and in some respects & unpleasant duty to perform, but my reliance is, that truth is mighty & will forever prevail, and I knew Eaton was too pure a man to be guilty of acts charged against him   I have not been mistaken—

present me affectionately to Betsy & your amiable family, tell my son I hope to receive a letter from him soon, yr friend

Andrew Jackson

ALS, NHi (13-1440). AJ enclosed a copy of the October 30, 1818, letter to Calhoun, which he endorsed "copy of a letter from the late Governor Shelby & A. Jackson commissioners to treat with the Chickasaw Indians to J. C. Calhoune sec. of war dated the 30th of Octbr. 1818—Taken from the files of the war office, they sinatures the proper handwriting of Isaac Shelby & Andrew Jackson."

In 1818 AJ and former Kentucky governor Isaac Shelby (1750–1826) concluded a treaty with the Chickasaws for land cessions in Tennessee and Kentucky. The treaty included several payments and provisions for members of the influential Colbert family. One article gave chiefs Levi Colbert and James Brown custody of a valuable salt lick, which they subsequently leased to AJ's friend William B. Lewis. Another confirmed George and Levi Colbert's title to reservations of land, which the commissioners secretly arranged to be purchased from them for $20,000 by either the government or private parties. In their October 30 letter to Calhoun (Bassett, 2:399–401), AJ and Shelby explained that these inducements were necessary to buy off the Colberts and prevent their thwarting the negotiations, without exceeding the funds at the commissioners' disposal.

Charges that AJ had acted improperly to enrich his friends ensued and were revived in AJ's presidential campaigns. In 1828, AJ's opponents publicized assertions by Isaac Shelby's son Thomas Hart Shelby (1789–1869) and his son-in-law Charles S. Todd that Shelby had opposed AJ's profligacy and corruption in the negotiations. James Shelby (1784–1848), Isaac's eldest son, wrote AJ asking him to permit his friends to reveal the secret history of the treaty. AJ considered the request insulting and did not reply. Shelby had then sent Leslie Combs ("the Chickasaw ambassador") in October 1828 to confront AJ directly. In AJ's view this joint 1818 letter to Calhoun, which he apparently had just rediscovered in the War Department files, showed Isaac Shelby's entire concurrence with him in the negotiations and thus proved false the charges of misconduct.

1. During his 1828 visit to Tennessee, Combs sought to interview AJ's estranged former friend James Jackson (1782–1840), who had been a party in the arrangement to purchase the Colbert reservations. James Jackson refused to betray confidences by talking to him. Harry Lightfoot Douglass (1784–1854), mayor of Lebanon, Tenn., and Wilkins Tannehill (1787–1858), a Nashville banker, urged James Jackson to cooperate with Combs. Their report of his continued refusal, published by James Shelby in his pamphlet *Chickasaw Treaty* (Lexington, Ky., October 1828), suggested that Jackson knew AJ had something to hide. Lewis sent Coffee a copy of the 1818 letter to Calhoun on September 28, 1829. "Doctor Shelby" was Nashville physician John Shelby.

2. Abraham Bradley (1767–1838) had been assistant postmaster general and his brother Phineas Bradley (1769–1845) second assistant. In early September Abraham Bradley and Amos Kendall had quarreled publicly over the removal of Frankfort postmaster James W. Hawkins. Postmaster General Barry dismissed Bradley on September 14. Bradley rejoined with a letter to Barry, dated September 23 and published in the *US Telegraph* on September 28, asserting his "total unfitness" for office. Bradley accused Barry of incompetence, malfeasance, and indebtedness to the government, and demanded he resign. Phineas had previously written Barry on September 16, protesting his brother's abrupt removal. In October Phineas too was dismissed, and about October 12 Abraham wrote AJ a long letter detailing his charges against Barry. On September 12, just previous to Abraham's dismissal, Barry had issued new regulations directing postmasters to deposit their proceeds in banks rather than, as before, forwarding them on to the assistant postmaster general.

To Samuel Angus

Washington Sept. 29th. 1829

Sir,

I have carefully examined your case, and altho' it may be a very hard one, as I remarked to you when you first presented it, I am still of the opinion that I have no constitutional power to redress it. on the 1st of June 1824 it appears that you were dismissed from the service and your name struck from the register of the Navy by the order of the President of the United States.

Your restoration would amount to this, that I have the power to undo the constitutional acts of my predecessors—a power which has not been granted, and if it had been could not be exercised without destroying the symmetry of the Government, and producing the utmost confusion and disorder in all its operations. Such a power does not exist under our constitution, and I hope no President will ever attempt its exercise. I am very Respectfully yr. obt. sert.

Andrew Jackson

LS in AJ Donelson's hand, MA (13-1454); ALS draft, DLC (37); LC, DLC (60). Angus (1784–1840) had been a Navy captain. In April 1824, he wrote Navy secretary Southard a letter demanding a command that was so indecorous that President Monroe ordered his summary dismissal. Pleading temporary insanity to excuse the letter, Angus appealed for reinstatement to President Adams. Adams refused in April 1825, claiming he had no authority to overturn an act of his predecessor. On March 23, 1829, Angus wrote AJ begging reinstatement. On October 15 he wrote, again unsuccessfully, to request a new appointment.

To John Jolly

My Friend John Jolly chief ruler of my children, the cherokees on the Arkansas.

your father the President of the United States by Dr Baylor has received your talk—he received it as tho' we were standing face to face, shaking each other by the hand.

you say, "twelve years ago you came here to rest, but have no rest, you come here by my advice, and I am President, and you are glad."

It is true, you went where you are by my advice, and there you and your children may rest as long as grass grows or water runs.[1]

you say "you have no rest," but you do not tell your father how it is interrupted—Inform him what disturbs your rest, and if it is an improper interruption, or interference with your or your childrens rights secured by the agreement which placed you there, they will be removed, and you and your people, shall be at rest. you will be protected in all your Just rights and no encroachments suffered upon you, or your people.

I am happy Governor Houston, your son, is now with you. I regret, he left his State, but as he has, I am glad he is with his father, I am sure you will treat him kindly as a son—shake him by the hand for me, and wish him happy—Tell him, I have recd. the pipe, & tobaco pouch; I will keep them in remembrance of him, and smoke the pipe in friendship with you & your people.

My heart is near to you & your people, and I shake you by the hand with the affection of a father as tho', we were face to face

Andrew Jackson

ALS draft, DLC (13-1221). Army surgeon John W. Baylor left the Cherokee Agency in Arkansas for Washington in June. He returned to Arkansas in the fall with this letter in hand.

1. An 1817 treaty negotiated by AJ secured the territory of the Western Cherokees.

To Martin Van Buren

Septbr. 1829—

I herewith send enclosed two letters for your perusal & consideration

If Mr Dickerson request can, with propriety, be granted, it would be serving a very worthy man, for such is Judge Leib represented, but I have no information on the subject of the conduct of either of the incumbents in the offices alluded to—

I do not believe there is any power to remove the Judges, if there were I would like to be informed, for surely, one ought to have been removed long ago, for his tyranny[.] yr friend

Andrew Jackson

ANS, DNA-RG 59 (M639-14). AJ enclosed Mahlon Dickerson's July 31 letter recommending John L. Leib, and probably a complaint about the Michigan or Florida territorial judges. The incumbent Michigan officers were territorial secretary James Witherell and district attorney Daniel Le Roy.

Memorandum on Nicholas Biddle's Letter

[In 1816 Congress chartered the second Bank of the United States (BUS) for twenty years. The Bank was to be headquartered in Philadelphia, with power to establish branches throughout the states. Its capital stock was set at $35 million, one-fifth held by the federal government and the rest by private investors. The president of the United States, with Senate consent, also appointed five of the Bank's twenty-five directors. In addition to its private commercial business, the Bank served as the federal government's fiscal agent. It brokered federal loans, received, stored, transmitted, and disbursed federal funds, and issued banknotes which were legal tender. In 1823 Nicholas Biddle (1786–1844) became the Bank's third president.

In the summer of 1829, New Hampshire Jacksonians leveled charges of partisan and capricious management against the new president of the Portsmouth branch of the BUS, former senator Jeremiah Mason. Senator Levi Woodbury complained about Mason to Treasury secretary Ingham, who forwarded his letter on to Biddle. Remarking on the Bank's vast financial power, Ingham admonished it to avoid even the appearance of political favoritism in its lending. Biddle in reply defended Mason, rejected the imputation of bias, and proclaimed the Bank's rigorous abstention from politics and its complete independence from all outside influence. Questioning this blanket declaration of innocence, Ingham further pressed Biddle to

investigate affairs at Portsmouth. Biddle answered on September 15.
He again pronounced the charges against Mason "entirely groundless,"
asserted the Bank's absolute autonomy from the executive, and suggested
that Ingham himself was attempting an improper political interference
(HRRep 460, 22d Cong., 1st sess., pp. 438–56, Serial 227). This memo-
randum by Jackson, probably written around the end of September, com-
ments on Biddle's letter and on Ingham's projected reply.]

Biddles letter—
    repeats their good feelings to the new administration & their great aid
afforded to it in the payment of the late sum of public Debt—¿Why this so
often mentioned—answer for ~~public~~ political effect—& newspaper slang
&c¿[1]

The act of Congress their guide—true, but if that charter is violated, is
there no power in the goverment to inquire & correct if true. The duties
exclusively the directors without controle of the Executive or any of his
officers &c &c &c—(Trusting to the variety of the directors)[2]
    The Bank is strong enough to sustain itself & officers—

Sec *answer*— The reply as to the purity of the Branch directors *well said.*
The suggestion of purity of all Judicial bodies Banks included—[3]

Extract from P. of the Bank—I deem it my duty to state to you in a manner perfectly respectful to your official & personal character, yet so clear
as to leave no possibility of misconception that the board of directors of
the Bank of the U. States and the boards of directors of they branches of
the Bank of the U. States, acknowledge not the slightest responsibility of
any description whatsoever to The secratary of the Treasury touching
the political opinions & conduct of their officers—that being a subject
on which they never consult & never desire to know the views of any
administration.[4]

☞ note—The Secratary must note, & reply to that part of the P. which
relates to Mr Hills note & the N. H. memorial—and to relieve the executive from any interference with The Bank, but remark, he reserves his
constitutional powers to be exercised through Congress, to redress all
grievances complained of by the people of the interference by the Branches
with the local elections of the states, & all their interference with party
politicks, in every section of our country, where those complaints have
reached the Executive.[5]

[Endorsed by AJ:] notes on the letters of Mr Biddle and the Sec of the
Treasury—

AN, DLC (13-1387). Ingham wrote Biddle on October 5. Charging that Biddle had distorted his meaning, he disclaimed political interference but affirmed that the Bank was a public institution properly subject, by terms of its charter, to executive oversight (*HRRep* 460, 22d Cong., 1st sess., pp. 456–69, Serial 227).

1. To show the Bank's disinterested and nonpartisan public service, Biddle had dwelt on its help in making a large payment on the public debt in July, which Ingham had complimented.

2. Biddle had cited the variety of the Bank's directors as a safeguard against abuse.

3. Biddle answered Ingham's first request to investigate Mason with a sweeping avowal of faith in the integrity of the Bank's five hundred national and branch officers. Ingham had rejoined that this declaration of "universal purity" was not credible as it belied the fallibility of human nature and of all human institutions.

4. From Biddle's September 15 letter.

5. Signing himself as second comptroller of the Treasury, Isaac Hill had sent Biddle petitions against Mason from Portsmouth businessmen and New Hampshire legislators. Hill complained of Mason's oppression of "the friends of General Jackson in New Hampshire." Biddle's letter of September 15 reproved this as overt political meddling. Ingham's reply disavowed knowledge or approval of Hill's action.

Andrew Jackson Donelson to Ezra Stiles Ely

My Dear Mr. Ely.

I recd. in proper time & manner your ~~confidential~~ two communications, ~~the first in relation to what you had learned from Mr F~~ which I consider confidential the first explaining a part of your action here upon the *object of your visit,* the last giving your views upon some topics of national concern.[1]

In reference to the last, I offer you my sincere thanks, without the power to assure you whether I shall be able to apply them in the manner contemplated. ~~It may be that I~~ If I shall due credit will be given to their disinterested source.

No doubt your mind has been much disturbed by the apprehension of mischief ~~likely~~ possibly to grow out of the controversy between Mr. C & Mr. E. I wish I could say that there was no cause for it; but I cannot to you. Its ~~inflammable nature~~ combustible qualities can be ignited in so many different ways, the keys to some of which are in the hands of our enemy, that sooner or later, we must anticipate an explosion; and all that wisdom can now do is to give it as much as possible the direction which a private affair ought to have; to separate it as far as possible from the Governmnt, and to rely on Providence for the aversion of the individual calamities which both sides ~~of the question~~ may sustain.

I beg that you will pardon my delay in answering your letters, ~~I wish not to speak on matters~~ and ascribe it to any thing else than a want of confidence in your sincere regard for the Genl, and tender concern for me. These ties are strengthened by the trials to which you have been recently exposed[.] yr. friend

Andrew J Donelson

ALS draft, DLC (37).

1. In three letters to Eaton of September 15, 16, and 22 (DLC-75), Thomas Fillebrown, Jr., charged Ely with misrepresenting what he had told him about the Eatons and then failing to correct his acknowledged error.

Memorandum Book

[These September and October entries in Jackson's memorandum book directly follow those above from June and July.]

Project for adding security to our revenue & improve our Navy &c.

The Revenue Cutters to be built in our Navy yard & not by contract— When the Sec, of the Treasury wants a Cutter, to make requisition on the Navy Dept. the expences of which to be charged to the Revenue Service— They Cutters ought to be the very best sailers, & to be such, must be of the very best models, and can be built of refuse timber, left from our 74rs., frigates, & Sloops of war—This would be good oconomy—besides, it is alledged that our Cutters are of a poor class & dull sailers which is injurious to the safety of our revenue, as they are outsailed by almost all bay craft, and merchantmen

Lieutenants of the Navy ought to be given the command of our Cutters & their subordinate officers taken from the midshipmen, and when detailed for this duty be under the exclusive command, orders, & controle of the Secratary of the Treasury—This would be guarding our revenue much better than the present mode, whilst we are improving the Navy, the great the strong arm of our national defence—whilst we are by this change, producing a great pecuniary saving to the nation, we are giving much employment to our Navy officers, where they will be improveing their seamanship and gaining knowledge of our coasts & inlets, & when not employed in the active duty watching of guarding our revenue, can be usefully employed in survaying the Coasts, harbours, & inlets of their respective crusing ground—

Sent this 16th. of Septbr. to the secretary of the Treasury for his consideration

A Jackson[1]

Message—Bankrupt Law—quere its policy, if recommend, to be general, embracing every one, from the porest laboured, to greatest merchant, never permitting the debt arising from the revenue to be included, only the security of the body, released, by the insolvant or Bankrupt law—To include debtors to the Goverment, would open so many doors to fraud & perjury, that would destroy all security in the collecting our revenue &c &c, too dangerous to the morales of our citizens to be enacted by Congress or sanctioned by the Govt.[2]—But the change from the credit system to cash duties, the warehouse system may be well recommended, as it will afford more[3]

☞ October 3rd. 1829—(note sent substance as below)

Mr Ingham will please to furnish the President with the amount of losses by failure to pay bonds at the custom Houses, since the year of 1789—part of this information, can be easily obtained from the reports on file of former Secretaries of the Treasury—Also the amount paid for rent of store, or ware Houses, for the last six years.[4]

It appears to me that it would be a great saving, as well as great security to our revenue, if all Collectors were made salary officers, as then their emoluments would not depend upon the amount of goods bonded—This being the case, the Collectors would be more exact in the enquiry as to the real situation & solvency of the bondsmen, to the revenue bonds. Where they receive a percentage, the object is, to get the goods bonded which secures to the Collectors their percentage—The case at amboy elucidates this—[5]

AN, DLC (64).

1. AJ wrote Ingham about this project on September 16 (above).

2. Congress had recently considered enactment of a national bankruptcy law. AJ's first annual message did not broach the subject. He did, however, recommend permitting the release of insolvent debtors to the government from their debts when their conduct had been clear of fraud.

3. Importers of foreign articles were allowed credit on their payment of customs duties. They gave security by posting bonds or by depositing a portion of their goods, which customs collectors then stored in rented warehouses. To reduce losses from defaulters, AJ contemplated switching to a system of cash duties, with all goods to be lodged in government warehouses until payment.

4. AJ queried Ingham to this effect on October 3, hoping, as he said, to "draw a contrast" between the cash and credit systems. Ingham replied on October 10. He remarked that switching to cash duties and government storage would incur a massive expense for warehousing, present a shock to the commercial system, dampen trade by tying up capital, and restrict the importing business to a few very large capitalists who could command bank credit. To reduce revenue losses, Ingham instead suggested shortening the two-year credit allowed on Asian imports (chiefly tea) to a year or less. He also proposed building government warehouses sufficient to replace the present rentals. AJ included both recommendations in his first annual message to Congress (Richardson, 2:452–53).

5. Customs collectors were compensated by a combination of salary and fees on customs duties. Ingham in his October 10 reply cautioned that putting collectors on straight salary might relax their vigilance against smuggling. The "case at amboy" was that of failed China trading firm Thomas H. Smith & Son.

October

To Moses Dawson

(private)

Washington 1rst. of Octbr. 1829—

My Dr. Sir

I enclose you a letter written by the late Govr. Shelby & myself as commissioners appointed to hold a treaty with the chikisaw Indians in the year 1818 and addressed to the then Secratary of War J. C. Calhoun and which accompanied the treaty, we had concluded with that nation. That the Sec of War Barber & Mr Clay should have concealed this letter from public view, when I was assailed by the Shebys, is not surprising, as their object was to conceal truth, & assail me with falshoods; but that none of my friends who knew this letter was on file in the war office, did not call for, & have it published; astonishes me

It is enclosed to be used by you as your Judgt. may direct—If published leave out the Colberts names, in blank. With my kind salutations to you & your family I am respectfully yr friend

Andrew Jackson

P.S. a copy certified by major Barry the Signature to the handwriting of Govr Shelby, has been sent to Mr Ficklin Lexington—[1]

ALS, OCHP (14-0063). AJ enclosed a copy of the October 30, 1818, letter to Calhoun, which he endorsed "copy of a letter from the late Govr. Isaac Shelby & Andrew Jackson commissioners to treat with the chikisaw Indians to J. C. Calhoune sec of war dated 30th. of Octbr. 1818—Taken from the files of the war office. They signatures the proper handwriting of Isaac Shelby & Andrew Jackson." Dawson printed the letter in his *Cincinnati Advertiser* on October 10.

1. Joseph Ficklin (1775–1859) was postmaster at Lexington and former editor of the *Kentucky Gazette*.

From James Dell, Simon Beckham, and Thomas Harn

Sir

Acting as a Committee appointed at a meeting of the citizens of Alachua County for the purpose of communicating with the General Government concerning the helpless and unprotected condition in which the Inhabitants are left, in relation to the Indians, by the removal of the garrison from Fort King, we beg leave to hand a Memorial signed by its citizens.

Your good sense will no doubt enable you readily to perceive from the tenor of this memorial the necessity which exists, of our being protected by an adequate force, and that too promptly; for already has report reached us, tho' not yet properly confirmed, that a family of the name of Howard have been butchered at Suwanney Old Town by the Indians—They are moreover buying up all the powder they can get at unusually high prices[1]

It may be proper to mention that our settlements are scattered from the northern boundary line of the Seminoles to the Suwanney and St. Marys River. From the manner in which the settlements are generally located, the junction of the males of any two families at the house of either would leave entirely exposed the property and family of the other—From this you may conclude what would be the consequence if all the men were ordered out; Our force would be too weak to permit its being divided, so that it could be efficient but at one point at the same moment—while the rest of the county, through which would be scattered their respective families, would be without the smallest shadow of protection. And what must be the result of this fact? Why, that in a case of danger every man will be compelled to remain at home to protect to the best of his ability with his single arm, the objects most dear to him; thus leaving it in the power of an enemy to cut us off peicemeal, or as it were, in detail, with little or no hazard to themselves.

The only remedy for this state of circumstances which presents itself to our veiw, is that proposed in the Memorial above referred to. To wit. That a garrison of four companies of United States troops be stationed at Micanopia in this County—By this means whenever an alarm occured, the Inhabitants from every part of the County would flock to it with their families, and having deposited them thus in a place of safety, would be unburthened of his chief care, and be then ready to fight the battles of his country. Which would be rendered more effectual, by the power, which the adoption of this plan would afford of cooperating with the regular forces.

These advantages were not afforded by the station at Fort King—being located so far within the boundaries, that in time of war, no man would have risqued his family through an anemy's country to have reached; while it had but little power of restraining the Indians from roaming at large in the Territory of the Whites, for from their situation it was rendered troublesome to send detachments among us—and when such detachments were sent, they could stay but so short a time that the Indians had it in their power to conceal themselves until the danger was past, without the least possibility of detection.

Micanopia is situated about twenty five miles north of the Agency[2]— and thirty East of the Suwanney Old Town—it is well watered—a high and healthy situation. The land carriage to the St. Johns would be between forty and fifty miles—one half the distance that was required for the delivery of the stores at Fort King, until shortly before their removal—nor will the cost of the Beef and grain required for their consumption amount to half the expence which was found necessary for its obtainment at that station.

The situation of Micanopia is such that with all ease and convenience detachments might be constantly kept on duty, which will be the only possible means of keeping the Indians within their boundary and of putting a stop to their depredations—while in time of danger it would be of easy access to all parts of the country—

Again with regard to the arms requested to be sent among us. We stand Sir in actual need of them. There are not more in our opinions than one Tenth of our men who could bring into action guns proper to be used there. Besides which our Regiment is almost universally desirous of forming into volunteer uniformed companies, which are generally the most efficient arm of the Militia, being better disciplined, but are prevented from doing so, by their being unable to obtain regular arms—there being but few public arms at the seat of Government.

The major part of the force at present stationed at Tampa Bay might with propriety be removed to this part of the country—At Tampa they are of little use or benefit, which will appear to you by a reference to the map of this country

We might enlarge, Sir, our veiws to a considerable extent on the subject on which we have the honor of adressing you, but have concluded that in resigning the matter, with the few remarks above submitted, entirely to your own good judgement, we shall have no reason to fear its reception of proper attention—Yet permit us, Sir, to add one remark—That we are an integral part of the citizens of the United States, and stand in need of protection from the General Governt. We have the Honor to be Sir With the highest esteem your fellow citizens

James Dell
S. Beckham
Thomas Harn

LS, DNA-RG 108 (14-0069). *TPUS*, 24:282–84. Dell (1784–1848) was a member of Florida's legislative council. A public meeting at Micanopia (now Micanopy) on August 22 had authorized the enclosed memorial and appointed the committee (St. Augustine *Florida Herald*, Sep 2).

The garrison at Fort King, now Ocala, Fla., had been withdrawn in July. AJ referred this communication on October 23 to Eaton, who referred it to Army commanding general Alexander Macomb. Macomb declined to redeploy troops from the Cantonment Brooke garrison at Tampa Bay, but on November 30 instructed its commander, Colonel Duncan L. Clinch, to protect the interior settlements by sending out armed detachments on any word of trouble. Clinch in reply complained that this was unfeasible and recommended reoccupying Fort King (*TPUS*, 24:297–98, 319-21). Fort King was reoccupied in 1832.

1. Suwannee Old Town was on the west bank of the Suwannee River, where AJ had destroyed an Indian village in 1818. On September 15 Florida Governor William P. Duval notified Eaton of alleged Indian depredations at Howard's, though he mentioned only destruction of property (*TPUS*, 24:267). On November 14 James Gadsden wrote AJ disclaiming the reports (below). Florida Indian agent Gad Humphreys was at this time absent in Washington to answer charges of misconduct. On January 15, 1830, acting agent Daniel C. H. Sims reported to him that there had been no raid at Howard's and that such stories were generally groundless. Sims accused whites who complained of Indian intrusions of themselves luring the Indians into the settlements to trade (DNA-RG 75, M234-287).

2. The Florida Indian Agency was adjacent to Fort King.

[Enclosure]

General Andrew Jackson, President of the United States of America

We, the Undersigned, Inhabitants of the County of Alachua, in East Florida, beg leave Respectfully to represent, That we regret the necessity of being again compelled to call the attention of the General Government to the subject of the Florida Indians.

Scarcely three years has elapsed since some of our peaceable Inhabitants were butchered by these savages without respect to age or sex and altho' their hostility was soon subdued, thier depredations on our property and lawless conduct have been continued from time to time.[1]

We have repeatedly complained to the proper authorities of the Territory of the impropriety of many of the priveledges granted to these people; but we are sorry to say without effect. Our situation at present is alarming, and rendered still more so by a leave of absence for six months which we are sorry to learn has been granted the agent. Within a few days parties of them have been detected in the fact of plundering our stock, in the very heart of our settlements, and fifty or sixty miles beyond their boundary.

About four weeks since a deputation from the Creek Nation visited these Indians—their business unknown but certain it is, that their conduct while here was calculated to produce alarm. Since which time we have been informed that a party of one or two hundred of them have come among the Seminoles, and still remain there. We have further, from the acting agent Mr. Sims, information that the Chiefs of the Seminoles were to hold a Council, for what object unknown, and that their deportment is hostile.[2]

For the protection of our frontiers, and to quell the fears of the people, we would beg leave Respectfully to request that a garrison of four Companies of U. S. Troops be stationed at Micanopia, in this County. Tho' we admit that the company recently stationed at Fort King had its influence, yet in case of difficulty their efforts to check the Indians would have been of little avail being twelve miles within the boundary, and affording no possibility of protection to our families, or of cooperation with our Militia.

We would beg leave further to request That, One Thousand stand of Arms with ammunition, may be sent to the Col. of the sixth Regiment of the Florida Militia in this County, to be distributed to those who may not be supplied with arms.

All which we respectfully submit to your consideration.

> Wiley Brooks
> Francis Richard Jr
> John Fleming
> William Branning
> Charles Woolf

[121 names follow.]

The original signatures are in possession of the Committee.

Copy, DNA-RG 108 (14-0073). *TPUS*, 24:284–87.
1. In 1826 Alachua and other counties mobilized their militias in response to the killing of six people on the west side of the Aucilla River.
2. Sims had spoken at the August 22 meeting.

From Ninian Edwards

Though as anxious as any man in America that you should again be a candidate for the Presidency, & elected by an increased majority,

Though neither intending to ask, nor expecting any thing from you for myself, & as anxious as any man in the Union that, you should permit your friends to run you again for the Presidency, & be elected by an increased majority, yet finding myself compelled in self defense to resist the influence of the patronage of your administration within this state, I have felt restrained by the delicacy of my situation, & a very obvious liability to have my motives misunderstood, from writing to you about the affairs of this state, as I would have wished to do, under different circumstances. And hence I have determined to deny myself that pleasure till after having proved, as I certainly can, my ability to overcome my enemies with all the assistance they can get, I can offer you my support without affording the possibility of any ground to question my disinterestedness.

Could I however have a personal interview with you in which it would be so much easier to guard against misconception, I should have much to say, & I would say it freely—for I have long believed there is no man whose friends can, in a proper manner, use greater freedoms with him, than yours can with you, & I have on former occasions fearlessly acted upon this opinion. It was probably owing to the confidence with which I expressed it, that in a general consultation among your friends, at the time of the Seminole discussion, when you were so justly excited, & had determined to go to the House, I was unanimously selected to communicate to you their views & wishes on the subject of your determination—and while others shrunk from it who might have been supposed to have the least reason to do so, I never undertook any thing with more alacrity, nor had less reason to regret that I had done so.[1] But I know too well the difference between ~~what may be said in~~ a letter & a personal interview to suppose that as much be hazarded in the one, as the other.

There are however, some things which have so awakened my own apprehensions that I deem it my duty to communicate them to you. Sensible of my limited means of knowing enough about them, and of the possibility that they may never even have been thought of out of the limits of this & an adjoining state, I know that I run some risk of the imputation of weakness & credulity for attaching to them more importance than they may deserve—but as it can do you no harm to put you on enquiry, & your sagacity will soon detect any errors into which, from the remoteness of my situation from the great political arena, I may have been betrayed, I will not hesitate to submit to your consideration, however they may be received some views that have been forced upon mine.

By some means or other it has got to be understood that Mr Crawford will be a candidate for the Presidency. This suggestion I think was originally made with a view to affect Mr Calhoun by showing division in the south & a greater practicability of uniting upon a northern man. Higher calculations however are now made, but to what extent I can not pretend to say. According to these, you are, if possible, to be constrained to decline a reelection—and if not, it is calculated upon with great certainty, that Virginia, which is said never to have supported you very cordially, either by taking exception to some of your future measures, or assuming the ground that no President ought to be elected more than once yielding to her predilection for Mr Crawford, will come out in his favor; that the south generally from the present tariff excitement may be induced to unite upon him as more favorable to their political notions; that if your course should prove satisfactory to the south, it will displease Pensylvania; that Mr Inghams enemies, the dissatisfied tariff men, Mr Crawfords old friends, & the opposition in the latter state will all combine in his favor; that Mr Clay who has recently mentioned him several times in his speeches, finding no chance for himself will eventually support him; that the friends of Mr Adams throughout New England who are presumed to prefer any man in the world to yourself will do the same; that even Mr Van Buren can not undo all that he has heretofore done for him in New York; that the Adams & Clay men uniting with his old friends in that state, will constitute a majority in his favor; & that he will every where get all his old friends with all those opposed to you. All these operations however, are probably to depend upon Virginia who is expected to take a leading part with the additional view of healing her present internal divisions, & reproducing that general concert & unity of action that have hitherto distinguished her.[2]

Certain it is the hopes of Mr Crawfords friends in this quarter have recently become very much revived—all of them return from the city of Washington proclaiming it as certain that you are not to be a candidate for reelection. They have great reason to congratulate themselves upon their success in this state, for though they were the smallest of all the presidential parties, they have contrived to retain in office every officer of that party that opposed your election, and there are several of them who did so, and to obtain every appointment that has been made within this state since your administration commenced, and I am confident there is not one of them who would not now as they all did heretofore prefer Mr Crawford to yourself. Mr Kane who was the head of that party, and Mr Kinney, a very illiterate man who cannot write a line of English, and who was till lately a very low subaltern in it, have the credit of having produced all these events. The latter boasting of having advised you to turn all the officers who opposed your election "like he would whip dogs out of a meat house" is now presenting himself before the people of this state as the administration candidate for Governor, & with great success endeavoring to produce the impression that no one who opposed you can be permitted to retain his place, contrary to his & Mr Kane's wishes, & that no appointment can be obtained from you but through the one or the other of them. ~~Successfull however, as he undoubtedly is in those attempts we should be able to defeat him, with an original Jackson man of little personal popularity, by an overwhelming majority—~~[3]

But if I am altogether wrong in reference to Mr Crawford, it is certain that no one who is really your friend should prematurely agitate the question as to who shall be your successor, much less should any department of the executive government attempt to build up the pretensions of any one of the asparants to that station. Such a course would more readily produce a division in the party, so ardently desired by your enemies, than any other that could be adopted. Is there not then something in the course of the removals & appointments that have taken place in this state calculated to produce a tendency to this unfortunate result? Your own original & uniform friends, two of whom Colo: Kimmil & Mr Pell who were recommended by all or nearly every member of the Legislature; & many other highly respectable & influential individuals, have all been overlooked.[4] Removals have been made since the adjourment of the Senate, at the instance our Crawford Senator, which Mr McLain, our other senator & as warm a friend as you have in the nation, positively asserts were in violation of an explicit promise to him that nothing of the kind should be done without previously apprizing him of the Intention to do so, appointments have been made to fill the vacancies thus produced without affording him or the Representative of the state any opportunity of recommending their friends, & every individual appointed, like Mr Kane himself, would prefer Mr Van Buren to either Mr Calhoun or yourself.[5] They are all, without exception, of that breed of Jackson men to which, as you will eventually be convinced, a decided majority of your active supporters at the two last elections are more opposed than to any other politicians in the state. Mr Calhoun cannot long remain ignorant that they have owed their success to the influence of men who are now & ever have been opposed to his pretensions, & in favor of those of another. He will doubtless know that one of his warmest friends who was appointed by Mr Monroe, on the recommendation & personal application of the whole delegation from Vermont, a man whose capability & correctness are unquestioned, whose honesty is universally admitted, & has been recently testified to as proverbial in a letter from Colo Benton to Mr Ingham, has been removed to make way for John Taylor, who is utterly incapable of doing the business himself, & was & still is a public defaulter of record to the County of Sangamo for moneys collected for it as sheriff.[6] If Mr Calhoun should find nothing in so many removals & appointments thus made to complain of at present, he has too much sagacity not to perceive the effects which the continuance of such a course must necessary produce upon himself, & it would not be wonderful if neither he nor his friends should be satisfied with it.

I have no disguise upon this subject. I would myself prefer Mr Calhoun to any other man as your successor—but strong as is my partiality for him, so far from wishing to raise up a distinct interest in his favor calculated to impair the success, or interrupt the tranquility & harmony of your administration, I have all along felt disposed to keep your successor entirely out of view, and to be satisfied with whatever individual the party shall ultimately select for that purpose. But, sir, others are determined to take the start, and there is but one way to prevent their premature efforts from doing much harm, and this, is, to yield to the wishes of your friends & permit them to put an end to the uncertainty as to your willingness to serve the nation another term.

In this case your friends should look less to the passed, & more to the coming election. Executive patronage judiciously managed is capable of accomplishing much, & doubtless was intended to enable the Executive, the weakest branch of the government to sustain itself. The advantage of patronage however consists much less in giving an office, than in having the power to confer one. So long as it remains unfilled an hundred expectants may be kept on their good behavior, the moment it has been conferred, one man only has been gratified & ninety nine may remain dissatisfied. It is therefore, somewhat surprizing, if Mr McLean is not mistaken in regard to the promise which he insist was made to him, that there should have been so much hurry on the part of the administration in making the removals & appointments that have been referred to—particularly, in reference to Mr West who publicly declares, he was not even a candidate for, and did not expect the office conferred upon him.[7]

That Mr Kinney should have been in a hurry to have these appointments made is natural enough, since he well knew that if they had been anticipated the most powerful objections against every one would have been submitted to your consideration.

It is right, I think, that you should be informed of the management & contrivances of this man & his party. Intending to obtain appointments for men of a description and standing which would necessarily render it extremely difficult for them to obtain the requisite security, their first object appears to have been to secure a district attorney who would not be too scrupulous for their purposes. With this view they united their exertions in favor of Mr Samuel McRoberts, a man who had been beaten by an overwhelming majority for a similar state office, in our late Jackson Legislature, by an Adams man; And never did any party select with more judgment, for, with a sense of obligation to them fresh & vigorous, the securities he has approved as far as they are known are so notoriously insufficient that his conduct is the standing jest of the country, & an exalting reproach to the administration.[8] As I know of the securities in two of the cases only, I shall confine my remarks to them, wishing it to be distinctly understood that I hold myself responsible for any thing that I may say in regard to either.

First then, as to Emanuel J. West. This man was a candidate for the last Legislature and beaten in a Jackson county by an Adams man. He is generally considered a bankrupt, & I officially know him to be a defaulting debtor to the state, & have good reason to believe he will always remain so. In the winter of 1826.'7 he became a candidate for the clerkship of our Senate, appealed to the sympathies of the members in regard to the debt he owed the state, professed that his object in seeking the appointment was to enable him to pay it, promised to appropriate his pay in that way, was elected, received his compensation, & never paid a cent of it according to his promise, nor has he yet paid any thing towards that debt in any other way.[9]

Professing to have no desire to remain in the state, nor to receive any office within it, he was fortunate enough to entrap some of our misguided citizens into a cooperation to obtain him an appointment in some foreign land which cooperation was rendered exclusively with a hope of getting rid of him altogether. With a view to keep up an impression that had been found so serviceable to him, & to elude an opposition which he had too much reason to expect, it was given out, when he & Mr Kinney returned from Washington city, that he had the promise & was in the constant expectation of a foreign appointment, and when his commission of Receiver of the land office arrived he professed to be amazed, affected to hesitate whether he would accept it or not, & openly declared that he had never been a candidate for it, that it had been conferred upon him without solicitation, & that he had expected it to have been given to another individual.

Now, Sir, I personally know the securities which this man, so highly distinguished if his own story be true, has given, & I pledge you my honor that the whole of their property at a fair valuation is not worth one half of the amount required. Other respectable individuals, minutely informed on the subject, do not believe it worth more than about half the sum I have stated—but my object is such extreme caution as to preclude the possibility of any question as to my statement. It is believed that some of these same securities have also been taken for another of those officers—but of this I have no personal knowledge, & if true, the files of the Treasury Department will shew it.[10]

Secondly—As John Taylor. This man was also a candidate for the last Legislature in a Jackson county which elects three representatives, lost his election, & was beaten by an Adams man. He is incompetent to the duties of his office, is too conscious of it to attempt to execute them himself, and, as before observed, was at the time of his appointment & continues to be a public defaulter of record to the county of Sangamo for moneys collected for it as sherriff. His securities, I unhesitatingly assert are not worth the one fifth part of the amount required, nor does any one else that I have conversed with believe that the one tenth of that amount could be made out of the whole of them I however intend only to answer for my own statement, which is purposely made with the caution, and for the object before observed in reference to the case of Mr West.[11]

It would thus appear that while public defaulters are so justly proscribed at Washington city, they are pushed into office within this state without even exacting the requisite security from them, while the man for whose benefit all this is generally supposed to have been done, is going about through the state making the impression that the administration is disposed to do much more, to secure his election to the office of Governor: One instance of which, has been communicated to Mr Barry, & I regret that I am not, *now,* at liberty to communicate a still more extraordinary one to you.

Half is not told, yet there is enough, I should think, to satisfy you, on reflection, that it must be difficult to prevent a reaction that cannot fail to be injurious. If there be any foundation whatever for even a suspicion that Mr Crawford wishes to be a candidate, you must perceive how well calculated your measures have been to encourage him & his friends to that determination. Every one of your own friends have been overlooked. Some of them have been rendered so dissatisfied that it has been extremely difficult to keep them in your ranks. You have given the Marshall's office to one of his most thorough going friends, in preference to Colo Kimmil, a vastly superior man, who was your earliest, boldest, & most persevering advocate in this state, who temporarily edited a paper, with great spirit, for no other purpose than to support you at the former election, whose father, then a wealthy man in Pensylvania, boldly advocated your pretensions in preference to Mr Monroe has continued inflexibly devoted to you ever since, & raised a numerous & highly respectable family all in the same faith.[12] You have given the office of District Attorney to one of Mr Crawfords most zealous partizans. Every [land] officer in his favor, who opposed your election, has been retained in office, all the new appointments have been given to his party, & they confidently calculate upon filling every new vacancy & with the patronage of the General goverment to obtain the unrivalled control of the state. Elated with their anticipations, there is not one of them as I verily believe, that is not determined to put down Green, or that does not encourage the belief, & felicitate himself with the hope that you will not be a candidate for reelection. Mr McLaughlin, Genl Duncan's Uncle, & the last one that has returned from Washington city, brings the news & spreads it far & wide, that, "it is well understood at Washington that you are not to be a candidate."[13]

If however all suspicion as to Mr Crawfords wishes are without any just foundation, still such a course of appointments can hardly fail to generate discontents & jealousies highly unpropitious to that unanimity with which all your true friends would rejoice to see you reelected.

But these appointments are calculated to affect you injuriously in another point of view. In our local parties we are divided on the question of slavery the only one which can materially control the presidential question in this state. It has been an all absorbing subject & is likely to be so again. Mr Kinney owes all his consequence to the fermentation which its agitation produced. He is the great Champion in favor of it, and it so happens that all those officers referred to as having been retained, & all those newly appointed, are of what is denominated the slave party. Upon a fair trial this party has heretofore been proved to be much the weakest, & the other side have been constantly gaining ground by new accessions of population that concur with them.[14] Nothing therefore could be more unfortunate than a suspicion of an intention to aid the cause of the former by the patronage of the administration, and it will be well if Mr Kinneys ignorance vanity precipitancy, & zeal in favor of this measure, do not produce an impression so much to be deprecated.

I have written more than I intended. I shall not trouble you again till after the first day of next August.[15] If my present frankness offends, all I have to say, is that, while nothing under the sun shall restrain me from defending myself against my own enemies, such is my view of the approaching crisis, that nothing which you can do towards me personally shall prevent me from affording you my most efficient support, because I do verily believe the political salvation of the nation greatly depends upon your reelection. I have the honor to be with the highest esteem & respect most unfeignedly yr friend & Obt St

Ninian Edwards

There can be no coalition between Mr Clay & Judge McLean[16] and I am always sorry to see such a suggestion in the papers that support you. They both look to the Presidency at a future day, & neither would wish to see another western President elected before himself. The former never will support a western man for that station. The latter though very popular has but little transferable interest & many motives to prefer you to any other man. Mr Clay will doubtless have steps taken to keep himself advantageously before the nation, but he can only be formidable for the Presidency seven years hence. This will depend upon his course in the mean time. He will naturally look to a coalition with some man in the south, or in New York. The tarriff question will interpose no obstacles. The policy of the nation in regard to that matter will be settled within the ensuing seven years. If Virginia can be got to take the lead, there is no man on whom the opposition can rally with more prospects of success than Mr Crawford, who is an ultra on the politics of your southern friends, & would be preferred by many of them if he were not. ~~The elements of dissatisfaction~~ There is in the present state of things such an obvious tendency to adverse coalitions, that nothing probably can prevent their becoming formidable but an early declaration that you are willing to be reelected, & a determination on your part to sustain your own friends, & to discountenance & put down every thing that has a tendency to divide your party into distinct interests in favor of this or that man as your successor.

Descending from this general view to our own little state. I invite your attention to the Vandalia paper.[17] It is & ever has been the most distinguished Clay paper in the state. You will find it the most zealous in the support of Mr Kinney for Governor. I wrote a long letter to Mr Ingham, last winter, giving a true account of the state of parties among us, which I expected to have been shown to you. You may depend upon it, there is no indisposition on the part of the Adams men in this state to support you and they will do so, if not driven from it, by the most impolitic proscription. a proscription which to punish the passed totally overlooks the future. This party have always been opposed to your principal enemies—and Mr Adams being now out of the way I verrily believe they would prefer you to any other man. But suppose they have even done wrong, can it be good policy to reject their proffered future support? Would it not rather be the part of wisdom to invite it? but I am going beyond the limits that I had prescribed to myself & will stop—

ALS draft, ICHi (14-0077). Illinois's leading politician, Edwards had been territorial governor and U.S. senator before becoming governor in 1826. He was a brother-in-law to Duff Green, father-in-law of former Illinois congressman Daniel Pope Cook, and the first cousin of brothers John and Nathaniel Pope, the latter federal district judge for Illinois.

1. Edwards had been a senator during Congress's investigation of AJ's Seminole campaign in early 1819, when AJ came to Washington and friends feared he would assault his accusers.

2. Edwards's and Calhoun's political antagonism to William H. Crawford ran back years. In 1823–24 Edwards had charged Crawford, then Treasury secretary, with official misconduct. The charges were not sustained. Crawford, who was Virginia-born, carried Virginia in the 1824 presidential election. Martin Van Buren managed his campaign in New York.

3. Elias Kent Kane (1794–1835) was a U.S. senator. William Kinney (1781–1843), a Baptist preacher, had been elected lieutenant governor in 1826 on a ticket opposing Edwards's. Kinney lost gubernatorial races in 1830 and 1834. In the 1830 campaign, already underway, Edwards supported his successful opponent, state representative John Reynolds (1788–1865).

4. Singleton Husband Kimmel (1797–1868) was a Jackson County state legislator. A January 16 address to AJ signed by thirty-nine legislators headed by Thomas Mather had recommended him for office. Mr. Pell was probably Gilbert Titus Pell, a state representative from Edwards County.

5. John McLean (1791–1830) was Illinois's other U.S. senator and Joseph Duncan (1794–1844) was its sole congressman. McLean claimed to have a pledge from Ingham that there would be no removals in Illinois without prior notice.

6. Pascal Paoli Enos (1770–1832) was appointed receiver of the Sangamo (later Springfield) land office by Monroe and reappointed by Adams. AJ had removed him for John Taylor (d. 1849), former Sangamon County sheriff and an 1828 Jackson elector.

7. Backed by Kinney and the Illinois congressional delegation, former Madison County representative Emanuel J. West (d. 1830) had sought a diplomatic post. AJ had appointed him land office receiver at Edwardsville in July. On October 22 West was appointed chargé d'affaires to Peru. He resigned the receivership, to which AJ appointed Edwards's brother Benjamin. West died before taking up his new post.

8. On December 20, 1828, George Forquer (1794–1837) defeated former judge and state senator Samuel McRoberts (1799–1843) for Illinois attorney general by a vote in the legislature of 32 to 21. In April 1829 AJ appointed McRoberts federal district attorney for Illinois.

9. West ran third in the 1828 election for Madison County representative, behind William Jones and George Churchill.

10. The sureties for West's $15,000 bond included Jacob C. Bruner, Theophilus W. Smith, John Y. Sawyer, Daniel Meeker, Samuel Whiteside, William Gillham, and Emanuel J. Leigh. In August Samuel McRoberts had vouched that West's security was good.

11. Taylor ran fourth in Sangamon County, behind Jonathan H. Pugh, Peter Cartwright, and William F. Elkin. On September 23, twenty individuals joined to guarantee Taylor's bond of $50,000.

12. In April AJ had appointed Charles Slade (d. 1834) federal marshal for Illinois. Kimmel's father, Peter (1771–1843), had moved from Pittsburgh to Shawneetown, where he published the *Illinois Emigrant* and *Illinois Gazette*.

13. State senator Robert K. McLaughlin (1779–1862) ran unsuccessfully for governor in 1834.

14. In 1824 Illinois voters had defeated a referendum, supported by Kinney, for a constitutional convention whose presumed object was to legalize slavery in the state.

15. The gubernatorial election was August 2.

16. Supreme Court justice John McLean of Ohio.

17. The *Illinois Intelligencer*, edited by state treasurer James Hall.

To John Kintzing Kane, Robert M. Lewis, and William Platt

Washington Octbr. 2nd. 1829—

Gentlemen

I have received your very polite note of the 29th. ult. inviting me to be present at the opening of the Chesapeake and Delaware Canal and to participate with you in the celebration of the labours that have accomplished this happy event; at any day of this month which I might designate.

The importance of the occasion and the flattering reference to my convenience of the period for its celebration, furnish the greatest inducements for my compliance with your wishes; but great as they are, the urgency of my public duties forces me to forego them. The few days which I spent at the Rip Raps, and the accumulation of business during my late indisposition, admonish me, that I shall have no time to spare between this and the approaching Session of Congress: and that I must decline both the honor of appointing the day for the celebration, and the pleasure of rejoicing with you at the completion of a work which promises so much good to the Union. you will have, however, my fervent wishes for its success, and for that of all *other internal,* similar, improvements.

Accept I pray you a tender of my sincere respect for the body which you represent on this occasion, and for yourselves individually, Gentlemen, the assurance of my great regard. I have the honor to be yr most obdt. servt.

Andrew Jackson

ALS, TNJ (14-0090); LS draft, DLC (37). *Nat. Intelligencer,* October 19. The fourteen-mile Chesapeake and Delaware Canal crossed the neck of the Delaware peninsula between Chesapeake Bay and Delaware Bay, linking Philadelphia to Baltimore and the Susquehanna valley. Begun early in the century, the project resumed in the 1820s with funding from the federal government and the states of Pennsylvania, Maryland, and Delaware. Festivities hailing its completion, including a ceremonial barge passage and an oration by Nicholas Biddle, were held on October 17. Kane (1795–1858), Lewis (d. 1855), and Platt (1790–1863), all of Philadelphia, were canal directors.

To Samuel Delucenna Ingham

Washington, Oct. 3, 1829

I sent for Mr. Hill yesterday & had an interview with him & he afforded me no just ground for his removal—I sent to your office & you not being there I was fearful you were indisposed, & entered on an inquiry as to the demeanor of Mr. Smith, and find—it has been decorous & correct through out. This removal is one well calculated to injure us there being no good cause only that he is brother in law to Mr. Adams, which from Delicacy, if no good cause exist, ought to retain him—Whilst on the one hand we ought, & must, drive out spies & traito[rs] from our camp, and default-ers from the guard of our Treasury, we must shield the honest, & well behaved, Justice to ourselves & others require this—and as this has been a very incou[r]teous and badly advised movement on Mr. Hill, we must repair—not by restoring Mr. Smith to Mr. Hills Department, for this would not do well, as Mr. Hills feelings might be implicated But by transferring Mr. Smith to Mr. Hagners office & Mr. R. Reed to the 2nd comptrollers. Their respective salaries are equal and I suppose their duties much the same. This will be restoring Mr. Smith, saving the feelings of Mr. Hill & restoring quietude again and Justice to all.

Extract, Charles Hamilton Galleries catalog, 1974 (14-0098). William Steuben Smith (1787–1850), at one time John Q. Adams's private secretary, had been a Treasury clerk on and off since 1817. He was both Adams's nephew (the son of his sister Abigail and William Stephens Smith) and the husband of Adams's wife's sister. Smith had been dismissed from his post in second comptroller Isaac Hill's office on September 30. On October 12 he was given a clerk-ship in the General Land Office, where he served until 1836. Robert Read remained as a clerk in the office of third auditor Peter Hagner. AJ wrote Ingham on October 12 declaring his satisfaction with the arrangement.

To John Coffee

Washington Octbr. 4th. 1829—

My Dr. Genl

It has become necessary for the goverment of the United States, from the urgent complaints of the cherokee Indians on the one hand, & the Executive of Georgia on the other, that we should cause to be assertained the true and ancient line between the cherokees & Creek Indians—and to have this done at as early a day as possible, & by a commissioner whose standing & character will give satisfaction to all parties concerned—for the accomplishment of this desirable object, we have been induced to call upon you to execute this high trust, for the Goverment, & I hope and trust, it will be in your power to exccute the same for us. Both par-ties have become importunate with their demands for the removal of intruders   The Executive of Georgia, under a Legislative Act, having appointed a commissioner with powers to take testimony, assertain the line dividing the creek boundery from that of the cherokees, which has upon exparte evidence been run, & which includes about one million of acres of what the cherokee Indians claim as their ancient boundery—The Georgians have taken possession of it, & want the cherokees removed from this land, & the cherokees complain of this intrusion, & require the removal of the Georgians; all this confusion is occasioned by the restless spirit of Georgia, whilst the Govt. is taking means to have the Indians peaceably removed beyond the Mississippi and which we must effect, to preserve them.[1] This I have always told them would be the case—I therefore hope you will undertake this commission, as we want this business done quickly, and by a character who, will ensure entire satisfaction to all parties from the confidence reposed in him; and in looking round it is dificulty to select one, except yourself, who will give general confidence to the parties.

Major Eaton has been directed to write you on this subject, to inclose your commission, and instructions, with a power to obtain the funds for its completion—I hope you will undertake, as it is important that we should have this boundery settled, at as early a day as possible— The cherokees claim as far down the chatahootche river, as the Buzzard Roost—The Georgians up to the Suwannee old Towns—These are marked on the plan that will be furnished you, and all you will have to do, is, to notify the parties, take testimony & decide this question—The lower line is contended by Georgia to be a line agreed on by the cherokees & Creeks about 1820—and contend that they had no right to alter their boundery without the consent of Georgia & the United States, as the U. States was bound to extinguish the Indian claim, & if the Indians had that right they might when compelled from interest or other cause to relinquish their claim, might transfer it to another tribe, & forever prevent a relinquishment—This is solid ground & must be the legal decision when made, & in your report—note the date of the agreement between the Indians of this lower line, & the upper, of the ancient boundery.[2] With my respects to all friends in haste yours—

Andrew Jackson

P.S. I inclose this under cover to Mr McLamore, to deliver or forward you as it may reach you at Nashville—

ALS, Anonymous (14-0099).

1. Georgia claimed ownership of all the former Creek domain within the state, including an area that the Creeks and Cherokees had recognized as belonging to the latter in a boundary agreement of 1821. Under the December 1828 resolution of the Georgia legislature, Governor Forsyth had appointed Samuel A. Wales (c1798–1858) to ascertain and mark what Georgia claimed as the historic Creek-Cherokee boundary. White settlers followed Wales into the disputed territory, and the Cherokees complained of intrusion, while Forsyth demanded federal aid in clearing off the Indians from state land (Forsyth to AJ, Jun 23, above). Citing the unsettled boundary, Eaton on August 18 had ordered Cherokee agent Hugh L. Montgomery to "forbear any harsh and rigid proceedings" against intruders for the moment. On September 15 he wrote Forsyth of AJ's hope to remove all the Indians and his "earnest desire" that Georgia would avoid precipitous action, as "a conciliatory course may do much good, a compulsory one much harm" (*HRDoc* 89, 21st Cong., 1st sess., Serial 197).

2. Eaton wrote Coffee on October 10 (DNA-RG 75, M21-6). He also on October 9 ordered Cherokee agent Montgomery to remove intruders, but later countermanded the order pending Coffee's report. Eaton informed Forsyth of Coffee's appointment on October 14. Reviewing the controversy at length, he reiterated AJ's hopes for a general Indian removal and his agreement with Georgia's assertion of sovereignty over her Indian lands. Concurring that if the Creeks had once held the disputed territory they probably had no right to convey it to the Cherokees without state and federal consent, he still urged Georgia's "patience and forbearance" until the true historic boundary could be determined (*HRDoc* 89, 21st Cong., 1st sess., Serial 197).

Memorandum concerning Moses Myers

Octbr. 5th. 1829—

Mr Inghams note inclosing Mr Giles & Mr Loyalls letters answered, & inclosed a remonstrance to him against the removal of the Collector at Norfolk—asking him to arrange & present me all the papers on this subject, we will consult & come to a final result in this case—A J.

ANS, NHi (14-0109). Moses Myers (1753–1835) was appointed customs collector at Norfolk, Va., by Adams in 1827. On October 3 Ingham had forwarded letters from Governor William B. Giles and from George Loyall (1789–1868) of Norfolk calling for his removal. Objections to Myers included his politics and his continued indebtedness to the government from the failure of his merchant firm in 1819. On July 18 Myers had sent AJ a memorial for his retention from Norfolk and Portsmouth residents. In March 1830 AJ removed him for Conway Whittle.

To Martin Van Buren

(Private)

Octbr. 6th. 1829—

My Dr. Sir

I have been much pestered lately by Col Owens, now at Mr Browns, and his friends, daily calling upon, & urging me to appoint him to office.[1]

I named to you the other day the visit of Genl Green on his behalf, to whom I had repeatedly said we had no means to send charges abroad, & to whom I had said that on the urgent solicitations of respectable merchants we had agreed to send Mr west to Peru on their making him the advances &c. On yesterday the Col Called upon me and urged his appointment to Guatemala, I answered, we had no funds, nor was it determined upon to send any person as charge de affairs to that place, that until we received advices from South america, from its unsettled state, we would make no appointment, & if it was necessary we could make none for the want of funds—Col Owens who I suppose Genl Green had whispered the appointment of Mr West, observed that he had friends, *merchants,* who would make the advance for him—that he had been writing the history of Texas, & wished to travel through that country to Guatemala, to observe whether his chart of that Country made, was correct or not—I replied to him again, that under the Existing circumstances in South america, we did not think it proper to send any minister to Guatemala; but I would advise with you to day on that subject—to get clear of this mans importunities & his friends, will it not be well for you, to address him a note informing him, that for the present, no charge de affairs to Guatemala will be appointed—I said he should receive a note to day.

I have just seen Commodore Porter, who informs he has been the bearer of despatches from Mr Poinsett[2]—I am yrs

Andrew Jackson

ALS, DLC-Van Buren Papers (14-0113).
    1. Thomas Deye Owings (1776–1853), a former Army colonel and Kentucky legislator, had written AJ on September 30 asking to be made chargé to Guatemala. He was not appointed. Guatemala had joined with El Salvador, Nicaragua, Honduras and Costa Rica in the United Provinces of Central America, whose government was in turmoil. "Mr. Browns" was probably the Indian Queen Hotel, run by Jesse Brown (c1768–1847).
    2. David Porter had resigned his command in the Mexican navy and returned to the U.S. He reached Washington on October 6, bringing August dispatches from Poinsett.

To William Donelson

Washington Octbr. 8th. 1829—
My Dr. William
This moment I was gratified with the receipt of your kind letter of the 25th. ult. mailed, Nashville, 28th. for which I sincerly thank you—I can easily forgive you for any neglect in writing, when I know how much you have been engaged in your own concerns—it, surely would afford me great pleasure to hear from you often, the kind attention of Elisabeth to her dear aunt has endeared her much to me, and I shall always be happy to hear of your & her welfare—An evidence of my *regard* for Elisabeth, was my leaving with her *poor poll* the *favorite* of my *Dear departed wife*—whether this bird still lives you have not said—present my best love to Elisabeth, and ask her for my sake, to preserve her for me if she can, until I return, as I intend to foster the bird & prolong its life as long as I live for the fondness my Dear wife had for her—when you write say whether it lives.

I sincerely thank you for the information given of the state of my negroes, stock, & farm, and your opinion of Mr Steel as an overseer—I have written him, often reminding him of his engagement to treat my negroes with humanity—I hope he will comply with this part of his engagement, as well as all others—for surely if he does not I will send him away forthwith upon receipt of the information—The deaths, & sickness of negroes this year, which has exceeded any thing before, since I settled there, has filled me with fear that his treatment has been severe, and that he has been inattentive to their health & comfort. I have wrote Mr. Love, in answer to a letter from him, on the subject of my employing him another year, I can make no contract with him until Mr Donelson & him are clear of the present contract, which, I observe from your letter, you understand[1]—If he appears to conduct himself with humanity to my negroes, careful of my stock, by keeping my mares & colts in good order, and attentive to his business, and correct in all his conduct, then I shall employ him again, subject to the same conditions as before—but if you will have the goodness to give some attention to those things, and if you find him deviating from these rules, I will surely send him away, I will have an honest humane man, to attend to my business, or none—The wages I give, is sufficient to command the best talents, honesty, industry, and humanity & the latter he must possess, with honesty, or he remains not with me—please say to him, that I have requested you to observe whether proper humanity is exercised towards my negroes, and attention to my stock, that my *young horses,* I expect to be *fed & raised as tho I was present*—that my colts are not be permitted to be poor, but well fed & attended to—and that having been thus requested, that on your finding a deviation by him from these instructions, you will communicate it—that you are not placed over him as a secrete spy, but as an open observer, as a friend, & neighbour of mine, and a friend of his Steels, so far as he will faithfully perform his duty, and extend humanity to my negroes, which I have so often enjoined upon him. This open conduct, *if he has proper feelings,* will, have a good effect upon him—you can say to him, this I have requested & it is all you will have to do in the business, unless, he Steel, should apply to you for advice, that you understand I have requested Colo. Love & Mr McLamore occasionally to ride up & if necessary counc[il] him.

My Dr. William I will thank you to do so much for me as I have requested—I am well aware you have anough to do to take care of your own business—but being so near you can occasionally step over & see the stock, & observe *particularly,* as to his treatment of my negroes, for *as sure as he exercises inhumanity to them he shall go*—subordination must be maintained by him, but this can be accomplished, without cruelty—I have lost more stock & negroes, this year than I have ever done before in ten years; there must be something wrong—still Mr. Steel may not be to blame—Dr Hogg acquits him of any blame of Jims death.

I have but a moment to write, for I am laboured from light in the morning, until late at night, and I have no leisure for private business, or friendship   I will be happy to hear from you—when you have leisure—I wish you to see Mr Steel and say to him what I have written you; present me affectionately to Mr McLamore, & say I have not time, at present, to write him, but near the close of the year, I will, if he and other of my friends approve & recommend it—employ Mr Steel for the next year giving him five hundred dollars to be paid out of the proceeds of the crop when sold, and I would not give him another cent—Indeed this is too high by one hundred & fifty dollars a year, and I could get *here,* plenty of the best characters as overseers, at this sum, but I know how dificult it is to get an honest man, and as Steel is there, if he will comply with his instructions, treat my negroes humanely & act honestly, I would rather continue, than change him—I would like to hear if my pork will be sufficient for the supply of my hands the ensuing year—if this is not the case, then ought Mr Steel to be removed—give my respects to your father mother Stockly & lady Mr Martin Kitty & family,[2] & all friends, in haste yr sincerely

Andrew Jackson

ALS, DLC-Donelson Papers (14-0115).
 1. Love had written AJ Donelson on August 22 that Steele wished to remain with AJ but not to continue on Donelson's farm for an additional $100. He acquitted Steele of mistreating AJ's slaves (Donelson Papers, DLC).
 2. William's brother Stockley and wife Phila Ann Lawrence (1809–51), and his sister Catherine and husband James G. Martin.

To *the Marquis de Lafayette*

Washington Octbr. 8th. 1829—
My Dr. Sir
 I read with the greatest pleasure your kind letter of the 4th. of August last from the place of your birth in the Mountains of Auvergne, and avail myself of the opportunity which the visit of Mr. D. C. Croxall to Marseilles affords of sending by him this reply to it. He is a highly respected Gentleman of Newjersey whom we have appointed consul for the Port of Marseilles, and to whom, I can safely refer you for such particulars of this country as may interest you, and which the news papers cannot supply. His intelligence, good manners, & patriotism cannot but please you.[1]
 I read with great attention and much profit the excellent address you delivered in the House of ~~delegates~~ deputies on the question of the credits called for by the regular commission. The liberal policy upon which you based your votes meets the approbation of your friends upon this side the Atlantic, and we think, will soon be found to be the only one by which the States of Europe can preserve their harmony, and secure the prosperity, and good Goverment of the people.[2]
 I am happy to learn, that you have anticipated with pleasure the arrival of Mr Reeves. He is indeed an excellent man, and before this can reach you will I hope, have satisfied you that his appointment does not convay

the slightest censure upon the conduct or character of Mr. Brown. I entertain the highest personal regard for Mr. & Mrs. Brown.[3] Have the goodness to offer, with my best wishes for yourself and amiable family, those
of Mr & Mrs. Donelson, who are now with me; and believe me as usual
your sincere friend & grateful servt.

Andrew Jackson

ALS, NIC (14-0122).
 1. Daniel Carroll Croxall (c1793–1877), of Burlington, N.J., had been commissioned as
consul at Marseilles in July.
 2. On July 9, Lafayette spoke in the Chamber of Deputies on a credit of 52 million
francs that the French ministry had requested, in part to support the regime in Greece.
Denouncing the foreign interventions of European powers, he declared against absolutism
and oppression and in favor of national independence and self-government in Greece and
elsewhere (*Niles,* Sep 5).
 3. AJ had appointed William C. Rives minister to France in place of James Brown
(1766–1835), a former senator from Louisiana. Brown's wife, Ann Hart (d. 1830), was the
sister of Henry Clay's wife, Lucretia.

From David W. Haley

Browns Hotel
8 October 1829

Sir
 I have thought it my duty to mention to you by letter who those
Gentlemen are that have written to me on the subject of the removal of
the choctaws which letters I have had the honor this day to hand to you
for inspection.
 Rev. Alexander Tally is a Methodist missionary sent by that society
from Mississippi to reform the indians. he is a Gentleman of high standing in that country. he resides with Col Leflore and in his letter he speaks
the views of that chief. Leflore sees the fate of his nation unless something
is done for them and there is but few of us (general) who are willing to
give up our own lives to save others. the chiefs cannot prepair the indians
for a Treaty   this must be done by the Goverment through some person
that the indians are well acquainted whith who has influence with them.
this person must go through the nation and call the indians in council,
in the different Towns and reason with them, and be plain and positive.
this power must should be directly from you, which would autherise this
counciler to assure them that his talk was the words of your lips. this
would sende the indians to their chiefs to know what should be done to
save them. then the chiefs could come out and tell them, they must go to
the country they now own west of the Mississippi or come under the laws
of the states, and by those laws they can only be treated as free persons
of Colour, and on that point alone your counciler can fetch the whole

nation to reflection. General I have contracted for the mail through the choctaw nation for a number of years, and believe I know what points the indians should be taken on to effect a refformation in their present views, as respects their remaining in quietude where they now are. (General) I have received many acts of Kindness and the strongest marks of friendship from a number of them and their chiefs amongst that number which gives me a feeling intrest for their happiness and prosperity which I know will be imposible to secure to them where they now reside. I am at your servis (General) at all times to give you my humble aid in facilitation your views in promoting the happiness of our Common Country, and the unfortunate Aborigines of america[.] I have the honor to be your obt sevt.

D. W. Haley

PS. Mr Reuben Harris who writes one of the letters is a brother in law to Col Leflore and a man who has influence and standing in the nation.[1]

ALS, DNA-RG 75 (M234-432). Haley (1793–1857) was a mail contractor in Mississippi. He enclosed letters to himself of September 18 from Reuben Harris (d. 1832), a mail contractor, and from Alexander Talley (1789–1835), a Methodist missionary to the Choctaws. Both men reported the Choctaws' unwillingness to submit to Mississippi's laws and their uncertainty at AJ's position. Harris and Talley believed the Indians would accept removal only if AJ would address them directly, leave no choice, offer good terms, and appoint a trusted friend such as Haley to accompany them as agent. Both warned that any Choctaw, including chief Greenwood Leflore (1800–1865), who dared advocate removal except under evident necessity would be endangering his life (DNA-RG 107, 13-1360; M222-26). AJ endorsed Talley's letter: "choctaw *nation*   Major Hailey to be seen & conversed with on the within subject—Three copies of my talk to the cherokees & creek Indians to be made out & forwarded by him, one to David Fulsome one to Peachlen & one to Laflour—A J." David Folsom (1791–1847) was a Choctaw chief and John Pitchlynn (d. 1835) an interpreter.
    1. Harris, a white man, was married to Leflore's sister Sylva (b. c1797).

From William Kinney

Mount Pleasant Octr. 8th. 1829

Dear Sir

In the enclosed "Thumb paper" you will see the letter written by the Hon. John McLean when a Senator in Congress on the subject of the charges made by Mr Kremer against H. Clay: For his letter written to John H. Eaton, see the United States Telegraph Extra, May 10th. 1828 page 197. No. 13[1]

The removals made in this State accord with the wishes of all the true hearted Republicans or Jackson-men here as far as I have been able to ascertain—Mr McKee the Register at Edwardsville is one of the men who called on Governor Coles to come out with his cock and goose story about the opinions of Mr Jefferson.[2] There are thousands of people in this country who have families to support, and have not the means of procuring a piece of land for homes, who are waiting with great anxiety in expectation that you will recommend to Congress to make some provision whereby the industrious poor may become the owners, each of a piece of land, by actual settlement on, and improving the same.

This is a subject upon which I have for some time reflected with much anxiety of mind, in as much as I know it will produce a twofold benefit. first the benefit of the poor people and secondly it will add much to the prosperity and physical strength of the nation and it is a measure which my heart would rejoice to see adopted. May God bless and preserve you in good health to preside over this great republic is the prayer of your most obedient Servant

William Kinney

N.B. I have been creditably informed that Governor Edwards says he has written as many as 10 or 15 pages on the subject of Reform, to prevent any further removals in this State and that he believes, he has convinced you of the *impropriety* of your *course*

William Kinney

[Endorsed by AJ:] Mr Kinney of Illanois inclosing a paper of 1825—

ALS, DLC (37).

1. Pennsylvania congressman George Kremer (1775–1854) had been the first to publicly charge a corrupt bargain between Henry Clay and John Q. Adams in January 1825. The Shawneetown *Illinois Gazette* on February 26, 1825, printed a February 3 letter from Senator John McLean of Illinois saying, "No man, I think, believes that there is the least foundation for the accusation against Mr Clay." In the letter to Eaton extracted in the May 10, 1828, *United States' Telegraph Extra,* McLean said that he had then disbelieved the charges against Clay despite hearing that Clay told the Kentucky congressional delegation before the presidential vote that a Jackson administration would oppose him personally but that Adams would not.

2. Land office register William Patton McKee (1800–1835) was appointed by Monroe and reappointed by Adams and AJ. Edward Coles (1786–1868) was governor of Illinois, 1822–26, and a friend of Thomas Jefferson. Responding to a call from McKee and seven others, Coles affirmed, in a letter published in the Vandalia *Illinois Intelligencer* on December 1, 1827, that Jefferson had opposed AJ for the presidency and had repeatedly disparaged his abilities, saying there were one hundred more qualified men in Albemarle County and that AJ's popularity made him doubt the survival of the republic. Coles offered in evidence a letter from Thomas W. Gilmer which quoted Jefferson saying, "one might as well make a sailor of a cock, or a soldier of a goose, as a president of Andrew Jackson."

To Martin Van Buren

[This undated memorandum was prompted by the receipt of Joel R. Poinsett's August dispatches from Mexico on October 6. It likely preceded the October 10 instructions to Anthony Butler below, which treated the decision to invite Poinsett home as settled.]

Mr. Poinsett & Mexico—

From the best consideration I have been able to give to this subject, I have come to the following result.

Mr. Poinsett's situation at Mexico must be very unpleasant & mortifying —The secratary of Foreign relations his enemy and at the head of the strong minority who he wields to his purposes & in hostility to Mr P. by which he overaws the Executive of Mexico who is friendly to our goverment, & to our minister[1]—under these circumstances we cannot reasonably to expect through Mr Poinsett to effect either, a commercial Treaty, or the Settlement of our limits, or cession of Territory in Texas. In proof of this we find, that the President failed, (after being requested by Mr Poinsett) to notify the Congress when he convened them that one object would be to ratify the commercial treaty that had been returned by this Goverment, and not being thus notified, the congress could not act on it[2]—This to my mind is sufficient proof that the executive of Mexico is overawed by the minority with the secratary of Foreign relations at their head—Therefore let Mr Poinsett with his secratary be invited home, (recalled) in such away as will preserve his feelings and give no cause for exultation by this minority or his enemies. In a firm but decorous language, breathing the best feelings to the mexican goverment; But observing that this goverment cannot but be alive to the insult ~~intended~~ offered to our goverment by the insult intended by the public act of the Legislature of one of the states of Mexico, by their resolution passed by that body calling upon their chief Executive to banish from Mexico our minister, without making to this goverment any representation of his improperly interfering with the interior concerns of their goverment,[3] as well as the deep rooted Jealousy, & hostility expressed in their public acts published to the world against our Goverment; whilst all the acts of ours, displayed the most sincere friendship & good will to theirs, & our instructions to our minister was to give every assurance of our friendship & good will for the republics, of the south, & particularly Mexico—But to preserve our minister from those continued insults of the minority & to foster, & continue our friendship & good understanding with the Republic of Mexico, we have withdrawn our minister & his secretary, & has charged Col Butler to represent our Goverment at Mexico, as charge de affairs with full powers to carry into effect any commercial regulations, and the settlement of our boundery &c &c &c and to cultivate the most friendly relations with that Goverment—with the assurance that whenever Mexico, thinks proper to send a minister here we will receive &c &c—

Andrew Jackson

ADS, DLC-Van Buren Papers (14-0186).
1. In dispatches of August 2 through 22 (DNA-RG 59, M97-5), Poinsett reported that Mexican foreign relations secretary José María Bocanegra (1787–1862) had pressed complaints of U.S. unfriendliness and military designs against Mexico, which Poinsett vehemently denied. Poinsett traced these accusations, and the violent public hostility to himself, to an oligarchic faction seeking the overthrow of Mexico's republican government. He regarded President Vicente Ramón Guerrero (1782–1831) as friendly but weak.
2. A commercial treaty with Mexico was signed and ratified by the U.S. in 1828, but remained unratified by Mexico. Contrary to Poinsett's expectation in July, Guerrero did not bring it before the special session of the legislature in August.
3. On July 29, the legislature of the state of Mexico adopted resolutions that attributed Mexico's internal discords to Poinsett's interference and demanded his expulsion. The resolutions accused the U.S. of implacable hostility toward Mexico. Poinsett reported that President Guerrero deplored such attacks but lacked firmness to stop them.

To Anthony Butler

(Confidential)

Washington Octbr. 10th 1829—

My Dear Sir,

From late advices forwarded by Mr. Poinsett exhibiting the state of parties at Mexico, in which the Secretary of her Foreign relations is understood to have adopted the factious feelings of those, who pretend to be jealous of the views of this Goverment and who, on this account, have treated, with great indecorum, Mr Poinsett, we have determined to recall him, unless the instructions which are transmitted with this letter should find him successfully engaged in the prosecution of the views of which you were the bearer. Those instructions will be shewn to you by Mr Poinsett, who, in the event of his determination to return, will hand you a commission of charge de affairs with full powers to conclude, with the Govt. of Mexico, a Treaty of commerce, and also one of *Limits*, according to the instructions to Mr Poinsett, by which you will be governed.[1]

Unless the aspect of affairs should be very much changed at that Court, when this letter reaches you, we suppose that Mr. Poinsett will gladly avail himself of an opportunity to leave it, and that you will accordingly enter upon the delicate, and highly important negotiations, with which he was charged. In doing so, it will be scarcely necessary to say to you, that the utmost prudence and caution should mark your conduct. A careful avoidance, on the one hand, of every thing calculated to keep alive the *jealousies* of the party opposed to us, and a discreet exhibition, on the other, of the respect due to the govering majority of the Republic, with which it is our wish, and interest, to cultivate the most friendly relations, may enable you to win the confidence of both, or at least, to favor the return of better feelings as it regards themselves, as well as us. A spirit of contrition generally succeeds the indulgence of bad passions, and unless Mr Poinsetts conduct has been greatly misunderstood by us, there is but little doubt that his withdrawal will furnish an abundant occasion for the operation of this spirit. It will be seen that his mighty agency in their political concerns had no foundation in fact, and that the ~~violent~~ consequences of his fancied influence, are only the natural effects of their own institutions with which he had nothing to do. It will be your business to watch this spirit.

With the minister of Foreign relations you must remember, you will be obliged to negotiate, and, in order to win and retain his good graces, that it will be necessary to study the character and the influence of the minority, which he is understood to direct. Let a listening ear, a silent tongue and a stedfast heart, the three jewels of wisdom, guard every advance which you make on the subject of *Texas*. The acquisition of that Territory is becoming every day an object of more importance to us, and if any reliance can be placed on the illiberal speculations which they already ascribe to us, in connection with it, a still stronger argument, for the cession, can be based upon them; for it is obvious, if they really believe that we have ten thousand troops on that frontier, watching an opportunity for the conquest of the Territory, any attempt to chastise the Indian hostilities there herafter, may endanger the peace of the two countries.[2] A conjecture so idle can only emanate from a consciousness of their weakness, and inability to assert their power in that province—a disposition upon which the arguments contained in the instructions, furnished to Mr Poinsett, may be pressed with every hope of success; for nations, like individuals, are never nearer a bargain, than when its conclusion can be clearly proved to be to their interests.

Their complaints, also, upon this subject, inform us of the danger to which we shall be exposed, in the event of an effort, on the part of the inhabitants of that Province, to set up an independant Govt.—one which they undoubtedly look to as problematical, and the responsibility of which, it seems, they are anxious before hand to ascribe to the agency of the United States. The indulgence of such a calculation, and ~~much more,~~ the unwise publication of such unjust reflections upon this Goverment, you cannot but perceive, are likely to hasten the very event which it should be, & no doubt is, their interest to avert. Unless they are determined upon breaking off all harmonious intercourse with this Goverment, I can put no other construction upon such conduct than a wish to create a negotiation by which they hope to effect a transfer of the country, before the power of disposing of it, is lost by the course of a revolution, in which event they may anticipate our possession of it, in some other manner than by that of purchace.

These suggestions are thrown out for your consideration. I will only add another, which has occurred since the arrival of Commodore Porter who has informed me, that the mexican minister for Foreign affairs, or the Secretary of the Treasury, perhaps both, has obtained a large grant of land in Texas, 20 leagues East & west, by three degrees north.[3] *This circumstance may be made to favour the negotiation for the cession*, by stipulating for the surrender of this grant to the United States, *at a fair price*, as a part of the five millions proposed to be given for the whole province. This must be an honest transaction however, not a violation of your general instructions, to regard no grant as legalised, which at the time of the cession, shall have any condition to be complied with. A provision of this character will be absolutely necessary to prevent fraud—The want of such a one in the Florida Treaty, made that country the Theatre for fraud and corrupt speculations. I scarcely ever knew a spaniard who was not the slave of averice, and it *is not improbable* that this *weakness* may be *worth a great deal to us, in this case.*

Be cautious, and while you profess great confidence in them around you, and with whom you have to act, be the possessor of your own secretes.

Wishing you great success in the matters confided to you, believe me very respectfully your most obedt. servant

Andrew Jackson

P.S. The general instructions which will be forwarded by the Secretary of State, & handed over to you by Mr Poinsett, you are at liberty to shew, *very confidentally,* and as a mere voluntary act of your own, to the President of Mexico, or other high functionaries of that Goverment.[4] When you read them you will discover there is nothing said about the purchase of Texas—You are refered to the instruction sent out by you, to Mr. Poinsett, for your Government on that subject, and being left out of your general instructions, nothing but good can grow out of *confidentially* shewing to the President these general instructions as a mark of your own confidence in him. It is all important, that these instructions are shewn to them of your own mere *will,* & begging at the same time that it may not be known to us—but in such a manner as to induce a belief that it must be kept a profound secrete from your own goverment, as on that event, it would destroy you.

When you have read this P.S. and my private letter you will burn them both, first, if you please, taking notes from them—not being accustomed to diplomacy these might be stolen from you & made a handle of against this Goverment. A. J.

[Endorsed by Butler:] remarkable communication

ALS, TxU (14-0130); LC, DLC (60).

1. Van Buren's August 25 instructions to Poinsett, pursuant to AJ's August 13 memo to Van Buren, had laid out the arguments for a Texas cession (DNA-RG 59, M77-152). His final instructions, dated October 16 and sent with this letter, directed Poinsett to resign and return unless the Mexican attitude toward him had completely reversed (*HRDoc* 351, 25th Cong., 2d sess., pp. 35–38, Serial 332).

2. On August 2 Poinsett reported that Mexicans credited a fanciful story of 15,000 Americans massing on the border for an invasion.

3. Manuel Lorenzo Justiniano de Zavala (1788–1836), secretary of the treasury from April until October, had received in March an empresario contract to settle 500 families on a huge land grant in southeast Texas. In 1830 he transferred rights to the Galveston Bay and Texas Land Company of New York City. Zavala later became vice president of the Republic of Texas.

4. Van Buren's instructions to Butler of October 16 reviewed the history of American aid and sympathy toward Mexico as a sister republic and reproached Mexico's unfriendliness in return (*HRDoc* 351, 25th Cong., 2d sess., pp. 40–53, Serial 332).

From Samuel Fisher Bradford

Philadelphia 10th. Oct. 1829.

Dear Sir

In compliance with your request, I now put on paper what I know relative to the wicked report against the character of Major and Mrs. Eaton.

Sometime since, conversing with a gentleman in this City on the subject, he mentioned a report which he had heard in Washington, and which he hoped and believed could be contradicted. I told him that I intended to go to New York the next day, and would make enquiry of the lady to whom he referred me

The report was, that Major Eaton, when in New York with Mrs. Timberlake, asked the lady of the house, where they boarded, to have a lock taken off, which was on a door that opened from Major Eaton's bed chamber to Mrs. Timberlake's, the key having been lost.

On my arrival in New York, I waited on the lady referred to, (with whom I was well acquainted) and she assured me that there was not a word of truth in the story—no such occurrence ever had taken place in her house.

I also understood that Mrs. Timberlake's Father and Husband were with her at the time—The gentleman who had requested me to enquire into the matter was much pleased to find so positive a denial of so injurious a tale.

It is now more than six years since I became acquainted with Mrs. Eaton, then Mrs. Timberlake—I have resided from one to two weeks, every year since, until he Mr Oneale moved to his farm—In that time, I have often seen Major Eaton and Mrs. Timberlake, and know that the most cordial friendship and confidence existed between them—The house was conducted, in the most perfect order, by the amiable and pious Mrs. O'Neal, who is, I believe, a sincere and exemplary member of the Methodist Church—Her husband assisted in regulating the affairs of the family, and a better conducted one, I have seldom, if ever, seen.

Major Eaton's conduct to every member of the family, was kind, respectful & delicate; and I never saw any improper familiarity between him and Mrs. Timberlake. Mrs. Timberlake was generally very gay and sometimes volatile—She is a lady who as the French say "porte le coeur dans la main" (carries her heart in her hand) thereby, in unguarded moments, laying herself open to the envious remarks of those who cannot attain her naiveté or sprightliness and charm of conversation[.] With great respect I have the honor to be Your friend & Servant

(Signed) Saml. F Bradford.

Copy, DLC (75).

To James Gadsden

Octr. 12th. 1829

Dear Sir,

I take pleasure in acknowledging the receipt of your letter of the 8th. ulto., in which I find your usual frankness & the spirit of that cordial friendship which has been uninterrupted since our first acquaintance, and I hope will ever continue so.

On the subject of the supposed outrage every effort will be made by the Dept in future to prevent the recurrence of such causes for it as those which you have described, growing out of the absence of the agent and the want of a sufficient force in the neighbourhood of the Indians. If the agent has been absent without leave he will be removed, and at any rate he will be ordered to his post and injoined to use the greatest vigilance in the discharge of his duty. Should it be true that a murder has been committed, two companies will be ordered to the old Towns on the Suwanne to keep the Indians in check, but we shall wait a few days for more particular accounts in as much as there will be some inconvenience in making this transfer of the companies on account of the want of funds in the quarter Master Dept. As a general rule I wish not to exceed the specific appropriation made by congress without a real necessity, such as that afforded by this case if there is reason to believe that the Indians have become hostile.

you may rest assured that I shall adhere to the just and humane policy towards the Indians which I have commenced. In this spirit I have recommended them to quit their possessions on this side the Mississippi, and go to a country in the west where there is every probability that they will always be free from the mercenary influence of white men, and undisturbed by the local authority of the states: under such circumstances the General Government can exercise a parental control over their interests and possibly perpetuate their race.

you shall hear from me again on this subject. In the mean time accept these assurances of my usual friendship and sincere regard for Mrs. G. as well as your self—your friend

Andrew Jackson

LS in AJ Donelson's hand, DLC (37). Gadsden (1788–1858) had been AJ's military aide before settling in Florida. He married Susanna Gibbes Hort (1786–c1858) in 1827. The "supposed outrage" was the purported murder of the Howard family at Suwannee Old Town.

To Hugh Lawson White

WASHINGTON, *Oct'r* 12*th,* 1829.

MY DEAR SIR:—

I have rec'd your letter from Nashville, 26th ult., and am pleased to learn from it your determination to remain in the Senate a little longer. Your services there, for the present, is all-important to your country, and your continuance in the Senate very gratifying to me. The severe affliction by the loss of so many of your children, I was aware, made public life a burden to you; still, I knew the high estimation in which your public services were held by your country, and that you would find it difficult to obtain the consent of your constituents to retire; am truly happy that you have consented to continue, for I had a hope that I would have your aid in the Senate so long as I remained in the executive. Both of us, I do suppose, would be more contented and happy in private life; but the lord hath willed it, and we must submit.

How grateful I feel to you for your kind and friendly visit to the Hermitage, where lies all that made life desirable to me, and whose loss I can never cease to mourn, and over whose tomb I would like to spend the remnant of my days in solitude, preparing to meet her in a happier and a better world.

Be pleased to present me kindly to every branch of your family, and believe me your friend,

ANDREW JACKSON.

Printed, Nancy N. Scott, ed., *A Memoir of Hugh Lawson White* (Philadelphia, 1856), p. 267 (14-0150). White had been re-elected to a full Senate term beginning in 1829. He had lost six children since 1826.

From Henry Miller Shreve

Louisville Ky Octr. 13th. 1829

Sir,

In July 1828, I was authorised by the Secretary of War, to have constructed a Steam Boat for removing the obstructions to the navigation of the Mississippi river. That boat has been completed and is now in full operation. Her success has been equal to my most sanguine expectations; she breaks down the largest snags or planters in that river, with great ease. Since I have seen the power and effect of that boat in breaking down trees of sound timber, of seven feet in diameter, I have been impressed with the belief, that such a Boat, or one of a similar construction, would be a valuable machine for harbour defence. A Boat of this kind can be so built and manoeuvred as to run down, and sink any ship that ever floated. She could be so constructed, as not to expose either the Crew or any part of her steam Engines to the fire from an enemy's ship. The blow would be struck immediately at the water line, the effect of which would be equal to a cannon shot of seven tons weight. The whole weight of such a vessel with her engines and apparatus, would be about 1200 tons, & moving at the rate of ten miles an hour, will produce an effect equal to a shot of at least 14000 pounds weight, one tenth of which would be instant destruction to any vessel, with which it might come in contact. Of the practicability of such a plan as above described I have no doubt, & have therefore deemed it my duty to communicate my ideas on the subject to you, which I hope will be a sufficient apology for troubling you with this communication. I am Sir Very Respectfully Your Obedient Servant

Henry M Shreve

[Endorsed by AJ:] Refered to the Secretary of the Navy—for his opinions & that of the Navy board—whether such a vessel could be built, & wielded—& whether, the shock, & recoil from a Seventy four, would not sink the boat, or destroy her   such a Boat, as within refered to, would, *surely,* be a sufficent *defence of our coasts & harbours*—but my faith is not strong enough for belief; still, the power of steem is not yet fully known & great strength may be added to a Boat—A. J—

ALS, DNA-RG 45 (M124-121). Shreve (1785–1851), a noted inland navigator and entrepreneur, had been appointed superintendent of western river improvements in 1826. The War Department had paid him $11,000 to build the snagboat *Heliopolis.*

To David W. Haley

Washington. Octbr. 15th. 1829

Sir

you have kindly offered to be the bearer of any communications to the Indians amonghst whom you will pass on your return Home. I place in your hands, copies, of a talk made by me last spring, to the Creeks; I wish you to shew them to the chiefs of the Choctaws, as you pass, and say to them, as far as this talk relates to their situation with their white brothers, and my wishes for them to remove beyond the Mississippi; it contains my sentiments towards the Choctaw, & Chikesaw Indians, and if they wish to be happy, and to live in quiett, and preserve their Nation, they will take my advice, and remove beyond the Mississippi.

Say to them as friends & brothers, to listen to the voice of their father, and their friend: where they now are, they and my white children are too near to each other, to live in harmony and peace. Their game is destroyed, & many of their people will not work, & till the earth. Beyond the great river Mississippi, where a part of their nation have gone, their father has provided a country, large enough, for them all, and he advises them to remove to it. There their white brethern will not trouble them; they will have no claim to the land, and they can live upon it, they and all their children, as long as grass grows or water runs, in peace and plenty. It will be theirs forever. For any improvements in the country where they now live, and for any stock which they cannot take with them, their father will stipulate, in a treaty to be holden with them, to pay them a fair price.

Say to my red choctaw children, and my chikesaw children, to listen —my white children of Mississippi have extended their laws over their country, If they remain where they now are they will be subject to those laws—If they remove across the Mississippi river they will be free from those laws of the state, and only subject to their own laws, and be under the care of their father the President of the united States—where they now are, say to them, their father cannot prevent them from being subject to the laws of the State of Mississippi. They are within its limits, and I pray you to explain to them that so far from the united States having a right to question the authority of any State, to regulate its affairs within their own limits, the General goverment will be obliged to sustain the States in the exercise of this right. Say to the chiefs and warriors that I am their friend, that I wish to act as their friend but they must, by removing from the limits of the States of Mississippi, and Alabama, and by being settled on the lands I offer them, put it in my power to be such—There, beyond the limits of any State, in possession of land of their own, which they shall possess as long as Grass grows or water runs, I can, and will protect them and be their friend & father.

That the chiefs and warriors may fully understand this talk, you will please go amonghst, & read it to, and fully explain it to them.

Tell them, it is from my own mouth you have recd it, and that I never speak with a forked Tongue—Whenever they make up their minds to exchange their lands where they now are for land across the river Mississippi, that I will direct a treaty to be holden with them, and assure them, that every thing that is liberal will be extended to them in that treaty—Improvements will be paid for, stock if left will be paid for, and all who wish to remain as citizens, shall have reservations laid out for them to cover their improvements; and every Justice due from a father to his red children, will be awarded to them & the chikesaws—again, I beg you to tell them to listen—The plan proposed is the only one, by which they can be perpetuated as nations & where can be extended to them, the right of living under their own laws.[1] I am very respectfully your friend & the Friend of my choctaw & chikesaw brethern

Andrew Jackson

ALS draft, DLC (37); Copy, MH-H (mAJs). Haley conveyed AJ's message to Choctaw chief David Folsom on November 24. Folsom replied rejecting removal on December 14 (*The Missionary Herald*, March 1830).

1. In the copy, this sentence continues "& be benefited by the care & humane attention of the United States."

To Tench Ringgold

Octbr 15th. 1829

The President with compliments to the Marshal of the District of Columbia wishes to have an interview with him at his office informs him that complaints have been made, that the Keeper of the prison in this District have placed individuals *convicted on criminal charges,* in rooms in the prison, other than those assigned for *criminals,* and these persons are seen in the debtors apartments, which have been assigned for the honest, but unfortunate individuals who are unable to pay ther debts; it would seem from the complaints made that these *convicted criminals* are treated as the honest debtor, altho condemned *as criminals,* and confinement, as *such, awarded,* as part of their punishment.

The Marshall will make report to the president the facts of the cases complained of, and whether any person *convicted upon a criminal charge,* have been, or are now confined in any other apartment of the prison other, than those, set apart for the confinement of *convicted criminals*[1]

AD draft, DLC (37). On October 9, the *US Telegraph* accused Ringgold of showing political favoritism to Tobias Watkins by moving debtors at the prison in with common criminals so that Watkins, a convicted criminal, could have their rooms. Richard R. Burr, keeper of the prison, replied in the *Telegraph* on October 13. He acknowledged lodging Watkins upstairs in debtors' quarters but denied giving him special treatment or mingling debtors with criminals.

1. Ringgold reported in the *National Journal* on November 2 that he had met with AJ. Crediting AJ with motives of humanity toward debtors rather than vengeance against Watkins, he said AJ was satisfied with Watkins's treatment and merely ordered him to "designate by proper indexes the separate apartments of debtors and criminals."

From Comstick et al.

October 15th. 1829

Our Father and president of the United States

We the Seneca Chiefs residing on Sandusky River and state of Ohio wish you to open your ears to your red Children in this plase our agents have long since told us that there was a good cuntry in the west and plenty of game where the Indians could live well and be out of the way of bad white men and from strong drink which has destroyed so many of our people, some of our young chiefs and some of our wariors have visited Misouri and Arkansaw and have returnd much pleased with the cuntry and particularly with that part of the cuntry where cherakees have lately took there seats

We therefore for our selves and for our nation request the President and government of the United States to make arangements to hold a treaty with us and prepare and secure a home for us by the side of our Brothers the cherakees in the west, we want cash for our Improvements and cash to meete the expense nessary to remove our people to the west and the Balance of the value of our reservation to be paid to us in land, it is our wish to moove next fall if possible We therefore for our selves and for our nation pledge our selves to be the friends of the president and people of the United States

Comstick his X
George curley Eye his—X
Seneca Steel his—X
Tall Chief his mark X
Wipeing stick his mark X
captain good hunt his mark X
Bluejacket his mark—X
Hardhicky his mark—X
Segow his mark—X
Captain Smith his mark X
Small cloud Spicer his mark X
Thomas Brant his mark X
Martin Lane Interpreter

I certify that the within aplycation of the chifes was sined of thir frei will and volluntary act and that the same was writen by their request

James Montgomery
assistant agent for the Senecas[1]

The number of Indians residing on the Seneca reservation is 337

DS, DNA-RG 75 (14-0161). *HRDoc* 47, 21st Cong., 1st sess., pp. 2–3 (Serial 196). Comstick (also Cornstick or Coonstick) was principal chief of the Senecas on Sandusky. He and Seneca Steel, his brother, had returned in 1828 from three years in the western country. This document was forwarded to Washington by Indian agent John McElvain, who reported that a council of Ohio tribes had been held October 8–10 at which only the Senecas favored removal. Receiving no answer, the chiefs petitioned AJ again in September 1830. They signed a treaty in 1831 and removed to Oklahoma.

1. Seneca subagent James Montgomery (d. 1830) was also a Methodist minister.

To *Vicente Ramón Guerrero*

Private & Confidential

Washington City October 18th. 1829

Respected & dear Sir,

The representative of your Exccllency's Government near to that of the United States, Mr. Montoya, has recently requested, in the name of your Excellency, the recall of Mr. Poinsett the duly accredited minister of this Government to yours. Deeply anxious to preserve the harmonious intercourse which it is the interest of both countries to cultivate, I have without hesitation yielded to your wishes on this subject, being unwilling to adopt an impression that any considerations besides those which your Chargé has declared to us have prompted a movement so unpleasant. Events in the relations of nations are often beyond the controul of those sentiments of exact justice and reciprocal rspect by which it should be the wish of all to distinguish them; and should never terminate a friendly intercourse when their cause can be traced to unavoidable circumstances that suspend rather the power of proper action, than indicate a wish to apply it prejudicially. It is thus that we look upon those that have produced the necessity under which you have acted in requesting the recall of Mr. Poinsett, who, we are constrained to think, from the many assurrances he has given us, has had no agency in their origin or direction; and of course that the imputations to which they have subjected his Government, of an improper interference with the concerns of yours, have grown out of misapprehension & error. Without intending therefore to cast a censure upon Mr. Poinsetts conduct, I had, before the receipt of your Excellency's wish for his recall appointed a Chargé de affaires to relieve him, from a belief that in the present posture of the affairs of your Excellency's Government, his continuance near it could not do justice to the feelings and sentiments which the people and authorities of this country really entertain towards yours, and to remove every obstacle to so desireable an object is now my motive in addressing this note to your Excellency personally; ~~in which I beg permission to assure you that in consequence of congress not being at this time in session it is not in my power to send a minister of equal grade to Mr. Poinsetts'. But that the Gentleman,~~ Col Butler who will deliver you this, in the character of charge de affaires, is appointed with full powers to negotiate upon the many points of common interest to the two countries.

I take this occasion ~~in this unofficial form to present~~ to recommend him to you as the gallant commander of one of our Regts of infantry in the last war of the United States with great Britain, and as a soldier & citizen of the highest honor and respectability, well entitled to your confidence.

Trusting that your Excellency will see in this departure from the ordinary forms of communication between nations the evidence of an anxious wish to do all in my power to preserve that good understanding which is so necessary to the permanent interest of the two republics, and so important to the character of free government, I offer your excellency those sentiments of profound respect which are due to your exalted situation, & to your distinguished personal merits. I have the honor to subscribe myself yr. obt. & Humble servant

[Endorsed by AJ Donelson:] copy to the President of the republic of Mexico

[Endorsed by AJ:] to be copied by A. J.

Draft in AJ Donelson's hand, DLC (37). The previous day, October 17, José María Montoya, Mexico's chargé d'affaires in Washington, delivered a formal request for the recall of minister Joel Poinsett. AJ assented in an official message to Guerrero the same day, and Van Buren added postscripts to his October 16 instructions to Poinsett and Butler confirming the former's recall and latter's appointment (*HRDoc* 351, 25th Cong., 2d sess., pp. 38–39, 52–53, 638–39, Serial 332).

To Anthony Butler

Confidential

Washington October 19th. 1829

My Dear Sir

On the eve of the departure of our messenger to Mexico with the dispatches referred to in my private & confidential letter to you of the 10th inst, Mr. Montoya has communicated to us a request from the President of Mexico, couched in the most friendly terms, for the recall of Mr. Poinsett. This, on a full view of the whole subject, we have determined to gratify. Mr Poinsett under existing circumstances could not possibly effect the objects we have in view and as these are no doubt with him as they are with us paramount to any private feeling, we have accordingly by the messenger requested his recall and you will of course enter upon the high & important duties which have been embraced in the previous instructions to Mr. Poinsett, and those which will be borne by the messenger on this occasion.[1] That you may be well known to President Guerrero, I have enclosed to you a letter to him unsealed, which you will please after reading, seal and deliver on your introduction in your official character as Charge de affaires.

With this introduction, and the hints contained in my letter of the 10th, I confide much in your ability to conduct the negotiation for the purchase of Texas, which is very important to the harmony and peace of the two republics. Unless we obtain that Territory we shall be in constant danger of the jealousy which the nature of its population is so well calculated to create. Its inhabitants will make an effort to set up a free Government the moment they have the power, and we shall be charged with aiding this movement altho all our constitutional powers may be employed to prevent it. Keep these considerations constantly in view, and if Mexico *understands well* her true interest, they will prevail[2]

you know the confidence I repose in you; & I am sure that you will endeavor to merit a continuation of it. your friend, & obt. sert.

Andrew Jackson

LS in AJ Donelson's hand, TxU (14 0194); ALS draft, DLC (37).
1. Marine lieutenant Andrew Ross was the messenger.
2. In AJ's draft this paragraph reads: "With this introduction, and the hints given you, in my confidential letter of the 10th. instant, & the powers & instructions sent to you, I have full confidence, you will effect the purchase of Texas, so important for the perpetuation of that harmony & peace, between us and the Republic of Mexico, so desirable to them & us to be maintained forever, & if not obtained, so sure to bring us into conflict, owing to their jealousy, and the dissatisfaction of those americans now settling Texas under the authority of Mexico—who will declare themselves independent of Mexico the moment they acquire sufficient numbers; This our government will be charged with fomenting, altho all our constitutional powers will be exercised to prevent. you will keep this steadily in view, and their own safety if it is considered will indunce them to yield *now* in the present reduced state of their finance."

From John Nicholson Campbell

Washn. City, Oct. 19. 1829

Sir,

The exigency of the circumstances referred to in this communication must furnish my apology for addressing you on this occasion after what has already occurred between us. I have reason to fear that a conversation lately held between Genl. Green & myself upon the subject of the unfortunate affair in which the Secretary of War & myself are involved, has been misunderstood.[1] Under ordinary circumstances, however, I should not interfere to rectify any mistake which may exist in reference to this matter, but should patiently await that developement of the truth which, sooner or later, always occurs. But to my great regret I learn that my excellent friend Col. Towson, than whom, I believe, a more high-minded & honorable man does not live, has been assailed by Majr. Eaton, and that the principal charge brought against him is the fact that he has been my friend and counseller: Now I cannot but see that any mistake in regard to the ground I at present occupy may be greatly injurious to him; and I feel myself impelled therefore by an imperative sense of duty to inform you that I have never for a moment changed the attitude I assumed before your Cabinet at that meeting of it, which, at your request, I attended, and that I have never in any manner nor in any measure retracted any thing that I have said. I did nothing more in my interview with Genl Green, who waited on me, as he said, for the purpose of accommodating matters if he could, than express my sorrow for the results which the affair alluded to had already produced & was likely still to produce, assure him of my willingness that it should die away forever and agree to be silent at all times about it, provided, neither my person, my character nor my friends were attacked on account of it. I had hoped that the conditions of this arrangement might be so observed on both sides that I at least might be forever set free from a concern most uncongenial both to my taste & my pursuits   I am truly sorry to be disappointed. But as it is I am absolved from all obligation to maintain neutrality, and for my friend's sake as well as for my own, I shall feel myself bound, as soon as it shall become necessary, vigourously to employ those means for our common defence, which the Providence of that God who ever defends the innocent & injured, has placed in my hands. I am, Respectfully, Yours

J. N. Campbell

ALS copy, PHi (14-0198).
   1. Campbell wrote Duff Green this same day to reiterate what he had told him earlier: that the pledge of silence he had given regarding Mrs. Eaton was conditional, and that the attack on Nathan Towson voided it and freed him to speak. Green replied that Campbell had misconstrued Green's position as intermediary and the purport of their conversation. While he had approved Campbell's intent to drop the matter, Eaton never had. Rather he was determined to trace the stories about his wife to a responsible source, and Campbell's refusal to speak and his security from challenge as a minister compelled Eaton to hold Towson accountable instead. Green urged Campbell to relieve Towson and clear the air by revealing all his evidence against Mrs. Eaton (DLC-75).

From Ralph Eleazar Whitesides Earl

Nashville (Tenn)
19th: Octr. 1829

Dr. Genl.

I regret it was not in my power to have accompanied your son Andrew on to the City as I would have wished and antisipated at the time I wrote to you last—It will however be but *very* shortly before I shall follow him.

It is impossible to tell in the line of my business how much is to be done where you have been engaged twelve or thirteen years, if you wish to make an honorable completion until you are about to move.

I will assure you my dear friend my heart is with you, and the only pleasure I have in this life is identified with that of yours.

I am much pleased to see the great work of Reform which you have undertaken for the people going on so well, and the Watkins case is a fine example to the rising generation of office holders. There is some grumbling amongst the Coalition, but that is as it should be, if they were satisfied I would think there was somthing wrong.

No Administration for its time has ever given more general satisfaction then that of yours, and may God grant you with health to go through with this ardious task of reform, is the prayers of yours sincerely

R. E. W. Earl

P.S. When I wrote to you last I stated that Judge Anderson had withdrawn from the Senatorial ~~Election~~ contest—why that report was put in to circulation I cannot ~~tell~~ say—but be that as it may Mr Grundy is elected senator. Genl. Purdy desires to be very kindly remembered to you

R E W E

ALS, William C. Cook (mAJs).

To Samuel Delucenna Ingham

Octbr. 20th. 1829—

My Dr. Sir

Having read the inclosed I return them to you; should you have occasion to write to him, you will please say, we have lived too long to be imposed upon by our enemies, we listen to no slanders on our friends, unless, coming from creditable witnesses[.] yrs respectfully

Andrew Jackson

ALS, CLjC (mAJs).

From John Henry Eaton

21. Octo 29

Dr Genl.

The Pension fund as I before stated to you will be greatly deficient: not less than $100,000   It is probable however that during the present quarter, not more than 30, or 40,000 may be necessary to meet the demands that will be made. You will perceive from the enclosed letter of N Biddle President US Bank that an advance is offered to be made. Shall it be accepted; & shall I so write him?[1] Very truly yours

J. H Eaton

You will perceive by the letter of Mr Edwards to which Biddles is a reply, that no application was made for a loan from this Dept. The offer being voluntary might I suppose be accepted, they resting on the faith of the Govt—[2]

I have a letter to day from Scott atto for Alabama   He says the suit of Jno Smith T has been decided in favor of the united States[3]

E

ALS, ViHi (14-0224).
1. Eaton accepted Biddle's offer of an advance on October 26 (DNA-RG 107, M6-12). The pension laws offered stipends to disabled or needy Revolutionary veterans. On December 26, 1828, Adams's secretary of war Peter B. Porter issued a directive easing the eligibility requirements to allow holders of modest property to claim a pension. On March 27 Eaton revoked Porter's order, but a number of new pensioners had already qualified. AJ in his annual message estimated the shortage in pension funds for 1829 at over $50,000. In February 1830 Congress appropriated $101,700 to cover the deficiency.
2. James L. Edwards was a War Department clerk.

3. John Smith T (1770–1836), formerly of Tennessee, was a frontier entrepreneur, duelist, judge, and land speculator now resident in Missouri. His case against the United States involved claims to land in north Alabama arising out of a 1795 grant from Georgia to Zachariah Cox and others associated as the Tennessee Company. In early October the federal district court for northern Alabama upheld the soundness of Smith's title but ruled that an 1816 Mississippi Territory statute of limitations on land claims barred him from recovery. Smith appealed to the Supreme Court while also soliciting Congress to buy out his claim for $100,000.

To Benjamin Garrison Jansen

WASHINGTON, Oct. 22d, 1829

Dear Sir—

I take great pleasure in thanking you for the complimentary terms of your note of the 3d instant, presenting me with copies of your Elementary Lessons in Natural History, which are received.

I shall endeavor to dispose of them in the manner best calculated to promote the objects of the author, for the success of which every patriot must feel a deep interest.

In this republic, education is inseparably connected with virtue and liberty; and he that improves its sources deserves the highest place in the rank of public servants.

Very respectfully, your obed't servant,

ANDREW JACKSON

Printed, *New-York Evening Post*, October 29 (mAJs). *Niles*, November 21 (14-0234). Jansen (1791–1855) was a New York City printer and bookseller.

From William Branch Giles

Richmond, October 22nd. 1829—

My Dear Sir,

I now do myself the honor of presenting you with a volume of Political Miscellanies, compiled by myself; and I hope you will do me the higher honor of accepting it. I have been induced to present you this volume, Sir, as well from my most respectful and friendly regards for your person and approbation of your public conduct and services, both civil and military, as because I conceive you are now placed in a station, big with the fates, not only of the American People, but of the whole human race. I cannot, however, entertain a hope, Sir, that you will have a sufficient exemption from your arduous official duties, to take even a superficial view of the contents of this volume; but, if by any fortuitous circumstance, it should so happen; that any thing contained therein, should come into your view, and should suggest a hint as to the proper course of measures to be pursued, in the great work of reformation, loudly called for at your hands by an abused and indignant People, the thought of having contributed the smallest mite towards this great work, would afford me the most heartfelt gratification, until the last moment of my life. In my judgement, your two last predecessors in Office have completely converted the great political principles, discovered by our Forefathers and introduced into all our fundamental institutions, as the only safe guarantees of human liberty, into the doctrines of despotic Governments, the dread guarantees of governmental liberty—which they tell us, is governmental power; and which, in its consequences, is individual slavery. They have, in practice, not only disavowded the great principles, that private property is the gift of God to individual man, and that all rightful governments are founded upon mans' consent, but have claimed the whole proceeds of the labour of the whole nation, as governmental property, to be distributed, for bettering the condition of man, according to their own fantastical, unlimited will, unrestrained by the will of the individual owners. They have, in the same spirit of usurpation, set at nought all the restraining provisions of the Constitution, by deriving powers from sources, paramount the consent of the American People, as solemnly ordained and established in the Constitution; thus substituting the principle of despotic Governments, for the Republican one. Your high destiny has placed you in a condition which enables you to contribute greatly to reinstate the Federal Constitution in its original energy & purity; and thus, to restore to the American People their usurped liberties. So high a destiny has perhaps, never yet fallen to the lot of man. Should it be your good fortune to effect this desirable object, you will be hailed, as the greatest benefactor of mankind, that has ever yet appeared upon the theater of human action; not only by the American People, but by the whole human race; not only by the present generation, but by all posterity, in all time to come. I rely with perfect confidence upon your best efforts to effect this third revolution in the administration of the Federal Government, upon which essentially depends all future political blessings to mankind. I have full confidence that your wisdom is abundantly sufficient to select the proper means for this great end; and your firmness abundantly sufficient for carrying them into effect. That wisdom & firmness combined, must ensure their complete success. That this may become your distinguished destiny, is the most fervent prayer of my heart, and I have no doubt that it will be that of millions now born, and yet unborn.

Be pleased, Sir, to accept assurances of my high considerations, and sincere personal regards, with my most fervent prayers for the complete success of your patriotic labors—for your health, prosperity and happiness during a long, useful life, which I pray God to preserve for many years yet to come.

Wm. B. Giles

ALS, DLC-Donelson Papers (14-0227). Giles had been a prominent Virginia congressman and senator before becoming governor in 1827. *Political Miscellanies* (Richmond, 1829) collected his speeches and writings, including essays from the *Richmond Enquirer* in 1824–27 criticizing John Q. Adams, protective tariffs, and ambitious national internal improvements.

From Felix Grundy

Nashville, Octr 22nd 1829—

Dear General—

Unless I were to prepare a Bill in all its details I doubt whether I can make a single suggestion which has not occurred to you on the subject of a National Bank—The following however would be the outline of a plan I should prefer—

The basis should be, the revenue of the U States. Say the Capital should be forty millions, the principal Bank located in Philadelphia, with all the powers, over the Brances, usual in such institutions—

The Directors of the principal Bank to be elected by Congress   the power placed either in the Executive or elsewhere would be dangerous—

Divide, for example, twenty millions of the Capital among the States, according to their representation in Congress, and establish a Branch in each State—here arises a great difficulty, how are the Directors of these Branches to be appointed? To authorise the Directors of the principal Bank to appoint them, would be to give them an alarming power—To say that the whole Congress should do it, would destroy every thing like accountability, in making the selections—To say that the State Legislatures should do it, is a very unstatesmanlike Idea, because over and above the imprudence of putting the money of the U States into the hands of others to manage—in times of emergency the very means necessary to sustain the Genrl. Government might be withheld or used to its injury, by reason of the disaffection of some of the States—

I would therefore say, that the representation in Congress from each State, should choose the Directors of the Branches—of the respective States—

~~The other twenty millions of Capital~~

The profits arising from this portion of the Capital might be applied to making such internal improvements in each State, as might be directed by Congress and agreed to by each State respectively, so that none of the profits of any Branch would be withdrawn from the State and in all cases of such internal improvements being made, the sovereignty and ownership to be in the States respectively—

The seat of Government in each State, would generally be fixed on in the Charter for the location of the Branches not in all cases—

The other twenty millions, allowing Philadelphia first to retain a sufficient amount, should be used by Branches established in the ~~commercial~~

large Cities to aid the Commerce of the Country, and its revenue—The Directors of the Branches last spoken of, might be appointed by the Directors of the principal Bank—

The above is a mere outline, If I go further, I shall have to go into matters, which the Congress alone and not the Executive has to regulate—

I hope to be in Washington a week or ten days before Congress convenes—and will loose no time before I see you—I intend to set out to Richmond on the 25th instant to see the Virginia Convention in Session—thence to the City—[1]

So soon as you receive this, will you be so good as to drop me a line to Richmond, stating the condition of your health—it is a subject which gives us all uneasiness in this quarter

You have seen the result of the Senatorial Election here—It was no contest, I was the second choice of both Andersons & Browns friends, so that I could have obtained two votes to one against either—[2]

Your family connections are all well, so far as I can learn—

The Comtee of the House of Representatives or rather the Managers are preparing Articles of Impeachment against Judge Williams—[3]

Mrs Grundy and Mrs Randal McGavock send their best wishes to you[4]—yr friend

Felix Grundy

[Endorsed by AJ:] Mr Grundy on Bank—

ALS, DLC (37).
   1. A convention to revise Virginia's state constitution had convened on October 5.
   2. Grundy was elected senator on the second ballot, with 31 votes to 17 for William E. Anderson and 12 for William L. Brown.
   3. The Tennessee house had voted to impeach circuit judge Nathaniel W. Williams (c1779–1833), an enemy of AJ's, on grounds of judicial negligence and partiality and of falsifying a record to defraud a woman of her property. Williams escaped conviction when two-thirds of the voting senators, but not of the entire senate, found him guilty on the fraud charge. His defenders charged that the impeachment was politically motivated.
   4. Sarah Dougherty Rodgers McGavock (1786–1854), wife of former Nashville mayor Randal McGavock, was Mrs. Grundy's sister.

From William Hendricks

Madison October 22 1829.

Sir,

By this mornings mail I recd. through the medium of the General Land Office, your order of sale, for the disposal, at Jeffersonville and Vincennes, on the second and third mondays in December next of all lands within those districts, which have been relinquished to the U.S. prior to the 4th day of July 1829; or which, previous to such sales, may have reverted to the U. S.; and the object of this letter is, most respectfully, though very earnestly, to request you to postpone those sales, until congress shall have time to deliberate on the subject.[1] The number of reversions or forfeitures in this state must be great, and the persons interested are the most needy of the whole class, for which the relief system was originally enacted; the persons heretofore unable to take the benefits of that system. They are no less meritorious than others who have completed their payments. Generally living on the lands thus reverted and cultivating small farms which they have made on them, they are daily becoming more and more able to meet the demands of the Government, and surmount their own embarrassments. It seems hardly possible that Congress will permit this class of citizens alone to suffer; to lose their lands and the monies paid for them. Should a disinclination to open the accounts under the credit system prevail, still it is in accordance with the most certain justice towards the General Government, to authorize a patent issue for a quantity proportioned to the money paid, or to issue to such persons scrip for the amount paid, and give for a limited period, a preference in becoming the purchasers at private sale. In either of these ways, it would generally be in the power of occupants, to retain their improvements.[2] I can assure you, that this class of citizens have been looking, with much anxiety to the next session of Congress, and in the confident expectation, that in the mean time the matter would rest. This expectation too is most certainly based on your own knowledge of the Western country and your devotion to its best interests

I flatter myself, that you will accord with this view of the subject, and come to the conclusion so desirable and so necessary to this portion of the country[.] With great respect your obt serv

William Hendricks

ALS, DNA-RG 49 (14-0231). Hendricks (1782–1850) was a U.S. senator and former governor of Indiana.

1. The post-1820 land relief laws had allowed purchasers under the old credit system the option to complete their payments over a period of years, with the time proportioned to what fraction of the purchase price they still owed. July 4, 1829, was the deadline for the last and most indebted class to complete payment or forfeit their lands. A September 30 presidential proclamation announced the resale of previously forfeited and relinquished lands in Indiana. On November 4 George Graham wrote Hendricks refusing to suspend the sale, while noting that lands just forfeited by purchasers failing the July 4 deadline were already exempted to give Congress time to intercede. On November 20 Graham, under AJ's authority, broadened the exemption to all lands forfeited within the last four years (DNA-RG 49, M25-25).

2. A relief law of March 31, 1830, entitled forfeiters to repurchase their lands at the current $1.25 per acre minimum, complete their original purchase at a discounted cash price, or draw land-office scrip for the amount previously paid on a forfeited purchase.

To Samuel Delucenna Ingham

Octbr. 23rd. 1829.

My Dr Sir

I have recd. today the enclosed letter from Col. J. A. Hamilton of N. Y. atto for the u states in the case of the British ship *Loyalist.*

This case requires great consideration and the view taken by the atto. from the view I have taken of, I think well founded in law. Should you upon a full examination not agree with Col. H. I think you had better consult Mr Van Buren & the atto. Genl on this subject—under our present circumstances with great Britain whilst we should do nothing to irritate, still, nothing ought to induce us to forget ourselves, or what relates to our national character. we must execute the law first, and then extend all the ~~possible~~ lenity to this case, that the Executive power may authorize[.] very respectfully your

Andrew Jackson

ALS, NjMoHP (14-0242). The *Loyalist,* a British vessel sailing from Tobago to London with a cargo of rum and sugar, docked at New York in September after suffering severe storm damage. The ship was seized by government officials but subsequently restored, and it left New York in November.

From John Henry Eaton

War Office 28 Octo 29

Sir

I submit to you the case of Major Whistler of the U S army, dismissed the service for whipping Dr. Foot asst Surgeon. For doing this he justifies himself thus, as is established by the testimony of Col. Lawrence. That Dr. Foot had circulated reports against his daughter & to the prejudice of his wife. That Miss Whister was pregnant, & that Mrs. Whister wished to obtain from him laudenum to destroy life. This is about the entire amount of the case, as you will see by the testimony of Col Lawrence at the 7th. page of the record. Dr. Foot as will appear by the same testimony circulated a report that Maj Whistler had for his own personal benefit sold 20 dollars worth of the public property   The chastisment tho appears to have been on account of the slanders against his family

J. H Eaton

ALS, DNA-RG 153 (14-0253). Major William Whistler (1780–1863) served at Fort Howard, Green Bay, Michigan Territory, under Colonel William Lawrence (d. 1841). Whistler had married Mary Julia Fearson (1787–1878); their daughter was Julia Ann. In September a court-martial convicted Whistler of conduct unbecoming an officer for his assault on assistant surgeon Lyman Foot (d. 1846). The court ordered Whistler dismissed from the service, and Army commander Alexander Macomb recommended confirming the sentence (Macomb to Eaton, Oct 6, DNA-RG 108, M857-1). AJ elicited opinions on the case from Macomb (Oct 29 and 30) and Berrien (Nov 3), particularly concerning the court's having allowed Foot to introduce new evidence after the defense had concluded. On November 6 Eaton for AJ ordered the verdict approved, but the sentence reduced to six months' suspension from duty because of Foot's provocations to Whistler's attack and the "gross irregularity" in the court's procedure (DNA-RG 153).

From Joel Barlow Sutherland

Philada October 28th 1829

Dear Genl.

Allow me to beg the favour of your not acting upon the subject of the *Mint appointments, before* the meeting of Congress. I have a view upon the subject of the appointments, *here* that I wish to present to your consideration, that I am sure will be beneficial to the party in this state, & at the same time subserve the interests of the public. I have sent you this in haste, as I have understood, that some changes were expected to be made by the Govt in a few days; that in my judgment can be as well delayed for a month or so at least. Our Govrs election, you will see is over & Mr Wolf is elected by about 26,000, the *largest majority* ever given to an opposed Govr in *this State.*[1] That worthless political profligate Binns, is trying to make it appear, that there is a defection in the Jackson Ranks in Penna. because Mr Wolf has not the *50,000 Majority* that you had. The *first* reply to this is, that about 40,thousand Jackson voters did not go to the polls as the election of *Geo Wolf,* was considered *so certain,* which if added to his 26,000 would show an increase of the Jackson strength in Penna. We say the 40,thousand that remained *at home,* were Jacksonians because the *Ritner* party, moved every thing out, that could be obtained, as their plan is clearly disclosed now, to have been to take a *snap* judgment of us. But independent of this fact, it is worthy of notice, that *Ritner* was all through the *Western* part of Penna electioneered as a Jackson Democrat & his letter to his constituents, just before his last attempt to get into the state legislature, was published & circulated every where in the West, in which he *wrote* that he was for Genl Jackson as President.[2] Besides all this he was supported in the West as a *Western candidate* aided by a german feeling upon the subject of *Masonry.* In Lancaster, Represented by Mr Buckannan, & in Dauphin & Lebanon, they circulated German Almanacks, with figures representing the Masons throwing Morgan into the Niagara[3] An Almanack is the most direct way of influencing the german population, as it is a stand-by book of reference for both *good* & *bad weather* with them & they read it through very frequenty. This scheme, secret & powerful operated to our disadvantage. Yet with all these insidious devices, our Candidate, has gone into office with a great majority, & could not have been less than 60,000 thousand if it had been thought, they intended contesting the question of Govr. Binns & Miner think, that they have achieved wonders because in some of the counties, that gave you a majority, where the anti masonic fever raged, have not gone for Ritner, that therefore the great Republican party of Penna is on the decline.[4] In Mercer County a small county by the way, but a *Western* one Mr *Ritner beat* Mr Wolf & Binns calls this a falling off. But there Ritner, was voted for as a Western man & a Jacksonian   To prove that *Mercer* stands unchanged as to the *present* Administration of the genl Govt. of the U. States, is is only necessary to advert to the fact that in *Mercer* county the *Jackson Senator, Genl Cunningham* has been elected by an overwhelming majority. And throughout the state, I know of but 2 persons, *one* in Lehigh & one in Pittsburg, who were *Adams* men at the last Election, who have got into the assembly *in Jackson Counties* this year. The first the one from Lehigh (a german county) *crawled* in by a small majority upon the anti Masonic fever. The other one in Pittsburg was got upon what was called the *regular* ticket in Pittsburg, & succeeded by a most *lean* majority. It is said that a disappointed *Jackson* man, was behind the curtain in that affair & trick'd *Craft* the Adams candidate on the ticket in Pittsburg.[5] In Philada & elsewhere they tried the same scheme, of getting up an amalgamation, & letting Binns & Co in the ranks but *we* kept *off* the *impurities* & ran alone.

AL, TNJ (14-0256).

1. George Wolf (1777–1840) was a Pennsylvania congressman before being elected governor on October 13 over the Anti-Masonic candidate, former Pennsylvania house speaker Joseph Ritner (1780–1869).

2. In a public letter of August 22, 1827, Ritner had declared his past and present support for Jackson (*US Telegraph,* Sep 7, 1827).

3. William Morgan (1774–1826?) of Batavia, N.Y., was planning to publish secret rituals of the Order of Freemasonry when he was abducted and disappeared, never to be seen again, in 1826. Charges of a Masonic conspiracy to murder Morgan and cover up the crime sparked a popular furor against Masonry that spread through several northern states and assumed political form as the Anti-Masonic Party.

4. Former Pennsylvania congressman Charles Miner (1780–1865) published the West Chester *Village Record.*

5. Thomas Scott Cunningham (1790–1855) had represented Mercer County in the legislature since 1825 and was elected to the state senate in October. James S. Craft (1796–1870), a Pittsburgh lawyer and businessman, was elected to the house from Allegheny County, and Peter Kneppley (1772–1855) from Lehigh County.

To Martin Van Buren

washington Octbr. 29th 1829

My Dr. Sir,

I have recd. Mr Barnet letter with a copy of Genl Lafayetts which you inclosed me—The information given presents a new question for consideration—first, the constitutional power to apply funds to this object, of relief, it being one unknown to any branch of appropriations by law. Second, *the policy,* if the power existed. ?would it not be introducing a precedent, that the Goverment would relieve & bring back all individuals altho not citizens who have been, or may hereafter be, enticed abroad by such men as Delany, who may, or may not, be a citizen of the United States, when those vile seducers have made, as I have no doubt *Delany has,* a fortune by them, & now wishes to throw them from him—my feelings say, relieve the poor & distressed, & bring them back to their country & friends—my Judgt. tells me, I have not the constitutional or legal power to put my hand into the national chest, & take from thence, the means to restore them to their country; but will freely contribute out of my private means to bring them home.[1] I will converse with you on this subject when we meet to day, in haste yrs.

Andrew Jackson

P.S. I have just recd information that Grundy is elected by a large plurality over his opponents—

ALS, DNA-RG 59 (M179-67). In 1827 David Delaunay, a former French officer and later resident of St. Louis, had brought six Osage Indians to Europe to exhibit for profit. They created a sensation, but by summer of 1829 the Indians were abandoned and destitute, and Lafayette and American consul at Paris Isaac Cox Barnet (d. 1833) were trying to raise funds to get them home. On October 26 Barnet's son Charles Barnet, who was in Washington, transmitted to Van Buren his father's appeal for the government to pay their passage (DNA-RG 59, T181-1).

1. The Osages returned to the U.S. in 1830 on funds raised in France. The War Department assisted their journey west to Osage territory.

From Martin Van Buren

W. October 31. 1829

My dear Sir

Young Mr Barnett who was removed from the Consulate at Antwerp to which Mr Patterson was appointed is still here & has pressed me anxiously but very respectfully for employment. He bears his removal so well & appears to be so clever—that I should for that reason as well as to soften these matters a little wherever that can be done with propriety like to do something for him.

I have however given him no encouragement. The office of consul at Venice has for a long time been vacant because it was worth nothing. It is understood that that has been made a free port and with that explanation I have offered it to several who were applicants but have not found one to take it. I was therefore upon the point of offering it to Mr Barnett when he told me that he understood the place was vacant—that his friends in Nyork & New Jersey would help him to goods & that with the collateral advantages of the Consulate he would attempt to make a business there. I told him I would speak to you & give him an answer. If you approve I will offer it to him—Yours cordially

M Van Buren

P.S. I should like to give him an answer in the morning.
P.S. I have read the *found* papers & shall be egregiously disappointed if the Majors bitterest enemies can make any thing discreditable out of them[1]

[Endorsed by AJ:] Mr VB on the subject of appointing Mr Barnett consul &c post script on the impressions made by reading the *found letters*

ALS, DLC (14-0286). Charles Barnet was appointed consul at Antwerp in 1823. In July AJ had replaced him with William Daniel Patterson (c1768–1836) of New York.

1. John B. Timberlake had died an apparent defaulter to the government. In October an anonymous tip to the Navy Department charged that Timberlake's records, then being reviewed by fourth auditor Amos Kendall, would reveal that he had been suspiciously remitting funds to Eaton while serving as purser. Kendall found three Eaton letters from 1824–27 among Timberlake's papers. They showed the two engaged in financial transactions but, as Kendall reported to the House of Representatives in 1830, revealed no evidence of impropriety or basis for holding Eaton accountable for Timberlake's liabilities (*HRDoc* 116, 21st Cong., 1st sess., Serial 198).

To Martin Van Buren

Octbr. 31rst. 1829.

My Dr. Sir

I have just recd your note on the subject of young Mr Barnett, and have no objections to your wishes with regard to him, would barely suggest to you that you would say to him that he should have the consulate at Venice, but pospone the appointment until he should be ready to leave the U States, as it might be viewed by our political enemies that we were unstable in our proceedings—however this is only a mere hint, for your consideration, after which make the appointment as soon as you please—

by posponing it a little until he left the city would be establish this rule, that men need not remain here for appointment[.] yrs respectfully—*In great haste*

Andrew Jackson

P S. I am pleased to hear your views on the found letters—

ALS, DLC-Van Buren Papers (14-0290). Charles Barnet was appointed consul at Venice in June 1830.

To *[John Henry Eaton]*

paymaster & surgeon General
These officers by law are placed on the same footing as to compensation, and if the annual salary attached by law, to each, does not exclude them from *all other* emoluments, they are entitled not only to their fuel, and quarters, but to their rations, and forrage—

The act of 28th. of May 1798 authorises the appointment of Q. Master Genl, phician Genl & paymaster Genl with the emoluments to each of Lt Col—By the 15th. section of the act of 3rd of March 1799, the paymaster to be quartered near the army, his pay $80 per month with the rations & forage of a Major—By the act of the 16 of March 1802, fixing the military peace establishment, one paymaster General, seven paymasters & assistants &c &c &c   The act of 18th. of april 1814 enacts that the paymaster shall receive an annual salary of $2000 to be paid quarter yearly at the Treasury &c &c the assistants the pay & emolument of Capt of Infantry—By the act of the 24 of april 1816, it provides that the pay Department shall consist of one paymaster Genl with the *annual salary of $2500.* By the act of the 2nd of March 1821 it is enacted that there shall be one paymaster Genl, with the *present compensation* &c—To determine what this was we have to turn to the act of april 1816 which tells us it is an *annual salary of $2500*—When we pass in review all the ~~acts~~ enactments on the subject of the paymaster General we find his pay & emoluments increased from time to april 1814 when it is changed to an annual salary of $2000, in 1816, at the reduction of the army to a peace establishment we find his *annual salary* increased to $2500 at which it has remained to this time.

It would seem to me, that Congress by adopting the language *annual salary* intended it, as a full compensation for his services, as much so, as if Congress had been annexing a salary to any other officer of the Goverment—it is the same language as used in other cases, & Congress, *surely has the same power,* to define the compensation of military men to *salaries,* as to civil officers. In the case of the Surgeon Genl., & paymaster

Genl., I think congress so intended the salary as a full compensation for their services as such, & in full of all other ~~compensation~~ emolument—If I am mistaken in this, then they are both entitled, in addition to their annual salary, to fewal & Quarters, Rations, and forage—and if congress so intended by their enactments, it will afford me pleasure to see them & every other officer of the army & Navy of the U States, receive for their services a fair & liberal equivalent, and I trust Congress will so regulate the pay and emoluments of the army & marine corps that it cannot be mistaken, but the real sense of Congress fairly & explicitly expressed that the feelings of they officers may be preserved and accounting officers ~~receive a fair compensation for their services, prescribed~~ be able clearly to understand the compensation intended by congress to be bestowed

That Justice may be done to the paymaster & Surgeon General you will suspend all emolument but the annual salary to the meeting of Congress; When I intend to bring it before that body in my communication by refering to your report—Before this is done I wish to ask the attorney Genl to review this part of his report—

AD draft, DLC (14-0059). Army Surgeon General Joseph Lovell had drawn $473.50 in annual fuel and quarters allowance in 1828 and 1829, while Paymaster General Nathan Towson's allowance was suspended in 1827. Berrien reported to AJ in favor of both allowances on July 18, and Towson pressed his claim to AJ on October 14. In his December annual message AJ asked Congress to clarify the matter (Richardson, 2:455–56). Eaton's accompanying annual report argued, as AJ did here, that by plain reading of the present law neither officer could claim the allowance, but that if one received it the other should too as they stood on the same legal ground (*SDoc* 1, 21st Cong., 1st sess., pp. 22–23, Serial 192). Towson's allowance was restored on January 1, 1830, and a law of March 1832 recompensed him for the time missed (*HRRep* 77, 23d Cong., 2d sess., p. 27, Serial 276).

From Willie Blount

Near Turnersville Post Office Robertson Coty. Tenn. Octr. 1829

Dear Sir,

Recollecting, when writing to you the other day by Mr. Johnson, that you once told me that you knew not how funds to equip Tenn. troops for service had been raised, or how funds had been furnished, I, in that letter took the liberty of asking your patience to read the supplement to my Memorial; & did so, to the end, that you might see, thereby, how, and to what extents, & under what circumstances, & from what motives, funds were raised by me, whether by authority, in part amt., or whether without authority for, by far, the greater amt. or whether remittances had been recd by me, how paid over, & how, when, & how often I had acctd., & again, reacctd. therefor, under enjoined, & again, under imposed responsibilities on me both as a, once, state officer, & then, on me, as a private citizen, &c. &c.: and I so requested of you to read that paper, that you might see the irregular mode of conducting funds for such uses, and how state officers were, or had been unjustly burthened with cares & responsibilities enjoined, or imposed, beyond the right of the Genl. Govt or of its officers of dept. to burthen them, either in raising, in receiving, in paying over, or in enjoining on them responsibilities to account for funds, who, owe no duties, services, responsibilities, or accountabilities to the Genl. Govt. or to its service about funds, in any sense, such, being the duties of others, to wit of the Genl. Govt. & of the officers of its service: and who, state officers, cannot have any such services packed on them, without a violation, thereby offered, of the Constitution of the U. S. & of those of the states, nor without a violation of state sovereign rights, nor without a violation of the independent rights & privileges of state officers, & of those of state private citizens, rights & privileges held to be, or should be, of sacred character, & are so provided for to be under our political fabri[c]s: and further, that you might see the abuses and misrule growing out of such practices about funds as are stated in that supplement to have prevailed last war, & ever since, in my case: & I thus called your attention thereto, with a hope, that such abuses & misrule might, for the future, be checked, & that the mode of conducting funds might be better regulated, for the advantage of the Genl. Govt., & for the greater security of state rights, & of the independent rights & privileges of state officers, & for the greater security of the rights, liberty & property of private citizens: & that some better general regulations, to guard against misrule, should be made, for the ease, relief, & benefit of state officers in general & special cases about service rendered beyond duty, in times of need, about funds & if a Governor should from necessity raise funds, at risk, that he may be well treated therefor, & that his official representations concerning such as he may raise, ~~surely are~~ should be entitled to credence, and should not be suffered to be disregarded, by an Auditor: and I trust that the manner I have treated those subjects, will meet your approbation: I have carefully, & faithfully examined these subjects on constitutional grounds, & from proper motives, wishing only to be correct, & with a hope of being useful: all abuses & misrule are serious evils: & if so, should be checked, & I hope that such abuses leading to every misrule & evil, will be corrected thro' your judicious recommendation of a correct course of proceeding about the proper general manner of conducting of funds, for the future: it is time they were checked, by making it unlawful to request of a state officer to raise, or to receive, or to pay over, or to be made accountable for funds to promote the service, or to place him under any responsibility for, or concerning funds, as no state officer owes to the Genl. Govt. any such service, or any such responsibilities, they being due from the officers of the Genl. Govt & from officers of its service, & from them only: to wit, in the case before us, from the Q. Masters of the U. S. service, in whose hands funds are expected to be placed, & to be acctd. for, on their own responsibility, without trouble or responsibility of a state officer: and if so regulated, as respectfully suggested, by law, abuses would be checked, for the relief of state officers, & for the benefit of the Genl. Govt., & thereby, the absurdity of state officers being erroneously, to the discredit of Govt., rendered arrearable to the Genl. Govt., of which, they are not officers, would, in all future time, be avoided, & their rights, privileges, liberty & property safe from the touch of arbitrary misrule[.] I don't know a greater relief to them, nor a greater benefit to Govt. than such regulation would be: they are valuable men: I voluntarily incurred heavy risks & liabilities, or no equipments for the willing sons of Tenn. would have been afforded[.] I fully & correctly acctd., & for doing so, with good motives, have been treated as if a dog defaulter, without cause: serious evil:[1]

Neither you, nor any other person, except myself, know the hundredth part of the particulars which embarrassed my situation about funds I raised, at risk, to promote the service you so signally and usefully commanded during the late war: many of which however, are stated in the supplement above alluded to: I acctd. for all the funds that passed thro' my hands, at the date of each transaction, a more than common prompt accountability, but it is so and documents on file show it to be so: & then, had after accountabilities imposed on me, for no cause: & without a referrence to that supplement those circumstances could not be known to any but myself, & could not be known to others, inasmuch as, altho' I did all I could, to aid the service, at risk, & shrunk from no hazardous responsibility, if by acting I could but be correctly, tho' at risk, useful, & altho' the doing so, was very embarrassing to my situation, as well as jeopardizing the safety of my property, & rendered more & more so, by after accountabilities, for no cause, imposed on me, yet, I made no song about my perilous situation, nor did I dwell in telling any persons, even my nearest friends & neighbours, to this day, of the many risks I incurred, nor of the many responsibilities I had imposed on me about funds to promote the service to the extent I acted: But such was my situation, that it was truly perilous, all the war, & it has been rendered additionally so, & more, & more burthensome, on an innocent man, ever since the war; & I have had to bear the burthen, & to stagger under it, as I could, whilst too, most people erroneously believed, that I acted by authority, or that Govt. furnished the funds, or that I raised them, under the Act of the Tenn. Assembly, Septr. 1813, erroneously thinking too, that that Act related to the equipment of all Troops who entered service, from Tenn, all the war, that is, to the tens of thousands who entered service beyond the number of 3500 men, when to that number of 3500, it only related: and thus, they erroneously believed, without troubling themselves to ascertain that the facts were directly the reverse, to wit, that Govt. did not advance funds, by remittances, to its Q. Masters in Tenn., nor to me, nor did it give authority to raise any, except $10,000, & except, towards the close of the war, when, its Treasury Note remittances came to hand, & then, too late to be of any use in equipping of Troops, and as to the Act of the State of Septr. 1813, I did not find it practicable to raise any funds on the credit of the state, even to equip the 3500 men it related to, as no person was found, on trial, willing to lend on the terms of that act: & every one knows that troops cannot enter & perform active service without being equipped for it: & hence, rather than witness a total inactivity of service, I interested myself, at risk, without authority, & on my liability to Banks & Individuals to raise funds, & of whom, & not of Govt. I got funds, without pledging the faith or credit of either the Genl, or state Govt., & did so act without the aid of the authority of either to protect me from damage—the first risks, were all mine to bear, & they were increased, by the protest of sundry of my Bills, &c., as stated in that supplement: but notwithstanding those facts, known to me, & not known to many others the above alluded to erroneous impressions prevailed, that is, the common, tho' unfounded opinion was, that Govt., in due time, remitted to me funds to promote the service, or that it had given me authority to raise them, or that that Act of the Tenn. Assembly had enabled me to raise them, without risk: & such erroneous impressions, together with the further erroneous one among inconsiderate people, that it was the duty of a Governor to raise funds, any how, & to pay them over, & to account for them too, as fully, as if he had been empowered, and under as strict responsibility to do so, as if he was an officer of the Genl. Govt. or of its service, & as if under bond to do so: & as above said, I did correctly & fully account for every cent, passed thro' my hands, & did so, at the date of each transaction: but from the after accountabilities imposed on me, those erroneous impressions, as well as the further erroneous one, that I had not acctd, or the auditor would not have reported me a defaulter, they, as well as the Auditor, most erroneously thought, that Bills drawn, at risk, & without authority, & without any refund of their amt. to me, amounted to an authority to act; & such erroneous impressions, together with the auditor's reported deficit against me, as a defaulter, as he errone-ously alleged me to be for my own advances, acctd. for, & never refunded to me, altho' acctd. for long before the date of that reported deficit, for no cause made, were very embarrassing to one who had acted, at risk, both usefully & correctly, & who had acctd. during the war, as I had done; & those erroneous impressions altogether, & those, together with the sacri-fices made of my property, thro' the force and effect of that unfounded, unjust, & oppressive reported deficit on my private credit, & that, together with the auditor's not giving me due credits on my vouchers filed in full of that reported deficit of vouchers due from others, & not from me, & these, with the delay also in not granting my just claim all contributed to the peril of my situation, & have embarrassed my situation which was before good, in private life, & all, for no cause, of default, & for no cause for such treatment; & independent of such treatment, there was no cause for my experiencing any sacrifice of property; but it was thus, & thus only forced, & it was thus forced, for if, that reported deficit, & those delays to render me justice had not been made, my credit and property would have remained unimpaired & unsacrificed: all which embarrassments, & sacrifices, for no cause, are great, & greater, than known to any person, but myself: they amount to grievances, & to a violation of the rights of person, & of the property of a private citizen: but thro' respect for Govt. & its officers I have borne them, in silence:

The facts and particulars respecting that unfounded reported deficit, made against me, by the Auditor, for my own advances, probably was made thro his misconception of the true character of those advances; & if so, he is not to blame, nor do I blame, tho' I regret his error, and the more so, as he acts by advice, as I suppose, of some comptroller, who, might have been under a similar delusion: but those facts &c. are fully, correctly, and I trust satisfactorily stated, and so, as to convince you & other friends, who read that supplement containing them, that I never was a defaulter; & I trust you know me well enough, to believe me incapable of being one: I have thought it my duty, to myself, thus fully to state those facts, that others might be convinced, that I never was a defaulter, & that I never had any opportunity of being one: & I hope, that my friends know, that I never was necessitated to be one, nor mean enough, to be one, under any circumstances: I always put a higher value on the little character I ever had, than to give it for the base pleasure of being a defaulter: I have from the date of my first advances, in 1812 to this day, been a constant creditor to Govt., to the amount of a just claim, and to the amount of due credits claimed, and to the amt. of large savings by me made for Govt's benefit, as fully shewn in that supplement, & which, contains nothing I would not verify on oath: & moreover, those facts are supported by documents on file, fully & honestly explained, & placed there, under official signature, at their date, shewing, that I did then pay over, and fully acct. for the very sum & Items of it that I was, without cause, reported a defaulter for: I could not have paid it over, & at the same time have kept it: nor could I be a debtor for my own advances—and I recd. no advances from Govt., all the war: The T. Note remittances came to hand too late, & I acctd. for them—

I delight, as much as any man, in witnessing strict accountability performed by those who owe it: I also abhor, as much as any man, any unjust attempt to force undue accountability, & trust I have had experience enough in life to be a judge of what is either due, or undue, accountability, & how it, when due, should be performed: & I have the pleasure to know, that I have ever performed all that was on any account due from me, & as I hope correctly, & in due time too: I acctd. promptly at the date of my advances: we will now turn to other matters—

My view of the manner of conducting funds &c., is shewn in the supplement alluded to, & I acted in a manner, as may be inferred, therefrom, in support of state interest, & not without asking, that Govt. should raise funds without violation of state rights &c.; & on those heads, no more need be said, here—

I need not say, I approve your policy, in support of state rights, with respect to a removal of the Indians, and concerning relief for them: have ever thought with you, on those subjects: & when in executive office, I endeavored to get the Govt. to remove them, on the same grounds you take: my letters to the Secy War, on those heads, are on file in the war dept., in the years 1810.1811—God grant you success in your undertaking: I worked at it six years, most zealously—[2]

I need not say your course persued, in making removals, is approved by me: go on: the slang of offenders only unites & rivets your friends most closely to you, & more & more so, if possible: it adds tens of thousands to your former well merited good standing: go on, & don't stop short of a full reform—It is believed, that Major Eaton is the most popular Secy War who has filled that Dept.: I am truly glad of it: well done Tenn: her people will do their duty as it should be done—

I should like to spend the time, of the coming session, at Washington: but desire is all: have not funds to enable me to do so: here, am contented, in choice retirement, & am not idle: my love for good Govt., keeps me busy, in trying to know how, & in acting in support of its measures, founded in proper policies—I read and write my own impressions of them to friends: my correspondence is extensive—

If the Russian should whip the Turk, I shall rejoice: Hope the Greeks may become independent, but not to be placed under a monarchy; I have no wish to see should be freemen, dogs, to any King—

Mexico, it is hoped, will be too hot for the Spaniards: Mr. Shaler will be a useful man to our Govt., at Cuba: he understands what he and others are about: I saw him once at Nashville, in 1814: If we had Texas back again, I should like it: but you understand such great matters best—I suspect, that the British would like to have a foothold there; & so much the worse for us—

It would seem, that the Hartford Convention has, of late, found out, that another Story is added to their House, with a new doorkeeper, Austin—it is the dead coming to life, to die again.[3]

It is understood, that Mr. Clay was so late, cutting down his cornstalks & mending up his fences, that his crop will not be good this year, notwithstanding he has Crittenden for an overseer: it is believed, they spend too much time, uselessly, on the stumps trying to improve in Oratory:[4] If by some wonderful change in ~~intellectual~~ endowment, & of heart, such men should ever become wise, and good, they will see the folly of such stump oratory, and learn to do better, than in going about the Country vomiting forth vindictive rages, founded only in disappointed, unhallowed ambition: but until such change does take place, it will be nothing strange to see those men, who erroneously imagine themselves to have been born great, laboring under such delusion, & trying to convince others of their vainly imagined superiority over men of greater worth, and more wisdom: an adage is, that it may be good fortune to have been, or to be, born great, but that it is, on the other hand, a misfortune to be unable to convince any body of it: if I had nothing else to do, I would not go about making stump ta[lks:] enemies to good men will, by such a course, throw themselves in the ditch, if let alone—but should be looked *[to]*

The new term, American System, predicated on the idea, that it is right, by laws, to regulate every man's industry and its proceeds, subjecting them too, to tariff protection, partial in its operation, and in its effects, as I understand the policy of the late Administration to have been, will never do for a republican people to subscribe to as wise, or useful, nor safe to state rights, & state interests: and it seems too, that there is like to be a stir, in Rhode Island, whether Mr. Burgess, or Mr. Clay shall be President to enforce such a system[.] Rhode Island surely ought to have a President to regulate state matters: it is a great state!:[5]

Am glad to believe, that under our present Administration, State rights will be safe, and that the crooked parts of the tariff will be put straight: that our commerce will be well regulated, for its great improvement, & for the advancement of agriculture, simply by such general & equal protection of its great interests, in either sense, as will cause their benefits to flow, untrammelled, among the people, thro' their own enterprize & industry: that Manufactures will flourish thro' the application of the means of capitalists concerned in them internal improvement is a state right for states, & not a Genl. Govt. object, & my hope is, that internal improvements will flourish, by the aid of state funds, & state appropriation of them: and I will further say, that if such funds, & if manufacturing capital, can be constituonably aided by our Govt.'s appropriation of any surplus money, to be made to the use of the states, severally, to be loaned out by the states, to companies, for promoting internal improvements, or to manufacturing capitalists, for terms of years, on interest, to be paid annually, & the amt. of loan to be returned, at the end of the term, such appropriations, if constituonal, would, under state, & not U. S. Govt. regulation, the right of making internal improvement being a state, & not a U. S. right to make, would produce benefits to the public interest, promote manufactures, & put an end to all squabbling about tariff protection: but the Constituonal right to make such appropriations of money, I am not sure of; however, if desireable to the states to be granted to the Genl. Govt. (that is, to make appropriation of surplus money, but not to levy taxes to raise funds therefor) but if gra[nted] under the above restrictions, the object could be attained by an amendment: but that amendment should not grant a power to the Genl. Govt. to levy taxes, or controul internal improvements in the states: Tariffs, can never protect one great interest, to the exclusion of others, without injuriously affecting other important interests: these are my views and desires on the above several heads—

And again, I hope, that our Militia will be well organized, under some uniform system, & well armed and disciplined, under a like uniform system to be devised & to operate throughout the States: that our Judiciary sy[s]tem will be extended, in the West: that Indian affairs, will be better regulated: that the vacant Territory of the U. S, will be better regulated, for the benefit of individual states: that the trade & commerce of the West, will be so ordered, as that a western system of commercial regulations may be seen in operation here, as like systems are seen, in other sections: and that our state elections, will be kept pure, & free from all federal executive influences, & free from all intrigueing & understrapping coalitions, of extraneous kind—such are my hopes, expressed to distant correspondents, hoped to be realized, thro' the attention of our present rulers; & I give them, as mine, without knowing theirs[.] I hope your health is good, & that it will remain so: my respects to your family & inquiring Tenn. friends, & am your sincere friend

Willie Blount

ALS, THi (14-0005).
1. As governor of Tennessee, Blount had been involved in financing southern military operations during the War of 1812. He borrowed money under state authority to pay and equip Tennessee troops, raised funds by issuing drafts on the War Department, and transmitted federal payments to the armies. The federal government covered all this expense, but in the postwar reckoning of accounts it and Blount disagreed over who owed whom. In 1822 the Treasury third auditor found a balance against Blount of nearly $2,400. Arguing that he deserved compensation for assuming risks and responsibilities that went beyond his official duties, Blount claimed a commission on the federal monies he had handled, making him the government's creditor, not debtor. Beginning in December 1822, Blount repeatedly memorialized Congress, whose committees reported variously on his claims. The most recent report, in 1828, was decidedly negative (SDoc 110, 20th Cong., 1st sess., Serial 166). In 1836, a year after Blount's death, Congress awarded his heirs $3,750, minus his still outstanding balance.
2. Blount's letters to Secretary of War William Eustis in 1810–11 advocated a strict stance toward the Indians. In a lengthy letter of April 24, 1811, Blount warned of the disloyalty of the southern tribes, repudiated their claim to independent nationality, and urged their removal west of the Mississippi as soon as possible (DNA-RG 107, M221-34).
3. Supreme Court Justice Joseph Story (1779–1845) was inaugurated on August 25 to a Harvard University law professorship endowed by and named for Nathan Dane of Massachusetts. In the course of praising Dane at the inaugural dinner, Story and James Trecothick Austin (1784–1870), a noted Boston attorney, both spoke kindly of the Hartford Convention, of which Dane had been a member. The Boston Statesman's critical account, reprinted by other Jackson papers, was headed "Lazarus Coming Forth."
4. In a speech at Lexington on May 16, Henry Clay explained his retirement from public life: "My private affairs want my attention. Upon my return home, I found my house out of repair; my farm not in order, the fences down, the stock poor, the crop not set, and late in April the corn stalks of last year's growth yet standing in the field" (Clay Papers, 8:53). Clay and John J. Crittenden spoke together at Russellville, Ky., on September 17.
5. Tristam Burges (1770–1853) was a pro-tariff congressman from Rhode Island. In a July 4 speech at Clayville he had accused AJ's administration of opposing the American System.

Memorandum on Pay and Allowances for the Paymaster and Surgeon General

The Journals—Mr. Cocke of congress moved to strike out the appropriation bill for fuel & quarters—in 18–19–20—[1]

Whilst paid at the Treasury quarterly viewed as a civil officer, untill allowed transportation   In the quartermaster department by Mr Monroe   The became a military officer—account for transportation to Col Towson—allowed by Mr Munroe until Mr. *Cutts decision,* after this a military officers—enquire.[2]

Surgeon Genl—The law stiles them 1799—phician general—a full compensation for his services—1813—for the better regulation—there shall be a phician & Surgeon Genl. with annual salary of 2500—regulations in 1814—quarters & fuel—Surgeon Genl 2. rooms & kitchen—1815. this office expired—in 1818—This office was renewed under the title of S. Genl one S. Genl. 2500—Sec of War order that surgeon Genl &c sec of wars order dated 10th. of August—1818—[3]

[Endorsed by AJ:] case of the surgeon & paymaster Genl. The record sent from Genl Jessup within to be returned.[4] The rules & regulations for the army promulgated by Adjt Genl from 1816. to 2 of March makes no allowance for fuel & quarters to the pay master or Surgeon Genl

AN, THer (14-0003).
    1. John Cocke (1772–1854) was a Tennessee congressman, 1819–27. He favored reducing military spending and in 1821 reported a bill to give Army officers a flat salary rather than pay and emoluments.
    2. Richard Cutts, second comptroller of the Treasury.
    3. A law of 1798 (not 1799) authorized a "physician-general," and an 1813 law reorganizing the Army created a "physician and surgeon general" at an annual salary of $2,500. The *Military Laws and Rules and Regulations* (Washington, 1814) allotted quarters of two rooms and a kitchen to certain officers, not mentioning the surgeon general. The 1815 law setting the peacetime military establishment eliminated the office of surgeon general, but an 1818 law revived it with a salary of $2,500. A War Department order of August 10, 1818, allowed fuel and quarters to several officers including the surgeon general (*Calhoun Papers,* 3:21–22).
    4. Thomas Sidney Jesup (1788–1860) was quartermaster general of the Army.

Memorandum on Reforming Customs Collections

Great losses have been sustained in the customs from the Collectors holding up the bonds after they have become due, & for want of a proper accountability of atto.'s & marshalls after the bonds are put into suit &c &c—To remedy these evils I propose the following corrective to congress

1rst. that all collectors on bonding the customs forthwith make deposit of them in some Bank designated by the Secretary of the Treasury for collection, taking the receeipt of the cashier for the same—by producing the cashiers receipt, the amount be carried to the credit of the collector & the Bank charged with the amount.

Should the bonds when they become due not be punctually paid to be regularly protested, and the cashier to hand them over to the District atto. for the U. States for suit, taking his receipt for the same then the Bank to be creditted, & the atto. charged with the amount of the same   so soon as payment is made to, or Judgt recovered by the atto. a report to be made to the sec. of the Treasury, and the Executions handed over to the marshall, taking his receipt for the same, endorsing on the clerks docket the amount of each Judgt & Execution, and on that receipt being produced the atto. to be creditted & the marshall charged with the same—When any mony is received by the atto. or marshall to be forthwith deposited in the Bank & receipts taken for the same & reported to the Sec of the Treasury—The attos. & marshalls to make reports quarterly to the Sec of the Treasury & at the rise of each court—The Districts

[Endorsed by AJ:] notes on the guards necessary for the better security of the collection of customs—

AN, DLC (37). At about this time Ingham submitted a proposal to improve accountability for customs collections, to which this and another undated AJ memorandum (both placed by DLC at October 10) may be responses or *vice versa*. Ingham suggested that unpaid bonds pass directly from collectors to district attorneys for suit and then to marshals for execution, with each officer held financially responsible for bonds in his custody and reporting quarterly on their status to the first auditor of the Treasury. In his other memorandum, AJ said that collectors should deposit customs bonds in local branches of the Bank of the United States, to be held there until paid or delivered to the attorney for suit.

November

To Ninian Edwards

Mr Crawford will not as I believe be bought again before the nation—nor I do I believe *now* that Virginia could be brought to support him, unless indeed, his mental faculties were to be restored, which is believed to have been very much impaired &c.[1]

Mr Kinney & Mr Kanes boasted influence we are unacquainted with here—in all Mr Kinney recommendations which has been acted on there were others that we relied on united in his recommendations

☞ no such thing exists here in the Cabinet as a policy to promote the views of any one aspirant to the executive chair—the moment that such a thing would unmask itself, I would throw it from my Cabinet—and one thing ought to have convinced you of this fact, that is, Mr Ingham being secratary of the Treasury all the appointments in your state as yet is under his Dept., & you know he is not in favor of Mr Crawford.

enquire into the fact—Senator McLean would recommend no removals whatever—The Senators, divided, &c&c—no promise of the kind named—enquire of Mr Ingham

But this answer may be made, that if they are honest & capable men that are appointed, I care not who they may prefer at the next Presidential Election—leaving as I intend that question to the unbiassed choice of the people—and from your statement, it is time for the Executive to seek information from other than partizan members of Congress, as my appointments are made for the public good, to execute their offices for the public benefit, & when found wielding them for any political effect, they will be removed regardless who may have recommended them.

Mr West has lately been appointed, to the Goverment of Peru—therefore this complaint is done away, & Mr West stands more highly recommended, than most men before the goverment, by members of Congress

& other well known citizens, in almost every state in the union—no proscriptions, we want honesty first, then capacity—reform where office has been abused for political purposes—

AL draft, DLC (14-0350).
1. William H. Crawford had been rarely seen in public since suffering a stroke in 1823.

From Spoliation Claimants

DEAR SIR:

The undersigned avail themselves of the privilege which our estimable institutions have secured to them, in common with their fellow citizens, to confer directly with the Chief Magistrate of the Nation, on matters of interest to themselves, whether of a pecuniary or political character.

The subject to which they beg leave to invite your attention, will be the more readily and candidly considered from the circumstance that the National Honor is concerned:—there was a time when no other incentive to prompt action need be whispered to ensure your full devotion, and it is believed that period has not passed.

Looking back to the early history of our revolution, it will be recollected, that, in 1778, the United States and France entered into Conventional engagements of alliance and Commerce, to which was added a further engagement of privileges to Consuls, in 1788. The several stipulations in our favour, and at the most gloomy period of our history, were much more than performed. During the war of the French Revolution which followed, the French were denied the benefits of the mutual stipulations which we had enjoyed through our war:—the guaranty of her West India Islands was left unexecuted; and her use of our ports and harbours denied to a serious extent.

We plead the hazard of a war with England as our excuse; with whom we soon after concluded a highly offensive treaty. But France would not consider us absolved from our engagements. She plundered our citizens of their property, confessedly without the shadow of justice; and in the end, the United States, after proceeding to every step short of actual war, concluded in 1800 a new system of Conventional law, by which all the old treaties together with the pecuniary and political claims under them, were virtually purchased out from France, in consideration of the claims of our citizens upon her—and that, too, after she had refused to sell out a part of her claims for the whole of ours, which, as well as a further offer of a purchase for large sums of money (also refused) we had offered.

France in no instance it is believed denied her obligation for said claims; but, on the contrary, uniformly professed her willingness to satisfy them; and the United States found, during the negotiations in 1800, that said claims were of more avail to her than an equal amount in money, since some of the differences were of a nature which money could not reach. It can be readily seen, that the chivalrous chief at the head of that nation[1] would not, during his then war with Great Britain, be willing to exchange the exclusive use of our ports as applicable to belligerent purposes for any sum of money that could be offered by us, especially as that use and to the like extent would immediately inure to Great Britain (her enemy,) under our treaty with her of 1794, the moment France should abrogate the exclusive use she had long possessed and enjoyed.

The Senate, by the suppression of the second article of the Convention, in effect offered the claims in question, to discharge our government from the onerous treaties and the liabilities under them, which was reluctantly accepted by France. Speaking of this suppression, the Secretary of State, previous to the final ratification of the instrument, thus writes, as instructions to our Minister in Paris, Mr. Livingston, on the 18th December 1801. (vide Doc: 446 of the collection communicated to the Senate by the President on the 20th May 1826.) "I am authorized to say that the President does not regard the declaratory clause as more than a legitimate inference from the rejection by the Senate of the second article, and that he is disposed to go on with the measures due under the compact to the French Republic."[2]

The Bargain (whether good or bad is not now in question—and it is not doubted was of incalculable benefit to the United States,) was of our own seeking; and on being agreed to, France was completely absolved from all further responsibility.

The history of these negotiations was placed among the secret archives of the State Department, and the grounds on which the claims were bargained away were not disclosed to the suffering parties. Recently, however, the documents containing the manner and motives for the exchange have been made public, since when the two Houses of Congress, and particularly the Senate, have evinced a laudable desire to do justice in part to, what may be justly termed, the government creditors: a bill for that object was reported to that body at the last session for two millions of dollars, which is regarded as a mean to effect the liquidation of the claims, and will doubtless realize that object, tho' the aggregate amount cannot be far short of eight millions of dollars.

These claims have their origin with the Hydra party rage which convulsed this country, and continued in active operation through every administration up to the last seven years; during that whole period, though they were at no time permitted to sleep, still it was not convenient to Congress to discharge them, and therefore inconvenient to discuss them.

In 1824, a more just disposition existed in our Councils; the documents were called for and published, and the obligation upon the United States being found free from all doubt, various favourable reports have been made to the two Houses of Congress—with all which it is presumed you are familiar.

It may be remarked, that the claims arise out of the exercise of the treaty making power, of which, the President, being the head, should take the lead in any measure tending to their final adjustment. It is very probable that the predecessor of Mr. Jefferson, under whose administration the Convention was concluded, and that Mr. Jefferson himself, by whom it was finally ratified, would have taken such lead, but that the party rage before mentioned, was then at its height; and the name of France of all things odious. Besides there has not been heretofore, and for the same reason, that clear indication of the favorable disposition of Congress which now happily exists, and which seems to invite some expression of opinion from the Executive branch of the government. It would appear, therefore, that the case was reserved for your participation, and which is now most respectfully solicited.

While the lapse of time in ordinary cases, operates to prejudice the pretensions of individuals, in this it excites strong motives for liberal justice, since they offer no proof whatever, and rely upon that which the ravages of time have left in the possession of the government:—If the sufferers are willing to rely on that proof under such evident disadvantages, surely the Government cannot do less.

It will not escape your notice, that the acts referred to, have prostrated to the dust many of our best citizens, scattering with a profuse hand poverty and ruin to their suffering families, (and affixing a scar upon the national affections of their children extending to many generations,) while the government has profited by the use of their capital, and gained advantages from its application which cannot be estimated. Surely there is a time to terminate this state of things:—Surely there is a time at which the inviolability of private property shall be respected,—a principle departed from ceases to be a principle;—surely there is a time when the Constitution thus infringed will not be passed in silence.

It is believed that no claims exist of so early a date for like acts, between any of the civilized nations of the earth; and it does not seem to comport with the high character we claim, that such an act should stand in constant judgment against us upon our recorded history. Posterity will owe us no gratitude for handing down such blemishes—and the finger of time may be already pointing to the act, superinduced thereto by the negotiations now pending in France and elsewhere, in which the foul blot may be used as a pretext for a denial of justice for similar though later violences.[3]

A hope is entertained that the time is not distant when the policy of our government will be to do, and to do promptly, ample justice to all her citizens—and that the rule shall be made so absolute that no man shall doubt it. Not only does constitutional obligation and moral duty point to such course, but sound policy in reference to foreign nations, from whom we shall always be the receivers, and not payers of maritime wrongs. The civic prize for such a moral victor should be "The Just."

While the undersigned address you with all the frankness of a friend and fellow citizen, they mean, and they trust they have evinced, nothing short of the full measure of respect due to the Chief Magistrate of their choice—in whose wisdom, intelligence and sense of justice, they are willing to rely for whatever merit their claims may possess. With high consideration And profound respect, We are, dear Sir. Your fellow citizens,

Printed and Draft in the hand of James H. Causten, DLC-Causten-Pickett Papers (mAJs; 14-0342). Causten (1787–1874), a Baltimore lawyer and businessman, was acting as agent for the claimants. Beginning in early November similar memorials, some with identical language, were sent from Baltimore, New Haven, Philadelphia, Providence, Hartford, and other cities.

The U.S. and France had signed commercial and alliance treaties in 1778, during the American Revolution. Among other provisions, they guaranteed French possessions in the Americas and gave French warships and privateers free access to U.S. ports. American neutrality in the war between Britain and revolutionary France that began in 1793 in effect abrogated the alliance, and after the Jay treaty between the U.S. and Britain in 1794 the French committed depredations on American shipping that led to naval warfare between the two countries in 1798–1800. The Convention of 1800, negotiated under President John Adams and finally ratified under Jefferson, ended hostilities.

The Convention's second article confessed disagreement and pledged further negotiation over the present status of the previous treaties and over indemnities claimed under them by either side. The U.S. Senate struck out this article, effectually terminating the previous treaties, and France concurred provided that both sides "renounce the respective pretentions which are the object of the said article." American acceptance of this clause mooted all past claims between the two countries.

American spoliation claimants then sought redress from their own government. The Senate called for the diplomatic record concerning the claims in 1824 and published it in 1826 (SDoc 102, 19th Cong., 1st sess., Serial 129). Committees reported favorably to the claimants, and a Senate bill in 1829 proposed to pay them $2 million.

1. Napoleon Bonaparte, then First Consul of France.

2. SDoc 102 (Serial 129), p. 703. James Madison was Jefferson's secretary of state and Robert R. Livingston (1746–1813) was then minister to France.

3. The U.S. was pursuing spoliation claims against Spain and Denmark, as well as against France for depredations committed after 1800.

From the Arkansas Territory General Assembly

To the President of the United States of America

The memorial of the general assembly of the Territoy of Arkansas, respectfully represents, the expediency of vesting in the executive of the Territory of Arkansas, a general superintendancy over the indian tribes bordering upon, and adjacent to, *the Territory of Arkansas*. In recomending to the president the propriety of the measure herein proposed, the general assembly would beg leave to state, that there are numerous tribes of indians residing on our frontiers, and that they are daily increasing by the migration of those who heretofore lived east of the mississippi. The nearness of their situation to the inhabitants of the Territory, give them ample scope to commit depredations on the property of the citizens. The defferrences and colisions (a consequence resulting therefrom) between the indians and citizens of the Territory, are refered, for adjustment and adjudication to the respective indian agensts, who recognise no superior with out the district of Columbia. Naturally independant, this circumstance emboldens them and they are, too apt, to be partial to the indian cause. This not infrequently produces delay and injustice. Situated as the agents are, in the midst of the indians, their own safetey depends upon the attachment of the tribes. The remoteness of Arkansas from the seat of government, forbids the idea of an application to the propper officers there, for an adjustment of their difficulties. An appeal from the decission of the agents is placed entirely beyound their attainment. Place a superintendant, within their reach, and justice in all cases will be obtained. The general assembly therefore earnestly desire and request the President of the united states to make the executive of the Territory the organ of communication between the indian tribes in our neighbourhood, and the executive authorities of the union, and to subject the indian agents of those tribes, to the control of the Territorial executive, which this general assembly conceive will be greatly conducive to the maintenance of that peace and harmony, which ought to exist between the white inhabitants of our Territory and their indian neighbours. And your memorialits as in duty bound will ever pray.

> John Wilson Speaker of the
> House of Representatives
> Chas. Caldwell President of
> The Legislative Council

Approved November 2nd. 1829.

> John Pope

DS, DNA-RG 107 (M222-26). John Wilson (d. 1865) and Charles Anthony Caldwell (1785–1844) were from Hempstead County and Pulaski County respectively. The 1819 law creating Arkansas Territory made its governor *ex officio* superintendent of Indian affairs. In June Pope had inquired of Eaton about his stipend for this duty and suggested that tribes and their agents who resided near the territory be put under his authority. Eaton replied in July that, as no Indians now remained in Arkansas itself, Pope had no duties and would receive no stipend (*TPUS*, 21:46, 61). In his October message to the legislature, Pope lamented that confining his authority within territorial boundaries left him with no power or influence over Arkansas's Indian neighbors (*Arkansas Gazette*, Oct 13).

From the Arkansas Territory General Assembly

To the President of the United States

The memorial of the General assembly of the Territory of Arkansas, Respectfully represents that in the winter of Eighteen hundred & twenty eight & nine, an order was directed by the Secratary at War General Porter to the Governor of this Territory directing him so soon as a valuation of the farms obtained by the recent Cherokee treaty could be obtained to expose all that had been valued to two hundred dollars or more to rent at the highest bidder, and if the inhabitants omitted or refused to give a fair rent for the land so offered, then to cause a fair estimate to be put upon the arable land, and compel the occupant either to leave the land, or to pay the sum so assessed, and that this year was included in the order.[1] Your memorialists confidently believe that the order above alluded to, would never have passed the War Department, had the then President understood the peculiar situation of the occupants of those farms, many of those persons originally emigrated to the country ceded to the Choctaws in Eighteen hundred & nineteen, A part of the country in which they settled had been surveyed and advertised for sale, with this implied assurance they were induced to open and improve farms, after the treaty with the Choctaws, many of them resided as Tenants at will until permission was granted by the Government of the United States, to settle Lovelys Purchase. To that country they immediately removed with their famalies fondly believing that they had then permanent homes. In the spring of Eighteen hundred & twenty eight, the entire County of Lovely was ceded to the Cherokee Indians, and its citizens again became wanderers. The munificent design of the Government in granting each sufferer Three hundred & twenty Acres of Land, as a home to which he might remove when compelled to leave his farm in Lovelys purchase has been inoperative for the purpose designed, either from the ambiguity of the law or the misapprehension of those whose duty it was to construe its provisions, and as a consequence when those settlers were constrained to move east of the line they had no immediate means of obtaining land. The time limited for their removal was the month of march eighteen hundred & twenty nine, and the only possible means of breading their famalies for the present year was in obtaining for valuable considerations the farms late the property of the Cherokees. The Indians were permitted to remain upon their old farms until the sixth of July, our citizens were compelled to abandon theirs in March, and thus constrained to purchase out the Indian farms at any price or starve.[2] And yet under all those distressing circumstances and after a valuable consideration had been paid the Indians for this years rent, they having the right of possession for half the year, the Government agent has been directed to call upon those people and assess a fair rent, which he is to compel them to pay. Your memorialists respectfully solicit your Excellency to interpose your authority to arrest a measure so oppressive and unjust as well as ruinous to the unfortunate people interested. They are unapprised of a single precedent for the course heretofore adopted by the Government in relation to this subject. They know of no solitary instance in which money has been coerced from the citizen for a residence upon the public lands unless they contained minerals, or salt water. And they can see nothing in the brief history they have given of the sacrifices and sufferings of this people, to exclude them from the benevolent usage of the Government for the last fifty years. Your memorialists earnestly solicit your Excellency not only to rescind the present order but to permit our unfortunate fellow citizens to occupy their habitations for the future unmolested. Some of the lands are now ordered for survey, and may yet be returned in time to enable the people interested to locate the land they occupy with the claim derived from the munificence of their Government.[3]

John Wilson Speaker of the
House of Representatives
Chas. Caldwell President of
The Legislative Council

Approved Novr. 2nd. 1829.

John Pope

DS, DNA-RG 107 (M222-26).
1. In a treaty of May 6, 1828, the Western Cherokees exchanged their lands in Arkansas Territory for a seven-million acre domain beyond the territory's newly drawn western boundary, in present Oklahoma. The Indians were given fourteen months, until July 1829, to remove, and the government pledged to pay for all improvements they left behind and to clear their new homeland of whites. In November 1828, Secretary of War Porter instructed that former Cherokee farms in Arkansas valued at more than two hundred dollars should be leased out at competitive bid, pending their further disposition by Congress. On protest from acting governor Crittenden, the order was amended in January to assess and charge occupants a "fair rent" (*TPUS*, 20:782, 819–20, 840–41).
2. Lovely's Purchase, ceded by the Osages in September 1818, lay astride the Arkansas-Oklahoma border, largely within the new Cherokee domain. By 1828 many whites had moved in, some from lands given to the Choctaws in the 1820 Treaty of Doak's Stand. In May 1828 Congress granted 320 acres in Arkansas to every settler displaced by the Cherokee treaty. A proclamation by Crittenden in January 1829 required whites to remove from the Cherokee country within ninety days (*TPUS*, 20:827–28).
3. Following further protests by Pope, Eaton halted the collection of rents in November 1830 (*TPUS*, 21:288).

From Arthur Peronneau Hayne

Private.

Charleston 3rd. Novr. 1829.

Dear General:
    On the 8th. of January last, before a large assemblage, of the people of my native City, with *one voice,* I was called upon, to give your character. I now enclose you the result. Its perusal, I am sure, will afford you pleasure. Show it to Judge White on his arrival at Washington. I look upon the Judge as one of the best specimens of Western character that we have. I have been long anxious to know him personally. When on a visit to the Hermitage four years ago, you gave me a letter to Judge W__ but on my arrival at Knoxville, I found the Court in Session, & the Judge in

the midst of a most important Land Case, and I feared the presentation of your letter, at the particular time in question, would have *produced inconveniece, and I passed on.*

Mrs. Hayne has been extremely ill for the last six weeks—her life at one time dispaired of—but thank God she is now Convalescent. She begs to be remembered affectionately to you. Our Daughter sends you a kiss—she is the express image of her sainted Mother. I remain, Dear General, your faithful friend.

A. P. Hayne

ALS, DLC (37). Hayne (c1788–1867) was a South Carolina legislator and brother of U.S. Senator Robert Y. Hayne. A former Army colonel, he had served with AJ at New Orleans and in the Seminole campaign. Hayne married Elizabeth Laura Alston (1799–1867) in 1822. Frances Duncan Hayne (b. c1819) was Hayne's daughter by his first wife, Frances G. Duncan (c1797–1820).

[Enclosure]

Celebration of the *"8th. of Jany."* 1829 at Charleston, South-Carolina.

While the Company were Assembled at the Festive Board, the following Toast having been given—

"Coll. Arthur P. Hayne—the gallant associate of the illustrious Jackson."

Coll. Hayne rose and spoke as follows:

Mr. President.

All, I can say on this joyous accasion, is, I thank you, from the *bottom* of my *heart,* for the kind and corteous sentiment, just expressed, in honor to myself. Sir—If during a long course of military life, it has been my good fortune, to have rendered some service, to our common Country, *I feel, that I stand this day more than rewarded.*
Fellow-Citizens.

South-Carolina, has cause, to be proud, of General Jackson. South-Carolina, has cause, to be proud of the *"8th. of January."* She is the Parent of the Great and good Man, destined to the chief Magistracy of our Republic, and whose wonderful deed we this day celebrate. But fellow-citizens, through another trying conflict have we just passed—another heart swelling victory has been won—*and proud* am I to believe that the *high moral character,* and distinguished talents of South-Carolina, *combined with the power—the generous patriotism—and wisdom of Pennsylvania,* have contributed more than any other causes, to effect the glorious political triumph, which by the blessing of God, the People in their Sovereign capacity, have so happily achieved.

Mr. President

The character of Andrew Jackson, is scarcely yet understood, *even in our own Country.* General Jackson's capacity as a Statesman *is even greater than his ability as a Soldier.* This is my deliberate opinion, formed after a personal intercourse of upwards of fourteen years. A simple fact will at once illustrate and justify this idea. It is known to us all, that General Jackson has devoted only a few years of his eventful life, to the acquisition of military knowledge—while he has devoted upwards of *forty years* to the acquisition of political and Constitutional knowledge. Again—I have seen General Jackson surrounded by the most Scientific and talented Soldiers in our Country—and on all such accasions, with that *frankness* which belongs to *true greatness,* he has acknowledged his want of early military education. I have seen him encircled by the most brilliant Statesmen of our Country—by Madison, Monroe, Calhoun, Crawford, Dallas, and last tho' not least in our estimation, *our own ever to be lamented Lowndes*[1]—but it is due to truth—it is due to Genl Jackson to say, that when compared with these great men, I never could discover any want of ~~knowledge~~ wisdom, any the least inferiority. Our distinguished fellow-Citizen, the Vice-President of the U. States, of whom we are all proud—and who in *colloquial eloquence* stands this day without a rival—Sir, I have seen *him* in company with this *"man of plain sense and plain integrity,"* and even Mr. Calhoun has listened with *instruction* and *admiration.*
Fellow-Citizens.

Bear with me a moment longer, while I briefly remind you of a few facts connected with the *"Man of Orleans."* Upon the all important subject of *State-rights,* it is known to us, that Genl. Jackson's *views* are *happily in strict accordance with our own.* Is this nothing? It is known to us that General Jackson is a Slave-holder. Is this nothing? It is known to us that Genl. Jackson derives his *revenue* and *subsistence* from the same *agricultural production upon which we depend.* Is this nothing? *Above all* General Jackson is our com-patriot—a native of South-Carolina.

"Breathes there a man, with soul so dead,
"Who never to himself hath said,
"This is my own my native Land."[2]

And now fellow-Citizens, in all these things, General Jackson stands completely identified with us, and I rejoice it is so.

One word more and I have done. You all remember during the first Presidential contest with Mr. Adams, that General Jackson held a seat in the Senate of the U. States. It was *then* he was so delicately, so critically situated. It was then that his bitterest enemies with their *implacable Chieftain Clay* at their head, left nothing undone to *rob* him of his *good name.* But thank God his very enemies on that occasion were obliged to Confess, that *Washington* himself could not have acted with more *dignity* and *Wisdom.* Indeed—it has been a *Vision,* with which my imagination has often indulged itself—that in the *person* of this *venerable patriot, by*

a most delightful association of Ideas, we were permitted by the God of the Quick and of the Dead, to behold once again on Earth, all that was divine—all that was endearing in our own immortal Washington. And fellow-Citizens, I now ask you—I now put the question to the World, on what occasion has General Jackson proved less than equal to the highest expectations formed of him. We will all therefore indulge the fond hope, that in the *hands of a Kind Providence, Jackson's administration of the Government like the Sun in its daily course will prove a common blessing to our Common Country.*
Mr. President.

I beg to propose a sentiment.
The *People of the U. States—In the late Presidential Election,* they have *nobly done their duty—they have covered themselves with immortal glory, and we may safely abide in their unbiassed Decision.*

AD in Hayne's hand, DLC (36).
1. Congressman William Lowndes (1782–1822) of South Carolina.
2. From the sixth canto of Sir Walter Scott's *The Lay of the Last Minstrel* (1805).

To Samuel Swartwout

(confidential)

Washington Novbr. 4th 1829.

My Dr Sir

I have Just recd. your letter of the 30th. ult. and hasten to reply to it.

Whatever our mutual friend Major Smith[1] may have communicated to you, only from your quotations, I cannot say—The Major read to me a letter from a confidential friend in Newyork, stating that he was fearful your expressions relative to Mr Van Buren would lead to raising up opposition to you, as collector &c &c—recollecting the good old adage, "never to break shins over stools, that were not in the way," induced me to say to him that I was sure Mr V. B. was not now your enemy, but was willing not only to harmonise with, but be your friend; and for your own quiett to cease any political enmity, that was not necessary in self defence. You Judge rightly of me when you believe that no influence or views of political preferment could swerve me from my duty, or occasion me to desert a high minded, virtuous, & independant friend—*This has been tried*—The struggle has passed away, and altho, I fully approve of your high minded & independant feelings, still, I repeat, it is useless "to break our shins over stools not in our way: and requested Major Smith thus to write you. My feelings you have a right to believe are such towards you as they ever will be to all high minded honorable men; but in your situation, unless in self defence, you ought to have no desire to multiply enemies, and I have every right to believe that Mr. V. B. has no wish *now,* to be unfriendly with you—receive this as a hint dictated by friendship, and just take it for what, upon your own good reflection, you may think it worth.

I am happy to hear you are getting on *well,* and I never for one moment doubted your success—I have just received a very interesting letter from our friend ogden, Liverpool, he will be of great advantage there to the revenue, and do honor to himself, & benefit to the nation.[2] In great haste yr Friend

Andrew Jackson

P.S. I must add, when one is crown*[ed]* with success, & puts down his ene*[mies,]* then, he ought to rest contented, a[nd] *act only on the defensive* A. J.

ALS, Clermont State Historic Site (mAJs).
 1. Thomas L. Smith, register of the Treasury.
 2. Francis Barber Ogden (1783–1857), appointed consul at Liverpool in June in place of James Maury.

From John B. Duncan

Tuscumbia Al
5th Novr. 1829

Sir

 Near two years has now passed away since I have been seeking an opportunity to show to the world that one of the public functionarys of the Govt has been acting in bad faith. But as yet all my efforts has been to no effect time after time have I made specific charges agst Majr. Benj F. Smith Agent for the Chickasaws. Prayer that the Govt. would order an investigation open and public to the world, so that all parties concerned might receive justice and *[not]* subject the inocent to the loss of Executive favor except upon a manifest proof of his unworthiness I charge Majr. Benj F Smith of being guilty of *many shamful acts of Peculations upon the Govt* I also charge him of official Treachery such as never before disgraced a public officer. If the charges which I have heretofore and at presant submit in refference to Majr. Smith should be credited it would deprive him of the confidence of the Govt, as well as blast his character for ever Therefore you may rest assured I did not act without deliberation. No Sir I acted with feelings of the most dispasionate cast, and I now am willing to stake my character my fortune and evry thing else that is dear to a man on supporting my accusations against him I am well apprised that my character is labouring under some imputation at Washington from the fact of Majr. being able to procure statements from various persons disproving my evidence given on charges prefered against him by the chiefs of the chickasaws. But Sir to a man of your experience it will only be necessary for me to explain one fact to convince you that if I am not inocently per[se]cuted that it is possible I may be. Majr. Smith obtained his exculpetory evidence last winter while I was engaged in conducting the exploring party of chickasaws west of the Mississippi river.[1] Their was not a single confronting question asked his witnesses he had a skillful Lawyer to draw up his response & in this way he made his path as white as snow at Washington when at home he has been told to his face by several respectable men that he *was a rogue a dishonest villian &c* and he fails to make an effort [to] vindicate himself by having a fair open and unbiased investigation into his official acts If you could spear the time to examin my several communications to the dept you will see I have been most shamfully treated by Mr. Eaton. I addressa letter to Mr Porter Secretary of War asking an investigation into Majr. Smiths official acts and stated if the dept would not grant the investigation that they might receive it as a resignation of my office This letter was afterwords answred by Mr. Eaton (stating that the dept acceded to my proposition of resigning and that an other would be appointed in my place) not even Condecending to say to me that the dept would not grant me an investigation so as to afford me an opportunity to honorably resign But acknoledges a resignation that he had not received Thus writing to me a base falsehood which he knew to be such and which must be considered as such by any person who may hereafter see it.[2] In conclusion I am compeld by that natural regard which evry man feels for his own character to publish to the world the circumstances which I have here submitted unless by the timely interference of your Excellency I have long posponed it from several causes one is that I wish not to commence a paper war which might in the least degree go to show an inconsistency in the course pursued by the present men in power, As I have ever belonged to their party I wish Mr. Eaton to know that I have a letter from Majr. T. P. Moore stating that he Mr. Eaton had given him his word to afford me a fair trial and the next day from the dates of the letters he tells me in substance I cant have a trial. I have seen a copy of one of Majr. Smiths late communic[ations to Mr.] McKenney of the War office in which he most bountifully heaps his slanders upon me and remarks that if the dept should doubt in the least the truth of his statements that he would refer them to Genl Coffee and Col John J. Winston who would confirm the fact.[3] Now I am willing that these men be called on to state what my Character is they are honorable men. But to convince you that this refference has been made at random and with the belief that these men would not be called on you can see on file in the War office a letter from Col. J. J. Winston asking for me an appointment of considerable responsibility. In perusing this letter you may find some sentiment which may be offensive to your feelings when not properly construed which difficulty to remove I say I believe you are disposed to do justice to all parties and not as Majr. Smith says support him under any circium-stances[.] I have the honor to be very Respectfuly yr obt Servt

Jno. B. Duncan

ALS, DNA-RG 75 (M234-135). Duncan had been a Chickasaw subagent since 1826. In 1828–29 the War Department investigated charges of misconduct against agent Benjamin F. Smith brought by Duncan and others, including Chickasaw chiefs. Smith submitted a lengthy defense discrediting Duncan and backed by testimony from more than a dozen witnesses (M234-135). In March 1829 Smith was cleared and Duncan was dismissed as subagent. His successor John L. Allen afterward joined Duncan in accusing Smith of swindling the Indians and the government, a charge they continued to pursue after Smith resigned in December.
    1. Duncan had led the Chickasaws on a western exploring trip in the winter of 1828–29.
    2. Duncan wrote Porter on January 19, 1829 (M234-135). Eaton replied on March 17 that as Smith had been cleared, Duncan would be removed had he not already offered to resign (DNA-RG 75, M21-5).
    3. Smith to McKenney, August 4, 1829 (M234-135). John J. Winston (b. 1785) resided in north Alabama.

From William Southerland Hamilton

Sir,
    Mr. Graham will inform you that I have declined the appointmt. with wh. you were pleased to honor me; & if he shd. not think proper to lay before you the letter of declension, may I request that you will ask him for it, that I may be justified in yr. opinion.
    You will therein observe an allusion to a confidential letter, & if Mr. Graham shd. not lay that before you, be pleased to ask for that also. My object in separating the two letters will be evident to yourself. It was not designed to keep either from your view. Indeed I presume Mr. G. will of course submit both to yr. inspection, & this will save me from an apparent impropriety in forwarding copies to yourself copies of both.
    Genl. R__ is a Yankee, & like almost every one of that Nation, who has ever come in contact with me, I think cold, selfish, & cunning. I care not about opposing him for Congress, but he distrusted, & instead of a free & candid conversation, he set to work like a Burr or a Clay, to manage & to master. To spare yr. time on this subject, if you will ask my old Friend & school mate the Secy. of war for two letters addressed to him the first in Feby. & the 2nd. in June, you will perceive my meaning.[1]
    I could not Sir but consider myself flattered by the tender of an office subject to yr. orders. That I decline, you will attribute to the proper motive, an unwillingness to remove from Louia. to a decent regard for the welfare of my Family, & to a preference for a life of less drudgery & more action. I think I can be more valuable useful to my State & my Country in other situations. Any how I am not in a situation condition to be exposed

to greater pecuniary embarassments than those under which (like most Planters of Cotton) I at present labor.

~~I am most grateful Sir, as a Citizen of this State, for your military exertions. I have great & well founded hopes, of the sound & practical energy & wisdom wh. as the Chief of the Nation you will direct to its affairs foreign & domestic. I respect your private virtues. In one word I admire & venerate your character. That you shd. have a good opinion of me makes me think better of myself. I cd. shd. not but take pleasure in conducting any branch of the Administration wh. you might confide to me, if I did not believe others cd. serve you as well. I regret the circumstances wh. compel my declension, and (trust that you will approve of my motives.) (I most sincerely sympathise in your domestic misfortune, & cd. ardently wish that men were more after yr. model, so that all might labor for the welfare of the Country as the chief good, instead of involving your sensitive feelings & your patriotic aspirations in continual difficulty & harassments. That energy however which has shed such honor on yr. name & such glory on the U. States, will carry you through all the contests & idle debates wh. will occur at the Federal City, and at other Places of inferior note, and)~~ I trust that Providence may long spare you among men that you may witness the welfare of your country, the almost unanimous applauses of your Fellow Citizens, & the improved condition of the human race.

Allow me Sir to assure you of my continued attachment, & veneration, and to subscribe myself ~~yr. Friend~~ yr obt Svt.

W. S. Hamilton

[Endorsed by Hamilton:] Copy To Adw. Jackson 5th. Novr. '29—

ALS draft, LU (mAJs). William Southerland Hamilton (1789–c1867) of West Feliciana was a Louisiana legislator and a former Army lieutenant colonel under AJ. He ran unsuccessfully for governor in 1830.

1. Hamilton wrote two letters to George Graham on November 5. The first declined his appointment as surveyor of public lands in Mississippi and Louisiana. In it Hamilton accused Eleazar Wheelock Ripley (1782–1839) of promoting his appointment to compel him to remove to the surveyor's office in Mississippi and thus bar him from competing with Ripley for a Louisiana congressional seat. Ripley was a New Hampshire native, onetime Massachusetts legislator, and an Army brigadier general in the War of 1812. He won election to Congress in 1834. Hamilton's second, confidential, letter warned Graham of possible tampering with their correspondence at the post office (Hamilton Papers, LU).

To Graves W. Steele

That an overseer is accountable to his employer *for all losses sustained through his neglect*—and I do assure you, I would not if I could, make you answerable for any thing else. Nor can you believe that I am very suspicious, when you take into view the great losses in stock and negroes

I have lost since I left my plantation under your charge & management—Therefore you see the necessity of forwarding to me agreable to your obligation, & instructions, a full account of your guardianship with the loss of my property, & with the cause that has lead to it.

I have been truly astonished to hear my beacon was nearly gone, this to me was unaccountable, because I stood by & saw a large supply as usual for my white & Black family salted in my smoke house. In your Statement I have asked you to forward, I shall expect you to furnish me with an explanation how this has happened—There can be no mistake in the quantity, for I took it down as weighed—I have wrote you before to advise me whether we would have a sufficent supply of Pork for the plantation for the next year—my son informs me, he is very doubtful whether you will raise a sufficient supply of Pork—[1]

It will surely be an evidence of bad management, if such a stock as I left, will not support the plantation—and if that turns out to be the fact, the sooner I break it up; the better must it be, for my interest.

I have been advised by some not to continue you, by others to try you another year—The latter I have concluded to do, as I am aware the injury it would be to you to leave the business under present rumors—But when I say I have concluded to retain you another year, it is on the express conditions that you treat my negroes with humanity, & attention when sick; & not work them too hard, when well—that you feed & cloath them *well*, and that you *carefully attend to my stock* of all kinds, & particularly to my mares & colts, & see that they are well taken care of & the colts kept in good growing order, & the mares in good condition to raise & suckle their colts. This I have a right to expect from you for the wages I give you—I have been offered here a first rate overseer for $350 pr year   I have been offered in Tennessee a well experienced, & well recommended overseer, for four hundred dollars   I give you five hundred which is equal to $1000 when cotton was at 14 cents pr pound—I engaged to give you this liberal wages because I had confidence in your honesty, your industry, your care & vigilence, over my stock & every other matter belonging to my business and farm—I gave it to you, because I expected you would treat my negroes with that humanity & care, that you by your articles was bound to do, and I now engage you again, because I believe what property, if any, that has been lost for want of proper care, that you, as an honest man, will truly report, & pay for, & that another year you will in all things strictly comply with your engagements in every respect

I shall expect to receive your answer to every part of this letter in all respects on its receipt and shew to all that my confidence in you was not misplaced[.] I am very respectfully yrs

Andrew Jackson

P S. send me the amount of the cotton picked out & the probable amount you will make this crop

[Endorsed by AJ:] copy of a letter to Graves Steele overseer at the Hermitage Tennessee Dated 7th. Novbr 1829 under cover to Wm. Donelson by him to be delivered—

ALS draft, DLC (37).
   1. AJ Jr. had just arrived in Washington from Tennessee.

From Senacheewane

[November 8]

Talk of Senacheewane, Chief of the United tribe of the Illinois River, to the President of the United States
   Listen to the prayers of your red children   I for them will tell you how we have been treated by those very same men you sent to speak to your children—
   Father, you call on us to meet you at Rock Island as you wish to buy our land—The next word, while preparing was we must meet you at Prairie du chien, a distance of 300 miles from our home   Father, all were ready and some had started to meet you at R Island, our woomen and children would also have been glad to have seen you there.
   Father, A few of us could have gone to Prairie du chien, but it would have been of no use as the nation, is determin never to sell their land, unless the whole of them be present, had we been call simply to receive presents we like the St Joseph Indns. could have raised a party of young men; But we were call to sell our lands—which can not be sold by a few, and much less by the agent of Cheecagoo, with a parcel of Indns. he hired to sell you our lands.[1]
   Father, Look at the treaty we made with *clark Edwards* & *Chouteau* you will see that the St Joseph Indns. took no part with us—[2]
   Father how comes it, that those very same Indns. who are strangers to us, should sell you our lands—It is not them Father: It is the agent at Cheecagoo, with those men you sent to buy our lands, that deprived us of those rights, those lands which the great Sperit gave us, and which you know be ours—
   Father, when we met you at Green bay last year you askd us, to meet you at R Island, then we should stipulate, concerning the purchase of some of our lands, at the same time, you promised us $10,000 in goods to clothes our women and children[3]—Was there an agent of Cheecagoo—or were there a single Indn. of St Joseph to make that agreement with you; no not one of them, we alone, of the Illinois as bro[t]hers—took you by

the hand and said that we should see you again at R Island, and we should have done so, if you had not disappointed us.

Father, where are those $10,000 to clothes our women and children, here we are about six hundred almost in a state of nakedness, shivering with cold, with no other hopes left, but that of our hunt, see Father how we are, cheated by those men you sent to speak to us, and that bad man at cheecagoo—

Father, We wish to be shaded by one tree—The black cloud, has long since disappeared—and we were in hopes, it should never return It is Father in your hand to keep it off, let the Influence of that great tree keep us in unity & friendship to go away from our home, is hard—but to be driven off without any hopes of finding a home again is to hard think of and the thought is equal to death—you do not know Father our situation for if you did, you would pitty us—for these very Same woods, that once made our delight, have now become the woods of danger, This River we once paddle our Canoes uncontroeled, has become the River of alarm and of blood. Several of my yung men have been killed by your white children & nothing has been done to cover the dead.

Father, We can not go away—this is our land this is our home, we sooner die, come Father speek to us and we shall try to please you, I am done, may the great Sperit above, give you health and a long life—is the wish of all your red children   I speak for my people, who are maney—

Senacheewane his   X   mark

in presence of
Peter Menard
U S S Indn. agent
J. Ogee[4]
U S Indn. Interpreter

DS, DNA-RG 75 (M234-749). Senacheewane (c1744–1831) was a Potawatomi chief residing near the Indian subagency at Peoria, Ill. An August 1828 treaty at Green Bay had planned a negotiation the next year for the cession of tribal lands on the upper Mississippi. Its location was changed from Rock Island to Prairie du Chien at the behest of Winnebago chief Naw-Kaw (Mar 14, above). In June Senacheewane complained to the Indian subagent at Peoria, Pierre Menard, Jr. (1797–1871), that his people were too poor to go so far (DNA-RG 75, T494-2). In July, Chippewas, Ottawas, and Potawatomis from the St. Joseph River in Michigan signed a treaty at Prairie du Chien surrendering lands in Illinois and Wisconsin in return for a perpetual annuity of $16,000 and other gifts. One of the U.S. commissioners, Pierre Menard, Sr. (1766–1844), objected to the proceedings as unfair to the absent Illinois Potawatomis, and on November 23 William Clark forwarded this protest by Senacheewane to the War Department. The treaty stood, but in 1830 the Illinois Potawatomis were included in the annuity.

1. Alexander Wolcott, Jr. (1790–1830), a former Army surgeon, was Indian agent at Chicago.

2. In 1816, territorial governors William Clark and Ninian Edwards and trader René Auguste Chouteau (1749–1829) concluded a treaty with the Potawatomis guaranteeing

them land in northwest Illinois and southwest Wisconsin. The 1829 Prairie du Chien treaty ceded this tract to the United States.

3. The 1828 Green Bay treaty pledged $20,000 in goods, payable at the pending cession treaty, to the tribes as compensation for white incursions on their lands. The goods were distributed at Prairie du Chien to the Indians present.

4. Joseph Ogee (1750–1833) operated a ferry over Rock River and served as interpreter for the Peoria subagency.

From Samuel Delucenna Ingham

Treasury Department 9 November 1829

Sir

I have the honor to lay before you a communication from Isaac T Preston Esqr, who was directed, in conformity with your order, to investigate the evidence on which certain claims to land in Arkansas, founded on French or Spanish grants, had been adjudicated by the courts of that territory, under the Act of 26 May 1824.

The circumstances detailed by Mr. Preston seem to be conclusive, that gross frauds have been perpetrated by means of forgery and perjury.

In consequence of suspicions entertained at this Department, I had directed the commissioner of the Genl Land office, to suspend the issuing of patents on the claims confirmed by the court, until a report of the above mentioned investigation should be received; this period having now arrived, it may be proper to decide, finally, as to the course to be adopted by the Executive power of the governments in relation to these patents.

A considerable number of claims have been finally decided on by the court of Arkansas, according to the forms of the Act of Congress beforementioned. And it may be doubted, whether the Treasury Department would be authorised by a further exercise of discretionary power to refuse the patents.

But it is respectfully submitted to the consideration of the President, whether in a case of such gross, and palpable fraud, the high obligation to cause the laws to be faithfully executed may not justify an order by him, to that effect; at least until Congress shall have time to act upon the subject.

It is not less a matter of regret, than surprise; that frauds so palpable, supported by evidence so impossible should have escaped the notice of the Registers & Receivers, the District Attorney, and Judges of the Court of Arkansas.

Should it be determined to withold the patents, it may be proper to give public notice of the fact, as early as possible. I have the honor with very great respect

S D Ingham

LS, DNA-RG 49 (14-0437). A law of 1824 authorized the superior court of Arkansas Territory to adjudicate and confirm claims to land based on old French and Spanish grants.

On August 6 AJ had appointed Isaac Trimble Preston (1793–1852), the land office register at New Orleans, to investigate suspected frauds. Preston reported on October 10 (*TPUS*, 21:72–80) that the court in 1827 had confirmed claims to more than 60,000 acres based on obviously forged Spanish documents brought from Louisiana by James Bowie (1796–1836), later of the Alamo, and his brother John J. Bowie (1785–1859).

To George Graham

Washington Novbr. 9th. 1829—

Dr. Sir,

I have recd. and carefully examined the report of Col. Isaac T Preston of the 10th. Octr. last; and have decided that it will be best for you forthwith to give instructions to the Atty of the U States for the Territory of Arkansas, that he cause to be made out and forwarded to you a transcript of the records of all claims confirmed by the court of Arkansas from the 19th. to the 24th of December 1827 by judgement, the case of claims called Bowie's, and also the record of all similar claims confirmed by the said court; and that this transcript be accompanied by the deposition of Col Isaac T Preston in whose possession the journals of Govr. Miro & Gayoso (the surveys & *requêtes* recorded by them) are—together with the testimony of Charles Tessier of Baton Rouge, and Jean Mercier of New orleans, touching the forgery of these *requêtes & concessions,* for which purpose the Attorney should apply to the court for a *dedimus potestatem,* and give due notice to the counsel of the claimants, or the claimants themselves personally if it can be done, of the time and place of taking such depositions.[1]

You will further instruct the atty to move the court for a rehearing in all these cases where an appeal has not been taken; and also direct the registers & surveyers to receive no entries on these claims, and make no surveys on them until such record is furnished, upon which further instructions from you will be given. And you will also please cause it to be made public that no grants will be issued on those claims until further investigation is had into the frauds that have been suggested in their acquirement.[2] I am respectfully yr. obt. sert

Andrew Jackson

LS, DNA-RG 49 (14-0430); ALS draft, DLC (37).
1. On November 10 Graham instructed Arkansas district attorney Samuel Calhoun Roane (1793–1852) pursuant to this directive (*TPUS*, 21:96–97). Esteban Rodríguez Miro y Sabater (c1744–95) was governor of Louisiana, 1782–91. Manuel Luis Gayoso de Lemos y Amorin (1747–99) was the Spanish governor of the Natchez district, 1787–97, and of Louisiana, 1797–99. Charles Tessier (c1776–1852) and Jean Mercier were land clerks under Gayoso. The "requêtes" were the initial requests for land directed to Spanish authorities before 1804. A "dedimus potestatem" is a commission to take testimony.

2. Graham instructed the land officers at Little Rock and Batesville accordingly and reviewed the situation for Congress in his annual report of November 21 (*SDoc* 1, 21st Cong., 1st sess., pp. 316–17, Serial 192). A law of May 8, 1830, suspended the patenting of claims and authorized the Arkansas court to rehear and reverse its previous decrees in cases of fraud. Under that authority the Arkansas supreme court annulled the Bowie claims in February 1831.

To Samuel Delucenna Ingham

Novbr. 10th. 1829—

The President with respects to the Secretary of the Treasury—sends to enquire after his health—If sufficiently restored, will be happy to see him at his office, when it may best suit his leisure. The President will thank him to send the amount paid of the national debt the present year[1]

The President wishes to converse with the Secretary, on the subject of Mr Key, who complains of injury & loss, by his employment against Watkins, thinks he ought to receive more than awarded him—The president really believed the allowance were doing liberal justice—but if we have not, he is willing Justice be done[2]

AN, PU (14-0524).
1. AJ announced in his annual message that $12,405,005.80 of the national debt was paid off in 1829.
2. Attorney Francis S. Key, who helped prosecute Tobias Watkins, had complained on October 15 that he was receiving less pay for more government work than in years past. AJ endorsed Key's note, "This to be submitted again to Mr Van Buren & Mr Ingham, the question—will it not be well to raise it to the average within, and be done with it."

From Thomas Graves

Cherokee Nation 12th. Novr. 1829.

My great Father

I have called upon a white man who can put my words on paper, & send them to you—I am old—I have seen the leaves, green & yellow, sixty three times in my life—I can no longer chase the game of the woods—My frame is feeble, but I still recollect the promises of my Father.

In the last treaty between the Cherokees, and your people, you promised to give me $1200: for harm which had been done to me—I wanted the money as I was poor, but I have not got it—I called on the Agent Mr. Duval for it & he only gave me 30$—But he does not pity the poor, for the Chiefs of our nation, & I was one of them, gave a share of our annuity to the very old, poor, blind & crippled part of our people—The agent said "give me the money, I am going to Orleans, and I will buy Blankets & such things very cheap, as the poor need & give to them." We gave him the money, and he gave small and mean Blankets to some of them; and to others he gave presents out of his store, but I dont think he gave them half the worth of their money—He keeps a store and sells goods high to the Indians, & when he pays our annuities, he counts out the money, and says to one man "so much money is yours," and then he says "your account in the store is so much," and draws the money off the table into his Box, and this makes the Indian's heart heavy, for we have heard that you dont allow your agents to sell goods to the Indians—But it may be that our great Father has changed his laws since he sent Colonel Meigs to us on Hiawassee—If my great Father would tell Colonel Arbuckle to pay me, I think I could get my money[.]¹ Your friend & Brother

Thoms Greaves his X mark

Jno. Brown Interpreter

LS, DNA-RG 75 (M234-432). Graves was a Western Cherokee chief and a signer of the treaty of May 1828, which awarded him $1,200 for his arrest and confinement by Arkansas authorities in 1823 on a charge of murdering Osage prisoners. Graves was acquitted at trial. The War Department recorded a requisition to pay him $1,200 in 1828, and another in July 1830.

1. Agents were barred by law from trading with the Indians. Return Jonathan Meigs (1740–1823) had been Cherokee agent in Tennessee. Edward Washington Duval (1789–1830) became agent to the Western Cherokees in 1823. In January 1830 he was dismissed for failing to settle his accounts regularly.

To Samuel Delucenna Ingham

Novbr. 14th. 1829—

My Dr Sir

Judge Berrien having differed from you on the subject, where it is best for the interest & security of the revenue, to vest the powers of the agent for the Treasury; I have thought it right to lay his views before you, and ask you to inform me, whether his reasoning has produced a change in your views to me on this subject—and whether, if his reasoning has not convinced you of the propriety of throwing this duty on the atto. Genl, whether a law agency would not be better than to throw it on the first auditor.

When you have leisure to attend to this subject, please to return to me the inclosed papers—yrs

Andrew Jackson

P.S. I have such a pain in my head I can scarcely write

ALS, John C. Wood, Jr. (14-0460).

From Samuel Delucenna Ingham

14 Nov 29

My dear Sir

I have recd Judge Berriens report and will give it an attentive examination as soon as I get home from the office—I can especially sympathise with you in your affliction with head ache being more unwell again myself I have sent up Mr Wheelers report on Rogersons case—but there is no occasion for your examining it untill we have information enough to make the appointment of a successor[.][1] very sincerely yours

S D Ingham

ALS, NjP (14-0461). In his first annual message, AJ recommended transferring "supervisory power over suits brought by the public" from the Treasury to the attorney general and making the latter head of a full government department responsible for all legal matters civil and criminal. The Treasury would retain control over accounts until they were reported for suit (Richardson, 2:453–54). Congress instead on May 29, 1830, created the new office of solicitor of the Treasury, with the supervisory authority over collectors, attorneys, and marshals in suits involving the U.S. that Ingham had proposed for the first auditor. The law directed the attorney general to advise the solicitor and raised his salary $500.

1. Asa Rogerson (d. 1832), customs collector at Elizabeth City, N.C., was reported in default for more than $30,000. AJ shortly removed him for Stephen Charles.

From James Gadsden

Wascissa
14th Novr. 29

My Dear General

Your letter of the 12th. Ulto was received by the last mail, and it gave me much satisfaction to find that my frankness and friendship are still acceptable to you. My letter on the subject of a supposed Indian outrage at or near the Sewaney river was predicated, as I intimated in that communication, on the statement of the Individual who preferred the complaint.[1] I was not disposed at the time to give full credence to his representations, and I have no doubt you have received from the Executive of the Territory a correct narative of the circumstance before this. My principal object in writing was to draw your attention to the subject of our Indian affairs, which in my opinion have not been managed with much judgement in this quarter. In adverting to your order for the removal of the Creeks west of the Mississippi its probable consequences to us struck me forcibly. You are better acquainted than myself with the intimate relations subsisting between the Creeks & Seminoles, their intercourse has always been [unin]terrupted, and the disaffected of the former nation have invariably sought an asylum with the latter whenever their irregularities above, exposed them to chastisement. It seems therefore to me more than probable that all those who are unwilling to emigrate west will seek a refuge in Florida; thus not only increasing the evils under which we labor from having an Indian population in the center of our country, but augmenting the obstacles to their final removal from our Territory. Messengers have already passed from the Creeks to the Seminoles & consultations held with the latter on the subject of their receiving into their country those Creeks who may be unwilling to go West. This object can be only defeated by the positive orders from yourself & by the vigilance of our agent. But at this particular crisis he is absent, the garrison at the agency broken up; & the agency confided to a young man not in any way qualified for the office.[2] The agent himself, is in my opinion, not qualified for the station. He has very little knowledge of the Indian character & his repeated absences from the Territory & the agency for months together, have been the fruitful source of most of the difficulties which have occurred with the Indians in this quarter. You may recollect I was one of the Commissioners who formed the Treaty with the Seminoles; & to your letters & advice were we greatly indebted for the success which attended that negotiation. Steadily adhering to your policy & looking ahead to the final removal of the Indians from the country east of the Mississippi, as one of the means to the accomplishment of this object, we endeavoured to confine the Indians to the most limited boundary that could sustain them. Unacquainted however with the country in which they were to be located; the consent of the Indians to the country allotted, could not be obtained without the additional stipulation that it should be enlarged, if inadequate to their support. Commissioners were however to be appointed to ascertain the fact & their report was to be final. I was appointed by the then President & my report recommended a small extension; not from the fact that the country allotted them was insufficient, for I thought otherwise but that the boundary designated approached too near one of their Towns. My report was approved & the boundary line run accordingly[3]

On your predecessors coming into office a Deputation of Indians were taken to Washington by the agent & their representations so far believed as to authorise them to retain the Big Swamp within their boundaries. It was an act of Mr Adams & not sanction[ed] by the Treaty.[4] I should have previously mentioned however, the agent never took the Indians within the limits mark[ed] out for them, but on his own responsibility permitted them to form settlements 20 miles north of their boundary & on a hammock which was then covered by a Spanish grant & which grant has been reported on favourably by the Land Commissioners. I mention this fact as it will enable you, should you think fit so to do, to present to the Seminole Indians the alternative of moving west of the Mississippi or of going within the limits marked by me and which alone is guaranteed to them under the

Treaty of Camp Moultrie. The Claimants of the Swamp, now in possession of the Indians by the permission, if not the order, of Mr Adams, will expect & will be entitled to payment from government should the Courts of our Country sanction their claim. The probability is with them, as their claim goes forward with the recommendation of the Commissioners authorised to examine into its validity. I have written you a long letter, which you will ascribe to the deep interest I feel in seeing your policy towards the Indians carried into effect before the expiration of your administration. I apprehended some difficulty in this Territory; as I believed the Indians would not by Treaty consent to emigrate & I saw not how you could present to them the same alternative you did to the Creeks. The fact of *their unauthorised occupation of a grant from the Spanish government,* seems to me to offer an opportunity which may be improved to our advantage. Order the agent within the limits marked by me & direct the Indians to follow or move west, and you may rest assured they will soon be found pliable instruments in your hands. I remain your friend

J Gadsden

[Endorsed by AJ:] Col Gadsden on the subject of Indians & Indian agent in Florida

ALS, DNA-RG 75 (M234-806).
1. Ambrose Cook had reported the alleged raid on his own farm and Howard's to Governor Duval (*TPUS,* 24:267).
2. Daniel C. H. Sims.
3. The 1823 Treaty of Camp Moultrie, signed by Gadsden, designated a reservation for Florida's Indian tribes, but provided for expanding its limits northward if a survey found it to contain insufficient tillable land for the Indians' support. Gadsden was commissioned to run the survey and recommended extending the boundary northward several miles. In February 1825 President Monroe approved Gadsden's line with a further extension "to embrace the Big Hammock, or Swamp" (*TPUS,* 22:905–7, 23:192–93). These were later clarified to be two different places, with the Big Swamp still lying outside the boundary. Governor Duval and others reported that without the Big Swamp the Indians still lacked enough tillable land. The War Department, over Gadsden's objections, concurred and allowed the Indians to provisionally occupy the area (*TPUS,* 23:343–44, 446–47, 482–83, 490–92, 531).
4. A Seminole delegation in Washington accompanied by agent Humphreys pressed their claims to the Big Swamp in May 1826. President Adams agreed and ordered the boundary redrawn (*TPUS,* 23:548, 557).

From Ishtehotopa et al.

Council House
Chickasaw Nation
November 14th 1829.

Father

We a portion of your Red children impressed with a belief, that it is your wish that we should be happy; consider it to be our duty to inform you directly, that we have for some time past suffered in character & National honor, owing to many false & malicious representations made to the War Department by our Agent Benjamin F Smith—[1]

We now rejoice to inform you, that he has left the Nation—He has said that he never will return: We sincerely hope that this will be the case. We hope that this communication will be the last in which there may be any necessity to mention his name—We wish to forget, that a heart so depraved ever resided amongst us—[2]

Father—The leaves have often fallen since we first saw you—We were then young   You were then our friend—We have now become old—Our hair is as the snow—We hope that you are yet our Friend—We talk to you as a friend—We speak as children to a Father—

Then Listen to us—

We had the honor in June last, to report our views consequent on our exploring expedition west of the Mississippi—We asked the favour of an early answer—We have received none—We have Respectfully to request an attention to our former letters—We hope that you will give the necessary instructions to that effect—[3]

We have understood that a great number of persons have applied for this Agency—some of whom we know—We believe that when an appointment is made, it is expected that the person will act correctly—that he will do justice to both *red & white;* This is sometimes the case—But we are compelled to believe that numbers are seeking this office, with the hope of becoming rich—They have seen that Major Smith has purchased near one hundred Negroes & an elegant & valuable sugar plantation through the medium of the perquisites of his office—We want a man accustomed to business—We wish him to do us justice—And if he does this—We are satisfied—You Sent Major John L. Allen to us as our Sub-Agent—and we are glad to tell you that since he has been here—he has attended faithfully to our business—he appears to be anxious to do us justice—And among all the Applicants for the Agency with whom we are acquainted, he is decidedly our choice—He appears to be qualified—He is amongst us & knows our wants & wishes—And if we are permitted to have a share in matters of this kind, he is Respectfully recommended to your notice—[4]

Father we are a great Distance apart—We would be glad to see you & talk togather—We remember that you have said that we shall not be imposed upon—We therefore hope that you will listen to our talk—Wishing that every breeze may bring Gladness to your heart—We conclude

Your Children—
Mingo his X mark King
Tishomingo X his mark
Levi his X mark Colbert
George his X mark Colbert
William his X mark MGilvery

[Seventeen additional names follow.]

We, whose names are herwith under written do certify that we were present at the Council when the above Letter to the President was acted upon, & that the Chiefs acknowledged it to be their act & deed. The chiefs consider a certificate of this kind, necessary as Major Smith has asserted to the War Department that Letters are frequently written from this Nation, purporting to be written from the Chiefs when in fact" he continues "*they are ignorant of their contents*"—

Given under our hands at the Council house of the Chickasaw Nation this 14th Day of November 1829—

G. W. Long
Hugh Wilson missiony
John Gattis[5]

November the 16th 1829. Council continued—

P.S.
Father
In addition to what we have said above we wish to say something relating to the extension of the Laws of the States of Mississippi & Alabam over us—

In the first place we would humbly enquire of the chief executive Authority of the United States, if the Congress has transfered the ~~right~~ power of regulating trade & intercourse with the Indian tribes, to the legislatures of the different States—

Secondly—Permit us to enquire if the Government of the United States are persuaded that the great Body of the Indians have sufficiently advanced in civilization to justify a measure of this kind—

Thirdly—We conceive it to be our duty to our country and to our children, to protest in the name of the chickasaw Nation against a procedure of this kind—We believe it to be unjust, unwise, & impolitic and a total departure from that magnanimity & generosity to the oppressed, of which the United States, have heretofore so justly boasted—

Fourthly—It is known to you that we are a small Nation that we possess not the means if we had the Disposition to be hostile to the United States   We have been taught to believe that the United States hold it as a maxim—that no nation possesses the right legally to impose Laws or taxes on an other without its consent—We yet confide in the integrity & justice of the federal Government—We hope that our Great Father will give our case a fair & honorable hearing—& that the collected wisdom of the United States will decide on equitable principles this interesting, & to us a painful question.

We are more than anxious, as old friends to see & converse with you face to face—We have a great deal to say to you & should be glad to visit Washington City this winter if the Goverment would permit it & defray our expenses, We hope that you will consider of the matter & permit four of us, togather with a white friend to visit you, in the event of which, we are persuaded that our business can be arranged with the Government—

DS, DNA-RG 75 (M234-135). The lead signatory, the Chickasaw King or "Mingo," was named Ishtehotopa (d. 1846). Tishomingo (c1736–1838) was the speaker and Levi Colbert (c1759–1834) the councillor of the Chickasaw Nation. George Colbert (c1764–1839), Levi's brother, was an influential trader. William McGillivray (c1754–1844), also known as "Red Cat," was a district chief who had served in both the American Revolution and the Creek War.

1. Smith had repeatedly represented the Chickasaw leaders to the War Department as stubborn, dishonest, and avaricious (M234-135).

2. Since 1826, Chickasaw chiefs had complained to the War Department, among other things, that Smith had failed to assist in recovering Chickasaw property stolen by whites, would not allow the Chickasaws a blacksmith of their own choosing, and had moved the agency to an inconvenient location (M234-135). Smith had left the Nation in October and resigned on December 16.

3. At the urging of Thomas McKenney, a party of Chickasaws had toured west of Missouri and Arkansas in 1828. In June 1829 they reported that the lands they saw were unsatisfactory, and asked instead to explore south of Red River (M234-135). McKenney's reply of October 21, which they had not yet received, said that no land there was available, but that there was plenty of good land north of the river that they had not seen (DNA-RG 75, M21-6).

4. John L. Allen (d. 1865) had replaced John Duncan as Chickasaw subagent. In February 1830 AJ appointed Benjamin F. Reynolds of Tennessee to succeed Smith as agent. Allen remained as subagent until 1837.

5. Gabriel W. Long (c1800–1853) served as acting Chickasaw subagent, 1824–26, and as Chickasaw agent, 1849–50. Hugh Wilson (1794–1868) was a Presbyterian missionary at Caney Creek, Ala., who ran a boarding school for Indian children. John Gattis was a blacksmith.

From Francis Baylies

Taunton November 17. 1829.

Sir.

I had the honour some months since, to address to you some communications on the subject of the appointments of the General Government in

Massachusetts but as those appointments for the most part (particularly in Boston) were made without regard to my ~~opinions~~ views, I supposed that some malign influence had ~~destroyed~~ changed that favourable opinion with which I well know. I was once regarded by the Cheif Magistrate of the Republic. Under this impression I abstained from all further interference, for I will not obtrude my advice on any one, and I endeavoured as well as I could to conceal the mortification and chagrin occasioned by the general disgust with which these appointments were received; ~~the odium of which was shared by all who had been your supporters.~~

I have witnessed some remarkable transactions. I have seen with astonishment a Post-Master appointed in this Village from amongst your most determined political enemies, from whom but a little more than a year since I was compelled to hear expressions extremely unpleasant to me for they were uttered against you—whose most active supporter was a person who was diligently employed ~~about that time~~ during the late Presidential controversy in writing articles nearly libellous against me for supporting you. I will however do the Post Master the justice to say that I beleive him well qualified for his place obliging, active, and hospitable. Of his hospitality I cannot speak from personal knowledge and therefore refer to that celebrated and unfortunate character Tobias Watkins ~~can attest~~ for he partook of it when on his travels in the North—~~How Sir~~ I have no~~t the least~~ disposition to disturb the Postmaster in his Office. I only mention this appointment as evidence brought home to my own door ~~that in this affair at least,~~ of some very strange influence ~~had been exerted,~~ or of some gross deception ~~practiced.~~[1] Notwithstanding this, ~~affair happened in my own neighbourhood~~ I remained silent—and silent I should have remained had not a case recently occurred of a character so flagrant that I think my social obligations as a member of society and as a good citizen compel me to interfere, and at least to try the extent of my influence for if I have any ~~to would be almost inexcuseable to~~ I should hold myself unworthy of the regard of honourable men, If I refrained any longer from its exercise—a silent acquicscence would justly expose me to the imputation of timidity, ingratitude and a reckless disregard of the ~~best interests of the society in which of which I am a member~~ public good. The Collector of Boston has within a few days removed from the office of Inspector of the Customs worth perhaps 10 or $1100 per annum the Hon William C Jarvis late Speaker of our House of Representatives. After ~~my predilections~~ I had been driven from Congress in consequence of my ~~well known and~~ avowed opinions on the Presidential question I was honoured by the people of my own Town with a seat in that Legislative Assembly in which Mr Jarvis presided. I received from him the most liberal and courteous treatment, and notwithstanding the general predjudices which then prevailed against all who supported you, he had the independence to place me at the head of the most important Legislative Committee ~~in the House.~~ For this act he was denounced in the Massachusetts Journal a paper of which you may have heard as being the vehicle of many slanders against you—and so much was his popularity at that time injured by this indication of partiality for a Jackson man that he came near losing his election as a Senator, when subsequently a candidate for that office in a County where his popularity until that time had been so firmly established, that it was thought impossible to shake it. Throughout the whole controversy for the Presidency his course was tolerant and liberal, and while he fairly supported his own candidate he was not so reckless of the moral obligation of truth as to deny to the other the most exalted patriotism, or so soured by party rancor as to refrain from acknowledgeing that he had illustrated the fame of his Country by acts of the most heroic virtue & valour.[2]

Now Sir when this gentleman became the victim of persecution ~~would you have justified me in remaining silent, and could I have done it~~ for political offences for I cannot learn that any other have been charged upon him & when ~~after~~ an appeal had been made to me on questions of fact could I have remained silent without displaying the most cold hearted indifference to the injuries of ~~a man~~ one who had exhibited ~~in a very~~ in a remarkable manner his good will to me, and his fairness to you under circumstances in which most men would have yielded to the violence of that predjudice which ~~was then propelling all things into its current~~ then admitted ~~no~~ neither excuse ~~and allowed no~~ or palliations for the slightest deviation from a prescribed course? There are circumstances which test the characters of men. He who can pass through the ordeals of political prosperity and adversity ~~and remain unchanged~~ and exhibit a mild forbearance in one situation and an unyielding firmness in the other gives some evidence of public virtue. ~~He who as~~ The head of a triumphant party (as Mr Jarvis in a manner was, in our State) who could refrain from crushing a political adversary ~~will not suffer one whom he thinks has some merit to be crushed to the earth for a difference in opinion and freely gives some proof of public virtue~~ and could honorably distinguish him before all others gives ~~some evidence of public virtue~~ more, far more than those characters who will not trust themselves in the fight when success is dubious but after the victory, will crowd around the camp to steal the ~~plunder~~ trophies.

The acceptance of this office by Mr Jarvis occasioned no little surprise. His talents and standing were such as would have justified him in the indulgence of an ambition of a more high reaching character. Such was the estimation in which he was held that but a few years since he received a respectable support for the office of Governor and amongst his supporters I believe this very Collector was numbered. It is certain that, at that time the columns of the Statesman were filled with his praises: but he says that he has learned that happy secret the essence of all true philosophy—to expect but little; and to be satisfied with little.[3] That such a man should have consented to serve *under* such a character as David Henshaw excites my special wonder! That such a man should have been superseded in office by Ephraim May Cunningham ~~a traitor to all the obligations of~~

~~social life, the betrayer of private correspondence a wretch who has had the audacity to proclaim his own shame bartered (as I beleive) confidential letters if not for money at least for reward, and gathered up the vile wages of his infamy from the grave of his father: who has violated every principle of honour which regulates the sanctity degrees of confidence amongst men, by bringing before the public the secrets which had been entrusted to his father by his father's kinsman the first President Adams entrusted too under the most solemn obligations of sacred fidelity~~—is such an outrage on public feeling that any Administration which countenances such transactions by sustaining such men will as surely lose the public confidence as though they had taken their Officers from the Penitentiaries; for Cunningham is a traitor to all the obligations of social life—the betrayer of private correspondence a wretch who has had the audacity to proclaim his own shame—bartered (as I beleive) confidential letters if not for money, at least for reward, and has gathered up the vile wages of his infamy from the grave of his father—and who by disclosing the secrets which under the most solemn engagements of fidelity, had been confided to his father by his father's friend and kinsman the first President Adams, has violated every principle of that chivalrous honor which holds sacred the reciprocal faith not only of friends, but of honourable enemies.[4]

Sir I must speak plainly Henshaw is but little better than Cunningham. That he a liar and slanderer I know. That he is universally odious & contemptible is notorious. That he never embraced your cause until your success was morally certain is equally notorious. That he will betray and desert you should you experience what I trust and hope you never will experience—the loss of popular favour—is a moral deduction founded on a knowledge of his character, almost as certain, as a fact already ascertained. If he is continued: if he is permitted to wreak his petty malignity upon honorable men for selfish purposes—for no other reason perhaps than this—that some of their connections did not suppose him a suitable person to manage a monied Institution in which they had some interest:[5] if it be the settled policy of the administration to hold out this man to the world as their trusted and confidential friend: the Administration will be left without support here, except from those venal sycophants who throng around this "puffed up and petty despot" to obtain offices.

These things I write in sorrow and not in anger. I pray you Sir to releive us from this man, who hangs like a mill-stone around the neck of the party and will inevitably carry all your disinterested supporters here to the bottom.

I have neither personal or party views to answer except in one way: I belong neither to the Statesman or the Bulletin as the Boston parties are called, but I have been steady in my fidelity to the great Administration party of the Union.[6] Nothing but my attachment to the true interests of that party induces me to take this step: an attachment which has been strengthened by having shared their toils when struggling in a minority to bring about an event auspicious as I had confidently hoped to the best interests of the nation. I wish to see the party great, respectable and powerful, winning and deserving the confidence of every man of worth in the community: and therefore it is that I entreat you not to force this man upon us. If none can be found in this state to whom you would be willing to give this office Give us a Collector from another, and we will be satisfied provided he is a man entitled to ~~your~~ our respect. I have the honour to be with great & sincere respect your obedient servant

Francis Baylies

ALS draft, MHi (14-0481). *Massachusetts Historical Society Proceedings*, 3d ser., 45 (1911–12): 169–72. Baylies (1783–1852) served in Congress, 1821–27, and the Massachusetts state legislature, 1827–32. He was the only New England congressman to support AJ in the 1825 House election. AJ had appointed him customs collector at New Bedford in March, but Baylies declined. He was appointed chargé to Argentina in 1832.

    1. Joseph L. Lord was the new Taunton postmaster. His "most active supporter" was *Boston Statesman* editor Nathaniel Greene.

    2. William C. Jarvis (c1786–1836), then speaker of the Massachusetts house of representatives, had put Baylies at the head of the judiciary committee in 1827. In 1828 Jarvis was elected a state senator. Made a custom house inspector in September 1828, he was removed by collector David Henshaw on November 7, 1829. On November 17, the same day Baylies wrote, Jarvis penned a public letter to AJ and the Senate protesting his dismissal and attacking Henshaw (*Boston Patriot*, Nov 21).

    3. In 1827 Jarvis was the gubernatorial and Henshaw a state senatorial candidate on a ticket opposing Governor Levi Lincoln's veto of a charter to the Warren Bridge Corporation for a free bridge across the Charles River. Despite publicly declining his nomination, Jarvis garnered nearly one-fifth of the vote.

    4. Henshaw had replaced Jarvis as inspector with Ephraim May Cunningham (1792–1852), the son of William Cunningham (1767–1823), a cousin of John Adams. Shortly after his father's death, Ephraim had published *Correspondence between the Hon. John Adams, Late President of the United States, and the Late Wm. Cunningham, Esq.* (1823). Issued by the printers of the *Boston Statesman*, it was intended to injure John Q. Adams by exposing his father's anti-republican opposition to the Jefferson and Madison administrations.

    5. On October 19 Henshaw failed for reelection as a director of the State Bank in Boston. William Jarvis of Weathersfield, Vt., a stockholder and relation of William C. Jarvis, had apparently voted against him.

    6. Boston's two Jackson factions were commonly designated by their respective newspaper organs, the *Boston Statesman* and the *Boston Evening Bulletin*.

To Samuel Delucenna Ingham

Novbr. 18th. 1829

Dr Sir

    I wish information upon the subject of the expenditures & application of the funds arising from the sale of our public lands

    Does the Commissioner of the General Land office draw on the receivers for mony under what authority, and what check, if any, are imposed by law—what sum of mony since 1821, has been drawn from receivers by checks, or draft, & upon what account, & under what authority—keeping each year seperate, & Distinct.

The above information is asked for, to see whether some further check than that which exists at present may not be necessary, for the proper security & application of the fund arising from the sale of public land—

I regret to call on you &c &c, but am not advised what officer audits these accounts—yr Fr.

A. J

[Endorsed by AJ:] Rough copy of a note to Sec. of Tr. on the subject of the manner mony is drawn from receivers—the amt since 1821—and by what authority the orders checks &c are drawn for what purpose & who settles these accounts—

ALS draft, DLC (37). The 1812 law establishing the General Land Office authorized its commissioner to audit and settle accounts, subject to review by the comptroller of the Treasury. Commissioner Graham answered AJ's queries in a November 20 letter to Ingham. He explained that land office receipts went to the Treasury except for certain specified types of administrative expenses which were paid directly by receivers on order of the commissioner. Records of such payments could be found in the receivers' quarterly accounts filed with the register of the Treasury (DNA-RG 49, M25-25).

From Deacon Sockbason and Sabattis Neptune

Pleasant Point Passamaquody
Nov 18. 1829

The Subscribers Deacan Sockbason & Sabattis Neptune in behalf of the Governor, Lieutenant Governor, Captains & the whole Tribe of the Passamaquody Indians and as a Deputation of said Tribe, met in full council, approach their Father the President of the United States.

The object of this memorial is to inform our Father the President that we are desirous of the arts of Civilization & the benefits resulting from instruction & knowledge. We have therefore to ask our Father the President for a School Master to instruct us & our Children and also for a Priest to minister to us & them & to lead us into the paths of Religion. We have also to inform our Father the President that our Tribe are Poor, that our fishing & Hunting have failed us as a means of support, that the trees on our lands are nearly all gone so that we cannot, without trespassing on our White neighbors, get bark for making our canoes or for Torches nor stuff for making Baskets & other articles for sale to buy us bread. We have therefore to ask our Father the President for more land on which to set our Wigwams, for wood to warm us & for bark & other materials for such articles as we are able to manufacture & for such other assistance or annuities as are given to other tribes, within the United States.

Deacon Sockbason
Sapatis Neptun

Eastport Nov 18. 1829

The undersigned, inhabitants of Eastport and vicinity respectfully represent that they are personally acquainted with the character and present condition of the Passamyquoddy Tribe of Indians; that they believe said tribe to stand in need of assistance for the reasons set forth in the memorial of their agents and they would therefore, recommend the subject of it to the favorable consideration of the President of the United States and through him to Congress that some provision may be made for the relief of this *Ancient* and *friendly* tribe.

J D Weston
Frederick Hobbs
Aaron Hayden

For many years I have been acquainted with Deacon Sockbason, one of the deputation within mentioned. He is one of the most intelligent Indians I have ever known; correct in his habits and honest in all his intercourse with the white population

While connected with the administration of the Government of this State, I saw much of him as the Representative of the Passamaquodies, and never, in a single instance, discovered the least defect in his moral character. The situation of the tribe, of which he is the Representative, is correctly set forth in the foregoing statement, signed by J. D. Weston and others, who are among the most respectable citizens in their vicinity, and with whom I unite in recommending the tribe and its Representative to the favourable consideration of the President of the United States

Albion K. Parris[1]

DS, DNA-RG 46 (14-0495). Passamaquoddy spokesman Deacon Sockbason was the son-in-law of governor Francis Joseph Neptune. He and Sabattis Neptune resided on a reservation in eastern Maine created in 1794 following a cession of lands to Massachusetts. Since 1824 the federal government had subsidized a Passamaquoddy school at Pleasant Point run by Congregational minister Elijah Kellogg. Funding was stopped in 1829 in response to tribal religious dissensions over the school, the Passamaquoddys being mainly Catholic. In December Sockbason and Neptune journeyed to Washington to petition AJ and Eaton in person. Indian superintendent McKenney informed them on December 14 that they would receive $300 annually, half for Kellogg's school and half for a priest of their choice (DNA-RG 75, M21-6). The next day, December 15, AJ forwarded this memorial to Congress and recommended the purchase of woodland adjoining the Passamaquoddy reservation to be held in trust for their use (Richardson, 2:463).

1. Albion Keith Parris (1788–1857) was a former governor and U.S. senator from Maine and at this time a judge of the state supreme court.

To John Henry Eaton

Novbr 19th. 1829

My Dr. Sir

I send inclosed, for your information & perusal, a letter from the Sec, of the Treasury, inclosing one from Mr Rush, which affords valuable information to the Sec of the Treasury, and realises information before received, and which I calculated upon, that the whole western country would be inundated with smuggled goods. This must if possible be checked. For this purpose you will order from such point where the Troops can be best spared, one company of infantry or Lieutenants command if a company cannot be spared from other points commanded by a discreet officer whose aid can be relied on in seconding the aims of the Govt. in detecting they smugglers, & supporting the custom House officers.

Have the goodness to return the inclosed letter, with the information at what Period the Troops can reach the destined point

[*Endorsed by AJ:*] Copy of order to Sec. of war Novbr. 19th. 1829—

AL draft, DLC (37). On November 20, General Macomb ordered a company from Cantonment Jesup in western Louisiana south to the Calcasieu River to interdict smuggling along the Gulf coast from Texas (DNA-RG 108, M857-1).

From Samuel Delucenna Ingham

My dear Sir

I enclose a letter from Col Mack giving reason for changing his Inspectors one of whom is Mr Trumbull for whom you were pleased to take some interest—Col. Mack says he is *good for nothing,* I fear that is the case with too many of our Border men but as Col Mack seems to enter into *his duties* with zeal, I shd be disposed to gratify him with his inspectors unless you think it expedient to retain either of them—with very great respect your obt srt.

S D Ingham

ALS, PU (14-0487). Andrew Mack, the new customs collector at Detroit, reported to Ingham on October 31 that he had complied with instructions to reduce his force of inspectors by dismissing the "indolent, and neglectfull" Edward A. Trumbull and two other slackers.

However, Mack believed he needed more, not fewer, inspectors to suppress smuggling in his district, and proposed new men for hire (DNA-RG 56, M178-33).

To *Samuel Delucenna Ingham*

Novbr. 19th. 1829—

The president with his respects to the Seccretary of the Treasury, acknowledges the receipt of his note enclosing Col Macks letter to him of the 31 of Octbr. last—which he has read with attention, and has to remark that the only solicitude the president has, is, that the revenue may be secured by the appointment of honest & industrious Inspectors, and Col Mack ought to be indulged in his selection, as he is responsible for the faithful execution of the revenue laws within his District.[1]

The president further adds, that the ideas The Sec of the T. sugested the other day, are consonant with those expressed by Col Mack, & ought to be embraced in his report, & recommended earnestly to be adopted by congress.[2]

AN, PU (14-0502).
1. Ingham replied to Mack on December 2, approving his personnel changes (DNA-RG 56, M175-2).
2. In his October 31 letter, Mack reported that most smuggling from Canada was in small shipments, which owners typically abandoned if seized. The cost of condemning such goods in court, as required by law, exceeded the proceeds from their sale. Mack recommended putting up small seizures for public sale without prior condemnation, unless their owners came forth to claim them. In his annual report of December 14, Ingham proposed that Congress authorize "the sale, without condemnation, of such goods as may be unclaimed, after a reasonable notice" (*HRDoc* 6, 21st Cong., 1st sess., pp.10–11, Serial 195).

From *Amos Kendall*

Nov. 20th '29

Dear Sir,

Inclosed you have the bank &c. With all my reflection, I can add but little to your own suggestions. I have labored to condense the subject into as narrow a compass as possible, deeming brevity on every subject most appropriate in your message. If preferred, I could amplify it a great deal, and throw in many considerations in relation to the *policy* and benefits of such an institution.

You were so kind as to request my views as to the plan. When suggested by you, it was almost new to me, and the field is so ample that I have not been able to investigate it all to my own satisfaction. It is a momentous subject; and speaking from my own feelings only, I could wish that a detailed plan of an institution like this, might not *as yet* be thrown before the public. I am not prepared to say that it is the best which can be de[*vi*]sed, although I have not been able to arrange a better, and in comparison with the present bank I should give it a decided preference. You have now my opinions *as they are*. With great respect

Amos Kendall

ALS, THer (14-0526).

[Enclosure]

The constitutionality of the present Bank of the United States has been maintained only on the ground that it is necessary to furnish a safe depository for the moneys of the United States and facilitate their transmission from one section of the Union to another. It may well be doubted, whether the people of the several states intended to delegate to the general government the power to create any corporation whatever, except within the District of Columbia for District purposes. That they did not intend to grant to this government the power to withdraw from the jurisdiction and taxing power of the states, persons or property located within their borders, by associating them with public officers or public property under any pretence whatever does not, in my mind, admit of a doubt.

In the present Bank of the United States, government owns one fifth of the stock and appoints one fifth of the directors. Four fifths of the stock are held and four fifths of the directors appointed, by private citizens. The whole bank is, therefore, under the control of private citizens and is managed with a view to private gains.

There are two leading features in this corporation, which, in my view, violate the constitution and the fundamental principles of our government. It is a grant of exclusive privileges. No other national bank can be established by the express terms of the charter. It grants to the stockholders a privilege to use their money in a business or in a mode from which the rest of the community is excluded. It gives them the special and exclusive countenance of the government, and affords them the use of the national revenue to augment their private gains. It withdraws the private property invested in it as stock from the jurisdiction and taxing power of the states. It has been decided, that this Bank and its branches are exempt from state taxation, to which every other bank, business and species of property is subject.[1] To the principle asserted in this exemption, there is no limit. The power which in the first Bank exempted eleven millions of dollars and in the present bank twenty eight, may, in a future bank, exempt three hundred. It is an unlimited and unchecked power to exempt private property and private business, within the states, from state taxation, in violation of the constitution and of the reserved rights of the states whose taxing power is rightfully sovereign.

If the argument be sound on which the constitutionality of a national bank is maintained, it does not follow that every species of national bank is constitutional. It must not, in any of its features, violate the reserved rights of the states or grant exclusive privileges to any man or body of men.

The charter of the present Bank expires in March 1836. If a bank be necessary as an appendage to the Treasury, care should be taken that the public interest does not suffer by its destruction. The government has within itself the means of furnishing a substitute for the present bank, which will afford all its facilities and not be subject to any of its constitutional objections. With the same propriety and upon the same principle, that the government holds seven millions of dollars of the stock of the present bank and appoints five of its directors, might it hold the whole stock and appoint all the directors. Ample means are found in our abundant revenue to furnish any amount of stock which the necessities of such an institution might require.

To obviate all inconvenience, therefore, which might arise from the dissolution of the present bank, let a bank (or Revenue Office) *purely national* be established and attached to the Treasury, based upon the revenue and public faith of the United States. A principal bank or office may be located in Philadelphia with branches (or auxiliary offices) in every state of the Union, among which the amount assigned for stock or the Treasury deposits may be distributed in such manner as may best promote the public interests. The President and directors of the principal bank may be appointed by the President and Senate of the United States[2]; and the Presidents and Directors of the several branches by the power in the states which elects Senators in Congress.[3] A power to remove any of these officers for cause, may be vested in the President, and the vacancy thus occasioned may be filled by the original appointing power or its lawful substitute. They may all be paid a regular salary for their services, and be subjected to heavy penalties for wilful mismanagement or peculation. Their power may extend only to dealing in exchange and discounting real transaction notes for short periods. It should be their chief business and duty to receive, safely keep, and when required, faithfully transmit the ~~revenues~~ moneys of the United States from one section of the Union to another and to foreign parts.

While such an institution would violate no ~~feature~~ provision of the constitution and trench upon no state right, it would increase the public revenues, afford the readiest means of transmitting it, afford an uniform circulating medium, and, in time of war, obviate the necessity of resorting to ruinous loans. The notes of the bank would be evidences of public debt, and, if thought expedient, by making them bear a moderate interest, they would be sought after and retained by citizens and foreigners who ~~seek~~ wish to invest their money in permanent public stocks.[4]

Such an institution checked by frequent investigations into its actual condition and entire publicity in its transactions, would afford a good substitute for the present bank and be attended with less evils and more advantages. The control given to the states in the choice of Presidents and Directors of the branches, would restrain the institution from abuses and counteract its tendency to strengthen the hands of the general government. But if any other constitutional ~~and safe~~ system can be devised, which shall answer the purposes of a safe depository of the public treasure and furnish the means of its ready transmission, so regulated and checked, as to strengthen this government as little as possible ~~the hands of the general government~~ and more effectually guard the rights of the states and the liberties of the people, it shall have my most hearty approbation and support.[5]

[Endorsed by AJ:] Mr Kendals letter & remarks on my plan of National Bank—

AD by Kendall with insertions by AJ, THer (14-0528).

1. The Supreme Court in *McCulloch* v. *Maryland* (1819) upheld the constitutionality of the BUS and denied the power of states to tax it.

2. AJ added here: "or in such a way as congress shall designate."

3. AJ added here: "with such restrictions as congress may require & impose."

4. AJ inserted here instead: "The notes of the Bank would be an evidence of Public debt and, if thought expedient in time of war, could be made to bear a moderate interest redeemable at the pleasure of the Government, they would be sought after and retained by our citizens and foreigners who might wish to invest their mony in public stocks."

5. AJ inserted here instead: "checked the more effectually to guard the rights of the states and the liberties of the people, it shall have my most hearty approbation & support."

From Tuskeneah et al.

Creek Nation November 20th 1829

President of the U S. Greeting

We the Chiefs Head men and Warriors of evry Town through out the Creek Nation, have this day assembled together to express to you our sentiments and wishes in relation to the removal of Coln. John Crowell from the office of Agent for I. A. of this Nation under the full belief that you will listen to your unhappy and much injured red children of the Creek Nation. Father listen we beseech you to hear us Coln. Crowell has been the Agent for this Nation a good many years, and within the last several years there has been large sums of money appropiated by Congress to pay the Creek Nation.[1] His Brother Thomas Crowell has been a merchant during the whole time, and from the various large sums of money we have received but a small proportion of it and some of our people have gotten some goods of the Agents Brother, they have become immensely rich and we have become poor, although the Agents Accts and Vouchers may appear to the Genl. Goverment to be fair and equitable. But Father listen, you know that we do not understand keeping accts of such magnitude therefor it is in the power of the Agent to defraud us, and this we unanimously believe has been done to a great extent, when we take into consideration the large appropriations that have been made by Congress and compare that with the small Amounts we have received, we cannot resist the belief that He has defrauded the Creek Nation of large sums of money and *Father*, as this belief is wholy [. . .] we have lost all confidence in the agent and his Brother the merchant and it can never be restored, and in various other, transactions we have been equally deceived. Father listen to your red children, we wish you to remove Coln John Crowell from the office of I. A. of this Nation and order Him and his Brother from the confines of the Creek Country[2] Some months ago there was a slanderous report in circulation on the frontiers of Georgia that the creeks intended to become hostile we believe that Coln. Crowell was the author of the report, to answer his own selfish aggrandizing purposes, as we endeavored to trace the authorship of the report and we could never trace it any farther than upon him, and this is the concurrant opinion of many disinterested white people both in Alabama and Georgia[3] Father sometime in the early part of last month we addressed you a communication wishing you to remove Coln Crowell from the office of Indian Agent and wished you to appoint Majr. William Triplett in his place and as we have not heard from you, that communication might have mislaid [. . .] and we have assembled together to address you again[4] Father listen, we here call your attention to Majr William Triplett and we wish you to appoint him Agent for I. A. of this Nation. He is a patriotic and meritorious Gentleman we have the utmost confidence in his honor and integrity and we think that an Agent of this Nation should have the full confidence of the Goverment the confidence of the people of the Creek Nation and also the confidence of the authorities of the State of Alabama so that all may move in an uninterrupted course of policy. And we repeat again He is the man of our choice. Father listen, we wish to say a word in relation to Capt. William Walker He has during his stay in Washington City written a letter to Mr. Mc.Kenny of the Indian Department. His letter is well calculated to deceive the people of the U. S. and the Goverment and we unhesitatingly say it was intended for no other purpose It is not founded on truth, He states that the most of our people would emigrate to the west if they were not held in fear of the Chiefs.[5] Father listen the common class of our people are as much opposed to leaving this Country as any of the Chiefs, as it is the general understanding among all classes of the people of the creek Nation that our Country has been secured to us by treaty and all we desire upon that subject, is the complete fulfilment of our various Treaties. Father listen. It has been a usage among our people from time immemorial, that there should be Chiefs and

Head men of our Nation, and we believe of other Indian Nations, and we believe that the same custom applys to all the civilized Nations of the Earth, that these Chiefs and Head men are placed in power to rule ov[e]r their people, to compell them to submit to the laws of their country. If their was no law what a scene of misery & degredation would there be among man kind, and more particularly among all those nations that have not advanced in the arts of civilization, therefore that part of Capt Walkers letter that relates to the cutting off the ears of two Indians that emigrated was slanderous in the extreme, It is true, their ears were cut off, but it was done for voilating the sacred laws of the creek Nation, and not for emigrating. We believe that the Chiefs of this Nation are as lenient and humane to the common class of our people as it is possible for them to be to have their laws obeyed. Father in closing this talk with you which is sharp but a plain statement of facts. we wish you a long happy and prosperous life and may that great Spirit, in whose hands, men and Empires are dust & ashes smile on your labours and when you depart this life here below may He crown you with immortal Joy

Tuskenehau his X mark
Nehor Micco his X mark
Tuskenehau his X mark
Nehorsloccohopee his X mark
Coosa Tutenuggy his X mark

[Fifteen additional names follow.]

test Wm. McGirth
Samuel Smith interpreter

LS, DNA-RG 75 (M234-222). Nehor Micco (d. 1836) was a former Seminole who became a principal chief of the lower Creek towns in 1829.

1. The 1826 Treaty of Washington and its 1827 supplement, which together completed the cession of Creek lands in Georgia, awarded the tribe cash payments of $217,600 and $27,491 respectively.

2. John Crowell remained as Creek agent until 1836. His brother Thomas Crowell (d. 1835) was employed at the agency in organizing Creek emigration.

3. Rumors of an impending Creek attack had prompted Governor Forsyth to mobilize the Columbus, Ga., militia in July. A widely reprinted account from the *Columbus Enquirer* reported Crowell as saying the Creeks in secret council had "resolved to stay and die upon their soil; that they had also resolved to kill him, the agent, and wage a war of extermination upon the frontiers, and assassinate every white west of the Flint river." Informants to Governor Forsyth attributed similar language to Crowell (DNA-RG 75, M234-222). Crowell denied the newspaper story, and a meeting of fifty Creek chiefs issued a public statement avowing their peaceful disposition (*Niles,* Aug 8 and 29).

4. Tuskeneah and other Creek chiefs had written AJ on October 12 asking him to replace Crowell with William M. Triplett, former Georgia state comptroller and brother of Creek subagent Thomas T. Triplett.

5. In an October 8 letter to Thomas L. McKenney, Creek subagent William Walker charged the Creek chiefs with terrorizing their people to prevent them from removing westward. In one instance a party led by the chief Nearnothla "actually cut off the ears of some

of the emigrants." Walker opined that three-fourths of the Creeks would gladly remove if not deterred by fear. Invoking Walker's letter to prove that the common Indians desired removal, McKenney sent it to Eli Baldwin of the New York Indian Board, who had it published in the *New-York Evening Post* on October 15.

To William Branch Giles

(Copy)

Washington November 21st. 1829

My Dear Sir,

I avail myself of the visit of Mr Campbell[1] to Richmond to thank you for your two favours of the 3d & 22d. of the last month[2]—the latter presenting me with a copy of your Political miscellanies which I should have acknowledged earlier had not the great pressure on my time interrupted so often the hasty examination which I was desirous of making, before I did. Having now completed this, I am enabled to express my cordial approbation of the leading principles which it discusses, and to assure you that I esteem it a great acquisition to the library of the Politician and Statesman.

I beg you, Sir, to believe that I accept it with á just sense of the obligation which it imposes as a token of your confidence in the success of my administration. All that I can offer in return is the guaranty of my past life, and an honest desire to obey those injunctions of the constitution which you have so uniformly and eloquently defended and illustrated. Wishing you every blessing I remain most respectfully yr. obt. servant.

A. Jackson

[Endorsed by AJ:] copy to Mr Wm B Giles Novbr. 21st 1829—

LS copy in AJ Donelson's hand, DLC (37).
    1. John Campbell, U.S. Treasurer.
    2. Giles had written AJ (on October 9, not 3) asking for aid in resolving the unsatisfied land claims of Virginia's Revolutionary veterans. AJ referred the subject to George Graham and noted "Gov. Giles to be answered with the assurance, of the cooperation of the executive in every thing that will procure ample Justice to the revolutionary officer & soldier." Graham reported adversely to the claimants on October 22.

From Robert Bean

Fort Smith Arkansas T. Nov the 23d. 1829.

Dear Genl.

I take the liberty of writing you a few lines the people in this Section of country have been moved by the government to give room to Indians that we are all easy alarmd. the Cherokees from the Old nation east of the Missipia have sent to thos in this country to lett them know what would be the best part for the Old Nation to exchange for and those is verry anxious to gett back the lands that was exchanged for loveleys purchase this country that they want is the best part of this Territory you know the disposition of Indians better than I can tell you but they never are satisfide I am in hopees the Government will not move us any more fore the Indians for we are at the Jumping off plaice now if we should have to leave this, the cherokees Is going on with G Houston I hope that we will not be moved to give way to the Indians thier is plenty of land in the cherokee nation in what is cald Lovesley purchase for all the Indians in this country and the Old Nation two. Genrl. Houston can give you more information about this country than I can write[.] I am dear Sir much Respect your friend,

Robert Bean

ALS, DNA-RG 107 (M222-25). *TPUS*, 21:117. Bean (1779–c1847), from Tennessee, had been speaker of the Arkansas Territory house of representatives in 1825. Samuel Houston left for Washington in December, bearing this letter.

To John Christmas McLemore

Washington Novbr. 24th. 1829—

My Dear Sir

By this days mail you will receive the papers which I long since promised to send you relating to the cruel persecution of Mrs. T. now Mrs. Eaton and the Major—These are but a part, and if you can rise from Perusing them without the greatest horror & disgust for a Clergyman, who professes to be the embassador of christ, but who, has, under the hypocritical cloak of religion become the secrete slandered of his neighbour, I can only say I will be much surprised.

You will discover, that every rumor has been traced, and to this day there has not been one individual who has said the knew of their own knowled one fact that could tarnish her virtue, and as for myself I have no doubt but the clergyman raised the villanous falshood about the abortion himself, no one else ever heard such *tale* from the lips of Doctor Craven, and the Revd. Mr Campbell I know will *lie*, and when you read Genl Duff Greens letter in reply to the Doctor, you will see there, that he will not only lie, but state falshoods for the basest purpose—I will add, the letter to Genl Green was to screen himself & his high chivalrick friend[1] from a dilemma into which they were placed with Major Eaton, from which this hero of the Revd. preacher, never will be able to extricate himself—Major Eaton in this instance has taken a stand worthy of himself, and will relieve him at least from the secrete slanders of Gentlemen worthy of his notice, as it is now understood, that they must account.

I wish you to let Judge Overton see them Mr Charles J Love & the family, Mr Barryhill and his, as from some whispers here, it may be, that as Miss *Harriet* only mixed with those who had been, and still are innimical to Major Eaton & his lady, and was in the midst of some of those who originated the slanders, & who, are interested in still having them believed, for their own credits sake, may have given false impressions—and indeed it might be well that Mr. H. Hill should also see them—

you will find that the first letter from my friend Dr Ely is private & confidential, this letter is only to be shewn to those who will view it as such—the others are not confidential may be shewn to any one, but is not intended for the press—as a time will come, but that is not yet, when these things will, as a part of the history of the times, be placed before the nation.

This persecution was founded in political views, looking to the future, Jelousy arose that Eaton might not be a willing instrument to those particular views, that his popularity was growing and it was necessary to put him out of the Cabinet & destroy him regardless what injury it might do me or my administration. But I thank my god, that truth is mighty and will prevail & it has recoiled upon the heads of the wicked engaged in it- the recoil is great, in Newyork the other day Mrs. Eaton was toasted at a public table at a dining given by the Mayor[2] to Major Barry at which Mr James Brown & Mr James Barbour with many others were present—from this you may infer, that the attempt *here* to put them down, has failed.

Present me to Betsy & your amiable little family, let me hear how my son[3] is coming on & believe me yr. friend

Andrew Jackson

ALS, NHi (14-0587); Photocopy of ALS, DLC (72).
1. Nathan Towson.
2. Walter Bowne (1770–1846).
3. Perhaps AJ's namesake Andrew Jackson McLemore (b. c1823).

At the end of 1829 the national debt of the United States stood at less than $49 million, down well more than half from its peak in 1815. The debt consisted of several types of securities paying varying rates of interest. Some $13 million in "3 per cent stock" tracing back to the Revolution was extinguishable at the pleasure of the government. So was $7 million at 5 per cent held by the Bank of the United States, with which the government had purchased its original $7 million share of Bank stock. The rest of the debt, paying rates between 4.5 and 6 per cent, would become "due," or available for redemption by the government, on dates set by terms of the individual loans.

To retire the debt Congress had created a "sinking fund" administered by five commissioners: the vice-president and chief justice of the United States, the secretaries of state and of the Treasury, and the attorney general. In 1817 Congress pledged a yearly $10,000,000 appropriation to the fund, as well as any annual Treasury surplus beyond a $2,000,000 reserve. After meeting interest payments and redeeming securities that came due, commissioners were authorized with presidential approval to use the fund to retire additional debt by purchasing securities on the open market, provided their prices remained below certain ceilings.

On November 15, BUS President Nicholas Biddle sent William B. Lewis a proposal to accelerate payment of the remaining debt (Biddle Papers, DLC). Biddle hinged his plan on a prompt renewal of the BUS charter, presently set to expire in 1836. The Bank would pay a $1.5 million bonus for recharter. It would exchange its $7 million in 5 per cent securities for the government's $7 million in Bank stock, retiring the former. Lastly, in return for a government payment of one-half their face value, it would assume responsibility for principal and interest on the 3 per cents. These transactions would allow the government to fully extinguish its debt by March 4, 1833, the end of Jackson's term.

On November 17 Biddle sent Lewis a table summarizing his plan. Within the next few days he met in person with Jackson in Washington. According to Biddle's memorandum of the conversation, Jackson thanked him for the plan but told him in frankness that he believed Congress had no power to charter a bank outside the District of Columbia (Biddle Papers, DLC; Reginald C. McGrane, The Correspondence of Nicholas Biddle Dealing with National Affairs, pp. 93–94).

Jackson passed Biddle's plan on to Treasury Secretary Ingham, who wrote Jackson three letters, all printed below. The first is a note of November 24 enclosing Biddle's tabular statement, followed by two undated letters evaluating his proposal.

From Samuel Delucenna Ingham

Ty Dpt 24 Nov 29

My dear Sir

I have the honor to enclose herewith Mr B's statement with the additional remarks—very respectfuly your

S D Ingham

[Endorsed by AJ:] Mr Ingham on the plan of Mr B for paying the public debt &c &c—

ALS, DLC (37).

Mode of discharging the Public debt

Years	Dates	Payments by the Govt.	Yearly appropriation to the Sinking Fund	Of Principal of Funded debt
1829	December 31st.	. . . . . .	. . . . . .	. . . . . .
1830	June 30th.	. . . . . .	. . . . . .	. . . . . .
	"	7,720,451.60	. . . . . .	6,648,124.72
	"	. . . . . .	. . . . . .	. . . . . .
	December 31st.	4,279,548.40	. . . . . .	3,581,665.26
	"	. . . . . .	12,000,000.00	. . . . . .
1831	June 30th.	7,643,534.33	. . . . . .	7,053,101.15
	"	. . . . . .	. . . . . .	. . . . . .
	"	. . . . . .	. . . . . .	. . . . . .
	"	. . . . . .	. . . . . .	. . . . . .
	"	. . . . . .	. . . . . .	. . . . . .
	"	. . . . . .	. . . . . .	. . . . . .
	December 31st.	4,356,465.67	. . . . . .	3,949,425.99
	"	. . . . . .	. . . . . .	. . . . . .
	"	. . . . . .	. . . . . .	. . . . . .
	"	. . . . . .	12,000,000.00	. . . . . .
1832	June 30th.	6,033,439.16	. . . . . .	5,717,809.82
	"	. . . . . .	. . . . . .	. . . . . .
	December 31st.	2,414,342.59	. . . . . .	2,227,363.97
	"	. . . . . .	. . . . . .	. . . . . .
	"	3,552,218.25	. . . . . .	3,552,218.25
	"	. . . . . .	12,000,000.00	. . . . . .
1833	March	2,145,036.04	of the Treasury receipts of the 1st quarter of	

By which it appears that the whole of the public debt will be paid off or absorbed by the Bank on the 1st of Jany. 1833 except $2,145.036.04, which might be paid to the Bank in Jany or Feby 1833, and thus discharge the entire debt. NB.

AD, DLC (14-0583).

before the 4th. of March 1833.

Of Interest on successive balances	Redemption of principal made or provided for.		Successive balances of debt unredeemed.
	Description of Stocks	Amounts to be redeemed	
. . . . . .	. . . . . .	. . . . . .	48,522,896.93
. . . . . .	Subscription 5 pCents	7,000,000.00	
. . . . . .	Three pCents . . .	13,296,249.45	20,296.249.45
1,072.326.88	. . . . . .	. . . . . .	28,226,620.48
. . . . . .	Six pCts of 1815	3, 581,665.26	3,581, 665.26
697,883.14	. . . . . .	. . . . . .	24,644,955.22
. . . . . .	Remainder of 6 pCts 1815	2,858,890.91	
. . . . . .	Two portions of Exc. 5 pCts	37,803.18	
. . . . . .	Exchanged 4½ pCts	1,539,336.16	
. . . . . .	Bank 5 pCts . . .	1,265,405.99	
. . . . . .	Bank 4½	1,351,664.91	7,053,101.15
590,433.15	. . . . . .	. . . . . .	17,591,854.07
. . . . . .	Third portion of Exc. 5 pCts	18,901.59	
. . . . . .	Five pCts of May 1820	999,999.13	
. . . . . .	4½ pCts	2,930,525.27	3,949,425.99
407,038.68	. . . . . .	. . . . . .	13,642,428.08
. . . . . .	Remainder of 4½ pCts	5,717,809.82	5,717,809.82
315,629.34	. . . . . .	. . . . . .	7,924,618.26
. . . . . .	Exchanged 4½ of 1824	2,227,363.97	2,227.363.97
186,978.62	. . . . . .	. . . . . .	5,697,254.29
. . . . . .	Remainder of 5 pCts of 1821, paymt. of which may be assumed by the Bank	3,469,890.31	
	Part of the residue of Exc. 4½ pCts of 1824— may be assumed also . .	82,327.94	3,552,218.25
. . . . . .	. . . . . .	. . . . . .	2,145,036.04
1833 would redeem the Remainder of Exch. 4½s. of 1824		2,145,036.04	
		48,522,869.93	

From Samuel Delucenna Ingham

My dear Sir

I have examined the Statement you were so good as to put into my hands. it does not contain any distinct proposition from the bank, except so far as one may be inferr'd from the Statement of the amount of debt to be paid in 1830 viz.

5 per cent Subscribn. Stock	$7,000,000
3 per cent—	13,296,249.45
Six per cents—	3,581,665.26
Interest—	1,770,210.02
total to be paid in 1830	25,648,124.73

To pay this sum the Govt. has at
command of Surplus Revenue, 12,000,000[1]
Bank stock <u>$7,000,000</u>
$19,000,000 <u>19,000 000 00</u>
to be provided for— 6,648,124 73

The Statement does not shew how this sum is to be provided, I am left therefore to suggest how it may be met—
If the Bank is rechartered the U S. Stock in it is worth 40 per cent advance instead of 24 per cent the present price—[2]
40 per cent on $7,000,000 is 2,800,000
a new Bonus for Charter of not less than that of 1816 <u>1,500 000</u>
$4,300 000
which deducted from $6,648,124.73 leaves $2,348 124.73
to be provided for—
~~If the Bank assumes to pay the 3 per cent upon receving~~
It may be observed that the payt. to be made in 1830 exclusive of the 3 per cent & Subscription to the Bank are

viz 6 pcts	$3,581,665 26
Int—	<u>1,770,210.02</u>
	$5 351 875.28

leaving unexpended of Sinking fund	<u>$6,648 124.72</u>
	$12,000 000 00

This sum ~~will~~ being paid to the bank together with the advance on sale of B. Stocks and the Bonus

viz.	$6,648,124.72
	2,800 000 00
	<u>1,500,000 00</u>
	10,948,124.72

The Bank may assume to pay the whole of the 3 per cents without any advance of money provided they can be redeemed at 82³/₁₀—and if the Bank were merely to assume and only pay at pleasure, the 3 per cents could no doubt be had for even less. The present price 88 is supported by the expectation that the Govt. will with its powerful sinking fund be soon obliged to redeem them at Par—[3]

The payments for the succeeding years viz 1831. 32. & 33 are I presume correctly stated, they only contemplate the employment of the actual Surplus revenue viz $12,000 000 a year—

This operation would leave the 3 per cents not *paid* but *assumed,* by the bank. The Govt. cannot be divested of its obligation to pay the debt nor can it properly be ~~divested~~ taken off the Trsy books—it would also leave the Govt. without any interest in the Bank—

Should it be thought advisable to dispose of the Surplus revenue ~~without~~ before the 3 per cents are paid—and to appropriate money enough to pay the Interest and a small sinking fund to be conditionally applied to pay the Principal, this stock could no doubt be redeemed at ~~even~~ less than 80—If 4 per cent be a regular interest for a perpetual stock, and I think it quite low enough—the stock should sell for 75—if 4½ per Cent be a fair interest it should sell for 66²/₃—

There can be no doubt if the price were limited to 80 under permanent arrangement of the sinking fund as proposed the whole could be obtained in a short time.[4]

AL, DLC (14-0579).

1. Biddle presumed $2 million in Treasury surplus each year for the sinking fund, making $12 million overall.

2. BUS stock sold at a premium above its par value, which would increase further upon the assurance of recharter.

3. Paying low interest, the 3 per cents circulated at discount. However, as the government's debt dwindled, their value increased in anticipation of redemption at par. The sinking fund commissioners could not retire the 3 per cents by open purchase, for their market price had risen beyond the ceiling of $65 for $100 in face value set by law in 1817. Biddle's proposal would defer the expected redemption and thus depress their value, allowing the Bank to buy them up at a savings.

4. Ingham here proposed that the government, rather than the Bank, stretch out the retirement of the 3 per cents in order to facilitate their purchase in market at a reduced price more reflective of their low yield than their par value.

From Samuel Delucenna Ingam

My dear Sir

I have carefully examined Mr Biddles whole project—and find it necessary to add very little to what has been already said—

He estimates the advance on the Bank Shares at—	$1,500,000
which is about 22½ per cent,	
he also proposes a Bonus of	1,500 000
	$3,000,000

which sum the Govt. will make by rechartering the Bank, and according to his proposition for redeeming the 3 per Cents—upon receiving the above sum of—

	$3,000,000
and ½ the amt of the 3 per cents	6 648,124
	$9,648 124

the Bank will assume the whole of the	
3 per cents viz.	$13,296,249.45
from which deduct as above	9,648 124
gain to the Govt.—	$3,648 125.45

by the redemption of the 3 per cents—provided it shd be otherwise obliged to redeem them at par—

The total gain by rechartering the bank according to Mr B's project is viz

Bonus—	1,500,000
advance on stock	1 500 000
Saved by the assumption of 3 per Cents	3,648 000
	$6,648 000

I am satisfied of the practicability of the operation so far as the bank is concerned because it will make a profit on the Bank Shares now held by U.S. of—

40 per cnt	$2,800,000
instead of 22	1 500 000
and gain—	1,300 000

and save by redeeming the 3 per cents at 80 a *further* sum of

	2,659,249
total saved by bank—	$3,959 249

The sum to be paid by the bank if the 3 per cents were redeemed at par is, as before

	3,648 000
the gain by the bank is	$311,249

Recapitulation

the Bank can therefore assume to pay one half the 3 per cents viz $6,648,000—in consideration of the profit on the bank shares

	2,800,000
Bonus—	1,500 000
	4,300 000
and save by redeeming the 3 per Cents at 80—	2,659 249
	$6,959,249
the sum assumed as above	6,648 000
gain to bank	$311,249

very respectfuly

S D Ingham

ALS, DLC (14-0585). Ingham figured roughly as follows. The government would pay over to the BUS $6,648,124, representing half the face value of the outstanding 3 per cents. It would also return the $1.5 million bonus the Bank paid for recharter, and swap its $7 million in BUS stock, worth $8.5 million at present premium, for the $7 million in government debt held by the Bank. In return, the Bank would wipe the $13,296,249 in total par value of the 3 per cents off the government's books. With the $9,648,124 realized from the government, and presuming a further $1.3 million in appreciation of the BUS stock thus acquired, the Bank could buy up the 3 per cents in market at 80% of par for $10,636,999 and come out ahead $311,125. (Ingham's figure of $311,249 came from rounding off a $124 in mid-tabulation.)

From Samuel Swartwout

New York 25th Nov 1829

Dr. Sir,

The bearer hereof Mr Isaac Kibbee goes to Washington on business with the Treasury Department   Being desirous however of paying his respects to the President, he has requested a line of introduction which I give with pleasure.

I am apprehensive, that owing to the severity of the Laws in relation to dishonored Bonds, Mr Kibbee may not succeed to his satisfaction with the Treasury Department. Nothing but a general Bankrupt Law can relieve merchants from the misfortune of a life of suffering who happen to be surety for an others Bonds. If a Law could be passed to relieve Merchants, leaving out Planters & Farmers, who can have but little to do with the Custom-House, it would be the greatest blessing ever confered upon a Commercial community. I am, Dr Sir, with great respect &c your obt Servt.

Saml. Swartwout

[Endorsed by AJ:] Mr Swartwout Introducing Mr Kibbee

ALS, DLC (37). Isaac Kibbe (1763–1845) was a merchant and former harbor master of the port of New York. Congress had enacted a general bankruptcy law in 1800, but repealed it in 1803. Though often discussed, another was not passed until 1841.

From Samuel Delucenna Ingham

[26 Nov 1829]

My dear Sir

I had the pleasure of receiving your note last evening on the subject of the W. India trade—The clause refered to will of course be inserted in the report agreeably to your wishes—[1]

I have been so engaged in examining the fiscal matter preparatory to ascertaining the balance in the Treasury that I have scarce had a moment to spare to think of the banks—

Your views as to promising a future message, are I think perfectly just whatever your purpose may be in that respect—you can select your own time unembarrassed by any commitment, as well or better than if a promise was given. The essential objects of a national bank are. 1. To preserve a sound currency *uniform* throughout the U. S. by which taxes shall be collected as well as levied *uniformly* thro the States—unless such a currency can be substantially maintained The Constitution is violated,[2] and it will be impossible for the Union to be preserved—In a case of great public exigency the people will submit to many grievances, but such a grievance made permanent must dissolve the Union.

2. To enable the Goverment to transfer its funds at pleasure from one extreme of the Union to another or wherever the public service may require;—This is necessary to the daily operations of the Treasury, but most essential in War—

3. That the Deposits of the Govt. should be safe—The outstanding debts due from state banks nearly all of which have occurred since the restoration of peace, prove that these banks are not safe depositories—

A National institution therefore seems indispensible; The Present Bank boasts that it has performed all these important functions—In the establishment of another, it will be highly important as well for the permanent character of your Admn. as to the nation, that it be equally as serviceable in all respects as the present bank, and not liable to the same objection in some particulars—

There are serious objections to placing the branches in the power of the States: a dissaffected State in time of war of which we have had examples, might frustrate a campaign or sacrifice an army upon some frivolous pretext for refusing the payt. of the Treasury draft—

The issues of paper by the branches to gratify the speculations of the Directors or their friends, might disturb the exchange between the various parts of the country and jeopardize the safety of the deposites. The Principle of responsibility in the head might be destroy'd by the want of Power to control the subordinate parts—

It appears to me that a bank founded solely on Govt. Capital must be *a bank of deposite only.* to be safe, its influence should rather be directed to the restraining issues of paper by other banks than be tempted to make large issues of its own—

I have taken the liberty of suggesting these remarks, altho too crude & undigested to be regarded as throwing any material light on the ~~subject~~ question; The subject is one of great magnitude, and require the most mature reflection, and I am obliged to acknowledge that I am not prepared to propose even a detailed outline of a plan that wd deserve your attention as it ought. Opinions are so various on the subject of banking operations, and yet it is necessary to compromise with public opinion in all such measures, in order to secure success, that it wd seem proper to reconnoitre the whole ground before any part is occupied—

we must be able if possible when called on for a plan to present some thing like demonstration, that the great objects of the Govt. will be secured;

you will excuse I am sure some appearance of solicitude on the subject and attribute it to the only proper motive That the Dept which you have assigned to my charge should be able to sustain with success your admn and that all its & your acts shd be remembered & refered to by posterity as redounding to the happiness & safety & durability of the Republic   I do apprehend sir that we have not time to enter safely upon this complicated question, whatever may be said in a Message to congress, will be difficult to change, and if it should not prove acceptable to public opinion it will increase instead of diminish the power of the present institution   excuse this long hasty letter & accept the assurance of the great respect of your.

S D Ingham

[Endorsed by AJ:] Mr. Inghams Ideas as far as he has had time to think upon the Bank question

ALS, DLC (37).
1. Ingham's annual Treasury report in December recommended customs adjustments to foster trade with the West Indies and encourage its opening to American shipping (*SDoc* 3, 21st Cong., 1st sess., p. 12, Serial 192).
2. Article I, section 8 of the Constitution required that "all Duties, Imposts and Excises shall be uniform throughout the United States."

From John Macpherson Berrien

Office of the Attorney General
27th Nov 1829—

The Attorney General presents his respects to the President of the United States, and Conforming to his request, has the honor to submit to his consideration the following suggestions—

The subject matter of the reference made to the Attorney General, includes two enquiries—*one*, which relates to the principles both of *constitutional law*, and of *finance*, connected with the *existing institution*, and *that which the message proposes to substitute for it*—and a *second*, which questions the *expediency* of making the proposed communication to Congress at this time—

The question of constitutional law which belongs to the first enquiry, relates to the power of the Federal Government, to establish a corporation for banking purposes, and to the right of the Legislature to grant exclusive privileges—

It is not to be denied that this question has heretofore occasioned much diversity of opinion, and it is not doubted that this diversity, still exists, although probably in a more limited degree. At the same time it must be admitted, that the existence of the power, has at various times, and in different forms, been affirmed by every department of the Government.

If this power is not granted by the Constitution, it is very certain, that no series of usurpations can give it a legitimate existence in that instrument. Since however an instution now exists, which results from the exercise of that power, it seems to me that the question of constitutional power may be wisely left to rest on the footing on which anterior decisions have placed it, so far as the Executive department is concerned, until that department shall be called to do some act, which will necessarily raise this question. If this view of the subject should not accord with the determinations of the President, the attorney General will cheerfully submit his opinion on the question of constitutional power, whenever it shall be desired

In the mean time I am bound to state respectfully to the President, my opinion that it is not expedient at this time, to make the proposed communication to Congress—

If this would be considered as falling within the scope of Executive *duty*, the question of *expediency* would not arise. What the *former* enjoins, could of course not be yielded to considerations springing from the *latter*—The Attorney General does not believe that any such obligation exists.

The charter of the present institution will not expire until *1836*. It is not proposed that the expression of the views of the President on this occasion, should interfere with that institution, except as they may affect the question of the renewal of the charter—Now it cannot be foreseen, as far as the Attorney General is advised, that the Executive and Legislature will be called to act upon that question, during the official term of the present President—The question may be raised in the course of the ensuing session of Congress—and the charter may expire during the continuance in office, of the present incumbent of the Executive chair—At this moment however, it is not believed that any fact is officially known, which calls for the immediate action of the Executive, or which renders it probable, that the Legislature will be called to the consideration of the subject—

Whenever that subject shall be presented to the Legislative body, it will without doubt occasion a strong sensation—It will divide many, who on other great questions, and indeed generally, are in harmonious concert of opinion. It will bring into active opposition to the administration, the institution whose legal existence is questioned, and those who from various causes, are interested in its welfare, or controuled by its influence—

I repeat the declaration—If the proposed communication were enjoined by duty, no considerations of this sort, could of course be permitted to interfere with its fulfilment—But since the question may not arise during the present official term of the Executive, and since if it does, ample time and opportunity will be afforded to communicate to Congress the views of the Executive, it does not seem to me to be expedient, by anticipating the agitation of the subject, to commence at this early day those exciting discussions, which unless they eventuate in the renewal of the charter, will without doubt be revived at each successive session, until some substitute institution exclusive in its character, shall be established—

The responsibilities of the administration must necessarily be great—and its indispensable duties during the approaching session of Congress, will be sufficiently arduous—As it advances in its official career, it will acquire by the judgment of a discerning people, on its zealous endeavors for the promotion of the public interests, an increase of strength, which will give increased effect to the just recommendations of the President—while a failure to obtain the support of Congress, to any measure which in this early stage he may recommend, may diminish its strength and capacity for advancing the great interests committed to its care—Respectfully submitted by

Jn. Macpherson Berrien

[Endorsed by AJ:] The atto. Genl on the inexpediency of bringing to the view of congress the Bank question—

ALS, DLC (37).

From Samuel Delucenna Ingham

Try Dept 27 Nov 1829

My dear Sir

In the memorandum submitted yesterday for your examination on the subject of the bank, my only purpose was to embody what I understood to be your own views on the subject, and to avoid as much as possible those details that would be likely to present points of discussion in which your political friends would be irresistably thrown into opposite sides—

But I do not find myself prepared to say that a bank founded on these principles could be successfully established   It is a subject of great moment and wd require very mature reflection, to enter upon a system entirely new for the disposition of so vast a sum of money as the public deposits—my time & thoughts have been so much given to other matters that I find myself wholly unprepared to render that assistance to you in this matter which you have a right to expect from the Dept which you have done me the honor to commit to my charge   I am fully persuaded that the fiscal affairs of the Govt. cannot be safely administered even in peace & much less in war without the U. S. Govt. can preserve a sound Currency and distribute its funds at pleasure at par with the Currency—Whether the present system could be so modified as to avoid the evils it is liable to and secure the benefits desired or whether it be best to make an experiment of a new & untried system are the first points to be considered, they are of great magnitude and your decision on them as well as the details of the plan that may be determined on, may involve at some future day the safety of the country—

It must be admitted to be a field of experiment, in which no certain results can be calculated upon   much care is therefore necessary in the preparation of a plan and not less in the effort to reconcile conflicting opinions, before any distinct ground is taken either as to the Principle to be adopted or the details—It therefore would seem advisable to have more time for that sort of reflection which is very necessary on such a subject, than can be now given before the message is prepared   I cannot therefore avoid indulging the hope that it may comport with your views of the public interest to defer a notice of the bank untill a future period—I am with the greatest your obt Svt

S D Ingham

ALS, DLC (37).

To Martin Van Buren

Novbr 28th. 1829—

The President with respects, returns Mr Crudners note, which he thought he had done yesterday, but accidently had omitted—Has the Sec of State passed in review the subject matter of Mr Poinsetts dispatch, it is of vital importance to the southern states, and we ought to have *evidence* of *record*, that we have acted promptly on the first intimation of the subject—but we must when we act, make our communication with much circumspection & deliberation—Think of this. yr friend.

Andrew Jackson

ANS, DLC-Van Buren Papers (14-0615). Paul Baron de Krudener (1784–1858) was the Russian minister to the United States. Poinsett had sent a dispatch on October 14 warning of Mexico's plan to foment a slave revolt in Cuba (DNA-RG 59, M97-5).

From Martin Van Buren

W. Nov. 28t 29

my dear Sir

I should have called on you last evening but was afraid to go out on account of my cold & am full of concerns to day as I suppose you are. I shall have a note to Col Butler prepared by monday morning for your consideration. I concur very fully in your views.[1] You will recollect that on one of our rides I suggested to you by my desire to make some improvement in the State Department to which you were good enough to tender your co-operation. I now enclose for your consideration a sketch of what I should like to have said upon that subject. My hope & intention is if the plan meets your approbation & that of Congress to get my friend Mr Butler to take the place. He would be eminently useful here in a thousand respects[2]   I cannot but think that Congress would without hesitation adopt the proposition as every body knows that something is necessary & I think the reflections in regard to the plan of a Home Department recommended by Messrs Madison Monroe & Madison would be well recvd. by the friends of State rights—Yours truly

M Van Buren

The great & constantly augmenting increase of business in the Department of State, forced itself, at an early period on the attention of the Executive. Thirteen years ago, it was made the subject of an earnest recommendation in Mr. Madisons last message to Congress; and his suggestions have been repeated by both his successors. This augmentation arises from many sources, not the least of which, is the increase in the family of independent nations, of late years very considerable, and attended with a corresponding multiplication of our foreign relations. The remedy which has been several times recommended, is, the establishment of a Home Department, a measure that does not appear to have met the views of the national Legislature. Believing that the leading objection to it, is, the apprehension that its tendency would be greatly and imperceptibly to increase the already strong bias of the Federal system towards the exercise of authority in matters that do not belong to it, I am not disposed to revive the recommendation. I am not the less impressed, however, with the urgent importance of enabling the head of that Department to devote more of his time to our foreign relations, by devolving upon some other officer the responsibility of many of its local concerns. This might be effected by the appointment of an under Secretary of State. averse to any augmentation of offices, not imperiously called for by the public business; I still deem it ~~my~~ our duty, when such real necessity exists, to provide for it. on its present footing, the Department of State does not appear to possess the advantages derived by the others from subsidiary bureaus, & clearly convinced that the public good will be materially promoted by the proposed measure, I deem it incumbent on me, respectfully to recommend it to your favourable consideration—[3]

[Endorsed by AJ:] Mr Van Buren reserved for a special message—A. J. Novbr. 28th 1829—second thought embraced it in my message

ALS, DLC-Van Buren Papers (14-0608).

1. On November 30 Van Buren instructed Anthony Butler to investigate Poinsett's report of Mexico's plan to incite a Cuban slave revolt and, if true, to remonstrate against it in the strongest terms (*HRDoc* 351, 25th Cong., 2d sess., pp. 54–55, Serial 332). Butler reported on February 19, 1830, that the new government in Mexico had disavowed the project (DNA-RG 59, M97-6).

2. Benjamin Franklin Butler (1795–1858) was Van Buren's former law partner and a New York state legislator. He became AJ's attorney general in 1833.

3. In addition to foreign affairs, the State Department had charge of general governmental business lying outside the specific provinces of the War, Navy, and Treasury Departments, including the patent office, the census, and the commissioning of marshals and attorneys. President Madison had recommended creating a new department in his last annual message in 1816, and Adams (though not Monroe) repeated the suggestion in 1825. AJ's first annual message incorporated most of Van Buren's suggested text nearly verbatim but dropped the concluding proposal for an undersecretary, merely asking Congress to alleviate the secretary's burden by "some suitable provision on the subject" (Richardson, 2:461–62).

From John Coffee

Cherokee Agency, 28th. Novr. 1829.

Dear Genl.

I have been here four days endeavouring to collect information touching the line between the Creeks and Cherokees. I have written the Secretary of War and informed him the state of things here in relation to this business.[1] I regret to find that neither the Govr. of Georgia, nor the Agent had taken any steps to forward the business, and the apology was, that the letter of the secretary of War did not reach here untill a very few days since, yet I find the letter of the Secretary of War to John Ross on the same subject has been published in the Cherokee Phoenix two weeks or more, but I do not intend to rely upon information to be furnished alone by the public authorities.[2] I must however in the first place call on them, and afterwards get all I can from other sourses, from private individuals who are disinterested—I have sent an express to the Govr. of Georgia, and I have sent for Ross and the other principal chiefs of this nation to come forward with their testimony   There is now here encamped near 300 emigrants for the Arkansas Country, and more is expected in before they are ready to start, their boats are not ready, and I suppose will not be ready for two weeks yet to come—indeed I saw waggons starting out today after some other Indian families who I understood had to go out upwards of one hundred miles and back before they could move down the river—Among the emigrants are several old men of the nation who has resided south of Hightowa river[3] from the earliest Cherokee settlements there, these men now seem to be entirely disinterested on the subject, and know a good deal about it, but they express fears to give written statements, least it would give offence to some one of the parties, but I shall try and get from them some usefull testimony in deciding the question. I shall attend to them while I am waiting a return of my express from Georgia which will be near a week yet to come, untill I learn more on the subject I cannot determine whether it will be necessary for me to go on the disputed territory, if I find that I can get any useful information by going there, I will certainly go—from some occurences that have come to my knowledge since here, I fear the Georgians are not disposed to come forward with their testimony in that open and frank manner that could be wished for, however I shall receive all the testimony offered, and give it the credit that it seems to merit, be it on either side—you will see the whole of it, as soon as I can collect it together[4]—I have just seen the Govrs. message, you will see from it, that they will be gratified if your decision is in their favour—but the honor of the state cannot be compromited by yielding their claim if given against them—I am sure they will have [fa]ir chance for justice if they will bring fo[rth] the evidence of their claim—[5]

I shall use all the diligence in my power to compleat this business and report to you at the earliest day possible, but I discover I cant hurry these people—I write you this hasty line that you may be advised of my movements—and not as an official letter—I send it by Mr. Lewis Ross who leaves here tomorrow morning for the city, & will probably reach there before the mail[6]—Dr. Genl. with great respect your friend & Servt.

Jno. Coffee

ALS, DLC (37).
1. Coffee's latest report to Eaton on November 28 explained delays in getting information from Governor Forsyth and his plans to start gathering evidence (DNA-RG 75, M234-73).
2. Eaton had written Forsyth on October 14, explaining Coffee's mission and asking Georgia's cooperation (*HRDoc* 89, 21st Cong., 1st sess., pp. 22–26, Serial 197). Thomas L. McKenney sent a copy to Cherokee chief John Ross. Both his letter and Eaton's appeared in the *Cherokee Phoenix* on November 18.
3. Hightower or Hightowah was the anglicized name for the Etowah River.
4. In December Coffee traveled through the disputed territory, collecting testimony and documents from whites and Indians. Finding evidence that the Cherokees had possessed the country long before 1821, he submitted a report to Eaton on December 30 sustaining most of their claim (*SDoc* 512, 23d Cong., 1st sess., vol. 2, pp. 226–29, Serial 245).
5. In his November 3 message to the Georgia legislature, outgoing Governor Forsyth said "the character of the state would be compromitted" by allowing federal adjudication of its unquestionable title to the land. Having asked federal assistance in removing the Indians, Georgia should "wait tranquilly" the result, but retained the right to assert sovereign authority over its entire Indian domain (*Niles,* Nov 21).
6. Lewis Ross (1792–1870), John Ross's brother, was one of six delegates recently named by the Cherokee Nation to present grievances in Washington.

To Robert Johnstone Chester

[This letter is available only in a published version.]

Washington, Nov. 30, 1829.

My Dr. Sir:

I have recd. your letter of the 8th instant and hasten to answer it. I seriously regret to hear of the persecution of your uncle and your distress. But your fortitude must rise superior to the purpose. always keep in view that economy and industry will overcome any and everything and bring you triumphant over your misfortunes. I am sure your amiable wife will aid you with her smiles and her industry, and when I can with propriety, it will afford me pleasure to assist you with an office agreeable to your merit. The office you ask I cannot give with propriety—before your application reached us, the influence of the citizens of the vicinity of Columbia and Nashville, with many other members of Assembly and the Governor of the State were presented in favor of Col. Reynolds in such manner, that it has precluded any others, and at least twenty others have applied. The office is not yet vacant.[1]

This may be fortunate for you, for if the Chikesaw Indians remove to the Mississippi as I expect, this Agency cannot be of long duration.

Upon the receipt of your letter I sent for the Secretary of War, whose feelings are of the most friendly kind to you, and the first office that presents itself you will not be forgotten, and it is probable ere long a better may.

Congress meets next Monday, and we will soon be able to judge what course it will adopt with regard to our Indian neighbours, and I expect soon to hear from Mexico, and as soon as I can see the whole ground I will write you again.

As the meetings of Congress Approaches, my labours increase. I am engaged preparing for them, and this with my other labours, employs me day and night. I can with truth say mine is a situation of dignified slavery. But my hope of hapiness fled with the severe bercavement I met with in the loss of my dear wife —the only consolation in this side of the grave, is, when I look forward to the time when I can again retire to the Hermitage, if God permits me, there to spend my latter days beside the tomb of the only solace of my life, set my house in order, and lay my bones beside her.

Present me kindly to my old friend, Mrs. Hays, say to her, that Saml. was to be married last tuesday, to a young lady of good family, and when she comes of age, of fortune, and every way accomplished—present me to Betsy, to Miss Norssee, Col. S. D. Hays and Lydia, Doctor Butler and Polley, and their sweet children. To Mrs. Hutchings and every branch of the family[2]—We are all in health here, and all join in kind salutation to all friends including you[r]self and believe me Sincerely yr. friend

Printed, John Spencer Bassett, ed., *Correspondence of Andrew Jackson*, 4:95–96 (14-0628). Chester (1793–1892), the postmaster at Jackson, Tenn., was married to Rachel Jackson's niece, Elizabeth ("Betsy") Hays (1805–41). He had written AJ Donelson on November 8 describing his financial difficulties and asking for an appointment (Donelson Papers, DLC). Chester was involved in a protracted legal contest with Robert Allen, his mother's brother-in-law and a former business partner. In 1831 he was ordered to pay a judgment in excess of $10,000.

1. Benjamin Franklin Reynolds (1788–1843), whom AJ appointed Chickasaw agent in February 1830 to replace Benjamin F. Smith, was a Tennessee state senator and had served under AJ as an Army captain in the Creek War.

2. AJ's sister-in-law Jane Donelson Hays (1766–1834), widow of Robert Hays and the mother of Betsy, was also mother to Stockley Donelson Hays (1788–1831), Martha Thompson ("Patsy") Hays Butler (1790–1857), Narcissa Hays (b. 1795), and Samuel J. Hays, who had just married Frances P. Middleton. Stockley's wife was Lydia Butler Hays (1788–1852), and Martha was married to William Edward Butler (1790–1882). Mrs. Hutchings was probably Catherine Donelson Hutchings (c1752–1834), another of AJ's sisters-in-law.

Draft by John Macpherson Berrien
on the Judicial System

In this general survey of the State and condition of the union, I consider it my duty, to call your attention to the present organization of the Judicial system. The uniform administration of public Justice, in the several States of the union, is certainly desirable, and existing as they do, in our Federal Union on the basis of perfect equality, each state has a right to expect, that the same privileges which in this regard are enjoyed by the citizens of other States should be extended to her citizens

The judicial system of the United States, [con]sisting as it does of a Supreme, Circuit, and district Courts exists, in all its efficiency, in only fifteen of the States of the Union—To three others the circuit courts, which compose an important part of that system, have been imperfectly extended—and to the remaining six, they [have] hitherto been denied[1]—The result has been [to] withhold from the citizens of the last mentioned States, the benefit of the protection afforded by the Supreme Court, to their fellow citizens of other States, in the whole extent of the criminal, and in much of the civil jurisdiction of the Federal Judiciary—That this state of things ought to be corrected, when it can be done consistently with the public welfare, is not I think, to be doubted, and neither is it to be disguised, that the proper organization of [our] Judicial System is at once difficult and delicate   To create a sufficient number of Judges to extend the circuit court system, equally throughout the different parts of the Union; and to avoid at the same time such a multiplication of those officers, as would incumber the Supreme appellate tribunal is the object which it is desirable to attain. Perhaps it might be accomplished, by dividing the Judges of that Court excluding the chief Justice, into two classes—and providing that the Supreme Court should be held by these classes alternately, the Chief Justice always presiding—

AD, THer (14-0740). AJ incorporated this text, slightly reworded, in his annual message (Richardson, 2:461).

1. The Judiciary Act of 1802 mandated that each federal circuit court consist of a Supreme Court justice and the local district judge. An 1807 act created a seventh Supreme Court justice and circuit court for the states of Ohio, Kentucky, and Tennessee, but subsequent growth had made that circuit unwieldy. The newer states of Louisiana, Indiana, Mississippi, Illinois, Alabama, and Missouri had not yet been incorporated into the circuit system.

Draft by John Henry Eaton
on the Bank of the United States

I consider the present a suitable occasion to bring to your consideration those principles which are involved in the establishment of the Bank of the U States, the charter of which will soon expire. ~~The constitutionality of its establishment~~ The propriety of its creation has been maintained on the ground that it is necessary to furnish a safe depository for the monies of the United States, & to fecilitate a transmission from one part of the Union to the other. It may well be doubted, if the people of the several states intended to delegate to the general goverment an ~~power~~ authority to create any corporation whatever, except within the District of Columbia. That they did not design to grant to this goverment under any pretence ~~whatever~~ a power to withdraw from the jurisdiction & taxing power of the States, persons or property located within their borders by associating them with public officers, or public property ~~under any pretence whatever,~~ does not in my mind admit of question

In the present US Bank the govermet owns one fifth of the Stock, & appoints a fifth of the directors: the rest of the Stock, & the appointment of the other directors ~~is~~ rests with private citizens. It is of course under the direction & control of ~~private citizens~~ individuals, & managed with a view to private gain

There are some leading features in this corporation which in my view, conflict with the constitution and the fundamental principles of our govermet. It is a grant of exclusive privileges; for by the express terms of the Charter, no other Bank can be established. It concedes the special & exclusive countenance of the Govt and affords the use of the national revenue to augment individual gain. ~~It withdraws~~ Private property, vested as stock, it withdraws from the jurisdiction & taxing power of the States, inasmuch as it has been decided, that the Bank & Branches are exempt from state taxation, to which every other ~~bank~~ business, bank, & species of property is subject. To the principle thus asserted, there is no limit The power which in the old Bank exempted Eleven millions of Dollars, & in the present twenty Eight, may in some future charter exempt three hundred millions, or any other amount. It is an unlimitted power acting; which ~~can~~ discharges private business, & property from taxation within a State ~~this being~~ a portion of original sovernty ~~in the States~~, which by the States has not yet been parted with

The charter of the present Bank ~~expires~~ ceases in March 1836. If it be necessary as an appendage of the Treasury to be continued, care should be taken, that the public interest does not suffer, by permitting it to expire; &

care be taken likewise that it shall contain no conceded privilege, which shall be considered adverse to any principle of the Constitution

The advantages to be derived through the operations of a Bank, in the transmission of funds to different parts of the Union, necessary to the use of the Goventment; & as affording facilities in a period of War, have been rendered manifest. To obviate the inconveniences which might arise from a dissolution of the present, might not a Bank, or revenue office, national in character, be established, & attached to the Treasury to be based upon the revenue, & public faith of the U States. By some of the states such a plan of banking has been tried with some success; & if it has not been found successful to the extent expected in the first formation, enough has been ascertained to show its entire practacability, under a system of proper organization and of salutary checks interposed. The faith & revenue of the Country would inspire confidence ~~in its favor,~~ and effectually sustain it under pressure. It would be only necessary to throw around it such cautions, as that while all encroachments upon the states thro' any power to be granted to the Executive, & which might improperly be used, should be guarded, such limitations might be imposed as to assure a correct & safe administration of its affairs. The Directors should be appointed ~~by the President & Senate~~ in such maner as Congress shall direct; to be made salary officers, & prohibited from receiving discounts or becoming endorsers: to be subject to gradual periodical changes; and to guard the better against Executive power, to permit changes to be made in no other way & at no other time than may be directed by the law, unless for misdemenors in office; with rigid & severe penalties for peculation or frauds committed by any one connected with the Bank

~~Whilst such an institution &c as in the original~~

ambition—repeal when you please

Such an institution, organised in a manner to trench upon no state rights, would increase the public revenue, afford readily the means of its transmission—introduce an uniform circulating currency, & in time of War, perhaps obviate the necessity of resorting to injurious loans. The notes of the Bank would exist as evidence of public debt, & in war might be made to bear an interest, until redeemed, & would thus partake of the character of our stocks, & be an inducement for our citizens to invest in them there capital. So modeled; & checked by frequent investigations of its condition; and publicity from time to time given to its transactions, banking benefits might be presented, free from the objections & complaints, which exist in reference to the present Bank of the US. Yet if any more acceptable & secure plan shall be devised, to attain the objects of public interest, & give security to the States & people, it shall receive my approbation

In offering these considerations, I have felt the weight of the responsibility imposed; but in justice to my self, and a Country which possesses my devotion I could not do less, or say less. It is a common remark, and a correct one, that monied institutions in a Country without proper guards interposed are dangerous to liberty. The generation which gave us the blessings we enjoy, has not ~~yet~~ passed away. The govemt we have, is even yet but experimental; and care & caution is to be consulted, that nothing of departure shall be witnessed in our day, least we leave the legacy impaired which has been given us. The time may come when an aspireing ~~ambitious~~ Chief Magistrate, prefering self, to other & higher considerations, may be presented; & in this event, how important is it that no facilties from legislative enactmets shall be afforded, by which his ambitious views shall be assisted. Terrible will it be, when the sword & the purse of any Country, shall form an alliance against the liberties of the people; it would be a powerful impulse of patriotism indeed, that could resist them. One advantage on this head through the monied institution proposed, is, that should it be found at all dangerous to liberty, a repeal can follow, because connected with nothing of contract. In that Country where liberty & the rights of man are regarded, too great vigilance cannot be maintained.

An attempt, ere long, most probably will be made by those interested in the Stock of the U States Bank, to obtain a renewal of its Charter. It is a fit occasion then, to suggest this important & interesting question to the consideration of Congress. Altho the Charter does not expire until 1836, yet to avoid precipitancy in so essential a measure, I should consider, that it could not too soon receive the attention of the Legislature. Opportunity should be afforded for discussion & reflection, that by timely notice to those who are interested justice may be done. It is well known that the Constitutionality of the law, which charters the present Bank has, by some been denied, & by many its expediency ~~has been~~ questioned. From various parts of the Union, dissatisfaction has been expressed as to the decision of the Supreme Court, which maintained a power granted by the Charter, to locate branches without the authority of a State to impose a tax upon the Capital. Besides this, it has been objected, that it is a monopoly, conceding to one portion of citizens, certain ~~defined~~ enlarged privileges for a given time, in exclusion to other members of the confederacy. It permits also, a power hazardous to liberty, the holding of large landed interests   These, & a denial of the right of taxation, on the part of the States, has excited a general apprehension of the absorbing power of the general goverment, which those interested for the liberties of the Country are so desireous to restrain.

I would suggest, if to avoid these objections and to silence all complaints, it might not be advisable to create a bank which in its character should prove purely national—the faith & revenue of the govt lay pledged; a bank which should claim exemption from all the objections, as to the infringement of state authority which exists in relation to the present— one which would place the Directors, under such restrictions, as might be conceived wholesome & proper—which should make them salary officers, with an exclusion for all participancy in its affairs, whether as principal or as endorser; a prohibition to become owners of real estate, and with severe penalties annexed, for any thing of practised misconduct. Through such a measure the inconveniences & objections at present complained of might be removed—the revenue aided—facilties in war obtained—ruinous loans avoided—the whole, not a few made participants; & by proper cautions interposed an ambitious Executive, who, in some future time might prefer self advancement to principle, be restrained from uniting together the purse & the sword of the Country   These will prove important considerations, & if under such checks & balances some plan can be suggested, whether in creating a new, or amendatory of the present charter of the present Bank, & thereby to guard against anticipated evils, & to secure permanently the blessings we enjoy, such a plan shall receive my consent & approbation

[Endorsed by AJ:] Majors E & B. remarks

AD, DLC (14-0317).

Memorandum on the Bank of the United States

The principles and interests involved in the Bank of the United States and the approaching expiration of its charter, present questions of grave importance which, perhaps cannot too soon engage the attention of Congress. Since the charter of that Bank was granted, its constitutionality has been affirmed by the Supreme court of the United States. The ground on which it was granted by congress and has been sustained by the Supreme Court, is, that a Bank is a necessary agent of this government in executing its delegated powers.

Nevertheless, doubts exist in the minds of many, whether it was the intention of the people to delegate to this government directly or indirectly, the power to create any corporation whatever, except within the District of Columbia for District purposes. Others maintain, that, admitting the correctness of the reasoning—which maintains the necessity of a national bank, it does not sustain the present institution in its details. The power of taxation being reserved to the States in the most unlimited manner, it is asserted, that a national bank, to be constitutional, must not exempt persons, property or business, within the limits of the States from the unrestrained exercise of that power. Nor must such a bank, it is affirmed, grant exclusive privileges, or extend to one Citizen of a State or of the united States, special advantages or exemptions, in his person, property or business, which are prohibited or denied to other citizens.

The present Bank, it is maintained, does in its details, violate these constitutional and fundamental principles. By the terms of its charter, no other national Bank can be established during its existence. It has been decided, that the States cannot tax it. Whatever benefits it may render to the government, its stock are principally owned by private citizens; it is subject to their controul; and its business is mainly conducted with a view to private gain. Citizens of a State who hold its stock, are enabled to carry on the business of banking within the limits of the state, exempt from those burdens to which other citizens in the same State, engaged in the same business are subject, These privileges, it is asserted, are exclusive, and are directly prohibited by the constitution. Complaints are also made, of the interference of the Bank in political contests, and dangers to the liberties of the people are apprehended from its monopoly of real estate, its control over the currency and the power it concentrates.

If congress deem a national Bank necessary as an agent of the Goverment, care should be taken, in the establishment of a future bank, to guard against these objections to the present institution. With this view, I recommend a careful enquiry, whether a bank, *purely national*, may not be established, so organised as to yield all the benefits of the existing institution, and subject to none of its objections. The Government needs not the capital of private citizens to endow its agent, and I would hope, it does not require the stimulant of the broker to secure their fidelity. It would seem, that by a pledge of the revenue and faith of the government, a bank or agent might be created, adequate to all the requisite purposes of the Treasury and competant to sustain the public credit in war, without the humiliation of a copartnership with private citizens. In the wisdom of congress the country may repose for the organisation of such an institution on principles which shall secure the fidelity of its managers, furnish all those aids to the Government which make a bank necessary; and at the same time, guard as far as practicable, against that executive control which might enable an ambitious President, by an union of the purse and the sword, to subvert the liberties of his country

[Endorsed by AJ:] on the Bank—

AD, DLC (14-0297).

Memorandum regarding James Alexander Hamilton

Majors. Eaton & Barry & Mr Kendal, with my own views, on the Bank question—for Col Hamiltons consideration—A. J.
also atto. Genl & Mr Inghams

ANS, DLC (14-0712). AJ apparently gave to Hamilton his own, Kendall's, and Eaton's drafts for the annual message on the Bank of the United States, together with the critiques of

Berrien and Ingham (all above). Hamilton produced his own draft (below, with the annual message).

Memorandum regarding Charles Pendleton Tutt

answer to Col Tutt—His letter recd; will see the Sec. of the Navy and write him as to the request for leave of absence to remove his family —which will be granted if the clouds in the south & west does require his constant attention there from the addition about to be made to West India Squadron—[1]

The request of Mr Fitzgerald must be made to the Collector of Mobile, as the collector nominates, and the secratary of the Treasury approves, all such subordinate appointments & the President has no controle on such appointments

Mr Fitzgerald will have less persecution, as Col Clinch is ordered to Tamp Bay & the quartermaster to some other post—Therefore the Tyranny of a monied aristocracy will no longer domineer over him[2]

The President can say nothing to you encouraging as to another appointment at present—

AD, DLC (37). Tutt (1780–1832), from Virginia, had been appointed Pensacola navy agent in May.

1. The full complement of the West Indies and Gulf of Mexico squadron in September 1829 was five frigates and two sloops. In October one of the sloops, the *Erie,* then in Norfolk, was ordered to Pensacola to rejoin the squadron. In February 1830, the frigate *Brandywine* was assigned to the squadron.

2. John Fitzgerald (b. c1801), former publisher of the *Nashville Republican,* was appointed postmaster at Pensacola in June. On May 20 he had written Eaton accusing Florida officials of malfeasance and fraud. Fitzgerald charged the Army quartermaster at Pensacola, Daniel E. Burch (c1796–1833), with peculation and with putting his commanding officer, Colonel Duncan L. Clinch, under his influence with a $10,000 loan (DNA-RG 107, M222-25). Fitzgerald's charges, which Clinch attributed to political malice, led to an Army court of inquiry which cleared Burch (Clinch to Eaton, Aug 24, DNA-RG 94, M567-42; *TPUS,* 24:302). Burch was reassigned to New Orleans in October, and in November Clinch was transferred from Pensacola to command Cantonment Brooke at Tampa Bay.

Memorandum Book

[These entries in Jackson's memorandum book, probably from around late November, directly follow those above from September and October.]

☞ I would draw the attention of Congress to a review of the pension laws, and barely remark, that whilst every revolutionary soldier who aided in procuring the blessings of that liberty we now enjoy, and is in want, has imperious claims upon his country that he should be sustained in comfort, in his decline of life; great care ought to be taken, that none but those who did aid in that glorious strugle, should be entitled to the munificence of their goverment—To those, might be added, all who in the late war by wounds & privations have been rendered unfit to sustain themselves by manuel labour, if any there are who are not provided for under existing laws—This review of the pension laws has become the more necessary from a very late order of the sec of war under the late administration extending the ~~field~~ terms of admission on the pension rolls incompatible with the former construction of the law, & the rules promulgated under them by his predecessor executive—This new regulation was viewed by me as an act of legislation, not within the constitutional powers, of the Executive, and as soon as made known to me, I ordered its suspension, & a strict adherence to the law & the former rules established under it, that had been so long the guide of the Executive Goverment, in placing soldiers on the pension rolls—But before this suspension, a debt had accrued under this late rule, to the amount of $_____ for which there had been no appropriation or requisition for one—and the requisition made by the late Sec. of war, for the payment of pensions list, as it existed at the time the requisition was made, has fell short of the amount due for the year 1829 $_____   I therefore call the immediate attention of Congress to this subject that an appropriation may be made to meet this arrearage—[1]

☞ *The Revenue,* where a reduction of duties are recommend to congress, if any is, let it be gradual—

[These notes appear together out of chronological sequence at the rear of the memorandum book.]

on this 13th. Novbr 1829. I enquired of the first comptroller of the Treasury whether he had written to Genl P. B Porter on the subject of the ballan[c]e due the U. States—He answered he had not—that he had & was waiting for the account of Mr Vaness to be closed before he could—that this account was still open, & required that the sec. of State should draw in favour of Mr Vaness for the ballance due U.S. before it could be closed as Mr. V. had not personally called himself—see the Sec of State on this subject so soon as he returns[2]

A. J

James Findly son of Govr. F. recommended by Mr Ingham—for atto. for western Pensylvania—This not to be overlooked when the subject is taken up—A. J.[3]

Judge Gibson—named for Judge of the U. States—Henry Baldwin, Mr. Wilkins, Mr. Binney, Mr Ross & Cheves—& Genl Wall—[4]

Mr Calhoune recommends, Mr John A. Dix, late of the army of the U. States for charge De affairs to *Europe*—⁵

AN, DLC (64).

1. Eaton had informed AJ of the pension deficiency on October 21 (above). A revised version of this passage, stating the shortage at more than $50,000, appeared in AJ's first annual message (Richardson, 2:456).

2. Cornelius P. Van Ness and New York congressman Peter Buell Porter (1773–1844), later Adams's secretary of war, had served as commissioners under the Treaty of Ghent to determine the boundary between the United States and Canada. Both men had challenged the validity of an 1821 law that set their annual salaries below what they claimed the treaty itself required. In June 1829, Van Ness, while still contesting the law's constitutionality, agreed to waive his claims and accept a closing settlement of his account. On August 10, first comptroller Joseph Anderson demanded the return from Porter of $9,440 in overpaid salary. Porter refused on September 4 (Porter Papers, NBuHi). Queried by AJ on September 26, Van Buren reported against Porter's claims on September 28. AJ afterward rendered a formal decision against Porter, which Van Buren communicated to him on November 26. The government unsuccessfully pursued Porter through the courts for repayment until 1835.

3. William Findlay (1768–1846), father of James Findlay, had been governor of Pennsylvania, 1817–20.

4. Supreme Court Justice Bushrod Washington died on November 26. AJ nominated Henry Baldwin to replace him on January 4, 1830. John Bannister Gibson (1780–1853) was chief justice of the Pennsylvania supreme court; Horace Binney (1780–1875) was a Philadelphia lawyer; John Ross (1770–1834) was a Pennsylvania judge and former congressman; and Langdon Cheves (1776–1857) had been speaker of the U.S. House of Representatives and president of the Bank of the United States.

5. John Adams Dix (1798–1879), later a U.S. senator and governor of New York, had resigned as an Army captain in 1828.

December

To a Cabinet Member

Decbr 2nd. 1829—

Dr. Sir,

I wish you & Major Barry to come over at 2 oclock if you can to read over that part of the Message, that relates to our foreign relations—It has Just underwent a pruning by the rest of the heads of Departments, and I wish it in the hands of the copiest—will you send your messenger for Major Barry & be here at 2 oclock—yrs

Andrew Jackson

ALS, James F. Ruddy (14-0795).

From David McClellan

Western Choctaw Agency
December 2d. 1829

Dear Sir

you will pardon me for taking the liberty to address you, but I feel it a duty that I owe to my Government. The cherokees are about to send another delegation to washington this winter to get more lands. they are the most intrigueing set of people I have ever known. I am informed they wish the Genl Government to purchase all that tract of country lying on the Arkansas & Canadian Rivers which belongs to the choctaws for them. which if done, would completely take away from the choctaws all their best navigation and greatly invalidate the ballence of their country here, and probably put an end to their migration west of Mississippi. Those people (the cherokees) have been so much fostered by Government where will they find a stopping place. I hope shortly, they are so sanguine of getting the Government to purchase that tract of country for them, their agent is about building his Agency on the choctaw lands[1]

I am of the opinion if I was authorised to go to the choctaw nation with funds, that I could bring a great many over to their lands west of the Mississippi. There are a great many of the choctaws settled in Louisana that could be brought to their lands here if measures were taken for that purpose. would it not be advisable to instruct the Governor of Louisana to order them out of that state to their lands on Red River and also the Governor of Arkansas to order those that are in the Territory to those lands also.

I reported myself to Majr. Duval the cherokee agent on the 12th. of September last and stated to him the necessity of having those white people that are settled on the choctaw lands removed and also the cherokees. they have caused a great deal of murmer and discord here, he promised me that he would give me orders to that amount, but I have never received such orders yet; I have discovered that an agent presiding over two different nations has a tendency to create a jealousy between the two tribes. If it would meet your approbation I would much rather have the controul of the choctaws myself, and not subject to the order of the cherokee agent, and so soon as there are Indians sufficient here to authorise the appointment of an agent I would be thankful for the appointment. I think I could manage those people so as to meet the views of Government as well as any other person, & that appointment would enable me to assisst the family of my brother (the late agent) to get along through the days of their pilgrimage easier[.][2] I have the Honor to be Respectfully your Obt Servt

D. McClellan
Sub Agent for the choctaws
west of mississippi

ALS, DNA-RG 75 (M234-184). McClellan (1783–1858), from Tennessee, was subagent for the western Choctaws.

1. The treaties of Doak's Stand in 1820 and Washington in 1825 secured to the Choctaws the lands west of Fort Smith between the Canadian and Arkansas Rivers to the north and the Red River to the south. The Western Cherokee treaty of May 1828 called for relocating their agency to the new Cherokee domain north of the Choctaw lands. Cherokee agent Edward W. Duval remained at the old agency in Arkansas until his dismissal in 1830.

2. Choctaw agent William McClellan had died on May 24, and David became subagent under the Cherokee agency. The Choctaw removal treaty of Dancing Rabbit Creek in 1830 mandated a full agent, and AJ appointed Francis W. Armstrong in 1831. McClellan continued as subagent.

From John Jolly

Wigwam Illinois C. N.
3d Decr 1829.

Great Father,

Your kind talk sent by Doct Baylor has been received by me, and has made my heart glad. Like a Father you ask me to let you know what my troubles are. That you may take them far from me I will tell you what they are, and some of them have rested on my heart for a long time. You will believe the talk which I now send to you. It is true, and tho' it true, I hope the causes of it will not long remain. More than a year ago, the last Treaty made by the great Father and my Nation, was to have been made good, and all the promises in it complied with, and it is not yet done—the lines are not run to shew my people where to make their Houses, and clear their fields![1]

The Osage Missionaries yet live on the land given to my people, and, also a number of Osage families live near to them. I wish them all removed. The Cherokees have Missionaries of their own, and want no more![2]

Several years since an Osage killed one of my young men, and no satisfaction has been given; but when my people were last at the City our Father promised, that the Cherokees should have satisfaction—They have no prospect of it. nothing is doing by the Agents of Goverment to have the Osage given up, to be punished—My young men say they will have blood for blood; The *clan* of the slain warrior have waited, along time, but say they can wait no longer, but will lay the murderer or some of his relations to rest with the dead. I do not want the innocent to suffer for the guilty! My people say it will be so, unless satisfaction is given. I wish the hands of my young men to be clean; and unstained with blood! The Osages say that *Dutch* a cherokee killed one of their people, but my Father can see, if he will look at the talk made by the Delegation last at Washington, to the Sec'y of War, all about the situation of Dutch![3]

By the last Treaty between the U. States & the cherokees, the country containing the Reservations, granted to Colo. Chouteau and others, was ceded to the cherokees. They are in the midst of our country and many white people are settled upon them, and I now hope my Father will have them bought up, and given to the cherokees—If it is not done I will have no peace, for troubles will arise with those white men who have *no laws*, & my people, and blood may be shed, and my people blamed when not in fault.[4]

I want my Father to send my people to me from the old Nation, but I want him to give them land to settle upon when they do come, for I have no more land here than is necessary for my children who are here—If more land is not given for them there will not be room for them, and they will not be happy. If land is given to them here, they will soon come to it and be at peace, & happy![5]

My son (Genl Houston or) the Raven came to me last spring. I was glad to meet him, and my heart embraced him. When he arrived at my Wigwam, he rested with me, and was, as my own son; He has walked straight, and my heart has rejoiced in him. His path is not crooked, nor has he walked in hidden ways. He is now leaving me to meet his *white* Father, Genl Jackson, and look upon him, and I hope he will take him by the hand and keep him as near his heart as I have done. He is beloved by all my people, who are here! When he returns to me from my Great Father, happiness will be in my Wigwam!

When you look upon this letter I wish you to feel, as though we *smoked* the pipe of peace together, and held each other by the hand, and felt, as one man. We are far a part, but I send my heart to *my* friend Jackson, and the Father of my people!

John Jolly his   X   mark

[Endorsed by AJ:] Indian Talk from King Jolly by Genl Houston refered to the Sec of war for his report on the Subject of the Indians, killed, and the satisfaction promised—that the President may answer his friend Jollys' *talk* A. J.

LS in Samuel Houston's hand, DNA-RG 107 (M222-26). Eaton referred Jolly's letter to Thomas McKenney, who reported back to Eaton on January 21, 1830 (DNA-RG 75, M21-6).

1. In the May 1828 treaty with the Western Cherokees, the U.S. promised to run the lines of their new homeland "without delay, say not later than the first of October next," and to immediately remove all unwanted persons. McKenney confirmed to Eaton that the running of the lines had been delayed and was still unfinished.

2. The Union Mission in present Mayes County, Okla., and the nearby Osage farm settlement at Hopefield Station lay within what was now Cherokee territory. The Osage cession treaty of 1825 had provided for relocating the mission, but it remained occupied in 1829, with Osage, Cherokee, and Creek children attending its school. McKenney assured Eaton that the few Osages left on Cherokee land would soon be removed. The Hopefield Osages left in 1830 and the Union Mission school closed in 1833.

3. The Western Cherokees and Osages had feuded for years. In 1822 an Osage killed a nephew of Cherokee chief Thomas Graves. Dutch, or Tahchee (c1790–1848), leader of a band of Cherokees who had moved south of Red River, killed an Osage in 1826. On February 28, 1828, the Western Cherokee delegates in Washington complained to Secretary of War Barbour that federal officials had allowed the Osage killer to go free after he was delivered up for execution. They denied responsibility for Dutch, who had left their territory and repudiated their authority (DNA-RG 75, T494-2; *TPUS*, 20:319–22).

4. The Osage cession treaty of 1825 prescribed individual square-mile reservations for a number of "half-breeds," including relatives of the fur trader Auguste Pierre Chouteau (1786–1838), in what was now Cherokee territory. The U.S. pledged to buy out the remaining titles for the Cherokees in the 1835 removal treaty of New Echota, which named Chouteau as agent or guardian for all the holders.

5. McKenney argued back to Eaton that Jolly was mistaken: his new homeland was meant for all Cherokees, Eastern and Western, as it had been obtained in exchange for Arkansas lands acquired by the whole Nation in 1817.

From Hall Jackson Locke

Mouth of the Piscataqua
New Castle N. H.
December 4th. 1829.

To General Andrew Jackson
President of the United States, and the Honorable Senate

Gentlemen,

Having for thirty years been attached to the republican cause of my beloved Country and seen the vile mechanations of its *Enemies* now partially subdued in this quarter, I hope nothing will be done to mar the good feelings of the genuine friends of the present *Administration*, many Animadversions have been made against the character of Colo. Decatur our present worthy collector of the customs but which only serves to raise him higher in the estimation of every *Democratical Republican* in this quarter of our Country, and I am positive when the cause of Democracy was desponding no *man* did so much to raise the drooping spirits as Colo. Decatur he opened his bosom to the shafts of battle and never tured back like many others to reap the laurels which he has won, I am confident he attends to the duties of his office with fidelity and honour, to himself, and Country, and gives good satisfaction to the Merchants, Ship Owners, fishermen and the publick generally, none oppose him but such as would in the hour of danger desert their post is a well known fact and sell their birthrights for a mess of pottage, yea, worse *Brittish Garlick,* but when such men a the Patriotic Governor Pierce, Hon. Elijah Hall, Hon. Wm. Gardner Hon. Isaac Hill, Hon. Wm. Badger, with all the other Heros of the State who do and will support him, and could the Illustrious Langdon rise from the tomb he would put his fist and say so long as the Decaturs have done so much for their beloved country let the present collector remain in said office as a small tribute of respect for his meritorious services.[1] Respecting Saml. Cushman Esqr. District Atty. I have been personally acquainted with him for fourteen years or more and believe him firmly inisiated in the faith of Republicanism and a highly qualified to fulfill the duties of said office, and has given good satisfaction to the public.

Accompanying this letter is another which will shew the cause of my soliciting your attention to the forgoing, having understood there is a remonstrance forwarded to your honours against our Collector of the Customs and I have only to say the movers of such a base project disgrace the ranks of *Democracy* and will be found in any ranks for the sake of Office. With sentiments of due respect I remain your humble Servt.—

Hall Jackson Locke.

[Endorsed by AJ:] Recommendations of Col Decatur

ALS, DNA-RG 46 (14-0798). Locke (c1779–1836), of New Castle, had been a delegate to the New Hampshire state Jackson convention in June 1828.
  1. Elijah Hall (1746–1830) was naval officer for the Portsmouth customs district. William Gardner (1751–1834) of Portsmouth was a former state treasurer and federal loan commissioner. William Badger (1779–1852), an Adams elector in 1824, presided over the 1828 New Hampshire Jackson convention and was later governor, 1834–36. Revolutionary patriot John Langdon (1741–1819) had been a member of the Continental Congress and the constitutional convention of 1787, a U.S. senator, and governor of New Hampshire.

From Ambrose Hundley Sevier

Washington City Decr 7th 1829.

Dear Sir,
  I would with great respect recommend to the president the removal from the office of judge of the superior court for the Territory of Arkansas, *William Trimble,* the brother of David Trimble, formerly a member of congress from the state of Kentucky—The judge has become verry obnoxious to the presidents friends in Arkansas, in consequence of his activity and zeal in the recent elections in Arkansas—He was busily engaged in the court yard, electioneering against the presidents friends, the whole day of the election—got drunk and when he found himself in the minority *cried like a stupid child*—I am pledged to the presidents friends to effect his removal from office if possible—and to *obtain the appointment, for Edward Cross,* (a gentleman whom the president may perhaps recollect,) formerly a citizen of Tennessee and for several years back, a citizen of Arkansas and of the county in which judge Trimble resides—I can say with great truth and the people of our Territory will I believe almost unanimously bear me out in it, that Cross is a good lawyer and would make a good judge, that he is a democrat in his principles—possesses unexceptionable morals—and is in every sense of the word, a high minded and honorable man—In the event of Trimble's removal, in which I hope the president will gratify his friends, I can assure the president, that no other appointment would be as popular as that of Cross. Mr Adams & Mr Monroe, during their administrations, with but one exception selected our judges from amoung our citizens—a different practice might be used, with effect, by des[i]gning men to the injury of Genl. Jacksons friends—By reference to the law, the president will discver that the judges of our Territory hold their commissions for the term

of four years *unless sooner removed by the president.* [So] far from wishing the president to assume the responsibility of his removal—I take upon myself the responsibility of the measure—provided the president will act upon my recommendation—With great respect I am sir, your most obedient and most humbl servant

A. H. Sevier.

ALS, DNA-RG 46 (14-0816). Sevier (1801–48), a Tennessee native and grand-nephew of late governor John Sevier, was the Arkansas Territory delegate in Congress. William Trimble (c1797–1853) was appointed judge by Monroe in 1824 and reappointed by Adams in 1828. AJ removed him and appointed Edward Cross (1798–1887), later a congressman, in May 1830. David Trimble (1782–1842), an opponent of AJ, had been a Kentucky congressman, 1817–27.

First Annual Message to Congress

[The Twenty-first Congress convened for its first session on December 7, and on December 8 Jackson sent in his first annual message. Signed manuscript copies, accompanied by annual reports of the executive departments and their subsidiary bureaus, were delivered to both houses and printed by their order (DSs, DNA-RG 46 and RG 233 [14-0820]; SDoc 1, 21st Cong., 1st sess. [Serial 192]). The message was widely published and appears in Richardson, 2:442–62.

In Jackson's papers in the Library of Congress (DLC-76) are many handwritten drafts of the message and its component parts. Some are in Jackson's hand, others by his secretary Andrew Jackson Donelson, Treasury fourth auditor Amos Kendall, James A. Hamilton, and Cabinet members Berrien, Eaton, Ingham, and Van Buren. State Department clerks Nicholas P. Trist and Aaron Vail served as scribes, copying out the successive revisions and the final texts delivered to Congress. Printed here are all the drafts written by Jackson and the most significant versions by others.]

Draft by Andrew Jackson

[This comprehensive text by Jackson apparently preceded other drafts and furnished the basis for subsequent revision. Despite many changes, the message in final form retained much of its substance and tone.]

It affords me pleasure to congratulate you on your safe arrival at this city, to enter upon a discharge of these important duties which have been assigned by your country and I offer up to the almighty ruler of the universe my fervent thanks for the peace and prosperity he has been pleased to bestow upon our favored country, and implore him at a throne of grace for a continuation of these blessings, and that he may endow by his spirit the councils of the nation with wisdom to discern, and united harmony to enact all laws that may tend to promote the prosperity of his Kingdom, and the best interests of the union. In communcating with you for the first time, since I entered upon the execution of those high trusts which the people of this Republic have confided to me, it gives me great satisfaction to state, that nothing has arisen to interupt those friendly relations which it is our policy & shall be my constant anxiety to maintain with foreign nations. Acting upon what is known to be the wishes of the people of this country, I have not failed to offer in their behalf the assurance, of an earnest desire to cultivate a good understanding and to maintain peace & friendship with all.

The late period at which our ministers to England & France left the U. States, & which on several accounts was unavoidable, places it out of my power, at this early period, to communicate what has been done, in the matter of negotiation which have been directed to be brought to the consideration of those goverments respectively: resting however upon the Justice of the applications submitted, and on the reciprocal good feelings which are believed to be cherished, a hope is entertained, that every thing may ~~presently~~ eventuate in a manner satisfactory to all. At home there has been nothing to produce disquiet: every where peace & harmony has prevailed.

Acting in obedience to the requirements of the constitution to advise you from time to time of the state of the Union, I cannot forbear to bring to your consideration, as first in importance, the propriety of so amending the constitution of the U. States, as ~~that~~ the choice of the chief magistrate of the country shall in no wise or in any event devolve upon the House of Representatives. After the numerous able discussions, which have taken place on this subject on the floor of Congress & elsewhere, I might be ~~pardoned~~ excused for omitting any thing in detail on the subject; to enforce its necessity.

The goverment of the U. States was one of experiment; opening for the contemplation of more new and untried principles. Differing so widely from all other modes and forms which had preceded, it was not to be expected that the system could at once be rendered perfect. Our greatest cause of wonder is, that in a theory so new, our success should have been so ample! From time to time, as the science of our goverment is improved, disclosing to us imperfections not previously anticpated, does it become our imperative duty; to guard & strengthen our posts, that every actual, or even expected danger may be avoided. A country so prosperous, & a goverment so well calculated to secure the happiness of the people, should leave nothing to chance and accident, but carefully guard every avenue, thro which possibly danger may be anticipated

There is no point at which, perhaps, we are more at risk, than in the choice of a chief magistrate; and none at which stronger guards ~~ought to~~ should be interposed   Looking to the nature, to the character, & feelings of the american people, one thing seems evident, that watchful and jealous of their rights, as they ever should be, they will never be satisfied with any ruler who is not the selection & choice of themselves; and he will never fail to have an unpleasant administration, who may obtain the direction of our national affairs, by any other means, than the free, unbiassed opinions of the people. For a single individual of the House of Representatives to give a descision in behalf of a million of people, which frequently may be done, apart from the sugestions of a sound Judgment, can seldom fail to excite suspicion, jealousy, & distrust in the minds of a people vigilant, and attentive to the maintainance of their own rights. It is submitted therefore, to the consideration of Congress to devise some mode by which this evil may be remedied for the future. It is due to the people to place this subject before them for descision, while it should be a matter of solicitude to the Representative in congress to remove far from him the exercise of a trust which is so well calculated, to expose him to censure & reproach. The people, it is believed, desire these changes to take place—the quiet & interest of the country evidently demand it. Composed as our confederacy· is, of so many indcpendant states, and of worthy intelligent & qualified ~~individuals~~ men, it is a reasonable inference, that in some future time, many, the favorites of particular sections of our Country, may be urged as candidates so that a majority of the whole people will seldom or ever be obtained; but if after the first trial a failure shall take place, let the amendment of the constitution be so framed as to demand a reference, under sufficient notice given of the two highest on the list, again to the people; & on their second attempt the descision will be certain.

Connected with this subject, and which might be embraced as part of the amendment, is that of securing to the people the priviledge of voting immediately, & by name, for the person prefered for chief magistrate. A fair expression of the public will, free from ~~anything of~~ management, is of the highest importance in popular elections: Elections loose their value & purity, if by intrigue & fraud, the priviledge of voting may be so affected as by possibility to change the result, & impair thereby the choice of the elector—There can be neither propriety or necessity, in requiring that to be performed by ~~another~~ agent, which can be as well done by the party himself, at the polls.

But should Congress entertain adverse sentiments on this subject, & be indisposed to submit, those salutary alterations to the examination of the people, then it is worthy to be considered, if, in future when the question who shall be chosen President, is submitted & decided upon in the House of Representatives, it should not be prohibited to every one, being a member of that congress, from holding during the administration any office, whatever, or profit or trust, whereby to remove from them every ~~thing of~~ suspicion or imputation, that his Representative vote was given from improper motives—through considerations of self alone.

Resting in connection with this subject, is another worthy of particular examination; it is to limit the service of the President of the U. States to a single term; whether of 4 or 6 years seems not material; the latter might perhaps be preferable, as corresponding with the tenure of service for which the senate are chosen. The chief magistrate of a free people, should never be found seeking & manoevring to possess himself of the office. Full of care & responsibility, the merit of its possession is taken away, when obtained thro any channel or means, other than the voluntary expression of the peoples will. When any shall be thus selected, and the constitution of the country, inhibit an extension of the trust beyond a single term, every thing of management & motive will be removed and an honorable, honest & faithful discharge of the duties confided, will alone have influence, & constitute his motive of action. Nor is it, ~~alone~~ that the term of the chief magistrate only should be limited; it occurs to me, as matter worthy of reflection if every office bestowed by the general goverment, even the clerks in the Depts. should not by some Legislative enactment be limited in their tenure. It has heretofore been the case, that the incumbents of office have not looked to the possession as temporary, but that in which they had an almost unqualified property. General opinion, has partially followed in the same tract, tending to produce improper & incorrect impressions on the public mind. One of the leading policies in our goverment wherein it differs from others, is, that no man was made for office; & offices created for no one; Encourage the idea, thro force of public sentiment, that an individual is entitled of right to his place, & that to remove him is cause of censure, and the effect & example, presently, to be produced may prove highly injurious to the forms & principles of our goverment. To declare by law that office shall continue for life, or during good behaviour, would be contrary to our free institutions, & stern opposition would at once rise up as the consequence; but in what consists the difference, between a law producing such a result, and that course of thought & action, which shall presently ~~produce~~ constitute public opinion, more dificult of repeal, & change, than even legal enactment. To counteract this too prevailing sentiment, and to preserve the government from that clamour & censure which is ever attendant on removals, I suggest, whether it would not be well to declare that the offices shall become vacant at stated periods, whereby the dishonest faithless & undeserving might quietly retire, and the honest meritorious & well qualified, be retained by reappointment. The effect would be to restrain in a great degree irritation & feeling always the effects of removals—to open something ~~of~~ like rotation in office, and to induce ~~to~~ that economy which would arise from the certainty that the tenure of office in this country is not to be considered as permanant.

There is another subject of interest which I avail myself of the occasion thus presented to bring to the consideration of Congress, that ~~they~~ it may determine upon the propriety of submitting it as a further amendatory provision. The framers of our constitution were sensible of the necessity of preserving to the uttermost, the purity of Congress. Acting upon this, they prohibited any member from being eligible to the holding of an office which had been created, or the emoluments of which had been increased, during the period for which he was elected: but it did not proceed far anough, and that deficiency ought now to be remidied.

The opinion by me formerly entertained & expressed, was that members representing the interests of the states & people, in the general goverment, during the period for which they were elected, should be excluded from every office except such as purtained to the Judiciary.[1] A post where life, liberty, & property were to be adjudged & disposed of, did not appear to be one, which should stand under any restriction whatever; but be left open for selection of the best talents the country could furnish. There are other offices which from their character and importance might merit the same exception. The Cabinet of the Executive, which is to be considered his staff, should be selected not alone on account of intelligence; but from such knowledge of them, as that they might deserve & receive in all things his entire confidence. The selection of ministers to forcign Courts ought to be made in reference to the same considerations—Of what avail would it be; what benefit or service could be derived, if charged with our countrys interest abroad, if our ministers should be wanting in proper zeal; or that the entire confidence which should exist between them & the chief magistrate of the country could not be reposed. For such places & such offices, nothing of no restriction should be imposed; the country and a proper representation of its interest demands that the Executive should have afforded to him the widest range for the selection of talents, & such other qualifications as would meet his unqualified approval. These are my opinions in reference to the duties which lie before me. The zeal which is felt, that nothing may be done, or omitted, which may secure to posterity that form of goverment, & those blessings, which we are possessed of, urges me to the suggestion. Ardently desiring that our institutions may permanently endure; and being without any thing of motive or self to serve, I shall omit no occasion to declare candidly & freely whatsoever views & opinions I may entertain calculated to afford security to those high priviledges of goverment we enjoy.

With the exceptions here sugested would it not be wise & proper by constitutional provisions, to restrain members of congress during the time for which they shall be elected, from holding any office whatever within the gift of the President—The necessity of extending the inhibition to a period beyond their time of service, will be wholly taken away, if the right of deciding the presidential election in future be taken away from the House of Representatives. Such a restriction will produce the effect, which every true patriot should desire. Congress is the great source, whence emanates arrangements for the important defences of the country at large. They are the practical expounders of the constitution, as to those powers which may be asserted & enforced by the general, over the goverment of the states. Composed of men standing aloof from every ~~thing of~~ motive, & looking only to a correct discharge of their duties, they will prove a staff of reliance & security; but a rod of affliction to their country if ever to be influenced by selfish considerations. The interposed checks & balances, of our constitution have widely established, that the different functionaries of the goverment shall be left distinct & sepeorate, each acting independantly in his own particular sphere—To maintain that purity, the President ought to be denied the priviledge of assigning office to members whereby in some future time inducements may be offered to swerve them from a faithful performance of duty to their constituents, and their country. As you value liberty, & hope to preserve it to your children, let the legislative hall of the country, be maintained pure, and ever free from temptation. While this shall be the case, dangers to our free institutions may be talked of, & may be anticipated; but need never to be feared: it is motive, & selfishness, and the evils consequent therefrom, in our public men, which extending their corrupting influence to the people, is to be feared, dreaded, & avoided. For myself I am now advanced in years, with a constitution enfeebled by those days & nights of toil, & watchfulness, which in the prime of life I encountered for my country. I am not a father only by adoption, to be concerned for the fate of my children. No other wish on this side the grave remains to me, but that my country may be prosperous, & happy, and that she may have preserved to her, her liberties unimpaired forever.

It is proper to call your attention to the Tariff of 1828, regulating the duties on imports with a view to the enquiry, if its provisions and details, are not of a character, to impair, rather, than foster the great interests of this country. If nations could be brought to adopt a free & friendly ~~intercourse &~~ interchange, of the labour, & industry of each other, very many of the inconveniencies arising from duties on imports, would be avoided; but as this is not the case, nor probably can never be rendered so, we have no other means left, of securing to our citizens a fair competition than to impose on the labour of other nations, burthens similar, or equal to that which they impose on ours. It is in this view, upon the principle of fair retaliation that one nation when its labour is taxed, must retort a similar imposition upon its exacting neighbor. This principle however should be asserted with proper guards & limitations. So far as the duties to be imposed on articles of foreign growth or manufactures, are needful in producing ~~some thing of~~ equality between the labor of this & other countries, so far a healthy action to the community may be the consequence; but to exceed that, is to produce injury. The tariff being one of those important & delicate subjects of legislation which in every change of its provisions, gives rise to speculations, and produces to some class of our citizens injury, should be seldom approached, and then always with care, deliberation, & harmony, & apart from every thing but regard for the mutual benefits of the whole united states: at such a moment, & on such a subject local feelings, & political prejudices, should be merged in the important enquiry, what does the public ~~good~~ interest, & the general good require?

By refering to the report from the Treasury Department which accompanies this communication it will be perceived that the revenue of the present year has been progressive. Besides the expenditure on numerous works of internal improvement in progress under the direction of the several acts of Congress, and meeting the ordinary expences of the Govt. there has been ~~paid~~ during the year twelves millions of principle & interest of the public debt discharged. This state of the finance may be expected to continue. With a progressive increase of population, & a commerce that finds its way into every sea, our prosperity will require no other aid, than that which leaves the Citizen untramelled & free to pursue, his interest, where his enterprise may open the way—with these facts before us, the certainty is presented, that in a few years, preserved in a state of peace, we shall present this marvellous picture to the world, a nation free from debt, and capable of applying all its resources to the great end & purpose, of executing those interior improvements, and maratime defences which in peace will constitute the prosperity, & in war, the defence & safety of the country. Over the one, the constitutional power of Congress to act is not contested, & hence may be proceeded in, as propriety & necessity may ~~seem to~~ require, free from those objections, which have affected the other.

[2]That which should early engage the attention of Congress, looking forward to the period when the sinking fund will be no longer required to meet our public debt, will be to reduce the duties on such articles of importation as do not come in competition with the labour & industry of this country, & which from habit are considered articles of necessity, of which Coffee, & tea, as entering largely into the consumption, may be considered as of first importance—such a regulation will operate ~~most~~ equally every where by extending & defusing its benefits extensively with the consumption of these articles—when this reduction takes place I would recommend it to be gradual that the stock on hand on which the high duties have been paid might find a markett before others could be introduced which would prevent an act of injustice and great injury to those who under the enactment of Govt. have paid the high duties on their stock on hand & must be injured by the act of the Government unless the gradual reduction be placed at a distant day—Government ought always to act Justly to its people. I would further suggest it as worthy of enquiry whether warehouses ought not to be provided by the Government sufficient to receive all goods voluntarily offered for deposit in security for duties, as well as all goods entered for debenture. These goods ought always to remain in custody of an officer of the Customs until removed for reexportation. For *this purpose* stores ought to be constructed under the directions of the seretary of the Treasury, and the merchants making the deposit to pay for their storage. No person unless accompanied by an

officer of the Customs ought to be permitted to have access to them. With these securities, and a priority of the Government secured by law—the long credits Judiciously reduced, there would be great safety given to the Revenue, and but few losses sustained to the customs.

At present the great losses sustained in the revenue chiefly arise from the long credits on wares imported from beyond the cape of good hope. I would therefore recommend that they be shortened to six, nine & twelves months. This can be done without injury, and ought to go hand & hand with a Judicious and gradual reduction of the Tariff on such articles as are become, from habit, of first necessity.

By a reference to the Books of the Treasury it appears there are many outstanding accounts, which from year to year have been reported as unsettled debts due to the Govt. and which it is likely never can be adjusted & paid.

These for the most part arise from the confusion which are necessarily incident to a state of war; and which produces unkind feelings in the citizen from being constantly held forth as a public defaulter   I would suggest therefore if some enlarged & liberal policy should not be adopted to enable the Govt. to get rid of those ballances. The act of 1823 is insufficient for this purpose; its provisions is too limitted requiring of the Departments to adjudge all such cases upon that kind of testimony *only* as would be admissable in courts of law.

Standing in connection with this subject is another description of debts which require the intervention of Legislative enactment. The interest of the Government, as well as Individuals, renders it necessary. It frequently happens that persons who become indebted on custom house bonds fail through misfortunes of their own, or from those they have become bound as security; and that compromises for the purpose of obtaining discharges are offered. No power resting with the Executive to enter into any arangement; the consequence is, that oftentimes the debt both principle & interest are lost. Would it not be proper under such instructions and regulations as might be deemed advisable to guard against any improper influence of Executive authority, to place a well regulated power somewhere, to compromise and arrange all such cases; by such a regulation the Govt. would be benefitted, and individuals who otherwise might sink dispiritted into a state of inaction, might be roused to efforts conducive to the public good and by again entering into business add to the resources of the country, and contribute to the maintainance of their own families. All experience teaches that to retain men in debt destroys every spirit of enterprise, and the enquiry is, if it be not more important to the wellfare and happiness of the people, that being the end object of all goverments, to release on all proper[3]

~~The fact cannot be denied, that there are certain great undertakings of a national character, calculated to interest the whole country.~~ The public debt discharged, the finance of the country within limited periods, may be considered fully adequate to the ~~beginning~~ commencement & completion of such great national works of internal improvement in which the whole nation are interested & which may be considered entirely national and of first importance to its prosperity. But in what mode shall this be effected? Hitherto a portion of the community questioned even the expediency of such undertakings. There is another which proceeds upon the ground, that it is one of the ungranted powers; & hence not within the competancy of Congress to be exercised. Added to this, is a third class of objections presented, that the agency of Congress in such matters, may have a tendency to impair that independence, & freedom of thought & action, so essential to wholesome legislation. In this aspect of the question, it behoves us to consider in what manner, objects so desirable, may be obtained without violence to the feelings of those, who may be influenced, either by constitutional scruples, or objections, arising on the score of expediency. It will become a question for deliberation, if some other better, & more harmonising mode cannot be devised by the Representatives of the states, & the people respectively.

After your tariff law, shall be considered, & judiciously arranged, in reference to these principles already suggested, it is a matter not to be questioned, that our public debt being paid, there will remain a surplus in the Treasury. In this situation of things, should the constitution be found to sanction the exercise of the power, would it not be salutary to make such apportionment of the surplus revenue amonghst the states, for the purpose of internal improvement as may be found to be, a fair, federal and ~~useful~~ Just disposition of it. One essential benefit to result from such a disposition, would be to create within the states respectively, an expenditure somewhat in proportion to the public demands made upon them and remove thereby, much of the Jelousy & complaints, which now, exists as to an unequal distribution amonghst them. Above all, those temptations, which must arise to members from local influence, & which it should be desirable to be relieved from, will be avoided.

The condition of the Indians within the limits of the U. States is of a character to awaken our Sympathies, & induce the enquiry if something cannot be done to better their situation. The policy of the goverment has been gradually to open to them the ways of civilisation; and from their wandering habits, to ~~draw~~ entice them to a course of life calculated to present fairer prospects of comfort and happiness. To effect this a system should be devised for their benefit—kind & liberal, & gradually to be enlarged as they may evince a capability to enjoy it. It will not answer to encourage them to the idea of exclusive self goverment. It is impracticable. No people were ever free, or capable of forming & ~~putting~~ carrying into execution a social compact for themselves until education & intelligence was first introduced. There are with those tribes, a few educated & well informed men, possessing mind & Judgment, & capable of conducting public affairs to advantage; but observation proves that the great body of the Southern tribes of Indians, are erratic in their habits, & wanting in those endowments, which are suited to a people who would direct themselves, & under it be happy & prosperous. With these disabilities to free & self goverment existing, our tribes on this side the Mississippi have been told, that while the U. States are kindly disposed toward them, and anxious for their prosperity, it cannot be conceded to them to continue their efforts at independence within the limits of any of the States. It would be a source of great pleasure if encouragement could be given, and success be attained in an undertaking so praiseworthy; and which every humane mind should desire to see fully effected: Not however by attempts to be made within the[4] jurisdictional limits of a state, where difficulties must be met; & where an opposing right to govern cannot be assented to or maintained; but by passing beyond the Mississippi   There thro' the fostering & protecting care of the goverment aided by their own exertions, a hope may be entertained, that in the end their best expectations may be realised.

Recollecting that these unfortunate people, were once the uncontroled & indisputable owners of this immense region of country, & that they have generally retired, yielding from time to time to the solicitations of their white brethern, until they are only to be found far in the interior, it is but Justice that a proper degree of sympathy should be awakened in their behalf. It is a subject of great interest, and deserves so to be considered that posterity may do Justice both to our motives & our actions towards them.

But while a generous feeling is entertained towards this race, it should not be at the sacrafice of principle, and of the interests of others concerned. The states of this Union are Sovereign. Certain rights they have parted with to the General Goverment for mutual security and defence. They have not agreed however, that any other authority than their own, shall be asserted within their confines; and when such an attempt shall be made, the state within whose limits it takes place will possess not only the right to resist, but a right to demand of the U. States to sustain her in that resistance. Upon this subject, there would remain no discretion, because over it there is no power granted. The states or the Indians, must be Sovereign, because in such a case power can not be concurrent. But our red friends, acting under erroneous impressions, have conceived the idea, that the states within which they reside, are incapable of extending over them their legislative acts, & that with entire independence, they may proceed within their limits to all the exercised priviledges which belong & apperrtain to sovereignty. Until better advised the Executive cannot consider itself authorised to concede what is assumed; and accordingly has disclosed to them through the secratary of war that which he believed the rights of the states and their own interest unequivocally demanded.

What then is to be done? Let the plan of removal beyond the Mississippi

AD, DLC (76).

1. In his address to the Tennessee legislature resigning from the Senate in 1825, AJ proposed a constitutional amendment to make members of Congress ineligible for non-judicial federal office during and for two years after their elected terms (*Jackson Papers*, 6:110).

2. The text that begins here is from a separate sheet that AJ marked for insertion in the manuscript.

3. The inserted sheet ends here.

4. A new sheet of the manuscript begins here. John Eaton supplied an alternative continuation from this point forward (below).

Draft by Amos Kendall

[Working from Jackson's original and a subsequent draft by Andrew J. Donelson, Amos Kendall produced this text. Sequential reworkings from this draft of the sections on federal offices and the tariff were written out by Donelson, Hamilton, Vail, and Trist and corrected by Berrien, Van Buren, and Eaton to reach their final form (Richardson, 2:447–450). The foreign relations section underwent a more thorough overhaul. From Kendall's text Van Buren produced an expanded draft, including a portion on Mexico which he later rewrote. Van Buren's version furnished the basis for copies by Trist and Vail which were amended to reach the finished text.]

It affords me pleasure to congratulate you on your safe arrival in this City for the purpose of entering upon the discharge of the important duties which are assigned to you by the constitution of our country. Twenty four sovereign states and twelve millions of happy people recognize you as their national Legislature and in obedience to the injunctions of the constitution and in imitation of my illustrious predecessors, it is incumbent on me to call your attention to such measures as I may deem necessary to promote the objects of our federal union.

In communicating with you for the first time, it affords me unfeigned satisfaction, and will be a cause of mutual gratulation and devout thanksgiving to a benignant Providence, that we are at peace with all ~~the world~~ mankind, and that our country exhibits, in its internal condition, the most illustrious example of general comfort and progressive improvement, which the world has ever witnessed.

In our intercourse with foreign nations nothing has occurred since the last session of Congress, to interrupt those friendly relations which it is our true policy and shall be my constant aim, to cultivate and preserve. Upon the nations of the old world and the communities springing into existence in the new, we look without any other interest than an ardent desire to see mankind, in the enjoyment of peace, health and plenty, advancing in knowledge, in freedom, and in social comfort.

The late period at which our ministers to England and France, on account of delays on many accounts unavoidable, left the United States, renders it impossible for me, at this early day, to inform you what has been done on the subjects which have been brought to the consideration of those governments. Relying upon the nature of the interests and the justice of the claims which we have committed to negotiation, as well as on the reciprocal good feelings which characterizes all our intercourse with those courts, we have scarcely room to doubt the most satisfactory adjustment of every existing difference, and nothing is indicated in the policy of those powerful nations which threatens any future breach in our friendly relations. With Great Britain whose courage we have proved and whose attainments in the arts of peace and war have spread her fame around the globe, we may look forward to many years of honorable and elevated competition; with France, our antient ally, associated as she is in the grateful remembrances of our revolutionary struggle, we rejoice in the establishment of her constitutional government and of religious tolera-tion. That 'wonderful people' emerging from the waves of revolution and war which shook the world, profit by misfortunes and reap advantages from defeats.[1] In her constitution, in her representative body, in the more general distribution of property and in the liberty of the press, she has made advances which compensate for the blood she has shed and the toil she has endured. We have now a right to expect from her that forbear-ance and justice in all her intercourse with foreign powers which become a powerful, intelligent and magnanimous ~~people~~ nation.

From the want of experience and a general diffusion of knowledge, the Southern Republics have not made safe that liberty for which they have been so long contending. In some of them, one political system after another has been overturned by internal convulsions, the throes of which have not yet ceased; in others, the force and influence of the mother coun-try are yet exerted to retard the progress of liberal principles and prevent the establishment of republican governments. We trust, however, that the day is fast approaching, when the restoration of peace and internal quiet under permanent systems of government which shall secure the liberty of the citizen and promote human improvement, will enable us to salute them as brethren in principle and peaceful rivals in all that is truly glori-ous and great.

With the other powers, our intercourse though more limited in extent, is of the most friendly character. In Russia whose territorial extent, numer-ous population, great power and merited fame place her in the front rank of nations, the United States have always found a steadfast friend. Although we have looked upon her recent invasion of Turkey with no other interest than a lively sympathy for all those who suffer from the casualties and desolations of war, we cannot but anticipate that its results will favour the cause of civilization and the progress of human happi-ness. The independence of Greece will be permanently established and the returning day of art and science will cast its increasing light upon her shores. With a lively enthusiasm the people and public functionaries of the United States hail reviving Greece, and are anxious to welcome the establishment, by her present sons, of institutions worthy of the ancestors, whose country they inherit.

In the indulgence of similar feelings, many of them look also ~~with attachment~~ to Holland, Germany, Scotland and Ireland, which, in addition to other ground of attachment are the lands of their ancestors and the homes of their kindred.

As a government, we regard all nations alike and acknowledge our obligation to treat all with equal kindness and equal justice.

I consider it one of the most urgent of my public duties to bring to your attention the propriety of amending that part of our constitution which relates to the election of President. Our system of government was considered by its framers an experiment and they wisely provided in the fundamental law, a mode of correcting its errors and supplying its defects. If through reverence of our fathers, we ~~refuse~~ neglect to profit by the admonitions of reason and the lights of experience, we shall ~~refuse to~~ render useless their precautions and deny their wisdom.

To the people belongs the right of electing their own Chief Magistrate. The interposition of electors, and, in a certain contingency, ~~the~~ reference of the election to the House of Representatives, could not have been intended to defeat the choice of the people. To say that our fathers contemplated such a result, would be to deny them republican principles and stigmatize their memories. Experience has proved what reason teaches, that in proportion as agents are ~~introduced between the people and~~ employed to execute the will of the people, in the same proportion is there danger ~~of~~ that the popular choice will be defeated. Some of those agents may be unfaithful; some corrupt; and all are liable to err. So far, therefore, as the people can with convenience speak, it is safer for them to express their own will. The people of New York vote for thirty six electors and those of every other state for more than one. Would it not be more convenient as well as more safe for them to vote directly for President and Vice President? Convenience, safety and I may add economy all ~~proclaim~~ conspire to recommend an election directly by the people.

So many are the aspirants to the Presidency and so different the interests which may hereafter constute the basis of their claims, that we have little reason to expect an election by the people or their electors in the first instance. In that event the election devolves on the House of Representatives. There the chances of unfaithfulness and corruption are more than redoubled. As the members vote by states, there are but twenty four votes, and it often happens that each of many of the number is controlled by a single man. We ought not so far to rely on human virtue as to suppose that candidates will never offer and members of Congress will never accept a portion of those offices and honors which the Presidency commands, as the price of votes.

But without corruption in the Representative body the will of the people is constantly liable to be misrepresented in such an election. Some may err from ignorance of the wishes of their constituents; other from a belief that it is their duty to consult their own opinions only in relation to the fitness of the contending candidates. Even if all be honest and faithful, a minority may often make the president in an election where a million of people in one state have no more weight than a ~~hundred~~ few thousands in another. When a minority makes the president, no matter whether the election be pure or corrupt, what have we to expect but a struggle on the part of the majority to regain their power and place in the Executive chair the candidate of their choice? It cannot be anticipated that a President elected by a minority will ever be permitted to administer the government in peace. He cannot do the good he would, and he has an ever active inducement to use the power and patronage of the government to increase the number of his supporters and thus endeavor to receive a reelection by the voice of a majority.

True policy as well as correct principle requires that the public will should flow freely in ~~all popular~~ this important election. Every obstruction is calculated to breed parties and promote dissention. The will of a powerful ~~and~~ people cannot be ~~safely~~ peaceably and safely thwarted. In despotic governments it seeks its ~~accomplishment~~ ends, in bloody revolutions; in Republics it accomplishes its purposes through the exercise of suffrage. In the former it is sometimes conquered by mercenary bayonets; in the latter it is often assailed by the arts of corruption and deceit. ~~In the latter,~~ Its conquest ~~is the~~ in Republic is a sure sign of the decay of public virtue; its victory is often achieved at the expence of social harmony. Let us then so amend our system as, in the election of Chief Magistrate, to let it run unobstructed. If there be any who doubt whether the people have the intelligence which would enable them to make a judicious choice, let them think, not how they be deprived of their rights, but how than can be qualified to use them with discretion. Let such statesmen turn all their energies to the establishment of schools in their several states and ~~of~~ the dissemination of that knowledge which shall enable the humblest of their fellow citizens to understand their rights and know how to preserve them.

Actuated by these views I earnestly recommend such an amendment of the constitution as will remove all intermediate agency in the election of President and Vice President and submit the question directly to the people. The mode may be so regulated as to preserve to each state its present relative weight in the election, and in case there be no choice in the first instance let it be again referred to the people to decide between the two highest candidates.

If Congress should doubt the wisdom or salutary effects of such a change, it is worthy of consideration whether every member of Congress who may vote for a President ought not to be disqualified by a constitutional provision from holding any office of trust or profit under his appointment. Corruption and suspicion would thus be removed from the members of Congress when acting as electors, and if the President himself were made ineligible for a second term much would be done to obiate the dangers which threaten our institutions.

There are perhaps few men who can long possess office and power without being more or less corrupted. If they do not sell their integrity for money, they acquire a habit of looking with indifference upon the public interests and tolerate practices at which an unpracticed man would revolt. Office becomes in their minds a kind of property and government is viewed more as a means of administering to their individual interests than as an institution created solely for the happiness of the people. Corruption in some and a perversion of right feelings and principles in others producing almost all the evils of corruption, pervert government from its legitimate ends and make it an engine for the support of the few at the expense of the many. The duties of all the public officers are or ought to be, so simple and plain that men of intelligence may soon learn to perform them. I cannot but think that more is lost by the long continuance of men in office than can possibly be gained by their experience, and I submit it to your consideration whether the security of the public offices would not be better preserved, industry and economy promoted and the treasury made more safe by limiting the appointments of the heads of bureaus and of Clerks to fixed periods and making them ineligible to the same offices thereafter.

In a country where offices are created solely for the benefit of the people one man has no more intrinsic right to an office than another. They are not created to give support to particular men at the expence of the people, but that every citizen may, under the protection of a free and cheap government, acquire by honest industry, the means of supporting himself and family. No wrong is done to him who is removed; for the [. . .] was given to him not on his own account. He was made an officer that the public good might be promoted. When the public good requires his removal his private interest is not to be consulted. The people have a right to complain when a bad officer is substituted for a good one; but not the removed officer. He has the same means of obtaining a living under the protection of government which are possessed by the millions who never held office. Limited terms would destroy the idea of property in an office now so prevalent, would obviate the clamor about removals and whatever of distress may be produced by them, would give healthful action to the system of government and would promote that rotation in office which constitutes a leading article in the republican creed.

While members of Congress can be constitutionally appointed to offices of profit and trust it will be the practice and perhaps is the duty of the Executive so select them for such stations whenever he honestly believes they will render better service to the public than other citizens. But it would doubtless tend to secure the purity of our government if they were excluded from all appointments to be bestowed by the President whose election they may have promoted. The nature of the judicial offices and the necessity of securing the best talents and experience in members of the Cabinet and the highest grade of foreign ministers, should perhaps, exclude those places from the prohibition.

No considerable change has occurred since the last session of Congress either in our agriculture, commerce, or manufactures. The operation of our Tariff has not yet proved so injurious to our agriculture and commerce nor so beneficial to our manufactures as by many was expected. Foreign merchants were induced by it to press into our market a larger amount than usual of middling and low priced goods; and many of our own capitalists anticipating largely increased profits upon the same species of domestic fabrics, vested their capital and extended their credit in enlarging the old and creating new manufactories. The natural consequences have followed—a market overstocked—depression of prices, extensive embarrassment and partial bankruptcy. That such establishments as are based on a solid capital and are prudently arranged, will survive the shock and become profitable to their owners there is no reason to doubt.

To balance justly between the interests of agriculture, commerce and manufactures so as to promote equally the ~~interests~~ prosperity of all, is one of the most difficult operations of government. Were the world in a state of perpetual peace and did every government consult the true interests of the human race, no other duty should be laid on the import or export of produce or manufactures than such as are ~~designed solely~~ necessary to furnish a revenue for the support of government. But unhappily we are obliged to anticipate wars and we must always expect selfish legislation in other nations. Not to provide the means of defence within ourselves would be as indiscreet as not to provide a weapon when we know that we shall meet an assassin; and to admit unrestricted the manufactures of a country which excludes by her laws all the products of our labor, would be as imprudent as to purchase clothing of our neighbors who will take in return neither our wool nor our provisions. Of what avail is it to raise produce for which we have no market, and is it not a mockery to tell us you will sell us cheap goods when you know that we have not the means to purchase and refuse even a liberal exchange for the produce of our lands?

In relation to the means of defence a provident nation will not stop short of providing them, if possible, within her own borders. In relation to duties on imports intended to countervail the legislation of foreign nations or promote any species of home manufacture, care should be taken that it does not on the whole produce more injury to one interest that it does good to another. The leading interest of the country is undoubtedly agricultural. It is the basis of every other, to which commerce and manufactures are but auxiliary. To place the auxiliary before the leading interest of the country would be as destructive of the public prosperity as it would be unnatural. No wise statesman or real republican wishes to see the farmer made poor that the manufacturer may become rich. ~~On the contrary,~~ Many honest and able men maintain that such is the effect of the present Tariff. If it be there is not a man among us who would not wish it modified or repealed. In its present form it seems not to be acceptable either to the manufacturer, the merchant or the farmer. I therefore recommend it to your careful revision with a view of adjusting it as far as possible to every interest in the community.

It is hardly necessary in this recommendation to caution you not to overlook the interests of the farmer. It is only as manufacturers increase the value of his products and add to his comforts that they are worthy of the fostering care of government. Who could wish to see multitudes of his fellow beings penned in villages and confined in manufactories unless they can produce some essential good to the farming interest which constitutes the bone and sinew of our Republic. It is on the farm and not in towns and workshops, that virtue thrives and freedom looks for supporters. It is to the pure air, the pure morals, the robust bodies and sturdy minds of our farming brethren in the North, the South and the West that we are to look for the preservation of liberty and the perpetuity of our happy institutions. ~~The good states~~ From them spring our best soldiers, our purest patriots and our ablest men. The good statesman will not jeopardize their interests for all the manufactories which the thousands of rivers that intersect our country could put in motion.

AD, DLC (76).
    1. President Washington had used the phrase "wonderful people" in accepting the presentation of a French tricolor from minister Pierre Adet on January 1, 1796.

Drafts by Martin Van Buren on the tariff

[Van Buren's two tariff drafts here were not based on the Kendall text. The first version was mostly discarded. The second appeared in the message nearly intact (Richardson, 2:450).]

among the subjects which have heretofore occupied the attention of Congress there is no one of more importance or more deserving of its most anxious care than that which concerns the regulation of our Tarriff with a view to the encouragement of domestic manufactures. It comports alike with my personal feelings as with my views of public duty to observe the utmost frankness in all my communications with the co-ordinate Departments of the Government upon public affairs, and least of all could I stoop the observance of the least reserve in regard to this confessedly the most delicate of our official public duties.

The policy of ~~extending~~ affording a liberal encouragement to the home manufacture of such article as are necessary to make us independent of foreign nations in time of war & its judicious extension to productions of a different character so far forth, as that can be done without imposing unreasonable and consequently oppressive burthens upon those who have no other than a general interest in the subject, has been the fixed opinion of my life—

In its indulgence as well as in acting upon it I have never been insensible to considerations of deep interest and great embarrassments that belong to it. They consist in the important bearing which every material alteration of the existing tariff must unavoidably have upon many of the most important interests of our fellow Citizens and in the unpleasant and embarrassing circumstance that in the present condition of the manufacturing interest of the Country the advantages derived from its Legislative encouragement are in a great degree local and the burthens thereby imposed consequently unequal. To the obligations resulting from this consideration to avoid frequent or ill advised changes no good citizen can be insensible. This is matter of the gravest import & most intense interest and cannot be too earnestly impressed upon our minds as well as upon those of our constituents. The most deleterious consequences must unavoidably result from the subjection of the Legislation of the country in this respect either to the ever varying speculations of political economists or the sinister requirements of insatiate avarice. Equally destructive to the best interests of the country must it be to mingle this subject with the political & party contests of the day. There is but too much reason to fear that our public councils have heretofore been too much under the influence of such feelings for their useful action &, it surely is the bounden duty of every honest man who prefers the interest of the Country to his own to discountenance all attempts to distract the public mind and to frustrate all designs which look to the acquisition of political power by raising & fomenting pretensions upon this subject which a just regard to the rights of all forbid & which the sober sense of the community will never sanction. He is unworthy of a public trust who can be induced by any consideration to minister to unjust pretensions whether the result of ambitious personal design or of overweaning avarice rather than expose himself to the current of public feelings however high it may for a season be ~~raised~~ have been raised. There is an abiding good sense and active patriotism abounding among the people of these States upon which those who in their discharge of their public trusts pursue only justifiable objects by pure motives may with confidence repose themselves.

Every attempt to connect them with the party conflicts of the day are of necessity injurious & should be discountenanced. our action upon them should be under the controul of higher & purer motives. Legislation subjected to such influences can never be just & will not long receive the sanction of a people whose active patriotism is not bounded by sectional limits.

AD, DLC (76).

Draft by Andrew Jackson on Treasury reforms

[Copies by Donelson and Trist polished this original text by Jackson into final form (Richardson, 2:453–54).]

~~Looking~~ Refering to the records of the Treasury I have been forcibly struck with the large amount of public mony which appears to be outstanding. A considerable portion of the sum, thus due from individuals to the Govt. is unquestionably *desperate,* and in many instances has probably been rendered so, by negligence, or want of skill on the part of the agents employed in collecting it, and perhaps for the want of a proper system of accountability on all & every agent of the govt. employed in its collection. A great part of this outstanding debt may yet be recovered by proper exertions. Whatever may be the respective proportions of these two classes of debts—how much may be beyond hope, & how much may yet be recoverable, it behoves the Government to know the real state of the facts—This can only be made known by the adoption of Judicious measures for the collection of such as by proper exertions may be made available—It is believed that a large amount of what is, or may be lost, has arisen from inadequacy of the means provided for the collection of debts due to the public, and this inadequacy has chiefly arisen from the want of legal skill habitually employed in the direction of the professional and other agents engaged in this service— I think it must be admitted that the Supervisary power over the public suits, which is now vested in an *accounting* officer of the Treasury, and not selected with a view to his *legal knowledge,* and charged & encumbered as he is, with numerous other duties is not favorable to the public Interest

It is important that the agents employed in the collection of the public dues, should be subjected to the supervision of professional skill, which will give efficiency to the exertions of the officers & agents employed— This supervision ~~I would~~ might be given to the attorney General of the U. States with such aids & assistants as may be found necessary to enable him faithfully to perform the duties that may be thought proper to be assigned to him, & which the agent of the Treasury is now charged with, and which will give efficiency to the professional operations of collecting debts by legal process, and an attentive superintendance over the District attos. & marshalls of the different states ~~which must~~—this will give action to the recovery of all debts due to the Govt. & its speedy payment into the Treasury

The expence which will be incurred by such a modification of the executive department as will be necessary to accomplish this, ~~will~~ be justified by the soundest principles of a liberal oconomy. I recommend therefore that the duties now assigned to the Agent of the Treasury so far as relates to superintending and ordering & directing legal proceedings be transfered to the atto. Genl & such aid as may be thought necessary to give promptness in the performance of the duties assigned, to him from the Treasury department—To these duties might be added the super-intendance of all criminal prosecutions for offences against the United States, and his personal attendance where it ~~was~~ is practicable—as well as the power of remitting penalties, where this power is now vested in the Secretary of the Treasury—and also the duty of investigating, the solvancy of all those reported as public defaulters to the Govt. report their ~~real~~ situation to congress, that by Legislative enactment, some mode may be pointed out by which those who have become really insolvant may be exonerated from the liability of his debt—In the transfer of the power from the Treasury Department to the attorney general great care ought to be had that no power which purtains to the Treasury Department nec-essary for its security & facilities and which it now possesses, up to the auditing the account & handing it over to the agent for suit ought to be disturbed, least the harmony of the system might be injured

AD, DLC (76).

Draft by Amos Kendall on Treasury frauds

[This passage, referring in part to the prosecution of Tobias Watkins, was included in the message after slight revision by Donelson (Richardson, 2:454).]

Since the last session of Congress, various frauds on the Treasury have been discovered which I thought it my duty to bring under the cognizance of the United States Court for this District by a criminal prosecution. It was my opinion and that of able counsel who were consulted, that the cases came within the penalties of the act of Congress entitled an act ____ passed for the express purpose of securing the treasury from such depre-dations.[1] Either from some defect in the law or in its administration, every effort to bring the ~~culprit~~ accused to trial under its provisions, proved ineffectual, and the government was driven to the necessity of resorting to the vague and inadequate provisions of the common law. It is therefore my duty to call your attention to the laws which have been passed for the protection of the Treasury. If indeed there is no law by which those who may be unworthily entrusted with its guardianship, can be punished for the ~~most dishonorable and~~ most flagrant violations of duty, extending even to the fraudulent appropriation of its contents to their own use, it is time to remedy so dangerous an omission. Or, if the law has been per-verted from its original purposes, and criminals intended to be punished under its provisions, have been rescued by legal subtleties, it ought to be made so plain, by amendatory provisions, as to baffle the arts of perver-sion and accomplish the ends of its original enactment.

In one of the most flagrant cases, the Court decided that the prosecution was barred by the statute which ~~requires that~~ limits prosecutions for fraud to two years. In this case, all the evidences of the fraud, and indeed all knowledge that a fraud had been committed, were in possession of the party accused until after the two years had elapsed. Surely the statute ought not to run in favor of any man while he retains all the evidences of his crime in his own possession, and least of all in favor of a public officer who contrives to defraud the treasury and conceal the transaction for the brief term of two years. I would therefore recommend such an alteration of the law as will give to the injured party and the government, two years after the disclosure of the fraud, or after the accused is out of office, to commence their prosecution.

In connection with this subject, I call the attention of Congress to the propriety of appointing a committee to enquire into and report, as far as it can be ascertained, the real state of the government at the commencement of the present administration. To them might be assigned the duty of ascertaining what retrenchments can properly be made, and of recommending such specific changes in the laws as may protect the Treasury from future depredations.

[Endorsed by Andrew J. Donelson:] Wadkins case

AD, DLC (76).
1. The official text supplies the blank with "the act of the Seventeenth Congress approved 3d March, 1823."

Drafts by Andrew Jackson on the Seneca annuity

[Jackson had been concerned about unauthorized overpayment of the annual Seneca annuity since receiving War Department clerk Charles Nourse's March 18 report on the subject, from which he drew the figures in these drafts. The message in final form reduced Jackson's text to a brief paragraph referring Congress to the accompanying annual report of the War Department (Richardson, 2:456). That report by Eaton closely followed Jackson's second draft (SDoc 1, 21st Cong., 1st sess., p. 28, Serial 192).]

Seneca Indians
The investment of this $100,000 was made agreable to the stipulations in the treaty in the U States Bank in March 1798—the dividend received by the U.S. ~~& paid to this tribe~~ on this stock annually averaged about $7000 pr annum ~~and~~ which was paid to them annually Except $8,430 which was invested in fifteen additional shares in February 1804 March 1806 & March 1807.

In the year 1811 the charter of the U. S. bank expired and the capital amount of 220 shares of stock was recd. by U.S. in dividends at different periods $77.200— of which was in 1812 and amounted $95,000 of this amount $93,060 was invested in $93,602⁶⁶/₁₀₀ 6 prcent stocks and $1980 was carried to the Indian appropriation.

The 6 prcent stock produced an interest of $5,618 pr annum which was recd. by the U States until it was paid off.

The proceeds—$93,602⁶⁶/₁₀₀ was invested by direction of the President of the U. States in $112,853 78/ 3 prcent stock. The stock produces now but $3,385 59/ pr annum the dividends were drawn by the late sec of war up to the 1rst of Octbr. 1828, and carried as all the dividends have been since 1812 to the credit of the Genl Indian appropriation

At the expiration of the charter, of the U. Bank The seneca Indians expressed some uneasiness as to this annuity, but was informed by the then incumbent of the war Department, that there would be no interruption of it; & since 1812 the sum of $6000 has been drawn from the Indian appropriation & remitted regularly to them annualy thro' their agent as interest upon the stock held by the President of the United States in trust for them. I can find no law authorising this assurance & not being able to see any power given by any law, to the Executive to pay more than what the Trustee recd. as interest annually accruing on the Dividend of their stock, having, as he believes, no Legislative power, but merely ~~an~~ executive *to see the laws duly executed,* he directed the sec of war, his legal appointed agent to pay over the amount of the interest only due on this stock, & no more, until congress by some enactment might direct otherwise, for which purpose he has brought it to your view—

When I came into the executive office, there were transfered to me by my predecessor, in trust for the Seneca tribe of Indians the amount of $112,853 of three prcent stock, which produces an annual interest of $3,385⁵⁹/₁₀₀. It appears from the history of this transaction, that as early as 1798, the sum of ~~one~~ $100,000 was invested, agreable to the stipulations of a Treaty with the Seneca tribe by Robert Morris in the Bank of the U. States, & held by the President in trust for them—In the year 1811 the charter of the Bank of the United States expired, & up to this period the annual dividend averaged the sum of $7000, which was paid to them—the Trustee caused this $100,000 after the Bank charter expired to be invested in 6 prcent stock, which ~~was paid by~~ produced an annual interest of $5,618 which was paid to the United States & the government paid over to the Seneca tribe the annual sum of $6000, all the dividends since 1812, up to 1828, have been recd. by the secretary of war, and passed to the credit of the United States, and the annual sum of $6000, paid over ~~annually~~ to these Indians up to & including the year 1828. ~~to the Seneca tribe~~ At the expiration of the charter of the U. B. it appears, that assurances was given by the then sec. of war that there should be no interruption of this fund, and the annual sum of $6000, was continued to be paid to the Seneca tribe of Indians without any legislative enactment by congress—The stock when transfered to me was only producing the sum of $3,385.⁵⁹/₁₀₀ requiring the sum of $2614.⁴¹/₁₀₀ annually to be added from sums in the Treasury for which there ~~are~~ were no appropriation by law, to make up the $6000, which was annually paid by the trustee to the agent of the seneca tribe of Indians.

I have carefully examined, and can find no authority for the payment of this annual sum of $6000 to this tribe of Indians, or any sum but the real interest which the stock annually produces, nor no specific appropriation for it—~~and~~ The Executive having no legislative power, ~~all his powers being Executive to see that the laws shall be faithfully executed,~~ I directed the sec. of war, as trustee to the Seneca tribe of Indians to pay over to their agent the precise sum which had accrued in interest from the three prcent stock which had been transfered to me by my predecessor, & *no more*, until Congress should act upon this subject—It is Therefore brought to your consideration

~~These~~ Indians cannot be ~~made well to understand this matter, of Government stock &~~ dividends ~~they know nothing—It~~ as it is for congress to determine whether, ~~they~~ as heretofore the sum of $6000 shall be paid them annually, or only the ~~real~~ sum annually arising from the interest upon their stock—should ~~the~~ Congress direct by law that the sum of $6000 pr annum should be paid to them, then the sum of $2614⁴¹/₁₀₀ will be necessary to be appropriated for the present, & a like sum for the succeeding year—

[Endorsed by AJ:] The Seneca Indians—for message—

AD, DLC (76).

Draft by John Henry Eaton on Indian removal

[This text is an apparent continuation of the passage on Indian removal in Jackson's original draft above. Other drafts on Indian removal by Donelson and Kendall, the latter approximating the final text, did not follow Eaton in either language or content.]

the states respectively where they reside. To maintain a contrary doctrine, & to require the Executive to enforce it by the employment of a military force would be to place in his hands, a power to make war, and to trample upon the rights of the states and the liberty of the Country. It is a power which should be placed in the hands of no individual; the consequences & dangers to which it might lead, are so obvious that to reason on it, seems to ~~me~~ be uncalled for & unnecessary—

If indeed the Indians be a people seperate, & with distinct & independent rights, which they may exercise regardless of the interference of a state, much error has arisen in the practices of this govt towards them. Why is it, that they have been called upon to assist in our wars without any exercise of opinions & discretion on their part   If an independent people, they should as such ~~have been~~ be consulted & advised with. But this has not been the course adopted. In an order which issued to me from the War Department in Sept 1814 this language is employed. "All the friendly Indians should be organized, & prepared to cooperate with your other forces. There appears to be some dissatisfaction among the Choctaws—their friendship & services should be secured without delay. The friendly Indians must be fed & paid, *& made to fight when, & where, their services may be required.*[1] To an independent & foreign people, this would seem to be, assuming I should suppose rather too lofty a ~~ground~~ tone; & one which this govermt would not have assumed, if they had considered them in that light

The practice of restraining intrusion upon Indian lands ~~to the South~~ had its origin with the commencement of our govermt, became a subject of particular & special legislation in 1802 Tho' with the reservation, which previously had been ~~the case~~ regarded, as to the rights, & authority of the states. The same course, & construction in the South have continued nearly to the present time So Carolina alone excepted. She uniformly has regulated Indian affairs within her limits. But in the other states it has remained unquestioned & undisputed. And why? because until lately the jurisdiction of the states, as it respects these people, was dormant; no attempt on their part, having been made, to render the Indians within their limits subject to their policy, & answerable to their laws. Georgia materially concerned, had forborne to spread her legislation farther than she found her own white citizens to be settled. But perceiving within her jurisdictnl limits recently a people, who claimed to be capable of self govemt sitting in legislative debate, organizing Courts, & adminstrng justice; it occured to her as proper, and she extended her laws throughout her limits. When this took place, an altered aspect of things, was presented; but not a new one, for it had been anticipated by the proclamation of 1783, and was afterwards ~~adopted~~ distinctly looked to by the 19th. section of the act of 1802   In the language & meaning of that section, the tribes to the South & So west are not only "surrounded by setelments of the Citizens of the U States"; but are also "within the ordinary jurisdiction of the individual states"   In fact they are now, within their actual & asserted & declared jurisdiction. They became so from the moment the laws were extended over them and are consequently within the exception & *[terms]* contained in the 19th. section. Why is it, that the US have omitted to interfere with Indian trade & intercourse in the Northern & middle states, the only conjecturable & probable reason, is that they have been considered within the exception which is reiterated in the 19 section of the act referred to.[2] Georgia Alabama & Missi. having now avowed a right of jurisdiction throught their respective limits, they are entitled to claim, in behalf of their soverignty that the same course shall be pursued towards them, which heretofore has been conceded to other states of the Union

Towards this race of people I entertain no feelings of unkindness. However strong the sympathies of many well meaning persons towards them may be, mine are not less than theirs. Nor are the principles ~~upon~~ which I now ~~act~~ avow, recent with me. They have long been entertained. Years since I stated to these tribes, my impression & belief that when the States choose to extend their laws & jurisdiction over the Country it would not be in the power of the general govermt to prevent it. My opinion remains the same. And to relieve them from this state of things, what is proposed? Nothing that bears the stamp of injustice! ~~Give~~ It is proposed that they give obedience to the laws as others residing in the states must do; or if dissatisfied to remove to the west, where ~~you~~ they can be maintained under ~~your~~ their own customs. ~~Remove,~~ On Consenting to remove! The US in a spirit of kindness ~~will defray your~~ agree to defray their expenses, supply the means of transportation, & grant supplies to ~~your~~ their families for a year, until ~~your~~ their farms can be opened & agriculture spring up. Either of these courses promises quiet & harmony, & opening prosperity; while a contest between the general & state govermts, can give assurance of nothing that is agreeable or cheering. At every step threatning dangers must be attendent on such a course. We should forbear violence & prejudice, & cleave to the plain common sense meaning of the Constitution. That ~~plain~~ rational mode of interpretation must admit, that conflicts & collisions with the states are to be avoided; & ~~nothing~~ no power be assumed by general govermt, which the states have not ~~parted with~~ consented to part with. Such a course, with kind feelings entertained, & mutual forbearance practiced, in relation to honest differences of opinion, can not fail to lead us on to prosperity & happiness; a different one, may endanger every thing, of which our country has so many & such abundant causes for rejoicing.

AD, DLC (76).
 1. Secretary of War James Monroe to AJ, September 7, 1814 (*Jackson Papers*, 3:128).
 2. The Indian Intercourse Act of 1802 tightly regulated white dealings with Indian tribes and individuals. Section 19 exempted from its prohibitions "any trade or intercourse with Indians living on lands surrounded by settlements of the citizens of the United States, and being within the ordinary jurisdiction of any of the individual states."

Draft by Andrew Jackson on the Navy and other topics

[In this text Jackson addressed subjects not covered in his draft above. Donelson and Trist produced later versions. In final form the passage on officers' pay was shifted to the War Department section, the praise for Postmaster General Barry was replaced with other text, and the penitentiary note was omitted (Richardson, 2:455–56, 459–61).]

The Report of the Secretary of the Navy, and Navy Board of commissioners here with communicated, will shew the dilapidated state of our ships of war in ordinary, and the necessity that exists for an appropriation for their repair, & to put them under cover to preserve them from utter ruin

The Navy is Justly viewed by the nation, as it strong arm of defence; to preserve it as such, its organization must be changed as I view the system entirely defective—In every part of which, the want of a proper responsibility for its oconomy is evident; we have been building more ships of war than has been needed for the protection of our commerce & those not wanted for service afloat, has been permitted to moulder & decay in the harbours, without covers, or proper attention for their preservation. Several of our finest vessels of war, which have been for years launched, remain unfinished & will take large sums to place them in the same state as when first ~~launched~~ convayed into their proper element. This shews the necessity of a change of a system so destructive to the welfare of this arm of our national defence. I would therefore recommend that we cease for the present bulding ships of war of the first & second class, and convert our attention & resources, to the procurement of ship timber & other materials, seasoning & preserving them, until the period may arise, that may make it necessary for our national defence, & protection of our commerce, to increase our Naval force, when, we can by uniting & concentrating our means, and our force, at two Navy yards Judiciously selected we can build ships faster than they can be manned—for the proper points for establishing those two Navy yards & two auxiliaries, I would refer you to the Judicious report of the Navy Board on this subject, as fully meeting my views ~~on that point~~.

The yard at this city, having all its machinery compleat for every branch of machanical art necessary for ship building will be competent to furnish the materials for all the ships that may become necessary on any emergency to be added to our Navy, and it would be useless to encounter the expence of similar machinery at any other point, as the transportation is so easy, & convenient, from the Navy yard at Washington, to the other points recommended, to be maintained as Navy yards.

I would recommend that the Navy Board as at present established undergo an entire change, and a similar organization as exists in the war be established in the Navy Department. This could be advantageously done by establishing in the Navy Department three Bureaus each Bureau having its specific duties assigned to it, & the head of each made responsible for the faithful performance of the duties assigned to it, and placing one of the commissioners of the Navy Board at the head of each, with such subordinate officers, taken from the Navy not on active service as the duties might require. The heads of these Bureaus, when called on by the Secretary of the Navy, as a board, or seperately bound to give their opinions on the subject submitted to them. This would throw the responsibity of each Bureau upon its own head—now as the board consists of three, the responsibility is divided, & where divided none feels its proper responsibility.

The Marine corps ought to be amalgamated with the infantry, as at present organised, it is an expensive useless corps; One Regt. commanded by a Lt Col commandant, & five Lt Cols. by Brevet receiving the pay & emoluments as such, without rendering any valuable service to the country. From the infantry when amalgamated with it might be detailed as occasion might require such number as might be necessary as marines afloat which would conduce to the interest of the service and be a great saving of expence to the Govt. I would also recommend a review of the laws regulating Brevet pay, & urge with earnestness Legislative enactment on this subjectt so explicit, that the military & the accounting officers, might clearly understand the pay & emoluments that each officer by law was to receive, without calling in the aid of the atto. Genl for the U. States. for his oppion; this will protect the feelings of the military officer from the imputation of asking more emolument than he is entitled to by law; and enable the accounting officers to settle & close all accounts agreable to law—The enactment ought to be clear, & explicit, prcisely stating the sum each officer was to receive, & to add emphatically the words no more. The case of the surgeon & paymaster General clearly elucidate the necessity of the amendment of the laws in this particular as recommended—The law gives to each, an annual salary of $2,5,00, the surgeon general has been allowed, & in the constant receipt of fuel & quarters, the paymaster has recd. it some times, and at others witheld from him—There can be no doubt but if one is entitled to emoluments above his annual salary, the other is als—and if to fuel & quarters, why not to forage & rations—Let the pay be liberal & adequate to the grade of officer but specific & certain, and much benefit to the service will follow—

Our squadrons afloat, for the suppression of piracy & the protection of our commerce, have been vigilent & attentive, and have in every instance faithfully performed their duty, our commerce have been every where protected and piracy has been put down upon the Gulph of Mexico & the west India seas, and in every other quarter where our squadrons have been ordered to cruise

With the amendment to our Naval system recommended, and the assiduity & great attention of its head, I have no doubt but the morale of our Navy will not only be much improved, but in a short time will be what the nation wish it "the strong arm of our national defence."

The Report of the Postmaster Genl is likewise communicated, which presents in a most lucid & satisfactory manner the high results that have already been produced from an honest, vigorous, efficient and oconomical administration of that department. Wherever it has appeared that abuses had crept into this department they have been promptly, & with energy reformed—The report of the Postmaster general is full evidence of the great ability with which it is managed, and the great confidence in the capacity & integrity of its head, the expedition with which information is convayed thoughout every section of our union—the increased expedition which has been given to it under the agency of its present head gives evidence of the talent & great attention the P. M. Gnl gives to the duties assigned him

The Penitentiary—The officers appointed agreable to the act of Congress 3rd. of March 1829—cannot go into opperation without further legislation. call for report from directors—[1]

[Endorsed by AJ:] Notes on Navy Dept   Post office   Penitentiary

AD, DLC (76).

1. A March 3, 1829, law directed the president to appoint five inspectors who were to oversee the District of Columbia penitentiary and report annually to Congress in January. The law provided no payment for their service. On February 1, 1830, AJ transmitted the inspectors' report and asked Congress to grant them compensation (Richardson, 2:473).

Draft by James Alexander Hamilton on the Bank of the United States

[This text probably drew on the several drafts concerning the Bank that AJ collected and turned over to Hamilton in late November (above).]

As the Charter of the Bank of the United States ~~will shall~~ will expire in 1836, and its Stockholders will most probably apply for a renewal of their privileges; ~~I feel~~ in order to avoid the evils resulting from precipitancy in a measure involving such important principles and such deep pecuniary interests I feel that I cannot in justice to our constituents and to the parties interested too soon present it to the deliberate consideration of the Legislature and ~~that~~ the people ~~in order that it may receive all the discussion reflection and discussion~~

The constitutionality of this Law has been well questioned because ~~among other reasons~~ it infringes State rights by ~~li controuling limiting~~ controuling their illimitable power of taxing ~~the proper~~ all private property within their ~~boundaries~~ Jurisdiction and because it grants to those ~~interested in it an~~ who hold the Stock exclusive ~~right to privileges~~ privileges of a dangerous tendency; ~~and power~~ Its expediency ~~Its expediency~~ is denied by a large portin of our Citizens while others insist that its operation is extensively injurious to ~~a large portion~~ various parts of our Country and it is believed none will deny that it has failed ~~to~~ in the great end of establishing a uniform and sound currency throughout the United States

AD, DLC (76).

Draft by Andrew Jackson Donelson on the Bank of the United States

[This draft was a reworking of Hamilton's. A further draft by Hamilton put the passage in nearly final form (Richardson, 2:462).]

Take this in at *Bank* af[. . .] Department

As the charter of the Bank of the Uni[ted States] expires in 1836, and its stockholders will most [*probably apply*] for a renewal of their privileges, in order to [*avoid the evils*] resulting from precipitancy in a measur[*e involving*] such important principles and such deep pecuniary interests, I feel that I cannot in justice ~~to our constituents and~~ to the parties interested too soon present it ~~to you for~~ to the deliberate consideration ~~of the Legislature and the people~~ of the Legislature and the People. The constitutionality of the law creating this Bank has been questioned because it infringes state rights by controulling their illimitable power of taxing all private property within their jurisdiction and because it grants to those who hold the stock exclusive privileges of a dangerous tendency. Its expediency is denied by a large portion of our citizens while others insist that its operation is exclusively injurious to various parts of our country: and it is believed that none will deny that it has failed in the great end of establishing a uniform and sound currency throughout the United States.

Under these circumstances if such an institution is deemed essential to the fiscal operations of the Govt. I submit to the wisdom of the Legislature whether a national ~~institution~~ one founded upon the credit of the Govt and its revenues might [not be dev]ised which would avoid all constitutional [difficul]ties, and at the same time secure all the [advant]ages to the Govt. and the country that were [*expected*] to result from the present Bank

AD, DLC (76).

Introductory and concluding drafts by Andrew Jackson

[*These drafts of the message's first and last paragraphs were composed together.*]

Fellow citizens of the Senate and House of Representatives

It affords me great pleasure to renew the tender of my friendly greetings to you on the occasion of your again assembling at the seat of Government to enter upon those important duties to which you have been called by the voce of your constituents and I take this occasion to congratulate you on the prosperous and happy state of our beloved Country; in the midst of plenty; at peace with all nations and general good health & prosperity pervading our land are blessings for which we ought render thanks to the great disposer of events and ~~continue~~ to offer up our supplications at a throne of gracce for a continuance of those blessings

(conclusion)

I now fellow citizens recommend you to the protection & guidance of almighty god, in a full reliance on his goodness for the maintainance of our free institutions, with an earnest and constant appeal to him, that whatever errors I may commit in discharge of the important duties which devolve on me may find a corrective in the united harmony and wisdom of your deliberations

AD, DLC (76).

To Hardy Murfree Cryer

Washington Decbr. 8th. 1829.

My Dr Sir

The Congress met yesterday formed quorums in both Houses, & I communicated my message to them at 12 oclock and I now enclose you a copy & will be glad to hear your opinion of it.

I have been without any information direct from you since the receipt of your letter advising me that you were on your way to Virginia to purchase from Mr. Johnston for you & Major Alexander a fine stud horse—on the receipt of your letter I wrote Mr. Johnston giving him your & Major Alexanders character & standing—whether you have been successful in your intentions I have not, but would be glad to hear.[1]

I have a fine stud colt at home 3 years old next spring, that I would like to have something done with   can I ask the favor of you to call at the Hermitage, look at my mares & colts & inform me how you like them and if you think the looks of the 3 year old would Justify the expense of training him, try & get Col Elliott to train him or have it done by Mr. Williams   I will give fifty dollars to have him trained if Col Elliott thinks his form would promise benefit from it. he is got by constitution his dam by Moors Diomede, by Bellair, he is a colt of great action out of hand & his bottom can only be known by trial—[2]

My health has improved, but my labour has been great—Having got matters before Congress, I hope I will have some ease—but why should I think so; the public dinners if nothing else, is laborious, and for me, who has lost all taste for society, irksome, still it is my duty, & I yield to it—I wish I could see you. I have much to say to you—I thought I had a knowledge of the depravity of the world—I did not believe that corruption had crept under the fair Ermine of the priesthood, altho the conduct of Sam. K. Blythe induced suspicion, that religion was sometimes a cloak for wickedness of the most depraved kind,[3] & lately it has been discovered here to exist in a regular licensed clergyman of the Presbaterian order, in the case of Major Eaton & his lady of the blackest depravity—still he has his supporters, which really has induced me to believe that there is as much corruption & less religion here than in any place I have ever been—still there are here many, very many, Presbyterian & Methodist & other clergymen, pure embassadors of Christ—There are several senators waiting & I must close with the request that you present me affectionately to your lady & family & believe me yr friend

Andrew Jackson

ALS, Anonymous (mAJs).
1. William Ransom Johnson (1782–1849) was a sometime Virginia state legislator and a renowned horseman. His stud horse Arab stood at Cryer's stable in 1830. "Major Alexander" may have been William Locke Alexander of Hartsville, a major of Tennessee volunteers in the War of 1812.
2. Cryer visited the Hermitage and sent AJ an assessment of the racing stock on March 4, 1830. He reported that the Constitution colt was too short and heavy for racing, and that Sumner County horsebreeder George Elliott (1780–1861) declined to train AJ's horses. Elliott had served under AJ as lieutenant colonel of Tennessee volunteers in the Seminole campaign. Williams was likely Green Berry (or Greenberry) Williams (b. 1778), another Sumner County horseman. AJ had put three mares to Constitution, owned by John Shute, in 1826.
3. Samuel K. Blythe (d. 1837) was a Sumner County Presbyterian minister. AJ had testified in a lawsuit between him and Cryer in 1825. In a July 1828 letter, published in the *National Banner and Nashville Whig* of August 2, Blythe accused AJ of past trafficking in slaves.

From Martin Gordon

New Orleans. 10. Decr. 1829.

Duplicate

Sir,

I consider no preamble or apology necessary in addressing you as the chief magistrate of the nation on the matters which form the subject of this Letter.

My appointment to office was the signal for bringing into action all the forces of the regularly organised party in this portion of the Country, determined right or wrong to find fault and oppose with all their means every act of your administration.

The first announcement of my appointment was marked by an immediate appeal to party feeling, and as you may have observed, a public meeting was instantly resorted to for the purpose of complimenting my predecessor, passing a censure upon the act of the Government in removing him, and keeping alive the excitement of their party and friends.[1]

This was shortly followed up by threats and menaces towards myself of prosecutions for the vigilance with which my sence of duty prompted me to watch over the public interest and to inforce the due execution of the laws.

Finding that these measures failed to have the desired effect, they were succeeded by insults in my very office, and threats of personal violence:

Subsequent events convinced me that all this was the result not alone of the deep rooted hatred and malignant hostility towards the Government such as it had lately been established by the voice of the people, but that this feeling was combined with another, which had the personal interest of the most prominent actors in all these scenes for its basis.

Shortly after coming into office I found that those persons had for a number of years been engaged in maturing a system in direct hostility to the public interest, to the great danger of the revenue of the Country and in open defiance of the most ancient, long established and important laws in relation to commerce.

I found that these dangerous infractions of the law had been acquiesced in or overlooked by the collector who proceded me, and therefore ceased to be surprised at the dissatisfaction which had been expressed at his removal from office. I myself entertained very different views of my duty and my powers. I did not feel myself authorized to interfere with legislation of the Country, to usurp and exercise a dispensing power not comtemplated or vested in me by law, and which would have an obvious tendency to introduce great evils and embarrassments into the administration of the revenue laws. I therefore determined to base my conduct on the express provisions of those laws, to administer them fairly and honestly, without favor or partiality, and to make an example of the most prominent among those who should persist in their violation

In accordance with this view of the subject I was soon called upon to act, and caused the ships Kentucky, Illinois and Azelia to be seized and prosecuted for a most flagrant violation of the act of Congress of the 18th. February 1793, upon the due execution of which act you cannot fail to perceive depends the very existence of the revenue, and if it be permitted to become a dead letter there is no limit to the frauds and impositions which may be practised; if it be permitted to become a dead letter all other laws in relation to the customs will be virtually repealed and rendered of no effect.[2]

These Ships happen to belong to the very description of persons who for so long a time have been indulged in an habitual disregard of the laws, whose convenience and interest required that those abuses should not be reformed, and whose malignant hatred and bitter curses are dispensed unceasingly and unsparingly upon those who have in the most humble degree been instrumental in exposing them and producing a change.

This feeling they have carried with them into every ramnification of Society, and it has grown up into a systematic hostility and oppression of all who are friendly to the present organization of the Government, who have the mis-fortune to find themselves within the reach of their influence

But finding that their threats of suits, their gross violation of the sanctity of my Office, their insults and menaces of personal violence had no effect upon me and that the law was taking its silent but steady course under the direction of the legal authorities of the Country, they have thought proper to acknowledge their violation of the law, to attempt to make out a case of pretended ignorance, and petition the Secretary of the Treasury for a remission.

And this is the point to which it is my principal object to call your attention: here we are completely at issue, and it remains to be seen whether such men shall be permitted to triumph over the law and those who administer it on an appeal to him who is comprehended in their universal malediction of all who are connected with the present administration.

To effect their purposes with the Secretary, they have resorted and will resort to every insidious artifice, every wily stratagem, and mode of influence which they so well know how to avail themselves of.

I shall not be surprised if they have induced some members of our party both here and in New York to combine with them and their friends to labor for the accomplishment of the common object of prevailing upon the Secretary to absolve them from the penalty of their wilful violation of the laws.

But if the Secretary should be so prevailed upon, and induced to extend his relief to those persons and remit the forfeiture they have incurred, it will be considered here as a victory gained over the officer who had only sought to fulfil his oath and his duty by a just execution of the laws, it will be regarded as a mark of disapprobation upon his conduct, and will be as much exulted in as would have been the acquittal of Watkins or any other public peculator. It will heighten their standing and increase their consequence in the eye of the public, it will enable them to make proselytes and to carry into complete effect their system of proscription, to the ruin and prostration of those who coincide with us from principle in this community: they will continue to violate the laws, and to set at defiance those whose duty it is to watch over and restrain them, under a full confidence (not unfounded should they succeed in their present application) that the equitable powers vested in the Secretary of the Treasury will be exercised in all future cases to exempt them from punishment.

It is to avoid if possible such a state of things that I have taken the liberty to address you personally upon the subject, with the hope that it may be of some avail in preventing that which cannot be viewed in any other light than as a calamity.

To bring the case more fully under your observation I respectfully refer to your attentive perusal and examination the argument against a remission and the other documents in relation to this matter, which have been transmitted to the Secretary of the Treasury.[3] I have the Honor to be Very Respectfully, Sir Your most obt Hbl Sevt

Martin Gordon

LS duplicate, TNJ (14-0985).

1. Gordon's predecessor as customs collector at New Orleans was Beverly Chew (1773–1851), appointed in 1817. A meeting at the Exchange Coffee House on May 16 had deplored his removal. Jacksonians countered with a May 18 meeting applauding AJ's appointments policy and declaring confidence in Gordon.

2. The 1793 law regulating ships engaged in the coasting trade required them to carry customs manifests listing in detail all imported goods or distilled spirits on board, under pain of forfeiture of both goods and vessel. The requirement had recently not been strictly enforced. Gordon seized the *Azelia, Illinois,* and *Kentucky,* all operating out of New York, for carrying foreign goods not listed on their manifests.

3. Gordon had written Ingham to explain his course on November 7 and 21. In January 1830 the Treasury Department remitted the forfeitures, instead assessing fines totaling $320. On February 4, Gordon, naval officer Peter K. Wagner, and surveyor Samuel Spotts protested to Ingham that such indulgence invited further offences. Ingham in reply defended leniency in cases of inadvertent rather than willful violation of the law (DNA-RG 56, M178-16).

From Tuskeneah et al.

Creek Nation Decr. 10th. 1829

Genl. Andrew Jackson
President of the U. States Greeting

We the chiefs and Head men of the Creek nation do hereby nominate constitute and appoint a delegation to visit you at the City of Washington and have appointed Opoithleholo and Tuckabatcha Hargo as principal of said delegation, we have instructed them to call upon you as our Father to fullfill all the provissions of our various treaties in which the faith of the U States is pledged   Father, they particularly are instructed to ask of you to interpose in our behalf to prevent the further opperation of the laws of Alabama and to prevent the Citizens of the U States from Settling within our limits   To these subjects they are instructed to attend particularly to and we indulge ourselves with the pleasing anticipation that your aid will be extended towards our nation in such manner as is in accordance with our Treaties and Father there is a large sum of money due us on acct of property lost during the war and also on account of the sum of Two Hundred and fifty thousand Dollars that was set apart for the payment of claims of the Citizens of Georgia the residue of that sum is due to our nation[1] and Father we wish you *not* to let any more money be placed in the Hands of Col Crowell for this nation but let be placed in the Hands of his Sucessor this deligation has no instructions or power to enter into any arrangement or Contract with regard to a further extinguishment of title to any lands belonging to the Creek nation as all the Country we now own has been secured to us by Treaty and we expect of the Goverment of the U States the complete fulfillment of our various Treaties the delegation is composed of Opoithliho Tuckabatcha Hargo Tuckabatcha Mico,

Tutunugy Emarthla Smut-Eye, Cohchu Tustenugy, Coosahtustenagy, Nimrod Doyl to accompany them

Tuskenahaw his X mark
Nehau Mico his X mark
Samuel Smith his X mark
Tuskenahaw of the lower contry his X mark
Nerharlockcohopie his X mark
Coosa Tustenuggy his X mark
John Steadham his X mark

John Ridge & Wm McGirth Secretarys
Danl Asbury clk
Saml. Smith Interpreter
test
Wm. McGirth

DS in John Ridge's hand, DNA-RG 75 (M234-222). The delegation arrived in Washington in January 1830. On February 3, citing federal treaty guarantees, they memorialized Congress for protection against the "grasping rapacity and tyranny" of Alabama (*HRRep* 169, 21st Cong., 1st sess., Serial 199). The War Department limited its discussions with the delegation, Indian superintendent McKenney claiming that in opposing emigration and complaining of Crowell it did not legitimately speak for the Creek nation. McKenney charged that John Ridge (1803–39), the delegation's secretary, had crafted this credentialing letter without its signatories' approval so as to expand the delegation's membership and enlarge its powers (DNA-RG 75, M21-6). Ridge was a Cherokee, son of the chief Major Ridge.

1. Congress in 1817 had appropriated $85,000 to compensate friendly Creeks for property destroyed by hostile Creeks in the War of 1812. In the 1821 Treaty of Indian Spring, the U.S. pledged in return for a cession of land to pay the Creeks $200,000 directly and to assume up to $250,000 in claims of Georgia citizens against the Creeks for property damages incurred before 1802. The approved claims came to less than half that sum, and the Creeks contended that the remainder, as part of the total price for the cession, should go to them. Congress however in 1834 designated the remaining $141,055.91 to satisfy further potential Georgia claimants, and in 1835 it was paid in a lump sum to Georgia. The Creeks protested, and in 1848 Congress paid them also the same amount.

To Robert Johnstone Chester

Washington Decbr. 11th. 1829—

Dr. Sir

In my last I intimated that it might be fortunate for you that the chikesaw agency was so pressed upon another that with propriety it could not be given to you—you will receeive from the Secretary of War a notification of your appointment as Indian agent to the tribes in Florida, where you will be near to Col Butler[1] & through his kindness may be able to obtain some *sugar land,* that in time, will be valuable—the salary is *$1500*—the other only *$1300*

The goverment is endeavouring to concentrate the Indians west of the Missysippi and you must turn all your energies to this object—in the cause of which, some more profitable business may present itself—on the receipt of your appointment you must repair forthwith to the agency as part of the cause of the removal of the Indian agent now there in office was his continued absence & promptness in your taking poss[es]sion of the office will be expected—

With our united salutions to Betsy & all our friends in haste yrs

Andrew Jackson

ALS, THi (14-1003). Chester wrote Eaton declining the appointment on January 6, 1830, citing his need to attend to business in Tennessee (DNA-RG 75, M234-433). Chester recommended his wife's brother Stockley Donelson Hays. In March AJ appointed John Phagan, replacing Gad Humphreys.

1. Robert Butler (1786–1860), formerly AJ's adjutant general, was the surveyor of public lands in Florida. He was married to Rachel Hays, Rachel Jackson's niece and Elizabeth Chester's sister.

To Samuel Delucenna Ingham

Decbr. 11th. 1829—

Dr. Sir

I return to your office the recommendations of sundry Gentlemen presented for the office of receiver of Public moneys at Edwardsville Illanois with the endorsement that Dr B. Edwards will be sent to the Senate—

If there are any recommendations for the Registers office Neworleans, will you please send them to me; I am not informed whether Col Piere will accept that office, therefore, hesitate to appoint him

If the recommendations are filed with you for the Survayer Genl Mississippi & Louisiana, I would like to see them as I wish to send it to the Senate with others on Monday next, with any others that you may have to present[.] yrs respectfully

Andrew Jackson

Facsimile of ALS, Christie's catalog, 1995 (mAJs). On December 14, AJ nominated Benjamin Franklin Edwards (1797–1877), a physician and brother of Ninian Edwards, for land office receiver at Edwardsville, Hilary B. Cenas for register at New Orleans, and Joseph Dunbar for surveyor of public lands south of Tennessee. Henry D. Peire had declined a New Orleans customs appointment in May. AJ's draft of the December 14 nomination named him for the register's office.

To Deacon Sockbason

Dec. 15, 1829.

Friend and Brother:—

When you return to your venerable Governor "Francis of the Quoddy tribe," say to him, that you are the bearer of my best wishes for his health and happiness, and that of his people, and that I return him, through you his friend, my sincere thanks for his kind benediction, by you presented to me—and, in return, assure him that I hold him and his people's hand fast in friendship, as his great father Washington did in former days; and my earnest desire is, that the chain of friendship may long continue bright between us.

ANDREW JACKSON.

Printed, Eastport, Maine, *Northern Light*, January 13, 1830 (mAJs). Francis Joseph Neptune (c1735–1834), the *sakom* or governor of the Passamaquoddy nation, had aided the Americans in the Revolution. In 1776 George Washington offered the Passamaquoddys "the chains of friendship," which they in turn vowed to keep "bright and unbroken" (*Papers of George Washington*, Ser. B, 7:433–34).

To the United States House of Representatives

[On December 15, Jackson recommended the purchase of land for the benefit of the Passamaquoddy Indians. Below is his draft of the message. Subsequent drafts by Andrew J. Donelson (DLC-37) tightened the wording and omitted the close of the first paragraph. The final text is in Richardson, 2:463.]

To the Speaker & House of Representatives

A Deputation from the Passamaquoddys—an ancient tribe of Indians (residents of Main) have arived here & presented a memorial of their chiefs Captains & whole tribe which is herewith transmitted soliciting of the Government to extend assistance to enable them to obtain a comfortable support. During the Revolutionary war they were our friends & fought with us for the liberty we now enjoy. These red children once numerous & the proud & unrestrained owners of the Surrounding forest now reduced, ~~to weakn~~ their number scarcely four hundred, supplicating for a small portion of the bark & timber of what was once their own native wields to sustain them in existence—What a spectakl & reverse of fortune is here presented?

It is represented that from Individuals adjoining their present small possession at a cheap rate land can be obtained, should congress in their wisdom & discretion, think it expedient so to direct. To that end therefore, I lay their application before you with the accompanying documents for your consideration that a tract of land two or three miles square may be authorised & directed to be purchased by the united States, adjoining them, to be held for them in trust during their existence as a tribe

AD draft, DLC (37).

From Stephen Decatur Miller

Executive Department
Columbia 15 Decr 1829

My dear Sir

The State of South Carolina has a claim against the United Sates for advances made during the late war.

I have been directed by Resolution of the Legislature to request the friendly consideration of this claim by the President and his recommendation to Congress for its payment, should it comport with his views of justice.

Alexander Speer Esquire our principal Fiscal officer is constituted a special agent to attend at Washington and superintend the investigations incident thereto, to whom you are referred for information

It cannot have escaped your recollection how imminent was the danger of the whole Southern country during the late war when the British Fleet hovered on the coast after the Capture of Washington. The United States were under the most solemn and Constitutional obligation to protect this State, which they were unable to do and left us to our own resources. In the liquidation of advances made by us, interest was withheld and many items rejected, on account of their informality.

The immense sacrifice which is made to the General Government during peace, for protection during War, ought to induce a liberal course in the part of that Government which omitted to do what the Constitution enjoined upon it.

It was entirely uncertain for some time whether Charleston or Savannah or New Orleans should be the object of the attack of the British when they left the Chesepeake   That a deep solicitude should have been felt and the most energetic means devised by South Carolina in this crisis was to have been expected, but that the accounts of this State should be subject to such a rule as would exclude many bona fide belligerent expenses, could not be rationally anticipated. To your own knowledge of the difficulties as well as to a sense of justice, and pledged faith of the Federal Government we appeal for a prompt and final liquidation of the Balance still due—With great Consideration I am dear Sir Your most obt.

Stephen D. Miller

[Endorsed by AJ:] The Executive of So. Carolina on the subject of a claim for advances made during the late war—To be considered. A. J. refered to the Sec of War for his report thereon—A. J.

LS, DNA-RG 46; Copy, ScU (14-1045). *SDoc* 12, 21st Cong., 1st sess., p. 2 (Serial 192). Miller (1787–1838) was governor of South Carolina. In the War of 1812, South Carolina had advanced funds to finance its defense. The federal government later reimbursed the state, but in 1828 South Carolina memorialized Congress for repayment of certain expenses that Treasury auditors had disallowed. It also asked for interest on its advances. Congress did not comply, and the South Carolina legislature directed Miller and state comptroller Alexander Speer (1790-1856) to present the claims again and to seek AJ's assistance. Speer delivered this letter to AJ on December 23. Eaton reported to AJ on January 2, 1830, and on January 4 AJ commended the claims to Congress, transmitting Miller's letter and Eaton's report. In March 1832 Congress authorized paying the claims, which came to about $200,000.

To Charles Jones Love

Washington Decbr. 17th. 1829.

My Dr. Sir

I have recd. your letter Postmarked 3rd. instant, but dated thro mistake the 15th. I regret to learn that Moses is dangerously ill, but never will charge you or Doctor Hogg with neglect; I feel under too many obligations to you for your kind attention to my business, & interest; and assure you, it will be long & gratefully remembered by me—I am truly astonished at Mr Steels neglect of my negroes when taken sick & shall write to him on this subject, for the last time. Should I be left without an overseer I will turn him away unless he pays more attention to their health, by sending for Doctor Hogg in due time after they are taken sick—and my Dr Sir I authorise you to assure him of this fact.[1]

I rejoice to hear that little Joe is still living but am fearful he is too much trouble to Mrs. Love & you, he may with care out grow the complaint, be this as it may when I know he has been carefully attended to, & has not suffer in his sickness, then, I will be satisfyed with whatever result providence may will.[2]

I wrote you some days ago, on the subject of a sale proposed by Capt Peter Mosely to me of one hundred & fifty acres of land adjoining My Winston tract on the north[3]—from the letter I wrote Capt Mosely & enclosed for your inspection, you will find that he has computed my crop of cotton this year at 160,000 in the seed—I am fearfull his calculation is too large, and my crop may not meet my [acc]ount with Mr Josiah Nichol on the 27th of Novbr. 1829 as pr account rendered is 1995 72½, add to this five hundred dollars my part of Steels wages as overseer for Major A J. Donelsons farm & my farm one hundred dollars to be paid out of A. J. Donelsons will make two thousand four hundred and ninety five dollars & seventy two & a half cents—I am thus particular, as I want this account of Mr Nichols closed & receipt taken that I may be able here after to look at the account of the overseer alone, & be more able to judge of his oconomy therefore I have concluded that it will be best to let Messhrs. Hill & Nichol have my whole crop at nine cents   close this account with Mr Nichol including five hundred to Steel for this years wages, let them pay to Mosely the amount of the ballance of the cotton & then if it does not amount to the price of the land, to draw upon me for the ballance if not over five hundred dollars—But if my crop should fall still short of meeting the purchase of the land & the payment of this account more than $500 then I cannot buy the land—you will see from all this that I am determined not to go in debt for land or any thing else to encumber myself—and the account with Mr Nichol *must be* closed with my crop. I have therefore wrote Mr Nichol that my cotton, with Mr Donelson will be sold to Nichol & Hill at 9 cents pr lb. if they will take it at that, if not then twenty thousand will be sold to Capt Mosely, if he will take it at nine cents & the ballance sold in Nashvill if it can, & if not be delivered to them to be shipped to Maunsal White N. Orleans, to be sold & amount remitted to them the ballance they will draw on me for—[4]

with my kind salutations to Mrs Love & all your family I am sincerely yr friend.

Andrew Jackson

ALS draft, DLC (37).

1. Moses was probably the eighteen-year-old son of Tom and Molly listed on the January 1829 Hermitage slave inventory. Love reported on January 15, 1830, that his health was improving.

2. The slave Joe, son of Peter, died in February 1830 at about age fourteen.

3. On September 3, AJ had written Peter Guerrant Moseley (1776–1858) of Wilson County, declining Moseley's offer of a different property and instead suggesting this purchase when his finances would permit. In February 1830 Love bought the 150-acre tract from Moseley for AJ.

4. Maunsel White (1783–1863), captain of a volunteer company in the Gulf campaign, was AJ's cotton factor at New Orleans. AJ's 1829 crop was ultimately consigned to him and sold in April 1830, with proceeds of $2,246.39 paid to Nichol & Hill as AJ's agents. They in turn paid $1975.72½, the correct balance due in AJ's November 27 account, to Josiah Nichol & Son. Another payment in August 1830 of $324.52 to Nichol & Son for subsequent purchases closed AJ's account.

Thomas Hart Benton to Andrew Jackson Donelson

Dowson's no. 2.
Dec. 17th. '29.

Dr. Sir,

Please to shew the enclosed paper to the President as it relates to a subject in the message which is new, and upon which all information may be desirable. Yours respectfully,

Thomas H. Benton.

[Endorsed by AJ:] Col Benton inclosing the view of Mr Jno Randolph & Mr Simpsons views of a substitute for the U.S. Bank—to be filed—The general ideas are good—A. J.

ALS, DLC (37). Stephen Simpson's separate letter of this same day proposed a national exchequer to replace the BUS. Alfred R. Dowson (c1783–1850) ran two adjacent boarding houses on A Street.

[Enclosure: John Randolph to Benton]

"you will search in vain "Congressional History" for the *project* mentioned by Hall, to whom I spoke of it more than once.[1] It was a creature of my own devise—shewn only to two friends, one of whom is long since dead—but never brought forward in publick.

Soon after Mr. Jefferson's accession, looking forward to the termination of the United States' Bank, and being much opposed to that, or any similar institution,[2] I turned my thoughts to the subject and devised a plan which, as I conceived, would supply all the duties and Offices of the United States' Bank so far as Government was concerned. It is obvious that the discounting of private paper has no connection with the transfer of public monies, or a sound paper currency. My plan was to make the great custom houses branches of our great National Bank of deposit—a sort of Loan Office if you will. Upon the deposits and monies received for duties, Treasury notes receivable in all taxes &c: of the U. S. to issue. The details you can easily conceive. The whole under the Secretary of the Treasury and other great Officers of State.

At the time I speak of, the Land Offices were not in the receipt of sufficient sums to make them depositaries similar to the great Custom Houses—but whenever large dues to Government were payable the plan would be extended. This would give one description of paper bottomed upon substantial capital, and whensoever Government might stand in need of a few millions, instead of borrowing their own money from a knot of Brokers, or the credit of said Brokers, it might, under proper restrictions, issue its own paper in anticipation of future revenues, or taxes to be laid. Such notes to be cancelled within a given time.

I have written with much difficulty and hope you may be able to read it and to supply my omissions—"

Copy, DLC (37).

1. Perhaps Samuel H. Smith's *History of the Last Session of Congress, Which Commenced on the Seventh of December, 1801* (Washington, 1802). It covered the first session of Jefferson's presidency, when Randolph was in the House of Representatives.

2. The first Bank of the United States was incorporated in 1791 despite the opposition of Jefferson, then secretary of state. Its charter was not renewed and it expired in 1811.

To *James Alexander Hamilton*

Washington Decbr. 19th. 1829—

My Dr. Sir,

I have been in the receipt of your letter of the 13th. instant, for four days & it is the first time since it came to hand, that I could seize a moment of lesure to reply to it.

It is a source of much gratification to me, that the message has been, so generally, well received both by my friends, & a great portion of my political enemies—I have recd. from Virginia North & South Carolina, Pennsylvania, Newyork & ohio, very flattering congratulations on this subject

I was aware that the Bank question would be disapproved by all the sordid, & interested, who prised self interest more than the perpetuity of our liberty, & the blessings of a free republican government—I foresaw the powerful effect, produced by this monied aristocrasy, upon the purity of elections, and of Legislation; that it was daily gaining strength, & by its secrete operations was adding to it, by pushing its branches every where; and, by its management, silencing opposition, by its corrupting influence, & preparing for a renewal of its charter, which I viewed as the death blow to our liberty—under such circumstances as these, I viewed it my duty to act fearless of consequences to myself—I thought the safety of our institutions required it—The confidence reposed by my country dictated to my conscience that now was the proper time, and altho, I disliked to act contrary to the opinion of so great a majority of my Cabinett I could not shrink from a duty so imperious, to the safety & purity of our free institution, as I conceived this to be—I have brought it before the people & I have confidence that they will do their duty.

I will thank you for your ideas on the details of my proposed national Bank, first as a Bank of Deposit, for the facility of the transfer of public moneys & the establishment of a sound & uniform currency; making if you please the Custom Houses, branches to this national Bank, and attaching it to the Treasury Department—The other of a mixed character, which may fulfil all the purposes of a Bank and be free from the infringe-ment of state rights, & our constitution—so soon as your Leisure will permit, I will thank you for your views upon this important subject, that I may use them when it may become necessary in the way you have sug-ested.

I am happy to hear that on your return you found your amiable family well, to whom I pray you to present me and all my houshold most respect-fully—I write in great haste am interrupted without having time to look over or correct it—sincerely yr friend

Andrew Jackson

ALS, NN (14-1072). Extract, Hamilton *Reminiscences*, pp. 151–52. Hamilton wrote back proposing a substitute for the BUS on January 4, 1830.

From William Donelson

December 20th 1829

Dear General

I received your kind letter of the 7th Nov—on the Sixth of this month, it had remained in the post office at the fountain of health 6 or 8 days before I heard of it   I delivered the letter enclosed to Mr Steel on the 9th after having taken a coppy of it,[1] and doing in all other respects as you requested me, and indeed Gen you need not be afraid of troubling of me about your business it will give me pleasure to do you a favour whenever it is in my power to do so, my greatest fault is in not letting you know in time what is doing, and about to be done here in all other things I believe I am prompt to your call—

From the tenor of your letter, I discover that you are very much dissat-isfyed with the great loss of property, and surely when one takes a view of the great amount of it, you have just cause to be so; how it has happened, I am unable to say, but believe much of it has happend through ignorance and the want of proper experiance, particularly so in regard to the work horses; for I think I have seen them hard worked when there was no need for it, and when the earth was so completely soaked with rain that it was purfect mud, and the water would follow in the channel after the plow

I did not fail to warn him of the risk he was runing of the loss and breaking down of horses, and the consequent loss of the crop, how far he took my advice I am unable to say, but do not think he regarded it much, yet notwithstanding all this it is very possible that the horses may have died of natural diseases; of your stock of hoggs you have the same reason to complain that the rest of the neighbourhood have (a scarcity of bacon hoggs) an evil that afflicts us all, and the cause of the scarcity being gener-ally attributed to the same thing, leaves no room for doubt, not that we do not rais enough for our use but that they are tken away after they are raised by unknown hands, and distroyed, this I am confidant is the cause of my scarcity, and believe it to be the same throughout the neighbourhood—with good economy Mr Steel may get through the year, with the supply of poark hoggs that he has up for killing, which I believe is 120 that will average a 120 pounds each, with this supply he may get through the year—your stock at this time looks tolerably well I have noticed you brood mares and young colts in paticular they are in good order—the work horses look tolerably well and your stock generally except the sheep, they look sickly and are in bad plight—

Our crops in this cuntry are turning out very well—corn in particular of which we will have an abundant supply—of cotton the crops will not be so good as was antisipated. on this part of the crop, I perhaps have chainged my mind as often as any body els; in the summer when the incets was making great distruction among it—I thought we would scarcely make any thing—in the fall when it began to open it looked so rich and flourishing, and the weather so favourable for it, that I thougt we would make great crops, but in this I was disappointed as well as in the other, we will make an average crop rainging from 7 to 8 hundred, a frost which fell about 14th Oct succeeded by an occational shower of rain for a week or two damaged our cotton very much and shortened the crop conciderably —and indeed it has been a very bad fall for picking of cotton, owing to this circumstance and the buildings that Mr Steel had on hand, will make him late in getting out your crop, if the weather continues as good as it is now, he may get it out and housed by the 10th January—From the vigilence and industry that Steel is using at this time, and if he continues to use it there is no doubt of his doing well next year. I am in hopes from the many admonitions that he has received, and his character as an overseer at stake that he will do beter next year—I understood the other day that your gin had come near taking fire I went over to inquire and see the cause of it on examination I found the brush conciderably out of rapair, the far end of the axel had worn flat on one side, which caused it to jostle thump very much in turning, and create great friction he Steel had it sent to the gin maker and repaired the next day it is now doing very well—

It is with pain that I am compeled to inform you of the misfortune that has befallen my dearest mother,[2] she has her other arm broken by a fall from the steps of the door, it is as near as possible broken in the same way that the other was, the only differance is, both bones of this arm are broken higher up, the wrist joint bruised and mashed in the same way she complains of much more pain from this fracture than she did from the first—Dr Hadly was called in immediatly, and dressed her arm correctly,[3] from its being attended to beter in the first instance I am in hopes she will not suffer so much in the end—the rest of the family are all well—and poor Poll too is doing well she is as fat and saucy as ever from her continud good health I think she will live to be an old Bird—

Elizabeth desires to be remembered affectionately to you and sais that she will insure Pollys life till you return[.] Yours sincerely

William Donelson

ALS, Stanley F. Horn (14-1077).
    1. AJ to Graves W. Steele, November 7 (above). The Fountain of Health was a spa and postal station near the Hermitage.
    2. Mary Purnell Donelson.
    3. John Livingston Hadley (1788–1870), a University of Pennsylvania medical graduate, had practiced in Davidson County since 1815.

From James Alexander Hamilton

Newyork
Decr. 22nd. 1829—

My dear Sir,

I enclose a letter received by me from our friend Genl. Green and beg leave to call your particular attention to the last paragraph.

This letter was received late on Saturday, on Monday I called upon the Editor of the Daily Advertiser to examine his files (for I had not heard of the paragraph referred to.) I did so and enquired of the Editor, whether any allusion was intended to be made to me? He assured me unhesitatingly that he had no such intention; that I had not been mentioned or referred to as in the remotest degree connected with the speculations commented upon; and this he repeated to a friend of mine who interrogated him on the subject. (Indeed, the paragraph itself does not allude to any person whatever). In addition to this I think it due to myself to declare in the most unreserved manner; that I never had any connection with the Bank of the United States; that I never bought, or sold, or speculated in its Stock directly or indirectly; and that I never afforded any information, of any kind, to any person whatever in relation to the Bank with a view to speculations in the Stock.

I feel that it is due to myself thus to meet and put down the slightest intimation of such an abuse of the confidence you have honored me with in relation to this Subject.

I have taken the liberty to make use of my daughters pen to write this letter. Your letter of the 19 int is at hand. I have the hnr to be with the truest attachment your friend & Svt

James A Hamilton

[Endorsed by AJ:] Mr Hamilton enclosing Genl Greens to be noted—

LS, DLC (37). Hamilton *Reminiscences*, p. 152. On December 12 the *New York Daily Advertiser*, edited by Theodore Dwight (1764–1846), had reported a rumor that persons in New York City knew AJ's message would oppose rechartering the BUS and had used the information to speculate in its stock. AJ replied to Hamilton on January 1, 1830, assuring him of "my exalted opinion of your virtue & honesty" and remarking his astonishment at Nicholas Biddle's mendacity.

[Enclosure: Duff Green to Hamilton]

Washington Decr. 16th. 1829

Dear Sir

When you were here I explained to you the causes which make it desirable that I should complete the negociation, of which you were so kind as to take charge, at an early day—Relying on the successful issue, I have not made other arrangements to meet the engagements soon to fall due, & which, if unprovided for, will produce unpleasant embarasments. Will you do me the favor to inform me of your prospects of success, and let me ask you to advise me *now* if you think the funds cannot be had in New York.[1]

I anticipate from what I see in the New York Daily that *you* will be charged with a speculation on the Presidents Message   Upon this subject I learn that after Mr Biddle had ascertained the president's views in relation to the Bank he represented him to be the *friend* of the present institution & that a consequent rise of six per cent on the price of stock ensued!! Would it not seem that this was done for fraudulent purposes? May I ask the favor of an early Answer? yours

D. Green

ALS, DLC (37). Hamilton *Reminiscences*, pp. 152–53.
1. Green had been looking for investors in the *United States' Telegraph* since the dissolution of his partnership with Russell Jarvis in 1828.

To John Test

Decbr. 24th. 1829—

Dr Sir.

The Deed which you have presented to me for approval signed by Rebecca Burnett with the papers which accompanied it, is returned to you.

If the Deed presented was for the interest of Rebecca Burnett only, I should have no objection to approve it, as the Treaty requires; but there are various other tracts contained in the Deed which she claims as heir. In the papers presented, there is nothing to shew that she is the heir. The courts of the Territory in which the lands are situated, are alone competant to settle this question[.] yours very respectfully

Andrew Jackson

ALS, DNA-RG 75 (14-1116). Test (1771–1849) was an Indiana congressman. Rebecca Burnett (1791–1841) was a niece of Potawatomi chief Topenebe. Treaties of 1818, 1821, and 1826 granted her and her six siblings each several sections of land, which could not be sold without presidential consent. Test had sent AJ a deed of sale of November 20, signed by Burnett, for a section and a quarter which she claimed as heir to her late brothers Abraham and Jacob. Test resubmitted the papers on January 28, 1831, with evidence that the heirs had subdivided the lands to make Burnett sole proprietor of the tracts she sold.

From Hardy Murfree Cryer

Gallatin. December 26th. 1829.

My Dear friend,

I wrote to you some ten or fifteen days ago, giving you a brief account of the situation of your affairs at the Hermitage, as well as my own temporal concerns—which letter you will have received before this reaches you. And I would not have written to you again so soon, knowing that your time is *precious,* and your mind is employed about the Weighty concerns of our common Country—But when you shall have read this letter you will not deem it amiss for me to have written you at this time

The young men to whom I sold your grey Colt in Kentucky—made a good season with him—all things considered. He meted something like *$570.* But as many young beginners in business—not satisfied with the prospects of a *moderate* lawful income they must needs close a race on him for $500, which was run on 25th. Novr. two mile heats—And owing doubtless to the *condition* of the turf—they lost the race—4 days previous to the race, there fell a very heavy rain—followed by a hard freeze —very unusual in this Country for the time of year—And on the morning of the race *a thaw* commenced—the *surface* was soft, and I am told by Col. Elliott who prepared the grey horse *"Tariff"* and attended the race—that every *jump* he went through the crust some times nearly to the knees—&C. which made the labour so great that the *difficulty* of breathing the *supposed* effects of colts distemper lost him the race—And Moore & Shaw lost a considerable sum, for them—As there are always some *poor wretches,* like summer flies not only given to defile the polished surface of a fair reputation, but would eat out the very cement of good society—So in this instance, there was not wanting the *officious* services of some *poor divils,* who endeavoured to impress the minds of Moore & Shaw that there was *fraud* practiced upon them in the sale of the horse—I am informed that my *English Daddy*—Foxall—publickly proclaimed that *I* had knowingly imposed upon the young men, selling them an unsound horse &C.¹ I was a little sprung at hearing *such lies*—called upon this *poor* vagabond immediately—& *he denied every word* of it—I then hastened over to see the *unfortunate* sportsmen—They were very much *under par,* in feeling & prospect—I was told by a mutual friend of your's & mine—that there might be a *difficulty* and a *long delay* in getting the pay for the horse—Some foul unmanly insinuations have been dropt—And knowing something of the influence of *party* spirit about the County of *Simpson & Logan*—I looked around for a *[little]*—And heard their proposition. One was to take the Horse at half the *purchase* price—the other was to give him up to me with the proceeds of the season allowing them a reasonable sum for expenses &C—I said to them in presense of several of your friends & mine—that I *would not act* on either of their propositions until every thing like fraud, imposition &C. be withdrawn—then I would proceed as your agent on the principle of *generosity*—that I knew you would much rather extend the hand of *relief* to the needy, than *oppress* the poor—all things being ready as above—I told Mr. Moore—as he had been *unfortunate*—and was like to become embarrassed—I would take back the Horse—with $370. of the season and he might have the ballance—to which proposition he agreed—He is to collect the money *forthwith*—and pay it over to me or order as your agent, &C—

The horse is in fine *heath* & spirits, plays and looks well, he is now in *the care* of old *Parson* Martin where he will remain until I hear from you²—If I have done wrong in this transaction I rely upon your *clemency for relief* and *forgiveness* both—Moore is *a newly* married man (the son in law of your old friend Gwin)³ and the loss of time from his daily avocation (a Clerk of the Court)—for the last 6 or 9 months—the losses he sustained on the race &C. would have *crippled* his circumstances very *materially* if not broken him up—which I knew you would not have wished or desired—I told him I knew you too well to think for a moment, that you would injure a *hair* of his head, *although* he was a strong Clay & Adams *Politician*—that you would rather give him the Colt—than see *him* & *family* injured to any considerable extent—Now sir what shall I do with this fine young horse—It may be, you may have an opening for sale to some of the *breeders* of Baltimore or Pensylvania—or shall I try to sell him in this Country? Dr. Wm. E. Butler was here a few weeks since looking for a horse for the Western District—I am pretty well assured there can be a sale made of him, so as to cover the sum of $800, including the $370, made or taken with him, which last mentioned sum will be available from 2 to 5 months from this time—An answer to the above I shall expect to receive from you as soon as circumstances will permit—The *presidents Message* is the subject of general conversation, and *Admiration* &C. Mrs Cryer & children beg leave to be presented you & for myself accept Sir the best wishes of my heart

H. M. Cryer

PS. Col. Elliott and his friends were very sanguine of winning—I am told they bet 2 & 3 to one on the grey's horse—and would have bet a great deal more if they could have gotten the opportunity—H M C.

[Endorsed by AJ:] The Revd. Hardy M Cryers letter Decbr 26th 1829—on the subject of taking back my stud colt Bolivar, by him called Tariff—his conduct approved—directed to place him in Col Elliot hand for training if he should advise it—otherwise place him at a stand— advertising him at $15 in the season or $20 out & insurance & the leap in proportion—If sold no less than $1000 in one, two & three years with interest—If a good stand cannot be got for him to stand at the Hermitage

ALS, DLC (37). The horse Bolivar, or Tariff, was sired by Oscar out of a Pacolet mare. AJ had sold him to Isham L. Moore, deputy clerk of the Simpson County, Ky., court, and his partner Shaw for $800. AJ replied to Cryer on January 10, 1830. He approved reclaiming Bolivar and proposed to either train him or put him to stud.
    1. Thomas Foxall (c1791–1835), from England, had married Cryer's widowed mother Mary in 1823. He was a Sumner County horseman.
    2. Probably Abram Martin (1774–1846), a Methodist minister of Sumner County.
    3. Moore had married Catherine P. Gwin, daughter of James Gwin.

To Samuel Delucenna Ingham

(Private)

Decbr. 29th. 1829—

Dr. Sir

Mr. Tyler waited upon me yesterday & made enquiry if Mr Biddle had resigned his appointment in the land office—of which I was not advised.[1]

The case of Mr Wm. E. Hayne of South Carolina I brought to your view the other day—I was informed that one of the appraisers for the Port of Charleston was intemperate, & ought to be removed—will you please make enquiry of the member from Charleston District on this subject[2]— [if] this appraiser is unworthy to be retained, the office would be well disposed of, by conferring it on Mr Hayne, who is presented to me as every way worthy, & needy; with an amiable family, & himself the only son of Isaac Hayne who fell a sacrafice to British cruelty in the Revolutionary war—I am yrs respectfully

Andrew Jackson

Facsimile of ALS, Max Rambod catalog, 1995 (mAJs). William Edward Hayne (1776– 1843) was the son of South Carolina militia colonel Isaac Hayne (1745–81), who was captured by the British, paroled, later recaptured, and executed without trial. William's wife, Eliza Peronneau Hayne, had written AJ on December 1 begging an appointment for him.

On January 6, 1830, AJ removed Charleston customs appraiser Andrew Smylie, who had held the post since 1818, and nominated Hayne in his place.

1. John Biddle (1792–1859), brother of Nicholas Biddle, was the present Michigan Territory delegate to Congress and also register of the Detroit land office, 1823–36.

2. William Drayton (1776–1846) was the congressman from Charleston.

From George Rockingham Gilmer

Executive Department
Milledgeville 29th Decr 1829

Sir

Early in the month of November information was received at this Department, that among the Cherokees about to emigrate beyond the Mississippi, were several very respectable men, who knew the manner in which their tribe had obtained possession of the strip of land claimed by the State of Georgia, and whose testimony could be obtained. By a resolution of the Legislature the Governor was authorized to appoint Commissioners for that purpose. The President will perceive from the instructions given to those Commissioners, that great care was taken not only to confine the examination of Witnesses to respectable persons, but that the manner of taking the testimony should be unexceptionable. The U States Agent was present, and witnessed each affidavit. The whole of the testimony thus taken is now forwarded to the President, together with an additional affidavit taken by the U States Agent of an Indian by the name of Rain crow, the affidavit of Majr. Ector a respectable member of the Legislature and the substance of a talk held by the Cherokees in 1818 at the request of the then U States Agent for the Creeks & by him communicated to this Department. I also communicate to the President a Message sent from this Department to the Legislature, together with the resolutions of that body upon the subject of the policy proposed to be pursued by him.[1] It is confidently believed that the testimony which is now sent to the President, when considered in connection with that which has heretofore been communicated from this Department upon the same subject will satisfy his mind as to the right of Georgia to the immediate possession of the territory in dispute. The account given in the Cherokee talk of the manner in which that tribe obtained permission of the Creeks to occupy the land of the latter is very much the same with that given by the Indian witnesses. That talk becomes very conclusive evidence when it is recollected that it was given by the Cherokees for the express purpose of satisfying the U States Agent of the right of the Creeks to the land south & west of the head of the Appalachee & between that river & the Chattahoochee & including a country similarly situated and occupied by the Cherokees to that which is now claimed by Georgia. That talk was held only two or three years before Genl McIntosh procured the dividing line between the two tribes to be established from the Buzzard Roost to the mouth of Wills

Creek and proves that in 1818 that line had not been understood among the Cherokees as their true boundery. The Commissioners of Georgia did not know when they took the testimony of the Indians, that such a talk had been delivered. The identity of its statements with the testimony of the Indians could only have arisen from the truth of both.[2] Independent of any knowledge derived from individuals, it is probable that we could have accounted for the change of possession of the disputed territory from the Creeks to the Cherokees, from the alteration of the habits of life which has been for a long time taking place in both tribes. Within the last thirty or forty years these tribes have gradually become less & less capable of subsisting by hunting. Very many of the individuals of each tribe became considerable herdsmen but even these were but little accustomed to provide by cultivating the earth, food for the support of their cattle during the winter, but rather trusted to the cane & other natural productions. Both tribes therefore inclined to progress to the South where the lands on the streams were richer & the cane more capable of sustaining their cattle. That portion of the Cherokee tribe in particular who inhabited the high mountainous cold & sterile country about the head waters of the Savannah & Chattahoochee would be disposed to leave it for one further to the south & more suitable to the change that was taking place in their habits. The truth of this opinion is verified by the talk delivered by the Cherokees in 1808 to the President of the U States, in which they represent the scarcity of game in that part of their country and their intention to leave it. In addition to the superior advantages of the more southern country for the support of their cattle, was added the inducement of approaching nearer their markets rendered important by the increased value of their stock.

It is probably known to the President from personal observation that the Country in dispute was formerly occupied by the Creeks entirely & that they gradually relinquished their possession until at the close of the late war there were very few of that tribe remaining and that at the same time & in the same manner the Cherokees by degrees obtained almost entire possession. The fact that all the streams & remarkable places in the disputed territory have Creek names, prove certainly that it was but lately occupied by the Creeks, and that there has been no general & simultaneous transfer of its possession from one tribe to the other, but that the Cherokees must have intermingled with the original inhabitants so as to have adopted their proper names. The Cherokee talk, the testimony of the Indians, and the information of the original white settlers on that frontier, prove that this occupation of the Country by the Cherokees was permissive on the part of the Creeks and so considered by the Cherokees until eighteen hundred & twenty when Genl McIntosh procured the consent of the Creeks to make it a matter of right. The Country was said to have been loaned by the Creeks to the Cherokees & the first claim of right of possession to it at all on the part of the latter tribe have been derived from their success at a ball play between the two tribes, at which the stake was the disputed Country & at which play the Cherokees were successful. This ball play if my information is correct took place at some time between the years 1816 & 1820.[3] I understand that the President is of the opinion that the U States Government are bound by their contract in 1802 with Georgia as well as upon general principles to permit no transfer of territory after that time from the Creeks to the Cherokees, or rather to disregard any contracts which may have been made between the two tribes upon that subject. That the Creeks were the rightful occupants of the country now claimed by Georgia in 1802 & were so admitted to be by the Cherokees until long after that time, is most conclusively proven, by the testimony which has been & is now submitted. The wisdom & prudence of the President will direct the time & manner in which the possession of the Country will be given to the Government of Georgia   We are desirous that the President should so manage this matter, as not to interfere at all with the efforts of his administration to obtain for Georgia through the measures proposed to be pursued by Congress during its present session the whole of its Indian territory. The people of Georgia and those who administer its Government are fully apprised of the delicate & difficult duty which the President has to perform in the management of Indian affairs. They know that in discharging his high duty in endeavouring to advance the real interest of the Indians, and securing the rights of the states, he will be opposed by the prejudices of ignorance, the sickly sensibility of affected philanthropists & the still more violent rage of party opposition. The Legislature of the state and its Executive have therefore endeavoured to pursue such a policy in relation to every thing connected with that subject as to aid the President in sustaining his measures. The President will be satisfied of this by the accompaniing report & Resolutions of the Legislature & the message of the Executive upon that subject.

It is my duty to state to the President that I have received information from a highly respectable source, that Genl. Coffee the U States Agent for taking testimony in relation to the disputed line will be subject to an attempt to have palmed upon him much corrupt testimony. Charles Gates Esqr. the Georgia Commissioner who lives immediately upon the line of the disputed territory writes me thus, "I am informed that Majr. Ridge a Cherokee has some old drunken Indians heretofore Chiefs drilling for a week and then introduced them to Genl Coffee as competent evidence"   The constant and active efforts of Ridge to thwart the views of the Government renders this account highly probable. It is however less regarded because it is believed that the President himself is well acquainted with the facts connected with the present possession of the Cherokees, the Indian habits & the character of their principal chiefs. I have requested Mr Gates to endeavour to procure some evidence in a more authentic form of the truth of the statement as to Ridges conduct.[4] Whilst Genl Coffee was at the Agency I received a letter from him requesting a copy of the testimony which was in the possession of this Department. All that had then been received was forwarded to him.[5] I feel more especially concerned that the testimony should satisfy the Presidents mind conclusively as to the right of the state to the land which she claims, because the Legislature was so entirely convinced that it would have that effect when taken in connection with other circumstances, that they declined expressing any opinion as to the course the Governor should pursue provided that should not be the case. A referance of our right as a contested or uncertain one to any tribunal was not anticipated. Georgia considers herself entitled to the immediate possession of the country claimed, but is willing to have that right postponed for the attainment of a more important object. If that object is not effected by the means adopted during the present session of Congress, she expects that the President will so far as his own power extends do her justice by having the Cherokees removed from so much of her territory as is included in the treaty lately made with the Creeks.

These remarks are submitted to the President, with sentiments of the most respectful consideration

George R Gilmer

LS, DNA-RG 75 (M234-73). LC, G-Ar; Copy, DNA-RG 46 (14-1138). *SDoc* 512, 23d Cong., 1st sess., vol. 2, pp. 214–16 (Serial 245). Gilmer (1790–1859) had succeeded John Forsyth as governor of Georgia on November 4. Eaton replied to him on January 13, 1830, that AJ would attend to the issue as soon as he received John Coffee's report (DNA-RG 75, M21-6).

1. Pursuant to resolutions of the Georgia legislature, Gilmer on November 11 had appointed Samuel A. Wales and Charles Gates commissioners to take testimony from emigrating Cherokees and others about the disputed boundary. Wales and Gates obtained affidavits, sworn in presence of agent Hugh Montgomery, from two native Cherokees and three intermarried whites. These, along with a statement by Hugh Walton Ector (c1798–1835) of Greenville, an affidavit by the Cherokee Raincrow, and a report by former Creek agent David Brydie Mitchell (1766–1837) of an 1818 talk by Cherokee chief Sour-mush, all supported Georgia's claim that the land in question had historically been Creek, not Cherokee. On December 11 Gilmer transmitted the evidence to the legislature. Affirming Georgia's right to the territory, he still deemed its immediate possession "comparatively of small importance" and urged forbearance while Congress considered AJ's recommendation to remove the Cherokees entirely from Georgia (Serial 245, pp. 216–24). On December 17 the Georgia legislature adopted resolutions approving AJ's policy of general Indian removal (DNA-RG 75, M234-73).

2. Both Sour-mush's talk, as reported by Mitchell, and the Cherokee affidavits said that Cherokees had been permitted by the Creeks to settle in the now disputed territory south of the Etowah but had never claimed ownership.

3. Ector's statement included the ball play story, as told to him by William McIntosh.

4. Major Ridge (c1770–1839), who had commanded auxiliaries under AJ in the Creek and Seminole wars, was a Cherokee chief and at this time a leading opponent of emigration.

5. Coffee had queried Gilmer on November 3, and Gilmer replied on November 30 (Serial 245, pp. 224–26).

From David Reed Mitchell

Montgomery December 30th 1829

Dr Sir

I hope you will excuse me for intruding on your time agane I have lernt that a delegation of eight or ten Indians started to Washington last week and Opothohola with the ballence who speaks the Spirrit of the Nation I mentained my suite aganst him and he is not worth any thing now and appeard verry much dejected before he started and told some of his friends that he was affraid his situation would make him unpopelar with his people and there is no doubt but if he could get a rise but he would sell his country as he is proud and ambitious and is determaned to mentain his popularity and he knows if the emmigration goes on the way it formaly has he will loss all his men and the McIntush party would have the assendency at Arkensaw. I think from every circumstance and I have had as good an oppertunity as any other person that if he can rase himself by a sale he will do so I recovered my Suite aganst him that is he has carriad it up to the Supream court and if I should recover it finally I shall be looser then as in the first place I was only Gardien in the case for my brothers two children and they only allowed me five hundred dollars for my expences and trouble and I spent near seven hundred dollars and near three years riding from Tennessee here and here together and I head to give my attorneys three hundred dollars and if Opothahola should sell I think nine tenths of the people would say who know the circumstance would say my suite aganst him was the moving cause and the way the emigration has went on it would take at the lowest calculation five year to take them of and if he dose make a sale they can all go in twelve months which on a fare calculation would be a saving to govermant of from fifty to one hundred thousand dollars or more and if I have done my country a favour in what I have done which eavery man aught to do when he has it in his power, if my govermant should think it proper to return it in any way It would be gratefully received I am poor and considerably in debt mostly owing to my having so much trouble about this case Dixen H. Lowis was one of my attorneys in this case who can give you any other information you may ask[1] James Polk is from the County I live in and is a friend of mine I shall write to Esqs Lowis and Polk on the same subject excuse the length of these lines with the well wishes of your H. St.

D. R. Mitchell

ALS, DNA-RG 75 (M234-222). Opothle Yoholo was a member of the Creek delegation that had recently left for Washington. He later signed the 1832 Treaty of Washington, by which the Creeks ceded all their land east of the Mississippi in return for various payments and reservations—a result which Mitchell, in his appeals for congressional compensation, claimed that his lawsuit had prompted (*Polk Correspondence*, 2:241–42).

1. Dixon Hall Lewis (1802–48) was an Alabama congressman.

To John Overton

copy
(*Private*)

Washington Decr. 31st. 1829

My D. Sir,

I have been anxiously awaiting the acknowledgement of my Message to Congress, forwarded to you, with such remarks as its subject matter might suggest; but, as yet, I have not heard from you. As far as I have seen it commented on, in the public Journals, it has been well received—except in the Abbeville District, So. Carolina, where it has been severely attacked. It is an old addage that—"straws show which way the wind blows." I assure you this has some what astonished, tho' I cannot say it has *surprised* me, because I had hints that some of my old friends had changed, and the case of Major Eaton was thought to present a fair opportunity of *destroying him,* and *injuring me,* by circulating, *secretly,* foul and insiduous slanders against him and his family. Be it so; I shall pursue the even tenor of my ways, consulting only the *public good*—not the *popularity* of any individual.

Congress is progressing with its labours, and I think I see in the commencement a little *new* leven trying to mix itself with the *old* lump, but I believe the old will be hard to mix with the new.

I regret, also, to say there is some little feeling still existing in a part of my Cabinet. I am in hopes, however, that harmony will be restored; and that union of feeling and of action, which so happily prevailed when this administration was first organized, will be again revived. I do not think I have been well treated by those members who have been instrumental in introducing discord into my counsels. They knew as well before, as they did after their appointment who were to compose my Cabinet. If they had any objection to associating, upon terms of equality, with any of the other members, they should have had candor enough to say so, before they accepted the offer of a seat in the Cabinet. I still hope, however, that I shall not be driven to extremities; but should *action* become necessary, on my part, to produce harmony, you may rest assured I shall not hesitate when the public interest requires it. It gives me pleasure to inform you that the most cordial good feeling exists between Mr. Van Buren, Major Barry, and Major Eaton. These gentlemen I have always found true, harmonious, and faithful—they not only most cheerfully cooperate with me in promoting the public weal, but do every thing in their power to render my situation, *personally,* as pleasant and comfortable as the nature of my public duties will admit.

Permit me here to say of Mr. Van Buren that I have found him every thing that I could desire him to be, and believe him not only deserving *my* confidence, but the *confidence* of the *nation.* Instead of his being selfish and intriguing ~~in his disposition~~, as has been represented by some of his opponants, I have ever found him frank, open, candid, and manly. As a counsellor he is *able* & *prudent*—Republican in his principles and one of the most pleasant men to do business with I ever saw. He, my dear friend, is not only well qualified, but deserves to fill the highest office in the gift of the people who, in him, will find a true friend and safe depository of their rights and liberty. I wish I could say as much for Mr. Calhoun and some of his friends. You know the confidence I once had in that gentleman—However, of *him* I desire not now to speak; but I have a right to believe that most of the troubles, vexations, and difficulties I have had to encounter, since my arrival in this City, have been occasioned by his friends—But for the present let this suffice.

I find Mr. Calhoun objects to the apportionment of the surplus revenue among the several states, after the public debt is paid—he is also, silent on the Bank question, and is believed to have encouraged the introduction and adoption of the Resolutions in the South Carolina Legislature relative to the Tariff.[1] I wish you to have a few numbers written on the subject of the apportionment of the surplus revenue, after the national debt is paid. It is the only thing that can allay the jealousies arising between the different sections of the union, and prevent that flagicious *logg-rolling-legislation,* which must, in the end, destroy every thing like harmony, if not the Union itself. The moment the people see that the surplus revenue is to be divided among the states, (when there shall be a surplus) and applied to internal improvement and education, they will instruct their members to husband the revenue for the payment of the national debt, so that the surplus, afterwards, may be distributed in an *equal ratio* among the several states. If this meets your views, by giving it an impulse before the people, in a few well written numbers, you will confer on your country a blessing, that will be hailed as no ordinary Boon by posterity, who must feel its benefits.[2] I feel the more anxious about this, because I have reason to believe a decided stand will be taken by the friends of Mr. Calhoun, in Congress, against the policy, if not the constitutionality, of such a measure.

Let me hear from you on the receipt of this. Present me affectionately to your amiable family and believe me to be, Your friend

Andrew Jackson

[Endorsed by AJ:] copy of a letter to the Honble John Overton near Nashville Tennessee

LS copy in William B. Lewis's hand, NN (14-1192).

1. In his annual message, AJ had recommended distributing surplus federal revenues to the states once the national debt was discharged, on the premise that any acceptable tariff revision would still yield a revenue well beyond the needs of government (Richardson, 2:451–52). Calhoun was the secret author of an anti-tariff report which was coupled with formal legislative resolutions protesting the tariff and published by the South Carolina legislature in December 1828 as *Exposition and Protest.* Deeming purely protective duties "unconstitutional, oppressive, and unjust," the Carolina resolutions demanded reducing the revenue to meet the bare wants of government, which would leave no surplus to distribute (*Calhoun Papers*, 11:442–539).

2. Overton may have been "Publius," author of a series titled "Internal Improvement—Surplus Revenue of the State and United States" that ran in the *Nashville Republican and State Gazette* from February 26 to March 26, 1830.

[Note by William Berkeley Lewis]

The foregoing letter was written under the circumstances and for the purposes stated in the following remarks—

All through the summer and fall of 1829, General Jackson was in very feeble health and in December, of the same year, his friends became seriously alarmed for his safety. Indeed his whole physical system seemed to be totally deranged—his feet and legs, particularly, had been *very much swoln* for several months and continued to get worse every day, until his extreme debility appeared to be rapidly assuming the character of a *confirmed dropsy.* The General himself was fully aware of his critical and alarming situation, and frequently conversed with me upon the subject. These conversations occasionally led to another subject in which I took a deep interest—to wit—the election of Mr Van Buren as his successor. This I thought highly important for the purpose of carrying out the principles upon which the General intended to administer the government; but, if he were to die so soon after his advent to power, I greatly feared this object would be defeated. However, even in that event I did not entirely dispair of success. It occurred to me that Genl Jackson's *name*, tho' *he* might be dead, would prove a powerful *lever,* if judiciously used, in raising Mr Van Buren to the presidency. I therefore determined to get the General, if possible, to write a letter to some friend, to be used at the next succeeding presidential election, (in case of his death,) expressive of the confidence he reposed in Mr. Van Buren's abilities, patriotism, and qualifications for any station, even the highest, within the gift of the people. Having come to this resolution I embraced the first favourable opportunity of broaching the subject to him, and was happy to find that he was not disposed to interpose the slightest objection to the proposition. He accordingly wrote a letter to his old friend, Judge Overton, of which the ~~enclosed~~ preceding is a duplicate, and handed it to me to copy, with authority to make such alterations as I might think proper. After copying it, (having made only a few verbal alterations,) I requested him to read it and, if satisfied with it, to sign it—He read it and said it would do, and then put his name to it—remarking, as he returned it to me—"If I die you have my permission to make such use of it as you may think most advisable."

I will barely add, that the General wrote this letter to his old and confidential friend, Judge Overton, at my particular request and with a full knowledge of the object for which I wished it written. He has, fortunately for the country, however, recovered his health and there will now, I hope, be no necessity for using it—In conclusion I will further remark that both the signature and endorsement, as will be perceived, are in *Genl. Jackson's own proper hand writing*.

WB Lewis.

ADS, NN (14-1197).

To Martha Jefferson Randolph

December 31st. 1829

Genl Jackson presents his respectful compliments to Mrs. Randolph, and acknowledges the receipt of the cane she has had the goodness to present to him with feelings of deep sensibility as a testimonial of her esteem derived from the venerated hands of her father, no expression of his can measure its value, or describe the satisfaction with which he will deposit it among the most precious of his *reminiscences*

AN, DLC-Thomas Jefferson Papers (14-1209). Randolph (1772–1836) was the daughter of Thomas Jefferson and widow of Thomas Mann Randolph.

To Martin Van Buren

Decbr. 31rst. 1829—

Dr. Sir

The enclosed appears a ~~real~~ case of real Systemactic Smuggling, and for which imprisonment is a fit punishment & more particularly where the individual in unable to pay the penalty—Therefore the prayer of the Petitioner cannot be granted—and I have thus endorsed on the petition & return the papers to your office yours respectfully

Andrew Jackson

ALS, DNA-RG 59 (14-1218). In January 1829, customs officers at Waterford, Vt., seized a variety of trade goods, including a thousand pounds of nutmegs, belonging to Christopher H. Sterns, or Stearns, of Plymouth, N.H. The goods were condemned and sold, and Sterns was tried and convicted for smuggling from Canada and fined $2,800 and costs. Unable to pay, he was jailed at Burlington about December 1. On December 11 he petitioned AJ for pardon, claiming destitution but arguing neither innocence nor special circumstance. In 1832, while resisting another arrest for smuggling, Sterns killed a man at Canaan, Vt., and fled to Canada.

From Susan Wheeler Decatur

George Town, Dec. 31st 1829—

My Dear General,

I have been watching the Newspapers, with *intense* anxiety to see the Report of the Naval Committee upon my claim; for I am afraid it will be thrown so low on the Docket, that it may share the same fate it has hitherto done from being taken up on the last days of the Session; and rejected more from the *hurry* and *impatience* of the members than from any decided objection to the Bill—The Naval committee consists of the same members who compos'd it last year, and who weigh'd all its merits, and I hope there can be no *new* stumbling block thrown in the way—May I therefore entreat you, My Dear General, to remind Mr Hoffman (the Chairman) of it, and of the great importance it is to me to have it settled as speedily as possible—for I can with truth assure you that I have not a single dollar! and I implore you to use all your influence to have me reliev'd from such a painful and humiliating situation!

I take the liberty to send you the enclos'd epistle, to let you see what a malicious and vindictive community is contain'd within the ten mile Square!

I beg you, My Dear General, to accept my best wishes for many years of health and happiness to yourself, and of increasing usefulness to your Country; and I pray you to accept the assurance of my cordial esteem and gratitude and to believe always most sincerely and respectfully yours

S. Decatur

[*Endorsed by AJ:*] Mrs. D. enclosing an anonymous letter—I think it is known who, is the author—we will examine—a copy of my answer within A J

ALS, DLC (37). Decatur enclosed a letter signed "A. B. C. & Z." and dated December 12: "Madam—I take the liberty to tell you that you will injure your *cause* by associating with Mrs. E—your best friends are *her enemies.*" AJ replied on January 2, 1830, pledging help with Decatur's claim and denouncing Mrs. Eaton's traducers. On January 7, Michael Hoffman (1787–1848) of New York, chairman of the House Committee on Naval Affairs, reported a bill in favor of Decatur's claim. The bill died in the House on May 1.

From Israel Beach, Isaac Morse, and Elihu Morse

Canandaigua, Ontario county N.y.

Sire:

the memorial of a very few of the yet remaining revolutionary patriots who ever have been, and still are of genuine republican principles and firm supporters of all such who hold these sentiments in righteousness, as given to us by the God of Independence, wish to remark, that to have those principles of government fully acted upon, have been strong advocates for you, to place you in the presidential chair, that justice and judgment may be done to all the people. We view your military fame, begining in early youth and continuing to the close of the last war, against a proud, powerfull and domineering nation, as true military fame and glory, divinely sanctioned by the Lord of hosts, as indisputeable at the memorable battle of New Orleans, and almost or quite unparalleled in the annals of history. Feeling ourselves greatly abused by a former administration on a military scale; it calls up that old spirit of war, at which vision we stand astonished at ourselves at the hazard we ran against odds infinitely unequal together with our sorrows and unequalled hardships through an eight years war, and mostly on our own private expence—we exclaim energeticly, and yet with a conscience void of offence against the injustice, partiality and ingratitude of those rulers.

We believe from your own experience in the hardships and horrors of war, and when feebly supported by a parsimonious, divided and distracted country, that you will warmly advocate the righteous cause of those few old soldiers yet living, who may not have any thing, scarce one of them less than seventy years old, whose brow of care and anxiety ought to be relieved, and the way made more plain for their crippled frames to totter into the tomb.

Sire—we wish still to remark, that we feel constrained to say, that the pension law as it now stands and operates is unjust and partial. Were we not all equal sufferers in that war? were we not side by side in every battle? did we not leave our homes, our families, our freinds and dearest connections, and the cultivation of our little properties to go to rack and ruin? O! my country and government, in the name of that Almighty power which gave our nation the victory—why reward me for services, when my tent mates, my fatigue mates, my right and left hand companions in battle, in watchings by night and day, in hunger cold and nakedness, may not have anything? The pension law as now framed, in some points, really defeats its own purpose—in demanding a nine months service at one time, or more, to intitle them to the pay—When a campaign opened in the spring, we had many inlistments from five to eight months, at the close of the campaign those troops would return home and be at no expence to government through the winter, and on opening it again in the spring would inlist for another term—thus loosing two summers at home instead of one, and doing the country more service than the inlistments for nine, ten or twelve months at one time, and loosing only one summers work—

Father—we humbly ask your patience a little longer. Inlistments were kept up untill very near the close of the war on the principle of during the war. Witness Gen. Washington's anxiety to keep his ranks as full as possible to the last, notwithstanding the previous prospects of a speedy peace. Many therefore inlisted during the war, who did not serve more than from six, down to three months &c, and draw full pay yearly. It is wholly impossible for the rational mind to see how the injustice and partiality of those rulers is removed, notwithstanding the little addition made to the pension roll—Nay, how easy it is to see that it remains just the same—[1]

The campaigns of 1775, 1776, and part of 1777 untill Burgoyne was taken, was by far the most disastrous of any through the whole war, especially the one in lower Canada, a great part of whom lost their lives there: The number of that army in 1776, was about 15000, all inlisted for one year.[2] There are a small number, comparatively speaking, of troops of the above said campaigns yet remaining, of whom the signers of this took an active part, who had their constitutions ruined by starvation, p[r]ison and wounds in the British prison ships jails and dungeons, by which means many of them became wholly unable to take any active part in the remaining campaigns of the war, and were discharged as such from farther military duty. These are all refused any compensation for services, except on the ground of sworn pauperism, and this made sacred as proof of holy writ—[3]

Sire—on the principle here under consideration, a memorial was sent to president Adams while he was in office, and signed by six or seven of the most substantial revolutionary patriots, that he would warmly advocate our cause in his message to Congress. Total silence on the subject, as far as we could learn, evinces how little he cares for the war-worn veterans—and no wonder! We do not beleive that one drop of military blood ever circulated in his veins—[4]

Sire—We wish to make one more remark, and then we have done. The United voice of the people of America is this, viz—that if government give anything to one of those revolutionary soldiers as a reward for services, they are in duty bound to reward them all, in order to run clear of downright partiality and injustice—

Concerning the pension awarded to a part of those old soldiers, and not to all, who are equally meritorious, and more so, Congress have had it in agitation for a long time, and last winter it passed the house of representatives by a large majority. Can the senate refuse to sanction this law which has been so long under much consideration, (by the whole people of america) without showing an act of disrespect and contempt to the judgement and principles of the lower house, who are in point of abilities and merit equal to themselves—

Should the senate eventually refuse to confirm this law; the voice of the people will frown upon them most severely—yea; it has a long time done so—

Should the President agree with us on the principle under consideration, he will instantly have the united voice of the people as a sanction to the compleat justice done to th[e] country. The voice of the people therefore, will be a most sure guaranty to the president, and other correct benevolent rulers, for their future continuance and prosperity in office.

Much respected President—and freind of the war-worn, aged and decriped soldier, We do humbly pray as in duty bound, that our request may be granted.

Israel Beach
Isaac Morse
Elihu Morse

DS, DNA-RG 107 (M222-28). The pension law of 1818 offered stipends to needy Revolutionary veterans who had served until the end of the war or for any term of nine months or longer. The three memorialists had all been privates in the Connecticut line. Israel Beach (1759–1836), who served for a year in 1776–77, qualified under the law and was granted a pension in 1818. Brothers Isaac Morse (1756–1849) and Elihu Morse (1758–1845) were ineligible, each having served for a total of more than two years in 1775–78 in multiple short enlistments of up to six months.

A bill to extend pensions to needy veterans who had at least nine months' total service or had been taken prisoner passed the House by 111 to 67 in February 1829, but failed in the Senate. In his December annual message AJ recommended pensioning "every Revolutionary soldier who aided in establishing our liberties, and who is unable to maintain himself in comfort" (Richardson, 2:456). An 1832 law granted to all Revolutionary veterans, including state troops and militia and regardless of their present circumstances, pensions of full pay for life for those with two years' total service and lesser stipends for those with at least six months. Under this law Isaac and Elihu Morse applied for and received pensions in 1832.

1. In 1778, during the war, Congress pledged a payment of $80 at the end of the war to those who would enlist for its duration. A law of 1828 granted full pay for life, retroactive to 1826, to every soldier covered by this provision and not already drawing a pension.

2. An American invasion of Canada in 1775 collapsed after a failed assault on Quebec. In 1776 and 1777 the British defeated Washington repeatedly and captured New York City and Philadelphia. The surrender of British General John Burgoyne (1723–92) and his army at Saratoga, N.Y., in October 1777 brightened American fortunes.

3. An 1820 law, modifying that of 1818, required pensioners to prove their "indigent circumstances" by submitting an inventory of their assets and swearing before a judge.

4. Adams recommended revision of the pension laws in his first three annual messages.

From Joseph Lancaster

New York No 10 Prince St Bowery

Honored Friend

Accompanying this letter and enclosure is a book, being the 14 report of the Society for promoting the education of the poor of Ireland—allow me to recommend the list of Schools for 100,000 children to thy notice. I am happy to say that this society originated myself and the late Lord Londonderry told me that he was the peer, who had carried the Question in the Cabinet for a Parliamentary grant in its aid in consequent of which its last report details an expenditure of £41,000 in one year for promoting Education in Ireland.[1]

Thou wilt perceive the immense importance of this to the United States—considering the immense emigration from Ireland to this country —How much the newcomers settle down and blend with the interior population, how greatly must the country be enriched by an instructed population instead of one as formerly—unhappily destitute of these advantages.

Yet this is only one specimen of the advantages of my system of Education—hundreds of thousands of dollars have been saved, or children educated by hundreds were they could otherwise only be educated by scores   I have published my inventions to mankind when I could by taking a patent have enriched myself—To this generous error, as some think it, in my early life and enthusiastic commencement of my benevolent labours, and to my losses and sufferings in South America and the terrible sickness of my wife and family in the United States last year, I owe that we have as a family been in much want and difficulty.

At present my wife, has her constitution so much impaired by many sufferings and sicknesses, that we can hardly hope she will have strength to bear up against any summer or autumnal sickness—we have only one way to renovate her broken constitution and prevent ~~her~~ our children becoming motherless—to return to England in hopes that the moderate heat of summer, in her native air will preserve her life—[2]

For this purpose we have only one hundred dollars in the world, and the sale or rather sacrifice of a little household furniture & will not much increase it. Her health, and the tender age of our three children require plain comfortable accommodations and we have no way to obtain them but by asking in this mann[er] the pecuniary aid of a few benevolent and Eminent persons—

Allow me therefore to solicit at thy hands the favor of such pecuniary assistance as thy kindness may dispose thee in this case to give—I refer thee to T. L. Smith Esq now auditor at Washington for further information on my case and I have no doubt he will be pleased to have any opportunity of speaking what is has heard in the state Legislature and city of New York respecting my usefulness to mankind[3]

Thus am I reduced to the painful necessity of seeking benevolent aid which formerly I have been very extensively accustomed to give yet at this time I can look around on many nations, which profess to feel the highest obligation to my talents and benevolent exertions—a like instance, has hardly any existence among mankind—

As the American nation has been greatly benefitted by my system I think surely they will not allow my family to return to England or Ireland uncomfortably destitute & pennyless[.] Hoping thy kind answer I remain with High consideration & respect thy friend—

Joseph Lancaster

[Endorsed by Lancaster:] 1829 unanswered

ALS draft, PHi (12-0372). Lancaster (1778–1838), an English Quaker educational reformer, was a pioneer of the monitorial system of schooling, which provided basic mass instruction through drills administered by students. In 1818 Lancaster came to the United States, where he opened schools, lectured, and published tracts. He went to South America in 1824 to operate a monitorial school at Caracas, Venezuela, but returned in debt in 1827 after falling out with his patron, Simón Bolívar. An attempted school in Trenton, N.J., failed in 1828 and left Lancaster destitute. In September 1829 he settled in Montreal.

1. The Society for Promoting the Education of the Poor of Ireland was founded in 1811. Its fourteenth annual report was published in Dublin in 1826. Robert Stewart (1739–1821), the first Marquess of Londonderry, was an Irish peer.

2. In 1827 Lancaster married the widow Mary Robinson, mother of three children.

3. Treasury register Thomas L. Smith had been a New York state legislator. The New York City Common Council presented Lancaster with $500 in 1828 for his contributions to education, and in early 1829 Lancaster petitioned the state legislature for funds.

Memorandum on a Pamphlet by William Martin

[The 1828 campaign revived an old controversy over Jackson's refusal in December 1813 to discharge the first brigade of Tennessee volunteers. The troops had been taken into federal service under a February 1812 law binding them "to continue in service for the term of twelve months after they shall have arrived at the place of rendezvous, unless sooner discharged." Jackson mustered the brigade at Nashville on December 10, 1812, for a march to New Orleans. In February 1813, Secretary of War John Armstrong aborted the campaign and ordered the troops "dismissed from public service." Jackson returned his force to Tennessee and disbanded it, issuing certificates to the volunteers on April 20 that they were "hereby discharged." Whether this constituted a formal discharge under the law soon became a point of controversy. Jackson held that his certificates were merely contingent, issued on the recipients' pledge to

*return upon notice, and phrased to entitle the men under a provision of
the enrollment law to keep their arms and equipment should they not be
recalled to duty.*

*In September 1813, Jackson summoned the volunteers back into ser-
vice against the Creeks. The troops complied. But on December 4, at
Fort Strother on the Coosa River, Lieutenant Colonel William Martin
(1765–1846), commander of the brigade's second infantry regiment, wrote
Jackson that his men expected to be discharged on December 10, one year
from their initial muster. Jackson construed the law differently, holding
that the soldiers were obliged to perform a year's worth of actual duty
in the field. Since they had been idle from April to September, Jackson
believed they owed several months more. Convinced that the brigade
was in a state of mutiny, Jackson had it paraded and disarmed on
December 9. On December 13, following the arrival at Fort Strother
of new troops under John Cocke, Jackson ordered the brigade back to
Nashville.*

*In 1827 Martin came out against Jackson's presidential candidacy,
and Jacksonians replied with charges that he had incited mutiny in 1813.
Martin presented his defense in the July 25, 1828,* National Banner and
Nashville Whig; *Jackson responded under the pseudonym "A Volunteer"
in the* Nashville Republican *of August 5. In January 1829 Martin pub-
lished a pamphlet,* The Self Vindication of Colonel William Martin,
Against Certain Charges and Aspersions Made Against Him, by Gen.
Andrew Jackson and Others, in Relation to Sundry Transactions in the
Campaign against the Creek Indians, in the Year 1813. *It reprinted his
Banner article, backed by further documentation. The following undated
memorandum, likely penned in 1829 after Jackson arrived in Washington,
was his response to Martin's pamphlet.]*

Col Martin says in page 16—pamphlet that the volunteers thought themselves absolved from the obligation the had come under by their tender—
This cannot be true —for the Colo. being appointed one of a committee
to wait on the Genl in Septbr. 1813, he had been advised of the construction given by Sec of War, that he could not discharge them nor did he
believe the Pt. could, and to be informed of him whether the Genl would
assume upon himself the responsibility of ordering these vollunteers into
service, the governor having no right to do so without the orders from the
President; The Governor being one of the committee assuring me if I did,
that if not sanctioned by the President they should be viewed as part of the
5000 ordered by the Legislature against the creeks for & during the campaign—nothing said at that time by Col Martin about the time of the men
expiring on the 10th. of Decbr. no because the militia was directed for the
campaign against the creeks & it was an after electioneering thought of
the Col & his coactors—[1]

That it is a positive untruth that the General ever did say that the Volunteers were entitled to there discharge on 10th. of Decbr. 1813[2]

view the phrasaology of this certificate   it proves ~~all that I ever alleged—that~~ much[3]

court martials composed of officers engaged in the same cause was a poor resort—This had been tried in Col Alcorn case—[4]

It is stated they marched by the Genl order—It is true after the mutiny of the 9th. of Decbr was put down & a pledge given that they would not attempt to go without an order from the Genl—They had entered into a solemn pledge to each other not to cross the Coosa—When informed of this by Genl Hall I ordered him to march them to Nashville & receive the Govr order[5]

Why did he not call on Col Williamson in his life for his [s]tatement, because the Colo. knew that Williamson knew all about the matter, and had at Ft Strother refused to march off on the 10th. of Decbr & gave the information of his first Seargeants conduct that led to his immediate arrest & confinement—& Genl Halls report[6]—Now Col Martin says Col Williamson came off with them—This is positively untrue—Colo. then Capt Williamson remained until ordered into the interior to raise other volunteers, & returned with a Regiment[7]

There is no such order as the one purporting to be sent from the Sec of War thro Wilkerson it was believed at the time that the word "*discharge*" introduced in that sent to Wilkerson instead of *dismiss* was intended to produce the dispersement of the soldiers there that his officers might enlist them—[8]

AN, DLC (37).

1. In September 1813, a delegation of officers and citizens including William Martin had met with AJ and Governor Blount to devise measures against the Creeks. AJ told them that Secretary Armstrong had ruled that the volunteers were still liable for service: they had not been finally discharged in April and could not lawfully be so by anyone, even the president, before their year's commitment ended (*Self Vindication*, p. 17). Martin afterwards held that this statement had persuaded the officers that their service time was still running and would expire December 10. On September 24, the Tennessee legislature authorized Blount to raise 3,500 militia to fight the Creeks, which with 1,500 volunteers gave AJ a force of 5,000.

2. Martin offered a statement from ten officers and soldiers of the first brigade that they had heard AJ say on November 18, 1813, that "the volunteers should be discharged on the tenth" (*Self Vindication*, p. 20).

3. As quoted by Martin, the certificates AJ issued on April 20, 1813, read: "I certify that A B enrolled himself as a volunteer under the acts of Congress of February sixth, eighteen hundred and twelve, and July sixth, eighteen hundred and twelve, and that he has served as such, under my command, on a tour to the Natchez country, from the tenth of December, eighteen hundred and twelve, to the twentieth April, eighteen hundred and thirteen, and is hereby discharged" (*Self Vindication*, p. 11).

4. In his pamphlet Martin asked why, if AJ had really thought him guilty of exciting mutiny, he did not court-martial him as he had Lieutenant Colonel John Allcorn (1769–1829), commander of a cavalry regiment. Allcorn was arrested and tried for mutiny on November 14, 1813, for purportedly threatening to lead his men home if an officer under his command was granted a furlough. The court acquitted him and rebuked the charge.

5. Martin contended that there was no mutiny and that his men had never deserted or disobeyed, but returned to Tennessee "under a regular order" from AJ (*Self Vindication*, p. 40). On December 13 AJ ordered Brigadier General William Hall (1775–1856) to march the brigade back to Tennessee. Permission for their discharge having arrived from Governor Blount, Hall dismissed the brigade at Fayetteville on December 25.

6. Captain Thomas Williamson (1767–1825) commanded a company in Martin's regiment. AJ had his first sergeant, Andrew Baldridge, arrested on December 9, the day that, according to AJ, Hall told him the brigade was in a state of mutiny.

7. Countering AJ's contention that Williamson had "remained firm at his post, and would not return with the troops when they retrograded," Martin in his pamphlet said that Williamson "did return with the troops, and with the rest was dismissed at Fayetteville" (*Self Vindication*, p. 40). On December 13, before dispatching the brigade, AJ had addressed the troops and appealed to them to stay on. Only Williamson among the officers stepped forward. On December 17 AJ ordered him back to Nashville on recruiting duty. He was promoted to major in January 1814 and later to colonel.

8. When Armstrong in February 1813 ordered AJ's troops "dismissed from public service," he also notified Major General James Wilkinson (1757–1825), commanding at New Orleans, that they were "discharged from further service" (*Jackson Papers*, 2:361, 394). Martin invoked the latter notice, which AJ had seen, to prove AJ knew the brigade had been "completely discharged" and "completely and fully absolved" from their engagement (*Self Vindication*, p. 44).

Calendar, 1829

Jan 1	*To Francis Preston Blair, Preston Samuel Loughborough,*	3
	and Charles Scott Bibb.	
Jan 1	To [Thomas Miller]. Abstract, *Richmond Enquirer,* Jan 29	
	(mAJs). Declines invitation to visit Virginia legislature.	
Jan 1	From Henry Conwell. ALS, THer (12-0423). Charleston *United*	
	States Catholic Miscellany, Jan 16, 1830; *Niles,* Feb 27, 1830.	
	Congratulates AJ on his election.	
[cJan 1]	From Mary Middleton Rutledge Fogg. ANS, THer (12-0426).	
	Sends condolences on Rachel's death and a copy of James	
	Abercrombie's *The Mourner Comforted.*	
Jan 1	From David Bailie Warden. ALS, DNA-RG 59 (M639-25).	
	Complains of his unjust removal as consul at Paris in 1814	
	and solicits reappointment.	
Jan 2	*Bill of sale of slaves from James Rucker Donelson.*	4
Jan 2	Receipt from Thomas Ivey for wages as overseer in 1828.	
	DS by Ivey and William Donelson, DLC (36).	
Jan 3	To Calvin Blythe et al. Printed, Harrisburg *Pennsylvania*	
	Reporter, and Democratic Herald, Jan 27 (mAJs). Declines	
	invitation to visit Harrisburg.	
Jan 3	To Robert Breckinridge et al. Printed, *Louisville Public*	
	Advertiser, Jan 14; *Niles,* Jan 31 (mAJs; 12-0430). Declines a	
	specific engagement, but intends to pass through Louisville on	
	the way to Washington.	
Jan 3	*To Katherine Duane Morgan.*	5
Jan 3	From Auguste Genevieve Valentin Davezac. Extract, American	
	Art Association Sale, 1926 (12-0431). Offers condolences on	
	Rachel's death.	
Jan 3	From Samuel Herrick et al. LS, TNJ (12-0432). Hail AJ's	
	election and invite him to Zanesville.	
Jan 3	*From Edward Livingston.*	5
Jan 4	*To James Ronaldson.*	6
Jan 5	*To William Polk.*	7
Jan 5	To Guilford D. Young. LS, NN (12-0451). Encourages Young's	
	claim against Mexico on account of his deceased father Guilford	
	Dudley Young.	
Jan 5	From Peter Johnston. Printed, *Richmond Enquirer,* Jan 20	
	(12-0445). Extends condolences of a meeting of Abingdon, Va.,	
	citizens on Rachel's death.	
Jan 5	From Sarah Buchanan Campbell Preston. Printed, *Richmond*	

	Enquirer, Jan 17 (mAJs; 12-0450). Offers condolences of Abingdon, Va., ladies on Rachel's death.	
Jan 5	*Inventory of Hermitage slaves and property.*	8
Jan 5	Receipt from Hardy Murfree Cryer for Sir William's stud fees. ADS, DLC (36).	
Jan 6	From Tunstall Quarles. ALS, DNA-RG 59 (M639-22). Recommends Elisha Smith for secretary of proposed Huron Territory.	
Jan 6	Memorandum of settlement of blacksmith accounts with James T. Carruth. DS in AJ's hand, DLC (36).	
Jan 6	Receipt from Thomas Ivey for payments to seamstress Nancy Ivey. DS, DLC (36).	
Jan 6	Receipt from Miles Blythe McCorkle for payment of medical bills. DS in AJ's hand, DLC (36).	
Jan 6	Supplemental inventory of William Donelson's (1758–1820) estate, signed by executors Jacob D. Donelson, AJ, and John Donelson (1755–1830). Copy, TNDa (mAJs).	
Jan 7	From Samuel Ramsay et al. Printed, *Cincinnati Advertiser,* Jan 14 (mAJs; 12-0453). Offer condolences on Rachel's death.	
Jan 8	To Worden Pope et al. Printed, *Louisville Public Advertiser,* Jan 21 (mAJs). Thanks Louisville citizens for condolences on Rachel's death.	
Jan 8	From Caleb Stark. Copy in Isaac Hill's hand, DLC (36). Introduces Hill and recommends him for office.	
Jan 8	From Tammany Hall. Printed, DLC (36). Toasts at celebratory Jan 8 dinner.	
Jan 9	To James Ruple, John Grayson, and William Hunter. Typed copy, DLC (12-0454). Acknowledges invitation and expects to pass through Washington, Pa.	
Jan 9	From Benjamin Franklin Currey to William Berkeley Lewis or AJ. DS, DLC (36). Requests payment to John Cain for a horse purchased for AJ from William C. Smartt. Receipted Jan 16.	
Jan 11	Receipt from William Donelson for purchase of a horse. DS in AJ's hand, DLC (36).	
Jan 11	George G. Barrell to Samuel B. Barrell. ALS, DNA-RG 59 (M639-2). Asks not to be removed as consul at Malaga, Spain. Endorsed by AJ.	
Jan 12	From Edward Condict et al. DS, DNA-RG 59 (M639-6). New Jersey legislators recommend Zephaniah Drake for marshal.	
Jan 12	From Robert Morrison et al. LS, DNA-RG 59 (M639-2). Recommend John J. Crittenden and William T. Barry for the cabinet.	
Jan 12	From New York City Common Council. Printed, *US Telegraph,* Jan 16 (12-0455). Offer condolences on Rachel's death.	
Jan 12	*From Benjamin Pierce.*	11
Jan 12	From William B. Speers. ALS, DNA-RG 94 (M688-61). Seeks appointment to West Point.	
Jan 13	From Ethan Allen Brown. ALS, DNA-RG 59 (M639-25). Recommends Joseph Watson for governor of proposed Huron Territory.	

Jan 15	From Edward Daniel et al. DS, DNA-RG 59 (12-1230). Urge the release of Martin H. W. Mahon, imprisoned in Nashville for stealing a lottery ticket from the mail.	
Jan 15	From Calvin Jones. ALS, DLC (36). *North Carolina Historical Review* 14 (Oct 1937): 365–66. Offers condolences on Rachel's death.	
Jan 16	From Thomas Mather et al. DS, DNA-RG 59 (M639-13). Illinois legislators recommend Singleton H. Kimmel for office.	
Jan 16	Charles Chitty, Jacques LaFosse, and P. Gondree to Edward Livingston. DS, DNA-RG 59 (12-1039). Request pardons for piracy. Endorsed by AJ.	
Jan 17	*Receipts from Ralph Eleazar Whitesides Earl and George Ament.*	12
Jan 17	*To John Coffee.*	12
Jan 17	*To Mary Middleton Rutledge Fogg.*	14
Jan 19	From James Gordon. ALS, DNA-RG 59 (M639-6). Recommends John M. Davis for marshal in Pennsylvania.	
Jan 19	From Daniel Sturgeon et al. Printed, Harrisburg *Pennsylvania Reporter, and Democratic Herald,* Jan 20 (mAJs). Pennsylvania legislators offer condolences on Rachel's death.	
Jan 19	*Contract with Graves W. Steele.*	15
Jan 20	AJ's resignation in Davidson County Court as guardian of Andrew J. Donelson (1815–61), son of William and Charity. Abstract, TNDa (12-0466).	
Jan 21	*From Charles Coffin.*	16
Jan 21	From [John Pine Decatur]. AL, TU (mAJs). Offers condolences on Rachel's death.	
Jan 21	John Coffee memorandum of AJ's accounts as guardian of Andrew Jackson Hutchings. DS, THi (12-0468). Runs to Apr 8, 1831.	
Jan 22	From Charles John, King of Sweden. Copy, DNA-RG 59 (M60-2). Announces the birth of a grandson.	
Jan 22	From Ezra Child et al. DS, DNA-RG 59 (M639-13). Indiana legislators recommend George L. Kinnard for marshal.	
Jan 22	From Timothy Gard et al. Copy, DNA-RG 46 (12-0473). Illinois legislators recommend Samuel McRoberts for office.	
Jan 22	From John Telemachus Johnson, Thomas Marshall et al. LS, DNA-RG 59 (M639-18). Kentucky legislators recommend John Pope for attorney general.	
Jan 22	From Hugh McPheeters et al. DS, DNA-RG 59 (M639-15). Indiana legislators recommend William Marshall for marshal.	
Jan 22	From James Brown Ray. LS, DNA-RG 59 (M639-13). Recommends George L. Kinnard for marshal in Indiana.	
Jan 24	From William McBride. ALS, DNA-RG 59 (M639-15). Asks to be appointed marshal in Kentucky.	
Jan 24	From John L. Woolf et al. DS, DNA-RG 59 (M639-12). Recommend Charles J. Jack for marshal in Pennsylvania.	
Jan 24	Samuel McRoberts to Andrew Jackson Donelson. ALS, DNA-RG 59 (M639-26). Recommends Emanuel J. West for office.	

Jan 25   From James A. Swaney. ALS, DNA-RG 59 (M639-23). Requests
                a diplomatic post.
Jan 26   *From Thomas Gillespie.*   18
Jan 26   From James G. Hardy et al. DS, DNA-RG 59 (M639-21).
                Kentucky legislators recommend Lewis Sanders, Jr., for marshal.
Jan 27   *From Ingoldsby Work Crawford.*   19
Jan 27   From Auguste Genevieve Valentin Davezac. ALS and LS (dated
                Jan 28), DNA-RG 59 (M639-4). Recommends Henry Carleton
                for district judge in Louisiana.
Jan 28   *From Ezra Stiles Ely.*   20
Jan 28   *Resolutions of the Louisiana legislature.*   22
Jan 28   From Nathan Reid, Jr. ALS, DNA-RG 59 (M639-25).
                Recommends Giles Ward for office in proposed Huron Territory.
Jan 28   From Bela P. Spalding. ALS, DNA-RG 59 (M639-26).
                Recommends Joel W. White for marshal in Connecticut.
Jan 29   From Caleb Atwater. ALS, DLC (72). Laments Rachel's death
                and asks to be her biographer.
Jan 29   From Charles Harryman. ALS, DLC (36). Reports Indian
                depredations on the Santa Fe trail and requests an Army escort.
Jan 29   From Andrew Thompson Judson. ALS, DNA-RG 59 (M639-
                26). Recommends Joel W. White for marshal in Connecticut.
Jan 29   *From Joseph Saul.*   23
Jan 30   From James M. Bradford, from Robert Haile, and from James J.
                Weems. ALSs, DNA-RG 59 (M639-21). Recommend Lafayette
                Saunders for district attorney in Louisiana.
Jan 30   From Lafayette Saunders. ALS, DNA-RG 59 (M639-21). Asks
                to be appointed district attorney in Louisiana.
Jan 31   From Alexander Barrow. ALS, DNA-RG 59 (M639-21).
                Recommends Lafayette Saunders for district attorney in
                Louisiana.
Jan   From Samuel Judah et al. DS, THi (12-0416). Indiana legislators
                recommend Israel T. Canby for office.
[Jan]   From John Taliaferro McKinney et al. DS, DNA-RG 59 (M639-
                15). Indiana legislators recommend Abner McCarty for marshal.
[Jan]   From Arthur St. Clair et al. DS, DNA-RG 107 (12-0419).
                Indiana legislators recommend Jonathan McCarty for
                Cumberland Road superintendent.
[Jan]   AJ memorandum of receipts from 1828 and Jan 1829.
                AN, DLC (12-0415).
[Jan-Feb]   *From Thomas Patrick Moore et al.*   25
Feb 1   *From Thomas Marshall.*   28
Feb 2   From Ezra Stiles Ely. ALS, DNA-RG 59 (M639-1).
                Introduces and commends James Akin.
Feb 2   From John W. Rathbun. LS, DNA-RG 59 (M639-19).
                Solicits an office.
Feb 3   From John L. Allen. ALS, DNA-RG 59 (M639-13).
                Recommends George L. Kinnard for marshal in Indiana.
Feb 3   From Jeremiah Chamberlain. ALS, DNA-RG 59 (M639-21).
                Recommends Lafayette Saunders for district attorney in
                Louisiana.

Feb 11   From Reasin Beall and John Thomson. LS, DNA-RG 59 (M639-17). Recommend John Patterson for marshal in Ohio.

Feb 11   From Humphrey Howe Leavitt et al. LS, DNA-RG 59 (M639-10). Ohio legislators recommend John Hamm for chargé d'affaires or consul.

Feb 11   James P. Turner to George Graham. ALS, DNA-RG 49 (M1329-4). Asks that AJ confirm his appointment of William Brown as principal deputy surveyor for the St. Helena, La., land district. AJ approves Apr 18.

Feb 12   To Edward George Washington Butler. LS, NNPM (mAJs). Declines an invitation to visit.

Feb 12   From David Daggett. ALS copy, CtY (12-0506). Recommends Simeon Baldwin for customs collector at New Haven.

Feb 12   From Joseph Hiester. ALS, PHi (12-0508). Recommends John M. Taylor of Philadelphia for office.

Feb 12   From Sebastian Hiriart. ALS, DNA-RG 59 (M639-4). Recommends Henry Carleton for district judge in Louisiana and Henry D. Peire for New Orleans postmaster.

Feb 12   From Samuel Houston. ALS, DNA-RG 59 (M639-18). Encloses Isaac T. Preston's application for district attorney in Louisiana, Jan 21, and William C. Bradley's letter discussing Cabinet appointments, Jan 5 (M639-3).

Feb 12   From Jeremiah McLene et al. NS, DNA-RG 59 (M639-10). Recommend John Hamm for chargé d'affaires or consul.

Feb 12   Account with Tucker & Thompson for clothing. DS, DLC (72). Runs to Jun 5.

Feb 12   AJ bank books for personal account with the Bank of the United States. ADS running to Mar 31, 1833, and D running to Jun 4, 1833, DLC (78).

Feb 13   From John Carney. ALS, DNA-RG 59 (M639-25). Recommends continuing John Vawter as marshal in Indiana.

Feb 13   From Charles Carroll. ALS, DNA-RG 59 (M639-26). Recommends Charles H. W. Wharton for a State Department clerkship.

Feb 13   From Lawrence T. Dade et al. DS, DNA-RG 59 (M639-24). Virginia legislators recommend Robert T. Thompson for office.

Feb 13   From Isaac Trimble Preston. ALS, DNA-RG 59 (M639-18). Asks to be appointed district attorney in Louisiana and recommends Henry Carleton for judge.

Feb 14   To David Campbell (1779–1859). LS, NcD (12-0511). Thanks him for condolences on Rachel's death.

Feb 14   From Theodorick Bland. ALS, DLC (36). Introduces Nicholas Martin.

Feb 14   From Adolphus F. Hubbard. ALS, DNA-RG 59 (M639-11). Hails AJ's election and asks for office in proposed Huron Territory.

Feb 14   Lucien J. Feemster to Andrew Jackson Donelson. ALS, DNA-RG

Feb 23 Homer Johnson to Andrew Jackson Donelson. ALS, DNA-RG 59 (M639-16). Encloses Ratliff Boon et al. to AJ, Feb 5, recommending Thomas P. Moore.

Feb 23 James Taylor, Jr., to Andrew Jackson Donelson. ALS, DNA-RG 59 (M639-2). Recommends William T. Barry for Supreme Court justice.

Feb 24 From Alexander Cook. ALS, DNA-RG 107 (12-0576). Asks to be appointed Treasurer of the U.S.

Feb 24 From Joseph Desha. ALS, DNA-RG 59 (M639-2). Recommends Thomas R. Benning for secretary of proposed Huron Territory.

Feb 24 From Joseph Desha. ALS, DNA-RG 59 (M639-21). Recommends George Shannon for governor of proposed Huron Territory.

Feb 24 From Jonathan Harvey et al. LS, DNA-RG 46 (12-0579). Recommend Daniel D. Brodhead for navy agent at Boston.

Feb 24 From Charles J. Jack. ALS, DNA-RG 59 (M639-7). Recommends William J. Duane for district attorney in Pennsylvania.

Feb 24 From David Marchand. ALS, DNA-RG 59 (M639-1). Recommends John B. Alexander for district judge in Pennsylvania.

[Feb 24] From Thomas Pollock et al. NS, DNA-RG 59 (M639-1). Recommend John B. Alexander for district judge in Pennsylvania.

Feb 24 From Jonathan Robinson et al. DS, DNA-RG 59 (M639-4). Ask that Richard K. Call be appointed counsel in Florida land cases.

Feb 24 From Thomas Shepherd. ALS, DNA-RG 59 (M639-7). Recommends Andrew Dunlap for district attorney in Massachusetts.

Feb 24 From Joseph M. White. ALS, DNA-RG 59 (M639-4). Recommends Henry Carleton for district judge in Louisiana.

Feb 25 From Joseph Anderson. ALS, DNA-RG 107 (12-0581). Recommends William Booker for Cumberland Road superintendent in Ohio.

Feb 25 From William Ashmead. ADS, DNA-RG 46 (12-0585). Recommends Walter Colton for naval chaplain.

Feb 25 From Allan Ditchfield Campbell. ALS, DLC (36). Encloses Benjamin Bakewell to Campbell, Feb 25, denying that Henry Baldwin was lukewarm in support of AJ.

Feb 25 From Thomas Chilton et al. LS, DLC (mAJs). Recommend Thomas Griffith for Indian agent.

Feb 25 From Townshend Stuart Dade. ALS, DLC (36). Introduces Dr. Oldham.

Feb 25 From James C. Johnston. ALS, DNA-RG 59 (M639-18). Recommends Garrett E. Pendergrast for consul at Havana.

Feb 25 From James Noble. ALS, DNA-RG 59 (M639-10). Recommends Alexander Hamilton [Dill] for marshal in Indiana.

Feb 25 From James Noble. ALS, DNA-RG 59 (M639-13). Recommends George L. Kinnard for marshal in Indiana.

Feb 25	From James Noble. ALS, DNA-RG 59 (M639-22). Recommends Ross Smiley for marshal in Indiana.
Feb 25	*From Spencer Darwin Pettis.* 62
Feb 25	From Reuben Post. ALS, DNA-RG 46 (12-0587). Recommends Walter Colton for naval chaplain.
Feb 25	From John Rowan. ALS, DNA-RG 59 (M639-10). Recommends Samuel H. Harper for district judge in Louisiana.
Feb 25	From Lewis Sanders, Jr., Francis Preston Blair et al. DS, DNA-RG 59 (M639-2). Recommend William T. Barry for Supreme Court justice.
Feb 25	Joseph Ficklin to Andrew Jackson Donelson. ALS, DNA-RG 59 (M639-2). Recommends Thomas R. Benning for Huron Territory secretary and William T. Barry for the Supreme Court.
Feb 26	From Noyes Barber et al. LS, DNA-RG 46 (12-0590). Connecticut congressmen recommend Walter Colton for naval chaplain.
Feb 26	From A. Cunningham. ALS, DNA-RG 59 (M639-17). Recommends John Patterson for marshal in Ohio.
Feb 26	From James Fenner. ALS, DNA-RG 59 (M639-7). Recommends Andrew Dunlap for district attorney in Massachusetts.
[Feb 26]	From James Alexander Hamilton. Printed, Hamilton *Reminiscences,* p. 100 (mAJs). Suggests judicial appointments including William T. Barry for the Supreme Court.
Feb 26	From Samuel H. Harper. ALS, DNA-RG 59 (M639-10). Encloses letters (M531-4) to aid his candidacy for district judge in Louisiana.
Feb 26	From Jonathan Harvey. ALS, DNA-RG 46 (12-0591). Recommends John P. Decatur for customs collector at Portsmouth, N.H.
Feb 26	*From John Johnston.* 63
Feb 26	From the Marquis de Lafayette. Extract, John Spencer Bassett, *The Life of Andrew Jackson,* p. 407 (12-0597). Offers sympathy on Rachel's death.
Feb 26	From George Merkle. Printed, *New-York Evening Post,* Apr 2; *Niles,* Apr 11 (mAJs; 12-1099). Presents a gift of beef from the ox Grand Canal.
Feb 26	From Alden Partridge. ALS, DNA-RG 46 (12-0598). Recommends Walter Colton for naval chaplain.
Feb 26	From James Ronaldson. ADS, PHi (12-0601). Recommends John M. Taylor of Philadelphia.
Feb 26	From John Tipton. ALS, DNA-RG 59 (M639-15). Recommends William Marshall for marshal in Indiana.
Feb 26	From Garret Dorset Wall et al. DS, DNA-RG 59 (M873-19). Recommend Daniel C. Croxall for office.
Feb 26	*From William Whiteley et al.* 65
Feb 26	Check to Edward Livingston for $133.00. DS, DLC (36).
Feb 27	From William Taylor Barry. ALS, DNA-RG 59 (M639-11). Recommends Charlton Hunt for marshal in Kentucky.
Feb 27	From Christopher Dudley, Jr., et al. Printed, Raleigh *Star and North Carolina State Gazette,* Jun 4 (mAJs). New Hanover

County, N.C., Jackson Association congratulates AJ on his election.

Feb 27   From Martin Gordon, John Nicholson, and Samuel H. Harper. Copy, DCU (mAJs). Recommend Jehiel Brooks for Indian agent at Red River.

Feb 27   From William Hammond Marriott. ALS, DNA-RG 59 (M639-4). Forwards William Whiteley et al. to AJ, Feb 26, recommending Dabney S. Carr.

Feb 27   From Epaphras Porter et al. DS, DNA-RG 59 (M179-67). Recommend Asa Child for district attorney in Connecticut and denounce Adams appointee Nathan Smith.

Feb 27   From Arthur H. Snowden. ALS, DNA-RG 59 (M639-3). Asks that Sidney Breese not be removed as district attorney in Illinois.

Feb 27   From Martin Van Buren. Extract, Hamilton *Reminiscences,* pp. 102–3 (12-0602). Asks to remain in Albany until April and suggests James A. Hamilton for interim secretary.

Feb 28   *From Caleb Atwater.*   67

Feb 28   From John Chandler. ALS, DNA-RG 46 (12-0603). Recommends Daniel D. Brodhead for navy agent at Boston.

Feb 28   From George Graham. LC, DNA-RG 49 (M25-23). Encloses recommendations for John C. Scott.

Feb 28   From William Hendricks. ALS, DNA-RG 59 (M639-13). Encloses recommendations for George L. Kinnard for marshal in Indiana.

Feb 28   From William Hendricks. ALS, DNA-RG 59 (M639-15). Encloses and seconds recommendations for William Marshall for marshal in Indiana.

Feb 28   From William Hendricks. ALS, DNA-RG 59 (M639-25). Encloses and seconds recommendations to reappoint incumbent Indiana marshal John Vawter.

Feb 28   From Thomas Kennedy. ALS, DNA-RG 59 (M639-13). Asks to be appointed dispatch bearer to Europe.

Feb 28   From William Cabell Rives. ALS, DNA-RG 46 (12-0606). Recommends George Vashon for office.

Feb 28   From Lemuel Sawyer. ALS, DNA-RG 59 (M639-21). Recommends his brother Matthias E. Sawyer for superintendent of the Patent Office.

Feb 28   *From Stephen Simpson.*   69

[Feb]   From George Washington Campbell et al. DS, DNA-RG 59 (12-1246). Urge the release of Nashville prisoner Martin H. W. Mahon.

[Feb]   From Samuel Fulton et al. LS, DNA-RG 59 (M639-16). Kentucky legislators recommend Thomas P. Moore for a Latin American mission.

Feb   From Henry Horn et al. DS, DNA-RG 59 (M639-18). Recommend Zalegman Phillips for office.

[Feb]   From Preston Samuel Loughborough. ANS, DNA-RG 59 (M639-2). Recommends George M. Bibb or William T. Barry for Supreme Court justice.

[Feb]   From Alexander McEwen. DS with ANSs by Samuel McKean and John Chandler, DNA-RG 107 (12-0478). Asks to be appointed Cumberland Road superintendent.

[Feb] From N. F. Slaughter. ALS, DNA-RG 59 (M639-21). Recommends Lafayette Saunders for district attorney in Louisiana.

Feb From Oliver Hampton Smith. ALS, DNA-RG 59 (M639-6). Recommends Alexander H. Dill for marshal in Indiana.

Feb From Oliver Hampton Smith. ALS, DNA-RG 59 (M639-15). Recommends Abner McCarty as second choice for marshal in Indiana.

Feb From Jonas Stanbery et al. NS, DNA-RG 59 (M639-10). Recommend John Hamm for chargé d'affaires or consul.

[Feb] From Samuel Sullivan et al. DS, DNA-RG 59 (M639-11). Recommend Samuel Herrick for district attorney in Ohio.

Feb From John Tappan et al. DS and copy, DNA-RG 59 (M639-8). Recommend Stephen Fessenden for consul at Liverpool.

[Feb] *Memorandum on administration policy.* 69

[cMar 1] From Thomas Patrick Moore et al. DS, DNA-RG 59 (M639-20). Kentucky congressmen recommend Atkinson H. Rowan for secretary of legation.

Mar 1 From James McPherson Russell et al. DS, DNA-RG 59 (M639-14). Recommend John Lyon for district judge in Pennsylvania.

[cMar 1] From Andrew Stevenson et al. DS, DNA-RG 59 (M639-24). Virginia congressmen recommend Robert T. Thompson for office.

[cMar 1] From Jacob Barge Weidman et al. DS, DNA-RG 59 (M639-14). Recommend John Lyon for district judge in Pennsylvania.

Mar 1 Alexander Scott to Andrew Jackson Donelson. ALS, DLC (36). Requests the return of letters from James Monroe and William Wirt to John C. Calhoun, recently enclosed to AJ.

Mar 2 To John Caldwell Calhoun. ALS, DNA-RG 46 (12-0817); LC, DLC (60). Richardson, 2:436; *Calhoun Papers*, 10:562. Proposes inaugural arrangements to the Senate.

Mar 2 *To John Marshall.* 72

Mar 2 From Walter Colton. ALS, DNA-RG 46 (12-0820). Requests a naval chaplaincy.

Mar 2 From William Finley. ALS, DNA-RG 59 (M639-9). Hails AJ's election and recommends John Grayson for postmaster and John M. Davis for marshal in Pennsylvania.

Mar 2 From Thomas Hamilton. ALS, DNA-RG 59 (M639-10). Asks to be appointed district attorney in Pennsylvania.

Mar 2 From Isaac Hill. ALS, DNA-RG 46 (12-0822). Recommends John P. Decatur for customs collector.

Mar 2 From Thomas Kennedy. ALS, DNA-RG 59 (M639-22). Recommends Samuel Smith for minister to Britain.

Mar 2 From Isaac Mills. ALS, DNA-RG 59 (M639-16). Asks to be appointed marshal in Ohio.

Mar 2 From James Noble. ALS, DNA-RG 59 (M639-15). Recommends William Marshall for marshal in Indiana.

Mar 2   From Robert Purdy. ALS, DNA-RG 59 (M639-15).
               Recommends his nephew John McElvain for marshal in Ohio.
Mar [2]   From James P. Stuart et al. DS, DNA-RG 59 (M639-10).
               Recommend Thomas Hamilton for district attorney in
               Pennsylvania.
Mar 2   From George Vashon. ALS, DNA-RG 46 (12-0824). Asks to be
               appointed auditor.
Mar 2   James Shannon to Andrew Jackson Donelson. ALS, DNA-RG
               59 (M639-11). Recommends Charlton Hunt for marshal in
               Kentucky.
Mar 3   From Nathaniel Herbert Claiborne. ALS, DNA-RG 59 (M639-
               25). Recommends Giles Ward for judge in proposed Huron
               Territory.
Mar 3   From Robert Desha. ALS, DNA-RG 59 (M639-18).
               Recommends James C. Pickett for secretary of legation.
Mar 3   From Richard Mentor Johnson. ANS, DNA-RG 59 (M639-10).
               Recommends John Hamm for a diplomatic post.
Mar 3   From William Russell. ALS, DNA-RG 59 (M639-4).
               Recommends John W. Campbell for district judge in Ohio.
Mar 3   From Charles Pendleton Tutt. ALS, DNA-RG 46 (12-0836).
               Asks to have letters recommending him for a clerkship deleted
               from his file.
[Mar 3]   From Thomas White et al. DS, DNA-RG 59 (M639-1).
               Recommend John B. Alexander for district judge in
               Pennsylvania.
[cMar 3]   From Lewis Williams et al. DS, DNA-RG 59 (M639-3).
               Recommend Hutchins G. Burton for governor of Arkansas
               Territory.
Mar 3   From Levi Woodbury. AN, DNA-RG 46 (12-0839).
               Recommends Daniel D. Brodhead.
Mar 3   Bill from Stephen R. Kean for servant's clothing. AD, DLC (72).
Mar 4   *From William Polk et al.*   72
Mar 4   *To William Polk et al.*   73
Mar 4   *Inaugural Address.*   74
Mar 4   To James Alexander Hamilton. LS, NN (12-0847); LC, DLC
               (60). Bassett, 4:13. Appoints him acting head of the State
               Department.
Mar 4   From John Strode Barbour, Andrew Stevenson, and William
               Cabell Rives. Copy, DNA-RG 59 (M639-24). Recommend
               William M. Thompson.
Mar 4   From Ezra Stiles Ely. ALS, DNA-RG 46 (12-0841).
               Recommends Walter Colton for naval chaplain.
Mar 4   From Nathaniel Garrow et al. DS, DNA-RG 59 (M639-23).
               Congressmen recommend John G. Stower for territorial judge.
Mar 4   From Henry Hosford Gurley. ALS, DNA-RG 59 (M639-18).
               Recommends Isaac T. Preston for district attorney in Louisiana.
Mar 4   From William Hendricks. AN, DNA-RG 59 (M639-25).
               Encloses a recommendation for Indiana marshal John Vawter.
Mar 4   From James Iredell. ALS, DNA-RG 59 (M639-3). Recommends
               Hutchins G. Burton for governor of Arkansas Territory.

[cMar 4]	From Charles J. Jack. ALS, DNA-RG 59 (M639-12). Asks to be appointed marshal in Pennsylvania.
Mar 4	From Richard Mentor Johnson. ALS, DNA-RG 107 (12-0849). Introduces the mother of dismissed War Department clerk William M. Stewart.
Mar 4	From Aaron Kerr et al. DS, DNA-RG 59 (M639-6). Pennsylvania legislators recommend John M. Davis for marshal.
Mar 4	From William Marshall et al. DS, DNA-RG 107 (12-0851). Recommend Jonathan McCarty for Cumberland Road superintendent in Indiana.
Mar 4	From Robert Lytle McHatton et al. DS, DNA-RG 59 (M639-23). Congressmen recommend John G. Stower for district attorney in Florida.
Mar 4	From William Mooney. ALS, DNA-RG 107 (12-0853). Asks for a clerkship.
Mar 4	From James Noble. ALS, DNA-RG 59 (M639-15). Recommends Abner McCarty for marshal in Indiana.
Mar 4	From Campbell Patrick White. Copy, DNA-RG 59 (M639-5). Recommends Jonathan I. Coddington for customs surveyor at New York.
Mar 4	*From Daniel W. Wright.* 79
Mar 5	From Stephen Barlow. ALS, DNA-RG 59 (M639-2). Asks to be appointed marshal in Pennsylvania.
Mar 5	From John Conrad. ALS, DNA-RG 59 (M639-13). Recommends Thomas Kittera for district attorney in Pennsylvania, and John Pemberton and Jacob Holgate for office.
Mar 5	From John M. Davis. ALS, DNA-RG 59 (M639-6). Forwards petitions for his appointment as marshal in Pennsylvania.
Mar 5	From Joseph Ficklin. ALS, DNA-RG 59 (M639-11). Recommends Charlton Hunt for marshal in Kentucky.
[cMar 5]	From Isaac Fisher et al. DS, DNA-RG 59 (M639-6). Recommend John M. Davis for marshal in Pennsylvania.
Mar 5	From George Graham. LC, DNA-RG 49 (M25-23). Advises on the appointment of a surveyor for the Virginia Military District in Ohio.
Mar 5	From James Alexander Hamilton. Printed, Hamilton *Reminiscences*, p. 114 (12-0855). Advises asking Senate consent to exchange ratifications of the commercial treaty with Prussia after the expired deadline.
Mar 5	From William Hendricks. ALS, DNA-RG 59 (M639-6). Endorses Alexander H. Dill for marshal in Indiana.
Mar 5	From William Hendricks. ALS, DNA-RG 59 (M639-15). Endorses Abner McCarty for marshal in Indiana.
Mar 5	From William Hendricks. ALS, DNA-RG 107 (12-0856). Recommends John Milroy for Cumberland Road superintendent in Indiana.
Mar 5	From William Hendricks. ALS, DNA-RG 59 (M639-22). Endorses Ross Smiley for marshal in Indiana.
Mar 5	From Benjamin Chew Howard. ALS, DNA-RG 59 (M639-15). Recommends James J. McLanahan for consul at Havana.

Mar 5	From Joshua Marriott. Printed, *US Telegraph*, Mar 6 (mAJs; 12-0858). Presents a hickory goblet.
Mar 5	From Charles Fenton Mercer. Copy, DNA-RG 59 (M639-24). Recommends William M. Thompson.
Mar 5	From James Noble. ALS, DNA-RG 59 (M639-6). Recommends Samuel Downing for marshal in Indiana.
Mar 5	From James Noble. ALS, DNA-RG 107 (12-0859). Urges AJ to appoint John Milroy Cumberland Road superintendent in Indiana.
Mar 5	From William Ramsey. ALS, DLC (12-0861). Recommends Russell Jarvis for naval officer at Boston.
Mar 5	From William Cabell Rives et al. LS, DNA-RG 59 (M639-16); Copy, DLC (mAJs). Recommend Thomas P. Moore for a Latin American mission.
Mar 5	*From Samuel Rogers.* 81
Mar 5	From Alexander Smyth. ALS, DNA-RG 59 (M639-22). Recommends Harold Smyth for secretary of legation or a chief clerkship.
Mar 5	Check to Richard Keith Call for $100. DS, DLC (36).
Mar 6	To the United States Senate. DS, DNA-RG 46 (12-0877); LC, DLC (60). Richardson, 2:439; *Senate Executive Proceedings*, 4:6. Withdraws John Quincy Adams's nominations to office not acted upon in the previous Congress.
Mar 6	To the United States Senate. DS, DNA-RG 46 (12-0870); LC, DLC (60). *Senate Executive Proceedings*, 4:6. Nominates Cabinet secretaries, judges, and district attorneys.
Mar 6	To the United States Senate. DS, DNA-RG 46 (12-0873); LC, DLC (60). Richardson, 2:439; *Senate Executive Proceedings*, 4:7. Asks Senate consent to exchange ratifications of the commercial treaty with Prussia after the expired deadline.
Mar 6	From John Anderson. ALS, DNA-RG 59 (M639-6). Recommends John Davis of Maine.
Mar 6	From William Burke. ALS, DNA-RG 59 (12-0864). Recommends James H. Looker and Sackett Reynolds for public printers in Cincinnati.
Mar 6	From Lewis Cass. ALS, DNA-RG 107 (M222-25). *TPUS*, 12:27–28. Recommends John R. Williams, Charles Larned, and John Stockton for Michigan militia generals.
Mar 6	From Nathaniel Pope Causin. ALS, DNA-RG 59 (M639-4). Asks to be appointed auditor.
Mar 6	From Richard Coulter. ALS, DNA-RG 59 (M639-14). Recommends John Lyon for district judge in Pennsylvania.
Mar 6	From John Fletcher. ALS, DNA-RG 59 (M639-6). Recommends John M. Davis for marshal in Pennsylvania.
Mar 6	From William Hendricks and James Noble. LS, DNA-RG 107 (12-0866). Recommend James Blake for Cumberland Road superintendent in Indiana.
Mar 6	From William Kinney et al. DS, DNA-RG 59 (M639-26). Recommend Emanuel J. West for a South American diplomatic post.

[cMar 6]	From Gawn Logan et al. DS, DNA-RG 59 (M639-6). Recommend John M. Davis for marshal in Pennsylvania.
Mar 6	From James J. McLanahan. ALS, DNA-RG 59 (M639-15). Asks to be appointed consul at Havana.
Mar 6	From Francis Barber Ogden. ALS, DNA-RG 59 (M639-17). Asks to be appointed consul at Liverpool.
Mar 6	*From John Ross et al.* 82
Mar 6	From Joseph W. Scott. ALS, DNA-RG 59 (M639-21). Asks to be appointed district attorney in New Jersey.
Mar 6	From Anthony Simmons. ALS, DNA-RG 59 (M639-11). Recommends Horatio Hubbell for consul at Algiers.
Mar 6	From Daniel Steenrod. ALS, DNA-RG 75 (M234-432). Recommends his son-in-law Hugh F. Feeny to supply Indian annuities in Indiana.
Mar 6	From John Peter Van Ness. ALS, DNA-RG 59 (M639-25). Recommends his brother Cornelius P. Van Ness for minister to the Netherlands.
Mar 6	Andrew Jackson Donelson to Samuel Delucenna Ingham and to Martin Van Buren. LC, DLC (60). Encloses Senate confirmation of their appointments to the Cabinet.
Mar 6	Account from William Langton to William Berkeley Lewis for White House kitchenware purchase and repairs. DS, DNA-RG 217 (M235-701). Runs to Mar 31.
Mar 7	From John Anderson. ALS, DNA-RG 46 (12-0879). Recommends John Chandler or David Henshaw for customs collector at Boston.
Mar 7	From Thomas Chilton. ALS, DNA-RG 59 (M639-6). Recommends John Daviess for marshal in Kentucky and William Douglass for Louisville postmaster.
Mar 7	From Susan Wheeler Decatur. ALS, DNA-RG 59 (M639-20). Recommends Navy clerk William G. Ridgely for higher office.
Mar 7	From Thomas Gohagan. ADS, DNA-RG 59 (12-1029). Requests a pardon for assault and battery.
Mar 7	From Martin Gordon, Samuel H. Harper, and John Nicholson. DS, DNA-RG 59 (M639-15). Recommend James J. McLanahan for consul at Havana.
Mar 7	From Martin Gordon et al. DS, DNA-RG 59 (M639-17). Recommend Francis B. Ogden for consul at Liverpool.
Mar 7	From Jacob C. Isacks. ALS, DNA-RG 59 (M639-13). Recommends Andrew Kinnard for secretary of legation.
Mar 7	*From Roley McIntosh et al.* 83
Mar 7	From John Nicholas. ALS, DNA-RG 59 (M639-17). Asks for an office.
[cMar 7]	From Joseph S. Riley et al. NS, THi (12-0885). Recommend John Shaw for commissary general of purchases.
[cMar 7]	From Thomas Russell et al. DS, THi (12-0882). Recommend John Shaw for commissary general of purchases.
Mar 7	From John Shaw. ALS, DNA-RG 107 (12-0884). Asks to be appointed commissary general of purchases.

[cMar 7]   From John Shaw. LS, THi (12-0885). Asks to be appointed
               commissary general of purchases.
Mar 7   From Stephen Simpson. ALS, DNA-RG 59 (M639-11).
               Recommends Horatio Hubbell for consul at Algiers.
Mar 7   From Samuel Smith. ALS, DNA-RG 107 (12-0887).
               Recommends Mr. Allison.
Mar 7   From Benjamin Taylor. ALS, DNA-RG 59 (M639-11).
               Recommends Charlton Hunt for marshal in Kentucky.
Mar 7   From Robert N. Verell. ALS, DNA-RG 59 (12-0889). Asks to be
               appointed public printer in North Carolina.
Mar 7   Henry Rozer Dulany to Andrew Jackson Donelson. ALS, DNA-
               RG 59 (M639-11). Recommends Alexander Hunter for marshal
               in the District of Columbia.
Mar 8   From William Montgomery Crane. ALS, DNA-RG 59 (M46-2).
               HRDoc 250, 22d Cong., 1st sess., Supplement p. 25 (Serial
               221). Reports David Offley's intent to break off deadlocked
               commercial negotiations with Turkey.
Mar 8   From Molton Cropper Rogers. ALS, DNA-RG 59 (M639-18).
               Recommends George B. Porter for customs collector in
               Philadelphia.
Mar 8   From Charles Pendleton Tutt. Copy, DNA-RG 59 (M639-24).
               Recommends William M. Thompson for a clerkship.
Mar 9   To the United States Senate. DS, DNA-RG 46 (12-0919); LC,
               DLC (60). *Senate Executive Proceedings*, 4:8. Nominates
               Cabinet secretaries.
Mar 9   To the United States Senate. DS, DNA-RG 46 (12-0917); LC
               (dated Mar 10), DLC (60). *Senate Executive Proceedings*, 4:8.
               Nominates territorial militia generals.
Mar 9   To the United States Senate. LC, DLC (60). *Senate Executive
               Proceedings*, 4:8. Nominates William T. Barry for postmaster
               general and John Pope for governor of Arkansas Territory.
Mar 9   To the United States Senate. DS, DNA-RG 46 (12-0921); LC,
               DLC (60). *Senate Executive Proceedings*, 4:9. Nominates a
               marshal and land office officials.
Mar 9   From Richard Alsop et al. DS, DNA-RG 59 (M639-17).
               Recommend Francis B. Ogden for consul at Liverpool.
[Mar 9]   From Gustavus Beall et al. DS, DNA-RG 77 (12-0893).
               Recommend David Shriver, Jr., for superintendent of
               Cumberland Road repairs.
Mar 9   From Thomas Holdsworth Blake. ALS, DNA-RG 107 (12-
               0897). Recommends James Blake for Cumberland Road
               superintendent in Indiana.
Mar 9   From Arthur Lee Campbell. ALS, DNA-RG 59 (M639-4). Asks
               to be appointed marshal in Kentucky and for his sons' admission
               to West Point to reward his father's Revolutionary service.
Mar 9   From John Davis. ALS, DNA-RG 107 (12-0899). Requests an
               office.
Mar 9   From Daniel Pickering Drown et al. Copy, DNA-RG 46 (mAJs).
               Urge AJ not to appoint John P. Decatur customs collector at
               Portsmouth, N.H.

Mar 9	From Joseph Duncan. ALS, DNA-RG 59 (M639-15). Recommends James J. McLanahan for consul at Havana.
Mar 9	From George Graham. LS, DNA-RG 49 (12-0901); LC, DNA-RG 49 (M25-23). *TPUS*, 24:161. Recommends engaging extra counsel to procure Spanish documents concerning the Forbes and Arredondo Florida land claims.
Mar 9	From Duff Green. ALS, DNA-RG 59 (M639-15). Recommends Jeremiah Matlock for office.
Mar 9	*From James Alexander Hamilton.* 86
Mar 9	From James Alexander Hamilton. Printed, Hamilton *Reminiscences,* pp. 117–18 (12-0909). Draft of a presidential message (not sent) to the Senate submitting the Northeast boundary arbitration proceedings.
Mar 9	From James Alexander Hamilton. Printed, Hamilton *Reminiscences,* p. 118 (12-0911). Reports that the 1828 boundary treaty with Mexico must be resubmitted to the Senate, as previous ratifications were not exchanged within the agreed time.
Mar 9	*From Richard Mentor Johnson.* 87
Mar 9	From Elias Kent Kane, John McLean (Ill.), and Joseph Duncan. LS, DNA-RG 59 (M639-26). Recommend Emanuel J. West for a South American diplomatic post.
Mar 9	From Edward Livingston. ALS, DNA-RG 59 (M639-17). Recommends Francis B. Ogden for consul at Liverpool.
Mar 9	From John McLean. ALS, DNA-RG 59 (12-0912). Accepts appointment to the Supreme Court and resigns as postmaster general.
Mar 9	From John McLean (Ill.). ALS, DNA-RG 59 (M639-13). Recommends Singleton H. Kimmel for office.
Mar 9	From James Wheelock Ripley. ALS, DNA-RG 46 (12-0914). Recommends Daniel D. Brodhead for navy agent at Boston.
Mar 9	From James Ronaldson. ALS, DNA-RG 59 (M639-7). Recommends William J. Duane for district attorney in Pennsylvania.
Mar 9	From Jared I. Sample. ALS, DNA-RG 59 (M639-21). Asks to be appointed marshal in Alabama.
Mar 9	From Robert Smith. ALS, DNA-RG 59 (M639-22). Discusses appointments, the tariff, harbor defenses, and his claims against various persons. (Endorsed "a madman.")
[Mar 9]	From William Thomson et al. DS, DNA-RG 59 (M639-19). Recommend Almon H. Read for marshal in Pennsylvania.
Mar 9	John Sommerville to Andrew Jackson Donelson. ALS, DNA-RG 59 (M639-22). Asks him to introduce Maxwell Sommerville to AJ.
Mar 10	To the United States Senate. DS, DNA-RG 46 (12-0931). *Senate Executive Proceedings,* 4:10–12. Nominates customs officials.
Mar 10	To the United States Senate. DS, DNA-RG 46 (12-0934). *Senate Executive Proceedings,* 4:13. Nominates naval pursers.
Mar 10	*From John Brown.* 89
Mar 10	*From Mary Conner.* 90

Mar 10   From Richard Coulter. ALS, DNA-RG 59 (M639-12). Recommends Alexander Johnston for marshal in Pennsylvania.

Mar 10   From John Pine Decatur and Isaac Hill. DS, DNA-RG 59 (M639-9). Recommend Charles B. Goodrich for New Hampshire district attorney in place of Daniel M. Christie.

Mar 10   From William Dewees. ALS, DNA-RG 107 (12-0924). Encloses recommendations for George W. Dewees for Cumberland Road superintendent in Indiana.

Mar 10   From John Henry Eaton. LC, DNA-RG 107 (M127-2). Submits Army promotions.

Mar 10   From Martin Gordon. ALS, DNA-RG 59 (M639-14). Recommends Jasper Lynch for secretary of legation.

Mar 10   From Henry Jackson. ALS, DNA-RG 59 (M639-12). Seeks a State Department job.

Mar 10   From S. Jones. ALS, DNA-RG 59 (M639-12). Requests a diplomatic post.

[cMar 10]   From Rebecca Clifford Pemberton. ALS copy, PHi (12-0928). Extends an invitation to AJ Jr.

Mar 10   From John Pemberton. ALS copy, PHi (12-0926). Encloses his wife's letter.

Mar 10   From James Chamberlayne Pickett. ALS, DNA-RG 59 (M639-18). Withdraws his application for secretary of legation if it will compete with Atkinson H. Rowan's.

Mar 10   From John Robb. ALS, DNA-RG 59 (M639-20). Asks for an office.

Mar 10   From John Taliaferro. ALS, DNA-RG 59 (12-0929). Requests clemency, refused by President Adams, for mail carrier Leland B. Rose, convicted of theft.

Mar 10   From Jesse Wilkinson. LS, DNA-RG 45 (M625-405). Asks to be restored to his proper seniority among naval officers.

Mar 10   From John S. Williams. ALS, DNA-RG 107 (12-0937). Asks to be appointed Cumberland Road superintendent in Ohio despite his support for Adams.

Mar 10   Check to Andrew Jackson, Jr., for $500. DS, DLC (36).

Mar 11   To John Henry Eaton. LS, DNA-RG 153 (12-0943). Approves the court-martial of Army lieutenant George W. Mountz.

Mar 11   To the United States Senate. DS, DNA-RG 46 (12-0948). *Senate Executive Proceedings,* 4:12–13. Nominates naval officers for promotion.

Mar 11   From John Henry Eaton. LS, DNA-RG 46; LC, DNA-RG 94 (12-0941). LC, DNA-RG 107 (M127-2). *Senate Executive Proceedings,* 4:13. Submits Army nominations.

Mar 11   To the United States Senate. DS, DNA-RG 46; LC, DNA-RG 94 (12-0951). Richardson, 2:439; *Senate Executive Proceedings,* 4:13–14. Criticizes brevet promotion for faithful service and submits Army nominations.

Mar 11   To the United States Senate. DS, DNA-RG 46 (12-0957). *Senate Executive Proceedings,* 4:14–15. Nominates Army officers for brevet rank.

Mar 11   To the United States Senate. DS, DNA-RG 46 (12-0963). *Senate*

Executive Proceedings, 4:15–16. Nominates Army officers for brevet rank.

Mar 11   From William Campbell. ALS, DNA-RG 107 (12-0939). Asks to be appointed lead mine agent at Galena, Ill.

Mar 11   From Susan Wheeler Decatur. ALS, M & S Rare Books (mAJs). Laments her straitened circumstances and presses her plea for William G. Ridgely's promotion.

Mar 11   *From John Forsyth.*   91

Mar 11   From John Miles. ALS, DNA-RG 59 (M639-16). Asks to be appointed district attorney in Pennsylvania.

Mar 11   *From Katherine Duane Morgan.*   92

Mar 11   *From John Rowan.*   92

Mar 11   From Peter S. Townsend. ALS, DNA-RG 59 (M639-24). Requests a diplomatic appointment.

Mar 11   From John Tyler. ALS, DNA-RG 59 (M639-8). Recommends John Floyd for minister to Mexico or Brazil.

Mar 11   From Garret Dorset Wall. ALS, DNA-RG 59 (M873 19). Recommends Daniel C. Croxall for consul at Algiers.

Mar 11   Henry Lee to Andrew Jackson Donelson or William Berkeley Lewis. Copies, DNA-RG 59 (M639-20). Introduces and recommends Jeremy Robinson for office.

Mar 12   From AJ et al. to John Gadsby. Printed, *Nat. Intelligencer,* Apr 8 (12-0974). Guests of the National Hotel compliment its owner.

Mar 12   To Littleton Waller Tazewell. AN, NjMoHP (12-0982). Asks to see him.

Mar 12   To the United States Senate. Printed, *Senate Executive Proceedings,* 4:18–19 (12-0994). Nominates Army officers for brevet rank.

Mar 12   To the United States Senate. DS, DNA-RG 46 (12-0984). *Senate Executive Proceedings,* 4:19. Nominates a Navy commissioner and navy agents.

Mar 12   To the United States Senate. Printed, *Senate Executive Proceedings,* 4:20 (12-0993). Nominates Thomas P. Moore for minister to Colombia.

Mar 12   To the United States Senate. DS, DNA-RG 46 (12-0987). *Senate Executive Proceedings,* 4:20. Nominates Thomas Griffith for Indian agent and James Hampson for Cumberland Road superintendent in Ohio.

Mar 12   To the United States Senate. DS, DNA-RG 46 (12-0989). *Senate Executive Proceedings,* 4:20. Nominates naval officers for promotion.

Mar 12   To the United States Senate. DS, DNA-RG 46 (12-0991). *Senate Executive Proceedings,* 4:20. Nominates Allen Latham for surveyor of the Virginia Military District in Ohio.

Mar 12   To the United States Senate. Printed, *Senate Executive Proceedings,* 4:22 (12-0995). Nominates Myles Elliott, Jr., for customs surveyor at Hertford, N.C.

Mar 12   To Unknown. LS, MLexM (12-0996). Introduces Mr. Janes, a young lawyer from Virginia.

[Mar 12]   From Stephen Collins et al. DS, DNA-RG 59 (M639-5).
Recommend William A. Collins for messenger.

Mar 12   From Samuel Dexter et al. LS, DLC (12-0971). Recommend
Benjamin H. Norton for office.

[cMar 12]   From Davis Dimock et al. DS, DNA-RG 59 (M639-19).
Recommend Nathan Raynor for consul.

Mar 12   From Charles Edward Dudley. ALS, DNA-RG 59 (M639-13).
Recommends Elias Kane for consul at Liverpool.

Mar 12   From William Duncan. ALS, DNA-RG 59 (M639-11).
Recommends Horatio Hubbell for consul at Algiers.

Mar 12   From John Floyd. ALS, DNA-RG 59 (M639-24). Recommends
Robert T. Thompson for office.

Mar 12   From John Floyd. ALS, DNA-RG 46 (12-0972). Recommends
Thomas L. Smith for second auditor of the Treasury.

Mar 12   From Edmund Pendleton Gaines. ALS, DNA-RG 107 (M222-
25). Recommends George Vashon for naval purser.

Mar 12   From James Linsey. ALS, DLC (36). Relates his travails and
religious persecutions and requests an office.

Mar 12   From Benjamin Pendleton. ADS, DNA-RG 45 (M124-117).
Requests payment for losses and expenses in selling his brig
Seraph to the Navy for the South Seas exploring expedition.

Mar 12   From Samuel Chester Reid. ALS, DNA-RG 59 (M639-19). Asks
to be appointed marshal or customs surveyor in New York.

Mar 12   From James Wheelock Ripley. ALS, DNA-RG 59 (M639-15).
Recommends John D. McCrate for secretary of legation.

Mar 12   From William Robinson. ALS, DNA-RG 59 (M639-20).
Recommends William R. Rose for a job as librarian.

Mar 12   From John Rowan. ALS, DNA-RG 59 (M639-16). Recommends
Thomas B. Monroe for district attorney in Kentucky.

Mar 12   From Samuel Smith. AL Draft, DLC (mALs). Clarifies his letter
of Feb 16 recommending Christopher Hughes.

Mar 12   From John M. Snowden. ALS, DNA-RG 59 (12-0978). Asks to
be appointed public printer at Pittsburgh and for a clerkship for
his son William.

Mar 12   From John D. Woolverton et al. LS, DNA-RG 59 (M639-26).
Recommend Emanuel J. West for chargé d'affaires in South
America.

Mar 12   Ratification of the May 1, 1828, commercial treaty with Prussia.
DS, DNA-RG 11 (12-0975).

Mar 13   To the United States Senate. DS, DNA-RG 46 (12-1003). *Senate
Executive Proceedings*, 4:22. Nominates a Marine lieutenant.

Mar 13   *From James Akin.*   94

[cMar 13]   From William Armstrong. Copy, DNA-RG 59 (M639-20).
Recommends Jeremy Robinson for office.

Mar 13   From Jonathan Inslee Coddington. ALS copy, DNA-RG 59
(M639-5). Asks to be appointed customs surveyor at New York.

Mar 13   From Charles Kitchel Gardner. ANS, DNA-RG 59 (M639-22).
Attests to Thomas L. Smith's early support for AJ.

Mar 13   From Elijah Hall et al. DS, DNA-RG 59 (M639-4). Recommend
William Claggett for district attorney in New Hampshire.

Mar 17 From John Norvell. ALS, DNA-RG 59 (M639-19). Relates Joseph Ray's persecution by the Brazilian government and urges reinstating him as consul at Pernambuco.

Mar 17 From Ebenezer Smith Thomas. Printed, Thomas, *Reminiscences of the Last Sixty-Five Years,* 2:95–96 (mAJs). Requests government patronage for his Cincinnati *Commercial Daily Advertiser.*

Mar 18 From Isaac Dutton Barnard. ALS, DNA-RG 59 (M639-18). Recommends Augustus J. Pleasonton for secretary of legation in Colombia.

Mar 18 *From John Caldwell Calhoun.*   *100*

Mar 18 From Charles John, King of Sweden. Copy, DNA-RG 59 (M60-2). Announces the death of his aunt.

Mar 18 *From Ezra Stiles Ely.*   *101*

Mar 18 From Stephen Fessenden. ALS, DNA-RG 59 (M639-8). Asks to be appointed consul at Liverpool.

Mar 18 From John W. James, Nathaniel Greene, and Isaac Hill. DS, DLC (12-1033). Recommend Daniel D. Brodhead for navy agent at Boston in place of Richard D. Harris.

Mar 18 Statement by Charles Josephus Nourse on the disposition and yield of $100,000 invested in trust for the Senecas in 1797. ADS, DNA-RG 75 (M234-808).

Mar 18 From Philip Reed. ALS, DNA-RG 59 (M639-19). Asks to be appointed marshal in Maryland.

Mar 18 From James Ronaldson. ALS, DNA-RG 59 (M639-7). Recommends William J. Duane for district attorney in Pennsylvania and William B. Hunt for office.

[cMar 18] From John K. Simpson et al. Copies, DNA-RG 59 (M639-8). Recommend Stephen Fessenden for consul at Liverpool.

Mar 18 From Henry Sims. DS, DNA-RG 59 (12-1127). Seeks a pardon for larceny, as he has been punished by whipping and is imprisoned for inability to pay court costs.

Mar 18 From Albert Smith et al. DS, DNA-RG 59 (M639-15). Recommend John D. McCrate for secretary of legation.

Mar 18 From Samuel Swartwout. ALS, DNA-RG 59 (M639-5). Recommends Cadwallader D. Colden for district attorney in New York.

Mar 18 Pardon for Thomas Gohagan. Copy and LC, DNA-RG 59 (12-1027; T967-1).

Mar 18 Pardon for juvenile mail thief George Q. Patch. LC, DNA-RG 59 (T967-1).

Mar 18 Proclamation of a Dec 1828 commercial treaty with Brazil. DS, DNA-RG 11 (12-1024). *Niles,* Apr 11.

Mar 18 Check to Andrew Jackson Donelson for $750. DS, DLC (36).

Mar 18 Charles Stewart to John Branch. Printed extract with AJ endorsement, Swann Galleries catalog, Nov 6, 1986 (mAJs). Recommends Francis G. McCauley for naval purser.

Mar 19 To [Alvan Coe]. Copy, DLC (12-1050). Grants permission to establish a Presbyterian mission to the Chippewas.

Mar 19 *To John Coffee.*   *104*

Mar 19   To James Alexander Hamilton. LS, MHi (12-1056). Directs him to obtain Turkish negotiation documents and Seneca and Wyandot trust fund stock certificates from John Q. Adams.

Mar 19   To Richard Smith. DS (signature removed), DNA-RG 217 (12-1063). Power of attorney to BUS cashier to receive AJ's salary as president.

Mar 19   From John Branch. LC, DNA-RG 45 (M472-1). Submits naval commissions for signature.

Mar 19   From Dabney Smith Carr. ALS, DNA-RG 59 (M639-3). Recommends James M. Buchanan for secretary of legation.

Mar 19   From Betsey Hawley. ALS, DNA-RG 59 (T229-1). Complains that Franklin Litchfield, consul at Puerto Cabello, has obstructed her efforts to recover payment due her late brother Isaac P. Hawley from the Colombian government.

[Mar 19]   From Charles Scudder & Co. et al. DS and Copy, DNA-RG 59 (M639-8). Recommend Stephen Fessenden for consul at Liverpool.

Mar 19   From John Vining. ALS, DNA-RG 59 (M639-16). Recommends Benjamin T. Moore for marshal in Alabama.

Mar 19   Pardon for Charles Chitty, Jacques La Fosse, and P. Gondree. Copy and LC, DNA-RG 59 (12-1037; T967-1).

Mar 20   From John Branch. LC, DNA-RG 45 (M472-1). Submits officers' commissions for signature.

Mar 20   From Byrd Brandon and William Brandon. LS, DNA-RG 59 (M639-16). Recommend Benjamin T. Moore for marshal in Alabama.

Mar 20   From William Brown. ALS, DNA-RG 59 (M639-3). Recommends James M. Buchanan for office.

Mar 20   From James G. Carroll. ALS, DNA-RG 59 (M639-4). Asks to be appointed marshal in Alabama.

Mar 20   From William John Duane. ALS, DNA-RG 107 (12-1065). Recommends Charles J. Jack for marshal in Pennsylvania.

Mar 20   From Thomas J. Sumner. ALS, DNA-RG 59 (M639-16). Recommends Benjamin T. Moore for marshal in Alabama.

Mar 20   From Samuel Swartwout. ALS, DNA-RG 59 (M639-22). Recommends Thomas L. Smith.

Mar 20   *From Tuskeneah et al.*   *106*

Mar 20   From Peter Aaron Van Dorn. ALS, DNA-RG 59 (M639-25). Recommends Joseph W. E. Wallace for consul in Texas.

Mar 20   From Joseph Washington Elliot Wallace. ALS, DNA-RG 59 (M639-25). Asks to be appointed consul at San Antonio, Texas.

[Mar 20]   Andrew Jackson Donelson to Samuel Delucenna Ingham. LC, DLC (60). Transmits a Senate request for data on land granted to states, federal expenses within states, and value of exports.

Mar 20   Andrew Jackson Donelson to Martin Van Buren. LC, DLC (60). Transmits a Senate request for the 1817 journal of the Passamaquoddy Bay boundary commissioners.

Mar 21   From John Catron. ALS, DNA-RG 59 (M639-1). Recommends William T. Arnold for secretary of legation in Mexico or Colombia.

Mar 23	From William Ingalls. ALS, DNA-RG 59 (M639-1). Recommends Joseph H. Adams for consul at Liverpool.
Mar 23	From Edward Livingston. ALS, DNA-RG 59 (M639-17). Recommends William D. Patterson for a consulate.
Mar 23	From George Mason. ALS, DNA-RG 59 (M639-15). Asks to be appointed District of Columbia marshal.
Mar 23	*From John Pemberton.* 120
Mar 24	To George Merkle. Printed, *New-York Evening Post,* Apr 2; *Niles,* Apr 11 (mAJs; 12-1099). Thanks him for a gift of beef.
Mar 24	From Isaac Dutton Barnard. ALS, DNA-RG 107 (12-1092). Recommends Richard H. Bell for office.
Mar 24	From Rudolph Bunner. ALS, DNA-RG 59 (M639-7). Urges AJ not to remove New York district attorney John Duer.
Mar 24	From Nicholas Dean. ALS, DNA-RG 46 (12-1094). Recommends Thomas L. Smith for office.
Mar 24	From Mahlon Dickerson. ALS, DNA-RG 59 (M639-17). Recommends William D. Patterson for consul in Europe.
Mar 24	*From Edward Digges.* 121
Mar 24	From John Freeman Schermerhorn. ALS, DNA-RG 59 (M639-7). Advises against removing New York district attorney John Duer.
Mar 24	From Lewis Warrington. ALS, DNA-RG 107 (mAJs). Recommends Richard H. Bell for office.
Mar 25	From Samuel York Atlee. ALS, DNA-RG 45 (mAJs). Asks to be appointed midshipman.
Mar 25	From Isaac Dutton Barnard. ALS, DNA-RG 107 (12-1100). Recommends Richard Bennett for office.
Mar 25	From John Yates Cebra. ALS, DNA-RG 46 (12-1104). Recommends Thomas L. Smith for office.
Mar 25	*From John Crowell.* 122
Mar 25	From Ogden Hoffman, from Oliver M. Lownds, from John Jordan Morgan, from Mordecai Manuel Noah, from Richard Riker, and from Campbell Patrick White. ALSs, DNA-RG 46 (12-1106, 12-1108, 12-1118, 12-1120, 12-1122, 12-1132). Recommend Thomas L. Smith for office.
Mar 25	From Joseph Kille et al. DS, DNA-RG 59 (M873-19). Recommend Daniel C. Croxall for consul at Algiers.
Mar 25	From Jasper Lynch. ALS, DNA-RG 59 (M639-14). Asks to be appointed secretary of legation at London or Paris.
Mar 25	From Elijah Hunt Mills. ALS, DNA-RG 56 (12-1111). Recommends reinstating Russel Freeman as New Bedford, Mass., customs collector.
Mar 25	From William Shaler. ADS and DS copy, DNA-RG 59 (M639-21). Asks to be appointed consul at Havana.
Mar 25	From Benjamin Taylor. ALS, DNA-RG 59 (M639-24). Asks to be appointed marshal in Kentucky.
Mar 25	Discharge for prisoner Henry Sims. Copy and LC, DNA-RG 59 (12-1125; T967-1).
Mar 25	Jared I. Sample to Andrew Jackson Donelson. ALS, DNA-RG 59

	(M639-21). Asks his aid in securing appointment as marshal in Alabama.
Mar 26	From Saul Alley et al. DS, DNA-RG 46 (12-1135). Recommend Jeromus Johnson, Jonathan I. Coddington, and William S. Coe for New York City customs offices.
Mar 26	From Moses Dawson. ALS, DNA-RG 59 (12-1137). Asks to be appointed public printer at Cincinnati.
[Mar 26]	From John Denney. ALS, DNA-RG 75 (M234-432). Passamaquoddy Indians request financial aid to return home from Washington; so ordered by AJ.
Mar 26	From George Gillasspy et al. DS, DNA-RG 59 (M873-19). Recommend Daniel C. Croxall for consul at Algiers.
Mar 26	From James Alexander Hamilton. DS, DNA-RG 59 (M800-1). Hamilton *Reminiscences,* pp. 587–611 (12-1139). Presents a synopsis of current American foreign relations.
Mar 26	From G. G. & S. Howland et al. DS, DNA-RG 59 (M639-13). Recommend James L. Kennedy for consul in Mexico.
Mar 26	From John S. Lytle. ALS, DNA-RG 59 (M639-11). Recommends Horatio Hubbell for consul at Algiers.
Mar 26	From William M. Price and from John Targee. ALSs, DNA-RG 46 (12-1152, 12-1154). Recommend Thomas L. Smith for office.
Mar 26	From Stephen Simpson. ALS, DNA-RG 59 (M639-11). Recommends Jonas Horwitz to superintend the Patent Office.
Mar 26	From Aaron Ward. ALS, DNA-RG 46 (12-1155). Recommends Thomas L. Smith for U.S. Treasurer.
Mar 26	Check to Andrew Jackson, Jr., for $100. DS, DLC (36).
Mar 27	*To John Branch.* 124
Mar 27	To [John Henry Eaton]. ANS, DNA-RG 107 (M221-109). Revokes War Department order of Feb 18 granting Army quartermasters a commission on disbursements outside their regular duties.
Mar 27	To Martin Van Buren. ADS, DNA-RG 59 (12-1157). Appoints inspectors for the District of Columbia penitentiary.
Mar 27	From John Brown. ALS, DNA-RG 59 (M639-3). Asks to be appointed marshal in Tennessee.
Mar 27	From Daniel H. Ellis et al. DS, DNA-RG 59 (M873-19). Recommend Daniel C. Croxall for office.
Mar 27	Denial of Captain Thomas F. Hunt's appeal for reinstatement in the quartermaster department. LC, DLC (60).
Mar 28	To John Henry Eaton. DS, DNA-RG 153 (12-1162); LC (dated Mar 25), DLC (60); Copy, DNA-RG 107 (M221-109). Remits the death sentence against private Nicholas Dale.
Mar 28	*To Samuel Delucenna Ingham.* 124
Mar 28	*From John Macpherson Berrien.* 125
Mar 28	From John Branch. LC, DNA-RG 45 (M472-1). Reports no midshipman's vacancy at present for John Martin of Kentucky.
Mar 28	From William Burke, Robert Punshon, and Moses Dawson. LS, DNA-RG 59 (12-1159). Recommend Richard C. Langdon for public printer at Xenia, Ohio.

Mar 28   From Charles Chauncey et al. DS, DNA-RG 59 (M639-3).
          Recommend James M. Broom.
Mar 28   From John M. Davis. ALS, DNA-RG 59 (M639-6). Asks to be
          appointed marshal in Pennsylvania.
Mar 28   From William McCreery. ALS, DNA-RG 59 (M639-6).
          Recommends John M. Davis for marshal in Pennsylvania.
Mar 28   From John Jordan Morgan. ALS, DNA-RG 59 (M639-6).
          Recommends John A. Dix for a diplomatic post in Europe.
Mar 28   From John Simpson. ALS, DNA-RG 59 (M639-21). Asks to be
          appointed superintendent of the Patent Office.
Mar 28   From Thomas Swann. ADS, THi (12-1168). Recommends
          William E. Hunton for a clerkship.
Mar 29   From L. Gasperi. ALS, DNA-RG 107 (12-1170). Requests
          employment and complains of his dismissal as inspector of
          fortifications.
Mar 29   From William M. Stewart. ALS, DNA-RG 59 (M639-23).
          Requests employment and complains of his unjust removal as a
          War Department clerk in 1827.
Mar 29   [Samuel Jackson Hays to Stockley Donelson]. AL draft, DLC
          (12-1173). Discusses the inauguration, the Cabinet, Henry
          Clay and the opposition, the clamor for office, and Washington
          social life.
Mar 29   Charles J. Jack to Andrew Jackson Donelson. ALS, TNJ (12-
          1177). Urges his appointment as marshal in Pennsylvania.
Mar 30   To John Macpherson Berrien. Printed, Tallahassee *Floridian,*
          May 11, 1833 (12-1180). Requests Florida land case papers for
          William Wirt, engaged as U.S. counsel.
Mar 30   From John Armstrong. Copy, DNA-RG 59 (M639-9).
          Recommends Charles K. Gardner for a chief clerkship.
Mar 30   From Jonas Horwitz. ALS, DNA-RG 59 (M639-11). Asks to be
          appointed Patent Office superintendent or consul.
Mar 30   From William E. Hunton. ALS, TNJ (12-1181). Requests the
          clerkship promised him by John S. Barbour.
Mar 30   From Thomas Kittera. ALS, DNA-RG 59 (M639-13). Asks to be
          appointed district attorney in Pennsylvania.
Mar 30   From Henry Lee. Printed, Robert Mayo, *Political Sketches of
          Eight Years in Washington,* p. 48 (12-1184). Recommends
          Robert Mayo for librarian of Congress.
Mar 30   From Virgil Maxcy. ALS, DNA-RG 59 (M639-3). Recommends
          James M. Broom for office.
Mar 30   From William Ramsey. ALS, DNA-RG 45 (M124-117).
          Recommends Jesse D. Elliott to command the West India
          squadron.
Mar 30   From Samuel Stevens. ALS, DNA-RG 59 (12-1185).
          Recommends John D. Green for public printer and postmaster
          in Talbot County, Md.
Mar 30   From Joseph Gardner Swift. AD, DLC (36). Complains of his
          replacement by Adams as New York City customs surveyor and
          requests reinstatement; refused by AJ.
Mar 30   From Littleton Waller Tazewell.   126

Mar 30   From Charles H. W. Wharton. ALS, DNA-RG 59 (M639-26).
                Requests a clerkship.
Mar 31   *From Martin Van Buren.*   *129*
Mar 31   *To Martin Van Buren.*   *132*
Mar 31   From John Branch. LC, DNA-RG 45 (M472-1). Reports that
                the *Natchez* sailed on Mar 28.
Mar 31   From James Madison Broom. ANS, DNA-RG 59 (M639-3).
                Transmits recommendations on his behalf.
Mar 31   From John Conrad. ALS, DNA-RG 107 (12-1187).
                Recommends Charles J. Jack for marshal in Pennsylvania.
Mar 31   From Isaac Eddy et al. DS, DNA-RG 26 (13-0450). Recommend
                Joshua Lane for lighthouse keeper at Portland, Maine.
Mar 31   From R. Lawrence. ALS, DNA-RG 59 (M639-13). Recommends
                G. Augustus Lawson for office in Philadelphia.
Mar 31   From William H. Low. ALS, DNA-RG 59 (M639-14). Asks to
                be appointed consul at Canton, China.
Mar 31   From John McLean. ALS, DNA-RG 59 (M639-21).
                Recommends Michael T. Simpson to bear dispatches to Europe.
Mar 31   From Henry H. Pfeiffer et al. LS, DNA-RG 59 (M639-6).
                Recommend John M. Davis for marshal in Pennsylvania.
Mar 31   From Joseph Saul. ALS, DLC (72). Requests an appointment
                for himself or his son Benjamin M. Saul.
[cMar]   From John Adlum. ALS, DNA-RG 59 (M639-1). Asks to be
                appointed marshal of the District of Columbia.
[cMar]   From Ezra Beales et al. DS, DNA-RG 77 (12-0614).
                Recommend James Bryant to superintend the Cumberland
                Road.
[cMar]   From Calvin Blythe, Samuel C. Stambaugh, and Samuel
                Douglas. LS, DNA-RG 77 (12-0620). Recommend Solomon G.
                Krepps to superintend the Cumberland Road.
Mar   From Bradford & Cooch et al. Copy, DNA-RG 46 (12-0623).
                Recommend continuing William B. Barney as naval officer at
                Baltimore.
[Mar]   From Joseph Carrol et al. DS, DNA-RG 107 (12-1102).
                Recommend James Bryant to superintend the Cumberland Road.
[cMar]   From Alexander Cook et al. DS, THi (12-0364). Recommend
                Charles J. Jack for marshal in Pennsylvania.
[cMar]   From Andrew Dempsy et al. DS, DNA-RG 77 (12-0630).
                Recommend Solomon G. Krepps to superintend the Cumberland
                Road.
Mar   From Hugh Ely et al. DS, DNA-RG 59 (M639-3). Maryland
                legislators recommend James M. Buchanan for secretary of
                legation.
[cMar]   From John Fuller et al. DS, DNA-RG 77 (12-0678).
                Recommend Valentine Giesey to superintend the Cumberland
                Road.
[Mar]   From William Goddard et al. DS, DNA-RG 59 (M639-1).
                Recommend Joseph H. Adams for consul at Liverpool.
[cMar]   From Martin Gordon et al. LS, DNA-RG 59 (M639-21).
                Recommend John Slidell for district attorney in Louisiana.

[cMar] From Isaac Hill et al. DS, DNA-RG 59 (M639-9). Recommend Charles B. Goodrich for district attorney in New Hampshire.

[Mar] From Henry Horn et al. DS, DNA-RG 59 (M639-7). Recommend Benjamin Evens for customs collector at Key West.

Mar From Thomas Irwin. ALS, DNA-RG 77 (12-0679). Recommends Solomon G. Krepps to superintend the Cumberland Road.

[cMar] From Joseph Lippincott et al. DS, DNA-RG 59 (M639-12). Recommend Alexander Johnston for marshal in Pennsylvania.

[cMar] From Edward Livingston and Martin Gordon. NS, DNA-RG 59 (M639-21). Recommend John Slidell for district attorney in Louisiana.

[cMar] From Thomson F. Mason. ALS, DNA-RG 59 (M639-11). Recommends Alexander Hunter for office.

Mar From Isaac McKim et al. DS, DNA-RG 59 (M639-15). Recommend James J. McLanahan for consul at Havana.

[cMar] From Ner Middleswarth et al. DS, DNA-RG 77 (12-0682). Pennsylvania legislators recommend Solomon G. Krepps to superintend the Cumberland Road.

[cMar] From Daniel H. Miller et al. DS, DNA-RG 59 (M639-19). Recommend Joseph Ray for consul at Pernambuco, Brazil.

[Mar] From John Mitchell. ALS, DNA-RG 59 (M639-17). Recommends Benjamin Patton, Jr., for secretary of legation.

[Mar] From Joseph Norton et al. DS, DNA-RG 59 (M873-19). Recommend Daniel C. Croxall for consul at Algiers.

[cMar] From Joseph Rankin et al. DS, DNA-RG 59 (M639-12). Pennsylvania legislators recommend Alexander Johnston for marshal.

[cMar] From Thomas Ringland et al. DS, DNA-RG 59 (M639-7). Pennsylvania legislators recommend Benjamin Evens for customs collector at Key West.

[Mar] From William Rotch, Jr., et al. Copy, DNA-RG 56 (12-0691). Recommend reinstating New Bedford customs collector Russel Freeman.

[cMar] From John Simpson. ALS fragment, DLC (12-0696). Offers his "Jackson Piano" for the White House; AJ Donelson recommends accepting.

[cMar] From Albert Smith et al. DS, DNA-RG 59 (M639-15). Maine legislators recommend John D. McCrate.

[cMar] From Joseph Michael Steck et al. DS, DNA-RG 59 (M639-12). Recommend Alexander Johnston for marshal in Pennsylvania.

[cMar] From John Targee et al. DS, DNA-RG 46 (12-0699). Recommend William S. Coe for New York City customs appraiser.

[Mar] From John M. Taylor. ALS, PHi (12-0702). Urges his claim to an appointment.

[cMar] From Peter S. Titus et al. DS, DNA-RG 46 (12-0706). New York legislators recommend Thomas L. Smith for office.

[cMar] From Charles Anderson Wickliffe. ANS, DNA-RG 77 (12-0816). Forwards an earlier recommendation for Solomon G. Krepps.

[cMar]   From Charles Anderson Wickliffe et al. DS, DNA-RG 77 (12-
              0815). Recommend Solomon G. Krepps for superintendent of
              Cumberland Road repairs.
[cMar]   From James A. Wilkinson et al. DS, DNA-RG 77 (12-0710).
              Recommend Valentine Giesey to superintend the Cumberland
              Road.
[Mar]   From Jacob M. Wise et al. DS, DNA-RG 59 (M639-12).
              Pennsylvania legislators recommend Alexander Johnston for
              marshal.
[cMar]   Andrew Jackson Donelson to [James Harvey Hook]. ALS, DNA-
              RG 192 (12-0676). Promises to look into complaints against
              newly appointed Ouachita, La., land officers John Hughes and
              Henry Bry.
[Mar–Apr]   *To Morgan Lewis.*   *134*
Apr 1   *From Jehiel Brooks.*   *135*
[cApr 1]   From John Henry Eaton. ALS, DNA-RG 59 (M639-22).
              Encloses recommendations for Thomas L. Smith.
Apr 1   From Elijah Hayward. ALS, DNA-RG 107 (12-1225); Copies,
              DCU (mAJs). Recommends Jehiel Brooks for an Indian agency.
Apr 1   From Michael T. Simpson. ALS, DNA-RG 59 (M639-21). Asks
              to be appointed dispatch bearer to Europe or Treasurer's chief
              clerk.
Apr 1   From Thomas Tenant. ALS, DNA-RG 59 (M639-15). Solicits
              office for his son-in-law James J. McLanahan.
Apr 1   Remission, on account of ill health, of remaining sentence for
              former Waynesboro, Tenn., postmaster Martin H. W. Mahon,
              imprisoned at Nashville for stealing a lottery ticket from the
              mail. Draft and LC, DNA-RG 59 (12-1228; T967-1).
Apr 2   *To Susan Wheeler Decatur.*   *136*
Apr 2   To Martin Van Buren. LC, DNA-RG 59 (M40-21). Orders an
              inquiry into charges of official misconduct against District of
              Columbia marshal Tench Ringgold.
Apr 2   From John Grayson. ALS, DNA-RG 59 (M639-6). Recommends
              John M. Davis for marshal in Pennsylvania.
Apr 2   From James B. Lowry. ALS, DNA-RG 26 (13-0452).
              Recommends Joshua Lane for lighthouse keeper at Portland,
              Maine.
Apr 2   From Nathaniel McLean and John McElvain. LS, DNA-RG 107
              (M222-26). Protest against rerouting the Cumberland Road
              through Newark, Ohio.
Apr 2   From Samuel Miller et al. DS, DNA-RG 59 (M639-8).
              Recommend Stephen Fessenden for consul at Liverpool.
Apr 2   From Henry Mason Morfit. ALS, DNA-RG 59 (M639-3).
              Recommends James M. Broom for district attorney in
              Pennsylvania.
Apr 2   From Robert I. Taylor et al. DS, DNA-RG 59 (M639-11).
              Recommend Alexander Hunter for District of Columbia marshal
              if Tench Ringgold is removed.
Apr 2   Bill from Nelson Davidson for coach repairs. ADS, DLC (72).
              Runs to May 15, 1830.

Apr 3   To Martin Van Buren. Abstract, DNA-RG 59 (M639-19).
     Requests attention to John Norvell's letter of Mar 17 about
     Joseph Ray.

Apr 3   From John Branch. LS, DLC (12-1257); LC, DNA-RG 45
     (M472-1). *North Carolina Historical Review* 14 (Oct 1937):
     366. Encloses sailing orders for the *Natchez*'s cruise against
     Cuban pirates and papers explaining its delay.

Apr 3   From Richard Keith Call. ALS, DNA-RG 59 (M639-3).
     Recommends Thomas Brown for secretary of legation in Britain.

Apr 3   From Dabney Smith Carr. ALS, DNA-RG 59 (M639-20).
     Recommends Thomas Russell for office.

Apr 3   From Ralph Eleazar Whitesides Earl. Extract, American Art
     Association catalog (12-1265). Describes Rachel Jackson's tomb.

Apr 3   From George Graham. LC, DNA-RG 49 (M25-23). Submits a
     land patent for signature.

Apr 3   From George Graham. LC, DNA-RG 49 (M25-23). Submits 583
     land patents for signature.

Apr 3   From Jean Baptiste Plauché. ALS, DNA-RG 94 (M688-63).
     Introduces his eldest son J. J. Alexander and solicits a West Point
     appointment for his son John Baptiste.

Apr 3   Commission for Richard Keith Call as agent to obtain Spanish
     documents concerning Florida land cases. Copy, FPeE (12-1263).

Apr 3   Order to the War Department setting terms for payments to
     civilian surgeons. LC, DLC (60).

Apr 3   John Coffee to Andrew Jackson Hutchings. ALS, DLC (36).
     Censures his irresponsible conduct and entreats him to reform.

Apr 4   To Walter Bowne. LS, NNMu (mAJs). *Niles,* May 2 (12-1266).
     Thanks the New York Common Council for Jan 12 condolences
     on Rachel's death.

Apr 4   To Samuel Delucenna Ingham. Extract, Parke-Bernet catalog
     2763 (mAJs; 12-1267). Approves William Wirt's $1,000 fee as
     counsel in Florida land cases.

Apr 4   From James Collinsworth. ALS, DNA-RG 59 (M639-5). Asks to
     be appointed district attorney in Tennessee.

Apr 4   From Thomas Crutcher. ALS, DNA-RG 59 (M639-2). Reports
     David Barrow's candidacy for district attorney in Tennessee.

Apr 4   From Thomas Crutcher. ALS, DNA-RG 59 (M639-5). Reports
     James Collinsworth's candidacy for district attorney in
     Tennessee.

Apr 4   From Thomas Crutcher. ALS, DNA-RG 59 (M639-2). Reports
     Henry Baldwin, Jr.'s candidacy for district attorney in Tennessee.

Apr 4   *From Ezra Stiles Ely.*   *137*

Apr 4   From Betsey Hawley. ALS, DNA-RG 59 (T229-1). Solicits AJ's
     personal attention to her complaint of Mar 19.

Apr 4   From Andrew Hays and Charles Jones Love. LSs, DNA-RG 59
     (M639-2). Recommend David Barrow for district attorney in
     Tennessee.

Apr 4   From J. Johnston. ALS, DNA-RG 59 (M639-6). Recommends
     George M. Dallas for district attorney and evaluates
     Philadelphia aspirants for office.

Apr 4   From Edward Livingston. ALS, DNA-RG 59 (M639-12).
            Introduces and commends Charles J. Ingersoll.
Apr 4   From Edward Livingston. ALS, DNA-RG 59 (M639-27).
            Introduces Benjamin C. Wilcocks, with information on
            American commercial interests in China.
Apr 4   From William McEllroy et al. LS, DNA-RG 59 (M639-6).
            Recommend John M. Davis for marshal in Pennsylvania.
Apr 4   From James Coffield Mitchell. ALS, DNA-RG 59 (M639-16).
            Urges John Callaway's removal as marshal in Tennessee and
            recommends Luke Lea.
Apr 4   From George Richards. Copy, DNA-RG 233 (12-1268). Presents
            the pension claim of Revolutionary veteran Daniel Coleman, a
            free man of color.
Apr 4   From John Peter Van Ness. ALS, DLC (12-1270). Recommends
            Russell Jarvis for office.
Apr 4   From Campbell Patrick White. ALS, DNA-RG 59 (M639-25).
            Recommends David B. Warden for consul or secretary of
            legation at Paris.
Apr 4   From Henry Alexander Wise. ALS, DNA-RG 59 (M639-7).
            Recommends Thomas A. Duncan for district attorney in
            Tennessee or secretary of legation in Colombia.
Apr 4   Check to Andrew Jackson Donelson for $1000. DS, DLC (36).
Apr 5   *From James Payne Clark.*   *139*
Apr 5   From David Craighead. ALS, DNA-RG 59 (M639-5).
            Recommends James Collinsworth for district attorney in
            Tennessee, reports AJ's farm in good order, and recalls AJ's
            defense of his father Thomas B. Craighead.
Apr 5   From Archibald W. Goodrich. ALS, DNA-RG 59 (M639-9).
            Asks to be appointed district attorney in Tennessee.
Apr 5   *From Henry Lee.*   *140*
Apr 5   *From Martin Van Buren.*   *141*
Apr 5   William A. Cook to [Andrew Jackson Donelson]. ALS, DNA-
            RG 59 (M639-5). Asks Donelson to recommend him for district
            attorney in Tennessee.
Apr 5   Henry Post, Jr., to Unknown. ALS, DLC (36). Applies for office
            and complains of Van Buren's proscription of AJ's Clintonian
            New York friends.
Apr 6   Address to the foreign ministers. LC, DLC (60). *New-York
            Evening Post,* Apr 20; Hamilton *Reminiscences,* p. 115.
            Promises friendship, reciprocity, and fair dealing.
Apr 6   To John Macpherson Berrien. LS, NcU (12-1276); LC, DLC
            (60). Offers the mission to Britain.
Apr 6   *To Littleton Waller Tazewell.*   *142*
Apr 6   From Benjamin Bailey. ALS, DNA-RG 59 (M639-22); Copy,
            CU-BANC (12-1275). Recommends Peter W. Spicer for office.
Apr 6   From Washington Barrow. ALS, DNA-RG 59 (M639-2).
            Recommends his brother David for district attorney in
            Tennessee.
Apr 6   From John Branch. LS, DNA-RG 45 (12-1280); LC, DNA-RG

	45 (M472-1). Reports three assistant naval surgeons' refusal to take their examination; AJ orders them dismissed.
Apr 6	From Morgan W. Brown. ALS, DNA-RG 59 (M639-3). Asks to be appointed district attorney in Tennessee.
Apr 6	From William Little Brown. ALS, DNA-RG 59 (M639-7). Recommends Thomas A. Duncan for secretary of legation in Colombia.
Apr 6	From William Little Brown. ALS, DNA-RG 59 (M639-5). Recommends his brother Morgan W. Brown or brother-in-law William A. Cook for district attorney in Tennessee.
Apr 6	From William A. Cook. ALS, DNA-RG 59 (M639-5). Asks to be appointed district attorney in Tennessee and recommends Thomas A. Duncan for secretary of legation in Colombia.
Apr 6	From Nathan Ewing. ALS, DNA-RG 59 (M639-2). Recommends David Barrow for district attorney in Tennessee.
Apr 6	From William W. Gault. ALS, DNA-RG 59 (M639-9). Asks to have the Cumberland Road routed through Newark and to be appointed marshal in Ohio.
Apr 6	From Vicente Ramón Guerrero. LS, DNA-RG 59 (M54-1). President of Mexico offers friendship.
Apr 6	From Washington L. Hannum. ALS, DNA-RG 59 (M639-10). Asks to be appointed district attorney in Tennessee.
Apr 6	From Benjamin Chew Howard. ALS, DNA-RG 59 (M639-20). Recommends Thomas Russell for librarian of Congress.
Apr 6	*From John Jack and Isaac Solomon.* 143
Apr 6	From Samuel Jones et al. DS, DNA-RG 59 (M639-1). Recommend Joseph H. Adams for consul at Liverpool.
Apr 6	From A. MacDonald. ALS, DNA-RG 59 (M639-15). Asks to be appointed justice of the peace in the District of Columbia.
Apr 6	From John Pemberton. ALS copy, PHi (12-1281). Thanks AJ for appointment as Philadelphia naval officer.
Apr 6	From Isaac Post et al. DS, DNA-RG 59 (M639-19). Pennsylvania legislators recommend Almon H. Read for superintendent of the Patent Office.
Apr 6	From Robert Purdy. ALS, DNA-RG 59 (M639-2). Recommends David Barrow for district attorney in Tennessee.
Apr 6	From Felix Robertson. ALS, DNA-RG 59 (M639-3). Recommends Morgan W. Brown for district attorney in Tennessee.
Apr 6	From Felix Robertson. LS, DNA-RG 59 (M639-10). Recommends Washington L. Hannum for district attorney in Tennessee.
Apr 6	*From John Ross et al.* 144
Apr 6	From Leverett Saltonstall, Benjamin Merrill, and Nathaniel Saltonstall. DS, DNA-RG 59 (M639-1). Recommend Joseph H. Adams for consul at Liverpool.
Apr 6	From Benjamin Tappan. ALS, DNA-RG 59 (M639-8). Recommends Stephen Fessenden for consul at Liverpool.
Apr 6	From John Travers. ALS, DNA-RG 59 (M873-19). Recommends Daniel C. Croxall for consul at Algiers.

Apr 6	From Campbell Patrick White. ALS, DNA-RG 59 (M639-22); Copies, CU-BANC (12-1291). Recommends Peter W. Spicer for office.
Apr 6	From John Campbell White. ALS, DNA-RG 59 (M639-25). Recommends David B. Warden for consul or secretary of legation at Paris.
[Apr 6]	From John Campbell White et al. DS, DNA-RG 59 (M639-25). Recommend David B. Warden for consul or secretary of legation at Paris.
Apr 6	Thomas A. Duncan to Andrew Jackson Donelson. ALS, DNA-RG 59 (M639-2). Recommends David Barrow for district attorney in Tennessee and asks to be appointed secretary of legation in Colombia.
Apr 7	To William Buell Sprague. ALS, DLC (75). Thanks him for sermons and promises a favor for Sprague's friend in England.
Apr 7	To Martin Van Buren. ANS, DNA-RG 59 (12-1300). Appoints George M. Dallas district attorney in Pennsylvania in place of Charles J. Ingersoll.
[Apr 7]	*To Martin Van Buren.* 146
Apr 7	From William E. Anderson. ALS, DNA-RG 59 (M639-4). Recommends James P. Clark for district attorney in Tennessee.
Apr 7	From Thomas H. Fletcher. ALS, DNA-RG 59 (12-1295). Resigns as district attorney in Tennessee and avows friendly feeling for AJ.
Apr 7	From Robert Monroe Harrison. ALS, DNA-RG 59 (M639-10). Congratulates AJ on his election.
Apr 7	From Samuel Hogg. ALS, DNA-RG 59 (M639-2). Recommends David Barrow for district attorney in Tennessee.
Apr 7	From Henry Lee. ALS, DNA-RG 59 (M639-11). Recommends Alexander Hunter for marshal of the District of Columbia.
Apr 7	Check to William Berkeley Lewis for $200. DS, DLC (36).
Apr 7	Temporary commission for George Mifflin Dallas as district attorney in Pennsylvania. DS, PPT (mAJs); LC, DNA-RG 59 (12-1294).
Apr 8	To Martin Van Buren. ANS, DNA-RG 59 (12-1307). *TPUS*, 21:13. Appoints William S. Fulton secretary of Arkansas Territory in place of Robert Crittenden.
Apr 8	To Martin Van Buren. ANS, DNA-RG 59 (12-1305). Appoints Henry Lee consul general at Algiers.
Apr 8	From William McLean Berryhill. ALS, DNA-RG 59 (M639-2). Recommends David Barrow for district attorney in Tennessee.
Apr 8	From Samuel Hervey Laughlin et al. LS, DNA-RG 59 (M639-2). Recommend Robert M. Burton for district attorney in Tennessee.
Apr 8	*From Enoch Parsons.* 147
Apr 8	From James Rucks. ALS, DNA-RG 59 (M639-5). Recommends James Collinsworth for district attorney in Tennessee.
Apr 8	From Joseph Warner et al. LS, DNA-RG 59 (M639-1). Recommend James Akin for superintendent of the Patent Office.
Apr 8	Temporary commission for William Savin Fulton as secretary of

	Recommends James C. Sprigg for secretary of Arkansas Territory.
Apr 11	From Uel Wilson. ALS, DNA-RG 59 (M639-27). Requests an office and complains of ill treatment by Duff Green and the administration.
Apr 11	Check to Andrew Jackson Donelson for $100. DS, DLC (36).
Apr 11	Warrant from Samuel Delucenna Ingham to U.S. Treasurer William Clark to pay AJ's monthly salary of $2,083.33 to BUS cashier Richard Smith. DS, DNA-RG 217 (12-1319).
Apr 12	From Frederick Watts Huling. ALS, DNA-RG 59 (M639-5). Recommends William A. Cook for district attorney in Tennessee.
Apr 13	*Introduction for Allan Ditchfield Campbell.* *155*
Apr 13	From John Henry Eaton. Abstract, Carnegie Book Shop catalog 132 (12-1333). Inquires about the Cherokees' protest against Georgia's extension of laws over them; endorsed by AJ that "the answer be well considered on constitutional grounds."
Apr 13	From George Fleming. ALS, DNA-RG 75 (M234-432). Conveys a report that the Chickasaws and Choctaws have decided to cede their lands to the U.S.
Apr 13	From John Hartwell Marable. ALS, DNA-RG 59 (M639-5). Recommends William A. Cook for district attorney in Tennessee.
Apr 13	From James Monroe Martin. ALS, DNA-RG 59 (M639-15). Asks to be appointed district attorney in Arkansas Territory.
Apr 13	From Morgan Neville. ALS, DNA-RG 59 (M639-17). Asks to be appointed minister to Mexico and complains that Ohio has been slighted.
Apr 13	From Nathan Reid. ALS, ViHi (12-1334). Recommends John E. Norvell for a position in the Navy.
Apr 13	From Thomas Swann et al. Printed, *Nat. Intelligencer,* Sep 17, 1831 (12- 1336). Urge AJ not to remove District of Columbia marshal Tench Ringgold.
Apr 13	From Stephen Woods. ALS, DNA-RG 59 (M639-6). Recommends John M. Davis for marshal in Pennsylvania.
Apr 13	Approval of Potawatomi Indian Madelaine Bertrand's location of her reserved land under the 1821 Treaty of Chicago. ANS, DNA-RG 75 (12-1323).
Apr 14	To Charles Richard Vaughan. AN by AJ Donelson, UkOxU-AS (12-1351). Thanks him for a gift of sherry.
Apr 14	From Henry Ashton. ALS, DNA-RG 59 (M639-1). Complains of President Monroe's failure to make him District of Columbia district attorney, and asks to be appointed in place of Thomas Swann.
Apr 14	From John Blair. ALS, DNA-RG 59 (M639-11). Recommends Jacob Howard for marshal in Tennessee in place of John Callaway.
Apr 14	From Churchill Caldom Cambreleng. ALS, DNA-RG 59 (M639-22); Copies, CU-BANC (12-1338). Recommends Peter W. Spicer for office.

Apr 22   To Samuel Delucenna Ingham. Extract, dealer catalog (13-0097). Appoints officers at New Orleans including Martin Gordon as customs collector.

Apr 22   From Charles Scott Bibb. ALS, DNA-RG 59 (M639-22). Recommends James C. Sprigg for secretary of Arkansas Territory.

Apr 22   From Samuel Daviess. ALS, DNA-RG 59 (M639-15). Recommends John M. McCalla for marshal in Kentucky.

Apr 22   From George Graham. LC, DNA-RG 49 (M25-23). Submits 622 land patents for signature.

Apr 22   From John M. Hewitt. ALS, DNA-RG 59 (M639-15). Recommends John M. McCalla for marshal in Kentucky.

Apr 22   From David Kizer. ALS, DNA-RG 59 (M639-13). Asks to be appointed consul at St. Thomas.

Apr 22   From Robert Breckinridge McAfee. ALS, DNA-RG 59 (M639-15). Recommends John M. McCalla for marshal in Kentucky.

Apr 22   From James Knox Polk. ALS, DNA-RG 59 (M639-27). *Polk Correspondence,* 1:257–58. Recommends Archibald Yell for secretary of Arkansas Territory.

Apr 22   From Nicholas Greenberry Ridgely. LC, MdHi (13-0102). Extract, ScCleU (mAJs); *Calhoun Papers,* 11:42. Recommends Virgil Maxcy for office.

Apr 22   From John J. Steele. ALS, DNA-RG 59 (M639-6). Urges John M. Davis for marshal in Pennsylvania and approves Valentine Giesey's appointment.

Apr 22   Power of attorney to John Henry Eaton to administer the government trust fund for the Seneca Indians. Copy, DNA-RG 75 (M234-808). Endorsed "Not executed."

Apr 22   Homer Johnson to Andrew Jackson Donelson. ALS, Stanley F. Horn (13-0098). Urges Samuel Judah for district attorney in Indiana in place of Charles Dewey; appointment ordered by AJ.

Apr 23   To Samuel Delucenna Ingham. LC, DLC (60). Approves equalizing compensation for physicians at the marine hospital before making new appointments.

Apr 23   To Samuel Delucenna Ingham. ALS, Colonel James S. Corbitt (13-0109). Introduces John Nicholson, who will carry commissions of office to New Orleans.

Apr 23   To Martin Van Buren. ANS, DNA-RG 59 (13-0111). Appoints James A. Hamilton district attorney in New York.

Apr 23   From Philip S. Butler. Abstract, Charles Hamilton catalog 127 (13-0104). Discusses financial matters.

Apr 23   From Richard Gilliam Dunlap. ALS, DNA-RG 107 (M222-25). Protests auditor Peter Hagner's rejection of his soldiers' claims for property lost in the Seminole campaign.

Apr 23   From Richard Gilliam Dunlap. ALS, DNA-RG 107 (M222-25). Presents further soldiers' claims for lost property rejected by Peter Hagner.

Apr 23   From John Forbes et al. LS, DNA-RG 59 (M639-16). Recommend Samuel R. Miller for marshal in Ohio.

Apr 23   *From Duff Green.*   *171*

Apr 27	From John Donelson (1787–1840). ALS, DNA-RG 59 (M639-15). Recommends James M. Martin for district attorney in Arkansas Territory and discusses his litigation with the Adams men and James Jackson.
Apr 27	From Catherine Fitzpatrick. ADS, DNA-RG 59 (M179-67). Requests that funds left by her dead husband in America be remitted to her in Ireland.
Apr 27	From Edmund Pendleton Gaines. ALS, InU (13-0160). Introduces and recommends Samuel C. Reid.
Apr 27	From William W. Gault. ALS, DNA-RG 59 (M639-9). Asks to be appointed marshal or Cumberland Road superintendent in Ohio.
Apr 27	From Alexander Hunter. ALS, DNA-RG 59 (M639-11). Asks to be appointed marshal of the District of Columbia.
Apr 27	From Richard Raynal Keene. ALS, DLC (37). Presents a copy of Robert Goodloe Harper's *Plain Reasons of a Plain Man for Preferring Gen. Jackson to Mr. Adams, as President of the U.S.* (Baltimore, 1825).
Apr 27	From Morgan Lewis. ALS and Copy, DNA-RG 59 (M639-19). Recommends Samuel C. Reid for office.
Apr 27	From Morgan Neville. ALS, DNA-RG 59 (M639-3). Recommends Theodore H. Burrows for territorial office.
Apr 27	Pardon for Henry Holt. Copy and LC, DNA-RG 59 (13-0164; T967-1).
Apr 28	To Amos Kendall. ANS, DNA-RG 45 (M124-140). Orders a review of Samuel T. Anderson's appeal of his accounts as naval supply contractor in the War of 1812.
Apr 28	*To Martin Van Buren.* 186
Apr 28	From Richard H. Bradford. LC, DNA-RG 45 (M472-1). Reports on Eleanor Wills's claim for a naval pension.
Apr 28	*From Richard Keith Call.* 187
Apr 28	From Richard Keith Call. ALS, DNA-RG 59 (M639-6). *TPUS,* 24:208. Recommends James Dell for marshal in Florida in place of Waters Smith.
Apr 28	From Charles Alexander Clinton. ALS, DNA-RG 45 (M124-118). Recommends John F. Sibell for office.
Apr 28	From Robert L. Cobbs. ALS, DNA-RG 59 (M639-5). Recommends James Collinsworth for district attorney in Tennessee.
Apr 28	From George Graham. LC, DNA-RG 49 (M25-23). Explains federal land surveyor James P. Turner's right to dismiss deputy surveyor James Allison.
Apr 28	From George Graham. LC, DNA-RG 49 (M25-23). Submits three land patents for signature.
Apr 28	From Peter Parsons. ALS, DNA-RG 59 (M639-15). Recommends Michael McCann for marshal in Tennessee.
Apr 28	From Washington G. Singleton. ALS, DNA-RG 28 (13-0171). Requests an office.
[Apr 28]	*Review of Abram Rall Woolley's court-martial.* 188
Apr 29	From John Chauncey. Printed, Washington *National Journal,*

Jun 20 (mAJs). Seeks AJ's confirmation that he spoke against the tariff at the Hermitage in 1828.

Apr 29   From John W. Cushman. ALS, TNJ (13-0182). Requests a record of the appointment of former Army paymaster Robert McClallen, being sued for defalcation.

Apr 29   From Thompson M. Rector. ALS, DNA-RG 59 (M639-21). Recommends Joseph Scott for district attorney in Alabama.

Apr 29   *From Samuel Swartwout.*   *189*

Apr 30   To Louis, Grand Duke of Baden. LC, DNA-RG 59 (13-0191). Offers condolences on the death of his sister-in-law.

Apr 30   To [Martin Van Buren]. ANS, DNA-RG 59 (13-0192). Appoints James Collinsworth district attorney in Tennessee.

Apr 30   From William Taylor Barry. ALS, DNA-RG 46 (13-0187). Encloses George Shannon's recommendation of Frederick R. Conway for land office register at Franklin, Mo.

Apr 30   From Elijah Hall. Copy, DNA-RG 45 (M625-405). Recommends his son-in-law John H. Sherburne for office.

Apr 30   From William Hamilton. ALS, DNA-RG 107 (M222-25). Requests government patronage for his improved firearms.

Apr 30   From Betsey Hawley. ALS, DNA-RG 59 (T229-1). Complains again of the conspiracy to deprive her of her dead brother's property.

Apr 30   Pardon for Joshua Winslow, imprisoned for inability to pay his fine for smuggling coffee. Copy and LC, DNA-RG 59 (13-0195; T967-1).

[cApr]   To Martin Van Buren. ANS, DNA-RG 59 (M179-67). Transmits a House request, Feb 4, for information on prisons in the District of Columbia.

[cApr]   From William B. Booker et al. DS, DNA-RG 59 (M639-15). Recommend John M. McCalla for marshal in Kentucky.

[cApr]   From Elias Brown, from Thomas M. Forman, from John Carlyle Herbert, from T. R. Johnson and Joseph Stone, from Patrick McCaulay, from Alexander McKim, from James Mosher, from John S. Sellman, and from Richard W. West. Extracts, ScCleU (mAJs); *Calhoun Papers,* 11:42. Recommend Virgil Maxcy for office.

[cApr]   From James Alexander Hamilton. ALS, DLC (12-0366). Withdraws a suggestion regarding his office because of Van Buren's disapproval.

[cApr]   From Isaac Hill. Cover, Michael Reese II (mAJs). Recommends John Laighton for navy agent at Portsmouth, N.H.

[cApr]   From Sewall Kendrick & Co. et al. DS, DNA-RG 59 (M639-1). Recommend Joseph H. Adams for consul at Liverpool.

[cApr]   From William Hammond Marriott. Extract, ScCleU (mAJs); *Calhoun Papers,* 11:42. Recommends Virgil Maxcy for Treasurer.

[cApr]   From John Montgomery. ADS, DNA-RG 59 (M639-5). Recommends William A. Cook for district attorney in Tennessee.

[cApr]   From William Shaler. AD with notes by Van Buren, DLC (12-1214). Advises on American relations with Algiers.

[May 1]   To John Henry Eaton. Facsimile of ALS, American Historical Auctions catalog, Jun 28, 1998 (mAJs); Abstract, DNA-RG 107 (M22-24). Asks him to search the War Department for Henri-Joseph Paixhans's *Nouvelle Force Maritime.*

May 1   To [Martin Van Buren]. ANS, DNA-RG 59 (13-0237). Reappoints Samuel H. Smith and six others to the levy court for Washington County, D.C.

May 1   From James Leander Cathcart. ADS, DNA-RG 46 (13-0228). Appeals for payment of his claims against the government.

May 1   From Duff Green. LC, DLC (13-0236). Withdraws his recommendation of John S. Meehan for librarian of Congress.

May 1   From Samuel B. Moore. ALS, DNA-RG 59 (M639-21). Recommends Joseph Scott for district attorney in Alabama.

May 2   From Richard Henry Bradford. LC, DNA-RG 45 (M472-1). Submits information on applicants for navy agent and storekeeper, and reports no vacancies.

May 2   From David Kizer. ALS, DNA-RG 59 (M639-13). Asks again to be appointed consul at St. Thomas.

May 2   From Morgan Lewis. ALS, DNA-RG 59 (M639-24). Recommends John C. Tillotson for consul at Havre.

May 2   From Enoch Lincoln. ALS, DNA-RG 59 (M639-4). Introduces and recommends Charles Q. Clapp.

May 2   From Levi Woodbury. ALS, DNA-RG 59 (M639-4). Recommends his brother-in-law Charles Q. Clapp for office.

May 3   From Samuel K. Colebridge. ALS, DNA-RG 59 (M639-20). Recommends Benjamin W. Richards for consul at Liverpool.

May 3   From Arthur Peronneau Hayne. ALS, DNA-RG 59 (M639-10). Asks to be appointed consul at Liverpool.

May 3   From Edward Livingston. ALS, DLC (13-0244). Regrets that his unsettled affairs require declining the mission to France.

May 4   To Richard Henry Bradford. LC, DLC (60). Orders a surgeon and surgeon's mate sent to the Mediterranean squadron.

May 4   From John Anderson. ALS, DNA-RG 59 (M639-4). Introduces and recommends Charles Q. Clapp.

May 4   From Richard Henry Bradford. LC, DNA-RG 45 (M472-1). Transmits recommendations of Daniel D. Brodhead for navy agent at Boston.

May 4   From Cotton Brown Brooks et al. DS, DNA-RG 76 (13-0253). Request a special mission to pursue spoliation claims against France.

[May 4]   From Martha Ann Crouch. ADS, DNA-RG 94 (M567-42). Indigent widow requests an Army discharge for her son Samuel W. Crouch. Favorably endorsed by AJ.

May 4   From George Mifflin Dallas. ALS, DNA-RG 59 (M639-17). Recommends Morgan Neville for minister to Mexico or governor of Arkansas Territory.

May 4   From George Graham. LC, DNA-RG 49 (M25-23). Submits land patents for signature.

May 4   *From Joseph Scott.*   205

May 4   From Joseph Scott. ALS, DNA-RG 59 (M639-21); AJ endorsement, Heritage Collectors' Society catalog, Spring 1987 (mAJs). Encloses his recommendations.

May 5   To Israel Cole. Printed, *History of Berkshire County, Massachusetts, with Biographical Sketches of Its Prominent Men* (New York, 1885), 1:623 (mAJs). Thanks him for a gift of cheese and voices confidence in American naval power.

May 5   From Samuel Fisher Bradford. ALS, DNA-RG 45 (M124-118). Recommends naval purser Francis B. Stockton for sea duty.

May 5   From Richard Keith Call. ALS, DNA-RG 59 (M639-4). Recommends John K. Campbell for district attorney in Florida.

May 5   From John M. Conn. ALS, DNA-RG 94 (M688-68). Requests a West Point appointment for his son.

May 5   From William H. Elting. ALS, DNA-RG 94 (M567-47). Forwards indigent widow Hannah Snow's request for an Army discharge for her son Oliver F. Snow.

May 5   From John P. Norton et al. DS, DNA-RG 46 (13-0256). Massachusetts legislators recommend Daniel D. Brodhead for navy agent at Boston.

May 5   From Robert D. Richardson. ALS, DNA-RG 107 (13-0258). Recites his political and military services and asks for an office in Louisiana.

May 5   From John Spear Smith. ALS, DNA-RG 59 (M639-2). Recommends retaining Reuben G. Beasley as consul at Havre.

[May 5]   From Adam Whann et al. DS, DNA-RG 59 (M639-23). Recommend Henry Stump for district attorney in Florida or Louisiana.

May 5   Check to Andrew Jackson Donelson for $1,079. DS, DLC (37).

May 6   From François Campau (Nowokeshik). DS, DNA-RG 75 (13-0262). Chippewa Indian asks permission to sell his reserved land under the 1819 Treaty of Saginaw.

May 6   From George Graham. LC, DNA-RG 49 (M25-23). Submits land patents for signature.

May 6   From William Pitt Preble. ALS, DLC (37). Encloses Portland, Maine, *Eastern Argus,* Dec 22, 1818, defending AJ's proceedings against Arbuthnot and Ambrister. Note by AJ "To be filed with my private papers."

May 7   To David Ritter. Printed, *National Banner and Nashville Whig,* Jul 7 (13-0264); *Nat. Intelligencer,* Aug 29. Thanks him for the gift of a razor strop.

May 11   From John Randolph Grymes. ALS, DNA-RG 59 (M639-9).
           Asks to be appointed minister to Mexico.
May 11   From Charles Hood et al. DS, DNA-RG 46 (13-0278).
           Recommend Daniel D. Brodhead for navy agent at Boston.
May 11   *From Samuel Houston.*   *212*
May 11   From Louis Marchand. ALS, DNA-RG 59 (M639-15). Offers to
           serve on a special mission to settle spoliation claims against
           France.
May 11   From John Christmas McLemore. ALS, DNA-RG 59 (M639-2).
           Recommends Henry Baldwin, Jr., for secretary of legation.
[May 11]   From William Thompson Nuckolls, William Dickinson Martin,
           and Robert Young Hayne. DS, DNA-RG 107 (13-0308).
           Recommend Wilson Nesbitt for Indian agent in Arkansas.
May 11   From John Pope. ALS, DNA-RG 59 (M639-21). Departs for
           Arkansas Territory and recommends William B. Slaughter for a
           diplomatic or consular post.
May 11   *From William Robinson.*   *214*
May 11   From William Banks Slaughter. ALS, DNA-RG 59 (M639-21).
           Requests an office.
May 11   From Samuel Smith. ALS, DNA-RG 59 (M639-3). Recommends
           James T. Brice for a clerkship.
May 11   Proclamation suspending discriminating tonnage duties on
           Austrian vessels. Draft and DS, DNA-RG 59 (T1223-1); Copy,
           DNA-RG 59 (13-0276). Richardson, 2:440.
May 12   From Isaac Hill. ALS, DLC (37). Requests a brief leave from his
           duties as second comptroller.
May 12   From John Mullowny. ALS, DNA-RG 59 (T61-4). Proposes
           international measures to suppress Barbary piracies.
May 13   To Hussein, Dey of Algiers. LC, DNA-RG 59 (13-0310). Presents
           Henry Lee, succeeding William Shaler as U.S. consul general.
May 13   *To Thomas Miller.*   *216*
May 13   From John Branch. LC, DNA-RG 45 (M472-1). Submits
           Pensacola navy agent Charles P. Tutt's commission for signature.
May 13   From John McNeil. ALS, DNA-RG 59 (M639-13).
           Recommends Asahel Langworthy for office.
May 13   From Stephen Pleasonton. LS and LC, DNA-RG 26 (13-0311).
           Recommends replacing Stony Point, N.Y., lighthouse keeper
           Cornelius W. Lansing with Robert Parkinson. Approved by AJ.
May 13   From William Sterrett. ALS, DLC (37). Requests an office and
           remarks on Ohio postal appointments.
May 14   To Garret Garretson. LS, NjR (mAJs). Thanks him for honorary
           membership in the Philoclean literary society of Rutgers College.
May 14   From Stephen Pleasonton. ANS, DNA-RG 26 (13-0325).
           Submits Cornelius P. Van Ness's request to replace Burlington,
           Vt., lighthouse keeper Frederick A. Sawyer with Malachi
           Corning, and Sawyer's protest against removal.
May 14   To Stephen Pleasonton. ANS, DNA-RG 26 (13-0334). Appoints
           Malachi Corning lighthouse keeper at Burlington in place of
           Frederick A. Sawyer.

May 20	From Lawrence Tremper. ALS, DNA-RG 59 (M639-18). Recommends James Points for marshal in Virginia.
May 20	From Martin Van Buren. ALS, NNPM (13-0363). Introduces William J. Worth.
May 20	From Garret Dorset Wall. ALS, DNA-RG 59 (M639-25). Recommends Henry L. Waddell for consul at Liverpool.
May 20	Order of remission and release for prisoner Richard Shackleford. Copy and LC, DNA-RG 59 (13-0355; T967-1).
May 21	From John Branch. DS and LC (dated May 20), DNA-RG 45 (13-0365; M472-1). Summarizes naval purser Lewis Deblois's unpaid debts to the U.S. AJ orders his dismissal May 27.
May 21	From Collin McDaniel. ALS, DNA-RG 94 (M688-68). Recommends his son Alfred W. for continuance as land office receiver in Mississippi, his nephew Clement McDaniel for cadet at West Point, and himself for customs collector at Magnolia, Fla.

May 22	From Henry H. B. Hays. ALS, THi (13-0375). Asks to succeed Creek agent John Crowell, reportedly deceased.
May 22	From Arsène Lacarrière Latour. ALS, DNA-RG 59 (M639-13). Recommends strengthening ties with Cuba and asks to be appointed consul at Havana.
May 22	From Aaron Lummus et al. DS, DNA-RG 46 (13-0377). Recommend Daniel D. Brodhead for navy agent at Boston.
May 22	From Jasper Lynch. AD, DNA-RG 59 (M639-14). Asks to be appointed secretary to the French mission.
May 22	From Roger Brooke Taney. Copy, DNA-RG 59 (M639-11). Recommends William Hebb for a clerkship.
May 22	From Peter S. Townsend. ALS, DNA-RG 59 (M639-24). Asks to be appointed secretary of legation at Paris or Madrid.
May 22	From Gulian Crommelin Verplanck. Copy, CU-BANC (13-0381). Introduces and recommends Peter W. Spicer.

May 22	Bill from Tucker & Thompson to Andrew Jackson Donelson for clothing. DS, DLC (37). Runs to Dec 17.

May 23	To Martin Van Buren. ANS, DNA-RG 59 (13-0409). Appoints John S. Smith district attorney and John M. McCalla marshal in Kentucky.
May 23	From John Branch. LC, DNA-RG 45 (M472-1). Submits naval chaplain William Ryland's commission for signature.
[May 23]	From James Conner. DS, DNA-RG 75 (13-0395). Asks permission to sell land granted him under the Potawatomi treaty of 1826.
May 23	From John Maul. ALS, DNA-RG 107 (13-0401). Recounts his military services and sacrifices and requests employment.

May 23   From William McCoy. ALS, DNA-RG 59 (M639-18).
                Recommends James Points for marshal in Virginia in place of
                Benjamin Reeder.
May 23   Remission of forfeiture of the schooner *Anna Maria,* owned by
                John Allen and John Polk. Draft and Copy, DNA-RG 59 (13-
                0383); LC, DNA-RG 59 (T967-1).
May 23   Alexander Barrow to Andrew Jackson Donelson. ALS, DNA-RG
                59 (M639-10). Recommends Archibald Haralson for consul at
                Havre or Bordeaux.
May 23   Joseph Grinnell to Andrew Jackson Donelson. ALS, DNA-RG
                59 (M639-26). Recommends John Whitehead for consul at
                Havana.
May 24   James Ramage to John Henry Eaton. ALS, DLC (37). Appeals
                to AJ not to approve his Navy court-martial, the product of
                political persecution.
May 25   To Joel Barlow Sutherland. Extract, Charles Hamilton Galleries
                catalog (13-0428). Brands as false a May 5 Philadelphia
                Democratic Press report that he had recently confronted
                Sutherland for calling him a murderer in the 1824 campaign.
May 25   To James Hervey Witherspoon. LS, ScLan; Copy, WHi (13-
                0429). E. Don Herd, *Andrew Jackson, South Carolinian*
                (Lancaster, S.C., 1963), p. 47. Returns greetings from his
                birthplace.
May 25   From Francis Wells Armstrong. ALS, DNA-RG 59 (M639-11).
                Recommends retaining Henry Hitchcock as district attorney in
                Alabama.
May 25   From Thomas Butler. ALS, DNA-RG 59 (M639-10).
                Recommends Archibald Haralson for consul in France.
May 25   From Benjamin Clements. ALS, DNA-RG 45 (M124-118).
                Reports that the live oak plantation at Pensacola is a waste of
                government funds.
May 25   From John Coffee. ALS, DNA-RG 59 (M639-20). Recommends
                Neil B. Rose for marshal in Alabama.
May 25   From William Duncan. ALS, DNA-RG 59 (M873-19).
                Recommends Daniel C. Croxall for consul at Havre.
May 25   From James Gadsden. ALS, DNA-RG 59 (M639-4).
                Recommends John K. Campbell for district attorney in Florida.
May 25   From James Herron. ALS, DNA-RG 59 (M639-11). Asks to be
                appointed consul at Wexford, Ireland.
May 25   From Samuel McPherson Janney. ALS, TNJ (13-0416). Arranges
                for delivery to AJ of two pipes of Madeira wine.
May 25   From James Cresap Sprigg. ALS, DNA-RG 59 (M639-2).
                Recommends Charles S. Bibb for district attorney in Kentucky.
May 25   From Joel Barlow Sutherland. ALS, DLC (37). Forwards *The
                Jackson Wreath, or National Souvenir* (Philadelphia, 1829), a
                gift from Jacob Maas.

May 25	From John Whitehead. ALS, DNA-RG 59 (M639-26). Asks to be appointed consul at Havana.
May 25	Temporary commission for William Lytle as surveyor general for Ohio, Indiana, and Michigan Territory. LC, DNA-RG 59 (13-0422).
May 25	Bill from Tucker & Thompson for clothing. DS, DLC (37). Bassett, 4:104. Runs to Dec 17.
May 25	Bill from Tucker & Thompson for Samuel J. Hays's clothing. DS, DLC (37). Runs to Dec 17.
May 26	To Martin Van Buren. ANS, DNA-RG 59 (13-0441). Appoints John Campbell U.S. Treasurer in place of William Clark.
May 26	To Martin Van Buren. ANS, DNA-RG 59 (13-0443). Appoints Robert Getty justice of the peace for Washington, D.C.
May 26	From Isaac Dutton Barnard. ALS, PPAmP (13-0433). Recommends Henry Kenyon for naval hospital superintendent or storekeeper at Philadelphia.
May 26	From Christopher Blockberger. ALS, DNA-RG 45 (M124-118). Offers to supply buoys to the government.
May 26	*From Susan Wheeler Decatur.* 243
May 26	From John Pemberton. ALS copy, PHi (13-0439). Encloses a letter from Benjamin W. Richards.
May 26	From Joel Barlow Sutherland. ALS, DLC (37). Introduces Joshua Shaw, inventor of a new percussion lock for artillery.
May 26	From Ross Wilkins. ALS, DNA-RG 94 (M688-60). Recommends James McFarland for cadet at West Point.
May 26	Temporary commission for John Campbell as U.S. Treasurer. LCs, DNA-RG 50 and DNA-RG 59 (13-0435).
May 26	Temporary commission for Robert Getty as justice of the peace in Washington, D.C. LC, DNA-RG 59 (13-0438).
May 27	From Stephen Pleasonton. LC, DNA-RG 26 (13-0447). Transmits applicant files for lighthouse keeper at Portland Harbor, N.Y., and recommends Joshua Lane.
May 27	To Stephen Pleasonton. ANS, DNA-RG 26 (13-0445). Appoints Joshua Lane lighthouse keeper at Portland Harbor, N.Y.
May 27	From John Branch. LC, DNA-RG 45 (M472-1). Encloses Charles G. Ridgely's reports of May 4 (M125-137) and May 9 (M125-136) explaining and defending his operations against Cuban pirates.
May 27	From John Branch. LC, DNA-RG 45 (M472-1). Submits naval purser Francis G. McCauley's commission for signature.
May 27	From Benjamin Ruggles. ALS, DLC (37). Recommends Thomas Rigdon for office.
May 27	From R. F. Slaughter. ALS, DNA-RG 59 (M639-10). Recommends Archibald Haralson for consul general in France.
May 28	To Isaac Anderson. LS draft, DLC (13-0460). *Morning Courier and New–York Enquirer,* Jun 11. Thanks him for the gift of a hickory walking cane.
May 28	To Charles John, King of Sweden. LS, Royal Ministry for Foreign Affairs, Stockholm, Sweden; Draft, DLC; LC, DNA-RG 59 (13-0465). Offers congratulations on the birth of a grandson.

May 28 To Martin Van Buren. ANS, DNA-RG 59 (13-0488). Appoints Richard C. Allen law agent and James W. Exum marshal in Florida.

May 28 To Martin Van Buren. NS, DNA-RG 59 (13-0490). Appoints John Silva Meehan librarian of Congress.

May 28 From James Andrew John Bradford. ALS, DNA-RG 107 (13-0463). Recommends retaining William Armistead as sutler at Fortress Monroe, Va.

May 28 From William C. Kelly. ALS, DNA-RG 107 (M221-109). Complains of his dismissal for corruption as clerk to Army paymaster David Gwynne in 1824.

May 28 From Thomas P. Moore. ALS, DNA-RG 59 (M639-7). Urges removing Edwin S. Duncan as district attorney in Virginia.

May 28 From Stephen Pleasonton. ANS, DNA-RG 26 (13-0471). Submits papers concerning a dispute over locating a lighthouse in Connecticut on Long Island Sound.

May 28 From Unknown. AL fragment, DLC (13-0484). Hails AJ's triumph over the monied aristocracy, decries the evils of alcohol, and urges AJ to set an example against its use.

May 28 Temporary commission for John Silva Meehan as librarian of Congress. DS, DLC (13-0470).

May 29 To Charles John, King of Sweden. LS, Royal Ministry for Foreign Affairs, Stockholm, Sweden; LC, DNA-RG 59 (13-0496). Offers condolences on the death of his aunt.

May 29 From John Brahan. ALS, DNA-RG 59 (M639-20). Recommends Neil B. Rose for marshal in Alabama.

[May 29] From Joaquín Campino. D, DNA-RG 59 (M73-1). Takes leave as Chilean minister to the United States.

May 29 From George W. Churchwell. ALS, DNA-RG 59 (M639-4). Asks to be appointed district attorney in Tennessee in place of John A. McKinney.

May 29 From William Hutchings, Jr., et al. DS, DNA-RG 59 (M639-24). Recommend Jonathan Thayer for marshal in Maine.

May 29 From Charles S. Morgan et al. LS, DNA-RG 59 (M639-10). Recommend William A. Harrison for district attorney in Virginia.

May 29 From James C. Patton. ALS, DNA-RG 59 (M639-10). Recommends Robert Haile for office.

May 29 John Thomas to William Berkeley Lewis. ALS, DNA-RG 45 (M124-118). Recommends a survey for a dockyard in the Harlem River. Endorsed by AJ.

May 30 To Samuel Delucenna Ingham. ANS, DNA-RG 59 (13-0507). Appoints Thomas L. Smith register of the Treasury in place of Joseph Nourse.

May 30 To Martin Van Buren. LS, DNA-RG 59 (M179-67). Proposes that librarian of Congress John S. Meehan should post bond in the same amount as his predecessors.

[cMay]   From Warren Preston et al. and from Edwin Smith et al. DSs,
              DNA-RG 59 (M639-24). Recommend Jonathan Thayer for
              marshal in Maine.
[Jun]   *Memorandum book.*   261
Jun 1   To Ferdinand VII, King of Spain. Copy, DNA-RG 59 (13-0534).
              Announces Alexander H. Everett's replacement by Cornelius P.
              Van Ness as minister to Spain.
Jun 1   To [Martin Van Buren]. NS, DNA-RG 59 (13-0546). Makes
              diplomatic appointments.
[Jun 1]   From George Mifflin Dallas, Edward King, et al. DS, DNA-RG
              59 (M639-10). Recommend Isaac A. Hayes for consul at Rio
              Grande, Brazil.
[cJun 1]   From James Devereux et al. DS, DNA-RG 76 (13-0531). Ask
              help in pursuing their claim against Portugal for seizure of the
              brig *Osprey*'s cargo at Bahia in 1823.
Jun 1   *From Tomlinson Fort.*   262
Jun 1   From Rosewell Saltonstall. ALS, DLC (37). Warns of plots
              against himself and Samuel Swartwout, requests a consulship,
              and asks to have his Biblical explanation of the tides printed.
Jun 1   From S. S. Smith et al. Copy, DNA-RG 59 (M639-25).
              Recommend Jesse Waln for consul at Tangier.
Jun 1   Temporary commissions for diplomats Charles Carroll Harper,
              Washington Irving, William Pitt Preble, and Cornelius Peter Van
              Ness. LCs, DNA-RG 59 (13-0543, 13-0548).
Jun 1   Robert D. Richardson to Thomas Deye Owings. ALS, DLC (37).
              Asks for a copy of a recommendation left with AJ and for AJ's
              attention to his claim against the government.
Jun 2   To Louis McLane. LS, ViW (mAJs). *New York Genealogical and
              Biographical Record* 23 (1892):154 (13-0549). Offers
              condolences on the death of his father Allan McLane and
              introduces Francis B. Ogden.
Jun 2   To Francisco Antonio Pinto Diaz. LS, Gallery of History, Inc.
              (mAJs); LC, DNA-RG 59; Draft, DLC (13-0550). Commends
              departing Chilean minister Joaquín Campino.
Jun 2   *To Martin Van Buren.*   265
[Jun 2]   From Martin Van Buren. ANS, DNA-RG 59 (M179-67).
              Suggests requiring an opinion from district attorney Nathaniel
              Williams before issuing a nolle prosequi for Elias H. Merryman.
Jun 2   *To Martin Van Buren.*   266
Jun 2   To Martin Van Buren. ANS, MHi (mAJs). Returns letters with
              assurance to John Chandler that Mr. H.'s influence has not
              shaken his good opinion of William P. Preble.
Jun 2   To Martin Van Buren. AN, MHi (mAJs). Returns a letter.
Jun 2   From Robert Butler. ALS, DNA-RG 59 (M639-21).
              Recommends John S. Shepard for secretary of Florida Territory.
Jun 2   From Richard Keith Call. ALS, DNA-RG 59 (M639-7). *TPUS,*
              24:222–23. Reports on Florida Spanish land claim cases, praises
              law agent Samuel Brents, and recommends James A. Dunlap for
              district attorney in place of James G. Ringgold.

Jun 2   From Richard Keith Call. ALS, DNA-RG 59 (M639-21). Recommends John S. Shepard for secretary of Florida Territory.

Jun 2   From Charles Alexander Clinton. ALS, DNA-RG 59 (M639-4). Recommends Nathaniel H. Carter for consul at Marseilles.

Jun 2   From William Pope Duval. ALS, DNA-RG 59 (M639-2). Recommends Abraham Bellamy for secretary of Florida Territory.

Jun 2   From John Andrew Graham. LS, DNA-RG 59 (M639-4). Recommends Nathaniel H. Carter for consul at Marseilles.

Jun 2   From Aaron Leggett. ALS, DNA-RG 59 (M639-4). Recommends Nathaniel H. Carter for consul at Marseilles.

Jun 3   To Unknown. LS, NNPM (mAJs). Explains that preference for a New Englander to present the Northeastern boundary case precluded considering Cadwallader D. Colden for minister to the Netherlands.

Jun 3   From Christopher Andrews. ALS, DNA-RG 59 (M639-11). Recommends Alexander Hunter for marshal of the District of Columbia.

Jun 3   From John Strode Barbour. ALS, DNA-RG 59 (M639-11). Recommends Alexander Hunter for office.

Jun 3   From James Gadsden. ALS, DNA-RG 46 (13-0560). *TPUS,* 24:226–27. Recommends reappointing Florida district attorney Benjamin D. Wright.

Jun 3   From George Graham. LC, DNA-RG 49 (M25-24). Submits land patents for signature.

Jun 3   From William Lytle. ALS, DNA-RG 59 (M639-3). Recommends Theodore H. Burrows for a southern territorial office.

Jun 3   From Joshua Stoney. ALS, DNA-RG 107 (13-0563). Asks to be made an Army captain.

Jun 3   From Samuel Swartwout. ALS, DNA-RG 59 (M639-4). Recommends Nathaniel H. Carter for consul.

Jun 3   From Nathaniel Williams. ANS, DNA-RG 59 (M179-67). Forwards and concurs in the grand jury's request for a nolle prosequi for Elias H. Merryman.

Jun 3   Check to Andrew Jackson, Jr., for $75. DS, DLC (37).

Jun 3   Proclamation suspending discriminating duties on goods imported in Austrian vessels. DS, DNA-RG 59 (T1223-1); Copy, DNA-RG 59 (13-0557). Richardson, 2:441–42.

Jun 4   *To Martin Van Buren.*   266

Jun 4   To Martin Van Buren. ALS, DNA-RG 59 (M179-67). Introduces Ebenezer J. Hume, to deliver instructions to George Watterston to relinquish the Library of Congress.

Jun 4   To Martin Van Buren. ANS, DNA-RG 59 (M179-67). Orders a nolle prosequi for Elias H. Merryman.

Jun 4   To Martin Van Buren. ANS, DNA-RG 59 (M179-67). Tells him where to find the order for a nolle prosequi for Elias H. Merryman.

Jun 4   From John Branch. LC, DNA-RG 45 (M472-1); Copy, DNA-RG 217 (13-0566). Asks for authority to advance funds to naval officials; approved by AJ.

Jun 4	From Henry Conner. DS, DNA-RG 75 (13-0568). Asks permission to sell land granted him under the Potawatomi treaty of 1826.
Jun 4	From Frances Howard. DS, DNA-RG 94 (M567-43). Indigent widow requests an Army discharge for her son George W. Howard.
Jun 4	From James Coffield Mitchell. ALS, DNA-RG 59 (M639-21). Recommends Joseph Scott for district attorney in Alabama in place of Harry I. Thornton.
Jun 4	From Samuel Swartwout. ALS, DLC (37). Introduces and recommends Charles Wilkes.
Jun 4	Check to John Henry Eaton for $1,521. DS, DLC (37).
Jun 4	Treasury warrant from Samuel Delucenna Ingham to John Campbell to pay AJ's monthly salary. DS, DNA-RG 217 (13-0570).
Jun 4	Thomas Lilly Smith to Andrew Jackson Donelson. LC, DNA-RG 39 (13-0572). Encloses documents pertaining to James Livingston's Revolutionary pension claim.
Jun 5	To Martin Van Buren. ALS, DNA-RG 59 (M179-67). Agrees to see [Thomas L.?] "McKennee" and returns a document.
Jun 5	From Elizabeth Langdon Elwyn. ALS, DNA-RG 45 (M124-119). Requests a berth on the frigate *Constellation* for her son, midshipman Thomas O. L. Elwyn.
Jun 5	*From Samuel Craig Lamme.* 267
Jun 5	From John Pope. ALS, DNA-RG 46 (13-0578). Recommends Wharton Rector for Choctaw agent.
Jun 5	From James G. Ringgold et al. LS, DNA-RG 59 (M639-7). *TPUS*, 24:227–28. Recommend John P. Duval for secretary of Florida Territory.
[Jun 5]	From James Robertson. ADS, DNA-RG 59 (13-0854). Petitions for release from prison, where he is held for inability to pay his fine and costs for assault and battery. AJ orders pardon Jul 15.
Jun 5	Maxwell Sommerville to Andrew Jackson Donelson. ALS, DNA-RG 59 (M639-22). Encloses John Sommerville's Mar 9 letter introducing him.
Jun 6	To Martin Van Buren. ALS, DNA-RG 59 (M179-67). *TPUS*, 24:228. Directs him to instruct Florida district judge James Webb to remove to Key West.
[Jun 6]	To [Martin Van Buren]. NS, DNA-RG 59 (13-0585). Appoints marshals and district attorneys.
Jun 6	From Calvin Blythe. ALS, DNA-RG 46 (13-0581). Recommends Sterrett Ramsey for naval purser.
Jun 6	From James Bradford. ALS, DNA-RG 59 (M639-3). Recommends James M. Bradford for governor of Arkansas Territory.
Jun 6	From Jehiel Brooks. ALS, DNA-RG 59 (M639-3). Requests a consulate if he cannot get an Indian agency.
[Jun 6]	From John Frost. DS, DNA-RG 59 (13-0644). Petitions for remission of penalties for carrying an excess of passengers on the British brig *Emma*. Approved by AJ.

Jun 6	From George Graham. LC, DNA-RG 49 (M25-24). Submits land patents for signature.	
Jun 6	From Henry Horn. ALS, DNA-RG 59 (M639-19). Recommends Joseph Ray for consul at Pernambuco.	
Jun 6	From Maxwell Sommerville. ALS, DNA-RG 59 (M639-10). Recommends William A. Harrison for district attorney in Virginia.	
Jun 6	Temporary commission for John Dean as marshal in Florida Territory. Copy, DNA-RG 59 (mAJs); *TPUS*, 24:229 (13-0584).	
Jun 7	*To John Donelson.*	268
Jun 7	Dentist's bill from James S. Gunnell. ADS, DLC (72). Runs to Aug 7.	
Jun 8	*To John Overton.*	270
Jun 8	*To Frances Walton Pope.*	272
Jun 8	From Elihu Hall Bay. ALS, DLC (72). Recommends his son Andrew for office in South Carolina.	
Jun 8	From John Branch. LC, DNA-RG 45 (M472-1). Submits naval purser William A. Slacum's commission for signature.	
Jun 8	From William Cox. ALS, DNA-RG 59 (M639-11). Recommends Alexander Hunter for marshal of the District of Columbia.	
Jun 8	From John H. Hall. ALS, DNA-RG 107 (M222-25). Encloses an 1819 Army report endorsing his breech-loading rifles.	
Jun 8	From James Taylor. ALS, DNA-RG 107 (M222-26). Recommends his brother-in-law James W. Moss for Iowa Indian agent; referred by AJ to Eaton's *"particular attention."*	
Jun 8	Temporary commission for Isaac Austin Hayes as consul at Rio Grande, Brazil. DS, DNA-RG 76; Copy, DNA-RG 59 (13-0593).	
Jun 9	To Simón Bolívar, President of Colombia. LC, DNA-RG 59 (13-0602). Presents American minister Thomas P. Moore.	
Jun 9	*From Martin Van Buren.*	273
Jun 9	*To Martin Van Buren.*	274
Jun 9	From Thomas Jefferson Green. ALS, DNA-RG 59 (M639-17). Recommends William B. Nuttall for secretary of Florida Territory.	
Jun 9	From Samuel Gardner Perkins et al. DS, DNA-RG 76 (mAJs). Boston merchants urge settlement of their spoliation claims against France.	
Jun 9	From William Lucius Storrs. ALS, CtHi (13-0605). Recommends William T. Williams for office.	
Jun 9	From Thomas Underwood. ALS, DNA-RG 15 (13-0609). Inquires why Revolutionary veteran James Hooper's approved claim for pay has not been paid.	
Jun 9	Temporary commission for James Chamberlayne Pickett as secretary of legation in Colombia. LC, DNA-RG 59 (13-0604).	
[Jun 9]	Memorandum by Andrew Jackson Donelson of the offer of return transportation to William H. Harrison. ANS, DLC (60).	
Jun 10	To Charles X, King of France. LC, DNA-RG 59 (13-0611). Presents American minister William C. Rives.	
Jun 10	To George IV, King of Great Britain. LC, DNA-RG 59 (13-0618). Presents American minister Louis McLane.	

Jun 12   From John Pope. ALS, DNA-RG 59 (M639-20). Recommends Samuel Q. Richardson for district attorney in Kentucky.

Jun 12   From William McFarland Saul. ALS, DLC (37). Requests a consulate to escape political persecution in New Orleans.

Jun 12   From the Misses Stark. AN, DLC (37); AN copy, Joseph M. Maddalena (mAJs). Granddaughters of Revolutionary general John Stark present a gift of watch paper.

Jun 12   From James Diament Westcott, Jr. ALS, DNA-RG 59 (M639-26). *TPUS,* 24:237. Asks to be appointed secretary of Florida Territory.

Jun 12   Remission of penalties against John Frost, master of the British brig *Emma.* Copy and LC, DNA-RG 59 (13-0635; T967-1).

Jun 13   To John Macpherson Berrien. ALS, DNA-RG 60 (13-0649); LC, DLC (60). Asks if he can legally advance funds to departing minister to Colombia Thomas P. Moore beyond the amount of his outfit; encloses former attorney general William Wirt's opinion of Oct 14, 1823 (DNA-RG 60, T412-2).

Jun 13   From Freeman Brady. ALS, DNA-RG 107 (M222-25). Complains of fraud and asks fair payment of his expenses for repairing the Cumberland Road.

Jun 13   From David Keller. ALS, DNA-RG 59 (M639-4). Recommends James G. Carroll for marshal in Alabama.

[Jun 13]   From Joel Whitney et al. DS, DNA-RG 59 (M639-24). Recommend Jonathan Thayer for marshal in Maine.

Jun 14   From Charles Carroll. ALS, DLC (37). Thanks AJ for appointing his grandson Charles C. Harper secretary of legation at Paris and invites a visit.

Jun 15   To Daniel Garland. ANS, Robert Icenhauer-Ramirez (mAJs). Promises delivery to Virginia of recaptured prison escapee John Dungey upon payment of fees.

Jun 15   To Joseph Jackson et al. ALS, MNS (13-0663); Draft, DLC (37). Trenton *Emporium,* Jul 18; *Niles,* Aug 1. Thanks New Jersey legislators for congratulations on his election.

Jun 15   To [Martin Van Buren]. ANS, DNA-RG 59 (13-0668); LC, DLC (60). Appoints James D. Westcott, Jr., secretary of Florida Territory.

Jun 15   To Martin Van Buren. ALS, DNA-RG 59 (M639-6). Introduces Auguste G. V. Davezac.

Jun 15   To Martin Van Buren. ALS, DNA-RG 59 (M639-18). Introduces Henry D. Peire and recommends him for a consulate.

Jun 15   From John Macpherson Berrien. ALS, DNA-RG 59 (M179-67); LC, DNA-RG 60 (T412-3). *HRDoc* 123, 26th Cong., 2d sess., pp. 678–79 (Serial 387). Opines that AJ may legally advance funds to American diplomats abroad.

Jun 15   From James Cowan. ALS, DNA-RG 75 (M234-73). Asks to be

Jun 18	From John Macpherson Berrien. LC, DNA-RG 60 (T412-3). *HRDoc* 123, 26th Cong., 2d sess., pp. 680–82 (Serial 387). Advises against pardoning counterfeiter Jacob K. Boyer.
Jun 18	From Upton S. Heath et al. DS, DNA-RG 59 (M639-11). Recommend Ralph Higginbotham for a West Indian consulate; referred favorably by AJ to Van Buren.
Jun 18	From Augustus Hoch. ALS, Stanley F. Horn (13-0673). Presents a poem honoring the Fourth of July.
Jun 18	From Jeromus Johnson. Copies, CU-BANC (13-0676). Introduces Peter W. Spicer.
Jun 18	*From Stephen Simpson.* 292
Jun 18	Check to William Berkeley Lewis for $357.25. DS, DLC (37).
Jun 18	Temporary commission for Jesse Moore as justice of the peace in the District of Columbia. LC, DNA-RG 59 (13-0678).
Jun 18	Temporary commission for Francis Barber Ogden as consul at Liverpool. Copy, DNA-RG 59 (13-0679).
Jun 19	From Harrison & Sterett. LS, THer (13-0684). Announce the arrival of sugar and lemons for AJ from New Orleans.
Jun 19	From John Prentiss Kewley Henshaw et al. DS, DNA-RG 45 (M124-119). Episcopal clergymen recommend naval chaplain John P. Fenner for shore duty.
Jun 19	From Samuel Delucenna Ingham. ALS, DNA-RG 59 (13-0751). Recommends a release for John Smith, jailed for unpaid debts to the U.S.; endorsed favorably by AJ.
Jun 19	From Pedro I, Emperor of Brazil. DS and translation, DNA-RG 59 (M49-1); Copy, DNA-RG 84 (13-0686). Announces a regency in the name of his daughter Maria II to govern Portugal in place of his usurping brother Miguel.
Jun 19	From Henry Duvivier Peire. ALS, DNA-RG 59 (M639-18). Asks again to be appointed consul at Havana.
Jun 19	From Henry Stark. ALS, DLC (37). Encloses the Jun 12 letter and gift from the Misses Stark.
Jun 20	*To Joseph Elgar.* 293
Jun 20	*To William Pitt Preble.* 293
[Jun 20]	From William Boswell. DS, DNA-RG 59 (13-0728). Petitions for remission of penalties and release of his ship *William Shand*, seized for carrying excess passengers.
Jun 20	From James Gadsden. ALS, DNA-RG 59 (M639-9). Recommends William J. Gibson for district attorney and Lackland M. Stone for marshal in Florida.
Jun 20	From James Morgan. ALS, DNA-RG 59 (M639-20). Urges removing Thomas M. Rodney as consul at Havana.
Jun 20	From Levi Woodbury. AN, DNA-RG 46 (13-0694). Recommends Walter Colton for naval chaplain.
Jun 20	Refusal of pardon for convicted counterfeiter Jacob K. Boyer. LC, DLC (60).
Jun 20	Receipt from Jeremiah James for purchase of linen. DS by Thomas Hurley, DLC (37).
Jun 20	John Randolph to Martin Van Buren. ALS, DNA-RG 59 (M639-

Papers, 1:165–66. Forwards records of Cherokee lawsuits dismissed due to agent Hugh Montgomery's negligence.

Jun 24   From Squire Streeter. ALS, DNA-RG 59 (M639-23). Asks to be appointed customs collector at St. Augustine or marshal in Florida.

Jun 25   To Samuel Delucenna Ingham. ALS, The Raab Collection (mAJs). Rejects a proposed customs change because it would entrust revenue to merchants' clerks instead of sworn officers.

Jun 25   From Charles Biddle. ALS, DNA-RG 59 (M639-8). Recommends Samuel R. Fisher for consul.

Jun 25   From Samuel Houston. ALS, DNA-RG 75 (M234-236). Gives credence to the Creek complaints against David Brearley and urges an inquiry.

Jun 25   From John Christmas McLemore et al. LS, DNA-RG 59 (M639-8). Recommend Samuel R. Fisher for consul at Cadiz.

Jun 25   From Henry Stark. ALS, DLC (37). Thanks AJ for his acceptance of a gift of watch paper.

Jun 25   From Martin Van Buren. ALS, DNA-RG 59 (13-0714). Recommends renewing Woodbridge Odlin's commission as consul at St. Salvador, Brazil; approved by AJ.

Jun 25   *Order for remission of penalties against William Boswell.*   *301*

Jun 25   Temporary commission for Woodbridge Odlin as consul at St. Salvador, Brazil. Copy, DNA-RG 59 (13-0713).

Jun 25   John Christmas McLemore to Andrew Jackson Donelson. ALS, DNA-RG 59 (M639-8). Recommends Samuel R. Fisher for consul at Cadiz.

Jun 26   From Benjamin Bailey. ALS, DNA-RG 59 (M639-20). Endorses George Robertson's request to transfer from consul at Tampico to another station.

Jun 26   From George Graham. LC, DNA-RG 49 (M25-24). Submits land patents for signature.

Jun 26   From John L. Harris. ALS, DNA-RG 59 (M873-19). Recommends Daniel C. Croxall for consul.

Jun 26   From William Seal et al. DS, DNA-RG 59 (M639-10). Recommend Samuel Harker for marshal in Delaware.

Jun 26   From John Smith. DS, DNA-RG 59 (13-0753). Requests release from his imprisonment at Hartford for debts to the U.S.; approved by AJ.

Jun 27   *To Stephen Simpson.*   *301*

Jun 27   *From Logan Davidson Brandon.*   *302*

Jun 27   From James Gadsden. ALS, DNA-RG 59 (M639-9). Introduces William H. Allen to recommend William J. Gibson for district attorney in Florida.

Jun 27   From George Graham. LC, DNA-RG 49 (M25-24). Submits land patents for signature.

Jun 27   From James McKenzie. ALS, DLC (13-0735). Recommends A. Orlando Newton for consul at Matanzas, Cuba.

Jun 27   From Washington G. Singleton. ALS, DNA-RG 59 (M639-21). Urges AJ not to appoint James Ship marshal of the District of Columbia.

be made a cadet at West Point and complains of exclusivity in
the appointments.

Jul 9	From Robert B. Stark et al. Printed, Norfolk *American Beacon,* Jul 10 (mAJs); *Niles,* Jul 18 (13-0832). Invite AJ to Norfolk, Va.; AJ accepts.
Jul 10	From James DeWolf. ALS, DNA-RG 59 (M639-6). Asks that his son-in-law Joshua Dodge be retained as consul at Marseilles.
Jul 10	From Arthur Emmerson et al. Printed, Norfolk *American Beacon,* Jul 11 (mAJs); *Nat. Intelligencer,* Jul 15 (13-0833). Invite AJ to Portsmouth, Va.; AJ accepts but declines a public dinner.
Jul 10	*From John Hanson Good.* 330
[Jul 10]	From John E. Holt. Printed, Norfolk *American Beacon,* Jul 13 (mAJs); *Niles,* Jul 18 (13-0834). Norfolk mayor welcomes AJ; AJ replies.
Jul 10	From Samuel M. Osbourne. ALS, DNA-RG 107 (13-0835). Asks for a clerkship in Washington.
Jul 11	From T. Child. ADS, DNA-RG 75 (M234-185). Reports that the Choctaws are eager to remove to Texas if it can be obtained from Mexico.
Jul 11	From Alphonso Wetmore. ALS, DNA-RG 107 (13-0839). Asks to be appointed superintendent at Harpers Ferry.
Jul 12	*From Richard Gilliam Dunlap.* 332
Jul 12	From William Hall. ALS, DNA-RG 59 (M639-9). Recommends John P. Graham for district attorney in Alabama in place of Joseph Scott.
Jul 13	From Asa Child. ALS, DNA-RG 59 (13-0894). Recommends amending the Jun 30 release for prisoner John Smith to allow him to keep his equity in a Cuban plantation.
Jul 13	From James Gadsden. ALS, DNA-RG 59 (M639-6). Recommends John K. Campbell for district attorney and James Dell for Indian agent in Florida.
Jul 13	From William Hume. ALS fragment, ICHi (13-0844). Reports on conditions at the Hermitage.
Jul 13	From Anthony B. Shelby. ALS, DNA-RG 45 (M124-119). Seeks a contract to supply meat to the Brooklyn and Norfolk navy yards.
Jul 13	From Robert Smith. ALS, DLC (37). Discusses canals and national defense.
Jul 14	*To Andrew Jackson, Jr.* 333
Jul 14	From Benjamin Evens. ALS, DNA-RG 59 (M639-7). Asks to be appointed consul at Leghorn, Italy.
Jul 14	From Benjamin Evens. ALS, DNA-RG 59 (M639-7). Further explains his request for a consulship.
Jul 14	From George Graham. LC, DNA-RG 49 (M25-24). Submits eight land patents for signature.
Jul 14	From Sylvanus Seeber et al. DS, DNA-RG 59 (M639-14). Recommend Thomas T. Loomis for Michigan Territory judge in place of James D. Doty.
Jul 14	From John Speed Smith. ALS, DNA-RG 94 (M688-59). Recommends Clarendon Peck for appointment to West Point.
Jul 15	To James Alexander Hamilton. LS, NN (13-0847). Hamilton *Reminiscences,* p. 142. Acknowledges his confidential letter of Jul 10, which he has forwarded to Ingham.

Jul 15	From William Taylor Barry. ALS, DNA-RG 59 (M179-67). Encloses a letter asking AJ's intercession for the release of American trappers held prisoner in California.
Jul 15	To Martin Van Buren. ANS, DNA-RG 59 (M179-67). Asks him to write the Mexican authorities in California about American prisoners held there.
[cJul 15]	From John Henry Eaton. Abstract, *American Book-Prices Current*, 1931 (13-0765). Asks to authorize sending Thomas L. McKenney to New York to organize the Indian Board for the Emigration, Preservation, and Improvement of the Aborigines of America; approved by AJ.
Jul 15	From Benjamin Franklin Gard. ALS, DNA-RG 107 (M222-25). Complains of persecution which drove him from West Point and asks for reinstatement in the Army.
Jul 15	From Jesse Haskell. ALS, DNA-RG 59 (M639-10). Asks to be appointed consul at Cape Verde.
Jul 15	From Peter Robinson. ADS, DNA-RG 59 (M639-10). Recommends Samuel Harker for marshal in Delaware.
Jul 15	From Conrad Smith. ALS, DNA-RG 107 (M222-26). Recommends Colonel William Lindsay to command the Second Artillery Regiment.
Jul 15	From John Peter Van Ness. ALS, DNA-RG 59 (M639-7). Recommends Robert P. Dunlop for marshal of the District of Columbia.
Jul 16	To Littleton Waller Tazewell, Jr. Printed, Stan V. Henkels catalog, 1929 (13-0859). Thanks him for the gift of a sprig of weeping willow.
Jul 16	From James Madison Buchanan. ALS, DNA-RG 59 (M639-3). Asks the fate of his application to be secretary of legation.
Jul 16	From George Graham. LC, DNA-RG 49 (M25-24); Copies, DNA-RG 45 and DNA-RG 49 (13-0849). Reports on preservation of federal live oak timberlands in Florida.
Jul 16	From Edward King. ALS, DNA-RG 59 (M639-16). Recommends John S. Meircken for consul at Valparaiso.
Jul 16	From William M. Pardue. ALS, DNA-RG 59 (M639-17). Asks to be appointed marshal and urges the removal of Adams partisans in Mississippi.
Jul 16	Alexander G. Morgan to Andrew Jackson Donelson. ALS, DNA-RG 59 (M639-15). Urges James W. McClung or Harry I. Thornton for Alabama district attorney in place of Joseph Scott, recommends his brother Samuel D. Morgan for register of the Huntsville land office in place of Benjamin S. Pope, and warns against the Brandons.
Jul 16	Release for prisoner James Robertson. LC, DNA-RG 59 (T967-1; 13-0853).
Jul 16	Temporary commission for John Adams Smith as secretary of legation at St. Petersburg. LC, DNA-RG 59 (13-0858).
Jul 17	From John Devereux DeLacy. ALS, DNA-RG 107 (M221-110). Demands a fair settlement of James R. Mullany's accounts as

	Army quartermaster general and accuses third auditor Peter Hagner of oppression and fraud.
Jul 17	From Samuel Delucenna Ingham. ALS, DNA-RG 59 (13-0897). Seconds Asa Child's Jul 13 proposal to amend the release for prisoner John Smith; approved by AJ.
Jul 17	From John Milner et al. DS, DNA-RG 59 (M179-67). American merchants at Buenos Aires urge AJ not to downgrade the U.S. legation to a consulate.
Jul 17	From Johnson F. Newlon et al. LS, DNA-RG 59 (M639-19). Request Benjamin Reeder's removal as marshal in Virginia.
Jul 17	From Charles Rhind. ADS copy, DNA-RG 59 (M639-20). Asks to be appointed consul at Odessa.
Jul 18	*To John Henry Eaton.* 334
[Jul 18]	To Samuel Delucenna Ingham. LS, DNA-RG 49 (13-0889). *TPUS,* 24:250–51. Discusses arrangements for Richard K. Call's mission to Havana to procure Spanish documents concerning Florida land claim cases.
Jul 18	From John Macpherson Berrien. LC, DNA-RG 60 (T412-3). AD fragment, DLC; Extract, DNA-RG 45 (13-0862). *HRDoc* 123, 26th Cong., 2d sess., pp. 691–704 (Serial 387). Answers AJ's Jun 11 query with opinion on pay and allowances for brevet officers, the surgeon and paymaster general, and the Marine Corps.
Jul 18	*From Richard Keith Call.* 334
Jul 18	From Moses Myers. AL Draft, ViW (mAJs). Defends his conduct as customs collector at Norfolk and encloses a petition opposing his removal.
Jul 18	Amended release for prisoner John Smith, exempting his Cuban property from surrender. LC and Draft, DNA-RG 59 (T967-1; 13-0893).
[cJul 18]	Memorandum that the War Department in 1827 had unlawfully allowed brevet pay to officers commanding below their brevet rank. AN, THer (13-0881).
Jul 19	To Ralph Eleazar Whitesides Earl. Photocopy of ALS, Early American History Auctions catalog, Jun 10, 2000 (mAJs). Laments his lonesomeness with AJ Jr. away and looks forward to Earl's arrival.
Jul 20	To John Branch. ANS, DNA-RG 45 (M124-120). Refers for inquiry a request for extension on a naval contract.
Jul 20	*To Andrew Jackson, Jr.* 336
Jul 20	From William M. Boggs et al. and from Johnson F. Newlon et al. DSs, DNA-RG 59 (M639-2). Recommend Thomas Bland for marshal in Virginia in place of Benjamin Reeder.
Jul 20	From Richard Henry Bradford. LS and LC, DNA-RG 45 (M124-119; M472-1); Copy, DNA-RG 217 (13-0904). Requests authority to advance funds to the American agent in Africa for receiving blacks repatriated from seized slave ships; granted by AJ.
Jul 20	From Joel W. Jouet. ALS, DNA-RG 94 (M567-44). Asks for a commission in the Army.

Jul 20	From Young King et al. DS, DNA-RG 75 (M234-832). Seneca chiefs and warriors request that Jasper Parrish be retained as subagent.
Jul 21	*To John Coffee.* *337*
Jul 21	To Martin Van Buren. AN, Mr. James Stahlman (13-0910). Transmits an application.
Jul 21	*From John Macpherson Berrien.* *338*
Jul 21	From James McCally. ALS, DNA-RG 59 (M639-2). Recommends Thomas Bland for marshal in Virginia in place of Benjamin Reeder.
Jul 21	From John Howe Peyton. ALS, DNA-RG 59 (M639-18). Recommends his son William M. Peyton for district attorney in Virginia.
Jul 21	From George Bryan Porter. ALS, DNA-RG 59 (M639-7). Recommends Benjamin Evens for consul at Leghorn.
Jul 21	From Charles Rhind. ALS, DNA-RG 59 (M639-20). Encloses his proposal for a negotiating strategy with Turkey for access to the Black Sea.
Jul 21	From John Stuart Skinner. ANS, DNA-RG 107 (M222-26). Transmits Conrad Smith's letter of Jul 15.
Jul 21	From Alphonso Wetmore. ALS, DNA-RG 107 (M222-26). Urges his superior claims to be appointed superintendent at Harpers Ferry.
[Jul 21]	Joshua Harding to John Davis. DS, DNA-RG 59 (13-1276). Petitions for remission of penalties against his brig *Bethiah* for carrying excess passengers from New Brunswick. Approved by AJ.
Jul 22	*To Andrew Jackson, Jr.* *340*
[Jul 22]	To Martin Van Buren. ANS, DNA-RG 59 (13-0914). Refuses clemency to John Ranaca, convicted of murdering Lieutenant John Mackenzie at Prairie du Chien.
[Jul 22]	From David Henshaw et al. LS, DNA-RG 59 (M639-6). Recommend Auguste G. V. Davezac for secretary of legation in the Netherlands.
Jul 22	From Roswell Lee. ALS, DNA-RG 107 (13-0911). Corrects an error in his testimony to the character of Harpers Ferry master armorer Armistead Beckham.
[Jul 22]	From Beverley Roy. ALS, DNA-RG 59 (M639-20). Asks to be appointed marshal in Virginia in place of Benjamin Reeder.
Jul 22	From William Vandegriff. ALS, DNA-RG 59 (M639-25). Asks for a consulate in France or other office.
Jul 23	*From Richard Keith Call.* *341*
Jul 23	From Thomas P. Moore. ALS, DNA-RG 59 (M639-12). Accuses Virginia marshal candidate Joseph Johnson of being an Adams man.
Jul 23	Lemuel Mead to Andrew Jackson Donelson. ALS, DNA-RG 59 (M639-21). Recommends Jared I. Sample for marshal in Alabama or other office.
Jul 24	From George Graham. LC, DNA-RG (M25-24). Submits three land patents for signature.

Jul 24   From William McCoy. ALS, DNA-RG 59 (M639-18).
          Recommends William M. Peyton for district attorney in
          Virginia.
Jul 24   From John W. Murdaugh. Copy, ViNC (mAJs). Recommends
          John S. Middleton for command of a revenue cutter.
Jul 24   From Neil B. Rose. ALS, DNA-RG 107 (13-0927). Relates his
          misfortunes and asks for an office.
Jul 25   From James W. Anderson. ALS, DNA-RG 59 (M639-1). Asks if
          he has been appointed consul at Baracoa, Cuba.
Jul 25   From Joseph Davis et al. DS, DNA-RG 59 (M639-2).
          Recommend Thomas Bland for marshal in Virginia.
Jul 25   From B. Downing. ALS, DLC (37). Describes the Mississippi
          valley and recommends navigational improvements.
Jul 25   From Lewis Maxwell. ALS, DNA-RG 59 (M639-2).
          Recommends Thomas Bland for marshal in Virginia.
Jul 26   *To Andrew Jackson, Jr.*   345
Jul 26   From Robert Irvin. ALS, DNA-RG 49 (13-0932). Asks
          permission on behalf of Poas Haujo, a Creek, to exchange his
          reservation under the 1814 Treaty of Fort Jackson for a better
          tract.
Jul 26   From William Tharp. ALS, DLC (13-0937). Accuses Eaton,
          Berrien, and Peter Hagner of unjustly rejecting his claims as
          Army sutler.
Jul 26   From William Vandegriff. ALS, DNA-RG 59 (M639-25). Still
          desires a French consulate despite his appointment as customs
          inspector at New Orleans.
Jul 27   To Charles Jones Love. ANS, DLC (37). Asks him to repay to
          Nichol & Hill the $200 AJ advanced to Love's wife when she
          left Washington.
Jul 27   To Martin Van Buren. ANS, DNA-RG 59 (13-0944). Appoints
          consuls.
Jul 27   From Samuel B. Davis. ALS, DNA-RG 59 (M873-19).
          Recommends Daniel C. Croxall.
Jul 27   From Benjamin Reeder. ALS, DNA-RG 59 (M639-19). Asks to
          be continued as marshal in Virginia and to know on what
          grounds his removal is urged.
Jul 27   From D. Urquhart. ALS, DNA-RG 59 (M639-21). Recommends
          Jared I. Sample for marshal in Alabama.
Jul 27   *Statement by Barnard O'Neill.*   346
Jul 27   Temporary commission for Daniel Carroll Croxall as consul at
          Marseilles. Copy, DNA-RG 59 (13-0940).
Jul 27   Temporary commission for John Jackson as consul at
          Martinique. Copy, DNA-RG 59 (13-0941).
Jul 27   Temporary commission for Samuel Milroy as register of the
          Crawfordsville, Ind., land office. DS, InHi (13-0942).
Jul 27   Temporary commission for William Daniel Patterson as consul
          at Antwerp. Copy, DNA-RG 59 (13-0943).
Jul 28   To Richard Drummond. Photocopy of LS, DLC (13-0947).
          Thanks him for a gift of figs and peaches and advice on raising
          seamen for the Navy.

Jul 28	From Sisters of the Visitation. LS, DLC (13-0950). Burke, 1:201. Invite AJ to an exhibition at the Ladies' Academy.
Jul 28	From Alphonso Wetmore. ALS, DNA-RG 107 (M222-26). Protests his reassignment as Army paymaster from Missouri to Florida.
Jul 29	To Thomas Handy Gilliss. LC, DNA-RG 59 (13-0991). Appoints him acting fourth auditor during Amos Kendall's absence.
Jul 29	From James Bennett. ALS, DNA-RG 59 (M639-2). Recommends Thomas Bland for marshal in Virginia.
Jul 29	From John Thomas Brown et al. LS, DNA-RG 59 (M639-19). Defend Benjamin Reeder and recommend his retention as marshal in Virginia.
Jul 29	From George Graham. LS, DNA-RG 45 (M124-119); LC, DNA-RG 49 (M25-24). Encloses information on reserved naval live oak timberlands in Louisiana.
Jul 29	Remission of penalties against Manuel de Cala, owner of the schooner *Rebecca and Eliza*. LC and Draft, DNA-RG 59 (T967-1; 13-0954).
Jul 29	Release for prisoner Abram B. Fickle. LC and Draft, DNA-RG 59 (T967-1; 13-0963).
Jul 29	Remission of penalties against James McGown, owner of the schooner *Albion*. LC and Draft, DNA-RG 59 (T967-1; 13-0993).
Jul 29	Remission of penalties against Francisco Vigué, owner of the Mexican schooner *Dorotea*. LC and Draft, DNA-RG 59 (T967-1; 13-1001).
Jul 30	*To Daniel Brent.* 348
Jul 30	From John Forbes. ALS, DNA-RG 59 (M179-67). Warns that John Hamm and Elijah Hayward are unfit for high office.
Jul 30	From George Graham. LC, DNA-RG 49 (M25-24). Submits eight land patents for signature.
Jul 30	From Henry Greenfield Sothoron Key. ALS, DNA-RG 94 (M688-64). Recommends Lewis J. Ford for appointment to West Point or the Navy.
Jul 30	From John Patterson et al. DS, DNA-RG 59 (M873-19). Recommend Daniel C. Croxall for consul.
Jul 30	From Pershapaho et al. Copy, DNA-RG 75 (M234-728). Sac and Fox chiefs ask for a survey of lands reserved for half-breeds by the 1824 Treaty of Washington.
Jul 30	From Joseph Lee Smith. ALS, DNA-RG 92 (13-1008). Asks that the Army rebuild the military bridge into St. Augustine or allow the city to do it.
Jul 30	From Daniel Stringer. ALS, DNA-RG 59 (M639-2). Recommends Thomas Bland for marshal in Virginia.
[cJul 30]	From Henry Weeks. D, DNA-RG 59 (13-1026). Petitions for release from prison, being unable to pay fine and costs after his whipping for larceny. Approved by AJ.
Jul 30	Account with Tucker & Thompson for clothing. DS, DLC (72). Runs to Aug 3.

Aug 3	From Samuel Delucenna Ingham. ANS, DNA-RG 49 (13-1034); LC, DNA-RG 56 (M733-1). Recommends appointing someone conversant with Spanish land titles to examine Louisiana land claims.
[cAug 3]	From William N. Jarrett et al. DS, DNA-RG 59 (M639-13). Recommend Henry Lazier for marshal in Virginia.
Aug 3	From Charles S. Morgan. ALS, DNA-RG 59 (M639-6). Recommends James Dougherty for marshal in Virginia and warns against appointing Joseph Johnson.
Aug 3	From Barnard O'Neill. ALS, DNA-RG 45 (M124-120). Encloses evidence for his charges of corruption and favoritism at the Gosport, Va., navy yard.
Aug 3	From James Ronaldson. ALS, DNA-RG 46 (13-1036). Recommends John L. Leib for office in Michigan Territory.
Aug 4	From Henry Hosford Gurley. ALS, DNA-RG 59 (M639-10). Recommends Archibald Haralson for a diplomatic appointment.
Aug 4	Check to Nichol & Hill for $5,500. DS, DLC (37).
Aug 4	Burgess Ball Long to Andrew Jackson Donelson. ALS, DNA-RG 59 (M639-14). Asks to be appointed consul at Tangier.
Aug 5	From Samuel H. Berry. ALS, DNA-RG 45 (M124-120). Asks for an extension of time on his contract to supply timber to the Brooklyn navy yard.
Aug 5	From George Graham. LC, DNA-RG 49 (M25-24). Submits land patents for signature.
Aug 5	From Daniel H. Miller. ALS, DNA-RG 46 (13-1038). Recommends John L. Leib for Michigan Territory office.
Aug 6	To John Forsyth. Typed copy, G-Ar (mAJs); LC dated Aug 7, DLC (60). Says that he did not receive Forsyth's letter of Jun 23.
Aug 6	To Samuel Delucenna Ingham. ANS, DNA-RG 49 (13-1040); LC, DNA-RG 56 (M733-1). Appoints Isaac T. Preston commissioner to examine Arkansas land claims.
Aug 6	Check to Andrew Jackson Donelson for $690. DS, DLC (37).
Aug 7	*To [F. J. Naylor?].* 355
Aug 7	From French S. Evans. ALS, DNA-RG 59 (M639-13). Encloses recommendations for Henry Lazier for marshal in Virginia.
Aug 7	From Alexander S. Withers. ALS, DNA-RG 59 (M639-12). Accuses Virginia marshal candidate Joseph Johnson of political duplicity.
Aug 7	Temporary commission for Charles Rhind as consul at Odessa. Copy, DNA-RG 59 (13-1041).
Aug 8	From James Buchanan. ALS, DNA-RG 59 (M639-7). Introduces and recommends Benjamin Evens.
Aug 8	*From John Miller.* 355
Aug 8	From Theodore Owens. Copy, DNA-RG 56 (M178-38). *TPUS*, 24:256–58. Accuses John Jackson, commander of the revenue cutter *Marion*, of election fraud and other misdeeds in Florida.
Aug 8	From John M. Taylor. ALS, DNA-RG 59 (M639-16). Recommends Benjamin T. Moore for marshal in Alabama.
Aug 8	Andrew Jackson Donelson to [Duff Green?]. ALS, NjMoHP (13-

1042). Explains that Norfolk navy agent Miles King's removal is contemplated on grounds of malfeasance, not politics.

Aug 9   From James Gadsden. ALS, DNA-RG 94 (M688-63). Recommends John Sanders for appointment to West Point.

Aug 9   *From William Ingalls.*   *357*

Aug 9   From William Ingalls. Copy, DNA-RG 46 (13-1048). Encloses Charles H. Stedman's denial of profiting on drug purchases for the Boston marine hospital.

[Aug] 9   From Charles Jones Love. ALS, DLC (37). Explains that he had already paid to AJ's credit the $200 to cover AJ's advance to his wife.

Aug 9   From David Offley. ALS, DNA-RG 59 (T238-1); Copy, DNA-RG 233 (13-1057). *HRDoc* 250, 22d Cong., 1st sess., pp. 73–74 (Serial 221). Reports on prospects for renewing commercial negotiations with Turkey and requests instructions.

Aug 10   From John Branch. LC, DNA-RG 45 (M472-1). Submits Nash Legrand's commission as Norfolk navy agent for signature.

Aug 10   From Darius Bullock. ADS, DNA-RG 59 (M639-14). Recommends Ellis Lewis for district judge in Pennsylvania.

Aug 10   From George D. Dillon. ALS, DNA-RG 59 (M179-67). Applies for American citizenship.

Aug 10   From William Garrison et al., from George P. Ross et al., from Joseph Woods et al., and from Noah Zane et al. DSs, DNA-RG 59 (M639-18). Recommend James Pemberton for marshal in Virginia.

Aug 10   From George Graham. LC, DNA-RG 49 (M25-24). Submits land patents for signature.

[cAug 10]   *From David Henshaw.*   *358*

Aug 10   From Samuel Delucenna Ingham. ALS, DNA-RG 46 (13-1106). Introduces John L. Leib.

Aug 10   From James McCrory. LS, DNA-RG 15 (13-1066). Presents his claim to a Revolutionary pension.

Aug 10   From James W. Roper. Abstract, DNA-RG 156 (13-1070). Recommends Marcus C. Buck for an appointment at Harpers Ferry.

Aug 10   From Daniel Steenrod. ALS, DNA-RG 59 (M639-18). Recommends James Pemberton for marshal in Virginia.

Aug 11   From Byrd Brandon. ALS, DNA-RG 59 (M639-16). Again recommends Benjamin T. Moore for marshal in Alabama.

[cAug 11]   From Anthony Butler. ADS, DLC (13-1073). Describes Texas and urges its prompt acquisition by the United States.

Aug 11   From Joel W. Jones. ALS, DNA-RG 107 (13-1104). Requests a commission in the Army.

Aug 11   From Samuel Leake. ALS, DNA-RG 59 (M639-14). Asks to be appointed marshal in Virginia or to some other office.

Aug 11   From Thomas B. Reily. ALS, DNA-RG 59 (M639-1). Recommends Henry Ashton for marshal or district attorney in the District of Columbia.

Aug 11   Temporary commission for Auguste Genevieve Valentin Davezac as secretary of legation in the Netherlands. LC, DNA-RG 59 (13-1103).

Aug 12   *To Martin Van Buren.*   363

Aug 12   From John Hanson Good. ALS, DNA-RG 59 (M639-18). Recommends James Pemberton for marshal in Virginia.

Aug 12   From Solomon King, Jonas Crumbacker, and William Webb. LS, DNA-RG 59 (M639-18). Recommend James Pemberton for marshal in Virginia.

Aug 12   From Solomon King et al. and from Philip Reilly et al. DSs, DNA-RG 59 (M639-18). Recommend James Pemberton for marshal in Virginia.

Aug 12   From William Cabell Rives. ALS copy, DLC (13-1108). Tenders his respects on departing for France.

Aug 12   From Daniel Steenrod. ALS, DNA-RG 59 (M639-18). Transmits Alexander Caldwell's endorsement of James Pemberton for marshal in Virginia.

Aug 12   From William Lucius Storrs. ALS, CtHi (13-1110). Recommends William T. Williams for customs collector at New London, Conn.

Aug 13   To Martin Van Buren. ALS, MHi (mAJs). Encloses a document, after a delay caused by headache.

[cAug 13]   *Notes for instructions to Joel Roberts Poinsett.*   364
Aug 13   *To Martin Van Buren.*   365

Aug 13   From Alexander Campbell. ALS, DNA-RG 59 (M639-6). Recommends James Dougherty for marshal in Virginia.

Aug 13   Robert Mayo to Andrew Jackson Donelson. ALS, Benjamin H. Caldwell, Jr. (37-0503). Urges his appointment to office, details abuses at the Richmond post office, and encloses his response to the *Richmond Whig*'s criticism of AJ.

Aug 14   *To Martin Van Buren.*   367

Aug 14   To Martin Van Buren. ANS, DNA-RG 59 (13-1134). Appoints Augustus Jones marshal and George Shannon district attorney in Missouri.

Aug 14   *From Eli Baldwin.*   368
Aug 14   *From Easter Charco Micco et al.*   369

Aug 14   From John Forsyth. AL fragment, DLC (37); LC dated Aug 17, G-Ar (13-1130). Promises to resend documents accompanying his lost letter of Jun 23.

Aug 14   From George Gillespie. ALS, DNA-RG 75 (M234-432). Asks to be appointed commissioner to appraise Indian improvements.

[cAug 15]   *To Martin Van Buren.*   370
[cAug 15]   From Henry Lee. Copy, PHi (13-1136). Recommends James McCrea for Brooklyn naval storekeeper in place of Tunis Craven.

Aug 15   From John McKinley. ALS, DNA-RG 59 (M639-16). Recommends Benjamin T. Moore for marshal in Alabama.

Aug 15   From Robert Mills. ALS, DNA-RG 77 (mAJs). Bess Glenn and A. S. Salley, eds., *Some Letters of Robert Mills, Engineer and Architect* (Columbia, S.C., 1938), pp. 13–15 (13-1138). Presents his atlas and statistical history of South Carolina and asks to be appointed an Army topographical engineer.

[Aug 18]	From Chesed P. Montgomery. ANS, TNJ (13-1149). Demands an immediate answer to his letter.
Aug 18	From Beverley Roy. ALS, DNA-RG 59 (M639-20). Asks to be appointed marshal in Virginia.
Aug 18	Check to self for $200. DS, DLC (37).
Aug 18	Archibald Haralson to Andrew Jackson Donelson. ALS, DNA-RG 59 (M639-10). Submits Henry H. Gurley's Aug 4 recommendation and explains that his endorsements from AJ's political opponents were unsolicited.
Aug 18	Joel Roberts Poinsett letter of transit for David Porter. DS, DNA-RG 59 (M179-67). Certifies that Porter has resigned his Mexican navy commission, remains a U.S. citizen, and is carrying official dispatches to Washington. Endorsed by AJ.
Aug 19	*To Andrew Jackson, Jr.* *384*
Aug 19	To William Berkeley Lewis. LC, DNA-RG 59 (13-1177); Copy, DNA-RG 45 (M124-120). Appoints him acting secretary of war during Eaton's absence.
Aug 19	*To Chesed P. Montgomery.* *385*
Aug 19	From Ezra Stiles Ely. ALS, CtHi (13-1175). Recommends William T. Williams for customs collector at New London, Conn.
Aug 19	From J. Goodwin et al. DS, DNA-RG 59 (M639-14). Recommend Ellis Lewis for district judge in Pennsylvania.
Aug 19	Andrew Jackson Donelson to Martin Van Buren. ALS, DNA-RG 59 (M179-67). Asks him to look up Joseph W. E. Wallace's full name on his recommendations.
Aug 20	*To Andrew Jackson, Jr.* *386*
Aug 20	*To Andrew Jackson Donelson.* *387*
Aug 20	From Richard Frisby. ALS, DNA-RG 94 (M688-64). Introduces Patrick Riley and recommends his son Bernard Riley for appointment to West Point.
Aug 20	From Charles J. Jack. ALS, DNA-RG 59 (M639-12). Denies that he is insolvent and asserts his readiness to assume office.
Aug 20	*From Henry Lee.* *388*
Aug 20	From Amasa Paine. Copy, DLC (75). Attests to John B. Timberlake's friendship for Eaton at the time of his death.
[Aug 21]	From John Jackson. Printed, Washington *National Journal*, Aug 21 (mAJs). Charges AJ with duplicity and tyranny in rescinding his appointment as consul.
Aug 21	From Everett H. Pierce. ALS, DNA-RG 75 (M234-73). At John Forsyth's direction, sends duplicates of documents concerning the Creek and Cherokee boundary line in Georgia.
Aug 21	Temporary commission for John S. Meircken as consul at Martinique. Copy, DNA-RG 59 (13-1180).
Aug 21	Bill from Marshall Parks for groceries. DS, DLC (37). Bassett, 4:64–65. Runs to Aug 31.
Aug 21	Chesed P. Montgomery to Andrew Jackson Donelson. ALS, TNJ (13-1181). Denounces Donelson, challenges him to a duel, and encloses a corrected copy of his Aug 18 letter to AJ.
Aug 22	*To Andrew Jackson Donelson.* *390*
Aug 23	From Jurutia Adjutant. ALS, DNA-RG 45 (M124-120). Begs for

the release from prison of her son George W. Adjutant, a Marine deserter.

Aug 23   From John Pryor Hickman. ALS, DNA-RG 59 (M639-17). Recommends Benjamin Patteson for marshal in Alabama.

Aug 23   From George French Strother. ALS, DNA-RG 107 (13-1199). Recommends Lewis Dent for a clerkship.

Aug 24   From Lewis Dent. ALS, DNA-RG 107 (13-1197). Asks for a clerkship.

Aug 24   From Charles S. Morgan. ALS, DNA-RG 59 (M639-6). Encloses a recommendation for James Dougherty for marshal in Virginia.

Aug 24   *From David Twopence.*   391

[Aug 25]   From Margaret G. Edmonston. ALS, DNA-RG 59 (13-1241). Asks to remit her son Theophilus's sentence of a fine and whipping for stealing. Approved by AJ Sep 2.

Aug 25   From David S. Hassinger. ALS, DNA-RG 59 (M639-23). Recommends Samuel C. Stambaugh for office.

Aug 25   From Horatio Hubbell. ALS, DNA-RG 59 (M639-11). Asks to be appointed consul at Trieste.

Aug 25   From William Trumbull Williams. ALS, InHi (13-1201). Asks to be appointed customs collector at New London, Conn.

Aug 25   Martin Van Buren to Joel Roberts Poinsett. LS, TxU (mAJs). Instructs him to open negotiations with Mexico to purchase Texas. Eaton note initialed by AJ cautions not to bring up Mexican constitutional obstacles to ceding territory, but be ready to counter them.

Aug 26   *From John Branch.*   392

Aug 26   From Charles Gouin, Pierre Gouin, and Therese Gouin. DS, DNA-RG 75 (13-1203). Miami Indians request permission to sell their reserved tracts under the Wabash Treaty of 1826.

Aug 27   *To Joel Roberts Poinsett.*   393

Aug 27   From Samuel Davies Heap. DS, DNA-RG 59 (M639-7). Recommends Paul Eynaud, vice-consul at Malta, for promotion. Endorsed favorably by AJ.

[Aug 27]   From Hyacinthe Lasselle. DS, DNA-RG 75 (13-1206). Asks permission to sell his reservation under the Potawatomi treaty of 1826.

Aug 28   From Lynde Catlin et al. DS, DNA-RG 59 (M639-21). Recommend Joseph Saul for consul at Havre.

Aug 28   From D. C. Porter et al. and from Francis B. Rhodes et al. DSs, DNA-RG 59 (M639-17). Recommend Nathaniel Niles for consul at Paris in place of Isaac C. Barnet.

Aug 29   From John Trucks. ALS, DNA-RG 15 (mAJs). Asks for an increase in his Revolutionary pension to cover his uncompensated militia service.

Aug 29   From Frederick G. Wolbert. ALS, DNA-RG 45 (M124-120). Points to his Navy court-martial for evidence on James Ramage's character and fitness for clemency.

Aug 30   From David Bannister Morgan. ALS, DNA-RG 45 (M124-120). Asks to have his son, midshipman David B. Morgan, Jr., reassigned to Mediterranean or Pacific sea duty.

Sep 4   From Philip Pendleton Barbour. Abstract, DNA-RG 156 (13-1255). Recommends Daniel Ward for paymaster at Harpers Ferry.

Sep 4   From John B. Beaubien. ALS, DNA-RG 75 (M234-315). Accuses Chicago Indian agent Alexander Wolcott of abusing his office.

Sep 5   Check to Andrew Jackson Donelson for $450. DS, DLC (37).

Sep 5   Andrew Jackson Donelson to Thomas B. Laighton. Copy, DNA-RG 46 (13-1258). Acknowledges Laighton's Aug 31 letter, to be referred to secretary Ingham.

Sep 6   From Josias Flannagan and Lewis Phillips. D, DNA-RG 107 (M222-25). Soldiers ask that their pay be continued during their imprisonment at hard labor.

Sep 6   From Gabriel Moore. ALS, DNA-RG 59 (M639-16). Recommends Benjamin T. Moore for marshal or land officer in Alabama.

Sep 7   From Benjamin Evens. ALS, DNA-RG 59 (M639-7). Asks again to be appointed consul at Leghorn and accuses Thomas Appleton of corruption. Referred by AJ to Van Buren for inquiry.

Sep 7   From George Graham. LC, DNA-RG 49 (M25-24). Submits nineteen land patents for signature.

Sep 7   From John Liggett. ALS, DLC (37). Complains of the appointments in Maryland and requests an office.

Sep 8   George Graham to Andrew Jackson Donelson. LC, DNA-RG 49 (M25-24). Advises against postponing Illinois land sales as requested by Joseph Duncan.

[Sep 8]   To Andrew Jackson Donelson. AN, DLC (13-1267). Declines Joseph Duncan's request to postpone Illinois land sales.

Sep 8   To John Henry Eaton. ANS, DNA-RG 46 (13-1268). Encloses David Campbell's May 29 letter and endorses his son John for Indian agent.

Sep 8   To Martin Van Buren. ANS, DNA-RG 59 (13-1287). Appoints William S. Hamilton surveyor of public lands south of Tennessee in place of James P. Turner.

Sep 8   From John M. Davis. ALS, DNA-RG 59 (M639-3). Recommends George W. Buchanan for district attorney in Pennsylvania in place of Alexander Brackenridge.

Sep 8   From James Gadsden. ALS, DNA-RG 26 (13-1270). Praises and recommends Gustavus Harrison, recently removed from command of the revenue cutter *Pulaski*.

Sep 8   From William Berkeley Lewis. ALS, DLC (37); ALS copy, NN

(13-1282). Asks what Mrs. Eaton and Richard K. Call told AJ of their encounter in 1824.

Sep 8   From John Rayner, Jr. ADS, DNA-RG 59 (13-1461). Asks to be released from imprisonment for his debts to the U.S. incurred as postmaster at South Reading, Mass. Approved by AJ Sep 26.

Sep 8   From Ross Wilkins. ALS, DNA-RG 59 (M639-3). Recommends George W. Buchanan for district attorney in Pennsylvania in place of Alexander Brackenridge.

Sep 8   Remission of penalties against Joshua Harding, master of the brig *Bethiah*. Draft and LC, DNA-RG 59 (13-1274; T967-1).

Sep 8   Temporary commission for William Southerland Hamilton as surveyor of public lands south of Tennessee. LC, DNA-RG 59 (13-1273).

Sep 8   Temporary commission for Sidney Mason as consul at San Juan, Puerto Rico. Copy, DNA-RG 59 (13-1284).

Sep 8   Temporary commission for William Shaler as consul at Havana. DS, DLC; Copy, DNA-RG 59 (13-1285).

Sep 9   From Thomas Miller. ALS, DNA-RG 59 (M639-16). Advises that Benjamin T. Moore is unfit to be marshal in Alabama.

Sep 10   From John Macpherson Berrien. LS, DNA-RG 59 (M179-67); LC, DNA-RG 60 (T412-3). *HRDoc* 123, 26th Cong., 2d sess., pp. 718–19 (Serial 387). Renders opinion that the U.S. cannot arrest Rodney French for a murder at sea, as requested by Britain, without firsthand testimony from witnesses.

[cSep 10]   From John Branch. LC, DNA-RG 45 (M472-1). Informs AJ of James Ramage's promotion to master commandant in Mar 1829.

Sep 10   From Henry Saunders. ALS and ALS copy, DNA-RG 107 (M222-26; M222-31); ALS copy, DNA-RG 94 (M567-55). Asks for a retroactive brevet promotion to captain for his part in the defense of Fort Bowyer in 1814.

Sep 10   Bill from Matilda Smith Bedford for wool for Andrew J. Hutchings's farm; receipted Oct 13. DS, THi (13-1289).

Sep 11   From Richard Ward. LS copy, DNA-RG 59 (M179-67). Proposes sending a ship equipped with his armaments to Turkey.

Sep 11   Remission of fine and order of release for prisoner Rosetta Williams. Draft and LC, DNA-RG 59 (13-1305; T967-1).

Sep 12   From William Gragroy. ALS, DNA-RG 49 (13-1310). Asks AJ's help in procuring a patent for his military bounty land claim.

Sep 12   From Barnard O'Neill. LS, DNA-RG 45 (M124-120). Recommends Marshall Parks to supply brick for the navy yard wall at Gosport, Va.

Sep 12   From Henry Wilson. LS copy, DNA-RG 59 (M639-27). Protests his removal as marshal in Florida.

Sep 12   From John Worrall. Printed, Philadelphia *Aurora & Pennsylvania Gazette*, Sep 19, 1829 (mAJs). Presents a song

Sep 21   From Matthew Harvey. ALS and Copy, DNA-RG 59 (M639-6). Recommends John A. Dix for a diplomatic post.

Sep 21   From Samuel Delucenna Ingham. ANS, NjP (13-1397). Reports that recommendations favor Sylvester R. Hazard for lighthouse keeper on Conanicut Island, R.I.

[Sep 21]   From John Pickrell et al. DS, DNA-RG 59 (13-1399). Recommend John A. King for justice of the peace in the District of Columbia; appointed by AJ.

Sep 21   Appointment for Joseph Mechlin as agent on the coast of Africa to receive blacks liberated from illegal slave ships. LC, DNA-RG 45 (M205-1).

Sep 21   Andrew Dunlap to Samuel Delucenna Ingham. ALS, DNA-RG 59 (13-1465). Recommends releasing insolvent public debtor John Rayner, Jr., from prison. Approved by AJ.

Sep 22   From John Branch. LCs, DNA-RG 45 (M472-1; M205-1). Submits Joseph Mechlin's appointment for signature.

Sep 22   From Joseph Guerard Nancrede. ALS, DNA-RG 59 (M639-17). Recommends his father Joseph Nancrède for consul at Paris.

Sep 22   Thomas Fillebrown, Jr., to John Henry Eaton. Copy, DLC (75). Relates his history with Timberlake and Mrs. Eaton and his efforts to correct Ezra S. Ely's false version of what he had said about them.

Sep 22   Daniel Parker to William Berkeley Lewis. Copy, DLC (75). Defends Mrs. Eaton's character and traces the slanders against her to the late John H. Henshaw.

Sep 23   From John Henry Eaton. Copy, DNA-RG 46 (13-1406). Proposes releasing the goods of Cherokee traders Peter A. Carnes and William Duval, seized by Colonel Mathew Arbuckle for alleged illegal liquor dealing, if they will forego damage claims against the government.

Sep 23   *To John Henry Eaton.*   *448*

Sep 23   From Joseph Inslee Anderson. LC, DNA-RG 217 (13-1404). Submits and approves an auditor's report rejecting the claim of William Otis, former collector at Barnstable, Mass.

Sep 23   From George Graham. LC, DNA-RG 49 (M25-24). Submits 843 land patents for signature.

Sep 23   AJ memorandum to send the *Kentucky Gazette* a copy of Isaac Shelby and AJ to John C. Calhoun, Oct 30, 1818, explaining the Colbert reservations in the Chickasaw cession treaty. ANS, DLC (13-1414).

Sep 24   To John Henry Eaton. Abstract, DNA-RG 107 (M22-25). Recommends James C. Williamson for cadet at West Point.

Sep 24   *To Samuel Delucenna Ingham.*   *449*

Sep 24   From Nathaniel L. Griswold et al. LS, DNA-RG 59 (M639-27). Recommend Asa Worthington for consul at Lima, Peru, in place of William Radcliff.

Sep 24   From William Lorman & Son et al. LS, DNA-RG 59 (M639-18). Recommend Theodore Privat for consul at Cette, France.

Sep 24   From Bernard Marigny. ALS and ALS copy, DNA-RG 59

(M639-4). Recommends Henry Carleton for the Supreme Court if a new seat is added.

Sep 24   From John Randolph. ALS, DLC (37); Copies, NcD, Nc-Ar, PHi (13-1422); LC, DLC (mAJs). Heiskell, 3:463–64. Accepts the post of minister to Russia.

Sep 25   To John Henry Eaton. ANS, DNA-RG 94 (M688-60). Presents Adam R. Wager, recommended by Samuel F. Bradford for cadet at West Point.

Sep 25   From Nathaniel Pitcher. ALS, TNJ (13-1427). Recommends John Sproull for office.

Sep 25   *Statement by Mary B. O'Neale Randolph.*   449

Sep 26   To Martin Van Buren. ALS, DLC (13-1434). Asks his opinion on Peter B. Porter's dispute with the Treasury over his salary as former Canadian boundary commissioner.

Sep 26   *From John England.*   450

Sep 26   From Chesed P. Montgomery. ALS, TNJ (13-1429). Accuses Darius Clagett of inciting him to attack AJ and asks for a loan of $100 to pay his debts to avoid prison.

Sep 26   Temporary commission for Theodore Privat as consul at Cette, France. Copy, DNA-RG 59 (13-1432).

Sep 26   Temporary commission for Frederick Schillow as consul at Stettin, Prussia. Copy, DNA-RG 59 (13-1433).

Sep 27   *To [Samuel Swartwout?].*   452

Sep 28   *To John Christmas McLemore.*   454

Sep 28   From Francis I, King of the Two Sicilies. LS and Copy, DNA-RG 59 (13-1436); translation, DLC (37) Announces the marriage of his daughter Maria Christina to King Ferdinand VII of Spain.

Sep 28   From Edgar Macon. ALS, DNA-RG 59 (M639-15). Asks to be appointed Florida district attorney if John G. Stower resigns.

Sep 28   From John Pemberton. ALS copy, PHi (13-1448). Introduces Robert Pettit.

Sep 28   From William Ryland. Copy, DLC (75). Reproves the slanders against the Eatons.

Sep 28   From Martin Van Buren. ALS draft, DLC (13-1450); Extract, Paul C. Richards Autographs catalog 246 (mAJs). States his opinion that Peter B. Porter is not entitled to the salary he claims as former Canadian boundary commissioner.

Sep 29   *To Samuel Angus.*   456

Sep 29   From Moses Dawson. ALS, DNA-RG 59 (M639-21). Recommends Robert Simms for consul at Belfast.

Sep 29   From John Kintzing Kane, Robert M. Lewis, and William Platt. LS, DLC (37). *Nat. Intelligencer,* Oct 19. Invite AJ to the opening of the Chesapeake and Delaware Canal.

Sep 29   From John Kintzing Kane. ALS, DLC (37). Proposes arrangements for AJ's attendance at the Chesapeake and Delaware Canal opening.

Sep 30   From Edward Chandler. ALS, DNA-RG 59 (M639-4). Asks to be appointed Florida district attorney if John G. Stower resigns.

Sep 30   From Chesed P. Montgomery. ALS, TNJ (13-1457). Asks again for a loan of $100.

Oct 4   From John Pemberton. ALS draft, PHi (14-0104). Introduces
             Thomas M. Taylor, an applicant for naval purser.
Oct 5   From Patrick Mulvany. ALS, DNA-RG 59 (M639-3).
             Recommends retaining Pennsylvania district attorney Alexander
             Brackenridge or appointing George W. Buchanan.
Oct 5   From John K. Smith. ALS, DNA-RG 46 (14-0110).
             Recommends Edward Chandler for district attorney in Florida.
Oct 5   *Memorandum concerning Moses Myers.*   479
Oct 5   Checks to Andrew Jackson Donelson for $100 and $651. DSs,
             DLC (37).
Oct 5   James Harvey Hook to Andrew Jackson Donelson. ALS, DNA-
             RG 107 (14-0106). Recommends Luther Leonard.
Oct 5   William Berkeley Lewis to James L. Edwards. Copy, DLC (75).
             Asks if he has a letter from John H. Henshaw attacking Mrs.
             Eaton's character.
[cOct 5]   James L. Edwards to William Berkeley Lewis. Copy, DLC (75).
             Denies any knowledge of a John H. Henshaw letter attacking
             Mrs. Eaton.
Oct 6   *To Martin Van Buren.*   479
Oct 6   From John Branch. LC, DNA-RG 45 (M472-1). Submits naval
             purser Nathaniel Wilson's commission for signature.
Oct 6   George Beale to John Henry Eaton. Copy, DLC (75). Describes
             Mrs. Eaton's 1814 or 1815 letter to him as friendly and proper,
             and offers to find and show it to Eaton.
Oct 6   John Christmas McLemore to Andrew Jackson Donelson. ALS,
             DNA-RG 59 (M639-1). Recommends Adam R. Alexander for
             surveyor general of public lands.
Oct 7   From Pedro I, Emperor of Brazil. Copy, DNA-RG 59 (M49-2).
             Announces his marriage to Princess Amelia of Leuchtenberg.
[cOct 7]   Statement by Philip Grymes Randolph. Copy, DLC (75).
             Recounts an Oct 7 interview between George Beale and Eaton,
             in which Beale cleared Mrs. Eaton of impropriety but declined
             to show her old letter for fear of embarrassing himself.
Oct 8   *To William Donelson.*   480
Oct 8   *To the Marquis de Lafayette.*   482
Oct 8   From Gaston Davezac. ALS, DLC (37-0295). Thanks AJ for his
             appointment to command the revenue cutter *Pulaski.*
Oct 8   *From David W. Haley.*   483
Oct 8   *From William Kinney.*   484
Oct 9   From James Barron. LS, NHi (14-0126). Recommends Robert
             Pettit for naval purser.
Oct 9   From William Branch Giles. LS, DLC (37). Asks AJ's aid in
             satisfying Ohio land claims of Virginia's revolutionary veterans.
             AJ agrees.
Oct 9   From John Johnson. ALS, TNJ (14-0128). Encloses a letter from
             Mr. Lamb.
Oct 9   Check to Samuel Jackson Hays for $100. DS, DLC (37).
Oct 9   James L. Edwards to John Henry Eaton. Copy, DLC (75).
             Denies having or knowing of a purported John H. Henshaw
             letter containing charges against Eaton.

Oct 13   From William Curtin. ADS, DNA-RG 59 (14-0156). Convicted thief, unable to pay fine and court costs, requests release from prison; approved by AJ.

Oct 13   From Thomas Raffles. Typed copy, THer (14-0153). Presents his *Lectures on Some Important Branches of Christian Faith and Practice* (London, 1825).

Oct 13   *From Henry Miller Shreve.*   493

Oct 13   Certification by AJ of Yves LeMonnier's meritorious service as military surgeon in the campaign of 1814–15. DS, LNT (14-0151).

[Oct 14]   From William Ingalls. ALS, DNA-RG 59 (M639-1). Recommends Joseph H. Adams for consul at Havre.

Oct 14   From Nathan Towson. LC, DNA-RG 99 (14-0159). Maintains that Army regulations support Berrien's Jul 18 opinion favoring his fuel and quarters allowance.

Oct 14   Pardon for William Curtin. Draft and LC, DNA-RG 59 (14-0154; T967-1).

Oct 14   Statement by John Hopkins Houston. Copy, DLC (75). Recounts an Oct 8 interview in which John N. Campbell refused to answer questions put to him by John H. Eaton.

Oct 14   John Connell to Martin Van Buren. ALS, DNA-RG 59 (M179-67). Suggests noting progress in claims negotiations with Denmark in annual message in order to prod further concessions; AJ agrees.

Oct 15   *To David W. Haley.*   494

Oct 15   *To Tench Ringgold.*   495

Oct 15   To James Simonton. ANS, Robert R. Hudson (14-0170). Encloses a communication for Vincent Gray's son.

Oct 15   From Joseph Inslee Anderson. Copy, DLC (75). Testifies to Mrs. Eaton's good character and reproves her traducers.

Oct 15   From Samuel Angus. ALS, DNA-RG 45 (M124-121). Asks to be appointed a Navy captain.

Oct 15   *From Comstick et al.*   496

Oct 15   From Alexander E. McConnell. ALS, DNA-RG 94 (M567-54). Asks to be appointed sutler at Baton Rouge or New Orleans.

Oct 15   From Samuel Nelson et al. LS, DNA-RG 59 (M639-6). Recommend John A. Dix for chargé d'affaires.

Oct 15   From Francisco Ramón Vicuña Larraín. LS, DNA-RG 59 (M73-1). President of Chile praises departing American chargé Samuel Larned.

Oct 15   Appointment of John Hooper as lightboat keeper in Maryland. ANS, NjP (14-0164).

Oct 15   Temporary commissions for consuls Silas K. Everett at Panama and James Lenox Kennedy in Mexico. Copies, DNA-RG 59 (14-0163; 14-0165).

Oct 15   Alexander Hunter to Andrew Jackson Donelson. ALS, DNA-RG 59 (M639-11). Asks to be appointed marshal of the District of Columbia.

Oct 15   Francis Scott Key to [Samuel Delucenna Ingham]. AD, DLC (14-0167). Complains of his reduced fees as U.S. attorney. AJ proposes restoring his previous rate.

Oct 24	From Samuel Hanna. DS, DNA-RG 75 (14-0244). Asks permission as Abraham Burnett's executor to sell land granted him in the 1826 Potawatomi treaty.
Oct 24	From Simon Kinney. ALS, DNA-RG 59 (M639-14). Recommends Ellis Lewis for district judge in Pennsylvania.
[Oct 24]	From Simon Kinney et al. LS, DNA-RG 59 (M639-14). Recommend Ellis Lewis for district judge in Pennsylvania.
Oct 25	From Clayton Talbot. ALS, DNA-RG 94 (M688-64). Recommends his grandson, son of John P. Oldham, for appointment to West Point.
Oct 26	From William Pope Duval et al. LS, DNA-RG 59 (M639-23). *TPUS*, 24:281. Recommend Lackland M. Stone for marshal in Florida.
Oct 26	From Unknown. AL, DLC (14-0247). European friend writes Joel R. Poinsett praying for his safety and asks AJ to forward it to him.
Oct 27	From John Henry Eaton. ALS, DNA-RG 217 (14-0249); LC, DNA-RG 107 (M127-2). Asks AJ to authorize a transfer of $50,000 from the subsistence to the quartermaster department. Approved by AJ.
Oct 27	From George Vashon. ALS, DNA-RG 75 (14-0250). Recommends a salary increase for Indian interpreter Anthony Shane.
Oct 27	Temporary commission for Joseph Washington Elliot Wallace as consul at San Antonio. Copy, DNA-RG 59 (14-0252).
Oct 27	Daniel Todd Patterson to John Branch. ALS, DNA-RG 59 (M179-67). Recommends a special thanks to Spain for Governor Joseph Taverner of Mahon's services to the Mediterranean squadron. Referred by AJ to Van Buren.
Oct 28	To Samuel Delucenna Ingham. DS, DNA-RG 217 (14-0255); LC, DNA-RG 107 (M127-2). Orders $50,000 transferred from the subsistence to the quartermaster department.
Oct 28	From John Branch. LC, DNA-RG 45 (M472-1). Recommends dismissing Navy midshipman James B. Glentworth for misconduct.
Oct 28	*From John Henry Eaton.* 508
Oct 28	From Payton Gay. ALS, DNA-RG 59 (M639-9). Requests a transfer from Tenerife to a more lucrative consulate.
Oct 28	*From Joel Barlow Sutherland.* 509
Oct 28	AJ memorandum of the transfer of $50,000 of War Department funds from the subsistence to the quartermaster department. ANS, DNA-RG 107 (M222-26).
Oct 29	*To Martin Van Buren.* 511
Oct 29	From Alexander Macomb. LCs, DNA-RG 108 (14-0260). Upholds the accuser's right of reply against the defense in military courts-martial.
Oct 29	From Bernard Marigny et al. DS, DNA-RG 233 (14-0263). Ask AJ to recommend congressional recognition of their Spanish land titles in West Florida.
Oct 30	From Alexander Macomb. LCs, DNA-RG 108 (14-0271). Cites

precedents for the accuser's right of reply in military courts-martial.

	107 (M222- 26). Requests that the garrison at Cantonment Gibson be moved to Fort Smith and reinforced.
Nov 2	From Edward Pannell, Jr. ALS, DNA-RG 59 (M639-2). Recommends John H. Baker for marshal of the District of Columbia in place of Tench Ringgold.
Nov 2	Check to John Scrivener for $25. DS, DLC (37). Subscription for a pew in Congress Street Methodist Church.
Nov 3	From Baltimore merchants. Copy, DNA-RG 59 (M179-67). Urge payment of their claims for French spoliations before 1800.
Nov 3	From John Macpherson Berrien. LS, DNA-RG 153 (14-0352); LC, DNA-RG 60 (T412-3). *HRDoc* 123, 26th Cong., 2d sess., pp. 730–32 (Serial 387). Submits opinion that the court-martial of William Whistler allowed the accuser too broad a right of reply, and that AJ has power to mitigate the sentence.
Nov 3	From Samuel W. Day. ALS, DNA-RG 107 (14-0396). Asks to be appointed commissary general of purchases in place of Callender Irvine.
Nov 3	*From Arthur Peronneau Hayne.* 532
Nov 3	From Edwin Lewis. ADS, DNA-RG 49 (14-0400). Complains of officials' corrupt frustration of his family land claim in former West Florida.
Nov 3	From John Pemberton. ALS copy, PHi (14-0408). Introduces Samuel Archer.
Nov 3	From Henry S. Sanderson. ALS, DNA-RG 59 (M639-2). Recommends John H. Baker for marshal of the District of Columbia in place of Tench Ringgold.
Nov 3	Temporary commission for John W. Bowyer as consul at Guazacualco, Mexico. Copy, DNA-RG 59 (14-0395).
Nov 3	John Macpherson Berrien to Martin Van Buren. Copy, UkLPR (14-0360). *HRDoc* 123, 26th Cong., 2d sess., pp. 732–36 (Serial 387). Submits opinion that former Portuguese chargé d'affaires Joaquim Barrozo Pereira still held diplomatic immunity on Oct 30.
Nov 4	*To Samuel Swartwout.* 535
Nov 4	From Thomas Green Davidson. ALS, DNA-RG 59 (M639-4). Recommends Henry Carleton for district judge in Louisiana.
Nov 4	Check to Andrew Jackson Donelson for $1,073. DS, DLC (37).
Nov 5	To [James] Miller. Printed, American Art Association catalog, Jan 22, 1926 (mAJs). Invites him to dinner.
Nov 5	From Arkansas Territory General Assembly. DS, DNA-RG 107 (M222-26). Asks for troops and an agent to protect southwest Arkansas against Indian incursions.
Nov 5	*From John B. Duncan.* 536
Nov 5	From Preserved Fish. ALS, DNA-RG 46 (14-0410). Encloses a New Bedford testimonial for Lemuel Williams for customs collector.
Nov 5	From William J. Leiper. ALS, DNA-RG 59 (M639-15). Recommends Daniel S. McCauley for a Mediterranean consulate.

Nov 27	Receipted bill from William Butler for boots for Charles. DS, DLC (37).	
Nov 27	Receipted bill from Josiah Nichol & Son for plantation supplies. DS with AJ notes, DLC (38). Runs to Aug 20, 1830.	
Nov 28	*To Martin Van Buren.*	*581*
Nov 28	*From Martin Van Buren.*	*581*
Nov 28	From Simón Bolívar. LS and translation, DLC (37). Welcomes American minister to Colombia Thomas P. Moore.	
Nov 28	From Alexander E. Brown, William L. Sebring, and Daniel W. Burke. Printed, *Easton Centinel,* Jan 8, 1830 (mAJs). Hickory Club of Easton, Pa., presents a cane cut from its 1828 campaign pole.	
Nov 28	*From John Coffee.*	*583*
Nov 28	From Thomas Patrick Moore. Copy, DNA-RG 233 (14-0606). *HRDoc* 31, 21st Cong., 1st sess., p. 2 (Serial 196). Sends AJ a gold medal from the Colombian government.	
Nov 28	From William H. D. C. Wright. ALS, DLC (14-0618). Asks to be retained as consul at Rio de Janeiro.	
Nov 30	*To Robert Johnstone Chester.*	*584*
Nov 30	From John Henry Eaton. DSs, DNA-RG 46 and DNA-RG 233 (14-0631); LC, DNA-RG 107 (M127-2). *SDoc* 1, 21st Cong., 1st sess., pp. 21–32 (Serial 192). Submits the annual report of the War Department.	
Nov 30	From Charles Kennan. Abstract, DNA-RG 107 (M22-28). Asks to be appointed commissioner to treat with the Cherokees.	
Nov 30	From Frances H. Williamson. Abstract, DNA-RG 107 (M22-28). Requests a cadet's appointment at West Point for her son James C. Williamson.	
Nov 30	Temporary commission for John G. Boker as consul general to Switzerland. Copy, DNA-RG 59 (14-0627).	
Nov 30	Francis Barber Ogden to John Henry Eaton. Copy, DLC (75). Encloses John E. Hyde's Nov 26 denial of making derogatory remarks about Mrs. Eaton.	
[cNov]	From Martin Waltham Bates et al. DS, DNA-RG 59 (M639-10). Recommend Abel Harris for marshal in Delaware.	
[cNov]	*Draft by John Macpherson Berrien on the judicial system.*	*586*
[cNov]	From Samuel Cooper et al. DS, DNA-RG 59; printed copy of AJ endorsement, Julia Sweet Newman catalog (14-0310). Recommend John H. Offley for consul at Trieste.	
[cNov]	From John G. Coster et al. DS, DNA-RG 76 (14-0313). Urge payment of their claims for French spoliations before 1800.	
[cNov]	*Draft by John Henry Eaton on the Bank of the United States.*	*587*
[cNov]	From Samuel Green. LS, DLC (14-0326). Urges payment of his claims for French spoliations before 1800.	
[cNov]	From Moses L. Neal et al. DS, DNA-RG 46 (14-0714). Applaud John P. Decatur's appointment as Portsmouth, N.H., collector.	
[cNov]	From Nathan Walden et al. DS, DNA-RG 46 (14-0339). Approve John P. Decatur's appointment as Portsmouth, N.H., collector.	

Dec 11   To Samuel Delucenna Ingham. AN, PU (14-1009). Decides land office nominees to be sent to the Senate.

Dec 11   From Jonathan Harvey et al. DS, DNA-RG 46 (14-1006). Congressmen recommend Daniel D. Brodhead for navy agent at Boston.

Dec 11   From John Owen. ALS, TNJ (14-1011). Recommends John A. Cameron for a foreign appointment.

Dec 11   From Christopher H. Sterns. DS, DNA-RG 59 (14-1219). Asks for remission of his fine for smuggling goods from Canada and for release from prison. AJ refuses Dec 31.

Dec 11   Order for remission of mail thief Orrin Shearman's prison sentence. ANS, Mrs. Lawrence E. Nostrand (14-1016).

Dec 12   To Edward Livingston. AN, NjP (mAJs). Asks to see him on business.

Dec 12   From John Branch. LC, DNA-RG 45 (M472-1). Reports the *Brandywine* can be readied for sea in twenty days and submits a statement of Navy Department finances.

Dec 12   From John Henry Eaton. LS, DNA-RG 233 (14-1026); LC (dated Dec 11), DNA-RG 107 (M127-2). *HRDoc* 7, 21st Cong., 1st sess., p. 1 (Serial 195). Submits reports of internal improvement surveys by Army engineers.

Dec 12   Pardon for mail thief Orrin Shearman. LC, DNA-RG 59 (T967-1).

Dec 13   From Walter Hampden Overton. ALS, DNA-RG 59 (M639-9). Transmits John R. Grymes's application to be appointed minister to Mexico.

[cDec 14]   To Nicholas Philip Trist and Virginia Jefferson Randolph Trist. N, DLC (14-1031). Invitation to dinner Dec 17.

Dec 14   To the United States Senate. DS, DNA-RG 46 (14-1036). *Senate Executive Proceedings*, 4:28. Nominates John Wambersie for consul at Rotterdam.

Dec 14   To the United States Senate. DS, CtNlCG (14-1032); LC, DLC (60). Richardson, 2:463; *Senate Executive Proceedings*, 4:28. Transmits the journal of the Passamaquoddy Bay boundary commissioners under the Treaty of Ghent.

Dec 14   To the United States Senate. DS, DNA-RG 46 (14-1034); LC, DNA-RG 59 (M40-21). Richardson, 2:463; *Senate Executive Proceedings*, 4:28. Submits a commercial treaty with Austria for ratification.

Dec 14   To the United States Senate. DS, DNA-RG 46; ADS draft, NjP (14-1038). *Senate Executive Proceedings*, 4:29. Nominates land officers.

Dec 14   From Thomas S. Slaughter. ALS, TNJ (14-1028). Urges Richard M. Hannum's claim to an office.

Dec 14   From Charles Pendleton Tutt. ALS, DLC (37). Urges retaining Pensacola as a naval depot, proposes coastal waterway improvements, and warns of Senate plots to oppose removals.

Dec 14   John Henry Eaton to Andrew Jackson Donelson. ALS, DLC (36). Suggests inserting into AJ's message transmitting the

Dec 18   Order to release insolvent public debtor Timothy Aldrich. LC,
              DNA-RG 59 (14-1061).
Dec 18   Andrew Jackson Donelson to Martin Van Buren. ALS, DNA-RG
              59 (M179-67). *TPUS,* 21:135. Says to tell Ambrose Sevier that
              AJ will not appoint a joint commissioner to run the Arkansas
              Territory boundary until Louisiana does also.
Dec 19   *To James Alexander Hamilton.*   642
Dec 19   John Watson Simonton to William Berkeley Lewis. Copy, DLC
              (75). Reports his neighbor Mrs. Williams's defense of Mrs.
              Eaton's character to John N. Campbell.
Dec 20   From John Strode Barbour and from Philip Pendleton Barbour.
              ALSs, DNA-RG 59 (M639-8). Recommend William S. Field for
              marshal in Virginia.
Dec 20   *From William Donelson.*   643
Dec [20]   From Samuel Rodman et al. DS, DNA-RG 56 (14-1081). Ask
              for Russel Freeman's reinstatement as New Bedford customs
              collector.
Dec 20   John Strode Barbour to Andrew Jackson Donelson. ALS, DLC
              (14-1075). Sends his and Philip P. Barbour's recommendations
              for William S. Field for marshal in Virginia. Endorsed by AJ,
              "There are more papers than this please look for them."
Dec 20   Moses Dawson to William Berkeley Lewis. ALS, DLC (37).
              Proposes his son Washington for land office receiver in his stead,
              to defeat Charles Hammond's opposition on grounds of his
              improper naturalization; praises the annual message and
              department reports.
Dec 21   From George Graham. LC, DNA-RG 49 (M25-25). Submits 54
              land patents for signature.
Dec 21   From Michael Cresap Sprigg. ALS, DNA-RG 156 (14-1085).
              Encloses Thomas B. Dunn's recommendation of Edward Lucas
              for paymaster at Harpers Ferry.
Dec 21   Check to Unknown for $220. DS, DLC (37).
Dec 21   Daniel Brent to Andrew Jackson Donelson. LC, DNA-RG 59
              (M40-21). Asks AJ's attention to pardon petitions, especially
              from mail robbers denied clemency by Adams.
Dec 22   To Edward Everett. AN, MHi (14-1092). Agrees to see Everett
              and his aged constituent Mr. Wood.
Dec 22   To the United States Senate. DS, DNA-RG 46 (14-1094); Copy,
              DLC (37). Richardson, 2:464; *Senate Executive Proceedings,*
              4:30. Submits a Chippewa, Ottawa, and Potawatomi treaty of
              Jul 29 and Winnebago treaty of Aug 1 for ratification.
Dec 22   From Maria Brooks. ALS, DNA-RG 94 (M688-72). Requests a
              West Point appointment for her son Horace.
Dec 22   From Charles Daubeville Dutillet. ALS, DNA-RG 94 (M688-
              56). Requests a West Point appointment for his son Charles.
Dec 22   *From James Alexander Hamilton.*   645
Dec 22   From Frederick May. ALS, DNA-RG 59 (M639-21). Repels
              charges of misconduct against George W. Slacum, consul at
              Buenos Aires.
[Dec 22]   Check to Andrew Jackson, Jr., for $50. DS, DLC (14-1093).

Dec 22	Refusal of clemency for shipowner William Williams. ANS, DNA-RG 59 (14-1096).
Dec 22	Andrew Jackson Donelson to Martin Van Buren. ALS, DNA-RG 59 (14-1088). Encloses John Wambersie's Senate confirmation as consul at Rotterdam.
Dec 23	To Alexander E. Brown, William L. Sebring, and Daniel W. Burke. Printed, *Easton Centinel,* Jan 8, 1830 (mAJs); Drafts, DLC (37; 72). Thanks the Easton, Pa., Hickory Club for its gift of a cane.
Dec 23	To James Eakin. LC, DNA-RG 59 (14-1101). Appoints him acting second auditor during William B. Lewis's absence.
Dec 23	From Alexander Speer. ALS, ScU (14-1102). Presents Stephen D. Miller's Dec 15 letter pressing South Carolina's claim for payment of War of 1812 expenses.
Dec 24	*To John Test.* 646
Dec 24	From Robert Gourlay. ALS, PPPrHi (14-1104). Presents his project of mass emigration to America and universal reform.
Dec 24	From John Harvey et al. DS, DNA-RG 59 (M639-17). Recommend Joshua Nelson for justice of the peace in the District of Columbia.
Dec 24	From John McNeil. LS, CtY (14-1108). Recommends George W. McLean for naval purser.
Dec 24	Order to release customs violator Israel Moses and remit his fine. LC, DNA-RG 59 (14-1109).
Dec 25	From Ferdinand VII, King of Spain. LS and Copy, DNA-RG 59 (14-1119). Announces his marriage to Maria Christina of Naples.
Dec 25	From Worden Pope. ALS, DLC (37). Presents his ideas on national defense, internal improvements, judiciary reform, the BUS, and acquiring Texas and Cuba; requests a West Point appointment for his son Curran Pope.
Dec 26	*From Hardy Murfree Cryer.* 647
Dec 26	Order for the release of Gamaliel King, held for nonpayment of a judgment as surety of late Brooklyn postmaster Thomas Kirk. LC, DNA-RG 59 (14-1126).
Dec 27	From James Earickson. ALS, DNA-RG 46 (14-1132). Introduces and commends Willis M. Green.
[cDec 27]	From Robert William Wells. ALS, DNA-RG 46 (14-1255). Recommends Willis M. Green for office.
Dec 28	From John Henry Eaton. LC, DNA-RG 107 (M127-2). Transmits a Delaware Indian treaty of Aug 3 for submission to the Senate.
Dec 29	*To Samuel Delucenna Ingham.* 649
Dec 29	To the United States Senate. DS, DNA-RG 46 (14-1158); Draft, DLC (37). Richardson, 2:464; *Senate Executive Proceedings,* 4:30. Submits the Delaware treaty for ratification.
Dec 29	To Martin Van Buren. ALS, Paul S. Zamostien (mAJs); Abstract, Carnegie Book Shop catalog, 1954 (14-1160). Proposes to reappoint Richard W. Greene as Rhode Island district attorney.

Dec 29   From David Crockett. ALS, MoSM (14-1134). Recommends
             George W. McLean for naval purser.
Dec 29   From John Henry Eaton. LS, DNA-RG 233 (14-1135); LCs,
             DNA-RG 77 (14-1136; M65-3) and RG 107 (M127-2). Submits
             a survey report by Army engineers on a canal and railroad to
             link the Tennessee and Altamaha rivers.
Dec 29   *From George Rockingham Gilmer.*   *650*
[cDec 29]   From George Taylor Graham. DS, DNA-RG 59 (14-1153).
             Pardoned watch thief, still confined for court costs which he is
             unable to pay, asks for release.
Dec 29   Order for release of prisoner George Taylor Graham. LC, DNA-
             RG 59 (14-1151).
Dec 29   Account with Josiah Nichol. Abstract, American Art Association
             catalog, 1926 (14-1157).
Dec 30   To the United States House of Representatives. DS, DNA-RG
             233 (14-1161); Draft, DLC (37). Richardson, 2:464. Transmits
             the survey of a canal and railroad route between the Tennessee
             and Altamaha rivers.
Dec 30   Martin Van Buren to Andrew Jackson Donelson. ALS, DLC
             (37). Asks him to correct Thomas Finley's nomination from
             district attorney to marshal in Maryland.
Dec 30   To the United States Senate. DS, DNA-RG 46 (14-1163); DS
             draft, DLC (37). *Senate Executive Proceedings,* 4:31–32.
             Nominates district attorneys and a marshal.
Dec 30   *From David Reed Mitchell.*   *654*
Dec 30   From Martin Van Buren. AN, DLC (37). Asks AJ to set a time
             to receive the Chevalier de Regina, consul general of the Two
             Sicilies; AJ selects Jan 4, 1830.
Dec 31   To John Branch. ALS, MoSM (14-1165). Encloses
             recommendations for George W. McLean for naval purser.
Dec 31   *To John Overton.*   *655*
Dec 31   *To Martha Jefferson Randolph.*   *658*
Dec 31   To the United States Senate. DS, DNA-RG 46 (14-1210). *Senate
             Executive Proceedings,* 4:34–35. Nominates customs officers.
Dec 31   To the United States Senate. DS, DNA-RG 46 (14-1212). *Senate
             Executive Proceedings,* 4:34. Nominates customs officers.
Dec 31   To the United States Senate. DS, DNA-RG 46 (14-1215). *Senate
             Executive Proceedings,* 4:33–34. Nominates land officers.
Dec 31   *To Martin Van Buren.*   *658*
Dec 31   *From Susan Wheeler Decatur.*   *659*
Dec 31   From John Henry Eaton. ALS, DNA-RG 46 (14-1167).
             Transmits a supplementary article to a Delaware treaty of 1818
             for submission to the Senate.
Dec 31   From John Henry Eaton. LS, DNA-RG 46 (14-1169). *Senate
             Executive Proceedings,* 4:35–37. Submits brevet promotions in
             the Army.
Dec 31   From John Henry Eaton. LS and Copy (dated Dec 7), DNA-RG
             46 (14-1178). *Senate Executive Proceedings,* 4:37. Submits
             Trueman Cross's brevet promotion to major.

Dec 31   From John Henry Eaton. LS, DNA-RG 46 (14-1183). *Senate Executive Proceedings*, 4:38–41. Submits Army promotions and appointments.

Dec 31   From Louisa Harvey. DS, DNA-RG 59 (14-1302). Requests a pardon for stealing a tablecloth and piece of lace while intoxicated; granted by AJ, Jan 1, 1830.

Dec 31   From Richard Harwood. ALS, DNA-RG 94 (M567-44). Transmits an abstract of the Maryland militia return for 1829.

Dec 31   From Jackey Spencer Hitt. Copy, DNA-RG 94 (M688-70). Requests a West Point appointment for his nephew Jesse H. Spurgin.

Dec 31   From Pedro Velez, Luis Quintana, and Lucas Alaman. DS and translation, DNA-RG 59 (M54-1). Mexican government acknowledges AJ's recall of minister Joel R. Poinsett.

[cDec]   From Archibald Nisbet and Mary Nisbet. DS, DNA-RG 94 (M567-46). Request an Army discharge for private Archibald Nisbet, who enlisted when intoxicated and underage.

[cDec]   From Paul Ratell et al. DS, DNA-RG 59 (M639-20). *TPUS*, 12:104–5. Oppose removing Michigan Territory marshal Thomas Rowland.

Dec   From Benjamin F. H. Witherell et al. DS, DNA-RG 59 (M639-20). *TPUS*, 12:103–4. Michigan Territory lawyers oppose removing marshal Thomas Rowland.

[1829]   *From Israel Beach, Isaac Morse, and Elihu Morse.*   660

[1829]   From John Black et al. and from William Paulding et al. DSs, DNA-RG 59 (M639-11). Recommend Robert R. Hunter for consul at Liverpool.

1829   *From Joseph Lancaster.*   663

[c1829]   From Arthur Dobbs Montjoy. ADS, THer (12-0379). Presents a poem.

[1829]   From Jacob Odell and John Targee. LS, DNA-RG 59 (M639-11). Recommend Robert R. Hunter for consul at Liverpool.

1829   From Walter Smith. Abstract, DNA-RG 156 (12-0387). Applies for a captaincy in the ordnance corps.

1829   From James Taylor. Abstract of AJ's endorsement, Argosy Book Stores catalog, 1983 (12-0393). Recommends Mr. Jones for midshipman.

[1829]   *Memorandum on a pamphlet by William Martin.*   664

[1829–1831]   List of books purchased by Andrew Jackson, Jr., and of books and miscellany presented to AJ and given by him to AJ Jr. in 1829–31. D, DLC (78).

[c1829]   Note praising the Chesapeake & Ohio Canal. D, DLC (12-0362). Endorsed by AJ as the substance of a possible message on internal improvements.

[c1829]   School composition by Andrew Jackson Hutchings. ADS fragment, DLC (75).

Index

Page numbers between 669 and 782 refer to the Calendar. An index reference to a single page of the Calendar may represent more than one item on that page. *Bold italic* page numbers immediately following a name represent documents written by or to that person and printed in the volume.